Fodor's 2009

FLORIDA

D0067521

**Where to Stay and Eat
for All Budgets**

**Must-See Sights
and Local Secrets**

Ratings You Can Trust

Fodor's Travel Publications   New York, Toronto, London, Sydney, Auckland
www.fodors.com

FODOR'S FLORIDA 2009

Editors: Eric B.Wechter, Paul Eisenberg

Editorial Contributors: Lynne Helm, Jennie Hess, Susan MacCallum-Whitcomb, Gary McKechnie, Alicia Callanan Mandigo, Julia Neyman, Kerry Speckman, Rowland Stiteler, Mary Thurwachter, Christina Tourigny, Jim Tunstall, Chelle Koster Walton

Editorial Production: Astrid deRidder

Maps & Illustrations: David Lindroth, *cartographer*; Bob Blake, Rebecca Baer, and William Wu *map editors*

Design: Fabrizio LaRocca, *creative director*; Guido Caroti, Siobhan O'Hare, *art directors*; Tina Malaney, Chie Ushio, Ann McBride, *designers*; Melanie Marin, *senior picture editor;* Moon Sun Kim, *cover designer*

Cover Photo (Sanibel Island): Visit Florida

Production/Manufacturing: Matthew Struble

ISBN 978–1–4000–1949–6

ISSN 0193–9556

SPECIAL SALES

This book is available at special discounts for bulk purchases for sales promotions or premiums. Special editions, including personalized covers, excerpts of existing books, and corporate imprints, can be created in large quantities for special needs. For more information, write to Special Markets/Premium Sales, 1745 Broadway, MD 6-2, New York, New York 10019, or e-mail specialmarkets@randomhouse.com.

AN IMPORTANT TIP & AN INVITATION

Although all prices, opening times, and other details in this book are based on information supplied to us at press time, changes occur all the time in the travel world, and Fodor's cannot accept responsibility for facts that become outdated or for inadvertent errors or omissions. So **always confirm information when it matters,** especially if you're making a detour to visit a specific place. Your experiences—positive and negative— matter to us. If we have missed or misstated something, **please write to us.** We follow up on all suggestions. Contact the Florida editor at editors@fodors.com or c/o Fodor's at 1745 Broadway, New York, NY 10019.

PRINTED IN THE UNITED STATES

10 9 8 7 6 5 4 3 2 1

Be a Fodor's Correspondent

Your opinion matters. It matters to us. It matters to your fellow Fodor's travelers, too. And we'd like to hear it. In fact, we need to hear it.

When you share your experiences and opinions, you become an active member of the Fodor's community. That means we'll not only use your feedback to make our books better, but we'll publish your names and comments whenever possible. Throughout our guides, look for "Word of Mouth," excerpts of your unvarnished feedback.

Here's how you can help improve Fodor's for all of us.

Tell us when we're right. We rely on local writers to give you an insider's perspective. But our writers and staff editors—who are the best in the business—depend on you. Your positive feedback is a vote to renew our recommendations for the next edition.

Tell us when we're wrong. We're proud that we update most of our guides every year. But we're not perfect. Things change. Hotels cut services. Museums change hours. Charming cafés lose charm. If our writer didn't quite capture the essence of a place, tell us how you'd do it differently. If any of our descriptions are inaccurate or inadequate, we'll incorporate your changes in the next edition and will correct factual errors at fodors.com immediately.

Tell us what to include. You probably have had fantastic travel experiences that aren't yet in Fodor's. Why not share them with a community of like-minded travelers? Maybe you chanced upon a beach or bistro or B&B that you don't want to keep to yourself. Tell us why we should include it. And share your discoveries and experiences with everyone directly at fodors.com. Your input may lead us to add a new listing or highlight a place we cover with a "Highly Recommended" star or with our highest rating, "Fodor's Choice."

Give us your opinion instantly at our feedback center at www.fodors.com/feedback. You may also e-mail editors@fodors.com with the subject line "Florida Editor." Or send your nominations, comments, and complaints by mail to Florida Editor, Fodor's, 1745 Broadway, New York, NY 10019.

You and travelers like you are the heart of the Fodor's community. Make our community richer by sharing your experiences. Be a Fodor's correspondent.

Happy traveling!

Tim Jarrell, Publisher

CONTENTS

MAPS

ABOUT THIS BOOK

Our Ratings

Sometimes you find terrific travel experiences and sometimes they just find you. But usually the burden is on you to select the right combination of experiences. That's where our ratings come in.

As travelers we've all discovered a place so wonderful that its worthiness is obvious. And sometimes that place is so experiential that superlatives don't do it justice: you just have to be there to know. These sights, properties, and experiences get our highest rating, **Fodor's Choice**, indicated by orange stars throughout this book.

Black stars highlight sights and properties we deem **Highly Recommended**, places that our writers, editors, and readers praise again and again for consistency and excellence.

By default, there's another category: Any place we include in this book is by definition worth your time, unless we say otherwise. And we will.

Disagree with any of our choices? Care to nominate a place or suggest that we rate one more highly? Visit our feedback center at www.fodors.com/feedback.

Budget Well

Hotel and restaurant price categories from ¢ to $$$$ are defined in the opening pages of each chapter. For attractions, we always give standard adult admission fees; reductions are usually available for children, students, and senior citizens. Want to pay with plastic? **AE, D, DC, MC, V** following restaurant and hotel listings indicate whether American Express, Discover, Diners Club, MasterCard, and Visa are accepted.

Restaurants

Unless we state otherwise, restaurants are open for lunch and dinner daily. We mention dress only when there's a specific requirement and reservations only when they're essential or not accepted—it's always best to book ahead.

Hotels

Hotels have private bath, phone, TV, and air-conditioning and operate on the European Plan (aka EP, meaning without meals), unless we specify that they use the Continental Plan (CP, with a Continental breakfast), Breakfast Plan (BP, with a full breakfast), or Modified American Plan (MAP, with breakfast and dinner), or are all-inclusive (including all meals and most activities). We always list facilities but not whether you'll be charged an extra fee to use them, so always ask.

Many Listings
- ★ Fodor's Choice
- ★ Highly recommended
- ✉ Physical address
- ✦ Directions
- ⬤ Mailing address
- ☎ Telephone
- 🖷 Fax
- ⊕ On the Web
- ✉ E-mail
- 🎟 Admission fee
- ☉ Open/closed times
- Ⓜ Metro stations
- ▭ Credit cards

Hotels & Restaurants
- 🏨 Hotel
- 🛏 Number of rooms
- ♨ Facilities
- ⧧ Meal plans
- ✕ Restaurant
- ⟋ Reservations
- ⟍ Smoking
- BYOB
- ✕🏨 Hotel with restaurant that warrants a visit

Outdoors
- 🏌 Golf
- ⛺ Camping

Other
- ☺ Family-friendly
- ⇨ See also
- ✉ Branch address
- ☞ Take note

Experience Florida

St. Joseph Peninsula State Park

WORD OF MOUTH

"For a real Florida feel, Vero Beach on the Atlantic side is wonderful. It's absolutely beautiful with quiet beaches. Sebastian Inlet which is just to the north is the most popular surfing location in Florida."

—ildiko

WHAT'S WHERE

The following numbers refer to chapters.

2 The Panhandle. The underappreciated Panhandle is a colorful place, dubbed the Emerald Coast because of its green Gulf waters.

3 Northeast Florida. This corner scores points for diversity. Time seems to rewind in St. Augustine, America's oldest continuously inhabited city. But it's on fast-forward in Daytona Beach and the Space Coast.

4 Walt Disney World & Orlando. Although Walt Disney World is the granddaddy of attractions, it doesn't hold a monopoly on fun. SeaWorld offers animal encounters and Universal packs a punch in terms of thrills.

5 Palm Beach & the Treasure Coast. Boca Raton to Jupiter is known for its golden sand and the golden bank accounts of its rich residents. Travelers who favor the unspoiled over the spoiled can turn inland to Lake Okeechobee or north to the Treasure Coast.

6 Fort Lauderdale & Broward County. The "Suds and Sun Capital of the Universe" has grown up. The beaches that first attracted college crowds are now complemented by a refurbished waterfront with luxe

hotels and upscale entertainment options.

7 Miami & Miami Beach. Art Deco buildings, towering palms, and white-as-bleached-teeth beaches set the scene here. Prepare for power shopping, club-hopping and fab Floribbean cuisine.

8 The Florida Keys. This slender necklace of landfalls, strung together by a 110-mi highway, marks the southernmost edge of the continental U.S. Divided into Upper, Middle, and Lower, the islands are nirvana for anglers, divers—even literature lovers.

9 The Everglades. Covering more than 1.5 million acres, the fabled "River of Grass" is Florida's greatest natural treasure.

10 The Lower Gulf Coast. This region serves up sandy beaches and pockets of untouched beauty, ranging from cypress swamps to mangrove-fringed barrier islands.

11 The Tampa Bay Area. Busch Gardens, Ybor City, and Tampa's other urban attractions are only part of the bay area's appeal. Culture vultures flock to St. Pete Beach and Sarasota for concerts and museums; while outdoorsy types veer northward for the Manatee Coast.

Gulf of Mexico

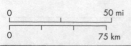

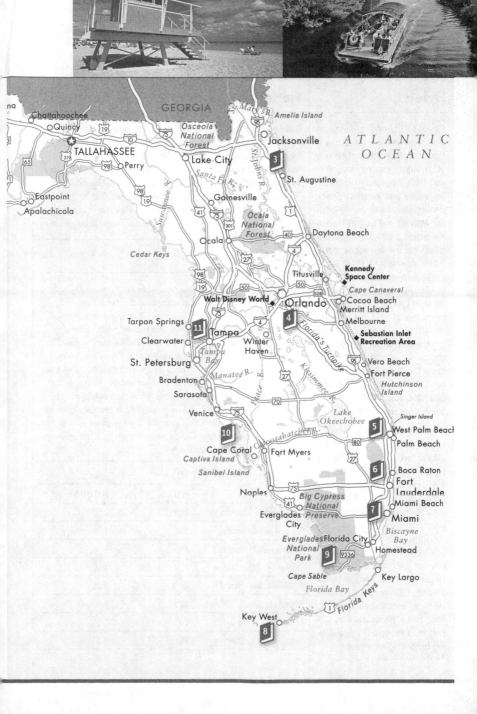

FLORIDA PLANNER

Flying

Florida's 21 commercial airports give travelers lots of choices. Most begin and end their trip at Orlando International Airport (MCO). Destinations like St. Augustine and Kennedy Space Center, plus beaches on both the Atlantic and Gulf of Mexico are within a 100-mi radius. The state's second-busiest airport is Miami International (MIA). But if you're destined for the north side of Miami-Dade, try flying instead into Fort Lauderdale–Hollywood International (FLL), a 40-minute drive away. Its smaller size usually means easier access and shorter security lines. Moreover, lower landing costs attract budget carriers—among them jet-Blue, Midwest, Southwest, and Spirit—that don't serve MIA.

Checking out alternate airports elsewhere can also yield benefits in terms of time or money saved. For instance, savvy flyers bound for the popular Tampa Bay area should investigate St. Petersburg–Clearwater International (PIE) as well as the larger Tampa International (TPA): they're within a 20-minute drive of each other. The state's Department of Transportation Web site (⊕ www.dot.state.fl.us/ aviation/commercialairports. htm) has a handy click-on airport map that makes researching further options easy.

Florida Travel

Before finalizing your dream itinerary, study a map to see how easy it will be to connect the dots. Since Florida is a long, lean peninsula anchored to the mainland by a "panhandle," the distances may surprise you. Panama City, for example, is closer to New Orleans than to Orlando; and Tallahassee, though only 8 mi from the Georgia border is a whopping 465 mi from Miami Beach. Key West, similarly, is 494 mi from Jacksonville, yet only 90 from Cuba.

Driving

You'll likely become acquainted with the three main highways that run into, then through, Florida: the I-95, I-75, and I-10. The first two (originating in Maine and Michigan respectively) extend south; the last (starting in California) extends west. Prefer to get off these well-beaten paths? Florida Tourism has developed a series of self-guided driving tours that cover scenic byways and themed routes, like the Florida Lighthouse Trail or African-American Heritage Trail. Its Web site also has helpful tools, including a fuel-cost calculator and downloadable maps. More are available at Florida's online information portal (⊕ www.stateofflorida. com). Its Transportation Guide has everything from mileage charts to details on turnpike tolls.

Typical Travel Times

	MILES	HOURS
Jacksonville–Tallahassee	165	2:50
Gainesville–Orlando	115	1:50
Orlando–St. Petersburg	105	1:50
Orlando–Ft. Lauderdale	210	3:10
Ft. Lauderdale–Miami	28	0:35
Miami–Naples	125	2:00
Miami–Kay Largo	64	1:15
Key Largo–Key West	98	2:00

GREAT ITINERARIES

3 to 4 Days: Orlando

Anyone can easily spend a week "doing the attractions." (Remember, Walt Disney World alone is roughly the size of San Francisco!) But unless you're a die-hard ride hound, a few days will let you sample them and still enjoy some of Orlando's other amenities. The hard part is deciding where to start. The Magic Kingdom has the greatest concentration of classic sites, and Epcot proves this really is "a small world." Film buffs can "get reel" at Disney's Hollywood Studios or Universal Studios, and thrill seekers can get their hearts pumping at Islands of Adventure. As for wildlife encounters, you can do like Dolittle at Disney's Animal Kingdom or SeaWorld. Want more? There are also enough water parks here to make you forget that Florida's beaches are only miles away. In Orlando itself, the collection of modern paintings at the Orlando Museum of Art is worth visiting; and flower fans can stop to smell the roses at the 50-acre Harry P. Leu Gardens. Boaters, moreover, can take advantage of the area's numerous lakes, and golfers can link up at some of the state's best courses.

2 to 3 Days: Panhandle

Let's be honest: people come to Florida's Panhandle primarily for those award-winning, sugar-white beaches. But it's possible to work on a tan and still work in some sightseeing. At Gulf Islands National Seashore, for instance, you can soak up the sun, cast a fishing net, take a hike, tour centuries-old forts, and have time left for a trip into historic Pensacola. Similarly, after beach time around Apalachicola Bay you can stop for oysters at a local raw bar (90% of Florida's haul comes from here); head north through the canopied roads around Apalachicola National Forest; then get a true taste of the Old South in moss-draped Tallahassee. Yet another day could be devoted to glorious Grayton Beach, where diving and kayaking can be followed up with a relaxing drive along Route 30A to cute (and controversial) communities like WaterColor and Seaside. When planning your trip, bear in mind that the Panhandle not only has its own time zone, but its own tourism season—and summer is prime time for beach-going.

2 to 3 Days: Space Coast

If you need proof that Florida was the first part of the U.S. to be settled, look no further than St. Augustine. It was founded by the Spanish in 1565, and visiting Castillo de San Marcos (its colonial-era fortress) or strolling the streets of the Old City that grew up around it allows you to experience life in the past lane. Taking in the educational (and entertaining!) sites at the 700,000-acre Kennedy Space Center has just the opposite effect. Although they may seem centuries removed, the nation's oldest continuously-inhabited city is less than two hours by car from our launch pad to the moon. Between them, you can lounge on the blissful beaches of Canaveral National Seashore, hear the call of the wild at Merritt Island National Wildlife Refuge, or catch a wave like surfing legend (and local hero) Kelly Slater. Racier options also await: just reset your GPS for Daytona Beach. Its International Speedway, which has hosted NASCAR's Daytona 500 every February since 1959, is a must-see for stock-car fans.

GREAT ITINERARIES

2 to 3 Days: Gold Coast & Treasure Coast

The opulent mansions of Palm Beach's Ocean Boulevard give you a glimpse of how the richer half lives. For exclusive boutique shopping, art-gallery browsing, and glittery sightseeing, sybarites should wander down "The Avenue" (that's Worth Avenue to non–Palm Beachers). The sporty set will find dozens of places to tee up (hardly surprising given that the PGA is based here), along with tennis courts, polo clubs, even a croquet center. Those who'd like to see more of the Gold Coast can continue traveling south through Boca Raton to Fort Lauderdale (justifiably known as the "Yachting Capital of the World"). But to balance the highbrow with the low-key, turn northward for a tour of the Treasure Coast. It was named for the booty spilled by a fleet of Spanish galleons shipwrecked here in 1715, and for centuries treasure kept washing ashore south of the Sebastian Inlet. These days you're more likely to find manatees and golden surfing opportunities. You can also look for the sea turtles that lay their own little treasures in the sands from May through August.

2 to 3 Days: Miami Area

Greater Miami lays claim to the country's most celebrated strand—South Beach—and lingering on it tops most tourist itineraries. (The Ocean Drive section, lined with edgy clubs, boutiques and eateries, is where the see-and-be-seen crowd gathers.) Once you've checked out the candy-colored Art Deco architecture, park yourself to ogle the parade of stylish people, or join them by browsing Lincoln Road Mall. Later, merengue over to Calle Ocho: the epicenter of Miami's Cuban community. Elsewhere in the area, Coconut Grove, Coral Gables, and the Miami Design District (an 18-block area crammed with showrooms and galleries) also warrant a visit. Since Miami is the sole U.S. city with two national parks and a national preserve in its backyard, it is also a convenient base for eco-excursions. You can take a day trip to the Everglades (if you've never seen an alligator eat a marshmallow or experienced an airboat ride, here's your chance!); get a spectacular view of the reefs from a glass-bottom boat in Biscayne National Park; then spot some rare wood storks in Big Cypress Swamp, which is best explored via Alligator Alley (Interstate 75).

2 to 3 Days: Florida Keys

Some dream of "sailing away to Key Largo;" others of "wasting away again in Margaritaville." In any case, almost everybody equates the Florida Keys with relaxation. And—assuming you survive the traffic—they live up to their reputation, thanks to off-beat attractions and that fabled come-as-you-are, do-as-you-please vibe. Key West, alternately known as the Conch Republic, is a good place to get initiated. The Old Town has a funky, laid-back feel. So take a leisurely walk; pay your regards to "Papa" (Hemingway, that is); then—if you haven't imbibed too much at one of the renowned watering holes—rent a moped to tour the rest of the island. Clear waters and abundant marine life make underwater activities another must. After scoping out the parrot fish, you can always head back into town and join local "Parrotheads" in a Jimmy Buffett sing-along. When retracing your route to the mainland, plan a last pit stop at Bahia Honda State Park (it has ranger-led activities plus the Keys' best beach) or John Pennekamp Coral Reef State Park,

which offers unparalleled snorkeling and scuba diving opportunities.

2 to 3 Days: Tampa Bay Area

Whether you bypassed Orlando's theme parks or simply want to add another one to your "I did it" list, Busch Gardens is a logical starting point. With hair-raising rides and more than 2,700 animals, it appeals to adrenaline junkies and 'fraidy cats alike. Later you can catch a pro sporting event (Tampa has Major League baseball, football, and hockey teams) or catch an act in the Spanish-inflected Ybor City entertainment district. If you're more interested in catching some rays, try the beaches of Caladesi Island State Park (to the west of the city) or Fort DeSoto Park (at the mouth of Tampa Bay). From there, culture lovers can visit St. Petersburg's museums; then push south to Sarasota, where a thriving arts scene is bolstered by a professional symphony, ballet and opera companies, more than 10 theaters, and dozens of galleries. Nature lovers, conversely, can proceed north to Crystal River to see—or even snorkel with—the gigantic but gentle manatees that congregate in the warm waters from November through March.

TIPS

Now that one-way airfares are commonplace, vacationers visiting multiple destinations can fly into and out of different airports. Rent a car in between, picking it up at your point of arrival and leaving it at your point of departure.

■ Break up a visit to Orlando with an overnight excursion to the Space Coast. Located less than an hour east, it has the beaches that the inland city lacks, plus boundless eco-opportunities and Kennedy Space Center.

■ Can't access the Everglades from the east? Try taking a tour out of Naples or Marco Island. Keep in mind that airboaters will have to stick to the fringes of Everglades National Park. Be sure to inquire about scheduled activities when visiting national or state parks and preserves. Many run free or low-cost ranger-led programs.

IF YOU LIKE

Beaches

Each of us defines the "perfect" beach differently. But whether you want to swim, surf, lounge, or leer, Florida has one to fit suit your preference. Best of all, in this skinny state—bounded by the Atlantic *and* Gulf of Mexico—the coast is never more than 60 mi away.

■ **Miami Beach.** Over the past 20 years, no American beach has generated as much buzz as the one that hugs Ocean Drive, and it's easy to see why. Fringed with palms, backed by Art Deco architecture, and pulsating with urban energy, South Beach is the place to stretch out or strut.

■ **Space Coast.** Canaveral National Seashore boasts pristine beaches, plus wetlands that attract endangered marine animals and people who admire them. Running from New Smyrna Beach to Titusville, the 24-mi preserve is undeveloped. So you relax in the shelter of dunes, not the shadow of high-rises.

■ **Panhandle.** Although northwest Florida has a surplus of Grade-A Gulf beaches, Grayton Beach is arguably the pick of the bunch. Halfway between Panama City and Pensacola, it has shockingly white sand and aqua-green water clear as any you'd find in the Keys or the Bahamas.

■ **Tampa Bay.** Sand comes with a side order of history at Fort DeSoto Park. Spread over five interconnecting islands southwest of St. Petersburg, the park's bountiful beaches have been added to the list of "America's Best" by Stephen Leatherman—otherwise known as Dr. Beach.

Animal Magnetism

Florida is home to one super-sized mouse and makes an ideal habitat for party animals. Yet there are other kinds of wildlife too. In terms of diversity, the state ranks third in the nation with more than 1,200 kinds of critters.

■ **Birds.** Located on two major migratory routes, Florida draws 470 species of birds—and the 2,000-mi Great Florida Birding Trail helps you find them. Through detailed guides and highway signs, it identifies sites where you might spy anything from bald eagles and burrowing owls to bubble gum–pink flamingos.

■ **Manatees.** They're nicknamed sea cows and resemble walruses. But Florida's official marine mammals are most closely related to elephants, which may account for their slow pace and hefty frames. In winter, scan the water for a telltale glassy patch (or "footprint") indicating a manatee swims below.

■ **Sea Turtles.** Ready for a late-night rendezvous with the leatherbacks and loggerheads that lumber onto Floridian beaches between May and October to lay eggs? Archie Carr National Wildlife Refuge, the world's second-largest sea-turtle nesting site, organizes free turtle watches in June and July.

■ **Alligators.** Florida has more than 1.5 million resident alligators. You can see them do tricks at places like Gatorland, but "gator spotting" in swamps or roadside waterways is a favorite pastime. Eating the official state reptile in nugget form is popular, too. Mmm…tastes like chicken.

Life in the Fast Lane

The Sunshine State has been satisfying visitors' need for speed ever since Henry Ford and his snowbird buddies started using Ormond Beach as a test track. Today roller coasters, stock cars, supersonic jets, and spaceships add momentum to your vacation.

■ **Tampa.** If you think the pursuit of happiness is a high-speed activity, head for Busch Gardens: Florida's premier roller-coaster location. SheiKra is one of the world's tallest dive coasters, Kumba features one of the world's largest vertical loops, and Montu (a gut-churning inverted coaster) delivers a G-force of 3.85.

■ **Daytona Beach.** Daytona 500, NASCAR's most prestigious event, pulls in legions of fans every February. But any time of year you can slip into a driving suit, then into the driver's seat of a Winston Cup–style stock car by signing up for the Richard Petty Driving Experience at Daytona International Speedway.

■ **Pensacola.** The National Museum of Naval Aviation displays 140-plus aircraft and has motion-based simulators that let you "fly" an F/A-18. Better yet, the U.S. Navy Precision Flight Team (commonly known as the Blue Angels) is based here, so you may get to see them in action at 700 mph.

■ **Kennedy Space Center.** Whether you're a fan of Buzz Aldrin or Buzz Lightyear, this spaceport has the right stuff. See a shuttle launch, admire the rockets, or take your own "giant leap" with the Astronaut Training Experience. The daylong program consists of realistic training exercises culminating in a simulated mission.

Something Old, Something New

You don't have to look far for "New Florida." It's evident in skyscrapers and sprawling suburbs, in malls, multiplexes, and condo complexes. Yet it's easy enough to find reminders of the state's rich past.

■ **St. Augustine.** Fortify yourself at Castillo de San Marcos. Built by the Spanish to defend "La Florida," this formidable 17th-century structure is America's oldest masonry fort. Even kids whose interest in architecture stops at Cinderella's Castle will be impressed by its turrets, moat, and double drawbridge.

■ **Apalachicola.** A booming cotton-and-lumber industry made this Panhandle town a bustling port in the 19th century. Now it's part of the Forgotten Coast. Hundreds of preserved buildings, ranging from antebellum warehouses to gracious Victorian-style homes, give it a time-warped appeal.

■ **Coral Gables.** You can soak up 1920s architecture in Miami Beach. But in nearby Coral Gables you can soak *in* it at the Venetian Pool: a vintage municipal "lagoon" fashioned from a quarry. Back in the day, it attracted Johnny Weissmuller, Esther Williams, and other legendary swimmers.

■ **Cross Creek.** The backwoods scrub immortalized by Marjorie Kinnan Rawlings in the 1930s hasn't changed much. Nor has the Cracker-style house where she wrote *The Yearling.* You can tour it October through July and visit the surrounding farm and grove year-round.

QUINTESSENTIAL FLORIDA

H2O

Spanish explorer Ponce de León didn't find the Fountain of Youth when he swung through Florida in 1513. But if he'd lingered longer, he could have located 7,800 lakes, 1,700 rivers and creeks, and more than 350 springs. Over the centuries, these have attracted Native Americans, immigrants, opportunists, and, of course, countless outdoor adventurers. Boaters come for inland waterways and a 1,200-mi coast, and anglers are lured by 700 species of fish. (Florida claims 700 world-record catches, too, so concocting elaborate "fish tales" is seldom necessary.) Snorkelers and divers eager to see what lies beneath can get face time with the marine life that thrives on the world's third-largest coral reef or bone up on maritime history in underwater archaeological preserves. Back on dry land, the beaches abutting the water are pretty impressive, too.

Food, Glorious Food

Geography and gastronomy go hand in hand in Florida. Seafood, for instance, is a staple almost everywhere, yet locals will point out that the way it's prepared changes considerably as you maneuver around the state. Northern restaurants show their regional roots with Cajun classics and Dixieland dishes. (It seems that any fish can be crusted with pecans and served with greens!) In southern Florida, menus highlight Floribbean cuisine, which marries Floridian, Caribbean, and Latin flavors. (Think mahimahi with mango salsa.) Inland, expect catfish, gator tails, and frogs' legs, all of which are best enjoyed at a Cracker-style fish camp with a side of hush puppies. In keeping with the regional emphasis, assorted seafoods—as well as peanuts, sweet corn, watermelons, and citrus fruits— merit their own down-home festivals.

Florida is synonymous with sunshine, and every year more than 84 million visitors come to revel in it. However, the people who live here—a diverse group that includes Mouseketeers, millionaires, and rocket scientists— know that the state's appeal rests on more than those reliable rays.

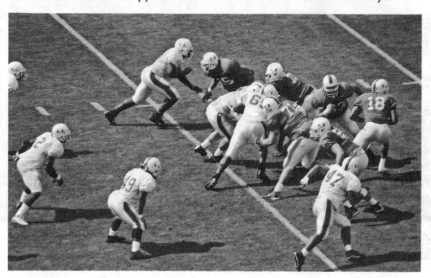

Theme Parks

Kids tend to think of Florida as a playland that's liberally sprinkled with pixie dust. And who can blame them? Orlando's theme parks are among the most popular—and most publicized—attractions on earth. Walt Disney World opened the first of its four Floridian parks in 1971. Competitors like SeaWorld and Universal followed suit, transforming a swampy cattle-and-citrus town into "Fun Central." Today dozens of smaller Orlando venues—including the Wet 'n Wild water park and a Christian park called Holy Land Experience—vie for visitors' dollars; and Busch Gardens in Tampa (85 mi southwest) scrambles for a piece of the pie with its own roundup of rides. Some locals love them. Others lament the dawn of the "Disney Era." Yet all recognize that theme parks are now a fact of life.

Superlative Sports

Panthers and Dolphins and Rays. Oh my! Florida is teeming with teams—and residents take the games they play *very* seriously. Baseball fans regularly work themselves into a fever pitch: after all, the state has a pair of Major League franchises and hosts another 16 in spring when the Grapefruit League goes to bat. Those with a preference for pigskin might cheer for NFL teams in Jacksonville, Miami, and Tampa. But the state is also home to top-rated college teams, and two (the Gators and 'Noles) have especially fervent followings. Basketball lovers, meanwhile, feel the "Heat" in Miami or the "Magic" in Orlando, and neophyte hockey fans (along with snowbirds needing a hockey fix) stick around to watch the Florida Panthers and Tampa Bay Lightning.

TOP FLORIDA ATTRACTIONS

Walt Disney World

(A) Like one of Snow White's dwarfs, Orlando was sleepy until Uncle Walt arrived. Today the city is booming—and so is Walt Disney World, which has grown into a sprawling 47-square mi complex with four separate parks, scores of hotels, and various satellite attractions.

Thanks, to innovative rides, dazzling Animatronics, and ubiquitous advertising, these feature prominently in every child's holiday fantasy. However, grown-ups don't have to channel their inner eight-year-old to enjoy themselves. That's because Walt Disney World also has decidedly adult amenities: including championship golf courses, seductive spas, sublime hotels, and even fine restaurants that consistently rank among North America's best.

South Beach

(B) Literally or figuratively, you can't miss the distinctive forms, vibrant colors, and extravagant flourishes of SoBe's architectural gems. The world's largest concentration of Art Deco edifices is right here; and the Art Deco District—with more than 800 buildings of significance—has earned a spot on the National Register of Historic Places. Needless to say, the neighborhood also has enough "beautiful people" to qualify for the Register of Hippest Places. The glitterati, along with assorted vacationing hedonists, are drawn in by über-trendy shops and a surfeit of celeb-studded clubs. South Beach's stellar eateries are the icing—umm, better make that the ganache—on South Beach's proverbial cake.

The Florida Keys

(C) These 800-plus islands are at once a unique landmass and a mass of contra-

dictions. Long years of geographic isolation not only allowed tropical flora and fauna to flourish here; it enabled locals to nurture a quirky culture. Unfortunately, increased traffic on the Overseas Highway linking the Upper, Middle and Lower Keys to the mainland has threatened both. So the Keys now have a split personality. On one hand they're a reef-rimmed paradise occupied by free-spirited folks; on the other they're a relatively mainstream realm comprised of traffic jams, shopping malls, and trailer parks. Avoiding the latter can be difficult. But the charm of the former is ample reward.

Kennedy Space Center
(D) Although there are enough wide-open expanses to justify the region's moniker, it was actually NASA that put the "space" in Space Coast—and this is its star attraction. Space memorabilia and aeronautic antiques, ranging from early Redstone rockets to the Apollo XIV command module, turn a visit here into a trip back in time for anyone who lived through the Space Race. Yet for today's kids the center opens up a "brave new world" filled with interactive bells and whistles. More down-to-earth types can also visit Merritt Island National Wildlife Refuge (created as a buffer for the space program) and the undeveloped Canaveral National Seashore.

Tampa
(E) As a vibrant city blessed with exceptional beaches, Tampa is perfect for indecisive folks who want to enjoy surf and sand without sacrificing urban experiences. Families will love Busch Gardens: a major zoo and theme park. Football and hockey fans, moreover, will relish the chance to see the Buccaneers and Tampa Bay Lightning in action. Baseball is big, too: the Rays are based here, and the Yan-

TOP FLORIDA ATTRACTIONS

kees descend annually for spring training. When you need a break from the big city, St. Pete Beach (famous for surreally beautiful strands) and St. Petersburg (home to the world's most comprehensive collection of Salvador Dalí's surrealist paintings) are a short drive away.

Go Fish

(F) Each October, Destin proves it is the "World's Luckiest Fishing Village" by inviting anglers young and old to compete in the month-long Destin Fishing Rodeo. However, if you'd prefer to throw fish than catch them, head to Pensacola in late April for the Interstate Mullet Toss. (Participants actually line up to throw dead fish across the Florida/Alabama state line). Epicures will be relieved to hear that Pensacola also stages a September Seafood Festival. As if fish fried, broiled, battered, and grilled weren't appealing

enough, gourmet options are added to the menu. Anyone for crawfish étouffée?

Say Boo

(G) In St. Augustine history comes alive. But it's the "undead" that some find most appealing. Ghosts are plentiful, thanks to all the pirates, plunderers, and other lost souls who formerly lived in this deceptively quiet city. To hear lurid lore about local haunts, sign on for one of the nightly "experiences" organized by Ghost Tours of St. Augustine. These 90-minute lantern-lit walks focus on well-researched stories full of goose bump–inducing details. Top off the spirited tour with an overnight stay at St. Francis Inn (St. Augustine's oldest hostelry) or Casablanca Inn: both are reportedly haunted.

Act Goofy

(H) If you have time for only one mega-park, choose the original: Walt Disney World's Magic Kingdom. Approached

with an open mind, it really can feel like the "happiest place on earth." Start by waving to Mickey on Main Street USA; then fly with Dumbo, take a spin in the Mad Hatter's Teacups, and catch the nighttime fireworks display over Cinderella's Castle. As an FYI, flume lovers can also have a blast on Splash Mountain: just be forewarned. Ride it more than once and you'll spend the rest of your trip humming Brer Rabbit's theme song.

Enjoy the High Life

(I) If money could talk, you'd hardly be able to hear above the din in Palm Beach. The upper crust started calling it home, during the winter months at least, back in the early 1900s. And today it remains a ritzy glitzy enclave for both Old Money and the nouveau riche (a coterie led by "The Donald" himself). Simply put, Palm Beach is the sort of place where shopping is a full-time pursuit and residents don't just wear Polo—they play it. Oooh and ahhh to your heart's content; then, for more conspicuous consumption, continue south on the aptly-named Gold Coast to Boca Raton.

Float Your Boat

(J) Mariners should set their compass for Fort Lauderdale (aka the "Venice of America"), where vessels from around the world moor along some two dozen finger isles between the beach and the mainland. Sailors can cruise Broward County's 300 mi of inland waterways by water taxi and tour boat, or bob around the Atlantic in a chartered yacht. If you're in a buying mood, come during October for the annual Fort Lauderdale International Boat Show. Billed as the world's largest, it has more than a billion dollars worth of boats in every conceivable size, shape, and price range.

TOP FLORIDA ATTRACTIONS

Live La Vida Local

(K) On the streets of Miami's Little Havana, just west of Downtown, salsa tunes blare and the smell of spicy chorizo fills the air. (You can get a good whiff of tobacco, too, thanks to the cigar makers who hand-roll their products here.) For more than 40 years, the neighborhood's undisputed heart has been Calle Ocho: the commercial thoroughfare that hosts Carnaval Miami each March. The festival's ten frenetic days culminate in the world's longest conga line. Ambience- and amenity-wise, it is as close as you'll get to Cuba without running afoul of the federal government.

Find Nemo

(L) Little wonder the Keys are a prime destination for divers and snorkelers: they boast the world's third-largest reef and aquarium-clear waters that are brimming with sea life. Under the surface lies a col-

orful world populated by 40 species of coral and over 600 of fish, which means you can spot purple sea fans, blue tangs, yellow-tailed snappers, green-finned parrot fish and more. Locals debate the premiere place for viewing them. But John Pennekamp Coral Reef State Park is high on everyone's list. Underwater excursions organized by park concessionaires let you put your best flipper forward.

Feel Swamped

(M) No trip to southern Florida is complete without seeing the Everglades. At its heart is a river—50 mi wide but only 6 inches deep—flowing from Lake Okeechobee into Florida Bay. For an up-close look, speed demons can board an airboat that careens through the marshy waters. Purists, alternately, may placidly canoe or kayak within the boundaries of Everglades National Park. Just remember to keep your hands in the boat. The crit-

ters that call this unique ecosystem home (alligators, Florida panthers, and cottonmouth snakes for starters) can add real bite to your visit!

Be Beachy Keen

(N) Ready to do something slightly more vigorous than applying SPF 45 and rolling over? Trade beach bumming for beachcombing in Sanibel, the "Shell Capital of the World." Conchs, cockles, clams, coquina: they're all here (the bounty is due to this barrier island's unusual east-west orientation). Of course, if you'd rather construct sand castles than do the "Sanibel Stoop," you need only cross the 3-mi causeway to Fort Myers Beach. It has the finest building material and, every November, professional and amateur aficionados prove it during the American Sandsculpting Championship.

Clown Around

(O) Sarasota (once winter headquarters for Ringling Bros. and Barnum & Bailey) is proud of its circus heritage, and several troupes are still based here, including Royal Hanneford, Walker Brothers, and Circus Sarasota. Visitors who can't get enough of sawdust and sequins can see an impressive collection of vintage costumes, props, and parade wagons at the Ringling Circus Museum. And the adjacent Tibbals Learning Center houses a mind-boggling ¾-inch scale miniature circus with almost a million pieces. Sarasota even has a "Circus Ring of Fame" honoring big top bigwigs.

WHAT'S NEW

Creature Comforts

Aquatica, SeaWorld's 60-acre water park in Orlando, opened with a splash in March of 2008. By sliding through a dolphin lagoon or floating in a fish-filled grotto, guests there can now immerse themselves (literally!) in the life aquatic. Landlubbers, on the other hand, can encounter exotic critters up close at Busch Gardens' new "Jungala" zone in Tampa. As part of the park's most ambitious expansion ever, Bengal tigers, orangutans, gibbons, and more were moved into naturalistic habitats that come complete with tree-top observation platforms and other cool viewing stations. New facilities at Floridian zoos (most notably Miami Metro-Zoo's $50-million "Amazon & Beyond" exhibit, opening late 2008) will also bring out the animal in you.

Oh Natural!

If you want to appreciate nature without buying pricey theme park passes, simply plot a course north to St. Marks River State Park. Located 20 mi outside Tallahassee, it is the newest of Florida's 161 state parks and offers almost 2,600 acres of recreational area for hikers, bikers and wildlife watchers. Boaters also have a new reason to celebrate now that the state tourism board has released a free "Florida Paddling Trails Guide," featuring details on designated waterways plus fold-out maps and outfitter info. Rather be under the water than on it? Florida Keys National Marine Sanctuary has good news for naval gazers. A 523-ft former U.S. Air Force ship (the *Vandenberg*) is slated to be scuttled south of Key West to create an artificial reef.

Tee Time

With more golf courses than any other state, Florida has always been a great place for swingers—and it just keeps upping its game. Take the Ginn Reunion Resort, near Orlando. Not content with having courses laid out by Tom Watson, Arnold Palmer, and Jack Nicklaus, it has added the Annika Academy: a golf school named for LPGA phenom Annika Sörenstam and overseen by her coach, Henri Reis. Other noteworthy upgrades include restorations of the highly regarded Dye Course at the PGA Golf Club in Port St. Lucie and the Donald Ross-designed Biltmore Golf Course in Coral Gables. The Fairmont Turnberry Isle Resort & Club in Aventura also decided to go fore it, having Raymond Floyd give its 36 holes a $30-million makeover.

Reel Life

Walt Disney World rolled out the red carpet in 2008, renaming its movie park Disney's Hollywood Studios and debuting attractions built around blockbuster films: among them an interactive *Toy Story* adventure designed to resemble a ride-through video game. Entertainment options starring characters from silver screen cartoons and the equally animated kids from *High School Musical* have also joined the daily lineup. Elsewhere in the state, set-jetting cinephiles can cue the action by following the "Map & Guide to Florida Movies" (available as a brochure through tourism board offices or online at (⊕ www.visitflorida.com/movies). It pinpoints the locations for films from cult classics like *Tarzan* and *Goldfinger* to the Academy Award–winning *Monster*.

It's Magic

Late 2009 will see the much-anticipated opening of "The Wizarding World of Harry Potter"—a magical 20-acre venue to be set within Universal's Islands of Adventure. In addition to the requisite rides, this new park will conjure up charming locales (like Hogwarts Castle and the Forbidden Forest), which are usually off-limits to mere Muggles. The shops and restaurants of Hogsmeade are to be replicated too, creating ample opportunities for wizard-themed merchandising. While waiting for Harry Potter to appear, Universal is relying on another boy wonder—Bart Simpson—to pull in crowds. He and the rest of the quirky Springfield crowd took over the old "Back to the Future" site when "The Simpsons" attraction launched in Spring 2008.

Eat, Sleep, and be Merry

Fine hotels and fine restaurants have long gone together, especially in South Florida (the Delano and the Blue Door? Hellooo!). Now that trend accelerates with the introduction of celeb chef Michael Mina's Bourbon Steak at the Fairmont Turnberry Isle Resort & Club. Michael Blum, meanwhile, has pulled up stakes and moved Michael's Kitchen from its original Hollywood location to the Newport Beachside Hotel & Resort in Sunny Isles. Also on the move: Norman Van Aken, who has closed his eponymous Coral Gables eatery and transferred his star power to the Tavern N Town at the new Beachside Resort in Key West. Next up is Daniel Boulud, who'll get cooking at the Miami Met Marquis when that hotel opens its doors in 2009.

Inn Flux

Proposals for countless condo complexes have been shelved because of the residential real-estate market's precipitous drop. However, it appears that many optimistic hotel builders are going ahead as planned with construction. Greater Orlando, as you might expect, will lead the pack in terms of quantity. Hoteliers there hope to unlock more than 10,000 new guest rooms by the end of 2009. Greater Fort Lauderdale, conversely, is a strong contender when it comes to quality. Having already opened upscale St. Regis, Hilton, and Crowne Plaza resorts in 2007, it welcomed the state's first W Hotel in 2008. Two further luxury projects (one from Trump International, the other affiliated with German-based WorldHotels) are in the works for 2009.

The Comeback Kids

Over the past 25 years Florida's New Urbanism movement has generated a lot of ink. The concept of newly-built but nostalgia-inducing towns filled with vernacular architecture was virtually invented here; and communities like Seaside are still New Urbanism's gold standard. Now, old urbanism is making headlines too, with cities statewide undergoing a renaissance of sorts. For instance, mixed-use developments and beautification projects in West Palm Beach are turning the Clematis District into a textbook example of downtown revitalization. Tampa's burgeoning Riverwalk, similarly, will get an added boost once the new History Center debuts in late 2008. An art museum, a children's museum, and enhanced green spaces will follow in 2009.

FAQS

I'm not crazy about spending seven nights in hotels. Any affordable alternatives? If you want to pretend you're lucky enough to live here, try a vacation rental. Aside from providing privacy, rentals let you set your own schedule and do your own cooking. The caveat is you'll likely have to rent in weekly—not nightly—increments. Several companies specialize in the Orlando area, Magical Memories (☎407/390–8200 or 800/736–0402 ⊕www.magicalmemories. com) being one reliable bet. However, in terms of coverage, geographically and price-wise, HomeAway (⊕www.home away.com) is the winner, listing more than 10,000 Floridian condos, cottages, beach houses, and villas. *See also* Apartment & House Rentals *under* Accomodations *in the* Essentials *chapter.*

How do I pick between Orlando's parks and Tampa's Busch Gardens? That's a tough call: especially now that both boast new must-see attractions, the most significant being Aquatica at SeaWorld and Jungala at Busch Gardens. The good news is you don't have to choose, because the Busch Gardens Shuttle Express (☎800/221–1339 ⊕www.mearstransportation.com) offers same-day round-trip service between designated locations in Orlando and the Tampa venue for only $10. When you buy a five-park Orlando Flex Ticket (good for 14 days unlimited admission to Universal, Islands of Adventure, SeaWorld, Wet 'n Wild, and Busch Gardens) the bus trip is complimentary.

What's the easiest way to reach Key West? Though it has its own international airport (☎305/296–7223 ⊕www.keywestinternationalairport.com), flights are frequently cancelled due to fuel costs and passenger counts. So driving via the 110-mi Overseas Highway (AKA US1) is preferred. Those unwilling to tackle the route's 43 bridges and peak-time traffic can take Greyhound's (☎800/231–2222 ⊕www.greyhound. com) Keys Shuttle, which has multiple daily departures from Miami International Airport. The Conch Republic can also be approached by cruise ship (it welcomes 660,000 passengers per year), or by high-speed catamaran (☎866/593–3779 ⊕www.seakeywestexpress.com) from Miami, Fort Meyers, and Marco Island.

Is Miami OK for families? Absolutely. Despite the attention paid to G-strings, it retains real G-rated appeal. Beyond the beaches, attractions like the interactive Children's Museum and the Museum of Science (which houses a planetarium plus hands-on exhibits) draw kids in droves. Want to go wild? Bypass the nightclubs and head to MetroZoo or Seaquarium. If you dream of being named "best parent ever," sign your offspring up for a junior zookeeper program at the former or a dolphin swim. Easy access to family-friendly adventures in the Everglades and Biscayne National Park is an added bonus.

Where can I find the real Florida? Well, if by "real" you mean untouristed, the state's northern reaches are a good place to start looking. Small towns like Apalachicola, Micanopy, and Quincy—where people still sip sweet tea on porch swings—are Florida's answer to classic Americana. There are larger centers, too, that remain off the radar despite their urban amenities. Take oh-so-Southern Tallahassee, with its historic buildings, grand canopy roads, and distinct antebellum charm. The city is hardly undiscovered: the state capital is here. Yet in tourism terms it appears to be "hiding in plain sight."

The Panhandle

Pensacola

WORD OF MOUTH

"The best beaches in Florida are on the Panhandle around Destin/Ft. Walton to Seagrove Beach and Seaside, FL. There is pretty good snorkeling off the jetties near the state park off the east end of Panama City Beach—lots of fish to be seen. There are crowded stretches, but there are also stretches relatively uncrowded for miles and miles."

—bkluvsNola

WELCOME TO THE PANHANDLE

TOP REASONS TO GO

★ **The Beaches:** Most of the Panhandle's Gulf Coast shoreline is relatively unobstructed by high-rise condos and hotels, and the white-powder sand is alluring.

★ **The History:** Spanish, Native American, and, later, French and English influences shaped the direction of this region and are well represented in architecture, historic sites, and museums.

★ **The Pace:** The Panhandle is sometimes referred to as "LA," Lower Alabama. Southern through and through, the pace here in some places is as slow as molasses—a fact Tallahassee plays up by claiming to be "Florida with a Southern accent."

★ **The Capital:** As the state capital (chosen because it was midway between the two earlier Spanish headquarters of St. Augustine and Pensacola), Tallahassee remains intriguing thanks to its history, historical museums, universities, and quiet country charm.

1 Around Pensacola Bay. By preserving architecture from early Spanish settlements, the city earns points for retaining the influence of these early explorers. The downtown district is compact and unique, plus there's the city's Naval Air Museum and its nearby beaches.

2 The Gulf Coast. The Eglin Air Force Base and adjoining nature reserve span thousands of square miles of Gulf Coast land, and they don't plan to surrender it anytime soon. Miles of shoreline between Pensacola and Destin is nearly void of development, and farther east even the urban areas like Destin, Panama City Beach, Seaside, and Apalachicola, has beaches that are well-preserved and inviting.

2

GETTING ORIENTED

The Panhandle is a huge area, and the lack of sufficient air service can make it tough to access. That said, two major east–west routes will introduce you to some fantastic back roads and waterfront drives. From Tallahassee, Highway 90 is an early byway that roughly parallels its modern cousin, Interstate 10, but goes through small Old Florida towns like Marianna, Chipley, and DeFuniak Springs on its way to Pensacola. From Pensacola, Highway 98 generally skirts along the Gulf of Mexico through seaside towns and communities like Fort Walton Beach, Destin, Panama City Beach, Seaside, and Apalachicola.

3 Inland Across the Panhandle. The shoreline gets most of the tourist business, so the areas north of it are lightly trafficked, giving this region great appeal with access to Old Florida's small towns, quiet roads, rolling hills, and deep forests.

4 Tallahassee. If you're visiting the Panhandle to see the old and new state capitol, the state's historical museum, attend an FSU football game, watch the famous FAMU Marching 100, or go for a country ride down canopy roads, Tallahassee is where you can do it all.

THE PANHANDLE PLANNER

When to Go

Peak season is Memorial Day to Labor Day, with another spike during Spring Break. Inland, especially in Tallahassee, high season is during the fall (football) and March–April. Vendors, attractions, and other activities will be in full swing in the summer. There's a "secret season" that falls around October and November. Things quiet down as students go back to school, but restaurants and attractions still keep normal hours and the weather is moderate. If you can time your trip for that period, you may enjoy the best of both worlds.

Flying In

None of Florida's major airports are in the Panhandle, but Pensacola, Tallahassee, and Panama City make do with their smaller airports. Many of the major carriers will stop by at least one of these facilities. The cost of flying in can be higher than arriving at a major hub—but it may compare to driving in from Orlando or Tampa or Jacksonville, which can be a far stretch. Pensacola is less than an hour's drive from Mobile, Alabama, and New Orleans is 200 miles (3 hours) away.

For more flight information see By Air in Essentials at the end of this chapter.

About the Restaurants

An abundance of seafood is served at coastal restaurants: oysters, crab, shrimp, scallops, and a variety of fish. Of course, that's not all there is on the menu. This part of Florida still impresses diners with old-fashioned comfort foods like meat loaf, fried chicken, beans and cornbread, okra, fried green tomatoes, and the like. You'll also find small-town seafood shacks where you can dine "Florida Cracker"–style on deep-fried mullet, cheese grits, coleslaw, and hush puppies. Restaurants, like resorts, vary their operating tactics off-season, so call first if visiting during winter months.

About the Hotels

Many of the lodging options here revolve around extended-stay options: resorts, condos, and time shares that allow for a week or more in simple efficiencies as well as fully-furnished homes. There are also cabins, such as the ones that rest between the dunes at Grayton Beach. In any case, these are great for families and get-togethers, allowing you to do your own housekeeping and cooking and explore the area without tour guides. Local visitors bureaus often act as clearinghouses for these types of properties, and you can also search online for vacation rentals. On the coast, but especially inland, the choices seem geared more toward mom-and-pop motels in addition to the usual line of chain hotels.

What It Costs

DINING & LODGING PRICE CATEGORIES

	¢	$	$$	$$$	$$$$
Restaurants	under $10	$10–$15	$15–$20	$20–$30	over $30
Hotels	under $80	$80–$100	$100–$140	$140–$220	over $220

Restaurant prices are per person for a main course at dinner. Hotel prices are for a standard double room, excluding 6% sales tax (more in some counties) and 1%–4% tourist tax.

By Gary
McKechnie

FLORIDA'S THIN, GREEN NORTHWEST CORNER snuggles up between the Gulf of Mexico and the Alabama and Georgia state lines. Known as the Panhandle, it's sometimes called "the other Florida," since in addition to palm trees what thrives here are the magnolias, live oaks, and loblolly pines common in the rest of the Deep South. As south Florida's season is winding down in May, action in the northwest is just picking up. The area is even in a different time zone: the Apalachicola River marks the dividing line between Eastern and Central time. Until World War II, when activity at the Panhandle air bases took off, this section of the state was little known and seldom visited. But by the mid-1950s, the 100-mi stretch along the coast between Pensacola and Panama City was dubbed the Miracle Strip because of a dramatic rise in property values. In the 1940s this beachfront land sold for less than $100 an acre; today that same acre can fetch hundreds of thousands of dollars. To convey the richness of the region, with its white sands and sparkling green waters, swamps, bayous, and flora, public-relations pros ditched the Redneck Riviera moniker that locals had created and coined the phrase Emerald Coast.

Politicians, developers, and community advocates haggle continuously over waterfront development, but despite unfortunate pro-growth realities, the Panhandle remains, for the time being, a land of superlatives: it has the biggest military installation in the Western Hemisphere (Eglin Air Force Base), many of Florida's most glorious white-sand beaches, and the most productive fishing waters in the world (off Destin). It has glitzy resorts, campgrounds where possums and deer invite themselves to lunch, and every kind of lodging in between. Students of the past can wander the many historic districts or visit archaeological digs. For sports enthusiasts there's a different golf course or tennis court for each day of the week, and for nature lovers there's a world of hunting, canoeing, biking, and hiking. And most anything that happens on water happens here, including scuba diving and plenty of fishing, both from deep-sea charter boats or the end of a pier.

EXPLORING THE PANHANDLE

There are sights in the Panhandle, but sightseeing is not the principal activity here. The area is better known for its rich history, military presence, and ample fishing and diving spots, and for being a spot to simply relax.

Florida's westernmost city, Pensacola, with its antebellum homes and historic landmarks, is a good place to start your trek through northwest Florida. After exploring the museums and preservation districts, head east on coastal Highway 98 to Fort Walton Beach, the Emerald Coast's largest city, and on to neighboring Destin, where

> **WORD OF MOUTH**
>
> "Depending on what part of the Panhandle you are going to, you could fly into either Pensacola or Tallahassee. If you go to the Grayton-Seagrove area, I think Pensacola might be closer."
>
> –cheryllj

sportfishing is king. Continuing along the coast, there are a dozen or so family-friendly communities collectively known as the Beaches of South Walton, where sugar-white, quartz-crystal sands and emerald-green waters make for some of the finest beaches in the country. This is also where you'll find some of the Panhandle's newest, most luxurious developments, such as WaterColor, where luxury meets modern seaside chic in smartly designed vacation homes and intimate inns. The next resort center along the coast is Panama City Beach—just look for the construction cranes—whereas to the far southeast is historic Apalachic-ola, the Panhandle's oyster-fishing capital. Just south of Apalachicola, St. George Island, a 28-mi-long barrier island bordered by the Gulf and Apalachicola Bay, has vacation homes on one end and a pristine state park on the other. Inland, a number of interesting towns and state parks lie along Interstate 10, which crosses the historic Suwannee River on its long eastward trek to the state capital, Tallahassee.

SCENIC ROUTE — Instead of Interstate 10, take Highway 90: it's the less-traveled, original, two-lane back road that takes you directly through the cute communities of Quincy, Marianna, Chipley, DeFuniak Springs, Crestview, and Milton.

AROUND PENSACOLA BAY

In the years since its founding, Pensacola has come under the control of five nations, earning this fine, old Southern city its nickname, the City of Five Flags. Spanish conquistadors, under the command of Don Tristan de Luna, landed on the shores of Pensacola Bay in 1559, but discouraged by a succession of destructive tropical storms and dissension in the ranks, de Luna abandoned the settlement two years after its founding. In 1698 the Spanish again established a fort at the site, and during the early 18th century control jockeyed between the Spanish, the French, and the British. Finally, in 1821 Pensacola passed into U.S. hands, although during the Civil War it was governed by the Confederate States of America and flew yet another flag. The city itself has many historic sights, however. Across the bay lies Pensacola Beach on Santa Rosa Island, an area still recovering from the devastation caused by Hurricane Ivan in 2004.

PENSACOLA

59 mi east of Mobile, Alabama.

Historic Pensacola consists of three distinct districts—Seville, Palafox, and North Hill—though they are easy to explore as a unit. Stroll down streets mapped out by the British and renamed by the Spanish, such as Cervantes, Palafox, Intendencia, and Tarragona. An influx of restaurants and bars is bringing new nightlife to the historic districts, but one-way streets can make navigation a bit tricky, especially at night. In late 2004 Hurricane Ivan blew through, downing many of the town's stately oak trees, severely damaging countless homes and commercial properties, washing out bayfront roadways and a stretch of Interstate

10, and scaring the heck out of residents. The Pensacola Bay area has made great strides rebuilding paradise after Ivan's hit-and-run, and years later, recovery efforts continue. One example is at the southern terminus of Palafox Street—the $2.3 million Plaza DeLuna, a 2-acre park with open grounds, interactive water fountains, and an amphitheater. A quiet place to sit and watch the bay, fish, or enjoy the city's Thursday evening sunset celebration, the park occupies the former site of the Bayfront Auditorium, which was wrecked by Ivan.

The best way to orient yourself is to stop at the **Pensacola Visitor Information Center,** at the foot of the Pensacola Bay Bridge. Pick up maps here of the self-guided historic-district tours. ✉*1401 E. Gregory St.* ☎*850/434–1234 or 800/874–1234* ⊕*www.visitpensacola.com.*

Established in 1559, the **Seville Square Historic District** is the site of Pensacola's first permanent Spanish colonial settlement, which beat St. Augustine's by six years. Its center is Seville Square, a live oak–shaded park bounded by Alcaniz, Adams, Zaragoza, and Government streets. Roam these brick streets past honeymoon cottages and homes set in an oak-filled parklike setting. Many of the buildings have been converted into restaurants, commercial offices, and shops that overlook broad Pensacola Bay and coastal road Highway 98, which you'll use to access the Gulf Coast and beaches. For information on home and museum tours, contact Historic Pensacola Village.

Within the Seville district is the **Historic Pensacola Village,** a complex of several museums and historic homes whose indoor and outdoor exhibits trace the area's history back 450 years. The Museum of Industry (✉*200 E. Zaragoza St.*), in a late-19th-century warehouse, is home to permanent exhibits dedicated to the lumber, maritime, and shipping industries—once mainstays of Pensacola's economy. A reproduction of a 19th-century streetscape is displayed in the Museum of Commerce (✉ *201 E. Zaragoza St.*). Also in the village are the Julee Cottage (✉*210 E. Zaragoza St.*), the "first home owned by a free woman of color," Dorr House (✉*311 S. Adams St.*), Lavalle House (✉*205 E. Church St.*), and Quina House (✉*204 S. Alcaniz St.*). Strolling through the area gives you a good look at many architectural styles, but to enter some of the buildings you must purchase an all-inclusive ticket at the Village gift shop in the Tivoli High House—which was once in the city's red-light district but now is merely a calm reflection of a restored home. Opt for the guided tour (11 AM, 1 PM, and 2:30 PM), and you'll experience the history of Pensacola as you visit the 1805 Lavalle House, the 1871 Dorr House, Old Christ Church, and the 1890s Lear-Rocheblave House. Tours last approximately 90 minutes to two hours. *Tivoli High House* ✉*205 E. Zaragoza St.* ☎*850/595–5985* ⊕*www.historic pensacola.org* 🎫*$6 includes tour and Wentworth Museum* ⊘*Mon.– Sat. 10–4* ☎*850/595–5993* ⊕*www.historicpensacola.org.*

☾ Even if you don't like museums, this is worth a look. The **T. T. Wentworth Jr. Florida State Museum,** housed in the elaborate, Renaissance Revival–style former city hall, has an interesting mix of exhibits illustrating life in the Florida Panhandle over the centuries. Mr. Wentworth was quite

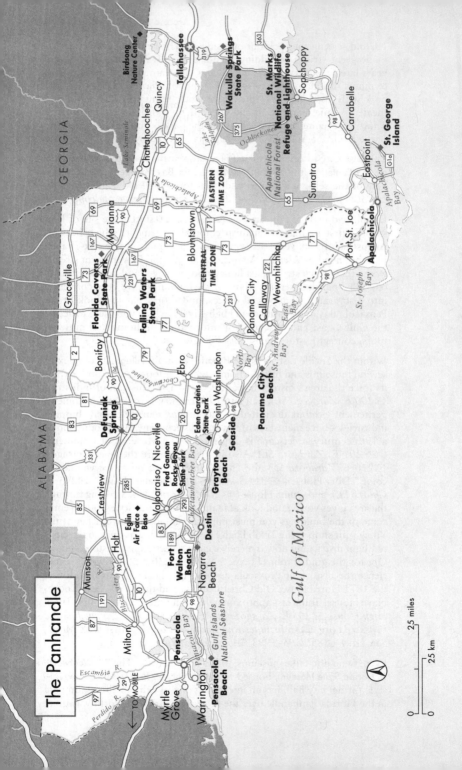

GREAT ITINERARIES

3 DAYS

History and nature are the two biggest calling cards of this part of the Sunshine State. Visit **Grayton Beach** and **Seaside** and take advantage of some of Florida's finest beaches. On Day 2 drive to the capital, **Tallahassee**, and soak up some of the state's past. On Day 3, make a trip to nearby **Wakulla Springs State Park**, where you'll find one of the world's deepest springs—perfect for sightseeing (the pontoon boat tour is a must) and swimming.

5 DAYS

Start with **Tallahassee**. Check out the local sights, including the State Capitol building, the Tallahassee Historic Trail, and Maclay Gardens State Park. Take another day day trip to head west on Interstate 10, visiting **Falling Waters State Park**

in Chipley in the morning and then exploring the cool, dark caves of the **Florida Caverns State Park** in Marianna in the afternoon when things heat up: you'll be amazed that such an extensive cave system exists anywhere in the Sunshine State. On Day 3, head south out of Tallahassee toward **Wakulla Springs State Park**, where you can explore the spectacular springs either with a mask and snorkel or from inside a glass-bottom boat. In the afternoon, head down to **St. Marks National Wildlife Refuge and Lighthouse** to hike, swim, or have a leisurely picnic. Eventually make your way to the coast and take Highway 98 west toward Apalachicola.

In **Apalachicola**, spend a day wandering around the historic downtown area and the waterfront, and spend another day on **St. George Island**.

a collector (as well as politician and salesman), and his eccentric collection includes a mummified cat (creepy) and the size 37 left shoe of Robert Wadlow, the world's tallest man (not creepy, but a really big shoe). Check out the exhibit that compares the devastating effects of 2004's Hurricane Ivan with a similarly destructive unnamed hurricane that blew through in 1926. Eerie. ⊠ *330 S. Jefferson St.* ☎ *850/595–5990* 🖃 *Free* ⊙ *Mon.–Sat. 10–4.*

Palafox Street is the main stem of historic downtown Pensacola and the center of the **Palafox Historic District.** The commercial and government hub of Old Pensacola is now an active cultural and retail district. Note the opulent Spanish Renaissance–style **Saenger Theater,** Pensacola's 1925 movie palace, which now hosts performances by the local symphony and opera, and the **Bear Block,** a former wholesale grocery with wrought-iron balconies that are a legacy from Pensacola's Creole past. On Palafox between Government and Zaragoza streets is a **statue of Andrew Jackson** that commemorates the formal transfer of Florida from Spain to the United States in 1821. While in the area, stop by Veterans Memorial Park, just off Bayfront Parkway near 9th Avenue. The ¾-scale replica of the Vietnam Memorial in Washington, D.C., honors the more than 58,000 Americans who lost their lives in the Vietnam War.

Pensacola's city jail once occupied the 1906 Spanish Revival–style building that is now the **Pensacola Museum of Art.** It provides a secure home (you can still see the actual cells with their huge iron doors) for the museum's permanent collection of paintings, sculptures, and works on paper by 20th- and 21st-century artists; traveling exhibits have focused on photography (Wegman, Leibovitz), Dutch masters, regional artists, and the occasional art-world icon, such as Andy Warhol or Salvador Dalí. ✉️*407 S. Jefferson St.* ☎️*850/432–6247* 🌐*www.pensacolamuseumofart.org* 💲*$5, free Tues.* 🕐*Tues.–Fri. 10–5, weekends noon–5.*

> **TOP GUN**
>
> The National Museum of Naval Aviation is one of only two locations nationwide that feature four real F-14 military flight-training simulators with all the actual controls. Experience mock air-to-air combat, practice carrier landings, or simply cruise over Las Vegas, Iraq, Miramar, California, and other simulated sites during a 20-minute joyride. The $25 experience includes "cockpit orientation training."

Locals almost unanimously suggest this as *the* must-see attraction of Pensacola. As you drive over to the **Pensacola Naval Air Station,** don't be alarmed if you're suddenly struck with the shakes—they're probably caused by the U.S. Navy's Blue Angel aerobatic squadron buzzing overhead. This is their home base, and they practice maneuvers here on Tuesday and Wednesday mornings at 8:30 from March to November. Public viewing is allowed from an area along the runway just behind the National Museum of Naval Aviation. So cover your ears as the six F/A-18s blast off in unison for 45 minutes of thrills and skill. Now that you're awake, you can fully appreciate the 300,000-square-foot **National Museum of Naval Aviation** (☎️*850/452–3604*), with examples of more than 140 aircraft that played important roles in aviation history. Among them are the NC-4, which in 1919 became the first plane to cross the Atlantic; the famous World War II fighter the F6 *Hellcat;* and the Skylab Command Module. Other attractions include an atomic bomb (they assure us it's defused), *Mercury* and *Apollo* capsules, and the restored Cubi Bar Café, a very cool former airmen's club transplanted here from the Philippines. Relive the morning's maneuvers in the 14-seat motion-based simulator as well as an IMAX theater playing *Fighter Pilot, The Magic of Flight* and other educational films, such as *Deep Sea* and *Hurricane on the Bayou.* ✉️*1750 Radford Blvd.* ☎️*850/453–2389, 800/327–5002, 850/453–2024 IMAX theater* 🌐*www.navalaviationmuseum.org* 💲*Free, IMAX film $8, two films for $13* 🕐*Daily 9–5.*

Dating from the Civil War, **Fort Barrancas** has picnic areas and a ½-mi woodland nature trail on its grounds. The fort, which is just northeast of the Museum of Naval Aviation, is part of the Gulf Islands National Seashore, maintained by the National Park Service. ✉️*Taylor Rd.* ☎️*850/455–5167* 💲*Free* 🕐*Nov.–Feb., daily 8:30–3:45; Mar.–Oct., daily 9:30–4:45.*

OFF THE BEATEN PATH

The ZOO. The local zoo, about 12 mi east of Pensacola, near Gulf Breeze, has more than 1,400 animals and assorted critters, including many endangered species. Kids especially enjoy the petting zoo, where they can touch most every style of live-stock on Old MacDonald's Farm. Other attractions yield tigers, zebras, and such unusual creatures as African wild dogs and pygmy hippos, and there's a tall platform where you can have face-to-face meetings with giraffes. The Safari Line Limited train runs through 30 acres of free-roaming animals in their natural habitats. ⊠*5701 Gulf Breeze Pkwy., Gulf Breeze* ☎*850/932–2229* ⊕*www.thezoonorthwest-florida.org* ☜*$11.50 (safari train $3 extra)* ☉*Daily 9–5 during standard time; daily 9–4 during daylight saving time.*

> **HEADS UP!**
>
> Watching the Blue Angels practice their aerobatics is one of the best "free" shows in all of Florida (your tax dollars are already pay-ing for these jets). The Naval Air Station's bleachers hold about 1,000 people and they fill up fast, so get here early. Then stay late—the pilots stick around after the show to shake hands and sign autographs.

WHERE TO EAT

$$$ ✕ **Global Grill.** When you have an appetite that begs for variety, con-sider this trendy yet friendly downtown Pensacola tapas restaurant. Come hungry and fill your eyes, plate, and belly from the selection of 45 different tapas, like the high-demand quick-fried calamari with gar-lic squash fries, the spicy seared tuna with five-pepper jelly, or the pork empanadas with cucumber cream. Wear an elastic waistband, because you may be tempted to try the 42 others. To jazz things up, entrées have been added as well, with filet mignon, Gulf shrimp, duck breast, grou-per, salmon, and NY strip competing with the light appetizers. ⊠*27 S. Palafox* ☎*850/469–9966* ☐*AE, MC, V* ☉ *Closed Sun. and Mon.*

$$–$$$ ✕ **Dharma Blue.** Geographically speaking, this trendy spot is in down-town Pensacola, on leafy Seville Square, but culinarily speaking it's all over the map. The menu roams from Asia (sushi and spring-roll appe-tizers) to Italy (panéed chicken) to Mexico (lime-roasted chicken quesa-dilla) to the American South (fried-green-tomato club sandwich)—but just stick close to home and you won't be disappointed. The lunch menu includes barbecued salmon with lemon coleslaw and Texas toast, focaccia BLT, or fish-and-chips. For dinner try tomato-crusted grou-per with caper cream sauce, the fish of the day (blackened, grilled, or tempura-fried), or Guinness-marinated sirloin with chipotle aioli. Dine inside under a collection of Southern folk art, or outside under café umbrellas and droopy oaks. ⊠*300 S. Alcaniz St.* ☎*850/433–1275* ☐*AE, MC, V* ☉*No lunch Sun.*

$$–$$$ ✕ **Fish House.** Come one, come all, come hungry, and come at 11 AM to witness the calm before the lunch storm. By noon the Fish House is packed with Pensacola's professionals, power players, and poseurs, all waiting for tables and the fresh fish brought in on the docks steps away. The wide-ranging menu of fish dishes served broiled, blackened, or fried is the bait—and when they're flavored with Asian and Euro-pean spices, it puts it over the top. The attentive service, bayfront set-

ting, and signature "Grits a Ya-Ya" dish (fresh gulf shrimp on a bed of smoked Gouda-cheese grits smothered with a portobello-mushroom sauce) keeps diners in the net. Steaks, delicious homemade desserts, a sushi bar, more than 300 varieties of wine, and a full-service bar don't hurt the extraordinary popularity of this restaurant either. The hot-ticket table is one out on the deck at sunset. ☒ *600 South Barracks St.* ☎*850/470–0003* ☐*AE, MC, V.*

$$–$$$ ✗ **McGuire's Irish Pub.** Since 1977 this authentic Irish pub has promised its patrons "feasting, imbibery, and debauchery" seven nights a week. And the floor-to-ceiling decor does wonders for the experience, suggesting that you may actually be dining in Dublin. A sense of humor pervades the place, evidenced by the range of prices on hamburgers—from $10 to $100 depending on whether you want it topped with cheddar or served with caviar and champagne. Beer is brewed on the premises, and the wine cellar has more than 8,500 bottles. Menu items include corned beef and cabbage and a hickory-smoked prime rib. In an old firehouse, the pub is replete with antiques, moose heads, Tiffany-style lamps, and Erin-go-bragh memorabilia. As for the "richness" of the decor, on the walls and ceiling are more than 550,000 dollar bills signed and dated by "Irishmen of all nationalities." ☒ *600 E. Gregory St.* ☎*850/433–2849 or 850/433–6789* ☐*AE, D, DC, MC, V.*

$–$$$ ✗ **Mesquite Charlie's.** Saddle up and head on over to this Wild West saloon, with brick walls, arched doorways, mounted game, and a second-floor balcony overlooking the lobby. All that's missing are the swinging doors. The 32-ounce porterhouse is large enough to satisfy a posse of cowboys and, in a publicity schtick lifted straight from a *Simpsons* episode, the monster-size 76-ounce sirloin is free if you finish it—along with your baked potato, baked beans, salad, and bread—in less than an hour (otherwise you'll pay $49.99). All steaks are charbroiled with 100% mesquite charcoal and seasoned with natural spices. ☒ *5901 N. W St.* ☎*850/434–0498* ☐*AE, D, MC, V.*

$–$$ ✗ **Ragtyme Grille.** Downtown's historic Economy Shoe Repair building now houses this intimate corner eatery that's become a favorite of local journalists (the *Pensacola News-Journal* offices are across the street). Choose from standard deli sandwiches (Reubens, corned beef), po'boys, and grilled fish specials; salads—with fresh fish, fruit, or chicken—and burgers round out the menu. Grab a table inside, or relax over a beer, margarita, or glass of wine on the covered patio. ☒ *201 S. Jefferson St.* ☎*850/429–9655* ☐*AE, MC, V.*

WHERE TO STAY

$$–$$$ ⊞ **Crowne Plaza–Pensacola Grand Hotel.** The Crowne Plaza is on the site of the restored historic Louisville & Nashville (L&N) railroad passenger depot, which now houses the lobby, lounges, shops, and 7,500 square feet of meeting space. After a complete smackdown by Hurricane Ivan in 2004, it took this local institution two years to shake itself off and reopen its doors. Its rich heritage remains: A 15-story glass tower, attached to the train depot by a glass atrium, features guest rooms with all new furniture, and incredible views of historic Pensacola. Bi-level penthouse suites have whirlpool baths. **Pros:** Great location near downtown, amenities perfect for business travelers. **Cons:** Aside from the historic station, it's a box; there are more intimate choices closer to downtown. ✉ *200 E. Gregory St.,* ☎ *850/433–3336 or 800/348–3336* ⊕ *www.pensacolagrandhotel.com* ⤳ *200 rooms, 10 suites* ⚷ *In-hotel: restaurant, bar, pool, gym, airport shuttle* ⊟ *AE, D, DC, MC, V.*

★ **$$-$$$**   ☷ **New World Inn.** If you like your inns small, warm, and cozy, with the bay on one side and a short two-block walk to the downtown historic area, then this is the inn for you. A complete makeover of the rooms was completed in 2007, with new bedding, carpeting, and wallpaper sprucing up rooms reflecting five periods of Pensacola's past: French and Spanish provincial, early American, antebellum, and Queen Anne. Several rooms have four-poster mahogany beds, and the rooms are large and comfortable, but the old-style furnishings might benefit from a little new-world dusting. A complimentary breakfast consists of pastries and boxed cereals. The lobby's collection of signed portraits of famous (and formerly famous) guests is a hoot. **Pros:** Perfect location downtown, with the unique decor of a boutique hotel. **Cons:** Could use a spring cleaning atop the room renovations. ✉ *600 S. Palafox St.* ☎ *850/432–4111* ⊕ *www.newworldlanding.com* ⤳ *14 rooms, 1 suite* ⚷ *In-room: hair dryers, iron and ironing board, coffee maker, Wi-Fi. In-hotel: restaurant, wine and martini bar, free continental breakfast* ⊟ *AE, MC, V* ⊙ *CP.*

$$-$$$ ☷ **Residence Inn by Marriott.** In the downtown bayfront area, this immaculately kept all-suites hotel is perfect for extended stays, whether for business or pleasure. The location is ideal for exploring Pensacola's historic streets on foot—rooms in the back have views of the bay—and families will especially appreciate the extra sleeper sofa, fully equipped kitchens, and free grocery delivery. Breakfast and evening social hour are complimentary. **Pros:** Self-serve meal and dining options make a family retreat easier. **Cons:** Ordinary hotel style. ✉ *601 E. Chase St.,* ☎ *850/432–0202* ⊕ *www.residenceinn.com* ⤳ *78 suites* ⚷ *In-room: kitchen, refrigerator. In-hotel: tennis court, pool, gym, some pets allowed (fee)* ⊟ *AE, D, DC, MC, V.*

NIGHTLIFE & THE ARTS

THE ARTS   Most cultural and arts offerings in town are conveniently centered around the historic district. The **Pensacola Little Theatre** (✉ *400 S. Jefferson St.* ☎ *850/432–2042* ⊕ *www.pensacolalittletheatre.com*) is a popular little venue for locals, with plays and musicals presented year-round. **Pensacola's Symphony Orchestra** (✉ *205 E. Zaragoza St.* ☎ *850/435–2533* ⊕ *www.pensacolasymphony.com*) offers more than 17 concerts each season at the Saenger Theatre and other locations. Productions at the restored 1925 **Saenger Theatre** (✉ *118 S. Palafox St.* ☎ *850/595–3880* ⊕ *www.pensacolasaenger.com*) include touring Broadway shows and three locally staged operas a year. Additional details can be found at ⊕ www.pensacolaopera.com.

NIGHTLIFE   There's almost as much to do after dark as there is during daylight hours. **Hub Stacey's** (✉ *312 E. Government St.* ☎ *850/469–1001* ⊕ *www.hubstaceys.com*), on the corner by Seville Square, is the friendly neighborhood locale with 55 types of bottled beer, sidewalk tables, and a good vibe. **McGuire's Irish Pub** (✉ *600 E. Gregory St.* ☎ *850/433–6789* ⊕ *www.*

mcguiresirishpub.com) is a restaurant and microbrewery that welcomes those of Irish descent, or anyone else who enjoys cold home-brewed ales, beers, or lagers. Their 8,500-bottle wine cellar includes vintages ranging in price from $14 to $20,000. If you want a quiet drink, steer clear on Friday and Saturday nights—or when Notre Dame games are televised. **Mesquite Charlie's** (⊠*5901 N. W St.* ☎*850/434–0498*) offers country music and all the Western trappings. **New York Nick's** (⊠*9–11 S. Palafox St.* ☎*850/469–1984* ⊕*www.enorthshore.com/nyn*) is a sports bar, rock-and-roll club, shrine to Bruce Springsteen, and popular downtown bar and grill. It's an "A+" spot for all the best "B's" in life—beer, billiards, burgers, and the Boss. **Starbuck's Billiards** (⊠*22 S. Palafox St.* ☎*850/438–9818*) is always hopping, with players lined up at the 20 billiards tables until 2:30 AM. The **Seville Quarter** (⊠*130 E. Government St.* ☎*850/434–6211* ⊕*www.rosies.com*) has nine rooms, seven fabulous bars, and two courtyards, offering everything from disco to dueling pianos, Motown acts, blues bands, and rockabilly trios—you name it. College students pack the place on Thursday, tourists on the weekend, and military men and women from six nearby bases are stationed here nearly all the time. In the heart of the historic district, it's Pensacola's equivalent of New Orleans's French Quarter.

SPORTS & THE OUTDOORS

CANOEING & KAYAKING
Adventures Unlimited (⊠*Rte. 87* ☎*850/623–6197 or 800/239–6864* ⊕*www.adventuresunlimited.com*), on Coldwater Creek, rents light watercraft as well as campsites and cabins along the Coldwater and Blackwater rivers in the Blackwater State Forest. Canoe season lasts roughly from March through mid-November, but they rent year-round. Canoe and kayak rentals for exploring the Blackwater River—the purest sand-bottom river in the nation—are available from **Blackwater Canoe Rental** (⊠*6974 Deaton Bridge Rd., Milton* ☎*850/623–0235 or 800/967–6789* ⊕*www.blackwatercanoe.com*), northeast of Pensacola off Interstate 10 Exit 31.

DIVING
It's called the "Mighty O," but it was formerly known as the **USS** *Oriskany* (⊕*www.mbtdivers.com*).The retired aircraft carrier was sunk 24 mi off the Pensacola Pass in 2006, and now the superstructure is the world's largest artificial reef. The "island" is accessible just 67 feet down, and the flight deck can be reached at 137 feet. Visibility and water temperatures are ideal for a visit, and divers from around the world are jumping in to explore the wrecked reef.

DOG RACING
Rain or shine, year-round there's live racing (as well as simulcast races) at the **Pensacola Greyhound Track.** Lounge and grandstand areas are fully enclosed and air-conditioned and have instant-replay televisions throughout. ⊠*951 Dog Track Rd., West Pensacola* ☎*850/455–8595* ⊕*www.pensacolagreyhoundpark.com* ⊡*Free* ☉*Racing Wed.–Sat. at 7 PM, weekends at 1.* Only simulcast racing on Wed.–Thurs.

FISHING
For a full- or half-day deep-sea charter ($75–$100 per person) that heads 10–20 mi into the Gulf, try the **Beach Marina** (⊠*655 Pensacola Beach Blvd.* ☎*850/932–8466*), which represents several charter outfits. Bottom fishing is best for amberjack and grouper, offshore trolling

trips are searching for tuna, wahoo, and sailfish, and inshore charters are out to hook redfish, cobia, and pompano. For a complete list of local fishing charters, visit ⊕*www.visitpensacola.com.*

GOLF   There are several outstanding golf courses in and around Pensacola, with the fees listed below reflecting a wide range that changes with the season. **The Club at Hidden Creek** (⊠*3070 PGA Blvd., Navarre* ☎*850/939–4604,* ⊕*www.hiddengolf.com*) is an 18-hole course in Santa Rosa County, 20 mi from Pensacola; greens fee $15/$66 with cart. **The Moors Golf Club** (⊠*3220 Avalon Blvd., Milton* ☎*850/994–2744* ⊕*www. moors.com*) is a public, 18-hole, par-70, Scottish links–style course. Greens fee $39/$49. The course was designed by John LaFoy. In Perdido, the **Perdido Bay Golf Club** (⊠*1 Doug Ford Dr.* ☎*850/492–1223,* ⊕*www.perdidobaygolf.com*) has a well-kept 18-hole course. Greens fee $45/$69 with cart. Also in Perdido is the **Lost Key Golf Club** (⊠*625 Lost Key Dr., Perdido Key Beach* ☎*850/492–1300* ⊕*www.lostkey. com*), a public, par-71, 18-hole Arnold Palmer Signature Design Course that was the first golf course in Florida—and the world—to be certified as an Audubon International Silver Signature Sanctuary. Greens fee $70/$99 with cart. **Tiger Point Golf & Country Club** (⊠*1255 Country Club Rd., Gulf Breeze* ☎*850/932–1330,* ⊕*www.tigerpointclub.com*) is a semiprivate 36-hole club. Greens fee $50/$60 with cart.

TENNIS   There are fine public tennis courts in more than 30 locations in the Pensacola area. The **Pensacola Racquet Club** (⊠*3450 Wimbledon Dr.* ☎*850/434–2434,* ⊕*www.pensacolaracquetclub.com*) has 10 Rubico (soft) and 2 hard courts, plus a junior-size Olympic pool with a baby pool and restaurant.

SHOPPING

The Palafox District is an enjoyable area for browsing. The **Quayside Art Gallery** (⊠*17 E. Zaragoza St.* ☎*850/438–2363* ⊕*www.quaysidegallery.com*), the largest co-op art gallery in the Southeast, reopened in November 2005, after Ivan's devastation, with new displays and items by local artists in a variety of mediums. Other shops here display art glass, wood, metal, paintings, and jewelry. Ten miles north of the historic district is the **Cordova Mall** (⊠*5100 N. 9th Ave.* ☎*850/477–5563*), anchored by three department stores, with more than 150 specialty shops and a food court. **Harbourtown Shopping Village** (⊠*913 Gulf Breeze Pkwy., Gulf Breeze*) has trendy shops and the look of a wharfside New England village.

PENSACOLA BEACH

5 mi south of Pensacola via U.S. 98 to Rte. 399 (Bob Sikes) Bridge.

After Hurricane Opal tore across this skinny barrier island in 1995, the damaged areas were redeveloped, sand was brought in to fill the eroded beachfront, and beach facilities and parking were added to what came to be known as the "Opal Day Use Area," named in honor of the hurricane responsible for the destruction. A local bartender even invented a potent but short-lived concoction called a "Raging Opal" to commemorate the storm.

It's doubtful, however, that any public parks or cocktails will be named after Hurricane Ivan, which devastated the area in 2004. The Category 4 storm wasn't an event that anyone around here cares to remember. The storm's tidal surge washed completely over the island in several places, and the obvious reminders of Ivan's visit—washed-out roads, devastated homes, uprooted lives, and erased sand dunes—are still visible and may well be for years to come.

> **WORD OF MOUTH**
>
> "Pensacola Beach has come a long way since Ivan (when most of the damage to the beach occurred, one year before Katrina). The beaches were renourished, the fishing pier rebuilt, and all of the hotels, restaurants and shops are up and running. There is, however, a lot of construction on the island. But, I wouldn't let that stop you from visiting. It's definitely less crowded than Destin!"
>
> –AustinTraveler

Since the national media focused its attention on Pensacola Beach for not much longer than it took the storm to do its damage, the scope of the disaster might come as a surprise to many visitors: nearly half of the island's homes were destroyed; all of the island's hotels were closed for months (some will never reopen); and the miles of sea oat–covered, pristine dunes that protected the island from winter storms and gave the area its laid-back Florida look were leveled in hours. In short, Pensacola Beach is a city changed.

But locals here know the post-hurricane drill: dig in, dig out, and move on. Several hotels have reopened after complete renovations, homes and condos have been demolished or are being rebuilt (such as a new seaside $500 million, 700-hotel/condo unit complex), and city and state crews have made significant progress in reconnecting roads to areas of the island rendered inaccessible by the storm. As of Spring 2008, most roads are open, although the main road that reaches Fort Pickens is still buried under tons of sand. If that's your goal, it's best to call to check on the status before paying the $1 toll to cross the bridge to reach Pensacola Beach.

Dotting the 150-mi stretch between Destin, Florida, and Gulfport, Mississippi, is **Gulf Islands National Seashore** (☎ 850/934–2600 ⊕ www. nps.gov/guis), managed by the National Park Service. The Gulf Islands National Seashore, which bookends Pensacola beach on the east and west with miles of unsullied, undeveloped beach, has reopened, and the main road—buried under 5 mi of sand after Ivan—is expected, as of this writing, to be cleared by mid-2009. Once accessible (call to verify) Fort Pickens Road will permit access to Fort Pickens (see below), a pre-Civil War–era brick fortress. At **Opal Beach Day Use Area** (✉ Rte. 399, 5 mi east of Pensacola Beach) you'll find pristine coastline, barbecue areas, covered picnic facilities, and restrooms. At the western tip of the island and part of the Gulf Islands National Seashore, **Fort Pickens** dates to 1834. Constructed of more than 21 million locally made bricks, the fort once served as a prison for Apache chief Geronimo. A National

2

Park Service plaque describes the complex as a "confusing jumble of fortifications," but the real attractions here are the beach, nature exhibits, a large campground, an excellent gift shop, and breathtaking views of Pensacola Bay and the lighthouse across the inlet. It's the perfect place for a picnic lunch and a bit of history, too. ⊠ *Ft. Pickens Rd.* ☎*850/934–2635* ⊠*$8 per car* ⊙*Daily 7–sunset.*

The 1,471-foot-long **Pensacola Beach Gulf Pier** touts itself as the longest pier on the Gulf of Mexico. This peerless pier hosts serious anglers who find everything they'll need here—from pole rentals to bait—to land that big one, but those looking to catch only a beautiful sunset are welcome, too. Check the pier's Web site for the latest reports on what's biting. ⊠*41 Ft. Pickens Rd.* ☎*850/934–7200* ⊕*www.fishpensacola beachpier.com* ⊠*Observers $1, fishing $6.50.*

WHERE TO EAT & STAY

$–$$$ ✕ **Flounder's Chowder and Ale House.** The wide and peaceful Gulf spreads out before you at this casual restaurant where, armed with a fruity libation, you're all set for a night of "floundering" at its best. Funkiness comes courtesy of an eclectic collection of objets d'art; tastiness is served in specialties such as seafood nachos and the shrimp boat platter. Most signature dishes are charboiled over a hardwood fire, and to cater to those who love the sea but not seafood, the extensive menu reveals more choices. Live entertainment is presented every night in season, with performances limited to weekends off-season ⊠*800 Quietwater Beach Blvd.* ☎*850/932–2003* ⊟*AE, D, DC, MC, V.*

$$–$$$ ▥ **Perdido Sun.** If you plan a stay of more than a few days, consider the all-inclusive offerings of a one-, two-, or three-bedroom decorator-furnished condo. A fully-equipped kitchen and majestic balconies with spectacular seaside views give you your personal paradise right on the water. Individual ownership means each unit offers unique decor and varied options such as double, queen, and king beds, videos and games (or not); and whichever unit you reserve you can count on cleanliness. Unlike a hotel, however, daily maid service is not included in the room rate, which can vary widely depending on the number of rooms and season. Still, a small concession for a grand location. **Pros:** Almost like owning a waterfront home. Great location, all-inclusive. **Cons:** Units lack the simplicity of a basic room if you're just on an overnight; and on longer stays you'll be doing the housework. ⊠*13753 Perdido Key Dr., Perdido Key* ☎*850/492–2390 or 800/227–2390* ⊕*www.perdidosun.com* ⟺*93 condos* ♿*In-hotel: pools, gym, beachfront* ⊟*AE, D, MC, V.*

THE GULF COAST

On U.S. 98, several towns, each with its own personality, are strung along the shoreline from Pensacola southeast to St. George Island. The twin cities of Destin and Fort Walton Beach seemingly merge into one sprawling destination and continue to spread as more condominiums, resort developments, shopping centers, and restaurants crowd the skyline each year. The view changes drastically—and for the better—farther along the coast as you enter the quiet stretch known as the Beaches of

South Walton, scattered along Route 30A, the main coastal road. Here building restrictions prohibit high-rise developments, and the majority of dwellings are privately owned homes, most of which are available to vacationers. A total of 19 beach communities cluster along 30A. Many are little more than a wide spot in the road, and all are among the least known and least developed in the Gulf Coast area, even though Grayton Beach is regularly ranked among the country's top 20 beaches. Seaside, which reached its quarter-century mark in 2006, is a thriving planned community with old-fashioned Victorian architecture, brick streets, restaurants, retail stores—and a surfeit of art galleries.

Continuing southeast on U.S. 98, you'll find Panama City Beach, whose "Miracle Strip," once crammed with carnival-like amusement parks, junk-food vendors, T-shirt shops, and go-kart tracks, is in the middle of a building frenzy that will double the number of condominiums and give the area a much-needed face-lift. Farther east, past the up-and-coming sleeper cities of Port St. Joe and Mexico Beach (these days, the din of construction drowns out the sounds of surf all along this coast), you'll come to the quiet blue-collar town of Apalachicola, Florida's main oyster fishery. Watch oystermen ply their trade, using long-handled tongs to bring in their catch. Cross the Apalachicola Bay via the Bryant Patton Bridge to St. George Island. This unspoiled 28-mi-long barrier island offers some of America's most scenic beaches, including St. George Island State Park, which has the longest beachfront of any state park in Florida.

FORT WALTON BEACH

46 mi east of Pensacola.

This coastal town dates from the Civil War, but had to wait more than 75 years to come into its own. Patriots loyal to the Confederate cause organized Walton's Guard (named in honor of Colonel George Walton, onetime acting territorial governor of West Florida) and camped at a site on Santa Rosa Sound, later known as Camp Walton. In 1940 fewer than 90 people lived in Fort Walton Beach, but within a decade the city became a boomtown, thanks to New Deal money for roads and bridges and the development of Eglin Field during World War II. The military is now Fort Walton Beach's main source of income, but tourism runs a close second. Don't miss a chance to waddle out to the end of the Okaloosa Island Pier. It costs only a buck to walk the plank, $6.50 if you'd like to fish.

Encompassing 724 square mi of land, **Eglin Air Force Base** includes 10 auxiliary fields and a total of 21 runways. Jimmie Doolittle's Tokyo Raiders trained here, as did the Son Tay Raiders, a group that made a daring attempt to rescue American POWs from a North Vietnamese prison camp in 1970. Off-limits to civilians, there are private tours for ROTC and military reunion groups. ⊠ *Rte. 85* ☎ *850/882–3931* ⊕ *www.eglin.af.mil.*

★ The collection at the **Air Force Armament Museum,** just outside the Eglin Air Force Base's main gate, contains more than 5,000 armaments from World Wars I and II and the Korean and Vietnam wars. Included are uniforms, engines, weapons, aircraft, and flight simulators; larger craft such as transport planes are exhibited on the grounds outside. A continuously-playing 32-minute movie, Arming the Future, features current weapons and Eglin's history and its role in their development. ⊠*Rte. 85, Eglin Air Force Base* ☎*850/882–4062* ⊒*Free* ⊙*Mon.– Sat. 9:30–4:30.*

John C. Beasley Wayside Park is Fort Walton Beach's seaside playground on Okaloosa Island. Across the dunes, a boardwalk leads to the beach, where there are a dozen covered picnic tables, pavilions, changing rooms, and freshwater showers. Lifeguards are on duty in summer. ⊠*Okaloosa Island* ☎*No phone.*

☼ At the fascinating **Heritage Park and Cultural Center** you can learn all about the prehistoric peoples who inhabited northwest Florida up to 10,000 years ago. Local tribes built this large earthen mound as a center of religious, political, and social activity but now it's a reminder of a lost world. A small museum explains the mound and the people who built it, showcasing prehistoric Native American artifacts and weaponry as well as a few hands-on exhibits that are a reminder of the area's previous inhabitants. A single fee provides admission to the museum and to a restored post office and schoolhouse on the site. ⊠*139 Miracle Strip Pkwy. SE (U.S. 98)* ☎*850/833–9595* ⊒*$5* ⊙*Weekdays 10–4, Sat. 9–4.*

☼ In the style of several modest oceanographic attractions, the **Gulfarium** tosses in an assortment of sealife-themed shows and exhibits. Its main attraction is the Living Sea, a 60,000-gallon tank that simulates conditions on the ocean floor, and there are campy performances by trained porpoises, sea-lion shows, and marine-life exhibits (a multispecies act includes dolphins and sea lions in the same show). Among other species here are otters, penguins, alligators, harbor seals, and sharks, which means that feeding time is always a crowd pleaser. Don't overlook the old-fashioned Dolphin Reef gift shop, where you can buy anything from conch shells to beach toys. There's also a dolphin-interaction program, but you don't swim with them. Instead, you sit in a pool as spotted dolphins swim up to your lap. ⊠*U.S. 98 E* ☎*850/243–9046 or 800/247–8575* ⊕*www.gulfarium.com* ⊒*$18.75, dolphin interaction $125* ⊙*Sept.–May, daily 9–4; June–Aug., daily 9–6.*

WHERE TO EAT

$$–$$$$ ✕ **Staff's.** Since 1913 folks have been coming to this garage-turned-eatery for steaks and seafood dishes like Florida lobster and char-grilled amberjack. Sip a Tropical Depression or a rum-laced Squall Line while you peruse a menu tucked into the centerfold of a tabloid-size newspaper filled with snippets of local history, early photographs, and family memorabilia. The grand finale is a trip to the delectable dessert bar; try a generous wedge of cherry cheesecake. ⊠*24 Miracle Strip Pkwy. SE* ☎*850/243–3482* ▭*AE, D, MC, V.*

★ **$$-$$$** ✕ **Pandora's Steakhouse and Lounge.** On the Emerald Coast the name Pandora's is synonymous with prime rib. Steaks are cooked over a wood-burning grill, and you can order your prime rib regular or extra-cut; fish aficionados should try the char-grilled yellowfin tuna or one of the daily fish specials. Cozy up in an alcove to enjoy your meal in peace or head to the lounge, where the mood turns a bit more gregarious with live entertainment Wednesday through Saturday. ⊠ *1226 Santa Rosa Blvd.* ☎ *850/244–8669* ▭ *AE, D, DC, MC, V* ☉ *Closed Mon.*

$-$$ ✕ **Angler's.** Unless you sit in the water, you can't dine any closer to the Gulf than at this casual beachside bar and grill next to the Gulfarium. Located at the entrance to Okaloosa Island Pier (and within a complex of other nightclubs and restaurants), Angler's houses the requisite sports bar with a million or more televisions (in the elevators and bathrooms even) broadcasting an equal number of sports events. Outside, a volleyball net tempts diners onto the sands to work up an appetite. When you do, snack on nachos and quesadillas, or sample the fresh-catch dishes such as seared tuna wasabi, spicy shrimp pow pow, and steamed snow crab legs. ⊠ *1030 Miracle Strip Pkwy. SE* ☎ *850/796–0260* ▭ *AE, D, MC, V.*

WHERE TO STAY

$-$$$ ▦ **Ramada Plaza Beach Resort.** If your family loves the water, splash down at this beachside extravaganza. Activity here revolves around a 194,000-gallon pool (allegedly the area's largest) with a separate grotto pool and bar and spectacular swim-through waterfall that tumbles down from an island oasis; there's also a separate kiddie pool, as well as an 800-foot private beach. Standard rooms have refrigerators, coffeemakers, and two double beds (a few have kings), in-room safes, and free high-speed Internet; beachfront units come with microwaves. It's a popular spot for conventions, Spring Break, and families on a budget: there's no charge for additional guests under 18, and roll-away beds are only an extra $10 per night. For an extra-special evening, book an odd-numbered room between 1133 and 1143—the back door of each opens right into the pool. **Pros:** Extravagant offerings for a family-friendly vacation—the pool may please the kids more than the Gulf. **Cons:** May be too busy for romance travelers or seniors seeking peace and quiet. ⊠ *1500 Miracle Strip Pkwy. SE,* ☎ *850/243–9161 or 800/874–8962* ⊕ *www.ramadafwb.com* ↝ *309 rooms, 26 suites* ⌂ *In-room: refrigerator. In-hotel: restaurant, bars, pools, gym, beachfront, no elevator (some)* ▭ *AE, D, DC, MC, V.*

NIGHTLIFE & THE ARTS

THE ARTS To appreciate dancing skills that go beyond your own tiptoeing on hot sands, visit the **Northwest Florida Ballet** (☎ *850/664–7787* ⊕ *www. nfballet.org*). Based in Fort Walton Beach, they have presented classical and contemporary dance performances to audiences along the Gulf Coast since 1969. Call for season schedule and ticket information as well as their current performance venue.

NIGHTLIFE Dueling pianos ((Tuesday through Sunday only) and a beachfront bar fuel the furious sing-alongs that make **Howl at the Moon** (⊠ *1450 Miracle Strip Pkwy.* ☎ *850/301–0111*), at the Boardwalk on Okaloosa Island, one of Fort Walton's most popular evening entertainment spots. The show starts at 8 PM, and rocks every night until 2, although the Comedy Zone—featuring stand-up comedians—takes over on Sundays.

SPORTS & THE OUTDOORS

MULTI-SPORT **Eglin Air Force Base Reservation** is the size of Rhode Island—1,045 square mi, 463,448 acres—and has 810 mi of creeks and plenty of challenging, twisting wooded trails. Outdoor enthusiasts hunt, fish, canoe, and swim here, and for $10 you can buy a day pass to camp or hike or mountain-bike on the Timberlake Trail, which is open from 7 AM to 4:30 PM Monday through Saturday. Permits can be obtained from the **Jackson Guard** (✉ *107 Rte. 85 N, Niceville* ☎ *850/882–4164*).

FISHING **Harbor Walk Marina** (✉ *66 U.S. 98 E, Destin* ☎ *850/337–8250* ⊕ *www.harborwalk-destin.com*) is a rustic-looking waterfront complex where you can get bait, gas, tackle, food, and anything else you might need for a day of fishing. Party fishing-boat excursions cost as little as $40, a cheaper alternative to chartering or renting your own boat.

GOLF The **Fort Walton Beach Golf Club** (✉ *Rte. 189* ☎ *850/833–9529*) is a 36-hole municipal course whose links (Oaks and Pines) lie about 400 yards from each other. The two courses are considered by many to be among Florida's best public layouts. Greens fee: $32/$40 with a shared cart. **Shalimar Pointe Golf & Country Club** (✉ *302 Country Club Dr., Shalimar* ☎ *850/651–1416* ⊕ *www.shalimarpointe.com*) has 18 holes with a pleasing mix of water and bunkers. Greens fee: $45/$59 with cart.

SCUBA DIVING Take diving lessons, arrange excursions, and rent all the necessary equipment at the **Scuba Shop** (✉ *348 Miracle Strip Pkwy.* ☎ *850/243–1600* ⊕ *www.thescubashopfwb.com*)where the specialty is wreck diving. Although visibility here isn't on par with the reefs of the Atlantic coast, local divers can also explore artificial reefs and a limestone shelf. The views are about 50 feet and diving depths up to 90 feet. A two-tank dive costs $75.

DESTIN

8 mi east of Fort Walton Beach.

Fort Walton Beach's neighbor lies on the other side of the strait that connects Choctawhatchee Bay with the Gulf of Mexico. Destin takes its name from its founder, Leonard A. Destin, a Connecticut sea captain who settled his family here sometime in the 1830s. For the next 100 years Destin remained a sleepy little fishing village until the strait, or East Pass, was bridged in 1935. Then recreational anglers discovered its white sands, blue-green waters, and abundance of some of the most sought-after sport fish in the world. More billfish are hauled in around Destin each year than from all other Gulf fishing ports combined, giving credence to its nickname, the World's Luckiest Fishing Village. But you don't have to be the rod-and-reel type to love Destin. There's plenty to entertain the sand-pail set as well as senior citizens, and there are many nice restaurants, which you'll have an easier time finding if you remember that the main drag through town is referred to as both U.S.

98 and Emerald Coast Parkway. The name makes sense, but part of what makes the gulf look so emerald in these parts is the contrasting whiteness of the sand on the beach. Actually, it's not sand—it's pure, powder-soft Appalachian quartz that was dropped off by a glacier a few thousand years back. Since quartz doesn't compress (and crews clean and rake the beach each evening), your tootsies get the sole-satisfying benefit of soft, sugary "sand." Sand so pure it squeaks.

☺ In addition to a seasonal water park, **Big Kahuna's Lost Paradise** has year-round family attractions, including 54 holes of miniature golf, two go-kart tracks, an arcade, thrill rides for kids of all ages, and an amphitheater. ⊠ *U.S. 98 E* ☎ *850/837–4061* ⊕ *www.bigkahunas.com* ▣ *Grounds free, water park $33, miniature golf $5, go-karts $5.50, combination ticket (water park, golf, and two go-kart tickets) $41* ⊙ *Water park: May–Labor Day, weekends 10–5; Labor Day–mid-Sept., daily 10 AM–midnight.*

WHERE TO EAT & STAY

★ $$$–$$$$ ✕ **Marina Café.** A harbor view, impeccable service, and sophisticated fare create one of the finest dining experiences on the Emerald Coast. The ocean motif is expressed in shades of aqua, green, and sand accented with marine tapestries and sea sculptures. The chef calls his creations contemporary continental, offering diners a choice of classic creole, Mediterranean, or Pacific Rim dishes. One regional specialty is the popular pan-seared yellowedge grouper with a blue crabmeat crust. A special sushi menu is available, and the wine list is extensive. ⊠ *404 U.S. 98 E* ☎ *850/837–7960* ▤ *AE, D, DC, MC, V* ⊙ *No lunch.*

$–$$$ ✕ **Louisiana Lagniappe.** In Louisiana when you say *lagniappe,* it means you're getting a little something extra—here it's the extra zing fresh local seafood gets when transformed into Cajun-style cuisine. You can't go wrong ordering Cajun standards like shrimp creole, crab bisque, and crawfish étouffée. Locals love the chef's innovations, such as grouper Cocodrie, sautéed and topped with fried crawfish, artichoke hearts, and a rich béarnaise sauce. There's outside dining overlooking Destin Harbor, but whether you're dining inside or out, the sunset views are delicious. ⊠ *775 Gulf Shore Dr., at Sandpiper Cove* ☎ *850/837–0881* ⩘ *Reservations not accepted* ▤ *AE, D, DC, MC, V* ⊙ *No lunch.*

$$$$ ▦ **Sandestin Golf and Beach Resort.** Almost a city in itself, and certainly Fodor'sChoice its own little world. Newlyweds, conventioneers, and families all find ★ their fit in this 2,400-acre resort with more than 1,400 accommodation offerings spread across five areas: Beachfront, Beachside, Village, Bayside, and Dockside. Each of the five neighborhood clusters offers a unique locale with villas, cottages, condominiums, boat slips, and an inn. All rooms have a view, either of the Gulf, Choctawhatchee Bay, a golf course, a lagoon, or a natural wildlife preserve. This resort accommodates an assortment of tastes, from the simple to the extravagant (the dial-up to the Wi-Fi), but the gigantic suites at the Westwinds are a cut above the rest. Baytowne Wharf has art galleries, wine stores, and a "festival marketplace" of shops and restaurants, so once you get here, you won't need—or want—to leave. **Pros:** Has everything you'd ever need in a resort—and more; it is a city; **Cons:** It is a city; lacks the

2

personal touches of a modest retreat. ✉*9300 Emerald Coast Pkwy. W,* ☎*850/267–8000 or 800/277–0800* ⊕*www.sandestin.com* ⟿*175 rooms, 250 condos, 275 villas* ☼*In-room: kitchen (some), refrigerator (some), Wi-Fi. In-hotel: 10 restaurants, bars, golf courses, tennis courts, pools, gym, beachfront, public Internet* ▤*AE, D, DC, MC, V.*

★ **$$–$$$$** ☷ **Bluewater Bay Resort.** A nice find that offers vacation rentals ranging from motel rooms to villas to patio homes, the resort is also popular for its 36 holes of championship golf (on courses designed by Jerry Pate and Tom Fazio). This upscale resort is 12 mi north of Destin via the Mid-Bay Bridge, on the shores of Choctawhatchee Bay. Tennis courts are privately owned, but you can use them for a special rate. **Pros:** Variety is the spice here; rooms for every taste, and many with kitchens or kitchenettes for a self-sufficient stay. **Cons:** On the bay, not the Gulf, so you'll have to drive to the seaside. ✉*1940 Bluewater Blvd., Niceville* ☎*850/897–3613 or 800/874–2128* ⊕*www.bwbresort.com* ⟿*23 rooms, 22 suites* ☼*In-hotel: restaurant, bar, golf course, tennis courts, pools* ▤*AE, D, DC, MC, V.*

$$–$$$$ ☷ **Holiday Inn Destin.** The hotel's towering, circular design ensures most rooms get a great view of the Gulf, which is only a few steps away. The location offers the chance to lounge on sugar-white sands, get to several golf courses with ease, and walk to some of Destin's amusement parks. Common areas jazzed up with skylights and greenery are spacious and eye-pleasing. The standard rooms are uniformly bright and well kept; prices vary depending on the view. Family-friendly, there are kiddie pools and "kids' suites" (with bunk beds) and magic shows and nature talks. **Pros:** Has one of the best locations right on the Gulf, and kids' programs make it a one-stop shop for families. **Cons:** Generic cookie-cutter hotel interiors; not every room has a Gulf view. ✉*1020 U.S. 98 E* ☎*850/837–6181* ⊕*www.hidestin.com* ⟿*233 rooms* ☼*In-room: Wi-Fi. In-hotel: restaurant, bar, pools, beachfront, laundry facilities* ▤*AE, D, DC, MC, V.*

NIGHTLIFE

Folks come by boat and car to **AJ's Club Bimini** (✉*116 U.S. 98 E* ☎*850/837–1913* ⊕*www.ajs-destin.com*), a supercasual bar and restaurant overlooking a marina. Nightly live music means young, lively crowds pack the dance floor. **Harbor Docks** (✉*538 U.S. 98 E* ☎*850/837–2506* ⊕*www.harbordocks.com*) is another favorite with the local seafaring set. Here since 1979, the incredibly casual feel is marked by picnic tables and Hibachi grills, Destin's first sushi bar, and live music Thursday-Saturday. The **Hog's Breath Saloon** (✉*541 U.S. 98 E* ☎*850/837–5991*), a chain hot spot with other locations in Key West and Destin, presents good live music Wednesday through Sunday. The food—steaks, burgers, salads—isn't bad, either. Not only is **Night Town** (✉*140 Palmetto St.* ☎*850/837–7625* ⊕*www.nightown.com*) the largest dance club in northwest Florida, it provides two clubs under one roof, a mighty generous 14,000-square-foot lighted dance floor, a beach bar, live music, pool tables—and it stays open seven nights a week until 4 AM.

SPORTS & THE OUTDOORS

FISHING   If you come to Destin and don't fish, you're missing out, since the city has the largest charter-boat fishing fleet in the entire state. You can also pier-fish from the 3,000-foot-long Destin Catwalk and along the East Pass Bridge. For a charter, check with **Adventure Charters** (✉ *East Pass Marina, 288 U.S. 98 E* ☎*850/654–4070*), which offers deep-sea, bay-bottom, and light-tackle fishing excursions. **East Pass Bait and Tackle** (✉ *East Pass Marina, 288 U.S. 98 E* ☎*850/837–2622*) sells bait, tackle, and most anything else you'd need for a day of fishing.

GOLF   The **Indian Bayou Golf & Country Club** (✉ *1 Country Club Dr. E, off Airport Rd., off U.S. 98* ☎*850/650–2284* ⊕*www.indianbayougolf. com*) has a 27-hole course; greens fee $55/$75 with cart. The 18-hole **Kelly Plantation Golf Club** (✉ *307 Kelly Plantation Dr.* ☎*850/650–7600* ⊕*www.kellyplantationgolf.com*), designed by Fred Couples and Gene Bates, is a semiprivate course that runs along Choctawhatchee Bay. Greens fee $142 with cart. There's an 18-hole, semiprivate course at **Regatta Bay Golf & Country Club** (✉ *465 Regatta Bay Blvd.* ☎*850/337–8080* ⊕*www.regattabay.com*). Greens fee $69/$89. For sheer number of holes, the **Sandestin Golf and Beach Resort** (✉ *9300 U.S. 98 W* ☎*850/267–8211* ⊕*www.sandestin.com*) tops the list, with 72. There are four courses: **Baytowne Golf Club at Sandestin**, greens fee $105/$125; **Burnt Pines Course**, greens fee $109/$155; **Links Course**, greens fee $65/$115; and the **Raven Golf Club**, greens fee $75/$135.

SCUBA DIVING   Scuba-diving and snorkeling instruction and outings are available through **Emerald Coast Scuba** (✉ *110 Melvin St.* ☎*850/837–0955 or 800/222–0955* ⊕*www.divedestin.com*). An appropriately named center, **The Scuba Shop** (✉ *348 S.W. Miracle Strip Pkwy. #19* ☎*850/243–1600* ⊕*www.thescubashopfwb.com*), offers dives and lessons as well.

SHOPPING

Don't call it a mall. **Destin Commons** (✉ *Mid-Bay Bridge and Hwy. 98, Destin* ☎*850/337–8700,* ⊕*www.destincommons.com*) is an "open-air lifestyle center." More than 70 high-end specialty shops are here, as well as a 14-screen theater, Hard Rock Cafe, a miniature train and a nautical-theme park for kids, and a 49-tap soda-pop fountain. The **Market at Sandestin** (✉ *9300 Emerald Coast Pkwy. W, Sandestin* ☎*850/267–8092*) has about two dozen upscale shops that peddle such goods as expensive chocolates and designer clothes in an elegant mini-mall in a courtyard setting. **Silver Sands Factory Stores** (✉ *10562 Emerald Coast Pkwy. W* ☎*850/654–9771* ⊕*www.silversandsoutlet.com*) is one of the Southeast's largest retail designer outlets. More than 100 shops sell top-name merchandise that ranges from gifts to kids' clothes to menswear.

GRAYTON BEACH

18 mi east of Destin.

The 26-mi stretch of coastline between Destin and Panama City Beach is referred to as the Beaches of South Walton. From the middle of this mostly residential stretch of the Panhandle you can see the monolithic condos of Destin and Panama City Beach in either direction, like massive bookends in the distance, flanking the area's low-slung, less imposing structures. A decidedly laid-back, refined mood prevails in these parts, where vacation homes go for millions and selecting a dinner spot is usually the day's most challenging decision. Accommodations consist primarily of private-home rentals, the majority of which are managed by local real-estate firms. Also scattered along Route 30A are a growing number of boutiques selling everything from fine art to unique hand-painted furniture, to jewelry, gifts, and clothes. Inland, pine forests and hardwoods surround the area's 14 dune lakes, giving anglers ample spots to drop a line and kayakers a peaceful refuge. Grayton Beach, the oldest community in this area, has reached its 100-year mark. You can still see some of the old weathered-cypress homes scattered along narrow, crushed gravel streets. The town has taken off with the addition of adjacent WaterColor, a high-end development of vacation homes with a stylish boutique hotel as its centerpiece. The architecture is tasteful, development is carefully regulated—no buildings taller than four stories are allowed—and bicycles and kayaks are the preferred methods of transportation. Stringent building restrictions, designed to protect the pristine beaches and dunes, ensure that Grayton maintains its small-town feel and look.

Fodor's Choice ★ The 2,133-acre **Grayton Beach State Park** is one of the most scenic spots along the Gulf Coast. Composed primarily of untouched Florida woodlands, it also has salt marshes, rolling dunes covered with sea oats, crystal-white sand, and contrasting blue-green waters. The park has facilities for swimming, fishing, snorkeling, and camping, and there's an elevated boardwalk that winds over the dunes to the beach. Even if you are just passing by, the beach here is worth the stop. Thirty fully equipped cabins are available for rent (⇨ *Where to Stay* below). ⊠*357 Main Park Rd. (off 30A)* ☎*850/231–4210* ⊠*$4 per vehicle, up to 8 people* ⊙ *Daily 8–sunset.*

OFF THE BEATEN PATH

Eden Gardens State Park. Scarlett O'Hara might be at home here on the lawn of an antebellum mansion amid an arcade of moss-draped live oaks. Tours of the mansion are given every hour on the hour, and furnishings inside the spacious rooms date as far back as the 17th century. The surrounding grounds—the perfect setting for a picnic lunch—are beautiful year-round, but they're nothing short of spectacular in mid-March, when the azaleas and dogwoods are in full bloom. ⊠*Rte. 395, Point Washington* ☎*850/231–4214* ⊠*Gardens $3, mansion tours, $3* ⊙ *Daily 8–sunset, mansion tours hourly Thurs.–Mon. 10–3.*

WHERE TO EAT

$$$–$$$$ ✕ **Criollas.** Inventive, contemporary, and constantly changing fare continues to win raves for this popular spot. You might choose to experience Island Hopping—a three-course dinner focusing on a particular Caribbean region—or stick closer to home with Southern-inspired fare (the owner is paying tribute to his Louisiana heritage) like crawfish callaloo soup, creole panfried oysters, or barbecue shrimp. The menu changes seasonally, so returning diners can sample a different cuisine each visit—perhaps one reason why a major state magazine consistently

places Criolla's in Florida's Top 20. ⊠*170 E. Hwy. 30A* ☎*850/267–1267* ☰*AE, D, MC, V* ⊘ *No lunch. Closed Sunday except on Memorial, Labor, and Independence Day weekends*

$$$–$$$$
Fodor'sChoice
★

✕ **Fish Out of Water.** Time your appetite to arrive at sunset here and you'll witness the best of both worlds: sea oats lumbering on gold-dusted dunes outside, and a stylish interior that sets new standards of sophistication for the entire Panhandle. Colorful, handblown glass accent lighting that "grows" out of the hardwood floors, plush taupe banquettes, oversize handmade lamp shades, and a sleek bar area that screams New York (complete with a cloud-white curtain-wall) create an atmosphere worthy of the inventive cuisine. Influences range from Asian (Thai-style grouper with lobster-coconut broth) to Southern (Low Country shrimp and scallops with creamy grits) to classic continental (porcini-crusted osso buco), but all are convincingly wrought and carefully presented. The extensive wine list keeps pace with the menu offerings. ⊠*34 Goldenrod Circle, 2nd fl. of WaterColor Inn* ☎*850/534–5008* ☰*AE, D, DC, MC, V* ⊘*No lunch.*

$–$$

✕ **Picolo Restaurant & Red Bar.** You could spend weeks here just taking in all the funky-junky, eclectic toy-chest memorabilia—from Marilyn Monroe posters to flags to dolls—dangling from the ceiling and tacked to every available square inch of wall. The contemporary menu is small, changes daily, and is very Floridian. A baked eggplant dish stuffed with shrimp, scallops, and grilled vegetables is a popular entrée. Blues and jazz musicians play nightly in the Red Bar. ⊠*70 Hotz Ave.* ☎*850/231–1008* ☰*No credit cards.*

WHERE TO STAY

$$$$
Fodor'sChoice
★

🏨 **WaterColor Inn.** Nature meets seaside chic at this boutique property, the crown jewel of the area's latest—and largest—planned community. Rooms are done in seashell tones with sea-blue comforters and accents; stylish armoires and desks look as natural and unfinished as driftwood. Dune-level bungalows have private courtyards with outdoor showers, whereas upper rooms have huge balconies and walk-in showers with windows overlooking the Gulf. Standard rooms come with a king-size bed and a queen sleeper-sofa, but consider one of the three Rotunda rooms for something larger and more spectacular. **Pros:** Perhaps the ultimate vacation experience on the Gulf; upscale and fancy. **Cons:** Again, upscale and fancy; you may feel like it caters exclusively to Ivy Leaguers and CEOs, which might make it hard to relax on a relaxing Gulf vacation. ⊠*34 Goldenrod Circle,* ☎*850/534–5000* ⊕*www.watercolorvacations.com* ⊅*60 rooms* ♿*In-room: safe, refrigerator, Wi-Fi. In-hotel: restaurant, pool, beachfront, public Internet, airport shuttle, no-smoking rooms.*

★ **$$**

🏨 **Cabins at Grayton Beach State Park.** Back-to-nature enthusiasts and families love the opportunity to retreat to stylish accommodations set among the sand pines and scrub oaks of this pristine state park. The two-bedroom duplexes (each named after a different species of tree found in the park) have tin roofs, white trim, and tropical wooden window louvers, and the beach is a leisurely five-minute walk away via a private boardwalk. Modern conveniences include central heat and air-conditioning and full-size kitchens complete with pots and pans.

There is no daily maid service—fresh linens are provided, however—and no room phones or televisions, but gas fireplaces, barbecue grills, and screen porches add a homey touch. They're often booked solid as much as 11 months in advance, so call to check for cancellations. **Pros:** The rare and welcome preservation of Old Florida, with pure peace and quiet; what a Gulf vacation is meant to be. **Cons:** If you're accustomed to abundant amenities, you won't find them here. ⊠*357 Main Park Rd.* ☎*800/326–3521 for reservations* ⊕*www.reserveamerica.com* ⇨*30 cabins* ⌂*In-room: no phone, kitchen, no TV* ⊟*AE, MC, V.*

NIGHTLIFE

The **Red Bar** (⊠*70 Hotz Ave.* ☎*850/231–1008*), the local watering hole, presents red-hot blues or jazz acts every night. On Friday and Saturday nights it's elbow-to-elbow at the bar.

SHOPPING

Gaffrey Art Gallery (⊠*21 Blue Gulf Dr., 3 mi west of Grayton Beach, Santa Rosa Beach* ☎*850/267–0228* ⊕*www.gaffreyart.com*) displays the contemporary and colorful folk art of Billie and Justin Gaffrey. **Grayton Beach House of Art** (⊠*26 Logan La.* ☎*850/231–9997* ⊕*www. house-of-art.com*) specializes in the works of Gordie Hinds, who gave up charter fishing and picked up a paintbrush in 2003. He paints what he knows best: fishing, seashores, piers, and marshes. Under the shade trees of Grayton Beach, **Magnolia House** (⊠*2 Magnolia St.* ☎*850/231–5859*) sells gift items, bath products, and accessories for the home. The **Shops of Grayton** (⊠*Rte. 283 [Grayton Rd.], 2 mi south of U.S. 98* ☎*No phone*) is a colorful complex of eight Cracker-style cottages selling gifts, artwork, and antiques. At **Woodie Long Folk Art Gallery** (⊠*1066 B. North Bay Dr./Rte. 283, Santa Rosa Beach* ☎*850/231–9961*), in the living room of the artist's residence, you'll find a few of the 10,000 artworks the quirky local claims to have painted (a feature in *Smithsonian* magazine put Woodie on the art-world map). His folk paintings can be seen at the Cooperstown Museum, the Philadelphia Museum of Art, and on CD jackets and book covers.

SEASIDE & ROSEMARY BEACH

2 mi east of Grayton Beach.

This community of Victorian-style homes is so reminiscent of a storybook town that producers chose it for the set of the 1998 film *The Truman Show,* starring Jim Carrey. The brainchild of Robert Davis, **Seaside** was designed to promote a neighborly, old-fashioned lifestyle, and there's much to be said for an attractive, billboard-free village where you can park your car and walk everywhere you need to go. Pastel-color homes with white picket fences, front-porch rockers, and captain's walks are set along redbrick streets, and all are within walking distance of the town center and its unusual cafés and shops.

The community has come into its own in the last few years, achieving a comfortable, lived-in look and feel that had escaped it since its founding in the 1970s: some of the once-shiny tin roofs are starting to rust around the edges, and the foliage has completely matured, creating pockets of privacy and shade. Still, while Seaside's popularity continues to soar, it retains a suspicious sense of *Twilight Zone* perfection that can weird out some visitors. Summer months can be crowded with the retired-CEO and prep-school-student-and-parent sets, so if you're seeking a little solitude, you might prefer visiting during the off-season—between Labor Day and Memorial Day.

Farther east down Highway 30A is **Rosemary Beach,** a fledgling development that is, like eleventy-million other new coastal communities, a variation on the theme pioneered by Seaside's founders. A few restaurants and shops have opened, and a super-luxe boutique hotel is under construction, so investors are snatching up the snazzy beach houses as fast as they're built (in many cases, even before they are built). Despite the growth, the focus here is still on preserving the local environment (the landscape is made up completely of indigenous plants) and maintaining its small-town appeal. You can already see a nascent sense of community sprouting at the Town Green, a perfect patch of manicured lawn fronting the beach, where locals gather with their wineglasses to toast the sunset.

WHERE TO EAT

$$$-$$$$　✕ **Bud & Alley's.** This down-to-earth beachside bistro (named for a pet cat and dog) has been a local favorite since 1986. Tucked in the dunes by the gulf, the rooftop Tarpon Club bar makes a great perch for a sunset toast (guess the exact moment the sun will disappear and win a drink). Daily salad specials are tangy introductions to such entrées as pan-roasted stuffed pork loin chop with andouille sausage, rosemary roasted potato, wilted spinach and tomato, and the grilled venison leg with a butternut squash puree. ✉*Rte. 30A, Santa Rosa Beach* ☎*850/231–5900* ▤*MC, V* ☺*No lunch.*

$$$-$$$$　✕ **Café Thirty-A.** In a beautiful Florida-style home with high ceilings
★　and a wide veranda, this restaurant has an elegant look—bolstered by white-linen tablecloths—and impeccable service. The menu changes nightly and includes such entrées as wood-oven roasted wild king salmon, sesame-crusted rare yellowfin tuna, and grilled Hawaiian butterfish. Even if you're not a Southerner, you should try the appetizer of grilled Georgia quail with creamy grits and sage fritters. With nearly 20 creative varieties, the martini menu alone is worth the trip. ✉*3899 E. Hwy. 30A, Seagrove Beach* ☎*850/231–2166* ▤*AE, D, DC, MC, V* ☺*No lunch.*

$$-$$$　✕ **The Great Southern Cafe.** Created by Jim Shirley, founder of Penscaola's very popular Fish House, he's brought the Grits a Ya Ya here as well, along with regional fare including Gulf shrimp, Apalachicola oysters, and fresh vegetables such as collards, okra, black-eyed peas, fried green tomatoes, and sweet potatoes. Po'boys stuffed with shrimp or oysters bring a little of N'awlins to Seaside. Beer and wine are served, to boot. ✉*83 Central Sq.* ☎*850/231–1950* ▤*AE, MC, V.*

2

WHERE TO STAY

$$$$ ⚐ **The Pensione at Rosemary Beach.** A spotless, eight-room inn on the town's main square, one block from the Gulf of Mexico. In keeping with the true *pensione* concept, rooms (all with queen beds) are basic, almost dorm-style, yet comfortable—those in front have views of the Gulf across the street—and thoughtful touches like chocolates, whimsical murals, and picture guides to local butterflies add a touch of homeyness. You're guaranteed peace and quiet here: children under 16, Spring Breakers, and overzealous wedding parties are not allowed. Continental breakfast is included in the room price. Onano, a "neighborhood café," occupies the inn's first floor. **Pros:** Wonderful location. **Cons:** For a pensione, the prices approach Relaix and Chateau status; you can't access the inn itself, only the reservation service. ⊠*78 Main St., Rosemary Beach* ☎*850/231–1790* ⊕*www.cottagerentalagency.com* ↪*8 rooms* ⅋*In-room: DVD. In-hotel: no kids under 16, no-smoking rooms* ▤*AE, D, MC, V* ⎮⊙⎮*CP.*

★ **$$$$** ⚐ **Seaside Cottage Rental Agency.** When residents aren't using their homes, they rent out their pricey one- to six-bedroom, porticoed, faux-Victorian cottages furnished with fully equipped kitchens, TV-VCR/DVDs, and vacuum cleaners—a perfect option for a family vacation or a large group. Gulf breezes blowing off the water remind you of the unspoiled sugar-white beaches a short stroll away. ⊠*Rte. 30A, Box 4730* ☎*850/231–1320 or 800/277–8696* ⊕*www.cottagerentalagency. com* ↪*275 units* ⅋*In-room: kitchen. In-hotel: tennis courts, pools, bicycles, no elevators.* ▤*AE, D, MC, V.*

NIGHTLIFE

Courtyard Wine and Cheese (⊠*66 Main St., Rosemary Beach* ☎*850/231–1219* ⊕*www.courtyardwineandcheese.com*) is a sophisticated wine bar (with free Wi-Fi) that opens onto a Tuscan-style courtyard and stocks 150 wines, fine cheeses, and artwork, too. It's closed Monday. The upstairs, open-air bar at **Bud & Alley's** (⊠*Rte. 30A* ☎*850/231–5900*) draws a friendly crowd for sunset, and the festivities usually continue until the wee hours.

THE OUTDOORS

An 8-foot-wide pathway covering 18 mi of scenic Route 30A winds past freshwater lakes, woodlands, and beaches. **Butterfly Bike & Kayak** (⊠*3657 E. Rte. 30A* ☎*850/231–2826*) rents bikes and kayaks and has free delivery and pick-up. In Seaside, consult the **Cabana Man** (☎*850/231–5046*) for beach chairs, umbrellas, rafts, kayaks, and anything else you might need for a day at the beach. If there's no answer, just head to the beach and you'll find him there.

SHOPPING

Seaside's central square and open-air market, along Route 30A, offer a number of unusual and whimsical boutiques carrying clothing, jewelry, and arts and crafts. **Perspicacity** (⊠*178 Market St.* ☎*850/231–5829*), an open-air market, sells simply designed women's clothing and accessories perfect for easy, carefree beach-town casualness. "Perspicacity," by the way, means "keenness of insight." So there. At **Ruskin Place Artist**

Colony, in the heart of Seaside, a collection of small shops and artists' galleries has everything from toys and pottery to fine works of art.

PANAMA CITY BEACH

21 mi southeast of Seaside.

The dizzying number of high-rises under construction on the Miracle Strip—about two dozen in total—has led to the formation of a new moniker for this stretch of the Panhandle: the "Construction Coast." But the vast majority of the new buildings are condominiums, not hotels, and many of the older mom-and-pop motels that once gave this town its beach-resort flavor have fallen victim to the wrecking ball. Invasive growth has turned the main thoroughfare, Front Beach Road, into a dense mass of traffic that peaks in spring and between June and August when college students descend en masse from neighboring states. The bright side of the changing landscape is that land values have risen so dramatically in the last few years that many of the attractions that gave parts of this area a seedy reputation (i.e., strip joints and dive bars) have been driven out, replaced by new retailers and the occasional franchise "family" restaurant or chain store.

The one constant in this sea of change, however, is the area's natural beauty that, in some areas at least, manages to excuse its gross overcommercialization. The shoreline in town is *17 mi* long, so even when a mile is packed with partying students, there are 16 more miles where you can toss a beach blanket. What's more, the beaches along the Miracle Strip, with their powder-soft sand and translucent emerald waters, are some of the finest in the state; in one sense, anyway, it's easy to understand why so many condos are being built here. Cabanas, umbrellas, sailboats, Wave Runners, and floats are available from any of dozens of vendors along the beach. For an aerial view, for about $30 you can strap yourself beneath a parachute and go parasailing as you're towed aloft behind a speedboat a few hundred yards offshore. And St. Andrews State Park, on the southern end of the beaches, is treasured by locals and visitors alike.

The area's incredible white sands, navigable waterways, and plentiful marine life that attracted Spanish conquistadors today draw invaders of the vacationing kind—namely families, the vast majority of whom hail from nearby Georgia and Alabama.

■**TIP**➜**When coming here, be sure to set your sights for Panama City** *Beach.* **Panama City is its beachless inland cousin.**

Once part of the now-defunct Miracle Strip Amusement Park operation, **Shipwreck Island,** a 6-acre water park, offers everything from speedy slides and tubes to the slow-moving Lazy River. ■**TIP**➜**Oddly enough, admission is based on height: 50 inches $29; between 35 and 50 inches, $24; under 35 inches, free. Wear flats.** ✉ *12000 Front Beach Rd.* ☎ *850/234–0368* ⊕ *www.shipwreckisland.com* 🎟 *$29* ☉ *Mid-Apr.–May, weekends 10:30–5; June–early Sept., daily 10:30–5.*

2

At the unique **Museum of Man in the Sea,** see rare examples of breathing apparatuses and diving equipment, some dating as far back as the 1600s, in addition to exhibits on Florida's historic shipwrecks. There are also treasures recovered from famous wrecks, including artifacts from the Spanish galleon *Atocha,* and live creatures found in the area's coastal waters. ⊠ *17314 Panama City Beach Pkwy.* ☎ *850/235–4101* ⬚ *$5* ⊙ *Daily 10–4.*

It's certainly no SeaWorld, but **Gulf World,** the resident marine park, with a tropical garden, tropical-bird theater, plus alligator and otter exhibits, is still a winner with the kids. The stingray petting pool and the shark-feeding and scuba demonstrations are big crowd pleasers, but the old favorites—performing sea lions, otters, and bottle-nosed dolphins—still hold their own. If you're really nautically minded, consider the Trainer for a Day program, which allows you to go behind the scenes to assist in food preparation and training sessions and make an on-stage appearance in the Dolphin Show. ⊠ *15412 Front Beach Rd.* ☎ *850/234–5271* ⊕ *www.gulfworldmarinepark.com* ⬚ *$24* ⊙ *Late May–early Sept., daily 9 AM–5:30 PM; call for hrs at other times of year.*

Fodor'sChoice ★ At the eastern tip of Panama City Beach, **St. Andrews State Park** includes 1,260 acres of beaches, pinewoods, and marshes. Complete camping facilities are here, and a snack bar, too, as well as places to swim, pier-fish, or hike on clearly marked nature trails. Board a ferry to **Shell Island**—a 700-acre barrier island in the Gulf of Mexico with some of the best shelling north of Sanibel Island. A rock jetty creates a calm, shallow play area that is perfect for young children. Come to this spectacular park for a peek at what the entire beach area looked like before developers sank their claws into it. ⊠ *4607 State Park La.* ☎ *850/233–5140* ⊕ *www.floridastateparks.org* ⬚ *$5 per vehicle, up to 8 people* ⊙ *Daily 8–5.*

WHERE TO EAT

$$$ ✕ **Capt. Anderson's.** Come early to watch the boats unload the catch of the day on the docks, and to beat the long line that forms each afternoon in this noted restaurant. Here since 1953, it doesn't seem to have changed much. A nautical theme is reinforced by tables made of hatch covers in the attached bar, which attracts longtime locals. The Greek specialties aren't limited to feta cheese and shriveled olives; charcoal-broiled grouper, amberjack, and yellowfin tuna, crab-stuffed jumbo shrimp, stuffed filet of grouper, whole oven-broiled stuffed Florida lobster, and steaks have a prominent place on the menu as well. If you're visiting in the off-season, call to make sure they are adhering to the posted hours before venturing out. ⊠ *5551 N. Lagoon Dr.* ☎ *850/234–2225* ⚓ *Reservations not accepted* ▭ *AE, D, DC, MC, V* ⊙ *Closed Sun. and Nov.–Jan. No lunch.*

$$–$$$ ✕ **Boars Head.** An exterior that looks like an oversize thatch-roof cottage sets the mood for dining in this ersatz-rustic restaurant and tavern. Prime rib has been the number one people-pleaser since the house opened in 1978, but blackened seafood and broiled shrimp with crab-meat stuffing are popular, too. ⊠ *17290 Front Beach Rd.* ☎ *850/234–6628* ▭ *AE, D, DC, MC, V* ⊙ *No lunch.*

$$-$$$ ✕ **The Boatyard.** The same folks who operate Schooners on the beach side opened this larger, more stylish establishment overlooking a marina on the Grand Lagoon. For starters, try Gulf shrimp and corn chowder, or Key West conch fritters with hot-pepper jelly and wasabi mayonnaise. For dinner, choose from the five-spice seared tuna, spicy bow tie pasta with shrimp and tasso, or the aptly named Fried Shrimp You Can't Live Without. The coconut-and-plantain-crusted grouper is a knockout, as is the pan-roasted catch with bacon, mushrooms, and grits (this is definitely the South). There are a kids' menu, an extensive wine list, and a full bar, and the upstairs deck area is a great place to get away from the beach for a long, lazy lunch or romantic sunset dinner. Be aware that the Boatyard kicks into high gear at sundown, transforming into one of the hottest nightspots in town. ⊠ *5325 N. Lagoon Dr.* ☎ *850/249–9273* ▭ *AE, D, DC, MC, V.*

$$ ✕ **Montego Bay.** A tiki-style bar is the focal point at this former beach cottage where you're guaranteed friendly service and reasonably priced seafood, chicken, and steak dishes. Appetizers include deep-fried Cajun crawfish and "gator bites" (if you've never eaten fried alligator tail, try it here: it's nowhere near as exotic as you might think), calamari, coconut shrimp, and chicken wings (tastes like alligator). Main courses range from fresh fish (fried, sautéed, or grilled) to caramelized ribs, grilled sirloin, and Jamaican jerk chicken. There's a special menu just for kids, and beer, wine, and frozen specialty drinks for adults. ⊠ *4920 Thomas Dr.* ☎ *850/234–8686* ▭ *AE, D, DC, MC.*

$$ ✕ **Schooners.** Billing itself as the "last local beach club," and more boldly, "the best place on earth," this beachfront spot is a perfect place for a casual family lunch or early dinner: kids can have burgers and play on the beach while Mom and Dad enjoy grown-up drinks and more substantial fare such as homemade gumbo, steak, or simply prepared seafood. Late-night crowds pile in for live music and dancing. ⊠ *5121 Gulf Dr.* ☎ *850/235–3555* ▭ *AE, D, MC, V.*

¢–$$ ✕ **Billy's Steamed Seafood Restaurant, Oyster Bar, and Crab House.** Roll up your sleeves and dig into some of the Gulf's finest blue crabs and shrimp seasoned to perfection with Billy's special recipe. Homemade gumbo, crawfish, and the day's catch as well as sandwiches and burgers round out the menu. The taste here is in the food, not the surroundings, but you can eat on an outdoor patio in the cooler months. ⊠ *3000 Thomas Dr.* ☎ *850/235–2349* ▭ *AE, D, MC, V.*

¢ ✕ **Coram's.** Don't feel slighted if you're the only one in the place the waitress doesn't know by name—she'll know it by the time you leave (and "Hon" will do in the meantime). More than a local institution, this plain-Jane, diner-style restaurant with parking-lot views makes up in taste and price for what it lacks in atmosphere. Locals flock here for hearty breakfasts—the fluffy omelets are ample enough for two— lunchtime salads and sandwiches, and a dinner menu that includes barbecued pork, fish specials, and steaks and roast beef preparations served with mashed potatoes. For solid food at criminally low prices 24/7, you just can't beat this place. ⊠ *2016 Thomas Dr.* ☎ *850/234–8373* ⚏ *Reservations not accepted* ▭ *No credit cards.*

WHERE TO STAY

$$$-$$$$ 🏨 **Legacy by the Sea.** Every room at this 14-story, pastel-peach hotel has a private balcony with commanding Gulf views. Rooms are designed with families in mind, from the fully equipped kitchens to the two televisions and waterproof sofa cushions, to the door that conveniently separates the bedroom area from the rest of the unit. There's a Gulf-front pool and hot tub area (with a kiddie pool), and freebies include continental breakfast, daily newspaper, local calls, and an airport shuttle. Shopping, dining, and attractions are within walking distance, and a variety of water-sport options, including parasailing and jet-skiing, is offered by on-site concessionaires. The hotel's closed-circuit cable channel, airing nothing but live security camera feeds (inside the elevator, around the pool, in the common areas), makes keeping an eye on the kids a breeze—and keeping an eye on unsuspecting adults a hoot. **Pros:** On the Gulf with all the amenities a family (or college kids) need. **Cons:** In the heart of a crowded and congested district—can be difficult to access during peak seasons. ✉*15325 Front Beach Rd.* ☎*850/249–8601 or 888/886–8917* ⊕*www.legacybythesea.com* ⇆*278 rooms, 78 suites* ☖*In-room: kitchen, Wi-Fi. In-hotel: pool, airport shuttle* ▭*AE, D, DC, MC, V.*

$$$-$$$$ 🏨 **Marriott Bay Point Resort Village.** Across the Grand Lagoon from St. **Fodor's**Choice Andrews State Park, this expansive property exudes sheer elegance. ★ The tropical-chic feel starts in the light-filled lobby, with its polished marble floors, glowing chandeliers, potted palms, and colorful floral paintings. Quiet guest rooms continue the theme with light-wood furnishings and armoires, floral-print fabrics, and private balconies or patios overlooking the lush grounds and peaceful bay. Rooms on the upper floors of the main building have expansive views of the bay and the gulf beyond, and villas are a mere tee-shot away from the hotel. A meandering boardwalk (which doubles as a jogging trail) leads to a private bayside beach where an open-air bar and water sports await. The 12,000 square foot Serenity Spa offers massages, facials, manicures, pedicures, and waxing. **Pros:** Quiet and away from the madness of Panama City Beach; complete range of services and activities **Cons:** May be too expansive and generic for those seeking a small, intimate resort. ✉*4200 Marriott Dr.* ☎*850/236–6000 or 800/874–7105* ⊕*www.marriottbaypoint.com* ⇆*316 rooms, 78 suites* ☖*In-room: refrigerator (some), Wi-Fi. In-hotel: 5 restaurants, bars, golf courses, pools, gym, airport shuttle* ▭*AE, D, DC, MC, V.*

★ **$$-$$$$** 🏨 **Edgewater Beach Resort.** You can sleep at least four and as many as eight in the luxurious one-, two-, and three-bedroom apartments in beachside towers and golf-course villas. Rooms are elegantly furnished with wicker and rattan, and the resort centerpiece is a Polynesian-style lagoon pool with waterfalls, reflecting ponds, footbridges, and more than 20,000 species of tropical plants. With plenty of swimming and sporting options, this is a good beachfront option for longer stays or family vacations. **Pros:** A variety of lodging options and 110- acres of beautiful beach. **Cons:** May be overwhelming for those looking for a quiet getaway. ✉*11212 Front Beach Rd.* ☎*850/235–4044 or 800/874–8686* ⊕*www.edgewaterbeachresort.com* ⇆*520 apartments*

&In-hotel: 2 restaurants, bars, golf course, tennis courts, spa, beach-front, public Internet =D, DC, MC, V.

$$-$$$ **Holiday Inn SunSpree Resort.** The pool area at this expansive, kidney-shape beachfront resort has waterfalls, faux-rock formations, lush foliage, thatch-roof huts, and Jamon, billed as the resort's own "Polynesian Islander," who lights the poolside torches every night. You might see why this tiki schtick appeals to Spring Breakers, who flock to the place in huge numbers, but if peace and quiet are your thing in spring, this is the wrong place—and the wrong town. The rest of the year, though, it's a pleasant enough retreat for families: kids enjoy the myriad planned activities of the Splash Around Kids Club and the beachfront game room, and parents can simply relax at the in-pool grotto bar. All rooms have terra-cotta tile floors, tropical-print bedspreads, wicker furnishings, and private balconies with views of the Gulf. If you want a decent place to plant the whole family without having to leave the grounds for food or entertainment, this is it. **Pros:** Designed with the needs of families in mind—there won't be a shortage of activities to keep kids occupied. **Cons:** If you're traveling sans children, you may find adult-oriented hotels and resorts more appealing. ⊠11127 Front Beach Rd. ☎850/234–1111 ⊕www.holidayinnsunspree.com ⚲337 rooms, 4 suites &In-room: safe, refrigerator, Wi-Fi. In-hotel: restaurant, bars, pool, gym, beachfront, children's programs (ages 3–18), laundry facilities =AE, D, DC, MC, V.

NIGHTLIFE & THE ARTS

THE ARTS   Broadway touring shows, top-name entertainers, and concert artists are booked into the **Marina Civic Center** (⊠8 Harrison Ave., Panama City ☎850/769–1217 or 850/763–4696 ⊕www.marinaciviccenter.com). The **Martin Theatre** (⊠409 Harrison Ave., Panama City ☎850/763–8080) is host to traditional plays and concerts throughout the year.

NIGHTLIFE   **The Boatyard** (⊠5325 North Lagoon Dr. ☎850/249–9273) is a multi-level, indoor-outdoor waterfront nightclub and restaurant that presents a regular lineup of bands, ranging from blues to steel drums to classic rock and beyond (DJs round out the entertainment roster).**Pineapple Willy's** (⊠9875 S. Thomas Dr. ☎850/235–0928) is an eatery and bar geared to families and tourists—as well as sports fans.

SPORTS & THE OUTDOORS

CANOEING   Rentals for a trip down Econofina Creek, known as Florida's most beautiful canoe trail, are supplied by **Econofina Creek Canoe Livery.** Kayaks can be rented for $25, canoes for $35. (⊠Strickland Rd., north of Rte. 20, Youngstown ☎850/722–9032).

DIVING   Snorkeling and scuba diving are extremely popular in the clear waters here. If you have the proper certification, you can dive among dozens of ships sunk by the city to create artificial reefs. The **Panama City Dive Center** (⊠4823 Thomas Dr., Panama City Beach ☎850/235–3390 ⊕www.pcdivecenter.com) offers instruction, rentals, and charters.

DOG RACING   Find pari-mutuel betting year-round and live greyhound racing five nights and two afternoons a week at the **Ebro Greyhound Park.** They're also cashing in on the poker craze with poker matches going from noon to midnight. Simulcasts of Thoroughbred racing from the Miami area are also shown throughout the year. Schedules change periodically, so call for details. ⊠*Rte. 79 and Hwy. 20, Ebro* ☎*850/234–3943* ⊕*www.goebro.com* ⊑*$2, clubhouse $2 extra.*

GOLF The **Hombre Golf Club** (⊠*120 Coyote Pass* ☎*850/234–3673* ⊕*www. hombregolfclub.com*) has a 27-hole course that occasionally hosts professional tours; greens fee $69/$89 with cart. **Marriott Bay Point Resort** (⊠*4200 Marriott Dr.* ☎*850/235–6950 or 850/235–6949* ⊕*www. baypointgolf.com*) has a country club with two courses open to the public: the **Nicklaus Course** and the **Meadows Course**. Greens fee $59/$99 each.

TENNIS The tennis center at **Marriott Bay Point Resort** (⊠*4200 Marriott Dr.* ☎*850/235–6910*) has 10 Har-Tru tennis courts.

SHOPPING

Stores in the **Manufacturer's Outlet Center** (⊠*105 W. 23rd St., Panama City*) offer well-known brands at substantial discounts. The **Panama City Mall** (⊠*2150 Martin Luther King Jr. Blvd., Panama City* ☎*850/785–9587*) is the only true mall within an hour's radius, and has a mix of some 100 franchise shops and national chain stores.

APALACHICOLA

65 mi southeast of Panama City Beach.

It feels like a long haul between Panama City Beach and here. Add an odd name and a town's below-the-radar reputation to that long drive and you may be tempted to skip Apalachicola. But you shouldn't. It's a weirdly fascinating town that, for some reason, has a growing cosmopolitan veneer. And that makes it worth a visit.

Meaning "land of the friendly people" in the language of its original Native American inhabitants, Apalachicola—known in these parts as simply Apalach—lies on the Panhandle's southernmost bulge. European settlers began arriving in 1821, and by 1847 the southern terminus of the Apalachicola River steamboat route was a bustling port town. Although the town is now known as the Oyster Capital of the World, oystering became king only after the local cotton industry flagged—the city's extra-wide streets, built to accommodate bales of cotton awaiting transport, are a remnant of that trade—and the sponge industry moved down the coast after depleting local sponge colonies. But the newest industry here is tourism, and visitors have begun discovering the Forgotten Coast, as the area is known, flocking to its intimate hotels and bed-and-breakfasts, dining at excellent restaurants, and browsing in unique shops selling everything from handmade furniture to brass fixtures recovered from nearby shipwrecks. If you like oysters or want to go back in time to the Old South of Gothic churches and spooky graveyards, Apalachicola is a good place to start.

Drive by the **Raney House**, circa 1850, and **Trinity Episcopal Church**, built from prefabricated parts in 1838. The town is at a developmental turning point, pulled in one direction by well-intentioned locals who want to preserve Apalachicola's port-town roots and in the other by longtime business owners who fear preservation will inhibit commercial growth. For now, however, the city exudes a refreshing authenticity—think Key West in the early 1960s—that many others in the Sunshine State lost long ago, one that might be lost to Panama City Beach–style overdevelopment unless local government institutes an official historic-preservation committee.

Stop in at the **John Gorrie Museum State Park,** which honors the physician credited with inventing ice-making, and almost inventing air-conditioning. Although he was hampered by technology, later air-conditioning patents used Gorrie's discoveries. Exhibits of Apalachicola history are displayed here as well. ⊠ *Ave. D and 6th St.* ☎ *850/653–9347* ☜ *$1* ⊘ *Thurs.–Mon. 9–5.*

WHERE TO EAT

$$–$$$ ✗ **Boss Oyster.** Located at the Apalachicola River Inn, this is where you can eat your oysters fried, Rockefeller-style, on the half shell, or Greek, Mexican, English, with garlic, with shrimp, with crab, with hot peppers, with…oh, just eat 'em with gusto at this laid-back eatery overlooking the Apalachicola River. In addition to oysters, they lay down jumbo Gulf shrimp, blue crabs, bay scallops, and fresh Gulf grouper. Eat alfresco at picnic tables or inside in the busy, rustic dining room, but don't let the modest surroundings fool you—oysters aren't cheap here or anywhere in Apalach. The menu also includes such staples as steak and pizza. ⊠ *125 Water St.* ☎ *850/653–9364* ▤ *AE, D, DC, MC, V.*

★ $$–$$$ ✗ **Magnolia Grill.** Chef-owner Eddie Cass has earned local and regional acclaim from major food critics who have discovered the culinary pearl in this oyster town. In addition to meat dishes such as char-grilled pork tenderloin served with raspberry bordelaise sauce, Eddie pays tribute to local seafood with a broiled seafood feast that includes three of the freshest market fish served with locally harvested shrimp, scallops, and Apalachicola Bay oysters. Dinners here tend to be leisurely events (this is the South, after all), and the stellar desserts—anything chocolate will wow you—deserve an hour of their own. The restaurant is small, so reservations are recommended. ⊠ *99 11th St.* ☎ *850/653–8000* ▤ *MC, V* ⊘ *Closed Sun. No lunch.*

$–$$$ ✗ **Owl Café.** Located in a behemoth clapboard building on a prime corner in downtown Apalachicola, this old-fashioned, charming lunch and dinner spot pleases modern palates, both in the white-linen elegance of the dining room and in the colorful garden terrace. The food is an artful blend of old and new as well: Grandma's chicken wrap seems as much at home on the lunch menu as the crab quesadillas. Dinner seafood specials are carefully prepared, but special requests are sometimes met with resistance from the kitchen. Fine wines for adults and special menu selections for children along with a cluttered gift shop make this a family-friendly place. At night, with a full liquor bar the mood shifts to a casual lounge setting. ⊠ *15 Ave. D* ☎ *850/653–9888* ▤ *AE, MC, V* ⊘ *No dinner Sun.*

2

★ $-$$$ ✕ **Tamara's Cafe Floridita.** Tamara, a native Venezuelan, brings the food and warmth of her homeland to this colorful bistro, which mixes Florida flavors with South American flair. For starters, try the creamy black-bean soup or the pleasantly spicy oyster stew; for dinner choose from seafood paella, prosciutto-wrapped salmon with mango-cilantro sauce, or margarita chicken and scallops with a tequila-lime glaze. All entrées come with black beans and rice, fresh vegetables, and focaccia bread, but if you still have room for dessert, try the fried banana split or the *tres leches* (cake soaked in three types of milk), a South American favorite. The chef, who keeps watch over the dining room from an open kitchen, is happy to accommodate most any whim. ✉*17 Ave. E* ☎*850/653–4111* ▤*AE, D, MC, V.*

$ ✕ **Avenue Sea.** Hobnob with Apalachicola aristocracy as you eat in a serene, Edwardian-style dining room at the Gibson Inn, the town's traditional hotel. A sea change came in 2006 when Chef David Carrier, an alum of the French Laundry, arrived to infuse a strong focus on fresh, local seafood and worldly wines. Entrées, though, are not your usual portions. Each is served as a 4-ounce course—much like a tapas menu—and you can order as many as you prefer. Sit at the cozy wooden bar for an after-dinner drink, a piece of key lime pie, and a taste of Apalachicola of yesteryear. ✉*51 Ave. C* ☎*850/653–2193* ▤*AE, MC, V.*

WHERE TO STAY

$$$-$$$$ ▥ **The Consulate.** These four elegant suites, on the second story of the former offices of the French consul, range in size from 650 to 1,650 square feet and combine a 19th-century feel with 21st-century luxury. Exposed wooden beams and brick walls, 13-foot ceilings, hardwood floors, and antique architectural details add more than a hint of charm, and custom-built kitchens, full-size washers and dryers, and cordless room phones make living easy. The two front units share an expansive balcony, where you can take in the constant parade of fishing vessels headed out the intracoastal waterway. The homelike amenities make this a popular spot for families, larger groups, and even wedding parties, and discounts are given for stays longer than two nights. The Grady Market, a locally owned art and clothing boutique, occupies the building's first floor. **Pros:** Large rooms and more character than you'd find in a chain hotel. **Cons:** Cons. A bit pricey, even for Apalachicola. ✉*76 Water St.,* ☎*850/653–1515 or 877/239–1159* ⊕*www.consulatesuites.com* ☙*4 suites* ⌂*In-room: kitchen, DVD. In-hotel: no elevator* ▤*AE, MC, V.*

$$-$$$ ▥ **Coombs House Inn.** A combination of neighboring homes and a carriage house, this is an entire complex created with a Victorian flair. Nine fireplaces and an ornate oak staircase with lead-glass windows on the landing lend authenticity to this restored 1905 mansion. No two guest rooms are alike, but all are appointed with Victorian-era settees, four-poster or sleigh beds, English chintz curtains, and Asian rugs on polished hardwood floors. A full breakfast is served in the dining room. Eighty steps away, you can stay in the villa (aka Coombs House East), and beyond that a renovated carriage house. Popular for weddings and receptions, these may be the most elegant homes in Apala-

chicola. Free tours are offered in the afternoon if the accommodations are not in use. **Pros:** Clean, comfortable; on-site, friendly owner whose happy to assist with travel tips and suggestions. **Cons:** Be prepared to meet and greet other guests at the inn; if you favor complete privacy, a hotel may suit you better. ⊠*80 6th St.,* ☎*850/653–9199* ⊕*www. coombshouseinn.com* ⇆*18 rooms* ⟨*In-hotel: bicycles, no-smoking rooms* ▤*D, MC, V.*

$–$$$ ⊞ **Gibson Inn.** One of a few inns on the National Register of Historic Places still operating as a full-service facility, this turn-of-the-20th-century hostelry in the heart of downtown is easily identified by its wraparound porches, intricate fretwork, and captain's watch. Large rooms are furnished with period pieces like four-poster beds, antique armoires, and pedestal lavatories. Extremely popular for weddings and special events, the inn equally impresses overnight visitors with its cleanliness, style, service, and rocking-chair-rich wraparound porch. Add chills to your thrills and ask for the haunted room. **Pros:** Smack dab in the center of town; easy to walk to every downtown site, then rest on the veranda afterwards. **Cons:** May get a little busy when weddings or celebrations are taking place in the main lobby or Avenue Sea. ⊠*51 Ave. C,* ☎*850/653–2191* ⊕*www.gibsoninn.com* ⇆*30 rooms, 2 suites* ⟨*In-hotel: restaurant, bar, no elevator, some pets allowed* ▤*AE, MC, V.*

$–$$ ⊞ **Best Western Apalach Inn.** Basic but impeccably kept, this modern property 1 mi from the downtown waterfront area has everything you need for a convenient, inexpensive overnight. Standard guest rooms—each with two queens or a king bed—are done in earth tones with wicker headboards and burgundy-print curtains and bedspreads. A large swimming pool, free local calls, and a complimentary continental breakfast are unexpected bonuses. **Pros:** Functional and practical. **Cons:** Practical can equal uninspiring. Out of walking distance to downtown. ⊠*249 U.S. 98 W* ☎*850/653–9131* ⊕*www.bwapalachinn.com* ⇆*42 rooms* ⟨*In-room: Wi-Fi. In-hotel: pool, no elevator* ▤*AE, D, MC, V* ⦿*CP.*

$–$$ ⊞ **Rancho Inn.** This mom-and-pop operation—the owners live on-site—prides itself on its homeyness and personalized service. Rooms are spotless, if a little dated in their beige-and-brown color schemes (a few have undergone recent renovations), but 27-inch color TVs (complete with HBO and other premium channels), in-room coffeemakers, refrigerators, and microwaves make it a hard-to-beat option for those on a budget. The owners advertise "never-smoked-in rooms"—and impose fines of $100 for guests who light up in them. Trained pets can share accommodations for a fee. Unless they smoke. **Pros:** All in all, an inexpensive option. **Cons:** Cut and dry. It's a motel. ⊠*240 U.S. 98 W* ☎*850/653–9435* ⊕*www.ranchoinn.com* ⇆*31 rooms, 1 suite* ⟨*In-room: refrigerator, Wi-Fi. In-hotel: pool* ▤*AE, D, MC, V.*

SHOPPING

The **Tin Shed** (⊠*170 Water St.* ☎*850/653–3635*) has an impressive collection of antiques and knickknacks, from antique brass luggage tags to 1940s nautical charts to sponge-diver wet suits to hand-glazed tiles and architectural elements salvaged from demolished buildings.

Closed Sunday. The **Grady Market** (✉ *76 Water St.* ☎ *850/653–4099*), on the first floor of the Consulate Inn, is a collection of more than a dozen boutiques, including several antiques dealers and the gallery of Richard Bickel, known for his stunning black-and-white photographs of local residents. **Avenue E** (✉ *15 Ave. E* ☎ *850/653–1411*) is a stylish store specializing in reasonably priced antique and reproduction pieces, including furniture, lamps, artwork, and interior accessories.

2

ST. GEORGE ISLAND

8 mi southeast of Apalachicola.

Pristine St. George Island sits 5 mi out into the Gulf of Mexico just south of Apalachicola. Accessed via the Bryant Patton Bridge off U.S. 98, the island is bordered by both Apalachicola Bay and the Gulf, offering vacationers the best of both. The rich bay is an angler's dream, whereas the snowy-white beaches and clear Gulf waters satisfy even the most finicky beachgoer. Indulge in bicycling, hiking, canoeing, and snorkeling, or find a secluded spot for reading, gathering shells, or bird-watching. Accommodations mostly take the form of privately owned, fully furnished condos and single-family homes, which allow for plenty of privacy.

Fodor'sChoice ★ **St. George Island State Park** gives you Old Florida at its undisturbed best. On the east end of the island are 9 mi of undeveloped beaches and dunes—the longest beachfront of any state park in Florida. Sandy coves, salt marshes, oak forests, and pines provide shelter for many species, including such birds as bald eagles and ospreys. Spotless restrooms and plentiful parking make a day at this park a joy. ☎ *850/927–2111* ⊕ *www.floridastateparks.org/stgeorgeisland* ☒ *$4 per vehicle, up to 8 people* ⊙ *Daily 8–sunset.*

WHERE TO EAT

$$-$$$ ✕ **Blue Parrot.** You'll feel like you're sneaking in the back door as you climb the side stairs leading to an outdoor deck overlooking the Gulf. Or if you can, grab a table indoors. During special-event weekends, the place is packed, and service may be a little slow. The food is hard to beat if you're not looking for anything fancy. Baskets of shrimp, oysters, and crab cakes—fried or char-grilled and served with fries—are more than one person can handle. Daily specials are listed on the blackboard. ✉ *68 W. Gorrie Dr.* ☎ *850/927–2987* ▭ *AE, D, MC, V.*

$-$$$ ✕ **That Place on 98.** This place used to be as folksy and unassuming as its name suggests—that is, until the owner decided on an eye-popping turquoise-and-pink color scheme. Lucky for you, though, because now you *can't* miss it, washed up on the shores of Apalachicola Bay like a Benjamin Moore shipwreck. Nonetheless, it's one of the most authentic seafood shacks on the entire Gulf Coast, and it's *the* place to go if you're looking for fresh oysters. Get them any way you like them: on the half-shell, steamed, fried, Rockefellered, or 98'ed (baked with bacon, onions, garlic, and mozzarella). Fresh fish dishes, chicken, beef, and Greek salads round out the menu. ✉ *500 Hwy. 98* ☎ *850/670–9898* ⊙ *Closed Sun.*

¢　✕ **BJs.** In any other locale you might think twice before dining at a restaurant that advertises "kegs-to-go" on the menu, but this is an island, so establishments tend to wear several hats (some even sell live bait). Fear not. This simple beach shack serves solid, if predictable, sandwiches (grilled chicken, turkey club, BLT), salads (Caesar, tuna, fried chicken), and appetizers (buffalo wings, cheese sticks, onion rings), but the pizza is definitely worth stopping for. Pies range from white pizza with chicken and bacon to shrimp-and-mozzarella, to build-your-own personal pie (choose from 15 toppings). Beer and wine are available, and there are pool tables to pass the time while you wait for your order. ✉*105 W. Gulf Beach Dr.* ☎*850/927–2805* ⚓*Reservations not accepted* ▭*MC, V.*

WHERE TO STAY

¢-$$　▦ **St. George Inn.** A little piece of Key West smack in the middle of the Panhandle, this cozy inn has tin roofs, hardwood floors, wraparound porches—even a widow's walk. Personal touches like private porches and in-room coffeemakers keep things homey. Both beach and bay are within view, and several restaurants and a convenience store are within walking distance. Two larger suites have full kitchens, and the pool is heated for year-round swimming. Specials are posted on the inn's Web site during off-season, when prices can drop by more than half. **Pros:** Recreating Old Florida in a modern way. **Cons:** The area is sparsely populated; you may miss access to modern conveniences—and people. ✉*135 Franklin Blvd.,* ☎*800/824–0416* ⇥*15 rooms, 2 suites* ⚭*In-room: kitchen (some), refrigerator. In-hotel: pool* ▭*MC, V.*

THE OUTDOORS

BOATING　For a **boat tour** (☎*850/697–3989*) of St. George Sound and Apalachicola Bay, call charter captain A.P. Whaley. He's famous in these parts for his uncanny ability to attract dolphins to the stern of his boat, the *Gat V.*

INLAND ACROSS THE PANHANDLE

Farther inland, where the northern reaches of the Panhandle butt up against the back porches of Alabama and Georgia, you'll find a part of Florida that goes a long way toward explaining why the state song is "Swannee River" (and why its parenthetical title is "Old Folks at Home"). Stephen Foster's musical genius notwithstanding, the inland Panhandle area is definitely more Dixie than Sunshine State, with few lodging options other than the chain motels that flank the Interstate 10 exits and a decidedly slower pace of life than you'll find on the tourist-heavy Gulf Coast. But the area's natural attractions—hills and farmland, untouched small towns, pristine state parks—make for great day trips from the coast should the sky turn gray or the skin red. Explore underground caverns where eons-old rock formations create bizarre scenes, visit one of Florida's up-and-coming wineries, or poke around small-town America in DeFuniak Springs. Altogether, the inland area of the Panhandle is one of the state's most satisifyingly soothing regions.

DEFUNIAK SPRINGS

28 mi east of Crestview.

This scenic spot has a rather unusual claim to fame: at its center lies a nearly perfectly symmetrical spring-fed lake, one of only two such naturally circular bodies of water in the world (the other is in Switzerland). In 1848 the Knox Hill Academy was founded here, and for more than half a century it was the only institution of higher learning in northwestern Florida. In 1885 the town was chosen as the location for the New York Chautauqua educational society's winter assembly. The Chautauqua programs were discontinued in 1922, but DeFuniak Springs attempts to revive them, in spirit at least, by sponsoring a countywide Chautauqua Festival in April. Christmas is a particularly festive time, when the sprawling Victorian houses surrounding the lake are decorated to the nines. There's not a tremendous amount to see here, but if you have the good sense to travel Highway 90 to discover Old Florida, at least take the time to travel Circle Drive to see its beautiful Victorian homes.

By all accounts, the 16-by-24-foot **Walton-DeFuniak Public Library** is Florida's oldest library continuously operating in its original building. Opened in 1887, the original space has been added to over the years. The library now contains nearly 30,000 volumes, including some rare books, many older than the structure itself. The collection also includes antique musical instruments and impressive European armor. ⊠*3 Circle Dr.* ☎*850/892–3624* ⊙*Mon. and Wed.–Sat. 9–5, Tues. 9–8.*

The **Chautauqua Winery** opened in 1989, and its vintages have slowly won respect from oenophiles wary of what was once considered to be an oxymoron at best: "Florida wine." But the state has history on its side: according to historical records, the first wine produced by Europeans in the New World was made in Florida in 1562 by French Huguenots (obviously, this predated their little-known Siege of Napa Valley). Take a free tour to see how ancient art blends with modern technology; then retreat to the tasting room and gift shop. ⊠*I-10 and U.S. 331* ☎*850/892–5887* ⊕*www.chautauquawinery.com.*

Some of the finest examples of Victorian architecture in the state can be seen while you are walking or motoring around **Circle Drive**, the road that wraps around Circle Lake. The circumference is marked with beautiful Victorian specimens like the Walton-DeFuniak Public Library, the Dream Cottage, and the Pansy Cottage. Most of the

PARK IT HERE

You can now buy a Florida State Park Annual Express Pass to alleviate individual park admissions. For $40 per person—or $80 for a family—you'll have entrance into any Florida state park (except Homosassa Springs and the Skyway Fishing Pier in St. Petersburg) for a full year. Even though you may not be here that long, it's worth considering if you plan to hit several state parks, which usually charge $4 per carload, and especially if you plan to return to Florida within the year. You can buy a pass at any state park, or buy one via their Web site at ⊕ *www.floridastateparks.org.*

other notable structures are private residences, but you can still admire them from the street.

WHERE TO STAY

¢-$ ⌹ **Hotel De Funiak.** You can't miss this Depression-era two-story red-brick structure on a quiet corner a few blocks from peaceful Lake DeFuniak—just look for the two-tone 1937 Buick permanently moored out front. Each room has a different theme decor, from Oriental to Art Deco to French Country, and contains a combination of period antiques and reproductions, many of which can be purchased on the spot. At the hotel restaurant, **Bogey's** (☎850/951–2233), the dinner menu centers around fresh Gulf seafood, yet also includes chicken and veal. It's an unusual find in a small town, and one of the nicer places to stay in this part of the Panhandle. Pros: Applause for the owners who created a sweet little retreat in the heart of downtown. Cons: DeFuniak can be eerily empty and quiet at night. ⌂400 E. Nelson Ave., ☎850/892–4383 or 877/333–8642 ⊕www.hoteldefuniak.com ☞7 rooms, 3 suites ♿In-hotel: restaurant, public Wi-Fi, no-smoking rooms ▭AE, D, MC, V ⦿CP.

FALLING WATERS STATE PARK

35 mi east of DeFuniak Springs.

This site of a Civil War–era whiskey distillery and, later, an exotic plant nursery—some imported species still thrive in the wild—is best known for also being the site of one of Florida's most notable geological features—the Falling Waters Sink. The 100-foot-deep cylindrical pit provides the background for a waterfall, and there's an observation deck for viewing this natural phenomenon. The water free-falls 67 feet to the bottom of the sink, but where it goes after that is a mystery. ⌂Rte. 77A, Chipley ☎850/638–6130 ⊕www.floridastateparks.org/falling-waters ⛟$4 per vehicle, up to 8 people ⊙Daily 8–sunset.

FLORIDA CAVERNS STATE PARK

13 mi northeast of Falling Waters off I–10 on U.S. 231.

Marianna is a cute and pristine community, and a short drive from the center of town you can see what's behind, or—more accurately—what's beneath it all. Take a ranger-led cave tour to see stalactites, stalagmites, soda straws, columns, rimstones, flowstones, and "waterfalls" of solid rock at these underground caverns where the temperature hovers at an oh-so-pleasant 68°F year-round. Some of the caverns are off-limits to the public or open for scientific study only with a permit, but you'll still see enough to fill a half day or more—and you'll be amazed that caverns of this magnitude exist anywhere in the Sunshine State. Between Memorial Day and Labor Day, rangers offer guided lantern tours on Friday and Saturday nights. There are also hiking trails, campsites, and areas for swimming, horseback riding, and canoeing on the Chipola River. ⌂3345 Caverns Rd. (off Hwy. 90 on Rte. 166), Marianna ☎850/482–9598, 800/326–3521 for camping reservations ⊕www.

floridastateparks.org/floridacaverns ⊠*Park $4 per vehicle, up to 8 people; caverns $5* ⊙*Daily 8–sunset; cavern tours daily 9–4.*

TALLAHASSEE

61 mi southeast of Florida Caverns.

Tallahassee is Florida with a Southern accent, a preserved part of the past and the only Southern capital spared in the Civil War. For such an active city, the pace here seems unusually slow, perhaps because of the canopies of ancient oaks and spring bowers of azaleas that line many streets. Along with Florida State University, the perennial Seminoles football champions, and FAMU's fabled "Marching 100" band, the city also has more than a touch of the Old South. Tallahassee maintains a tranquillity quite different from the sun-and-surf hedonism of the major coastal towns. Vestiges of the city's colorful past are found throughout. For example, in the capitol complex, the turn-of-the-20th-century Old Capitol building is strikingly paired with the New Capitol skyscraper. Tallahassee's tree-lined streets are particularly memorable—among the best "canopy roads" (as they are called) are St. Augustine, Miccosukee, Meridian, Old Bainbridge, and Centerville, all dotted with country stores and antebellum plantation houses. This is easily one of Florida's most pleasing cities.

DOWNTOWN

WHAT TO SEE

Downtown Tallahassee Historic Trail. A route originally mapped and documented by an eager Eagle Scout as part of a merit-badge project, this trail has become a Tallahassee sightseeing staple. The starting point is the New Capitol, where you can pick up maps and descriptive brochures at the visitor center. You'll walk through the **Park Avenue and Calhoun Street historic districts,** which will take you back to Territorial days and the era of postwar reconstruction. The trail is dotted with landmark churches and cemeteries, along with outstanding examples of Greek Revival, Italianate, and prairie-style architecture. Some houses are open to the public. The **Brokaw-McDougall House** (⊠*329 N. Meridian St.* ⊠*Free* ⊙*Weekdays 9–3*) is a superb example of the Greek Revival and Italianate styles. The **Meginnis-Monroe House** (⊠*125 N. Gadsden St.* ⊠*Free* ⊙*Tues.–Sat. 10–5, Sun. 2–5*) served as a field hospital during the Civil War and is now an art gallery.

Museum of Florida History. If you thought Florida was founded by Walt Disney, stop here. Covering 12,000 years, the displays explain Florida's past by highlighting the unique geological and historical events that have shaped the state. Exhibits include a mammoth armadillo grazing in a savanna, the remains of a giant mastodon found in nearby Wakulla Springs, and a dugout canoe that once carried Native Americans into Florida's backwaters. Florida's history also includes settlements by the Spanish, British, French, and Confederates who fought for possession of the state. Gold bars, weapons, flags, maps, furniture,

A GOOD TOUR

The downtown area is compact enough so that most sights can be seen on foot, although it's also served by a free, continuous shuttle trolley. Start at the capitol complex, which contains the **Old Capitol** and its counterpoint, the **New Capitol.** Across the street from the older structure is the restored **Union Bank Building,** and two blocks west of the new statehouse you'll find the **Museum of Florida History,** with exhibits on many eras of the state's history and prehistory. If you really want to get a feel for Old Tallahas-

see, walk the **Downtown Tallahassee Historic Trail** as it wends its way from the capitol complex through several of the city's historic districts.

TIMING

You can't do justice to the capitol complex and downtown area in less than two hours. Allow four hours to walk the 8-mi stretch of the historic trail. If you visit between March and April, you'll find flowers in bloom, the legislature in session, and the Springtime Tallahassee festival in full swing.

steamboats, and other artifacts underscore the fact that although most Americans date the nation to 1776, Florida's residents had been building settlements hundreds of years earlier. If this intrigues you, one floor up is the **Florida State Archives and Library,** where there's a treasure trove of government records, manuscripts, photographs, genealogical records, and other materials. ⊠ *500 S. Bronough St.* ☎ *850/245–6400, 850/245–6600 (library and archives)* ⊕ *www.flheritage.com* ✉ *Free* ⊙ *Weekdays 9–4:30, Sat. 10–4:30, Sun. noon–4:30.*

★ **New Capitol.** In the 1960s, when there was talk of relocating the capital to a more central location like Orlando, Panhandle legislators got to work and approved the construction of a 22-story modern skyscraper that would anchor the capital right where it was. It's perfectly placed at the crest of a hill, sitting prominently behind the low-rise Old Capitol. The governor's office is on the first floor, and House and Senate chambers on the fifth floor provide viewer galleries for when the legislative sessions take place (March to May). Catch a panoramic view of Tallahassee and the surrounding countryside all the way into Georgia from the fabulous 22nd-floor observation deck. Also on this floor is the Florida Artists Hall of Fame, a tribute to Floridians such as Ray Charles, Burt Reynolds, Tennessee Williams, Ernest Hemingway, and Marjorie Kinnan Rawlings. To pick up information about the area, stop at the Florida Visitors Center, on the plaza level. There are guided tours from 9 to 3 on the hour (except at noon), booked in advance. ⊠ *400 S. Monroe St.* ☎ *850/488–6167* ✉ *Free* ⊙ *Visitor center weekdays 8–5.*

★ **Old Capitol.** The centerpiece of the capitol complex, this 1842 structure has been added to and subtracted from several times. Having been restored, the jaunty red-and-white-stripe awnings and combination gas-electric lights make it look much as it did in 1902. Inside, it houses a must-see museum of Florida's political history as well as the old Supreme Court chambers and Senate Gallery—a very interesting peek

2

into the past. ⊠*S. Monroe St. at Apalachee Pkwy.* ☎*850/487–1902* 🖃*Free* ☉*Self-guided or guided tours weekdays 9–4:30, Sat. 10–4:30, Sun. noon–4:30.*

Union Bank Building. Chartered in 1833, this is Florida's oldest bank building. Since it closed in 1843, it has played many roles, from ballet school to bakery. It has been restored to what is thought to be its original appearance and currently houses Florida A&M's Black Archives Extension, which depicts black history in Florida. Call ahead for hours, which are subject to change, and directions. ⊠*Calhoun St. at Apalachee Pkwy.* ☎*850/487–3803* 🖃*Free* ☉*Weekdays 9–4.*

AWAY FROM DOWNTOWN

WHAT TO SEE

Alfred Maclay Gardens State Park. Starting in December, the grounds at this 1,200-acre estate are afire with azaleas, dogwood, Oriental magnolias, spring bulbs of tulips and irises, banana shrubs, honeysuckle, silverbell trees, pansies, and camellias. Allow half a day to wander past the reflecting pool into the tiny walled garden, and around the lakes and woodlands. The Maclay residence (open January through April only) is furnished as it was in the 1920s; picnic areas, gardens, and swimming and boating facilities are open to the public. ⊠*3540 Thomasville Rd.* ☎*850/487–4556* ⊕*www.floridastateparks.org/maclaygardens* 🖃*$4 per vehicle, up to 8 people; extra $4 per person for garden admission Jan.–Apr.; free rest of year* ☉*Daily 8–sunset.*

Lake Jackson Mounds Archaeological State Park. While the waters here can make bass anglers weep, the real find are the half-dozen temple mounds (and one possible burial mound), the largest of which is nearly 300 feet square at its base and 35 feet high. Inside these mounds, archaeologists have found pre-Columbian artifacts including jewelry, copper breastplates, and cloaks. Also on the site are the ruins of an early-19th-century plantation built by Colonel Robert Butler, adjutant to General Andrew Jackson during the siege of New Orleans. ⊠*3600 Indian Mounds Rd.* ☎*850/562–0042* 🖃*$2* ☉*Daily 8–sunset.*

San Luis Archaeological and Historic Site. Long before New England's residents began gaining a foothold in America, the native Apalachee Indians as well as Spanish missionaries were settled down here. On the site of a 17th-century Spanish mission and Apalachee Indian town sites, this museum focuses on the archaeology of the late 1600s, when the Apalachee village here had a population of at least 1,400. By 1704, however, threatened by Creek Indians and British forces, the locals burned the village and fled. Although you can take self-guided tours and watch scientists conducting digs daily, it's more fun to hook up with one of the dozen or so living-history guides who offer tours and insights every day from 10 AM–2 PM. ⊠*2020 W. Mission Rd.* ☎*850/487–3711* ⊕*www.missionsanluis.org* 🖃*Free* ☉*Tues.–Sun. 10–4.*

☺ **Tallahassee Museum.** About 20 minutes from downtown, this bucolic park showcases a peaceful and intriguing look at Old Florida. Although called a museum, this is really a working 1880s pioneer farm that offers daily hands-on activities for children, such as soap making and blacksmithing. A boardwalk meanders through the 52 acres of natural habitat that make up the zoo, which has such varied animals as panthers, bobcats, white-tailed deer, bald eagles, red wolves, hawks, owls, otters, and black bears—many of which were brought here injured or orphaned. Also on-site are nature trails, a one-room schoolhouse dating from 1897, and an 1840s Southern plantation manor, where you can usually find someone cooking on weekends. It's peaceful, pleasing, and educational. ✉3945 Museum Dr. ☎850/576–1636 ⊕www.tallahasseemuseum.org ☎$9 ☉Mon.–Sat. 9–5, Sun. 12:30–5.

Fodor'sChoice ★ Known for having one of the deepest springs in the world, the very picturesque and highly recommended **Wakulla Springs State Park** remains relatively untouched, retaining the wild and exotic look it had in the 1930s, when the films *Tarzan* and *Creature from the Black Lagoon* were shot here. Take a glass-bottom boat deep into the lush, jungle-lined waterways to catch glimpses of alligators, snakes, nesting limpkins, and other waterfowl. It costs only $50 to rent a pontoon boat and go it alone. It may be worth it, since an underground river flows into a pool so clear you can see the bottom more than 100 feet below. The park is 15 mi south of Tallahassee on Route 61. If you can't pull yourself away from this idyllic spot, spend the night in the 1930s Spanish-Mediterranean lodge (see below). ✉550 Wakulla Park Dr., Wakulla Springs ☎850/926-0700 ⊕www.floridastateparks.org/wakullasprings ☎$4 per vehicle, up to 8 people; boat tour $6 ☉Daily 8–sunset, boat tours hourly 9:30–4:30.

As its name suggests, **St. Marks National Wildlife Refuge and Lighthouse** is of both natural and historical interest. Natural salt marshes, tidal flats, and freshwater pools that nourished Paleo Indians 10,000 years ago and Apalachee Indians in the 1500s set the stage for the once-powerful Fort San Marcos de Apalache that was built nearby in 1639. Stones salvaged from the fort were used in the lighthouse, which is still in operation. In winter the 100,000-acre-plus refuge on the shores of Apalachee Bay is the resting place for thousands of migratory birds of more than 300 species, but the alligators seem to like it year-round (keep your camera ready and you're bound to get a photo op). The visitor center has information on more than 75 mi of marked trails, some of which wend through landscapes with foliage more reminiscent of North Carolina than Florida. Hardwood swamps and pine woodlands also provide habitat for wood ducks, black bears, otters, raccoons, deer, armadillos, coyotes, feral hogs, fox squirrels, gopher tortoises, and woodpeckers. Twenty-five miles south of Tallahassee, the refuge can be reached via Route 363. ✉ *1255 Lighthouse Rd., St. Marks* ☎ *850/925–6121* ⊕ *saintmarks.fws.gov* ✑ *$5 per vehicle* ⊙ *Refuge daily sunrise–sunset; visitor center weekdays 8–4, weekends 10–5.*

WHERE TO EAT

$$-$$$$ ✕ **Andrew's 228.** Part of a smart complex in the heart of the political district, this two-story "urban Tuscan villa" (contradiction noted) is the latest of owner Andy Reiss's restaurant incarnations to occupy the same space (the last was Andrew's Second Act). Leaning toward upscale, the menu includes a range of chicken, steak, pasta, and fish dishes such as grouper picatta, penne shrimp afelia, chicken marsala, and double-cut pork chops. If you're so inclined, a specialty is the $6 martini. ✉ *228 S. Adams St.* ☎ *850/222–3444* ▤ *AE, D, MC, V.*

$$-$$$ ✕ **Chez Pierre.** You'll feel as if you've entered a great-aunt's old plantation home in this restored 1920s house set back from the road in historic Lafayette Park. Since 1976, its warm, cozy rooms, gleaming hardwood floors, and large French doors separating dining areas have created an intimate place to go for authentic French cuisine. Try the tournedos of beef or one of the special lamb dishes. The Sunday brunch is one of the most popular around. ✉ *1215 Thomasville Rd.* ☎ *850/222–0936* ▤ *AE, D, MC, V.*

¢-$ ✕ **Rice-Bowl Oriental.** Bamboo woodwork and thatched-roof booths lend an air of authenticity to this Asian-hybrid spot tucked away in a Tallahassee strip mall. Chinese, Japanese, Thai, and Vietnamese favorites are all represented here, from General Tso's chicken to fresh sushi to green curry and rice noodle dishes. The all-you-can-eat lunch buffet (Sunday to Friday, $6.95), complete with entrées, salads, soups, and fresh sushi, just might be one of the best deals in town. ✉ *3813 N. Monroe St.* ☎ *850/514–3632* ▤ *AE, D, DC, MC, V.*

¢ ✕ **Decent Pizza.** The name is terribly modest—the pizza here is much more than decent, and the prices are more than reasonable. A couple of Florida State University grads opened this simple pizzeria, which became an instant hit with those on an undergraduate budget: slices and salads start at $3.50 each, and at a buck each, half-pint draft beers are cheaper than sodas. Choose from more than 30 toppings for regular red-sauce, pesto, or white pies. ✉ *1026 N. Monroe St.* ☎ *850/222–6400* ✑ *Reservations not accepted* ▤ *MC, V.*

> ### COKE REWARDS
>
> Roughly 10 mi west of Tallahassee on Highway 90, the tiny slow-as-molasses town of Quincy may look rough on the surface, but there are reportedly more millionaires here per capita than any area in the nation. Why? Because a little more than 100 years ago a local banker suggested that his customers invest in an unknown soft drink a friend had created. Smart idea—and smart investors. The drink was Coca-Cola.

¢ ✕ **Hopkins' Eatery.** Locals in the know flock here for superb salads, homemade soups, and sandwiches—expect a short wait at lunchtime—via simple counter service. Kids will like the traditional peanut butter–and-jelly sandwich (with bananas and sprouts, if they dare); adults might opt for a chunky chicken melt, smothered beef, or garden vegetarian sub. The spearmint iced tea is a must-have, as is a slice of freshly baked chocolate cake. A second location on North Monroe Street offers the same menu. ✉ *1415 Market St.* ☎ *850/668–0311* ✉ *1840 N. Monroe St.* ☎ *850/386–1809* ☰ *AE, D, DC, MC, V* ⊘ *Closed Sun. No dinner Sat.*

WHERE TO STAY

★ $$-$$$$ ⬚ **Governors Inn.** Only a block from the Capitol, this plushly restored historic warehouse is abuzz during the week with politicians, press, and lobbyists. It's a perfect location for business travelers and, on weekends, for tourists who want to visit downtown sites. Rooms are a rich blend of mahogany, brass, and classic prints. **Pros:** A few steps from the great museums, restaurants, and the Capitol; plus, the rooms and lobby are warm and inviting. **Cons:** During session and football season, the district can get crowded and busy, and accessing the area may be a challenge. ✉ *209 S. Adams St.,* ☎ *850/681–6855 or 800/342–7717* ⊕ *www.thegovinn.com* ⇆ *29 rooms, 12 suites* ⅋ *In-hotel: no elevator, laundry service, parking (fee)* ☰ *AE, D, DC, MC, V* ⏐⊙⏐ *CP.*

$-$$$$ ⬚ **DoubleTree Hotel Tallahassee.** This hotel a mere two blocks from the Capitol hosts heavy hitters from the worlds of politics and media. Since it's also an easy walk from the FSU campus, it welcomes plenty of Seminoles fans during football season. Rooms, which overlook either a city park or the Capitol, are basic but clean, with beige wallpaper and occasional chairs, and green-and-yellow-stripe bedspreads. Half the rooms have queen beds, the other half kings. **Pros:** A business traveler's friend, and the location is in the heart of it all. **Cons:** If you'd prefer something with character, then the Governor's Inn may work better. ✉ *101 S. Adams St.,* ☎ *850/224–5000* ⇆ *243 rooms* ⅋ *In-room: Wi-Fi. In-hotel: restaurant, bar, pool, gym* ☰ *AE, D, DC, MC, V.*

¢-$ ⬚ **Super 8.** The quiet courtyard with its own pool and the darkly welcoming cantina (where a complimentary continental breakfast is served) convey the look of Old Spain. Rooms are furnished in heavy Mediterranean style—and come with two double beds or one king. Time it right: rates double on FSU football home-game weekends. **Pros:** Close enough to the Capitol, and at a great rate. **Cons:** It's a Super 8, so it lacks the character of high-priced lodging. ✉ *2801 N. Monroe St.,* ☎ *850/386–8286* ⊕ *www.super8.com* ⇆ *108 rooms, 23 suites* ⅋ *In-room: Wi-Fi. In-hotel: pool.* ☰ *AE, D, MC, V* ⏐⊙⏐ *CP.*

CAMPING Spreading north of Apalachicola and west of Tallahassee and U.S. 319 is the **Apalachicola National Forest,** with campsites, hiking trails, picnic areas, and plentiful lakes for old-fashioned swimmin'. Honor-system fees range from $3 admission to $8 camping. ☎ *850/643–2282.*

NIGHTLIFE & THE ARTS

THE ARTS If you're too shy to crash a frat party, here's a more civilized evening out: **Florida State University** (☎*850/644–4774 School of Music, 850/644–6500 School of Theatre ⊕www.music.fsu.edu*) plays host to more than 400 concerts and recitals annually in year-round performances by its School of Music, and many productions by its School of Theatre. About 30 miles northwest of the capital in the small town of Monticello, the **Monticello Opera House** (✉*185 W. Washington [U.S. 90 E], Monticello* ☎*850/997–4242*) presents concerts and plays in a restored gaslight-era opera house. The **Tallahassee Little Theatre** (✉*1861 Thomasville Rd.* ☎*850/224–8474* ⊕*www.tallahasseelittletheatre.org*) has a six-production season that runs from September through May. The season of the **Tallahassee Symphony Orchestra** (☎*850/224–0461* ⊕*www.tallahasseesymphony.org*) usually runs from October through April; performances are usually held at Florida State University's Ruby Diamond Auditorium.

NIGHTLIFE There are endless options for after-dark entertainment for Tallahassee's government and university populations. When you're in town, be sure to check the college newspapers for the latest developments. **Waterworks** (✉*1133 Thomasville Rd.* ☎*850/224–1887*), with its retro-chic tiki-bar fittings, attracts jazz fans and hipsters of all ages for cocktails and DJ-spun dance music. On Friday night there's a banjo player, a retro-cool treat. **Floyd's Music Store** (✉*666-1 W. Tennessee St.* ☎*850/222–3506* ⊕*www.floydsmusicstore.com*) hosts some of the hottest local and touring acts around, such as Daughtry and Kenney Chesney. Other performers, from dueling pianos to assorted DJs, round out the schedule.

THE PANHANDLE ESSENTIALS

TRANSPORTATION

BY AIR

CARRIERS

Pensacola Regional Airport (⊕*www.flypensacola.com)* is served by Air Tran, American Eagle, Continental, Delta, Northwest, and US Airways.

Okaloosa County Regional Airport (⊕*www.okaloosacountyairports. com)* is served by American Eagle, Delta Connection, Continental Express, and Northwest.

Panama City–Bay County International Airport (⊕*www.pcairport. com)* is served by Delta Connection, Northwest Airlink, and Chautauqua Airlines.

Tallahassee Regional Airport (⊕*talgov.com/airport)* is served by Continental, Delta, Northwest, and US Airways Express.

Contacts AirTran (☎*800/247–8726).* **American/American Eagle** (☎*800/433–7300).* **Continental** (☎*800/523–3273).* **Delta** (☎*800/221–1212).* **Northwest**

(☎ *800/225–2525*). **Northwest Airlink** (☎ *800/225–2525*). **US Airways/US Airways Express** (☎ *800/428–4322*).

AIRPORTS & TRANSFERS

A trip from Pensacola Regional Airport via Yellow Cab costs about $14 to downtown and $24 to Pensacola Beach. A ride from the Okaloosa County Regional Airport via Checker Cab costs $18 to Fort Walton Beach and $24 to Destin. Bluewater Car Service charges $15–$17 to Fort Walton Beach and $28 to Destin. Yellow Cab charges about $15–$27 from Panama City–Bay County International Airport to the beach area, depending on the location of your hotel. DeLuxe Coach Limo Service provides van service to downtown Panama City and to Panama City Beach for $1.25 per mile. Yellow Cab travels from Tallahassee Regional Airport to downtown for $13–$16.

Airport Contacts Okaloosa County Regional Airport (☎ *850/651–7160* ⊕ *www.okaloosacountyairports.com*). **Panama City–Bay County International Airport** (☎ *850/763–6751* ⊕ *www.pcairport.com*). **Pensacola Regional Airport** (☎ *850/436–5005* ⊕ *www.flypensacola.com*). **Tallahassee Regional Airport** (☎ *850/891–7800* ⊕ *talgov.com/airport*).

Airport Transportation Contacts Okaloosa County Airport: Gulf Coast Shuttle Service (☎ *850/642–1042*). **Panama City Beach: Affordable Limousine Service** (☎ *850/233–0029*). **Pensacola: All Airports Taxi and Shuttle** (☎ *850/865–5619* or *800/643–4711*).

Tallahassee: Capital Transportation There are two choices for cabs: **City Taxi** (☎ *850/562–4222*) or **Yellow Cab** (☎ *850/575–1022*).

BY BUS

Greyhound has stations in Crestview, DeFuniak Springs, Fort Walton Beach, Panama City, Pensacola, and Tallahassee. The Baytown Trolley serves Bay County, including downtown Panama City and the beaches ($1). In Pensacola, Escambia County Area Transit (ECAT) provides regular citywide bus service ($1), downtown trolley routes, tours through the historic district (25¢), and from Memorial Day to Labor Day free trolley service on Friday, Saturday, and Sunday.

Contacts Baytown Trolley (☎ *850/769–0557*). **Escambia County Area Transit** (☎ *850/595–3228*). **Greyhound Lines** (☎ *800/231–2222, 850/682–6922 in Crestview, 850/892–5566 in DeFuniak Springs, 850/243–1940 in Fort Walton Beach, 850/785–6111 in Panama City, 850/476–4800 in Pensacola, 850/222–4240 in Tallahassee*).

BY CAR

The main east–west arteries across the top of the state are Interstate 10 and U.S. 90. Pensacola is about an hour's drive east of Mobile. Tallahassee is 3½ hours west of Jacksonville. It takes about four hours to drive from Pensacola to Tallahassee. Driving along Interstate 10 can be monotonous, but U.S. 90 piques your interest by routing you along the main streets of several county seats. U.S. 98 snakes eastward along the coast, splitting into 98 and 98A at Inlet Beach before rejoining at Panama City and continuing on to Port St. Joe and Apalachicola. The view of the Gulf from U.S. 98 can be breathtaking, especially at sunset, but ongoing construction projects make it slow going most of the time. If you need to get from one end of the Panhandle to the other in a timely manner, you're better off driving inland to Interstate 10, where the speed limit runs as high as 70 mph in places. Even with the extra time it takes to drive inland, you'll wind up getting where you need to go much more quickly. Route 399 between Pensacola Beach and Navarre Beach was completely destroyed by Hurricane Ivan and, as of this writing, was not open. Major north–south highways that weave through the Panhandle are (from east to west) U.S. 231, U.S. 331, Route 85, and U.S. 29. From U.S. 331, which runs over a causeway at the east end of Choctawhatchee Bay between Route 20 and U.S. 98, the panorama of barge traffic and cabin cruisers on the twinkling waters of the Intracoastal Waterway will get your attention.

CAR RENTAL
Contacts **Alamo** (☎ *800/462–5266*). **Avis** (☎ *800/331–1212*). **Budget** (☎ *800/527–7000*). **Hertz** (☎ *800/654–3131*). **National** (☎ *800/227–7368*).

BY TRAIN
Amtrak (☎ *800/872–7245*)connects the Panhandle to the east and west coasts via the *Sunset Limited,* with stations in Pensacola, Crestview, and Tallahassee.

CONTACTS & RESOURCES

EMERGENCIES
Ambulance or Police Emergencies (☎ *911*).

24-Hour Medical Care **Destin Urgent Care and Diagnostic Center** (✉ *996 Airport Rd., Destin* ☎ *850/837–9194*). **Fort Walton Beach Medical Center** (✉ *1000 Mar-Walt Dr., Fort Walton Beach* ☎ *850/862–1111*). **Gulf Coast Medical Center** (✉ *449 W. 23rd St., Panama City* ☎ *850/769–8341*). **Tallahassee Memorial Hospital** (✉ *Magnolia Dr. and Miccosukee Rd., Tallahassee* ☎ *850/431–1155*). **West Florida Hospital** (✉ *8383 N. Davis Hwy., Pensacola* ☎ *850/494–4000*).

VISITOR INFORMATION
All local visitor information centers are open weekdays, and many are open Saturday—or all weekend—as well. In winter these hours might be curtailed, so call or check the Web sites listed below for schedules. The Panhandle is blessed with many beautiful areas that are being preserved as parks by the State of Florida. Check out the Florida Department of Environmental Protection's excellent parks Web site for hours and admission fees, as well as photos and brief histories of the parks.

Contacts **Apalachicola Bay Chamber of Commerce** (✉ *122 Commerce St., Apalachicola* ☎ *850/653–9419* ⊕ *www.apalachicolabay.org*). **Beaches of South Walton Visitor Information Center** (✉ *U.S. 331 and U.S. 98, Santa Rosa Beach* ☎ *850/267–1216 or 800/822–6877* ⊕ *www.beachesofsouthwalton.com*). **Destin Chamber of Commerce** (✉ *4484 Legendary Dr., Destin* ☎ *850/837–6241* ⊕ *www. destinchamber.com*). **Emerald Coast Convention & Visitors Bureau** (✉ *1540 Miracle Strip Pkwy. SE, Fort Walton Beach* ☎ *850/651–7131 or 800/322–3319* ⊕ *www.destin-fwb.com*). **Florida Department of Environmental Protection–**

Parks Division (☎ *850/245–2157 information line* ⊕ *www.dep.state.fl.us/parks*). **Panama City Beach Convention & Visitors Bureau** (✉ *17001 Panama City Beach Pkwy., Panama City Beach* ☎ *850/233–5070 or 800/722–3224* ⊕ *www. thebeachloversbeach.com*). **Pensacola Visitor Information Center** (✉ *1401 E. Gregory St., Pensacola* ☎ *850/434–1234 or 800/874–1234* ⊕ *www.visitpensacola. com*). **Tallahassee Area Convention and Visitors Bureau** (✉ *106 E. Jefferson St., Tallahassee* ☎ *850/413–9200 or 800/628–2866* ⊕ *www.visittallahassee.com*). **Walton County Chamber of Commerce** (✉ *95 Circle Dr., DeFuniak Springs* ☎ *850/892–3191* ⊕ *www.waltoncountychamber.com*).

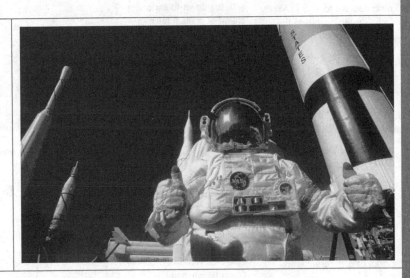

Kennedy Space Center, Cape Canaveral

WORD OF MOUTH

"There is plenty of things to see and do in St Augustine to occupy a couple of days. The Spanish Quarter, Lightner Museum, horse-drawn carriage tours, Old Village Museum, Alligator Farm, a visit to Amelia Island. Jacksonville is far more of a business center than a tourist destination, but its worth a visit if you have the time. Jacksonville Landing for shopping, Jacksonville Beach for swimming and relaxation, major sports events, world-class museums and exhibits, a Budweiser Brewery tour."

—hely5

WELCOME TO NORTHEAST FLORIDA

TOP REASONS TO GO

★ **Tee Time:** "Above par" describes the golf scene in these parts from award-winning courses to THE PLAYERS Championship to the World Golf Hall of Fame.

★ **A Need for Speed:** Few things will get racing fans as revved up as Daytona USA, the official attraction of NASCAR, and tours of Daytona International Speedway, home of the Daytona 500 and Pepsi 400.

★ **Northeast Florid-aaah:** Oceanfront destination spas like Ponte Vedra, The Shores Resort & Spa, and The Ritz-Carlton Spa, Amelia Island are amusement parks of a different kind.

★ **Seems Like Olde Times:** The nation's oldest city, St. Augustine, is a must-see for anyone interested in the discovery of the New World, the founding of Florida, and the birthplace of the tourist trap.

★ **Good Natured:** A wealth of state and national parks means canoeing, fishing, sunbathing, hiking, birdwatching, and camping opportunities are just a stone's throw away.

1 Jacksonville. With a population of 850,000, Jacksonville has the social and cultural appeal of a big city (think museums, nightlife, shopping, and dining) but with the down-to-earth charm of a small town (boiled peanuts, anyone?).

2 St. Augustine. You don't have to be a history buff to enjoy the Oldest City. Foodies, golfers, art lovers, and beach bums will find plenty to do here too (namely, eat, play, shop, and loaf).

3 Daytona Beach and the Space Coast. The Daytona 500, Bike Week, and Spring Break put it on the map, but Daytona Beach has become a popular family vacation destination; so, too, is the Space Coast, home to Canaveral National Seashore, Cocoa Beach, and the John F. Kennedy Space Center.

4 Inland Towns. Without beaches or theme parks, DeLand, Ocala, Gainesville, and Micanopy aren't what most folks picture when they think of Florida. And that's not necessarily a bad thing.

GETTING ORIENTED

Northeast Florida sits (big surprise) in the northeast corner of the state, just south of the Florida-Georgia border. The area is diverse, encompassing waterfront towns and inland cities like Fernandina Beach and Gainesville, as well as the area's "capital" of Jacksonville. About two hours south of Jacksonville on I–95, Titusville, home of the Kennedy Space Center, marks the northern perimeter of the Space Coast, which also includes Cocoa and Melbourne. Taking US 1 lengthens the trip, but the scenery makes up for the inconvenience.

NORTHEAST FLORIDA PLANNER

When to Go

It's not 90 degrees and sunny here every day. In winter the temperature can dip below freezing, and sudden thunderstorms are an almost daily occurrence during summer. For the most part, the weather is fair, averaging in the low 50s in Jacksonville and low 60s in Cocoa Beach in winter. Summer temperatures hover around 80, but the humidity makes it seem far hotter. March and April are good months to visit, since the ocean is beginning to warm up, and the beaches aren't yet packed.

Flying In

Jacksonville International Airport (JAX) is the main hub in the area with service to and from all major cities by the major carriers. Daytona Beach International (DAB) and Gainesville Regional (GNV) are smaller operations with fewer flights but may be more convenient in certain travel situations. Although Orlando isn't part of the area, visitors to northeastern Florida often choose to arrive at Orlando International Airport (MCO) since cheaper flights are often available; however, the headache isn't always worth the savings.

About the Restaurants

The ocean, the St. Johns River, and numerous lakes and smaller rivers are teeming with fish, and so, naturally, seafood dominates local menus. In coastal towns, catches are often from the restaurant's own fleet. Shrimp, snapper, swordfish, and grouper are especially prevalent. Northeast Florida also boasts a variety of award-winning fine-dining restaurants, ethnic eateries, and more barbecue joints than you can shake a hickory chip at.

About the Hotels

For the busy seasons—during summer in and around Jacksonville, and during summer holiday weekends all over Florida—always reserve well ahead for the top properties. Jacksonville's beach hotels fill up quickly for PGA's The Players Championship in mid-May. Daytona Beach presents similar lodging dilemmas during the Daytona 500 (mid-February), Bike Week (late February–early March), Spring Break (March), and the Pepsi 400 (early July). St. Augustine stays busy all year because of its historic character. Fall is the slowest season: rates are low and availability is high, but it is also the prime time for hurricanes.

What It Costs

DINING & LODGING PRICE CATEGORIES

¢	$	$$	$$$	$$$$
Restaurants				
under $10	$10–$15	$15–$20	$20–$30	over $30
Hotels				
under $80	$80–$100	$100–$140	$140–$220	over $220

Restaurant prices are per person for a main course at dinner. Hotel prices are for a standard double room, excluding 6% sales tax (more in some counties) and 1%–4% tourist tax.

Updated
by Kerry
Speckman

SOME OF THE OLDEST SETTLEMENTS in the state—indeed in all of the United States—are in northeastern Florida, although the region didn't get much attention until the Union army came through during the Civil War. The soldiers' rapturous accounts of the mild climate, pristine beaches, and lush vegetation captured the imagination of folks up north. First came the speculators and the curiosity seekers. Then the advent of the railroads brought more permanent settlers and the first wave of winter vacationers. Finally, the automobile transported the full rush of snowbirds, seasonal residents escaping from harsh northern winters. They still come to sop up sun on the beach, to tee up year-round, to bass-fish and bird-watch in forests and parks, and to party in the clubs and bars of Daytona, a popular Spring Break destination. The region is remarkably diverse. Tortuous, towering live oaks; plantations; and antebellum-style architecture recollect the Old South. The mossy marshes of Silver Springs and the St. Johns River look as untouched and junglelike today as they did generations ago. St. Augustine is a showcase of early U.S. history, and Jacksonville is a young but sophisticated metropolis. Yet these are all but light diversions from northeastern Florida's primary draw—its beaches. Hugging the coast are long, slender barrier islands whose entire eastern sides make up a broad band of spectacular sand. Except in the most populated areas, development has been modest, and beaches are lined with funky, appealing little towns.

EXPLORING NORTHEAST FLORIDA

The region defies any single description. Much of its tourist territory lies along the Atlantic coast, both on the mainland and on the barrier islands just offshore. A1A (mostly called Atlantic Avenue south of St. Augustine) is the main road on all the barrier islands, and it's here that you find the best beaches. Both Jacksonville, the region's only real highrise city, and the relatively remote Amelia Island, just south of the Georgia border, are in the far northeast. St. Augustine, about a 45-minute drive south of Jacksonville on Interstate 95, is the historic capital of this part of Florida. Farther south along the coast, the diversity continues among neighbors like Daytona Beach, where annual events are geared toward Spring Breakers, auto racers, and bikers; New Smyrna Beach, which offers quiet appeal; and Cocoa Beach, the ultimate boogie-board beach town. Inland are charming small towns, the sprawling Ocala National Forest, and Gainesville, home of the University of Florida.

JACKSONVILLE

399 mi north of Miami.

One of Florida's oldest cities and at 730 square mi the largest city in the continental United States, Jacksonville makes for an underrated vacation spot. It offers appealing downtown riverside areas, handsome residential neighborhoods, the region's only skyscrapers, a thriving arts scene, and, for football fans, the NFL Jaguars and the NCAA Gator

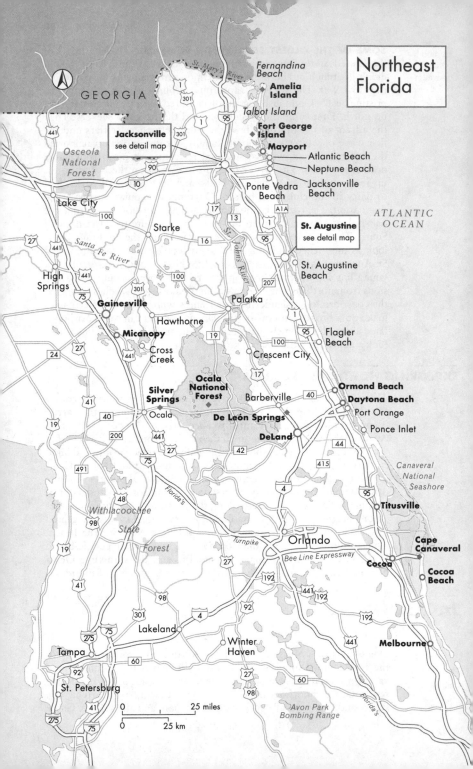

Bowl. Remnants of the Old South flavor the city, especially in the Riverside/Avondale historic district, where moss-draped oak trees frame prairie-style bungalows and Tudor Revival mansions, and palm trees, Spanish bayonet, and azaleas populate the landscape.

EXPLORING JACKSONVILLE

Because Jacksonville was settled along both sides of the twisting St. Johns River, a number of attractions are on or near a riverbank. Both sides of the river, which is spanned by myriad bridges, have downtown areas and waterfront complexes of shops, restaurants, parks, and museums. Some attractions can be reached by water taxi or Skyway Express monorail system—scenic alternatives to driving back and forth across the bridges—but a car is generally necessary.

Numbers in the margin correspond to the Jacksonville map.

WHAT TO SEE

❶ Alexander Brest Museum. Boehm and Royal Copenhagen porcelain and Steuben glass are among the collections at this Jacksonville University museum. Also on display are cloisonné pieces, pre-Columbian artifacts, and one of the finest collections of ivory anywhere from the early 17th to the late 19th century. ⊠ *Jacksonville University, Phillips Fine Arts Bldg., 2800 University Blvd. N* ☎ *904/256–7371* ⊕ *arts.ju.edu* ⊠ *Free* ⊙ *Weekdays 9–4:30; Sat. noon–5. .*

❿ Anheuser-Busch Jacksonville Brewery Tour. Beer lovers will appreciate this behind-the-scenes look at how barley malt, rice, hops, and water form the "King of Beers." Guided tours take guests through the entire brewing and bottling process. Or you can hightail it through the self-guided tour and head straight to the free beer tastings (for those guests 21 years and older, that is). ⊠ *111 Busch Dr.32218* ☎ *904/696–8373* ⊕ *www.budweisertours.com* ⊠ *Free* ⊙ *Mon.–Sat. 10–4; guided tours Mon.–Sat. 10–3 on the ½ hr.*

❹ Cummer Museum of Art and Gardens. The world-famous Wark Collection of early-18th-century Meissen porcelain is just one reason to visit this former riverfront estate, which includes 13 permanent galleries with more than 5,000 items spanning more than 8,000 years and 3 acres of riverfront gardens reflecting Northeast Florida's blooming seasons and indigenous varieties. For the kids, Art Connections allows them to experience art through hands-on, interactive exhibits. One of the museum's latest additions, the Thomas H. Jacobsen Gallery of American Art, focuses on works by American artists, including Max Weber, N.C. Wyeth, and Paul Manship. ⊠ *829 Riverside Ave.32204* ☎ *904/356–6857* ⊕ *www.cummer.org* ⊠ *$10 adults, $5 children over 5, free Tues. 4–9* ⊙ *Tues. 10–9, Wed., Thurs., Fri., and Sat. 10–5, Sun. noon–5.*

❻ Jacksonville Landing. During the week, this riverfront festival marketplace caters to locals and tourists alike, with more than 20 specialty shops with home furnishings, apparel, and toys, nine full-service restaurants—including a sushi bar, Italian bistro, and steak house—and an internationally flavored food court. On weekends the Landing hosts

A GOOD TOUR

Numbers correspond to the Jacksonville map.

Start your morning at the riverfront campus of Jacksonville University, site of the **Alexander Brest Museum ❶**. After browsing the collections, head south on University Boulevard and east on Arlington Expressway to **Kona Skatepark ❷**, where you can practice your sausage grinds or watch X-treme athletes riding the concrete wave. Next, head west on the Arlington Expressway over the Mathews Bridge onto State Street to Jefferson Street, then follow the signs for Riverside to get to the **Cummer Museum of Art and Gardens ❹**. After touring the museum and its grounds, head back on Riverside Avenue toward the Acosta Bridge and take the first exit, San Marco Boulevard. Two blocks north is the **Museum of Science and History ❺**. Walk a block south to the Automated Skyway Express station and take a monorail across the river to the **Jacksonville Landing ❻**,

where you can shop and grab some lunch. Afterward, walk four blocks north to the **Museum of Contemporary Art Jacksonville ❼**. Head back to the Landing to recross the river, but for the return trip, catch a water taxi. On the road again, go back over the Acosta Bridge and stay on Broad Street to First Street, where you'll find the **Karpeles Manuscript Library Museum ❽**. Next, proceed west on State Street to Interstate 95 north, then take the Heckscher Drive exit east to Zoo Road for the **Jacksonville Zoo ❾**. Finally, head back to Interstate 95 north and exit east at Dunn Avenue, which becomes Busch Road, and visit the **Anheuser-Busch Jacksonville Brewery ❿**.

TIMING

Jacksonville's sprawl dictates a generous amount of time for reaching and touring these sights. Allow at least two days, six hours a day (including driving time), budgeting at least an hour for each attraction, more for the zoo and art museums.

more than 250 events each year, ranging from the good clean fun of the American Cancer Society Duck Race to the just plain obnoxious Florida/Georgia game after-party, as well as live music (usually of the local cover band variety) in the courtyard. ⊠2 *Independent Dr.32202* ☎*904/353–1188* ⊕*www.jacksonvillelanding.com* ☎*Free* ☉*Mon.–Thurs. 10–8, Fri. and Sat. 10–9, Sun. noon–5:30; some restaurants open earlier and close later.*

❾   **Jacksonville Zoo and Gardens.** Encompassing more than 120 acres on
Fodor'sChoice   Jacksonville's north side, this midsize zoo is home to thousands of
★   amphibians, birds, invertebrates, mammals, and reptiles, from barking tree frogs and Madagascar hissing cockroaches to dusky pygmy rattlesnakes and giant anteaters. Among the zoo's outstanding exhibits are its collection of rare waterfowl and the Serona Overlook, which showcases some of the world's most venomous snakes. The Florida Wetlands is a 2½-acre area with black bears, bald eagles, white-tailed deer, and other animals native to Florida. The African Veldt has alligators, elephants, and white rhinos, among other species of African birds and mammals; and the Range of the Jaguar, winner of the Association of Zoos and Aquarium's Exhibit of the Year, includes 4 acres of exotic

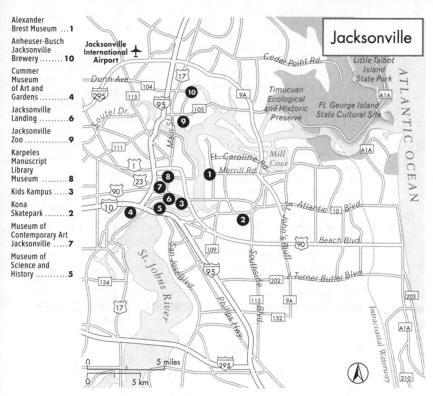

big cats as well as 20 other species of animals. One of the zoo's newest
additions is its Play Park, complete with a splash park, forest play area,
maze, and discovery building. ⊠*370 Zoo Pkwy., off Heckscher Dr.
E* ☎*904/757–4463* ⊕*www.jaxzoo.org* ⊠*$12 adults, $7.50 children
3–12* ☉*Daily 9–5.*

❽ **Karpeles Manuscript Library Museum.** File this one under "hidden treasure," because the majority of folks who live in Jacksonville have never
even heard of, let alone visited, Karpeles. That's too bad, because this
museum, in a 1921 neoclassical building on the outskirts of downtown,
has displayed some priceless documents, such as the original draft of
the Bill of Rights, the Emancipation Proclamation signed by Abraham
Lincoln, handwritten manuscripts of Edgar Allan Poe and Charles
Dickens, and musical scores by Beethoven and Mozart. Manuscript
exhibits change every three months or so and coincide with monthly
art exhibits. Also on the premises are an antique-book library, with
volumes dating from the late 1800s, and a children's museum. ⊠*101
W. 1st St.32206* ☎*904/356–2992* ⊕*www.rain.org/~karpeles/jax.html*
⊠*Free* ☉*Tues.–Sat. 10–4, Sun. noon–4 .*

❸ **Kids Kampus.** Directly on the St. Johns River adjacent to Metropolitan
Park, this 10-acre recreational facility, developed by local educators,
encourages children's natural curiosity with climbing and sliding appa-

ratuses and colorful playscapes, mini-representations of Jacksonville landmarks like Bay Street, Kings Road, and the main post office, and a splash park. It's not exactly Disney World, but parents looking for a way to entertain the kids for a couple of hours, especially in the sweltering Florida heat, report that it just might be the happiest place on earth. The "kampus" also has a picnic pavilion and jogging trail. ⊠*1410 Gator Bowl Blvd.32202* ☎*904/630–5437* ☐*Free* ⊙*Mar.–*

> **SIZE ISN'T EVERYTHING**
>
> It's nearly impossible to visit Jacksonville without hearing locals brag that their city is the largest in the U.S. Too bad it's not true. In fact, the River City's 841 square miles pales in comparison to the actual title holder: 4,710-square-mile Sitka, Alaska. More accurately, Jacksonville is the largest city in the continental U.S.

Oct., Mon.–Sat. 8–8, Sun. 10–8; Nov.–Feb., Mon.–Sat. 8–6, Sun. 10–6.

🖐 ❷ **Kona Skatepark.** Built back in the '70s—before most of its patrons were even born—this X-treme sport outpost still has its original bowls, plus updates like an 80-foot-wide vertical ramp, two street courses, and one of the area's few snake runs (a high-speed downhill run with banked turns). Skateboard legend Tony Hawk digs the park's retro feel so much that he named it one of his five favorite U.S. skate parks. The park, which also caters to in-line skaters, rents boards, skates, and safety equipment (required of all skaters) and offers lessons. Reduced rates are available on weekdays. And as proof that you're never too old to skate, skaters over 30 get half off every Wednesday night and those over 65 skate free every day. ⊠ *8739 Kona Ave.32211* ☎*904/725–8770* ⊕*www.konaskatepark.com* ☐*$5–$10* ⊙*Weekdays 1–9, Sat. 10–10, Sun. noon–9.*

❼ **Museum of Contemporary Art Jacksonville.** In this loftlike downtown build-
Fodor's Choice ing, the former headquarters of the Western Union Telegraph Company,
★ a permanent collection of 20th-century art shares space with traveling exhibitions. The museum encompasses five galleries and ArtExplorium, a highly interactive educational exhibit for kids, as well as a funky gift shop and Café Nola, open for lunch, Sunday brunch, and dinner on Wednesday. MOCA Jacksonville (previously known as the Jacksonville Museum of Modern Art) also hosts film series, lectures, and workshops throughout the year. Big-city visitors often remark that they're impressed with the facility and exhibitions, but with MOCA Jacksonville comprising just 14,000 square feet (compared with the 630,000 at New York's Museum of Modern Art), they wonder where the rest is. Sunday is free for kids and their accompanying adults. ⊠*Hemming Plaza, 333 N. Laura St.* ☎*904/366–6911* ⊕*www.mocajacksonville. org* ☐*$8, free Wed. 5–9 and Sun.* ⊙*Tues. and Thurs.–Sat. 10–4, Sun. noon–4, Wed. 10–9; hrs subject to change.*

🖐 ❺ **Museum of Science and History.** You won't find any mad scientists here, but you'll probably find lots of giggling ones. Targeted at the elementary and middle school set, MOSH aims to educate and entertain kids about science and history through a variety of interactive exhibits like the JEA Science Theatre, where they'll participate in live experiments related to electricity and electrical safety; the Florida Naturalist's Center, where they can explore Northeast Florida wildlife (like American alligators, gopher turtles, and various native snakes and birds); and the Universe of Science, where they'll learn about properties of physical science through hands-on demonstrations. Other permanent exhibits include Atlantic Tails, a hands-on exploration of whales, dolphins, and manatees; Currents of Time, chronicling 12,000 years of Northeast Florida history; and Prehistoric Park, featuring a life-size Allosaurus skeleton. The Alexander Brest Planetarium hosts daily shows on astronomy (request your seating pass from the front desk 30 minutes before any showing) and, on weekends, Cosmic Concerts, 3-D laser shows set to pop music. ⊠*1025 Museum Circle32207* ☎*904/396–6674* ⊕*www.themosh.org* ⊠*$9 adults, $7 children 3–12, Cosmic Concerts $7–$9* ⊗ *Weekdays 10–5, Sat. 10–6, Sun. 1–6.*

WHERE TO EAT

$$$-$$$$
FodorsChoice
★

✕**Matthew's.** Local foodies sing Chef Matthew Medure's praises not only for his culinary creativity but also his dazzling presentation, which stands out quite strikingly against the very spare decor of stainless steel, polished bronze, and terrazzo flooring. The menu changes nightly, but might include lemon-roasted Amish chicken with honey-truffle spaghetti squash, or herb-roasted rack of lamb with mustard pistachio crust. Complement your meal with one of 450 wines (topping out at more than $1,000 per bottle), then dive into one of the warm soufflés for dessert. ⊠*2107 Hendricks Ave., San Marco* ☎*904/396–9922* ▤*AE, D, DC, MC, V* ⊗*Closed Sun. No lunch.*

★ $$-$$$$

✕**Bistro Aix.** When a Jacksonville restaurant can make Angelinos feel like they haven't left home, that's saying a lot. With its slick black-leather booths, 1940s brick work, velvet drapes, and intricate marbled globes, Bistro Aix (pronounced "X") is just that place. Regulars can't get enough of the creamy onion soup, crispy calamari, and house-made potato chips with warm blue-cheese appetizers or entrées like oak-fired fish Aixoise, grilled salmon, and filet mignon. Aix's resident pastry chef ensures no sweet tooth leaves unsatisfied. For the most part, waitstaff are knowledgeable and pleasant, though some patrons find their demeanor snooty, except, of course, the ones from L.A. Call for preferred seating. ⊠*1440 San Marco Blvd., San Marco* ☎*904/398–1949* ⌦*Reservations not accepted* ▤*AE, D, DC, MC, V* ⊗*No lunch weekends.*

★ $$-$$$

✕**bb's.** Sleek yet cozy, this hip bistro is as popular with corporate muckety-mucks looking to close a deal as it is with young lovebirds seemingly on the verge of popping the question (though shouting the question might be more appropriate, considering how loud the dining room gets on weekends). The concrete floors and a stainless-steel wine bar provide an interesting backdrop for comfort food-inspired entrées and daily specials that might include char-grilled beef tenderloin, prosciutto-wrapped pork chops, or mushroom triangoli ravioli. On the lighter side, grilled pizzas, sandwiches, and salads, especially warm goat-cheese salad, are favorites. Although a wait is practically guaranteed, you can pass the time sizing up the display of diet-destroying desserts. ✉ *1019 Hendricks Ave., San Marco* ☎ *904/306–0100* ⚐ *Reservations not accepted* ☰ *AE, D, DC, MC, V* ⊘ *Closed Sun.*

$-$$$ ✕ **Biscottis.** The local artwork on the redbrick walls is a mild distraction from the jovial crowds (from yuppies to soccer moms to metrosexuals) jockeying for tables in this midsize restaurant. Elbows almost touch, but no one seems to mind.

The menu offers the unexpected: wild-mushroom ravioli with a broth of corn, leek, and dried apricot; or curry-grilled swordfish with cucumber fig bordelaise. Be sure to sample from Biscottis' decadent dessert case (we hear the peanut-butter ganache is illegal in three states). ✉ *3556 St. Johns Ave., Avondale* ☎ *904/387–2060* ⚐ *Reservations not accepted* ☰ *AE, MC, V.*

$-$$$ ✕ **Clark's Fish Camp.** It's out of the way and hard to find, but every mile and missed turn will be forgotten once you step inside this former bait shop overlooking Julington Creek. Clark's has one of the largest menus in town, with more than 160 appetizers and entrées, including the usual—shrimp, catfish, and oysters—and the unusual—ostrich, rattlesnake, and kangaroo. In keeping with the more bizarre entrées is the decor, best described as early American taxidermy: hundreds of stuffed birds and critters gaze upon you in the main dining room, and preserved lions, gazelles, baboons, even a rhino, keep a watchful eye in the bar. One person's kitschy may be another's creepy. Reservations accepted for parties of eight or more. ✉ *12903 Hood Landing Rd., Mandarin* ☎ *904/268–3474* ☰ *AE, MC, V* ⊘ *No lunch weekdays.*

$-$$ ✕ **Taste of Thai.** Ravenous regulars dominate the tightly packed tables at this warm family-owned restaurant in a nondescript strip mall down the street from Memorial Medical Center (which would explain the proliferation of diners in scrubs). For 10 years, proprietress Aurathai Sellas, who might just be the most cheerful person in the entire restaurant business, has prepared the exotic dishes of her homeland, including *pla lad prig* (hot and spicy fish), *goog thod* (crispy shrimp), and chicken peanut sauce, as well as pad thai. There may be fancier Thai restaurants in town, but none has the service and loyalty of this one. Reservations are accepted for parties of six or more. ✉ *4317 University Blvd. S, Southside 32216* ☎ *904/737–9009* ☰ *AE, D, MC, V* ⊘ *Closed Sun. No lunch Mon.*

¢-$$ ✕ **Mossfire Grill.** The tongue-in-cheek name of this Southwest-inspired restaurant speaks to the sassy waitstaff and the patrons who frequent it (the city's Great Fire of 1901 was started when a mattress factory, which processed moss, ignited). Dinner entrées range from fish tacos and crab-cake salad to New York strip loin and pecan chicken. The dimly lighted upstairs lounge has a coffeehouse vibe—with a handful of cozy booths, two-tops, and leather couches—and has the city's only tequila bar. Local bands perform Friday and Saturday night. ✉ *1537*

3

Margaret St., Riverside ☎*904/355–4434* ⚹*Reservations not accepted* 🍽*AE, MC, V.*

¢–$ ✗**Al's Pizza.** Although it fits the criteria of a neighborhood pizza joint—cheap, casual, and frequented by locals—this funky-chic pizzeria looks more like a hipster hangout than Jacksonvillians low on dough (pardon the pun). The main draw is the pizza, particularly Al's gourmet white pie, but eggplant parmigiana, stuffed shells, and lasagna are also good. The Riverside location caters to its more upscale clientele with table service and a separate bar area, but for some reason the folks in the kitchen don't grasp the concept of getting all of a table's orders to come out at the same time. ✉*1620 Margaret St. #201, Riverside* ☎*904/388–8384* ✉*14286 Beach Blvd., Intracoastal West* ☎*904/223–0991* ✉*8060 Philips Hwy., Southside* ☎*904/731–4300* ⚹*Reservations not accepted* 🍽*AE, D, MC, V.*

★ ¢–$ ✗**European Street Cafe.** Wicker baskets and lofty shelves brimming with European confections and groceries like Toblerone and Nutella fill practically every inch of space not occupied by café tables. The menu is similarly overloaded, with nearly 100 deli sandwiches and salads. Notable are raspberry-almond chicken salad and the "Blue Max," with pastrami, corned beef, Swiss cheese, sauerkraut, hot mustard, and blue-cheese dressing. This quirky spot is favored by area professionals looking for a quick lunch, as well as the under-40 set doing 23-ounce curls with one of the restaurant's 20-plus beers on tap (plus more than 100 in bottles). Entertainment-wise, the San Marco location offers live music Thursday nights. ✉*2753 Park St., Riverside* ☎*904/384–9999* ✉*1704 San Marco Blvd., San Marco* ☎*904/398–9500* ✉*5500 Beach Blvd., Southside* ☎*904/398–1717* ⚹*Reservations not accepted* 🍽*AE, D, MC, V.*

¢ ✗**Burrito Gallery.** There are no paintings of tortillas stuffed with beef and rice adorning the walls of this downtown hot spot. Instead, original artwork, mostly by local painters, livens up this otherwise nondescript restaurant, and tasty burritos, tacos, quesadillas, and nachos decorate your plate. Head down the narrow hallway after dinner and you'll find the hidden Urb Garden Bar with a collection of local characters and a unique view of downtown. ✉*21 E. Adams St., Downtown* ☎*904/598–2922* ⚹*Reservations not accepted* 🍽*AE, D, MC, V* ⊗*Closed Sun. No dinner Mon.*

¢ ✗**The Loop Pizza Grill.** Standing in line to place their orders, first-time diners may think this Jacksonville-based chain is just another fast-food joint. But one look at the menu, chock-full of designer salads, specialty pizzas, and upscale sandwiches, not to mention the stylish dining room complete with upholstered booths, funky light fixtures, and tiled floors, and they'll think they're in McDreamland. The big sellers here are the burgers (the Loop 'N Cheddar and Loop 'N Blue, in particular) and pizzas (both California-thin and Chicago-thick), but sandwiches like the portobello mushroom and Cajun chicken merit special mention. The salads can be a bit blah, but the onion rings and milk shakes are among the best in town. ✉*2014 San Marco Blvd., San Marco* ☎*904/399–5667* ✉*14444 Beach Blvd., San Pablo* ☎*904/223–6611* ✉*9965 San Jose Blvd., Mandarin* ☎*904/262–2210* ✉*4000*

*St. Johns Ave., Suite 21, Avon-
dale* ☎904/384–7301 ✉8221
Southside Blvd., Baymeadow s
☎904/645–7788 ⌧*Reservations
not accepted* ▤*AE, D, MC, V.*

¢ ✕**Tidbits.** Hearing locals speak of
Tidbits' best-selling side dish is a
little like listening to Homer Simpson talk about doughnuts ("Mmm,
potato salad")—dreamy and lust-
ful. Although not every item on the
menu has such a hypnotic hold on
its customers, the lunch-only res-

taurant has a devoted customer base, mostly San Marco and downtown worker bees, who gobble up the chicken supreme pita, French
dip, veggie surprise, and Tidbit Special, with seasoned chicken chunks
and pasta on a bed of lettuce topped with avocado and cheddar. It's
open fewer than 20 hours a week and there's almost always a line 10
deep. Don't be discouraged. It moves fast. ✉*1076 Hendricks Ave.,
San Marco* ☎904/396–0528 ⌧*Reservations not accepted* ☉*Closed
weekends. No dinner.* ▤*AE, MC, V.*

WHERE TO STAY

$$$$ ▦**Crowne Plaza Jacksonville Riverfront.** A staple on Jacksonville's south
bank for decades, the former Hilton Jacksonville Riverfront maintains
its commanding presence but now as a Crowne Plaza property. Its
location on the south side of the St. Johns River puts it within walking distance of restaurants, the Automated Skyway Express, and the
water taxi; Ruth's Chris Steak House is one of the on-site restaurants.
Guests wanting to live like a king can book the San Marco (aka the
Elvis Room), a premier suite with Jacuzzi tub and two balconies that
Presley called home during numerous trips to Jacksonville. Or rent out
the hotel's private yacht, the *Jacksonville Princess,* for a romantic cruise
down the river. **Pros:** Newly renovated rooms, riverfront balconies,
friendly staff. **Cons:** Small bathrooms, loud a/c units, no free parking.
✉*1201 Riverplace Blvd.,* ☎904/398–8800 ⊕*www.cpjacksonville.
com* ⥰*292 rooms, 30 suites* ⌂*In-room: refrigerator (some), Wi-Fi.
In-hotel: 2 restaurants, room service, bars, pool, gym, laundry service, concierge, executive floor, public Wi-Fi, parking (fee), no-smoking
rooms* ▤*AE, D, DC, MC, V.*

$$$$ ▦**Hyatt Regency Jacksonville Riverfront.** In Jacksonville it doesn't get much
more convenient than this downtown waterfront hotel. Perched on the
north bank of the St. Johns River, the 19-story property is within walking distance of the Jacksonville Landing, Florida Theatre, and Times-
Union Center, corporate office towers, and the county courthouse. The
former Adam's Mark Hotel has undergone some significant changes,
including the addition of the Plaza III Steakhouse and a complete room
overhaul with Florida-style decor, triple-sheeted beds, and sliding glass
doors. Since Northeast Florida's largest hotel encompasses 110,000
square feet of meeting space, chances are pretty good you'll share an

elevator with someone wearing a name tag (if you're not wearing one yourself). Pros: riverfront location, newly renovated, roof-top pool and gym. Cons: not all rooms are riverfront, slow valet service, no mini-bars. ⊠225 E. Coastline Dr., ☎904/588–1234 ⊕www.jacksonville. hyatt.com ↪966 rooms, 21 suites ⚷In-room: refrigerator (some), DVD (some), Ethernet. In-hotel: 3 restaurants, room service, bar, pool, gym, laundry facilities, laundry service, concierge, executive floor, public Wi-Fi, parking (fee), some pets allowed , no-smoking rooms ⊟AE, D, DC, MC, V

★ $$$$ ▦ **Omni Jacksonville Hotel.** The Omni has further cemented its reputation as Jacksonville's most luxurious and glamorous hotel with a multimillion-dollar makeover in 2006. Upgrades include "downtown urban style" guest rooms (think neutral grays and creams, dark wood, stainless steel, and flat-screen TVs), which they claim are the largest in the city, and an expanded fitness center. The splashy marble-floor lobby leads to the reception area, an upscale lounge—J Bar—and Juliette's Bistro, with cozy banquettes and tables that look up to a soaring atrium. Bell service is also exemplary: with many porters having 10-plus years on the job, they can, and will happily, help you find just about anything. Pros: Downtown location, large rooms, roof-top pool. Cons: Congested valet area, pricey on-site restaurant, chaotic when there's a show at the T-U Center across the street. ⊠245 Water St., ☎904/355–6664 or 800/843–666 ⊕www.omnijacksonville.com ↪326 rooms, 28 suites ⚷In-room: kitchen (some), Wi-Fi. In-hotel: restaurant, room service, bar, pool, gym, children's programs (ages 3– 10), laundry service, concierge, public Wi-Fi, parking (fee), some pets allowed, no-smoking rooms ⊟AE, D, DC, MC, V.

$$$ ▦**Riverdale Inn.** In the early 1900s Jacksonville's wealthiest residents built mansions along Riverside Avenue, dubbed "The Row": the three-story Riverdale Inn is only one of two such homes remaining. Previous owners took great care in preserving the home's original details, including heart-of-pine floors, crown moldings, and original shingle facade. Guest rooms, some with fireplaces, are individually decorated to evoke a turn-of-the-century feel. Some rooms have claw-foot tubs and shower combinations; others have only showers. The inn is within walking distance of numerous restaurants, the Cummer Museum of Art and Gardens, and Five Points. Or simply stumble downstairs to The Row Restaurant and Gum Bunch Pub. Pros: On-site restaurant and pub, proximity to area restaurants and shops, private bathrooms. Cons: Small rooms, restaurant and pub can be noisy, limited parking. ⊠1521 Riverside Ave.32204 ☎904/354–5080 ⊕www.riverdaleinn. com ↪7 rooms, 3 suites ⚷In-room: refrigerator (some), DVD (some), Wi-Fi. In-hotel: restaurant, bar, no elevator, public Wi-Fi, parking (no fee), some pets allowed, no kids under 12, no-smoking rooms ⊟AE, D, MC, V.

★ $$–$$$ ▦**The Inn at Oak Street.** Built in 1902 as a private residence, the three-story, 6,000-square-foot Frame Vernacular–style building was restored and reopened as a bed-and-breakfast popular for romantic weekends and girlfriend getaways. Rooms include the cozy and romantic Boudoir room, with four-poster bed and inlaid-tile fireplace, and the more modern St. John's Room, with cobalt-hue walls and a geometric bedspread. Each room has a private bath—some with whirlpool tubs and others with double-head showers—and second-story rooms offer balconies. Mornings start with a hearty breakfast in the dining room or on the enclosed porch; evenings wind down with wine and refreshments in the parlor. **Pros:** Meticulously clean, walking distance to restaurants, private bathrooms. **Cons:** Hardwood floors can be noisy, not for families with small children, no pool. ⊠*2114 Oak St.,* ☎*904/379–5525* ⊕*www.innatoakstreet.com* ⚓*6 rooms, 1 suite* ⚂*In-room: refrigerator, dial-up, Wi-Fi. In-hotel: gym, no elevator, concierge, public Wi-Fi, parking (no fee), no kids under 12, no-smoking rooms* ⊟*AE, D, MC, V* ◛*BP.*

NIGHTLIFE & THE ARTS

The **Alhambra Dinner Theatre** (⊠*12000 Beach Blvd., 32246* ☎*904/641–1212*) serves up professional theater along with a menu that's often altered with each new play. Northeast Florida's major presenter of professional national and international touring attractions is the **FCCJ Artist Series** (⊠*501 W. State St, .32202* ☎*904/632–3373*). **The Florida Theatre** (⊠*128 E. Forsyth St., 32202* ☎*904/355–2787*) presents concerts, dance productions, and special events, as well as a classic-movie series. The **Jacksonville Symphony Orchestra** (☎*904/354–5547*) performs at the Jacoby Music Hall in the Times-Union Center for the Performing Arts and gives outdoor concerts at downtown's Metro Park. Opened in 2003, the 16,000-seat **Jacksonville Veterans Memorial Arena** (⊠*300 A. Philip Randolph Blvd., 32202* ☎*904/630–3900*) is the latest addition to the city's entertainment complex. It hosts concerts, special events, and sporting events. **Metropolitan Park** (⊠*1410 Gator Bowl Blvd., 32202* ☎*904/630–0837*) is a 27-acre riverfront venue that hosts the city's major musical and cultural events, such as the Jacksonville Jazz Festival in April, and Freedom, Fanfare and Fireworks on July Fourth. Florida Community College at Jacksonville's South Campus is the site of the **Nathan H. Wilson Center for the Arts** (⊠*11901 Beach Blvd., 32246* ☎*904/646–2222*), a performing- and visual-arts facility showcasing multidisciplinary productions by students and professional artists. Dubbed "the Harlem of the South" in the 1920s, historic La Villa is the site of the **Ritz Theatre** (⊠*829 N. Davis St., 32202* ☎*904/632–5555*), which hosts musical and theatrical events of particular interest to the African-American community. One of the oldest continuously operating community theater in the United States, **Theatre Jacksonville** (⊠*2032 San Marco Blvd., 32207* ☎*904/396–4425*) presents outstanding productions ranging from Shakespeare to programs for children. The **Times-Union Center for the Performing Arts** (⊠*300 W. Water St., 32202* ☎*904/633–6110*) draws rock bands, musicals, and children's shows. The **University of North Florida Fine Arts Center** (⊠*4567 St. Johns Bluff Rd. S, Bldg. 45,* ☎*904/620–2878*) presents dance and comedy troupes and other shows.

Buffalo Wild Wings (⊠*9550 Baymeadows Rd. #26,* ☎*904/448–1293*), known as "BW3" to the locals, is *the* place to watch college and pro football. Inside the Ramada Inn Mandarin, the **Comedy Zone** (✉ *3130 Hartley Rd.,* ☎ *904/292–4242*) is the area's premier comedy nightclub. Crowds head to **Dave & Buster's** (✉ *7025 Salisbury Rd.,* ☎ *904/296–1525*) for its huge video-game room and for a part in the whodunit at the mystery theater Saturday night. Wine snobs, rejoice! You, too, have a place to hook up called **The Grotto** (✉ *2012 San Marco Blvd.,* ☎ *904/398–0726*). **Harmonious Monks** (✉ *10550 Old St. Augustine Rd.,* ☎ *904/880–3040*) claims to have "the world's most talented waitstaff," who perform throughout the night and encourage customers to dance on the bar. **Jack Rabbits** (✉ *1528 Hendricks Ave.,* ☎ *904/398–7496*) welcomes the latest and greatest indie bands and budding rock stars. Fans of Christian music flock to the **Murray Hill Theatre** (✉ *932 Edgewood Ave. S,* ☎ *904/388–7807*), a no-smoking, no-alcohol club. At 12,000 square feet, **Plush** (✉ *845 University Blvd. N,* ☎ *904/743–1845*) is certainly Jacksonville's largest nightclub; it's also the loudest. **Square One** (✉ *1974 San Marco Blvd.,* ☎ *904/306–9004*) hosts an upscale singles scene, with live music on weekends. The **Twisted Martini** (✉ *Jacksonville Landing, 2 Independent Dr.,* ☎ *904/353–8464*) is a glitzy meat market complete with designer martinis, chichi bar food, and a VIP area with bottle service.

> **PLAY BALL!**
>
> Jacksonville became Major League Baseball's first Spring Training location when the city hosted the Washington Statesmen in 1888. Spring Training has since moved south, but the baseball tradition has continued with some of the game's best players having done a stint on Jacksonville's farm league teams including Hank Aaron, Nolan Ryan, Tom Seaver, Randy Johnson, and Alex Rodriguez.

SPORTS & THE OUTDOORS

⏱ BASEBALL

The **Jacksonville Suns** (✉ *301 A. Phillip Randolph Blvd., 32202* ☎ *904/358–2846*), the AA minor-league affiliate of the Los Angeles Dodgers, play at the Baseball Grounds of Jacksonville, their $25 million ballpark.

DOG RACING

Jacksonville Greyhound Racing (☎ *904/646–0001*)encompasses three facilities: the **Orange Park Kennel Club** (✉ *455 Park Ave., , Orange Park,* ☎ *904/646–0001*) which runs greyhound races eight times a week throughout the year; **Jacksonville Kennel Club** (✉ *1440 N. McDuff Ave.,* ☎ *904/646–0001*), a simulcast-only track on the city's Westside;and The **"Best Bet" at St. Johns** (✉ *6322 Race Track Rd, .* ☎ *904/646–0001*), a simulcast-only facility that includes a 14,000-square-foot poker room.

FOOTBALL

Jacksonville Municipal Stadium (✉ *1 Stadium Pl., 32202* ☎ *904/633–6100*) is home to the NFL's **Jacksonville Jaguars** (☎ *904/633–6000, 904/633–2000 tickets*). Jacksonville kicks off each year with its own New Year's Day bowl game, the **Toyota Gator Bowl** (☎ *904/798–1700*), which usually hosts NCAA top-10 teams from the SEC, ACC, or Big East conferences. Billed as the "World's Largest Outdoor Cocktail Party," the **Florida/Georgia Game** (☎*904/630–3690*) celebrates one of college football's most heated rivalries—between the Florida Gators and Georgia Bulldogs every fall.

GOLF

Champions Club at Julington Creek (✉*1111 Durbin Creek Blvd., 32259* ☎*904/287–4653*) is well-maintained and reasonably priced; greens fee: $46–$56. The 6,891-yard course at **Cimarrone Golf Club** (✉*2800 Cimarrone Blvd., 32259* ☎*904/287–2000*) has a water or marsh feature on every hole; greens fee: $50–$60. **Deercreek Country Club** (✉*7816 McLaurin Rd., 32256* ☎*904/363–1604*) is a semiprivate, par-71 course with five different sets of tees; greens fee: $55–$70. The **Eagle Harbor Golf Club** (✉*2217 Eagle Harbor Pkwy., Orange Park* ☎*904/269–9300*) has an 18-hole, par-72 course designed by Clyde Johnston and has a driving range, club rentals, and discount packages; greens fee: $53–$64. **Magnolia Point Golf and Country Club** (✉*3670 Clubhouse Dr., Green Cove Springs* ☎*904/269–9276*) boasts a "player-friendly" course with beautiful scenery and wildlife; greens fee: $35–$70. **Panther Creek Golf Club** (✉*11209 Panther Creek Pkwy.,* ☎*904/783–2600*) is Northeast Florida's premier public course; greens fee: $40–$75. **Windsor Parke Golf Club** (✉*13823 Sutton Park Rd.,* ☎*904/223–4972*) has 18 holes (par 72) on tree-lined fairways and amid natural marshlands, greens fee: $45–$55.

SKYDIVING

The city's only drop zone, **Skydive Jacksonville** (✉*Herlong Airport, 9300 Normandy Blvd., 3 mi west of I–295* ☎*888/586–7529*), also boasts north Florida's highest tandem jump for $175 per person, including equipment rental and instruction. Or get certified with accelerated free-fall training (call for prices). Certified skydivers pay just $25 per jump. Video and photography services are available for an additional charge.

TENNIS

Boone Park Tennis Center (✉*3730 Park St., 32205* ☎*904/384–8687*) is a public tennis facility with hard and clay courts as well as picnic and restroom facilities. **Southside Tennis Complex** (✉*1539 Hendricks Ave, 32207* ☎*904/399–1761*) has hard and clay courts, picnic areas, and restrooms.

SHOPPING

At **Five Points** (✉*Intersection of Park, Margaret, and Lomax Sts., Riverside*) you'll find a small but funky shopping district of new and vintage clothing boutiques, shoe stores, and antiques shops, as well as a handful of eateries and bars, not to mention some of the most colorful characters in the city. **The Shoppes of Avondale** (✉*St. Johns Ave., between Talbot Ave. and Dancy St.*) highlight upscale clothing and accessories boutiques, art galleries, home-furnishing shops, a chocolatier, and trendy restaurants. **San Marco Square** (✉*Intersection of San Marco and Atlantic Blvds.*) has dozens of interesting apparel, home, and jewelry stores and restaurants in 1920s Mediterranean Revival–style buildings. One of Northeast Florida's newest shopping destination, **St. Johns Town Center** (✉ *4663 River City Dr., Southside* 🕾*904/642–8339*), is an outdoor "lifestyle center" with shops not found anywhere else in Northeast Florida, including Anthropologie, Apple, Lucky Brand Jeans, and Sephora, as well as The Cheesecake Factory, P. F. Changs, and Maggiano's Little Italy. Traditional malls (department stores, specialty shops, food courts, and the like) include **The Avenues** (✉*10300 Southside Blvd., Southside* 🕾*904/363–3060*), **Orange Park Mall** (✉*1910 Wells Rd., Orange Park* 🕾*904/269–2422*), and **Regency Square Mall** (✉*9501 Arlington Exp., Regency* 🕾*904/725–3830*).

JACKSONVILLE BEACHES

20 mi east of Jacksonville on U.S. 90 (Beach Blvd.).

Separated from the mainland by the Intracoastal Waterway, Jacksonville's main beaches run along the barrier island that includes the laid-back towns of Jacksonville Beach, Neptune Beach, Atlantic Beach, and Ponte Vedra Beach. The northernmost of Jacksonville's beaches, Atlantic Beach is more subdued but a favorite with local surfers. Adjacent Neptune Beach is largely residential and draws bicyclists and in-line skaters who cruise up and down First Street. Just south is Jacksonville Beach, which has a decidedly more active shoreline, with volleyballs and Frisbees buzzing through the air and portable radios blaring everything from Kanye West to Van Halen. With multimillion-dollar homes stretching for miles, Ponte Vedra is the most difficult beach to access, but makes for a lovely drive down A1A. Lifeguards are on duty on the more populated stretches of the beaches from 10 to 6 in summer.

WHAT TO SEE

☺ **Adventure Landing and Shipwreck Island Water Park.** With go-karts, two miniature-golf courses, laser tag, batting cages, kiddie rides, and arcades, Adventure Landing is more like an old-timey boardwalk than a high-tech amusement park. But when the closest theme park is more than two hours away, you make do. The largest family entertainment center in Northeast Florida also encompasses Shipwreck Island Water Park, which features a lazy river for tubing, a 500,000-gallon wave pool, and three extreme slides—the Rage, HydroHalfpipe, and Eye of the Storm. ✉*1944 Beach Blvd., Jacksonville Beach32250* 🕾*904/246–4386* ⊕*www.adventurelanding.com* ✇*Adventure Landing: free (fees for rides and games), Shipwreck Island: $25.99 adults, $21.99 children under 42"* ☉*Adventure Landing: Mon.–Thurs. and Sun. 10* AM*–10* PM*, Fri. and Sat. 10* AM*–midnight. Shipwreck Island: hrs vary (call for specific dates and times); Shipwreck Island closed late Sept.–late Mar.*

WHERE TO EAT

$$–$$$$ ✕**Restaurant Medure.** At more than 4,500 square feet, this chic Ponte
Fodor'sChoice Vedra restaurant is more spacious than its sister restaurant, Matthew's,
★ in Jacksonville. And with its uplit floor-to-ceiling wine cellars, concrete floors, overstuffed leather chairs, and room dividers constructed of oak branches and brushed aluminum, it's decidedly more urban.

What is a constant, however, are a 400-bottle wine list and Chef Matthew Medure's deliciously eclectic menu, including favorites like ahi tuna tartare, seared foie gras with huckleberry compote, and inventive variations on grouper and flounder. Those looking to cut corners would be wise to dine on Monday, when bottles of wine are half-price, or Wednesday, when you can enjoy appetizers and five featured wines for just $15 a person. ⊠ *818 N. A1A, Ponte Vedra Beach* ☎ *904/543–3797* ⊟ *AE, D, DC, MC, V* ⊙ *Closed Sun. No lunch.*

$$–$$$ ✗**Ocean 60.** Despite being located a block from the Atlantic Ocean, this lively restaurant–wine bar–martini room has gone largely undiscovered by tourists, who might think fine dining and flip-flops don't mix. Those who do stumble upon it, however, are pleasantly surprised to find that a casual aura befits Ocean 60's eclectic seasonal menu, with signature items like walnut-grilled salmon and Mayport prawns, Kona coffee–grilled rack of lamb, and Buddha's Delight, vegetables sautéed with cellophane noodles and Thai coconut and Kaffir lime broth. Things are anything but laid-back on Friday and Saturday nights, however, when live music and potent cocktails attract the party crowd, where you'll be more likely to wear your martini than drink it. ⊠ *60 Ocean Blvd., Atlantic Beach 32233* ☎ *904/247–0060* ⊙ *Closed Sun. No lunch.*

★ **$–$$$** ✗**Ragtime Tavern & Seafood Grill.** A New Orleans theme prevails at this loud place that attracts a lively crowd ranging in age from 21 to midlife crisis. Bayou bouillabaisse (lobster, shrimp, scallops, fish, crab, clams, and crawfish in a creole court bouillon) and Ragtime shrimp (deep-fried fresh shrimp rolled in coconut) are the true specialties here, along with microbrews made on the premises. If you aren't into creole and Cajun, try a po'boy sandwich or fish sizzled on the grill. ⊠ *207 Atlantic Blvd., Atlantic Beach* ☎ *904/241–7877* ⚇ *Reservations not accepted* ⊟ *AE, D, DC, MC, V.*

¢–$ ✗**Al's Pizza.** The beach locations of this popular restaurant defy all expectations of a neighborhood pizza joint. Bright colors and geometric patterns accent the dining room, which also takes on an industrial feel. The menu is fairly predictable; there's pizza by the slice and by the pie, plus standbys like lasagna and ravioli. The clientele, too, is typical Beaches, with lots of twentysomething surfer dudes and dudettes and sunburned families. ⊠ *303 Atlantic Blvd., Atlantic Beach* ☎ *904/249–0002* ⊠ *635 A1A N, Ponte Vedra Beach 32082* ☎ *904/543–1494* ⚇ *Reservations not accepted* ⊟ *AE, D, MC, V.*

¢–$ ✗**European Street Cafe.** After more than 25 years of dominance in Jacksonville, the colorful and quirky family-owned eatery finally lands at the beach with the same ambitious menu of sandwiches, salads, and soups; overflowing gourmet food section; mind-boggling beer list; and cookies big enough to knock someone unconscious. An impressive, hand-carved bar is a favorite hangout for thirsty locals who belly up for monthly beer tastings and one of the best happy hours, while the senior crowds prefer to sip their carafes of Zinfandel in the bustling dining room. ⊠ *992 Beach Blvd., Jacksonville Beach 32250* ☎ *904/249–3001* ⚇ *Reservations not accepted* ⊟ *AE, D, MC, V.*

WHERE TO STAY

$$$$ [🏨] **The Lodge & Club.** Inspired by a Mediterranean villa, this oceanfront
Fodor'sChoice resort—with its white-stucco exterior and Spanish roof tiles—is luxury
★ lodging at its best. Rooms are quite spacious and have cozy window
seats, appealing artwork, and private balconies overlooking the Atlantic Ocean. Some units include a whirlpool tub and gas fireplace. Guests
consistently praise staff for going the extra mile, whether it's accommodating special diets in the dining room or coordinating day trips
and shopping excursions. Relax in one of three pools or on the private
beach. Guests at the Lodge have full access to sports, recreation, and
spa facilities at sister property Ponte Vedra Inn & Club, less than 2
mi away. **Pros:** High-end accommodations, excellent service, private
beach. **Cons:** Overrated food, non-valet parking can be a hike, most
recreation facilities are off-site at the Inn & Club. ✉ *607 Ponte Vedra
Blvd., Ponte Vedra Beach* ☎ *904/273–9500 or 800/243–4304* ⊕ *www.
pvresorts.com* 📠 *42 rooms, 24 suites* ♿ *In-room: safe, kitchen (some),
refrigerators (some), Wi-Fi. In-hotel: 2 restaurants, room service, bars,
pools, gym, beachfront, water sports, bicycles, concierge, children's
programs (ages 4–12), laundry service, public Wi-Fi, airport shuttle,
parking (no fee), no-smoking rooms* ▤ *AE, D, DC, MC, V.*

$$$$ [🏨] **Ponte Vedra Inn & Club.** Considered Northeast Florida's premier
Fodor'sChoice resort for decades, this 1928 landmark continues to wow guests with
★ its stellar service and recently renovated rooms and common areas.
Accommodations are in a series of white-brick, Spanish-style buildings lining the beach; rooms are extra-large, and most have ocean
views. The main house holds the registration area and some common
spaces, including a big living room with fireplace. The inn's renowned
full-service spa, which recently got a face-lift of its own, still attracts
the rich and famous, including actors, supermodels, and former first
ladies. **Pros:** Accommodating and friendly staff, private beach, adults-
only pool. **Cons:** Small beds, charge for umbrellas and chaises on the
beach, crowded pool. ✉ *200 Ponte Vedra Blvd., Ponte Vedra Beach*
☎ *904/285–1111 or 800/234–7842* ⊕ *www.pvresorts.com* 📠 *205
rooms, 45 suites* ♿ *In-room: safe, kitchen (some), refrigerator (some),
DVD, VCR, Wi-Fi. In-hotel: 4 restaurants, room service, bars, golf
courses, tennis courts, pool, gym, spa, beachfront, bicycles, children's
programs (ages 2–12), laundry service, concierge, public Wi-Fi, parking
(no fee), no-smoking rooms* ▤ *AE, D, DC, MC, V.*

$$$$ [🏨] **Sawgrass Golf Resort and Spa, a Marriott Resort.** As the second-largest golf
resort in the country and home of the world-famous TPC at Sawgrass
Stadium Course, the Sawgrass Golf Resort and Spa has plenty to offer
golfers, including playing privileges on 99 holes of world renowned
courses (five, to be exact). This is truly a full-service resort, whether
you've come to laze about (the resort includes a 25,000-square-foot,
full-service spa and allows guests access to the Cabana Club, a private
beach club nearby) or get active playing an Arnold Palmer–designed
mini-golf course, swimming in one of four pools or fishing in freshwater lakes and ponds. A $16 million room-renovation project in
2007 has given the resort a face more befitting its name. **Pros:** Championship golf courses, readily available shuttle, efficient staff. **Cons:**

Beach not within walking distance, overrated food, no free parking. ✉*1000 PGA Tour Blvd., Ponte Vedra Beach* ☎*904/285–7777 or 800/457–4653* ⊕*www.sawgrass marriott.com* ➲*508 rooms, 24 suites* &*In-room: kitchen (some), refrigerator, Wi-Fi. In-hotel: 7 restaurants, room service, bars, golf, tennis, pools, gym, spa, bicycles, children's programs (ages 5–12), laundry facilities, laundry service, concierge, public Wi-Fi, airport shuttle, parking (fee), some pets allowed, no-smoking rooms* ⊟*AE, D, DC, MC, V.*

> ### GO FOR THE GREEN
>
> Guests of the Sawgrass Golf Resort and Spa in Ponte Vedra Beach have playing privileges on eight championship golf courses including the TPC at Sawgrass Stadium Course, home of THE PLAYERS Championship. Held in May, the tournament referred to as the "unofficial fifth major" features one of the toughest courses, biggest prize money, and best fields of the year. If you plan on going, get your tickets early: it will sell out.

$$$ **🏨Casa Marina Hotel.** Compared with nearby oceanfront inns, it's small. But Casa Marina's creature comforts and rich history—including a stint as military housing during World War II and host to Franklin Delano Roosevelt and Al Capone in its early days—make it a big hit with tourists and locals (especially of the wedding party kind) looking for a peaceful retreat with character. Rooms are spacious, with comfy beds, and most have some view of the ocean. Unwind in the large courtyard behind the hotel with a drink from the bar, or take a stroll on the beach. Take note that Friday and Saturday nights can get a little noisy with the Penthouse Lounge (and all those drunken groomsmen) in operation. **Pros:** Oceanfront location, comfortable beds, good alternative to chain hotels. **Cons:** No pool, inconsistent restaurant hours, room service on weekends only. ✉*691 1st St. N., Jacksonville Beach* ☎*904/270–0025* ⊕*www.casamarinahotel.com* ➲*7 rooms, 16 suites* &*In-room: refrigerator, Wi-Fi. In-hotel: 2 restaurants, room service (weekends only), bars, beachfront, public Wi-Fi, parking (no fee), no-smoking rooms* ⊟*AE, D, MC, V.*

$$$ **🏨Quality Suites Oceanfront.** The Breakers it ain't, but this simple, all-suites hotel, popular with families and couples alike, atones for its lack of designer decor and gourmet dining with clean and spacious rooms (each room has a bedroom and separate sitting area with pull-out sofa, microwave, refrigerator, and private balcony) and personable and down-to-earth staff. Budget-conscious travelers will appreciate the complimentary hot breakfast and weeknight manager's reception (with free drinks and hors d'oeuvres) and rates that won't "breakers" the bank. Room service is available only between 4 and 10, and it comes from Carabba's down the street. **Pros:** All rooms are oceanfront, pets allowed, clean. **Cons:** Small pool, slow elevators, no on-site restaurant or bar. ✉*11 N. First St., Jacksonville Beach* ☎*904/435–3535 or 800/294–2787* ⊕*www.qualitysuitesjacksonvillebeach.com* ➲*72 rooms* &*In room: safe, kitchen, public Wi-Fi. In hotel: room service, pool, gym, beachfront, laundry facilities, laundry service, parking (no fee), some pets allowed, no-smoking rooms.* ⊟*AE, D, MC, V*

3

$$ ⌂**Sea Horse Oceanfront Inn.** Lacking the hoity-toity decor and amenities of other beachfront properties, this bright pink and aqua '50s throwback (you check in at the motel office, not a grand lobby) caters to budget-minded guests seeking an ultracasual, laid-back vibe. Rooms are modestly decorated and equipped, but feature an ocean view with a private balcony or patio. The kidney-shaped pool and lounge chairs are pretty standard issue but make for a refreshing respite from the hot Florida sun. The Lemon Bar is a hot spot for locals and hotel guests. **Pros:** Beach access with private walk-over, popular bar on-site, walking distance to restaurants and shops. **Cons:** No-frills decor, no room service. ⊠*120 Atlantic Blvd., Neptune Beach* ☎*904/246–2175 or 800/881–2330* ⊕*www.seahorseoceanfrontinn.com* ⟳*39 rooms, 1 suite* ♿ *In-room: kitchen, refrigerator, Wi-Fi. In-hotel: bar, pool, beachfront, no elevator, public Wi-Fi, parking (no fee), no-smoking rooms* ⊟*AE, D, MC, V.*

NIGHTLIFE

A groovy, low-key lounge during the week, **The Atlantic** (⊠*333 N. 1st St., Jacksonville Beach* ☎*904/249–3338*) becomes jam-packed with twentysomethings on weekends.**Fionn MacCool's** (⊠*333 N. 1st St., Suite 150, Jacksonville Beach* ☎*904/242–9499*) is, first and foremost, an Irish pub, but its top-notch menu is nothing to shake a shillelagh at. Hoist a pint o' Guinness and sing along with Emerald Isle troubadours at **Lynch's Irish Pub** (⊠*514 N. 1st St., Jacksonville Beach* ☎*904/249–5181*). The beautiful people gather at the **Ocean Club** (⊠*401 N. 1st St., Jacksonville Beach* ☎*904/242–8884*) for dancing, flirting, and drinking, not necessarily in that order. The oldest bar in Jacksonville and the beaches, **Pete's Bar** (⊠*117 1st St., Neptune Beach* ☎*904/249–9158*) is notable for the cheapest drinks, cheapest pool tables, and most colorful clientele in town. Entertainment at the **Sun Dog** (⊠ *207 Atlantic Blvd., Neptune Beach* ☎*904/241–8221*) often includes acoustic guitarists. With nearly 80 TVs and an impressive menu (by sports-bar standards anyway), **Sneakers Sports Grille** (⊠*111 Beach Blvd., Jacksonville Beach* ☎*904/482–1000*) is the go-to sports bar at the beach. If you'd rather gawk at sports stars in person than on the tube, head out to the oceanfront **Penthouse Lounge** (⊠*Casa Marina Hotel, 691 N. 1st St., Jacksonville Beach* ☎*904/270–0025*), where local NFL and PGA stars have been known to congregate.

SPORTS & THE OUTDOORS

BIKING **Champion Cycling**(⊠*1303 N. 3rd St., Jacksonville Beach* ☎*904/241–0900*) rents beach cruisers by the hour and by the day.**Ponte Vedra Bicycles** (⊠*250 Solana Rd., Ponte Vedra Beach* ☎*904/273–0199*) includes free bike maps with your rental.

MAYPORT

20 mi northeast of downtown Jacksonville.

Dating back more than 300 years, this is one of the oldest fishing communities in the United States. It has several excellent and very casual seafood restaurants and a large commercial shrimp-boat fleet. It's also the home to the third-largest naval facility in the country, Naval Station Mayport.

Kathryn Abbey Hanna Park is a 450-acre oceanfront property just north of Atlantic Beach. It's filled with spectacular beaches, biking and hiking trails, wooded campsites, and a 60-acre freshwater lake, perfect for swimming, kayaking, and canoeing. The lake area also includes picnic tables, grills, and a quarter-acre water park with fountains and squirting hoses. Throughout the park there are restrooms, showers, and snack bars, open April through Labor Day, as well as lifeguards supervising all water activities during summer. Surfers in the know head to "the poles" for the best wave action in town. Camping fees range from $25 to $34 per day. ⊠ *500 Wonderwood Dr.* ☎ *904/249–4700* 🖙 *$3 per vehicle* ⊙ *Apr.–Oct., daily 8–8; Nov.–Mar., daily 8–6.*

EN ROUTE The arrival of the **St. Johns River Ferry** in 1948 represented a huge convenience to local residents, plus a fun activity to share with kids. The ferry (the *Jean Ribault*) continues to delight passengers young and old as they drive aboard the 153-foot vessel and embark on the 10-minute cruise across the river between Mayport and Fort George Island. ☎ *904/241–9969* ⊕ *www.stjohnsriverferry.com* 🖙 *$3 per motorcycle, $5 per car, $1 additional per axle, $1 for pedestrians and bicyclists* ⊙ *Departing from Mayport weekdays 6 AM–10 PM, Sat.–Sun. 7 AM–6:30 PM on the hour and half hour, from Fort George Island weekdays 6:10 AM–6:45 PM, Sat.–Sun. 7:10 AM–8:45 PM on the quarter after and quarter to the hour.*

FORT GEORGE ISLAND

25 mi northeast of Jacksonville.

One of the oldest inhabited areas of Florida, Fort George Island is lush with foliage, natural vegetation, and wildlife. A 4-mi nature and bike trail meanders across the island, revealing shell mounds dating as far back as 6,000 years.

Built in 1792 by Zephaniah Kingsley, an eccentric slave trader, the **Kingsley Plantation** is the oldest remaining cotton plantation in the state. The ruins of 23 tabby (a concretelike mixture of sand and crushed shells) slave houses, a barn, and the modest Kingsley home are open to the public via self-guided tours and reachable by ferry or bridge. ⊠ *A1A–Hecksher Dr., north of St. Johns River Ferry* ☎ *904/251–3537* ⊕ *www. nps.gov/timc* 🖙 *Free* ⊙ *Daily 9–5; ranger talks daily at 2.*

Talbot Island State Parks. The Talbot Island State Parks, including Big and Little Talbot islands, have 17 mi of gorgeous beaches, sand dunes, and golden marshes that hum with birds and native waterfowl. Come to picnic, fish, swim, snorkel, or camp. Little Talbot Island, one of the few undeveloped barrier islands in Florida, has river otters, marsh rabbits, raccoons, bobcats, possums, and gopher tortoises. A 4-mi nature trail winds across Little Talbot, and there are several smaller trails on Big Talbot. ⊠ *12157 Heckscher Dr. 32226* ☎ *904/251–2320* ⊕ *www.floridastateparks.org/littletalbotisland* 🖙 *$4 per vehicle, up to*

8 people; $3 per motorcycle, $1 for pedestrians and bicyclists ☉ Daily 8–sundown.

AMELIA ISLAND (FERNANDINA BEACH)

35 mi northeast of Jacksonville.

At the northeasternmost reach of Florida, Amelia Island has beautiful beaches with enormous sand dunes along its eastern flank, a state park with a Civil War fort, sophisticated restaurants, interesting shops, and accommodations that range from B&Bs to luxury resorts. The town of Fernandina Beach is on the island's northern end; a century ago casinos and brothels thrived here, but those are gone. Today there's little reminder of the town's wild days, though one event comes close: the Isle of Eight Flags Shrimp Festival, held during the first weekend of May in Fernandina.

★ The **Amelia Island Historic District,** in Fernandina Beach, has more than 50 blocks of buildings listed on the National Register of Historic Places; 450 ornate structures built before 1927 offer some of the nation's finest examples of Queen Anne, Victorian, and Italianate homes. Many date to the haven's mid-19th-century glory days. Pick up a self-guided-tour map at the chamber of commerce, in the old train depot—once a stopping point on the first cross-state railroad—and take your time exploring the quaint shops, restaurants, and boutiques that populate the district, especially along Centre Street.

Founded in 1859, **St. Peter's Episcopal Church** (✉ *801 Atlantic Ave., Fernandina Beach* ☎ *904/261–4293*) is a Gothic Revival structure with Tiffany glass–style memorials and a turn-of-the-20th-century L.C. Harrison organ with magnificent hand-painted pipes.

One of the country's best-preserved and most complete 19th-century brick forts is at

★ **Fort Clinch State Park.** Fort Clinch was built to discourage further British intrusion after the War of 1812 and was occupied in 1863 by the Confederacy; a year later it was retaken by the North. During the Spanish-American War it was reactivated for a brief time but no battles were ever fought on its grounds (which explains why it's so well preserved). Wander through restored buildings, including furnished barracks, a kitchen, and a repair shop. Living-history reenactments of Civil War garrison life are scheduled throughout the year. The 1,086-acre park surrounding the fort has camping, nature trails, carriage rides, a swimming beach, and surf and pier fishing. Nature buffs will enjoy the variety of flora and fauna, especially since Fort Clinch is the only state park in Northeast Florida designated by the Florida Fish and Wildlife Conservation Commission as a viewing destination for the eastern brown pelican, green sea turtle, and loggerhead sea turtle. ✉ *2601 Atlantic Ave., Fernandina Beach* ☎ *904/277–7274* ⊕ *www.floridastateparks. org/fortclinch* 🎫 *$5 per vehicle, up to 8 people, tours $2* ☉ *Daily 8–sundown.*

Amelia Island's eastern shore includes **Main Beach**, a 13-mi stretch of white-sand beach edged with dunes, some 40 feet high. It's one of the few beaches in Florida where horseback riding is allowed.

WHERE TO EAT

$$$$
Fodor'sChoice
★

✕**Salt.** The Ritz-Carlton, Amelia Island's restaurant continues to set the culinary standard in Northeast Florida with inventive cuisine highlighting seasonal ingredients that might include bison rib eye accompanied by corn five ways or wild salmon with sweet potato–and–goat cheese "ravioli." The impressive wine list has more than 500 bottles, service is nothing short of impeccable, and there's a view of the Atlantic Ocean from every table. For a unique dining experience, reserve A Seat in the Kitchen, a private dining room within the kitchen where you'll watch the chefs at work and enjoy a personalized five-course meal. Collared shirts are required. ⊠*Ritz-Carlton, Amelia Island, 4750 Amelia Island Pkwy.* ☎*904/277–1100* ⚶*Reservations essential* ▭*AE, D, DC, MC, V* ⊘*No lunch.*

$$–$$$$

✕**Verandah Restaurant.** Although located on Amelia Island Plantation, this family-friendly restaurant is open to nonresort guests, many of whom drive from Jacksonville to dine here. The dining room has a casual vibe to it, with floral prints and roomy booths, but the menu is all business. Fresh seafood dishes are a highlight, including red snapper with pecan, crab meunière, pasta paella, and surf and turf, as is the "famous" Verandah salad, a meal in itself. And if you luck out and find she-crab soup on the menu (it's seasonal and not always available), order yourself the biggest bowl or bucketful they have. ⊠*6800 1st Coast Hwy. 32034* ☎*904/321–5050* ⚶*Reservations not accepted* ▭*AE, D, MC, V* ⊘*No lunch.*

★ $$–$$$

✕**Beech Street Grill.** Housed in an 1889 sea captain's house, this highly regarded Fernandina Beach restaurant caters to locals who crave its comfort food–inspired dishes like tenderloin meat loaf with spinach, ham, and provolone cheese with shiitake-mushroom gravy and chive whipped potatoes, as well as visiting foodies who have heard its quiet buzz from miles away. Hardwood floors and marble fireplaces aside, one of Beech Street's most coveted fixtures is pianist John "If-you-can-hum-it-I-can-play-it" Springer, who has been entertaining diners for decades. A blackboard lists four or five fresh fish specials nightly. The outstanding wine list includes some coveted Californians. ⊠*801 Beech St., Fernandina Beach* ☎*904/277–3662* ⚶*Reservations essential* ▭*AE, D, DC, MC, V* ⊘*No lunch.*

WHERE TO STAY

$$$$
Fodor'sChoice
★

Amelia Island Plantation. The first-rate golf, tennis, and spa facilities are big draws at this sprawling, family-oriented resort where accommodations include full-service hotel rooms at the Amelia Inn as well as home and condo (or "villa") rentals. All hotel rooms are oceanfront with private balconies or patios, though first-floor rooms

WORD OF MOUTH

The Ritz on Amelia is absolutely gorgeous. You can't go wrong there." –Postal

"I'd do the Ritz Carlton, but you may want to look at the Elizabeth [Pointe] Lodge." –starrs

3

have a better view of the pool or golf course than the Atlantic. If the sound of waves crashing on the beach doesn't lull you to sleep, the pillow-top mattresses should do the trick. Villas are privately owned, meaning availability and amenities are inconsistent. With its ancient oaks, marshes, and lagoons, the resort is also a worthy destination for hiking, biking, and bird-watching, and is one of the few places in Northeast Florida to rent Segways. **Pros:** Family-friendly, variety of outdoor activities, shuttle service throughout property. **Cons:** Hotel far removed from other facilities (golf course, shops, tennis courts), quality of villas inconsistent, a hike to some hotel rooms. ⌂*6800 1st Coast Hwy.,* ☎*904/261–6161 or 800/874–6878* ⊕*www.aipfl.com* ⟳*249 rooms, 361 1-, 2-, and 3-bedroom villas* ⌂*In-room: safe, kitchen (some), refrigerator (some), DVD (some villas), VCR (some villas), Wi-Fi. In-hotel: 11 restaurants, room service, bars, golf courses, tennis courts, pools, gym, spa, beachfront, water sports, bicycles, children's programs (ages 3–10), laundry facilities (villas only), laundry service, concierge, some pets allowed, no-smoking rooms* ⊟*AE, D, MC, V.*

$$$$
Fodor'sChoice
★

The Ritz-Carlton, Amelia Island. Guests know what to expect from the Ritz-Carlton (namely, elegance, superb comfort, and excellent service), and the Amelia Island location is certainly no exception. All accommodations in the eight-story building have balconies and ocean views; suites and rooms are spacious and luxurious, and are furnished with heavy print draperies, plush carpet, framed prints, and beds so comfortable, you'll need a drag-out call instead of a wake-up call. Public areas are exquisitely maintained, and fine cuisine can be had at a choice of restaurants, including Salt. Room service is available 24/7. Recent additions include a 27,500-square-foot, state-of-the-art spa and Our Space, a social/recreational program for guests 12–19. **Pros:** Fine-dining restaurant, world-class spa, private beach access, accommodating staff. **Cons:** No self-parking, lack of nightlife, a drive to sites and restaurants. ⌂*4750 Amelia Island Pkwy.,* ☎*904/277–1100* ⊕*www.ritzcarlton. com/resorts/amelia_island* ⟳*444 rooms, 42 suites* ⌂*In-room: safe, Wi-Fi. In-hotel: 5 restaurants, room service, bars, golf course, tennis courts, pools, gym, spa, beachfront, bicycles, children's programs (ages 5–12), laundry service, concierge, executive floor, no-smoking rooms* ⊟*AE, D, DC, MC, V.*

$$$–$$$$

Ash Street Inn. It's only fitting that the sunny yellow historic homes that make up this precious inn are surrounded by a white picket fence. Just a block from the heart of downtown Fernandina Beach, rooms are spacious and individually decorated with bedspreads and fabrics, and, in some cases, window treatments and antiques. Some rooms have claw-foot tubs, others have whirlpools, and one has a working fireplace. The rate includes a three-course breakfast that can be enjoyed either in the bright dining room or out on the porch. Lemonade and fresh-baked cookies often appear on the porch in the afternoon. **Pros:** Walking distance to historic district, pets allowed in certain rooms, friendly staff, complimentary bicycles and beach gear (towels, umbrellas). **Cons:** May be boring for kids, small pool, not within walking distance of the beach. ⊠ *102 S. 7th St.,* ☎ *904/277–6660 or 800/277–6660* ⊕ *www.ashstreetinn.net* ⇦ *10 rooms, 1 suite* ⭕ *In-room: kitchen (some), refrigerator (some), VCR, Wi-Fi. In-hotel: pool, bicycles, public Wi-Fi, parking (no fee), some pets allowed, no-smoking rooms* ☐ *AE, D, MC, V* ⏐◎⏐ *BP.*

★ **$$$–$$$$** 🏨 **Elizabeth Pointe Lodge.** Guests at this oceanfront inn, built to resemble an 1890s sea captain's house, can't say enough about the impeccable personal service, beginning with its legendary gourmet breakfasts (dill scrambled eggs and French toast are among the crowd pleasers) and ending with social hour every evening with wine and hors d'oeuvres in the library. Oceanside units have great water views, albeit through disappointingly small windows, the Tradewinds Suite deemed the most romantic. A chair-lined porch offers everyone a chance to rock in ocean breezes, and on cold nights guests can cluster around the living-room fireplace. An adjacent cottage has additional rooms and a suite. **Pros:** Beachfront location, hospitable staff, 24-hour desk attendant. **Cons:** Pricey for a B&B, not all rooms are oceanfront, kids may be bored. ⊠ *98 S. Fletcher Ave.,* ☎ *904/277–4851 or 800/772–3359* ⊕ *www.elizabethpointelodge.com* ⇦ *24 rooms, 1 2-bedroom cottage* ⭕ *In-room: kitchen (some), DVD (some), Wi-Fi. In-hotel: beachfront, laundry facilities, concierge, public Wi-Fi, parking (no fee), no-smoking rooms* ☐ *AE, D, MC, V* ⏐◎⏐ *BP.*

$$$–$$$$ 🏨 **Hoyt House Bed & Breakfast.** Modeled after the Rockefeller Cottage in Jekyll Island, Georgia, this Queen Anne Victorian home is as warm and inviting today as it was when it was built a century ago. Inside, rooms show off antique and reproduction furniture, down quilts, and walls painted in rich hues, and a turn-of-the-century birdcage comes alive with colorful finches in the parlor. Relax in one of the rockers on the wide veranda, browse the fully stocked library, or practice on the lobby piano; just don't miss the wine and cheese reception every afternoon. **Pros:** Gourmet breakfast, pool and hot tub, walking distance to historic district. **Cons:** Two-night stay required most weekends, some small bathrooms, rooms near the kitchen can be noisy. ⊠ *804 Atlantic Ave.,* ☎ *904/277–4300 or 800/432–2085* ⊕ *www.hoythouse.com* ⇦ *10 rooms* ⭕ *In-room: DVD, Wi-Fi. In-hotel: pool, bicycles, no elevator, public Wi-Fi, parking (no fee), some pets allowed, no kids under 12, no-smoking rooms* ☐ *AE, MC, V* ⏐◎⏐ *BP.*

$$$ 🏨 **Amelia Hotel & Suites.** Across the street from the beach, this midsize inn is not only convenient but an economical and family-friendly alternative to the luxury resorts and romantic and kid-unfriendly B&Bs that populate the area. The beach and several restaurants are within walking distance, particularly convenient for families. Parents will also appreciate the hotel-wide no-smoking policy and continental breakfast served each morning in the lobby. Rooms are modestly furnished and have ocean views (provided you're not near-sighted) and pool views (considering the pool is practically in the parking lot, it's not much to look at). **Pros:** Complimentary breakfast, free Wi-Fi, 24-hour front desk. **Cons:** Small pool, not all rooms have balconies, no on-site restaurant. ✉*1997 S. Fletcher Ave.,* ☎*904/261–5735 or 877/263–5428* ⊕*www.ameliahotel.us* ⟿*90 rooms* ⚹*In-room: refrigerator, Wi-Fi. In-hotel: pool, public Wi-Fi, parking (no fee), no-smoking rooms* ▤*AE, D, MC, V* ⦿*CP.*

3

NIGHTLIFE

Located on Amelia Island Plantation, the 7,000-square-foot, aviation-themed **Falcon's Next** (✉*6800 1st Coast Hwy., 32034* ☎*904/261-6161*)features a dance floor and outdoor deck.It's St. Patrick's Day every day at **O'Kane's Irish Pub** (✉*318 Centre St., 32034* ☎*904/261-1000*). The oldest continuously operating bar in Florida, the **Palace Saloon** (✉*117 Centre St., 32034* ☎*904/491–3332*) entertained the Rockefellers and Carnegies at the turn of the 20th century, but now caters to common folk. Locals congregate on the outdoor deck at **The Surf** (✉*3199 S. Fletcher Ave., 32034* ☎*904/261–5711*) for drinks and good old-fashioned bar food (pizza, burgers, and wings).

SPORTS & THE OUTDOORS

HORSEBACK RIDING

Country Day Stables (✉*2940 Jane Lane, Hilliard* ☎*904/879–9383*) in Callahan offers individual and group rides, including private picnic outings, on its 40-acre ranch. Reservations are required. **Kelly Seahorse Ranch** (✉*7500 1st Coast Hwy., Amelia Island* ☎*904/491–5166*), located within the Amelia Isand State Park, takes guests on horseback rides on the beach.

KAYAKING

Kayak Amelia (✉*13030 Hecksher Dr., Amelia Island* ☎*904/251–0016*) takes adventurous types on guided tours of salt marshes and Fort George River and also rents equipment for those looking to create their own adventures. Reservations are required.

SHOPPING

Within the **Fernandina Beach Historic District** are numerous shops, art galleries, and boutiques, many clustered along Centre Street.

ST. AUGUSTINE

35 mi south of Jacksonville.

Founded in 1565 by Spanish explorers, St. Augustine is the nation's oldest city and has a wealth of historic buildings and attractions. In addition to the historic sites on the mainland, the city has 43 mi of beaches on two barrier islands to the east, both reachable by causeways. Several times a year St. Augustine holds historic reenactments, such as December's Grand Christmas Illumination, which commemorates the town's British occupation.

EXPLORING ST. AUGUSTINE

The core of any visit is a tour of the historic district, a showcase for more than 60 historic sites and attractions, plus 144 blocks of houses listed on the National Register of Historic Places. You could probably spend several weeks exploring these treasures, but don't neglect other, generally newer, attractions found elsewhere in town.

Numbers in the margin correspond to the St. Augustine map.

WHAT TO SEE

⑲ Anastasia State Park. With 1,700 protected acres of bird sanctuary, this Anastasia Island park draws families that like to hike, bike, camp, swim, and play on the beach. ⊠*1340 Rte. A1A S, Anastasia Island* ☎*904/461–2033* ⊕*www.floridastateparks.org/anastasia* ☜*$3–5 per vehicle, $1 for pedestrians or bicyclists* ☉*Daily 8–sundown.*

★ ⑤ Castillo de San Marcos National Monument. This massive structure is three centuries old, and it looks every second of it. The fort was constructed of coquina, a soft limestone made of broken shells and coral. Built by the Spanish to protect St. Augustine from British raids (English pirates were handy with a torch), the fort was used as a prison during the Revolutionary and Civil wars. Park rangers provide an introductory narration, after which you're on your own to explore the moat, turrets, and 16-foot-thick walls. Garrison rooms depict the life of the era, and special cannon-firing demonstrations are held on weekends from Memorial Day to Labor Day. Children under 16 are admitted free and must be accompanied by an adult. Save the receipt, since admission is valid for seven days. ⊠*1 S. Castillo Dr.* ☎*904/829–6506* ⊕*www.nps.gov/casa* ☜*$6* ☉*Daily 8:45–5:15.*

⑬ Cathedral Basilica of St. Augustine. The cathedral has the country's oldest written parish records, dating from 1594. Restored in the mid-1960s, the current structure (1797) had extensive changes after an 1887 fire. ⊠*40 Cathedral Pl. 32084* ☎ *904/824–2806* ⊕*www.thefirstparish.org* ☜*Donation welcome* ☉*Weekdays 9–4:30.*

② City Gate. The gate is a relic from the days when the Castillo's moat ran westward to the river, and the Cubo Defense Line (defensive wall) protected against approaches from the north. ⊠*St. George St.*

④ Colonial Spanish Quarter. Wander through the narrow streets at your own pace in this living-history museum depicting the lives of Spanish soldiers and their families in 1740s St. Augustine. Along the way you may see a blacksmith building his shop (a historic reconstruction) or artisans busy at candle-dipping, spinning, weaving, or cabinetmaking. The buildings themselves are reconstructed built on the original foundations. ⊠*33 St. George St., 32084* ☎*904/825–6830* ⊕*www.historicstaugustine.com* ☜*$6.95 adults, $4.25 children 6–17* ☉*Daily 9–5:30.*

A GOOD WALK

A good place to start is the **Visitor Information ❶** to pick up maps, brochures, and information. It's on San Marco Avenue between Castillo Drive and Orange Street. From there, cross Orange Street to reach the **City Gate ❷**, the entrance to the city's restored area. Walk south on St. George Street to the **Oldest Wooden Schoolhouse ❸**. Directly across from it is the **Colonial Spanish Quarter ❹**. Go out Fort Alley and cross San Marco Avenue to the impressive **Castillo de San Marcos National Monument ❺**. Now head west on Cuna Street and turn left on Cordova Street. Walk south three blocks to Valencia Street and turn right. At the end of the block is the splendid **Flagler Memorial Presbyterian Church ❻**. Head one block south on Sevilla Street and turn left on King Street to find the **Government House Museum ❼** and three more of Henry Flagler's legacies: the **Lightner Museum ❽**, **Flagler College ❾**, and the Casa Monica Hotel. Continue two blocks east on King Street and turn right onto St. George Street to reach the **Ximenez-Fatio House ❿**. Afterward, head a few blocks south down Aviles Street to St. Francis Street for a look at a microcosm of the city's history,

the **Oldest House ⓫** (not to be confused with the Oldest Wooden Schoolhouse). Head back north to the Bridge of Lions, the **Plaza de la Constitución ⓬** and the **Cathedral Basilica of St. Augustine ⓭**. You have to cross the Bridge of Lions to get to Anastasia Island and the historic **St. Augustine Lighthouse & Museum ⓮**, but it's worth the effort.

Several attractions are beyond this walk, including two of particular historic note: the **Mission of Nombre de Dios ⓯**, north of the visitor center, is the site of America's first Christian mass; and well north of the city's cluster of sights is the **Fountain of Youth National Archaeological Park ⓰**, marking the location of the famed spring. For recreation, also consider **Vilano Beach ⓱**, north of the city, as well as **St. Augustine Beach ⓲** and **Anastasia State Park ⓳**, both on Anastasia Island.

TIMING

Allot eight hours for the tour, covering it in two days if possible. Though most sights keep the same hours (daytime only), a few are not open on Sunday. Weekday mornings generally have the smallest crowds.

❾ **Flagler College.** Originally one of two posh hotels Henry Flagler built in 1887, this building—now a small liberal-arts college—is a riveting Spanish architecture structure with towers, turrets, and arcades decorated by Louis Comfort Tiffany. The former Hotel Ponce de Leon is a National Historic Landmark having hosted U.S. Presidents Grover Cleveland, Theodore Roosevelt, and Warren Harding. Tours are offered daily through Flagler's Legacy Tours. ✉ *74 King St. 32084* ☎ *904/829–6481, 904/823–3378 tour information* ⊕ *www.flagler.edu* 🎫 *Tours $6 per person* ⊙ *Tours daily at 10 and 2, additional hours during summer.*

❻ **Flagler Memorial Presbyterian Church.** To look at a marvelous Venetian Renaissance–style structure, head to this church, built by Flagler in

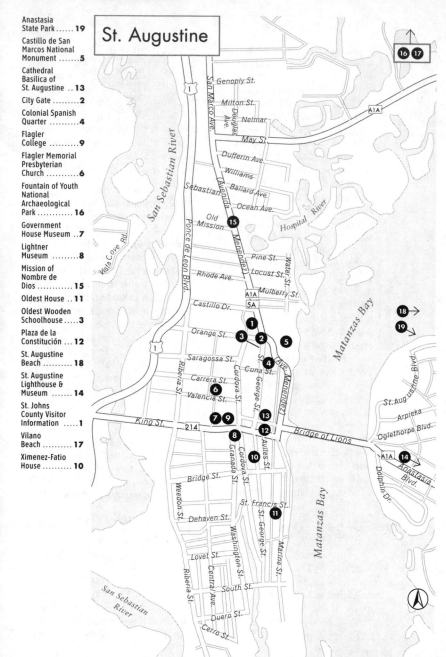

St. Augustine

1889. The dome towers more than 100 feet and is topped by a 20-foot Greek cross. ✉ *Valencia and Sevilla Sts. 32084* ☎*904/829–6451* ⊙ *Weekdays 8:30–4:30.*

3

HOPE SPRINGS ETERNAL

Whether or not the St. Augustine's world-renowned Fountain of Youth has actual curative powers is debatable. But visitors to North America's first historical site (Ponce de León's expedition landed in the vicinity in 1513) who are brave enough to drink the foul-smelling water will get a dose of 42 minerals, including iron and—not surprising—sulfur.

🔟 **Fountain of Youth National Archaeological Park.** Here's the thing about "North America's first historical site": you either love it, or you hate it. Fans of the grade-A tourist trap appreciate the kitsch factor. They laugh at the cheesy costumes and educational displays. They chuckle at the tired planetarium show. They sip from the legendary Fountain of Youth, if only to mock Ponce de León and his followers for believing such foul-tasting water could hold magical powers. If you don't, however, appreciate kitsch, you'll only be disappointed in the dated exhibits and disinterested employees and wish you had spent your seven bucks on a roast beef sandwich. ✉ *11 Magnolia Ave., 32084* ☎*904/829–3168 or 800/356–8222* ⊕*www.fountainofyouthflorida.com* 💲*$7 adults, $4 children 6–12* ⊙ *Daily 9–5.*

7 Government House Museum. With a collection of more than 300 artifacts from archaeological digs and Spanish shipwrecks off the Florida coast, this museum reflects five centuries of history. ✉ *48 King St., 32084* ☎*904/825–5033* 💲*$2.50 adults, $1 students* ⊙ *Daily 9–4:30.*

★ **8 Lightner Museum.** In his quest to turn Florida into an American Riviera, Henry Flagler built two fancy hotels in 1888—the Ponce de León, which became Flagler College, and the Alcazar, which now houses this museum. The building showcases three floors of furnishings, costumes, and Victorian art glass, plus ornate antique music boxes, which visitors say are not to be missed (demonstrations daily at 11 and 2). The Lightner Antiques Mall perches on three levels of what was the hotel's indoor pool. ✉ *75 King St., 32084* ☎*904/824–2874* ⊕*www.lightnermuseum. org* 💲*$10 adults, $5 children 12–18* ⊙ *Museum daily 9–4:30.*

15 Mission of Nombre de Dios. The site, north of the historic district, commemorates where America's first Christian mass was celebrated. A 208-foot-tall stainless-steel cross marks the spot where the mission's first cross was planted. ✉ *27 Ocean Ave., 32084* ☎*904/824–2809 or 800/342–6529* ⊕*www.missionandshrine.org* 💲*Donation requested* ⊙ *Weekdays 8–5, Sat. 9–5, Sun. 10–5.*

11 Oldest House. Known as the Gonzalez-Alvarez House, the Oldest House (technically, the oldest surviving Spanish Colonial dwelling in Florida), is a National Historic Landmark. The current site dates from the early 1700s, but a structure has been on this site since the early 1600s. Much of the city's history is seen in the building's changes and additions, from the coquina blocks—which came into use to replace wood soon after the town burned in 1702—to the house's enlargement during the

British occupation. Most visitors can't get over how small the house is. ⊠*14 St. Francis St., 32084* ☏*904/824-2872* ⊕*www.staugustine historicalsociety.org* ✉*$8 adults, $4 children 6–18* ☉*Daily 9–5.*

③ Oldest Wooden Schoolhouse. In another instance of exaggerated advertising in the Old City, the Oldest Wooden Schoolhouse is actually thought to be *one* of the nation's oldest schoolhouses. Nevertheless, the tiny 18th-century building of cypress and cedar has a fascinating history—told by automated mannequins of a teacher and students—including its having served as a guardhouse and sentry shelter during the Seminole Wars. ⊠*14 St. George St., 32084* ☏*888/653-7245* ⊕*www. oldestwoodenschoolhouse.com* ✉*$3.50 adults, $2.50 children 6–12* ☉*Mon.–Thur. 9–5, Fri.–Sat. 9–7:30, Sun. 9–6.*

⑫ Plaza de la Constitución. The central area of the original settlement was laid out in 1598 by decree of King Philip II, and little has changed since. At its center is a monument to the Spanish constitution of 1812, and at the east end is a public market dating from early American days. Just beyond is a statue of Juan Ponce de León, who "discovered" Florida in 1513. ⊠*St. George St. and Cathedral Pl., 32084*

⑱ St. Augustine Beach. This very popular strand is the closest beach to downtown. It's on the northern end of Anastasia Island, directly east of town. ⊠*1200 Rte. A1A S., 32084* ☏*No phone* ✉*Free.*

⑭ St. Augustine Lighthouse & Museum. Its beacon no longer guides ships to St. Augustine's shores, but the historic lighthouse continues to draw thousands of visitors each year. The 1874 structure replaced an earlier lighthouse built by the Spanish when the city was founded in 1565. The visitor center has an exhibit gallery and a store. With more than 200 steps from top to bottom, the winding staircase might be difficult for some, but those who make the journey say getting a little winded is well worth the trip. ⊠*81 Lighthouse Ave., 32080* ☏*904/829-0745* ⊕*www.staugustinelighthouse.com* ✉*$8 adults, $6 children under 11* ☉*Daily 9–6, last ticket sold at 5:45.*

❶ St. Johns County Visitor Information Center. Start your day of sightseeing here, where you can pick up maps and other information on local attractions and friendly hosts offer tips for getting around, dining, and accommodations. ⊠*10 Castillo Dr., 32080* ☏*904/825-1000* ✉*Free* ☉*Daily 8:30–5:30.*

⑰ Vilano Beach. Once-quiet Vilano Beach, just north of St. Augustine, is slowly blossoming into a bustling community with a town center, cozy restaurants and outdoor cafés, condos, and hotels. ⊠*3400 Coastal Hwy., across the St. Augustine Inlet* ☏*No phone* ✉*Free.*

⑩ Ximenez-Fatio House. Built as a merchant's house and store in 1797, the place became a tourist boardinghouse in the 1800s. It's been restored to look like it did during its inn days. ⊠*20 Aviles St., 32084* ☏*904/829-3575* ⊕*www.ximenezfatiohouse.org* ✉*$5 adults, $4 children 6–17* ☉*Tues.–Sat. 11–4.*

St. Augustine Alligator Farm Zoological Park. Founded in 1893, the Alligator Farm is one of Florida's oldest (and, at times, smelliest) zoological attractions and is credited with popularizing the alligator in the national consciousness and helping to fashion an image for the state. In addition to oddities like Maximo, a 15-foot, 1,250-pound saltwater crocodile, and a collection of rare albino alligators, the park is also home to Land of Crocodiles, the only place in the world to see all 23 species of living crocodilians. Reptiles are the main attraction, but there's also a wading bird rookery, an exotic birds and mammals exhibit, and nature trails. Educational presentations are held throughout the day, including live alligator feedings (not for the faint of heart). ⊠ *999 Anastasia Blvd., 32080* ☎*904/824–3337* ⊕*www.alligatorfarm.us* ☒*$19.95 adults, $10.95 children 3–11* ⊙ *Daily 9–5.*

OFF THE BEATEN PATH

World Golf Hall of Fame. This stunning tribute to the game of golf is the centerpiece of **World Golf Village,** an extraordinary complex that includes 36 holes of golf, a golf academy, several accommodation options, a convention center, and a variety of restaurants, including Murray Bros. Caddyshack. The Hall of Fame features an adjacent IMAX theater and houses a variety of exhibits combining historical artifacts and personal memorabilia with the latest in interactive technology. Stand up to the pressures of the TV camera and crowd noise as you try to sink a final putt, take a swing on the museum's simulator, or snap a photo as you walk across a replica of St. Andrews' Swilcan Burn Bridge. ⊠ *1 World Golf Pl., 32092* ☎*904/940–4123* ⊕*www.wgv.com* ☒*$19 adults, $8.50 children 3–12 (includes one IMAX film and one round on the putting course), IMAX film $8 adults, $5 children 3–12* ⊙ *Mon.–Sat. 10–6, Sun. noon–6.*

WHERE TO EAT

$$$–$$$$
Fodor$Choice
★

✕95 Cordova. Tucked away on the first floor of the Casa Monica Hotel, this restaurant serves classic cuisine with an international flair. Sup in one of three dining rooms, including the main room with intricate Moroccan-themed chandeliers, wrought-iron chairs, and heavy wood columns, or the Sultan's Room, a gold-dipped space accented with potted palms and a silk-draped ceiling. The exotic furnishings are inherently romantic, but still lend an appropriate feel to dinner with friends or business associates. Innovative dishes change seasonally and highlight local seafood and produce. The tasting menu offers diners six international courses paired with the restaurant's outstanding wines. ⊠ *95 Cordova St., 32084* ☎*904/810–6810* ⊟*AE, D, MC, V.*

$$$–$$$$

✕Collage. Foodies seeking a new dining experience in the Oldest City head to Collage for "artful global cuisine" in a warm and intimate setting. Tucked away on Hypolita street in the historic district, the 48-seat restaurant highlights local seafood with four fresh fish entrées each day and their signature dish, Florida bouillabaisse with littleneck clams, mussels, scallops, whitefish, and lobster. Pan-seared pork tenderloin, miso-glazed duck breast, chicken cordon bleu, and hand-cut steaks are also on the menu. For dessert, the bougainvillea, an original dessert inspired by the colorful flowering plants that frame the building, is made of strawberries, ice cream, and cabernet vanilla sauce served in a leaf-shaped phyllo cup. ⊠ *60 Hypolita St.,* ☏ *904/829–0055* ⊟ *AE, MC, V* ⊘ *No lunch.*

★ **$$–$$$** ✕**Columbia.** Arroz con pollo, fillet *salteado* (with a spicy sauce), and a fragrant seafood paella: this heir to the original Columbia, founded in Tampa in 1905 and still going strong, serves the same time-honored Cuban and Spanish dishes. Befitting its cuisine, the restaurant has a white stucco exterior and an atrium dining room full of palm trees, hand-painted tiles, and decorative arches. The wait can be off-putting, especially during summer, when the tourists are out in full force, but a glass of homemade sangria or a refreshing mojito usually manages to take the edge off. ⊠ *98 St. George St., 32084* ☏ *904/824–3341, 800/227–1905 in Florida* ⊟ *AE, D, DC, MC, V.*

★ **$$–$$$** ✕**Salt Water Cowboy's.** Rustic handmade twig furniture and 100-year-old hardwood floors are reminders that this spot, hidden in the salt marshes flanking the Intracoastal Waterway, began as a secluded fish camp (with more "fragrant" reminders at low tide). Clam chowder, oyster stew, barbecue ribs, and crispy fried chicken are standard fare, along with blackened and broiled seafood, steamed oysters, and steak. For more adventuresome palates, the menu includes frogs' legs, alligator, and cooter (fried soft-shell turtle rolled in seasoned bread crumbs). ⊠ *299 Dondanville Rd.,32080* ☏ *904/471–2332* ⚠ *Reservations not accepted* ⊟ *AE, D, DC, MC, V* ⊘ *Closed Tues. and Mon. in winter. No lunch.*

WHERE TO STAY

$$$$ ⌂**Casa de la Paz.** The cheery yellow three-story inn overlooking Matanzas Bay is apropos since the innkeepers are pretty darned sunny themselves. Committed to providing with the best possible service, George and Kathie Dann offer guests a two-course breakfast, afternoon wine socials, complimentary beverages, homemade desserts, and conveniences like a hair dryer, iron, and ironing board in every room. Antiques fill the inn without making it feel like your grandmother's house. The romantic setting (and lack of children) makes the inn a popular choice for honeymoons, anniversaries, and marriage proposals. Pros: Location, comfy beds, excellent service. Cons: Cancellation fee, supposedly haunted. ⊠ *52 Charlotte St.,* ☏ *904/829–3819 or 800/355–5508* ⊕ *www.casadelapaz.com* ➹ *7 rooms* ⚬ *In room: Wi-Fi. In hotel: no elevator, laundry facilities, public Wi-Fi, parking (no fee), no kids under 16* ⊟ *AE, D, MC, V.*

$$$$ ⌂**Casa Monica Hotel.** Hand-stenciled Moorish columns and arches, Fodor'sChoice hand-crafted chandeliers, and gilded iron tables decorate the lobby of ★ this late-1800s Flagler-era masterpiece. A retreat for the nation's wealthiest until the Great Depression put it out of business, it has returned to its perch as St. Augustine's grande dame. The turrets, towers, and wrought-iron balconies offer a hint of what's inside. Rooms—dressed in blues, greens, and whites—include wrought-iron two- and four-poster beds and mahogany writing desks and nightstands. The downtown location is within walking distance of many attractions. Guests also have access to the Serenata Beach Club, including three pools, private beach access, and beach-equipment rentals. **Pros:** Location, architecture and decor, service. **Cons:** Tourists clogging the lobby, expensive parking, extra charges, small rooms. ✉*95 Cordova St.,* ☎*904/827–1888 or 800/648–1888* ⊕*www. casamonica.com* ⇆*138 rooms, 14 suites* ♿*In-room: safe, kitchen (some), refrigerator, Ethernet. In-hotel: restaurant, room service, bar, pool, gym, laundry service, concierge, public Wi-Fi, parking (fee), no-smoking rooms* ▤*AE, D, DC, MC, V.*

> ## A HAUNTING WE WILL GO
>
> You may request a double-occupancy room, but don't be surprised if another guest joins you, since St. Augustine is reputed to be one of the most haunted cities in America. Many of the B&Bs, like Casa de Solana, Casablanca Inn, and St. Francis Inn, claim a resident ghost. But others prefer to keep their skeletons in the closet.

3

$$$$ ⌂**Hilton St. Augustine Historic Bayfront.** Travelers who want to stay in the heart of historic St. Augustine but don't want to be surrounded by antiques and chintz will find this Spanish colonial–inspired hotel (read: non-B&B) overlooking Matanzas Bay a comfortable and convenient alternative. Nineteen separate buildings make up the nontraditional Hilton property, most of which have water or city attraction views. Given its location in the thick of the Oldest City, the hotel caters to the tourist throngs with services such as in-room refrigerators, coin laundry, and cell-phone rentals. Staff are knowledgeable about the local attractions and dining options, and are happy to offer suggestions. **Pros:** Location, comfortable beds, great for families. **Cons:** 4 PM check-in, expensive parking, noise from the road. ✉*32 Avenida Menendez,* ☎*904/829–2277 or 800/445–8667* ⇆*72 rooms* ♿*In room: refrigerator, Ethernet. In hotel: restaurant, room service, bar, pool, gym, laundry facilities, laundry service, public Wi-Fi, parking (fee), no-smoking rooms.* ▤ *AE, D, MC, V.*

$$$–$$$$ ⌂**Inn on Charlotte.** Innkeeper Lynne Fairfield says guests comment that staying at her inn reminds them of visiting a friend or family member's home, assuming they offer gourmet breakfast every morning, truffles every afternoon, and cozy rooms with whirlpool tubs. Some rooms feature a private balcony, perfect for sipping complimentary lemonade or wine and people watching. The inn, situated on a quaint brick street, also hosts a variety of events throughout the year, such as cooking classes and book signings with local authors. **Pros:** Location, gourmet breakfast and afternoon refreshments, excellent service. **Cons:** Cancellation fee, street noise on weekends. ✉*52 Charlotte St.,* ☎*904/829–3819 or 800/355-5508* ⊕*www.innoncharlotte.com* ⇆*8 rooms* ♿*In room: Wi-Fi. In hotel: no elevator, concierge, public Wi-Fi, parking (no fee), no kids* ▤ *AE, D, MC, V.*

★ $$$ ⌂**Renaissance Resort at World Golf Village.** If you want to be within walking distance of all World Golf Village has to offer, this full-service resort is an excellent choice. Rooms and suites surround a soaring atrium, at the bottom of which is a restaurant set amid tropical foliage and streams. Units are oversize and are furnished in muted pastels. The hotel is adjacent to the World Golf Hall of Fame and borders a championship golf courses. And if you don't know the difference between a bogey and a birdie, not to worry; the PGA TOUR Spa Laterra is but a free shuttle ride away. Guests also have privileges at the private oceanfront Serenata Beach Club. **Pros:** Breakfast buffet, friendly staff, large bathrooms. **Cons:** Not much to do for nongolfers, small pool. ⊠*500 S. Legacy Trail,* ☎*904/940–8000 or 888/740–7020* ⊕*www. worldgolfrenaissance.com* ⤸*300 rooms, 28 suites* ⚭*In-room: safe, refrigerator, Wi-Fi. In-hotel: restaurant, room service, bar, golf, tennis, pool, gym, bicycles, laundry facilities, laundry service, concierge, public Wi-Fi, airport shuttle, parking (no fee), no-smoking rooms* ☱*AE, D, DC, MC, V.*

$$$ ⛉**St. Francis Inn Bed & Breakfast.** If the walls could whisper, this late-18th-century house in the historic district—and the oldest inn in the Oldest City—would tell tales of slave uprisings, buried doubloons, and Confederate spies. The inn, a guesthouse since 1845, offers rooms, suites, a room in the former carriage house, and a five-room cottage. Furnishings are a mix of antiques and just plain old. Guests these days rave about the friendly yet quiet atmosphere, gourmet food (there's a chef on property), and thoughtful extras like free admission to the Anastasia Athletic Club, beach house access, and nightly desserts. **Pros:** Warm hospitality, family-friendly cottage, Southern breakfast buffet. **Cons:** Small rooms, small pool, dated decor (and not in a good way). ⊠*279 St. George St.,* ☎*904/824–6068 or 800/824–6062* ☱*904/810– 5525* ⊕*www.stfrancisinn.com* ⤸*13 rooms, 4 suites, 1 2-bedroom cottage* ⚭*In-room: kitchen (some), refrigerator (some), DVD, Wi-Fi. In-hotel: pool, bicycles, no elevator, public Wi-Fi, parking (no fee), no kids under 10 in main house, some pets allowed, no-smoking rooms* ☱*MC, V* ⓘ*BP.*

$$-$$$ ⛉**Casablanca Inn Bed & Breakfast on the Bay.** Breakfast comes with sce-
Fodor's Choice nic views of the Matanzas Bay at this restored 1914 Mediterranean
★   Revival stucco-and-stone house, just north of the historic Bridge of Lions. Recently renovated rooms vary in size and shape; some have separate sitting rooms, some have views of the bay, and some have whirlpool tubs, but all are decorated with period and reproduction furniture and feature SleepNumber beds and flat-screen TVs. You can enjoy breakfast on the patio or in the sunny dining room. In the evening, you can sip complimentary sherry in the cozy parlor or pay up for something stronger in the Tini Martini Bar. **Pros:** Beds, friendly staff, complimentary snacks and beverages. **Cons:** Some rooms have no view, not for kids. ⊠*24 Avenida Menendez,* ☎*904/829–0928 or 800/826–2626* ⊕*www.casablancainn.com* ⤸*23 rooms, 13 suites* ⚭*In-room: kitchen (some), DVD, Wi-Fi. In-hotel: bar, no elevator, public Wi-Fi, parking (no fee), some pets allowed, no kids under 8, no-smoking rooms* ☱*AE, D, MC, V* ⓘ*BP.*

NIGHTLIFE

Live music haven **Cafe Eleven** (⊠*501 A1A Beach Blvd., St. Augustine Beach* ☎*904/460–9311*) specializes in catch-them-before-they-get-too-big bands. The very rustic **Mill Top Tavern** (⊠*19 St. George*

St., ☎*904/829–2329*) is famous for its live music. If you're staying on Anastasia Island, the "World Famous" **Oasis Deck and Restaurant** (✉*4000 Rte. A1A S, at Ocean Trace Rd., St. Augustine Beach* ☎*904/471–3424*) is your best bet for nightly entertainment, offering 24-ounce draft beers, beach access, and what many locals consider the best burgers in town. Something is always happening at **Scarlett O'Hara's** (✉*70 Hypolita St.,* ☎*904/824–6535*). Some nights it's blues or jazz bands; on others it might be disco, Top 40, or karaoke; and many nights the early and late-night entertainment are completely different. **Trade Winds** (✉*124 Charlotte St.,* ☎*904/829–9336*) showcases bands every night, from country and western to rock. **The White Lion** (✉*20 Cuna St.,* ☎*904/829–2388*) brings a taste of old England to this old city.

SPORTS & THE OUTDOORS

BIKING
Solano Cycle (✉*32 San Marco Ave., 32084* ☎*904/825–6766*) rents bicycles and scooters.

FISHING
K-2 Sport Fishing (✉*U.S. 1 and Rte. 207, 32084* ☎*904/824–9499*) offers 10- and 12-hour charters in addition to overnight and extended-stay trips. Charter the *Sea Love II* (✉*250 Vilano Rd., 32084* ☎*904/824–3328*), or sign up to join a half- or full-day fishing trip.

GOLF
Golfers looking for an economical round at Palm Coast can check out **Hampton Golf at Matanzas Woods** (✉*398 Lakeview Blvd., Palm Coast* ☎*386/446–6330*); greens fee $30–$80. **Pine Lakes at Hampton Golf** (✉*400 Pine Lakes Pl., Palm Coast* ☎*386/445–0852*) was designed by Arnold Palmer and Ed Seay and is reasonably priced; greens fee $40–$65. As part of its complex, **World Golf Village** (✉*21 World Golf Pl,* ☎*904/940–4000*) has two 18-hole layouts named for and partially designed by golf legends Sam Snead, Gene Sarazen, Arnold Palmer, and Jack Nicklaus. The courses are the **Slammer & Squire** (☎*904/940–6088*), greens fee $110; and the **King & Bear** (☎*904/940–6200*), greens fee $134–$160.

TENNIS
Ron Parker Park (✉*901 Pope Rd., St. Augustine Beach* ☎*904/209–0333*) has two lighted tennis courts and four paddleball courts. Public courts are available at **Treaty Park** (✉*2175 Wildwood Dr.,* ☎*904/209–0385*). It has six lighted tennis courts, eight paddleball and eight racquetball courts, and a skate park with ramps and jumps.

WATER SPORTS
Rent surfboards, skim boards, and body boards at the **Surf Station** (✉*1020 Anastasia Blvd., 32080* ☎*904/471–9463*). Or head off into the wild blue yonder, 1,400 feet over the ocean, with **Smile High Parasail** (✉*111 Avenida Menendez, 32164* ☎*904/819–0980*).

SHOPPING

Just north of St. Augustine, off Interstate 95, are the **St. Augustine Premium Outlets** (⊠*2700 State Rd. 16,32084* ☎*904/825–1555*), with 85 designer and brand-name outlets. **Prime Outlets** (⊠*500 Belz Outlet Blvd., 32084* ☎*904/826–1311*) has 60 name-brand stores. In town, be sure to walk along car-free **St. George Street** (⊠*Between Cathedral Pl. and Orange St.,*) to check out the art galleries and one-of-a-kind shops with candles, home accents, handmade jewelry, aromatherapy products, pottery, books, and clothing.

DAYTONA & THE SPACE COAST

This section of coast covers only 75 mi, but it offers considerable variety, from the unassuming bedroom community of Ormond Beach to the Spring Break capital of Daytona Beach, to the country's only launch site for the space shuttle in Cape Canaveral. On the northernmost tip of the coast sits Ormond Beach, established at the turn of the 20th century as a tourist haven for the rich and famous, now catering to families and seniors seeking a quiet escape. To the south is Daytona Beach. Primarily associated with auto racing and Spring Break, the World's Most Famous Beach is fronted with a mixture of tall condos and apartments, hotels, low-rise motels, and flashy nightclubs. Farther south is the small town of New Smyrna Beach, its beach lined with private houses, some empty land, and an occasional taller condominium. Just below it lie the Canaveral National Seashore and the John F. Kennedy Space Center. Still farther south, the laid-back town of Cocoa Beach attracts visitors on weekends all year, as it's the closest beach to Orlando. Although the hurricanes of 2004 and 2005 caused hundreds of millions of dollars in damage to the Daytona area, most commercial properties and many smaller family-owned properties have since reopened.

DAYTONA BEACH

65 mi south of St. Augustine.

Best known for the Daytona 500, Daytona has been the center of automobile racing since cars were first raced along the beach here in 1902. February is the biggest month for race enthusiasts, and there are weekly events at the International Speedway. During race weeks, bike weeks, Spring Break periods, and summer holidays, expect extremely heavy traffic along the strip as well as on the beach itself, since driving on the sand is allowed; areas marked NO CAR ZONES are less frenetic and more family-friendly. On the mainland, near the inland waterway, several blocks of Beach Street have been "street-scaped," and shops and restaurants open onto an inviting, broad brick sidewalk.

WHAT TO SEE

☾ **Daytona Lagoon.** Parents looking for a nonsandy way to occupy the kids for a few hours or a whole day may find their salvation at this colorful complex that features go-karts, miniature golf, laser tag, a video arcade with more than 100 games, and a water park with 10 different slides and a 500,000-gallon tidal wave pool. More adult entertainment—in the form of pool tables, dartboards, and plasma TVs—can be found in Gilligan's Sports Bar and Grill. ⊠ *601 Earl St., 32118* ☎ *386/254–5020* ⊕ *www.daytonalagoon.com* ✉ *Entertainment Center: free (fees for rides and games), Water Park: $27.99 adults, $19.99 children under 48" tall* ☉ *Family Entertainment Center: Sun.–Thurs. 10–10, Fri. and Sat. 10–midnight; Water Park: hrs vary (call for specific dates and times); Water Park closed Nov.–Feb.*

★ ☼ As the "official attraction of NASCAR," **Daytona USA** lets you experience the thrill of a race from the driver's seat with motion simulators like Dreamlaps and Accelerator Alley, a highly realistic head-to-head racing experience in an 80-percent-scale stock car at speeds reaching 200 mph. Participate in a pit stop on a NASCAR Winston Cup stock car or computer-design your own race car. There's also an exhibit of the history of auto racing with a rotating display of cars, an IMAX theater featuring "NASCAR 3D," and track tours. Daytona USA is also home to the **Richard Petty Driving Experience** (☎ 800/237–3889), where you can ride shotgun in or drive a stock car at Daytona International Speedway (call for prices). ⊠ *1801 W. International Speedway Dr., 32114* ☎ *386/947–6800* ⊕ *www.daytonausa.com* ✉ *$25 adults, $19 children 6–12* ☉ *Daily 9–7, last ticket sold at 5.*

One of only a dozen photography museums in the country ad, the internationally-renowned **Southeast Museum of Photography**, at Daytona Beach College, has changing historical and contemporary exhibits focusing on photojournalism, fashion, and new media. ⊠ *1200 W. International Speedway Blvd., Building 1200, 32114* ☎ *386/506–4475* ⊕ *www.smponline.org* ✉ *Donation welcome* ☉ *Wed. and Fri. 10–4, Tues. and Thurs. 11–5, weekends 1–5.*

The humanities section of the **Museum of Arts & Sciences**, one of the largest museums in Florida, includes displays of Chinese art, and glass, silver, gold, and porcelain examples of decorative arts. The museum also has pre-Castro Cuban art, Florida Native American items, pre-Columbian art, Indian and Persian miniature paintings, and an eye-popping complete skeleton of a giant sloth that is 13 feet long and 130,000 years old. ⊠ *352 S. Nova Rd., 32114* ☎ *386/255–0285* ⊕ *www.moas.org* ✉ *$12.95 adults, $6.95 children 6–17* ☉ *Mon.–Sat. 9–5, Sun. 11–5.*

★ **Daytona Beach**, which bills itself as the World's Most Famous Beach, permits you to drive your car right up to your beach site, spread out a blanket, and have all your belongings at hand; this is especially convenient for beachgoers who are elderly or have disabilities. However, heavy traffic during summer and holidays makes it dangerous for children, and families should be extra careful or stay in the designated car-free zones. The speed limit is 10 mph. To get your car on the beach, look for signs on Route A1A indicating beach access via beach ramps. Sand traps are not limited to the golf course, though—cars can get stuck.

**OFF THE
BEATEN
PATH**

Ponce Inlet. At the southern tip of the barrier island that includes Daytona Beach is this sleepy town with a small marina, a few bars, and casual seafood restaurants. Boardwalks traverse delicate dunes and provide easy access to the beach, although storms have caused serious erosion. Marking this prime spot is the bright-red, century-old **Ponce de León Lighthouse,** a historic monument and museum, the tallest lighthouse in the state and the second-tallest in the country. Climb to the top of the lighthouse tower for a bird's-eye view of Ponce Inlet. ⊠*4931 S. Peninsula Dr., 32127* ☎*386/761–1821* ⊕*www.ponce inlet.org* ⚟*$5 adults, $1.50 chil-*

> ### HURRY UP AND WAIT
>
> To snowbirds, a trip to Daytona Beach in mid-February might sound like a great idea. Just don't plan it for the weekend of the Daytona 500. Assuming you can even find a hotel room, it will probably cost you double the usual rate. If you plan on leaving your hotel room, you'll most likely get stuck in bumper-to-bumper traffic. And when you get to your destination, it might not be open. **Of course, you could give in and go to the race, but you'll never get a ticket.**

dren 11 and under ⊙*Memorial Day–Labor Day, daily 10–9; after Labor Day, daily 10–;6 last admission 1 hr prior to closing*

Listed on the National Register of Historic Places, the **Casements,** the restored winter retreat of John D. Rockefeller, is now a cultural center and museum. Take a tour through the period Rockefeller Room, which contains some of the family's memorabilia. The estate and its formal gardens host an annual lineup of events and exhibits; there's also a permanent exhibit of Hungarian folk art and musical instruments. ⊠*25 Riverside Dr.Ormond Beach 32176* ☎*386/676–3216* ⊕*www.obht. org/casements.htm* ⚟*Donations accepted* ⊙*Weekdays 8:30–5, Sat. 9–noon, tours 10–2:30.*

The scenic **Tomoka State Park,** 3 mi north of Ormond Beach, is perfect for fishing, camping, hiking, and boating. It is the site of a Timucuan Indian settlement discovered in 1605 by Spanish explorer Alvaro Mexia. Wooded campsites, bicycle and walking paths, and guided canoe tours on the Tomoka and Halifax rivers are the main attractions. ⊠*2099 N. Beach St.Ormond Beach 32130* ☎*386/676–4050, 800/326–3521 (Reserve America) for camping reservations* 🖷*386/676–4060* ⊕*www. floridastateparks.org/tomoka* ⚟*$5 per vehicle, up to 8 people, camping $20 per night* ⊙*Daily 8–sundown.*

WHERE TO EAT

$$-$$$$ ✕**Aunt Catfish's on the River.** Don't be surprised if your server introduces herself as your cousin, though you've never seen her before in your life. You see, everybody's "cousin" at Aunt Catfish's (as in, "Can I get you another mason jar of sweet tea, Cousin?"). The silly Southern hospitality is only one of the draws at this wildly popular seafood restaurant. The main lure, of course, is the food: fried chicken, fried shrimp, fried catfish, and crab cakes. Hot cinnamon rolls and hush puppies come with every entrée and can be a meal in themselves. Bring your appetite and your patience—a wait is practically guaranteed. Aunt Catfish's is

on the west bank of the Intracoastal Waterway (off U.S. 1, before crossing the Port Orange Causeway), just south of Daytona. ⊠*4009 Halifax Dr., Port Orange* ☎*386/767–4768* ⌲*Reservations not accepted* ⊟*AE, MC, V.*

★ $$–$$$$ ✕**Gene's Steak House.** Quiet and intimate, this family-operated restaurant and race-car-driver hangout has long upheld its reputation as the best place for steaks in the area (since 1948, to be exact) despite its nondescript exterior and somewhat out-of-the-way location west of town. Gene's has a decidedly old-school vibe, with classics like escargot, French onion soup, and Gene's special-recipe Roquefort dressing. Signature entrées include cooked-to-order filet mignons, sirloins, and porterhouses. Seafood is also on the menu, and the wine list is one of the state's largest, with bottles ranging in price from $19 to $1,200. ⊠*3674 W. International Speedway Blvd. (U.S. 92),* ☎*386/255–2059* ⊟*AE, DC, MC, V* ⊘*Closed Sun. and Mon. No lunch.*

$$–$$$ ✕**Martini's Chophouse.** Local beautiful people seem to flock to this trendy South Daytona Beach eatery and lounge as much for the scene as they do for the food. The bar area, done in tangerine with splashes of lime green, is a modern meeting place for the after-work crowd, and the outdoor deck and bar attract a livelier bunch. Those who do deign to dine will appreciate the chef's use of homegrown herbs and creative sauces in dishes such as marinated skirt steak with chimichurri sauce and barbecue-grilled Chilean salmon with cucumber and melon relish, which can be enjoyed in the sleek dining room or in the garden complete with a 20-foot lighted waterfall. ⊠*1815 S. Ridgeview Ave., South Daytona Beach 32119* ☎*386/763–1090* ⊟*AE, D, MC, V* ⊘*Closed Sun. and Mon.*

¢–$$ ✕**McK's Tavern.** Crowds fill up the bar, the tables, and the cozy booths in this lively tavern. The fare is simple, hearty, and generous, with American favorites like chicken wings, burgers, and steak served alongside Irish favorites like Guinness stew, shepherd's pie, and fish-and-chips, though the Guinness draft is practically a meal in itself. There's live music every weekend (usually of the Celtic variety). Plus, McK's is one of the few places in town—without a drive-through window—that serves food after midnight. ⊠*218 S. Beach St., 32114* ☎*386/238–3321* ⊟*AE, MC, V* ⊘*Closed Sun.*

WHERE TO STAY

$$$–$$$$ 🏨**The Shores Resort & Spa.** Rustic furniture and beds swathed in mos-
Fodor'sChoice quito netting lend themselves to the Old Florida decor at this 11-story
★ beachfront resort, but there's nothing primitive about the hotel's amenities, including a luxury four-poster bed and a 42-inch plasma TV in every room, the Indonesian-inspired spa Indulge, and Azure restaurant and bar overlooking the ocean. Rooms are spacious and have views of either the ocean or the Intracoastal Waterway. **Pros:** Beachfront location, spa, friendly staff. **Cons:** Only restaurant is expensive, pool can be crowded, not all rooms have balconies. ⊠*2637 S. Atlantic Ave., Daytona Beach Shores* ☎*386/767–7350 or 866/934–7467* ⊕*www.shores resort.com* ⇝*212 rooms, 1 suite* ⌂*In-room: safe, refrigerator (some), DVD, Wi-Fi. In-hotel: restaurant, room service, bars, pool, gym, spa,*

*beachfront, laundry service, concierge, public Wi-Fi, parking (no fee),
some pets allowed, no-smoking rooms* ☐AE, D, DC, MC, V.

$$–$$$$ 🏨**Wyndham Ocean Walk Resort.** Kids definitely won't be bored at this
high-rise beachfront resort that boasts four swimming pools, a water
slide, lazy river, game room, indoor miniature golf course, activities
center, and the only traffic-free beach in Daytona Beach. Guests also
appreciate the 1-, 2-, and 3-bedroom condominium-style units equipped
with kitchens (dishware and utensils included), washers, and dryers, as
well as the proximity to the shops and restaurants of Ocean Walk Vil-
lage. Because the property doubles as a hotel and time-share resort,
certain amenities such as room service and valet parking aren't offered.
Pros: Family-friendly, location, spacious accommodations. Cons: No
room service, very slow elevators. ⊠*300 N. Atlantic Ave., 32118*
☎*386/323–4800 or 800/347–9851* ⊕*www.oceanwalk.com* ⬎*200
1-, 2-, and 3-bedroom suites* ⚙*In-room: safe, kitchen, refrigerator,
DVD (some), VCR. In-hotel: restaurant, bars, golf course, pools, gym,
spa, beachfront, water sports, bicycles, children's programs age 5 and
up, laundry facilities, concierge, public Wi-Fi.* ☐AE, D, DC, MC, V.

★ $$$ 🏨**Hilton Daytona Beach Oceanfront Resort.** Perched on the only traffic-free
strip of beach in Daytona, this high-rise hotel is, ironically enough, as
popular with families as it is with couples. Every room has a great ocean
view, and the Old Florida decor (nostalgic prints, rattan headboards,
and sandy palettes) is warm and inviting. If beach bumming isn't your
thing, check out the spacious sundecks and two pools. Or take a stroll
down to the pier or boardwalk, both within walking distance. The hotel
is also connected to the Ocean Walk Shoppes via covered walkways.
Pros: Location, spacious rooms, beach access. **Cons:** Small pool, extra
charges, spotty valet service. ⊠*100 N. Atlantic Ave.,* ☎*386/254–8200
or 866/536–8477* ⊕*www.daytonahilton.com* ⬎*744 rooms, 52 suites*
⚙*In-room: refrigerators (some). In-hotel: 3 restaurants, room service,
bars, pools, gym, beachfront, laundry facilities, laundry service, concierge, no-smoking rooms* ☐AE, D, DC, MC, V.

$$$ 🏨**Perry's Ocean-Edge Resort.** Perhaps more than any other property
in Daytona, Perry's has a die-hard fan base, many of whom started
coming to the oceanfront resort as children, then returned with their
children and their children's children. Parents and kids alike are kept
happy with the free homemade doughnuts and coffee served in the
lush solarium every morning, and the clean indoor pool surrounded
by a 10,000-square-foot-atrium with a retractable roof. Two renova-
tions, after significant storm damage, added fun new features like a
pool tiki bar and spa (the largest in Daytona Beach), and spiffed up
the decor. Most rooms have kitchens and great ocean views. **Pros:** Spa-
cious rooms, helpful staff, nice pools, family friendly. **Cons:** Small bath-
rooms, slow elevators, limited TV channels. ⊠*2209 S. Atlantic Ave.,*
☎*386/255–0581 or 800/447–0002* ⊕*www.perrysoceanedge.com*
⬎*200 rooms* ⚙*In-room: safe, kitchen (some), Ethernet. In-hotel: res-
taurant, bar, pools, gym, beachfront, children's programs (ages 4–12),
laundry facilities, public Wi-Fi, parking (no fee), no-smoking rooms*
☐AE, D, DC, MC, V.

NIGHTLIFE & THE ARTS

THE ARTS Jazz, big band, blues, and folk acts perform at the outdoor, oceanfront **Daytona Beach Bandshell** (✉*250 N. Atlantic Ave., 32118* ☎*386/671–8250*). Internationally acclaimed orchestras and soloists appear as part of the **Daytona Beach Symphony Society** (✉*140 S. Beach St., Suite 107,* ☎*386/253–2901*). Affiliated with Bethune Cookman College, the 2,500-seat **Mary McLeod Bethune Performing Arts Center** (✉*698 W. International Speedway Blvd.,* ☎*386/481–2778*) showcases performing- and visual-arts productions by students and professional touring companies. The **Ocean Center at Ocean Walk Village** (✉*101 N. Atlantic Ave.,* ☎*386/254–4500 or 800/858–6444*) hosts concerts, conventions, boat shows, and rodeos, and is home to the Daytona ThunderBirds indoor football team. **Peabody Auditorium** (✉*600 Auditorium Blvd.,* ☎*386/671–3460*) is used for concerts and programs year-round. **Seaside Music Theater** (✉*221 N. Beach St.,* ☎*386/252–6200 or 800/854–5592*) presents musicals in two venues January through February and June through August.

NIGHTLIFE Despite its reputation as a biker bar, the **Boot Hill Saloon** (✉*310 Main St., 32118* ☎*386/258–9506*) welcomes nonbikers and even nonbiker tourists! **Ocean Deck** is the only oceanfront nightclub with live reggae music (✉*127 S. Ocean Ave., 32118* ☎*386/253–5224*). **Ocean Walk** (✉*250 N. Atlantic Ave., 32118* ☎*386/258–9544*) is a lively, always-hopping cluster of shops, restaurants, and bars right on the ocean, including **Adobe Gila's Margarita Fajita Cantina** (☎*386/481–1000*) and the **Mai Tai Bar** (☎*386/947–2493*). Spring Breakers congregate by the thousands at **The Oyster Pub** (✉*555 Seabreeze Blvd., 32118* ☎*386/255–6348*). At **Razzle's Nightclub** (✉*611 Seabreeze Blvd., 32118* ☎*386/257–6236*), DJs play high-energy dance music from 8 PM to 3 AM.

SPORTS & THE OUTDOORS

AUTO RACING The massive **Daytona International Speedway** (✉*1801 W. International Speedway Blvd., 32114* ☎*386/254–2700*), on Daytona's major east–west artery, has year-round auto and motorcycle racing, including the Daytona 500 in February and the Pepsi 400 in July.

DOG RACING There are more than 400 live races each year at the **Daytona Beach Kennel Club and Poker Room** (✉*2201 W. International Speedway Blvd., 32114* ☎*386/252–6484*).

FISHING **Finest Kind II Sport Fishing Charters** (✉*Inlet Harbor Marina, 133 Inlet Harbor Rd., Ponce Inlet* ☎*386/527–0732*) offers half-day, full-day, and night fishing excursions. **Sea Spirit Fishing** (✉*Inlet Harbor Marina, 133 Inlet Harbor Rd., Ponce Inlet* ☎*386/763–4388*) has four- to 10-hour private and group charters.

FOOTBALL The World's Most Famous Beach—more specifically, the Ocean Center at Ocean Walk Village—is home to **Daytona Beach ThunderBirds** (☎*386/254–4545*), of the AFL2 Arena Football League.

GOLF **Indigo Lakes Golf Club** (✉*312 Indigo Dr., 32114* ☎*386/254–3607*) has 18 holes of golf; green fee: $35–$50. The public courses at **LPGA Interna-**

tional (⊠*1000 Champions Dr., Daytona Beach* ☏*386/523–2001*) have 36 holes; greens fee $60–$90. **Pelican Bay South Country Club** (⊠*550 Sea Duck Dr.,* ☏*386/788–6496*) rents clubs and has a pro shop and a restaurant, in addition to 18 holes; greens fee $30–$40. There's an 18-hole course at **Spruce Creek Golf & Country Club** (⊠*1900 Country Club Dr., Port Orange* ☏*386/756–6114*), along with practice and driving ranges, rental clubs, a pro shop, and a restaurant; greens fee $39–$49.

WATER SPORTS
Catch air at **Daytona Beach Parasail** (⊠*Silver Beach Ramp, Silver Beach Ave. and US 1, 32118* ☏*386/334–2191*). Rent surfboards or boogie boards at **Salty Dog Surf Shop** (⊠*700 E. International Speedway Blvd., 32118* ☏*386/253–1234)* or **Maui Nix** (⊠*635 N. Atlantic Ave., 32118* ☏*386/258–0457).*

SHOPPING

Daytona Flea & Farmers Market (⊠*2987 Bellevue Ave., 32124* ☏*386/253–3330*) is one of the largest in the South. The **Volusia Mall** (⊠*1700 W. International Speedway Blvd., 32114* ☏*386/253–6783*) has more than 125 stores, including JCPenney and Dillard's.

TITUSVILLE

17 mi north of Cocoa.

It's unusual that such a small, easily overlooked community could accommodate what it does, namely the Kennedy Space Center, the nerve center of the U.S. space program, and the magnificent Merritt Island National Wildlife Refuge.

↻ Fodor'sChoice ★
The must-see **Kennedy Space Center Visitor Complex,** just southeast of Titusville, is one of Central Florida's most popular sights. Located on a 140,000-acre island 45 minutes outside Orlando, Kennedy Space Center is NASA's launch headquarters, where the space shuttle is prepared for flight, launched into space, and returns after its mission. The Visitor Complex gives guests a unique opportunity to learn about—and experience—the past, present, and future of America's space program.

Interactive programs make for the best experiences here, but if you want a low-key overview of the facility (and if the weather is foul) take the bus tour, included with admission. Buses depart every 15 minutes, and you can get on and off any bus whenever you like. Stops include the **Launch Complex 39 Observation Gantry,** which has an unparalleled view of the twin space-shuttle launchpads; the *Apollo/Saturn V* **Center,** with a don't-miss presentation at the Firing Room Theatre, where the launch of America's first lunar mission, 1968's *Apollo VIII,* is re-created with a ground-shaking, window-rattling liftoff; and the **International Space Station Center,** where NASA is building pieces of the Center; a mock-up of a "Habitation Module" is worth seeing.

Exhibits near the center's entrance include the **Early Space Exploration** display, which highlights the rudimentary yet influential *Mercury* and *Gemini* space programs; **Robot Scouts,** a walk-through exhibit of unmanned planetary probes; and the **Exploration in the New Millennium** display, which offers you the opportunity to touch a piece of Mars (it fell to the Earth in the form of meteorite). Don't miss the outdoor **Rocket Garden,** with walkways winding beside spare rockets, from early Atlas spacecraft to a *Saturn IB.* The redeveloped Children's Playdome enables kids to play among the next generation of spacecraft, climb a moon rock wall, and crawl through rocket tunnels. Astronaut Encounter Theater has two daily programs where NASA astronaut corps share their adventures in space travel and show a short film. The most moving exhibit is the **Astronaut Memorial**. The 70,400-pound black-granite tribute to astronauts who lost their lives in the name of space exploration stands 42½ feet high by 50 feet wide.

More befitting Walt Disney World or Universal Studios (complete with the health warnings), the **Shuttle Launch Experience** is the center's newest and most spectacular attraction. Designed by a team of astronauts, NASA experts, and renowned attraction engineers, the 44,000-square-foot structure uses a sophisticated motion-based platform, special-effects seats, and high-fidelity visual and audio components to simulate the sensations experienced in an actual space-shuttle launch, including MaxQ, Solid Rocker Booster separation, main engine cutoff, and External Tank separation. The journey culminates with a breathtaking view of Earth from space.

The only back-to-back twin **IMAX theater** in the world is in the complex, too. The dream of space flight comes to life on a movie screen five stories tall with dramatic footage shot by NASA astronauts during missions. Realistic 3D special effects will make you feel like you're in space with them. Films alternate throughout the year. Call for specific shows and times.

Add-on activities include **Lunch with an Astronaut** ($60.99, includes general admission), where astronauts talk about their experiences and engage in a good-natured Q&A; the typical line of questioning from kids—"How do you eat/sleep/relieve yourself in space?" **NASA Up Close** tour ($59, general admission included) brings visitors to sites seldom accessible to the public, such as the Vehicle Assembly Building, the shuttle landing strip, and the 6-million-pound crawler that transports the shuttle to its launchpad. Or see how far the space program has come with the **Cape Canaveral: Then and Now** tour ($59, includes general admission), which visits America's first launch sites from the 1960s and the 21st century's active unmanned rocket program. ⊠*S.R. 405, Kennedy Space Center* ☎*321/449–4444* ⊕*www.kennedyspace-*

center.com ☞*General admission includes bus tour, IMAX movies, Visitor Complex shows and exhibits, and the Astronaut Hall of Fame, $38* ☉*Space Center opens daily at 9, closing times vary according to season (call for details), last regular tour 3 hrs before closing; closed certain launch dates.*

The original *Mercury 7* team and the later *Gemini, Apollo, Skylab,* and shuttle astronauts contributed to make the **United States Astronaut Hall of Fame** the world's premium archive of astronauts' personal stories. Authentic memorabilia and equipment from their collections tell the story of human space exploration. You'll watch videotapes of historic moments in the space program and see one-of-a-kind items like Wally Schirra's relatively archaic *Sigma 7* Mercury space capsule, Gus Grissom's spacesuit (colored silver only because NASA thought silver looked more "spacey"), and a flag that made it to the moon. The exhibit **First on the Moon** focuses on crew selection for *Apollo 11* and the Soviet Union's role in the space race. Definitely don't miss the **Astronaut Adventure,** a hands-on discovery center with interactive exhibits that help you learn about space travel. One of the more challenging activities is a space-shuttle simulator that lets you try your hand at landing the craft—and afterward replays a side view of your rolling and pitching descent. If that gets your motor going, consider enrolling in **ATX (Astronaut Training Experience).** Held at the Hall of Fame, this is an intense full-day experience where you can dangle from a springy harness for a simulated moonwalk, spin in ways you never thought possible in a multi-axis trainer, and either work Mission Control or helm a space shuttle (in a full-scale mock-up) during a simulated landing. Veteran astronauts helped design the program, and you'll hear first-hand from them as you progress through your training. Space is limited (no pun intended), so call well in advance. Included in the $250 program is your astronaut gear, lunch, and a VIP tour of the Kennedy Space Center. ✉*S.R. 405, Kennedy Space Center,* ☎*321/449–4444, 321/449–4400 ATX* ⊕*www.kennedyspacecenter.com* ☞*$17 adults, $13 children 3–11* ☉*Hall of Fame opens daily at 9, closing times vary according to season (call for details).*

If you've ever wondered why cops deserve your respect, pay a visit to the **American Police Hall of Fame & Museum.** In addition to memorabilia like the Robocop costume and Blade Runner car from the films, there are informative displays on what cops face every day: drugs, homicides, and criminals who can create knives from dental putty and guns from a bicycle spoke (really). Other historical exhibits include invitations to hangings, police patches, how you collect evidence at a crime scene, and a rotunda where more than 7,000 names are etched in marble to honor police officers who have died in the line of duty. Cops, gun nuts, and curious tourists are taken by the 24-lane shooting range that provides rental guns (Tues.–Fri. noon–8, weekends noon–6). ✉*6350 Horizon Dr., 32780* ☎*32½64–0911* ⊕*www.aphf.org* ☞*$12 adults, $8 children 4–12* ☉*Daily 10–6.*

Although its exterior looks sort of squirrelly, what's inside the **Valiant Air Command Warbird Air Museum** is certainly impressive. Aviation buffs won't want to miss memorabilia from both world wars, Korea, and Vietnam, as well as extensive displays of vintage military flying gear and uniforms. There are posters used to identify Japanese planes, plus there's a Huey helicopter and the cockpit of an F-106 that you can sit in. In the north hangar it looks like activity day at the senior center as a volunteer team of retirees busily restores old planes. It's an inspiring sight, and a good place to hear some war stories. In the lobby gift shop they sell real flight suits, old flight magazines, bomber jackets, books, and T-shirts. ⊠*6600 Tico Rd., 32780* ☎*32½68–1941* ⊕*www.vacwar birds.org* 🖻*$12 adults, $5 children 4–12* ⊗*Daily 9–5.*

SPACE INVADERS

As fascinating as the exhibits and tours of Kennedy Space Center are, there's nothing like seeing a launch in person. Kennedy Space Center offers visitors two launch viewing options for witnessing blast-off, one from the Visitor Complex ($28–$38), and another from a restricted viewing site on NASA Causeway ($41–$51), the closest public viewing site to the launch pad. Ticket prices also include admission to the Visitor Complex. Check out ⊕www. kennedyspacecenter.com for launch schedules.

★ The 57,000-acre **Canaveral National Seashore** (☎*386/428–3384, visitor center*) is on a barrier island that's home to more than 1,000 species of plants and 300 species of birds and other animals. The unspoiled area of hilly sand dunes, grassy marshes, and seashell-sprinkled beaches is a large part of NASA's buffer zone. Surf and lagoon fishing are available, and a hiking trail leads to the top of a Native American shell midden at Turtle Mound. For an additional charge, visitors can take a pontoonboat tour ($20) or participate in the turtle-watch interpretive program ($14). Reservations required. A visitor center is on Route A1A. Weekends are busy, and parts of the park are closed before, during, and after launches, so call ahead.

At the opposite end of the seashore from New Smyrna Beach's Apollo Beach, remote **Playalinda Beach** has pristine sands and is the longest stretch of undeveloped coast on Florida's Atlantic seaboard. Its isolation explains why there are limited services (i.e., no phones, food service, drinking water, or lifeguards from September through May) and why a remote strand of the beach is popular with nude sunbathers. Aside from them, hundreds of giant sea turtles come ashore here from May through August to lay their eggs. Eight parking lots anchor the beach at 1-mi intervals. Take bug repellent in case of horseflies. To get here, take I–95 Exit 220 east and follow the signs. ⊠*Rte. 402/ Beach Rd.,* ☎*321/867–0677* ⊕*www.nps.gov/cana* 🖻*$3 per person* ⊗*Apr.–Oct., daily 6 AM–8 PM; Nov.–Mar., daily 6–6*

Fodor'sChoice
★ Owned by the Florida Fish and Wildlife Service and NASA, **Merritt Island National Wildlife Refuge,** which adjoins the Canaveral National Seashore, acts as a buffer around Kennedy Space Center, while protecting 500 species of wildlife, including 10 considered federally threatened or endangered. It's an immense area dotted by brackish estuaries and

marshes and patches of land consisting of coastal dunes, scrub oaks, pine forests and flatwoods, and palm and oak hammocks. You can borrow field guides and binoculars at the visitor center to track down various types of falcons, ospreys, eagles, turkeys, doves, cuckoos, loons, geese, skimmers, terns, warblers, wrens, thrushes, sparrows, owls, and woodpeckers. A 20-minute video about refuge wildlife and accessibility—only 10,000 acres are developed—can help orient you. You might take a self-guided tour along the 7-mi **Black Point Wildlife Drive.** The dirt road takes you back in time, where there are no traces of encroaching malls or mankind and it's easy to visualize the tribes who made this their home 7,000 years ago. On the **Oak Hammock Foot Trail** you can see wintering migratory waterfowl and learn about the plants of a hammock community. If you exit the north end of the refuge, look for the **Manatee Observation Area** just north of the Haulover Canal (maps are at the visitor center). They usually show up in spring and fall. There are also fishing camps scattered throughout the area. The refuge is closed four days before a shuttle launch. ⊠ *Rte. 402, across Titusville causeway,* ☎ *321/861–0667* ⊕ *www.fws.gov/merrittisland* ⊠ *Free* ⊙ *Daily sunrise–sundown; visitor center weekdays 8–4:30, weekends 9–5 (Nov.–Mar.).*

WHERE TO EAT & STAY

★ $$$ ✕**Dixie Crossroads.** This sprawling restaurant is always crowded and festive, but it's not just rustic setting that draws the throngs; it's the seafood. The specialty is the difficult-to-cook rock shrimp, which is served fried, broiled, or steamed. Diners with a hearty appetite can opt for the all-you-can-eat rock shrimp, small shrimp, tilapia, or catfish. Often the wait for a table can last 90 minutes, but if you don't have time to wait, you can order takeout or eat in the bar area. And a word to the wise: as tempting as those corn fritters dusted with powdered sugar are, don't fill up on them. ⊠ *1475 Garden St., 2 mi east of I–95 Exit 220,* ☎ *321/268–5000* ⚖ *Reservations not accepted* ⊟ *AE, D, DC, MC, V.*

$$-$$$ 🖃**Hampton Inn Titusville.** Proximity to the Kennedy Space Center and reasonable rates make this four-story hotel a top pick for visitors wanting to see a launch in person (though rates do generally go up just before launches). Guests deem the rooms clean, comfortable, and quiet (when the sky isn't reverberating with the sound of rocket thrusters, that is) and larger than those in comparable hotels. The property also scores points for conveniences like 24/7 coffee and tea service in the lobby and complimentary hot breakfast. **Pros:** Free shuttle, free Internet, extra-comfy beds. **Cons:** No coffeemakers in rooms, thin walls, no restaurant on-site. ⊠ *4760 Helen Hauser Blvd.,* ☎ *321/383–9191* ⥅ *86 rooms, 4 suites* ⚴ *In-room: refrigerator (some), Ethernet, Wi-Fi. In-hotel: pool, gym, laundry facilities, laundry service, public Wi-Fi, parking (no fee), no-smoking rooms* ⊠ *CP.*

CAPE CANAVERAL

5 mi north of Cocoa Beach.

This once-bustling commercial fishing area is still home to a small shrimping fleet, charter boats, and party fishing boats, but its main business these days is as a cruise-ship port. Cocoa Beach itself isn't the spiffiest place around, but what *is* becoming quite clean and neat is the north end of the port where the Carnival, Disney, and Royal Caribbean cruise lines set sail, as well as Sterling Casino Lines. **Port Canaveral** is now Florida's second-busiest cruise port, which makes this a great place to catch a glimpse of these giant ships even if you're not headed out to sea.

Jetty Park serves a wonderful taste of the real Florida. At Port Canaveral's south side, there are assorted restaurants and marine shops, a 4½-acre beach, more than 150 campsites for tents and RVs, picnic pavilions, and a 1,200-foot-long fishing pier that doubles as a perfect vantage point from which to watch a liftoff of the space shuttle. A jetty constructed of giant boulders adds to the landscape, and a walkway that crosses it provides access to a less-populated stretch of beach. Real and rustic, this is Florida without the theme-park varnish. ✉*400 E. Jetty Rd., Port Canaveral,* ☎*321/783-7111* ✆*$5 per car, $7 for RVs for fishing or beach; camping $18–$29 for basic, $22–$32 with water and electric, $25–$34 full hookup* ☉*Daily 7* AM–9 PM.

Sterling Casino Lines is like a mini–Las Vegas on the high seas with four casinos, five lounges, and cheesy celebrity impersonator shows, not to mention over-stimulated seniors wasting away their retirement savings one nickel slot at a time. The five-deck, 75,000-square-foot *Ambassador II,* which sets sail from Port Canaveral twice a day (afternoon cruises begin at 4, evening cruises at 7), features the standard casino table games, including blackjack, craps, and roulette, and more than 1,000 slot machines. Guests must be 21 to board, and reservations are highly recommended. ✉*Port Canaveral, 180 Jetty Dr., Terminal B, 32920* ☎*321/784-8558* ⊕*www.sterlingcasinolines.com* ✆*Free* ☉*Sun.–Thurs. 11–4 and 7–midnight; Fri. and Sat. 11–4 and 7–1.*

WHERE TO EAT & STAY

$-$$$ ✕**Rusty's Seafood & Oyster Bar.** Oysters, prepared raw, steamed, or casino-style, are just one of the draws at this ultracasual eatery. Daily happy hour (dollar drafts and two-for-one cocktails), outdoor dining on the deck, and waitresses sporting nylon short-shorts are undoubtedly among the others. Rusty's waterfront location gives diners an up-close-and-personal view of mammoth cruise ships leaving and returning to port. Rusty's quick service and proximity to the cruise ships also make it a favorite for those about to hit the high seas. Other menu items include seafood gumbo, spicy wings, steamed crab legs, burgers, and baskets of fish-and-chips, clam strips, or fried calamari. ✉*628 Glen Cheek Dr., 32920* ☎*321/783-2033* ▭*AE, D, MC, V.*

$$$ ⬚**Radisson Resort at the Port.** For cruise-ship passengers who can't wait to get under way, this splashy resort, done up in pink and turquoise, already feels like the Caribbean. Guest rooms have wicker furniture,

hand-painted wallpaper, tropical-theme decor, and ceiling fans. The pool is lushly landscaped and features a cascading 95-foot mountain waterfall, tiki bar, and occasional appearances by the "Radisson parrots," about a dozen renegade birds who call the resort home (can you blame them?). This resort, directly across the bay from Port Canaveral, is not on the ocean, but it does provide complimentary transportation to the beach, Ron Jon Surf Shop, and the cruise-ship terminals at Port Canaveral. **Pros:** Cruise ship convenience, pool area, free shuttle. **Cons:** Three-day cancellation policy, rooms around the pool can be noisy, loud a/c in some rooms. ✉ *8701 Astronaut Blvd., Cape Canaveral* ☎ *321/784–0000 or 888/201–1718* ⊕ *www.radisson.com/capecanaveralfl* ⤳ *284 rooms, 72 suites* ☐ *In-room: refrigerator (some), kitchen (some), Ethernet. In-hotel: restaurant, bar, tennis court, pool, gym, laundry facilities, laundry service, public Wi-Fi* ▤ *AE, D, MC, V.*

COCOA

50 mi east of downtown Orlando, 60 mi east of Walt Disney World.

Not to be confused with the seaside community of Cocoa Beach, the small town of Cocoa sits smack-dab on mainland Florida and faces the Intracoastal Waterway, known locally as the Indian River. There's a planetarium and a museum, as well as a rustic fish camp along the St. Johns River, a few miles inland.

Perhaps Cocoa's most interesting feature is restored **Cocoa Village.** Folks in a rush to get to the beach tend to overlook this Victorian-style village, but it's worth a stop. Within the cluster of restored turn-of-the-20th-century buildings and cobblestone walkways you can enjoy several restaurants, indoor and outdoor cafés, snack and ice-cream shops, and more than 50 specialty shops and art galleries. The area hosts music performances in the gazebo, arts-and-crafts shows, and other family-friendly events throughout the year. To get to Cocoa Village, head east on Route 520—named King Street in Cocoa—and when the streets get narrow and the road curves, make a right onto Brevard Avenue; follow the signs for the free municipal parking lot. ✉ *S.R. 520 and Brevard Ave., 32922* ☎ *321/631–9075* ⊕ *www.cocoavillage.com* ✉ *Free* ⊙ *Hours vary by store.*

As its name suggests, **Porcher House** was the home of E.P. Porcher (pronounced Por-*shay*), one of Cocoa's pioneers and the founder of the Deerfield Citrus groves. The Porcher home, built in 1916 and now a National Historic Landmark, is an example of 20th-century Classical Revival architecture incorporating local coquina rock. The house is open to the public for self-guided tours. ✉ *434 Delannoy Ave., Cocoa Village* ☎ *321/639–3500* ⊕ *www.cocoavillage.com/porcherhouse* ✉ *Donation welcome* ⊙ *Weekdays 9–5.*

☙ The **Brevard Community College Planetarium and Observatory,** one of the largest public-access observatories in Florida, has a 24-inch telescope through which visitors can view objects in the solar system and deep space. The on-campus planetarium has two theaters, one showing a changing roster of nature documentaries, the other hosting laser-light as well as changing planetarium shows. Science Quest Exhibit Hall has hands-on exhibits, including scales calibrated to other planets (on the moon, Vegas-era Elvis would have weighed just 62 pounds). The International Hall of Space Explorers displays exhibits on space travel. Show schedules and opening hours may vary, so it's best to call ahead. Travel 2½ mi east of Interstate 95 Exit 75 on Route 520, and take Route 501 north for 1½ mi. ⊠*1519 Clearlake Rd., Bldg. 19, 32922* ☎*321/433–7373* ⊕*www.brevardcc.edu/planet* ☞*Observatory and exhibit hall free; film or planetarium show $7 adults, $4 children 12 and under; both shows $11 adults, $6 children; laser show $7, triple combination $16* ☉*Call for current schedule.*

☾ To see what the lay of the local land looked like in other eras, check out the **Brevard Museum of History & Natural Science.** Hands-on activities for children are the draw here. Not to be missed is the Windover Archaeological Exhibit of 7,000-year-old artifacts indigenous to the region. In 1984, a shallow pond revealed the burial ground of more than 200 Native Americans who lived in the area about 7,000 years ago. Preserved in the muck were bones and, to the archaeologists' surprise, the brains of these ancient people. Don't overlook the hands-on discovery rooms and the collection of Victoriana. The museum's nature center has 22 acres of trails encompassing three distinct ecosystems—sand pine hills, lake lands, and marshlands. ⊠*2201 Michigan Ave., 32926* ☎*321/632–1830* ⊕*www.brevardmuseum.com* ☞*$6 adults, $4.50 children 5–16* ☉*Mon.–Sat. 10–4.*

If you haven't seen the swampy, alligator-ridden waters of Florida, then you haven't really seen Florida. **Twister Airboat Rides** takes guests on a unique and thrilling wildlife tour where eagles and wading birds coexist with water moccasins and gators. The Coast Guard–certified deluxe airboats hit speeds of up to 45 mph and offer unparalleled opportunities to photograph native species. The basic tour lasts 30 minutes, but 60- and 90-minute ecotours are also available. Twister Airboat Rides is inside the Lone Cabbage Fish Camp, about 9 mi west of Cocoa's city limits, 4 mi west of Interstate 95. ⊠*8199 Rte. 520 at the St. Johns River, 32926* ☎*321/632–4199* ⊕*www.twisterairboatrides.com* ☞*$20 adults, $12 children 12 and under* ☉*Daily 10–6.*

WHERE TO EAT

$$$–$$$$ ✕**Café Margaux.** Eclectic, creative, and international is the perfect way to describe the cuisine and the decor at this charming Cocoa Village spot. The menu blends French, Italian, and Asian influences with dishes like tenderloin of beef brochette, sesame-seared ahi with green tea and bamboo risotto, and braised veal scaloppine but also features more exotic fare such as duck and ostrich. The themed dining rooms are elaborately decorated with dramatic but not necessarily coordinating window treatments, wallpaper, and artwork. ⊠*220 Brevard Ave., 32922* ☎*321/639–8343* ☰*AE, D, MC, V* ☉*Closed Sun.*

★ $$–$$$ ✕**Black Tulip Restaurant.** Two intimate dining rooms invite romance at this Cocoa Village bistro, which takes pride in its 50-plus-label wine menu. Appetizers include tortellini with meat sauce and crab-stuffed mushrooms. Select such entrées as fettuccine primavera Alfredo; sautéed pork loin simmered with apples, brandy, and cream; roast duckling with peaches and cashews; or fillet medallions with artichoke sauce. Lighter lunch selections include sandwiches, salads, and quiches. Don't miss the chocolate mousse pie and the warm apple strudel. ⊠ *207 Brevard Ave., 32922* ☎ *321/631–1133* ☐ *AE, D, DC, MC, V* ⊘ *Closed Sun. and Mon.*

¢-$ ✕**Lone Cabbage Fish Camp.** The word "rustic" doesn't even begin to describe this down-home, no-nonsense restaurant (translation: you eat off paper plates with plastic forks) housed in a weathered old clapboard shack along with a bait shop and airboat tour company. Set your calorie counter for plates of catfish, frogs' legs, turtle, and alligator (as well as burgers and hot dogs). Dine inside or on the outdoor deck overlooking the St. Johns River with live music every Sunday. Who knows, you might even see your dinner swimming by. ⊠ *8199 Rte. 520, 32926* ☎ *321/632–4199* ⌔ *Reservations not accepted* ☐ *AE, MC, V.*

SHOPPING

You could spend hours browsing in the more than 50 boutiques and shops of **Cocoa Village** (⊠ *S.R. 520 and Brevard Ave., 32922* ☎ *321/631–9075*) along Brevard Avenue and Harrison Street, which has the densest concentration of shops. Although most are of the gift and clothing variety, the Village is also home to several antiques shops, art galleries, florists, bookstores, and even a tattoo parlor and a spa.

Shoppers looking for a bargain should check out the **Super Flea & Farmers Market** (⊠ *4835 W. Eau Gallie Blvd.,* ☎ *321/242–9124*)with its 900 booths and more than 300 dealers every Friday, Saturday, and Sunday.

COCOA BEACH

65 mi east of Orlando, 70 mi east of Walt Disney World.

Named for the former astronaut, **Alan Shepard Park** (⊠ *East end of S.R. 250, 32931* ☎ *321/868–3274*) is a 5-acre oceanfront park that, aptly enough, provides excellent views of shuttle launches. Facilities include 10 picnic pavilions, shower and restroom facilities, and more than 300 parking spaces (parking is $5 per day). Shops and restaurants are within walking distance.

After crossing a long and high bridge just east of Cocoa Village, you'll drop down upon a barrier island. A few miles farther and you'll reach the Atlantic Ocean and picture-perfect **Cocoa Beach** at Route A1A. This is one of the Space Coast's nicest beaches, with many wide stretches that are excellent for biking, jogging, power walking, or strolling. In some places there are dressing rooms, showers, playgrounds, picnic areas with grills, snack shops, and surf-side parking lots. Beach vendors offer necessities, and guards are on duty in summer. Cocoa Beach is considered the capital of Florida's surfing community.

Stretching far over the Atlantic, the **Cocoa Beach Pier** (⊠ *401 Meade Ave., 32931* ☎ *321/783–7549* ⊕ *www.cocoabeachpier.com*) is an everyday gathering spot as well as a beachside grandstand for space-shuttle launches. There are several souvenir shops, bars, and restaurants, as well as a bait-and-tackle shop. It costs $3 to park here, and another $1 for access to the fishing part of the pier that dangles 800 feet out into the Atlantic. Don't expect pristine Disney cleanliness here; this is a weather-beaten, sandy hangout for people who love the beach.

The 10-acre oceanfront **Sidney Fischer Park** (⊠*2100 block of Rte. A1A,* ☎*321/868–3252*) has showers, playgrounds, changing areas, picnic areas with grills, snack shops, and plenty of well-maintained, inexpensive surf-side parking lots. Beach vendors carry necessities for sunning and swimming. The parking fee is $5 for cars and RVs.

WHERE TO EAT

$$-$$$$ ✕**Bernard's Surf.** Since 1948 this family operation and Cocoa Beach institution has served astronauts, athletes, politicians, and celebrities a variety of fresh seafood entrées, from swordfish, cobia, and pompano to lobster and shrimp. The common folk also eat up the fresh catches that vary by the season and whim of the sea, but snapper under a creamy seafood sauce is the house specialty. Landlubbers can choose pork chops or steak. Try the tableside Caesar salad, and save room for the cheesecake. Bernard's sister restaurant located under the same roof, The Surf Bar & Grill, is a less expensive alternative. ⊠*2 S. Atlantic Ave., 32931* ☎*321/783–2401* ▭*AE, D, MC, V.*

★ $$-$$$$ ✕**Mango Tree Restaurant.** Candles, fresh flowers, and rattan basket chairs set a romantic mood in the intimate dining room designed to evoke the feel of a South Pacific plantation (a lush entryway with a koi pond with black-neck swans add to the dramatic effect). *Lobsterocki* (Maine lobster wrapped in bacon with teriyaki cream sauce), baked Brie, or rare seared tuna are good appetizer choices. For a main course, try Indian River crab cakes, roast Long Island duckling, or filet mignon stuffed with cream cheese and chives. ⊠*118 N. Atlantic Ave., 32931* ☎*321/799–0513* ▭*AE, MC, V* ☉*Closed Mon. No lunch.*

$$$ ✕**Heidelberg.** As the name suggests, the cuisine here is definitely German, from the sauerbraten served with potato dumplings and red cabbage to the beef Stroganoff and spaetzle to the classically prepared Wiener schnitzel. All the soups and desserts are homemade; try the Viennese-style apple strudel and the rum-zapped almond-cream tortes. Elegant interior touches include crisp linens and fresh flowers. There's live music Friday and Saturday evenings. You can also dine inside the jazz club, Heidi's, next door. ⊠*7 N. Orlando Ave., opposite City Hall,* ☎*321/783–6806* ▭*AE, MC, V* ☉*Closed Mon. No lunch Sun.*

$-$$ ✕**Oh Shucks Seafood Bar.** At the only open-air seafood bar on the beach, at the entrance of the Cocoa Beach Pier, the main item is oysters, served on the half shell. You can also grab a burger here (or Oh Shucks' most popular item, coconut beer shrimp), and there's live entertainment on Friday and Saturday. Some diners complain that the prices don't jibe with the ultracasual atmosphere (hello, plastic chairs!), but they're also paying for the "ex-Pier-ience." ⊠*401 Meade Ave., Cocoa Beach Pier,* ☎*321/783–7549* ▭*AE, D, MC, V.*

WHERE TO STAY

★ $$$ ▦**Hilton Cocoa Beach Oceanfront.** In 2004 the seven-story hotel sustained considerable hurricane damage, but thanks to a $15 million renovation, it's back as one of the best hotels in Cocoa Beach. Most rooms have ocean views, but for true drama get a room on the east end, facing the water. The hotel's best feature is its location, right on the beach. In season, a band plays poolside (on the 10,000-square-foot deck) on weekends, and activities directors keep kids busy with arts and crafts and surfing lessons. **Pros:** Beachfront, friendly staff, clean. **Cons:** No refrigerators in standard rooms, overpriced restaurant, small pool. ⊠*1550 N. Atlantic Ave.,* ☎*321/799–0003* ⊕*www.hiltoncocoabeach. com* ⇘*285 rooms, 11 suites* ⚷*In-room: refrigerator (some), Wi-Fi. In-hotel: restaurant, room service, bar, pool, gym, beachfront, laundry facilities, laundry service, executive floor, parking (no fee), no-smoking rooms* ⊟*AE, D, DC, MC, V.*

★ $$$ ▦**Inn at Cocoa Beach.** One of the area's best, this charming oceanfront inn has spacious, individually decorated rooms with four-poster beds, upholstered chairs, and balconies or patios; most have ocean views. Deluxe rooms are much larger, with a king-size bed, sofa, and sitting area; most also have a dining table. Jacuzzi rooms are different sizes. Included in the rate are afternoon socials in the breezeway, evening wine and cheese, and a continental breakfast. **Pros:** Quiet, romantic, honor bar. **Cons:** No on-site restaurant, "forced" socializing. ⊠*4300 Ocean Beach Blvd.,* ☎*321/799–3460, 800/343–5307 outside Florida* ⊕*www.theinnatcocoabeach.com* ⇘*48 rooms, 2 suites* ⚷*In-room: safe, VCR (some), Wi-Fi. In-hotel: pool, beachfront, public Wi-Fi, parking (no fee), no-smoking rooms* ⊟*AE, D, MC, V* ℗*CP.*

$$–$$$ ▦**Holiday Inn Cocoa Beach Oceanfront Resort.** When two adjacent beach hotels were redesigned and a promenade park landscaped between them, the Holiday Inn Cocoa Beach Resort was born. Standard rooms are modern, and designed in bright tropical colors. Suites and villas have a Key West feel, with louvered doors and rattan ceiling fans. Lodging options include standard and king rooms; oceanfront suites, which have a living room with sleeper sofa; villas; or bi-level lofts. Kids are given the royal treatment, with specially designed KidsSuites that feature bunk beds and video games, and a pirate-ship pool with water-blasting cannons. **Pros:** Beachfront, varied lodging options, fun pool area. **Cons:** Small bathrooms, loud a/c in some rooms. ⊠*1300 N. Atlantic Ave.,* ☎*321/783–2271 or 800/206–2747* ⊕*www.hi-cocoa. com* ⇘*500 rooms, 119 suites* ⚷*In-room: kitchen (some), refrigerator (some), Wi-Fi. In-hotel: 4 restaurants, bars, tennis courts, pool, gym, beachfront, laundry facilities, laundry service, parking (no fee)* ⊟*AE, D, MC, V.*

$$ **Doubletree Oceanfront Hotel Cocoa Beach.** After significant hurricane damage in 2004, this oceanfront hotel underwent an $8-million top-to-bottom renovation. Guest rooms are West Indies–inspired, with dark oak furniture, colorful tropical prints, and cheerful yellow walls. Most rooms are oceanfront, with superb water views and private balconies. The five-story hotel is a favorite of families as well as Orlandoans on weekend getaways, as are the chain's famous chocolate-chip cook-

ies. **Pros:** Private beach, refrigerator and microwave in every room, comfy beds. **Cons:** Extra charge for beach-chair rental, loud a/c in some rooms, roof views. ⊠*2080 N. Atlantic Ave.,* ☎*321/783–9222* ⊕*www.cocoabeachdoubletree.com* ⇥*148 rooms, 12 suites* ⚬*In-room: refrigerator, Wi-Fi. In-hotel: restaurant, room service, bar, pool, gym, beachfront, laundry facilities, laundry service, executive floor, public Wi-Fi, no-smoking rooms* ⊟*AE, D, DC, MC, V.*

NIGHTLIFE

The **Cocoa Beach Pier** (⊠*401 Meade Ave., 32920* ☎*321/783–7549*) is for locals, beach bums, surfers, and people who don't mind the weather-worn wood and sandy, watery paths. At the **Mai Tiki Bar** they claim that "No Bar Goes This Far," which is true, considering it's at the end of the 800-foot pier. Come to **The Boardwalk** Friday night for the Boardwalk Bash, with live acoustic and rock-and-roll music; drop in Saturday for more live music; and come back Wednesday evening to catch the reggae band. For great live jazz, head to **Heidi's Jazz Club** (⊠*7 Orlando Ave. N., 32931* ☎*321/783–4559*). Local and nationally known musicians (Boots Randolph and Mose Allison have taken the stage) play Tuesday through Sunday, with showcase acts appearing on weekends.

SPORTS & THE OUTDOORS

The **Cocoa Beach Recreation Complex** (⊠*5000 Tom Warriner Blvd., 32931* ☎*321/868–3352*) is actually an extensive public sports complex that's owned by the city and open to anyone. Facilities include an Olympic-size swimming pool; soccer, softball, and baseball fields; a restaurant and snack bar; and a riverside pavilion with picnic tables. The **Cocoa Beach Country Club** (☎*321/868–3252*) offers 27 holes of championship golf (greens fee: $30–$53) with an abundance of waterfowl and other birds, with species listed and information offered at each hole. The **Racquet Club** (☎*321/868–3224*) has 10 lighted tennis courts.

BIKING   Although there are no bike trails as such in the area, cycling is allowed on the beaches and the Cocoa Beach Causeway. Bikes can be rented hourly, daily, or weekly at **Ron Jon Surf Shop** (⊠*4151 N. Atlantic Ave., Rte. A1A* ☎*321/799–8888*). Locks are available.

FISHING   The **Cocoa Beach Pier** (⊠*401 Meade Ave. 32931* ☎*321/783–7549*) has a bait-and-tackle shop and a fishing area. Although most of the pier is free to walk on, there's a $1 charge to enter the fishing area at the end of the 800-foot-long boardwalk, and a $3.50 fishing fee. You can rent rods and reels here.

LIFE IMITATES ART

In the early 1960s Cocoa Beach was a sleepy, little-known town. But in 1965 the sitcom I Dream of Jeannie premiered. The endearing show centered around an astronaut, played by Larry Hagman, and his "Jeannie" in a bottle, Barbara Eden, and was set in Cocoa Beach. Though the series was never shot in Florida, creator Sidney Sheldon paid homage to the town with local references to Cape Kennedy (now known as the Kennedy Space Center) and Bernard's Surf.

3

KAYAKING   Specializing in manatee encounters, **Adventure Kayak of Cocoa Beach** (☎321/480–8632) takes guests on one- and two-person kayak tours of mangroves, channels, and islands.

SURFING   If you can't tell a tri-skeg stick from a hodaddy shredding the lip on a gnarly tube, then you may want to avail yourself of the **Ron Jon Surf School** (✉150 E. Columbia Lane, 32931 ☎321/868–1980). They teach grommets (dudes) and gidgets (chicks) from kids to seniors in groups and one-on-one. **Ron Jon Watersports** (✉4275 N. Atlantic Ave., 32931 ☎321/799–8888) rents surfboards, body boards, and wet suits, as well as kayaks and bikes. The building also houses the **East Coast Surfing Hall of Fame and Museum.**

SHOPPING

Merritt Square Mall (✉777 E. Merritt Island Causeway, Merritt Island ☎321/452–3272), the area's only major shopping mall, is about a 20-minute ride from the beach. Stores include Macy's, Dillard's, JCPenney, Sears, Steve & Barry's, Foot Locker, Island Surf and Skate, and roughly 100 others. There's a 16-screen multiplex, along with a food court and several restaurant chains.

Fodor'sChoice   It's impossible to miss the **Ron Jon Surf Shop** (✉4151 N. Atlantic Ave., ★   Rte. A1A, ☎321/799–8888). With a giant surfboard and an aqua, teal, and pink Art Deco facade, Ron Jon takes up nearly two blocks along A1A. What started in 1963 as a small T-shirt and bathing-suit shop has evolved into a 52,000-square-foot superstore that's open every day 'round the clock. The shop has water-sports gear as well as chairs and umbrellas for rent, and sells every kind of beachwear, surf wax, plus the requisite T-shirts and flip-flops. For up-to-the-minute surfing conditions, call the store and press 3 and then 7 for the **Ron Jon Surf and Weather Report.**

MELBOURNE

20 mi south of Cocoa.

Despite its dependence on the high-tech space industry, this town is decidedly laid-back. The majority of the city is on the mainland, but a small portion trickles onto a barrier island, separated by the Indian River Lagoon and accessible by several inlets, including the Sebastian Inlet.

It took 20,000 volunteers two weeks to turn 56 acres of forest and ☾ wetlands into the **Brevard Zoo,** the only American Zoo and Aquarium Fodor'sChoice Association–accredited zoo built by a community. Stroll along the ★   shaded boardwalks and get a close-up look at alligators, crocodiles, giant anteaters, marmosets, jaguars, eagles, river otters, kangaroos, exotic birds, and kookaburras. Alligator, crocodile, and river-otter feedings are held on alternate afternoons—although the alligators do not dine on the otters. Stop by Paws-On, an interactive learning playground where kids and adults can crawl into human-size gopher burrows, beehives, and spiderwebs; get cozy with several domestic animals in Animal Encounters; hand-feed a giraffe in Expedition Africa or a lorrikeet in the Australian Free Flight Aviary; and step up to the Wetlands Outpost, an elevated pavilion that's a gateway to 22 acres of wetlands through which you can paddle kayaks and keep an eye open for the 4,000 species of wildlife that live in these waters and woods. ⊠*8225 N. Wickham Rd., 32940* ☎*321–254–9453* ⊕*www.brevardzoo.org* ⊠*$11.50 adults, $8.50 children 2–12; train ride $3, kayaking $6* ⊘ *Daily 9:30–5.*

The **King Center for the Performing Arts** is one of the premier performance centers in Central Florida. Oddly enough, top-name performers often bypass Orlando to appear in this comfortable 2,000-seat hall. Call for a performance schedule. ⊠*3865 N. Wickham Rd., 32935* ☎*321–242–2219 box office.*

OFF THE BEATEN PATH

Satellite Beach. The beaches of this sleepy little community just south of Patrick Air Force Base, about 15 mi south of Cocoa Beach on A1A, are cradled between the balmy Atlantic Ocean and biologically diverse Indian River Lagoon. It's a popular spot for family vacations because of its slow pace and lack of crowds.

Paradise Beach. Small and scenic, this 1,600-foot stretch of sand is part of a 10-acre park north of Indialantic, about 20 mi south of Cocoa Beach on A1A. It has showers, restrooms, picnic tables, a refreshment stand, and lifeguards in summer.

SPORTS & THE OUTDOORS

BASEBALL Even though they play in our nation's capital during the regular season, the **Washington Nationals** (⊠*5800 Stadium Pkwy., Viera 32940* ☎*321/633–4487* ⊕*www.nationals.com*), formerly the Montreal Expos, use Melbourne's Space Coast Stadium for their spring-training site. Tickets are $10–$20. For the rest of the season, the facility is home to the **Brevard County Manatees** (☎*321/633–9200*), one of the Milwaukee Brewers' minor-league teams.

GOLF **Baytree National Golf Links** (⊠*8207 National Dr., 32940* ☎*321/259–9060*) is an 18-hole course; greens fee $39–$75. **Viera East Golf Club** (⊠*2300 Clubhouse Dr., Viera* ✛*5 mi from Melbourne* ☎*321/639–6500 or 888/843–7232*) has a public 18-hole course; greens fee $40–$60.

INLAND TOWNS

Inland, peaceful little towns are separated by miles of two-lane roads running through acres of dense forest and flat pastureland and skirting one lake after another. There's not much else to see but cattle, though you may catch a glimpse of the state's few hills. Gentle and rolling, they're hardly worth noting to folks from true hill country, but they're significant enough in Florida for much of this area to be called the "hill and lake region."

DELAND

21 mi southwest of Daytona Beach.

The quiet town is home to Stetson University, established in 1886 by hat magnate John Stetson. Several inviting state parks are nearby; as for activities, there's great manatee-watching during winter, as well as skydiving for both spectators and participants.

Soaring ceilings and neoclassical furnishings provide the backdrop at the **Duncan Gallery of Art,** on the Stetson University campus. The gallery hosts exhibits by southeastern and national artists and Stetson students. ✉*Stetson University, Sampson Hall, Michigan and Amelia Aves.,* ☎*386/822–7386* ⊕*www.stetson.edu/artsci/art* ✉*Donation welcome* ☾*Mon.–Sat. 10–4, Sun. 1–4.*

Located in the Cultural Arts Center across from Stetson University, the **Museum of Florida Art** highlights Florida artists and works of art pertaining to Florida, as well as hosting national traveling exhibitions (past shows have featured the work of Ansel Adams, William Wegman, and the Audubon Society). ✉*600 N. Woodland Blvd., 32723* ☎*386/734–4371* ⊕*www.delandmuseum.com* ✉*Donation welcome* ☾*Tues.–Sat. 10–4, Sun. 1–4.*

One of the most historically and scientifically significant collections of gems and minerals in the world can be found in the **Gillespie Museum,** on the Stetson University campus. ✉*Stetson University, Michigan and Amelia Aves.,* ☎*386/822–7330* ⊕*www.gillespiemuseum.stetson.edu* ✉*$2* ☾*Tue.–Fri.*

February is the top month for sighting sea cows at this designated manatee refuge, but they begin to head here in November, as soon as the water gets cold enough (below 68°F). (Your best bet for spotting a manatee is to walk along the boardwalk.) **Blue Spring State Park,** once a river port where paddle wheelers stopped to take on cargoes of oranges, also contains a historic homestead that is open to the public. Home to the largest spring on the St. Johns River, the park offers hiking, camping, and picnicking facilities. ✉*2100 W. French Ave., Orange City* ☎*386/775–3663* ⊕*www.floridastateparks.org/bluespring* ✉*$5 per vehicle, up to 8 people* ☾*Daily 8–sundown.*

Near the end of the 19th century, **De León Springs State Park** was promoted as a fountain of youth to winter guests. Today visitors are attracted to the year-round 72°F springs for swimming, fishing, canoeing, and kayaking. Nature trails draw hikers and outdoor enthusiasts. Explore an abandoned sugar mill at **Lake Woodruff National Wildlife Refuge**—accessible through De León Springs—which also has 18,000 acres of lakes, creeks, and marshes for scuba diving, canoeing, and hiking. ✉*601 Ponce de León Blvd., 6 mi. north of DeLand off U.S. 17, DeLeón Springs* ☎*386/985–4212* ⊕*www.floridastateparks.org/deleonsprings* ✉*$5 per vehicle, up to 8 people* ☾*Daily 8–sundown.*

3

WHERE TO EAT & STAY

$-$$$ ✕**Original Holiday House.** Don't be surprised if Holiday House makes you miss your Nana, since the DeLand institution has been preparing old-fashioned comfort food just like grandma used to make since 1959. The homey restaurant, located across from the Stetson University campus, is enormously popular with senior citizens, families, and college students who fill their bellies with turkey and dressing, roast beef, mashed potatoes, and plenty of veggies. Although the main draw is the buffet—salad only, salad and vegetables only, or the full buffet for $10.25—the menu also includes a short list of sandwiches and entrées. Holiday House uses only organic vegetables, bans MSG from all foods, and offers sugarless desserts. ⌂*704 Hwy. 17, 32720* ☎*386/734–6319* ⚑*Reservations not accepted* ▭*D, MC, V*

WORD OF MOUTH

"…The day continued with a trolley ride to the Fountain of Youth, America's oldest tourist trap! It's finely aged cheese, though, and an enjoyable way to spend a couple hours. There are 15 acres to explore."

–xrae

$-$$ ✕**Main Street Grill.** At first glance, this downtown restaurant looks like any nondescript, casual chain restaurant—with an uninspired menu to boot—but on closer inspection, the local favorite makes a name for itself with original twists on the expected like French onion steak sandwich, chicken cordon bleu pasta, and Southern fried shrimp. The extensive menu offers a variety of chicken, beef, and seafood entrées, as well as sandwiches and salads. Dine inside the historic brick building surrounded by colorful murals depicting downtown DeLand or outside on the patio by the manatee fountain. Regular diners praise the friendly and efficient waitstaff—and the cinnamon buns as big as your head. ⌂*100 E. New York Ave., 32724* ☎*386/740–9535* ⚑*Reservations not accepted* ▭*AE, MC, V.*

$ ▦**University Inn.** For years this older motel in historical DeLand has been the choice of business travelers and visitors to Stetson University. The inn is adjacent to campus, and has reasonable rates and a courteous staff. It also doesn't hurt that it's clean, well maintained, and has one of the largest pools in the area. **Pros:** Inexpensive, proximity to campus, clean. **Cons:** Only one suite, dated atmosphere. ⌂*644 N. Woodland Blvd.,* ☎*386/734–5711 or 800/345–8991* ⊕*www.universityinndeland. com* ⊜*57 rooms, 1 suite* ♿*In-room: refrigerator, Wi-Fi. In-hotel: pool, gym, no elevator, public Wi-Fi, parking (no fee), some pets allowed, no-smoking rooms* ▭*AE, D, MC, V* ⦿|CP.

THE OUTDOORS

BOATING & FISHING

Pontoon boats, houseboats, bass boats, and fishing-guide service for the St. Johns River are available from **Hontoon Landing Marina** (⌂*2317 River Ridge Rd., 32724* ☎*386/734–2474 or 800/248–2474*). One of the savviest guides to bass fishing in the St. Johns River and Central Florida lakes is Bob Stonewater of **Bob Stonewater's Trophy Bass Guide Service** (☎*800/835–2851*), who offers five- and nine-hour trips for solo or duo anglers.

SKYDIVING In addition to hosting competitions and offering accelerated free-fall training, DeLand has tandem jumping. You are literally attached to an experienced instructor-diver, which means that even novices are able to take their maiden voyage after one day. **Skydive DeLand** (✉*1600 Flightline Blvd., 32724* ☎*386/738–3539*), open daily 8 AM–sundown, offers lessons.

OCALA NATIONAL FOREST

Eastern entrance 40 mi west of Daytona Beach, northern entrance 52 mi south of Jacksonville.

This breathtaking 389,000-acre wilderness with lakes, springs, rivers, hiking trails, campgrounds, and historic sites has three major recreational areas (listed here from east to west): **Alexander Springs** (✉*Off Rte. 40 via Rte. 445 S*) has a swimming lake and a campground; **Salt Springs** (✉*Off Rte. 40 via Rte. 19 N.,*) has a natural saltwater spring where Atlantic blue crabs come to spawn each summer; **Juniper Springs** (✉*Off Rte. 40,*) includes a stone waterwheel house, a campground, a natural-spring swimming pool, and hiking and canoe trails. About 30 campsites are sprinkled throughout the park and range from bare sites to sites with electric hookups, showers, and bathrooms. Note that credit cards aren't accepted. ✉*Visitor center, 17147 E. Hwy. 40, Salt Springs* ☎*352/625–2520* ⊕*www.fs.fed.us/r8/florida* ✉*Alexander Springs, Salt Springs, Juniper Springs: $4.*

THE OUTDOORS

CANOEING The 7-mi **Juniper Springs run** is a narrow, twisting, and winding canoe ride, which, although exhilarating, is not for the novice. Canoe rentals and guided tours are available through **Juniper Springs Canoe Rentals** (☎*352/625–2808*) inside the park.

FISHING **Captain Tom's Custom Charters** (☎*352/236–0872*) allows you to charter fishing trips ranging from three hours to a full day, and offers sightseeing cruises as well.

HORSEBACK **JNB Horse Haven Farm** (✉*Hwy. 42 between Weirsdale and Altoona,*
RIDING *Lady Lake* ☎*352/821–4756 or 800/731–4756*), located within the Ocala National Forest, offers nature trail rides for beginners, intermediate, and advanced riders, as well as group and private lessons.

MICANOPY

36 mi north of Ocala.

Though this was the state's oldest inland town, site of both a Timucuan Indian settlement and a Spanish mission, there are few traces left from before white settlement, which began in 1821. Micanopy (pronounced micka-*no*-pee) does still draw those interested in the past, however. The main street of this beautiful little town has quite a few antiques shops, and in fall roughly 200 antiques dealers descend on the town for the annual Harvest Fall Festival.

★ A 20,000-acre wildlife preserve with ponds, lakes, trails, and a visitor center with a museum, **Paynes Prairie State Preserve** is a wintering area for many migratory birds where alligators, wild horses, and a herd of American bison also roam. There was once a vast lake here, but a century ago it drained so abruptly that thousands of beached fish died in the mud. The remains of a ferry stranded in the 1880s can still be seen. Swimming, boating, picnicking, and camping are permitted. ⊠ *Off U.S. 441 100 Savannah Blvd.,* ☏ *352/466–3397* ⊕ *www.floridastateparks.org/paynesprairie* ⊠ *$4 per vehicle, up to 8 people, $3 for singles* ⊙ *Daily 8–sunset.*

OFF THE BEATEN PATH

Marjorie Kinnan Rawlings State Park. The presence of Rawlings, whose works include *The Yearling* and *Cross Creek,* permeates this National Historic Landmark home where the typewriter rusts on the ramshackle porch, the closet where she hid her booze during Prohibition yawns open, and clippings from her scrapbook reveal her legal battles and marital problems. Bring lunch, and picnic in the shade of one of Rawlings's citrus trees. Then visit her grave a few miles away at peaceful Island Grove. ⊠ *18700 S. C.R. 325, Cross Creek* ☏ *352/466–3672* ⊕ *www.floridastateparks.org/marjoriekinnanrawlings* ⊠ *$2 per vehicle, up to 8 people; tours $3 adults, $2 children 6–12* ⊙ *Daily. 9–5; tours Thurs.–Sun. at 10, 11, and hourly 1–4 Oct.–July.*

WHERE TO EAT & STAY

¢ ✕**Blue Highway Pizzeria.** As proof that tasty pizza and friendly servers transcend all ages, income levels, and backgrounds, Blue Highway is as popular with locals and University of Florida students as it is with snowbirds and tourists. Pizza is, of course, the main attraction at the brightly colored building on the side of the highway, especially Frank's specialty pies like the Carne Combo with pepperoni, sausage, salami, and three kinds of cheese; and the Abruzzese with meatballs and sliced roasted garlic. But the menu also features sandwiches, calzones, panini, and salads with homemade dressings and a nice selection of beer and wine. ⊠ *204 NE Hwy. 441,* ☏ *352/466–0062* ⟳ *Reservations not accepted* ⊟ *MC, V.*

$-$$ ⊡**Herlong Mansion.** Spanish moss clings to the stately oak trees surrounding this restored mansion built in the 1800s. The imposing Greek Revival–style B&B has Corinthian columns and wide verandas perfect for relaxing in a rocker. Rooms and suites have period furniture, Oriental rugs, lead-glass windows, and claw-foot tubs; some rooms have whirlpools. A multicourse breakfast, which is included in the rate, is an event here. Emphasis is on personal attention without intrusion; guests appreciate the service without feeling rushed. **Pros:** Large private bathrooms, gourmet breakfast, evening wine and cheese reception. **Cons:** No phones in rooms, no TVs in some rooms, some small and windowless rooms. ⊠ *402 N.E. Cholokka Blvd.,* ☏ *352/466–3322 or 800/437–5664* ⊕ *www.herlong.com* ⟳ *12 rooms, 2 cottages* ⬭ *In-room: no phone, DVD (some), no TV (some) Wi-Fi. In-hotel: no ele-*

vator, public Wi-Fi, parking (no fee), no kids under 12, no-smoking rooms ▤AE, D, MC, V ⏹BP.

GAINESVILLE

11 mi north of Micanopy on U.S. 441.

The University of Florida anchors this sprawling town. Visitors are mostly Gator football fans and parents of university students, so the styles and costs of accommodations are primarily aimed at budget-minded travelers rather than luxury-seeking vacationers. The surrounding area encompasses several state parks and interesting gardens and geological sites.

On the campus of the University of Florida, the **Florida Museum of Natural History** has several interesting replicas, including a Mayan palace, a typical Timucuan household, and a full-size model of a Florida cave and mangrove forest. The collections from throughout Florida's history warrant at least half a day. ✉ *University of Florida Cultural Plaza, S.W. 34th St. at Hull Rd.,* ☎352/846–2000 ⊕*www.flmnh.ufl.edu* ▤*Free* ⏰*Mon.–Sat. 10–5, Sun. 1–5.*

About 10,000 years ago an underground cavern collapsed and created a geological treat. At **Devil's Millhopper Geological State Park,** see the botanical wonderland of exotic subtropical ferns and trees growing in the 500-foot-wide, 120-foot-deep sinkhole. You pass a dozen small waterfalls as you head down 232 steps to the bottom. Pets on a leash are welcome at the park. ✉*4732 Millhopper Rd., off U.S. 441,* ☎352/955–2008 ⊕*www.floridastateparks.org/devilsmillhopper* ▤*$2 per vehicle, up to 8 people, $1 for pedestrians and bicyclists* ⏰*Wed.–Sun. 9–5.*

WHERE TO EAT

$$$–$$$$ ✕**Melting Pot.** Eating is a group activity at this popular fondue spot; sit downstairs or upstairs in the cozy loft. Dip slivers of fish or steak in sizzling hot oil, or cubes of crusty French bread in pots of melted cheese. Save room for dessert—more fondue, naturally—pieces of fruit you dip into rich melted chocolate. By the time you leave, you might smell like a fry cook, but most diners agree it's worth any olfactory unpleasantries. ✉*418 E. University Ave., 32601* ☎352/372–5623 ▤AE, D, DC, MC, V ⏰*No lunch.*

$$$–$$$$ ✕**Paramount Grill.** You may be rubbing elbows with your neighbor, but the meal is definitely worth the inconvenience. Try one of the five house salads and such entrées as grilled Angus fillet served with shiitake-mushroom sherry-wine

LATER GATORS

Depending on what time of year you visit, Gainesville's population could be plus or minus 50,000. Home to one of the largest colleges in the country, the University of Florida, Gainesville takes on a different personality during the summer when the majority of students return home. During the fall and spring terms, the downtown streets are teeming with students on bikes, scooters, and foot, but in summer it's much more laid-back.

sauce and white truffle sauce or pan-roasted pork tenderloin with creamy blue-cheese polenta and apple-cider lemon-thyme sauce. If you miss dinner here, try the Sunday brunch. ✉ *12 S.W. 1st Ave., 32601* ☎ *352/378–3398* ▭ *AE, MC, V* ⊘ *No lunch Sat. and Sun.*

¢ ✕**Leonardo's by the Slice.** It's ironic that the kitschy pizza joint with a '50s flair is surrounded by a white picket fence, since most of its patrons and employees are far from conventional. College students, especially the pierced and tatted-up kind, flock to the Gainesville landmark not only because it's cheap but because it has the best pizza in town. Available in thick or thin varieties, by the pie and, of course, by the slice, Leonardo's pizza comes in a handful of varieties (like veggie, pepperoni, Greek, and spinach tomato). They also offer calzones, salads, and pasta such as baked ziti and spinach lasagna, with no entrée over $6. ✉ *1245 W. University Ave., 32601* ☎ *352/375–2007* ⚐ *Reservations not accepted* ▭ *AE, D, MC, V.*

WHERE TO STAY

$$$$ ▦**Hilton University of Florida Conference Center Gainesville.** With 25,000 square feet of meeting space, the University of Florida's flagship hotel caters most obviously to business travelers. Its location on the southwest corner of the campus also makes it a good choice for UF visitors. Guest rooms, which look like they came straight off the Rooms To Go show floor (blond-wood armoires, overstuffed couches with geometric-pattern throw pillows), have two phones with voice mail, large work desks, coffeemakers, MP3 players, and complimentary high-speed Internet. **Pros:** Proximity to college, free Internet, spacious rooms. **Cons:** 4 PM check-in, spotty service, overrated restaurant. ✉ *1714 S.W. 34th St.,* ☎ *352/371–3600* ⊕ *www.ufhilton.com* ⚐ *248 rooms, 3 suites* ⚘ *In-room: kitchen (some), Ethernet. In-hotel: restaurant, room service, bar, pool, gym, laundry service, public Wi-Fi, parking (no fee), some pets allowed, no-smoking rooms.* ▭ *AE, D, MC, V*

$$-$$$ ▦**The Magnolia Plantation Bed and Breakfast Inn.** You'll be within minutes of historic downtown and the University of Florida, and owners Joe and Cindy Montalto will welcome you like old friends, whether you stay in the main house or in one of the adorable cottages. The inn's unique French Second Empire architecture is one of only a handful of such examples in the southeastern United States. The lush gardens and gazebos offer quiet, shady spots to relax. A full breakfast is standard fare and is served in the formal dining room or in the privacy of your cottage. Children and pets are welcome with prior approval. **Pros:** Friendly service, breakfast, nightly social hour. **Cons:** Small rooms, seven-day cancellation policy, some uncomfortable beds. ✉ *309 S.E. 7th St.,* ☎ *352/375–6653 or 800/201–2379* ⊕ *www.magnoliabnb.com* ⚐ *5 rooms, 6 cottages* ⚘ *In-room: kitchen (some), DVD (some), VCR (some), no TV (some), Wi-Fi. In-hotel: laundry facilities, public Wi-Fi, parking (no fee), some pets allowed, no-smoking rooms* ▭ *AE, D, MC, V* ▯⊖|CP.

$-$$$ ▦**Sweetwater Branch Inn Bed & Breakfast.** You'll find such modern conveniences as data ports, hair dryers, and business services mixed with Southern charm and hospitality, all wrapped up in two grand Victorian homes surrounded by lush tropical gardens. Gleaming hardwood floors and antique furnishings lend a European flair to nicely appointed rooms. The Sweetwater is in historic downtown, adjacent to the University of Florida, and within walking distance of many of the area's better restaurants and entertainment venues. **Pros:** Southern breakfast, Jacuzzi suites, location. **Cons:** Spotty service, frequent on-site weddings. ✉625 E. University Ave., ☎352/373–6760 or 800/595–7760 ⊕www.sweetwaterinn.com ⇄12 rooms, 6 suites ♿In-room: kitchen (some), refrigerator (some), DVD (some), Wi-Fi. In-hotel: no elevator, public Wi-Fi, parking (no fee), some pets allowed, no-smoking rooms ⊟AE, MC, V ⦿CP.

SPORTS & THE OUTDOORS

AUTO RACING The **Gainesville Raceway** (✉11211 N. County Rd. 225, 32609 ☎352/377–0046, 626/914–4761 for National Hot Rod Association) is the site of professional and amateur auto and motorcycle races, including Gatornationals in March, as well as **Frank Hawley's Drag Racing School** (☎866/480–7223).

NORTHEAST FLORIDA ESSENTIALS

TRANSPORTATION

BY AIR

The main airport for the region is Jacksonville International (JAX). It's served by AirTran, American, Continental, Delta, Express Jet, Frontier, jetBlue, Midway, Northwest, Southwest, United Express, and US Airways. AirTran, Continental, Delta, US Airways, and Vintage Props & Jets serve Daytona Beach International Airport (DAB). Gainesville Regional Airport (GNV) is served by Continental, Delta, and US Airways. Although Orlando isn't part of the area, visitors to northeastern Florida often choose to arrive at Orlando International Airport (MCO) because of the huge number of convenient flights. Driving east from Orlando on the Beeline Expressway brings you to Cocoa Beach in about an hour. Reach Daytona, about a two-hour drive, by taking the Beeline Expressway to Interstate 95 and driving north.

Contacts AirTran (☎800/247–8726). **American** (☎800/433–7300). **Continental** (☎800/523–3273). **Delta** (☎800/221–1212). **Express Jet** (☎888/958–9538). **Frontier** (☎800/432–1359). **jetBlue** (☎800/538–2583). **Northwest** (☎800/225–2525). **Southwest** (☎800/435–9792). **United Express** (☎800/241–6522). **US Airways** (☎800/428–4322). **Vintage Props & Jets** (☎800/852–0275).

AIRPORTS & TRANSFERS At Jacksonville International, free shuttles run from the terminal to all parking lots (except the garage) around the clock. Taxi service is available from a number of companies, including Gator City Taxi and Yellow Cab, with fares to downtown approximately $30 and $55 to the beaches and Amelia Island. Shuttle service is available from Gator City Shuttle for approximately $32 for one to four people going downtown, $47 for one to four people going to the beaches and Amelia Island. Limousine service is available from Carey Jacksonville for approximately $89 to downtown and $96 to the beaches and Amelia Island

3

(one to four people), and reservations are required. From Daytona Beach International Airport, taxi fare to beach hotels runs about $18 to $25. Taxi companies include Yellow Cab and Checker Cab. DOTS Transit Service has scheduled service connecting the Daytona Beach and Orlando International airports, the Sheraton Palm Coast area, DeLand (including its train station), New Smyrna Beach, Sanford, and Deltona; fares are $35 one-way and $65 round-trip between the Daytona and Orlando airports, $32 one-way and $59 round-trip from the Orlando airport to DeLand or Deltona. From the Gainesville Regional Airport, taxi fare to the center of Gainesville is about $20; some hotels provide free airport pickup.

Airport Contacts Daytona Beach International Airport (*[DAB]* ☎ *386/248–8069* ⊕ *www.flydaytonafirst.com*). **Gainesville Regional Airport** (*[GNV]* ☎ *352/373–0249* ⊕ *www.gra-gnv.com*). **Jacksonville International Airport** (*[JAX]* ☎ *904/741–4902* ⊕ *www.jia.aero*). **Orlando International Airport** (*[MCO]* ☎ *407/825–2001* ⊕ *www.orlandoairports.net*).

Transfer Contacts Carey Jacksonville (☎ *904/992–2022*). **Checker Cab** (☎ *904/765–9999*). **DOTS Transit Service** (☎ *386/257–5411 or 800/231–1965*). **Gator City Shuttle** (☎ *904/741–6650*). **Gator City Taxi** (☎ *904/741–0008*). **Yellow Cab** (☎ *904/260–1111*).

BY BOAT

Connecting the north and south banks of the St. Johns River, in Jacksonville, the S.S. Marine Taxi runs between several locations, including the Crowne Plaza Jacksonville Riverfront and the Jacksonville Landing. The one-way trip takes about five minutes. During football season the water taxi also makes trips to Jacksonville Municipal Stadium on game days and for special events like the Florida/Georgia game. The ferry runs Sunday–Thursday 11 AM–9 PM; Friday and Saturday 11 AM–11 PM (except during rain or other bad weather), with special hours on game days and for special events. Round-trip fare is $5 adults, $4 children; one-way fare is $3 adults, $2 children.

Contacts S.S. Marine Taxi (☎ *904/733–7782* ⊕ *www.jaxwatertaxi.com*).

BY BUS

Greyhound Lines serves the region, with full-service terminals in Jacksonville, Daytona Beach, DeLand, Gainesville, Melbourne, Ocala, St. Augustine, and Melbourne. The Jacksonville Transportation Authority (JTA) serves Jacksonville and the beaches with weekday service to Orange Park, Palatka, and Green Cove Springs. Daytona Beach has an excellent bus network, Votran, which serves the beach area, airport, shopping malls, and major arteries, including service to DeLand and New Smyrna Beach and the Express Link to Orlando. Exact fare is required for Votran ($1–$2) and JTA ($1–$1.50).

Contacts Greyhound Lines (☎ *800/231–2222* ⊕ *www.greyhound.com*). **Jacksonville Transportation Authority** (☎ *904/630–3100* ⊕ *www.jtafla.com*). **Votran** (☎ *386/756–7496* ⊕ *www.votran.com*).

BY CAR

East–west traffic travels the northern part of the state on Interstate 10, a cross-country highway stretching from Santa Monica to Jacksonville. Farther south, Interstate 4 connects Florida's west and east coasts. Signs on Interstate 4 designate it an east–west route, but actually the road rambles northeast from Tampa to Orlando, then heads north–northeast to Daytona. Two interstates head north–south on Florida's peninsula: Interstate 95 on the east coast (from Miami to Houlton, Maine) and Interstate 75 on the west. If you want to drive as close to the Atlantic as possible and are not in a hurry, stick with A1A. It runs along the barrier islands, changing its name several times along the way. Where there are no bridges between islands, cars must return to the mainland via causeways; some are low, with drawbridges that open for boat traffic on the inland waterway, and there can be unexpected delays. The Buccaneer Trail, which overlaps part of Route A1A, goes from St. Augustine north to Mayport (where a ferry is part of the state highway system), through marshlands and beaches, to the 300-year-old seaport town of Fernandina Beach, and then finally into Fort Clinch State Park. Route 13, also known as the William Bartram Trail, runs from Jacksonville to East Palatka along the east side of the St. Johns River through tiny hamlets. It's one of the most scenic drives in north Florida—a two-laner lined with huge oaks that hug the riverbanks—very Old Florida. U.S. 17 travels the west side of the river, passing through Green Cove Springs and Palatka. Route 40 runs east–west through the Ocala National Forest, giving a nonstop view of stately pines and bold wildlife; short side roads lead to parks, springs, picnic areas, and campgrounds.

BY TRAIN

Amtrak schedules stops in Jacksonville, Daytona Beach, DeLand, Waldo (near Gainesville), Ocala, and Palatka. The Auto Train carries cars between Sanford (25 miles north of Orlando) and Lorton, Virginia (just south of Washington, D.C.). Schedules vary depending on the season.

Contacts Amtrak (☎ *800/872-7245* ⊕ *www.amtrak.com*).

CONTACTS & RESOURCES

EMERGENCIES

All of the following hospitals have 24-hour emergency rooms.

Emergency Services ☎911.

Hospitals Baptist Medical Center (⊠ *800 Prudential Dr., Jacksonville* ☎ *904/202-2000*). **Baptist Medical Center Beaches** (⊠ *1350 13th Ave. S., Jacksonville Beach* ☎ *904/627-2900*). **Halifax Medical Center** (⊠ *303 N. Clyde Morris Blvd., Daytona Beach* ☎ *386/254-4000*). **Orange Park Medical Center** (⊠ *2001 Kingsley Ave., Orange Park* ☎ *904/276-8500*). **Shands at AGH** (⊠ *801 S.W. 2nd Ave., Gainesville* ☎ *352/372-4321*). **Shands Jacksonville** (⊠ *655 W. 8th St., Jacksonville* ☎ *904/244-0411*). **St. Luke's Hospital** (⊠ *4201 Belfort Rd., Jacksonville* ☎ *904/296-3700*). **St. Vincent's Medical Center** (⊠ *1 Shircliff Lane, Jacksonville* ☎ *904/308-7300*).

TOURS

In Jacksonville, River Cruises has relaxing lunch and dinner-dancing cruises and private sightseeing charters aboard the *Annabelle Lee* and *Lady St. Johns* paddleboats; schedules vary with the season. The Jacksonville Historical Society arranges tours only for groups of 20 or more. On Amelia Island, Amelia River Cruises and Charters takes guests on a one-hour narrated tour of Fernandina's historic waterfront, salt marshes, and Cumberland Sound. In St. Augustine, Old Town Trolley Tours conducts fully narrated tours covering more than 100 points of interest. As the nation's oldest continually operated carriage company, the St. Augustine Transfer Company offers historic and ghost tours via horse-drawn carriage, as well as the Spirits of St. Augustine Ghost Walk. In Daytona Beach, A Tiny Cruise Line leaves from the public marina and explores the Intracoastal Waterway. Tour Time, Inc. offers custom group and individual motorcoach tours of Jacksonville, Amelia Island, and St. Augustine, as well as overnight trips to Silver Springs, Kennedy Space Center, Orlando, Okefenokee Swamp, and Savannah. Prior arrangements are required.

Contacts **River Cruises** (☎ *904/306–2200* ⊕ *www.jaxrivercruises.com*). **Jacksonville Historical Society** (☎ *904/665–0064* ⊕ *www.jaxhistory.com*). **Amelia River Cruises and Charters** (☎ *904/261–9972* ⊕ *www.ameliarivercruises.com*). **Old Town Trolley Tours** (☎ *904/829–3800* ⊕ *www.historictours.com/staugustine*). **St. Augustine Transfer Company** (☎ *904/829–2391* ⊕ *www.staugustinetransfer.com*). **A Tiny Cruise Line** (☎ *386/226–2343* ⊕ *www.visitdaytona.com/tinycruise*). **Tour Time, Inc.** (☎ *904/282–8500 or 800/822–4278* ⊕ *www.tourtimeinc.com*). **Florida Coastal Cruises** (☎ *386/428–0201 or 800/881–2628* ⊕ *www.manatee cruise.com*).

VISITOR INFORMATION

Most visitor information offices are open weekdays from 8 or 9 to 5. The St. Augustine Visitor Information Center is open daily 8:30 to 5:30.

Contacts **Amelia Island Tourist Development Council** (✉ *961687 Gateway Blvd., Suite G, Amelia Island* ☎ *904/261–6997 or 800/226–3542* ⊕ *www.amelia island.org*). **Cocoa Beach Convention and Visitor's Bureau** (✉ *400 Fortenberry Rd., Merritt Island* ☎ *321/454–2022 or 877/321–8474* ⊕ *www.visitcocoabeach. com*). **Daytona Beach Area Convention and Visitors Bureau** (✉ *126 E. Orange Ave., Daytona Beach* ☎ *800/544–0415* ⊕ *www.daytonabeach.com*). **Gainesville/Alachua County Visitors and Convention Bureau** (✉ *30 E. University Ave., Gainesville* ☎ *352/374–5260 or 866/778–5002* ⊕ *www.visitgainesville. net*). **Jacksonville and The Beaches Convention & Visitors Bureau** (✉ *550 Water St., Suite 1000, Jacksonville* ☎ *904/798–9100 or 800/733–2668* ⊕ *www. visitjacksonville.com*). **St. Augustine, Ponte Vedra & The Beaches Visitors & Convention Bureau** (✉ *88 Riberia St., Suite 400, St. Augustine* ☎ *904/829–1711 or 800/653–2489* ⊕ *www.getaway4florida.com*).

Walt Disney World & the Orlando Area

Walt Disney World, Orlando

WORD OF MOUTH

"My short list of must-dos to us would include: Magic Kingdom—Splash Mountain, Pirates of the Carib, Haunted Mansion, Buzz, Spectromagic (night parade), Wishes (fireworks) ; Epcot—Soarin', Test Track, American Adventure, Illuminations (night show) ; Universal Studios—the new stunt driving show, MuppetVision, Tower of Terror, Fantasmic (night show) ; Animal Kingdom—Safari, Lion King show, Everest, Nemo show."

—DancingBearMD

WELCOME TO WALT DISNEY WORLD & THE ORLANDO AREA

TOP REASONS TO GO

★ **A Little Bit of Fantasy:** There's nothing quite like passing beneath the WDW Railroad to enter the Magic Kingdom, leaving behind reality to enter a world of fantasy, filled with pastel, gingerbread-trim buildings, sparkling sidewalks, and chance encounters with your favorite characters.

★ **Thrills and Chills:** Tap into your inner daredevil and let your hair hang upside down on one of Central Orlando's many loop-de-loop roller coasters and water rides.

★ **'Round the World in 80 Minutes:** Take an entire day to stroll through Epcot's 11 countries, complete with perfect replicas of foreign monuments (the Doge's Palace, anyone?), intimate performances, and deliciously traditional cuisine.

★ **Animal Planet:** Go on safari in Disney's Animal Kingdom, let Shamu splash you at SeaWorld, kiss a dolphin at Discovery Cove, and watch gators wrestle at Gatorland.

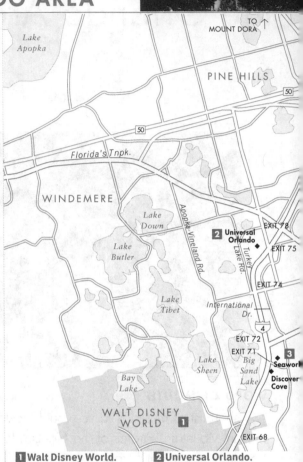

1 Walt Disney World.
Walt Disney's original decree that his parks be ever-changing, along with some healthy competition from Universal Studios and SeaWorld, has kept the Disney Imagineers dreaming up new entertainment and installing higher-tech thrills and attractions. Disney is still the king of all theme parks.

2 Universal Orlando.
While Disney creates a fantasy world for those who love fairy tales, Universal Orlando is geared to older kids, adults, and anyone who enjoys pop culture. Movie and TV fans will love this place.

GETTING ORIENTED

At 40 square mi, Disney World is twice the size of Manhattan, with four major theme parks—the Magic Kingdom, Epcot, Disney's Hollywood Studios, and Disney's Animal Kingdom—plus water parks, golf courses, and a host of other attractions. Straddling north and south Florida, Orlando is the point of arrival for many visitors. Aside from its proximity to all things Disney, it is about two hours from Tampa to the west, St. Augustine to the northeast, and it's within an hour of Kennedy Space Center and many Atlantic beaches.

4

3 SeaWorld & Discovery Cove. Less glitzy than Walt Disney World or Universal, SeaWorld and its sister park, Discovery Cove, are definitely worth a visit for a low-key, relaxing, ocean-theme experience. Of course, if you want to get more keyed up, pay a call on SeaWorld's new water park, Aquatica.

4 Away from the Parks. Once you've exhausted the theme parks, or have been exhausted by them, turn your attention to a wealth of other area offerings. There are museums, parks, and gardens galore, highlighting the cultural and natural heritage of this part of the South.

WALT DISNEY WORLD & THE ORLANDO AREA PLANNER

When to Go

For Walt Disney World avoid school holidays—essentially mid-June through mid-August, Christmastime, Spring Break, and holiday weekends like Presidents Day—which are the most crowded times in the parks. If you have school children, it's nice to avoid prime break times, but if you can't, then plan your itinerary a little more tightly. Spring and fall are the best times to visit.

Getting to & Around Orlando/Disney

All major and most discount airlines fly to Orlando International Airport (MCO). If you're booked into a Walt Disney World Resort, take advantage of the Magical Express Service that delivers you and your luggage, at no cost, from your home airport to your hotel and back again (you must book this service before departing on your trip). Disney's own fleet of buses, trams, boats, and monorail trains make it a breeze to travel throughout Mickey's world. To explore beyond the theme parks, be sure to have a good map—Orlando is a sprawling metropolitan area and some areas are tricky to traverse.

For more transportation info see the Essentials section at the end of this chapter.

About the Restaurants

Food in the parks ranges from fast to fabulous. Hamburgers, chicken fingers, and fries dominate at most of the counter-service places, but fresh sandwiches, salads, and fruit are available, too. Without reservations, you may find yourself having a burger for dinner, or having to leave Walt Disney World. Although some of Orlando's top restaurants are in Walt Disney World or Universal, many others are outside the parks. Sand Lake Road, International Drive, and Celebration all have excellent restaurants.

About the Hotels

Your basic options come down to properties that are (1) owned and operated by Disney on WDW grounds, (2) not owned or operated by Disney but on Disney property, and (3) not on WDW property. If you're coming to Orlando for only a few days and are interested solely in the Magic Kingdom, Epcot, and the other Disney attractions, the resorts on Disney property—whether or not they're owned by Disney—are the most convenient. But if you plan to spend time sightseeing in and around Orlando, it makes sense to look into the hotels on International Drive or in Kissimmee. Orlando hotels tend to be a little pricier than elsewhere in Florida.

What It Costs

DINING & LODGING PRICE CATEGORIES

	¢	$	$$	$$$	$$$$
Restaurants					
	under $8	$8–$15	$15–$20	$20–$30	over $30
Hotels					
	under $80	$80–$140	$140–$220	$220–$280	over $280

Prices are per person for a main course at dinner. Hotel price categories reflect the range between the least and most expensive standard double rooms in nonholiday high season, based on the European Plan (with no meals) unless otherwise noted. City and state taxes (10%–12%) are extra.

Revised by
Jennie Hess

THERE ARE TWO KINDS OF TRAVELERS TO WALT DISNEY WORLD.
There's the family that just shows up, trusting the reputation of Disney to guide them along the way. They'll arrive at the Magic Kingdom around 11, wander through Main Street and its stores, and then reach the other side of Cinderella's castle—wondering what to ride first. One child will want to go to Space Mountain, while another will start crying the farther the group gets from Dumbo, which now has a 90-minute line. This family might split up so each child can get in at least one preferred ride before lunch, or they might stick together, causing one child or the other to have a meltdown that ruins everyone's mood. Regardless, by the time they've struggled through the lines at rides and lunch counters, the late-afternoon sun will be beating down.

Other travelers do some research. They make their dining reservations in advance, and they decide which rides are must-sees for each person in their party. They learn the cardinal rule of Disney World touring—get there early—and they manage to avoid the worst lines. Above all, they remember that they can't do everything, and they relax long enough to enjoy their experience without stressing out about how much they need to do to merit the cost of their tickets.

Sure, the first family will still have fun at Walt Disney World, but they'll wait in more lines, probably spend more money, and stress out more than the second family.

EXPLORING WALT DISNEY WORLD

The secret to enjoying Disney with children is to have a good plan but be willing to take small detours when magical moments occur. You can probably persuade your children to rush to the big-deal rides early in the morning, when the timing matters most, but don't expect them to keep up that pace all day. Cushion your itinerary with extra time, and allow them to pause wherever they want as much as possible. When it comes to a Disney vacation with kids, let your mantra be "quality over quantity." It's better to tour the parks in a relaxed fashion than it is to antagonize your little ones by fleeing to Pirates of the Caribbean, passing up an opportunity to hobnob with Princess Jasmine along the way, only to find a 30-minute wait at the entrance to the ride. Jasmine definitely won't be there when you get out of the ride.

Finally, try to avoid building unrealistic expectations for yourself and your kids that may cause disappointment and tears. Let each family member choose one or two top rides or attractions for each park, and be sure those are part of your itinerary. Everything else should be icing on the cake. Run through the plan before you enter the park; if children know ahead of time that souvenirs are limited to one per person and that ice-cream snacks come after lunch, they're likely to be more patient than if they're clueless about your plans and dazzled by every snack and merchandise cart they discover. If you're towing an infant or toddler, be prepared to relax on a park bench while your little one snoozes in the stroller. Don't think about which ride you're missing while the rest of the family decides to ride and meet you later. Just kick back and soak up some of the remarkable detail that Disney's funmeisters have built into the enchanting scenery that surrounds you.

BEST WAYS TO SAVE

Don't buy a theme-park ticket for the day of your arrival or the day of your departure. It's not worth spending $60 for just a couple of hours in the parks. Instead, use those days to visit Downtown Disney, Disney's Boardwalk, or Universal CityWalk, or lounge around your hotel pool.

Buy your tickets as soon as you know you're going. Prices typically go up about once a year, so you might beat a price hike—and save a little money.

Avoid holidays and school vacation times, or go off-season. You can see more in less time, and lodging rates are lower.

If you plan to eat in a full-service restaurant, do it at lunch. Then have a light dinner. Lunchtime prices are almost always lower than dinnertime prices. Also look for "early bird" menus, which offer dinner entrées at reduced prices during late afternoon and early evening hours.

Watch your shopping carefully. Theme-park merchandisers are excellent at displaying the goods so that you (or your children) can't resist them. Most articles for sale are also available at home—for quite a bit less. One way to cope is to give every member of your family a souvenir budget. Another good option is to shop local CVS or Walgreens stores for cheap but cool souvenirs.

Bring essentials with you. Remember to pack your hat, sunscreen, camera, memory card or film, batteries, diapers, and aspirin. These items are all very expensive within the theme parks.

HOW LONG TO STAY

To have a rich and full Orlando resort experience, plan on a trip of seven or eight days. This gives you time to see all of the parks at Universal and WDW and to take in at least one water park, to sample the restaurants and entertainment, and to spend a bit of time around the pool. Figure on an additional day for every other area theme park you want to visit, and then add your travel time to and from home.

If you can, make time for shopping and for exploring Orlando. Central Florida has some great high-end and discount shopping and some visitor treasures like Green Meadows Farm in Kissimmee and the Charles Hosmer Morse Museum of American Art, with the world's largest collection of Tiffany glass, in Winter Park.

OPENING HOURS

The major area theme parks, including those in Walt Disney World, are open 365 days a year. Opening times vary, but generally hover around 9. Certain attractions within the parks may not open until 10 or 11 AM, however, and parks usually observe shorter hours during the off-seasons in January, February, April, May, September, and October. In general, the longest days are during prime summer months and over the year-end holidays, when the Magic Kingdom may be open as late as 10 or 11, later on New Year's Eve; Epcot is open until 9 or 9:30 in the World Showcase area and at several Future World attractions, the Studios until 7 or 8:30. At other times, the Magic Kingdom closes around 7 or 8—but there are variations, so call ahead. Most of the year, the Animal Kingdom closes at 5, though during peak holiday seasons it may open at 8 and close at 7 or 8.

The parking lots open at least an hour before the parks do. If you arrive at the Magic Kingdom turnstiles before the official opening time, you can often breakfast in a restaurant on Main Street, which usually opens before the rest of the park, and be ready to dash to one of the popular attractions in other lands at Rope Drop, the Magic Kingdom's official opening time.

Hours at Typhoon Lagoon and Blizzard Beach are 9 or 10 to 5 daily (until 7—occasionally 10—in summer).

The shops at Downtown Disney stay open as late as 11 PM in summer and during holidays.

You can check exact opening and closing times by calling the parks directly or checking their Web sites.

EXTRA MAGIC HOURS

The Extra Magic Hours program gives Disney resort guests free early and late-night admission to certain parks on specified days—call ahead for information about each park's "magic hours" days to plan your early- and late-visit strategies.

SEASONAL CLOSURES

Disney sometimes closes rides and attractions for refurbishment or maintenance during slower seasons. Before you finalize your travel schedule, call the theme parks to find out about any planned closures so you don't show up at the Magic Kingdom to find Peter Pan's Flight grounded for the week.

TAKING THE KIDS OUT OF SCHOOL

For many parents, it's worth avoiding the frustration of the crowds to take the kids out of school for a couple of days. We agree that this can make for a more enjoyable trip, but it's a good idea to consult with your child's teachers before making plans. Hopefully the teachers can advise you about the best time of year to go and help create a study plan to make certain your child's education isn't compromised. For elementary-school kids, there are ways of making the trip educational. For example, your child could write about the different countries featured at Epcot in lieu of a missed homework assignment. One last note: although it may be fine to take an elementary-school child out of school for a few days, missing several days of middle or high school could set your child back for the rest of the semester, so consider this option very carefully.

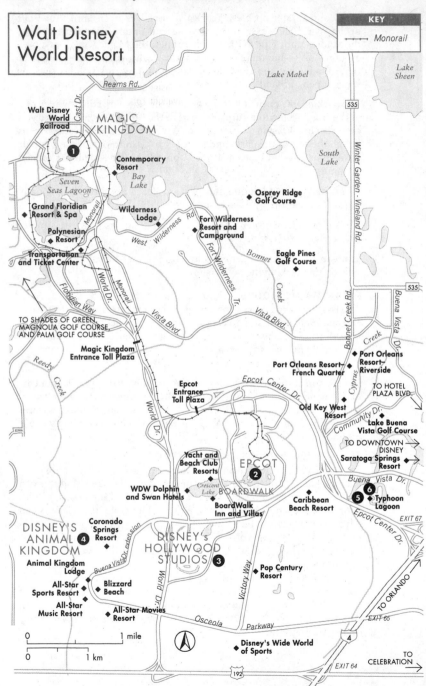

Walt Disney World Resort

KEY

←I—I—I→ Monorail

Reams Rd.

Lake Mabel

Lake Sheen

535

Cast Dr.

MAGIC KINGDOM

Walt Disney World Railroad

1

South Lake

Winter Garden - Vineland Rd.

Contemporary Resort

Bay Lake

Osprey Ridge Golf Course

Seven Seas Lagoon

Grand Floridian Resort & Spa

Wilderness Lodge

West Wilderness Rd.

Fort Wilderness Resort and Campground

Fort Wilderness Tr.

Bonnet Creek

Eagle Pines Golf Course

Polynesian Resort

Transportation and Ticket Center

Monorail

Floridian Way

World Dr.

Monorail

Vista Blvd.

Vista Blvd.

535

Bonnet Creek Rd.

Buena Vista Dr.

TO SHADES OF GREEN, MAGNOLIA GOLF COURSE, AND PALM GOLF COURSE

Reedy Creek

Magic Kingdom Entrance Toll Plaza

World Dr.

Epcot Center Dr.

Port Orleans Resort– French Quarter

Cyprus Creek

Port Orleans Resort– Riverside

TO HOTEL PLAZA BLVD.

Epcot Entrance Toll Plaza

Old Key West Resort

Community Dr.

Lake Buena Vista Golf Course

TO DOWNTOWN DISNEY

Yacht and Beach Club Resorts

EPCOT

2

Saratoga Springs Resort

Crescent Lake

BOARDWALK

Buena Vista Dr.

WDW Dolphin and Swan Hotels

BoardWalk Inn and Villas

Caribbean Beach Resort

5

6

Typhoon Lagoon

Epcot Center Dr.

EXIT 67

DISNEY'S ANIMAL KINGDOM

4

Coronado Springs Resort

DISNEY'S HOLLYWOOD STUDIOS

3

Buena Vista Dr. extension

Animal Kingdom Lodge

World Dr.

Pop Century Resort

TO ORLANDO

All-Star Sports Resort

Blizzard Beach

Victory Way

All-Star Music Resort

All-Star Movies Resort

EXIT 65

Osceola Parkway

0 _____ 1 mile
0 _____ 1 km

Disney's Wide World of Sports

4

EXIT 64

TO CELEBRATION

192

WDW WHAT'S WHERE

❶ The Magic Kingdom. What most people imagine to be Walt Disney World—the Magic Kingdom—actually is a small, but emblematic, part of it. For many of those who have grown up with Cinderella, Snow White, Peter Pan, Dumbo, and Pinocchio, it's a magical place. It's the site of such world-famous attractions as Space Mountain, Pirates of the Caribbean, Splash Mountain, and "it's a small world," as well as newer thrills like Stitch's Great Escape and Mickey's Philharmagic. *Take the Magic Kingdom–U.S. 192 exit (Exit 64) off I–4.*

❷ Epcot. Designed to promote enthusiasm for discovery and learning, WDW's Epcot is a sweeping combination of amusement park and world's fair. In Future World, the focus inside 10 landmark pavilions is on the fascinating discoveries of science and technology. Don't miss the funny, often startling, 3-D film and special-effects attraction *Honey, I Shrunk the Audience,* and if you can handle an intense simulation blast-off, try out the Mission: SPACE ride to Mars. In the second major area of Epcot, the World Showcase, you can tour 11 different countries without the jet lag. *Take the Epcot–Downtown Disney exit (Exit 67) off I–4.*

❸ Disney's Hollywood Studios. This is Disney's re-creation of Hollywood as it might have been in the good old days. Amazing attractions are the key to "The Studios'" success: there's the Rock 'n' Roller Coaster Starring Aerosmith, the Twilight Zone Tower of Terror, the classic Great Movie Ride, and two stunt shows. Other not-to-be-missed attractions include the closing show, *Fantasmic!,* and the Magic of Disney Animation. *Take the Disney's Hollywood Studios exit (Exit 64) off I–4.*

❹ Disney's Animal Kingdom. In the center of the park, the huge, sculpted Tree of Life rises 145 feet, towering over all the other trees in the park. Walkways encircle the tree, leading to attractions, including a water ride, a safari ride, and several shows in the Asia, Africa, and Dinoland areas of the park. With a 100-acre savanna and wildlife preserve, the Animal Kingdom is the largest of all the Disney parks. *Take the Disney's Animal Kingdom exit (Exit 65) off I–4.*

❺–❻ The Disney Water Parks. Blizzard Beach and Typhoon Lagoon are two separate water parks that are always jam-packed when the weather's steamy. The best ride—or is it the worst?—is the wild, 55-mph dead-drop to a splashy landing from Blizzard Beach's Summit Plummet, which feels as fast as it sounds. Water babies love Typhoon Lagoon's scaled-down Ketchakiddie Creek and Blizzard Beach's Tyke's Peak.

4

DINING AT DISNEY

CHARACTER MEALS

At special breakfasts, lunches, and dinners in many Walt Disney World restaurants, Mickey, Donald, Goofy, Chip 'n' Dale, Cinderella, and other favorite characters sign autographs and pose for snapshots. Universal's Islands of Adventure has a character breakfast, so your children can enjoy pizza or chicken fingers with Spiderman and their favorite Seuss characters. Talk with your children to find out which characters

GREAT ITINERARIES

Numbers correspond to the Orlando Area map.

4 DAYS

No stay in the area would be complete without a visit to the **Magic Kingdom**. The next day, take your pick between the more sophisticated **Epcot** and state-of-the-art **Universal Islands of Adventure**. On Day 3, see **Universal Studios** or the smaller and more manageable **Disney's Hollywood Studios**. On your fourth day go for **Disney's Animal Kingdom** or **SeaWorld Orlando**. Be sure to catch fireworks one night and one of the local dinner-show extravaganzas on another.

6 DAYS

Spend the first four days exploring in this order: **Magic Kingdom**, **Universal Islands of Adventure**, **Epcot**, and **Disney's Animal Kingdom** or **Universal Studios**. At night make sure you get to some fireworks, sample at least one of the now-ubiquitous themed dining experiences, and visit Pleasure Island, Downtown Disney, or **CityWalk at Universal**. After all that theme park-ing, you'll need a rest. Depending on your interests and the ages of your children, use Day 5 to relax and play at a Disney water park like **Typhoon Lagoon**, or venture into Orlando and Winter Park. Take a leisurely boat tour and visit the **Charles Hosmer Morse Museum of American Art** or the **Orlando Science Center** for its great interactive activities before relaxing at your hotel. The sixth day should be for **SeaWorld Orlando** or the more intimate **Discovery Cove**. On your last evening take in Cirque du Soleil's "La Nouba" or a dinner show, perhaps SeaWorld's luau, Disney's Hoop-Dee-Doo Revue, or Kissimmee's Arabian Nights show.

they most want to see; then call the Disney or Universal dining reservations line and speak with the representative about what's available.

Reservations are recommended because these hugging-and-feeding frenzies are wildly popular, but if you haven't reserved ahead, try showing up early and you may get lucky. It's a good idea to have your character meal near the end of your visit, when your little ones will be used to seeing these large and sometimes frightening figures; they're also a good way to spend the morning on the day you check out.

MEAL PLANS

If you book a package, you can add on a meal plan for more savings. The Magic Your Way Dining Plan allows you one table-service meal, one counter-service meal, and one snack per day of your trip at more than 100 theme-park and resort restaurants. You can add the plan to your package for $38.99 per adult, per day, and $10.99 per child age 3–9, per day (tax and gratuities included). When you consider that the average Disney table-service meal for a child runs about $10.99 *without* gratuity, you realize this plan is a steal. Another advantage of the plan is that you can swap two table-service meals for one of Disney's dinner shows or an evening at one of the high-end signature restaurants like California Grill.

RESERVATIONS

Make your dining reservations through the **WDW Reservation Center** (☎407/939–3463) before you leave home so you don't have to worry about finding a restaurant every night. Restaurants at Disney book up fast. Ask the reservationist about the cancellation policy—at a handful of restaurants, your credit card will be charged $10–$50 per person, depending on the restaurant, if you don't give 24-to-48 hours notice. Some dinner shows and other special dining events like the Mother's Day Brunch at Epcot charge the full cost to your card if you don't cancel within 48–72 hours. Make tee time reservations to play at any of Walt Disney World's six golf courses at ⊕ www.disneyworldgolf.com or by calling **WDW Golf Reservations** (☎407/939–4653).

WALT DISNEY WORLD ESSENTIALS

ADMISSION

Visiting Walt Disney World isn't cheap. Everyone 10 and older pays adult price. In addition, Disney changes its prices about once a year and without much notice. For that reason, you may save yourself a few bucks if you buy your WDW tickets as soon as you know for sure you'll be going.

DISCOUNT COUPONS

Coupon books, such as those available from **Entertainment Travel Editions** (☎800/445–4137 ⊕www.entertainment.com) for around $25 or $30, can be good sources for discounts on rental cars, admission to attractions, meals, and other typical purchases. Hotel and restaurant lobbies also often have racks with flyers that advertise business with coupons.

The **Orlando Magicard** (☎800/643—9492 ⊕www.orlandoinfo.com/magicard), offered for free by the Orlando–Orange County Convention & Visitors Bureau, provides discounts for many attractions, restaurants, and shopping-mall stores. Download it from the Web site or order it over the phone.

BUYING TICKETS

IN ADVANCE

You can get discounted three-or-more-day tickets from the **Orlando Convention & Visitors Bureau** at www.orlandoticketsales.com or 800/255–5786 or 407/363–5872.

IN ORLANDO

You can buy tickets at the Transportation and Ticket Center in the Magic Kingdom (also known as the TTC); at ticket booths in front of the other theme-park entrances; in all on-site resorts if you're a registered guest; at the Walt Disney World store at Orlando International Airport; and at various hotels and other sites around Orlando.

THE TICKETING SYSTEM

Once you've decided to take the plunge, Disney fortunately makes buying tickets easy and painless. The **Magic Your Way** ticketing system is all

The Most Important Advice You'll Get

If you remember nothing else, keep in mind these essential strategies, tried and tested by generations of Disney World fans. They're the Eight Commandments for touring Walt Disney World.

■ **Make dining reservations before you leave home, especially for character dining experiences.** If you don't, you might find yourself eating a hamburger (again) or leaving Walt Disney World for dinner. The on-site restaurants book up fast.

■ **Arrive at the parks at least 30 minutes before they open.** We know, it's your vacation and you want to sleep in. So go to the Caribbean. Or the mountains. Don't go to Walt Disney World, unless you've been there a hundred times and you plan to sit by the pool and play golf more than go on rides. If you're like most families and you want to make the most of your time and money, plan to be up by at least 7:30 every day. After transit time, it'll take you 10–15 minutes to park and get to the gates. If you know you want to use the lockers or ATMs, or rent strollers, get there 45 minutes in advance.

■ **See the top attractions first thing in the morning.** And we mean first thing. As in before 10 AM. Decide in advance which attractions you don't want to miss, find out where they are, and hotfoot it to them when the park opens. If you miss any in the morning, the other good times to see the most popular attractions are right before closing and during the parades. Otherwise, use Fastpass.

■ **Use Fastpass.** It's worth saying twice. The system is free, easy, and it's your ticket to the top attractions with little or no waiting in line.

■ **Build in rest time.** This is the greatest way to avoid becoming overly hot, tired, and grumpy. We recommend starting early and then leaving the theme parks around 3 or 4, the hottest and most crowded time of day. After a couple hours' rest at your hotel, you can have an early dinner and head back to the parks to watch one of the nighttime spectaculars or to ride a couple more of the big-deal rides (lines are shorter around closing time).

■ **Create a rough itinerary, but leave room for spontaneity.** Decide which parks to see on each day, and know your priorities, but don't try to plot your trip hour by hour. Instead, break up the day into morning, afternoon, and evening sections. If you're staying at a Disney resort, find out which parks are offering the Extra Magic Hours on which days, and plan to take advantage of the program.

■ **Eat at off hours.** Have a quick, light breakfast at 7 or 8, lunch at 11, and dinner at 5 or 6 to avoid the mealtime rush hours. Between 11:30 and 2:30 during high season you can wait in line up to 30 minutes for a so-called fast-food lunch in the parks.

■ **Save the high-capacity sit-down shows for the afternoon.** You usually don't have to wait in line so long for shows, and you'll be relieved at the chance to sit in an air-conditioned theater during the hottest part of the day.

about flexibility. You can tailor your ticket to your interests and desired length of stay. The more days you stay, the greater your savings on per-day ticket prices. A one-day ticket costs $71 for anyone age 10 and up, while a five-day ticket costs $215 or $43 per day.

Once you decide how many days to stay, you'll want to decide what options to add on. The **Park Hopper** option lets you move from park to park within the day and adds $45 to the price of your ticket, no matter how many days your ticket covers. So it's an expensive option for a one- or two-day ticket, but it can be well worth the cost for a four-day trip, especially if you know what you want to see at each park.

The **Water Parks & More** option allows a certain number of visits to the water parks and other Disney attractions: Typhoon Lagoon, Blizzard Beach, Pleasure Island, DisneyQuest, and Disney's Wide World of Sports complex. You pay $50 to add this option to your ticket, and you get 2 to 10 visits, depending on the length of your stay.

The **No Expiration** option can save you money if you know for sure you're coming back to Disney World again. For example, say you're planning a five-day trip one year, plus a weekend trip sometime the next year. You can buy a seven-day ticket, use it five days during your first trip and keep the remaining two-days' worth of theme-park fun for your next trip to Orlando. It will cost you $15 to $95 to add the No Expiration option to your two- to seven-day tickets.

Note that all Disney admission passes are nontransferable. The ID is your fingerprint. Although you slide your pass through the reader like people with single-day tickets, you also have to slip your finger into a special V-shape fingerprint reader before you'll be admitted.

HOTEL & TICKET PACKAGES   Disney's Magic Your Way value, moderate, and deluxe packages help families keep expenses in check by bundling hotel and theme-park expenses. For as low as $1,600, a family of four can plan a six-night, seven-day Magic Your Way Vacation that includes complimentary transportation from the airport and extra hours in the parks. Lower-end package rates offer value-resort accommodations; prices go up with moderate or deluxe accommodations. All Disney resort guests get free bus, boat, and monorail transportation across the property. Visit ⊕*www.disneyworld.com* to explore the different package options.

FASTPASS

Imagine taking a trip to Disney and managing to avoid most of the lines. Fastpass is your ticket to this terrific scenario, and it's included in regular park admission. Pocket your theme-park ticket upon entry, then insert it into a special machine at one of several Fastpass-equipped attractions at each Disney park. Out comes your Fastpass, printed with a one-hour window of time during which you can return to get into the fast line. *Don't forget to take your park ticket back, too.* While you wait for your Fastpass appointment to mature, enjoy other attractions in the park.

It's important to note that once you've made one Fastpass appointment you cannot make another until you're within the window of time for your first appointment. Smart guests save their Fastpass appointments for the most popular attractions, and they make new appointments as quickly as possible after their existing ones mature.

MONEY MATTERS

Be prepared to spend and spend—and spend some more. Despite relatively low airfares and car-rental rates, cash seems to evaporate out of wallets, and credit-card balances seem to increase on exposure to the hot Orlando sun. Theme-park admission is roughly $67 per day per person (for a family of two adults and two children ages 3–9)—not counting all the $2 soft drinks and $20 souvenirs. Hotels range so wildly—from $60 a night (at a few non-Disney hotels) to 10 or more times that—that you have to do some hard thinking about just how much you want to spend. Meal prices away from the theme parks are comparable to those in other midsize cities, ranging from $5 per person at a fast-food chain to $40 entrées at an upscale restaurant.

PARK BASICS: STROLLERS, FIRST AID, ETC.

BABY CARE

The Magic Kingdom's soothing, quiet **Baby Care Center** is next to the Crystal Palace, which lies between Main Street and Adventureland. The other three major Disney parks have similar baby care centers with nursing rooms furnished with rocking chairs. Low lighting levels make these centers comfortable for nursing, though it can get crowded in mid-afternoon in peak season. There are adorable toddler-size toilets (these may be a high point for your just-potty-trained child) as well as supplies such as formula, baby food, pacifiers, disposable diapers, and even children's pain reliever. Changing tables are in all women's rooms and most men's rooms.

BABY SWAP

Parents with small children under the height limit for major attractions have to take turns waiting in the long lines, right? Wrong. In what's unofficially known as the Baby Swap or Rider Switch, both of you queue up, and when it's your turn to board, one stays with the youngsters until the other returns; the waiting partner then rides without waiting again, and your young ones get to ride again with the other grown-up. This policy is not widely advertised at Disney, so it pays to ask attendants at individual rides if the swap is available. Universal Studios calls it a Baby Exchange and has areas set aside for it at most rides.

LOCKERS

Lockers are available near all the theme-park entrances ($5; plus $2 deposit). If you're park-hopping, you can use your locker receipt to acquire a locker at the next park you visit for no extra charge.

LOST CHILDREN

Losing a child in a crowded theme park is one of the most frightening experiences a parent can have, but the one thing to remember is that theme-park security is excellent and crime is practically nonexistent. Theme park staff members are trained to recover lost little ones

MAGIC YOUR WAY PRICE CHART

TICKET OPTIONS								
TICKET	**10-DAY**	**7-DAY**	**6-DAY**	**5-DAY**	**4-DAY**	**3-DAY**	**2-DAY**	**1-DAY**
BASE TICKET								
Ages 10-up	$225	$219	$217	$215	$212	$203	$139	$71
Ages 3-9	$187	$182	$181	$179	$178	$171	$117	$60

Base Ticket admits guest to one of the four major theme parks per day's use.
Park choices are: Magic Kingdom, Epcot, Disney-Hollywood Studios, Disney's Animal Kingdom.

ADD: Park Hopper	$45	$45	$45	$45	$45	$45	$45	$45

Park Hopper option entitles guest to visit more than one theme park per day's use. Park choices are any combination of Magic Kingdom, Epcot, Disney-Hollywood Studios, Disney's Animal Kingdom.

ADD: Water Parks & More	$50 6 visits	$50 7 visits	$50 6 visits	$50 5 visits	$50 4 visits	$50 3 visits	$50 3 visits	$50 3 visits

Water Parks & More option entitles guest to a specified number of visits (between 2 and 5) to a choice of entertainment and recreation venues. Choices are Blizzard Beach, Typhoon Lagoon, DisneyQuest, Pleasure Island, and Wide World of Sports.

ADD: No Expiration	$180	$95	$65	$60	$45	$20	$15	n/a

No expiration means that unused admissions on a ticket may be used any time in the future.
Without this option, tickets expire 14 days after first use.

MINOR PARKS AND ATTRACTIONS		
TICKET	**AGES 10-UP**	**AGES 3-9**
TYPHOON LAGOON OR BLIZZARD BEACH 1-Day 1-Park	$36	$30
DISNEYQUEST 1-Day	$37	$31
DISNEY'S WIDE WORLD OF SPORTS	$10.28	$7.71
CIRQUE DU SOLEIL'S *LA NOUBA*	$65–$114	$52–$91

and deliver them back to you safely. Disney cast members immediately accompany lost children to the Baby Care Center, where you can pick them up. But there are many ways you can avoid losing your child in the first place.

Have everyone in your family wear matching T-shirts or at least the same color, so you can easily find them and they can find you.

If you separate to use the bathroom or for any other reason, pinpoint a meeting location and time in the same area.

Hold tight to your children's hands after parades and during the massive exodus from the parks in the evening. The other times children can be easily separated are during character meet-and-greets, when parents are queuing up for Fastpass appointments, and when children are racing around play areas.

Explain to your kids ahead of time that, if they get lost, they should tell any Disney cast member right away. Cast members are easy to recognize, with their bright theme uniforms, and they always wear a name tag.

PACKAGE PICKUP
Ask the shop clerk to send any large purchase you make to Package Pickup, so you won't have to carry it around all day. Allow three hours for the delivery. The package pickup area is in Town Square next to City Hall.

TRANSPORTATON

CAR RENTAL
You should rent a car if you're staying at an off-site hotel; you want to visit sights or restaurants outside Walt Disney World; you're traveling in a group (four or more people); you like your independence. On the other hand, if you're staying at a Disney hotel and spending all or most of your trip at Disney World, you can rely on Disney's own very efficient transportation system.

RATES **Renting from Alamo, Avis, Budget, Dollar, or National can get you out of the airport the fastest because they have car lots on airport property, a short walk from baggage claim.** The other agencies offer courtesy shuttles to their lots.

EMERGENCY SERVICES
If you have a cell phone, dialing ***347** (***FHP**) will get you the Florida Highway Patrol. Most Florida highways are also patrolled by Road Rangers, a free roadside service that helps stranded motorists with minor problems and can call for a tow truck when there are bigger problems. The **AAA Car Care Center** (☎*407/824–0976*) near the Magic Kingdom is a full-service operation that will provide most emergency services, including free towing even for non-AAA members on Disney property, while it's open (weekdays 7 AM–7PM, Saturday 7 AM–4 PM). On Disney property you can flag a security guard any day until 10 PM for help with minor emergencies, such as a flat tire, dead battery, empty gas tank, or towing. Otherwise call 407/824–4777. You can also gas up

on Buena Vista Drive near Disney's BoardWalk and in the Downtown Disney area across from Pleasure Island.

Expect heavy traffic during rush hours, which are on weekdays 6–10 AM and 4–7 PM. To encourage carpooling, some freeways have special lanes for so-called high-occupancy vehicles (HOV)—cars carrying more than one passenger. The use of radar detectors is legal in Florida and its neighboring states, Alabama and Georgia. Although it's legal to talk on your cell phone while driving in Florida, it's not recommended. Dial *511 on a cell phone to hear traffic advisories for highways including I–4 and other major arteries.

TRANSPORTATION WITHIN THE PARKS

Walt Disney World has its own free transportation system of buses, trams, monorail trains, and boats that can take you wherever you want to go. If you're staying on Disney property, you can use this system exclusively. In general, allow up to an hour to travel between parks and hotels.

If you're park hopping, consider using your own car to save time. There can be 30-minute waits for park-provided bus transportation. Your parking pass is good at any of the theme parks, and parking is free if you're a resort guest.

DRIVING & PARKING IN WALT DISNEY WORLD

Sections of the Magic Kingdom lot are named for Disney characters; Epcot's parking lot highlights modes of exploration; those at the Studios are named Stage, Music, Film, and Dance; and the Animal Kingdom's sound like Beanie Baby names—Unicorn, Butterfly, and so on. Although in theory Goofy (row) 45 is unforgettable, by the end of the day, you'll be so goofy with eating and shopping and riding that you'll swear that you parked in Sleepy. ■ TIP➜ When you board the tram, write down your parking-lot location and keep it in a pocket. Trams make frequent trips between the parking area and the parks' turnstile areas. No valet parking is available for Walt Disney World theme parks.

For each major theme-park lot, admission is $11 for cars, $12 for RVs and campers, and free to those staying at Walt Disney World resorts. Save your receipt; if you want to visit another park the same day, you won't have to pay to park twice. If you have reservations at a Disney resort, check in early (leave baggage at the bell station if you wish) and ask for your free parking permit.

Parking is always free at Typhoon Lagoon, Blizzard Beach, Downtown Disney, and Disney's BoardWalk. You can valet park at BoardWalk for $10. Although valet parking is available at Downtown Disney, the congestion there is sometimes such that it may be faster to park in Siberia and walk. (Hint: arrive at Downtown Disney early in the evening—around 6 PM—and you'll get a much closer parking space; you'll also avoid long restaurant lines.) ■ TIP➜ At Disney's BoardWalk, you park in the hotel lot, where valets are available as well.

VISITOR INFORMATION

For general information for Walt Disney World call either the information number or the switchboard. For all accommodations and shows call the central reservations number. There's a single number for all dining reservations. To inquire about resort facilities, call the individual property. For child-care information call KinderCare. One of the easiest ways to get information is via the Web site ⊕ *www.disneyworld.com.*

Information WDW Information (☎ *407/824–4321, 407/827–5141 TDD*). **WDW Resort Reservations** (☎ *407/934–7639*). **WDW Dining reservations** (☎ *407/939–3463*).

UNIVERSAL ORLANDO

Updated by Gary McKechnie

Universal and Disney have been battling for years to attract attention and park-goers away from each other. From the outset it was a contest between Disney's Hollywood Studios and Universal to draw film fans and production crews. Disney opened earlier and had the lead, but Universal used the extra time to tweak old rides, design new ones, and within a few years it had hit its stride to out-dazzle Disney with Islands of Adventure. Then CityWalk was added to compete with Disney's Pleasure Island. When its three theme hotels opened, Universal became a complete resort destination and a serious Disney competitor.

Borrowing a concept from Walt Disney World Resort, which encompasses theme parks and hotels, Universal Orlando Resort refers to the conglomeration of Universal Studios Florida (the original theme park), Islands of Adventure (the second theme park), CityWalk (the dining-shopping-nightclub complex), and three fabulous on-property hotels.

Halfway between Walt Disney World and downtown Orlando, and just off heavily trafficked International Drive, Universal is surprisingly secluded. You drive into one of two massive parking complexes (at 3.4 million square feet they're the largest on earth) and take moving walkways to the theme parks. Or, if you're staying at a Universal hotel, you can take a motor launch or stroll to the entrance.

ADMISSION

TICKET	ADULTS	AGES 3–9
1 day, 1 park	$71	$60
1 day, 2 parks	$83	$73
2 days, 2 parks	$116.95 (second day expires within six days of first stamp; for unlimited expiration, add $10)	$106.95 (second day expires within six days of first stamp; for unlimited expiration, add $10)

For the most significant savings of time and money, buy your tickets online (at *www.universalorlando.com*) *or* on the phone ahead of time. You'll avoid the incredibly long and slow lines (even in low season) at the ticket booths at the park entrances and won't be subjected to the full-priced "at the gate" fees. Plus, there are no shipping costs because you can print your tickets directly from your computer. One such online-only bargain is the EarlyBird Exclusives Ticket. For about $85 you receive unlimited admission to both theme parks and CityWalk for seven consecutive days—quite a savings. Here are your other ticket options (tax not included).

You may also want to consider FlexTickets, which let you add visits to SeaWorld, Wet n' Wild, and Busch Gardens Tampa Bay onto visits to Universal. These FlexTickets are good for unlimited admission for 14 consecutive days.

People with a disability that limits enjoyment of the park are eligible for a 15% discount off the ticket price. Also, American Automobile Association members get 10% off, sometimes more, at AAA offices. There are discount coupons for most theme parks in tourist flyers distributed around Orlando, and if you buy tickets at the **Orlando/Orange County Convention & Visitors Bureau Orlando/Orange County Convention & Visitors Bureau**(✉ *8723 International Dr.* ☎ *407/363–5871*), you can save about $5 per adult ticket ($3 on children's prices).

TICKET	ADULTS	AGES 3–9
4-park FlexTicket	$194.95	$160.95
5-park FlexTicket	$239.95	$199.95

CHILD SWAP
All rides have Child Swap areas, so that one parent or adult party member can watch a baby or toddler while the other enjoys the ride or show. The adults then do the swap, and the former caretaker rides without having to wait in line all over again.

GETTING THERE & AROUND
Driving east on I–4 (from WDW and the Tampa area), get off at Universal Boulevard (Exit 75A). Then take a left onto Universal Boulevard and follow the signs.

Driving west on I–4 (from the Daytona and Jacksonville areas), take Universal Boulevard (Exit 74B). Turn right onto Hollywood Way and follow the signs.

HOURS
Universal Studios and Islands of Adventure are both open 365 days a year, from 9 to 7, with hours as late as 10 in summer and holiday periods.

INFORMATION
Call **Universal Orlando** (☎ *407/363–8000 or 888/331–9108* ⊕*www. universalorlando.com*) for tickets, hotel reservations, and information.

PARKING
Universal's parking garage complex, which serves both theme parks and CityWalk, is the world's largest. Definitely write down your parking space, because everything looks the same inside, and after a few go-rounds on the Hulk you might have a hard time remembering whether

MAGIC KINGDOM

NAME	Min. Height	Type of Entertainment	Duration	Suits	Crowds	Strategy
Main Street U.S.A.						
Walt Disney World Railroad	n/a	train	21 min.	All	Heavy	Board with small children for an early start in Toontown or hop on midafternoon.
Adventureland						
Enchanted Tiki Room	n/a	show	12 min.	All	30 min.	Go when you need a refresher in an air-conditioned room.
Jungle Cruise	n/a	boat	10 min.	All	Yes!	Go during the afternoon parade, but not after dark—you miss too much.
Pirates of the Caribbean	n/a	boat	10 min.	All	Less than 30 min.	A good destination, especially in the heat of the afternoon.
The Magic Carpets of Aladdin	n/a	thrill ride	3 min.	All	Fast lines	Visit while waiting for Frontierland Fastpass.
Swiss Family Treehouse	n/a	play area	Up to you.	All	Slow lines	Visit while waiting for Jungle Cruise Fastpass.
Frontierland						
★ Big Thunder Mountain Railroad	40"	thrill ride	4 min.	5 and up	Big crowds	Fastpass. Most exciting at night when you can't anticipate the curves.
Country Bear Jamboree	n/a	show	17 min.	All	Heavy	Visit before 11 AM. Stand to the far left lining up for the front rows.
★ Splash Mountain	40"	thrill ride	11 min.	5 and up	Yes!	Fastpass. Get in line by 9:45 AM or ride during meal or parade times. Bring a change of clothes.
Tom Sawyer Island	n/a	play area	Up to you.	5 to 13	ok	Afternoon refresher. It's hard to keep track of toddlers here.
Liberty Square						
Hall of Presidents	n/a	show	30 min.	9 and up	Light	Go in the afternoon for an air-conditioned break.
Haunted Mansion	n/a	thrill ride	8 min.	All	Fast lines	Nighttime adds extra fear factor.
Liberty Square Riverboat	n/a	boat	15 min.	All	ok	Good for a break from the crowds.
Fantasyland						
Ariel's Grotto	n/a	play area	Up to you.	Little kids	Yes!	Arrive 20 min. before autograph time.
Cinderella's Golden Carrousel	n/a	carousel	2 min.	All	Fast lines	Go while waiting for Peter Pan's Flight Fastpass, during afternoon parade, or after dark.

				Little kids	Slow lines	
Dumbo the Flying Elephant	n/a	thrill ride	2 min.			Go at Rope Drop. No shade in afternoon.
Fairytale Garden	n/a	show	25 min.	All	Midday	See during parade or Fantasyland Castle stage show.
it's a small world	n/a	boat ride	11 min.	All	Fast lines	Tots may beg for a repeat ride; it's worth it.
Mad Tea Party	n/a	thrill ride	2 min.	3 to 10	Slow lines	Go early morning. Skip if wait is 30 min. Spinning ride.
★ Mickey's PhilharMagic	n/a	3-D film	12 min.	All	Heavy	Fastpass or arrive early or during a parade.
Peter Pan's Flight	n/a	ride	2½ min.	All	Steady	Try evening or early morning. Fastpass first.
Snow White's Scary Adventures	n/a	thrill ride	3 min.	All	Steady	Go very early, during the afternoon parade, or after dark. May scare toddlers and pre-schoolers.
The Many Adventures of Winnie the Pooh	n/a	thrill ride	3 min.	All	Heavy	Fastpass. Go early, late in the afternoon, or after dark.
Mickey's Toontown Fair						
★ The Barnstormer at Goofy's Wiseacre Farm	35″	kid thrill ride	1 min.	3 and up	Steady	Go during evening if your child can wait.
Tomorrowland						
Astro-Orbiter	n/a	thrill ride	2 min.	All	Slow lines	Skip unless there's a short line.
Buzz Lightyear's Space Ranger Spin	n/a	thrill ride	5 min.	3 and up	Fast lines	Go early morning and Fastpass. Kids will want more than one ride.
Monster's Inc. Laugh Floor	n/a	interactive film	15 min.	All	Heavy	Go when you're waiting for your Buzz Lightyear or Space Mountain Fastpass.
★ Space Mountain	44″	thrill ride	2½ min.	7 and up	Yes!	Fastpass, or go at beginning or end of day or during a parade.
Stitch's Great Escape	40″	sim. exp.	15 min.	All	Large	Fastpass. Visit early after Space Mountain, Splash Mountain, Big Thunder Mountain, or during a parade.
Tomorrowland Indy Speedway	52″ to drive	racetrack	5 min.	Big kids	Steady	Go in the evening or during a parade; skip on a first-time visit.
Tomorrowland Transit Authority	n/a	tram	10 min.	All	ok	Go with young kids if you need a break.
Walt Disney's Carousel of Progress	n/a	show	20 min.	All	ok	Skip on a first-time visit unless you're heavily into nostalgia.

★ = FodorsChoice

EPCOT

NAME	Min. Height	Type of Entertainment	Duration	Suits	Crowds	Strategy
Future World						
Ellen's Energy Adventure (Universe of Energy)	n/a	ride	30 min.	All	ok	Best seats are to the far left and front of the theater.
★ Honey, I Shrunk the Audience (Imagination!)	n/a	show	14 min.	All	Yes!	Go early morning or just before closing. Take off the 3D glasses if little kids get scared
Innoventions	n/a	walk through	Up to you.	3 and up	at displays	Go before 10 AM or after 2 PM.
Journey into Imagination with Figment (Imagination!)	n/a	ride	8 min.	5 and up	Fast lines	Ride while waiting for Honey, I Shrunk the Audience Fastpass. Toddlers may be scared by darkness and scanner at end of ride.
Living with the Land (The Land)	n/a	boat	4 min.	Teens	ok	The line moves quickly, so go anytime.
Mission: SPACE	44"	thrill ride	4 min.	8 and up	Heavy	Get there before 10 AM or Fastpass. Don't ride on a full stomach.
★ Soarin' (The Land)	40"	sim. ride		5 and up	Heavy	Go early, Fastpass, or just before park closing. Mild flight ride.

					Morning	
Spaceship Earth	n/a	ride	15 min.	All		Ride while waiting for Mission: SPACE or just before closing.
Test Track	40″	thrill ride	5 min.	5 and up	Heavy	Go in morning with Fastpass. The ride can't function on wet tracks, so don't go after a downpour.
The Circle of Life (The Land)	n/a	film	20 min.	All	Steady	Go early or for your toddler's afternoon nap.
The Seas with Nemo & Friends	n/a	ride, film, interactive exhibits	Up to you.	All	Heavy	Get Nemo fans here early in the morning.
World Showcase						
Age of the Viking Ship	n/a	play area	Up to you.	3 and up	ok	Go anytime.
America Gardens Theatre	n/a	show	Varies	Varies	Varies	Arrive 30 min to 1 hr ahead of time for holiday and celebrity performances.
Gran Fiesta Tour Starring the Three Caballeros	n/a	boat	9 min.	All	Moderate	Good if you have small children.
Impressions de France	n/a	film	18 min.	7 and up	Steady	Come after dinner.
Maelstrom	n/a	thrill ride	10 min.	All	Steady	Fastpass for after lunch or dinner.
O Canada!	n/a	film	17 min.	All	late afternoon	Go when World Showcase opens or in the evening. No strollers permitted.
Reflections of China	n/a	film	19 min.	All	Yes!	Go anytime. No strollers permitted.
The American Adventure Show	n/a	show	30 min.	All	Fast lines	Arrive 10 min before the Voices of Liberty or the Spirit of America Fife & Drum Corps are slated to perform.

★ = Fodor'sChoice

DISNEY'S HOLLYWOOD STUDIOS

NAME	Min. Height	Type of Entertainment	Duration	Suits	Crowds	Strategy
Hollywood Blvd.						
Great Movie Ride	n/a	tour	22 min.	5 and up	Medium	*Go while waiting for Fastpass on another ride. Lines out the door mean 25-mins. wait.*
Sunset Blvd.						
Beauty and the Beast– Live on Stage!	n/a	show	30 min.	All	Yes!	*Go 30 min before showtime for good seats. Performance days vary, so check ahead.*
★ Rock 'n' Roller Coaster Starring Aerosmith	48″	thrill ride	3 min.	7 and up	Huge	*Ride early, then Fastpass for another go later.*
★ Twilight Zone Tower of Terror	40″	thrill ride	10 min.	7 and up	Yes!	*Fastpass. Go early or late evening. Plunging ride.*
Animation Courtyard						
Playhouse Disney– Live on Stage!	n/a	show	25 min.	toddlers & pre-schoolers	Afternoon	*Go first thing in the morning, when your child is most alert.*
★ The Magic of Disney Animation	n/a	tour	30 min.	All	Steady	*Go in the morning or late afternoon. Toddlers may get bored.*
Voyage of the Little Mermaid	n/a	show	15 min.	All	Yes!	*Go first thing in the morning. Otherwise, wait until after 5.*
Walt Disney: One Man's Dream	n/a	film	20 min.	10 and up	Heavy	*See this attraction while waiting for a Fastpass appointment.*
Mickey Avenue						
Studio Backlot Tour	n/a	tour	30 min.	All	Fast lines	*People sitting on the left get wet. Go early; it closes at dusk.*
Journey Into Narnia: Prince Caspian	n/a	tour	TBD	3 and up	TBD	*TBD as of this writing.*
Toy Story Mania	n/a	thrill ride	varies	All	Heavy	*Go early, use Fastpass.*

Streets of America

Honey, I Shrunk the Kids Movie Set Adventure	play area	n/a	Up to you.	All	Steady	Come after you've done several shows and your kids need to cut loose.
Jim Henson's Muppet*Vision 3-D	3-D film	n/a	20 min.	All	Moderate	Arrive 10 min early. And don't worry—there are no bad seats.
Lights, Motors, Action! Extreme Stunt Show	show	n/a	30 min.	All	Heavy	You should be able to get into the theater even if you arrive close to show time. For the best seats line up for the show while others are lining up for the parade.

Echo Lake

Indiana Jones Epic Stunt Spectacular!	stunt show	n/a	30 min.	All	Fast lines	Go at night, when the idols' eyes glow red. Sit up front to feel heat of truck on fire.
Sounds Dangerous Starring Drew Carey	show	n/a	30 min.	6 and up	steady	Arrive 15 min before show. You sit in total darkness.
Star Tours	sim. ride	40"	5 min.	3 and up	Fast lines	Go before closing, early morning or get a Fastpass. Keep to the left in line, for best seats.

Daily Performances

Block Party Bash	parade	n/a	25 min.	All	Heavy	Stake out your curb spot an hr early and hang on to it.
★ Fantasmic!	show	n/a	25 min.	6 and up	Heavy	Arrive at least 1 hr early and sit toward the rear, near the entrance/exit, or buy the Fantasmic! dinner package for preferred admission.
High School Musical 3: Senior Year	show	n/a	25 min.	All	Heavy	Stake out a spot 30–45 min early.

★ = Fodor'sChoice

ANIMAL KINGDOM

NAME	Min. Height	Type of Entertainment	Duration	Suits	Crowds	Strategy
Discovery Island						
★ Tree of Life—It's Tough to Be a Bug!	n/a	3-D film	20 min.	All but toddlers	Heavy	Do this after Kilimanjaro Safaris. Good photo op. Fastpass available. Small children may be frightened.
DinoLand U.S.A.						
Boneyard	n/a	play area	Up to you.	Under 9	Heavy	Play here while waiting for DINOSAUR Fastpass, or come late in the day.
Cretaceous Trail	n/a	walk through	Up to you.	All	ok	Stroll along here as you head toward Chester and Hester's for souvenirs or while you wait for the next Finding Nemo show.
Dinosaur	40"	thrill ride	4 min.	5 and up	Midmorning	Go first thing in the morning or at the end of the day, or use the Fastpass.
Fossil Fun Games	n/a	arcade	Up to you.	6 and up	ok	Bring a pocketful of change
Finding Nemo—The Musical	n/a	show	30 min.	All	Heavy	Arrive 40 min. before showtime. Take little kids here while big kids wait for Expedition Everest.
Primeval Whirl	48"	thrill ride	2½ min.	All	Heavy	Kids may want to ride twice. Take your first spin early, then Fastpass if the wait is more than 20 min. Spinning coaster.
TriceraTop Spin	n/a	thrill ride	2 min.	All	Heavy	Ride early while everyone else heads for the safari, or queue up while waiting for your Fastpass appointment for DINOSAUR.
Asia						
★ Expedition Everest	44"	thrill ride	2½ min.	7 and up	Yes!	Fastpass. This is the park's biggest thrill ride.
Flights of Wonder	n/a	show	30 min.	All	ok	Arrive 15 min before show time and find a shaded seat beneath one of the awnings–the sun can be brutal.
Kali River Rapids	38"	thrill ride	7 min.	4 and up	Yes!	Use your Fastpass, or go during the parade. You'll get wet.
Maharajah Jungle Trek	n/a	animal habitat walk	Up to you.	All	ok	Go anytime.
Africa						
★ Kilimanjaro Safaris	n/a	tour	20 min.	All	Morning	Do this first thing in the morning. If you arrive at the park late morning, save this for the end of the day, when it's not so hot.

Pangani Forest Exploration Trail	n/a	animal habitat walk	Up to you.	All	ok	Go while waiting for your safari Fastpass; try to avoid going at the hottest time of day, when the gorillas like to nap.
Rafiki's Planet Watch	n/a	walk through	Up to you.	All	Midmorning	Go in late afternoon after you've hit all key attractions.
Wildlife Express Train	n/a	train ride	7 min.	All	Steady	Head straight to Affection Section with little kids to come face-to-face with domesticated critters.
Camp Minnie-Mickey						
★ Festival of the Lion King	n/a	show	30 min.	All	ok	Arrive 15 min before showtime. Sit in one of the front rows to increase your kid's chance of being chosen.
Pocahontas & Her Forest Friends	n/a	show	12 min.	All	ok	May not be performed every day in low season; check entertainment guide map and arrive 15 min before showtime.
Entertainment						
★ Mickey's Jammin' Jungle Parade	n/a	parade	15 min.	All	Heavy	Choose your spot along the parade route early, as this is one of Disney's most creative parades, and you should try not to miss it.

★ = **Fodor'sChoice**

UNIVERSAL TIP SHEET

■ Get there early—at 8 AM if the parks open at 9. Seriously. Seeing the park with about 100 other people is far better than seeing it with thousands. Plus, it's cooler in the morning.

■ Try to visit on a weekday, as locals crowd the parks on weekends.

■ If you aren't a resort guest, arrive in the parking lot at least 45 minutes early.

■ Write down your parking location.

■ Don't forget anything in your car. The parking garage is at least a half mile from both park

■ entrances and a return round-trip will eat up valuable time.

■ If you're running late, skip the gargantuan parking garage and follow the signs to valet parking. For $18—almost twice the price of regular parking—you'll be in a lot just a few steps from the entrance to CityWalk and have a head start in reaching the parks.

■ If you're visiting during busy times, seriously consider buying the Universal Express PLUS Pass for an extra $15 and up (depending on the season and day of the week). It's well worth it to avoid waiting in line. Theme park food can be pricey. Consider the Universal Meal Deal ($19.99 for adults, $9.99 for kids), which pays for meals (one entrée platter and one dessert) at four specific restaurants per park throughout the day. Meal Deals for both parks are $23.99 for adults and $11.99 for kids. A souvenir cup for an additional $9.99 offers unlimited beverages. No sharing…

■ If you're in a hurry to reach the park and don't feel you can stop for a bite, don't worry—there's a Starbucks, a Cinnabon, and other quick-bite eateries at CityWalk. But we still recommend building in 10 minutes for a quick breakfast.

■ If you're overwhelmed by what to see and do, check with Guest Services, where Universal reps will create an itinerary for you, free of charge, based on your interests and available time.

■ One of the best perks of riding solo, if you don't mind breaking up your group, is the advantage of going into the fast-moving Single Rider line. Use it early and often anywhere it's offered.

■ If you're toting a baby around with you, check out the Child Swap areas. Although you won't be able to ride with your spouse, one parent can enter the attraction, take a spin, and then return to take care of the baby while the other parent rides without having to wait in line again.

■ Eat at off times, like 11 AM and 3 PM, to avoid the midday rush for food.

you parked at King Kong 104 or Jaws 328. Because your vehicle is covered, it's not so sweltering at the end of the day even when it's hot. The cost is $11 for cars and motorcycles, $12 for campers. Valet parking, which puts you just a short walk (and about 15 minutes closer) to the entrance of Universal Studios, is available for $18. Parking in the garage is free after 6 PM.

STAYING ON SITE

When you stay at one of Universal's resort hotels—the Portofino Bay, Hard Rock Hotel, or Royal Pacific—you receive early admission to the parks, unlimited access to the express lines at rides, and priority seating at some restaurants. And in minutes you can walk to CityWalk and the parks. All three resorts are luxurious, fantasy-theme palaces, with room rates to match (though bargains can be had in the off-season).

UNIVERSAL EXPRESS

The Universal Express Pass works much like Disney's Fastpass. You make appointments to get into the express line at certain popular attractions by inserting your theme-park ticket into a machine and getting a Universal Express Pass. The free pass is printed with the times between which you should show up for the ride, which means you'll likely wait no longer than 15 minutes for even the most popular attractions. Smart. You can't get another pass, or appointment, until your current one is used or the time expires.

With a Universal Express-PLUS-Pass, you get front-of-the-line access to rides and attractions without having to make or wait for an appointment. Prices vary depending on the season and number of days, but a one-day/one-park pass costs $15 and up; a two-day/two-park pass runs $25 and up. If you're a Universal hotel guest, you actually get this perk for free, or rather, as part of your room rate. You use your hotel key card to access the express lines.

ISLANDS OF ADVENTURE

The creators of Islands of Adventure (IOA) brought theme-park attractions to a new level. From Marvel Super Hero Island and Toon Lagoon to Seuss Landing, Jurassic Park, and the Lost Continent, almost everything is impressive, and the shows, attractions, and at times the rides can even out-Disney Disney.

The park's five theme islands, connected by walkways, are arranged around a large central lagoon. The waterside is a good place to relax, either as a way to escape crowds or to recuperate from an adrenaline-surging coaster.

BASIC SERVICES

HEALTH SERVICES There are two Health Services/First Aid centers at Islands of Adventure: one at the front entrance inside Guest Services, and the main center near Sindbad's Village in the Lost Continent.

INFORMATION **Guest Guest Services** (☎ *407/224–6350*) is just before the turnstiles on your right before you enter the park. Step through the turnstiles and

TOP ISLANDS OF ADVENTURE ATTRACTIONS

FOR AGES 8 & UP
The Amazing Adventures of Spider-Man.

Easily the best ride in town. Get ready to fight the bad guys and put your life in danger. You'll understand what all the brightest engineers and technology wizards are doing with their time after this one.

Dudley Do-Right's Ripsaw Falls. Prepared to be completely soaked on this log flume ride, which has an even scarier dive than Splash Mountain.

Dueling Dragons. Two floorless coasters go through multiple inversions at 120 mph. At times they come so close together you feel as though you're going to hit the passengers on the other track.

Eighth Voyage of Sindbad. Jumping, diving, punching—is it another Tom Cruise action film? No, it's a cool, live stunt show with a love story to boot.

Incredible Hulk. Florida's best and scariest coaster shoots you skyward and sends you on no less than seven inversions. It will be hard to walk straight after this one.

FOR AGES 6 & UNDER
The Cat in the Hat. Take a seat on a moving couch and see what it's like to have the Cat in the Hat come to babysit for a while. Ever wanted to enter a Dr. Seuss book? That's what this ride is like.

Popeye and Bluto's Bilge-Rat Barges. This tumultuous raft ride is perfect for kids under 7 who want to go on a big-deal ride but are too young for the Hulk and Dudley Do-Right's. It's not too scary—just wild and wet.

you'll find a rack of brochures and maps in French, Spanish, Portuguese, Japanese, and German, as well as English. If you have questions prior to visiting, call **Universal's main line** (☎ *407/363–8000*).

Studio Information Boards are at the Port of Entry in front of the Lagoon (where the circular walk around the park splits). The boards are posted with up-to-the-minute ride and show operating information—including the length of lines at the major attractions.

LOCKERS   There are $8-a-day lockers across from Guest Services at the entrance, with $10 family-size models available; you have unlimited access to both types throughout the day. Scattered strategically throughout the park—notably at Dueling Dragons, the Incredible Hulk Coaster, and Jurassic Park River Adventure—are so-called Smart Lockers that are free for the first 45 to 60 minutes, but are $2 per hour afterward and max out at $14 per day. Stash backpacks and cameras here while you're being drenched or going through the spin cycle.

STROLLER &   You can rent strollers ($11 per day for singles, $18 for doubles) man-
WHEELCHAIR   ual wheelchairs ($12 per day), and electric scooters ($40 per day) at
RENTALS   the Port of Entry to your left after the turnstiles. Photo ID or a $50 deposit on a credit card is required for either. If the wheelchair breaks down, disappears, or otherwise needs replacing, speak to any shop attendant. Since it's a long way between the parking garages and the

park entrance, you may want to rent a push wheelchair at the garages and upgrade to an ECV (electric convenience vehicle) when you reach the park entrance. Quantities are limited, so it's recommended that you reserve in advance.

UNIVERSAL STUDIOS FLORIDA

The park has 444 acres of stage sets, shops, reproductions of New York and San Francisco, and anonymous sound stages housing themed attractions, as well as genuine moviemaking paraphernalia. On the map, it's all neatly divided into six neighborhoods, which wrap themselves around a huge lagoon. The neighborhoods are **Production Central,** which spreads over the entire left side of the Plaza of the Stars; **New York,** with excellent street performances at 70 Delancey; the bicoastal **San Francisco/Amity; World Expo; Woody Woodpecker's KidZone;** and **Hollywood.**

Although the park looks easy to navigate on the map, a blitz tour through it can be difficult, since it involves a couple of long detours and some backtracking. Also keep in mind that some rides—and many restaurants—delay their openings until late morning, which may throw a kink in your perfectly laid plans. In fact, if you arrive when the gates open, it's kind of eerie walking around in a nearly deserted theme park where it's just you and the staff. To make sure you maximize your time and hit all the best rides, follow this chapter's Blitz Tour.

BASIC SERVICES

HEALTH SERVICES   Universal Studios' First Aid centers are between New York and San Francisco (directly across from *Beetlejuice's Graveyard Revue*) and at the entrance between the bank and the Studio Audience Center.

INFORMATION   Visit **Guest Services** (☎ *407/224–6350*) in the Front Lot to the right after you pass through the turnstiles, for brochures and maps in French, Spanish, Portuguese, Japanese, and German, as well as English. The brochures also lay out the day's entertainment, tapings, and rare film shoots. If you have questions prior to visiting, call **Universal's main line** (☎ *407/363–8000*) or Guest Services.

Studio Information Boards in front of Studio Stars and Mel's Drive-In restaurants provide up-to-the-minute ride and show operating information—including the length of lines at the major attractions.

LOCKERS   Locker rental charges are $8 for small lockers and $10 for family-size ones per day, and both offer unlimited access. The high-price lockers are clustered around the courtyard after you've cleared the turnstiles. Keep in mind it can be a long walk back to the gate when you're on the other side of the park. If you time it right, you may not need a locker here because Uni-

ON RAINY DAYS

Except during Christmas week, expect rainy days to be less crowded—even though the park is in full operation. (Coasters do run in the rain—although not in thunderstorms.) However, since most attractions are out in the open, you'll get very wet.

TOP UNIVERSAL STUDIOS ATTRACTIONS

FOR AGES 7 & UP
Revenge of the Mummy.

A pretty good indoor coaster that takes you past scary mummies and billowing balls of fire (really).

Universal Horror Make-Up Show.

This sometimes gross, often raunchy, but always entertaining demonstration merges the best of stand-up comedy with creepy effects.

FOR AGES 6 & UNDER
Animal Actors on Location!

A perfect family show starring a menagerie of animals whose unusually high IQs are surpassed only by their cuteness and cuddle-ability.

A Day in the Park with Barney.

Small children love the big purple dinosaur and the chance to sing along.

versal also has Smart Lockers at major thrill rides. These are free for up to 90 minutes.

STROLLERS &
WHEELCHAIRS
Strollers (singles $11, doubles $18), manual wheelchairs ($12 per day), and electric scooters ($40 per day) can be rented just inside the main entrance and in San Francisco/Amity. Photo ID or a $50 deposit on a credit card is required for either. If the wheelchair breaks down, disappears, or otherwise needs replacing, speak to any shop attendant. It's a long, long way from the parking garage to the entrance. Consider renting a push wheelchair from the central concourse between the parking garages. You can upgrade to an ECV (electric convenience vehicle, or scooter) when you reach the park entrance. Quantities are limited, so it's recommended that you reserve in advance.

DISABILITIES & ACCESSIBILITY

At each park's Guest Services desk, you can pick up a *Studio Guide for Guests with Disabilities* (aka *Rider's Guide*), which contains information for guests who require specific needs on rides and offers details on interpreters, braille scripts, menus, and assisted devices. During orientation, all employees learn how to accommodate guests with disabilities, and you can occasionally spot staffers using wheelchairs. All outdoor shows have special viewing areas for wheelchairs, and all restaurants are wheelchair accessible.

UNIVERSAL CITYWALK

CityWalk is Universal's answer to Downtown Disney. They've gathered theme retail stores and kiosks, restaurants, and nightclubs in one spot—here they're right at the entrance to both Universal Studios Florida and Islands of Adventure. CityWalk attracts a mix of conventioneers, vacationers, and what seems to be Orlando's entire youth market. You may be too anxious to stop on your way into the parks and too tired to linger on your way out, but at some point on your vacation you may drop by for a drink at **Jimmy Buffett's Margaritaville,** a meal at **Emeril's,** a concert at **Hard Rock Live,** take in the Blue Man Group,

UNIVERSAL BLITZ TOUR

BEST OF THE PARK

If you want to attempt to see everything in one day, arrive early so that you can take care of business and see the top attractions before the park gets very crowded. Another way to increase your attraction quota is to ignore the faux Hollywood streets and the gift shops. During peak seasons, you can avoid long waits at major attractions with the highly recommended Universal Express and Express PLUS Passes. These admit you to the attractions with little or no wait in line.

If you're one of the first people in the park and have plenty of early energy, circle the park twice to catch the A-list rides first, then pick up the B-list later. If you're dying to see *Shrek* **4-D,** you'll need to hit it first (it's straight ahead on the right), and then backtrack and turn left to follow up with *Terminator 2* **3-D.** Next, make tracks down the street to *The Simpsons Ride* while the lines are still at a minimum. As you continue counterclockwise, *Men in Black:* **Alien Attack** is next, followed by *Jaws, Disaster!,* then the must-see *Revenge of the Mummy* attraction

and, finally, back near the entrance to see *Twister* – **Ride It Out.** Anywhere along the line, if you time it right so you don't have to wait, consider dropping in to see the live action show, *Fear Factor Live.*

You've just circled the park, and chances are the crowds have arrived. Based on your preferences, you can backtrack to pick up other entertaining attractions like **Jimmy Jimmy Neutron's Nicktoon Blast,** *Animal Actors on Location!,* and the *Universal Horror Make-Up Show.* The remaining rides and attractions are up to you. If the lines are short, all that remains are the ride and show collection at **Woody Woodpecker's KidZone** and **Lucy: A Tribute.** It's been a full day. Go get some rest.

ON RAINY DAYS

Unless it's the week after Christmas, rainy days mean that the crowd will be noticeably thinner. Universal is one of the area's best bets in rainy weather—the park is fully operational, and there are many places to take shelter from downpours. Only a few street shows are canceled during bad weather.

or pick up a souvenir from one of several gift stores. Visiting the stores and restaurants is free, as is parking after 6 PM. The only price you'll have to pay is a cover charge for the nightclubs, or you can invest in the more sensible $9.95 Party Pass for admission to all the clubs all night long. Pay $13 and you can add a movie to your evening out. See Nightlife, below, for descriptions of CityWalk's bars and clubs.

SEAWORLD & DISCOVERY COVE

Updated by Gary McKechnie

Ten minutes from both Universal and Walt Disney World, SeaWorld and Discovery Cove are designed for animal lovers and anyone who prefers more natural pleasures. At SeaWorld you'll watch a series of high-energy circus shows involving dolphins, whales, sea lions, a huge walrus, and even cats and dogs. Plus, you can ride two thrilling roller

UNIVERSAL ORLANDO

NAME	Min. Height	Type of Entertainment	Duration	Suits	Crowds	Strategy
Universal Studios						
A Day in the Park with Barney	n/a	show	20 min.	Toddlers	ok	*Arrive 10-15 mins early on crowded days for a good seat-up close and in center.*
★ *Animal Actors on Location!*	n/a	show	20 min.	All	Peak times	*Come early for a good seat.*
Beetlejuice's Graveyard Revue	n/a	show	25 min.	5 and up	Fast lines	*Use Universal Express Pass here or go after dark on hot days.*
Curious George Goes to Town	n/a	play area	Up to you.	All	Midmorning	*Go in late afternoon or early evening.*
Disaster!	40"	thrill ride	20 min.	All	Heavy	*Come early, before closing or use Universal Express Pass. This is loud.*
E.T. Adventure	n/a	ride	5 min.	All	ok	*Go early morning or use Universal Express Pass.*
Fear Factor Live	n/a	show	25 min.	All	Fast lines	*Arrive 30 min. early for good seats. Or use Universal Express Pass. Toddlers may be bored.*
Jaws	n/a	thrill ride	7 min.	10 and up	Heavy	*Come after dark for a more terrifying ride.*
Jimmy Neutron's Nicktoon Blast	n/a	sim. ride	8 min.	All	Morning	*Come at end of day.*
Lucy: A Tribute	n/a	walk through	15 min.	Adults	ok	*Save this for a hot afternoon.*
Men in Black: Alien Attack	n/a	thrill ride	4½ min.	10 and up	Peak season	*Solo riders can take a faster line so split up. Spinning ride.*
Revenge of the Mummy	48"	thrill ride	3 min.	7 and up	Yes!	*Use Universal Express Pass or go first thing in the morning.*
Shrek 4-D	n/a	4-D film	12 min.	All	Yes!	*Very popular. Use Universal Express Pass.*
The Simpsons Ride	40"	thrill ride	6 min.	10 and up	Heavy	*Use Universal Express Pass.*
Terminator 2 3-D	n/a	3-D film	21 min.	7 and up	Yes!	*Go first thing in the morning or use Universal Express Pass.*
Twister . . . Ride It Out	n/a	sim. ride	3 min.	10 and up	Yes!	*Go first thing in morning or at closing.*
★ *Universal Horror Make-Up Show*	n/a	show	25 min.	All	Not daunting	*Go in the afternoon or evening. Young children may be frightened; older children eat up the blood-and-guts stories.*
Woody Woodpecker's Nuthouse Coaster	n/a	thrill ride	1½ min.	Toddlers	Midmorning	*Go at park closing, when most little ones have gone home.*

Universal Islands of Adventure

★ The Amazing Adventures of Spider-Man	40"	sim. ride	4½ min.	All	Yes!	Use Universal Express Pass or go early or late in day. See bad guys in the WANTED posters.
Camp Jurassic	n/a	play area	Up to you	All	ok	Go anytime.
Caro-Seuss-el	n/a	carousel	2 min.	All	Fast lines	Universal Express Pass or end day here.
The Cat in the Hat	n/a	thrill ride	4½ min.	All	Heavy	Universal Express Pass here or go early or at end of day.
Doctor Doom's Fearfall	52"	thrill ride	1 min.	10 and up	Fast lines	Universal Express Pass or go later in the day, on empty stomach.
★ Dudley Do-Right's Ripsaw Falls	44"	thrill ride	5½ min.	All	Summer	Go in late afternoon, to cool down, or at day's end. There's no seat where you can stay dry.
★ Dueling Dragons	54"	thrill ride	2¼ min.	10 and up	Yes!	Ride after dark or early morning. Go for the rear car of Fire Dragon
★ Eighth Voyage of Sinbad	n/a	show	25 min.	All	Fast lines	Come 15 min. before showtime. Don't sit too close up front.
Flying Unicorn	36"	thrill ride	1 min.	Under 7	Fast lines	Use Universal Express Pass if crowded.
High in the Sky Seuss Trolley Train Tour	34" to 48"	ride	3 min.	All	Heavy	Relatively new. You may have to wait.
★ Incredible Hulk Coaster	54"	thrill ride	2¼ min.	10 and up	Yes!	Come here first Effects best in the morning. The front row is best
Jurassic Park Discovery Center	n/a	walk through	Up to you	10 and up	ok	Go anytime.
Jurassic Park River Adventure	42"	thrill ride	6 min.	All	Yes!	Universal Express Pass. Toddlers may be scared.
One Fish, Two Fish, Red Fish, Blue Fish	n/a	ride	2+ min.	Toddlers	Yes!	Universal Express Pass or early or late in day.
Popeye & Bluto's Bilge-Rat Barges	42"	thrill ride	5 min.	All	Yes!	Come early morning or before closing.
Poseidon's Fury	n/a	show	20 min.	6 and up	Heavy	Come at end of day. Stay to the left for best spot. Get in first row each time
Pteranodon Flyers	n/a	ride	2 min.	All	Perpetual	Skip this on your first visit.
Storm Force Accelatron	n/a	thrill ride	2 min.	10 and up	ok	Go whenever—except after you've eaten.

★ = **Fodor'sChoice**

TOP SEAWORLD ATTRACTIONS

Kraken. SeaWorld's main thrill ride takes you on a high-speed chase with a dragon. But who's chasing who? Just don't disturb the dragon eggs on your way out.

Pets Ahoy. Anyone who has ever loved a pet, or wanted one, has to see the talented cats, dogs, birds, and pig in this show.

Journey to Atlantis. This somewhat dated Splash Mountain-esque ride still provides thrills on its last, steep, wet drop.

Believe. The park's flagship attraction and mascot are irresistible. In a show four years in the making, you'll see several Shamus performing graceful aquabatics that are guaranteed to thrill.

Clyde and Seamore Take Pirate Island. Head for Sea Lion & Otter Stadium to watch this slapstick comedy routine starring an adorable team of water mammals and their trainers.

coasters, one of which (Kraken) is considered one of the scariest rides in Florida.

Discovery Cove is more of a laid-back oasis. You change into your bathing suit and spend the day snorkeling among tropical fish, relaxing on the beach, and, for a short period, interacting with dolphins. You can also get up close to tropical birds in the aviary. For the luxury of visiting a faux tropical island, you'll pay roughly four times as much as a ticket to SeaWorld, but your ticket actually includes a pass to either SeaWorld or Busch Gardens in Tampa (which must be used within seven days).

Aquatica, which debuted in spring 2008, is a new rival for nearby Wet 'n Wild (as well as Disney's Blizzard Beach and Typhoon Lagoon), with water slides and lagoons and beaches created in a South Seas style. The park was still being evaluated by Fodor's (and our readers) as of this writing, so we have provided park highlights based on some initial visits to Aquatica.

SEAWORLD ORLANDO

There's a whole lot more to SeaWorld than Shamu. As the world's largest marine adventure park, SeaWorld celebrates all the mammals, birds, fish, and reptiles that live in and near the ocean.

Although SeaWorld can't rival Disney World when it comes to park design and attention to detail, it does offer a somewhat gentler and less-hurried touring experience governed mostly by show schedules. Every attraction is designed to showcase the beauty of the marine world and demonstrate ways that humans can protect its waters and wildlife. And because there are more exhibits and shows than rides—believe it or not, there are only three actual rides in the entire park—you can go at your own pace without that hurry-up-and-wait feeling.

ADMISSION

At this writing, regular one-day tickets to SeaWorld cost $67.95 for adults, and $57.95 for children ages 3 to 9, not including tax. For permission to bypass the admission line at the park, purchase and print out your tickets online at *www.seaworld.com*.

DISCOUNTS As SeaWorld, Discovery Cove, Aquatica, and Busch Gardens Tampa Bay (about an hour from Orlando on I–4) fall under the same corporate umbrella (Busch Entertainment Corporation), there are incentives for purchasing combination tickets to these parks as well as the Universal Orlando attractions Islands of Adventure, Universal Studios, and Wet 'n Wild. Visit www.seaworld.com for the pricing options.

BABY CARE

Diaper-changing tables are in or near most women's restrooms and in the men's restroom at the front entrance, near Shamu's Emporium. You can buy diapers at machines in all changing areas and at Shamu's Emporium. A special area for nursing is alongside the women's restroom at Friends of the Wild gift shop, equidistant from SeaWorld Theater, Penguin Encounter, and Sea Lion & Otter Stadium.

DISABILITIES & ACCESSIBILITY

With wide sidewalks and gentle inclines to the seats at shows, SeaWorld may be Florida's most accessible theme park.

GETTING THERE & AROUND

SeaWorld is just off the intersection of I–4 and the Beachline Expressway, 10 minutes south of downtown Orlando and 15 minutes from Orlando International Airport. Of all the Central Florida theme parks, it's the easiest to find. If you're heading west on I–4 (toward Disney), take Exit 72 onto the Beachline Expressway (aka Highway 528) and take the first exit onto International Drive and follow signs a short distance to the parking lot. Heading east, take Exit 71.

GUIDED TOURS

Unlike other theme parks, SeaWorld has created a variety of programs that—for a price—will get animal lovers up close and personal with their favorite creatures. Register for all tours and programs by calling the **Guided Tour Center** (☎*800/432–1178, 800/406–2244, or 407/363–2398 ⊕www.seaworld.com*). You can also go to the tour desk to the left of Guest Relations at the park entrance to see what's available that day.

HOURS

SeaWorld opens daily at 9 AM, but closing hours vary between 6 and 7 PM, and, during the holidays, as late as 11 PM. To be safe, call in advance for park hours.

INFORMATION

The **Main Information Center** is just inside the park, near the entrance. Pick up a map and showtime listing. You can also buy tickets for the luau, Discovery Cove, and guided tours here, as well as make dinner reservations. For general information, contact **SeaWorld Orlando** (☎*407/351–3600 or 800/327–2420 ⊕www.seaworld.com*).

SEAWORLD

NAME	Min. Height	Type of Ride	Duration	Suits	Crowds	Strategy
Aviary	n/a	aviary	Up to you.	All	ok	Be sure your camera has memory.
Beaches	n/a	pool	Up to you.	All	ok	Go to Discovery Cove for privacy.
Blue Horizon	n/a	show	30 min.	All	Heavy	Arrive 20 min early.
Clydesdale Hamlet	n/a	zoo	15 min.	All	ok	Go anytime.
Coral Reef	n/a	pool	Up to you.	All	ok	See barracudas and sharks here.
Dolphin Lagoon	n/a	pool	60 min.	6 and up	ok	Beware you'll be cajoled to buy photos.
Dolphin Nursery	n/a	touch pool	Up to you.	All	ok	Go during Shamu show so the kids can be up front.
Journey to Atlantis	42"	thrill ride	6 min.	7 and up	Large	Make a beeline here first thing or go about an hr before closing; this is best at night.
★ Key West at SeaWorld	n/a	touch pool		All	ok	If too crowded, wander until crowds disperse. Feed the dolphins
★ Kraken	54	thrill ride	6 min.	8 and up	Yes!	Get to the park when it opens and head straight to Kraken; otherwise, hit it close to closing.
Manatees: The Last Generation?	n/a	touch pool		All	ok	Go during a Shamu show and not right after a dolphin show.
Odyssea	n/a	show	30 min.	All	Fast lines	Arrive fifteen minutes before curtain for a choice of seats. Entertaining pre-show.
Pacific Point Preserve	n/a	sea lions	Up to you.	All	ok	Go anytime.
Penguin Encounter	n/a	touch pool	Up to you.	All	Yes!	Go during dolphin and sea lion shows, and before you've gotten soaked at Journey to Atlantis, or you'll freeze.
Ray Lagoon	n/a	pool	n/a	All	ok	Swim with barbless stingray.
★ Sea Lion & Otter Stadium	n/a	show	40 min.	All	ok	Sit toward the center for the best view, and don't miss the beginning.
★ SeaWorld Theater– Pets Ahoy	n/a	show	20–25 min.	All	Busy	Gauge the crowds and get there early if necessary.
★ Shamu Stadium	n/a	show	30 min.	All	Busy	Go 45 min early for early-afternoon show. Don't miss Close-up encounters.

		play area		Toddlers	Busy	
Shamu's Happy Harbor	n/a		Up to you.			Don't go first thing in morning or you'll never drag your child away; go midafternoon or toward dusk. Bring a towel to dry them off.
Shark Encounter	n/a	aquarium	20 min.	All	Sometimes	Go during the sea lion show.
Sky Tower	n/a	great view		All	ok	Look for a line and go if there's none.
Stingray Lagoon	n/a	aquarium	Up to you.	All	Moderate	Walk by if it's crowded, return before dusk.
Tropical Reef	n/a	aquarium	Up to you.	All	ok	Go at the end of the day—because it's near the entrance, most people stop here on their way in.
Tropical River	n/a	aquarium	Up to you.	All		Go anytime.
Turtle Point	n/a	zoo		All	ok	
Wild Arctic	42"	sim. ride		All	Peak season	Go during a Shamu show. You can skip the ride if you just want to see the mammals.

★ = **Fodor'sChoice**

SEAWORLD TIP SHEET

- Avoid a weekend visit or one during school holidays if you can, since those are the busiest times.

- Wear comfortable sneakers—no heels or slip-on sandals—since you may get your feet wet on the water rides.

- Pack dry clothes for yourself and your children if you intend to get wet by sitting close to the front at the Shamu show or riding Journey to Atlantis.

- If you prefer to take your own food, remove all plastic straws and lids before you arrive—they can harm fish and birds.

- Budget ahead for food for the animals—feeding time is a major part of SeaWorld charm. A small carton of fish costs $5.

- Arrive at least 30 minutes early for the Shamu show, which generally fills to capacity on even the slowest days. Prepare to get wet in the "splash zone" down front.

PARKING

Parking costs $10 per car, $12 for an RV or camper. Preferred parking, which costs $15, allows you to park in the six rows closest to the front gate.

DISCOVERY COVE

Moving away from the traditional theme-park format, SeaWorld took a chance when it opened Discovery Cove, a 32-acre limited-admission park that's a re-creation of a Caribbean island, complete with coral reefs, sandy beaches, and a signature experience, a dolphin encounter, for which you must be 6 or older (there is a park admission option that does not include the swim).

Here's how it works: after entering a huge thatch-roof tiki building, you register and are given a reserved time to swim with the dolphins, the highlight of your Discovery Cove day; the pre-appointed time also makes planning your day simple, as you can fill in with anytime-swims and meals or snacks before and after your dolphin time. With your admission, everything is included—food, lockers, snorkel & mask, wet suit or swim vest, fins (the use of which is discouraged, as they annoy the fish), and towels. Each guest is also issued a park-approved packet of sunblock: apply it early and often, especially to your face and shoulders. And if you've got a peckish and picky brood, it's a pleasure to go at will to the all-you-can eat cafeteria or simply walk up to snack stop and snatch some bottled water, chips, a hot pretzel, and other goodies.
■ TIP→ Since most of the rest of Orlando is not all-inclusive, it's probably best to grab snacks on behalf of your younger kids so they don't get used to the idea of theme-park snack stations being "free."

Once inside, you're confronted with rocky lagoons surrounded by lush landscaping, intricate coral reefs, and underwater ruins. Navigating the grounds is simple; posted signs point you toward swimming areas, cabanas, or the free-flight aviary, aflutter with exotic birds, which can

DISCOVERY COVE TIP SHEET

■ Make reservations three to four months in advance for peak seasons. Admission slots for June start selling out in March.

■ The masks Discovery Cove provides don't accommodate glasses, so wear contacts if you can. Otherwise, try to get one of the limited number of prescription masks. No deposit is required, but you will be responsible if they're lost or damaged.

■ Don't bother to pack your own wet suit or fins. Wet suits or vests are available here; the wet suit is the way to go for anyone in your party who thinks the water is cold regardless of its temperature.

■ You can leave your keys, money, and other personal belongings in your locker all day. The plastic passes you're given upon entering the park are all you need to pick up your meals and (nonalcoholic) drinks.

■ If it becomes an all-day thunder and lightning rainstorm on your reserved day, attempts will be made to reschedule your visit when you're in town. If that's not possible, you'll get a refund.

4

be reached by way of a quiet walkway or by swimming beneath a waterfall. Perhaps the most underhyped aspect of Discovery Cove are the snorkeling pools.

ADMISSION

If you're committed to visiting Discovery Cove, make reservations well in advance—attendance is limited to about 1,000 people a day. Tickets (with Dolphin Swim) start at $269 in the off-season and go up to $289 in summer. Prices drop by $100 if you choose to forsake the dolphin. Either fee includes unlimited access to all beach and snorkeling areas and the free-flight aviary; all meals and snacks; use of a mask, snorkel, swim vest, towel, locker, and other amenities; parking; and a pass for seven days of unlimited, come-and-go-as-you-please admission to Sea-World Orlando, Aquatica, or Busch Gardens in Tampa. For reservations and additional information, call **Discovery Cove** (☎*877/434–7268* ⊕*www.discoverycove.com*).

DISABILITIES & ACCESSIBILITY

Wheelchairs with wide, balloonlike tires that roll over the sand are available. Call to request one in advance so that they have one waiting for you at the reception.

AQUATICA

Sixty acres of waterpark just across I-Drive from SeaWorld, Aquatica is the new kid in town angling to lure water babies away from Disney's Typhoon Lagoon and Blizzard Beach. Aquatica's outfitted with the slides and thrills you'd expect from an Orlando water park, but with plenty of whimsical SeaWorld touches as well.

A tranquil South Seas look belies the active nature of the park; like its competition, key here is a series of super-fast water slides, coupled in this case with some serene crystal blue streams and white-sand beaches. Hidden grottos and waterfalls and brightly colored and quirky buildings topped with pitched roofs feed a laid-back feel. As at SeaWorld, wildlife plays a major role here, with black and white Commerson's dolphins (smaller dolphins that look a little like Shamu) and colorful fish figuring literally in a couple rides and prominently in Maori-style totem poles and fountains.

ADMISSION

Aquatica admission is $38.95 for adults and $32.95 for children 3 to 9, excluding tax. Visit *www.aquaticabyseaworld.com* for more details.

AWAY FROM THE PARKS

Revised by
Jennie Hess

Starting to feel irritable? Claustrophobic? It's called theme-park syndrome, and it often strikes four days or so into a vacation. You start to feel like you can't wait to get away from the crowds, hot pavement, and Candyland surroundings of the parks. If this sounds familiar and you need a break from the theme-park mania, or if you'd simply like to see more of Central Florida than what you can view from the top of a roller-coaster track, then this section is for you.

But take care—the sights listed below are fairly spread out from the northern suburbs to communities south of Disney World. Note their locations on a map before heading out to visit them.

Numbers in the margin correspond to points of interest on the Orlando Area map.

KISSIMMEE

10 mi southeast of WDW; take I–4 Exit 64A.

Long before Walt Disney World, there was **Gatorland.** This campy attraction near the Orlando–Kissimmee border on U.S. 441 has endured since 1949 without much change, despite competition from the major parks. A free train ride provides an overview of the park, taking you through an alligator breeding marsh and a natural swamp setting where you can spot gators, birds, and turtles. A three-story observation tower overlooks the breeding marsh, swamped with gator grunts, especially come sundown during mating season. For a glimpse of 37 giant rare and deadly crocodiles, check out the exhibit called **Jungle Crocs of the World.** To see eager gators leaping out of the water to catch their food, see the **Gator Jumparoo Show.** The most thrilling is the first one in the morning, when the gators are hungriest. There's also a **Gator Wrestlin' Show,** and although there's no doubt who's going to win the match, it's still fun to see the handlers take on those tough guys with the beady eyes. In the educational **Up Close Animal Encounters Show,** 30 to 40 rattlesnakes fill a pit around the show's host. This is a real Florida experience, and you leave knowing the difference between a gator and a croc. ⊠ *14501 S. Orange Blossom Trail, between Orlando and Kissimmee* ☎ *407/855–5496 or 800/393–5297* ⊕ *www.gatorland.*

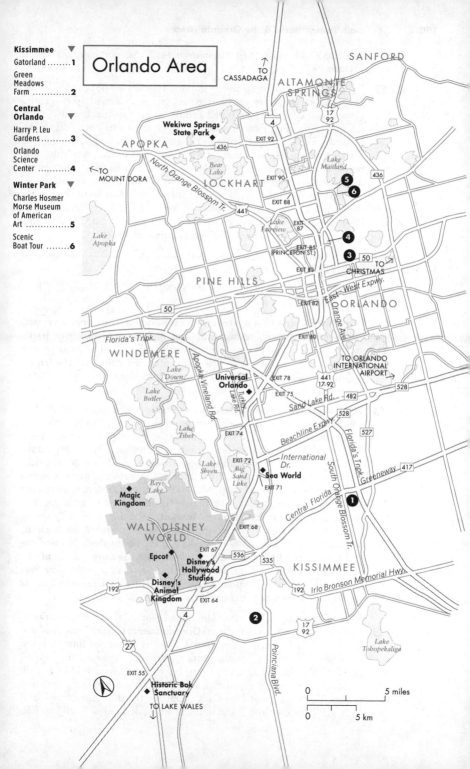

Orlando Area

TO
CASSADAGA

SANFORD

ALTAMONTE
SPRINGS

APOPKA

Wekiwa Springs
State Park

EXIT 92

Bear
Lake

Lake
Maitland

← TO
MOUNT DORA

LOCKHART

EXIT 90

436

EXIT 88

5

6

441

Lake
Fairview

EXIT
87

4

Lake
Apopka

EXIT 85
(PRINCETON ST.)

3

50

TO
CHRISTMAS

EXIT 83

PINE HILLS

EXIT 82

ORLANDO

50

East - West Expwy.

Florida's Tnpk.

WINDEMERE

EXIT 80

Lake
Down

Apopka-Vineland Rd.

Universal
Orlando

EXIT 78

441
17-92

TO ORLANDO
INTERNATIONAL
AIRPORT →

Lake
Butler

Turkey
Lake Rd.

EXIT 75

Sand Lake Rd.

182

528

527

Lake
Tibet

EXIT 74

Beachline Expwy.

528

Florida's Tnpk.

Greeneway

417

EXIT 72

International
Dr.

South Orange Blossom Tr.

Lake
Sheen

Sea World

EXIT 71

Big
Sand
Lake

Central Florida

1

Bay
Lake

Magic
Kingdom

EXIT 68

WALT DISNEY
WORLD

EXIT 67

536

535

KISSIMMEE

Epcot

Disney's
Hollywood
Studios

Irlo Bronson Memorial Hwy.

192

Disney's
Animal
Kingdom

EXIT 64

192

17
92

4

2

Poinciana Blvd.

Lake
Tohopekaliga

27

EXIT 55

Historic Bok
Sanctuary

TO LAKE WALES

0   5 miles

0   5 km

com $22.95 *adults,* $14.95 *children 3–12; discount coupons online* Daily 9–5.

★ ⏱ ❷ Friendly farmhands keep things moving on the two-hour guided tour of **Green Meadows Farm**—a 40-acre property with almost 300 animals. There's little chance to get bored and no waiting in line, because tours are always starting. Everyone can milk the fat mama cow, and chickens and geese are turned loose in their yard to run and squawk while city slickers try to catch them. Children take a quick pony ride, and everyone gets jostled about on the old-fashioned hayride. Youngsters come away saying, "I milked a cow, caught a chicken, petted a pig, and fed a goat." Take U.S. 192 for 3 mi east of I–4 to South Poinciana Boulevard; turn right and drive 5 miles. ✉ *1368 S. Poinciana Blvd.* 📞 *407/846–0770* 🌐 *www.greenmeadowsfarm.com* ✉ *$21; discount coupons online* Daily 9:30–5:30; last tour at 4 PM.

CENTRAL ORLANDO

15 mi northeast of WDW; take I–4 Exit 82C or 83B eastbound, or Exit 85 for Loch Haven Park sights.

Downtown Orlando is a dynamic area with high-rises, sports venues, interesting museums, restaurants, and nightspots. Numerous parks and lakes provide pleasant relief from the tall office buildings. A few steps away from downtown's tourist centers are delightful residential neighborhoods with brick-paved streets and live oaks dripping with Spanish moss.

❸ The **Harry P. Leu Gardens,** a few miles outside of downtown on the former lakefront estate of a citrus entrepreneur, are a quiet respite from the artificial world of the theme parks. On the grounds' 50 acres is a collection of historical blooms, many varieties of which were established before 1900. You can see ancient oaks, a 50-foot floral clock, and one of the largest camellia collections in eastern North America (in bloom November–March). **Mary Jane's Rose Garden,** named after Leu's wife, is the largest formal rose garden south of Atlanta. The simple 19th-century **Leu House Museum,** once the Leu family home, preserves the furnishings and appointments of a well-to-do, turn-of-the-20th-century Florida family. ✉ *1920 N. Forest Ave., North-Central Orlando* 📞 *407/246–2620* 🌐 *www.leugardens.org* ✉ *$7 adults, $2 children kindergarten–12th grade; toddlers and preschoolers free; also free to all Mon. 9–noon* Garden daily 9–5; guided house tours Aug.–June, daily on hr and half hr 10–3:30.

★ ⏱ ❹ With all the high-tech glitz and imagined worlds of the theme parks, is it worth visiting the reality-based **Orlando Science Center**? That depends. If you're into hands-on educational exhibits about the human body, mechanics, electricity, math, nature, the solar system, and optics, you'll really like the science center. It's in a gorgeous building with, besides the exhibits, a wonderful atrium that's home to live gators and turtles. There's a great DinoDigs room for the dinosaur-crazed, and Kids Town for children 7 and under is a wonderland of hands-on fun.

Titanic—The Experience will be featured through 2008 with a look at the history and science of the doomed cruise ship. The Dr. Phillips CineDome, a movie theater with a giant eight-story screen, offers large-format IWERKS films (Ub Iwerkswas an associate of Walt Disney's in the early days), as well as planetarium programs. On Friday and Saturday night you can peer through Florida's largest publicly accessible refractor telescope to view the planets and many of their moons, plus other galaxies and nebulas. ⊠*777 E. Princeton St.* ☎*407/514–2000 or 888/672–4386* ⊕*www.osc.org* ✉*$14.95 ($23 with Titanic) adults, $13.95 ($21 with Titanic) students and seniors with ID, $9.95 ($18 with Titanic) children 3–11; parking $4; tickets include all exhibits, films, and planetarium shows; additional admission charged for special exhibitions* ⊙*Sun.–Thurs. 10–6, Fri. and Sat. 10–9; Observatory Fri. and Sat. 6–9.*

WINTER PARK

20 mi northeast of WDW; take I–4 Exit 87 and head east 3 mi on Fairbanks Ave.

This peaceful, upscale community may be just north of the hustle and bustle of Orlando, but it feels miles away. You can spend a pleasant day here shopping, eating, visiting museums, and taking in the scenery along **Park Avenue,** in the center of town. This inviting brick street has chic boutiques, sidewalk cafés, restaurants, and hidden alleyways that lead to peaceful nooks and crannies with even more restaurants and shops. Park Avenue is definitely a shopper's heaven.

The world's most comprehensive collection of the work of Louis Comfort Tiffany, including immense stained-glass windows, lamps, watercolors, and desk sets, is at the **Charles Hosmer Morse Museum of American Art.** The museum's constant draws include exhibits on the Tiffany Long Island mansion, Laurelton Hall, and the 1,082-square-foot Tiffany Chapel, originally built for the 1893 world's fair in Chicago. It took craftsmen 2½ years to painstakingly reassemble the chapel here. Also displayed at the museum are collections of paintings by 19th- and 20th-century American artists, and jewelry and pottery, including a fine display of Rookwood vases. ⊠*445 N. Park Ave.* ☎*407/645–5311* ⊕*www.morsemuseum.org* ✉*$3 adults, $1 students, children under 12 free; Sept.–May, Fri. free 4–8* ⊙*Tues.–Sat. 9:30–4, Sun. 1–4; Nov.–Apr., Fri. until 8.*

From the dock at the end of Morse Avenue you can depart for the

★ ❻ **Scenic Boat Tour,** a Winter Park tradition that's been in continuous operation for more than 60 years. The relaxing, narrated one-hour pontoon boat tour, which leaves hourly, cruises by 12 miles of Winter Park's opulent lakeside estates and travels through narrow canals and across three lakes. ⊠*312 E. Morse Blvd.* ☎*407/644–4056* ⊕*www. scenicboattours.com* ✉*$10 adults, $5 children 2–11* ⊙*Daily 10–4.*

FodorśChoice
★

WEKIWA SPRINGS STATE PARK

13 mi northwest of Orlando, 28 mi north of WDW.

FodorsChoice
★

Where the tannin-stained Wekiva River meets the crystal-clear Wekiwa headspring, there's a curious and visible exchange—like strong tea infusing water. Wekiva is a Creek Indian word meaning "flowing water"; wekiwa means "spring of water."

Wekiwa Springs State Park sprawls around this area on 6,400 acres. The parkland is well suited to camping, hiking, and picnicking; the spring to swimming; and the river to canoeing and fishing. Canoe trips can range from a simple hour-long paddle around the lagoon to observe a colony of water turtles to a full-day excursion through the less-congested parts of the river that haven't changed much since the area was inhabited by the Timacuan Indians. Take I–4 Exit 94 (Longwood) and turn left on Route 434. Go 1¼ miles to Wekiwa Springs Road; turn right and go 4½ miles to the entrance, on the right. ⊠*1800 Wekiva Circle* ☎*407/884–2008* ⊕*www.myflorida.com* ⊠*$3–$5 per vehicle* ⊙*Daily 8–dusk.*

HISTORIC BOK SANCTUARY

57 mi southwest of Orlando; 42 mi southwest of WDW.

FodorsChoice
★

An hour's drive south of Kissimmee, the Historic Bok Sanctuary is an amazing sanctuary of plants, flowers, trees, and wildlife. Shady paths meander through pine forests in this peaceful world of silvery moats, mockingbirds and swans, blooming thickets, and hidden sundials. You'll be able to boast that you stood on the highest measured point on Florida's peninsula, a colossal 298 feet above sea level. The majestic, 200-foot Bok Tower is constructed of coquina—from seashells—and pink, white, and gray marble. The tower houses a carillon with 57 bronze bells that ring out each day at 1 and 3 PM during 30-minute live recitals, which may include early American folk songs, Appalachian tunes, Irish ballads, or Latin hymns. The landscape was designed in 1928 by Frederick Law Olmsted Jr., son of the planner of New York's Central Park. The grounds include the 20-room, Mediterranean-style **Pinewood Estate,** built in 1930. Take I–4 to Exit 55, and head south on U.S. 27 for about 23 miles. Proceed past Eagle Ridge Mall, then turn left after two traffic lights onto Mountain Lake Cut Off Road and follow signs. ⊠*1151 Tower Blvd., Lake Wales* ☎*863/676–1408* ⊕*www.boktower.org* ⊠*$10 adults, $3 children 5–12, 50% off admission Sat. 8–9; Pinewood Estate general tour $6 adults, $5 children 5–12; holiday tour prices higher* ⊙*Daily 8–6; check Web site or call for Pinewood Estate tour schedule, which varies seasonally; holiday tours late Nov.–early Jan.*

WHERE TO EAT

Revised by
Rowland
Stiteler

DRESS
Because tourism is king around Orlando, casual dress is the rule. Men need jackets only in the priciest establishments.

MEALTIMES
When you're touring the theme parks, you can save a lot of time by eating in the off-hours. Lines at the counter-service places can get very long between noon and 2, and waiting in line for food can get more frustrating than waiting in line for a ride. Try eating lunch at 11 and dinner at 5, or lunch at 2:30 and dinner at 9.

RESERVATIONS
All WDW restaurants and most restaurants elsewhere in greater Orlando take "priority seating" reservations. A priority-seating reservation is like a Fastpass to a meal. You don't get your table right away, but you should get the next one that becomes available. Say you make your reservation for 7 PM. Once you arrive, the hostess will give you a round plastic buzzer that looks sort of like a hockey puck. Then you can walk around, get a drink at the bar, or just wait nearby until the buzzer vibrates and flashes red. That means your table is ready and you can go back to the hostess stand to be seated. You will most likely be seated within 15 minutes of your arrival.

For restaurant reservations within Walt Disney World, call 407/939–3463 or 407/560–7277. And, although you can't make reservations online at *www.disneyworld.com*, you can certainly get plenty of information, like the hours, price range, and specialties of all Disney eateries. For Universal Orlando reservations, call 407/224–9255.

In reviews, reservations are mentioned only when they're essential or not accepted. Unless otherwise noted, the restaurants listed are open daily for lunch and dinner.

WINE & ALCOHOL
The Magic Kingdom's no-liquor policy, a Walt Disney tradition that seems almost quaint in this day and age, does not extend to the rest of Walt Disney World, and in fact, most restaurants and watering holes, particularly those in the on-site hotels, mix elaborate fantasy drinks based on fruit juices or flavored with liqueurs.

WALT DISNEY WORLD AREA

CHARACTER MEALS
At these breakfasts, brunches, and dinners staged in hotel and theme-park restaurants all over Walt Disney World, kids can snuggle up to all the best-loved Disney characters. Sometimes the food is served buffet style; sometimes it's served to you banquet style. The cast of characters, times, and prices changes frequently (although locations of performances remain fairly constant), so be sure to call ahead.

Reservations are always available and often required; some meals can fill up more than 60 days in advance. However, you can also book by phone on the same day you plan to dine, and it never hurts to double-check the character lineup before you leave for the meal. If you have your heart set on a specific meal, make your reservations when you book your trip—up to six months in advance. Smoking is not permitted.

BREAKFAST

Main Street, U.S.A.'s **Crystal Palace Buffet** (☎407/939–3463 $18.99 *adults, $10.99 children ages 3–9*) has breakfast with Winnie the Pooh, Eeyore, Tigger, Piglet, and friends daily from 8 AM to 10:30 AM. Disney–Hollywood Studios's **Hollywood & Vine** (☎407/939–3463 $22.99 *adults, $12.99 children ages 3–9*) hosts *Playhouse Disney* stars Jo Jo and Goliath from "Jo Jo's Circus" and June and Leo from "The Little Einsteins."

At Disney's Beach Club, characters including Goofy, Chip 'n'Dale, and Pluto are on hand at the **Cape May Café** (☎407/939–3463 $18.99 *adults, $10.99 children ages 3–9*) from 7:30 to 11 daily. At the Contemporary Resort, Chef Mickey, Goofy, and Chip 'n'Dale are on hand at **Chef Mickey's** (☎407/939–3463 $22.99 *adults, $12.99 children ages 3–9*),which has a no-holds-barred buffet from 7 to 11:15 daily. The Polynesian Resort's characters, including Lilo and Stitch, Pluto, and Mickey are on hand at **'Ohana** (☎407/939–3463 $18.99 *adults, $10.99 children ages 3–9*), which serves breakfast with Mickey and his friends daily from 7:30 to 11.

At the Swan, the weekend Good Morning Character Breakfast with Goofy and Pluto convenes at the **Garden Grove Café** (☎407/934–3000 $16.95 *adults, $8.50 children ages 3–9*) from 8 to 11. This location is typically not crowded, and makes a good place to take your kids if you can't get a character breakfast seating elsewhere.

At the Wyndham Palace Resort & Spa you can drop in Sunday from 8 to 10:30 am for a character meal at the **Watercress Restaurant** (☎407/827–2727 $24 *adults, $13 children ages 3–9*).

At the Covington Mill Restaurant at the Walt Disney World Hilton, a rotating cast of Disney characters appears Sunday from 8:30 to 11 am (☎407/827–4000 $18.50 *adults, $8.50 children ages 3–9*).

At the Regal Sun Resort (formerly the Grosvenor) on Disney Hotel Row, Pluto and Goofy appear from 8:30 am to 10:30 am on Tuesday, Thursday, and Saturday in what is one of the WDW area's least expensive character breakfasts(☎407/828–4444 $13 *adults, $6 children ages 3–9*).

BY RESERVATION ONLY

The Princess Storybook Breakfasts with Snow White, Sleeping Beauty, and at least three other princesses are held at Epcot Center in the Norway exhibit at **RoyalAkershus Banquet Hall** (☎407/939–3463 $22.99 *adults, $12.99 children ages 3–9*) in the Norway Pavilion from 8:30 to 10:30 daily. Donald Duck and his friends are at Donald's Breakfastosaurus 8:10 to 10 daily at the **Restaurantosaurus** (☎407/939–3463 $18.99 *adults, $10.99 children ages 3–9*), in Disney's Animal Kingdom. Mary Poppins and the Alice in Wonderland characters including

TOP DISNEY WORLD RESTAURANTS

Boma. African-inspired dishes like spiced chicken and banana-leaf–wrapped salmon are a hit with parents and kids at this casual buffet in the Animal Kingdom Lodge.

California Grill. This restaurant hits the top of the favorites list for most people for its innovative American cuisine and incredible views of the Magic Kingdom. Reserve months in advance for a window seat during the fireworks.

Jiko. Superb southern-African cuisine paired with an exceptional wine list and incredibly knowledgeable servers, Jiko is perfect for a romantic dinner for two.

Mama Melrose's. You can't go wrong with solid Italian pastas and secondi like osso buco. This casual *ristorante* in Disney–Hollywood Studios is great for families, and you get free drink refills if you sign up for the *Fantasmic!* dinner package.

Victoria & Albert's. Want to go all out? Treat yourself to a seven-course prix-fixe meal at the restaurant many consider to be Central Florida's best. The Victorian dining room and costumed servers transport you to another time and place, while every mouthful of the haute cuisine is a sensuous delight.

4

the Mad Hatter preside at **1900 Park Fare Restaurant** (☎*407/824–2383* ✉*$22.99 adults, $12.99 children ages 3–9*) in the Grand Floridian from 7:30 to 11:30 daily. Cinderella herself hosts Magic Kingdom breakfasts from 8:05 to 10 daily at

Fodor'sChoice   **Cinderella's Royal Table** (☎*407/939–3463* ✉*$31.99 adults, $21.99 chil-*
★   *dren ages 3–9*). This breakfast is extremely popular, so book six months in advance to be assured seating. (Prices jump to $36.99 for adults and $24.99 for children during holiday periods that include Thanksgiving, Christmas, and Easter.)

LUNCH

At Cinderella Castle, **Cinderella's Royal Table** (☎*407/939–3463* ✉*$33.99 adults, $22.99 children ages 3–9*) is a popular lunchtime option. Your picture is taken as you arrive, then presented to you—in a Cinderella frame, of course. (Prices jump to $39.99 for adults and $25.99 for children during holiday periods that include Thanksgiving, Christmas, and Easter.)

Winnie the Pooh, Tigger, and Eeyore come to the **Crystal Palace Buffet** (☎*407/939–3463* ✉*$20.99 adults, $11.99 children ages 3–9*) on Main Street U.S.A. from 11:10 to 2:30. This is a popular location for character meals, and reservations are essential here. Mickey, Pluto, and Chip 'n' Dale are on hand from noon to 3:50 at the **Garden Grill** (☎*407/939–3463* ✉*$20.99 adults, $11.99 children ages 3–9*) in the Land pavilion at Epcot.

The Princess Storybook Lunches with Snow White, Sleeping Beauty, and at least three other princesses are held at Epcot at the Norway Pavilion in **Royal Akershus Banquet Hall** (☎*407/939–3463* ✉*$24.99 adults, $13.99 children ages 3–9*) from 11:40 AM to 2:50 PM.

Jo Jo, Goliath, June, and Leo from *Playhouse Disney* make a comeback at Disney's Hollywood Studios' **Hollywood & Vine** (☎407/939–3463 ✉*$24.99 adults, $13.99 children ages 3–9*).

AFTERNOON SNACKS

For the *Wonderland* **Tea Party** (☎407/939–3463 ✉*$30 including tax*) at the Grand Floridian Resort, Alice and other characters preside over afternoon tea weekdays from 1:30 to 2:30. With the cast's help, children can bake their own cupcakes and then eat them at the tea party. Open only to children ages 3 to 10; all participants must be potty-trained.

DINNER

All character dinners require reservations.At Cinderella Castle, **the Dreams Come True Dinner** (☎407/939–3463 ✉*$40.99 adults, $25.99 children ages 3–9*) includes an appearance by the Fairy Godmother. Your evening concludes with the presentation of a framed photo of you and your child at the dinner. (Prices jump to $44.99 for adults and $27.99 for children during holiday periods that include Thanksgiving, Christmas, and Easter.)

Minnie Mouse, Goofy, Pluto, and friends (in this case not including Mickey) get patriotic during their evening appearance at the Liberty Square **Liberty Tree Tavern** (☎407/939–3463 ✉*$27.99 adults, $12.99 children ages 3–9*). A "revolutionary" feast of smoked pork, turkey, carved beef, and all the trimmings is served nightly from 4 PM to 8:40 PM. Farmer Mickey, along with Chip,'n' Dale and Pluto appear at the Land Pavilion at Epcot's **Garden Grill** (☎407/939–3463 ✉*$27.99 adults, $12.99 children ages 3–9*) from 4 to 8 daily. Winnie the Pooh and friends appear at a nightly buffet from 4 to 8:45 at the **Crystal Palace Buffet** (☎407/939–3463 ✉*$27.99 adults, $12.99 children ages 3–9*) on Main Street, U.S.A.

Every night at 8 (7 in winter), near Fort Wilderness's Meadow Trading Post, there's a **Character Campfire** (☎407/824–2727) with a free singalong. There are usually around five characters there, with Chip 'n' Dale frequent attendees.

Cinderella's Gala Feast is held at the Grand Floridian's **1900 Park Fare** (☎407/939–3463 ✉*$28.99 adults, $13.99 children ages 3–9*), for a buffet served from 4:30 to 8:20 daily. The Contemporary Resort hosts a wildly popular dinner starring the head honcho himself at **Chef Mickey's** (☎407/939–3463 ✉*$27.99 adults, $12.99 children ages 3–9*), from 5 to 9:15 daily. At the Walt Disney World Swan, you can dine with *Lion King* characters Monday and Friday from 5:30 to 10 at **Gulliver's at the Garden Grove** (☎407/934–1609). Known as the Garden Grove Café during the day, Gulliver's Grill hosts Goofy and Pluto the other five nights of the week. Dinner is $29.95 adults, $11.95 children ages 3 to 9.

The Princess Storybook Dinner, with Snow White, Sleeping Beauty, and at least three other princesses are held at Epcot Center at the Norway Pavilion in **Restaurant Akershus** (☎407/939–3463 ✉*$28.99 adults, $13.99 children ages 3–9*) from 4:20 to 8:40.

MAGIC KINGDOM

★ $$$$ ✕**Cinderella's Royal Table.** Cinderella and other Disney princesses appear at breakfast time at this eatery in the castle's old mead hall; you should book reservations up to 180 days in advance to be sure to see them. Breakfast and lunch are preplated meals. Breakfast, which includes scrambled eggs, sausages, bacon, Danishes, potatoes, and beverages is $32 for adults, $22 for children. Lunch, which includes entrées like herb-crusted pork tenderloin with mustard cheese grits and pan-seared salmon with saffron crab risotto, is $34 for adults, $23 for children. The prix-fixe dinner is $41 for adults, $26 for children. When you arrive at the Cinderella Castle, a photographer snaps a shot of your group in the lobby. A package of photographs will be delivered to your table during your meal. ⊠ *Cinderella Castle* ☎ *407/939–3463* ⚑ *Reservations essential* ▤ *AE, MC, V.*

$$–$$$ ✕**Crystal Palace.** Named for the big glass atrium surrounding the restaurant, the Crystal Palace is a great escape in summer, when the air-conditioning is turned to near meat-locker level. The buffet-style meal includes items like ancho-rubbed Atlantic salmon, rotisserie chicken, roasted adobo pork soups, pastas, fresh-baked breads, and ice-cream sundaes, all part of a one-price package (dinner price is $28 for adults). There's also a kids-only buffet with what many youngsters consider the basic food groups: macaroni and cheese, pizza, and chocolate chip cookies for $13 per child. The Crystal Palace is huge but charming, with numerous nooks and crannies, comfortable banquettes, cozy cast-iron tables, and abundant sunlight. It's also one of the few places in the Magic Kingdom that serves breakfast. Winnie the Pooh, Tigger, Piglet, and Eeyore visit at breakfast, lunch, and dinner. ⊠ *At Hub end of Main St. facing Cinderella Castle* ☎ *407/939–3463* ▤ *AE, MC, V.*

EPCOT

Epcot's World Showcase offers some of the finest dining in Orlando. Every pavilion has at least one and often two or even three eateries. Where there's a choice, it's between a relatively expensive full-service restaurant and a more affordable, ethnic fast-food spot, plus carts and shops selling snacks ranging from French pastries to Japanese ices—whatever's appropriate to the pavilion.

Lunch and dinner priority-seating reservations are essential at the full-service restaurants; you can make them up to 60 days in advance by calling 407/939–3463 or going in person to Guest Relations at the park (only on the day of the meal) or to the restaurants themselves when they open for lunch, usually at noon. No matter how you book, show up a bit early to be sure of getting your table.

$$ ✕**Biergarten.** Oktoberfest runs 365 days a year here. The cheerful, sometimes raucous, crowds are what you would expect in a place with an oompah band. Waitresses in Bavarian garb serve *breseln,* hot German pretzels, which are made fresh daily on the premises. The menu and level of frivolity are the same at lunch and dinner. For a single price ($20 for adults, $10.99 for kids ages 3–9 at lunch and $24 for adults

TOP OFF-SITE RESTAURANTS

Bonefish Grill. Standout seafood like grilled sea bass, tilefish, and rainbow trout is served in a casually elegant dining room.

Emeril's. Bam! Get kicked-up New Orleans food like andouille sausage, shrimp, and red beans at Emeril Lagasse's eponymous restaurant.

Le Coq au Vin. Souped-up French country fare, like bronzed grouper with roasted pecans and the namesake chicken with red-wine sauce, makes this fine little eatery in south-central Orlando worth seeking out.

Seasons 52. What's on the menu this month won't be on it next month at this new-concept restaurant where the ingredients in the dishes are served at the time of year when they are most ripe and flavorful. Besides flavor, you've got healthy here. Meats and fish tend to be grilled not baked. And the decadent desserts are served in shot-glass sizes.

and $12 for children at dinner), mountains of sauerbraten, bratwurst, chicken or pork schnitzel, German sausage, spaetzle, apple strudel, Bavarian cheesecake, and Black Forest cake await you at the all-you-can-eat buffet. And if you aren't feeling too Teutonic, there's also rotisserie chicken and roast pork. Patrons pound pitchers of all kinds of beer and wine on the long communal tables—even when the yodelers, singers, and dancers aren't egging them on. ⊠ *Germany* ⊟ *AE, MC, V.*

$$$$ ✕ **Bistro de Paris.** The great secret in the France pavilion—and, indeed, in
★ all of Epcot—is the Bistro de Paris, upstairs from Les Chefs de France. The sophisticated menu changes regularly and reflects the cutting edge of French cooking; representative dishes include pan-seared lobster, roasted rack of venison with black-pepper sauce, and seared scallops with truffle-potato puree. An excellent appetizer is smoked wild salmon dome with blue crab lemongrass vinaigrette and curry biscuit, a relative bargain at $13. Save room for the Grand Marnier flambéed crepes. Come late, ask for a window seat, and plan to linger to watch the nightly Epcot light show, which usually starts around 9 PM. Moderately priced French wines are available by the bottle and the glass. A good way to go here, especially if you like French cuisine but don't know much about it, is the six-course, prix-fixe meal, $75 per person without wine, or $120 with wine parings. ⊠ *France* ⊟ *AE, MC, V.*

$$$–$$$$ ✕ **Coral Reef Restaurant.** One of this restaurant's walls is made entirely of glass and looks directly into the 6-million-gallon Living Seas aquarium, where you can get tantalizingly close to sharks, stingrays, groupers, tarpons, sea turtles and even the occasional scuba diver. And with a three-tiered seating area, everyone has a good view. Edible attractions include seared Sterling salmon with ratatouille, grilled mahimahi with couscous, and Alaskan king crab legs with corn and an asparagus relish. If you prefer red meat, go for the 12-ounce New York strip with potatoes au gratin. Finish up with the butterscotch crème brûlée. ⊠ *The Living Seas* ⊟ *AE, MC, V.*

$$–$$$ ✕ **Le Cellier.** With the best Canadian wine cellar in the state, this charming eatery with stone arches and dark-wood paneling has a good selec-

tion of Canadian beer as well. Aged beef is king, although many steaks appear only on the dinner menu. If you're a carnivore, go for the herb-crusted prime rib ($25). Even though the menu changes periodically (gone are the buffalo steaks, alas), they've always got the pan-seared Canadian salmon ($22) and free-range chicken with a mustard marinade ($20).

For a light meal, try the Prince Edward Island mussels ($11), and a bowl of the hearty beef and barley soup ($6). Dessert salutes to the land up north include a crème brûlée made with maple sugar ($6) and the Canadian Club chocolate cake ($8). ⊠ *Canada* ⊟ *AE, MC, V.*

$$-$$$$ ✕ **Les Chefs de France.** What some consider the best restaurant at Disney was created by three of France's most famous chefs: Paul Bocuse, Gaston Lenôtre, and Roger Vergé. Classic escargots, a good starter, are prepared in a casserole with garlic butter; you might follow up with duck à l'orange or grilled beef tenderloin with a black-pepper sauce. Make sure you finish with crepes *au chocolat.* Best guilty pleasure: a sinful version of macaroni and cheese made with cream and Gruyère cheese, a bargain at $18. The nearby Boulangerie Pâtisserie, run by the same team, offers tarts, croissants, eclairs, napoleons, and more, to go. And if you want an oxymoron—inexpensive haute cuisine, try the three course, prix-fixe meal available until 7 pm for $40 per person. ⊠ *France* ⊟ *AE, MC, V.*

$$-$$$$ ✕ **Marrakesh.** Chef Abrache Lahcen of Morocco presents the best cooking of his homeland in this ornate eatery, which looks like something from the set of *Casablanca.* Your appetizer might be *harira,* a soup with tomatoes, lentils, and lamb that is traditionally served during Ramadan. From there, move on to the chicken, lamb, or vegetable couscous, Morocco's national dish. A good way to try a bit of everything is the Marrakesh Royal Feast ($42 per person), which includes chicken bastilla (chicken in phyllo pastry) and beef *brewat* (minced beef in a layered pastry dusted with cinnamon and powdered sugar), plus vegetable couscous and assorted Moroccan pastries. The best choice for dessert is a sweet bastilla in which the pastry is stuffed with vanilla cream and toasted almonds. Traditional belly dancers perform periodically throughout the day in a show that is completely G-rated. ⊠ *Morocco* ⊟ *AE, MC, V.*

$$-$$$$ ✕ **Mitsukoshi.** Three restaurants and a lounge are enclosed in this complex, which overlooks tranquil gardens. The complex was reburbished a bit in late 2007, and the menus tweaked a bit, but unchanged is the great cross-section of Japanse cuisine you can find here. **Yakitori House,** a gussied-up fast-food stand in a small pavilion, is modeled after a teahouse in Kyoto's Katsura Summer Palace. At the **Tappan Edo,** diners watch the chefs prepare sushi, sashimi, and tempura (batter-dipped deep-fried shrimp, scallops, and vegetables). In the five **Teppanyaki** dining rooms, chefs frenetically chop vegetables, meat, and fish and stir-fry them at the grills set into the communal tables. Specialties include Ueno (chicken breast and shrimp) and Asakusa (steak and shrimp). Tokyo Dining, the other restaurant in the same building, opened in 2007 with a menu that includes standouts like Hotate (cold water scallops tempura style), and Ginza Gozan (a tempura and shrimp combo). The **Matsu No Ma Lounge,** more serene than the restaurants, has a great view of the World Showcase Lagoon. It also offers one of Epcot's great bargains: a 12-piece sushi platter, with everything from tuna roll to salmon roe, for $21.75. Grown-ups might also go for the sake martini. ⊠*Japan*🖃*AE, MC, V.*

$$-$$$ ✕**Rose & Crown.** If you're an Anglophile and you love a beer so thick you could stand a spoon up in your mug, this is the place to soak up both the suds and the British street culture. "Wenches" serve up traditional English fare—fish-and-chips ($16), shepherd's pie ($13), and the ever-popular bangers and mash (sausage over mashed potatoes, $15). There are several traditional meat pies to choose from, including chicken-and-leek pie and cottage pie (with ground beef, mashed potatoes, and cheese), all served with a side of green beans. Vegetarians will even find an offering of curried veggies and tofu on the menu. For dessert try the sticky toffee pudding with rum-butter sauce ($5) or the chocolate Guinness torte ($7). If you're not driving soon after the meal, try the Imperial Ale sampler, which includes five 6-ounce glasses for $9.35. The terrace has a splendid view of IllumiNations. ⊠*United Kingdom*🖃*AE, MC, V.*

$$$ ✕**Royal Akershus Banquet Hall.** In recent years, this Norwegian restau-
★   rant has become the site of character buffets at all three meals, with an array of Disney princesses, including Arial, Belle, Jasmine, Snow White, Princess Aurora from Sleeping Beauty, Mulan, Mary Poppins, and even an occasional cameo appearance by Cinderella. The Norwegian buffet at this restaurant is as extensive as you'll find on this side of the Atlantic. Appetizers usually include herring, prepared several ways, and cold seafood, including gravlax (cured salmon served with mustard sauce) or *fiskepudding* (a seafood mousse with herb dressing). For your main course, you might try some hot sausages, venison stew, or grilled Atlantic salmon. The à la carte desserts include raspberry tarts, bread pudding, and chocolate mousse with strawberry sauce Breakfast prices average $23 for adults and $13 for kids 3–9; dinners run $29 for adults and $14 for kids. Call 407/939–3463 for reservations. ⊠*Norway*🖃*AE, MC, V.*

$$-$$$ ✕**San Angel Inn.** In the dark, grottolike main dining room, a deep purple, dimly lighted mural of a night scene in Central Mexico seems to envelop the diners. San Angel is a popular respite for the weary, especially when the humidity outside makes Central Florida feel like equatorial Africa. At dinner, guitar and marimba music fills the air. Start with the *sopa Azteca, (a traditional tortilla soup with avocado, cheese, and pasilla pepper)* and then try the authentic *filete motuleno* (grilled beef tenderloin over black beans and melted cheese, ranchero sauce, and poblano pepper strips) or the *puntas de filete* (tender beef tips sautéed with onions and chilies and accompanied by rice and refried

beans). For dessert, the flan is served with a piña colada sauce and topped with a fresh strawberry. ⊠ *Mexico* ⊟ *AE, MC, V.*

$$$–$$$$ ✕ **Tutto Italia.** After basically a generation as the culinary pillar of the Italy section at Epcot, L'Originale Alfredo di Roma Ristorante disappeared in summer 2007 and was replaced by Tutto, located in the same building, with the same formality—servers are wearing white shirts and black ties. Even though the typical diner is wearing shorts, T-shirt, and flip-flops, they're still welcome at the starched-tablecloth-covered tables, where you can enjoy a four-course Italian meal, as pricey as it is tasty. For instance, the "family table," a four-course dinner with two entrées, costs $60 for adults (which is anyone 10 years or older) and $18.50 for children 9 and under; à la carte dinner entrées run from $24 to $35. Offerings include a decent tortelloni stuffed with veal and served with white truffle cream, and a good slant on basic spaghetti and meat balls—these made with veal and pomodoro sauce. Desserts include mocha tiramisu and the cinnamon ricotta cheesecake, with raisins and apricot sauce. Expect a wait at peak lunch and dinner times; outdoor seating is also available. ⊠ *Italy* ☎ *407/939–3463* ⌂ *Reservations essential* ⊟ *AE, MC, V.*

DISNEY'S HOLLYWOOD STUDIOS

The Studios tend to offer more casual American cuisine than the other parks. In other words, it's cheeseburger city. However, there are some good, imaginative offerings, too. Where else but here can you watch '50s sitcoms nonstop while you devour veal-and-shiitake-mushroom meat loaf? Waits can be long. To make priority-seating reservations, call 407/939–3463 up to 180 days in advance, or stop in person at the restaurant or first thing in the morning at Hollywood Junction Restaurant Reservations. There are four ways to book dinner packages that include the *Fantasmic!* after-dark show: by phone, in person at a Disney hotel, at the park's Guest Relations, and at Hollywood Junction.

$–$$ ✕ **'50s Prime Time Café.** Who says you can't go home again? If you grew up in middle America in the 1950s, just step inside. While *I Love Lucy* and *The Donna Reed Show* play on a television screen, you can feast on meat loaf, pot roast, or fried chicken, all served on a Formica tabletop. At $15, the meat loaf is one of the best inexpensive dinners in any local theme park. Follow it up with angel food cake with whipped cream and fresh berries or an ice-cream soda—available in chocolate, strawberry, vanilla, even peanut butter and jelly. The place offers some fancier dishes, such as glazed, pan-seared salmon, which are good but out of character with the diner theme. If you're not feeling totally wholesome, go for Dad's Electric Lemonade (rum, vodka, blue curaçao, sweet-and-sour mix, and Sprite), worth every bit of the $9.50 price tag. Just like Mother, the menu admonishes, "Don't put your elbows on the table!" ⊠ *Echo Lake* ☎ *407/939–3463* ⊟ *AE, MC, V.*

$–$$$ ✕ **Hollywood & Vine.** This restaurant is designed for those who like lots of food and lots of choices. You can have everything from frittatas to fried rice at the same meal. Even though the buffet ($24 for adults, $12 for children ages 3–9) is all-you-can-eat at a relatively low price, it does offer some upscale entrées like oven-roasted prime rib, sage-rubbed rotisserie turkey, or grilled sirloin in a red wine demi-glace, plus a fresh fish of the day. There are plenty of kids' favorites, such as mac and cheese, hot dogs, and fried chicken. Minnie, Goofy, Pluto, and Chip 'n' Dale put in appearances at breakfast and lunch character meals. There's a Hollywood theme to the place; characters and servers are just hoping to be discovered by some passing Hollywood agent. Priority seating reservations are a must. ⊠ *Echo Lake* ☎ *407/939–3463* ▤ *AE, MC, V.*

$$-$$$ ✕ **Hollywood Brown Derby.** At this reproduction of the famous 1940s Hollywood restaurant, the walls are lined with movie-star caricatures, just like in Tinseltown, and the staff wears black bow ties. The house specialty is the Cobb salad, which by legend was invented by Brown Derby founder Robert Cobb; the salad consists of lettuce enlivened by loads of tomato, bacon, turkey, blue cheese, chopped egg, and avocado, all tossed table-side. And the butter comes in molds shaped like Mickey Mouse heads. Other menu choices include grilled salmon on creamy polenta and Gorgonzola with sun-dried tomatoes and baby arugula; and pan-roasted duck breast and venison sausage with celery root puree. For dessert, try the Brown Derby grapefruit cake, with layers of cream cheese icing. If you request the *Fantasmic!* dinner package, make a reservation for no later than two hours before the start of the show. ⊠ *Hollywood Blvd.* ☎ *407/939–3463* ▤ *AE, MC, V.*

$$-$$$ ✕ **Mama Melrose's Ristorante Italiano.** To replace the energy you've no
Fodor'sChoice doubt depleted by miles of theme-park walking, you can load up on
★ carbs at this casual Italian restaurant that looks like an old warehouse. Freshly baked breads with toppings such as arugula and chive pesto, sun-dried tomato, and garlic make great starters. Good main courses include Italian sausage with rigatoni pasta with tomato basil sauce and grilled salmon with sun-dried tomato pesto. Wood-fired flatbreads are available as an entrée choice here, with toppings ranging from pepperoni to grilled chicken with sun-dried tomato pesto. The sangria, available by the carafe, flows generously. Honey hazelnut ricotta cheesecake is the way to go for dessert. Kids' choices include a grilled chicken strips with macaroni and a three-item dinner that includes pizza or pasta. Ask for the *Fantasmic!* dinner package if you want priority seating for the show. ⊠ *Street of America* ☎ *407/939–3463* ▤ *AE, MC, V.*

$-$$ ✕ **Sci-Fi Dine-In Theater Restaurant.** If you don't mind zombies leering at you while you consume chef salads, barbecued pork sandwiches, charbroiled sirloin, and Milky-Way-Out Milk Shakes, then head to this enclosed faux drive-in, where you can sit in a fake candy-color '50s convertible and watch trailers from classics like *Attack of the Fifty-Foot Woman* and *Teenagers from Outer Space*. The menu includes choices like slow-roasted barbecue ribs, seared, marinated tuna, butcher-tendered steak in a red wine sauce, and shrimp penne pasta. The milk shakes are delicious. ⊠ *Echo Lake* ☎ *407/939–3463* ▤ *AE, MC, V.*

DISNEY'S ANIMAL KINGDOM

$$$-$$$$ ✕ **Yak & Yeti.** The location of this pan-Asian cuisine, sit-down eatery—the only full-service restaurant inside Disney's Animal Kingdom—certainly makes sense. It's just at the entrance to the Asia section, located in a two-story, 250-seat building that won't necessarily make you think you're somewhere on the outskirts of Bangkok, but is pleasantly faux-Asian, with cracked plaster walls, wood carvings, and tile mosaic tabletops. Standout entrées include the maple tamarind chicken, with coconut-ginger rice and stir-fried shiitake mushrooms, and the tempura pork or chicken from the wok, both cooked with broccoli, carrots, and a honey sauce. Also tasty, if not authentically Asian, are the baby back ribs with a hoisin barbecue sauce and sweet chili slaw. The grown-ups will like the Yak Attack, a mango daiquiri made with rum, and the Bonsai Blast, made with vodka, banana liqueur, schnapps, and curacao. The most worthy dessert is the combination of fried, cream cheese–filled wontons and pineapple wedges served on a skewer. ✉ *Disney's Animal Kingdom* ☎ *407/938–9100 or 407/939–3463* ▭ *AE, D, DC, MC, V* .

DOWNTOWN DISNEY

$$$-$$$$ ✕ **Fulton's Crab House.** Set in a faux riverboat docked in a lagoon between Pleasure Island and the Marketplace, this fish house offers fine, if expensive, dining. The signature seafood is flown in daily. Dungeness crab from the Pacific coast, Alaskan king crab, Florida stone crab: it's all fresh. Start with the crab and lobster bisque, then try one of the many combination entrées like the gulf shrimp and crab cake platter. If you have no budget constraints, go for Louis Fulton's Ultimate Crab and Lobster Experience for two, which includes generous servings of Alaskan king crab, snow crab, and golden crab, plus a 1.25-pound Maine lobster, for $42 a person. Or if you really want to shell out the bucks, try the king crab claws and lobster dinner ($52). Lobster can actually be added to any dish for $28. The cappuccino ice-cream cake is sublime, and one order is easily enough for two. Lunch is considerably less expensive than dinner here. ✉ *Marketplace* ☎ *407/934–2628* ▭ *AE, MC, V.*

$$$-$$$$ ✕ **Raglan Road Irish Pub.** Some would argue that the phrase "authentic Irish pub at Disney's Pleasure Island" is oxymoronic, particularly when that pub seats 600 people. But if Irish grub's your thing, Raglan's is on target: the shepherd's pie is prepared with the traditional beef, lamb, and mashed potatoes and jazzed up with house spices. And you don't have to settle for plain fish-and-chips here (though you can); there's also panfried lemon sole and chips ($28). You can also get lots of hearty soups and plenty of Irish beer and whiskey. Three massive and ornate bars, all imported from Ireland and all more than a century old, help anchor the pub. The entertainment (which runs from 9 am until 2 am Monday–Saturday) alone makes this place worth the visit. A good, four-person Irish house band, Tuskar Rock, performs nightly as does Danielle Fitzpatrick, herself an Irish import, who performs lively folk dances on stage each evening. ✉ *Pleasure Island, Downtown Disney* ☎ *407/938–0300* ▭ *AE, D, MC, V* .

$$$-$$$$　✕ **Wolfgang Puck.** There are lots of choices here, from wood-oven pizza at the informal Puck Express to five-course meals in the upstairs formal dining room, where there's also a sushi bar and an informal café; the café is quite literally a happy medium and may be the best bet for families hoping for a bit of elegance without the pressure of a formal dinner. At Express try the barbecue chicken pizza or spinach and mushroom pizza ($12–$14), or a real standout, Wolfgang's smoked salmon pizza. The dining room always offers inspired pastas with sauces sublimely laced with chunks of lobster, salmon, or chicken, like the "Wolf-fredo" fettucine with pan-roasted chicken. Always worth coming back for are the Asian hoisin barbecued ribs. Special five-course prix-fixe dinners ($110 with wine, $75 without) require 24-hour notice. ⊠ *West Side* ☎*407/938–9653* ▤*AE, MC, V.*

DISNEY'S BOARDWALK

$$-$$$$　✕ **Flying Fish.** One of Disney's better restaurants, this fish house's best dishes include potato-wrapped red snapper, and oak-grilled Alaskan king salmon. A tasty and creative light offering is the Maine lobster soup and sandwich. Save room for the citrus cheesecake or the molasses-laced tart with praline ice cream. ⊠*Disney's BoardWalk* ☎*407/939– 2359* ▤*AE, MC, V.*

$$-$$$　✕ **Spoodles.** The international tapas-style menu here draws on the best foods of the Mediterranean—from Italy to Greece to Lebanon—with dishes ranging from grilled steak kebabs with multigrain pilaf and harissa to Italian lemon-garlic shrimp linguine. Another good main dish is Israeli inspired, the pan-roasted red snapper filet with couscous, chorizo, wilted greens, and spicy tomato broth. Oak-fired flatbreads with such toppings as roasted peppers make stellar appetizers. For dessert, try the Greek baklava with almonds, walnuts, and dried fruit or the house-made Italian gelato. There's also a walk-up pizza window, where pizza by the slice is $4 and sangria by the glass is $7, if you prefer to stroll the boardwalk. ⊠*Disney's BoardWalk* ☎*407/939–3463* ▤*AE, MC, V.*

WDW RESORTS

$$$-$$$$　✕ **Artist Point.** If you're not a guest at the Wilderness Lodge, a meal here
　★　is worth it just to see the giant totem poles and huge rock fireplace in the lobby. The specialty is cedar-plank salmon and mashed potatoes with roasted fennel and truffle butter (worth its $34 price tag). Another good option: grilled buffalo sirloin with sweet potato–hazelnut gratin and sweet-onion jam. For dessert, try the wild berry cobble or the hazelnut chocolate torte. There's a good northwestern U.S. wine list, and wine pairings for the meal cost $28 per person. A fixed-price dinner, which offers a good cross section of the restaurant's cuisine, is available for $50 per person. ⊠*Wilderness Lodge* ☎*407/939–3463* ⚑*Reservations essential* ▤*AE, MC, V.*

$$$　✕ **Boma.** Boma takes Western-style ingredients and prepares them with
FodorsChoice　an African twist. The dozen or so walk-up serving stations have such
　★　entrées as spit-roasted pork, spiced roast chicken, pepper steak, and

banana leaf–wrapped sea bass or salmon. Don't pass up the soups, as the hearty chicken corn porridge is excellent. The zebra bones dessert is chocolate mousse covered with white chocolate and striped with dark chocolate. Breakfast includes choices from omelets to a vegetable-and-meat-lover's pizza to pap, a porridge made with white corn meal. All meals are prix-fixe (breakfasts are $17 for adults and $10 for kids 3–9; dinner is $26 for adults, $12 for children ages 3–9). The South African wine list is outstanding. Priority seating reservations are essential if you're not a guest at the hotel. ⊠*Disney's Animal Kingdom Lodge* ☎*407/939–3463* ⌔ *Reservations essential* ☐*AE, D, DC, MC, V* ⊘*No lunch.*

$$-$$$$ ✕**California Grill.** The view of the surrounding Disney parks from this
FodorsChoice rooftop restaurant is as stunning as the food, especially at night, when
★ you can watch the nightly Magic Kingdom fireworks from the patio. The menu changes periodically, but choices might include brick-oven flatbread with duck prosciutto and goat-cheese sausage, a sushi platter, oak-fired beef fillet with three-cheese potato gratin and tamarind barbecue sauce, or the linguini with lobster and crab Bolognese. Good dessert choices might include a pear tart with brown-sugar ice cream and quince syrup and a honey crunch cake with chantilly cream and roasted pineapple. ⊠*Contemporary Resort* ☎*407/939–3463* ⌔*Reservations essential* ☐*AE, MC, V.*

$$$ ✕**Chef Mickey's.** This is the holy shrine for character meals, with Mickey, Minnie, and Goofy always around for breakfast and dinner, so it's not a quiet spot to read the *New York Times.* Folks come here for entertainment and comfort food. The dinner buffet ($30 adults, $15 for kids 3–9) includes prime rib, baked ham, and changing specials like beef tips with mushrooms or baked cod with tarragon butter. The Parmesan mashed potatoes have been a popular menu item for years, but you can also get more unusual offerings like broccoli with black olives and feta. The all-you-can-eat dessert bar has sundaes and chocolate cake. ⊠*Contemporary Resort* ☎*407/939–3463* ☐*AE, MC, V.*

$$$-$$$$ ✕**Citricos.** Although the name implies that you might be eating lots of local citrus-flavor specialties, you won't find them here, aside from drinks like a "Citropolitan" martini, infused with lemon-and-lime liqueur, and a tropical fruit crème brûlée for dessert. Standout entrées include grilled swordfish Provençal with orzo pasta, grape tomatoes, and clams and sherry-roasted breast of chicken with chicken sausage and pasta. The wine list, one of Disney's most extensive, includes vintages from around the world. And wine pairings are available with dinner for $25.50 for three wines. ⊠*Grand Floridian* ☎*407/939–3463* ⌔ *Reservations essential* ☐*AE, MC, V.*

$$$-$$$$ ✕**Jiko.** The menu here is more African-inspired than purely African, but
FodorsChoice does include authentic entrées like jumbo scallops with golden brown
★ mealie pap (a porridge made from ground grain) and steamed golden bass with spicy chaka-laka (a mixture of baked beans, carrots, tomato, onions, and spices—a longtime menu favorite). The menu changes periodically, but typically includes such entrées as roasted chicken with mashed potatoes, and braised lamb shank with toasted couscous. After dinner, try a non-African treat: Jiko Dulce de Leche (pure Spanish for

"sweet milk," which is the house version of the very Latin dessert and is covered with what the menu calls "tres leches" sauce—maybe from the wrong continent, but quite tasty. ⊠ *Disney's Animal Kingdom Lodge* ☎ *407/939–3463* ♨ *Reservations essential* ▤ *AE, D, MC, V* ⊘ *No Lunch* .

$$$-$$$$ ✗**Narcoossee's.** The dining room here overlooks the Seven Seas Lagoon and is a great place to catch the Electric Water Pageant at night. Grilled salmon and grilled filet mignon are popular entrées, as is the traditional surf-and-turf centerpiece: Maine lobster and a tender filet mignon. Other good choices include filet mignon with peppercorn sauce and roasted chicken breast with truffle mashed potatoes. For dessert, don't miss the almond-crusted cheesecake with a cherry sauce and the key lime crème brûlée. ⊠ *Grand Floridian Resort* ☎ *407/939–3463* ▤ *AE, MC, V.*

$$$-$$$$ ✗**Todd English's bluezoo.** Celebrity chef Todd English opened this cutting-edge seafood eatery in late 2003. The sleek, modern interior resembles an underwater dining hall, with blue walls and carpeting, aluminum fish suspended from the ceiling, and bubblelike lighting fixtures. The menu is creative and pricey, with entrées like miso-glazed sea bass with spinach and pea-tendril salad or tuna steak wrapped in bacon. If you don't care for fish, alternatives include a beef fillet with fingerling potatoes, and a half chicken cooked in a cast-iron skillet. The chocolate fondue, into which you dip piece of pound cake, marshmallows, and berries, is worthy. ⊠ *Walt Disney World Dolphin* ☎ *407/934–1111* ▤ *AE, D, DC, MC, V* ⊘ *No lunch.*

$$$$ ✗**Victoria & Albert's.** At this Disney fantasy you are served by "Victoria"
FodorsChoice and "Albert," who recite the menu in tandem. There's also a sommelier
★ to explain the wine pairings. Everyone, of course, is dressed in period Victorian costumes. This is one of the plushest fine-dining experiences in Florida: a regal meal in a lavish, Victorian-style room. Perhaps because of this regal atmosphere, WDW made a policy change and in January 2008 and announced that it no longer allows children under 10 in the restaurant. The six-course, prix-fixe menu ($125; wine is an additional $60) changes daily. Appetizer choices might include chorizo-crusted duck or walnut oil-seared duck with hearts of palm and a cheese fondue; entrées may be napoleon of veal tenderloin with tomato fennel jus and artichokes or Kansas City Angus beef with candied potatoes. The restaurant also features a vegetarian menu with exotics such as rutabaga napoleon with melted leeks and ramps. Every female diner gets a long-stemmed rose. For most of the year, there are two seatings, at 5:45 and 9. In July and August, however, there's generally just one seating—at 6:30. The chef's table dinner event is $165 to $235 (with wine pairing) per person. Make your reservations at least 90 and up to 180 days in advance. ⊠ *Grand Floridian* ☎ *407/939–3463* ♨ *Reservations essential ,jacket required* ▤ *AE, MC, V* ⊘ *No lunch.*

UNIVERSAL ORLANDO AREA

$$$-$$$$ ✗**Emeril's.** The popular eatery is a culinary shrine to Emeril Lagasse,
FodorsChoice the famous Food Network chef who occasionally appears here. The
★ menu changes frequently, but you can always count on New Orleans treats like andouille sausage, shrimp, and red beans appearing in some

form or fashion. Entrées may include pecan-crusted redfish with crispy shoestring potatoes; hickory-smoked, lemongrass-roasted duck with ginger rice pilaf; and grilled beef fillet with bacon mashed potatoes and buttermilk-breaded onion rings. The wood-baked pizza, topped with exotic mushrooms, is stellar. Save room for Emeril's ice-cream parfait—banana-daiquiri ice cream topped with hot fudge, caramel sauce, walnuts, and a double-chocolate-fudge cookie. Reservations are usually essential, but there's a chance of getting a walk-in seating if you show up early for lunch (11:30) or dinner (5:30) ⊠ *6000 Universal Blvd.* ☎ *407/224–2424* ⚐ *Reservations essential* ▤ *AE, D, MC, V.*

$$$$ ✕ **Bice.** Pronounced "*beach*-ay"), Bice is an Italian nickname for Beatrice, as in Beatrice Ruggeri, who founded the original Milan location of this family restaurant in 1926. But the word "family" does not carry the connotation "mom and pop" at Bice, where white starched tablecloths set the stage for sophisticated cuisine. The restaurant retains its frescoed ceilings, marble floors, and, of course, picture windows overlooking great views of the artificial bay just outside. This restaurant is expensive, but some of the entrées that seem worth it are the osso buco with risotto and the baked scallops wrapped in prosciutto with a bechamel cream sauce ($36). While you're running up your tab, you may as well also try the tasty appetizer, the seafood risotto ($24). Desserts, ranging from tiramisu to baked apple tart with vanilla ice cream, are delicious. Outdoor seating overlooks a lake. ⊠ *Portofino Bay Resort, 5601 Universal Blvd.* ☎ *407/503–1415* ▤ *AE, D, DC, MC, V* ⊗ *No lunch.*

$$$-$$$$ ✕ **Tchoup Chop.** With its cathedral ceiling, the inside of this restaurant
★ looks almost churchlike, and the food at Emeril Lagasse's Pacific-influenced restaurant is certainly righteous. Following the theme of the Royal Pacific Resort, the decorators included a tiki bar with lots of bamboo, a couple of indoor waterfalls, and a long pool with porcelain lily pads running the length of the dining room. The menu combines Lagasse's own New Orleans–style cuisine with an Asian theme. Entrées change periodically, but representative dishes include pork osso buco with pasta and braised carrots, macadamia nut–encrusted salmon with ginger-soy butter sauce, and grilled New York strip steak with stir-fried vegetables. One of the mainstay dishes is fish steamed in a banana leaf and covered with a sake–soy sauce—something to give you that South Pacific feeling. For dessert try the bittersweet chocolate layer cake with banana sauce or the pecan pie with vanilla-bean ice cream. If you want an experience to remember, try the Teppenyaki Tasting, a limited seating event, held every second Saturday of the month, with a five-course, prix-fixe menu and a serving at which a staff chef presides. ⊠ *Royal Pacific Resort,6300 Hollywood Way* ☎ *407/503–2467* ⚐ *Reservations essential* ▤ *AE, D, DC, MC, V.*

CELEBRATION

If this small town with Victorian-style homes and perfectly manicured lawns reminds you a bit of Main Street, U.S.A., in the Magic Kingdom, it should. The utopian residential community was created by Disney, with all the Disney attention to detail. To get here take I–4 to Exit 64A and follow the "Celebration" signs.

$$–$$$$ ✗**Celebration Town Tavern.** This New England–cuisine eatery is operated by a family with Yankee roots, plus experience operating restaurants in South Florida, and the cuisine reflects both parts of their experience. For instance, on the appetizer menu you'll find plenty of Gulf shrimp to peel and eat, as well as Ipswich clams, and there's excellent clam chowder (New England style) at the Town Tavern. On the entrée menu there are heaping platters of fried clams and oysters, fried Boston scrod, or Florida stone crabs served in season (market price in the spring). Steak is not extremely expensive here. A filet mignon is $27, and you can dine on a steak and lobster combo for $38, roughly half of what you would pay at pricier restaurants. For dessert there's great—what else?—Boston cream pie. ⊠ *721 Front St.* ☎*407/566–2526* ⊟*AE, D, MC, V.*

ORLANDO METRO AREA

INTERNATIONAL DRIVE

A number of restaurants are scattered among the hotels that line manicured International Drive. Many are branches of chains, from fast-food spots to theme coffee shops and up. The food is sometimes quite good. To get to the area, take I–4 Exit 72 or 74A. Count on it taking about a half hour from the Kissimmee area or from WDW property.

$$$–$$$$ ✗**Café Tu Tu Tango.** The food here is served tapas-style—everything is appetizer-size but plentiful, and inexpensive. The eclectic menu is fitting for a restaurant on International Drive. If you want a compendium of cuisines at one go, try the black-bean soup with cilantro sour cream, mango duck quesadillas, the pan-seared pork pot stickers, or the baby chipotle lobster tails. The wine list includes more than 30 wines from half a dozen countries, both by the bottle and the glass. The restaurant is supposed to resemble a crazy artist's loft; artists paint at easels while diners sip drinks like Matisse Margaritas. ⊠*8625 International Dr.* ☎*407/248–2222* ⬧*Reservations not accepted* ⊟*AE, D, DC, MC, V.*

$$$$ ✗**Norman's.** Chef-entrepreneur Norman Van Aken brings impressive
★ credentials to the restaurant that bears his name, as you might expect from the headline eatery in the first and only Ritz-Carlton in Orlando. Van Aken's culinary roots go back to the Florida Keys, where he's credited with creating "Floribbean" cuisine, a blend that is part Key West, part Havana, part Kingston, Jamaica. In the '90s, Van Aken became a star in Miami with his Coral Gables restaurant. The Orlando operation is a formal restaurant with marble floors, starched tablecloths, waiters in black-tie, and a creative, if expensive, prix-fixe menu. The offerings change frequently, but representative selections include Florida Gulf pompano with ham hash, mahimahi with whipped potatoes and mussel chorizo salad, and grilled rib-eye steak with fingerling potatoes. For dessert, try the Pink Lady apple beignet with carmelized molassas ice cream. This place is not for those on a budget. The most frequent dinner option with most customers is a five-course, prix-fixe meal for $100 per person, with wine pairing for an additional $50 per person.

For those who want to go a step farther, there's a seven-course dinner for $140, with wine pairings for $75. ✉ *Ritz-Carlton Grande Lakes, 4000 Central Florida Pkwy.* ☎407/393–4333 ▭ *AE, D, DC, MC, V* ⊘ *No lunch.*

SAND LAKE ROAD

Over the past few years one of the most significant dining sectors in Orlando has sprung up along Sand Lake Road, Exit 74A, just about a mile west of crowded International Drive.

$$–$$$
Fodor'sChoice
★

✕ **Bonefish Grill.** After perfecting its culinary act in the Tampa Bay area, this Florida-based seafood chain has moved into the Orlando market with a casually elegant eatery that offers seafood from around the world. Anglers (waiters) serve standout dishes like wood-grilled grouper in mango sauce ($20), mahimahi piccata, and pistachio-crusted rainbow trout. Meat-lovers may prefer the center-cut, wood-grilled filet mignon. For the record, there's no bonefish on the menu. It's an inedible game fish, caught for sport (and usually released) in the Florida Keys. ✉ *7830 Sand Lake Rd., I–4 Exit 74A* ☎407/355–7707 ▭ *AE, D, DC, MC, V* ⊘ *No lunch.*

$$–$$$
Fodor'sChoice
★

✕ **Seasons 52.** Parts of the menu change every week of the year at this innovative restaurant, which began with the concept of serving different foods at different times, depending on what's in season. Meals here tend to be light, healthy, and very flavorful. You might have an oak-grilled venison chop with mashed sweet potatoes, pork tenderloin skillet with polenta, or salmon cooked on a cedar plank and accompanied by grilled vegetables, or if you prefer a light beef meal, go for the 6-ounce char-crust filet mignon with garlic mashed potato. An impressive wine list complements the long and colorful menu. Another health-conscious concept adopted at Seasons 52 is the "mini indulgence" dessert: classics like chocolate cake, butterscotch pudding, and rocky road ice cream served in portions designed not to bust your daily calorie budget. Although the cuisine is haute, the prices are modest—not bad for a snazzy, urbane, dark-wood-walled bistro and wine bar. It has live music nightly. ✉ *7700 Sand Lake Rd.* ☎407/354–5212 ✉463 E. Altamonte Dr., Altamonte Springs* ☎407/767–1252 ▭*AE, D, DC, MC, V.*

CENTRAL ORLANDO

$–$$
★

✕ **Alfonso's Pizza & More.** This is a strong contender for the best pizza in Orlando (in the non-wood-fired oven division). Since it's across the street from a high school, things get frenzied at lunch. The hand-tossed pizza's toppings range from pepperoni to pineapple—but the calzones and some of the pasta dishes, such as fettuccine Alfredo, are quite worthy as well. There are also subs and salads for lighter fare. The secret to the superior pizza is simple: the dough and all the sauces are made from scratch each and every day. For dessert, opt for the apple pie. Take I–4 Exit 84 to the College Park neighborhood area. ✉ *3231 Edgewater Dr., College Park* ☎407/872–7324 ▭*Reservations not accepted* ▭ *MC, V.*

¢–$ ✕ **Johnny's Fillin' Station.** In a building that once housed a gas station, this burger joint and sports bar is a monument to the fact that good eating can sometimes be had in extremely humble surroundings. Orlando residents rave about the burgers, which are straightforward half-pounders infused with what the management calls a "family recipe." Generous portions of onions, tomatoes, and other less common ingredients—like grilled mushrooms and peppers—make these burgers wonderfully sloppy. Make sure to grab extra napkins. The bacon-and-blue cheeseburger is the most popular item on the menu. Other options include chicken wings, cheesesteaks, and a worthwhile corned-beef sandwich. Best pick for dessert is an order of cheesecake bites with raspberry drizzle. This place is also a sports bar and can get pretty loud and crowded. ⊠ *2631 Ferncreek Ave., Central Orlando* ☎ *407/894–6900* ▭ *D, MC, V.*

$$–$$$$ ✕ **Le Coq au Vin.** Chef-owner Louis Perrotte is something of a culinary
Fodor'sChoice   god in Orlando, but he doesn't let it go to his head. He operates a
★   modest little kitchen in a small house in south Orlando, seating 100 people in three dining rooms. Perrotte's homey eatery is usually filled with locals who appreciate the lovely traditional French fare: roasted halibut with manchego cheese and ham crust on a bed of potatoes; rack of lamb with potatoes au gratin; and of course, the house namesake dish, coq au vin, braised chicken with red wine, mushrooms, bacon, and onion with creamed potatoes. The menu changes seasonally. But the house namesake dish is always available and always excellent. For dessert, try the Grand Marnier soufflé. One caveat: the menu somewhat patronizingly proclaims "We accept well-behaved children." ⊠ *4800 S. Orange Ave., South-Central Orlando* ☎ *407/851–6980* ▭ *AE, DC, MC, V* ☙ *Closed Mon..*

$–$$ ✕ **Little Saigon.** This local favorite is one of the best of Orlando's ethnic
★   restaurants. Even though there are more than 100 menu items, you can still create your own dish, and the good news is that everything is inexpensive. Sample the summer rolls (spring-roll filling in a soft wrapper) with peanut sauce, or excellent Vietnamese crepes (stuffed with shredded pork and noodles). Move on to the com heo xao bong cai (sautéed pork, onion, and broccoli over rice), or the traditional soup filled with noodles, rice, vegetables, and your choice of either chicken or seafood; ask to have extra meat in the soup if you're hungry, and be sure they bring you the mint and bean sprouts to sprinkle in. And if you have never experienced the strong, sweet Vietnamese iced coffee, it's almost like a dessert in itself. But if you prefer a dessert you can eat, go for the wuong xo hat luu. ⊠ *1106 E. Colonial Dr., South-Central Orlando* ☎ *407/423–8539* ▭ *MC, V.*

WINTER PARK

$ ✕ **Briarpatch Restaurant & Ice Cream Parlor.** With a faux country-store facade, this small eatery makes quite a contrast to its upscale neighbors, stores like Gucci and its ilk. But Briarpatch makes a great place to catch a hearty and inexpensive meal. The locals favor the thick burgers, which are topped with your choice of cheese, bacon, or mushrooms. Good breakfast choices include Belgian waffles, raisin-bread French

4

toast, and freshly made scones, and there is a wide variety of omelets, served with toast, home fries, or grits. About 30 flavors of ice cream are available to help cool off on those long strolls down Park Avenue. ✉*252 Park Ave.* N☎*407/628–8651* ⚞*Reservations not accepted* ⊟*AE, D, DC, MC, V.*

$$-$$$$ ✕**Chef Justin's Park Plaza Gardens.** Sitting at the sidewalk café and bar is like sitting on the main street of the quintessential American small town. But the locals know the real gem is hidden inside—an atrium with live ficus trees, a brick floor, and brick walls that give the place a Vieux Carré feel. Chef Justin Plank's menu combines the best of French and Italian cuisine with an American twist. Much of the dinner menu is composed of traditional continental fare, like rack of lamb or tenderloin topped with boursin cheese. One Florida touch is baked grouper with lemon jasmine rice and tomato ginger coulis. Lunch offerings are lighter, with selections like glazed salmon and a good blue-cheese burger. ✉*319 Park Ave.* S☎*407/645–2475* ⊟*AE, D, DC, MC, V.*

$$-$$$$ ✕**Luma on Park.** Park Avenue, once an ultra-upscale enclave, was itself
★   a tourist attraction decades before the advent of Walt Disney World. Although Luma on Park is a 21st-century place, serving what some call "new American cuisine," it's also very much in line with Winter Park's 19th-century past. The chic contemporary setting includes terrazzo floors accented by plush carpets and seating areas in alcoves that create a cozy feel. A high point is the wine cellar, which holds 95 varieties of fine wine. The menu changes periodically, but on recent visits standouts included two appetizers, the blue crab cannollini with peppercorn and sherry sauce, the wood-fired pizza with pear, smoked bacon, arugula, and bleu cheese, and a pair of entrées, flounder with truffled potato gnocchi, artichokes, and lobster cream, and pork tenderloin and Italian sausage with fingerling potatoes, brussel sprouts, and apple coulis. Save room for the warm chocolate truffle cake with banana ice cream and chocolate sauce. The restaurant offers an extensive wine list with vintages from all over the world, by the bottle or glass, and also offers a dinner with wine pairings for $45 per person. ✉*250 S. Park Ave.* ☎*407/599–4111* ⚞*Reservations essential* ⊟*AE, MC, V.*

¢-$$ ✕**Pannullo's.** The view of the tidy little downtown park across the street rivals the quality of the Italian cuisine when you dine in the sidewalk seating area. But when the rain or the heat drives you indoors, you've still got the consistently great cooking at this place, which includes an excellent veal piccata. Pizza-by-the-slice starts at $2.50—a good choice if you are in a hurry or on a budget. Perhaps the best entrée is the lobster-stuffed ravioli, but the fettucine Alfredo with chicken is excellent as well. ✉*216 Park Ave.* S☎*407/629–7270* ⊟*AE, D, DC, MC, V.*

WHERE TO STAY

Updated
by Rowland
Stiteler

Year in and year out, Orlando entertains almost 50 million visitors annually, making it the most popular tourism destination on this planet, and consequently it has a huge and complex inventory of hotel rooms at all price points, themes, color schemes, brands, plans—you name it.

If you're an on-site guest at a Disney lodging, you're guaranteed entry to parks even when they have reached capacity, as the Magic Kingdom, Disney's Hollywood Studios, Blizzard Beach, and Typhoon Lagoon sometimes do. You also get other perks like meal plans ($39 a day); the chance to enter Disney parks earlier and stay later than nonguests; and the ability to use the Magical Express service to check your bags through to the hotel from your home airport when departing for Orlando and back again on return.

Though rates are often better at non-Disney-owned hotels on Disney property (e.g., the Swan, the Dolphin, and the hotels on the so-called Hotel Row just outside Downtown Disney), the perks are fewer. Be sure to clarify what you'll get for the money at each type of property.

RESERVATIONS

Reserve your hotel several months in advance if you want to snag the best rooms during high season. You can book all on-site accommodations—including Disney-owned hotels, non-Disney-owned hotels, and the Hotel Row properties—through the **WDW Central Reservations Office** (*Box 10100, Suite 300, Lake Buena Vista 32830* 407/934–7639 *www.disneyworld.com*). People with disabilities can call **WDW Special Request Reservations** (407/939–7807) to get information or book rooms at any of the on-site Disney properties.

Packages, including airfare, cruises, car rentals, and hotels both on and off Disney property, can be arranged through your travel agent or **Walt Disney Travel Co.** (7100 Municipal Dr., Orlando 407/828–3232 *www.disneyworld.com*).

RATES

Rates are lowest from early January to mid-February, from late April to mid-June, and from mid-August to the third week in December.

Don't overlook the savings to be gained from preparing your own breakfast and maybe a few other meals as well, which you can do if you choose a room or suite with a kitchenette or kitchen.

WHAT TO CONSIDER FOR YOUR FAMILY

Walt Disney World has strong children's facilities and programs at the BoardWalk, Contemporary, Dolphin, Grand Floridian, Polynesian, Swan, Wilderness Lodge, and Yacht and Beach Club resorts. The Polynesian Resort's Neverland Club has an enchanting Peter Pan–theme clubhouse and youngsters-only dinner show. Parents also rave about the Sand Castle Club at the Yacht and Beach Club resorts. The BoardWalk's child-care facility, Harbor Club, provides late-afternoon and evening child care for children ages 4–12.

Many hotels have supervised children's programs with trained counselors and planned activities as well as attractive facilities; some even have mascots. Standouts are the Hyatt Regency Grand Cypress, near Downtown Disney, and the Camp Holiday programs at the Holiday Inn SunSpree Resort Lake Buena Vista.

East of International Drive, the connected JW Marriott and Ritz-Carlton Grand Lakes resorts have rooms with adjoining kids' suites, complete with miniature furniture and toys. Additionally, the JW Marriott has a 24,000-square-foot "lazy river" pool, and the Ritz-Carlton has a Kids Club with a play area and daily scheduled activities.

Nickelodeon Family Suites by Holiday Inn, in Lake Buena Vista, offers suites with separate kid-friendly bedrooms decorated with images of cartoon characters. Plus, there are scheduled breakfasts and shows featuring Nick characters.

4

BABYSITTING

The **Kid's Nite Out** (☎407/828–0920 or 800/696–8105 ⊕www.kids niteout.com) program works in participating hotels throughout the Orlando area, including the Disney resorts. It provides infant care and in-room babysitting for children ages 6 weeks to 12 years (a waiver must be signed for older children who are under the care of the sitter). Fees start at $14 an hour for one child, and increase by $2.50 for each additional child. There's a four-hour minimum, plus a transportation fee of $10 for the sitter to travel to your hotel room. When you make a reservation, you must provide a credit-card number. There's a 24-hour cancellation policy; if you cancel with less than 24 hours' notice, your credit card is charged the four-hour minimum fee ($56 for one child, higher rates for multiple children booked). The service recommends booking from two weeks to 90 days in advance.

THE DISNEY PARKS

Disney-operated hotels are fantasies unto themselves. Each is immaculately designed according to a theme (quaint New England, the relaxed culture of the Polynesian Islands, an African safari village, etc.) and each offers the same perks: free transportation from the airport and to the parks, the option to charge all your purchases to your room, special guest-only park-visiting times, and much more. If you stay on-site, you'll have better access to the parks and you'll be more immersed in the Disney experience.

MAGIC KINGDOM RESORT AREA

Take I–4 Exit 62, 64B, or 65. The ritzy hotels near the Magic Kingdom all lie on the monorail route and are only minutes away from the park. Fort Wilderness Resort and Campground, with RV and tent sites, is a bit farther southeast of the Magic Kingdom, and access to the parks is by bus.

$$$–$$$$ ▣ **Contemporary Resort.** You're paying for location, and perhaps tradition, when you stay here. This 15-story, flat-topped pyramid, the first hotel to open here more than 35 years ago, has been completely renovated several times. The 2006–07 upgrade brought work-station desks, flat-panel TVs, blond-wood furniture that is truly "contemporary,"

Perks for Disney Resort Guests

■ **Location! Location! Location!** You'll probably get to the parks faster than guests staying off-site, and if you plan to stay at Disney for your whole trip, you won't need to rent a car.

■ **Extra Magic Hour.** You get special early- and late-night admission to certain parks on specified days—call ahead for information about each park's "Magic Hours" days to plan your early- and late-visit strategies.

■ **Magical Express.** This perk answers that bothersome question, "How do I get there from the airport?" If you're staying at a Disney hotel, you don't need to rent a car, and you don't even have to think about finding a shuttle or taxi. Or picking up your luggage. With Disney Magical Express, once you get off your plane at Orlando International you're met by a Disney rep who leads you to a coach that takes you directly to your hotel. Your luggage is delivered separately and usually arrives at your hotel room an hour or two after you do. Participating airlines include American, Continental, Delta, JetBlue, Northwest, Southwest, and United. When you're ready to leave, the process works in reverse (though only on some participating airlines, so check in advance).

You get your boarding pass and check your bags at the hotel. Then you go to the airport and go directly to your gate, skipping check-in. You won't see your bags until you're in your hometown airport. Best of all, the service is free.

■ **Package Delivery.** Anything you purchase, whether at one of the parks, one of the hotels, or even in Downtown Disney, can be delivered to the gift shop of your Disney hotel free of charge. It's a big plus not to have to carry your packages around all day.

■ **Priority Reservations.** Hotel guests get priority reservations at Disney restaurants by calling 407/939–3463. Hotel guests also get the choicest tee times at Disney golf courses. Reserve them up to 30 days in advance by calling 407/939–4654.

■ **Charging Privileges.** You can charge most meals and purchases throughout Disney to your hotel room.

■ **Free Parking.** Parking is free for hotel guests, and that extends beyond hotel parking lots. Show your parking pass when you go to any of the Disney parks and you won't be charged for parking.

and marble bathroom vanities. The monorail runs through the lobby, so it takes just minutes to get to the Magic Kingdom and Epcot. Upper floors of the main tower (where rooms are more expensive) offer great views of all the activities in and around the Magic Kingdom, including the nightly fireworks. For the fireworks alone, at least one dinner at the California Grill (atop the building) is worth the pricey dinner tab. **Pros:** Easy access to Magic Kingdom; Chef Mickey's, the epicenter of the character-meal world; launching point for romantic sunset Bay Lake cruises. **Cons:** A mix of vacationers and conventioneers (there's an on-site convention center); sometimes too frenzied for the former and too staid for the latter. This can be among the most kid-intensive of the pricier Disney hotels, so if you don't like children around, look elsewhere. ☎407/824–1000 ✈1,013 rooms, 25 suites ♿In-room:

TOP 5 ON-SITE RESORTS

All-Star Movies Resort. Kids love the giant *Toy Story* figures and Disney-movie themes everywhere, and parents love the price.

BoardWalk Inn & Villas. The price is right and the location can't be beat for adults more interested in Epcot and nightlife than being close to the Magic Kingdom.

Grand Floridian Resort & Spa. If you want to be on the monorail line just minutes from the Magic Kingdom's gate and you can splurge

to stay in a gorgeous luxury hotel, the Grand Floridian is for you.

Wilderness Lodge. Close to the Magic Kingdom yet surprisingly secluded, this stunning retreat is perfect for families who prefer a lodge theme in a good location.

Yacht & Beach Club Resorts. With a man-made beach, spacious family suites, and a relaxed, luxurious, Ralph Lauren-esque feel, the Yacht and Beach clubs appeals to families looking for tranquility and beauty closer to Epcot.

4

safe, refrigerator, Ethernet. In-hotel: 3 restaurants, room service, tennis courts, pools, gym, beachfront, concierge, children's programs (ages 4–12), laundry facilities, laundry service, executive floor, public Wi-Fi, no-smoking rooms ☰AE, D, DC, MC, V.

$$$–$$$$ 🏕 **Fort Wilderness Resort Cabins.** This 700-acre campground is a resort in itself. With its dozens of entertainment options—including biking, outdoor movies, and singing around the campfire—and the very popular *Hoop-Dee-Doo Musical Review* character event, a family can have a truly memorable vacation. The campground is so big that you may want to rent a golf cart (about $45 a day) or a bike ($22 a day). There's a shuttle bus system, but it's about 20 minutes between departures. The larger cabins can accommodate four grown-ups and two youngsters; the bedroom has a double bed and a bunk bed, and the living room has a double sleeper sofa or Murphy bed. Each cabin has a fully equipped kitchen, and daily housekeeping is provided. **Pros:** Cabins don't constitute roughing it (they have air-conditioning); you can save a fortune by cooking, but you don't have to, thanks to the three-meals-a-day restaurant and nightly barbecue. **Cons:** Shuttle to Disney theme parks is free, but slow; coin-op laundry is pricey ($2 to wash, $2 to dry). ☎407/824–2900 🛏408 cabins ⌂In-room: kitchen, Ethernet. In-hotel: restaurant, tennis courts, pools, beachfront, bicycles, laundry facilities, no-smoking rooms ☰AE, D, DC, MC, V.

¢–$ 🏕 **Fort Wilderness Resort Campground.** Bringing a tent or RV is one of the cheapest ways to stay on WDW property, especially considering that sites accommodate up to 10. Tent sites with water and electricity are real bargains. RV sites cost more but are equipped with electric, water, and sewage hookups as well as outdoor charcoal grills and picnic tables. Even with just a good tent and cozy sleeping bag you'll be relatively comfortable, since the campground has 15 strategically located comfort stations where you can take a hot shower, as well as laundry facilities, restaurants, a general store—everything you need. There are many activities to keep you occupied, such as tennis and horseback rid-

TOP 5 OFF-SITE HOTELS

Gaylord Palms Resort. The interior of this place is like a Cecil B. DeMille movie—about Florida. Just walking around in the 4-acre atrium is an adventure in itself: the Everglades, old St. Augustine. The wow-factor isn't exclusive to the theme parks.

Hyatt Regency Grand Cypress Resort. A top-class resort with sprawling grounds almost on top of Walt Disney World property, the Hyatt is perfect for families who want to be near the Mouse but need to take a break from Disney each night.

Nickelodeon Family Suites by Holiday Inn. For the same amount you'd spend on a basic room at a Disney value resort, you get a suite with a separate area for the kids, a Nickelodeon-theme pool, and tons of kids' activities at this family-oriented hotel.

Ritz-Carlton Orlando Grande Lakes. Ultraluxurious rooms, restaurants, and spa programs, plus a championship golf course, make this resort one of the best in the Orlando area.

Royal Pacific Resort. Like roller coasters? Got teens? You might want to stay at Universal Orlando instead of Disney. A stay at this South Pacific-theme hotel gets you into the Express lines on an unlimited basis for free.

ing. Tents can be rented for $30 a night, so it's easy to camp here with virtually no gear of your own. **Pros:** Disney's most economical lodging; pets allowed ($5 nightly fee per campsite, not per pet). **Cons:** Amount of walking within the camp (to reach the store, restaurants, etc.) can be a little much; shuttle rides to Disney parks too long for some. Like every other place in Florida, the bugs can be a little much around twilight, except in winter. ☎407/824–2900 ⏤788 *campsites, 695 with full hookups, 90 partial hookups* ⏤*Pools, flush toilets, full hookups, dump station, drinking water, guest laundry, showers, picnic tables, food service, electricity, public telephone* ⊟*AE, D, DC, MC, V.*

$$$$
Fodor's Choice
★
🏨 **Grand Floridian Resort & Spa.** On the shores of the Seven Seas Lagoon, this red, gable-roof Victorian is all delicate gingerbread, rambling verandas, and brick chimneys. It's Disney's flagship resort: add a dinner or two at Victoria & Albert's or Cítricos and you may spend more in a weekend here than on your mortgage payment—but you'll have great memories. Although you won't look out of place walking through the lobby in flip-flops, afternoon high tea and a pianist playing nightly in the lobby are among the high-scale touches. The Mouseketeer Clubhouse on the ground floor offers children's programs until midnight daily. **Pros:** On the monorail; Victoria & Albert's, one of the state's best restaurants. If you're a couple with no kids, this can be among the least noisy of the on-property Disney hotels. **Cons:** Some say it's not ritzy enough to match the room rates; conference center and convention clientele lend stuffiness. Victoria & Albert's no longer seats kids 10 and under. ☎407/824–3000 ⏤900 *rooms, 90 suites* ⏤*In-room: safe, Ethernet, Wi-Fi. In-hotel: 5 restaurants, room service, tennis courts, pools, gym, spa, beachfront, concierge, children's programs (ages 4–*

12), *laundry facilities, laundry service, executive floor, no-smoking rooms ⊟AE, D, DC, MC, V.*

$$$$ 🏨**Polynesian Resort.** You may not think you're in Fiji, but it's not hard to pretend here, especially after downing a few of the tropical drinks available in the Great Ceremonial House—aka the lobby. In the three-story atrium lobby orchids bloom alongside coconut palms and banana trees, and water cascades from volcanic-rock fountains. At the evening luau, Polynesian dancers perform before a feast with Hawaiian-style roast pork. Rooms sleep five, since they all have two queen-size beds and a daybed. Most rooms also have a balcony or patio. Lagoon-view rooms—which overlook Magic Kingdom fireworks—are peaceful but costly. **Pros:** On the monorail; great aloha-spirit atmosphere. **Cons:** Pricey; not good for those bothered by lots of loud children. ☎407/824–2000 ⌖853 rooms, 5 suites ⚴In-room: safe, Ethernet. In-hotel: 4 restaurants, room service, bar, pools, gym, beachfront, children's programs (ages 4–12), laundry facilities, laundry service, concierge, executive floor, public Wi-Fi, no-smoking rooms ⊟AE, D, DC, MC, V.

$$$–$$$$ 🏨**Wilderness Lodge.** The architects outdid themselves with this seven-
Fodor's Choice story hotel modeled after the majestic turn-of-the-20th-century lodges
★ of the American Northwest. The five-story lobby, supported by towering tree trunks, has an 82-foot-high, three-sided fireplace made of rocks from the Grand Canyon and lighted by enormous tepee-shape chandeliers. Two 55-foot-tall hand-carved totem poles complete the illusion. Rooms have leather chairs, patchwork quilts, cowboy art, and a balcony or a patio. The hotel's showstopper is its Fire Rock Geyser, a faux Old Faithful, near the large pool, which begins as an artificially heated hot spring in the lobby. This hotel is a good option if you're a couple without kids looking for more serenity than is found at Disney's other hotels. **Pros:** High-wow-factor architecture. One of the restaurants, Artist Point, is among the best at Disney; boarding point for romantic Bay Lake sunset cruises. **Cons:** Ferry toots its horn at every docking; no direct shuttle to Magic Kingdom. ☎407/824–3200 ⌖728 rooms, 31 suites ⚴In-room: safe, Ethernet. In-hotel: 3 restaurants, room service, pool, beachfront, bicycles, children's programs (ages 4–12), laundry facilities, laundry service, concierge, executive floor, public Wi-Fi, no-smoking rooms ⊟AE, D, DC, MC, V.

EPCOT RESORT AREA

Take I–4 Exit 64B or 65. From the Epcot resorts you can walk or take a boat to the International Gateway entrance to Epcot, or you can take the shuttle from your hotel or drive to the Future World (front) entrance.

$$$$ 🏨**Beach Club Villas.** Each villa has a separate living room, kitchen, and one or two bedrooms; studios are more like hotel rooms. Interiors are soft yellow and green with white iron bedsteads. Private balconies on the upper levels or porches at street level ensure that you can enjoy your morning coffee in the sun with a view of the lake. The villas are marketed as time-share properties for Disney Vacation Club members, but available rooms are also rented on a per-night basis. You'll have

access to all the facilities of the adjacent Yacht and Beach Club resorts, including Stormalong Bay. The Studio Villas do not have full kitchens; the more expensive, one and two-bedroom villas, which cost up to $1,140 a night during high-season, have all the furnishings of a nice home. **Pros:** Short walk to Epcot's BoardWalk area; in-suite kitchens let you save money on meals. **Cons:** Can be noisy; not close to Magic or Animal Kingdoms. ☎407/934–8000 ⇌205 villas ⌂In-room: safe, Ethernet. In-hotel: restaurant, room service, tennis courts, pools, gym, beachfront, laundry service, concierge, public Wi-Fi, no-smoking rooms ☰AE, D, DC, MC, V.

$$$$ ▦ **BoardWalk Inn & Villas.** Disney's smallest deluxe hotel is a beauti-
★ ful re-creation of Victorian-era Atlantic City inn. Architectural master Robert A.M. Stern designed it to mimic 19th-century New England building styles. Rooms have floral-print bedspreads and blue-and-white painted furniture. Those overlooking Crescent Lake cost the most and are the noisiest. A 200-foot waterslide in the form of a classic wooden roller coaster cascades into the pool area. The property opens directly onto Disney's BoardWalk entertainment complex, where you can ride surrey bikes, watch a game at the ESPN Sports Club, or dine in some of Disney's better restaurants. The hotel is also a 15-minute walk from Disney's Hollywood Studios. **Pros:** Quick access to nighttime fun; rooms are larger than average (390 square feet). **Cons:** Shuttle to Magic Kingdom and other parks is slow. ☎407/939–5100 inn, 407/939–6200 villas ⇌370 rooms, 19 suites, 526 villas ⌂In-room: safe, Ethernet. In-hotel: 4 restaurants, room service, tennis court, pool, gym, concierge, children's programs (ages 4–12), laundry facilities, laundry service, public Wi-Fi, no-smoking rooms ☰AE, D, DC, MC, V.

$$–$$$ ▦ **Caribbean Beach Resort.** Six palm-studded "villages," all awash in
★ dizzying pastels and labeled with Caribbean names like Barbados and Trinidad, share 45-acre Barefoot Bay and its white-sand beach. Bridges connect to a 1-acre path-crossed play and picnic area called Parrot Cay. You can rent boats to explore the lake, or rent bikes to ride along the 1½-mi lakefront promenade. The Old Port Royale complex, decorated with cannons, statues, and tropical birds, has a food court, lounge, and pool area with falls and a big slide. Rooms, which have painted–wood furniture, are fresh and done in soft pastels like turquoise and peach. **Pros:** Restaurants sell Jamaica's Red Stripe beer; plenty of on-site outdoor activities, giving the place a lush "summer camp" feel; convenient to Epcot, Disney's Hollywood, and Downtown Disney. **Cons:** You don't truly feel swept away to a tropical island; the only crystalline and swimmable waters are in the pools; walks from your room to the beach or a restaurant can be up to 15 minutes. ☎407/934–3400 ⇌2,112 rooms ⌂In-room: safe, Ethernet. In-hotel: restaurant, room service, pools, beachfront, bicycles, no elevator, laundry facilities, laundry service, public Wi-Fi, no-smoking rooms ☰AE, D, DC, MC, V.

$$–$$$ ▦ **Coronado Springs Resort.** Because of its 95,000-square-foot convention center and the adjacent 84,000-square-foot exhibit hall, this is Disney's most popular convention hotel. But since the meeting space is in its own wing, the moderately priced resort is also popular with families who appreciate its casual Southwestern architecture, its lively, Mexican-

style food court, and its elaborate swimming pool, which has a Mayan pyramid with a big slide. There's a full-service health club and spa, and if you like jogging, walking, or biking you're in the right place—a pleasant path circles the lake. You can rent bikes, kayaks, canoes, and paddleboats. **Pros:** Great pool with a play area/arcade for kids and a bar for adults; lots of outdoor activities. **Cons:** Some accommodations are a half-mile from the restaurants; standard rooms are on the small side (314 square feet); kids may find the subdued atmosphere boring. ☎407/939–1000 ⬌1,967 rooms ♿In-room: safe, Ethernet. In-hotel: 2 restaurants, room service, bar, pools, gym, spa, bicycles, laundry service, public Wi-Fi, no-smoking rooms ☐AE, D, DC, MC, V.

$$$$ ★ ▥ **Yacht & Beach Club Resorts.** These big Seven Seas Lagoon inns seem straight out of a Cape Cod summer, if perhaps a tad institutional because of their sheer size. The five-story Yacht Club has hardwood floors, a lobby full of gleaming brass and polished leather, an oyster-grey clapboard facade, and evergreen landscaping; there's even a lighthouse on its pier. Rooms have floral-print bedspreads and a small ship's wheel on the headboard. At the Beach Club, a croquet lawn and cabana-dotted white-sand beach set the scene. Stormalong Bay, a 3-acre water park with slides and whirlpools, is part of this club. Both lodgings have "quiet pools," which are secluded and largely kid-free, albeit nondescript. **Pros:** Location, location, location—it's easy to walk to Epcot and the BoardWalk, and Disney's Hollywood is a fun, 20-minute ferry ride away. **Cons:** Distances within the hotel—like, from your room to the front desk—can seem vast; high noise factor. ☎407/934–8000 Beach Club, 407/934–7000 Yacht Club ⬌1,213 rooms, 112 suites ♿In-room: safe, Ethernet, Wi-Fi. In-hotel: 4 restaurants, room service, tennis courts, pools, gym, beachfront, bicycles, children's programs (ages 4–12), laundry service, concierge, public Wi-Fi, no-smoking rooms ☐AE, D, DC, MC, V.

ANIMAL KINGDOM RESORT AREA

Take I–4 Exit 64B. In the park's southwest corner, Disney's third resort area comprises the fabulous Africa-theme Animal Kingdom Lodge, plus two budget-price hotel complexes: All-Star Village, not far from U.S. 192, and the Pop Century Resort, on Osceola Parkway.

☾ $–$$ FodorsChoice ★ ▥ **All-Star Sports, All-Star Music & All-Star Movies Resorts.** Stay here if you want the quintessential Disney-with-your-kids experience, or if you're a couple that feels all that pitter-pattering of little feet is a reasonable tradeoff for a good deal on a room. (Hint: for a little peace, request a room away from pools and other common areas.) In the Sports resort, Goofy is the pitcher in the baseball-diamond pool; in the Music resort you'll walk by giant bongos; and in the Movies resort, huge characters like *Toy Story*'s Buzz Lightyear frame each building. Each room has two double beds, a closet rod, an armoire, and a desk. At 260 square feet, these are the smallest rooms in any Disney hotel, which helps keep the room rate down. The food courts sell standard fare, and you can have pizza delivered to your room. **Pros:** Unbeatable price for a Disney property. **Cons:** No kids' clubs or programs; distances between rooms and on-site amenities can seem vast. ☎407/939–5000 Sports,

407/939–6000 Music, 407/939–7000 Movies ⇋*1,920 rooms at each* ☜*In-room: safe, Ethernet. In-hotel: room service, bars, pools, laundry facilities, laundry service, public Internet, public Wi-Fi, no-smoking rooms* ⊟*AE, D, DC, MC, V.*

$$–$$$$ ⊞**Animal Kingdom Lodge.** Giraffes, zebras, and other wildlife roam three
★ 11-acre savannas separated by wings of this grand hotel. In the atrium lobby, a massive faux-thatched roof hovers almost 100 feet above hardwood floors with inlaid carvings. Cultural ambassadors give talks about their African homelands, the animals, and the artwork on display; evenings include storytelling sessions around the fire circle on the Arusha Rock terrace. All the romantic rooms (with drapes descending from the ceiling to lend a tentlike feel) have a bit of African art, including carved headboards, pen-and-ink drawings, or original prints. Most rooms also have balconies overlooking the wildlife reserve. **Pros:** Extraordinary wildlife and cultural experiences; Jiko and Boma restaurants serve authentic African cuisine. **Cons:** Shuttle to parks other than Animal Kingdom can take more than an hour; guided savannah tours available only to guests on the concierge level. ☎*407/934–7639* ⇋*1,293 rooms* ☜*In-room: safe, Ethernet. In-hotel: 3 restaurants, bar, pools, gym, spa, children's programs (ages 4–12), laundry facilities, laundry service, public Wi-Fi, no-smoking rooms* ⊟*AE, D, DC, MC, V.*

★ $–$$ ⊞**Pop Century Resort.** Giant jukeboxes, 65-foot-tall bowling pins, an oversized Big Wheel and Rubik's Cube, and other pop-culture memorabilia are scattered about the grounds. Items from mood rings to eight-track tapes are incorporated into the architecture; wall-mounted shadow boxes display toys, fashions, and fads from each decade since the 1950s. Brightly colored rooms of 260square feet are functional for families, with two double beds or one king. A big food court and a cafeteria serve reasonably priced fare. This megahotel was opened in 2003 after the All-Star Resorts at Disney proved that a low price point was a big draw for many families. **Pros:** Great room rates; the trip down memory lane; proximity to Wide World of Sports and Disney's Hollywood. **Cons:** Big crowds at the front desk; big crowds (and noise) in the food court; small rooms. ☎*407/934–7639* ⇋*2,880 rooms* ☜*In-room: safe, Ethernet. In-hotel: room service, bar, pools, gym, laundry service, public Wi-Fi, no-smoking rooms* ⊟*AE, D, DC, MC, V.*

DOWNTOWN DISNEY RESORT AREA
Take I–4 Exit 64B or 68. The Downtown Disney–Lake Buena Vista resort area, east of Epcot, has two mid-price resorts with an Old South theme, plus the upscale Old Key West Resort. From here shuttles are available to all of the parks.

$$$$ ⊞**Old Key West Resort.** A red-and-white lighthouse helps you find your way through this marina-style resort. Freestanding villas resemble turn-of-the-20th-century Key West houses, with white clapboard siding and private balconies that overlook the waterways winding through the grounds. The one-, two-, or three-bedroom houses have whirlpools in the master bedrooms, full-size kitchens, (which could save you a fortune on food if you shop at an off-site grocery store), washers and dryers, and patios. The 2,265-square-foot three-bedroom grand villas

accommodate up to 12 adults—so bring some friends. The resort is part of the Disney Vacation Club network, but rooms are rented to anyone when they're available. A ferry service will transport you across the lake to Downtown Disney, which can be a fun experience in itself. **Pros:** Quiet and romantic; abundance of accommodations with whirl-pool baths. **Cons:** Distances between rooms and restaurants, recreation facilities, bus stops, etc. ☎407/827–7700 ☞761 *units* ⚐*In-room: safe, Ethernet, Wi-Fi. In-hotel: restaurant, tennis courts, 4 pools, gym, spa, bicycles, laundry facilities, laundry service, no-smoking rooms* ☰*AE, D, DC, MC, V.*

$$–$$$ ▦**Port Orleans Resort–French Quarter.** Ornate Big Easy–style row houses with vine-covered balconies cluster around squares planted with mag-nolias. Lamp-lighted sidewalks are named for French Quarter thorough-fares. Because this place is relatively quiet, it appeals more to couples than families with kids. The food court serves Crescent City specialties such as jambalaya and beignets. Scat Cat's Lounge is a serene little bar. Doubloon Lagoon, one of Disney's most exotic pools, includes a clever "sea serpent" slide that swallows and then spits you into the water. **Pros:** Authentic, fun New Orleans atmosphere; lots of water recreation options, including boat rentals. "Standard View" rooms have a view of the parking lot, but in peak season they are $25 a night cheaper than the rooms with better views. **Cons:** Public areas can be quite noisy in this kid-attractive resort; shuttle service is slow; food court is the only on-site dining option. ☎407/934–5000 ☞1,008 *rooms* ⚐*In-room: safe, Ethernet. In-hotel: pool, bicycles, laundry facilities, laundry ser-vice, public Wi-Fi, no-smoking rooms* ☰*AE, D, DC, MC, V.*

$$–$$$ ▦**Port Orleans Resort–Riverside.** Buildings look like plantation-style mansions (in the Magnolia Bend section) and rustic bayou dwellings (in the Alligator Bayou section), and you can typically pick which sec-tion you want. Rooms accommodate up to four in two double beds and have wooden armoires, quilted bedspreads, and gleaming brass fau-cets; a few rooms have king-size beds. The registration area looks like a steamboat interior, and the 3½-acre, old-fashioned swimming-hole complex called Ol' Man Island has a pool with slides, rope swings, and a nearby play area. Recreation options here include fishing trips on the Sassagoula River, paddleboat and canoe rentals, and evening carriage rides. **Pros:** Carriage rides; river cruises; lots of recreation options for kids. **Cons:** Shuttle can be slow, no shortage of extremely noisy young-sters, if that's a concern. ☎407/934–6000 ☞2,048 *rooms* ⚐*In-room: safe, Ethernet. In-hotel: restaurant, pools, gym, bicycles, laundry facili-ties, laundry service, no-smoking rooms* ☰*AE, D, DC, MC, V.*

$$$$ ▦**Saratoga Springs Resort.** This large Disney Vacation Club has hun-dreds of units on 16 acres. Three- and four-story buildings, decorated inside and out to look like the 19th-century resorts of upstate New York, overlook a giant pool with artificial hot springs and faux boul-ders. Standard rooms, with 355 square feet, have microwaves and refrigerators; suites have full kitchens. Three-bedroom family suites—as big as most homes, with 2,265 square feet—occupy two levels and have dining rooms, living rooms, and four bathrooms. Rich woods, Early American–style furniture, and overstuffed couches lend a homey, country-chic look. You can walk to Downtown Disney in 10 minutes or take the ferry, which docks near Fulton's Crab House. **Pros:** In-room massage; abundance of rooms with whirlpool baths. **Cons:** It's a fair hike from some accommodations to the restaurant and other facilities. ☎407/934–7639 ⬅828 *units ⌂ In-room: safe, Ethernet. In-hotel: restaurant, tennis courts, pools, gym, spa, bicycles, public Wi-Fi, no-smoking rooms* ⊟*AE, D, DC, MC, V.*

OTHER ON-SITE HOTELS

Although not operated by the Disney organization, the Swan and the Dolphin just outside Epcot, Shades of Green near the Magic Kingdom, and the hotels along Hotel Plaza Boulevard near Downtown Disney call themselves "official" Walt Disney World hotels. While the Swan, Dolphin, and Shades of Green have the special privileges of on-site Disney hotels, such as free transportation to and from the parks and early park entry, the Downtown Disney resorts have their own systems to shuttle hotel guests to the parks.

MAGIC KINGDOM RESORT AREA

¢–$ ⬜ **Shades of Green.** Operated by the U.S. Armed Forces Recreation Center, the resort is open only to active-duty and retired personnel from the armed forces, as well as reserves, National Guard, active civilian employees of the Department of Defense, widows or widowers of service members, disabled veterans, and Medal of Honor recipients. Rates vary with your rank, but are significantly lower than at Disney hotels open to the public. You'll find a Tuscan-style restaurant, a ballroom for weddings and other events, 11 family suites that sleep up to eight adults each, and two swimming pools surrounded by expansive decks and lush, tropical foliage. **Pros:** Large standard rooms (480 square feet); on Disney's shuttle line; Army–Air Force Exchange store discounts deeply for people with military IDs. A little-known fact is that the resort is a short walk from the Polynesian, so it's easy to use the Monorail stop at the Polynesian to expedite your travels around Disney World. **Cons:** Three-night minimum stay. ☎407/824–3600 or 888/593–2242 ⊕*www.shadesofgreen.org* ⬅586 *rooms, 11 suites ⌂ In-room: safe, refrigerator, Ethernet. In-hotel: 4 restaurants, room service, bars, outdoor tennis courts, pools, gym, children's programs (ages 4–12), laundry facilities, laundry service, public Wi-Fi, no-smoking rooms* ⊟*AE, D, MC, V.*

EPCOT RESORT AREA
Take I–4 Exit 64B or 65.

$$$–$$$$ ⬜ **Walt Disney World Dolphin.** World-renowned architect Michael Graves designed the neighboring Dolphin and Swan hotels. Outside, a pair of 56-foot-tall sea creatures bookend this 25-story glass pyramid. The fabric-draped lobby resembles a giant sultan's tent. All rooms have either two queen beds or one king, and bright, beach-inspired spreads and drapes. The pillow-top mattresses, down comforters, and multitude of overstuffed pillows make the beds here some of the kingdom's most comfortable. Extensive children's programs include Camp

Dolphin summer camp and the five-hour Dolphin Dinner Club. **Pros:** Charge privileges and access to all facilities at the Swan; easy walk to BoardWalk; good on-site restaurants. **Cons:** Rooms only dip below $250 in off-season; self parking is $9 a day; Internet use is $12.75 a day ⊠*1500 Epcot Resorts Blvd., Lake Buena Vista* ☎*407/934–4000 or 800/227–1500* ⊕*www.swandolphin.com* ⇒*1,509 rooms, 136 suites* &*In-room: safe, Ethernet. In-hotel: 9 restaurants, room service, tennis courts, pools, gym, spa, beachfront, children's programs (ages 4–12), executive floor, concierge, public Wi-Fi, no-smoking rooms* ⊟*AE, D, DC, MC, V.*

$$$–$$$$ ▦**Walt Disney World Swan.** Facing the Dolphin across Crescent Lake, the Swan is another example of the postmodern "Learning from Las Vegas" school of entertainment architecture characteristic of Michael Graves. Two 46-foot swans grace the rooftop of this coral-and-aquamarine hotel, and the massive main lobby is decorated with a playful mix of tropical imagery. Guest rooms are quirkily decorated with floral and geometric patterns, pineapples painted on furniture, and exotic bird-shape lamps. Every room has two queen beds or one king, two phone lines (one data port), and a coffeemaker; some have balconies. The Grotto, a 3-acre water playground complete with waterslides, waterfalls, and all the trimming, is nearby, as is Disney's BoardWalk and the Fantasia Gardens miniature golf complex. You can walk for miles around here and always be in a super-pleasant Disney environment. **Pros:** Charge privileges and access to all facilities at the Dolphin; easy walk to BoardWalk; good on-site restaurants. **Cons:** Rooms only dip below $250 in off-season. ⊠*1200 Epcot Resorts Blvd., Lake Buena Vista* ☎*407/934–3000 or 800/248–7926* ⊕*www.swandolphin. com* ⇒*756 rooms, 55 suites* &*In-room: safe, Ethernet. In-hotel: 6 restaurants, room service, tennis courts, pools, gym, spa, beachfront, children's programs (ages 4–12), executive floor, concierge, public Wi-Fi, no-smoking rooms* ⊟*AE, D, DC, MC, V.*

DOWNTOWN DISNEY RESORT AREA

Take I–4 Exit 68. A number of non-Disney-owned resorts are clustered on Disney property not far from Downtown Disney, and several more sprawling, high-quality resorts are just outside the park's northernmost entrance. Several of these hotels market themselves as "official" Disney hotels, meaning that they have special agreements with Disney that allow them to offer their guests such perks as early park admission. The hotels on Hotel Plaza Boulevard are within walking distance of Downtown Disney Marketplace, though most offer shuttle service anyway.

$$–$$$ ▦**Buena Vista Palace Resort & Spa in the WDW Resort.** This hotel gets kudos as much for its on-site charms as for its location—100 yards from the Wolfgang Puck's in Downtown Disney. All rooms have patios or balconies, most with great views of Downtown Disney. As a guest, you receive free transportation to all Disney parks, the chance to sign up for Disney character meals, access to Disney golf courses, and early entrance to the Disney theme parks, just like in the Disney on-property hotels. **Pros:** Easy walk to Downtown Disney; huge spa. **Cons:** Inconvenient to Universal and downtown Orlando. ⊠*1900 Buena*

Vista Dr., Lake Buena Vista ☎*407/827–2727* ⊕*www.luxuryresorts. com* ⇨*1,014 rooms, 209 suites* ♿*In-room: safe, Ethernet. In-hotel: 4 restaurants, room service, tennis courts, pools, gym, spa, children's programs (ages 4–12), laundry facilities, laundry service, concierge, public Wi-Fi, no-smoking rooms* ▤*AE, D, DC, MC, V.*

$$–$$$$ ⊡**Doubletree Guest Suites in the WDW Resort.** The lavender-and-pink exterior that used to leap out at you, and not in a good way, has given way to a more sedate beige, and the interior has gotten a make-over as well. Comfortable one- and two-bedroom suites are decorated in tasteful hues, with blue carpeting and bedspreads and raspberry-colored furniture. Each bedroom has either a king bed or two doubles. Units come with three TVs, including one in the bathroom, and a wet bar, microwave, refrigerator, and coffeemaker. The small lobby has a charming feature—a small aviary with birds from South America and Africa. There's a special "registration desk" for kids, where they can get coloring books, balloons and oatmeal cookies. **Pros:** Within walking distance of Downtown Disney; free shuttle to all Disney attractions. **Cons:** Inconvenient to Universal and downtown Orlando. ✉*2305 Hotel Plaza Blvd., Lake Buena Vista* ☎*407/934–1000 or 800/222–8733* ⊕*www.doubletreeguestsuites.com* ⇨*229 units* ♿*In-room: safe, refrigerator, Ethernet. In-hotel: restaurant, room service, bars, tennis courts, pool, gym, laundry facilities, laundry service, public Wi-Fi, no-smoking rooms* ▤*AE, DC, MC, V.*

$$$–$$$$ ⊡**Hilton in the WDW Resort.** An ingenious waterfall tumbles off the covered entrance and into a stone fountain surrounded by palm trees. Although not huge, rooms are upbeat, cozy, and contemporary, and many on the upper floors have great views of Downtown Disney, which is just a short walk away. The hotel offers two good eateries: Andiamo Italian Bistro, specializing in pasta and grilled seafood, and a Benihana Steakhouse and Sushi Bar. Guests can enter Disney parks an hour before they officially open. **Pros:** Close to Downtown Disney; because this is an "official" Disney hotel (although not a Disney-operated one) you get the same early-entrance privileges to Disney Parks; free shuttle bus; kids program. **Cons:** Pricier than similar lodgings father from Disney; inconvenient to Universal and downtown Orlando. ✉*1751 Hotel Plaza Blvd., Lake Buena Vista* ☎*407/827–4000, 800/782–4414 reservations* ⊕*www.hilton.com* ⇨*814 rooms, 27 suites* ♿*In-room: safe, Ethernet. In-hotel: 7 restaurants, room service, pools, gym, children's programs (ages 3–12), laundry facilities, laundry service, public Wi-Fi, no-smoking rooms* ▤*AE, DC, MC.*

OFF-SITE HOTELS NEAR WALT DISNEY WORLD

LAKE BUENA VISTA AREA

Many people stay in resorts a bit farther northeast of Downtown Disney because, though equally grand, they tend to be less expensive than those right on Hotel Plaza Boulevard. If you're willing to take a five-minute drive or shuttle ride, you might save as much as 35% off your room tab.

$-$$ ▦**Buena Vista Suites.** In this all-suites property you get a bedroom, a living room with a foldout sofa bed, two TVs, two phones, and a small kitchen with a coffeemaker, sink, microwave, and refrigerator. King suites have a single king bed and a whirlpool bath. **Pros:** Free breakfast buffet; free Disney shuttle. **Cons:** Not much of interest within walking distance (but there is a convenience store across the street). ✉*8203 World Center Dr., Lake Buena Vista Area* ☎*407/239–8588 or 800/537–7737* ⊕*www.buenavistasuites.com* ⤳*280 suites* ⌂*In-room: safe, refrigerator, Ethernet. In-hotel: restaurant, room service, tennis courts, pool, gym, laundry facilities, public Wi-Fi, no-smoking rooms* ▤*AE, D, DC, MC, V* ▯O▮*BP.*

$ ▦**Holiday Inn SunSpree Lake Buena Vista.** This family-oriented hotel has a children's registration desk. Off the lobby you'll find the CyberArcade; a small theater where clowns perform weekends at 7 PM; and a buffet restaurant where kids accompanied by adults eat free at their own little picnic tables. Families love the Kidsuites: playhouse-style rooms within a larger room. **Pros:** Extremely kid-friendly; great deal for families. You can walk to some off-property restaurants without crossing the street. **Cons:** Too noisy at times for adults; street is a tad busy for pedestrians to try to cross, especially at night. ✉*13351 Rte. 535, Orlando* ☎*407/239–4500 or 800/366–6299* ⊕*www.kidsuites. com* ⤳*507 rooms* ⌂*In-room: safe, refrigerator, Ethernet. In-hotel: restaurant, bar, pool, gym, children's programs (ages 4–12), laundry facilities, laundry service, public Wi-Fi, no-smoking rooms* ▤*AE, D, DC, MC, V.*

$$$$ ▦**Hyatt Regency Grand Cypress Resort.** On 1,500 acres just outside Disney's north entrance, this spectacular resort has a private lake, three golf courses, and miles of trails for bicycling, jogging, and horseback riding. The 800,000-gallon pool has a 45-foot slide and is fed by 12 waterfalls. Tropical birds and plants and Chinese sculptures fill the 18-story atrium. All rooms have tasteful rattan furniture and a private balcony overlooking either the Lake Buena Vista area or the pool. Villas have fireplaces and whirlpool baths. Accommodations are divided between the hotel and the **Villas of Grand Cypress** (✉*1 N. Jacaranda Dr., Lake Buena Vista* ☎*407/239–1234 or 800/835–7377*), with 200 villas. **Pros:** Great Sunday brunch at La Coquina; huge pool; lots of recreation options, including nearby equestrian center. **Cons:** Pricey; inconvenient to Universal Orlando, SeaWorld, and downtown Orlando. ✉*1 Grand Cypress Blvd., Lake Buena Vista Area, Orlando* ☎*407/239–1234 or 800/233–1234* ⊕*www.hyattgrandcypress.com* ⤳*750 rooms* ⌂*In-room: safe, Ethernet. In-hotel: 5 restaurants, room service, 18-hole golf courses, 9-hole golf course, tennis courts, pools, gym, spa, bicycles, children's programs (ages 5–12), laundry service, public Wi-Fi, no-smoking rooms* ▤*AE, D, DC, MC, V.*

Fodor's Choice
★

$-$$ ▦**Marriott Village at Little Lake Bryan.** The private, gated Marriott Village has three hotels. The **Courtyard** welcomes both families and business travelers with 3,000 square feet of meeting space and large standard rooms decorated with yellow and green floral patterns and blond-wood furniture. Each room has a coffeemaker and Web TV, and the indoor-outdoor pool has a swim-up bar. At **SpringHill Suites,** accommodations have kitchenettes, separate sleeping and dining areas, and Sony Playstations. The **Fairfield Inn** is the least expensive of the three, but rooms are as bright and pleasant, if not quite as amenity-laden. It also has family suites with bunk beds and a Hawaiian theme that kids will love. Continental breakfast is included in the rates, and there are several chain restaurants in the complex. Best of all, there's an on-site Disney planning center where you can buy park tickets. **Pros:** Lots of informal dining options; lower room rates than hotels on the other side of I–4. You can walk to a few chain restaurants just off of the hotel property. **Cons:** Disney shuttle costs $5 per person round-trip (hotels across I–4 have free shuttles). ⊠ *8623 Vineland Ave., Orlando* ☎ *407/938–9001 or 877/682–8552* ⊕ *www.marriottvillage.com* ✒ *650 rooms, 450 suites* ⚷ *In-room: safe, refrigerator, Ethernet. In-hotel: 8 restaurants, room service, bars, pools, gym, children's programs (ages 4–12), laundry facilities, laundry service, public Wi-Fi, no-smoking rooms* ⊟ *AE, D, DC, MC, V* ⊚ *CP.*

☾ **$$–$$$$**
Fodor'sChoice
★
🗂 **Nickelodeon Family Suites by Holiday Inn.** The Nickelodeon theme extends everywhere, from the suites, where separate kids' rooms have bunk beds and SpongeBob wall murals, to the two giant pools built up like water parks. Kids will look forward to wake-up calls from Nickelodeon stars, character breakfasts, and live entertainment. You can choose between one-, two- and three-bedroom suites, with or without full kitchens. **Pros:** Extremely kid-friendly; free Disney, Universal Orlando, and SeaWorld shuttles; golf course. **Cons:** Not within walking distance of Disney or Downtown Disney; may be too frenetic for folks without kids. ⊠ *14500 Continental Gateway, I–4 Exit 67, Orlando* ☎ *407/387–5437 or 866/462–6425* ⊕ *www.nickhotels.com* ✒ *777 suites* ⚷ *In-room: safe, kitchen (some), refrigerator, Ethernet. In-hotel: 3 restaurants, room service, pools, 9-hole golf course, gym, children's programs (ages 4–12), laundry facilities, laundry service, public Wi-Fi, no-smoking rooms* ⊟ *AE, D, DC, MC, V.*

★ **$–$$**
🗂 **PerriHouse Bed & Breakfast Inn.** An eight-room bed-and-breakfast inside a serene bird sanctuary is a unique lodging experience in fast-lane Orlando. The PerriHouse offers you a chance to split your time between sightseeing and spending quiet moments bird-watching: the 16-acre sanctuary has observation paths, a pond, a feeding station, and a small birdhouse museum. It's attractive to bobwhites, downy woodpeckers, red-tail hawks, and the occasional bald eagle. The inn is a romantic getaway, with four-poster and canopy beds and some fireplaces. And the resort recently added a freestanding villa that can sleep six. The staff can book some interesting adventures—anything from bass-fishing trips to sessions at an Orlando skydiving simulator. You're free to use the kitchen. **Pros:** Intimate and private; great bird-watching. **Cons:** Not an easy walk to much of interest; need a rental car. ⊠ *10417 Vista Oak Ct., Lake Buena Vista* ☎ *407/876–4830 or 800/780–4830* ⊕ *www.perrihouse.com* ✒ *8 rooms* ⚷ *In-room: safe, Ethernet. In-hotel: pool* ⊟ *AE, D, DC, MC, V* ⊚ *CP.*

$$
🗂 **Sheraton Vistana Resort.** Consider this peaceful resort, just across I–4 from Downtown Disney, if you're traveling with a large family or group of friends. The spacious, tasteful, one- and two-bedroom villas and

town houses have living rooms, full kitchens, and washers and dryers. Tennis players take note: the 13 clay and all-weather courts are free to guests; private or semiprivate lessons are available for a fee. With seven outdoor heated pools, five kiddie pools, and eight outdoor hot tubs, you can spend the whole day just soaking up the sun. **Pros:** Kitchens let you save money on food; lots of on-site recreation options. **Cons:** Not within walking distance of Downtown Disney (across I–4); shuttles to Disney ($9 round-trip) and Universal and I-Drive ($11 round-trip) are slow. No-smoking rooms are not guaranteed. ⊠*8800 Vistana Center Dr., Orlando* ☎*407/239–3100 or 800/325–3535* ⊕*www.starwoodvo.com* ✑*1,700 units* ⚠*In-room: safe, kitchen, refrigerator, Ethernet. In-hotel: 2 restaurants, tennis courts, pools, gym, concierge, children's programs (ages 4–12), public Wi-Fi, no-smoking rooms* ▭*AE, D, DC, MC, V.*

KISSIMMEE
Take I–4 Exit 64A, unless otherwise noted.

One Kissimmee caveat: beware of the word "maingate" in many hotel names. It's a good 6 mi from Kissimmee's "maingate" hotel area to the Walt Disney World entrance. The "maingate west" area, however, is about 2 miles from the park. Of course, the greater the distance from Walt Disney World, the lower the room rates. A few additional minutes' drive may save you a significant amount of money, so shop around. And if you wait until arrival to find a place, don't be bashful about asking to see the rooms. It's a buyer's market.

¢–$ **Celebrity Resorts Kissimmee.** A collection of villas a few blocks south of U.S. 192, this resort puts you far enough from the highway to avoid the clutter of the tourist strip, but close enough to conveniently reach its shops and restaurants. And it's about 4 miles from the Walt Disney World entrance. As at the Celebrity Resort in Lake Buena Vista, accommodations here range from standard hotel rooms to two-bedroom deluxe suites that can sleep up to 10 people. Suites have living rooms with sofa beds and separate dining areas. **Pros:** Feels miles off the tourist strip; short drive to shops. **Cons:** Not within an easy walk of much; Disney shuttle costs $10 per person round-trip. There's a $4 daily "resort fee" for such standards as phone usage and self-parking. Two-night minimum during high season. ⊠*2800 N. Poinciana Blvd., Kissimmee* ☎*407/997–5000 or 800/423–8604* ⊕*www.celebrity resorts.com* ✑*311 suites* ⚠*In-room: safe, kitchen (some), refrigerator, Ethernet, Wi-Fi. In-hotel: restaurant, room service, tennis court, pools, gym, children's programs (ages 4–12), laundry facilities, laundry service, no-smoking rooms* ▭*AE, D, MC, V.*

★ $$–$$$$ **Gaylord Palms Resort.** Built in the style of a grand turn-of-the-20th-century Florida mansion, this resort is meant to awe. Inside its enormous atrium, covered by a 4-acre glass roof, are re-creations of such Florida icons as the Everglades, Key West, and old St. Augustine. Restaurants include Sunset Sam's Fish Camp, on a 60-foot fishing boat docked on the hotel's indoor ocean, and the Old Hickory Steak House in an old warehouse overlooking the alligator-ridden Everglades. Rooms carry on the Florida themes with colorful, tropical decorations. With extensive children's programs, two pool areas, and a huge Canyon Ranch spa, the hotel connives to make you never want to leave. The newest room amenity is Gaylord iConnect, complete with a 15-inch flat-screen monitor that connects you to the Internet plus a hotel network for booking dinner and activity reservations. **Pros:** You could have a great vacation without ever leaving the grounds; free shuttle to Disney. **Cons:** Rooms and meals are pricey; not much within walking distance (although the hotel is so big, you can take quite a hike inside the building). ⊠ *6000 Osceola Pkwy., I–4 Exit 65, Kissimmee* ☎ *407/586–0000* ⊕ *www.gaylordpalms.com* ⇖ *1,406 rooms, 86 suites* ♿ *In-room: safe, Ethernet. In-hotel: 5 restaurants, bars, pools, gym, spa, children's programs (ages 4–12), laundry service, public Wi-Fi, no-smoking rooms* ▭ *AE, D, DC, MC, V.*

$–$$ ▦ **Magical Memories Villas.** Despite the name, this resort is not affiliated with Disney, but you'll probably feel the magic anyway when you get your bill. Two-bedroom villas with full kitchens start at $89 a night. Three- and four-bedroom villas are also available. (But, the resort requires a three-night minimum stay.) Although the furnishings are standard, the villas are spacious and bright, with large windows and pastel pink walls. All the suites include a washer and dryer, and a set of linens. **Pros:** Sequestered and homey; free long-distance calls with mid-price and premium rooms. **Cons:** Not an easy walk to area shops or restaurants; extra charge for daily housekeeping (which is required). ⊠ *5075 U.S. 192 W, Kissimmee* ☎ *407/390–8200 or 800/736–0402* ⊕ *www.magicalmemories.com* ⇖ *140 villas* ♿ *In-room: kitchen, refrigerator, VCR, Ethernet. In-hotel: tennis court, pool, gym, laundry facilities, no-smoking rooms, some pets allowed (fee)* ▭ *D, MC, V.*

¢–$ ▦ **Seralago Hotel & Suites Maingate East.** It's within walking distance of the Old Town shopping and entertainment complex and 3 miles from Disney. Special kids' suites have a room designed to look like Wild West fort, with bunk beds, TVs, and video games. All rooms have VCRs and kitchenettes with refrigerators and microwaves. Kids under 12 eat free (with a paying adult) at the restaurant. **Pros:** Easy walk to shops and restaurants; pets are welcome ($40 nonrefundable deposit; dogs must be 40 pounds or less); free shuttle to all Disney parks. **Cons:** On a touristy strip of highway about as far from Walden Pond as you could imagine. ⊠ *5678 W. Irlo Bronson Memorial Hwy., Kissimmee* ☎ *407/396–4488, 800/366–5437, or 800/465–4329* ⊕ *www.orlando familyfunhotel.com* ⇖ *614 rooms, 110 suites* ♿ *In-room: kitchen, VCR. In-hotel: restaurant, room service, bar, tennis courts, 2 pools, children's programs (ages 3–12), laundry facilities, laundry service, no-smoking rooms* ▭ *AE, D, DC, MC, V.*

UNIVERSAL ORLANDO AREA

Take I–4 Exit 74B or 75A, unless otherwise noted.

$$ ▦ **Doubletree Hotel at the Entrance to Universal Orlando.** It's a hotbed of business-trippers that also attracts pleasure-seekers thanks to a location right at the Universal Orlando entrance. Don't worry about noisy conventioneers—the meeting and convention facilities are completely isolated from the guest towers. If you happen to stay here on business, though, note that the teleconferencing center lets you connect with points all over the world. **Pros:** Within walking distance of Universal and area shops and restaurants. **Cons:** On a fast-lane tourist strip; need a rental car to reach Disney, I-Drive, or downtown Orlando. ✉ *5780 Major Blvd., I–4 Exit 75B,* ☎ *407/351–1000* ⊕ *www.doubltree1. hilton.com* ⇨ *742 rooms, 15 suites* ♿ *In-room: safe, Ethernet. In-hotel: restaurant, room service, pool, gym, laundry facilities, laundry service, public Wi-Fi, no-smoking rooms* ▤ *AE, D, DC, MC.*

$$$$ 📷 **Hard Rock Hotel.** Inside the California mission–style building you'll find such rock memorabilia as the slip Madonna wore in her "Like a Prayer" video. Rooms have black-and-white photos of pop icons and serious sound systems with CD players. Stay in a suite, and you'll get a big-screen TV and a wet bar. Kid-friendly suites have a small extra room for children. Your hotel key card lets you bypass lines at Universal. The Kitchen, one of the hotel's restaurants, occasionally hosts visiting musicians cooking their favorite meals at the Chef's Table. **Pros:** Whort walk to Universal and CityWalk; preferential treatment at Universal rides. **Cons:** Rooms and meals are pricey; loud rock music in public areas may annoy some people. ✉ *5800 Universal Blvd., Universal Studios* ☎ *407/503–7625 or 800/232–7827* ⊕ *www.universal orlando.com* ⇨ *621 rooms, 29 suites* ♿ *In-room: safe, refrigerator, VCR, Ethernet. In-hotel: 3 restaurants, room service, bars, pools, gym, children's programs (ages 4–14), laundry service, public Wi-Fi, no-smoking rooms, some pets allowed (fee)* ▤ *AE, D, DC, MC, V.*

¢–$ 📷 **Holiday Inn Express Hotel & Suites Universal Orlando.** Rooms in this 11-story hotel have two double beds or one king; suites add full kitchens and a sofa bed. All baths have large walk-in showers. **Pros:** Within walking distance of Universal and area shops and restaurants; free shuttle to Universal, Sea World, and Wet 'n Wild. **Cons:** Need a rental car to reach Disney or downtown Orlando; no on-site restaurant or room service. ✉ *5605 Major Blvd., Orlando* ☎ *407/363–1333* ☎ *888/465-4329* ⊕ *www.hixuniversal.com* ⇨ *196 rooms, 40 suites* ♿ *In-room: safe, kitchen (some), refrigerator, Ethernet. In-hotel: pool, gym, laundry facilities, laundry service, no-smoking rooms* ▤ *AE, D, DC, MC, V* ⊙l *CP.*

★ $–$$ 📷 **Hyatt Place Orlando/Universal.** This new Hyatt Place is geared to support what Hyatt calls the "24/7" lifestyle, which means essentially that any of the hotel amenities that are available at 3 in the afternoon are also on tap for hotel guests at 3 in the morning. For instance, in the Gallery (aka the lobby) you can check in at a touch-screen kiosk, order hot food 24/7 in the Gallery Kitchen (casual restaurant), or watch a big-screen flat-panel TV in the Gallery Den while sipping espresso or wine. Rooms, done in gold and earth tones, have a pleasant, contemporary feel and have flat-panel TVs equipped with docking ports, to which you can hook up your own DVD, laptop, video game system, or MP3 player. **Pros:** Walking distance to Universal Orlando, and there's also a free shuttle; free high-speed wireless Internet access throughout the hotel. **Cons:** No kids' programs or babysitting service, no room service. ✉ *5859 Caravan Court, Universal Orlando area* ☎ *407/351-0627* ⊕ *www.orlando universal.place.hyatt.com* ⇨ *151 rooms* ♿ *In-room: safe, refrigera-*

tor, Ethernet. In-hotel: restaurant, room service, bar, pool, gym, laundry facilities, laundry service, public Wi-Fi, no-smoking rooms ☐AE, DC, MC, V.

$$$-$$$$ ⚏**Portofino Bay Hotel.** The charm and romance of Portofino, Italy, are conjured up at this lovely luxury resort. The illusion is so faultless, right down to the cobblestone streets, that you might find it hard to believe that the different-color row houses lining the "bay" are a

WORD OF MOUTH

"If you are planning to visit Universal parks then stay in one of their three on site hotels. That way you will gt automatic express access to all the park attractions by showing your room key. They are all Loews hotels and are great. The Portofino Resort is the most adult oriented." –schmerl

facade. Large, plush rooms here are done in cream and white, with down comforters and high-quality wood furnishings. There are two Italian restaurants, Mama Della's and Bice, and gelato machines surround the massive pool. The Feast of St. Gennaro (the patron saint of Naples) is held here in September, as are monthly Italian wine tastings. **Pros:** Incredible, Italian villa atmosphere; large spa; short walk or ferry ride to Universal Studios and Islands of Adventure; preferential treatment at Universal rides. **Cons:** Rooms and meals are noticeably expensive; in-room high-speed Internet access costs $10 a day. ✉*5601 Universal Blvd., Universal Studios* ☎*407/503–1000 or 800/232–7827* ⊕*www.universalorlando.com* ⚏*699 rooms, 51 suites* ⚐*In-room: safe, VCR, Ethernet. In-hotel: 3 restaurants, room service, bar, pools, gym, spa, children's programs (ages 4–14), laundry service, public Wi-Fi, some pets allowed (fee)* ☐AE, D, DC, MC, V.

$$-$$$$
Fodor's Choice
★
⚏**Royal Pacific Resort.** The entrance—a footbridge across a tropical stream—sets the tone for the South Pacific theme of this hotel, which is on 53 acres planted with tropical shrubs and trees, most of them palms. The focal point is a 12,000-square-foot, lagoon-style pool, which has a small beach and an interactive water-play area. Indonesian carvings decorate the walls everywhere. An $8.5 million makeover transformed all guest rooms in late 2007, with bright, tropical bed coverings, bamboo ceiling accents, and hot electronics that include iPod station clock radios and 32" flat panel televisions, plus in-room high speed wireless reception. Emeril Lagasse's restaurant, Tchoup Chop, draws crowds. The hotel hosts Polynesian-style luaus every Saturday. **Pros:** Emeril's restaurant; preferential treatment at Universal rides. **Cons:** Rooms can feel cramped; $10-a-day fee for Internet access unwarranted given rates. ✉*6300 Hollywood Way, Universal Orlando* ☎*407/503–3000 or 800/232–7827* ⊕*www.universalorlando.com* ⚏*1,000 rooms, 113 suites* ⚐*In-room: safe, VCR, Ethernet. In-hotel: 3 restaurants, room service, bars, pool, gym, children's programs (ages 4–14), laundry facilities, laundry service, executive floor, public Wi-Fi, no-smoking rooms, some pets allowed (fee)* ☐AE, DC, MC, V.

ORLANDO METRO AREA

INTERNATIONAL DRIVE

Take I–4 Exit 72, 74A, or 75A, unless otherwise noted.

$-$$$ ☶ **The Doubletree Castle.** You won't really think you're in a castle at this mid-price hotel, although the tall gold-and-silver spires, medieval-style mosaics, arched doorways, and British tourists may make you feel like reading Harry Potter. Take your book to either the rooftop terrace or the inviting courtyard, which has a big, round swimming pool. Rooms have gold-framed mirrors and black-velvet headboards. And then there's the legend of the castle's "creature." Don't worry, it won't scare your kids. Café Tu Tu Tango, one of the better restaurants in this part of Orlando, has a zesty, small-dish, multicultural menu, and Pointe Orlando, with lots of new dining options, is an easy walk. **Pros:** Kid-friendly; easy walk to I-Drive eateries and attractions; free theme-parks shuttle. **Cons:** On a congested stretch of I-Drive. ⊠*8629 International Dr., I-Drive Area, Orlando* ☎*407/345–1511 or 800/952–2785* ⊕*www.doubletreecastle.com* ⇴*216 rooms* ⌂*In-room: safe, refrigerator, Ethernet, Wi-Fi. In-hotel: 2 restaurants, room service, pool, gym, laundry service, public Wi-Fi, no-smoking rooms* ⊟*AE, D, DC, MC, V.*

$$$-$$$$ ☶ **JW Marriott Orlando Grande Lakes.** With more than 70,000 square feet of meeting space, this hotel caters to a convention clientele. But because it's part of a lush resort that includes a European-style spa and a Greg Norman–designed golf course, it also appeals to those looking to relax. Rooms are large (420 square feet), and most have balconies that overlook the huge pool complex. The good news about this place is that you get Ritz-Carlton amenities at JW Marriott prices. Wander down a long connector hallway to the adjoining Ritz-Carlton, where you can use your room charge card in the restaurants and shops. **Pros:** Pool is great for kids and adults; shares amenities with the Ritz. **Cons:** Things are spread out on the grounds; you need a rental car to reach Disney and other area offerings. ⊠*4040 Central Florida Pkwy., I-Drive Area, Orlando* ☎*407/206–2300 or 800/576–5750* ⊕*www.grandelakes.com* ⇴*1,000 rooms, 57 suites* ⌂*In-room: Ethernet. In-hotel: 4 restaurants, room service, bars, 18-hole golf course, pool, gym, spa, concierge, laundry service, executive floor, public Wi-Fi, no-smoking rooms* ⊟*AE, D, DC, MC, V.*

$-$$ ☶ **Marriott Residence Inn SeaWorld International Center.** The longish name hints at all the markets the hotel is attempting to tap: SeaWorld, I-Drive, and the convention center. All are within a 2-mile radius; all are served by hotel shuttles. Even the least expensive suites can sleep five people. A free breakfast is served daily, and several nearby restaurants will deliver to your room. The recreation area around the pool is like a summer camp, with a basketball court, playground equipment, picnic tables, and gas grills. Get a firm grip on directions if you're driving. The hotel is adjacent to I–4, but it's 2 miles from the interstate via two expressways, including Beachline Expressway. There's free shuttle service to Universal and SeaWorld. **Pros:** Well-equipped kitchens; free breakfast; pets allowed ($75 deposit); free shuttles to lots of places. **Cons:** Not much within walking distance; hard to find from I–4, even though you can see the hotel from the freeway. ✉ *11000 Westwood Blvd., I–4 Exit 72, I-Drive Area, Orlando* ☎ *407/313–3600 800/331–3131* ⊕ *www.residenceinnseaworld.com* ⌨ *350 suites* ⚹ *In-room: safe, kitchen, Ethernet, Wi-Fi. In-hotel: restaurant, bar, pool, gym, laundry facilities, laundry service, no-smoking rooms* ⊟ *AE, D, DC, MC, V* ⎮⊙⎮*BP.*

★ **$$$–$$$$**   ⊞**Peabody Orlando.** Every day at 11 AM the celebrated Peabody ducks exit a private elevator and waddle across the lobby to the marble fountain where they pass the day, basking in their fame. At 5 they repeat the ritual in reverse. Built by the owners of the landmark Peabody Hotel in Memphis, this 27-story structure resembles a trio of high-rise office towers, but don't be put off by the austerity. The interior impresses with gilt and marble halls. Some of the oversize upper-floor rooms have views of Disney. A lobby concierge can answer your questions about attractions and cultural events. You can leave your cares behind at the spa or health club. A round-trip shuttle to Disney or Universal is $10 per person. This hotel is about to double in size at the end of 2009, when a brand-new high-rise tower will be built and connected to the Orange County Convention Center. This will bring a new luxury spa, and plenty of conventioneers. **Pros:** Adjacent to convention center (business travelers take note); good spa; short walk to shops and restaurants. **Cons:** Pricey; adjacent to convention center (leisure travelers take note); on a congested section of I-Drive. ✉ *9801 International Dr., I-Drive Area, Orlando* ☎ *407/352–4000 or 800/732–2639* ⊕ *www. peabodyorlando.com* ⌨ *891 rooms* ⚹ *In-room: safe, Ethernet. In-hotel: 3 restaurants, room service, tennis courts, pool, gym, spa, concierge, public Wi-Fi, no-smoking rooms* ⊟ *AE, D, DC, MC, V.*

$$$$ ⊞**Ritz-Carlton Orlando Grande Lakes.** Orlando's first and only Ritz is a
Fodor'sChoice   particularly extravagant link in the luxury chain. Service is exemplary,
★   from the fully attended porte-cochere entrance to the 18-hole golf course and 40-room spa. Rooms and suites have large balconies, elegant wood furnishings, down comforters, and decadent marble baths (with separate showers and tubs). A lovely, Roman-style pool area has fountains and a hot tub. Make reservations for dinner at Norman's when you reserve your room (Norman's is hugely expensive, but if you can afford the Ritz, you can probably afford Norman's). An enclosed hallway connects the Ritz to the nearby JW Marriott Hotel, where you'll find more restaurants and a kid-friendly water park. **Pros:** Truly luxurious; impeccable service; great spa; golf course; shares amenities with Marriott. **Cons:** Pricey; need a rental car to reach Disney and area shops and restaurants. ✉ *4012 Central Florida Pkwy., I-Drive Area, Orlando* ☎ *407/206–2400 or 800/576–5760* ⊕ *www.grandelakes.com* ⌨ *520 rooms, 64 suites* ⚹ *In-room: Ethernet. In-hotel: 4 restaurants, room service, bars, 18-hole golf course, pool, gym, spa, concierge, children's programs (ages 4–12), laundry service, executive floor, public Wi-Fi, no-smoking rooms* ⊟ *AE, D, DC, MC, V.*

$–$$ ⊞**Wyndham Orlando Resort.** Two-story villas, palm trees, and romantic lagoons evoke a Caribbean getaway. There's a children's entertainment center and an upscale shopping court. The villas are comfortable, if not necessarily candidates for *Architectural Digest*. And you can't beat the location five minutes from Universal. If you choose the Family Fun Suites option, your youngsters get a separate room with bunk beds. There's a free shuttle to Universal and SeaWorld. **Pros:** Convenient to Universal, SeaWorld, I-Drive, and outlet malls; pets allowed ($50 nonrefundable fee, pets can't weigh more than 50 pounds and no more than two are allowed). **Cons:** No shuttle to Disney; about 30 minutes away. ⊠*8001 International Dr., I-Drive Area, Orlando* ☎*407/351–2420 or 800/996–3426* ⊕*www.wyndham.com* ☞*1,064 rooms* ⅋*In-room: safe, refrigerator, Ethernet. In-hotel: 3 restaurants, room service, tennis courts, jogging track, pools, gym, spa, massage, laundry service, public Wi-Fi, no-smoking rooms, some pets allowed (fee)* ▤*AE, D, DC, MC, V.*

4

DOWNTOWN ORLANDO

$-$$$

Fodor'sChoice

★

The Courtyard at Lake Lucerne. Four beautifully restored Victorian houses surround a palm-lined courtyard at this inn. Although it's almost under an expressway bridge, there's no traffic noise. You can sit on one of the porches and imagine yourself back in the time when citrus ruled and the few visitors arrived at the old railroad station on Church Street, six blocks away. Rooms have hardwood floors, Persian rugs, and antique furniture. A real treat is the Turret Room, which overlooks the lake across the street. **Pros:** Serenity; great Victorian architecture; the azaleas in this neighborhood are alive with color in spring and summer; short walk to Lake Eola and Church Street. **Cons:** Far from theme parks and I-Drive. ⊠*211 N. Lucerne Circle E, Downtown, Orlando* ☎*407/648–5188* ⊕*www.orlandohistoricinn.com* ☞*15 rooms, 15 suites* ⅋*In-room: Ethernet. In-hotel: no elevator, no-smoking rooms* ▤*MC, V* ⊚*CP.*

★ $$-$$$

Eō Inn & Urban Spa. The entrance is at the rear of the building, behind Panera Bread, the bakery–restaurant that occupies the ground floor. Consequently, this three-story boutique hotel in a 1923 building is an undiscovered charmer. The spa does a brisk business on its own, but as a hotel guest you can always get in for a Swedish massage or a beauty treatment. Rooms have black-and-white photographs, thick down comforters, and high-speed Internet connections. Best of all, Lake Eola, with its 1-mile walking path, is across the street—treat yourself to a king suite, with a balconyoverlooking the lake. **Pros:** Good spa; very short walk to Lake Eola; short walk to Thornton Park and Church Street; these areas have plenty of restaurants and are safe to walk to at night. **Cons:** You have to battle I–4 traffic; Disney is 30 minutes away. ⊠*227 N. Eola Dr., off E. Robinson St., Thornton Park, Orlando* ☎*407/481–8485 or 888/481–8488* ⊕*www.eoinn.com* ☞*17 rooms* ⅋*In-room: safe, Ethernet. In-hotel: spa, laundry service, public Wi-Fi, no-smoking rooms* ▤*AE, D, DC, MC, V.*

NIGHTLIFE

When you enter the fiefdom known as Walt Disney World, you're likely to see as many watering holes as cartoon characters. After beating your feet around a theme park all day, there are lounges, bars, speakeasies, pubs, sports bars, and microbreweries where you can settle down with a soothing libation. Everywhere you look, jazz trios, bluesmen, DJs, and rockers are tuning up and turning on their amps after dinner's done. Plus, two long-running dinner shows provide an evening of song, dance, and dining, all for a single price. Get information on WDW nightlife from the **Walt Disney World information hotline** (☎407/824–2222 or 407/824–4500) or check online at www.waltdisneyworld. com. Disney nightspots accept American Express, MasterCard, and Visa. And cash. Lots of it.

DISNEY'S BOARDWALK

The BoardWalk is Disney's version of a shoreside complex with restaurants, bars and clubs, souvenir sellers, surreys, saltwater taffy vendors, and shops. When the lights go on after sunset, the mood is festive in a family way, far more tranquil than at Downtown Disney. For information on events call the **BoardWalk entertainment hotline** (☎407/939–3492 or 407/939–2444).

Atlantic Dance Hall. This club started out as a hypercool room recalling the Swing Era, with martinis, cigars, and Sinatra soundalikes, but that didn't last, so it reopened as a Latin club. That didn't last either, so now it's a typical Top 40 dance club. These days it has a huge screen showing videos requested by the crowd. You must be 21 to enter. ☎407/939–2444 or 407/939–2430 🎫No cover ⊙Tues.–Sat. 9 PM–2 AM.

Big River Grille & Brewing Works. Disney World's first brewpub, Big River, has warm wood surfaces and intimate tables where brewmasters tend to their potions, adding to the charm of this retreat. Inside, stainless-steel vats brew a variety of beers, the most popular being Rocket Red Ale. But if you're not sure what you'd like best, order a $5 sampler that includes up to six 4-ounce shots of whatever they have on tap that day. The sidewalk café is a great place for people-watching and good conversation. ☎407/560–0253 🎫No cover ⊙Daily 11:30 AM–12:30 AM.

DOWNTOWN DISNEY

Fodor'sChoice
★
West Side **Cirque du Soleil—**_La Nouba._ This surreal show by the world-famous circus company starts at 100 mph and accelerates from there. The performance is 90 minutes of extraordinary acrobatics, avant-garde stagings, costumes, choreography, and a thrilling grand finale that makes you doubt Newton's law of gravity. ☎407/939–7600 _reservations_ ⊕_www.cirquedusoleil.com_ 🎫 _Front and center $121.41 adults, $96.92 children under 10; Category 1 seats (front sides) $105.44 adults, $84.14 children under 10; Category 2 seats (to the side and the back) $86.27 adults, $69.23 children under 10; Category 3 seats (to_

the far sides and very back) $69.23 adults, $55.38 children under 10 ⊙ *Performances Tues.–Sat. 6 and 9* PM.

Fodor'sChoice **House of Blues.** The restaurant hosts cool blues nightly (alongside its
★ rib-sticking Mississippi Delta cooking), but it's the HOB's concert hall
next door that garners the real attention. The hall has showcased local
and nationally known artists including Aretha Franklin, David Byrne,
Steve Miller, Los Lobos, the Roots, and even Journey. From rock to
reggae to R&B, this is arguably the best live-music venue in Orlando,
and standing a few feet from your guitar heroes is the way music should
be seen and heard. ☎407/934–2583 ☒*Covers vary* ⊙*Daily, performance times vary.*

PLEASURE ISLAND

4

Pleasure Island was Disney's initial and exciting foray into a nighttime complex, but that was 1989. Over the years they've tweaked
and adjusted things—as they should—and they're still at it. The 6-
acre park has clubs that draw an across-the-board mix of college kids,
young married couples, middle-age business folk, world travelers, and
moms and pops sneaking out for an evening. Weekends are the busiest,
although Thursday hops with Disney World cast members itching to
blow their just-issued paychecks. On the "street," video displays and
carnival games keep the atmosphere festive as you bounce from club
to club. Photo ID is required for the wristband that lets you purchase
alcoholic drinks. ☒*Off Buena Vista Dr.* ☎407/934–7781 or 407/824–
2222 ☒*$21.95 plus tax for all clubs; multiclub annual passes, $55.95
plus tax; access to shops and restaurants is free* ⊙ *Clubs daily 7* PM–2
AM; *shops and restaurants daily 10:30* AM–2 AM.

BET SoundStage Club. Backed by Black Entertainment Television, this
club pays tribute to all genres of black music through videos, live performances, and shows by BET's own dance troupe. As the evening
progresses, sounds shift from BET's Top 10 to old R&B to hip-hop—a
blend that's attracted legions of locals who proclaim this the funkiest
nightspot in Central Florida (perhaps also the loudest). Even if you're
dance-challenged, you might find it hard to resist shakin' your groove
thang to the beat-rich music. Go on, Spaulding. Bust a move. You must
be at least 21 to enter. ☎407/934–7666.

Fodor'sChoice **Comedy Warehouse.** At one of the island's most popular clubs, gifted
★ comedians perform various improv games, sing improvised songs, and
create off-the-cuff sketches based largely on suggestions from the audience. Each of the evening's five performances is different, but the cast is
usually on a roll no matter when you go. Lines for the free shows start
forming roughly 45 minutes before curtain, so get there early for a good
seat. It's well worth the wait to watch a gifted comedy troupe work
without profanity. The club is open to all ages. ☎407/828–2939.

8TRAX. In case the lava lamps and disco balls don't tip you off, the
'70s are back at this glittering club. Slip on your bell-bottoms, strap
on your platform shoes, and groove to Chic, the Village People, or
Donna Summer on disk. After a while, it might seem like you're in

your own Quentin Tarantino film. You must be at least 21 to enter. ☎*407/934–7160.*

Mannequins. How far has Disney veered off the family path since Walt died? Stop here and you'll find out. You can expect over-the-top floor shows complete with suggestive bump-and-grind moves at this New York–style dance palace that's patterned after a fashion district warehouse. Twentysomethings rule on the revolving dance floor, and the club also welcomes a gay clientele. Everyone grooves to Top 40 hits, elaborate lighting, and special effects like bubbles and snow. You must be at least 21 to enter. ☎*407/934–6375.*

Raglan Road. A low-key jazz club couldn't cut it here, so Disney found some folks who were ready to bring an authentic Irish pub to Orlando. A dramatic change has taken place. While dancers, storytellers, and musicians keep the pub thumpin', patrons are downing an assortment of Irish fare and beers, ales, and liquors served from four bars. Doors open nightly at 9 PM (and stay open until 2 AM). ☎*407/938-0300* ⊕*www.raglanroadirishpub.com.*

DISNEY'S DINNER SHOWS

★ **Hoop-Dee-Doo Revue.** Staged at Fort Wilderness's rustic Pioneer Hall, this show may be corny, but it's also the liveliest dinner show in Walt Disney World. A troupe of jokers called the Pioneer Hall Players stomp their feet, wisecrack, and sing and dance, while the audience chows down on barbecued ribs, fried chicken, corn on the cob, strawberry shortcake, and all the fixin's. There are three shows nightly, and the prime times sell out months in advance in busy seasons. But you're better off eating dinner too early or too late rather than missing the fun altogether—so take what you can get. If you arrive in Orlando with no reservations, try for a cancellation. Prices vary by seat selection. ⊠*Fort Wilderness Resort* ☎*407/939–3463 advance tickets, 407/824–2803 day of show* ⊞*$50.99–$59.99 adults, $25.99–$30.99 children 3–9, including tax and gratuity* ⊙*Daily 5, 7:15, and 9:30.*

Spirit of Aloha. Formerly the Polynesian Luau, this show is still an outdoor barbecue with entertainment in line with its colorful South Pacific style. Its fire jugglers and hula-drum dancers are entertaining for the whole family, if never quite as endearing as the napkin twirlers at the Hoop-Dee-Doo Revue. The hula dancers' navel maneuvers, however, are something to see. You should try to make reservations at least a month in advance. ⊠*Polynesian Resort* ☎*407/939–3463 advance tickets, 407/824–1593 day of show* ⊞*$50.99–$59.99 adults, $25.99–$30.99 children 3–9, including tax and gratuity. Prices vary by seat selection* ⊙*Tues.–Sat. 5:15 and 8.*

UNIVERSAL ORLANDO'S CITYWALK

Armed with a catchy headline ("Get a Nightlife"), CityWalk met the challenge of diverting the lucrative youth market from Disney and downtown Orlando. It did so by creating an open and airy gathering place that includes clubs ranging from quiet jazz retreats to over-the-top discotheques and, as of 2007, the fabulous and extremely popular Blue Man Group that performs in its own theater (formerly the Nickelodeon studios). On weeknights the crowd is a mix of families and conventioneers; weekends draw a decidedly younger demographic who are still arriving into the wee hours.

Although clubs have individual cover charges, it's far more economical to pay for the whole kit and much of the caboodle. You can buy a variety of admissions and accessories including a Party Pass (a one price–all clubs admission) for $11.99; or a Party Pass-and-a-Movie for $15.98 (plus tax); or a Movie-and-a-Meal for $21.95; or a Party Pass-and-a-Meal for $21. The movies are those at the Universal Cineplex 20, and the meals (tax and gratuity included) are served at City Walk restaurants including Jimmy Buffett's Margaritaville, the Hard Rock Café, NASCAR Sports Grille, and others. What makes these deals even better is the fact that after 6 PM the $11 parking fee drops to nothing. It is, however, a long walk from the parking garage to CityWalk (even longer when you stumble out at 2 AM and realize it's a ¼-mi walk to your car). Then again, you shouldn't be driving in this condition, so have a good time and call a cab. Taxis run at all hours. ☎407/224–2692, 407/363–8000 Universal main line ⊕www.citywalkorlando.com.

CityJazz/Bonkerz. Despite the name on the marquee, there's a serious mix of musical styles in this club. Early in the week there's high energy funk, R&B, soul, rock, Top 40, and "old school" dance; while Thursday, Friday, and Saturday kick off with Bonkerz Comedy Club, starring a litany of touring comics, and a comedy hypnosis show on Sundays. After the comedy, the music kicks in again. ☎407/224–2692, 407/224–2189, 407/629–2665 Bonkerz ◻$7, special performance ticket prices $6–$35 ☾Sun.–Thurs. 8 PM–1 AM, Fri. and Sat. 7 PM–2 AM. Bonkerz shows, Thurs.–Sat. 8 PM.

the groove. The very sound of this place can be terrifying to the uninitiated: images flicker rapidly on several screens and the combination of music, light, and mayhem appeals to a mostly under-30 crowd. Within the cavernous hall, every nook and cranny is filled with techno pop. If you need to escape, the dance floor leads to three rooms: the '70s-style Green Room, filled with beanbag chairs and everything you threw out when Duran Duran hit the charts; the sci-fi Jetson-y Blue Room; and the Red Room, which is hot and romantic in a bordello sort of way. Prepare yourself for lots of fog, swirling lights, and sweaty bodies. This is another 21-and-up club. ☎407/224–2692 ◻$7 ☾Daily 9 PM–2 AM.

Pat O'Brien's. A legend in pre-Katrina New Orleans, this exact reproduction of the original is doing all right in Orlando, with its flaming fountain, dueling pianists, and balcony that re-creates the Crescent City. The draw here is the Patio Bar, where abundant tables and chairs allow you to do nothing but enjoy a respite from the madding crowd—and drink a potent, rum-based hurricane. You must be 21 to enter. ☎407/224–2692 ⊕www.patobriens.com ◻$7 after 9 PM ☾Patio Bar daily 4 PM–2 AM; Piano Bar daily 6 PM–2 AM.

Red Coconut Club. Swank and hip, the interior of CityWalk's newest nightclub is an ultralounge that features a full bar, signature martinis, an extensive wine list, and VIP bottle service. Loaf around the Rat Pack–era lounge, hang out on the balcony, or mingle with the happening crowd at the bars. If you're on a budget, take advantage of the daily happy hours and a gourmet appetizer menu. A DJ and live music push the energy with tunes from rock to Sinatra. You must be 21 to enter. ☎407/224–2692 ⌨$7 after 9 PM ☉Sun.–Wed. 7 PM–2 AM, Thurs.–Sat. 6 PM–2 AM.

DOWNTOWN ORLANDO

Cheyenne Saloon. After an absence of many years, Cheyenne is back. The tri-level structure has a quarter-million board feet of golden oak rails, spindles, banisters, and balustrades, spiffed up Remington art and sculptures, fantastically elaborate cut-glass doors, and beautiful chandeliers. While it may sound like a museum, the purpose is to party with Grand Ol' Opry-style country music performed by the Cheyenne Stampede band. There's red-hot music, dancing, food, nickel beer Wednesday 5–7, and a poker parlor. There's a $5 cover charge. ✉128 West Church St. ☎407/839–3000 ☉Daily 4 pm–2 am; closed Mon.

Social. Perhaps the favorite live-music venue of locals, Social is a great place to see touring and local musicians. It serves full dinners Wednesday through Saturday and offers up live music seven nights a week. You can sip trademark martinis while listening to anything from alternative rock to rockabilly to undiluted jazz. Several now-national acts got their start here, including Matchbox Twenty, Seven Mary Three, and other groups that don't have numbers in their names. ✉54 N. Orange Ave. ☎407/246–1419 ⊕www.thesocial.org ⌨$5–$18, depending on entertainment ☉Sat.–Thurs. 8 PM–2 AM, Fri. 5 PM–2 AM.

SPORTS & THE OUTDOORS

Updated by Rowland Stiteler

There's more to an active Orlando experience than walking 10 miles a day in the theme parks. Northern travelers were flocking to central Florida's myriad lakes, streams, and golf resorts decades before there was a Disney World. There's nothing that can quite compare to an afternoon paddling down a Florida river, watching the alligators splash into the water, and the snowy egrets glide among the palm trees. You can find just about every outdoor sport in the Orlando area—unless it involves a ski lift.

BALLOONING

Fodor'sChoice ★

It's hard to imagine a more inspiring way to enjoy the beautiful Central Florida outdoors than with a hot-air balloon ride. **Bob's Balloons** offers one-hour rides over protected marshland and will even fly over Disney World if wind and weather conditions are right. You meet in Lake Buena Vista at dawn, where Bob and his assistant take you by van to the launch site. It takes about 15 minutes to get the balloon in the air and then you're off on an adventure that definitely surpasses Peter Pan's Flight in the Magic Kingdom.

From the treetop view you'll see farm and forest land for miles, along with horses, deer, wild boar, cattle, and birds flying *below* you. Bob may take you as high as 1,000 feet, from which point you'll be able to see Disney's landmarks: the Expedition Everest mountain, the Epcot ball, and more. Several other balloons are likely to go up near you— there's a tight-knit community of ballooners in the Orlando area—so you'll view these colorful sky ornaments from a parallel level. There are seats in the basket, but you'll probably be too thrilled to sit down.

Landing places are somewhat arbitrary, since your direction depends on the wind. You may even land on a private farm. Fortunately, Bob has a relationship with most of the landowners in the area. A private flight for two (should you, say, want to pop the question) is $475. ☎407/466–6380 or 877/824–4606 ⊕*www.bobsballoons.com* ✉*$165, $90 per child under 90 lbs or 12 yrs* ▭*D, MC, V.*

FISHING

WALT DISNEY WORLD

★ You can sign up for two-hour **fishing excursions** (☎407/939–7529)on regularly stocked Bay Lake and Seven Seas Lagoon. In fact, Bay Lake is so well stocked, locals joke that you can almost walk across the lake on the backs of the bass, so your chances of catching fish are quite good. The trips work on a catch-and-release program, though, so you can't take fish home.

These organized outings are the only way you're allowed to fish on the lakes. Reservations are required. Yacht and Beach Club guests and Boardwalk Hotel guests can book a similar fishing excursion on Crescent Lake for the same fee as the Bay Lake trip. Two-hour trips, which depart daily at 7, 10, and 1:30, cost $250 for the morning departures and $225 for the afternoon departure, plus $100 for each additional hour. Live bait is free.

GOLF

Golfpac (✉*483 Montgomery Pl., Altamonte Springs* ☎*407/260–2288 or 800/327–0878* ⊕*www.golfpactravel.com*)packages golf vacations and prearranges tee times at more than 78 courses around Orlando. Rates vary based on hotel and course, and at least 60 to 90 days' advance notice is recommended to set up a vacation.

WALT DISNEY WORLD

Where else would you find a sand trap shaped like the head of a well-known mouse? Walt Disney World has 99 holes of golf on five championship courses—all on the PGA Tour route—plus a 9-hole walking course. Disney provides a special perk to any guest at a WDW hotel who checks in specifically to play golf: free cab fare for you and your clubs between the hotel and the course you play. (It saves you from having to lug your clubs onto a hotel shuttle bus.) Ask at the front desk when you check into the hotel or call ☎407/939–7529.

GREENS FEES There are lots of variables here, with prices ranging from $20 for a youngster 17 or under to play 9 holes at Oak Trail walking course, to an adult nonhotel guest paying $169 to play 18 holes at one of Disney's newer courses in peak season. Disney guests get a price break. All have a twilight discount rate, $30–$80 for the 18-hole courses, which goes into effect at 2 PM from October 31 to January 14 and at 3 PM from April 1 to October 26. Note that golf rates change frequently, so double-check them when you reserve.

TEE TIMES & Tee times are available daily from 6:45 AM until dark. You can book
RESERVATIONS them up to 90 days in advance if you're staying at a WDW-owned hotel, 30 days ahead if you're staying elsewhere from May through December, and four days in advance from January through April. For tee times and private lessons at any course, call **Walt Disney World Golf & Recreation Reservations** (☎407/939–7529).

ORLANDO AREA

Celebration Golf Club course—in addition to its great pedigree (it was designed by Robert Trent Jones Jr. and Sr.)—has the same thing going for it that the Disney-created town of Celebration, Florida, has: it's just 1 mile off the U.S. 192 tourist strip and a 10-minute drive from Walt Disney World, yet it's lovely and wooded, and as serene and bucolic as any spot in Florida. In addition to the 18-hole course, driving range, and 3-hole junior course, the club includes a quaint, tin-roof clubhouse with a pro shop and restaurant, flanked by a tall, wooden windmill that is a local landmark. The club has golf packages, which include lodging at the nearby Celebration Hotel. ⊠ *701 Golf Park Dr., Celebration* ☎*407/566–4653* ⊕*www.celebrationgolf.com* ⅄*18 holes, 6,783 yards, par 72, USGA rating 73* ⊠*Greens fees $69–$145* ⌒*Restaurant, pro shop, private lessons, club rental.*

★ **Champions Gate Golf Club,** which has the David Leadbetter Golf Academy on its property, has courses designed by Greg Norman. The club is less than 10 miles from Walt Disney World at Exit 24 on I–4. The two courses have distinct styles; the 7,406-yard International has the feel of the best British Isles courses, whereas the 7,048-yard National course is designed in the style of the better domestic courses, with a number of par-3 holes with unusual bunkers. ⊠*1400 Masters Blvd., Champions Gate* ☎*407/787–3330 or 888/558–9301 Champions Gate, 888/633-5323 Ext. 23 Leadbetter Academy* ⊕*www.championsgategolf.com* ⅄*International: 18 holes, 7,406 yards, par 72, USGA rating 73.7; National: 18 holes, 7,048 yards, par 72, USGA rating 72.0* ⊠*Greens fees $65–$187* ⌒*Pro shop, golf school, private lessons, club rental.*

Grand Cypress Golf Club, fashioned after a Scottish glen, is comprised of four nines: the North, South, East, and New courses. In addition, the Grand Cypress Academy of Golf, a 21-acre facility, has golf lessons and clinics. The North and South courses have fairways constructed on different levels, giving them added definition. The New Course was inspired by the Old Course at St. Andrews, and has deep bunkers, double greens, a snaking burn, and even an old stone bridge. ✉*1 N. Jacaranda, Orlando* ☎*407/239–1909 or 800/835–7377* ⊕*www. grandcypress.com* ⚑*North: 9 holes, 3,521 yards, par 36; South: 9 holes, 3,472 yards, par 36; East: 9 holes, 3,434 yards, par 36; New: 9 holes, 6,773 yards, par 72. USGA rating 72* ◱*Greens fees $120–$190* ☞*Tee times 7:30* AM*–6* PM*. Restaurant, club rental, shoe rental, locker room, driving range, putting green, free valet parking.*

MINIATURE GOLF

☀ **Fantasia Gardens Mini-Golf** (☎*407/560–4870*), near Disney's Hollywood Studios and the Swan and Dolphin resorts, recalls Disney's *Fantasia* with a huge statue of Mickey in his sorcerer's outfit directing dancing broomsticks. Music from the film plays over loud speakers. Games cost $11.75 for adults, $9.75 for children ages 3 to 9, and there's a 50% discount for the second consecutive round played.

☀ **Winter Summerland Mini-Golf** (☎*407/560–7161*)has everything from
Fodor'sChoice sand castles to snowbanks, and is allegedly where Santa and his elves
★ spend their summer vacation. The course is close to Disney's Animal Kingdom and the Coronado Springs and All-Star resorts. Adults play for $11.75 and children ages 3 to 9 play for $9.75, including tax. A 50% discount applies to your second consecutive round.

WALT DISNEY WORLD SPORTS

★ **Disney's Wide World of Sports Complex** is proof that Disney doesn't do anything unless it does it in a big way. The 220-acre facility plays host to more than 170 amateur and professional events each year. The huge complex contains a 7,500-seat baseball stadium—housed in a giant stucco structure that from the outside looks like a Moroccan palace—a 5,000-seat field house, and a number of fan-oriented commercial ventures such as the Official All-Star Cafe and shops that sell clothing and other items sanctioned by Major League Baseball, the NBA, and the NFL. During spring training, the perennially great Atlanta Braves play here, and the minor-league Orlando Rays have games during the regular season. But that's just the tip of the iceberg. The complex hosts all manner of individual and team competitions, including big-ticket tennis tournaments. In all, some 30 spectator sports are represented among the annual events presented, including Harlem Globetrotters basketball games, baseball fantasy camps held in conjunction with the Braves at the beginning of spring training each year, and track events ranging from the Walt Disney World Marathon to dozens of annual Amateur Athletic Union (AAU) championships. The complex has softball, basketball, and other games for group events ranging from family reunions to corporate picnics. ✉*Osceola Pkwy.* ☎*407/828–3267 events information* ⊕*www.disneyworldsports.com.*

A key source for sports information on all things Disney is the **Sports Information and Reservations Hotline** (☎*407/939–7529*).

WATER SPORTS

WALT DISNEY WORLD

Boating is big at Disney, and it has the largest fleet of for-rent pleasure craft in the nation. There are marinas at the Caribbean Beach Resort, Contemporary Resort, Downtown Disney Marketplace, Fort Wilderness Resort and Campground, Grand Floridian, Old Key West Resort, Polynesian Resort, Port Orleans Resort, Port Orleans–Riverside Resort, and the Wilderness Lodge. The Yacht and Beach Club Resorts rent Sunfish sailboats, catamarans, motor-powered pontoon boats, pedal boats, and tiny two-passenger Water Sprites—a hit with children—for use on Bay Lake and the adjoining Seven Seas Lagoon, Club Lake, Lake Buena Vista, or Buena Vista Lagoon. Most hotels rent Water Sprites, but you should check each hotel's rental roster. The Polynesian Resort marina rents outrigger canoes. Fort Wilderness rents canoes for paddling along the placid canals in the area. And you can sail and water-ski on Bay Lake and the Seven Seas Lagoon; stop at the Fort Wilderness, Contemporary, Polynesian, or Grand Floridian marina to rent sailboats or sign up for waterskiing. Call 407/ 939–7529 for parasailing, waterskiing, and Jet Skis reservations.

Sammy Duvall's Water Sports Centre (⊠ *Disney's Contemporary Resort* ☎ *407/939–0754*)offers waterskiing, wakeboarding (like waterskiing on a small surfboard; usually done on your knees), and parasailing on Bay Lake. Boat and equipment rental is included with waterskiing (maximum of five people) and wakeboarding (maximum of four people), as are the services of an expert instructor. Parasailing is $95 single for an 8–10 minute ride, and $160 for tandem. Wakeboard is $75 per half hour and $125 per hour.

SHOPPING

Updated
by Alicia
Callanan
Mandigo

From fairy-tale kingdoms to Old West–style trading posts to outlet malls, Walt Disney World and Orlando have a plethora of shopping opportunities that won't leave you disappointed. The colors are bright and energetic, the textures soft and cuddly, and the designs fresh and thoughtful. Before you board any roller coaster or giggle at any show, you'll catch yourself window-shopping and delighting in the thought of making a purchase. And when it comes time to do some serious shopping, you may have a hard time deciding what to buy with all the options available. Of course, your best bet is to wait a couple of days before you buy anything; survey the scene a little before spending all the money in your budget. Better yet, save shopping for the last day of your trip.

WALT DISNEY WORLD

If you return home and realize that you've forgotten a critical souvenir, call WDW's Merchandise Mail Order service at 407/363–6200.

The number-one best store on Disney property is **World of Disney** in the Marketplace section of Downtown Disney. You could actually skip all of the stores in the theme parks and find everything you want here in an hour. And it may be a cliché, but there really is something for everyone, whether you're looking for a something small and inexpensive, like the $3 princess pen, or a Disney collectible, like a Mickey watch or figurine.

DOWNTOWN DISNEY

Fodor$Choice
★ **Mickey's Mart.** The sign proclaims "Everything Ten Dollars and Under," undoubtedly a welcome sight for those who've been reaching for their wallets a little too frequently. Look for the Surprise Grab Bags and the Item of the Week specials. ☎407/828–3864.

LEGO Imagination Center. An impressive backdrop of large and elaborate LEGO sculptures and piles of colorful LEGO pieces wait for children and their parents to build toy kitties, cars, or cold fusion chambers. ☎407/828–0065.

Once Upon A Toy. A joint venture by Disney and Hasbro, this huge toy store is the kind of place childhood dreams are made of. There are tons of classic games redesigned with Disney themes. You'll find Princess Monopoly and the Pirates of the Caribbean Game of Life, just to name a couple. Overhead are a massive Tinker Toy creation and an oversized toy train making the rounds on a suspended track. Toys in the main room seem to be mostly for boys, but another room has a huge faux-candy castle and a My Little Pony Creation Station. You can test-drive many of the toys and play with touch-screen computers. With so many things to do, this is one store that might let you escape without making a purchase. ☎407/934–7775.

World of Disney. You might make it through Once Upon a Toy without pulling out your wallet, but you probably won't be so lucky at World of Disney. For Disney fans, this is *the* Disney superstore. It pushes you into sensory overload with nearly a half-million Disney items from Tinker Bell wings to Tigger hats. But if you have girls in your party, it's the Princess Room that will get you into the most trouble. Five-foot-tall likenesses of Cinderella and Sleeping Beauty stand watch over hoards of little misses scrambling to pick out just the right accessories. Besides princess dolls, clothes, shoes, and jewelry, you can buy a Belle (or Cinderella or Sleeping Beauty) wig to complete the look. Be warned, if you have a princess-obsessed child, one of the dazzling $65 princess dresses is going to be a must-have in her eyes, and people will be plucking them off the racks left and right of her. Add to that the new Bibbidi Bobbidi Boutique, where girls just like yours will be receiving princess makeovers ranging in price from $45 to $180, and you could land your budget in a royal mess. Of course there are things in the $10 to $30 range, including some cute pajamas, but it's hard to compare with those dresses. For grown-ups there are elegant watches, limited-edition artwork, and stylish furniture pieces with a Disney twist. ☎407/828–1451.

4

Pin Traders. It's nice to know that you can visit the biggest and best location for pin collectors without paying park admission. The Marketplace location has not only the largest selection, it also sells many limited-edition pins that are hard to find elsewhere. There are enough pins lining the walls to make you go cross-eyed, but the employees in this shop know their inventory very well, so if you're looking for something in particular, be sure to ask. And if you're having trouble managing your collection, you can buy additional lanyards, pin bags, and corkboards, too. ☎407/828–1451.

Mickey's Pantry is the only store on property dedicated to cooking-related items. This is where you'll find Mickey Mouse waffle irons, fun Mickey coffee mugs, cookie cutters, and the like. ☎407/828–1451.

UNIVERSAL ORLANDO'S CITYWALK

Cartooniversal. Small but packed with great products, Cartooniversal is the place to pick up your kid's favorite cartoon hero: Spider-Man, SpongeBob, and the Cat in the Hat are everywhere. A big plush Scooby Doo goes for $29.95, and X-Men T-shirts go for $14.95. ☎407/224–2464.

Universal Studios Store. Although impressive in size, this store does not have all of the merchandise that's available in the individual park gift shops. Only the best-sellers are for sale here—T-shirts, stuffed animals, and limited-edition comic-book artwork. What's exclusive to this store are the mini movie posters, featuring some of Universal Studios greatest monster movies, priced at $11.99. It's also one of the few places on the property selling Universal trading pins. While you're here, be sure to check the back of the store for clearance racks. ☎407/224–2207.

THE ORLANDO AREA

FACTORY OUTLETS

★ **Prime Outlets Orlando.** Two malls and four annexes make Prime Outlets Orlando the area's largest collection of outlet stores. ✉5401 W. Oak Ridge Rd., at northern tip of International Dr. ☎407/352–9600 ⊕www.primeoutlets.com ⊙Mon.–Sat. 10–9, Sun. 10–6.

Lake Buena Vista Factory Stores. Although there's scant curb appeal, this is a nice gathering of standard outlet stores. The center is roughly 2 mi south of I–4 and includes Reebok, Nine West, Big Dog, Sony, Liz Claiborne, Wrangler, Disney's Character Corner, American Tourister, Murano, Sony/JVC, Tommy Hilfiger, Ralph Lauren, Jockey, Casio, Osh-Kosh, Fossil, and the area's only Old Navy Outlet. If you can, check the Web site before traveling as some stores post online coupons. Take Exit 68 at I–4. ✉15591 State Rd. 535, 1 mi north of Hwy. 192 ☎407/238–9301 ⊕www.lbvfs.com ⊙Mon.–Sat. 10–9, Sun. 10–6.

SHOPPING CENTERS & MALLS

INTERNATIONAL DRIVE AREA

★ **Florida Mall.** With 260-plus stores, this is easily the largest mall in Central Florida. Anchor stores and specialty shops include Nordstrom, Sears Roebuck, JCPenney, Dillard's, Saks Fifth Avenue, Restoration Hardware, J. Crew, Pottery Barn, Brooks Brothers, Cutter & Buck, Harry & David Gourmet Foods, and Swarovski. A 17-restaurant food court and four sit-down restaurants assure you won't go hungry. Stroller and wheelchair rentals are available, along with concierge services and, because the mall attracts crowds of Brazilian and Puerto Rican tourists, foreign-language assistance. The mall is minutes from the Orlando International Airport and 4½ mi east of I–4 and International Drive at the corner of Sand Lake Road and South Orange Blossom Trail. ⊠ *8001 S. Orange Blossom Trail* ☎ *407/851–6255* ⊕ *www. simon.com* ⊙ *Mon.–Sat. 10–9:30, Sun. 11–7.*

Fodor'sChoice **Mall at Millenia.** The best way to describe this mall is "high-end." Designers such as Gucci, Dior, Burberry, Chanel, Jimmy Choo, Hugo Boss, Cartier, and Tiffany have stores here. You'll also find Anthropologie, Neiman Marcus, Bloomingdale's, Bang & Olufsen, and Orlando's only Apple store. But in case you're thinking the shopping here is too high-end, there is also now a new freestanding IKEA store immediately adjacent to Bloomingdale's. A few minutes northwest of Universal, the mall is easy to reach via Exit 78 off I–4. ⊠ *4200 S. Conroy Rd.* ☎ *407/363–3555* ⊕ *www.mallatmillenia.com* ⊙ *Mon.–Sat. 10–9:30, Sun. 11–7.*

Pointe Orlando. Strategically located within walking distance of the Peabody Orlando and Orange County Convention Center, this impressive retail center along the I-Drive corridor has also undergone a massive renovation and upgrade designed to make it even more appealing to expense-account-rich conventioneers. In addition to WonderWorks and the enormous Muvico Pointe 21 theater, the complex houses more than 60 specialty shops. ⊠ *9101 International Dr.* ☎ *407/248–2838* ⊕ *www. pointeorlando.com* ⊙ *Sun.–Thurs. 10–10, Fri. and Sat. 10 AM–11 PM.*

THE ORLANDO AREA ESSENTIALS

TRANSPORTATION

BY AIR

CARRIERS

More than 20 scheduled airlines and more than 30 charter firms operate into and out of Orlando International Airport, providing direct service to more than 100 cities in the United States and overseas.

Major Airlines AirTran (☎ *800/247–8726* ⊕ *www.airtran.com*). **Alaska Airlines** (☎ *800/252–7522* ⊕ *www.alaskaair.com*). **American** (☎ *800/433–7300* ⊕ *www. aa.com*). **Continental** (☎ *800/523–3273* ⊕ *www.continental.com*). **Delta** (☎ *800/221–1212* ⊕ *www.delta.com*). **Northwest/KLM** (☎ *800/225–2525* ⊕ *www. nwa.com*). **United Airlines** (☎ *800/241–6522* ⊕ *www.united.com*). **US Airways/**

America West Airlines (☎ *800/428–4322* ⊕ *www.usairways.com*).

Smaller Airlines ATA (☎ *800/225–2995* ⊕ *www.ata.com*). **Frontier** (☎ *800/432–1359* ⊕ *www.frontierairlines.com*). **JetBlue** (☎ *800/538–2583* ⊕ *www.jetblue.com*). **Midwest Express** (☎ *800/452–2022* ⊕ *www.midwestairlines.com*). **Southwest** (☎ *800/435–9792* ⊕ *www.iflyswa.com*). **Spirit** (☎ *800/772–7117* ⊕ *www.spiritair.com*).

AIRPORTS & TRANSFERS

The Orlando airport (MCO on your baggage tag) is ultramodern, huge, and growing all the time. However, it's relatively easy to navigate. Just follow the excellent signs. Monorails shuttle you from gate areas to the core area, where you'll find baggage claim. The complex is south of Orlando and northeast of Walt Disney World.

Find out in advance whether your hotel offers a free airport shuttle. If not, you have a few options. Cab fare from the airport to the Disney World area runs $50–$60. If there are four or more people in your party, taking a taxi may cost less than paying by the head for an airport shuttle.

A shuttle service, the Mears Transportation Group, meets you at the gate, helps with the luggage, and whisks you away in either an 11-passenger van, a town car, or a limo. Vans run to Walt Disney World, International Drive, and along U.S. 192 in Kissimmee every 30 minutes; prices range from $19 one-way for ($15 for children 4–11) to $31 round-trip ($23 children 4–11). Limo rates run $60–$70 for a town car that accommodates three or four to $155 for a stretch limo that seats eight. Town & Country Transportation charges $150 one-way for a limo seating up to seven or eight people depending on luggage needs.

If you're staying at a Disney hotel (excluding the Walt Disney World Swan, Dolphin, and Downtown Disney Resort area hotels), make arrangements to use Disney's free Magical Express service, which includes shuttle transportation to and from the airport, luggage delivery, and baggage check-in at the hotel. You can't book the service once you've arrived at the airport, so be sure to reserve ahead.

Airport Contacts Orlando International Airport ((*MCO*) ☎ *407/825–2001*).

Transport Contacts Magical Express service (☎ *866/599–0951*). **Mears Transportation Group** (☎ *407/423–5566* ⊕ *www.mearstransportation.com*). **Star Taxi** (☎ *407/857–9999*). **Town & Country Transportation** (☎ *407/828–3035*). **Yellow Cab Co.** (☎ *407/422–2222*).

BY CAR

The Beeline Expressway (State Road 528) is the best way to get from Orlando International Airport to area attractions; however, it's a toll road, so expect to pay about $1.25 in tolls to get from the airport to Interstate 4. Interstate 4 is the main artery in central Florida, linking the Gulf Coast in Tampa to the Atlantic coast in Daytona Beach. Although Interstate 4 is an east–west highway, it actually follows a north–south track through the Orlando area, so traveling north on Interstate 4 through Orlando would actually be heading east toward

Daytona, and traveling south would actually be traveling west toward Tampa. So **think north when Interstate 4 signs say east, and think south when the signs say west.**

BY TAXI

Taxi fares start at $3.50 for the first mile and add $2 for each mile thereafter. Sample fares: to WDW's Magic Kingdom, about $25 from International Drive, $14 to $18 from U.S. 192. To Universal Studios, $10 to $14 from International Drive, $27 to $34 from U.S. 192. To Church Street or downtown, $22 to $28 from International Drive, $32 to $44 from U.S. 192. *For information on getting to or from the airport by taxi, see Airport Transfers.*

Contacts **A-1 Taxi** (☎ *407/328–4555*). **Checker Cab Company** (☎ *407/699– 9999*). **Star Taxi** (☎ *407/857–9999*).

4

CONTACTS & RESOURCES

EMERGENCIES

In an emergency, always call **911.**

Doctors & Dentists **Dental Emergency Service** (☎ *407/331–2526*).

Hospitals & Clinics The **Centra Care** (⊠ *12500 S. Apopka Vineland Rd., Lake Buena Vista* ☎ *407/934–2273*) near Downtown Disney provides free shuttle service from any of the Disney, Universal, and SeaWorld theme park's first-aid stations and from all Disney resort hotels and other area hotels. It's open weekdays 8–midnight, weekends 8–8.

For minor emergencies visit the **Main Street Physicians Clinic** (⊠ *8723 International Dr., Suite 115* ☎ *407/370–4881*). It's open Monday–Thursday 8–8, Friday 8–9, Saturday 9–9, and Sunday 9–5 .

In an emergency near Celebration, head to **Florida Hospital Celebration Health** (⊠ *400 Celebration Pl., Celebration* ☎ *407/303–4000*). If you're closer to Universal Studios, head to **Orlando Regional Medical Center/Sand Lake Hospital** (⊠ *9400 Turkey Lake Rd., International Drive Area, Orlando* ☎ *407/351–8500*). Hospital emergency rooms are open 24 hours a day.

VISITOR INFORMATION

Contacts **Kissimmee/St. Cloud Convention and Visitors Bureau** (⊠ *1925 Irlo Bronson Memorial Hwy., Kissimmee* ☎ *407/847–5000 or 800/327–9159*). **Orlando/Orange County Convention & Visitors Bureau** (⊠ *8723 International Dr., Orlando* ☎ *407/363–5871*). **Winter Park Chamber of Commerce** (⌂ *Box 280, Winter Park* ☎ *407/644–8281*).

Palm Beach & the Treasure Coast

Worth Avenue, Palm Beach

WORD OF MOUTH

"Walk Worth Ave. if you enjoy oggling fancy shops. There's a shopping mall in West Palm called CityPlace that also has some restaurants where you'll find some nightlife.... I don't think there's that much to see/do other than shop and relax in Palm beach."

—mclaurie

WELCOME TO PALM BEACH & THE TREASURE COAST

TOP REASONS TO GO

★ **Beautiful Beaches:** From Jupiter's sandy shoreline, where leashed dogs are welcome, to the broad stretches of sand in Delray Beach and Boca Raton, swimmers, sunbathers and surfers—and sea turtles looking for a place to hatch their eggs—all find happiness here.

★ **Exquisite resorts:** The Ritz-Carlton and the Four Seasons in Palm continue to sparkle with service fit for royalty. Two historic gems—The Breakers in Palm Beach and The Boca Raton Resort—perpetually draw the rich, famous and anyone else who can afford the luxury.

★ **Horse around:** Wellington, with its annual national horse show and its popular polo season, is often called the winter equestrian capital of the world.

★ **Have a reel good time:** From Lake Okeechobee, a great place to catch bass and perch, to the Atlantic Ocean, teeming with kingfish, sailfish, dolphin, and wahoo, fishermen will find the waters here a treasure chest.

1 Palm Beach. With Gatsby-era architecture, stone-and-stucco estates, extravagant landscaping, and highbrow shops, Palm Beach is a must-see for travelers to the area. Plan to spend some time on Worth Avenue, also called the Mink Mile, a collection of more than 200 shops, and Whitehall, once the winter retreat for Henry Flagler, Palm Beach's founder.

2 West Palm Beach. Bustling with its own affluent identity, West Palm Beach has much to offer. Palm Beach-style homes line lovely Flagler Drive and golf courses are abundant. Culture fans have much to cheer about, from the Kravis Center of the Performing Arts, to the Norton Museum of Art and The Armory Arts Center. Kids will love the Palm Beach Zoo.

3 South to Boca Raton. The territory from Palm Beach south to Boca Raton defines old-world glamour and new-age sophistication. Delray Beach boasts a lively downtown, with galleries, shops and restaurants. To the west are the Morikami Japanese Gardens and the headquarters of the American Orchid Society. Boca Raton's Mizner Park has tony boutiques, restaurants and the Boca Raton Museum of Art.

4 The Treasure Coast. Despite a growing number of malls and beachfront condominiums, much of the Treasure Coast's shoreline remains blissfully undeveloped. Along the coast, the broad tidal lagoon called the Indian River separates barrier islands from the mainland. Inland there's cattle ranching in tracts of pine and palmetto scrub, along with sugar and citrus production

GETTING ORIENTED

This South Florida region extends 120 miles from Sebastian to Boca Raton. The golden stretch of the Atlantic from Palm Beach south to Boca Raton defines old-world glamour and new age sophistication. North of Palm Beach, you'll uncover the comparatively undeveloped Treasure Coast, where towns and wide-open spaces along the road await your discovery. Altogether, there's a delightful disparity, from Palm Beach, pulsing fast with old-money wealth, to low-key Hutchinson Island and Manalapan. Ten miles west of Palm Beach you'll find the burgeoning equestrian community of Wellington, site of much of the county's new development.

ATLANTIC OCEAN

TO SEBASTIAN

Florida's Turnpike

Fort Pierce

Indian River

St. Lucie

Hutchinson Island (Jensen Beach)

Stuart

Sewalls Point

Florida's Turnpike

TO OKEECHOBEE

Jupiter Island & Hobe Sound

Indiantown

Tequesta

Jupiter

Port Mayaca

Juno Beach

Lake Okeechobee

Singer Island

Palm Beach Gardens

Riviera Beach

Palm Beach Shores

West Palm Beach

Palm Beach

Loxahatchee

Lake Worth

Wellington

Lantana

Manalapan

Boynton Beach

Gulf Stream

Delray Beach

Highland Beach

Boca Raton

Florida's Turnpike

0   10 miles

0   15 km

PALM BEACH & TREASURE COAST PLANNER

When to Go

The weather is optimum from November through May, but the trade-off is that roadways and facilities are more crowded and prices higher. In summer it helps to have a tolerance for heat, humidity, and afternoon downpours. Hurricane season runs from June through Nov. 30, not necessarily a bad time for a trip here as there is always plenty of warning for the big storms. For best rates for lodging, consider summer months or the early weeks of December. Make sure to bring insect repellent for outdoor activities.

Flying In

The best place to fly in is Palm Beach International Airport (PBIA), which is served by Air Canada, AirTran, American, Bahamasair, CanJet, Comair, Continental, Delta, Frontier, jetBlue, Laker Air, Northwest, Song, Southwest Airlines, Spirit Airlines, United, and US Airways/US Airways Express. PalmTran Routes 44 and 40 run from the airport to Tri-Rail's nearby Palm Beach airport station daily. Palm Beach Transportation provides taxi and limousine service from PBIA. Another option is Fort Lauderdale–Hollywood International Airport, 45 miles south of West Palm Beach.

About the Restaurants

Numerous elegant establishments offer upscale continental and contemporary fare, but the area also teems with casual waterfront spots serving affordable burgers and fresh seafood feasts. Grouper, fried or blackened, is especially popular here, along with the ubiquitous shrimp. An hour's drive west of the coast, around Lake Okeechobee, dine on catfish, panfried to perfection and so fresh it seems barely out of the water. Early-bird menus, a Florida hallmark, typically entice the budget-minded with several dinner entrées at reduced prices offered during certain hours, usually before 5 or 6.

About the Hotels

Palm Beach has a number of smaller hotels in addition to the famous Breakers. Lower-priced hotels and motels can be found in West Palm Beach and Lake Worth. To the south, the coastal town of Manalapan has the Ritz-Carlton, Palm Beach; and the posh Boca Raton Resort & Club is near the beach in Boca Raton. To the north in suburban Palm Beach Gardens is the PGA National Resort & Spa. To the west, small towns near Lake Okeechobee offer country-inn accommodations.

What It Costs

DINING & LODGING PRICE CATEGORIES				
¢	$	$$	$$$	$$$$
Restaurants				
under $10	$10–$15	$15–$20	$20–$30	over $30
Hotels				
under $80	$80–$100	$100–$140	$140–$220	over $220

Restaurant prices are per person for a main course at dinner. Hotel prices are for a standard double room, excluding 6% sales tax (more in some counties) and 1%–4% tourist tax.

Updated
by Mary
Thurwachter

THIS GOLDEN STRETCH OF ATLANTIC coast resists categorization for good reason. The territory from Palm Beach south to Boca Raton defines old-world glamour and new-age sophistication. North of Palm Beach you'll uncover the comparatively undeveloped Treasure Coast—liberally sprinkled with coastal gems—where towns and wide-open spaces along the road await your discovery. Altogether, there's a delightful disparity, from Palm Beach, pulsing fast with plenty of old-money wealth, to low-key Hutchinson Island and Manalapan. Seductive as the beach scene interspersed with eclectic dining options can be, you should also take advantage of flourishing commitments to historic preservation and the arts, as town after town yields intriguing museums, galleries, theaters, and gardens.

Long reigning as the epicenter of where the crème de la crème go to shake off winter's chill, Palm Beach continues to be a seasonal hotbed of platinum-grade consumption. Yes, other Florida favorites such as Jupiter Island actually rank higher on the per-capita-wealth meters of financial intelligence sources such as *Worth* magazine. But there's no competing with the historic social supremacy of Palm Beach, long a winter address for heirs of icons named Rockefeller, Vanderbilt, Colgate, Post, Kellogg, and Kennedy. Yet even newer power brokers, with names like Kravis, Peltz, and Trump, are made to understand that strict laws govern everything from building to landscaping, and not so much as a pool awning gets added without a town council nod. If Palm Beach were to fly a flag, it's been observed, there might be three interlocking Cs, standing not only for Cartier, Chanel, and Christian Dior but also for clean, civil, and capricious. Only three bridges allow access to the island, and huge tour buses are a no-no. Yet when a freighter ran aground near a Palm Beach socialite's pool, she was quick to lament not having "enough Bloody Mary mix for all these sailors."

To learn who's who in Palm Beach, it helps to pick up a copy of the *Palm Beach Daily News*—locals call it the Shiny Sheet because its high-quality paper avoids smudging society hands or Pratesi linens—for, as it is said, to be mentioned in the Shiny Sheet is to be Palm Beach. All this fabled ambience started with Henry Morrison Flagler, Florida's premier developer, and cofounder, along with John D. Rockefeller, of Standard Oil. No sooner did Flagler bring the railroad to Florida in the 1890s than he erected the famed Royal Poinciana and Breakers hotels. Rail access sent real-estate prices soaring, and ever since, princely sums have been forked over for personal stationery engraved with the 33480 zip code of Palm Beach. To service Palm Beach with servants and other workers, Flagler also developed an off-island community a mile or so west. West Palm Beach now bustles with its own affluent identity, even if there's still no competing with one of the world's toniest island resorts.

With Palm Beach proper representing only 1% of Palm Beach County's land, remaining territory is given over to West Palm and other classic Florida coastal towns, along with—to the west—citrus farms, the Arthur R. Marshall–Loxahatchee National Wildlife Refuge, and Lake Okeechobee, a bass-fishing hot spot and Florida's largest lake. Well worth exploring is the Treasure Coast territory, covering northernmost

Palm Beach County, plus Martin, St. Lucie, and Indian River counties. Despite a growing number of malls and beachfront condominiums, much of the Treasure Coast's shoreline remains blissfully undeveloped. Along the coast, the broad tidal lagoon called the Indian River separates barrier islands from the mainland. Inland there's cattle ranching in tracts of pine and palmetto scrub, along with sugar and citrus production. Shrimp farming uses techniques for acclimatizing shrimp from saltwater—land near seawater is costly—to freshwater, all the better to serve demand from restaurants popping up all over the region.

EXPLORING PALM BEACH & THE TREASURE COAST

Palm Beach, with Gatsby-era architecture, stone-and-stucco estates, extravagant landscaping, and highbrow shops, can reign as the focal point for your sojourn any time of year. From Palm Beach, head off in any of three directions: south via the Gold Coast toward Boca Raton along an especially scenic route known as A1A, back to the mainland and north to the barrier-island treasures of the Treasure Coast, or west for more rustic inland activities such as bass fishing and biking on the dikes around Lake Okeechobee.

PALM BEACH

78 mi north of Miami.

Setting the tone in this town of unparalleled Florida opulence is the ornate architectural work of Addison Mizner, who began designing homes and public buildings here in the 1920s and whose Moorish-Gothic style has influenced virtually all community landmarks. Thanks to Mizner and his lasting influence, Palm Beach remains a playground of the rich, famous, and discerning.

EXPLORING PALM BEACH

Numbers in the margin correspond to the Palm Beach & West Palm Beach map.

For a taste of what it's like to jockey for position in this status-conscious town, stake out a parking place on Worth Avenue or parallel residential streets, and squeeze in among the Mercedeses, Rolls-Royces, and Bentleys. Between admiring your excellent parking skills and feeling "car-struck" at the surrounding fine specimens of automobile, be sure to note the PARKING BY PERMIT ONLY and TWO HOUR parking signs, as a $25 parking ticket might take the shine off your spot. ■TIP➔**The best course for a half-day visit is to valet-park at the parking deck next to Saks Fifth Avenue.** Away from downtown, along County Road and Ocean Boulevard (the shore road, also designated as Route A1A), are Palm Beach's other defining landmarks: Mediterranean-style residences, some built of coral rock, that are nothing short of palatial, topped by barrel-tile roofs and often fronted by 10-foot ficus and sea-grape hedges. The low wall that separates the dune-top shore road from the sea hides shoreline that

A GOOD TOUR

Start at the **Henry Morrison Flagler Museum ❶**, a 55-room, 60,000-square-foot villa Flagler built for his third wife, to get your first look at the eye-popping opulence of the Gilded Age, which defined Palm Beach. From here, turn left on Cocoanut Row, and right onto Royal Poinciana Way—outdoor cafés on the left and the Breakers golf course to your right—then right onto North County Road. Head south and look for the long, stately driveway on the left that leads to the **Breakers ❷**, built by Flagler in the style of an Italian Renaissance palace. Parking costs $20 and there are ample valets under the porte cochere. Have your parking ticket validated while lunching at the Breakers and the parking fee is waived. Continue south on South County Road to **Bethesda-by-the-Sea ❸**, a Spanish Gothic Episcopal church. Keep driving south on South County Road until you reach Royal Palm Way; turn right, and drive a few blocks until you see the **Society of the Four Arts ❹**. Turn left back onto Royal Palm Way and drive until it ends at the ocean,

and turn right onto Ocean Boulevard until you reach famed **Worth Avenue ❺** on the right, which is a one-way street running east to west. Park, stroll, and ogle designer goods. Then drive south back on Ocean Boulevard to peek at magnificent estates, including **El Solano ❻**, designed by Addison Mizner, and the fabled **Mar-a-Lago ❼**, a Mediterranean Revival palace with a distinctive 75-foot tower, now owned by Donald Trump and operating as a private club. At this point, if you want some sun and fresh air, continue south on South County Road until you reach **Phipps Ocean Park ❽** and its stretch of beach, or head back toward town along South Ocean Boulevard to the popular **Mid-Town Beach ❾** at the east end of Worth Avenue.

TIMING

You'll need half a day, minimum, for these sights. A few shops and attractions are closed Sunday and May through October. From November through April, often-heavy traffic gets worse as the day wears on, so plan to explore in the morning.

varies in many places from expansive to eroded. Here and there, where the strand deepens, homes are built directly on the beach.

WHAT TO SEE

❸ **Bethesda-by-the-Sea.** Donald Trump and his wife Melania were married here in 2005, but this Spanish Gothic Episcopal church had a claim to fame upon its creation in 1925: it was built by the first Protestant congregation in southeast Florida. Guided tours follow some services. Adjacent are the formal, ornamental **Cluett Memorial Gardens.** ⊠ *141 S. County Rd.* ☎ *561/655–4554* ⊕ *www.bbts.org* ☾ *Church and gardens daily 8–5. Services Sept.–May, Sun. at 8, 9, and 11, Tues. at 8, Wed. and Fri. at 12:05; June–Aug., Sun. at 8 and 10. Call to confirm.*

❷ **The Breakers.** Built by Henry Flagler in 1896 and rebuilt by his descendants after a 1925 fire, this magnificent Italian Renaissance–style resort helped launch Florida tourism with its GildedAge opulence, attracting influential, wealthy northerners. The hotel, still owned by Flagler's

Fodor's Choice
★

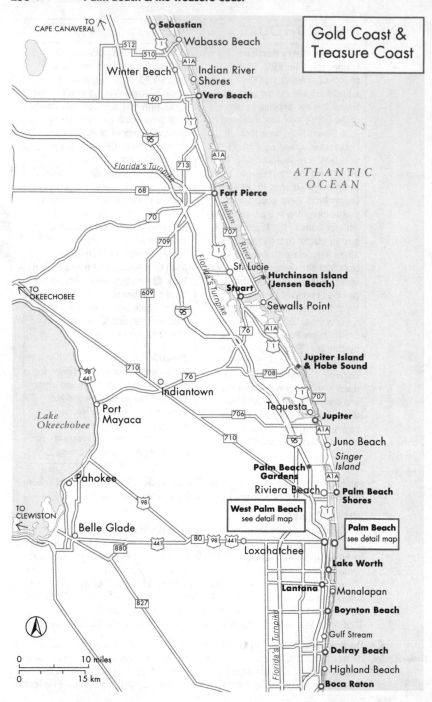

Gold Coast & Treasure Coast

TO CAPE CANAVERAL

Sebastian
Wabasso Beach
Winter Beach
Indian River Shores
Vero Beach

ATLANTIC OCEAN

Florida's Turnpike

Fort Pierce

TO OKEECHOBEE

St. Lucie
Hutchinson Island (Jensen Beach)
Stuart
Sewalls Point

Florida's Turnpike

Jupiter Island & Hobe Sound

Indiantown

Port Mayaca
Lake Okeechobee

Tequesta
Jupiter
Juno Beach
Singer Island

Pahokee

Palm Beach Gardens
Riviera Beach
Palm Beach Shores

TO CLEWISTON

Belle Glade

West Palm Beach see detail map

Palm Beach see detail map

Loxahatchee

Lake Worth

Lantana
Manalapan
Boynton Beach
Gulf Stream
Delray Beach
Highland Beach
Boca Raton

Florida's Turnpike

0   10 miles
0   15 km

heirs, is a must-stop even if you don't stay here. Walk through the 200-foot-long lobby, which has soaring arched ceilings painted by 72 Italian artisans and hung with crystal chandeliers, and the ornate Florentine Dining Room decorated with 15th-century Flemish tapestries. ✉*1 S. County Rd.* ☎*561/655–6611* ⊕*www.thebreakers.com.*

❻ El Solano. No Palm Beach mansion better represents the town's luminous legacy than the Spanish-style home built by Addison Mizner as his residence in 1925. Mizner later sold El Solano to Harold Vanderbilt, and the property was long a favorite among socialites for parties and photo shoots. Vanderbilt, like many of the socially attuned, would open his home to social peers to accommodate worthy causes. Beatle John Lennon and his wife, Yoko Ono, bought it less than a year before Lennon's death. It's still privately owned and not open to the public. ✉*721 S. County Rd.*

❶ Henry Morrison Flagler Museum. The opulence of Florida's Gilded Age **Fodor'sChoice** lives on at Whitehall, the palatial 55-room "marble palace" Henry ★ Flagler commissioned in 1901 for his third wife, Mary Lily Kenan. Architects John Carrère and Thomas Hastings were instructed to create the finest home imaginable, and they outdid themselves. Whitehall rivals the grandeur of European palaces and has an entrance hall with baroque ceiling similar to Louis XIV's Versailles. To create the museum, Flagler's granddaughter, Jean Flagler Matthews, in 1960 purchased the property, which had been operating as the Whitehall Hotel since 1929. You'll see original furnishings, a hidden staircase Flagler used to sneak · from his bedroom to the billiards room, an art collection, a 1,200-pipe organ, and Florida East Coast Railway exhibits, along with Flagler's personal railcar, the *Rambler,* showcased in an 8,000-square-foot Beaux Arts–style pavilion behind the mansion. Tours take about an hour and are offered at frequent intervals. The café, open after Thanksgiving through mid-April, offers snacks and afternoon tea. ✉*1 Whitehall Way* ☎*561/655–2833* ⊕*www.flagler.org* ✉*$15* ⊙*Tues.–Sat. 10–5, Sun. noon–5.*

❼ Mar-a-Lago. Breakfast-food heiress Marjorie Merriweather Post commissioned a Hollywood set designer to create Ocean Boulevard's famed Mar-a-Lago, a 118-room, 110,000-square-foot Mediterranean Revival palace. Its 75-foot Italianate tower is visible from most areas of Palm Beach and from across the Intracoastal Waterway in West Palm Beach. Owner Donald Trump has turned it into a private membership club. He and wife Melania held their wedding reception in the ballroom here after marrying at Bethesda-by-the-Sea Episcopal Church in 2005. ✉*1100 S. Ocean Blvd.*

❽ Phipps Ocean Park. In addition to the shoreline, tennis courts, picnic tables, and grills, this park has a Palm Beach County landmark in the **Little Red Schoolhouse.** Dating from 1886, it served as the first schoolhouse in what was then Dade County. No alcoholic beverages are permitted in the park. ✉*2185 S. Ocean Blvd.* ☎*561/832–0731* ✉*Free* ⊙*Daily dawn–dusk.*

④ Society of the Four Arts. Despite widespread misconceptions of members-only exclusivity, this privately endowed institution—founded in 1936 to encourage appreciation of art, music, drama, and literature—is funded for public enjoyment. A gallery building—designed by Addison Mizner, of course—artfully melds an exhibition hall, library, and the Philip Hulitar Sculpture Garden, which underwent a major renovation in 2006. Open from about Thanksgiving to Easter, the museum's programs are extensive, and there's ample free parking. The museum often presents free movie screenings in the auditorium on weekends. ⊠2 *Four Arts Plaza* ☎*561/655–7226* ⊕*www.fourarts.org* ⊠*$5* ☉*Galleries Dec.–mid-Apr., Mon.–Sat. 10–5, Sun. 2–5. Library, children's library, and gardens Nov.–May, weekdays 10–5, Sat. 10–1.*

★ **⑤ Worth Avenue.** Called the Avenue by Palm Beachers, this ¼-mi-long street is synonymous with exclusive shopping. Nostalgia lovers recall an era when faces or names served as charge cards, purchases were delivered home before customers returned from lunch, and bills were sent directly to private accountants. Times have changed, but a stroll amid the Moorish architecture of its shops offers a tantalizing taste of the island's ongoing commitment to elegant consumerism. Explore the labyrinth of eight pedestrian vias, on both sides of Worth Avenue, that wind past boutiques, tiny plazas, bubbling fountains, and the bougainvillea-festooned wrought-iron balconies of second-floor apartments. ⊠*Between Cocoanut Row and S. Ocean Blvd.*

WHERE TO EAT

$$$$ ✕ **Café L'Europe.** Even after 25 years, the favorite lunch stop of society's movers and shakers remains a regular stop on fine diners' itineraries. Management pays close attention to service and consistency of excellence here. Best sellers include rack of lamb, Dover sole, and Wiener schnitzel, along with creations such as crispy sweetbreads with poached pear and mustard sauce. Depending on your mood, the champagne-caviar bar can provide appetizers or dessert. ⊠*331 S. County Rd.* ☎*561/655–4020* ⚐*Reservations essential* ⊟*AE, DC, MC, V* ☉*No lunch.*

$$$$ ✕ **Leopard Supper Club and Lounge.** In the Chesterfield hotel, this enclave feels like an exclusive club. Choose a cozy banquette set off by black-and-red lacquer trim or a table near the open kitchen. Start with sweet-corn-and-crab chowder with Peruvian purple potato or a jumbo crab cake, moving on to an arugula or spinach salad followed by a prime strip steak or a glazed rack of lamb. As the night progresses, the Leopard turns into a popular nightclub for Palm Beach's old guard. ⊠*363 Cocoanut Row* ☎*561/659–5800* ⊟*AE, D, DC, MC, V.*

$$$–$$$$ ✕ **Bice Ristorante.** The bougainvillea-laden trellises set the scene at the main entrance on Peruvian Way, and weather permitting, many patrons prefer to dine on the outdoor patio on the narrow pedestrian walkway. A favorite of Palm Beach society and Hollywood celebs, both the restaurant and the bar become packed and noisy during high season. The aroma of basil, chives, and oregano fills the air as waiters bring out home-baked focaccia to accompany delectable dishes such as sea-

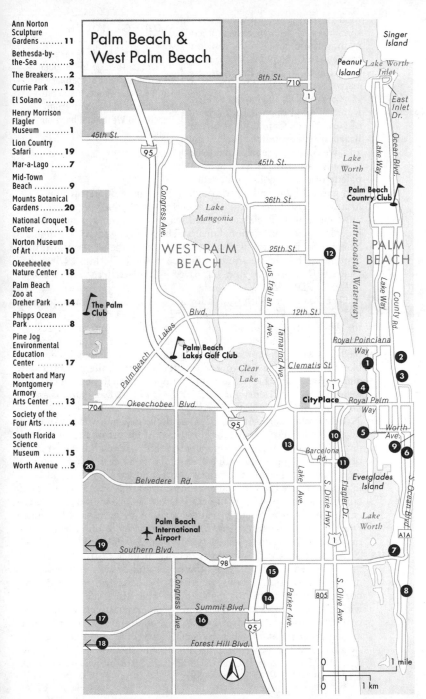

Palm Beach & West Palm Beach

Singer Island

Peanut Island

Lake Worth Inlet

East Inlet Dr.

8th St.

710

45th St.

95

45th St.

36th St.

Lake Mangonia

Lake Worth

Lake Way

Palm Beach Country Club

25th St.

WEST PALM BEACH

PALM BEACH

Intracoastal Waterway

Lake Way

County Rd.

The Palm Club

Palm Beach Lakes Golf Club

Blvd.

12th St.

Royal Poinciana Way

Clear Lake

Clematis St.

CityPlace

Royal Palm Way

Okeechobee Blvd.

704

95

Barcelona Rd.

Worth Ave.

Everglades Island

Belvedere Rd.

Lake Worth

A1A

Palm Beach International Airport

Southern Blvd.

98

805

S. Olive Ave.

Summit Blvd.

Forest Hill Blvd.

95

0   1 mile

0   1 km

food risotto, veal chops, and such specialties as duck breast sautéed in mushroom sauce with venison truffle ravioli. ⊠ *313½ Worth Ave.* ☎ *561/835–1600* ⚑ *Reservations essential* ▤ *AE, DC, MC, V.*

$$$-$$$$
Fodor's Choice
★

✕ **Café Boulud.** Celebrated chef Daniel Boulud opened his outpost of New York's Café Boulud in the Brazilian Court hotel. The warm and welcoming French-American venue is casual yet elegant, with a palette of honey, gold, and citron, and natural light spilling through arched glass doors opening to a lush courtyard. Lunch and dinner entrées on Boulud's signature four-muse menu include classic French, seasonal, vegetarian, and a rotating selection of international dishes. The lounge, with its backlighted amber glass bar, is the perfect perch to take in the jet-set crowd that comes for a hint of the south of France in South Florida. ⊠ *Brazilian Court, 301 Australian Ave.* ☎ *561/655–6060* ⚑ *Reservations essential* ▤ *AE, DC, MC, V.*

$$$-$$$$
Fodor's Choice
★

✕ **Chez Jean-Pierre.** With walls adorned with Dalí- and Picasso-like art, this is where the Palm Beach old guard likes to let down its guard, all the while partaking of sumptuous French cuisine and an impressive wine list. Forget calorie or cholesterol concerns and indulge in scrambled eggs with caviar or homemade duck foie gras, along with desserts like hazelnut soufflé or profiteroles au chocolat. Waiters are friendly and very attentive. Jackets are not required, although many men wear them. ⊠ *132 N. County Rd.* ☎ *561/833–1171* ⚑ *Reservations essential* ▤ *AE, DC, MC, V* ⊘ *Closed Sun. No lunch.*

$$-$$$$

✕ **Testa's Palm Beach.** Attracting a loyal clientele since 1921 and still owned by the Testa family, the restaurant offers breakfast, lunch, and dinner. Lunches range from burgers to crab salad, and dinner specialties include snapper Florentine and jumbo lump crab cakes. You can dine inside in an intimate pine-paneled room with cozy bar, out back in a gazebo-style room for large groups, or outside at tables with pink tablecloths next to planters of pink hibiscus, with a view of the Breakers in the distance. Friendly waiters greet many customers by name. Don't miss the signature strawberry pie made with fresh Florida berries. ⊠ *221 Royal Poinciana Way* ☎ *561/832–0992* ▤ *AE, MC, V.*

$$-$$$

✕ **Amici.** The town's premier celebrity-magnet bistro is a crowd pleaser: when it moved across the street and down the block from its original location, a consistent Palm Beach crowd followed. The northern Italian menu highlights house specialties such as rigatoni with spicy tomato sauce and roasted eggplant, potato gnocchi, grilled veal chops, risottos, and pizzas from a wood-burning oven. There are nightly pasta and fresh-fish specials as well. To avoid the crowds, stop by for a late lunch or early dinner. Lunch and brunch on Sunday. ⊠ *375 S. County Rd.* ☎ *561/832–0201* ⚑ *Reservations essential* ▤ *AE, DC, MC, V* ⊘ *No lunch Sun.*

★ **$$-$$$**   ✕ **Ta-boó.** This peach stucco 60-year-old landmark with green shutters attracts Worth Avenue shoppers looking for a two-hour lunch and a dinner crowd ranging from tuxed and sequined theatergoers to polo-shirted vacationers. Entrées include Black Angus dry-aged beef or roast duck, along with main-course salads, pizzas, and burgers, plus coconut lust, a signature dessert. Drop in late night during the winter season when the nightly music is playing and you'll probably spot a celebrity or two. There's a late-night menu Friday and Saturday. ⊠*221 Worth Ave.* ☎*561/835–3500* ☐*AE, DC, MC, V.*

¢-$ ✕ **Hamburger Heaven.** A favorite with locals since 1945, the quintessential diner with horseshoe-shaped counter as well as booths and tables is loud and casual and has some of the best burgers on the island. Vegetarian meals, fresh salads, sandwiches, homemade pastries, and daily soup and hot-plate specials featuring comfort foods like meat loaf and chicken potpie are also available. During the week, it's a popular lunch stop for working locals.The staff are friendly and efficient. ⊠*314 S. County Rd.* ☎*561/655–5277* ☐*MC, V* ⊙*Closed Sun.*

¢-$ ✕ **Pizza Al Fresco.** The secret-garden setting is the secret to the success of this popular European pizzeria (beer and wine only), where you can dine under a canopy of century-old banyans in a charming courtyard. Specialties are 12-inch hand-tossed brick-oven pizzas; calzones, salads, and sandwiches round out the selection. Slices are available with such interesting toppings as prosciutto, arugula, and caviar; there's even a dessert pizza topped with Nutella. Look for the grave markers of Addison Mizner's beloved pet monkey, Johnnie Brown, and Rose Sachs's dog Laddie (she and husband Morton bought Mizner's villa and lived there 47 years) next to the patio. Delivery is available, by limo, of course. ⊠*14 Via Mizner, at Worth Ave.* ☎*561/832–0032* ☐*AE, MC, V.*

WHERE TO STAY

★ **$$$$**   ⊞ **Brazilian Court.** A short stroll from Worth Avenue shopping, the yellow-stucco Spanish-style facade and red-tile roof, and lobby with pecky-cypress ceilings and stone floors, underscore this boutique hotel's Roaring '20s origins. All of the studio and one- and two-bedroom suites have rich limestone baths and showers, Sub-Zero wine refrigerators, and personal butler service. Bay windows look out into the impeccably maintained gardens and enchanting flower-filled courtyards. Amenities include video-conference capabilities in a state-of-the-art business center, a Frederic Fekkai hair salon and spa, and Café Boulud, a New York outpost from famed restaurateur Daniel Boulud; hotel guests reportedly have a better shot than outsiders at procuring a table. Don't feel like dressing up for a table? There's 24-hour in-room dining by Café Boulud. **Pros:** Connected to one of the best restaurants in town; attracts a young, hip crowd; close to Worth Avenue shopping and not far from the beach. **Cons:** Rooms are small and rooms near the restaurant can be noisy. ⊠*301 Australian Ave.* ☎*561/655–7740* 🖷*561/655–0801* ⊕*www.thebraziliancourt.com* ⬐*80 rooms* ⬧*In-room: refrigerator, VCR (some), dial-up. In-hotel: restaurant, room* *service, bar, pool, gym, spa, bicycles, laundry facilities, concierge, some pets allowed (fee), no-smoking rooms* ☰AE, D, DC, MC, V.

$$$$ 🏨 **The Breakers.** Dating from 1896 and on the National Register of
Fodor'sChoice Historic Places, this opulent Italian Renaissance–style resort, owned
★ by Henry Flagler's heirs, sprawls over 140 oceanfront acres. Cupids frolic at the main Florentine fountain, and majestic frescoes grace hallways leading to restaurants. More than an opulent hotel, the Breakers is a modern resort packed with amenities, from a 20,000-square-foot luxury spa and beach club to golf and tennis clubhouses that support the 10 tennis courts and two 18-hole golf courses. Jackets and ties are no longer required after 7 PM. **Pros:** Fine attention to detail throughout; beautiful room views; top-rate golf, tennis and croquet facilities. **Cons:** All this luxury comes with a big price! ⊠*1 S. County Rd.,* ☎*561/655–6611 or 888/273–2537* 🖶*561/659–8403* ⊕*www.thebreakers.com* ⇘*569 rooms, 57 suites* ⌂*In-room: dial-up. In-hotel: 5 restaurants, room service, bars, golf courses, tennis courts, pools, gym, spa, beachfront, children's programs (ages 3–12), concierge* ☰*AE, D, DC, MC, V.*

$$$$ 🏨 **The Chesterfield.** Two blocks north of Worth Avenue, the distinctive white stucco, European-style hotel with red-and-white-striped awnings offers inviting rooms ranging from small to spacious. All have plush upholstered chairs, antique desks, paintings, and marble baths. Settle on a leather couch near the cozy library's fireplace and peruse an international newspaper or classic book. A quiet courtyard surrounds a large pool where you can relax, and the Leopard Lounge draws a convivial crowd. **Pros:** Great location near Worth Avenue, elegant rooms, Leopard Lounge is a hot spot. **Cons:** Rooms close to the bar can be noisy. ⊠*363 Cocoanut Row,* ☎*561/659–5800 or 800/243–7871* 🖶*561/659–6707* ⊕*www.chesterfieldpb.com* ⇘*44 rooms, 11 suites* ⌂*In-room: refrigerator (some), VCR (some). In-hotel: restaurant, room service, bar, pool, concierge, public Internet* ☰*AE, D, DC, MC, V.*

$$$$ 🏨 **The Colony.** What distinguishes this legendary pale-yellow British colonial–style hotel is that it's only one short block from Worth Avenue and one block from a beautiful beach on the Atlantic Ocean. Having just celebrated its 60th birthday, the hotel's lobby and pool area has had a face-lift, with ornamental plants, fountains, new lighting, wicker furniture, and billowing white panels reminiscent of South Beach's luxurious Delano. An attentive staff, youthful yet experienced, is buzzing with competence and a desire to please. Guest rooms are decorated in Caribbean-colonial, with sunny yellow walls and dark mahogany desks, and pineapple-carved poster beds grace some rooms. Roomy suites and luxurious two-bedroom villas (rentable by the week or month) have laundry facilities and full kitchens. Reserve early for the dinner cabaret shows, which have featured entertainers such as Faith Prince and Andrea Marcovicci. **Pros:** Close to Worth Avenue and the beach. **Cons:** Elevators are small. ⊠*155 Hammon Ave.,* ☎*561/655–5430 or 800/521–5525* 🖶*561/659–8104* ⊕*www.thecolonypalmbeach.com* ⇘*64 rooms, 16 suites* ⌂*In-hotel: restaurant, bar, pools, spa, bicycles, concierge* ☰*AE, DC, MC, V.*

★ $$$$ ⊞ **Four Seasons Resort Palm Beach.** Relaxed elegance is the watchword at this four-story resort on 6 acres with a delightful beach at the south end of town, approximately 5 mi outside the heart of Palm Beach. Fanlight windows, marble, chintz, and palms are serene and inviting. Rooms are spacious, with separate seating areas and private balconies; many have ocean views. On weekends, piano music accompanies cocktails in the Living Room lounge. Jazz groups perform on some weekends in season. The restaurants are worth sampling, and all three have children's menus. **Pros:** Outstanding restaurants, great location on the ocean. **Cons:** At least 10 minutes away from nightlife in West Palm or Delray. ⊠*2800 S. Ocean Blvd.,* ☎*561/582–2800 or 800/432–2335* 🖷*561/547–1557* ⊕*www.fourseasons.com* ⇗*200 rooms, 10 suites* ⚐*In-room: safe, Ethernet. In-hotel: 3 restaurants, room service, bars, tennis courts, pool, gym, spa, beachfront, bicycles, children's programs (ages 3–12), laundry service, concierge, no-smoking rooms* ⊟*AE, D, DC, MC, V.*

$$$-$$$$ ⊞**Fairfield Inn Suites by Marriott.** The Fairfield Inn has a lighter, brighter look since it got a fresh coat of paint, new carpeting, framed art, bedding, and lampshades. Closer to Lake Worth than downtown Palm Beach, the Fairfield remains a good value for travelers who don't require room service or a fancy spa. It has centers for business and fitness and a outdoor pool and whirlpool. Breakfast is complimentary and boasts Jimmy Dean breakfast sandwiches. Those who crave something more elaborate in the morning need only cross the street to John G's, famous for stuffed French toast and eggs benedict. But be prepared to wait in line! **Pros:** Great location across the street from the beach and on the Intracoastal Waterway. **Cons:** Not a lot of closet space and a few miles from Worth Avenue. ⊠*2870 S. Ocean Blvd.,* ☎*561/582–2585 or 800/347–5434* ⊕*www.marriott.com/hotels/travel* ⇗*98 rooms, 20 suites* ⚐*In-room: refrigerator (some), cable TV, CD players, Ethernet* ⊟*AE, DC, MC, V.*

NIGHTLIFE & THE ARTS

THE ARTS

Society of the Four Arts (⊠*2 Four Arts Plaza* ☎*561/655–7226*) has concerts, lectures, and films December through March. Movie tickets can be purchased at time of showing; other tickets may be obtained a week in advance.

NIGHTLIFE

Palm Beach is teeming with restaurants that turn into late-night hot spots, plus hotel lobby bars perfect for tête-à-têtes. Popular for lunch and dinner, **Cucina Dell 'Arte** (⊠*257 Royal Poinciana Way* ☎*561/655–0770*) later becomes the in place for the younger and trendy set. The old guard gathers at the **Leopard Lounge** (⊠*363 Cocoanut Row* ☎*561/659–5800*) in the Chesterfield hotel for piano music during cocktail hour and later to dance until the wee hours. Thursday night happy hours spiked by Flirtinis and live jazz draw a local crowd to the lobby lounge and outdoor patios of the **Brazilian Court** (⊠*301 Australian Ave.* ☎*561/655–7740*).

SPORTS & THE OUTDOORS

BIKING

Bicycling is a great way to get a closer look at Palm Beach. Only 14 mi long, ½ mi wide, flat as the top of a billiard table, and just as green, it's a perfect biking place. The palm-fringed **Lake Trail** (⊠ *Parallel to Lake Way*) skirts the backyards of many palatial mansions and the edge of Lake Worth. The trail starts at the Society of the Four Arts, heading north 8 mi to the end and back—just follow the signs. A block from the bike trail, the **Palm Beach Bicycle Trail Shop** (⊠ *223 Sunrise Ave.* ☎ *561/659–4583*) rents by the hour or day. It's open daily.

DOG RACING

Since 1932 the hounds have raced year-round at the 4,300-seat **Palm Beach Kennel Club.** Across the bridge in West Palm Beach, the track also offers simulcasts of jai alai and horse racing, and wagering on live and televised sports. There's also a 30-table card room with high-stakes wagers, and fine dining in the Paddock Restaurant. ⊠ *1111 N. Congress Ave.* ☎ *561/683–2222* ☎ *50¢, terrace level $1, parking free* ☉ *Racing Mon.–Sat. at 12:40, Fri. and Sat. at 12:40 and 7:30, Sun. at 1. Simulcasts daily at 11:30 and 7:30.*

GOLF

Breakers Hotel Golf Club (⊠ *1 S. County Rd.* ☎ *561/659–8407*) has the historic Ocean Course and the Todd Anderson Golf Academy and is open to members and hotel guests only. A $205 greens fee includes range balls, cart, and bag storage at Breakers West or at the redesigned Ocean Course. The **Town of Palm Beach Golf Club** (⊠ *2345 S. Ocean Blvd.* ☎ *561/547–0598*) has 18 holes, including four on the Atlantic and three on the inland waterway; greens fee $39.

SHOPPING

★ One of the world's premier showcases for high-quality shopping, **Worth Avenue** runs ¼ mi east–west across Palm Beach, from the beach to Lake Worth. The street has more than 250 shops (more than 40 of them sell jewelry), and many upscale stores (Gucci, Hermès, Pucci, Saks Fifth Avenue, Neimen Marcus, Louis Vuitton, Emanuel Ungaro, Chanel, Dior, Cartier, Tiffany, and Tourneau) are represented, their merchandise appealing to the discerning tastes of the Palm Beach clientele. The six blocks of **South County Road** north of Worth Avenue have interesting (and somewhat less expensive) stores. For specialty items (out-of-town newspapers, health foods, and books), try the shops along the north side of **Royal Poinciana Way.** Most stores are closed on Sunday, and many go on hiatus in summer.

Calypso (⊠ *247-B Worth Ave.* ☎ *561/832–5006*), tucked into Via Encantada, is where owner Christiane Celle—known for handcrafted fragrances—has curated a lively collection of resort wear for the whole family. The thrift store **Church Mouse** (⊠ *374 S. County Rd.* ☎ *561/659–2154*) is where many high-end resale boutique owners grab their merchandise. **Déjà Vu** (⊠ *Via Testa, 219 Royal Poinciana*

Way ☎*561/833–6624*) could be the resale house of Chanel, as it has so many gently used, top-quality pieces. There's no digging through piles here; clothes are in impeccable condition and are well organized. **Giorgio's** (✉*230 Worth Ave.* ☎*561/655–2446*) is over-the-top indulgence, with 50 colors of silk and cashmere sweaters and 22 colors of ostrich and alligator adorning everything from bags to bicycles. Jewelry is very important in Palm Beach, and for more than 100 years **Greenleaf & Crosby** (✉*236 Worth Ave.* ☎*561/655–5850*) has had a diverse selection that includes investment pieces. **Hollywould** (✉*36 Via Mizner* ☎*561/366–9016*) stocks the Palm Beach It-Girl uniform of bright jersey dresses, shoes from slides to stilettos, and coordinating handbags. Collector and trader Edmund Lo packs the goods in this tiny shop. **Spring Flowers** (✉*337 Worth Ave.* ☎*561/832–0131*) has beautiful children's clothing, pajamas, and special-occasion outfits, from tiny to size 12. Little ones start with a newborn gown set by Kissy Kissy or Petite Bateau and grow into fashions by Cacharel and Lili Gaufrette. Holding court for more than 60 years, **Van Cleef & Arpels** (✉*249 Worth Ave.* ☎*561/655–6767*) is where legendary members of Palm Beach society shop for tiaras and formal jewels.

WEST PALM BEACH

Across the Intracoastal Waterway from Palm Beach.

Long considered Palm Beach's less-privileged stepsister, sprawling West Palm has evolved into an economically vibrant destination of its own, ranking as the cultural, entertainment, and business center of the entire county and territory to the north. High-rise buildings like the mammoth Palm Beach County Judicial Center and Courthouse and the State Administrative Building underscore the breadth of the city's governmental and corporate activity. The glittering Kravis Center for the Performing Arts is Palm Beach County's principal entertainment venue. One of the newest additions to the city is the enormous and extravagant Palm Beach County Convention Center, which cost more than $80 million to build; the 350,000-square-foot campus sits on almost 20 acres across from the Kravis Center and CityPlace.

DOWNTOWN

The heart of revived West Palm Beach is a small, attractive, easy-to-walk downtown area, spurred on by active historic preservation. Along five blocks of beautifully landscaped Clematis Street, which ends at the Intracoastal Waterway, are boutiques and outdoor cafés, plus the 400-seat Cuillo Center for the Arts, which features pre-Broadway shows and concerts; and Palm Beach Dramaworks, an intimate theater that often shows new plays. An exuberant nightlife has taken hold of the area. In fact, downtown rocks every Thursday from 6 PM on with Clematis by Night, a celebration of music, dance, art, and food at Centennial Square. Even on downtown's fringes there are sights of cultural interest.

WHAT TO SEE

⑪ Ann Norton Sculpture Gardens. This monument to the late American sculptor Ann Weaver Norton, second wife of Norton Museum founder Ralph H. Norton, includes a complex of art galleries in the main house and studio, plus 2½ acres of gardens, where you'll find 300 varieties of palm trees, seven granite figures, and six brick megaliths. The plantings were designed to attract native birdlife. ✉*253 Barcelona Rd.* ☎*561/832–5328* ✉*$5* ☼ *Wed.–Sun. 11–4; call ahead, as schedule is not always observed; or by appointment.*

⑩ Norton Museum of Art. Constructed

Fodor'sChoice   in 1941 by steel magnate Ralph H.

★   Norton, the museum has an extensive collection of 19th- and 20th-century American and European paintings—including works by Picasso, Monet, Matisse, Pollock, and O'Keeffe—and Chinese, contemporary, and photographic art. There's a sublime outdoor covered loggia, Chinese bronze and jade sculptures, and a library. Galleries, including the Great Hall, also showcase traveling exhibits. ■TIP→**One of the city's best-kept secrets is this museum's café, with its artfully presented dishes that taste as good as they look.** ✉*1451 S. Olive Ave.* ☎*561/832–5196* ⊕*www.norton.org* ✉*$8* ☼ *Mon.–Sat. 10–5, Sun. 1–5.*

⑫ Currie Park. Frequent weekend festivals, including an annual celebration of seafood, take place at the scenic city park next to the Intracoastal Waterway. Sit on one of the piers and watch the yachts and fishing boats pass by. Put on your jogging shoes—the park is at the north end of a 6.3-mi biking/jogging/skating path. ✉*N. Flagler Dr. at 23rd St.*

⑬ Robert and Mary Montgomery Armory Arts Center. Built by the WPA in 1939, the facility is now a visual-arts center hosting rotating exhibitions and art classes throughout the year. ✉*1703 Lake Ave.* ☎*561/832–1776* ✉*Free* ☼ *Weekdays 9–6, Sat. 9–5.*

MOLLY'S TROLLEYS

The relentless Florida sun can be merciless when you're loaded down with Macy's shopping bags and you still have all those other stores to visit. Molly's Trolleys to the rescue! Share space with local lawyers and shoppers on the free and frequent trolley service that makes continuous loops down Clematis Street, the city's century-old main street, and through CityPlace, a shopping-restaurant-theater district. Hop on and off at any of the seven stops—four on Clematis, one next to the Intracoastal Waterway, and two in CityPlace. The trolleys run Sunday–Wednesday 11 AM–9 PM and Thursday–Saturday 11 AM–11 PM. Call ☎561/838–9511.

AWAY FROM DOWNTOWN

West Palm Beach's outskirts, flat stretches lined with fast-food outlets and car dealerships, may not inspire, but are worth driving through to reach attractions scattered around the city's southern and western reaches. Several sites are especially rewarding for children and other animal and nature lovers.

A GOOD TOUR

Head south from downtown and turn right on Southern Boulevard, left onto Parker Avenue, and right onto Summit Boulevard to reach the **Palm Beach Zoo at Dreher Park** ⑭. In the same area (turn right onto Dreher Trail) and also appealing to kids, the **South Florida Science Museum** ⑮, with its Aldrin Planetarium and McGinty Aquarium, is full of hands-on exhibits. If a quick game of croquet intrigues you, head to the **National Croquet Center** ⑯, less than 2 mi from the museum, by turning onto Summit Boulevard from Dreher Trail north and proceeding to Florida Mango Road, where you will turn left. Backtrack to Summit Boulevard and go west to the 150-acre **Pine Jog Environmental Education Center** ⑰. For more natural adventure, head farther west on Summit until you reach Forest Hill Boulevard, where you turn right to reach the **Okeeheelee Nature Center** ⑱ and its miles of wooded trails. Now retrace your route to Summit Boulevard, drive east until you reach Military Trail, and take a left. Drive north to Southern Boulevard and turn west to reach **Lion Country Safari** ⑲, a 500-acre cageless zoo. For the last stop on this tour, backtrack to Military Trail and travel north to the **Mounts Botanical Gardens** ⑳.

TIMING

Tailor your time based on specific interests, because you could easily spend most of a day at any of these attractions. Prepare yourself for heavy rush-hour traffic, and remember that sightseeing in the morning (not *too* early, to avoid rush hour) will be less congested.

WHAT TO SEE

👐 ⑲ **Lion Country Safari.** Drive your own vehicle (with windows closed) on 8 mi of paved roads through a 500-acre cageless zoo with a thousand free-roaming animals. Lions, elephants, white rhinos, giraffes, zebras, antelopes, chimpanzees, and ostriches are among the wild things in residence. Lions are fenced away from roads, but there's a good chance you'll have a giraffe or two nudging at your window. Exhibits include the Kalahari, designed after a South African bush plateau and containing water buffalo and Nilgai (the largest type of Asian antelope), and the Gir Forest, modeled after a game forest in India and showcasing a pride of lions. A walk-through park area has bird feeding and a petting zoo, or take a pontoon boat tour. There's also paddleboating, miniature golf, a children's play area with rides and sports fields, a picnic pavilion, a restaurant, and a snack shop. No convertibles or pets are allowed. ⊠ *2003 Lion Country Safari Rd., at Southern Blvd. W., Loxahatchee* ☎ *561/793–1084* ⊕ *www.lioncountrysafari.com* ⊴ *$22.99; $4.50 parking fee* ☉ *Daily 9:30–5:30; last vehicle in by 4:30.*

★ ⑳ **Mounts Botanical Gardens.** Take advantage of balmy weather by walking among the tropical and subtropical plants here. Join a free tour or explore the 14 acres of exotic trees, rain-forest area, and butterfly and water gardens on your own. Many plants were significantly damaged during the 2004 and 2005 hurricanes, and new plantings will take years to reach maturity. There are lots of free brochures about tropical trees, flowers, and fruits in the main building. If you're feeling inspired, be sure to check out the gift shop's wide range of gardening books. ⊠ *531 N. Military Trail* ☎ *561/233–1749* ⊕ *www.mounts.org* ⊠ *Gardens free; tours $5 suggested donation* ☉ *Mon.–Sat. 8:30–4:30, Sun. noon–4; tours Sun. at 2.*

★ ⑯ **National Croquet Center.** The world's largest croquet complex, the 10-acre center is also the headquarters for the U.S. Croquet Association. Vast expanses of manicured lawn are the stage for fierce competitions—in no way resembling the casual backyard games where kids play with wide wire wickets. There's also a clubhouse with a pro shop and Café Croquet, with verandas for dining and viewing, and a museum hall. You have to be a member, or a guest of a member, to reserve a lawn every day but Saturday, when lessons are free and lawns are open to all. ⊠ *700 Florida Mango Rd., at Summit Blvd.* ☎ *561/478–2300* ⊕ *www.croquetnational.com* ⊠ *Free admission. Free lessons Sat. Full day of play $25 June–Sept., Oct.–May* ☉ *Court times June–Sept., Tues.–Sat. 9–5; Oct.–May, daily 9–5.*

☾ ⑱ **Okeeheelee Nature Center.** Explore 5 mi of trails through 90 acres of western Palm Beach County's native pine flatwoods and wetlands. A visitor center–gift shop has hands-on exhibits and offers guided walks by the center's volunteers. ⊠ *7715 Forest Hill Blvd.* ☎ *561/233–1400* ⊠ *Free* ☉ *Visitor center Tues.–Fri. and Sun. 1–4:35, Sat. 8:15–4:35; trails daily dawn–dusk.*

☾ ⑭ **Palm Beach Zoo at Dreher Park.** This wild kingdom is a 23-acre complex with 400-plus animals representing more than 125 species, from Florida panthers to the giant Aldabra tortoise, and the first outdoor exhibit of Goeldi's monkeys in the nation. The Tropics of America exhibit has 6 acres of rain forest plus Mayan ruins, an Amazon river village, and an aviary. This was a one-tiger zoo until late 2006, when a pair of Malayan tiger brothers were added to the mix. Also notable are a nature trail, the otter exhibit, a children's petting zoo, and a restaurant overlooking the river. ⊠ *1301 Summit Blvd.* ☎ *561/533–0887* ⊕ *www.palmbeachzoo.com* ⊠ *$12.95* ☉ *Daily 9–5.*

☾ ⑰ **Pine Jog Environmental Education Center.** The draw here is 150 acres of mostly undisturbed Florida pine flatwoods with one self-guided ½-mi trail. Formal landscaping around five one-story buildings includes native plants; dioramas and displays illustrate ecosystems. School groups use the trails during the week; special events include camping and campfires. Call for an event schedule. ⊠ *6301 Summit Blvd.* ☎ *561/686–6600* ⊕ *www.pinejog.org* ⊠ *Free* ☉ *Weekdays 9–5.*

☾ ⑮ **South Florida Science Museum.** Here at the museum, which includes the Aldrin Planetarium and McGinty Aquarium, there are hands-on exhibits with touch tanks, and laser shows with music by the likes of Dave Matthews. Galaxy Golf is a 9-hole science challenge. Weather permitting, you can observe the heavens Friday night through the most powerful telescope in South Florida. ⊠ *4801 Dreher Trail N* ☎ *561/832–1988* ⊕ *www.sfsm.org* ⊠ *$9, planetarium $4 extra, laser show $5 extra, galaxy golf $2 extra* ☉ *Weekdays 10–5, Sat. 10–6, Sun. noon–6.*

WHERE TO EAT

$-$$$ ✕ Bellagio. In the center of CityPlace in a former church built in 1926, this European-style bistro offers Italian specialties with a wide variety of Italian wines. The menu includes Italian classics like chicken parmigiana, risotto, and fettuccine Alfredo. Pizzas from the wood burning oven are especially good. Service is friendly and efficient, but the overall noise level tends to be high. Sit at the outdoor tables next to the main plaza's dancing fountains. ⊠*600 S. Rosemary Ave., CityPlace Plaza* ☎*561/659–6160* ⊟*AE, MC, V.*

¢-$$ ✕ Havana. Decorated with tile floors and vintage posters of its namesake city, this two-level restaurant serves such authentic specialties as Cuban sandwiches and chicken slowly cooked in Spanish sauce. Lunch and dinner dishes are enhanced by the requisite black beans and rice. Open until 1 AM Friday and Saturday, it attracts a late-night crowd. The popular 24/7 walk-up window serves strong Cuban coffee, sugary fried churros, and fruit juices, including mamey, mango, papaya, guava, and guanabana. ⊠*6801 S. Dixie Hwy.* ☎*561/547–9799* ⊟*AE, MC, V* ⊙*Open daily.*

¢-$$ ✕ Howley's Restaurant. Since 1950, this diner's eat-in counter and "Cooked in sight, it must be right" motto has made a congenial setting for meeting and making friends. Forgo the counter for the 1950s-style tables or sit out on the patio. The café attracts a loyal clientele for breakfast, lunch, and dinner with such specialties as turkey and dressing, burgers, and chicken salad. There's also a bar. ⊠*4700 S. Dixie Hwy.* ☎*561/833–5691* ⊟*AE, MC, V.*

¢-$ ✕ Middle East Bakery. This hole-in-the-wall Middle Eastern bakery, deli, and market fills at lunchtime with regulars who are on a first-name basis with the gang behind the counter. From the nondescript parking lot the place doesn't look like much, but inside, delicious hot and cold Mediterranean treats await. Choose from traditional gyro sandwiches and lamb salads with sides of grape leaves, tabbouleh, and couscous. ⊠*327 5th St., at Olive Ave.* ☎*561/659–7322* ⊟*AE, MC, V* ⊙*Closed Sun.*

WHERE TO STAY

$$$$ ⊞ Hampton Inn & Suites in Wellington. Taking its cues from the polo fields and the equestrian center nearby, the Hampton sports a handsome look and an equestrian theme. The new, four-story hotel 10 miles west of West Palm Beach has the feeling of a ritzy clubhouse, with rich dark woods, hunt prints, and elegant chandeliers. One-bedroom suites have king beds or two doubles, sleeper sofa, bar sink, refrigerator, and microwave. All rooms have coffeemakers and in-room movie channel. Some rooms have a lake view. **Pros:** Complimentary hot breakfast and high-speed Internet access; next to the Wellington Green mall. **Cons:** No in-house restaurant. ⊠*2155 Wellington Green Dr.* ☎*561/472-9696* ⊕*www.hamptoninn.com* ⇆*122 rooms, 32 suites* ⚒*In-hotel: pool, gym, public Internet* ⊟*AE, MC, V.*

$$$ ⊞ Hotel Biba. In the El Cid historic district, this 1940s motel has gotten a fun, stylish revamp from Barbara Hulanicki, designer of the 1960s Biba fashion line. Each room has a vibrant mélange of colors, along with handcrafted mirrors, mosaic bathroom floors, and custom mahogany furnishings. Luxury touches include Egyptian-cotton sheets, down pillows and duvets, and lavender-scented closets. The hotel is one block from the Intracoastal Waterway and about a mile from Clematis Street nightlife, and the lobby bar attracts a hip happy-hour crowd. **Pros:** Especially appealing to the young and hip crowd; close to nightlife on Clematis. **Cons:** Water pressure is weak and bathrooms are tiny; can be noisy on Wednesday nights when the bar is open late. ⊠*320 Belvedere Rd.* ☎*561/832–0094* 🖨*561/833–7848* ⊕*www.hotelbiba. com* ⇆*43 rooms* ♿*In-hotel: bar, pool, no elevator, no-smoking rooms* ▭*AE, DC, MC, V.*

★ **$$–$$$** ▦ **Grandview Gardens Bed & Breakfast.** This cheery yellow 1923 Spanish Mediterranean inn is the new kid on the B&B block in West Palm Beach. It is very conveniently located—next to Howard Park, across from the Armory Art Center, a short walk from the Convention Center, CityPlace, and the Kravis Center, and a 10-minute drive from the airport—and warmly decorated with terra-cotta floors, a coral-stone fireplace, and terraces overlooking a swimming pool and gardens. Each spacious room has its own Mediterranean flair, as well as a private entrance and French doors opening to private terraces overlooking the pool. **Pros:** Private entrances, owners are multilingual. **Cons:** Not close to the beach. ⊠*1608 Lake Ave.* ☎*561/833–9023* ⊕*www. grandview-gardens.net* ⇆*5 rooms and a Bermuda-style guest cottage* ♿*In-room: dial-up. In-hotel: pool, no elevator, airport shuttle* ▭*AE, DC, MC, V* ⊙*BP.*

NIGHTLIFE & THE ARTS

THE ARTS

★ Starring amid the treasury of local arts attractions is the **Raymond F. Kravis Center for the Performing Arts** (⊠*701 Okeechobee Blvd.* ☎*561/832–7469*), a 2,200-seat glass, copper, and marble showcase just steps from the restaurants and shops of CityPlace. Its 250-seat Rinker Playhouse has children's programming, family productions, and other events. The outdoor Gosman Amphitheatre is perfect for winter nights and holds 1,400 in seats and on the lawn. A packed year-round schedule unfolds here with drama, dance, and music—from gospel and bluegrass to jazz and classical, including performances of the Palm Beach Pops, New World Symphony, Ballet Florida, and Miami City Ballet. **Palm Beach Opera** (⊠*415 S. Olive Ave.* ☎*561/833–7888*) stages four productions each winter at the Kravis Center with English translations projected above the stage. The family opera series includes matinee performances such as *Hansel & Gretel*; tickets are $22 to $225. The **Cuillo Center** (⊠*201 Clematis St.* ☎*561/835–9226*) has a 377-seat theater on the main floor with off-Broadway shows and a 40-seat theater upstairs with small acting groups.

NIGHTLIFE

The **Palm Beach Casino Line** (⊠*1 E. 11th St., Riviera Beach* ☎*561/845–7447 or 800/841–7447*) runs a five-hour getaway aboard the *Palm Beach Princess,* sailing twice daily from the Port of Palm Beach. There are a 15,000-square-foot casino, assorted lounges, a sports booking bar with nine televisions, a gift shop, and entertainment, along with a prime-rib buffet in the evening. Sailings are at 11 AM and 6:30 PM daily, and you'll need to allow time for preboarding procedures. Fares are $25 to $35 per person. CityPlace comes alive at **Blue Martini** (⊠*550 S. Rosemary Ave., 2nd fl., across from Muvico* ☎*561/835–8601*), a bar with eclectic music that attracts a diverse crowd. **ER Bradley's Saloon** (⊠*104 Clematis St.* ☎*561/833–3520*) is an open-air, pavilion-style restaurant and bar where large groups of all ages congregate to hang out and socialize while overlooking the Intracoastal Waterway and the Meyer Amphitheatre. There are guitars hanging above the bar and a DJ booth made from a 1957 Chevy, plus a 7,500-square-foot dance floor at **Dr. Feelgood's Rock Bar & Grill** (⊠*219 Clematis St.* ☎*561/833–6500*). Vince Neil, Mötley Crüe's lead singer, is the owner.

SPORTS & THE OUTDOORS

GOLF

The **Palm Beach National Golf & Country Club** (⊠*7500 St. Andrews Rd., Lake Worth* ☎*561/965–3381*) has an 18-hole classic course with a Joe Lee championship layout; greens fee: $49/$75. The Joanne Carner Golf Academy is based here.

SHOPPING

If you're looking for a mix of food, art, performance, landscaping, and retailing, then head to renewed downtown West Palm around **Clematis Street,** which runs east–west from Dixie Highway to Flagler Drive. Water-view parks with attractive plantings and lighting—and fountains where kids can cool off—add to the pleasure of browsing, window-shopping, and resting at an outdoor café. Hip national retailers such as Design Within Reach, Ann Taylor Loft, and Z Gallerie blend in with restaurants, pubs, and nightclubs. The 55-acre, $550 million **CityPlace** (☎*561/366–1000*), a four-block-by-four-block commercial and residential complex centered on Rosemary Avenue, attracts people of all ages to enjoy restaurants, cafés, and outdoor bars, a 20-screen Muvico, the Harriet Himmel Theater, and a 36,000-gallon dance, water, and light show. This family-friendly dining, shopping, and entertainment complex has plenty to see and do. Among CityPlace's stores are popular national retailers Macy's, Armani Exchange, Pottery Barn, Lucky Brand Jeans, Nine West, Sephora, and Restoration Hardware, designer boutiques including Betsey Johnson, Kenneth Cole, and Nicole Miller, and several shops unique to Florida. Behind the punchy, brightly colored clothing in the front window of **C. Orrico** (☎*561/832–9203*) are family fashions and accessories by Lily Pulitzer and girlie casual gear by Three Dots and Trina Turk. **Rhythm Clothiers** (☎*561/833–7677*) attracts fashion-forward types with a stock of men's and women's clothing by Dolce & Gabbana, Catherine Malandrino, Diesel, Miss Sixty, and J. Lindeberg. The free downtown trolley runs a continuous loop linking Clematis Street and CityPlace, so you won't miss a shop.

★ West Palm's **Antique Row,** aka South Dixie Highway, is the destination for those who are interested in interesting home decor. From thrift shops to the most exclusive stores, it is all here—furniture, lighting, art, junk, fabric, frames, tile, and rugs. So if you're looking for an Art Deco or French Provincial or Mizner pièce de résistance, big or small, schedule a few hours for an Antique Row stroll. You'll find bargains during the off-season (May–November). Antique Row runs north–south from Okeechobee Road to Forest Hill Boulevard, although most stores are bunched between Belvedere Road and Southern Boulevard.

LAKE OKEECHOBEE

40 mi west of West Palm Beach.

Rimming the western edges of Palm Beach and Martin counties, the second-largest freshwater lake completely within the United States is girdled by 120 mi of road yet remains shielded from sight for almost its entire circumference. Lake Okeechobee—the Seminole's Big Water and the gateway of the great Everglades watershed—measures 730 square mi, roughly 33 mi north–south, and 30 mi east–west, with an average natural depth of only 10 feet (flood control brings the figure up to 12 feet and deeper). Six major lock systems and 32 separate water-control structures manage the water. Encircling the lake is a 34-foot-high grassy levee—locals call it "the wall"—and the Lake Okeechobee Scenic Trail, a segment of the Florida National Scenic Trail, an easy, flat ride for bikers. ■TIP➡There's no shade, so wear a hat, sunscreen, and bug repellent. Be sure to bring lots of bottled water, too, because restaurants and stores are few and far between. You are likely to see alligators in the tall grass along the shore, as well as birds, including herons, ibises, and bald eagles, which have made a comeback in the area. The 110-mi trail encircles the lake atop the 34-foot Herbert Hoover Dike. On the lake, you'll spot happy anglers from all over, themselves hooked on some of the best bass fishing in North America. There are 40 species of fish in "Lake O," including largemouth bass, bluegill, Okeechobee catfish, and speckled perch. You can fish from the shore or hire a guide for a half-day or all-day boat trip.

Small towns dot the lakeshore in this predominantly agricultural area. To the southeast is Belle Glade—motto: "her soil is her fortune"—playing a role as the eastern hub of the 700,000-acre Everglades Agricultural Area, the crescent of farmlands south and east of the lake. Southwest lies Clewiston, billing itself as "the sweetest town in America" thanks to the presence of "Big Sugar," more formally known as the United States Sugar Corporation. At the lake's north end, around Okeechobee, citrus production has outgrown cattle ranching as the principal economic engine, and still-important dairying diminishes as the state acquires more acreage in efforts to reduce water pollution. Set back from the lake, Indiantown is the western hub of Martin County, noteworthy for citrus production, cattle ranching, and timbering. The town reached its apex in 1927, when the Seaboard Airline Railroad briefly established its southern headquarters and a model town here.

WHAT TO SEE

Detailing city history, the **Clewiston Museum** tells stories not only of Big Sugar and the Herbert Hoover Dike construction but also of a ramie crop grown here to make rayon, of Royal Air Force pilots training at the Clewiston airfield, and of a World War II prisoner-of-war camp. ⊠*109 Central Ave., Clewiston* ☎*863/983–2870* ⊑*$4* ☉ *Weekdays 9–4.*

In the **Municipal Complex** are the public library and the **Lawrence E. Will Museum,** both with materials on town history. On the front lawn is a Ferenc Verga sculpture of a family fleeing a wall of water rising from the lake during the catastrophic hurricane of 1928. More than 2,000 people perished, and 15,000 families were left homeless by torrential flooding. ✉*530 Main St., Belle Glade* ☎*561/996–3453* ⌨*Free* ☺*Mon.–Wed. 10–8, Thurs.–Sat. 10–5.*

WHERE TO EAT

$-$$$ ✕ **Colonial Dining Room.** The Clewiston Inn's restaurant has ladder-back chairs, chandeliers, fanlight windows, and an attitude that's anything but fancy. The regional and continental dishes—chicken, pork, steak, and the ubiquitous catfish—are mighty tasty. ✉*108 Royal Palm Ave., at U.S. 27, Clewiston* ☎*863/983–8151* ⊟*MC, V* ☺*No dinner Sun.*

¢-$ ✕ **Lightsey's.** The pick of the lake, this lodgelike restaurant at the Okee-Tantie Recreation Area started closer to town as a fish company with four tables in a corner. Now folks gladly trek out here for lunch and dinner daily. Get most items fried, steamed, broiled, or grilled. The freshest are the catfish, cooter (freshwater turtle), frogs' legs, and gator. ✉*10430 Rte. 78 W., Okeechobee* ☎*863/763–4276* ⊟*D, MC, V.*

WHERE TO STAY

$-$$$ ⛻ **Clewiston Inn.** A classic antebellum-style country hotel in the heart of town, this inn was built in 1938. In 2007 a spa and business center were added as part of a major renovation. The cypress-paneled lobby, wood-burning fireplace, Colonial Dining Room, and Everglades lounge with a wraparound Everglades mural are standouts. The 57 rooms, six suites and seven efficieny apartments are furnished with furniture representative of the 1930s and 1940s. Rates include a full breakfast cooked to order. There's a pool across the street in the park. **Pros:** The oldest hotel in the Glades is full of charm and a good value; has the only spa in town. **Cons:** Far from the beach, no elevator. ✉*108 Royal Palm Ave., at U.S. 27, Clewiston* ☎*863/983–8151 or 800/749–4466* 🖶*863/983–4602* ⊕*www.clewistoninn.com* ⇌*48 rooms, 5 suites* ⚒*In-hotel: restaurant, bar, tennis courts, spa, no elevator, public Internet* ⊟*AE, D, DC, MC, V* ⎊*BP.*

¢-$$$ ⛻ **Pier II Resort.** This two-story motel on the rim canal has a five-story observation tower for peeking over the lake's levee. Large, motel-plain rooms arc niccly maintained. Out back are a 650-foot fishing pier and the Oyster Bar, one of the lake area's best hangouts for shooting pool or watching TV, attracting a mix of locals and out-of-towners. The suites were refurbished after Hurricane Wilma in 2005. **Pros:** Nice fishing pier and observation tower. **Cons:** If you're not a fisherman, the early morning get-up noise could be annoying. ✉*2200 S.E. U.S. 441, Okeechobee* ☎*863/763–8003 or 800/874–3744* 🖶*863/763–2245* ⊕*www.pier2resort.com* ⇌*83 rooms, 6 suites* ⚒*In-room: kitchen (some), refrigerator. In-hotel: bar, pool* ⊟*AE, D, DC, MC, V* ⎊*CP.*

$-$$ ⛻ **Seminole Inn.** Once the Seaboard Airline Railroad's southern headquarters, this two-story, Mediterranean Revival inn, with cypress ceilings and pine hardwood floors, was restored by Holman Wall. It's now run by the late Indiantown patriarch's daughter, Jonnie Wall Williams, a fifth-generation native. Carpeted rooms are done in country ruffles and prints, with comfy beds. Rocking chairs await on the porch, and there's Indiantown memorabilia in the lobby, a sitting area on the second floor, and good local art throughout. **Pros:** Restaurant has a good Sunday brunch. **Cons:** No elevators. ⊠*15885 S.W. Warfield Blvd., Indiantown* ☎*772/597–3777* 🖨*772/597–2883* ⊕*www.seminoleinn. com* ➪*22 rooms* ᴄ*In-hotel: 2 restaurants, pool, no elevator.* ⊟*AE, D, MC, V* ❘❍❘*CP.*

¢   🖵 **Okeechobee Inn.** Rooms in this simple, two-story, L-shaped motel, 2 mi west of Belle Glade, are done in green floral prints. Large windows let in plenty of light, and balconies overlook the pool. **Pros:** A good value, has a pool. **Cons:** Fishing and boat ramps are a mile away. ⊠*265 N. U.S. 27, South Bay* ☎*561/996–6517* ➪*115 rooms* ᴄ*In-hotel: pool, no elevator* ⊟*AE, D, DC, MC, V.*

SPORTS & THE OUTDOORS

FISHING

Since the **Okee-Tantie Recreation Area** (⊠*10430 Rte. 78 W., Okeechobee* ☎*863/763–2622*) has direct lake access, it's a popular fishing outpost, with two public boat ramps, fish-cleaning stations, a marina, picnic areas and a restaurant, a playground, restrooms, showers, and a **bait shop** (☎*863/763–9645*) that stocks groceries. In addition to operating the bridge to Torry Island (among Florida's last remaining swing bridges—it's cranked open and closed by hand, swinging at right angles to the road), brothers Charles and Gordon Corbin run **Slim's Fish Camp** (⊠*215 Marina Dr., Belle Glade* ☎*561/996–3844*).

GOLF

Belle Glade Municipal Country Club (⊠*Torry Island Rd. [W. Lake Rd.], Belle Glade* ☎*561/996–6605*) has an 18-hole golf course and restaurant open to the public; greens fee $25/$34.

SOUTH TO BOCA RATON

Strung together by Route A1A, the towns between Palm Beach and Boca Raton are notable for their variety, from high-rise condominiums to small-town public beaches. In one town you'll find a cluster of art galleries and fancy dining, and the very next town will yield mostly hamburger joints and mom-and-pop stores.

LAKE WORTH

2 mi south of West Palm Beach.

For years, tourists looked here mainly for inexpensive lodging and easy access to Palm Beach, since a bridge leads from the mainland to a barrier island with Lake Worth's beach. Now Lake Worth has several blocks of restaurants and art galleries, making this a worthy destination on its own.

Also known as Casino Park, **Lake Worth Municipal Park** has a beach, Olympic-size swimming pool, a fishing pier (as of this writing, still partially closed after hurricane damage), picnic areas, shuffleboard, restaurants, and shops. ⊠*Rte. A1A at end of Lake Worth Bridge* ☎*561/533–7367* 🎦*Pool $3, parking 25¢ for 15 mins* ☉*Daily 9–5.*

WHERE TO EAT

$-$$ ✕ **Bizaare Avenue Café.** Decorated with a mix of artwork and antiques, this cozy tapas bar–wine bar–bistro fits right into downtown Lake Worth's groovy, eclectic scene. Daily specials are available on both the lunch and dinner menus, where crepes, pizzas, pastas, and salads are the staples. ⊠*921 Lake Ave.* ☎*561/588–4488* 🖃*AE, D, DC, MC, V.*

¢-$ ✕ **John G's.** Count on a line here until the midafternoon closing. The menu is as big as the crowd: grand fruit platters, sandwich-board superstars, grilled burgers, seafood, eggs every which way, and the house specialty, French toast. Breakfast is served until 11, lunch until 3. ⊠*10 S. Ocean Blvd. (Lake Worth Casino)* ☎*561/585–9860* ⚘*Reservations not accepted* 🖃*No credit cards* ☉ *No dinner.*

¢ ✕ **Benny's on the Beach.** Perched on the Lake Worth Pier (and nearly wiped out in hurricanes France and Jeanne), Benny's has diner-style food that's cheap and nothing fancy, but the spectacular view of the sun glistening on the water and the waves crashing directly below is what dining here is all about. ⊠*10 Ocean Ave.* ☎*561/582–9001* 🖃 *MC, V* ☉ *No dinner.*

WHERE TO STAY

$$$-$$$$ 🏨 **Sabal Palm House.** Built in 1936, this historic two-story frame enclave ★ is a short walk from the Intracoastal Waterway and a golf course. Three rooms and a suite are in the main house, and three others are across a brick courtyard in the carriage house. Each room is inspired by a different artist—including Renoir, Dalí, Norman Rockwell, and Chagall—and all have oak floors, antique furnishings, and private balconies. There's an inviting parlor where afternoon tea and weekend wine and appetizers are served. A full breakfast is offered indoors or in the courtyard, under the palms. **Pros:** Fresh flowers in guest rooms, extra pillows, close to shops, restaurants and the beach. **Cons:** No pool. ⊠*109 N. Golfview Rd.* ☎*561/582–1090 or 888/722–2572* 🖷*561/582–0933* ⊕*www.sabalpalmhouse.com* 🛏*6 rooms, 1 suite* ⚭*In-hotel: no kids under 14* 🖃*AE, MC, V* �’○❘*BP.*

★ $$$ 🏨 **Mango Inn.** It's only a 15-minute walk to the beach from this white frame B&B built as a private house in 1915. The two ground-floor rooms have French doors opening onto a patio. A poolside cottage has two bedrooms and two bathrooms. Have your complimentary breakfast of homemade raspberry buttermilk pancakes on the veranda overlooking the heated pool, or in the courtyard next to the fountain. **Pros:** Great breakfasts served poolside. **Cons:** Some rooms are quite small with tiny bathrooms. ⊠*128 N. Lakeside Dr.* ☎*561/533–6900 or 888/626–4619* 🖷*561/493–3748* ⊕*www.mangoinn.com* 🛏*7 rooms, 3 suites, 1 cottage* ⚭*In-room: kitchen, refrigerator (some), VCR, dial-up. In-hotel: pool, no elevator, no kids under 16, no-smoking rooms* 🖃*AE, D, MC, V* ❘○❘*BP.*

SPORTS & THE OUTDOORS

The **Gulfstream Polo Club,** the oldest such club along the Palm Beaches, began in the 1920s and plays medium-goal polo (for teams with handicaps of 8–16 goals). Seven polo fields and stabling for more than 60 horses make up this facility on the western edge of Lake Worth. ⊠ *4550 Polo Rd.* ☎ *561/965–2057* ☒ *Free* ☉ *Games Dec.–Apr.*

The **Museum of Polo & Hall of Fame** is a good place to start if you're looking for an introduction to polo. See polo memorabilia, art, and a film on the history of the sport. ⊠ *9011 Lake Worth Rd.* ☎ *561/969–3210* ☒ *Free, but donations encouraged* ☉ *10–4 weekdays all year and 10–2 Sat. Jan.–Apr.*

LANTANA

2 mi south of Lake Worth.

Lantana—just a bit farther south from Palm Beach than Lake Worth—has inexpensive lodging and a bridge connecting the town to its own beach on a barrier island. Tucked between Lantana and Boynton Beach is **Manalapan,** a tiny but posh residential community crowned by a luxury Ritz-Carlton beach resort.

Ideal for sprawling, beachcombing, or power-walking, **Lantana Public Beach** is also worthy for its proximity to one of the most popular food concessions in town, the **Dune Deck Cafe.** Here the choices are standard, but the food is particularly fresh and the portions are hearty. Try an omelet with a side of potato fries and melon wedges, Greek salad, homemade yogurt with seasonal fruit topped with honey, or a side of banana nut bread. There are daily breakfast and lunch specials; dining is outdoors under yellow canopies perched over the beach. ⊠ *100 N. Ocean Ave.* ☎ *561/582–0472* ☒ *Parking 25¢ for 15 mins* ☉ *Daily 9–4:45.*

WHERE TO EAT

$$-$$$ ✕ **Station House Restaurant.** The best Maine lobster in South Florida might well reside at this delicious dive, where all the seafood is cooked to perfection. Sticky seats and tablecloths are an accepted part of the scene, so wear jeans and a T-shirt. Although it's casual and family-friendly, reservations are recommended, since it's a local favorite. Station Grill, across the street, is less seafood oriented, but every bite as good. ⊠ *233 Lantana Rd.* ☎ *561/547–9487* ☰ *AE, D, DC, MC, V.*

★ $$-$$$ ✕ **Suite 225.** On a quaint street with other shops and eateries is this stylish restaurant, an inviting older house that's been renovated into a sleek sushi bar. Glass doors and windows open up to outdoor dining areas, and a bar nestles under large banyan trees. Start with a sample platter from the extensive list of eclectic "suite rolls," which includes nearly 40 choices. Among the good non-seafood bets are grilled sake skirt steak with ginger barbecue sauce and pork chops with Asian-pear chutney. ⊠ *225 E. Ocean Ave.* ☎ *561/582–2255* ☰ *AE, D, MC, V* ☉ *No lunch Sun. and Mon.*

$–$$$ ✕ **Old Key Lime House.** Overlooking the Intracoastal Waterway, the 1889 Lyman House has grown in spurts over the years and is now a patchwork of shedlike spaces, housing an informal Old Florida seafood house with prime key lime pie—the house specialty. Although there's air-conditioning, dining is open-air most evenings. The panoramic water views are the main appeal here for adults—kids love to feed the fish and rock in the glider seats on the dock. ⊠ *300 E. Ocean Ave.* ☎ *561/533–5220* ▤ *AE, MC, V.*

WHERE TO STAY

$$$$ ▥ **Ritz-Carlton, Palm Beach.** Despite its name, this bisque-color, triple-★   tower landmark is actually in Manalapan, halfway between Palm Beach and Delray Beach. A huge double-sided marble fireplace dominates the elegant lobby and foreshadows the luxury of the guest rooms, which have rich upholstered furnishings and marble tubs. Most rooms have ocean views, and all have balconies. A $15 million room renovation and a $45 million expansion in 2006 added a 3,000-square-foot oceanfront terrace, a new seawall, a second pool, two restaurants, a beauty bar for big and little kids, a grand spa, and a program for teens. Coconut palms shade the pools and courtyard—all of which are served by attendants who can fulfill whims from iced drinks to cool face towels. **Pros:** Gorgeous rooms with magnificent ocean views; good theater and shops across the street. **Cons:** Not close to golf course; a 15-minute drive to nightlife in Delray or West Palm Beach. ⊠ *100 S. Ocean Blvd., Manalapan* ☎ *561/533–6000 or 800/241–3333* 🖷 *561/588–4555* ⊕ *www.ritz-carlton.com* ↘ *310 rooms* ♿ *In-room: dial-up. In-hotel: 4 restaurants, room service, bars, tennis courts, pools, spa, beachfront, water sports, bicycles, children's and teens' programs, laundry service, concierge, public Ethernet, no-smoking rooms* ▤ *AE, D, DC, MC, V.*

$$$–$$$$ ▥ **Palm Beach Oceanfront Inn.** Families seeking closer-to-earth prices gravitate to this casual two-story resort on the beach. Don't count on anything fancy, but large, adequately furnished rooms and suites face tropical gardens. Beach frontage is the draw here. A wide wooden sundeck surrounds the free-form pool, and both look to the ocean. The informal restaurant and outdoor bar also overlook the water. **Pros:** Good value for a seaside inn, and the restaurant and outdoor bar are lively hangouts. **Cons:** Rooms and bathrooms are small. ⊠ *3550 S. Ocean Blvd.* ☎ *561/582–5631 or 800/457–5631* 🖷 *561/588–4563* ⊕ *www.palmbeachoceanfrontinn.com* ↘ *50 rooms, 8 suites* ♿ *In-room: kitchen (some), refrigerator, VCR (some), dial-up. In-hotel: restaurant, room service, bar, pool, beachfront* ▤ *AE, D, MC, V.*

SPORTS & THE OUTDOORS

B-Love Fleet (⊠ *314 E. Ocean Ave.* ☎ *561/588–7612*) offers three deep-sea fishing excursions daily: 8–noon, 1–5, and 7–11. No reservations are needed; just show up 30 minutes before the boat is scheduled to leave. The cost is $35 per person and includes fishing license, bait, and tackle.

BOYNTON BEACH

3 mi south of Lantana.

In 1884, when fewer than 50 settlers lived in the area, Nathan Boynton, a Civil War veteran from Michigan, paid $25 for 500 acres with a mile-long stretch of beachfront thrown in. How things have changed, with today's population at about 118,000 and property values still on an upswing. Far enough from Palm Beach to remain low-key, Boynton Beach has two parts, the mainland and the barrier island—the town of Ocean Ridge—connected by two bridges.

An inviting beach, boardwalk, concessions, grills, a jogging trail, and playground await at **Boynton Beach Oceanfront Park.** Weekend evening concerts are held throughout the year. Parking costs more if you're not a Boynton resident. ⊠*6415 Ocean Blvd. (Rte. A1A)* 🕾*No phone* 🚗*Parking $10 per day in winter, $5 per day rest of yr* ⊗*Daily 9 AM–midnight.*

☺ ★ Boynton Beach's history is highlighted through interactive exhibits that make the **Schoolhouse Children's Museum** a kid and parent pleaser. In this 1913 schoolhouse children can milk a mock cow or pick and wash plastic vegetables at the Pepper Patch Farm. Kids can buy tickets and dress up for a "time travel" train ride that immerses them in Boynton's history. A great outdoor playground castle is adjacent to the museum. ⊠*129 E. Ocean Ave.* 🕾*561/742–6780* 🚗*$5* ⊗*Tues.–Sat. 10–5.*

OFF THE BEATEN PATH **Arthur R. Marshall–Loxahatchee National Wildlife Refuge.** The most robust part of the Everglades, this 221-square-mi refuge is one of three huge water-retention areas accounting for much of the Everglades outside the national park. These areas are managed less to protect natural resources, however, than to prevent flooding to the south. Start from the visitor center, where there is a marsh trail to a 20-foot-high observation tower overlooking a pond. The boardwalk takes you through a dense cypress swamp. There's also a 5½-mi canoe trail, best for experienced canoeists since it's overgrown. Wildlife viewing is good year-round, and you can fish for bass and panfish. ⊠*10119 Lee Rd., off U.S. 441 between Boynton Beach Blvd. (Rte. 804) and Atlantic Ave. (Rte. 806), west of Boynton Beach* 🕾*561/734–8303* 🚗*$5 per vehicle, pedestrians $1* ⊗*Daily 6:30 AM–6 PM; visitor center, weekdays 9–4, weekends 9–4:30.*

WHERE TO EAT & STAY

$$-$$$ ✕ **Nirvana.** Highly stylized dining attracts experimental foodies hungry for Indian food touched with Caribbean, American, and French flavors. Given its strip-mall location, the attentive service is an unexpected treat, as is the intimate interior: sheer fabrics drape from the ceiling, warm woods trim the perimeter, and terra-cotta-color floors and walls contrast with the crisp white tablecloths. ⊠*1701 N. Congress Ave.* 🕾*561/752–1932* 🖃*AE, MC, V* ⊗*No lunch.*

¢-$$ ✕ **Banana Boat.** A mainstay for local boaters, who cruise up and down the Intracoastal Waterway and dock here, Banana Boat has fish-and-chips, burgers, ribs, and raw seafood. On weekends, casual crowds clad in tank tops, flip-flops, and bikinis dance to live island music while downing frozen drinks. ⊠*739 E. Ocean Ave.* ☎*561/732–9400* ☰*AE, MC, V.*

$$$-$$$$ ☷ **Holiday Inn Express.** Conveniently perched right off Interstate 95, this four-story hotel has large rooms with purple-and-green fabrics, blond-wood furniture, and small sitting areas. A large sundeck surrounds the heated pool. Complimentary breakfast is served, and free beverages are on tap at the end of the day. The hotel completed a $1 million renovation in 2006, which included a new lobby and breakfast room, a fitness center, a convenience store, and new furniture in guest rooms. **Pros:** Good value and convenient to interstate. **Cons:** Noise from nearby Interstate 95. ⊠*480 W. Boynton Beach Blvd.* ☎*561/734–9100* 🖷*561/738–7193* ⊕*www.hiexpress.com* ⇱*100 rooms, In-room: dial-up. In-hotel: pool, laundry facilities* ☰*AE, DC, MC, V* ⏃⎸*BP.*

SPORTS & THE OUTDOORS

FISHING
Fish the canal at the **Arthur R. Marshall–Loxahatchee National Wildlife Refuge** (☎*561/734–8303*). There's a boat ramp, and the waters are decently productive, but bring your own equipment. On the other side of town, catch fish swimming between the Atlantic and Intracoastal at the **Boynton Beach Inlet Pier** (☎*No phone*).

GOLF
Links at Boynton Beach (⊠*8020 Jog Rd.* ☎*561/742–6500*) has 18-hole and 9-hole executive courses; greens fees: Champion course $25/$55, Family course $39/$49.

DELRAY BEACH

2 mi south of Gulf Stream.

A onetime artists' retreat with a small settlement of Japanese farmers, Delray has grown into a sophisticated beach town. Atlantic Avenue, the once dilapidated main drag, has evolved into a more-than-a-mile-long stretch of palm-dotted sidewalks, lined with stores, art galleries, and dining establishments. Running east–west and ending at the beach, it's a pleasant place for a stroll, day or night. Another active pedestrian way begins at the eastern edge of Atlantic Avenue and runs along the big, broad swimming beach that extends north to George Bush Boulevard and south to Casuarina Road.

WHAT TO SEE
Just off Atlantic Avenue, the **Old School Square Cultural Arts Center** has several museums in restored school buildings dating from 1913 and 1926. The **Cornell Museum of Art & History** offers ever-changing art exhibits. During its season, the **Crest Theatre** showcases performances by local and touring troupes in the restored 1925 Delray High School building. ⊠*51 N. Swinton Ave.* ☎*561/243–7922* ⊕*www.oldschool. org* ⎘*$6* ⏲*Tues.–Sat. 10:30–4:30, Sun. 1–4:30.*

A restored bungalow-style home that dates from about 1915, **Cason Cottage** serves as the Delray Beach Historical Society's offices. It's filled with Victorian-era relics, including a pipe organ donated by descendants of a Delray Beach pioneer family. Periodic displays celebrate the town's architectural evolution. The cottage is a block north of the cultural center. ⊠ *5 N.E. 1st St.* ☎ *561/243–0223* 🎫 *Free* ⊙ *Call for an appointment for tours.*

The chief landmark along Atlantic Avenue since 1926 is the Mediterranean Revival–style **Colony Hotel,** which is a member of the National Trust for Historic Preservation. Walk through the lobby to the parking lot of the hotel where original stable "garages" still stand—relics of the days when hotel guests would arrive via horse and carriage. ⊠ *525 E. Atlantic Ave.* ☎ *561/276–4123.*

Traditional and digital photography are on display at the **Palm Beach Photographic Centre,** in the Pineapple Grove section of town. There's a small museum, gallery, darkroom, and retail shop. ⊠ *55 N.E. 2nd Ave.* ☎ *561/276–9797* ⊕ *www.workshop.org* 🎫 *$3* ⊙ *Mon.–Sat. 9–5:30.*

Fodor'sChoice ★ Out in the boonies west of Delray Beach seems an odd place to encounter the inscrutable East, but there awaits **Morikami Museum and Japanese Gardens,** a cultural and recreational facility heralding the Yamato Colony of Japanese farmers. The on-site Cornell Café serves light Asian fare. If you don't get your fill of orchids, the American Orchid Society's 20,000-square-foot headquarters is across the street. ⊠ *4000 Morikami Park Rd.* ☎ *561/495–0233* ⊕ *www.morikami.org* 🎫 *$10* ⊙ *Tues.–Sun. 10–5.*

★ Enjoy many types of water-sport rentals—sailing, kayaking, windsurfing, Boogie boarding, surfing, snorkeling—or scuba diving at a sunken Spanish galleon less than ½ mi offshore at **Seagate Beach.** ⊠ *½ mi south of Atlantic Ave. at Rte. A1A.*

A scenic walking path follows the main stretch of the public **Delray Beach Municipal Beach.** ⊠ *Atlantic Ave. at Rte. A1A.*

WHERE TO EAT

★ $$–$$$$ ✕ **32 East.** Although restaurants come and go on a trendy street like Atlantic Avenue, 32 East is a consistent staple, if not the best restaurant on any given night in Delray Beach. A daily menu of wood-oven pizzas, salads, soups, seafood, meat, and desserts is all based on what is fresh and plentiful. Dark-wood accents and dim lighting make this large restaurant seem cozy. There's a packed bar in front and an open kitchen in back. ⊠ *32 E. Atlantic Ave.* ☎ *561/276–7868* 🗖 *AE, D, MC, V* ⊙ *No lunch.*

$$–$$$ ✕ **Kyoto.** An energetic crew, from the sushi chefs to the waitstaff, keeps this bustling restaurant running into the wee hours all week long. Sushi and sake are the main draw here, and the less traditional dishes still have Japanese influences. Indoor dining is in a stylish, contemporary setting with sleek black accents and multicolor lighting. You can dine among a bar crowd and watch your sushi being assembled, or take a table in the front courtyard and watch the crowds meander along hap-

pening Pineapple Grove. ⊠*25 N.E. 2nd Ave.* ☎*561/330–2404* ▤*AE, DC, MC, V* ⊘*No lunch weekends.*

¢-$$$ ✕ **Pineapple Grille.** A magnet for regulars, this informal tropical enclave serves dependable Caribbean fare. An extensive menu includes macadamia nut–crusted crab cakes and mango goat-cheese chicken, along with imaginative pizzas. There's also a good and affordable wine list and live music on weekends. ⊠*800 Palm Trail, in Palm Trail Plaza* ☎*561/265–1368* ▤*AE, MC, V* ⊘*Closed Mon. mid-May–mid-Sep.*

¢-$$ ✕ **Blue Anchor.** Yes, this pub was actually shipped from England, where it stood for 150 years as the Blue Anchor Pub in London's historic Chancery Lane. There it was a watering hole for famed Englishmen, including Winston Churchill. The Delray Beach incarnation has stuck to authentic British pub fare. Chow down on a ploughman's lunch (a chunk of Stilton cheese, a hunk of bread, and pickled onions), shepherd's pie, fish-and-chips, and bangers and mash (sausages with mashed potatoes). Don't be surprised to find a rugby game on TV. English beers and ales are on tap and by the bottle. It's a late-night place open until at least 2. ⊠*804 E. Atlantic Ave.* ☎*561/272–7272* ▤*AE, MC, V.*

★ ¢-$ ✕ **Old School Bakery.** Formerly in a much larger shop where they actually baked all the goodies, this purveyor of many restaurants' breads has moved its baking facilities off-site and concentrates on simple sandwich making at its best. Particularly worthy is the cherry chicken salad sandwich with Brie on multigrain. Apart from sandwiches and soups served for lunch every day, order from a diverse baked-goods menu with artisan breads, pastries, several kinds of cookies, and even biscotti. The bakery is primarily take-out, but there are a few small tables in an adjacent open-air courtyard. ⊠*814 E. Atlantic Ave.* ☎*561/243–8059* ▤*AE, MC, V* ⊘*No dinner.*

WHERE TO STAY

$$$$ ⊡ **Colony Hotel & Cabana Club.** In the heart of downtown Delray, this lovely and charming building underwent an exterior renovation that luckily did not do away with the stables in the back, which date back to 1926 when the hotel was built. Today it's listed on Delray's local Register of Historic Places and maintains an air of the 1920s with its Mediterranean Revival architecture. The Cabana Club is a separate property on the ocean about a mile away, with a private beach, club, and heated saltwater pool. A convivial bar and live music on weekend nights make the lobby area a great place to wind down. Fine shops selling leather goods, body products, and stationery fill the lower-level storefronts. ⊠*525 E. Atlantic Ave.* ☎*561/276–4123 or 800/552–2363* 🖷*561/276–0123* ⊕*www.thecolonyhotel.com* ⇲*70 rooms* ⚷*In-room: dial-up. In-hotel: bar, pool, beachfront* ▤*AE, DC, MC, V* ⎇⊙*CP.*

★ $$$$ ⊡ **Sundy House.** Just about everything in this bright, bungalow-style inn is executed to perfection. Guest rooms are luxuriously decorated and offer hotel-style amenities, the cottage has its own Jacuzzi and fireplace, and the apartments offer a full kitchen and laundry. Situated a few blocks south of Atlantic Avenue, the only downside is a hearty walk to the beach (although a complimentary beach shuttle lessens the inconvenience). Even if you do not stay here, come see the grounds, where rooms are hidden behind extraordinary tropical gardens. Dine at the exceptional restaurant De la Tierra ($$$–$$$$) under an expansive indoor canopy, or on the outside patios under trees and among koi ponds. This is a popular weekend wedding spot. **Pros:** Beautiful property with excellent restaurant, quiet area. **Cons:** Far from beach, some may prefer conventional pool. ⊠*106 Swinton Ave.* ☎*561/272–5678 or 877/434–9601* ⊕*www.sundyhouse.com* ⌨*11 rooms* ⌂*In-hotel: no elevator* ⊟*AE, DC, MC, V.*

$$$–$$$$　⊡ **Delray Beach Marriott.** A bright pink five-story hotel, this is by far the largest property in Delray, with a stellar location at Atlantic Avenue's east end, across the road from the beach and within walking distance of restaurants, shops, and galleries. Rooms and suites are spacious, and many have stunning ocean views. In 2006 the hotel added a spa. The giant, free-form pool is surrounded by a comfortable deck. **Pros:** Great location for beach, restaurants, and nightlife on Atlantic Avenue; great spa. **Cons:** Large resort, can be overwhelming. ⊠*10 N. Ocean Blvd.* ☎*561/274–3200* 🖶*561/274–3202* ⊕*www.delraybeachmarriott.com* ⌨*268 rooms, 88 suites* ⌂*In-room: safe, Ethernet. In-hotel: 3 restaurants, room service, bars, pool, gym, spa, beachfront, laundry facilities* ⊟*AE, DC, MC, V.*

NIGHTLIFE

Bistro 52 (⊠*110 E. Atlantic Ave.* ☎*561/274–7077)* is packed with local society and celebrity. The drinks flow as does the chatter, but there's no dancing, only posing. **Dada** (⊠*52 N. Swinton Ave.* ☎*561/330–3232)* presents live music in the living room of a historic house, and movies play on the wall. It's a place where those who don't drink will also feel comfortable. **Elwood's** (⊠*301 E. Atlantic Ave.* ☎*561/272–7427)* is a fun drinking establishment in a former service station. Harley Davidsons line up on the weekend as locals stop by for the jamming live music and occasional Elvis sighting. **Delux** (⊠*16 E. Atlantic Ave.* ☎*561/279–4792)* is where the young South Beach wannabe crowd goes to dance all night long.

SPORTS & THE OUTDOORS

BIKING

There's a bicycle path in Barwick Park and a special oceanfront lane along Route A1A. **Richwagen's Bike & Sport** (⊠*298 NE 6th Ave.* ☎*561/276–4234)* rents bikes by the hour or day and provides lock, basket, helmet, and maps.

TENNIS

Each winter the **Delray Beach Tennis Center** (⊠*201 W. Atlantic Ave.* ☎*561/243–7360)* hosts professional tournaments such as the Chris Evert Tennis Classic and trains top-ranked players—even Andy Roddick. It offers individual lessons and clinics, and you can practice or learn on 14 clay courts and five hard courts year-round. It's open 8 AM–9 PM weekdays, 8 AM–6 PM weekends.

WATERSKIING

At **Lake Ida Park** (⊠*2929 Lake Ida Rd.*) you can water-ski whether you're a beginner or a veteran. The park has a boat ramp, a slalom course, and a trick ski course.

SHOPPING

Street-scaped **Atlantic Avenue** is a showcase for art galleries, shops, and restaurants. This charming area, from Swinton Avenue east to the ocean, has maintained much of its small-town integrity. **Snappy Turtle** (⊠*1038 Atlantic Ave.* ☎*561/276–8088*) is a multiroom extravaganza where Mackenzie Childs and Lily Pulitzer mingle with other fun fashions for the home and family. A store in the historic Colony Hotel, **Escentials Apothecaries** (⊠*533 Atlantic Ave.* ☎*561/276–7070*) is packed with all things good-smelling for your bath, body, and home. **Murder on the Beach** (⊠*273 N.E. 2nd Ave.* ☎*561/279–7790*) specializes in new, used, and antiquarian mystery books, with an impressive selection from local authors. You can also purchase mystery games and puzzles.

5

BOCA RATON

6 mi south of Delray Beach.

Less than an hour south of Palm Beach and anchoring the county's south end, upscale Boca Raton has much in common with its fabled cousin. Both reflect the unmistakable architectural influence of Addison Mizner, their principal developer in the mid-1920s. The meaning of the name Boca Raton (pronounced boca rah-*tone*) often arouses curiosity, with many folks mistakenly assuming it means "rat's mouth." Historians say the probable origin is Boca Ratones, an ancient Spanish geographical term for an inlet filled with jagged rocks or coral. Miami's Biscayne Bay had such an inlet, and in 1823 a mapmaker copying Miami terrain confused the more northern inlet, thus mistakenly labeling this area Boca Ratones. No matter what, you'll know you've arrived in the heart of downtown when you spot the town hall's gold dome on the main street, Federal Highway.

WHAT TO SEE

★ ☺ In a spectacular building in the Mizner Park shopping center (⇨ *Shopping)*, the **Boca Raton Museum of Art** has an interactive children's gallery and changing exhibition galleries showcasing internationally known artists. Upstairs galleries house a permanent collection including works by Picasso, Degas, Matisse, Klee, and Modigliani, as well as notable pre-Columbian art. ⊠*501 Plaza Real* ☎*561/392–2500* ⊕*www.bocamuseum.org* ⊠*$8* ☉*Tues., Thurs., and Fri. 10–5, Wed. 10–9, weekends noon–5.*

> ### WORD OF MOUTH
>
> "It's interesting to see what a great job the townspeople did planning Boca—no billboards, parking lots at the beach hidden behind dunes, gas stations and shopping areas screened with lush landscaping—controlled growth and strict zoning and ordinances paid off. I think Boca is one of the nicest towns on the Gold Coast."–PrettyLake

☺ A big draw for kids, **Gumbo Limbo Nature Center** has four huge saltwater tanks brimming with sea life—from coral to stingrays—and a boardwalk through dense forest with a 40-foot tower you can climb to overlook the tree canopy. In spring and early summer, staffers lead nocturnal turtle walks: you can watch nesting females come ashore and lay eggs. ✉ *1801 N. Ocean Blvd.* ☎ *561/338–1473* ⊕ *www.gumbo-limbo.org* ✉ *Free; turtle tours $5; tickets must be obtained in advance* ⊙ *Mon.–Sat. 9–4, Sun. noon–4; turtle tours May–Aug., Mon.–Thurs. 9 PM–midnight.*

Built in 1925 as the headquarters of the Mizner Development Corporation, **2 East El Camino Real** is an example of Mizner's characteristic Spanish Revival architectural style,

> **THIS LIMBO ROCKS**
>
> Gumbo Limbo might sound like a Cajun dish or a party dance, but in Boca Raton, it's actually an environmental complex between Lake Wyman and the Atlantic Ocean. The name comes from the dominant tree in the park, sometimes called the tourist tree, because the bark resembles a peeling sunburn. A great hiking spot, the park has a sturdy boardwalk and a 40-foot observation tower. Spend a little time there and you're likely to see brown pelicans and osprey. Kids love the aquariums, insect tanks and butterfly garden. Gumbo Limbo is at 1801 N. Ocean Blvd., Boca Raton.

with its wrought-iron grilles and handmade tiles. As for Mizner's grandiose vision of El Camino Real, the architect-promoter once prepared brochures promising a sweeping wide boulevard with Venetian canals and arching bridges. Camino Real is attractive, heading east to the Boca Raton Resort & Club, but don't count on feeling like you're in Venice.

Within a shimmering golden dome, **Town Hall Museum** has a vital repository of archival material and special exhibits on the area's development. Tours and the gift shop are hosted by the Boca Raton Historical Society. One of IBM's first PCs is on display here. ✉ *71 N. Federal Hwy.* ☎ *561/395–6766* ⊕ *www.bocahistory.org* ✉ *Free, tours $7* ⊙ *Tues.–Fri. 10–4, Sat. 10–2; tour dates and times vary.*

A residential area behind the Boca Raton Art School on Palmetto Park Road, **Old Floresta** was developed by Addison Mizner starting in 1925 and landscaped with varieties of palms and cycads. It includes houses that are mainly in a Mediterranean style, many with upper balconies supported by exposed wood columns. Home tours are held twice a year.

☺ Hands-on interactive exhibits enliven the **Children's Science Explorium,** at Sugar Sands Park. Children can create their own laser-light shows, explore a 3-D kiosk that illustrates wave motion, and try assorted electrifying experiments. There are also wind tunnels, microscopes, and microwave- and radiation-experiment stations. ✉ *300 S. Military Trail* ☎ *561/347–3913* ✉ *Free* ⊙ *Weekdays 9–6, weekends 10–5.*

WHERE TO EAT

$$$-$$$$ 🍴**Truluck's.** The popular seafood chain landed in Boca's Mizner Park in 2007 and boasts its own fleet of 16 boats near Naples. Stone crabs are the signature dish and you can have all you can eat on Monday nights during the season (Dec.-May). Other recommended dishes

include jalapeño salmon topped with blue crab meat, hot and crunchy trout, crab cakes, and bacon-wrapped shrimp. In a spot formerly occupied by American Café, Truluck comes alive each night with its popular piano bar. ✉*351 Plaza Real, Mizner Park* ☎*561/391–0755* ⊕ *www. trulucks.com* ⊟*AE, D, MC, V.*

$$-$$$$ ✕ **Tiramisu.** The food is an extravaganza of taste treats; veal chops, tuna, and anything with mushrooms draw raves, but count on hearty fare rather than a light touch. Start with the portobello mushroom with garlic or the Corsican baby sardines in olive oil. For a main course, try ricotta ravioli; scaloppine of veal stuffed with crabmeat, lobster, and Gorgonzola; or Tuscan fish stew. ✉*855 S. Federal Hwy.* ☎*561/338–9692* ⊟*AE, DC, MC, V* ⊘*Dinner only on Sun.*

$$-$$$ ✕ **Uncle Tai's.** The draw at Boca's most upscale Chinese restaurant is some of the best Szechuan food on Florida's east coast. Specialties include sliced duck with snow peas and water chestnuts in a tangy plum sauce, and orange beef delight—flank steak stir-fried until crispy and then sautéed with pepper sauce, garlic, and orange peel. They'll go easy on the heat on request. Service is quietly efficient. ✉*5250 Town Center Circle* ☎*561/368–8806* ⊟*AE, MC, V* ⊘*No lunch Sun.*

★ $-$$ ✕ **La Tre.** An adventuresome menu distinguishes this simple Vietnamese eatery. Try the crispy eggplant and the happy pancake, a Vietnamese crepe stuffed with pork, shrimp, and vegetables. Tamarind squid is another winner. The restaurant's decor seems to date from the 1980s, with black lacquer furniture and an odd purple hue cast from fluorescent lighting. Don't anticipate a romantic dinner experience, but rather a very good Vietnamese dining experience. ✉*249 E. Palmetto Park Rd.* ☎*561/392–4568* ⊟*AE, DC, MC, V* ⊘*No lunch Sat.–Tues.*

WHERE TO STAY

★ $$$$ 🏨 **Boca Raton Resort & Club.** Addison Mizner built the Mediterranean-style Cloister Inn here in 1926, and additions over time have created this sparkling, sprawling resort with a beach accessible by shuttle. There are recreational activities here and many lodging options: traditional Cloister rooms are small but warmly decorated; accommodations in the 27-story Tower are more spacious; Beach Club rooms are light, airy, and contemporary; golf villas are large and attractive. In addition to a redesigned golf course, there's a two-story golf clubhouse, and the deluxe Tennis & Fitness Center. **Pros:** Beautiful, historical property; celebs stay here; close to beach and golfing. **Cons:** Older rooms are dated. ✉*501 E. Camino Real* ☎*561/447–3000 or 800/327–0101* 🖷*561/447–3183* ⊕*www.bocaresort.com* 🛏*840 rooms, 63 suites, 60 golf villas* ᾧ*In-room: safe, kitchen (some). In-hotel: 11 restaurants,* *room service, bars, golf course, tennis courts, pools, gym, beachfront, water sports, children's programs (ages 2–17), laundry service, concierge* ▭*AE, DC, MC, V.*

$$$$ **Radisson Bridge Resort of Boca Raton.** This pink mid-rise resort sits directly on the Intracoastal Waterway yet has views of the ocean that can't be beat, especially from the top-floor restaurant, which is open only for Sunday brunch (very popular with locals) and private parties. The ground-floor restaurant, Water Color, offers great views of passing boats. The beach is a five-minute walk away, as are restaurants, galleries, and boutiques. Comfortable accommodations, the kind of attentive service found at smaller resorts, and an amazing location are the draws. Rooms are decorated in typical Boca-style light woods and rattan and a watercolor palette—nothing spectacular, yet quite presentable. **Pros:** Next to Boca Raton Resort & Club with more affordable rates. **Cons:** Can be noisy if your room is next to the bridge. ✉*999 E. Camino Real* ☎*561/368–9500 or 800/333–3333* 📠*561/362–0492* 🌐*www.radisson.com* *110 rooms, 11 suites* *In-room: refrigerator (suites), dial-up. In-hotel: 2 restaurants, room service, bars, pool, gym, beachfront, laundry facilities* ▭*AE, DC, MC, V.*

$$ **Ocean Breeze Inn.** If golf is your game, this is an excellent choice. Inn guests can play the outstanding course at the adjoining Ocean Breeze Golf & Country Club, otherwise available only to club members. Rooms are in a three-story building, and most have a patio or balcony. Although the inn is nearly 30 years old, refurbished rooms are comfortable and contemporary. **Pros:** Great spot for golfers. **Cons:** Attracts older crowd. ✉*5800 N.W. 2nd Ave.* ☎*561/994–0400 or 800/344–6995* 📠*561/998–8279* 🌐*www.oceanbreezegolf.com* *46 rooms* *In-hotel: restaurant, golf course, tennis courts, pool, laundry facilities* ▭*AE, DC, MC, V.*

NIGHTLIFE

Drop by **Gatsby's Boca** (✉*5970 S.W. 18th St., Shoppes at Village Point* ☎*561/393–3900*) any night of the week to mingle with a lively crowd. Shoot pool at one of 18 tables or watch sporting events on several giant screens. **Pranzo** (✉*402 Plaza Real* ☎*561/750–7442*) has a happening weekend bar scene.

SPORTS & THE OUTDOORS

BEACHES

Red Reef Park (✉*1400 N. Rte. A1A*) has a beach and playground plus picnic tables and grills. Popular **South Beach Park** (✉*400 N. Rte. A1A*) has a concession stand. In addition to its beach, **Spanish River Park** (✉*3001 N. Rte. A1A*) has picnic tables, grills, and a large playground.

BOATING

For the thrill of blasting across the water at up to 80 mph, **Palm Breeze Charters** (✉*107 E. Palmetto Park Rd., Suite 330* ☎*561/368–3566*) offers weekly cruises and boat charters. Rates are quoted individually depending on boat and charter.

GOLF

Two championship courses and golf programs are at **Boca Raton Resort & Club** (⊠*501 E. Camino Real* ☎*561/447–3078*), greens fee $100/$195, includes cart. The Dave Pelz Golf School is at the Country Club course.

SCUBA & SNORKELING

Force E (⊠*2181 N. Federal Hwy.* ☎*561/368–0555*) has information on dive trips and also rents scuba and snorkeling equipment. It has PADI affiliation, provides instruction at all levels, and offers charters.

SHOPPING

Locals know that Boca strip malls contain great shops. While stopping for essentials at Publix, be sure to check out that unassuming consignment, shoe, or fashion boutique next door and you may discover one of Boca's better finds.

★ **Mizner Park** (⊠*Federal Hwy., 1 block north of Palmetto Park Rd.*) is a distinctive 30-acre shopping center with apartments and town houses among its gardenlike retail and restaurant spaces. Some three-dozen stores, including national and local retailers, mingle with fine restaurants, sidewalk cafés, galleries, a movie theater, museum, and amphitheater. **Town Center Mall** (⊠*6000 W. Glades Rd.* ☎*561/368–6000*) is an upscale shopping mall. Major retailers include Nordstrom, Bloomingdale's, Macy's, Lord & Taylor, Saks Fifth Avenue, and Neiman Marcus. The mall's specialty may be women's fashion, but there are more than 200 stores and restaurants.

THE TREASURE COAST

From south to north, the Treasure Coast encompasses the top of Palm Beach County plus Martin, St. Lucie, and Indian River counties. Although dotted with seaside communities, this coastal section is one of Florida's quietest. Beyond the Palm Beach County border, most towns are small, with plenty of undeveloped land in between. Vero Beach, the region's most sophisticated beach area, was hit hard by the hurricanes of 2004 and 2005. Recovery includes new condo-hotels, and refurbishing of fine-dining establishments and upscale shops. Beaches along here are also sought out by nesting sea turtles; join locally organized watches to view the turtles laying their eggs in the sand between late April and August. It's illegal to touch or disturb turtles or their nests.

PALM BEACH SHORES

7 mi north of Palm Beach.

Rimmed by mom-and-pop motels, this residential town is at the southern tip of Singer Island, across Lake Worth Inlet from Palm Beach. To travel between the two, however, you must cross over to the mainland before returning to the beach. This unpretentious community has affordable beachfront lodging and is near several nature parks.

In the Intracoastal Waterway between Palm Beach Shores and Riviera Beach, 79-acre **Peanut Island** was opened in 1999 as a recreational park. There's a 20-foot-wide walking path surrounding the island, a 19-slip boat dock, a 170-foot T-shape fishing pier, six picnic pavilions, a visitor center, and 20 overnight campsites. The small **Palm Beach Maritime Museum** (☎561/832–7428) is open daily except Friday and showcases the "Kennedy Bunker," a bomb shelter prepared for President John F. Kennedy (call for tour hours). To get to the island, you can use your own boat or take a water taxi (call for schedules and pickup locations). ☎561/540–5147 ⊕www.pbmm.org ✉Free, tours $10 ☉ Daily dawn–dusk for noncampers.

WHERE TO EAT & STAY

$-$$$ ✕ **Sailfish Marina Restaurant.** Once known as the Galley, this waterfront restaurant looking out to Peanut Island remains a great place to chill out after a hot day of mansion-gawking or beach-bumming. Sit inside or outdoors to order tropical drinks and mainstays like conch chowder, grouper, or meat loaf. More upscale entrées—this, after all, is still Palm Beach County—include lobster tail or baby sea scallops sautéed in garlic and lemon butter. Breakfast is a winner here, too. ✉98 Lake Dr. ☎561/842–8449 ▭AE, MC, V.

$$-$$$$ 🏨 **Sailfish Marina and Sportfishing Resort.** This one-story motel has a marina with 94 deepwater slips and accommodations that include motel-style rooms, small and large efficiencies, and even a three-bedroom house. All rooms open to landscaped grounds, although none are directly on the water. Units 9–11 have ocean views across the blacktop drive. Rooms have peaked ceilings, carpeting, king-size or twin beds, and stall showers; all have ceiling fans. From the seawall, you'll see fish through the clear inlet water. **Pros:** Inexpensive, on the Intracoastal and not far from the beach. **Cons:** Can be noisy, especially on weekends when waterway and Peanut Island are crowded with party animals; dated rooms. ✉98 Lake Dr., Singer Island ☎561/844–1724 or 800/446–4577 🖷561/848–9684 ⊕www.sailfishmarina.com ✎30 units ⚖In-hotel: 2 restaurants, bar, pool, no elevator ▭AE, MC, V.

SPORTS & THE OUTDOORS

FISHING

The **Sailfish Marina and Resort** (✉98 Lake Dr. ☎561/844–1724) has a large sportfishing fleet, with 28-foot to 60-foot boats and seasoned captains. Book a full- or half-day of deep-sea fishing for up to six people.

PALM BEACH GARDENS

5 mi north of West Palm Beach.

About 15 minutes northwest of Palm Beach is this relaxed, upscale residential community known for its high-profile golf complex, the PGA National Resort & Spa. Although not on the beach, the town is less than a 15-minute drive from the ocean.

Florida's Sea Turtles: The Nesting Season

From May to October it's turtle-nesting season all along the Florida coast. Female loggerhead, Kemp's ridley, and other species living in the Atlantic Ocean or Gulf of Mexico swim up to 2,000 mi to the Florida shore. By night they drag their 100- to 400-pound bodies onto the beach to the dune line. Then each digs a hole with her flippers, drops in 100 or so eggs, covers them up, and returns to sea.

The babies hatch about 60 days later. Once they burst out of the sand, the hatchlings must get to sea rapidly or risk becoming dehydrated from the sun or being caught by crabs, birds, or other predators.

Instinctively, baby turtles head toward bright light, probably because for millions of years starlight or moonlight reflected on the waves was the brightest light around, serving to guide hatchlings to water. But now light from beach development can lead the babies in the wrong direction, running to the street rather than the water. To help, many coastal towns enforce light restrictions during nesting months. Florida homeowners are requested theirlights be dimmed on behalf of baby sea turtles.

At night, volunteers walk the beaches, searching for signs of turtle nests. Upon finding telltale scratches in the sand, they cordon off the sites, so beachgoers will leave the spots undisturbed. Volunteers also keep watch over nests when babies are about to hatch and assist if the hatchlings get disoriented.

Males never, ever return to land, but when females attain maturity, in 15–20 years, they return to shore to lay eggs. Remarkably, even after migrating hundreds and even thousands of miles out at sea, most return to the very beach where they were born to deposit their eggs. Each time they nest, they come back to the same stretch of beach. In fact, the more they nest, the more accurate they get, until eventually they return time and again to within a few feet of where they last laid their eggs. These incredible navigation skills remain for the most part a mystery despite intense scientific study. To learn more, check out the Sea Turtle Survival League's and Caribbean Conservation Corporation's Web site at ⊕ *www.cccturtle.org.*

–Pam Acheson

WHERE TO EAT

★ $$$ ✕ **Café Chardonnay.** At the end of a strip mall, Café Chardonnay is surprisingly elegant inside. Soft indirect lighting, warm woods, and cozy banquettes set the scene for a quiet lunch or romantic dinner. Established by the Eucalitto husband-and-wife team, the restaurant consistently receives praise for its innovative menu and outstanding wine list. Starters include wild-mushroom strudel and truffle-stuffed diver sea scallops; entrées might include Gorgonzola-crusted filet mignon or pan-seared veal scaloppine with rock shrimp. ⊠ *4533 PGA Blvd.* ☏ *561/627–2662* ⊟ *AE, MC, V* ⊘ *No lunch weekends.*

$-$$$ ✕ **Spoto's.** If you like oysters, this is the place to go. Black-and-white photographs of oyster fisherman adorn the walls and the polished, dark-wood tables give the eatery a country club look. A local chain with a restaurant in downtown West Palm Beach, too, and another high-end eatery in the same PGA Commons (Spoto's Oakwood Grille), Spoto's serves up a delightful bowl of New England clam chowder and an impressive variety of oysters and clams. The prime rib Caesar salad with crispy croutons never disappoints. Sit outside on the patio to take advantage of Florida's perfect weather. There's a popular jazz brunch on Sundays. Open for lunch and dinner. ⊠ *4560 PGA Blvd.* ☏ *561/776-9448* ▭ *AE, MC, V,DC.*

WHERE TO STAY

★ $$$$ ⊡ **PGA National Resort & Spa.** New owners have launched a $25 million renovation of this 25-year-old resort, which has hosted more golf championship tournaments than any other golf destination in the country. A new 5,000-sq.-ft. outdoor pavilion will create meeting space, and members can look forward to a new interior in the huge, two-story clubhouse. Guest rooms have Asian maple wood furnishings, flat-screen TVs, marble bathrooms and private balconies. The entire resort is richly detailed, from the consistently updated rooms to the lavish landscaping to the extensive sports facilities to the excellent dining. The spa is in a building styled after a Mediterranean fishing village, and six outdoor therapy pools, dubbed Waters of the World, are joined by a collection of imported mineral salt pools. Flowering plants adorn golf courses and croquet courts amid a 240-acre nature preserve. Lodgings include two-bedroom, two-bath cottages with kitchens. Golf is key here and guests have access to a rotating selection of four of the resort's five private courses. **Pros:** A short drive to beaches in Juno and Jupiter and shopping at The Gardens mall and Downtown at The Gardens; excellent golf courses. **Cons:** Resort is undergoing renovations, so guests have to deal with construction. ⊠ *400 Ave. of the Champions, 33418* ☏ *561/627–2000 or 800/633–9150* ⊕ *www.pga-resorts.com* ⌁ *339 rooms and suites, 50 cottages* �ċ *In-room: safe, kitchen (some), refrigerator (some), Ethernet. In-hotel: 7 restaurants, room service, bars, golf course, tennis courts, pools, gym* ▭ *AE, D, DC, MC, V.*

SPORTS & THE OUTDOORS

AUTO RACING

If you yearn for drag racing action, the **Moroso Motorsports Park** (⊠ *17047 Beeline Hwy.* ☏ *561/622–1400*) awaits with weekly ¼-mi drag racing; monthly 2¼-mi, 10-turn road racing; and monthly AMA motorcycle road racing. These events and swap meets take place all year long. Spectator admission is $13 on Saturday, $15 on Sunday, and there's a $20 two-day pass.

GOLF

PGA National Resort & Spa (⊠ *1000 Avenue of the Champions* ☏ *561/627–1800*) has a reputedly tough 90 holes, which are available to hotel guests and members. Among them are the Champion Course, designed by Tom Fazio and Jack Nicklaus, greens fee $215/$345; the General Course, designed by Arnold Palmer, greens fee $215/$345; the Haig Course, the first course opened at the resort, greens fee $200/$300; the Estate Course, with a practice range and putting green, greens fee

$215/$345; and the Tom Fazio–designed Squire Course, greens fee $215/$345. Lessons are available at the Golf Digest Academy.

SHOPPING

Downtown at the Gardens (✉ *11701 Lake Victoria Gardens Ave.* ☎ *561/340–1600*) offers open-air shopping with a movie theater, Whole Foods Market, restaurants, and shops like Urban Outfitters, Smith & Hawken, and Sur La Table.

EN ROUTE

John D. MacArthur Beach State Park. Almost 2 mi of beach, good fishing and shelling, and one of the finest examples of subtropical coastal habitat remaining in southeast Florida are among the treasures here. To learn about what you see, take an interpretive walk to a mangrove estuary along the upper reaches of Lake Worth. Or visit the **William T. Kirby Nature Center** (☎ *561/624–6952*), open daily from 9 to 5, which has exhibits on the coastal environment. ✉ *10900 Rte. A1A, North Palm Beach* ☎ *561/624–6950* ⊕ *www.macarthurbeach.org* 🎟 *$4 per vehicle, up to 4 people* ⊗ *Daily 8–sundown.*

5

JUPITER

12 mi north of Palm Beach Shores.

Jupiter is one of the few little towns in the region not fronted by an island. Beaches here are part of the mainland, and Route A1A runs for almost 4 mi along the beachfront dunes and beautiful estates.

A beach is just one of the draws of **Carlin Park,** which has picnic pavilions, hiking trails, a baseball diamond, a playground, six tennis courts, and fishing sites. The Park Galley, serving snacks and burgers, is open daily 9–5. ✉ *400 Rte. A1A* ☎ *No phone* ⊗ *Daily dawn–dusk.*

Take a look at how life once was at the **Dubois Home,** a modest pioneer outpost dating from 1898. Sitting atop an ancient Jeaga Indian mound 20 feet high and looking onto Jupiter Inlet, it has Cape Cod as well as Cracker (Old Florida) design. Even if you arrive when the house is closed, surrounding **Dubois Park** is worth the visit for its lovely beaches and swimming lagoons. ✉ *Dubois Rd.* ☎ *561/747–6639* ⊕ *www.lrhs. org* 🎟 *$2; park is free* ⊗ *Tues. and Wed. 1–4; park daily dawn–dusk.*

Permanent exhibits at the **Loxahatchee River Historical Museum** review not only modern-day development along the Loxahatchee River but also shipwrecks, railroads, and steamboat-era, Seminole, and pioneer history. ✉ *805 N. U.S. 1, Burt Reynolds Park* ☎ *561/747–6639* ⊕ *www. lrhs.org* 🎟 *$7* ⊗ *Tues.–Fri. 10–5, weekends noon–5.*

Designed by Civil War hero General George Meade, the redbrick Coast ★ Guard **Jupiter Inlet Lighthouse** has operated here since 1860. Tours of the 105-foot-tall landmark unfold every half hour, and there's a small museum. The lighthouse has undergone significant change, courtesy of an $858,000 federal grant, transforming it from bright red to natural brick, the way it looked from 1860 to 1918. Children must be at least 4 feet tall to go to the top of the lighthouse. ✉ *500 Capt. Armour's Way*

(U.S. 1 and Beach Rd.) ☎*561/747–8380* ⊕*www.jupiterlighthouse.org* 🎫*Tour $7* ⊙*Tues.–Sun. 10–5; last tour at 3:15.*

Maltz Jupiter Theatre. This renovated 550-seat theater is open all year with comedy and dramatic performances, but the major shows, such as *Anna in the Tropics,* run from September to April. Shows have both evening and matinee performances, and tickets range from $35 to $50. ✉*1001 E. Indiantown Rd.* ☎*561/743–0714* ⊕*www.jupitertheatre.org.*

WHERE TO EAT

$-$$$ ✗ **Sinclairs Ocean Grill.** This popular spot in the Jupiter Beach Resort has French doors looking out to the pool, and a menu with a daily selection of fresh fish, such as cashew-encrusted grouper, Cajun-spice tuna, and mahimahi with pistachio sauce. There are also thick, juicy steaks—filet mignon is the house specialty—or chicken and veal dishes. Sunday buffet is a big draw. ✉*5 N. Rte. A1A* ☎*561/745–7120* ⊟*AE, MC, V.*

$-$$ ✗ **Food Shack.** This barlike shack filled with locals is a bit tricky to find, but worth the search. Fried-food standards typical of such a casual place are not found at the Food Shack; instead there are fried tuna rolls with basil and fried grouper cheeks with a fruity side slaw. A variety of beers are fun to pair with the creatively prepared seafood dishes that include wahoo, mahimahi, dolphin, and snapper. ✉*103 South U.S. 1* ☎*561/741–3626* ⊟*DC, MC, V* ⊙*Closed Sun.*

¢-$ ✗ **Lighthouse Restaurant.** Low prices match the plain look in this coffee shop–style building. The same people-pleasing formula has been employed since 1936: round-the-clock service (except 9 PM Sunday–6 AM Monday) and a menu that changes daily to take advantage of in-season market buys. Order chicken breast stuffed with sausage and vegetables, burgundy beef stew, crab cakes, and great pastries. ✉*1510 U.S. 1* ☎*561/746–4811* ⊟*D, DC, MC, V.*

WHERE TO STAY

$$$$ 🏨 **Jupiter Beach Resort.** Although unpretentious, this time-share resort had a multimillion-dollar makeover before 2004's hurricane season and then another refurbishing after, and it shows. Caribbean-style rooms with mahogany sleigh beds and armoires are within a nine-story tower. Most rooms have balconies, and those on higher floors have great ocean views. Plentiful activities and a casual approach draw families here, and the resort offers turtle watches in season, May through October. Snorkeling equipment and bicycles are available for rent. ✉*5 N. Rte. A1A* ☎*561/746–2511 or 800/228–8810* 🖶*561/747–3304* ⊕*www.jupiter beachresort.com* 🛏*88 rooms, 65 suites* ♿*In-room: dial-up. In-hotel: 3 restaurants, bars, tennis court, pool, gym, beachfront, diving, laundry facilities* ⊟*AE, D, MC, V.*

SPORTS & THE OUTDOORS

BASEBALL

Both the **St. Louis Cardinals and Florida Marlins** (✉*4751 Main St.* ☎*561/775–1818*) train at the $28 million Roger Dean Stadium, which seats 7,000 and has 12 practice fields.

CANOEING

Canoe Outfitters of Florida (⊠*9060 W. Indiantown Rd.* ☎*561/746–7053*) runs two- to three-hour trips (Thurs.–Mon.) and six-hour trips (weekends) along 8 mi of the Loxahatchee River, Florida's only government-designated Wild and Scenic River, where you can see animals in the wild, from otters to eagles. Canoe or kayak rental for two to three hours is $25, six hours $40, with drop-off and pickup.

GOLF

Abacoa Golf Club (⊠*105 Barbados Dr.* ☎*561/622–0036*), with 18 holes, is a recommended alternative to nearby private courses; greens fee: $65/$130, including cart. The **Golf Club of Jupiter** (⊠*1800 Central Blvd.* ☎*561/747–6262*) has 18 holes of varying difficulty; greens fee $49/$69, including cart. **Jupiter Dunes Golf Club** (⊠*401 Rte. A1A* ☎*561/746–6654*) has an 18-hole golf course named Little Monster and a putting green near the Jupiter River estuary; greens fee $36/$65.

5

JUPITER ISLAND & HOBE SOUND

5 mi north of Jupiter.

Northeast across the Jupiter Inlet from Jupiter is the southern tip of Jupiter Island, including a planned community of the same name. Here expansive and expensive estates often retreat from the road behind screens of vegetation, and at the north end of the island turtles come to nest in a wildlife refuge. To the west, on the mainland, is the little community of Hobe Sound.

WHAT TO SEE

In **Blowing Rocks Preserve,** within the 73-acre Nature Conservancy holding, are plant communities native to beachfront dune, coastal strand (the landward side of the dunes), mangrove, and hammock (tropical hardwood forests). The best time to visit is when high tides and strong offshore winds coincide, causing the sea to blow spectacularly through holes in the eroded outcropping. Park in the lot; police ticket cars parked along the road. ⊠*574 South Beach Rd. (Rte. 707), Jupiter Island* ☎*561/744–6668* 🕮*$2* ☉*Daily 9–4:30.*

Two tracts make up **Hobe Sound National Wildlife Refuge:** 232 acres of sand-pine and scrub-oak forest in Hobe Sound and 735 acres of coastal sand dune and mangrove swamp on Jupiter Island. Trails are open to the public in both places. Turtles nest and shells wash ashore on the 3½-mi-long beach, which has been severely eroded by 2004 and 2005 hurricanes' high tides and strong winds. ⊠*13640 S.E. Federal Hwy., Hobe Sound* ☎*772/546–6141* 🕮*$5 per vehicle* ☉*Daily dawn–dusk.*

Ⓒ Although on the Hobe Sound National Wildlife Refuge, **Hobe Sound Nature Center** is an independent organization. Its museum, which has baby alligators and crocodiles, and a scary-looking tarantula, is a child's delight. Interpretive exhibits focus on the environment, and a ½-mi trail winds through a forest of sand pine and scrub oak—one of Florida's most unusual and endangered plant communities. As of this writing, a new visitor center was nearing completion after the former structure was destroyed by Hurricanes Frances and Jeanne in 2004. ✉*13640 S.E. Federal Hwy., Hobe Sound* ☎*772/546–2067* 💲*Donation suggested* 🕐*Trail daily dawn–dusk; nature center weekdays 9–3, call to verify hrs.*

Once you've gotten to **Jonathan Dickinson State Park,** follow signs to **Hobe Mountain.** An ancient dune topped with a tower, it yields a panoramic view across the park's 10,285 acres of varied terrain, as well as the Intracoastal Waterway. The Loxahatchee River, part of the federal government's Wild and Scenic Rivers program, cuts through the park and harbors manatees in winter and alligators year-round. Two-hour boat tours of the river leave daily at 9, 11, 1, and 3. Among amenities are a dozen cabins for rent, tent sites, bicycle and hiking trails, a campground, and a snack bar. ✉*16450 S.E. Federal Hwy., Hobe Sound* ☎*772/546–2771* 💲*$4 per vehicle for up to 4 people, boat tours $14.50* 🕐*Daily 8–dusk.*

SPORTS & THE OUTDOORS
Jonathan Dickinson's River Tours (✉*Jonathan Dickinson State Park* ☎*561/746–1466*) offers boat tours of the river and canoe, kayak, and motor-vessel rentals for use around the park from 9 to 5 daily. The fee is $10 for the first two hours and $4 for each additional hour.

STUART

7 mi north of Hobe Sound.

This compact little town on a peninsula that juts out into the St. Lucie River has a remarkable amount of river shoreline for its size as well as a charming historic district. The ocean is about 5 mi east.

WHAT TO SEE
★ Strict architectural and zoning standards guide civic-renewal projects in **historic downtown Stuart,** which has antiques shops, restaurants, and more than 50 specialty shops within a two-block area. A self-guided walking-tour pamphlet is available at assorted locations downtown to clue you in on this once small fishing village's early days.

On the National Register of Historic Places, the **Lyric Theatre** (✉*59 S.W. Flagler Ave.* ☎*772/286–7827*) has been revived for performing and community events; a gazebo has free music performances.

The old courthouse has become the **Court House Cultural Center** (✉*80 E. Ocean Blvd.* ☎*772/288–2542*) and presents folk art and other art exhibits.

The George W. Parks General Store is now the **Stuart Heritage Museum** (✉*161 S.W. Flagler Ave.* ☎*772/220–4600*).

For information on the historic downtown, contact the **Stuart Main Street** (✉*201 S.W. Flagler Ave.,* ☎*772/286–2848*).

★ Linking the watery past with a permanent record of maritime and yachting events contributing to Treasure Coast lore, the **Maritime & Yachting Museum** is near a marina with many old ships as well as historic exhibits to explore. Ship modelers are usually on hand, too; call for an events and activities schedule. Among those leading Saturday tours is a retired ship captain who has many interesting stories to share. ⊠*3250 S. Kanner Hwy.* ☎*772/692–1234* ☒*Free* ⊗*Mon.–Sat. 11–4, Sun. 15.*

WHERE TO EAT

$$-$$$ ✕ **Bare Bones Grill & Brewery.** Located on the Manatee Pocket in Port Salerno, the popular restaurant chain (there's one in Ellicott City, Maryland, too) is surrounded by boatyards and a lively art-gallery scene. Sit outside on the covered dock and take in the breeze while your eating the tastiest crab cakes south of Chesapeake Bay. Besides crab cakes seasoned just right with Old Bay, Bare Bones serves up savory barbecued ribs, crispy salads, Cajun gumbo, steak, fish, chicken, home-brewed beers and sides, including smokey butter beans that are nearly impossible to resist. Open for lunch and dinner. ⊠*4817 S.E. Dixie Hwy,* ☎*772/286–3535* ☐*AE, MC, V.*

$$-$$$ ✕ **Courtine's.** A husband-and-wife team oversees this quiet and hospitable restaurant under the new Roosevelt Bridge. The Swiss chef's food represents French continental and American influences, from his seafood and poultry dishes to the grilled house special of filet mignon stuffed with Roquefort, fresh spinach, and a port wine–balsamic reduction. The formal dining room has subtle touches of elegance, such as soft lighting and fresh flowers on each table. A full bar and extensive wine list are available. A more casual and light menu is also available at the bar. ⊠*514 N. Dixie Hwy. (SR707)* ☎*772/692–3662* ☐*AE, MC, V* ⊗*Closed Sun. and Mon. No lunch.*

¢-$$ ✕ **The Ashley.** Despite the hanging plants and artwork, this restaurant still has elements of the old bank that was robbed three times early in the 20th century by the Ashley Gang (hence the name). Situated at the end of the main historic street in downtown Stuart, The Ashley is easy to spot because of its redbrick facade. Spacious tables, comfortable seats, and good service make this restaurant a consistently pleasant place to eat. The continental menu has lots of salads, fresh fish, and pastas, and all are served in large portions. Crowds head to the lounge for a popular happy hour. Live bands play regularly. Brunch is the only meal served on Sunday. ⊠*61 S.W. Osceola St.* ☎*772/221–1769* ☐*AE, MC, V.*

WHERE TO STAY

$$$ ▦ **Pirates Cove Resort and Marina.** On the banks of the St. Lucie River and the Intracoastal Waterway in the heart of Sailfish Alley, this cozy enclave is the perfect place to recoup after a day at sea. This midsize resort is relaxing and casual but packed with recreational activities for the day. The tropically furnished rooms are large, with balconies to enjoy the waterfront views. The few suites include microwaves and refrigerators. A continental breakfast is included. **Pros:** Pretty location, great for fishermen with boats. **Cons:** The Pirates Loft Lounge gets lively at night, but the restaurant can be rather dull during the day. ⊠*4307 S.E. Bayview St., Port Salerno* ☎*772/287–2500 or 800/332–1414* 🖷*772/220–2704* ⊕*www.piratescoveresort.net* ↩*48 rooms, 2 mini suites* ⟡*In-room: refrigerator, Wi-Fi. In-hotel: restaurant, room service, bar* ☐*AE, D, DC, MC, V.*

SPORTS & THE OUTDOORS

Deep-sea charters are available at the **Sailfish Marina** (⊠ *3565 S.E. St. Lucie Blvd.* ☎ *772/221–9456*).

SHOPPING

More than 60 restaurants and shops with antiques, art, and fashions have opened along **Osceola Street** in the restored downtown area. Operating for more than two decades, the **B&A Flea Market,** the oldest and largest such enterprise on the Treasure Coast, has a street-bazaar feel, with shoppers happily scouting for the practical and unusual. ⊠ *2885 S.E. Federal Hwy.* ☎ *772/288–4915* 🖃 *Free* ⊙ *Weekends 8–3.*

HUTCHINSON ISLAND (JENSEN BEACH)

5 mi northeast of Stuart.

Area residents have taken pains to curb the runaway development that has created the commercial crowding found to the north and south, although some high-rises have popped up along the shore. The small town of Jensen Beach, occupying the core of the island, stretches across both sides of the Indian River. Citrus farmers and anglers still play a big community role, anchoring the area's down-to-earth feel. Between late April and August more than 600 turtles come here to nest along the town's Atlantic beach.

WHAT TO SEE

★ The **Florida Oceanographic Coastal Center** consists of a coastal hardwood hammock-and-mangrove forest. Expansion has added a visitor center, a science center with interpretive exhibits on coastal science and environmental issues, and a ½-mi interpretive boardwalk. Guided nature walks through trails and stingray feedings are offered at various times during the day. Eco–boat tours are 1½ hours long and include a 20-minute stop at a bird sanctuary. Dolphins, manatees, and turtles are often seen on the boat tour, for which reservations are required. ⊠ *890 N.E. Ocean Blvd.* ☎ *772/225–0505* ⊕ *www.floridaoceanographic.org* 🖃 *$8; $22 boat tour* ⊙ *Mon.–Sat. 10–5, Sun. noon–4; guided nature walks Mon.–Sat. 11 and 3, Sun. at 2; boat tours Tues. and Thurs.–Sat. at 11 and Thurs. at 4.*

The pastel-pink **Elliott Museum** was erected in 1961 in honor of Sterling Elliott, inventor of an early automated addressing machine and a four-wheel cycle. The museum, with its antique cars, dolls, toys, and vintage baseball cards, is a nice stop for anyone fond of nostalgic goods. There are also antique fixtures from an early general store, blacksmith shop, and apothecary shop. ⊠ *825 N.E. Ocean Blvd.* ☎ *772/225–1961* 🖃 *$7* ⊙ *Mon.–Sat. 10–4, Sun. 1–4.*

Built in 1875, **Gilbert's House of Refuge Museum** on Hutchinson Island is the only remaining building of nine such structures built by the U.S. Life Saving Service (a predecessor of the Coast Guard) to aid stranded sailors. Exhibits include antique lifesaving equipment, maps, artifacts from nearby wrecks, and boatbuilding tools. ⊠ *301 S.E. MacArthur Blvd.* ☎ *772/225–1875* 🖃 *$5* ⊙ *Mon.–Sat. 10–4, Sun. 1–4.*

WHERE TO EAT

★ $$$ ✕ **11 Maple Street.** With a mere 16 tables, this spot is as good as it gets on the Treasure Coast, with a menu that changes nightly. Soft recorded jazz and friendly staff satisfy, as does food served in ample portions. Although the cuisine is progressive, the place is filled with antiques and many vintage collectibles. Appetizers run from panfried conch and crispy calamari to spinach salad, and entrées include panseared rainbow trout, wood-grilled venison with onion-potato hash, and beef tenderloin with white-truffle-and-chive butter. Desserts such as a white-chocolate custard with blackberry sauce are seductive, too. ✉*3224 Maple Ave.* ☎*772/334–7714* ⚓*Reservations essential* ▤*MC, V* ⊘*Closed Mon. and Tues. No lunch.*

$$–$$$ ✕ **Baha Grill.** Replacing the former Scalawags restaurant, but in a slightly different locale (the main dining room is now on the first floor), this spot serves breakfast, lunch, and dinner daily, though from a more limited menu than before. The food is basically the same—assorted soups, salads, and entrées consistent with most Marriott hotels. Standouts include a prime-rib buffet on Friday night and the all-you-can-eat Wednesday-evening seafood extravaganza with jumbo shrimp, Alaskan crab legs, clams on the half shell, marinated salmon, and fresh catch. The decor is also standard for a Marriott dining room—a tasteful assemblage of wood accents, floral patterns, and subtle hues. ✉*Marriott Beach Resort, 555 N.E. Ocean Blvd.* ☎*772/225–6818* ▤*AE, D, DC, MC, V.*

¢–$$ ✕ **Conchy Joe's.** This rustic Florida stilt house full of antique fish mounts, gator hides, and snake skins dates from the 1920s, although Conchy Joe's, like a hermit crab sliding into a new shell, moved up from West Palm Beach in 1983. It's a popular tourist spot, but its waterfront location, supercasual attitude, and seafood continue to attract locals, too. Staples are grouper marsala, broiled sea scallops, and fried cracked conch. There's live music Friday, heady rum drinks on Saturday, and a happy hour daily 3 to 6 and during NFL games. ✉*3945 N.E. Indian River Dr.* ☎*772/334–1130* ▤*AE, D, MC, V.*

WHERE TO STAY

$$$$ ▦ **Hutchinson Island Marriott Beach Resort & Marina.** With golf, tennis, a 77-slip marina, and a full water-sports program, plus many restaurants and bars, this 200-acre self-contained resort is excellent for families. Reception, some restaurants, and many rooms are in a trio of yellow four-story buildings that form an open courtyard with a large pool. Additional rooms and apartments with kitchens are spread over the property, some overlooking the Intracoastal Waterway and marina, others looking onto the ocean or tropical gardens. ✉*555 N.E. Ocean Blvd., Hutchinson Island* ☎*772/225–3700 or 800/775–5936* 🖷*772/225–0003* ⊕*www.marriotthotels.com* ➥*213 rooms, 70 suites, 70 condominiums* ⚑*In-room: kitchen (some). In-hotel: 3 restaurants, room service, bars, tennis courts, pools, gym, spa, beachfront, children's programs (2–12), laundry facilities, some pets allowed* ▤*AE, D, DC, MC, V.*

SPORTS & THE OUTDOORS

BEACHES

Bathtub Reef Park (⊠ *MacArthur Blvd. off Rte. A1A*), at the north end of the Indian River Plantation, is ideal for children because the waters are shallow for about 300 feet offshore and usually calm. At low tide bathers can walk to the reef. Facilities include restrooms and showers.

GOLF

Hutchinson Island Marriott Golf Club (⊠ *555 N.E. Ocean Blvd.* ☎ *772/225–6819*) has 18 holes for private-club members and hotel guests; greens fee: $60 for 18 holes. The PGA-operated **PGA Golf Club at the PGA Villages** (⊠ *1916 Perfect Dr., Port St. Lucie* ☎ *772/467–1300 or 800/800–4653*) is a public facility with the PGA Learning Center and three courses designed by Pete Dye and Tom Fazio; greens fee for North Course, South Course, and Dye Course: $55/$89, including cart.

FORT PIERCE

11 mi north of Stuart.

About an hour north of Palm Beach, this community has a distinctive rural feel, focusing on ranching and citrus farming. There are several worthwhile stops, including those easily seen while following Route 707.

WHAT TO SEE

☾ Once a reservoir, the 550-acre **Savannas Recreation Area** has been returned to its natural state. Today the semi-wilderness area has campsites, boat ramps, and trails. ⊠ *1400 E. Midway Rd.* ☎ *772/464–7855* ▨ *$1 per vehicle. RV hookups $20.* ☉ *Daily 8–6.*

A self-guided tour of the 3½-acre **Heathcote Botanical Gardens** takes in a palm walk, a Japanese garden, and subtropical foliage. There are also a pioneer house, orchid house, and gift shop with whimsical and botanical knickknacks. Guided tours are available Tuesday through Saturday by appointment. ⊠ *210 Savannah Rd.* ☎ *772/464–4672* ⊕ *www.heathcotebotanicalgardens.org* ▨ *$6* ☉ *Tues.–Sat. 9–5; Nov.–Apr., also Sun. 1–5.*

As the home of the Treasure Coast Art Association, the **A.E. "Bean" Backus Gallery** displays works of one of Florida's foremost landscape artists. The gallery mounts changing exhibits and offers exceptional buys on work by local artists. ⊠ *500 N. Indian River Dr.* ☎ *772/465–0630* ⊕ *www.backusgallery.com* ▨ *Free* ☉ *Tues.–Sat. 10–4, Sun. noon–4; summer hrs by appointment.*

Accessible only by footbridge, the **Ft. Pierce State Park** has 4 mi of trails around Jack Island. The 1½-mi Marsh Rabbit Trail across the island traverses a mangrove swamp to a 30-foot-tall observation tower overlooking the Indian River. ⊠ *Rte. A1A* ☎ *772/468–3985* ▨ *$3* ☉ *Daily 8–5:30.*

★ Commemorating more than 3,000 navy frogmen who trained along Treasure Coast shoreline during World War II, the **Navy SEAL Museum** has weapons and equipment on view and exhibits depicting the history of the UDTs (Underwater Demolition Teams). Patrol boats and vehicles are displayed outdoors. ⊠*3300 N. Rte. A1A* ☎*772/595–5845* ⊠*$6* ⊙*Mon.–Sat. 10–4, Sun. noon–4.*

The **St. Lucie Marine Station** is a facility of the Smithsonian Museum in Washington, D.C., and is where Smithsonian scientists come to study ecosystems. Inside are large fish tanks filled with ocean, river, and lagoon ecosystems and one special tank with "Nemo" the fish. The Station's parklike setting, where visitors picnic and children play, makes it an ideal stop when you visit the St. Lucie County Historical Museum, which is within walking distance. ⊠*1420 Seaway Dr.* ☎*772/462–3474* ⊠*$2, free Tues.* ⊙*Tues.–Sat. 10–4, Sun. noon–4.*

The 340 acres of the **Fort Pierce Inlet State Recreation Area** contain sand dunes and a coastal hammock. The park has swimming, surfing, picnic facilities, hiking, and a self-guided nature trail. ⊠*905 Shorewinds Dr.* ☎*772/468–3985* ⊠*$3 for 1 person, $5 for 2–8 people per vehicle* ⊙*Daily 8–dusk.*

WHERE TO EAT & STAY

$$–$$$ ✕ **Mangrove Mattie's.** Since opening in the 1980s, this upscale but rustic spot on Fort Pierce Inlet has provided dazzling waterfront views and delicious seafood. Dine on the terrace or in the dining room, and try the coconut-fried shrimp or the chicken and scampi. Or come by during happy hour (weekdays 5–8) for a free buffet of snacks. Sunday brunch. ⊠*1640 Seaway Dr.* ☎*772/466–1044* ⊟*AE, D, DC, MC, V.*

¢–$$$ ▥ **Dockside Harborlight Resort Inn.** Formerly two adjacent motels, this expanded resort is the pick of the pack of lodgings lining the Fort Pierce Inlet along Seaway Drive. Spacious units on two floors have a kitchen or wet bar and fresh furnishings. Some rooms have a waterfront porch or balcony. A set of four apartments is across the street, off the water. Overnight boat docking is available for an additional $25 per night. **Pros:** A good value, can dock your boat. **Cons:** Rooms have the basics, but nothing fancy. ⊠*1160 Seaway Dr.* ☎*772/468–3555 or 800/286–1745* ☎*772/489–9848* ⊕*www.docksideinn.com* ⇆*60 rooms, 4 apartments* ♿*In-room: refrigerator (some). In-hotel: pools, laundry facilities, no elevator* ⊟*AE, D, DC, MC, V.*

SPORTS & THE OUTDOORS

FISHING

For charter boats and fishing guides, contact the dockmaster at the **Dockside Harborlight Resort** (⊠*1152 Seaway Dr.* ☎*772/461–4824*).

JAI ALAI

Fort Pierce Jai Alai (⊠*1750 S. Kings Hwy., off Okeechobee Rd.* ☎*772/464–7500 or 800/524–2524*) operates April through May for live jai alai and year-round for off-track betting on horse-racing simulcasts. Admission is free, with games Wednesday and Saturday at noon and 7, Friday at 7, and Sunday at 1.

5

SCUBA DIVING

Some 200 yards from shore and ¼ mi north of the Navy SEAL Museum on North Hutchinson Island, the **Urca de Lima Underwater Archaeological Preserve** contains remains of a flat-bottom, round-bellied store ship. Once part of a treasure fleet bound for Spain, it was destroyed by a hurricane.

EN ROUTE To reach Vero Beach, you have two options—Route A1A, along the coast, or Route 605 (also called Old Dixie Highway), on the mainland. As you approach Vero on the latter, you'll pass through an ungussied landscape of small farms and residential areas. On the beach route, part of the drive is through an unusually undeveloped section of the Florida coast. Both trips are relaxing.

VERO BEACH

12 mi north of Fort Pierce.

Tranquil and charming, this Indian River County town has a strong commitment to the environment and the arts. There are plenty of outdoor activities here, even though many visitors gravitating to the training camp of the Los Angeles Dodgers opt to do little at all. In the town's exclusive Riomar Bay area, roads are shaded by massive live oaks, and a popular cluster of restaurants and shops is just off the beach.

Fodor'sChoice ★ On the National Register of Historic Places, the 18-acre **McKee Botanical Garden** is both a subtropical garden and a horticulture teaching museum. There's a 1,600-square-foot bamboo pavilion, gift shop, library, and the Hibiscus café, which serves tasty snacks and sandwiches and locally grown tea. This is the place to see spectacular water lilies. ⊠*350 U.S.Hwy. 1* ☎*772/794–0601* ⊕*www.mckeegarden.org* ⊠*$6* ⊙*Tues.–Sat. 10–5, Sun. noon–5.*

In addition to aquariums filled with Indian River Lagoon life, the **Environmental Learning Center,** on 51 acres, has a 600-foot boardwalk through the mangrove shoreline and a 1-mi canoe trail. The center is on the north edge of Vero Beach, on Wabasso Island, and the pretty drive is worth the trip. Some vegetation was lost after the hurricanes of 2004, and parts of the area are still wind-beaten. ⊠*255 Live Oak Dr.* ☎*772/589–5050* ⊕*www.elcweb.org* ⊠*Donation suggested* ⊙*Tues.– Fri. 10–4, Sat. 9–4, Sun. noon–3.*

WHERE TO EAT & STAY

$$-$$$ ✕ **Ocean Grill.** Opened by Waldo Sexton as a hamburger shack in 1938, the Ocean Grill combines its ocean view with Tiffany-style lamps, wrought-iron chandeliers, and paintings of pirates and Seminoles. Count on at least three kinds of seafood any day on the menu, along with pork chops, tasty soups, and salads. The house drink, the Leaping Limey—a curious blend of vodka, blue curaçao, and lemon—commemorates the 1894 wreck of the *Breconshire,* which occurred just offshore and from which 34 British sailors escaped. ⊠*Sexton Plaza, 1050 Ocean Dr.* ☎*772/231–5409* ⊟*AE, D, DC, MC, V* ⊙*Closed 2 wks after Labor Day. No lunch weekends.*

$$$-$$$$ 🏨 **Aquarius Oceanfront Resort.** Right on beautiful, uncrowded South Beach, the small unpretentious resort is owned by a local family and has loyal guests who book a year in advance. Ask for Rooms 125 and 126, which have balconies overlooking the beach. Other rooms, most with kitchens, face the parking lot. Walk across the street to the excellent Italian restaurant Monte's and to South Beach Pizza. **Pros:** Guests get all the basics, without froufrou; most rooms have kitchens; best of all, the location right on the beach! **Cons:** No elevators, so dragging your luggage up the stairs can be a pain. ✉ *1526 Ocean Dr.* ☎ *772/772-231-5218 or 877/7671526* 🖷 *772/234–4158* 🛏 *27 efficiencies with kitchens and 2 rooms without kitchens* ♿ *In-room: kitchen. In-hotel: pool, beachfront, no elevator, laundry facilities, no-smoking rooms.* 🞸 *AE, DC, MC, V.*

$$$-$$$$ 🏨 **Disney's Vero Beach Resort.** On 71 pristine oceanfront acres, this sprawling family-oriented retreat, operating both as a time-share and a hotel, is Vero's top resort. The main four-story building, three free-standing villas, and six beach cottages, all painted in pastels with gabled roofing in an approximation of turn-of-the-19th-century Old Florida style, are nestled among tropical greenery. Units, some with kitchens and many with balconies, have bright interiors with rattan furniture and tile floors. Shutters, one of two restaurants, has American food. Disney-wary adults need not worry; you have to go out of your way to track down a Disney character. **Pros:** Fun for families, lots to do for kids. **Cons:** Not the best place for couples traveling without children. ✉ *9250 Island Grove Terr.* ☎ *772/234–2000 or 800/359–8000* 🖷 *772/234–2030* ⊕ *www.dvc.disney.go.com* 🛏 *161 rooms, 14 suites, 6 cottages* ♿ *In-room: safe, kitchen (some), refrigerator (some), VCR. In-hotel: 3 restaurants, room service, bar, tennis courts, pool, gym, beachfront, bicycles, children's programs (ages 4–12), laundry facilities, no-smoking rooms* 🞸 *AE, MC, V.*

$$$-$$$$ 🏨 **Driftwood Inn.** Listed on the National Register of Historic Places, this unique 1935 inn was built entirely from ocean-washed timbers and decorated with such artifacts as cathedral and ship bells, Spanish tile, and a cannon from a 16th-century Spanish galleon. The time-share hotel complex includes nine buildings on the beach with both modern and historic rooms. The inn attracts guests from around the world, who sit in wooden rockers facing the beach. **Pros:** Great seaside location, near restaurants and shops. **Cons:** Older inn, rooms can be musty. ✉ *3150 Ocean Dr.* ☎ *772/231–0550* 🖷 *772/234–1981* ⊕ *www.thedriftwood. com* 🛏 *86 rooms, 12 1- and 2-bedroom suites, 2 cottages* ♿ *In-room: kitchen (some), refrigerator. In-hotel: restaurant, bar, pools, beachfront* 🞸 *AE, DC, MC, V.*

5

THE ARTS

The **Civic Arts Center** (✉*Riverside Park*), a cluster of cultural facilities, includes the **Riverside Theatre** (✉*3250 Riverside Park Dr.* ☎*772/231–6990*), which stages six productions each season in its 633-seat performance hall; and the **Agnes Wahlstrom Youth Playhouse** (✉*3280 Riverside Park Dr.* ☎*772/234–8052*), mounting children's productions.

Riverside Children's Theatre (✉*3280 Riverside Park Dr.* ☎*772/234–8052*) offers a series of professional touring and local productions, as well as acting workshops, at the Agnes Wahlstrom Youth Playhouse. **Vero Museum of Art** (✉*3001 Riverside Park Dr.* ☎*772/231–0707* ◷*Mon.–Sat. 10–4, Sun. 1–4:30*) is part of the Riverside Park's 26-acre campus dedicated to the arts. The museum is where a full schedule of exhibitions, art movies, lectures, workshops, and classes are hosted. The museum's five galleries and sculpture garden make it the largest art facility in the Treasure Coast.

SPORTS & THE OUTDOORS

BEACHES

Humiston Park (✉*Ocean Dr. below Beachland Blvd.* ☎*772/231–5790* ▨*Free* ◷*Lifeguards 9* AM–5 PM) is one of the beach-access parks along the east edge of town that have boardwalks and steps bridging the dunes. There are picnic tables and a children's play area. There are many services at **Treasure Shores Park** (✉*A1A, 3 mi north of County Rd. 510 at the Wabasso Bridge* ☎*772/581–4997*). **Wabasso Beach Park** (✉*County Rd. 510, east of A1A intersection, north of Disney Resort* ☎*772/581–4998*) is a good option for a day in the sun.

GOLF

Sandridge Golf Club (✉*5300 73rd St.* ☎*772/770–5000*) has two public 18-hole courses designed by Ron Garl; greens fee: Dunes Course or Lakes Course $47, including cart.

SHOPPING

Along **Ocean Drive** near Beachland Boulevard, a shopping area includes art galleries, antiques shops, and upscale clothing stores. The eight-block area of Oceanside has an interesting mix of boutiques, specialty shops, and eateries. Just west of Interstate 95, **Outlets at Vero Beach** (✉*1824 94th Dr.* ☎*772/770–6171* ◷*Stores open Mon.–Sat. 9–8, Sun. 11–6*) is a discount shopping destination with 85 brand-name stores, including Ann Taylor, Ralph Lauren Polo, Mikasa, Bombay, and Jones New York.

SEBASTIAN

14 mi north of Vero Beach.

One of few sparsely populated areas on Florida's east coast, this fishing village has as remote a feeling as you're likely to find between Jacksonville and Miami Beach. That adds to the appeal of the recreation area around Sebastian Inlet, where you can walk for miles along quiet beaches and catch some of Florida's best waves for surfing.

You'll really come upon hidden loot when entering **Mel Fisher's Treasure Museum.** See some of what was recovered in 1985 from the Spanish treasure ship *Atocha* and its sister ships of the 1715 fleet. The museum certainly piques one's curiosity about what is still buried at sea: treasures continue to be discovered each year. A similar museum in Key West is also operated by the late Mel Fisher's family. ✉*1322 U.S. Hwy. 1* ☎*772/589–9875* ⊕*www.melfisher.com* 🖅*$6.50* ☉*Mon.–Sat. 10–5, Sun. noon–5.*

Founded in 1903 by President Theodore Roosevelt as the nation's first national wildlife refuge, **Pelican Island National Wildlife Refuge** is in the Indian River Lagoon between Sebastian and Wabasso. The island is accessible only by boat. Public facilities—a boardwalk and observation tower, built for the refuge's centennial—enable visitors to see birds, endangered species, and habitats.

Because of the highly productive fishing waters of Sebastian Inlet, at the north end of Orchid Island, the 578-acre **Sebastian Inlet State Recreation Area** is one of the Florida park system's biggest draws. Both sides of the high bridge spanning the inlet—views are spectacular—attract plenty of anglers as well as those eager to enjoy the fine sandy shores, known for having some of the best waves in the state. A concession stand on the inlet's north side sells short-order food, rents various craft, and has a small apparel and surf shop. There's a boat ramp, and not far away is a dune area that's part of the **Archie Carr National Wildlife Refuge,** a haven for sea turtles and other protected Florida wildlife. ✉*9700 S. Rte. A1A, Melbourne Beach* ☎*321/984–4852* ⊕*www.floridastateparks.org* 🖅*$3 for single occupancy, $5 for more than 1 in vehicle* ☉*Daily; bait and tackle shop 7:30–6, concession stand 8–5.*

A National Historical Landmark, the **McLarty Treasure Museum** underscores the credo "Wherever gold glitters or silver beckons, man will move mountains." It has displays of coins, weapons, and tools salvaged from a fleet of Spanish treasure ships that sank in the 1715 storm, leaving some 1,500 survivors struggling to shore between Sebastian and Fort Pierce. The museum's last video showing begins at 3:15. ✉*13180 N. Rte. A1A* ☎*772/589–2147* 🖅*$1* ☉*Daily 10–4:30.*

WHERE TO EAT & STAY

$–$$$ ✕ **Capt. Hiram's Restaurant.** This family-friendly outpost on the Indian River Lagoon is easygoing, fanciful, and fun. Don't miss Capt. Hiram's Sandbar, where kids can play while parents enjoy drinks at stools and booths set in the sand and on wooden decks overlooking the water. Order the fresh catch, crab cakes, stuffed shrimp, raw-bar items, or a juicy steak. There's a weekday happy hour and nightly entertainment in season. ✉*1606 N. Indian River Dr.* ☎*772/589–4345* ▭*AE, D, MC, V.*

$$$ 🏨 **Capt. Hiram's Resort.** A Key West–style inn with a lobby embellished with a classic surfboard collection brings the Florida Keys to Sebastian's Riverfront, about 17 mi north of Vero at Marker 66 on the Intracoastal. All rooms have a private balcony and most have oak furnishings. Minisuites include microwave, refrigerator, and wet bar; deluxe suites also include dishwasher and stove. A heated pool has a tropical sundeck, shaded by tables with umbrellas. A continental break-

fast is included. **Pros:** Great location for fishing, boating, and sunbathing; a good price for a resort with these amenities. **Cons:** Rooms to the far eastern side of the property can be noisy when bands are performing in the restaurant. ⊠*1580 U.S. 1* ☎*772/388–8588* 📠*772/589–4346* ⊕*www.hirams.com* 🛏*56 rooms* ♿*In-room: kitchen (some), Ethernet. In-hotel: 2 restaurants, bar, pool* ⊟*AE, D, MC, V* ⫿○⫿*CP.*

SPORTS & THE OUTDOORS

CANOEING & KAYAKING

The boating stand at **Sebastian Inlet State Recreation Area** (⊠*9700 S. Rte. A1A, Melbourne Beach* ☎*321/724–5424*) rents canoes, kayaks, and powerboats daily.

FISHING

The region's best inlet fishing is at **Sebastian Inlet State Recreation Area** (⊠*9700 S. Rte. A1A, Melbourne Beach*), where the catch includes bluefish, flounder, jack, redfish, sea trout, snapper, snook, and Spanish mackerel. For bottom fishing, try **Incentive Charter Fishing** (⊠*Dock at Capt. Hiram's Restaurant* ☎*321/676–1948*). For sportfishing, try **The Big Easy Fishing Charters** (⊠*Dock at Capt. Hiram's Restaurant* ☎*772/664–4068*). Another good sportfishing choice is **Skipper Sportfishing Charters** (⊠*Dock at Capt. Hiram's Restaurant* ☎*772/589–8505*).

PALM BEACH & THE TREASURE COAST ESSENTIALS

TRANSPORTATION

BY AIR

CARRIERS

Palm Beach International Airport (PBIA) is served by Air Canada, AirTran, American, Bahamasair, CanJet, Comair, Continental, Delta, Frontier, jetBlue, Laker Air, Northwest, Song, Southwest Airlines, Spirit Airlines, United, and US Airways/US Airways Express.

Contacts Air Canada (☎*800/247–2262*). **AirTran** (☎*800/247–8726*). **American** (☎*800/433–7300*). **Bahamasair** (☎*800/222–4262*). **CanJet** (☎*800/809–7777*). **Comair** (☎*800/354–9822*). **Continental** (☎*800/525–0280*). **Delta** (☎*800/221–1212*). **Frontier** (☎*800/432–1359*)</S>. **JetBlue** (☎*800/538–2583*). **Northwest** (☎*800/225–2525*). **Song** (☎*800/359–7664*). **Southwest Airlines** (☎*800/435–9792*). **Spirit Airlines** (☎*800/772–7117*). **United** (☎*800/241–6522*). **US Airways/US Airways Express** (☎*800/428–4322*).

AIRPORTS & TRANSFERS

PalmTran Routes 44 and 40 run from the airport to Tri-Rail's nearby Palm Beach airport station daily. Palm Beach Transportation provides taxi and limousine service from PBIA. Reserve at least a day in advance for a limo. The lowest fares are $2 per mile, with the meter starting at $2.25. Depending on your destination, a flat rate (from PBIA only) may save money. Wheelchair-accessible vehicles are available.

Contacts **Palm Beach International Airport (PBIA)** (⌧ *Congress Ave. and Belvedere Rd., West Palm Beach* ☏ *561/471–7420*). **Palm Beach Transportation** (☏ *561/689–4222*). **Tri-Rail Commuter Bus Service** (☏ *800/874–7245*).

BY CAR

Interstate 95 runs north–south, linking West Palm Beach with Fort Lauderdale and Miami to the south and with Daytona, Jacksonville, and the rest of the Atlantic coast to the north. To access Palm Beach, exit east at Southern Boulevard, Belvedere Road, or Okeechobee Boulevard. Florida's Turnpike runs from Miami north through West Palm Beach before angling northwest to reach Orlando. U.S. 1 threads north–south along the coast, connecting most coastal communities, whereas the more scenic Route A1A ventures out onto the barrier islands. Interstate 95 runs parallel to U.S. 1 but a few miles inland. A nonstop four-lane route, Okeechobee Boulevard carries traffic from west of downtown West Palm Beach, near the Amtrak station in the airport district, directly to the Flagler Memorial Bridge and into Palm Beach. The best way to access Lake Okeechobee from West Palm is to drive west on Southern Boulevard from Interstate 95 past the cutoff road to Lion Country Safari. From there, the boulevard is designated U.S. 98/441.

CAR RENTAL

Contacts **Alamo** (☏ *800/462–5266*). **Avis** (☏ *800/331–1212*). **Budget** (☏ *800/527–7000*). **Hertz** (☏ *800/654–3131*). **National** (☏ *800/227–7368*).

BY TAXI

Palm Beach Transportation has a single number serving several cab companies. Meters start at $2, and the charge is $2.25 per mile. Some cabs may charge more.

Contacts **Palm Beach Transportation** (☏ *561/689–4222*).

CONTACTS & RESOURCES

EMERGENCIES

Ambulance or Police Emergencies (☏ *911*).

Late-Night Pharmacies CVS (⌧ ., *Palm Springs* ☏ *561/965–3367*). **Walgreens** (⌧ *1634 S. Federal Hwy., Boynton Beach* ☏ *561/737–1160* ⌧ *1208 Royal Palm Beach Blvd., Royal Palm Beach* ☏ *561/798–9048* ⌧ *1800 W. Indiantown Rd., Jupiter* ☏ *561/744–6822* ⌧ *2501 Broadway, Riviera Beach* ☏ *561/848–6464*).

TOURS

Jonathan Dickinson's River Tours runs two-hour guided riverboat cruises daily at 9, 11, 1, and 3. The cost is $14.50. Loxahatchee Everglades Tours operates airboat tours year-round from west of Boca Raton through the marshes between the built-up coast and Lake Okeechobee. The *Manatee Queen*, a 49-passenger catamaran, offers day and evening cruises November through May on the Intracoastal Waterway and into the park's cypress swamps for $24. *Pilgrim Belle* operates two-hour sightseeing cruises along the Intracoastal Waterway. Water Taxi Scenic Cruises has several different daily sightseeing tours in a 16-person launch. All include a close-up look at the mansions of the rich and famous. The southern tour passes Peanut, Singer, and Munyan islands, and Palm Beach mansions. A second tour runs solely along the shore of Jupiter Island. A third tour passes the Craig Norman estate and goes into Lake Worth and Sawgrass Creek.

DivaDuck amphibious tours run 75-minute tours of West Palm Beach/ Palm Beach in and out of the water. Cruises run two or three times a day for $25.

The Boca Raton Historical Society offers tours of the Boca Raton Resort & Club and trolley tours of city sites during season. The Indian River County Historical Society conducts walking tours of downtown Vero by reservation. Old Northwood Historic District Tours leads two-hour walking tours that include visits to historic home interiors. During season they typically start Sunday at 2, and a $5 donation is suggested. Tours for groups of six or more can be scheduled almost any day.

Contacts **Audubon Society of the Everglades** (Box 16914, West Palm Beach 33416 ☎ 561/588–6908). **Boca Raton Historical Society** (⊠ 71 N. Federal Hwy., Boca Raton ☎ 561/395–6766). **Indian River County Historical Society** (⊠ 2336 14th Ave., Vero Beach ☎ 772/778–3435). **Jonathan Dickinson's River Tours** (⊠ Jonathan Dickinson State Park, 16450 S.E. Federal Hwy., Hobe Sound ☎ 561/746–1466). **Loxahatchee Everglades Tours** (⊠ 15490 Loxahatchee Rd. ☎ 561/482–8026). **Manatee Queen** (⊠ Jonathan Dickinson State Park, 1065 N. Hwy. A1A, Jupiter ☎ 561/744–2191). **Old Northwood Historic District Tours** (⊠ 501 30th St., West Palm Beach ☎ 561/863–5633). Intracoastal Cruises (⊠ 801 E. Atlantic Ave., Delray Beach ☎ 561/243–0686). **DivaDuck tours** (Rosemary Ave and Hibiscus St., in CityPlace, West Palm Beach ☎ 561/832–5196 .

 Water Taxi Scenic Cruises (⊠ Panama Hatties Restaurant, 11511 Ellison Wilson Rd., North Palm Beach ☎ 561/775–2628).

VISITOR INFORMATION

Tourist Information **Belle Glade Chamber of Commerce** (⊠ 540 S. Main St., Belle Glade ☎ 561/996–2745). **Chamber of Commerce of the Palm Beaches** (⊠ 401 N. Flagler Dr., West Palm Beach ☎ 561/833–3711). **Clewiston Chamber of Commerce** (⊠ 109 Central Ave., Clewiston ☎ 863/983–7979). **Delray Beach Chamber of Commerce** (⊠ 64-A S.E. 5th Ave., Delray Beach ☎ 561/278–0424). **Glades County Chamber of Commerce** (⊠ 998 U.S. 27 SE, Moore Haven ☎ 863/946–0440). **Indian River Chamber of Commerce** (⊠ 1216 21st St., Vero Beach ☎ 772/567–3491). **Indiantown and Western Martin County Chamber of Commerce** (Box 602, Indiantown ☎ 772/597–2184). **Okeechobee County Chamber of Commerce** (⊠ 55 S. Parrott Ave., Okeechobee ☎ 863/763–6464). **Pahokee Chamber of Commerce** (⊠ 115 E. Main St., Pahokee ☎ 561/924–5579). **Palm Beach County Convention & Visitors Bureau** (⊠ 1555 Palm Beach Lakes Blvd., Suite 800, West Palm Beach ☎ 561/233–3000). **St. Lucie County Tourist Development Council** (⊠ 2300 Virginia Ave., Fort Pierce ☎ 800/344–8443). **Stuart/Martin County Chamber of Commerce** (⊠ 1650 S. Kanner Hwy., Stuart ☎ 772/287–1088). **Town of Palm Beach Chamber of Commerce** (⊠ 400 Royal Palm Way, Palm Beach ☎ 561/655–3282). **U.S. Army Corps of Engineers (Okeechobee area information)** (⊠ South Florida Operations Office, 525 Ridgelawn Rd., Clewiston ☎ 863/983–8101).

Fort Lauderdale & Broward County

Caribbean Mardi Gras Junior Carnival, Ft. Lauderdale

WORD OF MOUTH

"I love Fort Lauderdale. Tons of upscale shopping, dining and attractions. Make sure you head to Las Olas to eat. The Floridian is a treat for breakfast. Rainy day? Hit The Festival, a huge indoor flea market."

—GoTravel

WELCOME TO FT. LAUDERDALE & BROWARD COUNTY

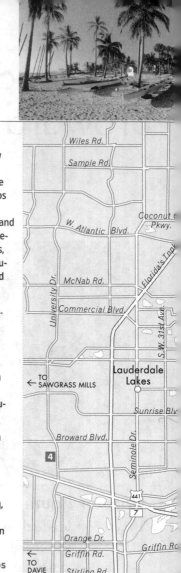

TOP REASONS TO GO

★ **Blue Waves:** Sparkling Lauderdale beaches—from Deerfield Beach and Pompano Beach through Dania Beach and Hollywood—are Florida's first to capture Blue Wave Beach status from the Clean Beaches Council in Washington, D.C.

★ **Inland Waterways:** More than 300 miles of inland waterways including downtown Fort Lauderdale's historic New River create what's known as the Venice of America.

★ **Everglades Access:** Just minutes from luxury hotels and golf courses, the rugged Everglades tantalize with alligators and other wildlife.

★ **Vegas-Style Gaming:** In 2008 Broward's Vegas-style slots selection extended to Hollywood's glittering Seminole Hard Rock Hotel & Casino.

★ **Cruise Gateway:** Port Everglades, a hop-skip from Fort Lauderdale Beach, hosts gleaming cruise ships from major lines that often partner with hotels for pre-/post-cruise packages.

1 Fort Lauderdale. Anchored by historic New River and its attractive Riverwalk, Fort Lauderdale embraces high-rise condos along with single-family homes, museums, parks, and attractions. Las Olas Boulevard, lined with boutiques, sidewalk cafes, and restaurants, links downtown and the beaches.

2 North on Scenic A1A. Stretching north on A1A, seaside attractions range from the high-rise Galt Ocean Mile to low-rise resort communities and a glimpse of a lighthouse, inspiration for the community of Lighthouse Point.

3 South Broward. From Hollywood's beachside Broadwalk and historic Young Circle, the latter transformed into an Arts Park, to Seminole gaming, South Broward provides grit, glitter and diversity in attractions.

4 The Western Suburbs & Beyond. From alligators in the Everglades to alligator handbags at nearby Sawgrass Mills, western Broward magnetism ranges from residential development to marathon shopping, golf, and outdoor adventure options.

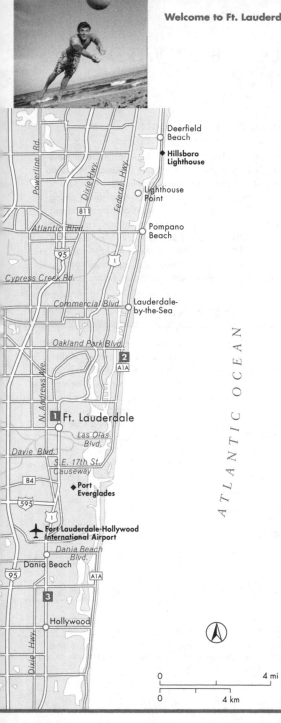

Deerfield Beach

♦ Hillsboro Lighthouse

Lighthouse Point

Pompano Beach

Lauderdale-by-the-Sea

1 Ft. Lauderdale

Las Olas Blvd.

♦ Port Everglades

✈ Fort Lauderdale-Hollywood International Airport

Dania Beach Blvd.

Dania Beach

3

Hollywood

Powerline Rd.

Dixie Hwy.

Federal Hwy.

811

Atlantic Blvd.

95

Cypress Creek Rd.

Commercial Blvd.

Oakland Park Blvd.

2

A1A

N. Andrews Ave.

Davie Blvd.

S.E. 17th St. Causeway

84

595

1

Dania Beach Blvd.

95

A1A

Dixie Hwy.

ATLANTIC OCEAN

0 — 4 mi

0 — 4 km

GETTING ORIENTED

Along the southeast's Gold Coast, Fort Lauderdale & Broward County anchor a delightfully chic middle ground between the historically elite Palm Beaches and the international hubbub of Miami. From downtown Fort Lauderdale, it's about a four-hour drive to either Orlando or Key West, but there's plenty to keep you in Broward. All told, Broward boasts 31 communities from Deerfield Beach to Hallandale Beach along the coast, and from Coral Springs to Southwest Ranches closer to the Everglades. Big—in fact, huge—shopping options await in Sunrise, home of Sawgrass Mills, the upscale Colonnade Outlets at Sawgrass, and the new IKEA Sunrise.

6

FT. LAUDERDALE & BROWARD COUNTY PLANNER

When to Go

Peak season runs Thanksgiving through March, when concert, art, and entertainment seasons go full throttle. Waits at restaurants are often shorter in summer, which can be rainy, hot, and humid. Summer moves into fall at a slow, sticky pace. Both 2004 and 2005 brought hurricane winds in August and September, although the past couple of seasons have been tranquil. Golfing tee-time waits are longer on weekends year-round. Even in cloudy weather and especially when reflected off water, Fort Lauderdale sunshine can burn.

Flying In

Serving more than 21 million travelers a year, Fort Lauderdale–Hollywood International Airport (FLL) is near Fort Lauderdale Beach, Port Everglades and situated just off U.S. 1 between downtown Fort Lauderdale and Hollywood. Other options include Miami International Airport (MIA), about 35 miles to the south, and the far less chaotic Palm Beach International Airport (PBI), about 45 miles to the north. All three airports link to Tri-Rail, a commuter train operating seven days through Palm Beach, Broward, and Miami-Dade counties.

For more flight information see By Air in the Essentials section at the end of this chapter.

About the Restaurants

References to "Fort Liquordale" from Spring Break days of old have given way to au courant allusions for the decidedly cuisine-oriented "Fork Lauderdale." Greater Fort Lauderdale offers some of the finest, most varied dining of any U.S. city its size, spawned in part by the advent of new luxury hotels and upgrades all around. From among nearly 4,000 wining-and-dining establishments in Broward, choose from basic Americana or cuisines of Asia, Europe, or Central and South America, and enjoy more than just food in an atmosphere with subtropical twists.

About the Hotels

Not as posh as Palm Beach or as Deco-trendy as Miami Beach, Fort Lauderdale has a growing roster of more than respectable lodging choices, from beachfront luxury suites to intimate bed-and-breakfasts to chain hotels along the Intracoastal Waterway. Relatively new on the luxury front are the Atlantic and the Hilton Fort Lauderdale Beach Resort, and more upscale accommodations are on the horizon. If you want to be *on* the beach, be sure to ask specifically when booking your room, since many hotels advertise "waterfront" accommodations that are actually on inland waterways or overlooking the beach from across the A1A highway.

What It Costs

DINING & LODGING PRICE CATEGORIES

	¢	$	$$	$$$	$$$$
Restaurants					
	Under $10	$10–$15	$15–$20	$20–$30	over $30
Hotels					
	Under $80	$80–$100	$100–$140	$140–$220	over $220

Restaurant prices are per person for a main course at dinner. Hotel prices are for a standard double room, excluding 6% sales tax (more in some counties) and 1%–4% tourist tax.

Updated by
Lynne Helm

COLLEGIATES OF THE 1960S NOW returning to Fort Lauderdale would be hard pressed to recognize the onetime "Sun and Suds Spring Break Capital of the Universe." Back then, Fort Lauderdale's beach-front was lined with T-shirt shops, and downtown consisted of a lone office tower and dilapidated buildings waiting to be razed. Today, the beach and downtown have exploded with upscale shops, restaurants, and luxury resort hotels equipped with enough high-octane amenities to light up skies all the way to western Broward's Alligator Alley. At risk of losing small-town 45-rpm magic in iPod times—when hotel parking fees alone threaten to eclipse room rates of old—Greater Fort Lauderdale somehow seems to be melding disparate eras into nouveau nirvana, seasoned with a little Gold Coast sand.

Credit the 1960 film *Where the Boys Are* for catapulting sleepy Lauder-dale environs onto that era's *Haute List* for spring-fling campus escape. The movie depicted college students—upward of 20,000—swarming into town for the Spring Break phenomenon. By 1985 the 20,000 had mushroomed to 350,000. Hotel owners bemoaned students cramming into standard-size hotel rooms by the dozen, with civility hitting new lows. Drug trafficking and petty theft proliferated, along with down-scale bars staging wet T-shirt and banana-eating contests. Fed up, city leaders cracked down with policies designed to encourage Spring Breakers to go elsewhere. They did, ushering in a new era attracting a far more sophisticated, affluent crowd.

A major beneficiary is Las Olas Boulevard, a shopping street once mori-bund after 5 PM, which reinvented itself as a hot venue, with a mix of trendy shops and eateries. Even so, a wave-capped shoreline with wide ribbons of golden sand for beachcombing and sunbathing remains the anchor draw for Fort Lauderdale and Broward County.

Tying all this together is a transportation system that, though less con-gested than elsewhere in South Florida, suffers from traffic overload. Interstate 595 connects the city and suburbs and provides a direct route to the Fort Lauderdale–Hollywood International Airport and Port Everglades, but be sure to avoid morning and evening rush hours, when lanes slow to a crawl. For a more scenic way to really see this canal-laced city, simply hop on a water taxi, now known as a Water Bus. None of this was envisioned by Napoleon Bonaparte Broward, Florida's governor from 1905 to 1909, for whom the county was named. His drainage schemes opened much of the marshy Everglades region for farming, ranching, and settling (in retrospect, an environ-mental disaster). It was for Major William Lauderdale, who built a fort at the river's mouth in 1838 during the Seminole Indian wars, that the city was named.

Incorporated in 1911 with just 175 residents, Fort Lauderdale grew rapidly during the Florida boom of the 1920s. Today its population is 150,000, and the suburbs keep growing—1.6 million live in the county's 31 municipalities and unincorporated areas. As elsewhere, many specula-tors busily flipping property here got caught when the sun-drenched real-estate bubble burst, leaving Broward's foreclosure rate to skyrocket.

6

Despite economic downturns, gaming has further rouged the area's complexion. Although South Florida's Indian tribes have long offered bingo, poker, and machines resembling slots—Hollywood's Seminole Hard Rock Hotel & Casino (where beleagured Anna Nicole Smith spent her final hours in 2007) ranks as the most glittering example. In 2005, Broward's electorate gave a thumbs-up to becoming Florida's first county to offer Las Vegas–style gambling with true slot machines at four wagering facilities: Gulfstream Park Racing & Casino, the Mardi Gras Racetrack & Gaming, Dania Jai Alai Casino, and The Isle Casino & Racing of Pompano Park. In 2008 the Seminole Hard Rock also cut a deal with the state and promptly replaced bingo-style machines with genuine Vegas-style slots.

EXPLORING FORT LAUDERDALE & BROWARD COUNTY

Numbers in the margin correspond to the Fort Lauderdale map.

The Fort Lauderdale metro area is laid out in a basic grid system, and only myriad canals and waterways interrupt the mostly straight-line path of streets and roads. Nomenclature is important here. Streets, roads, courts, and drives run east–west. Avenues, terraces, and ways run north–south. Boulevards can (and do) run any which way. For visitors, Las Olas Boulevard is one of the most important east–west thoroughfares from the beach to downtown, whereas Route A1A—referred to as Atlantic Boulevard, Ocean Boulevard, and Fort Lauderdale Beach along some stretches—runs along the north–south oceanfront. These names can confuse visitors, since there are separate streets called Atlantic and Ocean in Hollywood and Pompano Beach. Boulevards, composed of either pavement or water, give Fort Lauderdale its distinct "Venice of America" character. Honeycombed with some 300 mi of navigable waterways, the city is home port for about 44,000 privately owned boats. An easy, pleasant way to tour the canals is via Fort Lauderdale's water-taxi system, made up of motor launches carrying up to 70 passengers, providing transportation and quick, narrated tours. Larger, multiple-deck touring vessels and motorboat rentals for self-guided tours are other options.

TIMING

Tourists visit all year long, arriving in winter or summer, depending on budget, interests, hobbies, and the climate where they live. The winter season, roughly Thanksgiving through March, attracts the biggest crowds and regular "snowbirds"—seasonal residents showing up when snow starts up north. Concert, art, and entertainment seasons are at their height then, packing restaurants and roadways. In summer, waits at even the top restaurants are likely to be shorter, although some venues curtail hours. Summer can be rainy—although weather patterns have been less predictable in recent years—with showers arriving about midafternoon and typically soon gone. Heat and humidity do not quickly subside, and summer moves into fall at a slow, sticky pace.

⚠CAUTION. Avoid unguarded waters, and be aware of color codes. In Fort Lauderdale, double red flags mean water is closed to the public, often

GREAT ITINERARIES

Since many Broward County attractions are close, it's realistic to pack a lot into a day—if you have wheels. Catch the history, museums, and shops and bistros in Fort Lauderdale's downtown and along Las Olas Boulevard. Then if you feel like hitting the beach, head east to the intersection of Las Olas and A1A and you're there. Neighboring communities like Lauderdale-by-the-Sea and Pompano Beach (to the north) or Dania Beach and Hollywood (to the south) have attractions of their own, and you may not even be aware when you've crossed municipal lines. As a result, you'll be able to cover most high points in three days, and with seven to 10 days you can experience virtually all of Broward's mainstream charms.

3 DAYS

With a bigger concentration of hotels, restaurants, and attractions than its suburbs, Fort Lauderdale makes a logical base of operations for any visit. On your first day, see the downtown, especially Las Olas Boulevard between Southeast 3rd and Southeast 15th avenues. After lunch at a sidewalk café, head for the nearby Arts and Science District and the downtown **Riverwalk** ❻; enjoy it at a leisurely pace in half a day or less. On your second day, spend some time at the **Fort Lauderdale Beachfront** ⓫, shopping or having a cooling libation at an oceanfront lounge if heat drives you off the sand. Tour the waterways on the third day, either on a rented boat from one of the marinas along Route A1A, or via a sightseeing vessel or water taxi. Reachable by water taxi are attractions such as Gallery at Beach Place, Broward Center for the Performing Arts, Galleria Mall, Las Olas Boulevard shops, Las Olas Riverfront, and the **Museum of Art** ❸ and **Museum of Discovery and Science/AutoNation IMAX Theater** ❼; restaurants such as 15th Street Fisheries, Grill Room at Riverside Hotel, Shula's on the Beach, and dozens of others; and hotels such as the Hyatt Regency Pier Sixty-Six, and Bahia Mar Beach Resort.

5 DAYS

With additional time, see more of the beach and the arts district and still work in some outdoor sports— and you'll be able to rearrange your plans depending on weather. On the first day, visit the Arts and Science District and the downtown **Riverwalk** ❻ . Set aside the next day for an offshore adventure, perhaps a deep-sea fishing charter, a reef-diving trip, or some parasailing along the beach. Landlubbers might go for hiking at Markham Park or at Tradewinds Park (home of **Butterfly World**). On Day 3, shop, dine, and relax along the **Fort Lauderdale Beachfront** ⓫, and at the end of the day, sneak a peek at the Hillsboro Light, at **Lighthouse Point**. Day 4 can be spent at the **Hugh Taylor Birch State Recreation Area** ⓬. Enjoy your fifth day in **Hollywood**.

6

because of lightning or sharks; a lone red flag means strong currents; purple signals dangerous marine life such as men-of-war; green means calm conditions. In Hollywood, orange signals rip currents with easterly onshore winds; blue means dangerous marine life such as jellyfish; red means hazardous; green means good conditions.

FORT LAUDERDALE

Like many southeast Florida neighbors, Fort Lauderdale has been revitalizing for several years. In a state where gaudy tourist zones often stand aloof from workaday downtowns, Fort Lauderdale exhibits consistency at both ends of the 2-mi Las Olas corridor. The sparkling look results from efforts to upgrade both beachfront and downtown. Matching the downtown's innovative arts district, cafés, and boutiques is an equally inventive beach area, with hotels, cafés, and shops facing an undeveloped shoreline, and new resort-style hotels replacing faded icons of yesteryear. Despite wariness of pretentious overdevelopment, city leaders have allowed a striking number of glittering high-rises. Some nostalgia buffs fret over the diminishing vision of sailboats bobbing in waters near downtown, now that a boxy high-rise has erased one of the area's oldest marinas. Sharp demographic changes are also altering the faces of Greater Fort Lauderdale communities, increasingly cosmopolitan with more minorities, including Hispanics and people of Caribbean descent, as well as gays and lesbians. In Fort Lauderdale, especially, a younger populace is growing, whereas longtime residents are dying off or heading north, to a point where one former city commissioner likens the change to that of historic New River—moving with the tide and sometimes appearing at a standstill. "The river of our population is at still point, old and new in equipoise, one pushing against the other."

DOWNTOWN

The jewel of downtown along New River is the Arts and Entertainment District, with Broadway shows, ballet, and much more at the riverfront Broward Center for the Performing Arts. Clustered within a five-minute walk are the Museum of Discovery and Science, the expanding Fort Lauderdale Historical Museum, and the Museum of Art (MOA/FL), home to blockbuster touring exhibits like Princess Diana's wedding dress and "Tutankhamun and the Golden Age of the Pharaohs." (Ancient Egyptians surely rest easy knowing that the county has added free wireless broadband network or Wi-Fi hot spots downtown.) Restaurants, sidewalk cafés, bars, and blues, folk, jazz, reggae, and rock clubs flourish. Las Olas Riverfront, a multistory entertainment, dining, and retail complex along several waterfront blocks once owned by pioneers William and Mary Brickell, has been a retail disappointment to developers, and is evolving with more luxury housing. Tying this district together is the Riverwalk, extending 2 mi along the New River's north and south banks. Tropical gardens with benches and interpretive displays fringe the walk on the north, boat landings on the south.

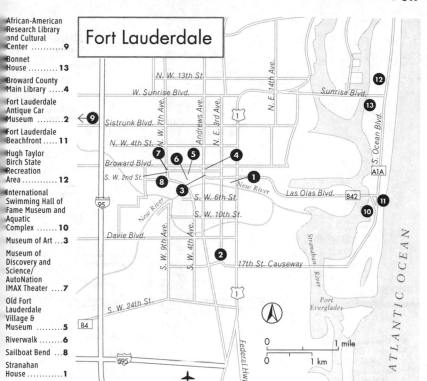

WHAT TO SEE

9 **African-American Research Library and Cultural Center.** A two-story, $14 million gem, a few miles west of downtown, this resource provides locals and researchers from around the world with more than 75,000 books, documents, and artifacts centering on experiences of people of African descent. There's a gift shop and a small café, and parking is free. ⊠*2650 Sistrunk Blvd.* ☎*954/625–2800* ⊕*www.broward.org/library/ aarlcc.htm* ☞*Free* ⊙*Mon.–Thurs. 10–9, Fri. and Sat. 10–6, Sun. 1–5.*

4 **Broward County Main Library.** One of more than 30 libraries in the Broward County system, this eight-story building of Florida limestone with a terraced glass facade that stood up remarkably well to Hurricane Wilma was designed by Marcel Breuer to complement the environment. Works are displayed here from Broward's Public Art and Design Program, including paintings, sculpture, photographs, and weavings by nationally renowned and Florida artists. A technology center has personal computers for public use and assistant/adaptive devices for patrons with disabilities. A 300-seat theater hosts productions from theater to poetry readings. ⊠*100 S. Andrews Ave.* ☎*954/357–7444, 954/357–7457 for self-guided Art in Public Places walking tour brochure* ⊕*www.broward.org/library* ☞*Free* ⊙*Mon.–Thurs. 9–9, Fri. and Sat. 9–5, Sun. noon–5:30.*

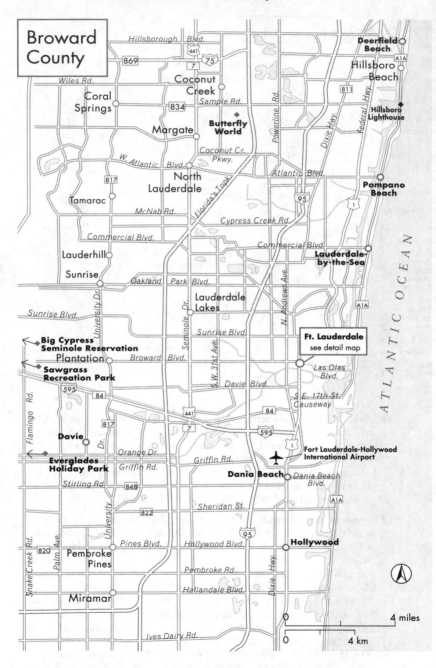

Don't miss Charcuterie Too (✉*100 S. Andrews Ave.* ☎*954/463–9578*), a cozy cafeteria on Broward County Main Library's second floor. Breakfast treats include muffins, scones, and coffee cakes, and a lunch menu has quiche, soups, salads, and entrées. Open weekdays from 8 to 2:30, it caters to library bookworms and downtown worker bees.

❷ Fort Lauderdale Antique Car Museum. Retired floral company owner Arthur O. Stone set up a foundation to preserve these eye-poppers. Nostalgia includes nearly two dozen Packards from 1900 to the 1940s, along with a gallery saluting Franklin Delano Roosevelt. Within a quick commute of both Port Everglades and the airport, this museum has everything from spark plugs and gearshift knobs to Texaco Oil signage, plus a new wing and an enlarged library. ✉*1527 S.W. 1st Ave.* ☎*954/779–7300* ⊕*www.antiquecarmuseum.org* ✉*$8* ⊙*Weekdays 10–4.*

★ ❸ Museum of Art. In an Edward Larrabee Barnes–designed building that's considered an architectural masterpiece, this newly renovated museum, which started in a storefront and now makes a habit of hosting world-class touring exhibits, has an impressive permanent collection of 20th-century European and American art, including works by Picasso, Calder, Dalí, Mapplethorpe, Warhol, and Stella, as well as works by celebrated Ashcan School artist William Glackens. ✉*1 E. Las Olas Blvd.* ☎*954/763–6464* ⊕*www.moafl.org* ✉*$7 and up, depending on exhibit* ⊙*Daily 11–7, Thurs. open until 9; closed Tues. mid-Dec.–Jan.*

★ ❼ Museum of Discovery and Science/AutoNation IMAX Theater. Open 365 days barring weather-related events, the aim here is to show children—*and* adults—the wonders of science in an entertaining fashion. The courtyard's 52-foot-tall Great Gravity Clock lets arrivals know a cool experience awaits. Inside, exhibits include Kidscience, encouraging youngsters to explore the world; and Gizmo City, a look at how gadgets work. Florida Ecoscapes has a living coral reef, plus sharks, stringrays, and eels. The AutoNation IMAX theater, part of the complex, shows films (some 3-D) on a five-story-high screen. ✉*401 S.W. 2nd St.* ☎*954/467–6637 museum, 954/463–4629 IMAX* ⊕*www.mods. org* ✉*Museum $15, includes one IMAX show* ⊙*Mon.–Sat. 10–5, Sun. noon–6.*

❺ Old Fort Lauderdale Village & Museum. Surveying city history from the Seminole era to more recent times, the museum has expanded into several adjacent historic buildings, including the King-Cromartie House, the Historical Society's Hoch Heritage Center, and the New River Inn. The research facility archives original manuscripts, maps, and more than 250,000 photos. Walking tours of the historic district depart from the New River Inn with reservations on Saturday, the $10 fee including admission and tours of the inn and King-Cromartie House. ✉*231 S.W. 2nd Ave.* ☎*954/463–4431* ⊕*www.oldfortlauderdale.org* ✉*$7* ⊙*Tues.–Sat. 10–5, weekends noon–5.*

★ ❻ Riverwalk. Fantastic views and entertainment prevail on this lovely, paved promenade on the New River's north bank. On the first Sunday of every month a free jazz brunch attracts visitors.

6

⑧ Sailboat Bend. Between Las Olas and the river lies a neighborhood with character reminiscent of Key West's Old Town and Miami's Coconut Grove, except there are no shops or services here.

❶ Stranahan House. The oldest residence in the city, increasingly dwarfed by high-rise development, was once home for businessman Frank Stranahan, who arrived in 1892. With his wife, Ivy, the city's first schoolteacher, he befriended Seminole Indians, traded with them, and taught them "new ways." In 1901 he built a store and later made it his home. After financial reverses, he tied himself to a concrete block and jumped into New River, leaving his widow to carry on. Ivy died in 1971, and now her home (at various times a post office, general store, and restaurant) is a museum, with many original furnishings, and tours. ✉335 S.E. 6th Ave., at Las Olas Blvd. ☎954/524–4736 ⊕www.stranahanhouse.org ⬚$12 ⊙Wed.–Sat. 10–3, Sun. 1–3.

EN ROUTE

North of Fort Lauderdale's 17th Street Causeway, within the gothic intrigue of **Evergreen Historic Cemetery**, lies a bird-watchers haven. The circa 1879 graveyard, shaded by gumbo limbo and strangler figs, doubles as a place of fleeting repose for Bahama mockingbirds and other species winging through urban Broward. Warblers are big here, and there are occasional sightings of red-eyed vireos, northern waterthrushes, and scarlet tanagers. Headstones of Florida pioneers include city founders Frank and Ivy Stranahan as well as legendary bar owner Crazy Gregg Newell, whose beer-soaked wet T-shirt contests helped launch the once-rousing Lauderdale Spring Break. ✉1300 SE 10th St. 33315 ☎954/745–2140 ⊕www.browardcemeteries.com ⬚

ALONG THE BEACH

Fort Lauderdale's increasingly stylish beachfront offers easy access not only to a wide band of beige sand but also to restaurants and shops. For 2 mi heading north, beginning at the Bahia Mar yacht basin along Route A1A, you'll have clear ocean views, typically across rows of colorful beach umbrellas, to ships passing in and out of nearby Port Everglades. If you're on the beach, gaze back on an exceptionally graceful promenade. Broad walkways line both sides of the beach roadway, and traffic has been trimmed to two gently curving northbound lanes, where in-line skaters skim past slow-moving cars. On the beach side, a low masonry wall doubles as an extended bench, separating sand from the promenade. At night the wall is accented with pretty ribbons of fiber-optic color, often on the blink despite an ongoing search for a permanent fix. The beach is most crowded between Las Olas and Sunrise boulevards.

NEED A BREAK?

Catch an orange-bottomed, yellow-topped Sun Trolley—running every 15 minutes, either free or for less than $1, depending on routes—and catch a break. Sun Trolley's *Convention Connection*, at 50¢ per person, runs roundtrip from Cordova Road's Harbor Shops near Port Everglades to past the Convention Center, over the 17th Street Causeway, and north along A1A to

Beach Place. Wave at trolley drivers—yes, they will stop—for pickups anywhere along the route. (☎ *954/761–3543* ⊕ *www.suntrolley.com*)

WHAT TO SEE

★ ⑬ **Bonnet House.** A 35-acre oasis in the heart of the beach area, this subtropical estate stands as a tribute to the history of Old South Florida. The charming home was the winter residence of the late Frederic and Evelyn Bartlett, artists whose personal touches and small surprises are evident throughout. Whether you're interested in architecture, artwork, or the natural environment, this is a special place. Be on the lookout for playful monkeys swinging from trees, a source of amusement at even some of the most solemn weddings on the grounds. Hours can vary, so call first. ✉ *900 N. Birch Rd.* ☎ *954/563–5393* ⊕ *www.bonnethouse. org* 💰 *$20 for house tours, $10 for grounds only* ⊙ *Wed.–Fri. 10–3, weekends noon–4.*

⑪ **Fort Lauderdale Beachfront.** A wave theme unifies the setting—from the low, white, wave-shaped wall between the beach and beachfront promenade to the widened and bricked inner promenade in front of shops, restaurants, and hotels. Alone among Florida's major beachfront communities, Fort Lauderdale's beach remains gloriously open and uncluttered. More than ever, the boulevard is worth promenading.

Fodor'sChoice ★

6

⑫ **Hugh Taylor Birch State Recreation Area.** Amid the tropical greenery of this 180-acre park, stroll along a nature trail, visit the Birch House Museum, picnic, play volleyball, or paddle a rented canoe. Since parking is limited on A1A, park here and take a walkway underpass to the beach (between 9 and 5). ✉ *3109 E. Sunrise Blvd.* ☎ *954/564–4521* ⊕ *www.floridastateparks.org* 💰 *$4 per vehicle with up to 8 people, $1 per pedestrian* ⊙ *Daily 8–sunset; ranger-guided nature walks Fri. at 10:30.*

⑩ **International Swimming Hall of Fame Museum and Aquatic Complex.** This monument to underwater accomplishments has two 10-lane, 50-meter pools that are open daily to the public, when not hosting international competitions. The exhibition building has photos, medals, and other souvenirs from major swimming events worldwide, as well as a theater that shows vintage films such as Esther Williams in *Million Dollar Mermaid.* ✉ *1 Hall of Fame Dr., 1 block south of Las Olas at A1A* ☎ *954/462–6536 museum, 954/828–4580 pool* ⊕ *www.ishof. org* 💰 *Museum $8, pool $4* ⊙ *Museum and pro shop mid-Jan.–late Dec., weekdays 9–7, weekends 9–5; pool mid-Jan.–late Dec., weekdays 8–4, weekends 9–5.*

WHERE TO EAT

AMERICAN

$$$–$$$$
Fodor'sChoice ★

✕ **Shula's on the Beach.** For anyone getting positively misty-eyed at mere mention of Don Shula's Miami Dolphins 17–0 Perfect Season of '72, the good news for steak—and sports—fans is that the staff here also turns out culinary winners. Certified Angus beef is grilled over a superhot fire for quick charring. Try Steak Mary Anne, named for

Cruising for a Taxi

Shout "Taxi! Taxi" in Fort Lauderdale, and look for your ship to come in.

Actually, you'll be catching a Water Bus or Water Taxi, depending on your point of view, since the original fleet of water taxis has been replaced by Water Buses carrying up to 70 passengers. Either way, they're floating "cabs" that you can "hail" along the Intracoastal Waterway and New River.

For sightseeing, the water-taxi-cum-bus can pick you up at any of several docking spots along the intracoastal or New River, and you can stop off at attractions like the Performing Arts Center, the Museum of Discovery & Science, Stranahan House, or the Gallery at Beach Place. For lunch, sail away to restaurants on Las Olas Boulevard or Las Olas Riverfront. As the sun disappears, water taxis are a superb way to head out for dinner or bar-hop, letting your pilot play the sober role of designated driver.

The water-transport venture was started by Bob Bekoff, a longtime Broward resident and outspoken tourism promoter, who decided to combine the need for transportation with one of the area's most captivating features: waterways that make Fort Lauderdale the Venice of America.

Ride all you want with a day pass from 10:30 AM to 12:30 AM for $11. Family all-day passes for two adults and up to four youths are $39, and after 7 PM passes are $8. Annual passes are $150. A dozen or so scheduled stops include the Bahia Mar, the Gallery at Beach Place, Galleria Mall, Seville Street, Pier 66, the Convention Center, and the historic Downtowner Saloon. The South Beach shuttle, a socko day-trip to the Art Deco District of Miami Beach ($22 Tuesday only), leaves Fort Lauderdale at 8:45 AM and Hollywood at 10 AM, returning to Hollywood at 5:45 PM and to Fort Lauderdale at 7 PM. For family reunions and such, group tours like the Sunset Cruise, or Mansions and Marinas are on tap. To get around town by Water Bus, call 954/467–6677 about 20 minutes ahead of pickup, or check out the schedule at ⊕ *www.watertaxi.com.*

—Lynne Helm

Shula's wife, consisting of two sliced fillets in a savory sauce. Seafood is excellent, too, as is the apple cobbler à la mode. Patio tables provide views of sand and ocean, and inside seating provides access to sports memorabilia and large-screen TVs. Complimentary valet parking is a nice alternative to pricey beach-area parking. ⊠*Sheraton Yankee Trader, 321 N. Fort Lauderdale Beach Blvd.* ☎*954/355–4000* ▭*AE, D, DC, MC, V.*

$$-$$$ ✕**Casablanca Cafe.** You'll get a fabulous ocean view and a good meal
Fodor\$Choice   to boot at this historic two-story Moroccan-style villa, built in the
★   1920s by local architect Francis Abreu. The menu is an American potpourri with both tropical and Asian influence (try the mussels in Thai curry sauce) along with North African specialties like lamb shank and couscous. There's a bar downstairs, and a deck for outside dining. Service is friendly. ⊠*A1A and Alhambra St.* ☎*954/764–3500* ▭*AE, D, MC, V.*

$$-$$$ ✕**Tropical Acres.** The Studiale family's sprawling icon restaurant has served up sizzling steaks from a fireplace grill since 1949—a millen-

nium by South Florida standards. Juicy prime rib is big here, and you'll find some of the best early-bird specials around. Choose from more than 40 entrées, including sautéed frogs' legs, rack of lamb, and boneless New York strip for two, or ask for recommendations. A wine list of some 60 labels ranges from under $20 to $70, with more than a dozen poured by the glass. ⊠*2500 Griffin Rd.* ☎*954/989–2500* ▤*AE, DC, MC, V.*

¢–$ ✕**Alligator Alley.** At this native Florida taproom and music hall big on nightly rockabilly to funk rock chefs ladle up memorable signature gumbo, and alligator ribs once featured on the Food Network. Wash down your beer with gator bites or Buffalo fingers. Vegetarians can stroke out on cheese fries or go with a garden salad. ⊠*1321 E. Commercial Blvd.* ☎*954/771–2220* ⊕*www.alligatoralleyflorida.com* ▤*AE, D, MC, V.*

¢–$ ✕**Elbo Room.** You can't go wrong wallowing in the past, lifting a drink, and exercising your elbow at the Elbo, a noisy, suds-drenched hot spot since 1938. This watering hole phased out food (except for light nibbles) a long time ago, but they kept their hokey sense of humor: upstairs a sign proclaims "We Don't Serve Women Here … You Have to Bring Your Own." ⊠*241 S. Fort Lauderdale Beach Blvd.* ☎*954/463–4615* ▤*AE, D, MC, V.*

DID YOU KNOW? The Elbo room is so revered as the last bar standing from a washed-out era that an impassioned coterie calling themselves "Sons of the Beach" wants the old joint anointed as an official historic city landmark.

¢–$ ✕**Floridian.** This Las Olas landmark with photos of Monroe, Nixon, and local notables past and present in a succession of brightly painted rooms with funky chandeliers dishes up some of the best breakfasts around, with oversize omelets that come with biscuits, toast, or English muffins, plus a choice of grits or tomatoes. With sausage or bacon on the side, the feast will make you forget about eating again soon. Count on savory sandwiches and hot platters for lunch, tempting meat-loaf plates for dinner, and friendly, efficient service. It's open 24 hours—even during hurricanes, as long as the power holds out. Feeling flush? Try the Fat Cat Breakfast (New York strip steak, hash browns or grits, toast, and a worthy champagne) or the Not-So-Fat-Cat, with the same grub and a lesser-quality vintage. ⊠*1410 E. Las Olas Blvd.* ☎*954/463–4041* ▤*No credit cards.*

¢–$ ✕**Lester's Diner.** Home to strong steaming coffee and a demanding skip-your-dinner dessert display, Lester's has stood as a 24-hour haven for the hungry along State Road 84 since 1967. Truckers head in here on their way to Port Everglades, as do workers from the area's thriving marine industry, suits from downtown toting briefcases, and tourists packing beach bags. Patronage gets even more eclectic in the wee hours. A stick-to-the-ribs menu includes breakfast anytime, homemade soups, sandwiches (try the Monte Cristo), salads, and dinners of generous portions. If your cholesterol count can take the hit, try the country-fried steak for less than $10 or the chicken-liver omelet (under $8). Smokers like the patio dining, under a red awning on the east side, but don't count on a view beyond what's in the parking lot. Two other

Lester's—in western Broward's Margate and Sunrise—close at mid-night on weeknights. ⊠*250 State Rd. 84* ☎*954/525–5641* ⊠*4701 Coconut Creek Pkwy., Margate* ☎*954/979–4722* ⊠*1399 N.W. 136th Ave., Sunrise* ☎*954/838–7473* ▤*D, MC, V.*

¢–$ ✕**Southport Raw Bar.** You can't go wrong at this unpretentious spot where the motto, seen on bumper stickers for miles around, proclaims EAT FISH, LIVE LONGER, EAT OYSTERS, LOVE LONGER, EAT CLAMS, LAST LONGER. Raw or steamed clams, raw oysters, and combos, along with peel-and-eat shrimp, are market priced. Hoagies, subs, and burgers are the ticket for less than $10. Side orders range from Bimini bread to key lime pie, with conch fritters, beer-battered onion rings, and corn on the cob in between. Order wine by the bottle or glass and beer by the pitcher, bottle, or can. Eat outside overlooking a canal, or inside at booths, tables, or the bars, in front and back. Limited parking is free, and a grocery store parking lot is across the street. ⊠*1536 Cordova Rd.* ☎*954/525–2526* ▤*MC, V.*

¢–$ ✕**Tom Jenkins.** Big portions of drippingly delicious barbecue are dispensed at this handy spot for eat-in or takeout, south of the New River Tunnel and north of the 17th Street Causeway. If you think you don't have time to stop, roll down your window and inhale on the way by, and you're likely to change your mind. Furnishings include an old Singer sewing machine and a wringer washer, and diners partake at picnic-style tables. Side dishes with dinners for less than $10 include baked beans, collards, and mighty tasty macaroni and cheese. For lunch, Tom's pork, beef, and catfish sandwiches are a surefire shortcut to satisfaction. Leave room for sweet-potato pie or apple cobbler. ⊠*1236 S. Federal Hwy.* ☎*954/522–5046* ▤*MC, V* ⊗*Closed Sun. and Mon.*

¢   ✕**Ernie's Barbecue.** Walls once plastered with philosophical quotes from a former owner have been scrubbed clean at Ernie's, where the menu proclaims CONCH IS KING, BARBECUE IS A WAY OF LIFE, AND THE BAR IS OPEN LATE. Fortunately for patrons, barbecue platters of pork or beef and conch chowder are as lip-smacking as ever. Bimini bread, thick-sliced for sandwiches, is also sold by the loaf to go, along with racks of ribs and conch chowder by the quart. Seafood, salads, and burgers also pass muster here, and there's a children's menu. Eat downstairs, or, if you don't mind the buzz of Federal Highway traffic, take the stairs to second-floor open-air patio tables near a couple of pool tables. ⊠*1843 S. Federal Hwy.* ☎*954/523–8636* ▤*AE, D, MC, V.*

¢   ✕**Georgia Pig.** When heading out to the area's western reaches, this postage-stamp-size outpost can add down-home zing to your day. Breakfast, including sausage gravy and biscuits, is served from 6 to 11 AM. But the big attraction is barbecue beef, pork, or chicken, on platters or in sandwiches. Alternatives include a spicy Brunswick stew and fried jumbo shrimp. There's apple, peach, cherry, and pecan pie, and a small-fry menu. Order takeout (25¢ extra) or eat at the counter, at wooden tables, or at a half dozen or so booths. ⊠*1285 S.W. 40th Ave. (State Rd. 7–U.S. 441, just south of Davie Blvd.)* ☎*954/587–4420* ▤*No credit cards.*

¢   ✕**Stork's Café.** In trendy Wilton Manors (a municipality in remarkable renaissance), Stork's Café stands out as a gay-friendly, straight-friendly, just plain friendly place to plot sightseeing strategy (or catch up on local papers). Sit indoors or outside under red umbrellaed tables. Custom Barbie Cakes (real dolls, edible ball gowns) are hot here. Divine baked goods range from croissants, tortes, cakes, and pies to Monster Cookies ($1.75 each), including gingersnap and snickerdoodle. The Pilgrim (turkey) or Hello Kitty (tuna) sandwiches go with salads or soups like Vegan Split Pea. Offshoot Stork's Las Olas is becoming the tail wagging the dog, with a similar menu, friendly staff, a great view of the Himmarshee Canal, and even gondola service promoted by owner Jim Stork. ⊠*2505 N.E. 15th Ave., Wilton Manors* ☎*954/567–3220* ⊠*1109 E. Las Olas Blvd., Fort Lauderdale* ☎*954/522–4670* ⊟*AE, D, MC, V.*

ASIAN

$$$ ✕ **Mai-Kai.** You'll think you've tripped off to the South Seas rather than South Florida upon arrival at this torchlighted landmark, anchoring Federal Highway since this particular stretch was a two-laner. Yes, it's touristy, yet somehow magnetic. Specialties include Peking duck, exotic tropical drinks, and a pulsating Polynesian dance review with a flaming finale. Valet parking is available. ⊠*3599 N. Federal Hwy.* ☎*954/563–3272* ⊟*AE, D, MC, V.*

$-$$ ✕ **Siam Cuisine.** Some locals claim that this eatery, tucked away in a small storefront in Wilton Manors, serves the best Thai in the Fort Lauderdale area, and they may be right. The family-run kitchen turns out appealing, flavorful delights from $10 to around $25 for a whole fish, usually red snapper. Curry dishes with chicken or shrimp are favorites, along with steamed dumplings and roast duck. ⊠*2010 Wilton Dr.* ☎*954/564–3411* ⊟*AE, MC, V.*

CONTEMPORARY

★ $$$-$$$$ ✕ **By Word of Mouth.** Unassuming but outstanding, this restaurant never advertises, hence its name. But word has sufficed for nearly a quarter century because locals consistently put this dining spot along the railroad tracks just off Oakland Park Boulevard at the top of "reader's choice" polls. There's no menu. Patrons are shown the day's specials to make their choice. Count on a solid lineup of fish, fowl, beef, pasta, and vegetarian entrées. Salads are served with dinner entrées, and there's a retail bakery for takeout. ⊠*3200 N.E. 12th Ave.* ☎*954/564–3663* ⊟*AE, D, MC, V.*

$$-$$$$ ✕ **Mark's Las Olas.** Mark Militello, a star among chefs in South Florida and beyond, commands this offshoot of north Miami's long-gone Mark's Place. Militello's loyal following remains enchanted with his Florida-style preparation, blending flavors from Caribbean, Mediterranean, and southwestern traditions. Entrées change daily, but patrons can count on signatures like crab-crusted black grouper. Appearing on occasion is Italian baby chicken grilled under a brick. And some patrons rave about the wild-mushroom polenta with roasted shallots and porcini oil. Dishes are occasionally paired off with combos of callaloo (West Indian spinach), chayote, ginger, jícama, and plantain. Be aware that substitutions are frowned upon, although servers are warmly hospitable. The wine list is mostly California, with many offered by the

FodorsChoice ★

glass. ⊠*1032 E. Las Olas Blvd.* ☎*954/463–1000* ⚑*Reservations essential* ⊟*AE, D, DC, MC, V* ⊘*No lunch weekends.*

$-$$$ ✗**Creolina's.** Since it moved to Himmarshee Village from a more modest storefront birthplace not far away, it's still not uncommon to see chef-owner Mark Sulzinski cooking up Cajun-creole delights for city power brokers, including the longtime mayor. Try Gumbo Ya Ya, crawfish rémoulade, or alligator piquant (tender strips crisp-fried) for starters. Also consider the catfish with pecans or plain old red beans and rice. Warm bread pudding with bourbon sauce is a worthy finale. Prices (up with the fancier digs) remain a good deal. ⊠*209 S.W. 2nd St.* ☎*954/524–2003* ⊟*AE, D, DC, MC, V.*

FRENCH

$$-$$$ ✗**Le Café de Paris.** Serving the classics for lunch and dinner under ownership of Swiss-born (and jeans-clad) Louis Flematti (former owner of the now-closed French Quarter), Le Café seats upward of 150 but keeps everything cozy with comfort foods like crusty bread, onion soup, and crepes, as well as duck, lamb, and beef dishes. There's also a mouthwatering pastry wagon. ⊠*715 Las Olas Blvd.* ☎*954/467–2900* ⊟*AE, D, DC, MC, V* ⊘*Closed Sun. No lunch Sat.*

GERMAN

$-$$$ ✗**Old Heidelberg Restaurant & Deli.** Likened to a Bavarian mirage plucked from the Alps and plopped along State Road 84 near airport and seaport, the Old Heidelberg's beer stein–cowbell–cuckoo clock decor accents the veal loaf, sauerkraut, and other specialties, from apple strudel to Black Forest cake. Owners Heidi Bruggermann and Dieter Doerrenberg hit South Florida to thaw out in 1984. After opening a wholesale sausage factory, they bought a onetime seafood eatery in 1991 for transformation into a German-style haven for dishes like stuffed roast pork with bread dumplings. For better or wurst in take-out, the Old Heidelberg Deli next door (open Tuesday through Saturday 9–6) stocks kielbasa, liver dumplings, Bitburger beer, breads, and nearly a dozen mustards. ⊠*900 State Rd. 84* ☎*954/463–6747 or 954/463–3880* ⊟*AE, D, MC, V* ⊘*Closed Mon. No lunch Sat.*

IRISH

¢-$ ✗**Maguire's Hill 16.** With the requisite lineup of libations and sandwiches, this comfortable and long-popular Irish pub has a very tasty potato soup, shepherd's pie, bangers and mash, corned beef and cabbage, and Irish stew. ⊠*535 N. Andrews Ave.* ☎*954/764–4453* ⊟*AE, D, DC, MC, V.*

ITALIAN

$$-$$$$ ✗**Primavera.** Tucked inside an ordinary shopping plaza is this extraordinary find. Apart from fresh pasta with rich sauces and risotto entrées, choose from creative fish, poultry, veal, and beef dinners. Among chef-owner Giacomo Dresseno's favorites is a double-cut veal chop. If you're in town for a while, check out the chef's lunch ($45) or dinner ($50) cooking classes. Ticket holders appreciate the pre-theater menu. ⊠*830 E. Oakland Park Blvd.* ☎*954/564–6363* ⊟*AE, D, DC, MC, V* ⊘*Closed Mon. No lunch.*

$-$$$$ **✕Casa D'Angelo.** Owner-chef Angelo Elia has re-created his former Café D'Angelo into a gem of a Tuscan-style white-tablecloth restaurant, tucked in the Sunrise Square shopping center. Casa D'Angelo's oak oven turns out marvelous seafood and beef dishes. The pappardelle with porcini mushrooms takes pasta to pleasant heights. Another favorite is the calamari-and-scungilli salad with garlic and lemon. Ask about the oven-roasted fish of the day. ⊠*1201 N. Federal Hwy.* ☎*954/564–1234* ⊟*AE, D, DC, MC, V* ☾*No lunch.*

¢-$$$ **✕Louie, Louie Bistro.** Some of the best pasta dishes on Las Olas are served at this friendly, tavern-style establishment with white twinkling lights out front, along with a few tables. Try thin-crust pizzas, sandwiches, or complete dinners. Fresh-fish specials are offered daily. Grouper, when available, is excellent. Wash it all down with any of eight on-tap beers, or select from the wine list. ⊠*1404 E. Las Olas Blvd.* ☎*954/524–5200* ⊟*AE, MC, V.*

MEDITERRANEAN

$$$-$$$$ **✕Trina.** You might well fill up on eyefuls of Fort Lauderdale Beach during breakfast or lunch at this spot on the ground level of the Atlantic hotel, but come dinnertime your focus will shift to the crackling activity in the open kitchen and among the well-heeled crowd. Trina, of course, is derived from Trinakria, a symbol of the three-legged medusa found on the flag of Sicily. Warm wood tones and minimalist fixtures mirror the Atlantic's restrained elegance, but there's a touch of New York fanfare on the menu, in part because Don Pintabona, former executive chef of Tribeca Grill, is running the kitchen. Seafood dominates, with some interesting results: scallops and sweetbreads mingle in one entrée, whereas Florida favorites like snapper and sole get Mediterranean touches. One successful leitmotif is flatbread: a tasty herbed variation with pancetta at breakfast, or with such toppings as rock shrimp or spicy Moroccan lamb at dinner. Another good bet is a Trina Trio, which might include an appetizer of tuna carpaccio, salmon tartare, and snapper ceviche, or a crème brûlée sampler including coffee, chocolate and, most worthy, coconut. Reservations are recommended. ⊠*601 N. Fort Lauderdale Beach Blvd.* ☎*954/567–8020* ⊟*AE, D, DC, MC, V.*

MEXICAN

$$$ **✕Carlos & Pepe's.** In a strip shopping center west of the 17th Causeway bridge, this favorite among locals, with its cozy booths and tables amid Mexican tile decor, has long been known for icy margaritas, chips and salsa, and tasty fare from omelets to Mexican pizza. On the downside, its icon margaritas for the past couple of years have been served in beer-style tumblers rather than stemmed margarita ware of old (management mumbles something about breakage and safety). On the upside, the Tuna Dip that goes so well with those libations has retained its luster. Open nightly for dinner and for lunch on Saturday and Sunday. ⊠*1302 S.E. 17th Street, Harbor Beach* ☎*954/467–7192* ⊟*AE, D MC, V.*

¢ **✕Tortilleria Mexicana.** With a machine about the size of an old home-style Mixmaster cranking out 1,000 pounds of cornmeal tortillas daily (double that on weekends) as you watch, the tiny hole-in-the-wall Tortilleria Mexicana, near Oakland Park City Hall, has authentic fare that attracts Broward's growing Mexican population and plenty of gringos to boot. Try such staples as tacos, tamales, chicken with rice and beans, enchiladas, quesadillas, and flautas with chicken, salad, and hot pepper slices. Owner Eliseo Martinez opened a second tortilla haven, in Pompano Beach, this one with a bakery and butcher shop. ⊠ *4115 N. Dixie Hwy., Oakland Park* ☎ *954/563–2503* ⊠ *1614 E. Sample Rd., Pompano Beach* ☎ *954/943–0057* ▤ *MC, V.*

SEAFOOD

★ **$$$–$$$$** ✕ **Blue Moon Fish Company.** Most tables have stellar views of the Intracoastal Waterway, but Blue Moon's true magic comes from the kitchen, where chefs Baron Skorish and Bryce Statham create moon-and-stars-worthy seafood dishes. Start with the raw bar, a sushi sampler, or pan-seared fresh-shucked oysters. Salads include a hydroponic Bibb with candied walnuts, and entrée favorites include lumb crab and corn roasted grouper with asparagus risotto ($30) or peppercorn-crusted big-eye tuna with sticky rice ($28). Carnivores might opt for prosciutto-stuffed veal tenderloin ($36). To wrap up an evening, indulge in the Tartelette of Bananas Foster Blue Moon. Book early, even in the off-season, for the popular Sunday champagne brunches ($29.95). ⊠ *4405 W. Tradewinds Ave.* ☎ *954/267–9888* ▤ *AE, D, DC, MC, V.*

$$–$$$$ ✕ **15th Street Fisheries.** A prime Intracoastal Waterway view is a big part of allure at this two-story seafood landmark alternately drawing praise and pans from patrons, some complaining about lackluster service during financial seminars—also known as plate lickers—booked upstairs. Now back under the original ownership, the old 15th is carrying on with spicy conch chowder, cold seafood salads, and homemade breads, a specialty, with a cheese-and-chive spread. Grilled mahimahi and alligator are among the more than 50 entrées. The key lime pie has an Oreo crust. Valet parking costs $2 at dinner, but it's free at lunch. ⊠ *1900 S.E. 15th St.* ☎ *954/763–2777* ▤ *AE, D, DC, MC, V.*

$$–$$$$ ✕ **Rustic Inn Crabhouse.** The late Wayne McDonald started with a cozy one-room roadhouse in 1955, when this stretch was a remote service road just west of the little airport. Now run by Wayne's family, the still-rustic place brags that it is still crackin' after 50 years. The ample menu once luring entertainer Arthur Godfrey, and more recently Johnny Depp and Dan Marino, features garlic crabs, with patrons banging crabs open with mallets on tables covered with newspapers, and peel-and-eat shrimp, served either with garlic and butter or spiced and steamed. Lunch includes a fine fish sandwich with fries and a soda for less than $5. Finish off with pie or cheesecake. ⊠ *4331 Ravenswood Rd.* ☎ *954/584–1637* ▤ *AE, D, DC, MC, V.*

SOUTHWESTERN

$$–$$$ ✕ **Canyon Southwest Cafe.** Southwestern fusion fare adventure helps you escape the ordinary at this small, stylish enclave (next to the Gateway movie theater at Sunrise Boulevard and Federal Highway) run for the past dozen years by owner and executive chef Chris Wilber. Take, for example, the ostrich skewers, smoked salmon tostada, or coriander-crusted tuna with sticky rice. Chipotle, wasabi, jalapeño, mango, and red chilies accent fresh seafood and wild game. Start off with Canyon's famous prickly-pear margaritas or choose from a well-rounded wine list or beer selection. ⊠ *1818 E. Sunrise Blvd.* ☎ *954/765–1950* ⊟ *AE, MC, V* ⊘ *No lunch.*

WHERE TO STAY

DOWNTOWN & BEACH CAUSEWAYS

$$$–$$$$
Fodor'sChoice
★
🏨 **Hyatt Regency Pier Sixty-Six.** Unfortunately, the trademark of this high-rise resort on the Intracoastal Waterway—the rooftop Pier Top Lounge—has closed, and is now a banquet-meeting space. Still, the 17-story tower dominates a lovely 22-acre spread that includes Spa 66, a full-service European-style spa. Each room has a balcony with views of the 142-slip marina, pool, ocean, or Intracoastal. Some guests prefer the ground-level lanai rooms. Lush landscaping and convenience to the beach, shopping, and restaurants add to overall allure. Hail the Water Bus at the resort's dock for access to downtown or the beach. **Pros:** Continuing upgrades over the decades have maintained quality. **Cons:** Spa (added long after hotel debut) is relegated to space that somehow has always seemed like an afterthought. ⊠ *2301 S.E. 17th St. Causeway* ☎ *954/525–6666 or 800/327–3796* 📠 *954/728–3551* ⊕ *www. pier66.com* 🛏 *380 rooms, 8 suites* ♿ *In-hotel: 6 restaurants, bars, tennis courts, pools, gym, spa, water sports* ⊟ *AE, D, DC, MC, V.*

$$$–$$$$
🏨 **Riverside Hotel.** On Las Olas Boulevard, just steps from boutiques, restaurants, and art galleries, Fort Lauderdale's oldest hotel was built in 1936, and within the past decade added luster with a $25 million renovation and expansion. Penthouse suites in the newer 12-story executive tower have balconies with sweeping views of Las Olas, New River, and downtown's skyline. Historic photos grace hallways, and rooms are outfitted with antique oak furnishings and framed French prints. Enjoy afternoon tea in the newly spruced-up lobby, and dine at Indigo, where American favorites include steaks and seafood, or the elegant Grill Room. The hotel's new Wine Room for private dining has a 1,500-bottle cellar, and a reservations-only English afternoon tea program (choose from Classic, Full, or Royal) uunfolds in the lobby. **Pros:** Historic appeal in the thick of action downtown. **Cons:** No quickie access to either beach or golf. ⊠ *620 E. Las Olas Blvd.* ☎ *954/467–0671 or 800/325–3280* 📠 *954/462–2148* ⊕ *www.riversidehotel.com* 🛏 *206 rooms, 11 suites* ♿ *In-hotel: 3 restaurants, bars, pool, no-smoking rooms* ⊟ *AE, DC, MC, V.*

$$$–$$$$
🏨 **Schubert Resort.** This restored 1950s Art Deco property is an all-male, clothing-optional boutique resort tucked into tropical landscaping within the Victoria Park neighborhood. Suites are oversize and have marble-and-granite baths; most have either a king-size bed or two double beds. Continental breakfast is served overlook-

6

> **WORD OF MOUTH**
>
> "If you want a really cool hotel, stay at the Riverside on Los Olas Boulevard. Plenty of upscale nightlife and shopping. IMO it's a much better spot than close to the beach."
>
> –Pugsly

ing the pool and Jacuzzi. The property feels secluded yet is a short walk from shopping and restaurants. **Pros:** Friendly, well-managed. **Cons:** Clean and tidy, but somewhat dated decor. ✉*855 N.E. 20th Ave.* ☎*954/763–7434 or 866/338–7666* 🖷*954/763–4132* ⊕*www. schubertresort.com* 🗨*30 rooms* ⚬*In-room: kitchen (some). In-hotel: pool* ☰*AE, DC, MC, V* ⦿*CP.*

ALONG THE BEACH

★ $$$$ ▦ **The Atlantic.** Functional but elegant is the principle behind this luxury condo hotel, a Starwood newcomer steps from Las Olas Boulevard and the Atlantic beyond. In lieu of having you hunch over the front desk, staffers check you in one-on-one while you sip an icy libation in the lobby, a marriage of marble and wood, beiges and browns. This British-colonial scheme is picked up in the spacious, unfussy rooms, which have simple, dark-wood furniture, ample marble kitchen areas, and creamy fabrics and plush carpeting that smartly frame rather than compete with the main event—balcony views of the city or ocean (go for the latter). Little in-room touches include Bose Wave CD/radio systems and a host of Internet connection options; among on-premises amenities are a European-style spa offering treatments and massages within the spa or in-room, and the tony Trina lounge and restaurant, or Spuma, for light fare with a pool view. **Pros:** Among Fort Lauderdale's most sophisticated options. **Cons:** It's across busy A1A from beach, not on beach. ✉*601 N. Fort Lauderdale Beach Blvd.* ☎*954/567–8020* 🖷*954/567–8040* ⊕*www.luxurycollection.com/atlantic* 🗨*61 rooms, 58 suites, 5 penthouses* ⚬*In-room: kitchen, refrigerator (some), dialup, Wi-Fi. In-hotel: 2 restaurants, bar, pool, gym, spa, concierge, laundry service, parking (fee), no-smoking rooms* ☰*AE, D, DC, MC, V.*

$$$–$$$$ ▦ **Best Western Pelican Beach.** On the beach and under new owner-
★ ☾   ship, this already lovely property has been transformed into an entirely new no-smoking resort with a restaurant and lounge, an old-fashioned ice-cream parlor, and Fort Lauderdale's only lazy river pool, allowing guests to float around a moatlike "river." For small fry, there's also a Funky Fish program. Of 156 rooms and one-bedroom suites in the new building, 117 are oceanfront. With the new building all aglow, the original Sun Tower has gotten a makeover. **Pros:** You can't get any closer to the beach in Fort Lauderdale. **Cons:** You'll need wheels to access Las Olas beach area action. ✉*2000 N. Atlantic Blvd.* ☎*954/568–9431 or 800/525–6232* 🖷*954/565–2622* ⊕*www.pelicanbeach.com* 🗨*180 rooms* ⚬*In-hotel: restaurant, bar, pools* ☰*AE, DC, MC, V.*

$$$–$$$$ ▦ **Hilton Fort Lauderdale Beach Resort.** Dominating a corner facing A1A and the ocean, this 26-story, amenity-packed sparkler has loads of retail space, and a spa that schedules poolside massages. A 25,000 square foot, sixth-floor pool deck features private cabanas and Ilios for casual fare. Aquinox, as an upscale seafood venue, was very near opening at press time. Count on a multilingual concierge staff, and deluxe turndown service. For a fee with advance notice, you can arrange with the grocery concierge to stock your quarters with favorites prior to check-in. Room amenities include marble flooring, marble bathroom vanities, and high-definition flat-screen televisions, and suites have washers and dryers. **Pros:** Ultra-friendly service to go with shiny new ameni-

ties. **Cons:** Despite "every room has an ocean view" marketing, some have only neck-craning, partial sea views. ⊠*505 N. Fort Lauderdale Beach Blvd.* ☎*954/760–7177* ⊕*www.fortlauderdalebeachresort. hilton.com* ⟿*333 units, from 186 studios to 1- to-3-bedroom suites* ⌂*In-hotel: restaurant, pools, spa* ▤*AE, D, DC, MC, V.*

WORD OF MOUTH

"Loved Lago Mar. The rooms are spacious and clean, nice pools and nice beach. Restaurant is very good. You would need a car to get to other places in Fort Lauderdale but I think it is worth it"

–lindafromNJ

★ **$$–$$$** ⊡ **Lago Mar Resort & Club.** The sprawling Lago Mar, owned by the Banks family since the early 1950s, has retained its sparkle thanks to significant upgrades. Most accommodations are suites, ideal for families. Suite highlights include a king-size bed, pull-out sofa, and full kitchen. All rooms have granite countertops, cordless phones, CD clock radios and Wi-Fi. Trellises and bougainvillea plantings edge the swimming lagoon, and you have direct access to a large private beach in an exclusive neighborhood. Acquario serves northern Italian cuisine nightly, although kids and the young-at-heart gravitate toward the Soda Shop, a combo gift shop, bakery, and ice-cream parlor. **Pros:** Secluded setting far from the madding crowds. **Cons:** Not the easiest to find if you don't have GPS, even if you're familiar with the property. ⊠*1700 S. Ocean La.* ☎*954/523–6511 or 800/524–6627* ▤*954/524– 6627* ⊕*www.lagomar.com* ⟿*52 rooms, 160 suites* ⌂*In-hotel: 3 restaurants, tennis court, pools* ▤*AE, DC, MC, V.*

$$–$$$ ⊡ **The Pillars Hotel at New River Sound.** Described as Fort Lauderdale's "small secret" by locals in the know, this gem is one block in from the beach on the Intracoastal. Its design recalls the colorful architecture of 18th-century British-colonial Caribbean plantations. Most rooms have views of the waterway or pool, with French doors opening to individual patios or balconies. Rooms have rattan-and-mahogany headboards, antique reproduction desks and nightstands, and lush draperies. Suites include wet bars with refrigerators and microwaves. **Pros:** Attentive, polished staff. **Cons:** When inclement weather curbs access to idyllic pool and grounds, small rooms can seem claustrophic. ⊠*111 N. Birch Rd.* ☎*954/467–9639* ▤*954/763–2845* ⊕*www.pillarshotel.com* ⟿*19 rooms, 4 suites* ⌂*In-room: refrigerator (some), VCR, Ethernet. In-hotel: room service, pool, no elevator, concierge, no kids under 12, no-smoking rooms* ▤*AE, D, DC, MC, V.*

$–$$$ ⊡ **The Alcazar Resort.** For decades known as the family-owned, family-oriented Sea Chateau, this property has been acquired by owners of the Worthington (next door), who transformed the two-story enclave about a block from the beach into a gay-friendly place. A 24-hour clothing-optional heated swimming pool and shaded courtyard are within the now-fenced property, and corner efficiencies with kitchenettes are now called junior suites. Most beds are king-size, although some rooms have pairs of queen-size beds. **Pros:** Architecture buffs may appreciate the Miami Modern (MiMo) effect on balcony rail overlooking pool. **Cons:** Close to water, but no view. ⊠*555 N. Birch Rd.* ☎*954/567–2525*

6

⊕*www.alcazarresort.com* ⇔*15 rooms, 5 suites* ⚄*In-room: kitchen (some), refrigerator. In-hotel: pool, no elevator* ☐*AE, D, DC, MC, V.*

NIGHTLIFE & THE ARTS

For the most complete weekly listing of events, check the "Showtime!" entertainment section and events calendar in the *South Florida Sun-Sentinel.* "Weekend," in the Friday Broward edition of *The Herald,* also lists area happenings. The weekly *City Link* is principally an entertainment and dining paper with an "underground" look. *New Times* is a free alternative weekly circulating a Broward–Palm Beach County edition. *East Sider* is another free weekly entertainment guide. Broward County's new Web site for **Arts & Entertainment** is www.broward. org/arts. Get tickets at individual box offices and through **Ticketmaster** (☎*954/523–3309*); there's a service charge.

THE ARTS
Broward Center for the Performing Arts (✉*201 S.W. 5th Ave.* ☎*954/462–0222*) is the waterfront centerpiece of Fort Lauderdale's arts district. More than 500 events unfold annually at the 2,700-seat architectural masterpiece, including Broadway-style musicals, plays, dance, symphony, opera, rock, film, lectures, comedy, and children's theater. An enclosed elevated walkway links to a parking garage across the street. **Cinema Paradiso** (✉*503 S.E. 6th St.* ☎*954/525–3456* ⊕*www.cinema paradiso.org*) operates as an art-house movie theater from a former church (south of New River). The space doubles as headquarters for FLIFF, the Fort Lauderdale International Film Festival. Screenings stretch from extreme sports to anime.

★ **Chef Jean-Pierre Cooking School** (✉*1436 N. Federal Hwy.* ☎*954/563–2700* ⊕*www.chefjp.com* ✉*$50 per class, $285 per series* ☉*10 AM–7 PM*) carries on from the long gone Left Bank by New River Tunnel, with Chef Jean-Pierre Brehier now presiding at his school and cookware shop. Teaching basics from boiling water onward to more than 7,000 avid learners since 1997, the enthusiastic Gallic transplant has appeared on PBS, NBC's *Today,* and CNN's *Larry King Live.* Chef J-P's fun cooking facility also sells nifty pots, pastas, oils, and other irresistibles. **Laffing Matterz.** Across from the Museum of Art in an old five-and-dime that still has its circa 1936 McCrory logo carved on the facade, all-American guffaws at this live musical comedy review target politics, sports, and celebrity machinations. Entrance, $45 to $54.50 for reserved tiered circular seating surrounding the stage, covers show, house salad, and entrées like beef tenderloin and teriyaki salmon. Appetizers, desserts, and libations such as the Laffing Martini ($8.95) are extra. Laffing Matterz promises that although it's fine to dress casual, you might get stares if you show up in bathing suits. Geared toward grown-ups, there's no kid's menu. ✉*219 S. Andrews Ave.* ☎*954/763–5236* ☐*AE, D, MC, V.*

An African-American Gem

West of downtown Fort Lauderdale's Arts & Sciences District, in the heart of the African-American community along Sistrunk Boulevard, lies a gem once discounted as a grand idea unlikely to get off the ground.

Yet in late 2002, Fort Lauderdale's African-American Research Library and Cultural Center soared into reality as a sparkling two-story, $14 million repository of history and heritage of African, African-American, and Caribbean cultures, with historic books, papers, and art, much of it pertaining to the African diaspora. There's a 300-seat auditorium, a story-time area, and 5,000 square feet of gallery space for exhibits. African symbols appear as part of the decor.

For Samuel F. Morrison, now-retired Broward County Library director, the center is the culmination of his dream, a vision to create a worthy showcase reflecting African-American heritage. Broward County anted up $5 million for the 60,000-square-foot center, and Morrison raised the rest.

Of the nation's three major African-American public research facilities, Fort Lauderdale's also has a Caribbean focus. Offerings include the Alex Haley Collection, with eight unfinished manuscripts. Other components range from Fisk University research of slave narratives to books on Jamaica. You'll also find the Kitty Oliver Oral Histories Collection on Broward and Okeechobee and the Niara Sudarkasa Collection of papers, artwork, and other materials of the former president of Lincoln University.

And there's the collection of Dorothy Porter Wesley—in some eyes the greatest of the black bibliophiles. Her collection includes about 500 inscribed and autographed books—some date to 1836—with personal narratives, histories, fiction, and reference works. Wesley's daughter, Constance Porter Uzelac, refers to "Mama's stuff." Wesley was known for going to the homes of the recently deceased to make sure nothing of value got tossed. Her daughter recalls, "She'd get to the house before the body was cold," heading straight to attics and basements to retrieve bits and scraps of history.

Passionate about his dream, Morrison also remains adamant about the library's widespread appeal, noting that "these pieces provide glimpses [into] the hearts and minds of people who have made a difference in the lives of not only people of color and African culture, but people of many colors and cultures."

—Lynne Helm

NIGHTLIFE

BARS & LOUNGES

Automatic Slims (⊠ *15 W. Las Olas Blvd.* ☎ *(954) 522–8585* ☎)is neon-lit and plenty loud; hordes jam in to do shots and hang out. I **Laguna Beach** (⊠ *The Gallery at Beach Pl.* ☎ *954/523-7377*) has stepped in and glammed up space previously occupied by the defunct Hurricane Bar & Grill, Crazy Louie's, and Cafe Iguana. **Howl at the Moon Saloon/Sloppy Joe's** (⊠ *The Gallery at Beach Place, 17 S. Fort Lauderdale Beach Blvd.* ☎ *954/522–5054*) has dueling piano players and sing-alongs Wednesday through Sunday. Sloppy Joe's, a take-off on the iconic Key West bar, is open nightly. **Maguire's Hill 16** (⊠ *535*

N. Andrews Ave. ☎954/764–4453) hosts live music in classic Irish-pub surroundings. **O'Hara's Jazz & Blues Café** (✉*722 E. Las Olas Blvd.* ☎954/524–1764) takes pride in giving good sax nightly, with live jazz, blues, R&B, and funk. Its crowd spills onto this prettiest of downtown streets. **Coyote Ugly** (✉*220 S.W. 2nd St.* ☎954/764–8459) continues a tradition of being one of the hottest spots in Broward. **Tarpon Bend** (✉*200 S.W. 2nd St.* ☎954/523–3233) specialties—food, fishing gear, and bands covering current hits—draw a casual, beer-drinking crowd. **Tavern 213** (✉*213 S.W. 2nd St.* ☎954/463–6213) is a small, no-frills club where cover bands do classic rock nightly. **Voodoo Lounge** (✉*111 S.W. 2nd Ave.* ☎954/522–0733) plays the latest in club music inside the nightclub and hip-hop on the elegant outside deck. There's a VIP room, and the scene here doesn't start until almost midnight.

SPORTS & THE OUTDOORS

BIKING

Among the most popular routes are Route A1A and Bayview Drive, especially in early morning before traffic builds, and a 7-mi bike path that parallels State Road 84 and the New River and leads to Markham Park, which has mountain-bike trails. ■ TIP→**Alligator alert: Do not dangle your legs from seawalls.**

FISHING

If you're interested in a saltwater charter, check out the **Radisson Bahia Mar Beach Resort** (✉*801 Seabreeze Blvd.* ☎954/627–6357 or 954/764–2233). Both sportfishing and drift-fishing bookings can be arranged.

GOLF

Ten miles from Fort Lauderdale in Dade County are two newly revamped 18-hole courses reflecting $100,000 of landscaping per hole, and a new driving range at Fairmont **Turnberry Isle Resort & Club** (✉*19999 W. Country Club Dr., Aventura* ☎305/933–6929 or 800/327–7028 ⊕*www.turnberryisle.com*); greens fee $95/$150.

SCUBA DIVING & SNORKELING

Lauderdale Diver (✉*1334 S.E. 17th St. Causeway* ☎954/467–2822 or 800/654–2073), which is PADI-affiliated, arranges dive charters throughout the county. Dive trips typically last four hours. Nonpackage reef trips are open to divers for around $50; scuba gear is extra. **Pro Dive** (✉*515 Seabreeze Blvd.* ☎954/761–3413 or 800/776–3483), a PADI five-star facility, is the area's oldest diving operation and offers packages with several hotels, including the Radisson Bahia Mar Beach Resort, from which its 60-foot boat departs. Snorkelers can go out for $29 on a two-hour snorkeling trip, including equipment. Scuba divers pay $45 using their own gear or $94 with full scuba and snorkel rental gear included.

TENNIS

With 22 courts (18 lighted clay courts, three hard courts, and a newer low-compression sand "beach" court), the **Jimmy Evert Tennis Center at Holiday Park** is the crown jewel of Fort Lauderdale's public tennis facilities. Chris Evert learned the sport here under the watchful eye of her father, Jimmy, who retired after 37 years as the center's tennis pro. ✉*701 N.E. 12th Ave.* ☎*954/828–5378* ⬛*$6 per person per hr* ⏱*Weekdays 8* AM*–9* PM*, weekends 8–6.*

SHOPPING

MALLS

Just north of Las Olas Boulevard on Route A1A is **The Gallery at Beach Place** (✉*17 S. Fort Lauderdale Beach Blvd. [A1A]*). Browse shops, have lunch or dinner at restaurants ranging from casual Caribbean to elegant American, or carouse at assorted nightspots—open late. Lower-level eateries tend toward the more upscale, whereas upper-level prices are lower (go figure), with superior ocean views. ■**TIP➔Beach Place has covered parking, but you can pinch pennies by using a nearby municipal lot.** Just west of the Intracoastal Waterway, the split-level **Galleria Mall** (✉*2414 E. Sunrise Blvd.*) entices with Neiman Marcus, Dillard's, Macy's, and Saks Fifth Avenue, plus 150 specialty shops for anything from cookware to exquisite jewelry. Chow down at Capital Grille, Blue Martini, Mama Sbarro's, and Seasons 52, or head for the food court, a decided cut above at this upscale mall open 10 to 9 Monday through Saturday, and noon to 5:30 Sunday. The **Swap Shop** (✉*3291 W. Sunrise Blvd.*) is the South's largest flea market, with 2,000 vendors open daily. While exploring this indoor–outdoor entertainment and shopping complex, hop on the carousel or stick around for Swap Shop drive-in movies.

SHOPPING DISTRICTS

When you're downtown, check out **Las Olas Riverfront** (✉*1 block west of Andrews Ave. along New River*), a shopping, dining, and entertainment complex. **Vogue Italia** (✉*Las Olas Riverfront, 300 S.W. 1st Ave.* ☎*954/527–4568*) is packed with trendy fashions by D&G, Ferré, Versus, Moschino, and Iceberg, among others, at wholesale prices. If only for a stroll and some window-shopping, don't miss **Las Olas Boulevard** (✉*1 block off New River east of Andrews Ave.*). The city's best boutiques plus top restaurants and art galleries line a beautifully landscaped street. **American Soul** (✉*810 E. Las Olas Blvd.* ☎*954/462–4224*) carries menswear from suits to socks, along with leather goods and gifts. **Casa Chameleon** (✉*619 E. Las Olas Blvd.* ☎*954/763–2543*) has antiques and beautiful things to top your table. The sweet smell of waffle cones lures pedestrians to **Kilwin's of Las Olas** (✉*809 E. Las Olas Blvd.* ☎*954/523–8338*), an old-fashioned confectionery that also sells hand-paddled fudge and scoops of homemade ice cream. **Lauderdale Lifestyle–A Lilly Pulitzer Signature Store** (✉*819 E. Las Olas Blvd.* ☎*954/524–5459*) specializes in the South Florida dress requisite—clothing and accessories in Lilly Pulitzer's signature tropical colors and prints. **Seldom Seen** (✉*817 E. Las Olas Blvd.* ☎*954/764–5590*) is a gallery of contemporary and folk art, including furniture, jewelry, ceramics, sculpture, and blown glass. **Zola Keller** (✉*818 E. Las Olas Blvd.* ☎*954/462–3222*) sells special-occasion dresses—cocktail dresses, evening gowns, vow-renewal apparel, and, yes, pageant dresses.

6

Victoria's Bridal Couture (✉ *E. Las Olas Blvd.* ☎*954/522–167*)attracts brides-to-be (or wannabes) with gowns by top designers including Manhattan's Judd Waddell.

SIDE TRIPS

THE WESTERN SUBURBS & BEYOND

West of Fort Lauderdale is ever-growing suburbia, with most of Broward's golf courses, attractions, and malls. As you head west, the terrain takes on more characteristics of the Everglades, and you'll occasionally see alligators sunning on canal banks. Cute as they appear, please refrain from feeding. Keep Fido out of sight, too, as gators find small dogs especially tasty. Iguanas, often discarded as pets (and comparatively harmless except for spreading salmonella when handled), are proliferating here as sunbathers.

As many as 80 butterfly species from South and Central America, the Philippines, Malaysia, Taiwan, and other Asian nations are typically found within the serenity of **Butterfly World**, a 3-acre site inside Tradewinds Park (itself a delight with fishing, an educational farm, horseback riding, and sports-equipment rental). A screened aviary called North American Butterflies is reserved for native species. The Tropical Rain Forest Aviary is a 30-foot-high construction, with observation decks, waterfalls, ponds, and tunnels where thousands of colorful butterflies flutter. Kids bug out on the bug zoo. ✉*3600 W. Sample Rd., Coconut Creek* ☎*954/977–4400* ⊕*www.butterflyworld.com* ✑*$21.95* ☉*Mon.–Sat. 9–5, Sun. 11–5.*

The 30-acre **Everglades Holiday Park** provides brag-worthy glimpses of the Everglades. Take an airboat tour, look at an 18th-century-style Native American village, or catch the alligator wrestling (not to be reenacted at home). A souvenir shop, a deli, a convenience store, and a campground with RV hookups ($24.40 per night) and tent sites ($22 nightly) are all here. ✉*21940 Griffin Rd.* ☎*954/434–8111* ⊕*www. evergladesholidaypark.com* ✑*Free, airboat tour $21* ☉*Daily 9–5.*

For an ever-so-thrilling Everglades experience, take an airboat ride at **Sawgrass Recreation Park.** You'll see all sorts of plants and wildlife, from birds and alligators to turtles, snakes, and fish. Besides the ride, your entrance fee covers admission to an Everglades nature exhibit, a native Seminole village, and exhibits about alligators, other reptiles, and birds of prey. A souvenir shop, food service, boat rental ($49 for for four hours), and an RV park with hookups are also at the park. ✉*U. S. 27 north of I–595* ☎*954/389–0202* ⊕*www.evergladestours.com* ✑*$19.50* ☉*Weekdays 7–6, weekends 6–6; airboat rides daily 9–5.*

A stretch from Fort Lauderdale's beaches, but worth the hour-plus drive, is the **Big Cypress Seminole Reservation** and its two very different attractions. At the **Billie Swamp Safari,** experience the majesty of the Everglades firsthand. Daily tours of the wetlands and hammocks, where wildlife abounds, yield sightings of deer, water buffalo, bison, wild hogs, hawks, eagles, alligators, and occasionally the rare Florida

CLOSE UP

Swap till You Drop

Just when you thought it was safe to head for the beach, the siren's song of dirt-cheap bargain-hunting draws you to a sprawling, sun-baked patch of land where you can park free, get in free, browse free, and load up with eclectic acquisitions or plain swell stuff for darned-near free.

From Barbie dolls to slightly used miter saws, here's a place where you can feel free to squeeze nickels until the buffalos moan. Fort Lauderdale's Swap Shop—among Florida's largest tourist draws long before the day of sub-prime mortgage havoc—is a 180,000-square-foot shopping-entertainment complex, on 88 acres and painted in screaming yellow, that makes it possible to find dollar-store items for a dime, hand-dipped mango incense for a couple of bucks, and fresh Florida produce on your way to the parking lot. Psychic readings are negotiable, and it's $15 for 15 minutes at the Chinese Backrub Booth, near a stall where you can get tailoring done while you wait. A small midway with a merry-go-round near the pedestrian walkway over Sunrise Boulevard houses a giant video arcade and eateries. You can hang around past dusk to catch flicks from Mad Money to Rambo at the Swap Shop Drive-In, now with 14 screens.

Established in 1963 by Betty and Preston Henn, the Fort Lauderdale

Swap Shop stems from what originally was known as the Thunderbird, one of America's then-ubiquitous drive-ins. By 1966, Henn started farming out his land as a weekend flea market. As drive-ins went bust, the Thunderbird held on, propped up by Swap Shop revenues. By 1979 Henn had put up a building as an open-air food court surrounded by vendors. In 1988 he walled it in, adding air-conditioning and a stage where local bands jammed at no charge. Next came a circus, later phased out in favor of a high-end auto display. In 1990 singer Ronnie Milsap kicked off a free-concert tradition. And the rest, as they say, is drive-in-movie-aficionado history.

Henn, a handsome devil now well into the un-sunny side of 70, made news in 2005 when he got into a scuffle with a tenant, after which Broward Sheriff's Office deputies took a notion to taser-gun the Swap Shop king. Henn bounced back with an ad campaign proclaiming "Crazy… Loco…Insane…Our Swap Shop prices are so low that they're tasering me." The Swap Shop pulls in more than 12 million visitors a year. Fort Lauderdale Swap Shop grounds are between Interstate 95 and Florida's Turnpike at 3291 E. Sunrise Blvd., 954/791–7927.

—Lynne Helm

6

panther. Animal and reptile shows are entertaining. Ecoheritage tours are conducted aboard motorized swamp buggies, and airboat rides are available, too. On the property is Swamp Water Café, serving gator nuggets, frogs' legs, catfish, and Indian fry bread with honey, along with burgers and more. ⊠*19 mi north of I–75 Exit 49* ☎*863/983– 6101 or 800/949–6101* ⊕*www.seminoletribe.com* ✉*Seminole Village reservation, free; combined ecotour, reptile or critter show, and airboat ride, $43* ⊙*Daily 8–5.*

Not far from the Billie Swamp Safari is the **Ah-Tah-Thi-Ki Museum,** whose name means "a place to learn, a place to remember." It is just that. The museum documents and honors traditions and culture of the Seminole Tribe of Florida through artifacts, exhibits, and reenactments of rituals and ceremonies. The 60-acre site includes a living-history Seminole village, nature trails, and a wheel-chair accessible boardwalk through a cypress swamp. ⊠*17 mi north of I–75 Exit 49* ☎*863/902–1113* ⊕*www.seminoletribe.com* ✎*$6* ⊙*Tues.–Sun. 9–5.*

WHERE TO STAY

$$–$$$$ 🖫 **Coral Springs Marriott Hotel, Golf Club and Convention Center.** Adjacent to the Heron Bay Golf Club, this resort's perch near the Sawgrass Expressway also makes it convenient to area attractions. Spacious, updated rooms are furnished with oak and cherrywood. There's an outdoor terrace and a game room. **Pros:** Golfing proximity. **Cons:** Frequent convention hubbub. ⊠*11775 Heron Bay Blvd., Coral Springs* ☎*954/753–5598* 🖷*954/753–2888* ⊕*www.marriott.com* ✐*224 rooms, 7 suites* ⚿*In-room: Wi-Fi. In-hotel: restaurant, bar, golf course, pool, gym* ▤*AE, D, MC, V.*

$$–$$$$ 🖫 **Hyatt Regency Bonaventure Conference Center Hotel & Spa.** Formerly
Fodor'sChoice   a Wyndham, the new name (along with a $100 million renovation)
★   asserts itself as a decidedly more upscale venue targeting conventioneers as well as leisure guests who value golf or the Everglades over beach proximity. Factor in the allure of a huge Elizabeth Arden's Red Door Lifestyle Spa (48,000 square feet with 30 treatment rooms) with a Pilates studio, Hot Yoga Room, and Zen Garden, and you'll understand why. Shop & Drop packages with free transport to nearby Sawgrass Mills extend the appeal to an even wider audience. Spacious guest rooms (and public areas) have a light British-colonial-amid-an-oasis look, with plentiful modern amenities, including clock radios with iPod docks. Banyan Restaurant serves American and continental fare, and the Bamboo Spa Café dishes up tasty, nutritional fare. Golf and tennis facilities adjacent to the hotel are independent of the 23-acre resort. **Pros:** "Pets Can Stay" in your room program (for a $50 fee) provides canines with a bone, temporary ID tag, and a dog-walk route. **Cons:** Traffic on I-595 can impede off-property exploration. ⊠*250 Racquet Club Rd., Westin* ☎*954/616–1234* 🖷*954/384–6157* ⊕*www. bonaventure.hyatt.com* ✐*501 rooms* ⚿*In-hotel: 3 restaurants, bars, golf courses, tennis courts, 4 pools, gym, spa* ▤*AE, D, DC, MC, V.*

SHOPPING

Surveys reveal that shopping is vacationers' number-one activity. With 26 million visitors annually, **Sawgrass Mills** (⊠*12801 W. Sunrise Blvd., at Flamingo Rd., Sunrise*), 10 mi west of downtown Fort Lauderdale, proves the point, ranking as Florida's second-biggest tourist attraction, after Disney. The ever-growing complex has a basic alligator shape, and walking it all amounts to about a 2-mi jaunt, making comfy shoes a near necessity. Count on 11,000 self-parking spaces (note your location, or you'll be working those comfysoles), valet parking, and two information centers. More than 400 shops—many manufacturer's outlets, retail outlets, and name-brand discounters—include Abercrombie & Fitch Outlet, assorted Gaps, Chico's Outlet, Polo Ralph Lauren Factory Store, Super Target, and Ron Jon Surf Shop. Restaurants such as Cajun Grill, Cheeburger Cheeburger, the Cheesecake Factory, Mangia La Pasta, Rainforest Cafe, and others are joined by the inevitable Starbucks and entertainment venues—Regal 23 Cinemas, GameWorks, and Wannado City, billing itself as the nation's first interactive empowerment environment for ages four to 11. While parents shop, kids can role-play as firefighters, reporters, doctors, chefs, archaeologists, even

> ### WORD OF MOUTH
>
> "The kids would probably like Wannado City inside Sawgrass Mills Mall, way west on Sunrise Blvd. They can go in and pretend they are a firefighter, chef, or a number of other jobs. The mall also has the interactive Rainforest Cafe, which to me is overpriced, but the kids will get a kick out of it. And of course, you and your aunt can go shopping there."
>
> —Safarichick

King Tut, the boy-king from Egypt, among occupations. For upscale shopping, the Mediterranean-inspired, open-air **Colonnade Outlets at Sawgrass,** caters to the well-heeled—and those who want to look that way—with a David Yurman jewelry outlet, along with Valentino, Burberry, Kate Spade, and Vilebrequin outlets, for tantalizing openers. To top it off, a Grand Lux Cafe serving lunch, dinner, and afternoon tea is near a Paul (à la Paris) bakery. An expanded Neiman Marcus Last Call Clearance and the Off 5th Saks Fifth Avenue Outlet have relocated from Sawgrass Mills proper to the Colonnade.

With sprawling interior spaces rivaling all outdoors, **IKEA SUNRISE** (*151 136th Ave., Sunrise* ☎*954/838-9292* ⊕*www.ikea.com* ⊗*Mon.-Sat. 10 AM to 9 PM; Sun. 11 AM to 8 PM; Closed Thanksgiving and Christmas*) can seem like a mini-trip to Sweden—and a tasty one at that, given the mountains of Swedish meatballs in nutmeg cream sauce dispensed inside. Prepare to be unimpressed if you want—besviken as the Swedes say—but don't count on remaining so. The 293,000-sq ft store's "natural path" takes you past some 10,000 home-furnishing items and gadgets, 50 room settings, and three model homes, providing enough design inspiration to last this millennium. There's Smalland, the supervised in-store playhouse where parents can drop off tykes before shopping for homey stuff from cheese graters to media centers. Signs invite abuse of furnishings, so feel free to unleash your inner Tom Cruise on couches. Plastic bags for purchases cost a nickel, with proceeds donated to nationwide tree planting, and industrial-strength Big Blue Bags (59¢) proclaim where you've shopped. As for caloric seduction, Ikea's sunny second-floor eatery does a 99-cent breakfast of scrambled eggs, potatoes, and two bacon strips. Swedish coffee and a cinnamon roll are $1.50, and a $4.99 plate heaps on 15 meatballs, mashed potatoes, gravy, and lingonberry sauce. Gotta have more for your hotel-room microwave? Meatballs come frozen in 2.5 pound bags for $7.99 at another food station near checkout.

6

NORTH ON SCENIC A1A

North of Fort Lauderdale's Birch Recreation Area, Route A1A edges away from the beach through a stretch known as the Galt Ocean Mile, and a succession of oceanside communities lines up against the sea. Traffic can line up, too, as it passes through a changing pattern of beach-blocking high-rises and modest family vacation towns and back again. Here and there a scenic lighthouse or park dots the landscape, and other attractions and recreational activities are found inland.

LAUDERDALE-BY-THE-SEA

5 mi north of Fort Lauderdale.

Just north of Fort Lauderdale's northern boundary, this low-rise family resort town traditionally digs in its heels at mere mention of high-rises. The result is choice shoreline access that's rapidly disappearing in similar communities, and Lauderdale-by-the-Sea (L-B-T-S) takes delight in enhancing the beachgoing experience, adding such amenities as showers and bike racks. Where Commercial Boulevard meets the ocean, **Anglin's Fishing Pier** (shored up by new owners after repeated storm damage) stretches 875 feet into the Atlantic. You can sit on nearby canopied benches to soak up pier atmosphere or grab a bite at restaurants clustered around the seafront plaza.

WHERE TO EAT

$$-$$$ ✕**Sea Watch.** For more than 25 years this nautical-themed restaurant with a prime beach location has catered to the crowds for lunch and dinner. Among appetizers are oysters Rockefeller, gulf shrimp, clams casino, and Bahamian conch fritters. Daily entrées might include oat-crusted sautéed yellowtail snapper with roasted red bell-pepper sauce and basil, or charbroiled swordfish or dolphin fillet marinated with soy sauce, garlic, black pepper, and lemon juice. Early-bird multicourse dinners are $17.95, and 6-pound Maine lobsters flown in are $93. ⊠*6002 N. Ocean Blvd. (Rte. A1A), Fort Lauderdale* ☎*954/781–2200* ▤*AE, MC, V.*

$-$$$ ✕**Aruba Beach Café.** A big beachside barn of a place—very casual,
Fodor$Choice always crowded, always fun—Aruba serves Caribbean conch chow-
★   der and a Key West soup loaded with shrimp, calamari, and oysters, plus fresh tropical salads, sandwiches, and seafood. For less than $10, Aruba serves a mighty juicy burger with custom toppings. A band performs day and night, so head for the back corner with eye-popping views of the beach if you want conversation while you eat and drink. ⊠*1 E. Commercial Blvd.* ☎*954/776–0001* ▤*AE, D, DC, MC, V.*

WHERE TO STAY

$$-$$$$ ▦ **Best Florida Resort.** Although the name might seem a bit cocky, this fenced two-story oasis a block or so from the beach seduces with subtropical palm-fringed landscaping, creative decor, and other whimsical touches, including a supply-room sign warning of a make-believe attack alligator. Rooms showcase fresh takes on classic rattan and bamboo. Hospitable owners Bozena and Tomasz Jurczak, fluent in several

languages, provide no-smoking, pet-free respite without Spring Break revelry. Besides wireless Internet access, there's a barbecue grill for guest use, and one apartment unit has a private patio. **Pros:** Attentive management. **Cons:** Sooner or later you'll probably need to forsake the whimsy and go home. ✉*4628 N. Ocean Dr.* ☎*954/772–2500* ⊕*www.bestfloridamotel.com* ☞*12 units, including 1- and 2-bedroom units* ☐*AE, D, MC, V.*

$$-$$$$ 🖵 **Tropic Seas Resort Motel.** It's only a block off A1A, yet this two-story property has a multimillion-dollar location—directly on the beach and two blocks from municipal tennis courts. Built in the 1950s and spiffed up in 2007, units are plain but clean and comfortable, with tropical rattan furniture and ceiling fans. Coffee and Danish rolls are served daily. **Pros:** Family-owned and -managed. **Cons:** To avoid any disappointment, reservations dates should be double-checked. ✉*4616 El Mar Dr.* ☎*954/772–2555 or 800/952–9581* 🖷*954/771–5711* ⊕*www. tropicseasresort.com* ☞*3 rooms, 6 efficiencies, 7 apartments* ♿*In-hotel: pool, beachfront, no elevator* ☐*AE, D, DC, MC, V.*

$$-$$$ 🖵 **Sea Lord Hotel & Suites.** You won't need to wonder "are we there yet," since Sea Lord is spelled out loud and clear in huge letters on this attractive oceanside building, along a stretch of private beach. Enjoy a complimentary continental breakfast by the pool overlooking the ocean. Efficiencies and one- and two-bedroom units all have coffee-makers and refrigerators, and some have full kitchens. The staff prides itself on creating a warm, hospitable environment. **Pros:** Terrific beach location. **Cons:** Depending on the time of year, market conditions, and area events, you may encounter a four-night or longer minimum stay requirement. ✉*4140 El Mar Dr.* ☎*954/776–1505 or 800/344–4451* 🖷*954/776–1505*✖*www.sealord.com* ☞*48 rooms* ♿*In-room: kitchen (some). In-hotel: pool, beachfront, laundry facilities* ☐*AE, D, MC, V* ⦿|*CP.*

$$-$$$ 🖵 **A Little Inn by the Sea.** Subtropical charm flourishes at this two-story inn, which caters to an international clientele—French and English are spoken here. Rooms have bamboo-and-rattan furniture and nice views from private balconies, many facing the beach. **Pros:** Smack on the beach shaded by palms. **Cons:** Along with casual housekeeping standards, towels can be in short supply. ✉*4546 El Mar Dr.* ☎*954/772–2450 or 800/492–0311* 🖷*954/938–9354* ⊕*www.alittleinn.com* ☞*10 rooms, 7 suites, 12 efficiencies* ♿*In-hotel: pool, beachfront, bicycles, no elevator* ☐*AE, D, DC, MC, V* ⦿|*BP.*

★ $$-$$$ 🖵 **High Noon Beach Resort.** Flanked by the Nautilus Resort to the north and the Sea Foam Resort to the south, High Noon—family-owned and -run—plays the central role for this resort trio on the beach, where you'll find a comfortable place to relax morning, high noon, or night. Accommodations, either poolside or oceanfront, range from rooms to efficiency apartments with kitchens, to apartments with separate bedrooms and one or two baths. Wicker furnishings and a color scheme of sea foam, sage, and beiges prevail at High Noon; Sea Foam rooms have terra-cotta tile, and High Noon and Nautilus rooms have beige tile. **Pros:** Smack on the beach. **Cons:** Given high return guest rate, you'll need to book early. ✉*4424 El Mar Dr.* ☎*954/776–1121 or*

6

800/382–1265 ☎954/776–1124 ☞40 rooms ♿In-room: kitchen (some), refrigerator (some). In-hotel: pool, beachfront, no elevator ▤AE, D, DC, MC, V.

$-$$$ 🏨 **Blue Seas Courtyard.** Innkeeper Cristie Furth, with her husband, Marc, runs this small one- and two-story motel in a quiet resort area across from the beach. Lattice fencing, fountains, and gardens of cactus and impatiens provide privacy around the brick patio and pool. A palm-fringed Mexican hacienda look predominates, and guest quarters have hand-painted and stenciled furnishings and terra-cotta tiles. **Pros:** South-of-the-border verve with an outdoor smoking area. **Cons:** You'll need a second-floor room for a good view of the ocean across the street. ✉4525 El Mar Dr. ☎954/772–3336 ☎954/772–6337 ⊕www.blue seascourtyard.com ☞12 rooms ♿In-room: kitchen. In-hotel: pool, no elevator, laundry facilities ▤MC, V.

¢-$$ 🏨 **Great Escape Hotel.** For comfortable accommodations retaining a well-kept look of yesteryear amid palms and other tropical plants in a poolside courtyard, this could be your great—and economical—escape, while staying connected with Wi-Fi Internet. Among the units are four hotel rooms, five efficiencies, and two one-bedroom apartments. **Pros:** You can walk to the beach. **Cons:** Location prevents an ocean view. ✉4620 N. Ocean Dr. ☎954/772–1002 ☎954/772–6488 ⊕www. greatescapehotel.com ☞11 units ♿In-hotel: pool, no elevator, laundry facilities ▤AE, MC, V.

¢-$$ 🏨 **Villa Orleans.** With a touch of New Orleans architecture, this beach-area property rests behind an inviting pool and well-groomed grounds. Rooms, each with a kitchen area, are spacious, and all face the courtyard. **Pros:** Owner lives on property. **Cons:** Beach is a block away. ✉4513 N. Ocean Dr. ☎888/301–2363 ☎954/491–2363 ⊕www. villaorleans.com ☞12 rooms ♿In-room: Ethernet. In-hotel: pool, no elevator, laundry facilities ▤AE, MC, V.

THE OUTDOORS

★ **Anglin's Fishing Pier** (☎954/491–9403), a longtime favorite for 24-hour fishing, has new ownership and a fresh, newly renovated appearance after sustaining repeated storm damage that has closed the pier at intervals. Its tiny coffee shop—with a friendly staff and seats inside and outdoors—has survived the damage and renovation.

POMPANO BEACH

3 mi north of Lauderdale-by-the-Sea.

As Route A1A enters this town directly north of Lauderdale-by-the-Sea, the high-rise scene resumes. Sportfishing is big in Pompano Beach, as its name implies, but there's more to beachside attractions than the popular Fisherman's Wharf. Behind a low coral-rock wall, Alsdorf Park extends north and south of the wharf along the road and beach.

WHERE TO EAT & STAY

★ **$$$-$$$$** ✗**Cafe Maxx.** New-wave epicurean dining had its South Florida start here in the early 1980s, and Cafe Maxx remains new. The menu changes nightly, showcasing tropical appeal with ancho-rubbed swordfish and citrus gnocci or jumbo stone-crab claws with honey-lime mustard sauce and black-bean and banana-pepper chili with Florida avocado. Appetizers include caviar pie and crispy sweetbreads. Desserts such as Hawaiian vintage chocolate soufflé cake stay the tropical course. Select from 300 wines by the bottle, and many by the glass. ⊠*2601 E. Atlantic Blvd.* ☎*954/782–0606* ▭*AE, D, DC, MC, V* ⊘*No lunch.*

$$-$$$ ▦ **Beachcomber Resort & Villas.** This property's beach location is central to most Broward County attractions and a mile from the Pompano Pier. Ocean views are everywhere, from the oversize guest-room balconies to dining rooms. Although there are also villas and penthouse suites atop the eight-story structure, standard rooms are spacious. The multilingual staff is attentive to guest requests. **Pros:** Think Old Florida with laid-back charm. **Cons:** Don't count on anything close to sparkling new. ⊠*1200 S. Ocean Blvd.* ☎*954/941–7830 or 800/231–2423* ⊞*954/942–7680* ⊕*www.beachcomberresort.com* ⤶*143 rooms, 9 villas, 4 suites* ⏚*In-room: Ethernet. In-hotel: restaurant, bar, pools, beachfront* ▭*AE, D, DC, MC, V.*

$$-$$$ ▦ **Fairfield Fairways of Palm-Aire Resort & Spa.** In its heyday (and hey, that's many a day ago), stars like Elizabeth Taylor checked in here to let loose and relax. Now a time-share, this resort has studios and one-, two-, and four-bedroom apartments that are individually owned but share similar decor. Some units have whirlpool tubs and washers and dryers; kitchens range from partial to full. Housekeeping is provided weekly, and more frequently for a charge. The spa and fitness complex has a sauna, a steam room, cardiovascular machines, weight equipment, fitness classes, and body treatments. Five championship golf courses at the Palm-Aire Country Club are just a chip shot away. The Tiki Hut serves lunch and drinks. **Pros:** Roll out of bed onto the golf course. **Cons:** Not prime for seeking cutting-edge chic. ⊠*2601 Palm-Aire Dr. N* ☎*954/972–3300* ⊞*954/968–2711* ⊕*www.efairfield.com* ⤶*298 units* ⏚*In-hotel: tennis courts, pools, gym, spa* ▭*AE, D, DC, MC, V.*

EN ROUTE About 2 mi north of Pompano Beach you are afforded a beautiful view across Hillsboro Inlet to **Hillsboro Lighthouse,** often called the brightest lighthouse in the southeast. Mariners have used this landmark for decades. When at sea you can see the light almost halfway to the Bahamas. Although the lighthouse is on private property inaccessible to the public, it's well worth a peek, even from afar. Tours are offered about four times a year; call 954/942–2102 for schedule and information.

SPORTS & THE OUTDOORS

FISHING

Pompano Pier (☎*954/773–1346*) extends more than 1,000 feet into the Atlantic and is getting a $12 million upgrade to add style and stability. A two-story Pompano Beach Pier & Promenade will have upscale seafood and steak restaurants, a tiki bar, and more, with completion planned for the city's 2008 centennial celebration. Admission is $3 to fish, $1 to sightsee; rod-and-reel rental is $5.25, plus $5 deposit and a driver's license. Anglers brag about catching barracuda, jack, and snapper here in the same sitting, along with bluefish, cobia, and, yes, pompano. For drift-fishing try *Fish City Pride* (⊠*Fish City Marina, 2621 N. Riverside Dr.* ☎*954/781–1211*). Morning, afternoon, and evening trips cost $35 and include fishing gear and bait. Arrange for a saltwater charter boat through the **Hillsboro Inlet Marina** (⊠*2629 N. Riverside Dr.* ☎*954/943–8222*). The 10-boat fleet offers half-day charters for $500, including gear for up to six people.

GOLF

Crystal Lake Golf Club South Course (⊠*3800 Crystal Lake Dr.* ☎*954/943–2902*) has 18 holes; greens fee $21/$69. **Palm-Aire Country Club** (⊠*3701 Oaks Clubhouse Dr.* ☎*954/978–1737, 954/975–6244 tee line*) has four golf courses, including an executive course with four extra practice holes; greens fee $25/$99.

HORSE RACING

The Isle Casino & Racing of Pompano Park, Florida's only harness track, has world-class trotters and pacers during its October through August meet. It now pulls the punters with Vegas-style slot machines. Casino sustenance can be had at Bragozzo for Italian fare, Farraddays' Steakhouse, the Isle Buffet for brunch, lunch or dinner, and Myron's deli. The track also has a poker room and afternoon and evening simulcast betting. ⊠*1800 S.W. 3rd St.* ☎*954/972–2000* ☒*Grandstand and clubhouse free* ☉*Racing Mon., Wed., Fri., and Sat. at 7:30* PM.

SHOPPING

Bargain hunters head to the **Festival Flea Market Mall** (⊠*2900 W. Sample Rd.* ☎*954/979–4555* ⊕*www.festivalfleamarket.com*), where more than 800 stores, booths, and kiosks sell new brand-name merchandise at discounts. For diversion, there's also an arcade, beauty salon, farmers' market, and food court. On acreage formerly occupied by Pompano Square Mall, **Citi Centre** (⊠*2001 N. Federal Hwy., at Copans Rd.*) is an indoor/outdoor retail hub with Lowe's, Macy's, JCPenney, and Sears, along with smaller enterprises, boutiques, fine dining, and casual outdoor cafés.

DEERFIELD BEACH

3½ mi north of Pompano Beach.

☺ The name **Quiet Waters Park** belies what's in store for kids here. Splash Adventure is a high-tech water-play system with slides and tunnels, among other activities. There's also cable waterskiing and boat rental on the park's lake, and a skate park. ⊠*401 S. Powerline Rd.* ☎*954/360–1315* ☒*Park $1 weekends, free weekdays; Splash Adventure $3* ☉*Apr.–Sept., daily 8–7; Oct.–Mar., 8–5:30; Splash Adventure May–Labor Day, daily 9:30–5:30; Labor Day–Apr., weekends 9:30–5:30.*

Deerfield Island Park, reached only by boat, is a group of coastal hammock islands. Officially designated an Urban Wilderness Area along the Intracoastal Waterway, it contains a mangrove swamp that provides a critical habitat for gopher tortoises, gray foxes, raccoons, and armadillos. Boat shuttles run Wednesday through Sunday 9 AM–5 PM.

Amenities include a boardwalk, coquina and mangrove trails, a six-slip marina, and an observation tower. ✉*1720 Deerfield Island Park* ☎*954/360–1320* ☜*Free.*

WHERE TO EAT & STAY

★ $$-$$$$ ✕**Brooks.** Long known as one of Broward's more elegant dining spots, thanks to French perfectionist Bernard Perron, Brooks is now run by Perron's son-in-law John Howe. Updated Continental meals are served in a series of rooms filled with replicas of Old Masters, cut glass, antiques, and floral wallpaper. Fresh ingredients go into distinctly Floridian dishes, including baked Atlantic swordfish or sautéed Key Largo yellowtail snapper. Put your order in early for the chocolate or Grand Marnier soufflé. ✉*500 S. Federal Hwy.* ☎*954/427–9302* ▤*AE, D, MC, V.*

★ ¢-$$$ ✕**Whale's Rib.** For a casual, almost funky nautical experience near the beach, look no farther. If you want to blend in, order a fish special with whale fries—thinly sliced potatoes that look like hot potato chips. Lesser appetites can choose from salads and fish sandwiches, or raw-bar favorites like Ipswich clams. ✉*2031 N.E. 2nd St.* ☎*954/421–8880* ▤*AE, MC, V.*

$$$-$$$$ ▦ **Ocean Club of Deerfield Beach.** This motel-turned-condominium, renting only by the week, is just south of the Palm Beach County line, across the narrow shore road from the beach. Large units—efficiencies and one- and three-bedroom, three-bath apartments—all have full-size kitchens and big balconies overlooking the sea. Units vary, some with new tile and newer rattan furnishings. A recently added fifth floor has two penthouse apartments. **Pros:** Panoramic view near fishing pier. **Cons:** Decor on the bland beige side. ✉*2080 E. Hillsboro Blvd.* ☎*954/421–7112* ▤*954/421–8693* ⊷*34 units* ⌂*In-room: kitchen. In-hotel: pool, laundry facilities* ▤*AE, D, DC, MC, V.*

$$-$$$$ ▦ **Royal Flamingo Villas.** A small community of houselike villas built in the 1970s reaches from the Intracoastal Waterway to the ocean on 7.5 acres of manicured grounds. Roomy one- and two-bedroom villas are decorated in Florida pastels, rattan, and wicker, all keeping with the tropical theme. If you don't need lavish public facilities, this is your upscale choice at a reasonable price. **Pros:** Serene atmosphere. **Cons:** Don't look for vibrant decor. ✉*1225 Hillsboro Mile (Rte. A1A), Hillsboro Beach* ☎*954/427–0660 or 800/241–2477* ▤*954/427–6110* ⊕*www.royalflamingovillas.com* ⊷*40 villas* ⌂*In-hotel: pool, beachfront, no elevator, laundry facilities* ▤*D, MC, V.*

$$ ▦ **Carriage House Resort Motel.** This tidy motel is one block from the ocean. The white, two-story, colonial-style property with black shutters is actually two buildings connected by a second-story sundeck. Steady improvements have been made to the facility, and kitchenettes are equipped with good-quality utensils. Rooms, with king or double beds, are quiet and have walk-in closets and safes. **Pros:** Friendly staff. **Cons:** High-speed Internet not in all rooms. ✉*250 S. Ocean Blvd.* ☎*954/427–7670* ▤*954/428–4790* ⊕*www.carriagehouseresort.com* ⊷*6 rooms, 14 efficiencies, 10 1-bedroom apartments* ⌂*In-room: Ethernet (some). In-hotel: pool, no elevator, laundry facilities* ▤*AE, D, DC, MC, V.*

SPORTS & THE OUTDOORS

FISHING

The **Cove Marina** (⊠*Hillsboro Blvd. and the Intracoastal Water-way* ☎*954/427–9747*) has a deep-sea charter fleet. In winter there are excellent runs of sailfish, kingfish, dolphin, and tuna. A half-day charter costs about $500 for six people. Enter the marina through the Cove Shopping Center, where The Cove Restaurant and Marina (☎954/421–9272), founded by the late Ken Gulden and still run by his family, does a spirited happy hour with a complimentary buffet.

GOLF

Off Hillsboro Boulevard west of Interstate 95, **Deer Creek Golf Club** (⊠*2801 Country Club Blvd.* ☎*954/421–5550*) has 18 holes. Greens fee $60/$50; there are six fee structures depending on the season.

SCUBA DIVING

One of the area's most popular dive operators, **Dixie Divers** (⊠*Cove Marina, Hillsboro Blvd. and the Intracoastal Waterway* ☎*954/420–0009*) has morning and afternoon dives aboard the 48-foot *Lady-Go-Diver,* plus evening dives on weekends. Snorkelers and certified divers can explore the marine life of nearby reefs and shipwrecks. The cost is $50; ride-alongs are welcome for $35.

SOUTH BROWARD

South Broward's roots are in early Florida settlements. Thus far it has avoided some of the glitz and glamour of neighbors to the north and south, and folks here like it that way. Still, there's plenty to see and do—excellent restaurants in every price range, world-class pari-mutuels, now gussied up with gaming on the side, and a new focus on the arts.

HOLLYWOOD

7 mi south of Fort Lauderdale.

Hollywood has had a face-lift, with more nips and tucks to come as Young Circle, plagued in recent times by derelicts, has become Broward's first Arts Park. Things didn't go smoothly for the revamp, given an unrealistic completion timetable and developer difficulties, but now the park is a delightful reality, the biggest criticism being not enough shade for extended stays on sunny days. On Hollywood's western outskirts, the flamboyant Seminole Hard Rock Hotel & Casino has permanently etched the previously downtrodden section of State Road 7/U.S. 441 corridor on the map of trendy excitement, drawing local weekenders, architecture buffs, and gamblers. But Hollywood's redevelopment effort doesn't end there: new shops, restaurants, and art galleries open at a persistent clip, and the city has spiffed up its Broadwalk—a wide pedestrian walkway along the beach—where Rollerbladers are as commonplace as snowbirds from the north. Trendy sidewalk cafés have opened, vying for space with mom-and-pop T-shirt shops. Downtown, along Harrison Street and Hollywood Boulevard, jazz clubs and still more fashionable restaurants draw young professionals to the scene.

The **Art and Culture Center of Hollywood** is a visual and performing-arts facility with an art reference library, outdoor sculpture garden, and arts school. It's just east of Young Circle, melding urban open space with a fountain, a 2,000-plus seat amphitheater, and an indoor theater. Nearby, on trendy Harrison Street and Hollywood Boulevard, are chic lunch places, bluesy entertainment spots, and shops. ✉*1650 Harrison St.* ☎*954/921–3274* 💲*$6, and free on the third Sunday of each month* ⏱*Tues., Mon. –Sat. 10–5, Sun. 12–4.*

Fodor'sChoice
★

With the Intracoastal Waterway nearby to its west and the beach and ocean immediately east, the newly spiffed-up 2[1//5]-mi paved promenade known as the **Broadwalk** has lured pedestrians and cyclists since 1924. Thanks to a $14 million makeover, this stretch has taken on new luster for the buff, the nubile, the laid-back, and the retired. Kids also thrive here: there are play areas, rental bicycles-for-two, trikes, and other wheeled, pedal-powered gizmos. Expect to hear French spoken along this scenic stretch that now has an 18-inch decorative wall separating sand and the promenade, since Hollywood Beach has been a favorite getaway for Québecois ever since Joseph Young hired French-Canadians to work here in the 1920s. Conversations in Spanish and Portuguese are also frequently overheard on this path.

Hollywood North Beach Park is at the Broadwalk's north end. No high-rises overpower the scene, and there's nothing hip or chic about the park. It's just a laid-back, old-fashioned place for enjoying the sun, sand, and sea. ✉*Rte. A1A and Sheridan St.* ☎*954/926–2444* 💲*Free; parking $5 until 2, $3 thereafter* ⏱*Daily 8–6.*

Comprising 1,500 acres at the Intracoastal Waterway, **West Lake Park** is one of Florida's largest urban nature facilities. Rent a canoe, kayak, or boat with an electric motor (no fossil fuels are allowed in the park) or take the 40-minute environmental boat tour. Extensive boardwalks traverse mangroves, sheltering endangered and threatened species. A 65-foot observation tower showcases the entire park. More than $1 million in exhibits are on display at the **Anne Kolb Nature Center,** named after the late county commissioner and leading environmental advocate. The center's exhibit hall has 27 interactive displays, an ecology room, and a tri-level aquarium. ✉*1200 Sheridan St.* ☎*954/926–2410* 💲*Weekends $1, weekdays and holidays free; exhibit hall $1* ⏱*Daily 9–5.*

At the edge of Hollywood lies **Seminole Native Village,** a reservation where you can pet a cougar, hold a baby alligator, and take in wildlife demonstrations. The Seminole also sell their art and crafts here.

WHERE TO EAT

$$$$ ✕**Nikki Marina Hollywood Restaurant & Bar.** As part of the growing global village of Nikki Beach outposts, stretching from St. Tropez to Sardinia, Marrakech to Miami Beach, Hollywood's own is situated at Diplomat Landing across from the Westin Diplomat Resort. This is a good spot

to sample sushi, sip mojitos, and gawk at mega yachts. At lunch, go for the Nikki Lobster Club ($15) or the Nikki Marina Salad ($10) with Stilton cheese, pears, grapefruit, toasted cashews, and greens. A dinner menu stretches from Cowboy Steak ($42) to paella ($40), with lobster, shrimp, clams, and mussels amid the saffron rice. High rollers can order Nikki's Delight of the Sea Platter ($200), loaded with crab legs, lobster, shrimp, and oysters. Sunday Brunch ($38) includes a raw bar. Arrive by vehicle or boat, and prepare to be upstaged by something a little bigger or snazzier than whatever you're steering. ⊠ *3660 S. Ocean Dr.* ☎ *954/602–8750.* ⊟ *AE, D, MC, V*

$$-$$$$ ✕ **Giorgio's Grill.** Good food and service are hallmarks of this 400-seat restaurant overlooking the Intracoastal Waterway. Seafood is a specialty, but you'll also find pasta and meat dishes, and a solid Sunday brunch ($19.95). A great water view and friendly staff add to the experience. A surprisingly extensive wine list is reasonably priced. ⊠ *606 N. Ocean Dr.* ☎ *954/929–7030* ⊟ *AE, D, DC, MC, V.*

$$-$$$ ✕ **Las Brisas.** Next to the beach, this cozy bistro offers seating inside or out, and the food is Argentine with Italian flair. A small pot, filled with *chimichurri*—a paste made of oregano, parsley, olive oil, salt, garlic, and crushed pepper—for spreading on steaks, sits on each table. Grilled fish is a favorite, as are pork chops, chicken, and pasta entrées. Desserts include a flan like *mamacita* used to make, and a *dulce con leche* (sweet milk pudding). ⊠ *600 N. Surf Rd.* ☎ *954/923–1500* ⊟ *AE, D, DC, MC, V* ⊘ *No lunch.*

$-$$ ✕ **Sushi Blues Café and Blue Monk Lounge.** Raw fish, burgers, and soul food complement the American roots music and vintage lamps at this hip (read: far from stodgy) Hollywood institution, open daily from 11:30 AM until the wee hours. It's operated by husband-and-wife team Kenny Millions and Junko Maslak. Japanese chefs prepare conventional and macrobiotic-influenced dishes, from sushi and rolls (California, tuna, and the Yozo roll, with snapper, flying-fish roe, asparagus, and Japanese mayonnaise) to steamed vegetables with tofu and steamed snapper with miso sauce. Poached pears steamed in cabernet sauce and cappuccino custard are popular desserts. The Sushi Blues Band performs many evenings. ⊠ *2009 Harrison St.* ☎ *954/929–9560* ⊟ *AE, MC, V.*

¢-$$ ✕ **Le Tub.** Formerly a Sunoco gas station, this place is now a quirky waterside saloon with an enduring affection for claw-foot bathtubs. Hand-painted tubs, sinks, and toilets are everywhere—under ficus, sea grape, and palm trees. If a potty doesn't appeal, there's a secluded swing facing the water north of the main dining area. Despite molasses-slow service and an abundance of flies at sundown, this eatery is favored by locals, and management seemed genuinely appalled when hordes of trend-seeking city slickers started jamming bar stools and tables after *GQ* magazine and Oprah declared its thick, juicy Angus burgers the best around. ⊠ *1100 N. Ocean Dr.* ☎ *954/921–9425* ⊟ *No credit cards.*

WHERE TO STAY

$$-$$$$ ⊞ **Seminole Hard Rock Hotel & Casino.** Springing up on flatlands of western Hollywood as if a virtual mirage, the Seminole Hard Rock Hotel & Casino has become a magnet for Vegas-style excitement, entertain-

ment, and dining with a subtropical appeal. The 4½-acre pool complex inspires a wow-reaction, where a rock mountain doubles as a backdrop to a 182-foot-long waterslide. A lazy river circulating pool, waterfalls, hot tubs, and a shallow play area are capped by a nearly 22,000-square-foot spa. Partially embracing this landscaping is a starkly white 12-story tower. Amenities include Tivoli stereos and ultra-luxe beds dressed in Egyptian cottons. Dining options include the memorabilia-packed Hard Rock Cafe Hollywood, the Council Oak, for steak and seafood, and the 24-hour Blue Plate, bordering casino action. The facility is designed in a somewhat dizzying fashion so that eateries, lounges, and elegant outlying lobby area form a peripheral map of sorts for the casino floor, where poker pulsates at 40 tables, to spectator delight, along with a phalanx of Vegas-style slots, including progressives. A ballroom theater just off the casino hosts stage extravaganzas; and "Hard Rock Live!," a 5,600-seat live performance venue, hosts performers like Prince, touring bands, theater, championship boxing, and rodeo. Seminole Paradise, an adjacent retail, restaurant, and live-entertainment district, will relieve you of any casino-floor winnings. Acres of free parking including the Lucky 7 garage accommodate wheels of any size. **Pros:** For entertainment, everything's here but beach and golf. **Cons:** Don't look for serenity except in your room, spa, or maybe by the pool. ⊠*1 Seminole Way* ☎*954/364–4171 or 800/937–0010* ⊕*www.hardrock.com* ⋐*500 rooms, including 100 suites* ♿*In-room: dial-up. In-hotel: 3 restaurants, bars, golf course, tennis courts, pools, gym, spa* ▤*AE, DC, MC, V.*

★ $$–$$$$ 🏨 **The Westin Diplomat Resort & Spa.** Opened in 2002 on the site of the original 1950s hotel of the same name, the Diplomat is a grand 39-story, dual-tower property. The hotel has a lobby-atrium area with ceilings soaring to 60 feet. A signature of the resort is its 120-foot bridged pool, extending from lobby to oceanfront. A Mediterranean-inspired spa offers fitness facilities and more than 20 luxury treatments. The Diplomat's country club, across the Intracoastal, has 60 guest rooms, golf, tennis, and spa. You'll have use of facilities at both properties; shuttle service is provided. **Pros:** Loads of pizzazz for the see-and-be-seen crowd. **Cons:** To offset erosion, a beach replenishment project seems a never-ending, if not a forever-losing, battle. ⊠*1995 E. Hallandale Beach Blvd.* ☎*954/457–2000 or 800/327–1212* ⊕*www. starwoodhotels.com* ⋐*900 rooms, 100 suites* ♿*In-room: dial-up, minibar. In-hotel: 3 restaurants, bars, golf course, tennis courts, pools, gym, spa,* ▤*AE, DC, MC, V.*

★ $$–$$$ 🏨 **Manta Ray Inn.** Canadians Donna and Dwayne Boucher run this immaculate, affordable two-story inn on a beach, perfect for a low-key getaway. Dating from the 1940s, the inn offers casual, comfortable beachfront accommodations with wicker or rattan furnishings and cable TV. Kitchens are equipped with microwaves, pots, pans, and serving utensils. One-bedroom apartments have marble shower stalls, and two-bedroom units also have tubs. **Pros:** On the beach. **Cons:** No pool. ⊠*1715 S. Surf Rd.* ☎*954/921–9666 or 800/255–0595* 🖷*954/929–8220* ⊕*www.mantarayinn.com* ⋐*12 units* ♿*In-room: VCR, Wi-Fi. In-hotel: beachfront, no elevator* ▤*AE, D, MC, V.*

$-$$$ 🖼 **Sea Downs.** Directly facing the Broadwalk, this three-story lodging is a good choice for efficiency or apartment living (one-bedroom units can be joined to make two-bedroom apartments). All but two units have ocean views. Kitchens are fully equipped, and most units have tub-showers and closets. Housekeeping is provided once a week. In between, fresh towels are provided daily and sheets upon request, but you'll need to make your own bed. **Pros:** Ocean proximity. **Cons:** Depending on season, multiple-night minimum stay required and credit cards not accepted. ✉2900 *N. Surf Rd.* ☎954/923–4968 🖨954/923–8747 ⊕*www.seadowns.com* ⇱*4 efficiencies, 8 1-bedroom apartments* 🖧*In-room: Wi-Fi. In-hotel: pool, no elevator, laundry facilities* ▤*No credit cards.*

$-$$ 🖼 **Driftwood on the Ocean.** Facing the beach at the secluded south end of Surf Road is this attractive late-1950s resort motel that clearly shows its age. The setting is what draws guests, but attention to maintenance and refurbishing efforts make it a value. Accommodations range from a studio to a deluxe two-bedroom, two-bath suite. Most units have a kitchen; all have balconies or terraces, and wireless Internet access. **Pros:** Wide ribbon of beachfront. **Cons:** Not all rooms face ocean. ✉2101 *S. Surf Rd.* ☎954/923–9528 *or* 800/944–3148 🖨954/922–1062 ⊕*www.driftwoodontheocean.com* ⇱*7 rooms, 9 2-bedroom apartments, 13 1-bedroom apartments, 20 efficiencies* 🖧*In-room: kitchen (some), Wi-Fi. In-hotel: pool, beachfront, bicycles, no elevator, laundry facilities* ▤*AE, D, MC, V.*

NIGHTLIFE & THE ARTS

THE ARTS
Harrison Street Art and Design District in downtown Hollywood has galleries featuring original artwork (eclectic paintings, sculpture, photography, and mixed media) and Costa Rica collectibles. Friday night the artists' studios, galleries, and shops stay open later while crowds meander along Hollywood Boulevard and Harrison Street. **Mosaica** (✉*2020 Hollywood Blvd.* ☎954/923–7006) is a design studio with handcrafted, one-of-a-kind mosaic tile tables, mirrors, and art.

NIGHTLIFE
Although Hollywood has a small-town feel, it has an assortment of coffee bars, Internet cafés, sports bars, martini lounges, and dance clubs. Downtown Hollywood is known for its live jazz and blues venues. **O'Hara's Hollywood** (✉*1903 Hollywood Blvd.* ☎954/925–2555) highlights top local jazz and blues talent six nights a week. Sushi café and wine bar **Sushi Blues** (✉*1836 Young Circle* ☎954/929–9560) serves up live blues Friday and Saturday nights starting at 9.

SPORTS & THE OUTDOORS

DOG RACING
Mardi Gras Racetrack & Gaming, long known as the Hollywood Greyhound Track before arrival of more than 1,200 Vegas-style slot machines, including progressives, has live dog racing during its December through May season and simulcasting every day. ✉*831 N. Federal Hwy., Hallandale* ☎954/924–3200 🎫*Admission and parking are free* ⊙*Racing nightly at 7:30, and Tues., Thurs., and Sat. at 12:30* PM.

BOATING

Adventure World at the Landing (✉*3570 South Ocean Dr.* ☎*954/457–9575*) provides Jet Ski, Air Cat, and other boat rentals, and runs fishing trips as well as kayak and canoe expeditions through the mangroves and lagoons of local parks. Electric bikes, all-terrain Segways, and bicycle rentals are also available.

FISHING

Sea Leg's III (✉*5400 N. Ocean Dr.* ☎*954/923–2109*) runs drift-fishing trips from 8 AM to 12:30 PM and 1:30 to 6 and bottom-fishing trips from 7 PM to midnight. Trips cost $35 to $38, including rod rental.

GOLF

The **Diplomat Country Club & Spa** (✉*501 Diplomat Pkwy., Hallandale* ☎*954/883–4000*) has 18 holes and a spa. Greens fee $69/$209. The course at **Emerald Hills** (✉*4100 N. Hills Dr.* ☎*954/961–4000*) has 18 holes. Greens fee $55/$175, depending on the season.

HORSE RACING

Gulfstream Park Racing & Casino is the winter home of top Thoroughbreds, trainers, and jockeys, and now the year-round home of slot machine action. After 37 years on Miami Beach, **Christine Lee's**, known for prime steaks and Asian specialties, has relocated here. The season is capped by the $1 million Florida Derby, with Kentucky Derby hopefuls. Racing unfolds January through April. ✉*901 S. Federal Hwy., Hallandale* ☎*954/454–7000 or 800/771–8873* 🎫*Grandstand $3, clubhouse $5* ⊙*Racing Wed.–Mon. at 1 and nightly simulcasting.*

DANIA BEACH

3 mi north of Hollywood, 4 mi south of Fort Lauderdale.

This town at the south edge of Fort Lauderdale is probably best known for its antiques dealers, but there are other attractions as well.

The once pine-dotted **John U. Lloyd Beach State Recreation Area** has lost significant shaded ambience, thanks to government-driven efforts to pull out all but indigenous plants, leaving taxpayers to gripe that myopic bureaucrats could have waited for Hurricane Wilma to decide what might stay and what should go. Disappointed shade-seeking park-goers are advised that, eventually, sea grape, gumbo limbo, and other native plantings will fill the uninspiring void. Meanwhile, gate attendance has declined appreciably, hurricane damage has closed the jetty pier for fishing, and erosion has done a number on what remains of the beach. Nature trails and a marina remain open, along with canoeing on Whiskey Creek. Despite setbacks, this is a prime spot for watching cruise ships enter and depart Port Everglades. ✉*6503 N. Ocean Dr.* ☎*954/923–2833* 🎫*$5 per vehicle with up to 8 people* ⊙*Daily 8–sunset.*

★ **IGFA Fishing Hall of Fame and Museum** is a shrine to the sport. Near the Fort Lauderdale airport at Interstate 95 and Griffin Road, the center is the creation of the International Game Fishing Association. Check out the World Fishing Hall of Fame, a marina, and an extensive museum and research library, where seven galleries feature fantasy fishing and other interactive displays. At the Catch Gallery, you can cast off via virtual reality to reel in a marlin, sailfish, trout, tarpon, or bass. ⊠ *300 Gulfstream Way, Dania Beach* ☎ *954/922–4212* ⊕ *www.igfa.org* ☞ *$6* ⊙ *Daily 10–6.*

WHERE TO EAT

¢-$ ✕ **Grampa's Bakery & Restaurant.** A magnet for local politicos, Grampa's provides a cheery, homey fix of comfort foods from the charbroiler, fryer, and grill. You won't go hungry with Grampa's chili with cheese, lox, eggs, an onion omelet, or biscuits and gravy. Check out the sweets, at the bakery counter up front. ⊠ *17 S.W. 1st St.* ☎ *954/923–2163* ▭ *MC, V.*

¢-$ ✕ **Jaxson's Ice Cream Parlor.** Across from the Dania United Methodist Church, the half-century-old Jaxson's whips up malts, shakes, and jumbo sundaes, plus sandwiches and salads, amid an antique-license-plate decor. Ice creams and toppings are prepared daily on premises. Owner Monroe Udell has trademarked the Kitchen Sink—a small sink full of ice cream, topped by sparklers—reserved for parties of four or more for $11.25 per person. Less-ambitious appetites lean toward Jaxson's Sampler (Junior or Senior), the Tin Roof Goober Special or the Banana Skyscraper. Chocoholics can ponder Chocolate Suicide. ⊠ *128 S. Federal Hwy.* ☎ *954/923–4445* ▭ *AE, D, MC, V.*

¢-$ ✕ **Tarks of Dania.** Started in 1966 as a small stand for clams, wings, and beer, Tarks hasn't changed much, with a counter and a few tables for neighbors and drop-ins to eat, drink, and rejuvenate. From Tarks's raw bar come topneck and littleneck clams along with raw oysters. From the fryer are clams (bellies or strips), oysters, scallops, shrimp, wings, and curly fries. For around $10 you can order a gator-tail dinner (gently marinated and deep-fried) or a tasty conch salad. Nightly specials include Alaskan snow crab on Friday. Tarks markets its own bottled "terminator" sauce, and there's a "Frequent Tarks Club" to accumulate points for special offers. ⊠ *1317 S. Federal Hwy.* ☎ *954/925–8275* ▭ *AE, D, MC, V.*

SPORTS & THE OUTDOORS

FISHING

The 920-foot, 24-hour **Dania Pier** (☎ *954/929–4887*) has gussied up with chickee huts, new restrooms, and the **Beach Watch** restaurant serving lunch and dinners including peel-and-eat shrimp, wings, pizza, and three-course Sun-Set Dinners (from $15.95). You can still get hot dogs at the bait shop. Fishing is $3 (with parking another $4 for the day), tackle rental $6, bait about $3, and spectators pay $1.

JAI ALAI

Dania Jai-Alai Casino has one of the fastest ball games on the planet, scheduled year-round. Simulcast wagering from other tracks and a poker room are also available, with slot machines on the very near horizon. ⊠ *301 E. Dania Beach Blvd.* ☎ *954/920–1511* ☞ *$1.50, reserved seats $2–$7* ⊙ *Games Tues. and Sat. at noon, Sun. at 1, nightly Tues.–Sat. at 7:15.*

MINIATURE GOLF

☺ **Boomers!** has action games for kids of all ages—go-kart and Naskart racing, miniature golf, batting cages, bumper boats, Lasertron, and a skycoaster. ✉*1801 N.W. 1st St.* ☎*954/921–1411* ☼*Mon.–Thurs. noon–11* PM, *Fri. noon–2* AM, *Sat. 10* AM–2 AM, *Sun. 10* AM–11PM.

ROLLER COASTER

☺ **Dania Beach Hurricane,** visible from Interstate 95, isn't the world's highest, fastest, or longest roller coaster, but it's near the top in all those categories, and it's the tallest wooden coaster south of Atlanta. This retro-feeling ride creaks like an old staircase while you race along 3,200 feet of track and plummet from a height of 100 feet at speeds up to 55 mph. Pay by the ride, or buy an all-day wristband ($13). ✉*1760 N.W. 1st St.* ☎*954/921–7433* ☜*$6.25* ☼*Sun.–Thurs. 11*AM–11 PM, *Fri. and Sat. 10* AM–1:30 AM.

SHOPPING

Despite moans over eBay competition encroachment, dozens of dealers along **Dania Antique Row** do business buying and selling everything from vintage knickknacks to furnishings of antiquity. You never know what you'll find here, but Depression-era glassware and old dolls seem plentiful, and shop owners are cordial. This two-square-block area is on Federal Highway (U.S. 1), ½ mi south of the Fort Lauderdale airport and ½ mi north of Hollywood. Take the Stirling Road or Griffin Road East exit off Interstate 95.

6

FORT LAUDERDALE & BROWARD ESSENTIALS

TRANSPORTATION

CARRIERS **BY AIR**

More than 40 scheduled airlines, commuters, and charters serve Fort Lauderdale–Hollywood International Airport.

Contacts Allegiant Air (☎*702/205-8888*) **Air Canada** (☎*888/247-2262*). **Air Jamaica** (☎*800/523-5585*). **AirTran** (☎*800/247-8726*). **American** (☎*800/433-7300*).**BahamasAir** (☎*800/222-4262*) **Continental** (☎*800/525-0280*). **Delta** (☎*800/221-1212*). **jetBlue** (☎*800/538-2583*). **Northwest** (☎*800/225-2525*). **Southwest** (☎*800/435-9792*). **Spirit** (☎*800/772-7117*). **TWA** (☎*800/221-2000*). **United** (☎*800/241-6522*). **US Airways** (☎*800/428-4322*).

AIRPORTS & TRANSFERS Fort Lauderdale–Hollywood International Airport is 4 mi south of downtown Fort Lauderdale. Broward County Mass Transit operates bus route No. 1 between the airport and its main terminal at Broward Boulevard and Northwest 1st Avenue, in the center of Fort Lauderdale. Service from the airport is every 20 minutes and begins daily at 5:40 AM; the last bus leaves the airport at 11:15 PM. The fare is $1.50. Airport Shuttle provides limousine service to all parts of Broward County. Fares to most Fort Lauderdale beach hotels are in the $25 range.

Airport Contacts Fort Lauderdale-Hollywood International Airport (☎ *954/359-6100*). **Airport Shuttle** (☎ *954/561-8888*). **Broward County Transit** (☎ *954/357-8400*).

BY BOAT & FERRY

Water Taxi, also known as Water Bus, provides service along the Intracoastal Waterway in Fort Lauderdale between the 17th Street Causeway and Oakland Park Boulevard daily from 10:30 AM until midnight.

Contacts Water Bus, Water Taxi (☎ *954/467-6677*).

BY BUS

Greyhound Lines buses stop in Fort Lauderdale. Broward County Transit bus service covers the county on 275 fixed routes and ventures into Dade and Palm Beach counties. The fare is $1.50, and BUZ pass options include unlimited daily ($3.50), weekly ($13), monthly ($52), and 10 rides for $10 any day, any time, sold at bus stations, libraries, and elsewhere. Route service starts at 5 AM and continues to 11:30 PM, except on Sunday. Call for route information. Fort Lauderdale's Sun Trolley is free on some routes or costs 25¢ to 50¢ per ride, depending on the route (flow of federal grant money, and whims of local transportation czars), and covers both the downtown loop and the beach area. The Courthouse Route generally runs every 10 minutes weekdays from 7:30 until 6. The Las Olas & Beach Route runs on the half hour 5:45 PM–1:45 AM.

Contacts Broward County Transit (*Main Bus Terminal* ✉ *Broward Blvd. at N.W. 1st Ave., Fort Lauderdale* ☎ *954/357-8400*). **Greyhound Lines** (✉ *515 N.E. 3rd St., Fort Lauderdale* ☎ *800/231-2222 or 954/764-6551*). **TMAX** (☎ *954/761-3543*).

CUTTING COSTS Broward County Mass Transit offers seven-day passes for $13 that are good for unlimited use on all county buses. Get passes at some hotels, Broward County libraries, and the main bus terminal.

BY CAR

Access to Broward County from north or south is via Florida's Turnpike, Interstate 95, U.S. 1, or U.S. 441. Interstate 75 (Alligator Alley, requiring a toll despite being part of the nation's interstate highway system) connects Broward with Florida's west coast and runs parallel to State Road 84 within the county. Except during rush hour, Broward County is easier than elsewhere in South Florida for driving. East–west Interstate 595 runs from westernmost Broward County and links Interstate 75 with Interstate 95 and U.S. 1, providing handy access to the airport and seaport. The scenic, slow Route A1A generally parallels the beach. The Sawgrass Expressway (also known as State Road 869 north of Interstate 595 and Interstate 75 south) is a toll road that links to Sawgrass Mills shopping and the ice-hockey arena, both in Sunrise.

CAR RENTAL **Contacts Alamo** (☎ *954/3592550*). **Avis** (☎ *954/359-3250*). **Budget** (☎ *954/359-4700*). **Dollar** (☎ *954/359-7800*). **Enterprise** (☎ *954/760-9888*). **Hertz** (☎ *954/764-1199*). **National** (☎ *954/359-8303*).

BY TAXI

It's difficult to hail a cab on the street. Sometimes you can pick one up at a major hotel. Otherwise, phone for taxi service. Meters run at a rate of $4.50 for the first mile and $2.40 for each additional mile; waiting time is 40¢ per minute, with rates likely to rise as fuel costs escalate. The major company serving the area is Yellow Cab.

Contacts Yellow Cab (☎ *954/565–5400*).

BY TRAIN

Amtrak provides daily service to the Fort Lauderdale station as well as other Broward County stops at Hollywood and Deerfield Beach. Tri-Rail operates train service daily 4 AM–11 PM (limited service on weekends) through Broward, Miami-Dade, and Palm Beach counties. Six Broward stations are west of Interstate 95: Hillsboro Boulevard in Deerfield Beach, Pompano Beach, Cypress Creek, Fort Lauderdale, Fort Lauderdale Airport, Sheridan Street in Hollywood, and Hollywood Boulevard.

Contacts Amtrak (✉ *200 S.W. 21st Terr., Fort Lauderdale* ☎ *800/872–7245*). **Tri-Rail** (☎ *800/874–7245*).

CONTACTS & RESOURCES

TOURS

Carrie B., a 300-passenger day cruiser, gives 90-minute tours on the New River and Intracoastal Waterway. Cruises depart at 11, 1, and 3 each day and cost $15.95. *Jungle Queen III* and *Jungle Queen IV* are 175-passenger and 527-passenger tour boats taking day and night cruises up New River through the heart of Fort Lauderdale. Sightseeing cruises at 9:30 and 1 cost $16.50, and the evening dinner cruise costs $36.95. Professional Diving Charters operates the 60-foot glass-bottom boat *Pro Diver II* for taking in offshore reefs. Daily two-hour sightseeing trips cost $22 to ride and $29 to snorkel.

Contacts Carrie B. (✉ *Riverwalk at S.E. 5th Ave., Fort Lauderdale* ☎ *954/768–9920*). **Jungle Queen III and Jungle Queen IV** (✉ *Radisson Bahia Mar Beach Resort, 801 Seabreeze Blvd., Fort Lauderdale* ☎ *954/462–5596*). **Professional Diving Charters** (✉ *515 Seabreeze Blvd., Fort Lauderdale* ☎ *954/761–3413*).

VISITOR INFORMATION

Contacts Chamber of Commerce of Greater Fort Lauderdale (✉ *512 N.E. 3rd Ave., Fort Lauderdale* ☎ *954/462–6000* ⊕ *www.ftlchamber.com*). **Greater Deerfield Beach Chamber of Commerce** (✉ *1601 E. Hillsboro Blvd., Deerfield Beach* ☎ *954/427–1050* ⊕ *www.deerfieldchamber.com*). **Greater Fort Lauderdale Convention & Visitors Bureau** (✉ *100 E. Broward Blvd., Suite 200, Fort Lauderdale* ☎ *954/765–4466* ⊕ *www.broward.org*). **Hollywood Chamber of Commerce** (✉ *330 N. Federal Hwy., Hollywood* ☎ *954/923–4000* ⊕ *www. hollywoodchamber.org*). **Lauderdale-by-the-Sea Chamber of Commerce** (✉ *4201 N. Ocean Dr., Lauderdale-by-the-Sea* ☎ *954/776–1000* ⊕ *www.lbts.com*). **Pompano Beach Chamber of Commerce** (✉ *2200 E. Atlantic Blvd., Pompano Beach* ☎ *954/941–2940* ⊕ *www.pompanobeachchamber.com*).

Miami & Miami Beach

Art Deco District, Ocean Drive, Miami Beach

WORD OF MOUTH

"When you're in South Beach, take a quick trip to Vizcaya, just south of Miami. It's an Italian Renaissance Villa and Gardens. Just beautiful. Built around 1912. Other options are Cuban food in Little Havana and the Venetian Pool in Coral Gables. South Beach has all the restaurants, bars, and clubs you could ever hope for."

–Cimbrone

WELCOME TO MIAMI & MIAMI BEACH

TOP REASONS TO GO

★ **The beach:** Miami Beach has been rated as one of the 10 best in the world. White sand, warm water, and bronzed bodies everywhere provide just the right mix of relaxation and people-gazing.

★ **The restaurants:** Miami's eclectic residents have transformed the city into a museum of epicurean wonders, ranging from Cuban and Argentine fare to fusion haute cuisine.

★ **The parties:** A 24-hour liquor license means clubs stay open until 5 AM, and after parties go until noon the following day. The strong chance of encountering a celebrity at the hottest local bar is just one more reason to venture out.

★ **The people:** Miami is a watering hole for the vain and beautiful of South America, Europe, and the Northeast. Watch them—or join them—as they strut their stuff on Lincoln Road, chow down in style at the Forge, and flaunt their tans on the white beds of the Shore Club hotel.

1 South Beach. People-watch from sidewalk cafés along Ocean Drive, lounge poolside at posh Collins Avenue hotels, and party till dawn at the nation's hottest clubs.

2 Downtown Miami. Weave through the glass-and-steel labyrinth of new condo construction to catch a Miami Heat game at the American Airlines arena or a ballet at the spaceship-like Adrienne Arsht Center for the Performing Arts.

3 Coral Gables. Dine and shop on family-friendly Miracle Mile, and take a driving tour of the Mediterranean-style mansions in the surrounding neighborhoods.

4 Coconut Grove. Catch dinner and a movie and listen to live music at CocoWalk, or cruise the bohemian shops and locals bars in this hip neighborhood.

5 Key Biscayne. Pristine parks and tranquillity make this upscale enclave a total antithesis to the South Beach party.

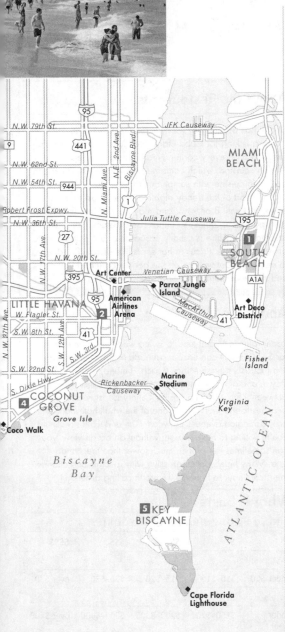

GETTING ORIENTED

Long considered the gateway to Latin America, Miami is as close to Cuba and the Caribbean as you can get within the U.S. The 36-square-mi city is located at the southern tip of the Florida peninsula, bordered on the east by Biscayne Bay. Over the bay lies a series of barrier islands, the largest being a thin, 18-square-mi strip called Miami Beach. To the east of Miami Beach is the Atlantic Ocean. A collection of islands called the Florida Keys extends 160 miles south and ends with Key West, the southernmost point in the United States.

7

MIAMI & MIAMI BEACH PLANNER

When to Go

Miami and Miami Beach are year-round destinations. Most visitors come October through April, when hotels, restaurants and attractions are busiest and each weekend holds a festival or event. "Season" kicks off in December with Art Basel Miami Beach, and hotel rates don't come down until after the college kids have returned from Spring Break. Summer is a good time for budget traveler; many hotels lower their rates considerably, and many restaurants offer discounts. Summer travel is promoted with Miami Restaurant Month in July and August.

Flying In

Miami is serviced by Miami International Airport (MIA) near downtown and Fort Lauderdale-Hollywood International Airport (FLL) 18 miles north. Many discount carriers, like Spirit Airlines, Southwest Airlines and Airtran, fly into FLL, making it a smart bargain if you are renting a car. Otherwise, look for flights to MIA on American Airlines, Delta, and Continental. MIA is extremely busy, and is undergoing renovation, so don't be surprised by delays and far walks to gates.

For more on Miami flight information *see* By Air under *Essentials* at the end of this chapter.

About the Restaurants

Miami has an array of sophisticated, tasty cuisine. Little Havana is king for Cuban fare; look for strong colada coffee served on every corner. Miami Beach is swept up with "fusion" cuisine, which combines Asian, French, American and Latin cuisine with sumptuous results. Since Miami dining is a part of the trendy nightlife scene, most dinners don't start until 8 or 9 PM, and may go well into the night. Hot spots fill up quick, so either come before 7 or make reservations. Attire is usually casual-chic, but patrons try to dress to impress. Prices in hot spots like Lincoln Road tend to stay high, but venture off the beaten path and you can find delicious Latin food for reasonable prices.

About the Hotels

Room rates in Miami tend to swing wildly: a room that goes for $150 in July can easily cost north of $400 in January. Most tourists stay on Miami Beach. If money isn't an object, stay in one of the glamorous hotels lining Collins Avenue between 15th and 21st streets. Otherwise, stay on the quiet beaches farther north, or in one of the small hotels on Collins or Washington avenues between 10th and 15th streets. If you're willing to have a room without an ocean view, you can sometimes get a price much lower than the standard rate. Many hotels are aggressive with specials and change their rates hour to hour, so it's worth calling around.

What It Costs

DINING & LODGING PRICE CATEGORIES				
¢	$	$$	$$$	$$$$
Restaurants				
under $10	$10–$15	$15–$20	$20–$30	over $30
Hotels				
under $150	$150–$200	$200–$300	$300–$400	over $400

Prices for restaurants are per person for a main course at dinner. Prices for hotels are for two people in a standard double room in high season, excluding 12.5% city and resort taxes.

Updated by
Julia Neyman

THINK OF MIAMI AS A teenager: a young beauty with growing pains, cocky yet confused, quick to embrace the latest fads, exasperating yet lovable. It may help you understand how best to tackle this imperfect paradise.

As cities go, Miami and Miami Beach really are young. Just a little more than 100 years ago, Miami was mosquito-infested swampland, with an Indian trading post on the Miami River. Then hotel builder Henry Flagler brought his railroad to the outpost known as Fort Dallas. Other visionaries—Carl Fisher, Julia Tuttle, William Brickell, and John Sewell, among others—set out to tame the unruly wilderness. Hotels were erected, bridges were built, the port was dredged, electricity arrived. The narrow strip of mangrove coast was transformed into Miami Beach. And the tourists started to come.

Greater Miami is many destinations in one. At its best it offers an unparalleled multicultural experience: melodic Latin and Caribbean tongues, international cuisines and cultural events, and an unmistakable joie de vivre—all against a frankly beautiful beach backdrop. In Little Havana the air is tantalizing with the perfume of strong Cuban coffee. In Coconut Grove, Caribbean steel drums ring out during the Miami/Bahamas Goombay Festival. Anytime in colorful Miami Beach restless crowds wait for entry to the hottest new clubs.

Many visitors don't know that Miami and Miami Beach are really separate cities. Miami, on the mainland, is South Florida's commercial hub. Miami Beach, on 17 islands in Biscayne Bay, is sometimes considered America's Riviera, luring refugees from winter with its warm sunshine; sandy beaches; graceful, shady palms; and tireless nightlife. The natives know well that there's more to Greater Miami than the bustle of South Beach and its Art Deco District. In addition to well-known places such as Coconut Grove and Bayside, the less reported spots, like the Museum of Contemporary Art in North Miami; the burgeoning Design District in Miami; and the mangrove swamps of Matheson Hammock Park, in Coral Gables, are great insider destinations.

EXPLORING MIAMI & MIAMI BEACH

If you had arrived here 40 years ago with a Fodor's guide in hand, chances are you'd be thumbing through listings looking for alligator wrestlers and you-pick strawberry fields or citrus groves. Well, things have changed. While Disney sidetracked families in Orlando, Miami was developing a grown-up attitude courtesy of the original *Miami Vice,* European fashion photographers, and historic preservationists. Nowadays the wildest ride is the city itself. Climb aboard and check out the different sides of Greater Miami.

To find your way around Greater Miami, learn how the numbering system works. Miami is laid out on a grid with four quadrants—northeast, northwest, southeast, and southwest—which meet at Miami Avenue and Flagler Street. Miami Avenue separates east from west, and Flagler Street separates north from south. Avenues and courts run north–south;

GREAT ITINERARIES

3 DAYS

Grab your lotion and head to the ocean, more specifically **Ocean Drive** on **South Beach,** and catch some rays while relaxing on the white sands. Afterward, take a guided or self-guided tour of the **Art Deco District** to see what all the fuss is about. Keep the evening free to socialize at Ocean Drive cafés. The following day drive through **Little Havana** to witness the heartbeat of Miami's Cuban culture on your way south to Coconut Grove's Vizcaya. Wrap up the evening a few blocks away in downtown **Coconut Grove,** enjoying its partylike mood and many nightspots. On the last day head over to **Coral Gables** to take in the eye-popping display of 1920s Mediterranean Revival architecture in the neighborhoods surrounding the city center and the majestic **Biltmore Hotel**; then take a dip in the fantastic thematic **Venetian Pool.** Early evening, set aside a little time to shop at Village of Merrick Park (at the corner of Ponce and Bird), and later that night have a fine meal in Coral Gables.

5 DAYS

Follow the suggested three-day itinerary, and on Day 4 visit the beaches of **Virginia Key** and **Key Biscayne.** Take a diving trip or fishing excursion, learn to windsurf, or just watch the water. On Day 5, step back to the 1950s with a cruise up **Collins Avenue** to some of the monolithic hotels, such as the **Fontainebleau Hilton** and **Eden Roc**; continue north to the elegant shops of **Bal Harbour**; and return to **South Beach** for an evening of shopping, drinking, and outdoor dining at **Lincoln Road Mall.**

streets, terraces, and ways run east–west. Roads run diagonally, northwest–southeast. But other districts—Miami Beach, Coral Gables, and Hialeah—may or may not follow this system, and along the curve of Biscayne Bay the symmetrical grid may shift diagonally. It's best to buy a detailed map, stick to the major roads, and ask directions early and often. However, make sure you're in a safe neighborhood or public place when you seek guidance; cabdrivers and cops are good resources.

SOUTH BEACH

The hub of South Beach is the 1-square-mi Art Deco District, fronted on the east by Ocean Drive and on the west by Alton Road. In recent years the story of South Beach has become a big part of the story of Miami. Back in the early 1980s the neighborhood's vintage hotels were badly run down. But a group of visionaries led by the late Barbara Baer Capitman, a spirited New York transplant, saw this group of buildings as architecturally significant and worth protecting from mindless urban renewal. Capitman was well into her 60s when she stepped in front of bulldozers ready to tear down the Senator, an Art Deco hotel. The Senator fell, but thanks to preservationists 40 others were saved. As the movement picked up, investors started restoring the interiors and repainting the exteriors of classic South Beach buildings. The area is now distinguished as the nation's first 20th-century district to be listed on the National Register of Historic Places, with 800 significant buildings making the roll.

Life along Ocean Drive now unfolds 24 hours a day. Beautiful people pose in hotel lounges and sidewalk cafés, tanned cyclists zoom past palm trees, and visitors flock to see the action. On Lincoln Road café crowds spill onto the sidewalks, weekend markets draw all kinds of visitors and their dogs, and thanks to a few late-night lounges the scene is just as alive at night.

You'll notice right away that several things are plentiful in South Beach. Besides the plethora of surgically enhanced bodies and cell phones, there are a lot of cars for a small area, and plenty of attentive meter maids. On-street parking is scarce, tickets are given freely when meters expire, and towing charges are high. Check your meter to see when you must pay to park; times vary by district. No quarters? Try the municipal lot west of the convention center; the 17th Street Garage between Pennsylvania and Meridian; the 16th Street Garage between Collins and Washington; or the 7th Street Garage at Washington and Collins. Better yet, take advantage of the South Beach Local shuttle—it costs only a quarter and runs until the wee hours of the morning.

TWO GOOD WALKS

South Beach is the most pedestrian-friendly part of Miami, so if you've got the time, spend a couple of days exploring it on foot. Work the southern end of the beach one day, savoring the Art Deco architecture along Ocean Drive, the local museums, and the shops of Española Way. The next day, set your sights on the many pleasures of Lincoln Road and its neighboring attractions.

Numbers correspond to the Miami Beach map.

DAY 1

Start this walk early (8 AM) if you want to watch the awakening city without distraction. At this hour you're also likely to see a fashion photo shoot in progress, since photographers like early morning light. If you're really up for a good walk, start your day at the up-and-comingest part of South Beach: SoFi, so called because it's South of Fifth Street. Here South Pointe Park is a good place to watch cruise ships glide by. Walk north on Ocean Drive and two blocks west (Washington Avenue) to the **Sanford L. Ziff Jewish Museum of Florida ❶** . From here return to Ocean Drive and head north, or, if you don't have the legs for it, begin your South Beach walking tour north of Fifth.

A bevy of Art Deco jewels hugs the drive here, and across the street lies palm-fringed Lummus Park. Cross to the west side of Ocean Drive and walk north, taking note of the Park Central Hotel (No. 640), built in 1937 by Deco architect Henry Hohauser. If you're in the vicinity of 10th Street after 10 AM, recross Ocean Drive to the beach side and visit the **Art Deco District Welcome Center ❷**. Rent a tape or hire a guide for an Art Deco District tour.

Look back across Ocean Drive and take a peek at the wonderful flying-saucer architecture of the Clevelander, at No. 1020. On the next block you'll see the late Gianni Versace's Spanish-Mediterranean Casa Casuarina. Graceful fluted columns stand guard at the Leslie (No. 1244) and the 1941 Carlyle (No. 1250); to their north is the much-photographed Cardozo. Walk two blocks west (away from the ocean) on 13th Street to Washington Avenue, and step inside the 1937 Depression moderne Miami Beach Post Office, designed by Howard Cheney, to see the rotunda and the Works Project Administration–era mural. Turn left on Washington and walk 2½ blocks south to the **Wolfsonian–Florida International University** ❸, where design and art used as propaganda from 1885 to 1945 are the focus.

Return north on Washington—without kids in tow—for a stop at the **World Erotic Art Museum** ❹, then continue past 14th Street, and turn left to end the tour on **Española Way** ❺. Return to Ocean Drive in time to pull up a chair at an outdoor café, order an espresso, and settle down for some people-watching, South Beach's most popular pastime. Or grab some late rays at the beach, which has unofficial gay, mixed, and family zones.

TIMING
To see only the Art Deco buildings on Ocean Drive, allow one hour. Schedule six hours for the whole tour, including a stop at a café and browsing time in the shops.

DAY 2
Start at **Lincoln Road Mall** ❻, three blocks north of Española Way, and part of must-see South Beach. Look beyond the lively parade of pedestrians and you'll find architectural gems.

The next main street north of Lincoln Road is 17th Street, and to the east is the Miami Beach Convention Center, where Muhammad Ali (then known as Cassius Clay) defeated Sonny Liston for the world heavyweight boxing championship in 1964. Walk behind the massive building to the corner of Meridian Avenue and 19th Street to see the chilling **Holocaust Memorial** ❼. Just east is the compact Miami Beach Botanical Garden.

On the east side of the Convention Center, you'll find Park Avenue, site of such architectural jewels as the Adams Tyler Hotel at 2030 Park and the Streamline-style Plymouth at 336 21st Street. Continue east through Collins Park and its enormous baobab trees to the **Bass Museum of Art** ❽. Then make a loop back to Lincoln for a tour-ending shopping spree (you don't want to lug bags all day) or grab a libation at the Delano Hotel or the National Hotel. If you have kids—and energy—make a beeline by cab or rental car for the **Miami Children's Museum** ❾ and **Parrot Jungle Island** ❿, two attractions right across the road from each other on MacArthur Causeway.

TIMING
Allow about four hours to amble down Lincoln Road and visit the museums, gardens, and architectural sights a few blocks to the north. It's worth planning the tour around a meal, given the abundance of Lin-

coln Road's outdoor dining options. Set aside an entire day to include a side trip to MacArthur Causeway.

WHAT TO SEE

② **Art Deco District Welcome Center.** Run by the Miami Design Preservation League, the center provides information about the buildings in the district. A gift shop sells 1930s–1950s Art Deco memorabilia, posters, and books on Miami's history. Several tours—covering Lincoln Road, Española Way, North Beach, and the entire Art Deco District, among others—start here. You can rent audiotapes for a self-guided tour, join one of the regular morning (Wednesday and Friday through Sunday) or Thursday-evening walking tours, or take a bicycle tour. All of the options provide detailed histories of the Art Deco hotels. Don't miss the special boat tours during Art Deco Weekend, in early January. ⊠ *1001 Ocean Dr., at Barbara Capitman Way (10th St.), South Beach* ☎ *305/531–3484* ☒ *Tours $20* ☉ *Sun.–Thurs. 10–7, Fri. and Sat. 10–6.*

⑧ **Bass Museum of Art.** The Bass, in historic Collins Park, is part of the Miami Beach Cultural Park, which includes the Miami City Ballet's Arquitectonica-designed facility and the Miami Beach Regional Library. The original building, constructed of keystone, has unique Maya-inspired carvings. The expansion designed by Japanese architect Arata Isozaki houses another wing and an outdoor sculpture garden. Special exhibitions join a diverse collection of European art. Works on permanent display include *The Holy Family,* a painting by Peter Paul Rubens; *The Tournament,* one of several 16th-century Flemish tapestries; and works by Albrecht Dürer and Henri de Toulouse-Lautrec. Special exhibits often cost a little extra. ⊠ *2121 Park Ave., at 21st St., South Beach* ☎ *305/673–7530* ⊕ *www.bassmuseum.org* ☒ *$8* ☉ *Tues.–Sat. 10–5, Sun. 11–5.*

⑤ **Española Way.** There's a decidedly bohemian feel to this street lined with
★ Mediterranean Revival buildings constructed in 1925. Al Capone's gambling syndicate ran its operations upstairs at what is now the Clay Hotel, a youth hostel. At a nightclub here in the 1930s, future bandleader Desi Arnaz strapped on a conga drum and started beating out a rumba rhythm. Visit this quaint avenue on a weekend afternoon, when merchants and craftspeople set up shop to sell everything from handcrafted bongo drums to fresh flowers. Between Washington and Drexel avenues the road has been narrowed to a single lane, and Miami Beach's trademark pink sidewalks have been widened to accommodate sidewalk cafés and shops selling imaginative clothing, jewelry, and art. ⊠ *Española Way, between 14th and 15th Sts. from Washington to Jefferson Aves., South Beach.*

⑦ **Holocaust Memorial.** A bronze sculpture depicts refugees clinging to a
★ giant bronze arm that reaches out of the ground and 42 feet into the air. Enter the surrounding courtyard to see a memorial wall and hear the music that seems to give voice to the 6 million Jews who died at the hands of the Nazis. It's easy to understand why Kenneth Triester's dramatic memorial is in Miami Beach: the city's community of Holocaust

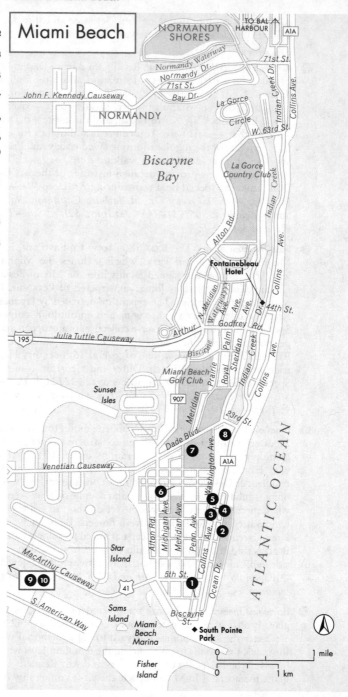

survivors was once the second-largest in the country. ⊠ *1933–1945 Meridian Ave., at Dade Blvd., South Beach* ☎ *305/538–1663* ⊕ *www.holocaustmmb.org* ☞ *Free, donations welcome* ⊙ *Daily 9–9.*

6 **Lincoln Road Mall.** A playful 1990s redesign spruced up this open-air pedestrian mall, adding a grove of 20 towering date palms, five linear pools, and colorful broken-tile mosaics to the futuristic 1950s vision of Fontainebleau designer Morris Lapidus. Some of the shops are owner-operated boutiques with a delightful variety of clothing, furnishings, garden supplies, and decorative design. Others are the typical chain stores of American malls. Remnants of tired old Lincoln Road—beauty-supply and discount electronics stores on the Collins end of the strip—somehow fit nicely into the mix. The new Lincoln Road is fun, lively, and friendly for people old, young, gay, and straight—and their dogs. Folks skate, scoot, bike, or jog here. The best times to hit the road are during Sunday morning farmers' markets and on weekend evenings, when cafés bustle, art galleries open shows, street performers make the sidewalk their stage, and stores stay open late.

Two of the landmarks worth checking out at the eastern end of Lincoln Road are the massive 1940s keystone building at 420 Lincoln Road, which has a 1945 Leo Birchanky mural in the lobby, and the 1921 mission-style Miami Beach Community Church, at Drexel Avenue. The Lincoln Theatre (No. 541–545), at Pennsylvania Avenue, is a classical four-story Art Deco gem with friezes. The New World Symphony, a national advanced-training orchestra led by Michael Tilson Thomas, rehearses and performs here, and concerts are often broadcast via loudspeakers, to the delight of visitors. Just west, facing Pennsylvania, a fabulous Cadillac dealership sign was discovered underneath the facade of the Lincoln Road Millennium Building, on the south side of the mall. At Euclid Avenue there's a monument to Lapidus, who in his 90s watched the renaissance of his whimsical creation. At Lenox Avenue, a black-and-white Art Deco movie house with a Mediterranean barrel-tile roof is now the Colony Theater (No. 1040), where live theater and experimental films are presented. ⊠ *Lincoln Rd., between Collins Ave. and Alton Rd., South Beach.*

FodorsChoice

★

THE OCEAN DRIVE HUSTLE

As you stroll by the sidewalk restaurants lining Ocean Drive, don't be surprised if you are solicited by a pretty hostess, who will literally shove a menu in your face to entice you to her café—which is exactly like every other eatery on the strip. Use the chance to bargain. Ask for a free glass of champagne with dinner, and you'll be surprised when you get a whole bottle!

NEED A BREAK?

Lincoln Road is a great place to cool down with an icy treat while touring South Beach. Try the homemade ice cream and sorbets—including Indian mango, key lime, and litchi—from the Frieze Ice Cream Factory (⊠ *1626 Michigan Ave., south of Lincoln Rd., South Beach* ☎ *305/538–2028*). Or try an authentic Italian gelato at the sleek glass-and-stainless-steel Gelateria

Parmalat (✉ *670 Lincoln Rd., between Euclid and Pennsylvania Aves., South Beach* ☎ *786/276–9475*). If you visit on a Sunday, stop at one of the many juice vendors, who will whip up made-to-order smoothies from mangos, oranges, and other fresh local fruits.

⑨ Miami Children's Museum. This Arquitectonica-designed museum, both imaginative and geometric in appearance, is directly across the MacArthur Causeway from Parrot Jungle Island. Twelve galleries house hundreds of interactive, bilingual exhibits. Children can scan plastic groceries in the supermarket, scramble through a giant sand castle, climb a rock wall, learn about the Everglades, and combine rhythms in the world-music studio. ✉ *980 MacArthur Causeway, Watson Island, Miami* ☎ *305/373–5437* ⊕ *www.miamichildrensmuseum.org* ✏ *$10, parking $1 per hr* ☉ *Daily 10–6.*

⑩ Jungle Island. South Florida's original tourist attraction, the park is home to more than 1,100 exotic birds, a few orangutans and snakes, a squadron of flamingos, a rare albino alligator, a liger (lion and tiger mix) and a 28-foot long "crocosaur," plus amazing orchids and other flowering plants. There's also the Hippo, but in this case, it's a three-story waterslide open on weekends. Kids enjoy the hands-on (make that wings-on) experience of having parrots perch on their shoulders. The Japanese garden that once stood on this site is next door—it's open on weekends and free to enter. ■ **TIP→You can eat at the indoor-outdoor lakeside café, overlooking the Caribbean flamingos, without paying the park's admission fee.** ✉ *1111 Parrot Jungle Trail, off MacArthur Causeway (I–395), Watson Island, Miami* ☎ *305/400–7000* ⊕ *www.parrotjungle.com* ✏ *$22.95 plus $7 parking* ☉ *Daily 10–6.*

❶ Sanford L. Ziff Jewish Museum of Florida. Listed on the National Register of Historic Places, this former synagogue, built in 1936, contains Art Deco chandeliers, 80 impressive stained-glass windows, and a permanent exhibit, MOSAIC: Jewish Life in Florida, which depicts more than 235 years of the Florida Jewish experience. The museum also hosts changing exhibits and events and has a museum store. ✉ *301 Washington Ave., at 3rd St., South Beach* ☎ *305/672–5044* ⊕ *www.jewishmuseum.com* ✏ *$6, free on Sat.* ☉ *Tues.–Sun. 10–5.* Museum store closed Sat.

★ ❸ Wolfsonian–Florida International University. An elegantly renovated 1927 storage facility is now both a research center and home to the 70,000-plus-item collection of modern design and "propaganda arts" amassed by Miami native Mitchell ("Micky") Wolfson Jr., a world traveler and connoisseur. Broad themes of the 19th and 20th centuries—nationalism, political persuasion, industrialization—are addressed in permanent and traveling shows. Included in the museum's eclectic holdings, which represent Art Deco, Art Moderne, Art Nouveau, Arts and Crafts, and other aesthetic movements, are 8,000 matchbooks collected by Egypt's King Farouk. ✉ *1001 Washington Ave., at 10th St., South Beach* ☎ *305/531–1001* ⊕ *www.wolfsonian.org* ✏ *$7, free after 6 on Fri.* ☉ *Mon., Tues., Sat., and Sun. noon–6, Thurs. and Fri. noon–9.*

4 **World Erotic Art Museum (WEAM).** The prudish can skip right on to the next stop, but anyone with an appreciation for the offbeat should check out whimsical, wonderful WEAM. The sexy collection, all owned by millionaire Naomi Wilzig, unfolds with contemporary and historical art of varying quality—there are amazing fertility statues from around the globe dating to 500 BC sharing the space with knickknacks that look like they came from the bawdiest yard sale on earth. An original phallic prop from Stanley Kubrick's *A Clockwork Orange* and an over-the-top Kama Sutra bed are worth the price of admission, but the real standout is "Miss Naomi," who is usually on hand to answer questions and provide behind-the-scenes anecdotes. Kids 17 and under are not admitted. ✉ *1205 Washington Ave., at 12th St., South Beach* ☎ *305/532–9336* ⊕ *www.weam.com* ✎ *$15* ⊙ *Daily 11 AM–midnight.*

DOWNTOWN MIAMI

Downtown Miami dazzles from a distance. The skyline is fluid, thanks to the sheer number of sparkling glass high-rises springing up between Biscayne Blvd. and the Miami River. Business is the key to downtown Miami's daytime bustle. Traffic congestion from the high-rise offices and expensive parking tend to keep the locals away, unless they're bringing out-of-town guests to touristy Bayside Marketplace. But change is in the air— the influx of condos and offices is starting to bring in shops and restaurants, most notably Mary Brickell Village, which serves as a culinary oasis for the starved business district. Thanks to the free Metromover, which runs inner and outer loops through Downtown and to nearby neighborhoods to the south and north, this is an excellent tour to take by rail. Attractions are conveniently located within about two blocks of the nearest station. If you're coming from north or east of Downtown, leave your car near a Metromover stop and take the Omni Loop downtown. If you're coming from south or west of Downtown, park your car at a Metrorail station and take a leg of the 21-mi elevated commuter system downtown.

Numbers correspond to the Downtown Miami map.

A GOOD TOUR

Make your way to the Metrorail/Metromover Government Center Station, board the southbound Brickell Avenue Loop, and get off at the Financial District stop. From the station, turn left and head up Brickell Avenue, where sleek high-rises, international banks, and a handful of restaurants have replaced the mansions of yesteryear. For retail therapy or a bite, take a left on Southeast 10th Street to check out Mary Brickell Village.

As you walk across the Miami River via the Brickell Avenue Bridge, check out the parcel of riverfront land on the right, the site of the Miami Circle. A multimillion-dollar development was halted here when archaeologists discovered a circular stone formation and other ancient artifacts. After crossing the bridge, go left to the Hyatt Regency Miami, adjacent to the James L. Knight Convention Center. Walk down Southeast 4th Street to an old yellow-frame house, Flagler Palm Cot-

Downtown Miami

TO AIRPORT
395
N. E. 15th St.
SCHOOL BOARD
N. W. 14th St.
N. E. 14th St.
OMNI
4
N. W. 13th St.
N. E. 13th St.
41
Causeway
Dolphin
N. W. 12th St.
TO MIAMI BEACH
Expressway
CULMER
N. W. 11th St.
N. E. 11th St.
BICENTENNIAL PARK
95
N. W. 10th St.
ELEVENTH STREET
N. E. 10th St.
Bicentennial Park
N. W. 9th St.
OMNI EXTENSION
N. E. 9th St.
AmericanAirlines Arena
METRORAIL
N. W. 8th St.
N. E. 8th St.
PARK WEST
South American
TO PORT OF MIAMI
N. W. 7th St.
OVERTOWN ARENA
N. E. 7th St.
N. W. 6th St.
STATE PLAZA/ ARENA
2
N. E. 6th St.
FREEDOM TOWER
Way
N. W. 5th St.
METROMOVER
COLLEGE NORTH
Bayside Marketplace
N. W. 4th St.
N. E. 4th St.
N. E. 3rd St.
COLLEGE BAYSIDE
N. E. 2nd St.
GOVERNMENT CENTER
N. E. 1st St.
FIRST STREET
3
W. Flagler St.
MIAMI AVE.
E. Flagler St.
S. W. 1st St.
THIRD STREET
S. E. 1st St.
BAYFRONT PARK
S. W. 2nd St.
KNIGHT CENTER
S. E. 2nd St.
S. W. 3rd St.
Biscayne Blvd. Way
S. W. 4th St.
S. E. 4th St.
S. W. 4th St.
Miami River
BRICKELL EXTENSION
Brickell Key
S. W. 5th St.
S. E. 5th St.
S. W. 6th St.
S. E. 6th St.
FIFTH STREET
Brickell Park
95
S. W. 7th St.
S. W. 7th St.
S. E. 7th St.
S. W. 8th St.
S. W. 8th St.
S. E. 8th St.
EIGHTH STREET
METRORAIL

0   1/4 mile
0   1/4 km

KEY
🅼 Metro stops
--- Metromover

tage, a 19th-century anachronism in this modern neighborhood. From the adjoining Bijan's on the River you can look out over the Miami River, a hub of Native American commerce hundreds of years ago (and, more recently, drug running).

From here you can reboard the Metromover at Riverwalk Station to ride past the following sights, or you can remain on foot and walk up Southeast 1st Avenue to Southeast 2nd Street. You'll instantly notice the proliferation of Brazilian flags in the storefronts. This lively part of Downtown draws crowds of South American shoppers. Turn right at Southeast 2nd Street and continue for three blocks, passing the towering 55-story Wachovia Financial Center, the second-tallest building in Florida; royal palms grace its 1-acre Palm Court plaza. Proceed until you reach Biscayne Boulevard at the southwest corner of Bayfront Park. Rising up in the corner of the park is the white *Challenger* Memorial, commemorating the space shuttle that exploded in 1986. Continue north on Biscayne on foot, past Plaza Bolivar, a tribute by Cuban immigrants to their adopted country. You'll reach the JFK Torch of Friendship, a plaza adorned with plaques representing all the South and Central American countries except Cuba, and Bayside Marketplace, the popular entertainment, dining, and retail complex. If you reboarded Metromover, get off at the College/Bayside Station to visit Bayside and to continue the next part of the tour on foot. From Bayside, cross Biscayne and walk up Northeast 3rd Street to Northeast 2nd Avenue, where you'll come upon Miami Dade College, home of two worthy art galleries. One block farther west stands the U.S. Courthouse, notable for the epic Depression-era mural inside that depicts Floridian progress.

Turn south on Northeast 1st Avenue and walk one block to Northeast 2nd Street. On the corner stands the 1922 Historic Gesu Church, one of South Florida's oldest. Return to Northeast 2nd Avenue; then turn right. Before you is the architectural clutter that characterizes downtown Miami: a cacophony of gaudy outlet shops, homely storefronts, and the occasional gem of a building. At 174 East Flagler, the landmark Gusman Center for the Performing Arts is a stunning movie palace that now serves as a concert hall. Now head west on Flagler Street, downtown Miami's commercial spine. You'll see the 1936 Streamline moderne building housing Macy's department store. After one more block on Flagler, the Dade County Courthouse comes into view. After crossing 1st Avenue you'll arrive at the **Miami-Dade Cultural Center** ❸, home of the Miami Art Museum, the Historical Museum of Southern Florida, and the Miami-Dade Public Library. From the adjacent Metrorail/Metromover Government Center Station, you can reboard the Metromover.

Continue north via metro mover's Omni Loop to get a close-up look at the **Freedom Tower** ❷, where the track heads north. To get an even closer view of the tower, once a processing center for Cuban refugees, walk north from College North Station to Northeast 6th Street, then two blocks east to Biscayne. The Omni Loop continues north over the MacArthur Causeway past the *Miami Herald* building, past the

Adrienne Arsht Performing Arts Center ❶, and on to Omni Center, which houses a hotel and defunct mall. Stay on the train for the return trip and a beautiful view of the American Airlines Arena, the architecturally progressive venue that replaced the Miami Arena as home of the Miami Heat.

TIMING

To walk and ride to the various points of interest, allow three hours. If you want to spend additional time eating and shopping at Bayside, allow at least five hours. To include museum visits, allow seven hours.

WHAT TO SEE

❶ **Adrienne Arsht Performing Arts Center.** The buzz associated with the new concert home for the Florida Grand Opera, Miami City Ballet, New World Symphony and Concert Association of Florida, and other local and touring groups has sparked development up and down Biscayne Boulevard. Designed by architect Cesar Pelli, the massive development contains a 2,400-seat opera house, 2,200-seat concert hall, a black-box theater, and an outdoor Plaza for the Arts. ⊠*1300 Biscayne Blvd., at N.E. 13th St., Downtown* ☎*305/949–6722* ⊕*www. carnivalcenter.org.*

❷ **Freedom Tower.** In the 1960s this imposing Spanish-baroque structure was the Cuban Refugee Center, processing more than 500,000 Cubans who entered the United States after fleeing Fidel Castro's regime. Built in 1925 for the *Miami Daily News*, it was inspired by the Giralda, an 800-year-old bell tower in Seville, Spain. Preservationists were pleased to see the tower's exterior restored in 1988. ⊠*600 Biscayne Blvd., at N.E. 6th St., Downtown* ☎No phone.

★ ❸ **Miami-Dade Cultural Center.** Containing three cultural resources, this fortresslike 3-acre complex is a Downtown focal point. The **Miami Art Museum** (☎ *305/375–3000* ⊕*www.miamiartmuseum.org*) is waiting to move into its new space in Museum Park, to be completed in 2010. Meanwhile, it presents major touring exhibitions of work by international artists, focusing on art since 1945. Open Tuesday–Friday 10–5 (until 9 the third Thursday of the month) and weekends noon–5, the museum charges $8 admission ($10 including the historical museum). At the **Historical Museum of Southern Florida** (☎*305/375–1492* ⊕*www. hmsf.org*) you'll be treated to pure South Floridiana, with exhibits celebrating Miami's multicultural heritage and history, including an old Miami streetcar, cigar labels, and a railroad exhibit, plus a display on prehistoric Miami. Admission is $8 ($10 including the art museum), and hours are Monday to Saturday 10–5, and Sunday noon–5. The **Main Public Library** (☎*305/375–2665*)—open Monday to Wednesday and Friday to Saturday 9–6, Thursday 9–9, plus Sunday 1–5 from August to May—contains nearly 4 million holdings and a Florida Department that includes rare books, documents, and photographs recording Miami history. It also has art exhibits in the auditorium and in the second-floor lobby. ⊠*101 W. Flagler St., between N.W. 1st and 2nd Aves., Downtown.*

4 **Wynwood Art District.** Just north of downtown Miami, the up-and-coming Wynwood Art District is peppered with galleries, art studios, and private collections that are open to the public. Visit during Wynwood's monthly gallery walk to maximize viewing of the smaller venues. Make sure a visit includes a stop at the

★ **Margulies Collection at the Warehouse** (✉ *591 N.W. 27th St., between N.W. 5th and 6th Aves., Downtown* ☎ *305/576–1051* ⊕ *www.marguarieswarehouse.com*). Martin Margulies's collection of vintage and contemporary photography, videos, and installation art in a 45,000-square-foot space makes for eye-popping viewing. It's free to enter and open from October to April, Wednesday to Saturday, 11 to 4. Fans of edgy art will appreciate the **Rubell Family Collection** (✉ *95 N.W. 29th St., between N. Miami Ave. and N.W. 1st Ave., Downtown* ☎ *305/573–6090* ⊕ *www.rubellfamilycollection.com*). Mera and Don Rubell have accumulated work by artists from the 1970s to the present, including Jeff Koons, Cindy Sherman, Damien Hirst, Keith Haring, and Ansel M. Kiefer. Admission is $5, and the gallery is open Wednesday to Sunday 10 to 6. ✉ *N.W. 10th St. to N.W. 37th St. between Biscayne Blvd. and N.W. 6th Ave., Wynwood Art District* ☉ *Times vary, approx. 10–5; gallery walks 2nd Sat. 7–10.*

LITTLE HAVANA

First settled en masse by Cubans in the early 1960s, after that country's Communist revolution, Little Havana is a predominantly working-class area and the core of Miami's Hispanic community. Spanish is the language that predominates, but don't be surprised if the cadence is less Cuban and more Salvadoran or Nicaraguan. The main commercial zone is bounded by Northwest 1st Street, Southwest 9th Street, Ronald Reagan Avenue (Southwest 12th Avenue), and Teddy Roosevelt Boulevard (Southwest 17th Avenue). Calle Ocho (Southwest 8th Street) is the axis of the neighborhood.

Some of the restaurants host traditional flamenco performances and Sevillaña *tablaos* (dances performed on a wood-plank stage, using castanets), and some clubs feature recently arrived Cuban acts. Intimate neighborhood theaters host top-notch productions ranging from Spanish classics to contemporary satire. Throughout the year a variety of festivals commemorate Miami's Hispanic heritage, and residents from no fewer than five countries celebrate their homeland's independence days in Little Havana. On the last Friday of every month Little Havana takes its culture to the streets for Cultural Fridays, between 6:30 and 11 PM on 8th Street from 14th to 17th avenues. Art expositions, music, and avant-garde street performances bring a young, hip crowd to the neighborhood.

Numbers correspond to the Miami, Coral Gables, Coconut Grove & Key Biscayne map.

7

A GOOD WALK

An ideal place to discover the area's flavor, both literally and figuratively, is along Calle Ocho (Southwest 8th Street), at the eastern end of Tamiami Trail between Southwest 12th and 27th avenues. You'll need to drive in, but definitely park, since the only way to really experience the neighborhood is on foot; metered spots are readily available, and it's not too hard to find a free spot on a side street. Start at **Cuban Memorial Boulevard** ❶ a section of Southwest 13th Avenue just south of Calle Ocho. Memorials to Cuban patriots line the boulevard, and the plaza here is the scene of frequent political rallies. On Mother's Day older women adorn a statue of the Virgin Mary with floral wreaths and join in song to honor her. Believers claim a miracle occurs here each midafternoon, when a beam of sunlight shoots through the foliage overhead directly onto the Christ child in the Virgin's arms.

On Calle Ocho to the east of the boulevard is El Aguila Vidente (The Seeing Eagle), one of many neighborhood *botánicas* (stores selling spiritual items). The shop welcomes the respectfully curious. A particularly worthwhile stop is next door at the **El Credito Cigar Factory** ❷. At this family-owned business, one of about a half-dozen cigar factories in the neighborhood, employees deftly hand-roll more than a million stogies each year. On Calle Ocho, between Southwest 13th and 17th avenues, you'll find the Walkway of the Stars. The Latin version of its Hollywood namesake, the strip of sidewalk embedded with stars honors many of the world's top Hispanic celebrities, among them the late salsa queen Celia Cruz, crooner Julio Iglesias, and superstar Gloria Estefan. Stop in at La Casa de los Trucos, a magic store where the owners sometimes demonstrate their skills. Farther west on Calle Ocho is Domino Park, at 15th Avenue. The game tables are always two deep with guayabera-clad men—it wasn't until the last decade that the park's male domino aficionados even allowed women into their domain.

TIMING

If a quick multicultural experience is your goal, set aside an hour or two to do this tour on foot. For real ethnic immersion, allow more time; eating is a must, as well as a peek at the area's residential streets lined with distinctive homes. Especially illuminating are Little Havana tours led by Dr. Paul George (✉ *101 W. Flagler St.* ☎ *305/375–1621*), a history professor at Miami Dade College and historian for the Historical Museum of Southern Florida.

WHAT TO SEE

❶ **Cuban Memorial Boulevard.** Two blocks in the heart of Little Havana are filled with monuments to Cuba's freedom fighters. Among the memorials are the *Eternal Torch of the Brigade 2506,* commemorating those who were killed in the failed Bay of Pigs invasion of 1961; a bust of 19th-century hero Antonio Maceo; and a bas-relief map of Cuba depicting each of its *municipios.* There's also a bronze statue in honor of Tony Izquierdo, who participated in the Bay of Pigs invasion, served in Nicaragua's Somozan forces, and interestingly enough was also on the CIA payroll. ✉ *S.W. 13th Ave., south of S.W. 8th St., Little Havana.*

2 **El Credito Cigar Factory.** Through the giant storefront windows you can see cigars being rolled. Many of the workers at this family business dating back three generations learned their trade in prerevolutionary Cuba. Today the tobacco leaf they use comes primarily from the Dominican Republic and Mexico, and the wrappers from Connecticut, making theirs a truly multinational product. A walk-in humidor has more than 40 brands favored by customers such as Arnold Schwarzenegger, Bill Clinton, Robert De Niro, and Bill Cosby. ⊠*1106 S.W. 8th St., near S.W. 11th Ave., Little Havana* ☎*305/858–4162* ☉ *Mon. –Sat. 9–4.* Factory is closed Saturdays.

NEED A BREAK?

Everywhere in Little Havana are walk-up windows peddling the quick energy of thimble-size *café cubano* for as little as 40¢. The locals call it *un cafecito* (literally, "a small coffee"), but be warned that it's high-octane and sure to keep you going through this tour. In the mood for something refreshing? Try Las Pinareños (⊠*1334 S.W. 8th St., Little Havana* ☎*305/285–1135*), a *fruteria* (fruit stand), for fresh cold coconut juice served in a whole coconut, mango juice, or other *jugos* (juices). For something a little more substantial, pop into Exquisito Restaurant (⊠*1510 S.W. 8th St., Little Havana* ☎*305/643–0227*), next to the Tower Theatre. The unassuming Cuban café serves up delectable yuca with garlic sauce and other traditional dishes.

COCONUT GROVE

Eclectic and intriguing, Miami's Coconut Grove can be considered the tropical equivalent of New York's Greenwich Village. A haven for writers and artists, the neighborhood has never quite outgrown its image as a small village. During the day it's business as usual in Coconut Grove, much as in any other Miami neighborhood. But in the evening, especially on weekends, it seems as if someone flips a switch and the streets come alive. Locals and tourists jam into small boutiques, sidewalk cafés, and stores lodged in two massive retail-entertainment complexes. For blocks in every direction, students, honeymooning couples, families, and prosperous retirees flow in and out of a mix of galleries, restaurants, bars, bookstores, comedy clubs, and theaters. With this weekly influx of traffic, parking can pose a problem. There's a well-lighted city garage at 3315 Rice Street, or look for police to direct you to parking lots where you'll pay $5–$10 for an evening's slot. If you're staying in the Grove, leave the car behind, and your night will get off to an easier start.

Nighttime is the right time to see Coconut Grove, but in the day you can take a casual drive around the neighborhood to see its diverse architecture. Posh estates mingle with rustic cottages, modest frame homes, and stark modern dwellings, often on the same block. If you're into horticulture, you'll be impressed by the Garden of Eden–like foliage that seems to grow everywhere without care. In truth, residents are determined to keep up the Grove's village-in-a-jungle look, so they lavish attention on exotic plantings even as they battle to protect any remaining native vegetation.

Numbers correspond to the Miami, Coral Gables, Coconut Grove & Key Biscayne map.

WHAT TO SEE

❺ Barnacle Historic State Park. A pristine bayfront manse sandwiched between cramped luxury developments, Barnacle is Miami's oldest house still standing on its original foundation. To get here, you'll hike along an old buggy trail through a tropical hardwood hammock and landscaped lawn leading to Bis-

cayne Bay. Built in 1891 by Florida's first snowbird—New Yorker Commodore Ralph Munroe—the large home, built of timber Munroe salvaged from wrecked ships, has many original furnishings, a broad sloping roof, and deeply recessed verandas that channel sea breezes into the house. If your timing is right, you may catch one of the monthly Moonlight Concerts, and the old-fashioned picnic on the Fourth of July is popular. ✉ *3485 Main Hwy., Coconut Grove* ☎ *305/442–6866* ⊕ *www.floridastateparks.org/thebarnacle* ✆ *$1, concerts $5* ☉ *Fri.–Mon. 9–4; tours at 10, 11:30, 1, and 2:30; group tours for 10 or more Tues.–Thurs. by reservation; concerts Sept.–May on evenings near the full moon 6–9, call for dates.*

❻ CocoWalk. This indoor-outdoor mall has three floors of nearly 40 name-brand (Victoria's Secret, Gap, Banana Republic, etc.) and independent shops that stay open almost as late as its popular restaurants and clubs. Kiosks with beads, incense, herbs, and other small items are scattered around the ground level; street entertainers hold court on weekends; and the movie theaters and nightspots are upstairs. If you're ready for an evening of touristy people-watching, this is the place. ✉ *3015 Grand Ave., Coconut Grove* ☎ *305/444–0777* ⊕ *www.galleryatcoco walk.com* ☉ *Sun.–Thurs. 11–10, Fri. and Sat. 11 AM–midnight.*

❹ Miami Museum of Science and Planetarium. This museum is chock-full of ☺ hands-on sound, gravity, and electricity displays for children and adults alike. A wildlife center houses native Florida snakes, turtles, tortoises, and birds of prey. Outstanding traveling exhibits appear throughout the year, and virtual reality, life-science demonstrations, and Internet technology are on hand every day. If you're here the first Friday of the month, stick around for a laser-light rock-and-roll show, presented in the planetarium at 9, 10 and 11, or just check out the Weintraub Observatory for free. ✉ *3280 S. Miami Ave., Coconut Grove* ☎ *305/646–4200* ⊕ *www.miamisci.org* ✆ *Museum exhibits, planetarium shows, and wildlife center $20, laser show $7* ☉ *Museum daily 10–6.*

③ **Vizcaya Museum & Gardens.** Of the 10,000 people living in Miami
Fodor'sChoice between 1912 and 1916, about 1,000 of them were gainfully employed
★ by Chicago industrialist James Deering to build this Italian Renaissance–style winter residence. Once comprising 180 acres, the grounds
now occupy a 30-acre tract that includes a native hammock and more
than 10 acres of formal gardens with fountains overlooking Biscayne
Bay. The house, open to the public, contains 70 rooms, 34 of which
are filled with paintings, sculpture, antique furniture, and other fine
and decorative arts. The pieces date from the 15th through the 19th
century and represent the Renaissance, baroque, rococo, and neoclassical movements. So unusual and impressive is Vizcaya that visitors have
included many major heads of state. Guided tours are available. Moonlight tours, in particular, offer a unique look at the gardens; call for
reservations. ⊠ *3251 S. Miami Ave., Coconut Grove* ☎ *305/250–9133*
⊕ *www.vizcayamuseum.org* ☜ *$12* ⊙ *Daily 9:30–4:30.*

CORAL GABLES

You can easily spot Coral Gables from the window of a Miami-bound
jetliner—just look for the massive orange tower of the Biltmore Hotel
rising from a lush green carpet of trees concealing the city's gracious
homes. The canopy is as much a part of this planned city as its distinctive architecture, all attributed to the vision of George E. Merrick
nearly 100 years ago.

The story of this city began in 1911, when Merrick inherited 1,600
acres of citrus and avocado groves from his father. Through judicious
investment he nearly doubled the tract to 3,000 acres by 1921. Merrick
dreamed of building an American Venice here, complete with canals
and homes. Working from this vision, he began designing a city based
on centuries-old prototypes from Mediterranean countries. Unfortunately for Merrick, the devastating no-name hurricane of 1926, followed by the Great Depression, prevented him from fulfilling many of
his plans. He died at 54, an employee of the post office. Today Coral
Gables has a population of about 43,000. In its bustling downtown,
more than 150 multinational companies maintain headquarters or
regional offices, and the University of Miami campus in the southern
part of the Gables brings a youthful vibrancy to the area. A southern
branch of the city extends down the shore of Biscayne Bay through
neighborhoods threaded with canals. The gorgeous Fairchild Tropical
Botanic Garden and beachfront Matheson Hammock Park dominate
this part of the Gables.

Numbers correspond to the Miami, Coral Gables, Coconut Grove &
Key Biscayne map.

WHAT TO SEE

⑫ **Biltmore Hotel.** Bouncing back stunningly from its dark days as an army
★ hospital, this hotel has become the jewel of Coral Gables—a dazzling
architectural gem with a colorful past. First opened in 1926, it was a
hot spot for the rich and glamorous of the Jazz Age until it was converted to an Army–Air Force regional hospital in 1942. The Veterans

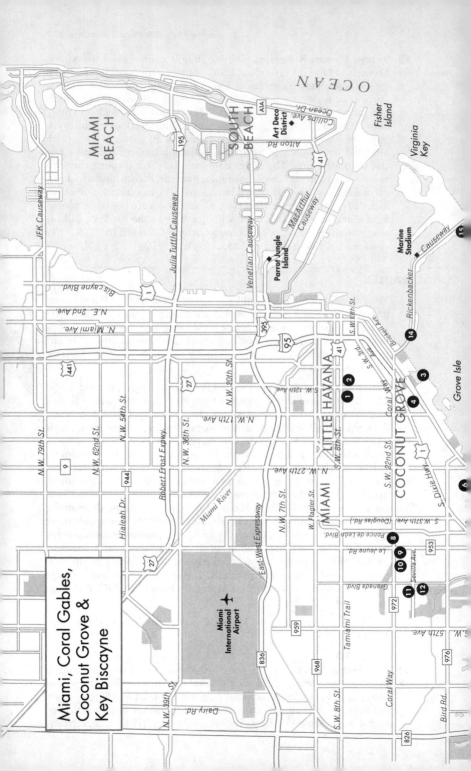

ATLANTIC

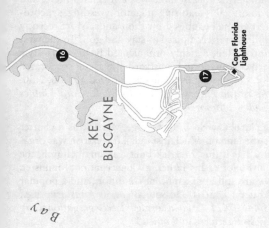

Biscayne Bay

KEY BISCAYNE

16

17

◆ Cape Florida
Lighthouse

5
7

CORAL GABLES

S.W. 72nd St.

Coral Gables

Sunset Dr.

Maynada St.

Ponce de León Rd.

Red Rd.

Cartagena Plaza

Waterway

Old Cutler Rd.

Ponce de León Blvd.

874

986

SOUTH MIAMI

13

0   3 km

0   3 miles

Administration continued to operate the hospital after World War II, until 1968. Then the Biltmore lay vacant for nearly 20 years before it underwent extensive renovations and reopened as a luxury hotel in 1987. Its 16-story tower, like the Freedom Tower in downtown Miami, is a replica of Seville's Giralda Tower. The magnificent pool, reportedly the largest hotel pool in the continental United States, is steeped in history—Johnny Weissmuller of Tarzan fame was a lifeguard there, and in the 1930s grand aquatic galas featuring alligator wrestling, synchronized swimming, and bathing beauties drew thousands. More recently it was President Clinton's preferred place to stay and golf. To the west is the Biltmore Country Club, a richly ornamented Beaux Arts–style structure with a superb colonnade and courtyard; it was reincorporated into the hotel in 1989. On Sunday free tours are offered at 1:30, 2:30, and 3:30. ✉ *1200 Anastasia Ave., near De Soto Blvd., Coral Gables* ☎ *305/445–1926* ⊕ *www.biltmorehotel.com.*

⓫ **Coral Gables Congregational Church.** With George Merrick as a charter member (he donated the land on which it stands), this parish was organized in 1923. Rumor has it that Merrick built this small church, the first in the Gables, in honor of his father, a Congregational minister. The original interiors are still in magnificent condition, and a popular concert series is held here. ✉ *3010 De Soto Blvd., at Anastasia Ave., Coral Gables* ☎ *305/448–7421* ⊕ *www.coralgablescongregational.org* ⊗ *Weekdays 8:30–5, Sun. services at 9 and 11.*

❾ **Coral Gables Merrick House and Gardens.** In 1976 the city of Coral Gables acquired Merrick's boyhood home. Restored to its 1920s appearance, it contains Merrick family furnishings and artwork. The breezy veranda and coral-rock construction are details you'll see repeated on many of the grand homes along Coral Way. ✉ *907 Coral Way, at Toledo St., Coral Gables* ☎ *305/460–5361* 🎫 *House $5, grounds free* ⊗ *House tours Wed. and Sun. at 1, 2 and 3; grounds daily 8–sunset.*

OFF THE BEATEN PATH

Everglades Alligator Farm. Here's your chance to see gators, gators, gators—2,000 or so—and other wildlife, of course, such as blue herons, snowy egrets, and perhaps a rare roseate spoonbill. You can also take in alligator wrestling, reptile shows, and other animal exhibits as well as an airboat ride (they're not allowed inside Everglades National Park). This place is a little over 30 mi south of Miami, just south of the former pioneer town of Homestead. ✉ *40351 S.W. 192nd Ave., Florida City* ☎ *305/247–2628* ⊕ *www.everglades.com* 🎫 *$13.50, $19 with airboat tour* ⊗ *Daily 9–6.*

⓭ **Fodor's**Choice ★ **Fairchild Tropical Botanic Garden.** With 83 acres of lakes, sunken gardens, a 560-foot vine pergola, orchids, bellflowers, coral trees, bougainvillea, rare palms, and flowering trees, Fairchild is the largest tropical botanical garden in the continental United States. The tram tour highlights the best of South Florida's flora; then set off exploring on your own. A 2-acre rain-forest exhibit showcases tropical rain-forest plants from around the world complete with a waterfall and stream. The conservatory, Windows to the Tropics, houses rare tropical plants, including the Titan Arum (*Amorphophallus titanum*), a fast-growing variety that attracted thousands of visitors when it bloomed in 1998. (It was only the sixth documented bloom in this country in the 20th century.) The Keys Coastal Habitat, created in a marsh and mangrove area in 1995 with assistance from the Tropical Audubon Society, provides food and shelter to resident and migratory birds. Check out the Montgomery Botanical Center, a research facility devoted to palms and cycads. Spicing up Fairchild's calendar are plant sales, afternoon teas, and genuinely special events year-round, such as the International Mango Festival the second weekend in July. The excellent bookstore–gift shop carries books on gardening and horticulture, and the Garden Café serves sandwiches and, seasonally, smoothies made from the garden's own crop of tropical fruits. ✉ *10901 Old Cutler Rd., Coral Gables* ☎ *305/667–1651* ⊕ *www.fairchildgarden.org* 🖅 *$20* ⊙ *Daily 9:30–5.*

OFF THE BEATEN PATH

Metrozoo. Don't miss a visit to this top-notch zoo, the only subtropical zoo in the continental United States. Its 290 acres, 14 mi south of Miami, are home to more than 900 animals that roam on islands surrounded by moats. Take the monorail for a cool overview, then walk around to take a closer look at such attractions as the Tiger Temple, where white tigers roam, and the African Plains exhibit, where giraffes, ostriches, and zebras graze in a simulated natural habitat. You can even feed veggies to the giraffes at Samburu Station. The Wings of Asia aviary has about 300 exotic birds representing 70 species flying free within the junglelike enclosure. There's also a petting zoo with a meerkat exhibit and interactive opportunities, such as those at Dr. Wilde's World and the Ecology Theater, where kids can touch Florida animals like alligators and opossums. An educational and entertaining wildlife show is given three times daily. In addition to standard fare, the snack bar offers local favorites such as Cuban sandwiches, *arepas* (corn pancake sandwiches), and Cuban coffee—and cold beer. ✉ *12400 Coral Reef Dr. (S.W. 152nd St.), Richmond Heights, Miami* ☎ *305/251–0400* ⊕ *www.miamimetrozoo.com* 🖅 *$13.95,$9.95 per child. 45-min tram tour $4.95* ⊙ *Daily 9:30–5:30; gates close at 4 pm. last admission at 4.*

⑧ Miracle Mile. Even with competition from some impressive malls, this half-mile stretch of retail stores continues to thrive because of its intriguing mixture of unique boutiques, bridal shops, art galleries, charming restaurants, and upscale nightlife venues. ✉ *Coral Way between S.W. 37th and S.W. 42nd Aves., Coral Gables.*

⑩ Venetian Pool. Sculpted from a rock quarry in 1923 and fed by artesian wells, this 825,000-gallon municipal pool remains quite popular because of its themed architecture—a fantasized version of a waterfront Italian village—created by Denman Fink. The pool has earned a place on the National Register of Historic Places and showcases a nice collection of vintage photos depicting 1920s beauty pageants and swank soirées held long ago. Paul Whiteman played here, Johnny Weissmuller and Esther Williams swam here, and you should, too (but no kids under three). A snack bar, lockers, and showers make this must-see user-friendly as well. ✉ *2701 De Soto Blvd., at Toledo St., Coral Gables* ☎ *305/460–5356* ⊕ *www.venetianpool.com* 🖅 *Apr.–Oct.,*

Fodor$Choice
★

7

$10; Nov.–Mar., $6.75, free parking across De Soto Blvd. ⊘*June–Aug., weekdays 11–7:30, weekends 10–4:30; Sept. and Oct., Apr. and May, Tues.–Fri. 11–5:30, weekends 10–4:30; Nov.–Mar., Tues.–Fri. 10–4:30, weekends 10–4:30.*

KEY BISCAYNE & VIRGINIA KEY

Once upon a time, these barrier islands were an outpost for fishermen and sailors, pirates and salvagers, soldiers and settlers. The 95-foot Cape Florida Lighthouse stood tall during Seminole Indian battles and hurricanes. Coconut plantations covered two-thirds of Key Biscayne, and there were plans as far back as the 1800s to develop the picturesque island as a resort for the wealthy. Fortunately, the state and county governments set much of the land aside for parks, and both keys are now home to top-ranked beaches and golf, tennis, softball, and picnicking facilities. The long and winding bike paths that run through the islands are favorites for in-line skaters and cyclists. Incorporated in 1991, the village of Key Biscayne is a hospitable community of about 10,500; Virginia Key remains undeveloped at the moment, making these two playground islands especially family-friendly.

Numbers correspond to the Miami, Coral Gables, Coconut Grove & Key Biscayne map.

WHAT TO SEE

17 ⓒ **Bill Baggs Cape Florida State Park.** Thanks to great beaches, sunsets, and a
Fodor'sChoice lighthouse, this park at Key Biscayne's southern tip is worth the drive.
★ It has boardwalks, 18 picnic shelters, and two cafés that serve light lunches. A stroll or ride along walking and bicycle paths provides wonderful views of Miami's dramatic skyline. From the southern end of the park you can see a handful of houses rising over the bay on wooden stilts, the remnants of Stiltsville, built in the 1940s and now dying a natural death. Bill Baggs has bicycle rentals, a playground, fishing piers, and guided tours of the **Cape Florida Lighthouse,** South Florida's oldest structure. The lighthouse was erected in 1845 to replace an earlier one destroyed in an 1836 Seminole attack, in which the keeper's helper was killed. Plantings around the lighthouse and keeper's cottage recall the island's past. The restored cottage and lighthouse offer free tours at 10 AM and 1 PM Thursday–Monday. Be there a half hour beforehand. ✉ *1200 S. Crandon Blvd., Key Biscayne* ☎ *305/361–5811 or 305/361–8779* ⊕ *www.floridastateparks.org/capeflorida* ✉ *$3 per single-occupant vehicle, $5 per vehicle with 2–8 people; $1 per person on bicycle, bus, motorcycle, or foot* ⊘ *Daily 8–dusk, tours Thurs.–Mon. at 10 and 1; sign up ½ hr beforehand.*

ⓒ **16** **Crandon Park.** This laid-back park in northern Key Biscayne is popular with families, and many educated beach enthusiasts rate the 3½-mi beach here among the top 10 beaches in North America. The sand is soft, there are no riptides, there's a great view of the Atlantic, and parking is both inexpensive and plentiful. Because it's a weekend favorite of locals, you'll get a good taste of multicultural Miami flavor: salsa and hip-hop, jerk chicken and barbecue ribs. **Crandon Gardens** at Cran-

A GOOD DRIVE

Day or night, there are few drives prettier than the one to Key Biscayne and Virginia Key. And if you're in a convertible on a balmy day—well, this kind of drive is what South Florida living is all about. You can also make this tour on in-line skates or bicycle.

From I–95 take the Key Biscayne exit to the Rickenbacker Causeway (a $1.25 toll covers your round-trip). If you plan to skate or bike, just park anywhere along the causeway after the tollbooth and take off. The beaches on either side of the causeway are popular for water sports, with sailboards, sailboats, and Jet Skis available for rental. The causeway bridge rises 75 feet, providing a spectacular if fleeting view of the cruise ships at the Port of Miami, to the north. You can also see the high-rises looming at the tip of South Beach to the northeast, the bright blue Atlantic straight ahead, and sailboat-dotted Biscayne Bay to the south. South of Powell Bridge you'll see anglers fishing off the **Old Rickenbacker Causeway Bridge** ⓮ among the hungry seabirds.

After the causeway turns southeast on Virginia Key, you can spy the gold geodesic dome of the **Miami Seaquarium** ⓯. Visit the undersea world of South Florida and beyond; then cross the Bear Cut Bridge

(popular for fishing) onto lush Key Biscayne. Past the marina on your right, winding Crandon Boulevard takes you to **Crandon Park** ⓰, home to one of South Florida's best-loved beaches. As you approach the village of Key Biscayne, take note of the iguana-crossing signs warning motorists of the many green reptiles that scamper about the area. As you drive through town, you'll see luxurious beachfront condos and smaller buildings on your left and single-family houses on your right. Peek down some of the side streets—especially those along waterways—and you can spot spectacular bayfront mansions. Crandon turns into Grapetree Drive as you enter **Bill Baggs Cape Florida State Park** ⓱, a 410-acre park with great beaches, an excellent café, picnic areas, and at its southern tip the brick Cape Florida Lighthouse and light keeper's cottage. After you've taken the sun, or perhaps a bicycle ride, in the park, backtrack on Crandon to the causeway. On your way to the mainland, there's a panoramic view of downtown Miami as you cross the bridge.

TIMING

Set aside the better part of a day for this tour, saving a few afternoon hours for Crandon Park and the Cape Florida Lighthouse.

don Park was once the site of a zoo. There are swans, waterfowl, and even hundreds of huge iguanas running loose. Nearby are a restored carousel (open weekends and major holidays), outdoor roller rink, and playground. At the north end of the beach is the free **Marjory Stoneman Douglas Biscayne Nature Center** (☎ *305/361–6767*), open daily 9–4. Here you can explore sea-grass beds on a tour with a naturalist; see red, black, and white mangroves; and hike along the beach and hammock in the Bear Cut Preserve. The park also sponsors hikes and tours. ✉ *4000 Crandon Blvd., Key Biscayne* ☎ *305/361–5421* ⊕ *www.biscaynenaturecenter.org* ✐ *Free, parking $5 per vehicle* ☉ *Daily 8–sunset.*

⑮ Miami Seaquarium. This classic but aging visitor attraction stages shows with sea lions, dolphins, and Lolita the killer whale. The Crocodile Flats exhibit has 26 Nile crocodiles. Discovery Bay, an endangered mangrove habitat, is home to indigenous Florida fish and rays, alligators, herons, egrets, and ibis. You can visit a shark pool, a tropical reef aquarium, and West Indian manatees. The big draw now is the Swim with Our Dolphins program. A two-hour session offers one-on-one interaction with the dolphins. It's expensive—$189 to touch, kiss, and swim with them—but the price does include park admission, towel, and snacks. Call for reservations. ■TIP→Book online and save $2 per ticket. ✉4400 Rickenbacker Causeway, Virginia Key, Miami ☎305/361–5705 ⊕www.miamiseaquarium.com ✒$29.95, and $22.95 for children. dolphin swim program $189, parking $7 ⊙Daily 9:30–6, last admission at 4:30; dolphin swim daily at 9:30, 11:30 and 2:30.

⑭ Old Rickenbacker Causeway Bridge. Here you can watch boat traffic pass through the channel, pelicans and other seabirds soar and dive, and dolphins cavort in the bay. Park at the bridge entrance, about a mile from the tollgate, and walk past anglers tending their lines to the gap where the center draw span across the Intracoastal Waterway was removed. On the right, on cool, clear winter evenings, the water sparkles with dots of light from hundreds of shrimp boats. ✉Rickenbacker Causeway south of Powell Bridge, east of Coconut Grove, Miami.

WHERE TO EAT

Restaurants listed here have passed the test of time, but you might double-check by phone before you set out for the evening. At many of the hottest spots, you'll need a reservation to avoid a long wait for a table. And when you get your check, note whether a gratuity is already included; most restaurants add between 15% and 18% (ostensibly for the convenience of, and protection from, the many Latin-American and European tourists who are used to this practice in their homelands), but reduce or supplement it depending on your opinion of the service.

BEST BETS FOR MIAMI DINING

With thousands of restaurants to choose from, how will you decide where to eat? Fodor's writers and editors have selected their favorite restauraunts by price, cuisine, and experience in the Best Bets lists below. In the first column, Fodor's Choice designations represent the " best of the best" in every price category. Find specific details about a restaurant in the full reviews, listed alphabetically by neighborhood.

Fodor'sChoice ★

Azul $$$-$$$$
Big Pink $-$$
Havana Harry's $-$$
Nemo $$$-$$$$
Pascal's on Ponce $$$-$$$$
The Forge $$$-$$$$
Timo $$$$

By Price

¢

Arnie and Richie's
Tobacco Road

$

Big Pink
Tutto Pasta

$$

Las Culebrinas
Novecento

$$$

Café Prima Pasta
Emeril's

$$$$

The Forge
Joe's Stone Crab

By Cuisine

American

The Forge $$$-$$$$
News Café $-$$$

ASIAN

SushiSamba Dromo $$-$$$$
Hy-Vong Vietnamese Cuisine ¢-$$

FRENCH

Le Bouchon du Grove $$$
Pascal's on Ponce $$-$$$

ITALIAN

Osteria del Teatro $$-$$$$
Café Prima Pasta $$$

Spanish/Cuban

Las Culebrinas $-$$
Versailles $-$$
Novecento ¢-$$

SEAFOOD

Joe's Stone Crab $$$-$$$$
Nemo $$$-$$$$

STEAKHOUSE

Prime One Twelve $$$$
Tuscan Steak $$-$$$$

By Experience

CHILD-FRIENDLY

Tutto Pasta $
Versailles $-$$

HISTORIC INTEREST

Versailles $-$$
The Forge $$$$

HOTEL DINING

Cioppino $$-$$$$
Blue Door at the Delano $$$-$$$$

HOT SPOTS

Michael's Genuine Food & Drink $$$
Novecento ¢-$$

LATE-NIGHT DINING

Big Pink $-$$
News Café $-$$$
Pizza Rustica $
Sushi Samba Dromo $$-$$$

MOST ROMANTIC

Café Prima Pasta $$-$$$
Nemo $$$-$$$$
Special Occasion
The Forge $$$$
Prime One Twelve $$$$

7

Where to Eat in the Miami Area

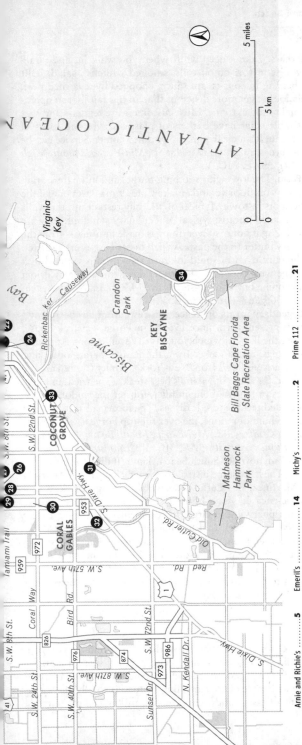

ATLANTIC OCEAN

Virginia
Key

Biscayne
Bay

Rickenbacker Causeway

Crandon
Park

KEY
BISCAYNE

Biscayne

Bill Baggs Cape Florida
State Recreation Area

COCONUT
GROVE

Matheson
Hammock
Park

CORAL
GABLES

Tamiami Trail

Coral Way

Bird Rd.

Red Rd.

Old Cutler Rd.

S. Dixie Hwy.

S.W. 57th Ave.

N. Kendall Dr.

Sunset Dr.

S. Dixie Hwy.

S.W. 72nd St.

S.W. 87th Ave.

S.W. 24th St.

S.W. 40th Ave.

S.W. 8th St.

S.W. 8th St.

S.W. 22nd St.

5 miles

5 km

MID-BEACH & NORTH

¢-$ **✗ Arnie and Richie's.** Take a deep whiff when you walk in, and you'll
DELICATESSEN know what you're in for: onion rolls, smoked whitefish salad, half-sour pickles, herring in sour-cream sauce, chopped liver, corned beef, pastrami. Deli doesn't get more delicious than in this family-run operation that's casual to the extreme. Most customers are regulars and seat themselves at tables that have baskets of plastic knives and forks; if you request a menu, it's a clear sign you're a newcomer. Service can be brusque, but it sure is quick. ⊠ *525 41st St., Mid-Beach, Miami Beach* 📞 *305/531–7691* 🖃 *AE, MC, V.*

★ $$–$$$ **✗ Café Prima Pasta.** The low light, soothing music, and intimate seating
ITALIAN on this restaurant's outdoor veranda make Café Prima Pasta one of the most romantic spots in town. Typical of a family restaurant, the walls are littered with faded photos; typical of a culinary standout, they are also littered with Zagat honors. Everything is made in-house—from the fragrant rosemary butter to the pasta, which tastes best as crab stuffed ravioli or as linguini dyed in squid ink and served with seafood in a lobster sauce. The wine is reliable, but order a cocktail made by Prima Pasta's award winning bartender instead. ⊠ *414 71st St., North Beach, Miami Beach* 📞 *305/867–0106* 🖃 *MC, V.*

$$$–$$$$ **✗ The Forge.** Legendary for its opulence, this restaurant has been wow-
CONTINENTAL ing patrons in its present form since 1968! The Forge is a steak house,
Fodor's Choice but a steak house the likes of which you haven't seen before. Antiques,
★ gilt-framed paintings, a chandelier from the Paris Opera House, and Tiffany stained-glass windows from New York's Trinity Church are the fitting background for some of Miami's best steaks. The tried-and-true menu also includes prime rib, bone-in fillet, lobster thermidor, chocolate soufflé, and Mediterranean side dishes. The focaccia bread is to die for. For its walk-in humidor alone, the over-the-top Forge is worth visiting. ⊠ *432 Arthur Godfrey Rd., Mid-Beach, Miami Beach* 📞 *305/538–8533* ⌕ *Reservations essential* 🖃 *AE, MC, V* ⊙ *No lunch.*

$$$$ **✗ Timo.** Located 5 mi north of South Beach, Timo (Italian for "thyme")
ITALIAN is worth the trip. The handsome bistro, co-owned by chef Tim Andriola
Fodor's Choice and Rodrigo Martinez, has dark-wood walls, Chicago brick, and a
★ dominating stone-encased wood-burning stove. Banquettes around the dining room's periphery and a large flower arrangement at its center add to the quietly elegant feel. Andriola has an affinity for robust Mediterranean flavors: sweetbreads with bacon, honey, and aged balsamic; artisanal pizzas; and homemade pastas. Wood-roasted meats and Parmesan dumplings in a truffled broth are not to be missed. Every bite of every dish attests to the care given. ⊠ *17624 Collins Ave., Sunny Isles* 📞 *305/936–1008* 🖃 *AE, DC, MC, V.*

SOUTH BEACH

$–$$ **✗ Big Pink.** The decor in this innovative diner may remind you of a
AMERICAN roller-skating rink—everything is pink Lucite, stainless steel, and campy
Fodor's Choice (think sports lockers as decorative touches). And the menu is a virtual
★ book, complete with table of contents. But the food is solidly all-American, with dozens of tasty sandwiches, pizzas, turkey or beef burgers,

and side dishes, each and every one composed with a gourmet flair. Customers comprise club kids and real kids, who alternate, depending on the time of day—Big Pink makes a great spot for brunch—but both like to color with the complimentary crayons. ✉*157 Collins Ave., South Beach* ☎*305/532–4700* ☰*AE, MC, V.*

$$$–$$$$
FRENCH
✗**Blue Door at the Delano.** In a hotel where style reigns supreme, this high-profile restaurant provides both glamour and solid cuisine. Acclaimed consulting chef Claude Troisgros combines the flavors of classic French cuisine with South American influences to create a seasonal menu that might include foie gras with berries, or lobster with caramelized banana. Equally pleasing is dining with the crème de la crème of Miami (and New York and Paris) society. Don't recognize the apparent bigwig next to you? Just eavesdrop on his cell phone conversation, and you'll be filled in pronto. ✉*1685 Collins Ave., South Beach* ☎*305/674–6400* ⚭*Reservations essential* ☰*AE, D, DC, MC, V.*

★ **$$$–$$$$**
ITALIAN
✗**Casa Tua.** To accommodate the demanding clientele of this exclusive boutique hotel as well as anyone willing to wait two weeks for a reservation, Casa Tua provides a charming restaurant. You can dine inside or alfresco under the trees. Either way, the idea is to make you feel as if you were at home in a Mediterranean beach house. The food is Italian—sophisticated yet simple dishes, such as truffle risotto and seared diver scallops with an artichoke puree. The service is seamless and relaxed. And the elegant experience is a peaceful respite from Miami Beach's dizzying energy. ✉*1700 James Ave., South Beach* ☎*305/673–1010* ⚭*Reservations essential* ☰*AE, MC, V.*

$$–$$$
SOUTHERN
✗**Emeril's.** "It's getting happy in here" is one of Emeril Lagasse's stock phrases, and now he has brought his brand of happy to Miami Beach. You can expect a different gumbo each day and other New Orleans specialties at Lagasse's ninth restaurant, which appears to have the winning formula down, though the seafood naturally shines in these parts (an andouille-crusted redfish signals the imported Lagasse touch) and the chef has his own take on mango pie and banana cream pie. As a bonus, the restaurant delivers without even a hint of South Beach attitude. ✉*1601 Collins Ave., South Beach* ☎*305/695–4550* ☰*AE, D, DC, MC, V.*

$$–$$$
AMERICAN
✗**Joe Allen.** Crave a good martini along with a terrific burger? Locals head to this hidden hangout in an exploding neighborhood of condos, town houses, and stores. The eclectic crowd includes kids and grandparents, and the menu has everything from pizzas to calves' liver to steaks. Start with an innovative salad, such as arugula with pear, prosciutto, and a Gorgonzola dressing, or roast duck salad with blue cheese and pears. Home-style desserts include banana cream pie and ice-cream-and-cookie sandwiches. Comfortable and homey, this is the perfect place to go when you don't feel like going to a restaurant. ✉*1787 Purdy Ave., South Beach* ☎*305/531–7007* ☰*MC, V.*

$$$–$$$$
SEAFOOD
✗**Joe's Stone Crab Restaurant.** In South Beach's decidedly new-money scene, the stately Joe's Stone Crab is an old school testament to good food and good service. South Beach's most storied restaurant started as a turn of the century eating house when Joseph Weiss discovered succulent stone crabs off the Florida coast. Almost a century later, the

7

restaurant stretches a city block and serves 2,000 dinners a day to local politicians and moneyed patriarchs. Stone crabs, served with legendary mustard sauce, crispy hash browns, and creamed spinach, remain the staple. But don't think you need a trust fund to eat here: Joe's serves sensational fried chicken for $5.95. Finish your meal with tart key lime pie, baked fresh daily. Joe's famously refuses reservations, and weekend waits can be three hours long, so come early or order from Joe's Take Away next door. ⊠*11 Washington Ave., South Beach* ☎*305/673–0365, 305/673–4611 for takeout, 800/780–2722 for overnight shipping* ⌂*Reservations not accepted* ⊟*AE, D, DC, MC, V* ⊘*Closed May–mid-Oct. No lunch Sun. and Mon.*

$-$$$
CHINESE

✕**Miss Yip Chinese Cafe.** As the most popular of only a handful of Chinese restaurants on South Beach, the hip Miss Yip serves up authentic dim sum and steaming fresh Cantonese dishes. Try the Peking duck and the "Princess Jade" sea bass, made of cubes of tender battered fish with Chinese mayo sauce. Then wash it down with one of Miss Yip's many specialty cocktails. A few favorites include the lychee mojito, the ginger martini, and the "Big Bamboo." But be forewarned—Miss Yip's monopoly over South Beach's Chinese scene means you won't be getting any $7.99 specials. ⊠*1661 Meridian Ave., South Beach* ☎*305/534–5488* ⊟*AE, D, DC, MC, V.*

$$$-$$$$
SEAFOOD
Fodor's Choice
★

✕**Nemo.** The SoFi (South of Fifth Street) neighborhood may have emerged as a South Beach hot spot, but Nemo's location is not why this casually comfortable restaurant receives raves. It's the menu, which often changes but always delivers, blending Caribbean, Asian, Mediterranean, and Middle Eastern influences and providing an explosion of cultures in each bite. Popular appetizers include citrus-cured salmon rolls with tobiko caviar and wasabi mayo, and crispy duck leg confit, served with lentils in a tangy pineapple sauce. Main courses might include wok-charred salmon or grilled Indian-spice pork chop. Hedy Goldsmith's funky pastries are exquisitely sinful. Bright colors and copper fixtures highlight the tree-shaded courtyard. ⊠*100 Collins Ave., South Beach* ☎*305/532–4550* ⊟*AE, DC, MC, V.*

$-$$$
AMERICAN

✕**News Café.** An Ocean Drive landmark, this 24-hour café attracts a crowd with snacks, light meals, drinks, and the people parade on the sidewalk out front. Most prefer sitting outside, where they can feel the salt breeze and gawk at the human scenery. Offering a little of this and a little of that—bagels, pâtés, chocolate fondue, sandwiches, and a terrific wine list—this joint has something for everyone. Although service can be indifferent to the point of laissez-faire, the café remains a scene. ⊠*800 Ocean Dr., South Beach* ☎*305/538–6397* ⌂*Reservations not accepted* ⊟*AE, DC, MC, V.*

★ **$$-$$$$**
ITALIAN

✕**Osteria del Teatro.** Thanks to word of mouth, this northern Italian restaurant is constantly full. Orchids grace the tables in the intimate gray-on-gray room with a low, laced-canvas ceiling, Deco lamps, and the most refined clink and clatter along Washington Avenue. Regulars know not to order off the printed menu, however. A tremendous variety of daily specials offers the best options here. A representative appetizer is poached asparagus served over polenta triangles with a Gorgonzola sauce. Stuffed pastas, including spinach crepes overflowing with ricotta, can seem heavy but taste light; fish dishes yield a rose-mary-marinated tuna or salmon in a rosemary shiitake lemon sauce. ✉*1443 Washington Ave., South Beach* ☎*305/538–7850* ⚓*Reservations essential* ▤*AE, DC, MC, V* ☉*Closed Sun. No lunch.*

$$$$
STEAK HOUSE
✗**Prime One Twelve.** This wildly busy steak house is particularly renowned for its highly marbleized prime beef (try the 30-ounce bone-in rib eye for two), creamed corn, truffle macaroni-and-cheese, and buzzing scene: while you stand at the bar awaiting your table (everyone has to wait—at least a little bit), you'll clamor for a drink with all facets of Miami's high society, from the city's top real-estate developers and philanthropists to striking models and celebrities (mentioning the names Lenny Kravitz, Jay-Z, and Matt Damon hardly scratches the surface). ✉*112 Ocean Drive, Miami Beach* ☎*305/532–8112* ▤*AE, D, DC, MC, V.* Elisa Gelb (pr)

$$$–$$$$
JAPANESE
✗**SushiSamba Dromo.** This sibling to the New York City SushiSamba makes an eclectic pairing of Japanese cuisine with Brazilian. The results are fabulous if a bit mystifying: miso-marinated sea bass, hamachi taquitos (basically a yellowtail tartar), mocqueca mista (Brazilian sea-food stew), and caramel passion-fruit sponge cake. Loaded with customers, SushiSamba has a vibe that hurts the ears but warms the trendy heart. ✉*600 Lincoln Rd., South Beach* ☎*305/673–5337* ⚓*Reservations essential* ▤*AE, MC, V.*

★ **$$$–$$$$**
AMERICAN
✗**Talula.** Husband and wife Frank Randazzo and Andrea Curto have each collected numerous awards and fabulous press. At Talula they are cooking together for the first time, while keeping their own styles: she, the cuisine she developed at Wish, joining Asian and tropical influences; he, from the Gaucho Room, grills with a Latin influence. Together they call their style "American creative." Florida wahoo ceviche, Barbe-cued quail, steamed mussels in a saffron broth, grouper with lime and chili, and a tender and moist barbecued pork tenderloin stand out. The key lime pie alone is worth a visit. ✉*210 23rd St., South Beach* ☎*305/672–0778* ▤*AE, MC, D, V.*

★ **$$–$$$$**
ITALIAN
✗**Tuscan Steak.** Dark wood, mirrors, and green upholstery define this chic, masculine place, where big platters of meats and fish are served family-style, assuming yours is a royal family. Tuscan can be as busy as a subway stop, and still the staff is gracious and giving. The chefs take their cues from the Tuscan countryside, where pasta is rich with truffles and main plates are simply but deliciously grilled. Sip red wine with a house specialty: three-mushroom risotto with white truffle oil, gnocchi with Gorgonzola cream, Florentine T-bone with roasted garlic puree, or filet mignon with a Gorgonzola crust in a red wine sauce. Portions are enormous. Bring your friends and share, share, share. ✉*433 Washington Ave., South Beach* ☎*305/534–2233* ▤*AE, DC, MC, V.*

DOWNTOWN MIAMI

$$$–$$$$
ECLECTIC
Fodor'sChoice
★
✗**Azul.** Azul has sumptuously conquered the devil in the details, from chef Clay Conley's exotically rendered Asian-Mediterranean cuisine to the thoughtful service staff who graciously anticipate your broader dining needs. Does your sleeveless blouse leave you too cold to properly

appreciate the Moroccan lamb and seared red snapper? Ask for one of the house pashminas, available in a variety of fashionable colors. Forgot your reading glasses and can't decipher the hanger steak with foie-gras sauce? Request a pair from the host. Want to see how the other half lives? Descend the interior staircase to Cafe Sambal, the all-day casual restaurant downstairs. ⊠*Mandarin Oriental Hotel, 500 Brickell Key Dr., Brickell Key* ☎*305/913–8288* ⌕*Reservations essential* ⊟*AE, MC, V* ⊘*Closed Sun. No lunch weekends.*

\$\$–\$\$\$
AMERICAN

✗**Michael's Genuine Food & Drink.** This sophisticated new eatery has finally put Miami's Design District on the culinary map. The ultrahip restaurant reflects its surroundings—beautifully arranged combinations like crispy beach cheek with whipped celeriac and sweet & spicy pork belly with kimchi explode with unlikely, but satisfying, flavor. Owner Michael Schwartz, famous for South Beach's popular Nemo Restaurant, aims for sophisticated American cuisine with a touch of Latin and Asian influence, and he gets it right. Portions are divided into small, medium, and large plates, and the smaller plates are more inventive. So order several and explore. ⊠*130 N.E. 40th St., Downtown* ☎*305/573–5550* ⊟*AE, MC, V.*

> ### CHEAP EATS ON SOUTH BEACH
>
> Miami Beach is notorious for overpriced eateries, but locals know better. **Pizza Rustica** (⊠ 8th St. and Washington Ave., 14th St. and Washington Ave., and on Lincoln Rd.) serves up humungous slices overflowing with mozzarella, steak, olives, and barbecue chicken until 4 AM. **La Sandwicherie** (⊠ 14th St. between Collins Ave. and Washington Ave.) serves gourmet French sandwiches, a mean prosciutto salad, and healthy smoothies. **Lime Mexican Grill** (⊠ Alton Rd. and 14th St.) serves fresh and tangy fish tacos and homemade guacamole.

\$\$–\$\$\$
MEDI-
TERRANEAN

✗**Michy's.** Miami's homegrown star chef Michelle Bernstein now has her own gig. The funky, blue, late 1960s–inspired dining room on the mainland's "Upper East Side" serves exquisite French- and Mediterranean-influenced seafood dishes at over-the-causeway (read: non-tourist-trap) prices. Plates come in half portions and full portions, which makes the restaurant even more of a deal. Can't-miss entrées include the blue cheese and fig croquetas, the beef short rib and the steak frite au poivre. ⊠*6927 Biscayne Blvd., Upper East Side* ☎*305/759–2001* ⊟*AE, D, DC, MC, V.*

\$–\$\$
ARGENTINE

✗**Novecento.** This Argentine eatery is the Miami financial district's answer to Ocean Drive: the people are still beautiful, but now they're wearing suits. Known for its empanadas (tender chicken or spinach and cheese), simple grilled meats (luscious grilled skirt steak with chimichurri), and the innovative Ensalate Novecento (grilled skirt steak, french fries, avocado, and greens), it's no wonder Novecento is Brickell Avenue's best power lunch and happy hour spot. Come for Sunday brunch and enjoy the signature parallida, a small grill with an assortment of steaks, sausages, and sweetbreads (not sweet bread, but rather the sweet pancreas of a lamb or calf). ⊠*1414 Brickell Ave., Downtown Miami* ☎*305/403–0900* ⊟*AE, D, DC, MC, V.*

$-$$$ **✕Perricone's Marketplace and Café.** Brickell Avenue south of the Miami
ITALIAN River is burgeoning with Italian restaurants, and this lunch place for
local bigwigs is the biggest and most popular among them. It's housed
partially outdoors and partially indoors in a 120-year-old Vermont
barn. Recipes were handed down from grandmother to mother to
daughter, and the cooking is simple and good. Buy your wine from
the on-premises deli, and enjoy it (for a small corking fee) with home-
made minestrone; a generous antipasto; linguine with a sauté of jumbo
shrimp, scallops, and calamari; or gnocchi with four cheeses. The
homemade tiramisu and cannoli are top-notch. ⌧*Brickell Village, 15
S.E. 10th St., Downtown* ☎305/374–9449 ▤AE, MC, V.

¢–$ **✕Tobacco Road.** If you like your food the way you like your blues—
AMERICAN gritty, honest, and unassuming—then this octogenarian joint will earn
your respect. The kitchen's open until 4 AM, and there's a live band
every day of the week, making this hangout one of Miami's low-key
gems. The Road-burger is a popular choice, as are the chili worthy of
a fire hose and appetizers such as nachos and chicken wings. Don't let
the rough-edged exterior deter you from finer dining. On Tuesday dur-
ing the season, Tobacco Road offers a Maine lobster special, and fine
single-malt scotches are stocked behind the bar. ⌧ *626 S. Miami Ave.,
Downtown* ☎305/374–1198 ▤AE, D, DC, MC, V.

LITTLE HAVANA

$$–$$$$ **✕Casa Juancho.** This meeting place for the movers and shakers of the
SPANISH Cuban *exilio* community is also a haven for lovers of fine Spanish
regional cuisine. Strolling balladeers serenade surrounded by brown
brick, rough-hewn dark timbers and hanging smoked meats. Try the
hake prepared in a fish stock with garlic, onions, and Spanish white
wine or the *carabineros a la plancha* (jumbo red shrimp with head and
shell on, split and grilled). For dessert, *crema Catalana* is a rich pastry
custard with a delectable crust of burnt caramel. The house features the
largest list of reserved Spanish wines in the States. Jackets are recommended for men. ⌧*2436 S.W. 8th St., Little Havana* ☎305/642–2452
▤AE, D, DC, MC, V.

★ $–$$ **✕Hy-Vong Vietnamese Cuisine.** Spring springs forth in spring rolls of
VIETNAMESE ground pork, cellophane noodles, and black mushrooms wrapped in
homemade rice paper. Folks'll mill about on the sidewalk for hours—
come before 7 PM to avoid a wait—to sample the fish panfried with
mango or with *nuoc man,* a garlic-lime fish sauce, not to mention the
thinly sliced pork barbecued with sesame seeds, almonds, and peanuts. Beer-savvy proprietor Kathy Manning serves a half-dozen top
brews (Double Grimbergen, Peroni, and Spaten, among them) to further inoculate the experience from the ordinary. Well, as ordinary as
a Vietnamese restaurant on Calle Ocho can be. ⌧*3458 S.W. 8th St.,
Little Havana* ☎305/446–3674 ▤AE, D, MC, V ⊘*Closed Mon. and
Tues. No lunch.*

¢–$ **✕Tutto Pasta.** Tourists might pay $30 for linguini elsewhere, but locals
ITALIAN are more likely to frequent Tutto Pasta, where they feast on the delicious homemade pasta for less than $15. The food is Italian, but with

distinctive Brazilian influence. Start with fresh-baked goat-cheese foccacia with truffle oil. Then try the famous lobster ravioli garnished with plantain chips, or the tilapia sautéed with shrimp, calamari, scallops, and tomato sauce. Hop over to Tutto Pizza next door to enjoy innovative Brazilian-inspired thin pizzas like the Portuguesa, topped with ham, mozzarella, black olives, eggs, and onions. Finish with Tutto chocolate cake or creamy Brazilian Pave. ⊠ *1751 S.W. 3rd Ave. at S.W. 18th Rd., Downtown Miami* ☎ *305/857–0709* ⊟ *MC, V.*

$-$$$ ✕ **Versailles.** To the area's Cuban population, Miami without Versailles
CUBAN   is like rice without beans. The storied eatery, where old émigrés opine daily about all things Cuban, is a stop on every political candidate's campaign trail, and it should be a stop for you as well. Enjoy the juxtaposition of plastic tables under ornate mirrors and gilded chandeliers. Order a heaping platter of *lechon asado* (roasted pork loin), *ropa vieja* (shredded beef) or *picadillo* (spicy ground beef), all served with rice, beans, and fried plantains. Battle the oncoming food coma with a cup of the city's strongest cafecito, which comes in the tiniest of cups but packs a lot of punch. ⊠ *3555 S.W. 8th St., between S.W. 35th and S.W. 36th Aves., Little Havana* ☎ *305/444–0240* ⊟ *AE, D, DC, MC, V.*

COCONUT GROVE & KEY BISCAYNE

★ $$$-$$$$ ✕ **Cioppino.** Choose your view: the ornate dining room near the exhi-
ITALIAN   bition kitchen or the alfresco area with views of landscaped gardens or breeze-brushed beaches. Then select your food, which may be even more difficult, given the many rich, luscious Italian options, including imported cheeses are flown in twice a week. Items range from creamy mozzarella with green beans to tantalizing risotto with lobster, white wine, and zucchini. Aria is fortunate to have a master sommelier, whose palate is impeccable and whose wine list is impossible to resist. ⊠ *Ritz-Carlton, Key Biscayne, 455 Grand Bay Dr., Key Biscayne* ☎ *305/365–4286* ⚄ *Reservations essential* ⊟ *AE, D, DC, MC, V.*

$$$ ✕ **Le Bouchon du Grove.** Waiters tend to lean on chairs while taking
FRENCH   orders, and managers and owners freely mix with the clientele, making Le Bouchon perhaps the last remaining vestige of the Grove's bohemian days. The result is one big happy family, all enjoying traditional French pâtés, gratins, quiches, chicken fricasse, mussels, duck leg confit, and steak frites. The supercharged atmosphere inside is equally matched by the throngs that tour the Grove outside the French doors. ⊠ *3430 Main Hwy., Coconut Grove, Miami* ☎ *305/448–6060* ⊟ *AE, MC, V.*

CORAL GABLES

$-$$ ✕ **Havana Harry's.** When Cuban families want a home-cooked meal but
CUBAN   don't want to cook it themselves, they come to this spacious, airy res-
Fodor'sChoice   taurant. In fact, you're likely to see whole families here, from babes
★   in arms to grandmothers. The fare is traditional Cuban: the long thin steaks known as *bistec palomilla,* roast chicken with citrus marinade, and fried pork chunks; contemporary flourishes—mango sauce and guava-painted pork roast—are kept to a minimum. Most dishes come

with white rice, black beans, and a choice of ripe or green plantains. The sweet ripe ones offer a good contrast to the savory dishes. This is an excellent value. ⊠*4612 Le Jeune Rd., Coral Gables* ☎*305/661–2622* ▤*AE, MC, V.*

¢-$$
SPANISH

✕ **Las Culebrinas.** At this Spanish *tapacería* (house of little plates), live each meal as if it were your last, though you may wait as long as some inmates do for an appeal. Tapas here are not small; some are entrée size: the succulent mix of garbanzos, ham, sausage, red peppers, and oil, or the Frisbee-size Spanish tortilla (omelet). Indulge in a tender fillet of crocodile, fresh fish, or the grilled pork stuffed with mashed bananas. For dessert there's *crema Catalana,* caramelized at your table with a blowtorch. This is a good time to remind your kids not to touch. ⊠*4700 W. Flagler St., at N.W. 47th Ave., Coral Gables* ☎*305/445–2337* ▤*AE, MC, V.*

$$-$$$$
CARIBBEAN

✕ **Ortanique on the Mile.** First, the place is gorgeous. Soft ochre walls and columns are hand-painted with cascading ortaniques, a Jamaican hybrid orange, creating a warm, welcoming, and soothing atmosphere. Next, the food is vibrant in taste and color, as delicious as it is beautiful. Though there is no denying that the strong, full flavors are imbued with island breezes, chef/partner Cindy Hutson's personal cuisine goes beyond Caribbean refinements. The menu centers on fish, since Hutson has a special way with it, and the Caribbean bouillabaisse is not to be missed. ⊠*278 Miracle Mile, Coral Gables* ☎*305/446–7710* ▤*AE, MC, V.*

$$$-$$$$
FRENCH
Fodor'sChoice
★

✕ **Pascal's on Ponce.** This French gem in the midst of the Coral Gables restaurant district is always full, thanks to chef-proprietor Pascal Oudin's assured and consistent cuisine. Oudin foregoes the glitz and fussiness usually often associated with French cuisine, and instead opts for a low-key, open atmosphere that won't overwhelm patrons. The equally sensible menu proves even dishes we can pronounce can be delicacies. Start with the supurb gnocchi appetizer, and ask for mushrooms on top. The main course is a tough choice between oven-roasted duck with poached pears, milk-fed veal loin, and diver sea scallops with beef short rib. Ask your expert waiter to pair dishes with a selection from Pascal's impessive wine list. ⊠*2611 Ponce de León Blvd., Coral Gables* ☎*305/444–2024* ▤*AE, D, DC, MC, V* ⊘*Closed Sun. No lunch Sat.*

7

WHERE TO STAY

In high season, which is January to May, expect to pay at least $150 per night. In summer, however, prices can be as much as 50 percent lower than the dizzying winter rates. You can also find great values between Easter and Memorial Day, which is actually a delightful time in Miami, and in September and October, the height of hurricane season.

SOUTH BEACH

Now that it's a scene of international celeb partying, synonymous with glamour and style, it's hard to imagine that South Beach was a derelict district 15 years ago. These days the hotels themselves are attractions to see, both outside and in, on a visit to Miami. The inventory of playful 1930s Art Deco buildings is unmatched anywhere in the world. What's different today from even 10 years ago is their total renovation into glistening, historic, architectural gems. Feel free to visit the hotels to explore their lobbies, restaurants, lounges, and bars, where you'll find much of the city's nightlife taking place.

BEST BETS FOR MIAMI LODGING

Fodor's offers a selective listing of quality lodging experiences in every price range, from the city's best budget beds to its most sophisticated luxury hotels. Here, we've compiled our top recommendations by price and experience. The very best properties—in other words, those that provide a particularly remarkable experience in their price range—are designated in the listings with the Fodor's Choice logo.

Fodor'sChoice ★

Acqualina $$$$
Biltmore Hotel $$$-$$$$
Circa 39 ¢
Delano Hotel $$$$
Fisher Island Hotel & Resort $$$$
Four Seasons Hotel Miami $$$$
Mandarin Oriental Miami $$$$
Miami River Inn ¢
Ritz-Carlton Key Biscayne $$$$
Sagamore $$$-$$$$
The National $$$-$$$$
The Tides $$$$
The Townhouse $$-$$$
Travelodge Monaco Beach Resort ¢

By Price

¢
Cadet Hotel
Circa 39

$
Catalina Hotel & Beach Club
Pelican

$$
Essex House Hotel
The Hotel

$
Sagamore
Bitmore Hotel

$$$$
Setai
Hotel De Soleil South Beach

By Experience

BEST POOL
Ritz-Carlton Miami Beach $$$$
Setai $$$$
The Standard $

BEST HOTEL BAR
The National $$$$
Sagamore $$$-$$$$
The Hotel $$-$$$$

BEST FOR ROMANCE
Mandarin Oriental Miami $$$$
The Standard $
Hotel De Soleil South Beach $$$-$$$$

BEST SERVICE
The Setai $$$$
Aqualina $$$$
Circa 39 ¢

BEST VIEWS

Mandarin Oriental Miami $$$$
Delano Hotel $$$$
Hotel Victor $$$$

HIPSTER HOTELS

Hotel Victor $$$$
Shore Club $$$$
Catalina Hotel & Beach Club $-$$

BEST LOCATION

The National $$$$
Sagamore $$$-$$$$
Pelican $-$$

BEST KEPT SECRET

Ocean Surf ¢
Circa 39 ¢
The National $$$$

NEW HOTELS

Hotel De Soleil South Beach $$$-$$$$
Aqualina $$$$
Eden Roc Renaissance Resort & Spa $$$-$$$$

7

Where to Stay in the Miami Area

ATLANTIC OCEAN

MIAMI BEACH

NORTH MIAMI BEACH

NORTH MIAMI

Miami International Airport

Miami River

Miami Gdns. Dr.
N. Miami Beach Blvd.
Biscayne Blvd.
Broad Causeway
Collins Ave.
JFK Causeway
Biscayne Blvd.
Julia Tuttle Causeway
Venetian Causeway
N.E. 6th Ave.
N.E. 135th St.
N.E. 103rd St.
N.E. 95th St.
N.E. 2nd Ave.
N. Miami Ave.
N.W. 54th St.
N.W. 62nd St.
N.W. 79th St.
N.W. 95th St.
N.W. 103rd St.
N.W. 135th St.
N.W. 27th Ave.
N.W. 36th St.
N.W. 20th St.
Robert Frost Expwy.
Hialeah Dr.
Gratigny Rd.
7th Ave.
8th Ave.
E. 49th St.
E. 25th St.
W. 4th Ave.
W. 49th St.
W. 72nd Ave.
N.W. 72nd Ave.
N.W. 57th St.
N.W. 58th St.
N.W. 87th Ave.
Dairy Rd.
Red Rd.
Okeechobee Rd.
Palmetto Expwy.
Florida's Turnpike
Miami Gdns. Dr.

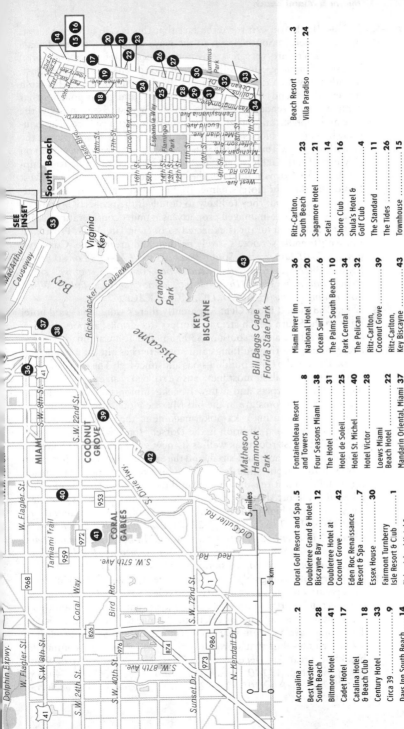

South Beach

SEE INSET

MacArthur Causeway

Bay

Biscayne Bay

Virginia Key

Rickenbacker Causeway

Crandon Park

KEY BISCAYNE

Biscayne

Bill Baggs Cape Florida State Park

Matheson Hammock Park

MIAMI

COCONUT GROVE

CORAL GABLES

Dolphin Expwy.

W. Flagler St.

Coral Way

Tamiami Trail

S. Dixie Hwy.

S.W. 57th Ave.

Red Rd.

Bird Rd.

Old Cutler Rd.

Sunset Dr.

N. Kendall Dr.

5 miles

5 km

7

★ ¢-$$ ⊞**Cadet Hotel.** You can trace the fact that this is one of the sweetest, quietest hotels in South Beach to the ways of its independent female owner. (There are very few privately owned hotels here anymore.) The placid patio-garden is the perfect spot to enjoy a full breakfast, included in your rate. Little touches, like candles in the lobby, fresh flowers all around, 600-thread-count sheets, and small pouches that contain fresh lavender or seashells, depending on the season, show the care and sophistication that are of utmost importance here. The boutique hotel is two blocks from Lincoln Road and the beach, across the street from Casa Tua, and yet you feel like a local resident when you stay here. Clark Gable stayed in Room 225 when he came to Miami for Army Air Corps training in the 1940s; he'd been enrolled at West Point, and thus the hotel's name. Right now the rates are an incredibly good value, but they're likely to double if the property becomes a Relais & Chateaux–managed property, as is under consideration. A 50-person French restaurant is expected to open in late 2008. **Pros:** Well run with friendly service, a lovely garden, and great value. **Cons:** No pool. ⊠*1701 James Ave., South Beach* ☎*305/672–6688 or 800/432–2338* ᕔ*305/532–1676* ⊕*www.cadethotel.com* ⬎*33 rooms, 3 suites* ♿*In-room: safe, Wi-Fi. In-hotel: bar, laundry service, public Wi-Fi, no-smoking rooms* ⊟*AE, D, DC, MC, V* ⃝❘*CP.*

★ $-$$ ⊞**Catalina Hotel & Beach Club.** Apparently there's value in a good hotel right on the South Beach strip that offers free drinks, airport shuttles, and bike rentals, all for south of $300 a night: The Catalina has taken over two neighboring buildings and now stretches almost a whole city block. Each of the three buildings has a distinct feel: The original Catalina (with the smallest, most inexpensive rooms) is an exercise in camp, with red shag carpets and a funky backgammon table in the lobby. The mid-range rooms are in the old Maxine Hotel, decorated in rock baroque and featuring a karaoke machine in the lobby. The newest, and most luxurious, addition is the Dorset Hotel, which now houses Catalina's biggest rooms as well as its new sushi restaurant, Kung Fu Chus. The rooms are good-sized, and the extra perks—free drinks from 7 to 8, a free airport shuttle, and free bike rental until 6 PM —make this hotel the most reasonable bet on the strip. **Pros:** Free drinks, free bikes, free airport shuttle, good people-watching. **Cons:** $15 wireless fee, service not a high priority, loud. ⊠*1732 Collins Ave., Miami Beach* ☎*305/674–1160* ᕔ*305/674–7522* ⊕*www.catalinahotel.com* ⬎*200 rooms.* ♿*In-room: safe, refrigerator, Wi-Fi. In-hotel: restaurant, bars, pool, bicycles, laundry service, public Wi-Fi, airport shuttle, parking (fee), some pets allowed, no-smoking rooms* ⊟*AE, D, DC, MC, V.*

$-$$ ⊞**Century Hotel.** Designed in 1939 by Art Deco master Henry Hohauser, the Century now garners an *InStyle* guest list. Like the Marriott across the street, it's a little south of the action, but that can be a good thing: the Century is a favorite of celebrities trying to keep a low profile. The rooms have a certain spartan warmth and definitely feel stylish, if a little remote—but that's probably the point. **Pros:** Free continental breakfast, great Art Deco exterior. **Cons:** Not in the heart of South Beach, no pool. ⊠*140 Ocean Dr., South Beach* ☎*305/674–8855 or 888/982–3688* ᕔ*305/538–5733* ⊕*www.centurysouthbeach.com*

⌨26 *rooms* ⌂*In-room: safe. In-hotel: wireless, restaurant, bar, parking (fee), no-smoking rooms* ⊟*AE, DC, MC, V* ⦿|*CP.*

¢ ⊞**Days Inn South Beach.** Wedged, improbably, in the space that should by sheer size and might belong to the Setai, which towers above and around it, this cheesy little Days Inn has managed to hold on to its claim to prime beachfront (*someone's* not selling). Unfortunately, it doesn't seem to be taking full advantage of its privileged location. The big pool, which should have amazing ocean views right next to the boardwalk, is fenced in so no views are possible. To reach the sand you have to walk back out through the lobby and down 30 steps. The lobby itself is like a bad parody of Miami Beach, with a big sunset mural, a bridge over a fountain, and a dozen old-fashioned lampposts. But if you're in the right frame of mind, meaning you're willing to put up with mediocre rooms and service, you can get beachfront accommodations for a little more than $100 a room. Spend a little extra for one of the 30 ocean-front rooms with balconies. **Pros:** Cheap beachfront rooms in a prime location. **Cons:** Cheesy, older hotel with spotty service. ⊠*100 21st St., South Beach* ☎*305/538–6631 or 800/451–3345* 🖷*305/674–0954* ⊕*www.daysinnsouthbeach.com* ⌨*172 rooms* ⌂*In-room: safe, refrigerator (some), Ethernet, Wi-Fi. In-hotel: bar, pool, beachfront, laundry facilities, laundry service, concierge, public Internet, public Wi-Fi, parking (fee), no-smoking rooms* ⊟*AE, D, DC, MC, V.*

$$$$ ⊞**Delano Hotel.** The decor of this grand hotel is inspired by Lewis
Fodor'sChoice Carroll's Alice in Wonderland, and as you make your way from the
★ sparse, busy, spacious lobby past cascading white curtains and through rooms dotted with strange, whimsical furniture pieces, you will feel like you are indeed falling down a rabbit hole. Brush by celebrities and expatriates as you make your way to the vast ocean-front gardens and enormous pool outside, where the rich and famous lounge in white cabanas. Like most hotels on South Beach's hottest strip, the Delano boasts glamour and wealth. Unlike some of the other hotels, the Delano's smartly designed rooms and helpful staff make the illusion a reality. Make sure to visit the hotel's brand new "Florida Room," an über-exclusive lounge designed by Lenny Kravitz with a glass baby grand piano that he plays whenever he's in town. **Pros:** Electrifying design, lounging among the beautiful and famous. **Cons:** crowded, scene-y, small rooms, expensive. ⊠*1685 Collins Ave., South Beach* ☎*305/672–2000 or 800/555–5001* 🖷*305/532–0099* ⊕*www.delano-hotel.com* ⌨*184 rooms, 24 suites* ⌂*In-room: safe, refrigerator, Wi-Fi. In-hotel: 3 restaurants, room service, bars, pool, gym, spa, beachfront, laundry service, concierge, public Wi-Fi, parking (fee), no-smoking rooms* ⊟*AE, D, DC, MC, V.*

★ $-$$ ⊞**Essex House.** You'll get your own South Beach people-watching perch on the outdoor patio at this wonderfully restored Art Deco gem. A favorite with Europeans, especially the British, Essex House has average-size rooms with midcentury-style red furniture and marble tubs. The suites, reached by crossing a lovely tropical courtyard, are well worth the price: each has a wet bar, king-size bed, pull-out sofa, 100-square-foot bathroom, refrigerator, and hot tub. The lobby mural was created in 1938 by artist Earl Le Pan, and touched up by him 50 years

7

later. **Pros:** A social, heated pool; great Art Deco patio; good service. **Cons:** Small pool. ✉*1001 Collins Ave., South Beach* ☎*305/534–2700 or 800/553–7739* 🖶*305/532–3827* ⊕*www.essexhotel.com* ✑*61 rooms, 19 suites* ⌂*In-room: Wi-Fi. In-hotel: bar, pool, laundry service, parking (fee)* ▭*AE, D, DC, MC, V.*

$$$$
Fodor'sChoice
★

🛏 **Fisher Island Hotel & Resort.** Want to explore Fisher Island? Assuming you don't have a private yacht, there are three ways to gain access to the island just off South Beach: you can either become a club member (initiation fee alone: $25,000), be one of the 750 equity members who have vacation places here (starting price: $8 million), or book a night at the club hotel (basic villa: $900 a night). Once you've made it, you'll be welcomed at reception with champagne. Considering you get a private house, a golf cart, and a fenced-in backyard with a hot tub, villas are a value for a memorable honeymoon or other lifetime event, if not a casual weekend. Families should stay in one of three former guest cottages of the former Italianate mansion of William K. Vanderbilt (in 1925 he swapped Carl Fisher *his* yacht for the island), which forms the centerpiece of this resort. A 9-hole golf course, the surprisingly affordable Spa Internazionale, and 18 lighted tennis courts (hard, grass, and clay), kids' programs, and 1 mi of very private (and very quiet) white sand beach imported from the Bahamas means there's plenty of sweet nothing to do here. Oh, and there are eight restaurants and a fun sunset tiki bar to choose from—Porto Cervo is the best Italian restaurant nobody knows about. The Garwood Lounge features nightly piano and seats just 16. Remarkably, this true exclusivity and seclusion is minutes from South Beach. **Pros:** Great private beaches, exclusive surroundings, varied dining choices. **Cons:** Expensive, ferry rides take time. ✉*1 Fisher Island Dr., Fisher Island, Miami* ☎*305/535–6000 or 800/537–3708* 🖶*305/535–6026* ⊕*www.fisherisland.com* ✑*5 junior suites 50 condo units, 6 villas, 3 cottages* ⌂*In-room; safe, refrigerator, DVD. In-hotel: 8 restaurants, golf course, tennis courts, pools, gym, spa, beachfront, water sports, children's programs (ages 4–12), laundry service, concierge, public Internet, parking (no fee), some pets allowed, no-smoking rooms* ▭*AE, D, DC, MC, V.*

$$$$

🛏 **Hotel De Soleil South Beach.** The newest addition to South Beach's glamorous high-end hotel strip doesn't disappoint. The Arquitectonica-designed suites are modern and huge—all span at least 500 square feet and boast humongous balconies. The furnishings are sleek but comfortable, with two flat-screen TVs and oversized marble-floored bathrooms. If you can, stay in one of the 27 rooftop suites: each has a private rooftop terrace complete with a Jacuzzi, plush chaise lounges, and a beautiful view of the South Beach skyline. If you ever make it out of the room, come downstairs and check out celebrity Chef Govind Armstrong's **Table 8** restaurant on the ground floor. **Pros:** Incredible balconies, huge rooms, brand-new. **Cons:** Gym is just a small "cardio room." No spa ✉*1437 Collins Ave., South Beach* ☎*305/672–4554* ✑*80 suites* ⌂*In room: safe, refrigerator, DVD, Wi-Fi. In-hotel: restaurant, room service, bar, pool, gym, concierge, public Wi-Fi, parking (fee), no-smoking rooms* ▭*AE, D, DC, MC, V.*

★ $$$$ ⊞ **Hotel Victor.** The Victor just took over two neighboring stores, making the Parisian designer Jacques Garci's Ocean Drive prize into a more versatile hotel, good for hipsters, families, and even business travelers. The first floor features Hotel Victor's signature jellyfish tank, but by far the coolest part of this deceptively big hotel is the second floor, which features an infinity-edge pool and a large outdoor terrace bar that's open until 2 AM. Don't forget to visit Ocean Drive's only subterranean spa, which offers Turkish hamams and coed steam rooms Most rooms are fairly small and overlook the second-floor pool and the ocean; ask for a room in one of the newly constructed wings, which have little balconies and better views. Instead of walls, drapes and sliding mirrors allow you to control the space in your room. Deep tubs in the middle of the rooms create intimacy. The Victor hosts the city's hottest Thursday-night party, a boon, since you're invited, but it stays noisy till 2 AM. **Pros:** Great design, views of Ocean Drive from the pool deck, high hip factor, good service. **Cons:** Small rooms, small pool. ⊠ *Ocean Dr., South Beach* ☎ *305/428/1234 or 800/327–7028* 🖷 *305/933–6560* ⊕ *www.hotelvictorsouthbeach.com* 🛏 *91 rooms.* ♿ *In-room: safe, kitchen (some), refrigerator, DVD, Wi-Fi. In-hotel: 2 restaurants, room service, bar, pool, gym, spa, laundry service, public Wi-Fi, parking (fee), some pets allowed, no-smoking rooms* ⊟ *AE, D, DC, MC, V.*

★ $$$$ ⊞ **Loews Miami Beach Hotel.** The oldest of South Beach's "new hotels," Loews Miami Beach is marvelous for families, businesspeople, and groups. The 800-room mega-hotel combines top-tier amenities, a massive new spa, a great pool, and a direct beachfront setting in its pair of enormous 12- and 18-story towers. When it was built in 1998, Loews managed not only to snag 99 feet of beach, but also to take over the vacant St. Moritz next door and restore it to its original 1939 Art Deco beauty. The entire complex combines boutique charm with updated opulence. How big is it? The Loews has 85,000 square feet of meeting space and an enormous ocean-view grand ballroom. Emeril Lagasse opened a restaurant here, and a three-story spa opened in 2007 with 15 treatment rooms and a state-of-the-art fitness center. In the grand lobby you'll find a dozen black-suited staffers behind the counter, and a half-dozen other bellboys and valets. Rooms are great: contemporary and very comfortable, with flat-screen TVs and high-end amenities. If you like big hotels with all the services, this is your choice in South Beach. **Pros:** Top-notch amenities include a beautiful oceanfront pool and immense spa. **Cons:** Intimacy is lost in the size of the place, and parking costs $30. ⊠ *1601 Collins Ave., South Beach* ☎ *305/604–1601 or 800/235–6397* 🖷 *305/604–3999* ⊕ *www.loewshotels.com/miamibeach* 🛏 *733 rooms, 57 suites* ♿ *In-room: dial-up. In-hotel: 3 restaurants, room service, bars, pool, gym, spa, beachfront, laundry service, concierge, public Internet, public Wi-Fi, parking (fee), some pets allowed, no-smoking rooms* ⊟ *AE, D, DC, MC, V.*

$–$$ ⊞ **Park Central.** Park Central operates as three side-by-side, much-photographed, Art Deco hotels on Ocean Drive: the Imperial, which has oceanfront and standard rooms; the Heathcote, which has 12 suites; and the seven-story, 1937 flagship building, also called Park Central, which has rooms in many categories. The crowning "blue jewel" of the three, it has wraparound corner windows, a sculpture garden, and a compact pool, the setting of much parading about in swimsuits. Black-and-white photos of old beach scenes decorate rooms in all three buildings. You'll also find mahogany furnishings from the Philippines and ceiling fans. There's a roof deck for sunning, where people also gather to watch movies shown here Thursday and Sunday nights all year, with free popcorn and soda. **Pros:** Spacious rooftop sundeck, comfy beds, perfect location for first trip to Miami. **Cons:** Small bathrooms, most rooms have limited views. ⊠ *640 Ocean Dr., South Beach* ☎ *305/538–1611 or 800/727–5236* 🖷 *305/534–7520* 🌐 *www.theparkcentral.com* 🛏 *115 rooms, 12 suites* ♿ *In-room: refrigerator, dial-up. In-hotel: 2 restaurants, room service, bars, pool, gym, laundry service, concierge, public Internet, public Wi-Fi, parking (fee), no-smoking rooms* ▭ *AE, D, DC, MC, V.*

$-$$ 🖵 **Pelican.** The spirit of Diesel clothing company, which owns this Ocean Drive boutique, permeates the hotel. Each room is completely different, fashioned from a mix of antique and garage-sale furnishings selected by the designer of Diesel's clothing display windows. Each room has its own name, and guests try to stay in a different one each time, or else fall in love with one room and request it for every stay. For example, the "Me Tarzan, You Vain" room has a jungle theme, with African wood sculptures and a stick lamp, and "Up, Up in the Sky" has a space theme, with a model rocket and off-kilter furniture. The best bet is to head down to the Pelican's porch-front restaurant, which offers one of the most extensive wine lists in town and a bar-none view of Ocean Drive's people parade. **Pros:** Unique, over-the-top design; central Ocean Drive location. **Cons:** Rooms are so tiny that the quirky charm wears off quickly, no no-smoking rooms. ⊠ *826 Ocean Dr., South Beach* ☎ *305/673–3373 or 800/773–5422* 🖷 *305/673–3255* 🌐 *www.pelicanhotel.com* 🛏 *28 rooms, 4 suites* ♿ *In-room: safe, refrigerator, Wi-Fi. In-hotel: restaurant, room service, bar, beachfront, laundry service, parking (fee)* ▭ *AE, D, DC, MC, V.*

★ $$$$ 🖵 **Ritz-Carlton South Beach.** A sumptuous affair, the Ritz-Carlton is the only truly luxurious property on the beach that *feels* like it's on the beach, because its long pool deck leads you right out to the water. There are all the usual high-level draws the Ritz is known for, that is, attentive service, a kids' club, a club level with five food presentations a day, and high-end restaurants. The spa has exclusive brands of scrubs and creams, and dynamite staff, including a "tanning butler" named Malcolm, who will make sure you're not burning, and will apply lotions in the hard-to-reach places. Thursday through Saturday, enjoy Grammy-nominated percussionist Sammy Figeuroa, who plays Latin Jazz by the pool. The **diLido Beach** club restaurant, believe it or not, is one of the very few places in Miami where you can get a beach-side meal. Overall, this landmarked 1954 Art Moderne hotel, designed by Melvin Grossman and Morris Lapidus, has never been hotter. **Pros:** Luxury rooms, beachside restaurant, fine spa. **Cons:** Too big to be intimate and the lobby feels corporate. ✉*1 Lincoln Rd., South Beach* ☎*786/276–4000 or 800/241–3333* 🖷*786/276–4100* ⊕*www.ritzcarlton.com* 🛏*375 rooms* △*In-room: safe, refrigerator, Wi-Fi. In-hotel: 4 restaurants, room service, bars, pools, gym, spa, beachfront, children's programs (ages 5–12), laundry service, concierge, executive floor, public Wi-Fi, parking (fee), some pets allowed, no-smoking rooms* ⊟*AE, D, DC, MC, V.*

$$$–$$$$
Fodor'sChoice
★

⛬**Sagamore.** This super-sleek all-white hotel in the middle of the action looks and feels more like a Chelsea art gallery, filled with brilliant contemporary art. Its restaurant, Social Miami, is one of the hottest reservations in town. With all the mind-bending hipness, you might expect some major flaw, like small rooms, but in fact they're all suites here, and some of the largest on the strip, starting at 525 square feet. All have full kitchens with big fridges, mini ovens, microwaves, and dishwashers. You can also expect huge flat-screen TVs and whirlpool baths. Hallways have artists' quotes lining the walls, and public restrooms have video installations. The poolside duplex bungalows make posh party pads on weekend nights, when the Sagamore is *the* place to be in all of Miami (no surprise there). Staying here saves you the long wait and the begging to get in. Don't worry—it's still safe for kids here, and they'll love the glass, flourescent-lighted swing in the lobby. A VIP kids card entitles them to unlimited free ice cream, hot dogs, and soda (what the heck, it's a vacation). **Pros:** Sensational pool, Friday and Saturday night parties, great location, quiet on weekdays, good rate specials. **Cons:** Basic rooms are not as stylish as public areas, noisy on weekends. ✉*1671 Collins Ave., South Beach* ☎*305/535–8088* 🖷*305/535–8185* ⊕*www.sagamorehotel.com* 🛏*93 suites* △*In-room: safe, kitchen, refrigerator, Wi-Fi. In-hotel: restaurant, room service, bars, pool, spa, beachfront, laundry service, concierge, parking (fee), no-smoking rooms* ⊟*AE, D, DC, MC, V.*

$$$$

⛬**Shore Club.** Unquestionably the destination for the young, the rich, and the ready to party, Shore Club is the perfect adult playground. Don't spend your time in the rooms—they're nothing special, and the white-on-white decor feels more cold than cool. Instead, venture to down to the lobby, where a peek behind the cascading white curtains can yield a celebrity, a scandal, or a makeout session. More debauchery awaits at **Sky Bar**, the glitziest outdoor bar on the strip. Step into Tuscan restaurant Ago, or Nobu (if you can afford it), and watch Hollywood royalty graze on Japanese-Peruvian delicacies. In terms of lounging, people-watching, and poolside glitz, this is the best of South Beach. **Pros:** Great outdoor lounge, good restaurants and bars, nightlife in your backyard. **Cons:** Uninviting rooms, snooty service. ✉*1901 Collins Ave., South Beach* ☎*305/695–3100 or 877/640–9500* 🖷*305/695–3299* ⊕*www.shoreclub.com* 🛏*322 rooms* △*In-room: safe, refrigerator, Wi-Fi. In-hotel: 2 restaurants, room service, bars, pools, gym, spa, beachfront, laundry service, concierge, public Wi-Fi, parking (fee), some pets allowed, no-smoking rooms* ⊟*AE, D, DC, MC, V.*

$$$$

⛬**Setai.** Even if you can't afford a stay at Miami's priciest hotel (rooms start at north of a thousand dollars), take time to visit the city's most beautifully designed space. The place feels like an Asian museum, serene and beautiful, with heavy granite furniture lifted by orange accents, warm candlelight, and the soft bubble of seemingly endless pools and ponds. The ocean-front gardens are expansive, lush, and painstakingly manicured. Three infinity-edge pools, heated to 75, 85, and 95 degrees lead to an ocean-front terrace and then, white sand. The rooms are as expansive as the premises, and furnished in an Asian style that is at once minimalist and cozy. **Pros:** Quiet and classy, beautiful grounds, perfection in rooms. **Cons:** Somewhat cold aura, TVs are far from the beds. ✉*101 20th St., South Beach* ☎*305/520–6000 or 888/625–7500* 🖷*305/520–6111* ⊕*www.setai.com* ⇘*110 rooms* ⟁*In room: safe, refrigerator, DVD, Wi-Fi. In-hotel: restaurant, room service, bars, pools, gym, spa, beachfront, laundry service, concierge, public Wi-Fi, parking (fee), some pets allowed, no-smoking rooms* ▭*AE, D, DC, MC, V.*

★ $$-$$$$ 🏨 **The Hotel.** Fashion designer Todd Oldham wanted to preserve the Art Deco roots of the Hotel, which inhabits the historic Tiffany building, while making it modern. So, he made it tie-dye. Everything in this quirky, romantic boutique, from the decor of four-star restaurant Wish to the bathrobes hanging in the small but cute bathrooms, is stained blue and green. Somehow the decor, paired with soft browns and whites and accented with the knowing eye of a mega-designer, works. Add soft lighting and two-person bathtubs, and you have all the makings of a romantic retreat. The hotel's most exquisite treat is a rooftop bar, a low-key hangout where locals and hotel guests lounge under the neon light of the Tiffany sign on Thursday, Friday, and Saturday nights. **Pros:** Great service, coolest roof deck bar in town, good for couples. **Cons:** Pool is tiny, rooms have no view. ✉*801 Collins Ave., South Beach* ☎*305/531–2222 or 877/843–4683* 🖷*305/531–3222* ⊕*www. thehotelofsouthbeach.com* ⇘*48 rooms, 4 suites* ⟁*In-room: safe, Wi-Fi. In-hotel: restaurant, room service, bar, pool, laundry service, concierge, public Internet, public Wi-Fi, parking (fee), no-smoking rooms* ▭*AE, D, DC, MC, V.*

$$-$$$ 🏨 **The National Hotel.** Most locals have partied everywhere on Miami's
Fodor's Choice   hot hotel strip—except for the National Hotel. That's because this lux-
★   urious hotel serves as a bastion of calm in the sea of white-on-white mod decor and raucous reveling usually reserved for the beachfront masterpieces lining Collins Avenue between 15th and 20th streets. Unlike its neighbors, the National hasn't parted with its Art Deco past. Most of the chocolate- and ebony-hued pieces in the lobby date back to the 1930s, and the baby grand piano beckons toward a throwback D-Bar Lounge. The most spectacular feature is Miami Beach's longest pool, which stretches from the tower to a duo of tropical tiki bars, a series of comfy black-and-white-striped cabanas and poolside tables, and then the beach. See that black-and-white striped hut on the sand? That's owned by the National as well, and staffed with runners who can bring you food from hotel restaurants. **Pros:** Stunning pool, perfect location. **Cons:** Rooms aren't stylistically impressive, $11 daily charge for Internet. ✉*1677 Collins Ave., South Beach* ☎*305/532–2311 or 800/327–8370* 🖷*305/534–1426* ⊕*www.nationalhotel.com* ⇘*143 rooms, 9 suites* ⟁*In-room: safe, DVD, VCR (some), Ethernet, Wi-Fi.*

In-hotel: 2 restaurants, room service, bars, pools, gym, beachfront, laundry service, concierge, public Internet, public W-Fi, parking (fee), some pets allowed, no-smoking rooms ⊟*AE, DC, MC, V.*

$ ⊡**The Standard.** An extension of André Balazs's trendy, budget hotel chain, the Standard is a Hollywood newcomer that set up shop a few minutes from South Beach on an island just over the Venetian Causeway. The message: we'll do what we please, and the cool kids will follow. The scene is trendy 30- and 40-year-olds interested in the hotel's many "do-it-yourself" spa activities, including mud bathing, scrubbing with sea salts, soaking in hot or arctic-cold waters, and yoga. An 8-foot, 103-degree cascade into a Roman hot tub is typical of the handful of adult pleasures spread around the pool deck. An informal restaurant overlooks the bay's Mediterranean-style mansions and the cigarette boats that float past. If you choose, you can go kayaking around the island. On the hotel facade you'll see the monumental signage of a bygone occupant, the Lido Spa Hotel, and the much smaller sign of its current occupant, hung, with a wink, upside down. The rooms are small and simple, though they have thoughtful touches like a picnic basket and embroidered fabric covers for the small flat-screen TVs. First-floor rooms have outdoor soaking tubs but very limited privacy, so few take that plunge. **Pros:** Interesting island location, free bike and kayak rentals, swank pool scene, great spa, inexpensive. **Cons:** Removed from South Beach nightlife, small rooms with no views, outdoor tubs are gimmicks, mediocre service. ⊠*40 Island Ave., Belle Isle, Miami Beach* ☎*305/673–1717* 🖷*305/673–8181* ⊕*www.standardhotel.com* ✍*104 rooms, 1 suite* ♿*In-room: safe, refrigerator, DVD, Ethernet. In-hotel: restaurant, room service, bars, pool, gym, spa, water sports, bicycles, laundry service, concierge, Wi-Fi, parking (fee), some pets allowed, no children under 14, no-smoking rooms* ⊟*AE, D, DC, MC, V.*

$$$$ ⊡**The Tides.** The newly designed Tides Hotel is fashioned after the
Fodor's Choice interior of a jewelry box, and this hotel may indeed be the jewel of
★ South Beach boutiques. Gone is the stark white-on-white minimalism, replaced with soft pinks and corals, gilded accents, and marine-inspired decor. The new "Coral Bar" boasts rums from around the world, and La Marea restaurant offers delectable seafood. The Tides' main competition is Hotel Victor, but this hotel's rooms all have direct ocean views. The rooms are small, but pretty, with pink and tan accents and cool tables made of petrified stumps. **Pros:** Superior service, great beach location, and ocean views from all suites plus the terrace restaurant. **Cons:** Small rooms, tiny elevator. ⊠*1220 Ocean Dr., South Beach* ☎*305/604–5070 or 866/438–4337* 🖷*305/604–5180* ⊕*www.the tideshotel.com* ✍*45 suites* ♿*In-room: safe, Ethernet, Wi-Fi. In-hotel: restaurant, pool, gym, beachfront, concierge, laundry service, parking (fee), no-smoking rooms* ⊟*AE, D, DC, MC, V.*

$$–$$$ ⊡**Townhouse.** Sandwiched between the Setai and the Shore Club—two of the hottest hotels on the planet—the Townhouse looks like an adult playhouse, and fits the bill as the most lighthearted hotel on South Beach. The rooms aren't as luxurious, and you won't find many amenities (no gym, no spa, no pool), but if you want to stay in the midst of the action for $250 a night, this may be a good choice. Enter through

7

a brightly lit lobby decorated with red plastic beach balls, red bicycles and, you guessed it, red furniture, and head to a small but freshly adorned white-and-red room. The coolest part of the hotel is a rooftop terrace with plush red lounge chairs, a funky DJ, and a breathtaking view of the strip. Townhouse Terrace is where weekend nights start for many on Miami's party circuit, so if you've primed to party but unsure of where to go, head upstairs and keep your ears open. A hip sushi restaurant, Bond St. Lounge, is downstairs, and delivers to rooms during restaurant hours. With its clean white backdrops and discounts for crew members, there's always a good chance a TV production or magazine shoot is happening. **Pros:** A great budget buy for the style-hungry. **Cons:** No pool, small rooms not designed for long stays. ⊠ *150 20th St., east of Collins Ave., South Beach* ☎ *305/534–3800 or 877/534–3800* 🖷 *305/534–3811* ⊕ *www.townhousehotel.com* 🛏 *69 rooms, 3 suites* ⚐ *In-room: safe, Ethernet, Wi-Fi. In-hotel: restaurant, room service, bar, bicycles, laundry facilities, laundry service, public Wi-Fi, parking (fee), no-smoking rooms* ⊟ *AE, D, DC, MC, V* ⏻ *CP.*

> ### WORD OF MOUTH
>
> "Bond St. [Lounge]: Located on 20th at the Townhouse Hotel. The food was definitely a highlight, everything was amazing. Service was also excellent. We got here at 8 PM on a Thursday night and thought we were hitting the early-bird special though. It definitely doesn't pick up until 9. I liked the atmosphere but it's in the basement so it's dark and lounge-y."
>
> –wyatt92

★ ¢–$ 🏨 **Villa Paradiso.** One of South Beach's best deals, Paradiso has huge floor-through rooms with kitchens, and a charming tropical courtyard with benches for hanging out at all hours. There's even another smaller courtyard on the other side of the rooms. Peeking out from a sea of tropical foliage, the hotel seems at first to be a rather unassuming piece of Deco architecture. But for all its simplicity, value shines bright. Rooms have polished hardwood floors, French doors, and quirky wrought-iron furniture. They are well suited for extended visits—discounts begin at 10% off for a week's stay. **Pros:** Great hangout spot in courtyard, huge rooms with kitchens, good value, great location. **Cons:** No wireless Internet, no pool, no restaurant. ⊠ *1415 Collins Ave., South Beach* ☎ *305/532–0616* 🖷 *305/673–5874* ⊕ *www.villaparadisohotel.com* 🛏 *17 studios* ⚐ *In-room: kitchen, refrigerator, dial-up. In-hotel: some pets allowed, no-smoking rooms* ⊟ *AE, D, DC, MC, V.*

MID-BEACH AND BAL HARBOUR

Where do South Beach end and Mid-Beach begin? With the massive amount of money being spent on former 1950s pleasure palaces like the Fontainebleau and Eden Roc, it could be that Mid-Beach will soon just be considered part of South Beach. North of 24th Street, Collins Avenue curves its way to 44th Street, where it takes a sharp left turn after running into the Fontainebleau Resort. The area between these two points—24th Street and 96th Street—is Mid-Beach. This stretch is undergoing a renaissance, as formerly run-down hotels are renovated and new hotels and condos are being built.

At 96th Street, the town of Bal Harbour takes over Collins Avenue from Miami Beach. The town runs a mere 10 blocks to the north before the bridge to Sunny Isles. Bal Harbour is famous for its outdoor upscale shops. If you take your shopping seriously, you'll probably want to stay in this area.

¢ 🏨**Circa 39.** This stylish boutique combines the smooth management of a big-budget hotel with the quaint little details of an Art Deco gem. A peek around each corner reveals a new delight, from a plush lip-shaped sofa to a lush courtyard connecting the two wings of the hotel, to a bar that offers free drinks every evening. The hotel is so focused on catering to your desires that they've even created a $10 "spoil me package" which includes European-style breakfast, cocktail hour, and two lounge chairs. Don't worry about asking for the package—it's added to your room rate. Rooms have wood floors and a cool, crisp look with white furnishings dotted with pale blue pillows. An in-room "spoil me basket" has everything you may need, from potato chips to condoms. The name Circa 39? It was built in 1939 and is on 39th Street. **Pros:** Affordable, chic, and intimate. **Cons:** You can't opt out of the $10 "spoil me package." ✉*3900 Collins Ave., Mid-Beach, Miami Beach* ☎*305/538–4900 or 877/8CIRCA39* 🖷*305/538–4998* ⊕*www. circa39.com* 🛏*82 rooms* ♿*In-room: safe, kitchen, refrigerator, Ethernet, Wi-Fi. In-hotel: restaurants, bar, pool, gym, concierge, public Wi-Fi, parking (fee), some pets allowed, no-smoking rooms* ▤*AE, D, DC, MC, V.*

FodorsChoice in the left margin; **★**

$$$-$$$$ 🏨**Eden Roc Renaissance Resort & Spa.** Like its next door neighbor, the Fontainebleau, this grand 1950s hotel designed by Morris Lapidus is undergoing a head-to-toe renovation, as well as the construction of a new wing and huge pool complex, both expected to open in late 2008. When they do, the Eden Roc will be one of the biggest hotels in the city. The public areas are landmarks and will retain their grand elegance, including monumental columns. The room renovations should renew the allure and perhaps return the swagger of a stay at the Eden Roc to the heights it had reached after opening in the 1950s. For a glimpse of the old glamour, visit Harry's Grille, which has murals of former guests, a veritable roll call of '50s and '60s stars. **Pros:** All-new rooms and facilities. **Cons:** Not on South Beach. ✉*4525 Collins Ave., Mid-Beach, Miami Beach* ☎*305/531–0000 or 800/327–8337* 🖷*305/674–5555* ⊕*www.edenrocresort.com* 🛏*631 rooms* ♿*In-room: safe, kitchen (some), refrigerator, Wi-Fi (fee). In-hotel: 3 restaurants, room service, bars, pools, gym, spa, beachfront, parking (fee), no-smoking rooms* ▤*AE, D, DC, MC, V.*

$$-$$$$ 🏨**Fontainebleau Resort and Towers.** Look out, South Beach. When Hilton reopens the Fontainebleau in July of 2008 as Miami's biggest hotel—twice the size of the Loews, with more than 1,500 rooms—it will be the fruit of the most ambitious and expensive hotel renovation project in the history of Greater Miami. The impact could be even more astonishing to the travel industry here than its original opening in 1954.

Planned are 11 restaurants, a huge nightclub, sumptuous pools with cabana islands, a state-of-the-art fitness center and a 40,000 foot spa, and more than 60,000 square feet of meeting and ballroom space—all of it built from scratch. A 36-story all-suites tower was completed in 2005 and remains open continuously during construction. Suites in the lavish tower offer a peek at the luxury to come in the rest of the resort, with full kitchens including dishwashers and outstanding views looking south over Miami Beach. You may have been wondering whether any part of the original hotel is left, and it is. Two Morris Lapidus–designed and landmarked exteriors and lobbies are being restored to their original state. All original rooms, however, were completely gutted, down to the beams, to create new, contemporary rooms. **Pros:** Historic design mixed with all-new facilities, fabulous pools. **Cons:** Away from the South Beach pedestrian scene, too big to be intimate. ⊠*4441 Collins Ave., Mid-Beach, Miami Beach* ☎*305/538–2000 or 800/548–8886* 🖷*305/673–5351* ⊕*www.fontainebleau.com* ⇱*1,504 rooms* ⌂*In-room: safe, kitchen (some), refrigerator, DVD (some), Wi-Fi. In-hotel: 11 restaurants, bars, pools, gym, spa, water sports, laundry service, public Internet, public Wi-Fi, parking (fee), no-smoking rooms* ▤*AE, D, DC, MC, V.*). 305-535-3240

★ ¢–$ 🛏**Ocean Surf.** Don't expect luxury in this colorful Art Deco lodge, but if you want a cheap stay and ideal beach access, you can't beat the tiny Ocean Surf hotel. Sure the beds look like they're 20 years old, and the hallways are small and humid, but where else will you stay across a parking lot from the beach for eighty bucks a night? The hotel has its charms—the 1940s pink and green pastels, soda-pop kitsch furnishings, and a conveniently located steak house next door put this hotel several notches above the Motel 6. The location off of 74th Street puts this quiet hotel well out of the reach of boisterous South Beach. Add in free continental breakfast, and you've got a great crash pad for a low-key vacation. **Pros:** Adorable Art Deco hotel, cheap, free continental breakfast. **Cons:** Basic rooms, no Internet, spotty service. ⊠*7436 Ocean Terr., North Beach, Miami Beach* ☎*305/866–1648 or 800/555–0411* ⊕*www.theoceansurfhotel.com* ⇱*49 rooms* ⌂*In-room: safe, refrigerator. In-hotel: beachfront, parking (fee), no-smoking rooms* ▤*AE, MC, V* ⦶*CP.*

★ $–$$$ 🛏**The Palms South Beach.** Stay here if you're seeking an elegant, relaxed property away from the noise but still near South Beach. Like its sister property, the National Hotel, to the south, The Palms has an exceptional beach, an easy pace, and beautiful gardens with a gazebo, fountains, soaring palm trees, and inviting hammocks. A 2008 renovation has left the rooms looking as fabulous as the grounds, and added a gym and 5,000-square-foot spa. There are more large palms inside, in the Great Room lounge just off the lobby, and designer Patrick Kennedy used subtle, natural hues of ivory, green, and blue for the homey, well-lighted rooms. **Pros:** Tropical garden, relaxed and quiet. **Cons:** No balconies, away from South Beach, city-view rooms feel detached. ⊠*3025 Collins Ave., Mid-Beach, Miami Beach* ☎*305/534–0505 or 800/550–0505* 🖷*305/534–0515* ⊕*www.thepalmshotel.com* ⇱*220 rooms, 22 suites* ⌂*In-room: safe, refrigerator, Wi-Fi. In-hotel: restaurant, room* *service, bars, pool, beachfront, laundry service, concierge, public WiFi, parking (fee), no-smoking rooms* ☰AE, D, DC, MC, V.

SUNNY ISLES, AVENTURA & MIAMI LAKES

Twenty minutes north of South Beach lies the newly fashionable stretch of beach hotels and condos in the formerly anonymous town of Sunny Isles. Because it's accessible to South Beach, but miles away in spirit, Sunny Isles is an appealing, calm, predominantly upscale choice for families looking for a beautiful beach.

There is no nightlife to speak of in Sunny Isles, and yet the half-dozen mega-luxurious skyscraper hotels that have sprung up here since 2005 have created a niche resort town from the demolished ashes of much older, affordable hotels. It's funny in this context to see the last remnant of the old, two-story, humble beach motels, the Monaco, wedged in between two monster luxury high-rises. That hotel's days are numbered, but things are just starting for the next generation.

$$$$
Fodor's Choice
★
🏨**Acqualina.** When it opened in 2006, this hotel raised the bar for luxury in Miami. You'll pay for it, too: Acqualina promises a lavish Mediterranean lifestyle with lawns and pool set below terraces that evoke Vizcaya, and Ferraris and Lamborghinis lining the driveway. There is much to love about the amenities here, including three private pools, the colossal ESPA spa, gorgeous pools, and the trendiest of restaurants, including one of only a handful in Miami to offer unobstructed beach views. And, upon arrival, you're escorted to your room for a personal, in-room check-in. Rooms are sinfully comfortable, with every conceivable frill. Even standard rooms facing away from the ocean seem grand; they have huge flat-screens that rise out of the foot of the bed, making recumbent TV watching seem like a theater experience. If you're planning to pop the big question on your vacation, a Proposal Concierge will help set the scene. **Pros:** In-room check-in, luxury amenities, huge spa. **Cons:** Guests have to pay an extra $40 to use the steam room or sauna. ✉*17875 Collins Ave., Sunny Isles* 📞*305/918–8000* 🖷*305/918–8100* ⊕*www.acqualinaresort.com* 📞*54 rooms, 43 suites* ♿*In-room: safe, refrigerator, Wi-Fi. In-hotel: 3 restaurants, room service, bars, pools, gym, spa, beachfront, water sports, children's programs (ages 5–12), laundry service, concierge, public Internet, public Wi-Fi, parking (fee), no-smoking rooms* ☰AE, D, DC, MC, V.

★ $$$$
🏨**Fairmont Turnberry Isle Resort & Club.** This lush resort doesn't just feel like a country club: the LPGA Tour hosts an annual tournament here every April. The sprawling 300-acre resort completed a $100 million renovation, and has got a tremendous winding lagoon pool, a three story spa and a delicious new restaurant called **Bourbon** to show for it. The rooms are also jumbo sized, decorated in calming tan hues and equipped with every amenity you could need. Add two Robert Trent Jones golf courses, four clay tennis courts, and a 117-boat marina, and you've got a corporate vacationer's dream. South Beach may seem a world away, but anyone who wants to delve into Ocean Drive madness can access to the resort's private Ocean Club at Collins Avenue and

7

17th Street. **Pros:** Lots of activity. **Cons:** No beach nightlife. ✉19999 *W. Country Club Dr., Aventura* ☎*305/932–6200 or 800/327–7028* 🖷*305/933–6560* ⊕*www.turnberryisle.com* 🖙*392 rooms, 41 suites* ⚒ *In-room: safe, kitchen (some), refrigerator, DVD (some), Wi-Fi. In-hotel: 4 restaurants, bars, golf courses, tennis courts, pools, gym, spa, water sports, bicycles, laundry service, executive floor, public Internet, public Wi-Fi, parking (fee), some pets allowed, no-smoking rooms* ▭*AE, D, DC, MC, V.*

¢–$$ 🏨 **Shula's Hotel & Golf Club.** In leafy Miami Lakes, about 14 mi northwest of downtown Miami, the hotel is part of the Main Street shopping, dining, and entertainment complex. The golf club, with par-72 senator and par-3 executive courses, is less than a mile away. Both wings have rooms with sports prints, and a shuttle runs between them and all around the 500-acre property. If you're not teeing off, you can work out or play tennis in the hotel's 40,000-square-foot athletic club. Need to fortify yourself with some protein? Don Shula's Steak House serves hefty cuts of prime beef in an atmosphere that can best be described as "football elegant." **Pros:** Good golf, fun sports atmosphere, unpretentious vibe. **Cons:** Suburban location, far from beaches. ✉*6842 Main St., Miami Lakes* ☎*305/821–1150 or 800/247–4852* 🖷*305/820–8071* ⊕*www.donshulahotel.com* 🖙*205 rooms, 16 suites* ⚒ *In-room: safe, refrigerator, Wi-Fi. In-hotel: 2 restaurants, bars, golf courses, tennis courts, pools, gym, spa, public Internet, public Wi-Fi, parking (no fee), no-smoking rooms* ▭*AE, DC, MC, V.*

¢
Fodor's Choice
★

🏨 **Travelodge Monaco Beach Resort.** Book a room here today, before the Monaco is demolished to make way for another high-rise luxury hotel. Peek inside the courtyard and you'll see older men and women playing shuffleboard. Some have been coming here for 50 years, and it seems almost out of charity that the Monaco stays open for them today. In high season rooms are only $100. Want a kitchen? Ten dollars more. Naturally the furnishings are simple, but they're clean, and the oceanfront wing literally extends out onto the sand. So there's no wireless Internet here—who needs it? Read a book under one of the tiki huts on the beach. You don't need to reserve them, and you don't pay extra. This is easily the best value of any hotel in Miami. **Pros:** Steps to great beach, wholly unpretentious, bottom-dollar cost. **Cons:** Older rooms, not service oriented. ✉*17501 Collins Ave., Sunny Isles* ☎*305/932–2100 or 800/227–9006* 🖷*305/931–5519* ⊕*www.monaco miamibeachresort.com* 🖙*110 rooms* ⚒ *In-room: safe, kitchen (some), refrigerator. In-hotel: restaurant, bar, pool, beachfront, public Wi-Fi (fee), parking (fee)* ▭*AE, D, DC, MC, V.*

DOWNTOWN MIAMI

$$–$$$ 🏨 **Doubletree Grand Hotel Biscayne Bay.** Like the Biscayne Bay Marriott, this elegant waterfront option is at the north end of downtown off a scenic marina, and near many of Miami's headline attractions: the Port of Miami, Bayside, the Arena, and the Carnival Center. Rooms are spacious, and most have a view of Biscayne Bay and the port. Some suites have full kitchens. You can rent Jet Skis or take deep-sea fishing

trips from the marina. **Pros:** Great bay views, deli and market on-site. **Cons:** Need a cab to get around. ✉*1717 N. Bayshore Dr., Downtown* ☎*305/372–0313 or 800/222–8733* 🖷*305/539–9228* ⊕*www. doubletree.com* 🛏*152 suites* ⚴*In-room: safe, kitchen (some), Wi-Fi (fee). In-hotel: restaurant, room service, bar, pool, gym, spa* ▭*AE, D, DC, MC, V.*

$$$$
Fodor's Choice
★

🏨**Four Seasons Hotel Miami.** Stepping off busy Brickell Avenue into this hotel, you see a soothing water wall trickling down from above. Inside, a cavernous lobby is barely big enough to hold the enormous sculptures—part of the hotel's collection of local and Latin American artists. A 2-acre pool terrace on the seventh floor overlooks downtown Miami while making you forget you're in downtown Miami. The hotel's best feature is the beautiful Sports Club/LA, complete with complementary yoga and exercise classes. Three heated pools include a foot-deep wading pool with 24 palm tree "islands." Service is tops for Miami. **Pros:** Sensational service, amazing gym and pool deck. **Cons:** No balconies. ✉*1435 Brickell Ave., Downtown* ☎*305/358–3535 or 800/819–5053* 🖷*305/358–7758* ⊕*www.fourseasons.com/miami* 🛏*182 rooms, 39 suites* ⚴*In-room: safe. In-hotel: restaurant, bars, pools, gym, spa, public Internet* ▭*AE, D, DC, MC.*

$$$$
Fodor's Choice
★

🏨**Mandarin Oriental, Miami.** If you can afford to stay here, do. The location, at the tip of Brickell Key in Biscayne Bay, is superb. Rooms facing west overlook the downtown skyline; to the east are Miami Beach and the blue Atlantic. There's also beauty in the details: sliding screens that close off the baths, dark wood, crisp linens, and room numbers hand-painted on rice paper at check-in. The **Azul** (⇨Where to Eat, above) restaurant, with an eye-catching waterfall and private dining area at the end of a catwalk, serves a mix of Asian, Latin, Caribbean, and French cuisine. The hotel has a 20,000-square-foot private beach and an on-site spa. **Pros:** Only beach (man-made) in downtown, intimate feeling, top luxury hotel. **Cons:** Small pool, few beach cabanas. ✉*500 Brickell Key Dr., Brickell Key* ☎*305/913–8288 or 866/888–6780* 🖷*305/913–8300* ⊕*www.mandarinoriental.com* 🛏*326 rooms, 31 suites* ⚴*In-room: safe, Ethernet. In-hotel: 2 restaurants, bars, pool, spa, gym, laundry service, children's programs (ages 5–12) concierge, parking (fee)* ▭*AE, D, DC, MC, V.*

¢
Fodor's Choice
★

🏨**Miami River Inn.** Billed as Miami's only bed-and-breakfast, this inn dispenses the attentive, personalized hospitality often lost in Miami Beach's gleaming Deco towers. The inn's four restored 1904 clapboard buildings are the only group of Miami houses left from that period. A glass of wine at check-in sets the tone. Rooms (some with tub but no shower) are filled with antiques, and many have hardwood floors. All have TVs and phones. The most popular rooms overlook the river from the second and third floors. The heart of the city is a 10-minute stroll across the 1st Street Bridge. The inn is eco-friendly and sponsors a community garden down the street. **Pros:** Free Continental breakfast, unusual but central location, quaint and inexpensive. **Cons:** Windows can't be opened. ✉*118 S.W. South River Dr., Little Havana,* ☎*305/325–0045 or 800/468–3589* 🖷*305/325–9227* ⊕*www.miami riverinn.com* 🛏*38 rooms* ⚴*In-hotel: pool, laundry facilities, public*

7

Wi-Fi, parking (no fee), some pets allowed, no-smoking rooms ⊟*AE, D, DC, MC, V* ⍥*CP.*

COCONUT GROVE

Coconut Grove is blessed with a number of excellent luxury properties. All are within walking distance of its principal entertainment center, Coco Walk, as well as its marinas. Although this area certainly can't replace the draw of Miami Beach or the business convenience of downtown, about 20 minutes away, it's an exciting bohemian-chic neighborhood with a gorgeous waterfront.

$-$$$ ⛉**Doubletree Hotel at Coconut Grove.** Along Coconut Grove's hotel row, which faces some of the best waterfront in the country, the Doubletree is a short walk from popular Grove shops and restaurants and a quick drive from Miami's beaches and business districts. Most rooms have terraces open to breezes from the bay, plus work desks, coffeemakers, movies, and complimentary Internet access. **Pros:** Cookies at check-in, nice marina views. **Cons:** Drab, older exterior. ⊠*2649 S. Bayshore Dr., Coconut Grove* ☎*305/858–2500 or 800/222–8733* 🖷*305/858–9117* ⊕*www.coconutgrove.doubletree.com* ⌨*196 rooms, 20 suites* ⌂*In-room: Wi-Fi. In-hotel: restaurant, room service, bars, pool, gym, parking (fee), no-smoking rooms* ⊟*AE, D, DC, MC, V.*

$$$-$$$$ ⛉**Ritz-Carlton, Coconut Grove.** Although it's the least exciting of the Ritz-Carlton's three properties in the Miami area, it provides the best service experience in Coconut Grove. Overlooking Biscayne Bay, rooms are appointed with marble baths, a choice of down or nonallergenic foam pillows, and private wraparound balconies. And there's a butler to solve every dilemma—technology butlers to resolve computer problems, travel butlers to meet your flight and guide you to the hotel, dog butlers to watch after your version of Tinkerbell, and shopping and style guides to make sure you don't drop while you shop. A 5,000-square-foot spa is on hand to soothe away stress, and the open-air Bizcaya is among Coconut Grove's loveliest dining spots. **Pros:** Best service in Coconut Grove, high-quality spa. **Cons:** Least exciting of the three Miami Ritz-Carltons. ⊠*3300 S.W. 27th Ave., Coconut Grove* ☎*305/644–4680 or 800/241–3333* 🖷*305/644–4681* ⊕*www.ritz carlton.com* ⌨*88 rooms, 27 suites* ⌂*In-room: safe, refrigerator, Ethernet, Wi-Fi. In-hotel: 2 restaurants, room service, bar, pool, gym, spa, laundry service, concierge, executive floor, public Internet, public Wi-Fi, parking (fee), some pets allowed, no-smoking rooms* ⊟*AE, D, DC, MC, V. Michele Payer*

KEY BISCAYNE

Key Biscayne is the southernmost barrier island in the country, yet it's only 5 mi from downtown Miami.

$$$$ ⛉**Ritz-Carlton, Key Biscayne.** There is probably no other place in Miami
Fodor's Choice where slowness is lifted to a fine art. On Key Biscayne there are no pres-
★ sures, there's no nightlife, and the dining choices are essentially limited

to the hotel. In this kind of setting, you'll appreciate the Ritz brand of pampering. Need something to do? The "tequilier" at the seaside Cantina Beach will educate you on the finer points of his native region's drink. Hitting the spa? In one of 21 treatment rooms, try the 42 Movement Minerale Massage. An 11-court tennis "garden" with tennis butler, a private beach, and beachside water sports are other options. In-room luxuries like robes, slippers, fine linens and toiletries, and scales are of course expected. The club level offers five food presentations a day, and the Ritz Kids club has full- and half-day, and Saturday night, programs. Borrow bikes here to explore Billy Baggs park and its lighthouse. **Pros:** Top tennis facility, private beach, good family retreat. **Cons:** Beach is gray sand, you have to drive to Miami for nightlife. ⊠*455 Grand Bay Dr., Key Biscayne* ☎*305/365–4500 or 800/241–3333* 🖷*305/365– 4505* ⊕*www.ritzcarlton.com/resorts/key_biscayne* ⇋*365 rooms, 37 suites* &*In-room: safe, DVD (some), VCR (some), Ethernet, Wi-Fi. In-hotel: 2 restaurants, room service, bars, tennis courts, pools, gym, spa, beachfront, water sports, bicycles, laundry service, concierge, executive floor, public Internet, public Wi-Fi, parking (fee), some pets allowed, no-smoking rooms* ▤*AE, D, DC, MC, V.*

CORAL GABLES

Coral Gables is a beautiful town, set around its beacon, the national landmark Biltmore Hotel. It also has a couple of big business hotels and one smaller boutique property. The University of Miami is nearby.

$$$-$$$$
Fodor'sChoice
★

🏨Biltmore Hotel. Built in 1926, this landmark hotel has had several incarnations over the years—including a stint as a hospital during World War II—and has changed hands more than a few times. Through it all, this grandest of grandes dames remains an opulent reminder of yesteryear, with its palatial lobby and grounds, enormous pool, and distinctive 315-foot tower, which rises above the canopy of trees shading Coral Gables. Fully updated, the Biltmore has on-site golf and tennis, a spa and fitness center, extensive meeting facilities, and the celebrated Palme d'Or restaurant. The $65 Sunday Brunch is a must. **Pros:** Historic property, possibly best pool in Miami, great tennis and golf. **Cons:** Far from Miami Beach. ⊠*1200 Anastasia Ave., Coral Gables* ☎*305/445–1926 or 800/727–1926* 🖷*305/913–3159* ⊕*www. biltmorehotel.com* ⇋*241 rooms, 39 suites* &*In-hotel: 4 restaurants, bars, golf course, room service tennis courts, pool, gym, spa, public Wi-Fi (fee)* ▤*AE, D, DC, MC, V.*

★ $-$$
🏨Hotel St. Michel. There is no other hotel quite like the St. Michel, where each room is individually decorated with antiques imported from England, Scotland, and France by the owner. Built in 1926, this historic and intimate inn has glass chandeliers suspended from vaulted ceilings in the public areas. Dinner at the superb Restaurant St. Michel is a must, but there is also a more casual bar and dining area behind the lobby, better suited for quiet breakfasts or late-night aperitifs. The St. Michel is nearly always fully booked, so reserve early. **Pros:** Personal service, good free continental breakfast, European sensibility. **Cons:** Slightly less than luxurious. ⊠*162 Alcazar Ave., Coral Gables*

7

☎*305/444–1666 or 800/848–4683* 🖨*305/529–0074* ⊕*www.hotelst-michel.com* ⇗*29 rooms* ⚘*In-room: Wi-Fi. In-hotel: restaurant, room service, bar, laundry service, parking (fee), no-smoking rooms* ▤*AE, D, DC, MC, V* ⦿*CP.*

NIGHTLIFE

Miami's pulse pounds with nonstop nightlife that reflects the area's potent cultural mix. On sultry, humid nights with the huge full moon rising out of the ocean and fragrant night-blooming jasmine intoxicating the senses, who can resist Cuban salsa, Jamaican reggae, and Dominican merengue, with some disco and hip-hop thrown in for good measure? When this place throws a party, hips shake, fingers snap, bodies touch. It's no wonder many clubs are still rocking at 5 AM.

FIND OUT WHAT'S GOING ON

The *Miami Herald* (⊕*www.herald.com*) is a good source for information on what to do in town. The "Weekend" section, included in the Friday edition, has an annotated guide to everything from plays and galleries to concerts and nightclubs. The "Ticket" column of this section details the week's entertainment highlights. You can pick up the free weekly tabloid *Miami New Times* (⊕*www.miaminewtimes.com*), the city's largest free alternative newspaper, published each Thursday. It lists nightclubs, concerts, and special events; reviews plays and movies; and provides in-depth coverage of the local music scene. "Night & Day" is a rundown of the week's cultural highlights. *Ocean Drive,* Miami Beach's model-strewn, upscale fashion and lifestyle magazine, squeezes club, bar, restaurant, and events listings in with fashion spreads, reviews, and personality profiles. Paparazzi photos of local party people and celebrities give you a taste of Greater Miami nightlife before you even put on your black going-out ensemble.

The Spanish-language *Nuevo Herald,* published by the *Miami Herald,* has extensive information on Spanish-language arts and entertainment, including dining reviews, concert previews, and nightclub highlights. *Spanish-language radio,* primarily on the AM dial, is also a good source of information about arts events. Tune in to WXDJ (95.7 FM), Amor (107.5 FM), or Radio Mambi (710 AM).

Much news of upcoming events is disseminated through flyers tucked onto windshields or left for pickup at restaurants, clubs, and stores. They're technically illegal to distribute, but they're mighty useful. And if you're a beachgoer, chances are that as you lie in the sun you'll be approached by kids handing out cards announcing the DJs and acts appearing in the clubs that night.

BARS & LOUNGES

One of Greater Miami's most popular pursuits is barhopping. Bars range from intimate enclaves to showy see-and-be-seen lounges to loud, raucous frat parties. There's a decidedly New York flair to some of the

THE VELVET ROPES

How to get past the velvet ropes at the hottest South Beach nightspots? First, if you're staying at a hotel, use the concierge. Decide which clubs you want to check out (consult *Ocean Drive* magazine celebrity pages if you want to be among the glitterati), and the concierge will e-mail, fax, or call your names in to the clubs so you'll be on the guest list when you arrive. This means much easier access and usually no cover charge (which can be upward of $20) if you arrive before midnight. Guest list or no guest list, follow these pointers: make sure there are more women than men in your group. Dress up—casual chic is the dress code. For men this means no sneakers, no shorts, no sleeveless vests, and no shirts unbuttoned past the top button. For women, provocative and seductive is fine; overly revealing is not. Black is always right. At the door: don't name-drop—no one takes it seriously. Don't be pushy while trying to get the doorman's attention. Wait until you make eye contact, then be cool and easygoing. If you decide to tip him (which most bouncers don't expect), be discreet and pleasant, not big-bucks obnoxious—a $10 or $20 bill quietly passed will be appreciated, however. With the right dress and the right attitude, you'll be on the dance floor rubbing shoulders with South Beach's finest clubbers in no time.

newer lounges, which are increasingly catering to the Manhattan party crowd who escape to South Beach for long weekends. If you're looking for a relatively unfrenetic evening, your best bet is one of the chic hotel bars on Collins Avenue.

SOUTH BEACH

B.E.D. Innocently standing for "beverages, entertainment, and dining," B.E.D. also offers king pillow–strewn beds in place of tables. ✉929 *Washington Ave., South Beach* ☎*305/532–9070.*

★ **Buck 15.** This secret lounge above popular Lincoln Road eatery Miss Yip Café is one of Miami's best-kept secrets. The tiny club manages to play amazing music—a rock-heavy mix of songs you loved but haven't heard in ages—and maintain a low-key, unpretentious attitude. The drinks are reasonable, and the well-worn couches are great to dance on. The club attracts local hipsters and some gay couples. ✉*707 Lincoln Road., South Beach* ☎*305/534–5488.*

Club Deuce. Although it's completely unglam, this pool hall attracts a colorful crowd of clubbers, locals, celebs—and just about anyone else. Locals consider it the best spot for a cheap drink. ✉*222 14th St., at Collins Ave., South Beach* ☎*305/531–6200.*

Laundry Bar. Do your laundry while listening to house music or quaffing a drink at the bar (you can leave your dry cleaning, too). It's mostly gay (with a ladies' night), but definitely straight-friendly. ✉*721 N. Lincoln La., 1 block north of Lincoln Rd., South Beach* ☎*305/531–7700.*

Lost Weekend. Players at this pool hall are serious about their pastime, so it's hard to get a table on weekends. The full bar, which has 150 kinds of beers, draws an eclectic crowd, from yuppies to drag queens to slumming celebs like Lenny Kravitz and the guys in Hootie and the Blowfish. ✉*218 Española Way, at Collins Ave., South Beach* ☎*305/672–1707.*

Mynt Ultra Lounge. The name of this upscale lounge is meant to be taken literally—not only are the walls bathed in soft green shades, but an aromatherapy system pumps out different fresh scents, including mint. Celebs like Enrique Iglesias, Angie Everhart, and Queen Latifah have cooled down here. ✉*1921 Collins Ave., South Beach* ☎*786/276–6132.*

> **WORD OF MOUTH**
>
> "Skybar at the Shore Club: Located on Collins, a couple of doors down from the Raleigh. This was our favorite lounge experience, we came here twice. The grounds are so extensive and so pretty (they have two pools). There's tons of loungers and outdoor seating so even when it's busy, it didn't feel crowded. The bartenders were also great. We corralled a bed and just people-watched, I really loved the vibe here." —wyatt92

★ **The National.** Don't miss a drink at the hotel's nifty wooden bar, one of many elements original to the 1939 building, which give it such a sense of its era that you'd expect to see Ginger Rogers and Fred Astaire hoofing it along the polished lobby floor. The adjoining Martini Room has a great collection of cigar and old airline stickers and vintage Bacardi ads on the walls. There's live jazz most nights. Don't forget to take a peek at the long, sexy pool. ✉*1677 Collins Ave., South Beach* ☎*305/532–2311.*

Fodor's Choice
★ **Rose Bar at the Delano.** The airy lobby lounge at South Beach's trendiest hotel manages to look dramatic but not cold, with long gauzy curtains and huge white pillars separating conversation nooks (this is where Ricky Martin shot the video for "La Vida Loca"). A pool table brings the austerity down to earth. There's also a poolside bar with intimate waterside cabanas. ✉*1685 Collins Ave., South Beach* ☎*305/672–2000.*

Fodor's Choice
★ **SkyBar at the Shore Club.** Splendor-in-the-garden is the theme at this haute spot by the sea, where multiple lounging areas are joined together. Daybeds, glowing Moroccan lanterns, and maximum atmosphere make a visit to this chic outdoor lounge worthwhile. Groove to dance music in the Red Room, or enjoy an aperitif and Japanese bar bites at Nobu Lounge. The Red Room, Nobu Restaurant and Lounge, Italian restaurant Ago, and SkyBar all connect around the Shore Club's pool area. ✉*1901 Collins Ave., South Beach* ☎*305/695–3100.*

Snatch. An upscale rock-and-roll bar with a sophisticated edge, this VIP mecca is where you can hear your favorite hard rock and hip-hop tunes from the '80s and '90s, swing on a stripper pole, and/or ride a mechanical bull. ✉*1439 Washington Ave., Miami Beach* ☎*305/604–8889.*

Santo Restaurant. This Lincoln Road lounge is where Miami's Latin crowd (and anyone who loves Latin music) comes to party. During the day, Santo serves eclectic flair with a Latin twist. At night, the back half of the venue turns into a stage for nightly live and DJ performances, ranging from Salsa to Raggaeton. ✉ *430 Lincoln Rd.., South Beach* ☎ *305/532-2882.*

DOWNTOWN MIAMI & DESIGN DISTRICT

Gordon Biersch. This financial district brew house is classier than most, with glass-enclosed copper pots cranking out tasty ales and lagers, an inspired menu, live music on Fridays, and a steady happy-hour crowd. ✉ *1201 Brickell Ave., Downtown* ☎ *786/425–1130.*

FodorsChoice **Tobacco Road.** Opened in 1912, this classic holds Miami's oldest liquor
★ license: No. 0001! Upstairs, in a space that was occupied by a speakeasy during Prohibition, local and national blues bands perform nightly. There are excellent bar food, a dinner menu, and a selection of singlemalt Scotches, bourbons, and cigars. This is the hangout of grizzled journalists, bohemians en route to or from nowhere, and club kids seeking a way station before the real parties begin. ✉ *626 S. Miami Ave., Downtown* ☎ *305/374–1198.*

COCONUT GROVE

Monty's in the Grove. The outdoor bar here has Caribbean flair, thanks especially to live calypso and island music. It's very kid-friendly on weekends, when mom and dad can kick back and enjoy a beer and the raw bar while the youngsters dance to live music. Evenings bring a DJ and reggae music. ✉ *2550 S. Bayshore Dr., at Aviation Ave., Coconut Grove* ☎ *305/858–1431.*

CORAL GABLES

Bar at Ponce and Giralda. One of the oldest bars in South Florida, the old Hofbrau has been reincarnated and now serves no-nonsense, live homegrown rock-and-roll and a non-touristy vibe. ✉ *172 Giralda Ave., at Ponce de León Blvd., Coral Gables* ☎ *305/442–2730.*

Globe. The centerpiece of Coral Gables' emphasis on nightlife draws crowds of twentysomethings who spill into the street for live jazz Wednesday through Saturday and a bistro-style menu nightly. Free appetizers and drink specials every weekday attract a strong happy-hour following. Outdoor tables and an art-heavy, upscale interior are comfortable, if you can find space to squeeze in. ✉ *377 Alhambra Circle, at Le Jeune Rd., Coral Gables* ☎ *305/445–3555.*

John Martin's Restaurant and Irish Pub. The cozy upscale Irish pub hosts an Irish cabaret on Saturday nights, with live contemporary and traditional music—sometimes by an Irish band—storytelling, and dancers. ✉ *253 Miracle Mile, at Ponce de León Blvd., Coral Gables* ☎ *305/445–3777.*

CABARET, COMEDY & SUPPER CLUBS

If you're in the mood for scantily clad showgirls and feathered head-dresses, you can still find the kind of song-and-dance extravaganzas that were produced by every major Miami Beach hotel in the 1950s. Modern-day offerings include flamenco shows, salsa dancing, and comedy clubs.

Casa Panza. The visionary Madrileñan owners of this Little Havana restaurant have energized the neighborhood with a twice-weekly tribute to *La Virgen del Rocío* (the patron saint of a province in Andalusia), in which the room is darkened and diners are handed lighted candles and sheet music. Everyone readily joins in the singing, making for a truly enjoyable evening. There is flamenco dancing on Tuesday, Thursday, Friday, and Saturday. ⊠*1620 S.W. 8th St., Little Havana, Miami* ☎*305/643–5343* ⊠*Free.*

Improv Comedy Club. This long-standing comedy club hosts nationally touring comics nightly. Comedy-club faithfuls will recognize Margaret Cho and George Wallace, and everyone knows Damon Wayans and Chris Rock, both of whom have taken the stage here. Urban Comedy Showcase is held Tuesday and Wednesday, with an open mike part of the evening on Wednesday. A full menu is available. ⊠*Streets of Mayfair, 3390 Mary St., at Grand Ave., Coconut Grove, Miami* ☎*305/441–8200.*

Lombardi's. You can shake it salsa-style or merengue until midnight to the music of three different bands on Friday, Saturday, and Sunday nights at this downtown restaurant and bar. ⊠*Bayside Marketplace, 401 Biscayne Blvd., Downtown, Miami* ☎*305/381–9580.*

DANCE CLUBS

SOUTH BEACH

Fodor'sChoice **Cameo.** One of Miami's ultimate dance clubs, Cameo, formerly known ★ as Crobar, has gotten a welcome face-lift. Gone is the industrial feel, but all-star DJs and plentiful dance space remain, and plush VIP lounges have been added. If you can brave the velvet rope, Saturday night parties are the best. ⊠*1445 Washington Ave. South Beach* ☎*305/532-2667.*

Nikki Beach Club. With its swell on-the-beach location, the full-service Nikki Beach Club has become a favorite pretty-people and celeb hangout. Tepees and hammocks on the sand, dance floors both under the stars and inside, and beach parties make this a true South Beach experience. ⊠*1 Ocean Dr., South Beach* ☎*305/538–1111.*

Opium Garden. Enter the Asian temple and behold a lush waterfall, lots of candles, dragons, and tapestries. Casually chic twenty- and thirtysomethings go for the exotic intrigue of the popular nightspot and dance to house music and hip-hop. The particularly stylish set should set their sights on the club's upstairs VIP lounge, Privé—a more intimate dance club and lounge experience. ⊠*136 Collins Ave., South Beach* ☎*305/531–5535.*

DOWNTOWN

Space. Want 24-hour partying? Here's the place. Created from four downtown warehouses, Space has three dance rooms, an outdoor patio, a New York industrial look, and a 24-hour liquor license. It's open on weekends only, and you'll need to look good to be allowed past the velvet ropes. ✉*34 N.E. 11th St., Downtown* ☎*305/375–0001.*

COCONUT GROVE

★ **Oxygen Lounge.** Latin and dance sounds dominate at this sleek, below-ground lounge. Water cascades down a wall, and blue neon light casts a glow over the crowd of mainly young professionals out for a good time and a little dancing. ✉*2911 Grand Ave., Coconut Grove* ☎*305/476–0202.*

GAY NIGHTLIFE

Aside from a few bars and lounges on the mainland, Greater Miami's gay action centers on the dance clubs in South Beach. That tiny strip of sand rivals New York and San Francisco as a hub of gay nightlife—if not in the number of clubs then in the intensity of the partying. The neighborhood's large gay population and the generally tolerant attitudes of the hip straights who live and visit here encourage gay-friendliness at most South Beach venues that are not specifically gay. In addition, many mixed clubs, like Cameo, have one or two gay nights. To find out what's going on, log on to *The Express* (⊕*www.express gaynews.com*) or OutInMiami.com (⊕*www.outinmiami.com*).

7

Twist. This longtime hot spot and local favorite with two levels, an outdoor patio, and a game room is crowded from 8 PM on, especially on Monday, Thursday (two-for-one), and Friday nights. Male dancers entertain seven nights a week. ✉*1057 Washington Ave., South Beach, Miami Beach* ☎*305/538–9478.*

Score. This popular bar is the see-and-be-seen central of Miami's gay community. DJs spin every night of the week except Sunday, a popular Karaoke night where everything goes. ✉*727 Lincoln Road., South Beach, Miami Beach* ☎*305/535–1111.*

LIVE MUSIC

★ **Jazid.** Thanks to a sleek interior design job in aqua tones, Jazid is an intimate, candlelighted standout on the strip. The music is jazz, with blues and R&B. Bands play downstairs in the cozy barroom and upstairs on an even tinier stage. Call ahead to reserve a table. ✉*1342 Washington Ave., South Beach, Miami Beach* ☎*305/673–9372.*

Fodor'sChoice **Tobacco Road.** Live blues, R&B, and jazz are on tap seven days a week
★ along with the food and drink at this Miami institution. ✉*626 S. Miami Ave., Downtown* ☎*305/374–1198.*

SPORTS & THE OUTDOORS

Sun, sand, and crystal-clear water mixed with an almost nonexistent winter and a cosmopolitan clientele make Miami and Miami Beach ideal for year-round sunbathing and outdoor activities. Whether the priority is showing off a toned body, jumping on a Jet Ski, or relaxing in a tranquil natural environment, there's a beach tailor-made to please. But tanning and water sports are only part of this sun-drenched picture. Greater Miami has championship golf courses and tennis courts, miles of bike trails along placid canals and through subtropical forests, and skater-friendly concrete paths amidst the urban jungle. For those who like their sports of the spectator variety, the city offers up a bonanza of pro teams for every season. The Miami Dolphins remain the only NFL team to have ever played a perfect season, the scrappy Florida Marlins took the World Series title in 2003, and the Miami Heat are the 2006 NBA champions. There's even a crazy ball-flinging game called jai alai that's billed as the fastest sport on earth.

In addition to contacting the venues below directly, get tickets to major events from **Ticketmaster** (☎ *305/358–5885* ⊕ *www.ticketmaster.com*).

AUTO RACING

★ For NASCAR Nextel Cup events, head south to the **Homestead–Miami Speedway,** which hosts the Ford 400 Nextel Cup Series season finale. The highlight of the speedway schedule, it's held the third Sunday in November in conjunction with the NASCAR Craftsman Truck Series season finale and other races. The speedway, built in 1995 and improved with steeper banking in 2003, is also home to the Toyota Indy 300 IRL season opener each February and other Indy-car racing. ✉ *1 Speedway Blvd., Exit 6 of Florida's Tpke. (Rte. 821) at S.W. 137th Ave., Homestead* ☎ *866/409–7223* ⊕ *www.homesteadmiamispeedway.com* ◷ *Weekdays 9–5* 🎫 *Prices vary according to event.*

BASEBALL

⟳ The **Florida Marlins** won't be playing at Dolphin Stadium much longer. In 2011 they will move into a brand new stadium being constructed on the grounds of Miami's famous Orange Bowl. Go see the team that came out of nowhere to beat the New York Yankees and win the 2003 World Series before they move. Home games are April through early October. ✉ *Dolphin Stadium, 2267 N.W. 199th St., 16 mi northwest of Downtown, between I–95 and Florida's Tpke., Miami* ☎ *305/626–7400 or 877/627–5467* ⊕ *http://florida.marlins.mlb.com* 🎫 *$9–$48, parking $10.*

BASKETBALL

The **Miami Heat,** the 2006 NBA champs, play at the 19,449-seat, waterfront AmericanAirlines Arena. The state-of-the-art venue has indoor fireworks, restaurants, a wide patio overlooking Biscayne Bay, and a silver sun-shape special-effects scoreboard with rays holding wide-screen TVs. During Heat games, when the 1,100 underground parking spaces are reserved for season-ticket holders, you can park across the street at Miami's Bayside Marketplace ($20), at metered spaces along Biscayne Boulevard, or in lots on side streets, where prices range from $5 to $25, depending on the distance from the arena (a limited number of spaces for people with disabilities are available on-site for non-season-ticket holders). Better yet, take the Metromover to the Park West or Freedom Tower station. Home games are held November through April. ✉*AmericanAirlines Arena, 601 Biscayne Blvd., Downtown* ☎*786/777–4328, 800/462–2849 ticket hotline* ⊕*www.nba.com/heat* 🎟*$10–$265.*

BEACHES

Almost every side street in Miami Beach dead-ends at the ocean. Sandy shores also stretch along the southern side of the Rickenbacker Causeway to Key Biscayne, where you'll find more popular beaches. Greater Miami is best known for its ocean beaches, but there's freshwater swimming here, too, in pools and lakes. Below are the highlights for the get-wet set.

MID-BEACH & NORTH

Let's cut to the chase. There are plenty of beaches in Miami, but only one lets you return home without a single trace of a tan line. Park in the North Lot of **Haulover Beach Park** to hit the clothing-optional stretch of sand. It's unofficial, but the gay crowd gathers to the left. The sections of beach requiring swimwear are popular, too, given the park's ample parking and relaxed atmosphere. Tunnels leading from the beach to the lots are less than pristine, but the park is nice for those who want to get to the water without a long march across hot sand. There are lifeguards on duty, barbecue grills, tennis, and volleyball, plus showers for rinsing off after a day in the sun and surf. Or check out the kite rentals, charter fishing excursions, and a par-3, 9-hole golf course. ✉*10800 Collins Ave., north of Bal Harbour, North Miami-Dade, Miami Beach* ☎*305/947–3525* 🎟*$5 per vehicle* ⊙*Daily sunrise–sunset.*

★ ☼ Across the Intracoastal Waterway from Haulover is **Oleta River State Park,** 1,033 acres of subtropical beauty along Biscayne Bay. Swim in the calm bay waters and bicycle, canoe, and bask among egrets, manatees, bald eagles, and fiddler crabs. Highlights include picnic pavilions, five on the Intracoastal and four adjacent to a man-made swimming beach; a playground for tots; a mangrove island accessible only by boat; mountain-bike trails; and primitive but air-conditioned cabins ($50.85 per night, reservations required) for those who wish to tackle the trails at night. In early 2007, the Historic Blue Marlin Fish House and Outdoor Experience, a casual café and self-guided interpretative center, opened on park land just west of the entrance. ✉*3400 N.E. 163rd St., North Miami Beach* ☎*305/919–1844* ⊕*www.floridastate parks.org/oletariver* 🎟*$1 per person on foot or bike; $3 for single-*

occupant vehicle; $5 per vehicle up to 8 people; $1 each additional. Free entrance if renting a cabin. ⊙ *Daily 8–sunset.*

Parlez-vous français? If you do, you'll feel quite comfortable at **Surfside Beach.** This stretch of beach is filled with the many French Canadians who spend the winter here. ✉ *Collins Ave. between 88th and 96th Sts., Surfside.*

SOUTH BEACH

Fodor's Choice ★ The stretch of beach along **Ocean Drive**—primarily the 10-block stretch from 5th to 15th streets—is one of the most talked-about beachfronts in America. The beach is wide, white, and bathed by warm aquamarine waves. Separating the sand from the traffic of Ocean Drive is palm-fringed Lummus Park, with its volleyball nets and chickee huts for shade. The beach also plays host to some of the funkiest lifeguard stands you'll ever see, pop stars shooting music videos, and visitors from all over the world. The beach at 12th Street is popular with gays. Locals hang out on 3rd Street beach, where they watch fit Brazilians play foot volley, a variation of volleyball that uses everything but the hands! Because much of South Beach has an adult flavor—women are often casually topless—many families prefer Mid- and North Beach. Unless you're parking south of 3rd Street, metered spaces near the waterfront are rarely empty. Instead, opt for a public garage and walk; you'll have lots of fun people-watching, too. ✉ *Ocean Dr., between 1st and 22nd Sts., South Beach, Miami Beach* ☎ *305/673-7714.*

KEY BISCAYNE & VIRGINIA KEY

Fodor's Choice ★ Beyond Key Biscayne's commercial district, at the southern tip of the island, is **Bill Baggs Cape Florida State Park,** a natural oasis with an excellent swimming beach frequently ranked among the top 10 in North America by the University of Maryland's esteemed sandman, Dr. Beach. Sea grass–studded dunes, blue-green waters, and plenty of native plants and trees add to the tranquil setting. The 410-acre park has a restored lighthouse, 18 picnic shelters, and a casual seafood restaurant, which also serves beer and wine. A stroll or bike ride along paths and boardwalks provides wonderful views of the bay and Miami's skyline. You can rent bikes, beach chairs, and umbrellas, and there are fishing platforms and a playground. ✉ *1200 S. Crandon Blvd., Key Biscayne* ☎ *305/361-5811 or 305/361-8779* 💲 *$1 per person on foot, bike, motorbike, or bus; $5 per vehicle up to 8 people* ⊙ *Daily 8–sunset, lighthouse tours Thurs.–Mon. 10 and 1.*

★ ☉ The 3½-mi-long beach at **Crandon Park** has a great view of the Atlantic, and parking is inexpensive and plentiful at several different entry points. On busy days be prepared for a long hike from your car to the beach. There are bathrooms, outdoor showers, plenty of picnic tables, and concession stands. The entire park is family-friendly and the sand is equally soft no matter where you place your towel, but the South Beach entrance has boredom-busting access to marine-theme play sculptures, a dolphin-shaped spray fountain, an old-fashioned outdoor roller rink, and a restored carousel (it's open weekends and major holidays 10–5, until 6 in summer, and you get three rides for $1). Then there's **Crandon**

Gardens, a former zoo site that's home to free-roaming swans, iguanas, and at least one American crocodile. Enter at North Beach for the weekend kayak-rental concession, bike path, and the $4 million **Marjory Stoneman Douglas Biscayne Nature Center** (☎*305/361–6767* ☯*daily 10–4*), home of interactive aquatic exhibits and walking trails through Bear Cut Preserve. Eco-tours can be arranged through the center as well. ✉*4000 Crandon Blvd., Key Biscayne* ☎*305/361–5421* 🔖*$5 per vehicle* ☯*Daily 8–sunset.*

BICYCLING

Perfect weather and flat terrain make Miami-Dade County a popular place for cyclists; however, biking here can also be quite dangerous. Be very vigilant when biking on Miami Beach, or better yet, steer clear and bike the beautiful paths of Key Biscayne. A big help is the free color-coded map that points out streets best suited for bicycles. Also available are printouts listing parks with multiuse paths and information about local bike clubs. The map is available from the **Miami-Dade County Bicycle Coordinator** (✉*Metropolitan Planning Organization, 111 N.W. 1st St., Suite 910, Miami* ☎*305/375–1647*), whose purpose is to share with you the glories of bicycling in South Florida. There's some especially good cycling to be had in South Miami-Dade. On Key Biscayne, **Key Cycling** (✉ *61 Harbor Drive, Key Biscayne* ☎*305/361–0061*) rents bikes for $15 for two hours, $20 for the day, and $60 for the week. On Miami Beach the proximity of the **Miami Beach Bicycle Center** (✉*601 5th St., South Beach, Miami Beach* ☎*305/531–4161*) to Ocean Drive and the ocean itself makes it worth the $24 per day (or $8 per hour), $80 for the week.

BOATING & SAILING

Boating, whether on sailboats, powerboats, or luxury yachts, Wave Runners or Windsurfers, is a passion in greater Miami. The Intracoastal Waterway, wide and sheltered Biscayne Bay, and the Atlantic Ocean provide ample opportunities for fun aboard all types of watercraft.

The best windsurfing spots are on the north side of the Rickenbacker Causeway at Virginia Key Beach or to the south at, go figure, Windsurfer Beach. Kitesurfing adds another level to the water-sports craze. The shallow waters off the parking lot in Matheson Hammock Park are like catnip for local kiteboarders. They also blast off from 87th Street in Miami Beach at North Shore Open Space Park.

MARINAS

Haulover Marine Center (✉*15000 Collins Ave., north of Bal Harbour, North Miami-Dade, Miami Beach* ☎*305/945–3934*), which has a bait-and-tackle shop and a 24-hour marine gas station, is low on glamour but high on service.

Near the Art Deco District, **Miami Beach Marina** (✉*MacArthur Causeway, 300 Alton Rd., South Beach, Miami Beach* ☎*305/673–6000* ⊕*www.miamibeachmarina.com*) has plenty to entice sailors and landlubbers alike: restaurants, charters, boat rentals, a complete marine-hardware store, a dive shop, excursion vendors, a large grocery store, a fuel dock, concierge services, and 400 slips accommodating vessels of up to 250 feet. There's also a U.S. Customs clearing station and a charter service, Florida Yacht Charters. Picnic tables along the docks make this marina especially visitor-friendly.

One of the busiest marinas in Coconut Grove is **Bayshore Landing Marina** (⊠*2560 S. Bayshore Dr., Coconut Grove, Miami* ☎*305/854–7997*), home to a lively seafood restaurant that's good for viewing the nautical eye candy.

RENTALS & CHARTERS

You can rent 18- to 68-foot powerboats through **Club Nautico** (⊠*Miami Beach Marina, 300 Alton Road, #112, South Beach, Miami Beach* ☎*305/673–2502* ⊕*www.clubnauticousa.com* ⊠*Crandon Park Marina, 5400 Crandon Blvd., Key Biscayne* ☎*305/361–9217*), a national powerboat-rental company. You can also get a 100-foot powerboat, but make sure to call a week in advance. Half- to full-day rentals range from $200 to $699. You may want to consider buying a club membership; it'll cost a bundle at first, but you'll save about 50% on all your future rentals. The family-owned **Florida Yacht Charters** (⊠*MacArthur Causeway, 390 Alton Rd., Suite A, South Beach, Miami Beach* ☎*305/532–8600 or 800/537–0050*), at the full-service Miami Beach Marina, will give you the requisite checkout cruise and paperwork. Then you can take off for the Keys or the Bahamas on a catamaran, sailboat, or motor yacht. Charts, lessons, and captains are available if needed.

Playtime Watersports (⊠*Collins Ave., Mid-Beach, Miami Beach* ☎*786/234–0184* ⊠*Eden Roc, 4525 Collins Ave.* ⊠*Miami Beach Resort and Spa, 4833 Collins Ave.* ⊠*Alexander Hotel, 5225 Collins Ave.*) sells and rents high-end water-sports equipment, including Wave Runners and wind-driven devices. **Playtime Events** (⊠*4833 Collins Ave., Mid-Beach, Miami Beach* ☎*305/216–6967*) offers boat rentals, corporate team-building events, and 50-foot catamaran sailing trips from the Ritz Carlton Key Biscayne and from the new Regent Hotel in Bal Harbour. In addition to renting equipment, the friendly folks at **Sailboards Miami** (⊠*Site E1 Rickenbacker Causeway, Key Biscayne* ☎*305/361–7245* ⊕*www.sailboardsmiami.com*) say they teach more windsurfers each year than anyone in the United States, and promise to teach you to windsurf within two hours—for $69. Rentals average $30 for the hour, and $25 for each additional hour.

FOOTBALL

Fodor'sChoice ★ The **Miami Dolphins** have one of the largest average attendance figures in the league. September through January, on home game days the Metro Miami-Dade Transit Agency runs buses to the stadium. ⊠*Dolphin Stadium, 2267 N.W. 199th St., 16 mi northwest of Downtown, between I–95 and Florida's Tpke., Miami* ☎*305/620–2578* ⊕*www. miamidolphins.com*.

GOLF

Greater Miami has more than 30 private and public courses. Costs at most courses are higher on weekends and in season, but you can save by playing on weekdays and after 1 or 3 PM, depending on the course—call ahead to find out when afternoon–twilight rates go into effect. To get a **"Golfer's Guide for South Florida,"** which includes information on most courses in Miami and surrounding areas, call ☎800/864–6101. The 18-hole, par-71 championship **Biltmore Golf Course** (✉ *1210 Anastasia Ave., Coral Gables* ☎*305/460–5364*), known for its scenic layout, has been restored to its original Donald Ross design, circa 1925. Greens fees in season range from $145 to $165 for non-residents. The optional cart is $27.

Overlooking the bay, the **Crandon Golf Course** (✉ *6700 Crandon Blvd., Key Biscayne* ☎*305/361–9129*) is a top-rated 18-hole, par-72 public course in a beautiful tropical setting. Expect to pay $150 for a round in winter, $33 in summer, cart included. Twilight rates from $40 apply after 3. **Don Shula's Hotel & Golf Club** (✉ *7601 Miami Lakes Dr., 154th St. Exit off Rte. 826, Miami Lakes* ☎*305/820–8106* ⊕*www.don shulahotel.com*), in northern Miami, has one of the longest championship courses in the area (7,055 yards, par-72), a lighted par-3 course, and a golf school. Greens fees are $134–$175, depending on the season. Hotel guests get discounted rates. You'll pay in the lower range on weekdays, more on weekends, and $45 after 3 PM. Golf carts are included. The par-3 course is $12 weekdays, $15 weekends. The club hosts more than 75 tournaments a year.

Among its five courses and many annual tournaments, the **Doral Golf Resort and Spa** (✉ *4400 N.W. 87th Ave., 36th St. Exit off Rte. 826, Doral, Miami* ☎*305/592–2000 or 800/713–6725* ⊕*www.doralresort. com*), just west of Miami proper, is best known for the par-72 Blue Monster course and the PGA's annual World Golf Championship. (The week of festivities planned around this tournament, which offers $8 million in prize money, brings hordes of pro-golf aficionados in late March.) Greens fees range from $95 to $325. Carts are not required. For a casual family outing or for beginners, the 9-hole, par-3 **Haulover Golf Course** (✉ *Haulover Beach Park, 10800 Collins Ave. North Miami-Dade, Miami Beach* ☎*305/940–6719*) is right on the Intracoastal Waterway at the north end of Miami Beach. The longest hole on this walking course is 120 yards; greens fees are only $7, plus $5 for parking. Hit the links in the heart of South Beach at the lovely 18-hole, par-72 **Miami Beach Golf Club** (✉ *2301 Alton Rd., South Beach, Miami Beach* ☎*305/532–3350* ⊕*www.miamibeachgolfclub.com*). The 2002 redesign from Arthur Hills took the course to the next level. Greens fees are $95 in summer, $200 in winter, including mandatory cart.

IN-LINE SKATING

Miami Beach's ocean vistas, wide sidewalks, and flat terrain make it a perfect locale for in-line skating. And don't the locals know it. Very popular is the **Lincoln Road Mall** from Washington Avenue to Alton

Road; many of the restaurants along this pedestrian mall have outdoor seating where you can eat without shedding your skates. For a great view of the Art Deco District and action on South Beach, skate along the sidewalk on the east side of **Ocean Drive** from 5th to 14th streets. In South Miami an often-traversed concrete path winds **under the elevated Metrorail** from Vizcaya Station (across U.S. 1 from the Miami Museum of Science) to Red Road at U.S. 1 (across from the Shops at Sunset Place). You don't have to bring your own; a number of in-line skate shops offer rentals that include protective gear. **Fritz's Bike, Skate and Surf** (⊠730 Lincoln Rd., South Beach, Miami Beach ☎305/532–1954) charges $10 an hour or $24 for 24 hours, which includes a helmet. A deposit of $150 is required.

POOL

★ ☪ The 820,000-gallon **Venetian Pool,** fed by artesian wells, is so special that it's on the National Register of Historic Places. The picturesque pool design and lush landscaping place it head and shoulders above typical public pools, and a snack bar, lockers, showers, and free parking make an afternoon here pleasant and convenient. Children must be at least 38 inches tall or three years old. ⊠2701 De Soto Blvd., Coral Gables ☎305/460–5306 ⊕www.venetianpool.com ☒$7–$10, free parking across De Soto Blvd. ⊙June–July, weekdays 11–7:30, weekends 10–4:30; Aug.–Oct. and Apr.–May, Tues.–Fri. 11–5:30, weekends 10–4:30; Nov.–Mar., Tues.–Sun. 10–4:30.

SCUBA DIVING & SNORKELING

Diving and snorkeling on the off-shore coral wrecks and reefs on a calm day can be comparable to the Caribbean. Chances are excellent you'll come face-to-face with a flood of tropical fish. One option is to find Fowey, Triumph, Long, and Emerald reefs in 10- to 15-foot dives that are perfect for snorkelers and beginning divers. On the edge of the continental shelf a little more than 3 mi out, these reefs are just ¼ mi away from depths greater than 100 feet. Another option is to paddle around the tangled prop roots of the mangrove trees that line the coast, peering at the fish, crabs, and other creatures hiding there.

☪ It's a bit of a drive, but the best diving and definitely the best snorkeling to be had in Miami-Dade is on the incredible living coral reefs in **Biscayne Underwater Park** (⊠9710 S.W. 328th St., Exit 6 of Florida's Tpke., Homestead ☎305/230–1100 ⊕www.nps.gov/bisc), in the rural southeast corner of the county. With 95% of its 173,000 acres underwater, this is the national park system's largest marine park. The huge park includes the northernmost islands of the Florida Keys and the beginning of the world's third-longest coral reef. Guided snorkeling and scuba trips, offered from the concession near the visitor center, cost $35.95 for a three-hour snorkel trip (daily 1:30–4:30), including equipment, and $54 for a 4½-hour, two-tank dive trip (weekends 8:30–1). Scuba equipment is available for rent.

Perhaps the area's most unusual diving options are its **artificial reefs** (⌧*1920 Meridian Ave., South Beach, Miami Beach* ☎*305/672–1270*). Since 1981, Miami-Dade County's Department of Environmental Resources Management has sunk tons of limestone boulders and a water tower, army tanks, and almost 200 boats of all descriptions to create a "wreckreational" habitat where divers can swim with yellow tang, barracudas, nurse sharks, snapper, eels, and grouper. Most dive shops sell a book listing the locations of these wrecks. Information on wreck diving can be obtained from the Miami Beach Chamber of Commerce.

Divers Paradise of Key Biscayne (⌧*5400 Crandon Blvd., Key Biscayne* ☎*305/361–3483* ⊕*www.keydivers.com*) has a complete dive shop and diving-charter service next to the Crandon Park Marina, including equipment rental and scuba instruction with PADI and NAUI affiliation. Dive trips are offered Tuesday through Friday at 1, weekends 8:30 and 1:30. Trip is $55. **South Beach Dive and Surf Center** (⌧*850 Washington Ave., South Beach, Miami Beach* ☎*305/531–6110*), an all-purpose dive shop with PADI affiliation, runs dives with instructors on Tuesdays, Thursdays, and Saturdays at 8 AM, night dives on Wednesday nights (departure at 5 PM), and wreck and reef dives on Sundays at 11:45 AM. The center also runs dives in Key Largo's Spiegel Grove, the largest wreck ever to be sunk for the intention of recreational diving, and in the Neptune Memorial Reef, which is made using the ashes of cremated bodies. Boats depart from marinas in Miami Beach and Key Largo, in the Florida Keys.

SHOPPING

Miami teems with sophisticated shopping malls and the bustling avenues of commercial neighborhoods. But this is also a city of tiny boutiques tucked away on side streets—such as South Miami's Red, Bird, and Sunset roads intersection—and outdoor markets touting unusual and delicious wares. Stroll through Spanish-speaking neighborhoods where shops sell clothing, cigars, and other goods from all over Latin America. At an open-air flea-market stall, score an antique glass shaped like a palm tree and fill it with some fresh Jamaican ginger beer from the table next door. Or stop by your hotel gift shop and snap up an alligator magnet for your refrigerator, an ashtray made of seashells, or a bag of gumballs shaped like Florida oranges. Who can resist?

MALLS

People fly to Miami from all over the world just to shop, and the malls are high on their list of spending spots. Stop off at one or two of these climate-controlled temples to consumerism, many of which double as mega–entertainment centers, and you'll understand what makes Miami such a vibrant shopping destination.

Fodor'sChoice **Bal Harbour Shops.** Local and international shoppers flock to this swank ★ collection of 100 high-end shops, boutiques, and department stores, which include such names as Christian Dior, Gucci, Hermès, Salvatore Ferragamo, Tiffany, and Valentino. Many European designers open their first North American signature store at this outdoor, pedestrian-friendly mall, and many American designers open their first boutique outside of New York here. Restaurants and cafés, in tropical garden settings, overflow with style-conscious diners. People-watching at outdoor café Carpaccio is the best in town. ⊠*9700 Collins Ave., Bal Harbour* ☎*305/866–0311* ⊕*www.balharbourshops.com.*

CocoWalk. This popular three-story outdoor mall is busier than ever after a beautiful renovation. Chain stores like Victoria's Secret and Gap blend with specialty shops like Koko & Palenki and Edward Beiner, blending the bustle of a mall with the breathability of an open-air venue. Kiosks with cigars, beads, incense, herbs, and other small items are scattered around the ground level, and restaurants and nightlife (The Cheesecake Factory, Fat Tuesday, and a 16-screen AMC theater, to name a few) line the upstairs perimeter. Hanging out and people-watching is somewhat of a pastime here. The stores stay open almost as late as the popular restaurants and clubs. ⊠*3015 Grand Ave., Coconut Grove, Miami* ☎*305/444–0777.*

Fodor'sChoice
★

Village of Merrick Park. At this Mediterranean-style shopping and dining venue Neiman Marcus and Nordstrom anchor 115 specialty shops. Designers such as Etro, Tiffany, Burberry, Carolina Herrera, and Gucci fulfill most high-fashion needs, and Brazilian contemporary-furniture designer Artefacto provides a taste of the haute-decor shopping options. International food venues like C'est Bon and a day spa, Elemis, offer further indulgences. ⊠*358 San Lorenzo Ave., Coral Gables* ☎*305/529–0200* ⊕*www.villageofmerrickpark.com.*

SHOPPING DISTRICTS

If you're over the climate-controlled slickness of shopping malls and can't face one more food-court "meal," you've got choices in Miami. Head out into the sunshine and shop the city streets, where you'll find big-name retailers and local boutiques alike. Take a break at a sidewalk café to power up on some Cuban coffee or fresh-squeezed OJ and enjoy the tropical breezes.

MIAMI DESIGN DISTRICT

★ Miami is synonymous with good design, and this visitor-friendly shopping district is an unprecedented melding of public space and the exclusive world of design. Covering a few city blocks around N.E. 2nd Avenue and N.E. 40th Street, the Design District contains more than 200 showrooms and galleries, including Kartell, Ann Sacks, Poliform, and Luminaire. Recent openings of Michael's Genuine Food & Drink and Domo Japones sushi make this trendy neighborhood a hip place to dine as well. Unlike most showrooms, which are typically the beat of decorators alone, the Miami Design District's showrooms are open to the public and occupy windowed, street-level spaces. Bring your quarters, as all of the parking is on the street and metered. The neighborhood even has its own high school (of art and design, of course) and hosts street parties and gallery walks. Although in many cases you'll need a decorator to secure your purchases, browsers are encouraged to consider for themselves the array of rather exclusive furnishings, decorative objects, antiques, and art. ⊠ *N.E. 36th St. to N.E. 42nd St. between N.E. 2nd Ave. and N. Miami Ave., Design District, Miami* ⊕ *www.miamidesigndistrict.net.*

MIRACLE MILE–DOWNTOWN CORAL GABLES

Lined with trees and busy with strolling shoppers, Miracle Mile is the centerpiece of the downtown Coral Gables shopping district, which is home to men's and women's boutiques, jewelry and home furnishing stores, and a host of exclusive couturiers and bridal shops. More than 30 first-rate restaurants offer everything from French to Indian cuisine, and art galleries and the Actors' Playhouse give the area a cultural flair. ⊠ *Douglas Rd. to LeJeune Rd. and Aragon Ave. to Andalusia Ave., Coral Gables* ☎ *305/569–0311* ⊕ *www.shopcoralgables.com.*

SOUTH BEACH–COLLINS AVENUE

★ Give your plastic a workout in shopping the many high-profile tenants on this densely packed two-block stretch of Collins Avenue between 5th and 10th streets. Think Club Monaco, MAC, Kenneth Cole, Barney's Co-Op, and A/X Armani Exchange. Sprinkled among the upscale vendors are hair salons, spas, cafés, and such familiar stores as the Gap, Urban Outfitters, and Banana Republic. Be sure to head over one street east and west to catch the shopping on Ocean Drive and Washington Avenue. ⊠ *Collins Ave. between 5th and 10th Sts., South Beach, Miami Beach* ☎ *305/672–1270.*

SOUTH BEACH–LINCOLN ROAD MALL

Fodor'sChoice
★ This eight-block-long pedestrian mall is the trendiest place on Miami Beach. Home to more than 150 shops, 20-plus art galleries and nightclubs, about 50 restaurants and cafés, and the renovated Colony Theatre, Lincoln Road is like the larger, more sophisticated cousin of Ocean Drive. The "see and be scene" theme is furthered by outdoor seating at every restaurant, where well-heeled patrons lounge and discuss the people (and pet) parade passing by. An 18-screen movie theater anchors the west end of the street, which is where most of the worthwhile shops are; the far east end is mostly discount and electronic shops. Sure, there's a Pottery Barn, a Gap, and a Williams-Sonoma, but the emphasis is on emporiums with unique personalities, like En Avance, Chroma, Base, and Jonathan Adler. ⊠ *Lincoln Rd. between Alton Rd. and Washington Ave., South Beach, Miami Beach* ☎ *305/672–1270.*

SPECIALTY STORES

Beyond the shopping malls and the big-name retailers, Greater Miami has all manner of merchandise to tempt even the casual browser. For consumers on a mission to find certain items—Art Deco antiques or cigars, for instance—the city streets burst with a rewarding collection of specialty shops.

ANTIQUES

Alhambra Antiques (✉*2850 Salzedo St., Coral Gables* ☎*305/446–1688*) houses a collection of high-quality furniture and decorative pieces acquired on annual jaunts to Europe.

★ **Architectural Antiques** (✉*2520 S.W. 28th La., Coconut Grove, Miami* ☎*305/285–1330*) carries large and eclectic items—railroad crossing signs, statues, English roadsters—along with antique furniture, lighting, paintings, and silverware, all in a cluttered setting that makes shopping an adventure.

Artisan Antiques Art Deco (✉*110 N.E. 40th St., Design District, Miami* ☎*305/573–5619*) purveys china, crystal, mirrors, and armoires from the French Art Deco period, but an assortment of 1930s radiator covers, which can double as funky sideboards, is what's really neat here.

★ **Senzatempo** (✉*1680 Michigan Ave., Ste. 1015, South Beach, Miami Beach* ☎*305/534–5588* ⊕*www.senzatempo.com*) was once a popular showroom but now operates as a warehouse, yet buyers can stop into their Lincoln Road area offices to place orders for great vintage home accessories by European and American designers of the 1930s through the 1970s, including electric fans, klieg lights, and chrome furniture. **Valerio Antiques** (✉*250 Valencia Ave., Coral Gables* ☎*305/448–6779*) carries fine French Art Deco furniture, bronze sculptures, shagreen boxes, and original art glass by Gallé and Loetz, among others

BEAUTY

Fodor'sChoice
★ **Brownes & Co.** (✉*841 Lincoln Rd., South Beach, Miami Beach* ☎*305/532–8703* ⊕*www.brownesbeauty.com*) provides luxurious products to those who appreciate them the most. Cosmetics include Molton Brown, Nars, Le Clerc, and others. It also sells herbal remedies and upscale hair and body products from Bumble and Bumble. Try to resist something from the immense collection of scented European soaps in all sizes and colors. A popular in-house salon, **Some Like It Hot** (☎*305/538–7544*), offers some of the best waxing in town. **The Fragrance Shop** (✉*612 Lincoln Rd., South Beach, Miami Beach* ☎*305/535–0037*) carries more than 800 perfume oils, including those that mimic famous brands, in a setting that resembles an 18th-century apothecary. The staff will customize a unique blend for you or sell you a handblown perfume bottle made by one of many international artisans.

BOOKS

Barnes & Noble (✉*152 Miracle Mile, Coral Gables* ☎*305/446–4152*), like others in the superstore chain, encourages customers to pick a book off the shelf and lounge on a couch. A well-stocked magazine and international news rack and an espresso bar–café make it even easier to while away a rainy afternoon here or at the Kendall, North Miami Beach, or South Miami locations.

Fodor'sChoice
★ **Books & Books, Inc.** (✉*265 Aragon Ave., Coral Gables* ☎*305/442–4408* ✉*933 Lincoln Rd., South Beach, Miami Beach* ☎*305/532–3222* ✉*9700 Collins Ave., Bal Harbour Shops, Bal Harbour* ☎*305/864–4241*), Greater Miami's only independent English-language bookshops,

specialize in contemporary and classical literature as well as in books on the arts, architecture, Florida, and Cuba. At any of its three locations you can lounge at a café or browse the photography gallery. All stores host regular poetry and other readings. ok./ 3/2008 **La Moderna Poesia** (✉*5739 N.W. 7th St., Little Havana, Miami* ☎*305/262-1975*), with more than 100,000 titles, is one of the region's largest and most complete sources for *los libros en español*.

CIGARS

El Credito Cigars (✉*1106 S.W. 8th St., Little Havana, Miami* ☎*305/858-4162*), in the heart of Little Havana, employs rows of workers at wooden benches. They rip, cut, and wrap giant tobacco leaves, and press the cigars in vises. El Credito cigars are known for their good quality and relatively low price. Dedicated smokers find their way here to pick up a $90 bundle or to peruse the *gigantes, supremos,* panatelas, and Churchills available in natural or *maduro* wrappers. **Macabi Cigars** (✉*3475 S.W. 8th St., Little Havana, Miami* ☎*305/446-2606*) carries cigars, cigars, and more cigars, including premium and house brands. Humidors and other accessories are also available.

CLOTHING FOR MEN & WOMEN

★ **Base** (✉*939 Lincoln Rd., South Beach, Miami Beach* ☎*305/531-4982*) is a constantly evolving shop with a cutting-edge magazine section, an international CD station with DJ, and groovy home accessories. Stop here for men's and women's eclectic clothing, shoes, and accessories that mix Japanese design with Caribbean-inspired materials. The often-present house label designer may help select your wardrobe's newest addition.

Genius Jones (✉*1661 Michigan Ave., South Beach, Miami Beach* ☎*305/534-7622*) is a modern design store for kids and parents. It's the best—and one of few—places to buy unique children's gifts on South Beach. Pick up furniture, strollers, clothing, home accessories, and playthings, including classic wooden toys, vintage rock T-shirts by Claude and Trunk, and toys designed by Takashi Murakami and Keith Haring. **Intermix** (✉*634 Collins Ave., South Beach, Miami Beach* ☎*305/531-5950*) is a modern New York boutique with the variety of a department store. You'll find fancy dresses, stylish shoes, slinky accessories, and trendy looks by sassy and somewhat pricey designers like Chloé, Stella McCartney, Marc Jacobs, Moschino, and Diane von Furstenberg.

Kristine Michael (✉*7271 S.W. 57th Ave., South Miami* ☎*305/665-7717*) is a local fashion institution with suburban moms and University of Miami students. The store's hip and up-to-the-minute selection of pieces from Theory, Alice & Olivia, Kors, and C & C California stands out from the national retailers across the street at the Shops at Sunset Place.

★ **MIA Jewels** (✉*1439 Alton Rd., Miami Beach* ☎*305/532-6064*) is an Alton Road jewelry and accessories boutique known for its colorful, gem- and bead-laden, gold and silver earrings, necklaces, bracelets, and brooches by lines such as Cousin Claudine, Amrita, and Alexis Bittar. This is a shoo-in store for everyone: you'll find things for trend

7

lovers (gold-studded chunky Lucite bangles), classicists (long, colorful, wraparound beaded necklaces), and ice lovers (long Swarovski crystal cabin necklaces) alike.

★ **Silvia Tcherassi** (✉ *350 San Lorenzo Ave., Coral Gables* ☎ *305/461–0009*), the Colombian designer's signature boutique, in the Village of Merrick Park, features feminine and frilly dresses and separates accented with chiffon, tulle, and sequins.

SHOES

Koko & Palenki (✉ *CocoWalk, 3015 Grand Ave., Coconut Grove, Miami* ☎ *305/444–1772*) is where Grovers go for a well-edited selection of trendy shoes by Calvin Klein, Casadei, Charles David, Stuart Weitzman, Via Spiga, and others. Handbags, belts, and men's shoes add to the selection. Koko & Palenki also has stores in the Aventura and Dadeland malls.

SWIMWEAR

Absolutely Suitable (✉ *1560 Collins Ave., South Beach, Miami Beach* ☎ *305/604–5281*) carries women's and men's swimwear and accessories for lounging poolside. The salespeople will put you in a suit that fits just right and dress you from sunhat to flip-flops. **Everything but Water** (✉ *Aventura Mall, 19501 Biscayne Blvd., Aventura* ☎ *305/932–7207*) lives up to its name, selling everything for the water (except the water itself). The complete line of women's and junior's swimwear includes one- and two-piece suits and tankinis (tank tops with bikini or high-top bottoms).

South Beach Surf & Dive Shop (✉ *850 Washington Ave., South Beach, Miami Beach* ☎ *305/531–6110* ⊕ *www.southbeachdivers.com*) is a one-stop shop for beach gear—from clothing and swimwear for guys and gals to wake-, surf-, and skateboards. The shop also offers multilingual surfing, scuba, snorkeling, and dive lessons and trips.

VINTAGE CLOTHING

★ **Consign of the Times** (✉ *1635 Jefferson Ave., South Beach, Miami Beach* ☎ *305/535–0811*) sells vintage and consignment items by top designers at pre-owned prices, including Chanel suits, Fendi bags, and Celine and Prada treasures.

★ **Fly Boutique** (✉ *650 Lincoln Rd., South Beach, Miami Beach* ☎ *305/604–8508*) is where South Beach hipsters flock for the latest arrival of used clothing. At this resale boutique '80s glam designer pieces fly out at a premium price, but vintage camisoles and Levi's corduroys are still a resale deal. Be sure to look up—the eclectic lanterns are also for sale.

FodorsChoice **Miami Twice** (✉ *6562 S.W. 40th St., South Miami* ☎ *305/666–0127*) has
★ fabulous vintage clothes and accessories from the last three decades. After all, everyone needs a leisure suit or platform shoes. Check out the vintage home collectibles and furniture, too.

JEWELRY

Beverlee Kagan (✉ *5831 Sunset Dr., South Miami* ☎ *305/663–1937*) deals in vintage and antique jewelry, including Art Deco–era bangles, bracelets, and cuff links. **Jose Roca Fine Jewelry Designs** (✉ *297 Miracle*

Mile, Coral Gables ☎*305/448–2808*) designs fine jewelry from precious metals and stones. If you have a particular piece that you would like to create, this is the place to have it meticulously executed. **Me & Ro** (⊠*Shore Club hotel, 1901 Collins Ave., South Beach, Miami Beach* ☎*305/672–3566* ⊕*www.meandrojewelry.com*) is a trendy New York–based jewelry shop run by Michele Quan and Robin Renzi, with a celebrity clientele that reads like a who's who. Designs are crafted from silver, gold, and semiprecious stones.

ODDS & ENDS

Condom USA (⊠*3066 Grand Ave., Coconut Grove, Miami* ☎*305/445–7729*) sells condoms by the gross, sexually oriented games, and other titillating objects. If you're easily offended, stay away, but if you're easily aroused, stay the night (or at least until closing—2 AM on Friday and Saturday, midnight the rest of the week). **La Casa de los Trucos (The House of Costumes)** (⊠*1343 S.W. 8th St., Little Havana, Miami* ☎*305/858–5029*) is a popular costume store that first opened in Cuba in the 1930s; the exiled owners reopened it here in the 1970s. When they're in, the owners perform for you. ■TIP→If you come any time near Halloween, expect to stand in line just to enter the tiny store.

ONLY IN MIAMI

ABC Costume Shop (⊠*575 N.W. 24th St., Design District, Miami* ☎*305/573–5657* ⊕*www.abccostumeshop.com*) is a major costume source for TV, movie, and theatrical performances. Open to the public, it rents and sells outfits from Venetian kings and queens to Tarzan and Jane. Hundreds of costumes and accessories, such as wigs, masks, gloves, tights, and makeup, are available to buy off the rack, and thousands are available to rent.

★ **Dog Bar** (⊠*1684 Jefferson Ave., South Beach, Miami Beach* ☎*305/532–5654*), just north of Lincoln Road's main drag, caters to enthusiastic animal owners who simply must have that perfect leopard-skin pet bed, gourmet treats, and organic food. **La Casa de las Guayaberas** (⊠*5840 S.W. 8th St., Little Havana, Miami* ☎*305/266–9683*) sells custom-made guayaberas, the natty four-pocket dress shirts favored by Latin men. Hundreds are also available off the rack. **Orchids International** (⊠*2662 S.W. 27th Ct. , Coconut Grove, Miami* ☎*305/665–3278*) will satisfy your yen for mysteriously beautiful varieties of orchids, bromeliads, and bonsai.

SPORTING GOODS

Bikes to Go (⊠*6600 S.W. 80th St., Miami* ☎*305/666–7702*) sells wheels and products that protect you from the hazards of biking but does not rent equipment.

★ **Miami Golf Discount Superstore** (⊠*111 N.E. 1st St., 2nd fl., Downtown* ☎*305/371–4554* ⊕*www.miamigolfdiscount.com* has 10,000 square feet of golf equipment, including clubs, balls, shoes, and clothing. A practice net lets you test your swing.

OUTDOOR MARKETS

Pass the mangos! Greater Miami's farmers' markets and flea markets take advantage of the region's balmy weather and tropical delights to lure shoppers to open-air stalls filled with produce and collectibles.

★ **Coconut Grove Farmers Market.** The most organic of Miami's outdoor markets specializes in a mouthwatering array of local produce as well as such ready-to-eat goodies as cashew butter, homemade salad dressings, and fruit pies. If you are looking for a downright granola crowd and experience, pack your Birkenstocks, because this is it. ⊠ *Grand Ave. and Margaret St., Coconut Grove, Miami* ☎ *305/238–7747.*

Coral Gables Farmers Market. Some 25 local produce growers and plant vendors sell herbs, fruits, fresh-squeezed juices, chutneys, cakes, and muffins at this market between Coral Gables' City Hall and Merrick Park. Artists also join in. Regular events include gardening workshops, children's activities, and cooking demonstrations offered by Coral Gables' master chefs. ⊠ *405 Biltmore Way, Coral Gables* ☎ *305/460–5311.*

Española Way Market. This market has been a city favorite since its debut in the heart of South Beach in 1995. Along a two-block stretch of balconied Mediterranean-style storefronts, the road closes to traffic, and vendors set up tables on the wide sidewalks as street musicians beat out Latin rhythms. You might find silver jewelry, antique lanterns, orchids, leather jackets, cheap watches, imports from India and Guatemala, or antique Venetian painted beads. Scattered among the merchandise, food vendors sell tasty but inexpensive Latin snacks and drinks. Park along a side street. ⊠ *Española Way between Drexel and Washington Aves., South Beach, Miami Beach* ☎ *305/531–0038.*

Lincoln Road Farmers Market. With all the familiar trappings of a farmers' market, this is quickly becoming a must-see event before or after visiting the Antique and Collectibles Market. It brings local produce and bakery vendors to the Lincoln Road Mall and often features plant workshops, art sales, and children's activities. This is a good place to pick up live orchids, too. ⊠ *Lincoln Rd. between Meridian and Euclid Aves., South Beach, Miami Beach* ☎ *305/673–4166.*

★ **Lincoln Road Antique and Collectibles Market.** Interested in picking up samples of Miami's ever-present modern and moderne furniture and accessories? This outdoor show offers eclectic goods that should satisfy post-impressionists, Deco-holics, Edwardians, Bauhausers, Goths, and '50s junkies. ⊠ *Lincoln and Alton Rds., South Beach, Miami Beach* ☎ *305/673–4991.*

MIAMI & MIAMI BEACH ESSENTIALS

TRANSPORTATION

Greater Miami resembles Los Angeles in its urban sprawl and traffic. You'll need a car to visit many attractions and points of interest. Some are accessible via the public transportation system, run by a department of the county government—the Metro-Dade Transit Agency, which maintains 650 Metrobuses on 70 routes; the 21-mi Metrorail elevated rapid-transit system; and the Metromover, an elevated light-rail system. Free maps and schedules are available.

BY AIR

Miami International Airport (MIA), 7 mi west of downtown Miami, is the only airport in Greater Miami that provides scheduled service. If you're destined for the north side of Miami-Dade County, though, consider flying into Fort Lauderdale International Airport. It is less crowded and more user-friendly, and you may also find greatly reduced fares on airlines that don't serve MIA. Approximately 32 million visitors pass through MIA annually, just less than half of them international travelers. Altogether, more than 80 airlines serve nearly 150 cities with nonstop or one-stop service from here.

Getting around MIA is easy if you envision a horseshoe or U-shaped terminal. Eight concourses extend out from the terminal; Concourse A is on the right or north side, E is in the center, and H is on the left or south side (a map of the airport is available on the MIA Web site (⊕ *www.miami-airport.com*). If you're headed from one concourse to another, **take the Moving Walkway** on the skywalk (third) level; it links all eight concourses and the parking garages. Skycaps are available for hire throughout the airport, but on busy days be prepared to wait. Within Customs, portage is free only from baggage claim to the inspection line. A better bet: **grab a luggage cart**—they're free within Customs and $3 elsewhere.

A Tourist Information Center, open 5 AM–9 PM, is on Level 2, Concourse E; free brochures here tell you everything you'd want to know about the airport. Long-term parking is $4 per hour for the first and second hour, $2 for the third hour, and a maximum of $15 per 24-hour period. Short-term parking is $2.50 per half hour, with a maximum of $30 per day.

International flights arrive at Concourses A, B, D, E, and F, as well as at the International Satellite Terminal ¼ mi west of the main terminal. International passengers can be met outside U.S. Customs exits on the lower level of Concourse E or on the third level of Concourse B.

Airport Contacts Miami International Airport (☏ *305/876–7000* ⊕ *www.miami-airport.com*). **Fort Lauderdale–Hollywood International Airport** (☏ *954/359–1200* ⊕ *www.fll.net*). **Miami International Airport Hotel** (✉ *Concourse E, upper level* ☏ *305/871–4100* ⊕ *www.miahotel.com*).

GROUND TRANSPORTATION

Taxi, shuttle, and limousine service are available outside baggage claim areas on Level 1. **Look for a uniformed county dispatcher** to hail a cab for you. On the mainland (i.e., west of Biscayne Bay) cabs cost $2.50 when the meter starts and $.40 for each 1/6 of a mile thereafter (plus a $2 surcharge for trips originating at MIA or the Port of Miami); the fare from the airport to downtown Miami averages $22, and from the Port it's a flat fare of $24.

Flat-rate fares are set for five zones along the barrier island generally referred to as Miami Beach. The long, thin stretch of beachfront actually encompasses not only Miami Beach proper but Indian Creek Village, Surfside, Bay Harbor Islands, Bal Harbour, Sunny Isles, Golden Beach, and adjacent unincorporated areas. The fare zones comprise five east–west bands bound on the east by the Atlantic Ocean and on the west by the mainland. Flat-rate fares run $32 (South Beach)–$52 (North Dade, Sunny Isles) per trip, not passenger; they include tolls and the airport surcharge, but no gratuity.

For taxi service to destinations in the immediate vicinity of the airport, **ask the dispatcher to call an ARTS (Airport Region Taxi Service) cab** for you. These blue cars offer a short-haul flat fare in two zones. An inner-zone ride costs $10; the outer-zone fare is $14. The area of service runs north to 36th Street, west to the Palmetto Expressway (77th Avenue), south to Northwest 7th Street, and east to Douglas Road (37th Avenue). Maps are posted in cab windows on both sides.

Limo service is available through prior arrangement only, but SuperShuttle vans transport passengers on demand between MIA and local hotels, the Port of Miami, the Greyhound terminal, and even individual residences on a 24-hour basis. Shuttles are available throughout the lower level of the terminal outside baggage claim areas. Service extends from Palm Beach to Monroe County (including the Lower Keys). It's best to **make reservations 24 hours in advance for the return,** although the firm will try to arrange pick-ups within Miami-Dade County on as little as four hours' notice. Per-person rates average $9–$25; additional members of a party pay a lower rate for many destinations, and children under three ride free with their parents. There's a pet transport fee of $5 for a pet less than 20 pounds, $8 for 20–50 pounds, or $10 for more than 50 pounds in kennels.

Greyhound offers two departures daily (1 PM and 9:50 PM) connecting the airport with a number of its local terminals, including its Bayside (downtown) terminal (1012 N.W. 1st Ave.). If those times don't work out, more routes are available from Greyhound's main hub (4111 N.W. 27th St.), a short taxi ride from the airport.

Contacts Greyhound (☎ 305/871–1810 ⊕ www.greyhound.com). Miami-Dade Transit, **Metrobus** (☎ 305/770–3131 ⊕ www.miamidade.gov/transit). **SuperShuttle** (☎ 305/871–2000 from MIA, 954/764–1700 from Fort Lauderdale, 800/258–3826 elsewhere ⊕ www.supershuttle.com). **Tri-County Airport Express** (☎ 954/561–8888 or 800/244–8252 ⊕ www.floridalimo.com) is a car service that leaves from Fort Lauderdale International Airport. **TriRail** (☎ 800/874–7245 ⊕ www.tri-rail.com).

BY BUS, AROUND MIAMI

Metrobus stops are marked with blue-and-green signs with a bus logo and route information. If you want to get around by bus or rapid transit, **call Miami-Dade Transit for exact bus routes.** It's staffed with people who can give you specific information and route schedules. If you call from your hometown, they can also mail you a map of Miami-Dade showing all the bus routes and their numbers.

The frequency of service varies widely from route to route, depending on the demand, so call in advance to **obtain specific bus schedules.** Buses on the most popular routes run every 10 to 15 minutes. The fare is $1.50 (exact change only). Transfers cost 50¢. Some express routes carry surcharges of $1.85.

Contacts Miami-Dade Transit, **Metrobus** (☎ 305/770–3131 ⊕ www.miamidade. gov/transit).

BY CAR

I–95 is the major expressway connecting South Florida with points north; State Road 836 is the major east–west expressway and connects to Florida's Turnpike, State Road 826, and I–95. Seven causeways link Miami and Miami Beach, I–195 and I–395 offering the most convenient routes; the Rickenbacker Causeway extends to Key Biscayne from I–95 and U.S. 1. **Remember U.S. 1 (aka Biscayne Boulevard)**—you'll hear it often in directions. It starts in Key West, hugs South Florida's coastline, and heads north straight through to Maine.

Road construction is constant; **pay attention to the brightly lighted, roadside Smart Signs that warn drivers of work zones and street closings.** During rainy weather be especially cautious of flooding in South Beach and Key Biscayne. The Web site ⊕ www.dot.state.fl.us lists roadwork updates for Florida's interstates.

SAFETY

Courtesy may not be the first priority of Miami drivers, who are allergic to turn signals and may suddenly change lanes or stop to drop off passengers where they shouldn't. **Watch out for short-tempered drivers** who may shout, gesticulate, honk, or even approach the car of an offending driver.

Even when your driving is beyond censure, you should **be especially careful in rental cars.** Despite the absence of identifying marks and the stepped-up presence of TOP (Tourist Oriented Police) patrols, cars piled with luggage or driven by hesitant drivers are prime targets for thieves. Keep car doors locked, and ask questions only at tollbooths, gas stations, and other evidently safe locations. Don't stop if your car is bumped from behind, you see a disabled vehicle, or even if you get a flat tire. Drive to the nearest gas station or well-lighted locale and telephone the police from there. It's a good idea to **bring or rent a cellular phone,** as well.

CAR RENTAL

The following agencies have booths near the baggage-claim area on MIA's lower level: Avis, Budget, Dollar, Hertz, National, and Royal. Avis and Budget also have offices at the Port of Miami. If money is no object, check out Excellence Luxury Car Rental. As the name implies, rent some wheels (a Ferrari, perhaps?) to cruise SoBe. If you can't find the excellent car you want, rent a Dodge Viper, BMW, Hummer, Jaguar, Porsche, or Rolls-Royce from Exotic Toys. Airport pickup is provided.

Contacts Alamo (☎*800/468-2583*). **Avis** (☎*800/331-1212*). **Budget** (☎*800/527-0700*). **Dollar** (☎*800/800-4000*). **Exotic Toys Car Rental** (☎*305/888-8448*). **Hertz** (☎*800/654-3131*). **National** (☎*800/227-7368*). **Royal** (☎*800/314-8616*).

PARKING

Many parking garages fill up at peak times. This is particularly true in Miami Beach and Coconut Grove, where streetside parking is impossible and spaces in municipal lots cost a fortune. Thankfully, these neighborhoods are the most pedestrian-friendly in Greater Miami. On Miami Beach valet parking is offered at most dining and entertainment venues (although it can cost as much as $20 on a busy weekend night). "Cabbing" it in South Beach is easy and inexpensive, but if you have to drive, call the **City of Miami Beach's Parking Hotline** (☎*305/673-PARK*) for garages convenient to where you're going. **Don't be tempted to park in a tow-away zone,** as the fees are high and you'll be surprised at how quickly the tow trucks arrive. If your car is towed, contact the municipality for details on how to retrieve your vehicle.

RULES OF THE ROAD

Drive to the right and pass on the left. Keep change handy, since tolls are frequent and can range from 75¢ to as much as $1.50. Right turns are permitted at red lights (after a complete stop), unless otherwise indicated. At four-way stop signs it's first-come, first-go; when in doubt, yield to the right. Speed limits are 55 mph on state highways, 30 mph within city limits and residential areas, and 55–70 mph on interstates and Florida's Turnpike. Be alert for signs announcing exceptions and school zones (15 mph).

All front-seat passengers are required to wear seat belts, and children under five must be fastened securely in child safety seats or boosters; children under 12 are required to ride in the rear seat. Florida's Alcohol–Controlled Substance DUI Law is one of the toughest in the United States. A blood alcohol level of .08 or higher can have serious repercussions even for the first-time offender. Cell phone use while driving is discouraged, although it's currently still legal.

BY TAXI

Except in South Beach, it's difficult to hail a cab on the street; in most cases you'll need to call a cab company or have a hotel doorman hail one for you. Fares run $4.50 for the first mile and $2.40 every mile thereafter; flat-rate fares are also available from the airport to a variety of zones. Fares are set by the board of county commissioners, so if you have a question or complaint, call the **Metro-Dade Passenger Transportation Regulatory Service** (☎*305/375–2460*), informally known as the Hack Bureau. There's no additional charge for up to five passengers or for luggage. Many cabs now accept credit cards; inquire when you call or before you get in the car.

Recent taxi-regulating legislation, hospitality training, and increased competition should rein in most surly drivers. But Greater Miami still has cabbies who are rude and in some cases even dishonest, taking advantage of visitors who don't know the area, so **try to be familiar with your route and destination.**

Taxi Companies Central Taxicab Service (☎*305/532-5555*). **Diamond Cab Company** (☎*305/545-5555*). **Flamingo Taxi** (☎*305/759-8100*). **Metro Taxi** (☎*305/888-8888*). **Society Cab Company** (☎*305/757-5523*). **Super Yellow Cab Company** (☎*305/888-7777*). **Tropical Taxicab Company** (☎*305/945-1025*). **Yellow Cab Company** (☎*305/633-0503*).

BY TRAIN, TO MIAMI

Amtrak provides service from 500 destinations to the Greater Miami area, including two trains daily from New York City. The trains make several stops along the way; north–south service stops in the major Florida cities of Jacksonville, Orlando, Tampa, West Palm Beach, and Fort Lauderdale. For extended trips, or if you want to visit other areas in Florida, come via Auto Train from Lorton, Virginia, just outside of Washington, D.C., to Sanford, Florida, just outside of Orlando. From there it's less than a four-hour drive to Miami. ■**TIP➔: you must be traveling with an automobile to purchase a ticket on the Auto Train.**

The Auto Train runs daily with one departure at 4 PM (however, car boarding ends one hour earlier). Fares vary depending on class of service and time of year, but expect to pay between $269 and $346 for a basic sleeper seat and car passage each way.

Train Information Amtrak (✉*8303 N.W. 37th Ave., Miami* ☎*800/872-7245* ⊕*www.amtrak.com*).

BY TRAIN, AROUND MIAMI

Elevated Metrorail trains run from downtown Miami north to Hialeah and south along U.S. 1 to Dadeland. The system operates daily 5 AM–midnight. Trains run every six minutes during peak hours, every 15 minutes during weekday mid-hours, and every 30 minutes after 8 PM and on weekends. The fare is $1.50; 50¢ transfers to Metromover or Metrobus must be purchased at the station where you originally board the system. Parking at Metrorail stations costs $4.

Metromover resembles an airport shuttle and runs on two loops around downtown Miami, linking major hotels, office buildings, and shopping areas. The system spans 4½ mi, including the 1½-mi Omni Loop, with six stations to the north, and the 1-mi Brickell Loop, with six stations to the south. Service runs daily, every 90 seconds during rush hour and every three minutes off-peak, 5 AM–midnight along all loops. There is no fee to ride; transfers to Metrorail are $1.50.

Tri-Rail, South Florida's commuter train system, offers daily service connecting Miami-Dade with Broward and Palm Beach counties via Metrorail (transfer at the TriRail–Metrorail Station at the Hialeah station, at 79th Street and East 11th Avenue). They also offer shuttle service to and from MIA from their airport station at 3797 N.W. 21st Street. Tri-Rail stops at 18 stations along a 71-mi route. Fares are established by zones, with prices ranging from $3.50 to $9.25 for a round-trip ticket.

Information Metrorail and **Metromover** (☎ 305/770–3131 ⊕ www.miamidade. gov/transit). **TriRail** (☎ 800/874–7245 ⊕ www.tri-rail.com).

CONTACTS & RESOURCES

E-MAIL SERVICE

Save the cost of phone calls and avoid the delays of postal service by using e-mail. If you're sans laptop and modem, get a free e-mail account from any of the larger service providers or try ⊕ www.hot-mail.com. You can log on free at the local library, or try Kafka's Kafe in South Beach. A used bookstore, newsstand, and cybercafé, it's very Europeanlike. High-speed access for 10 minutes is $1, for one hour $6; discounted rates available before noon and after 8 PM. If you're in one of the larger hotels, you can use their business center to send and receive e-mail.

E-mail Service Kafka's **Cybernet Kafe** (✉ 1464 Washington Ave., Miami Beach ☎ 305/673–9669).

EMERGENCIES

Doctors & Dentists Miami-Dade County Medical Association (☎ 305/324–8717) is open weekdays 9–5 for medical referrals. **South Florida District Dental Association** (☎ 305/667–3647 or 800/344–5860 ⊕ www.sfdda.org) is open weekdays 9–4:30 for dental referrals. After hours, stay on the line and a recording will direct you to a dentist. **Dental Referral Service** (☎ 800/577–7322) is open 24 hours for dental referrals. **Visitors Medical Hotline** (☎ 305/674–2273) is available weekdays 8:30–6:30 for medical referrals provided by Mt. Sinai Medical Center.

Emergency Services Dial 911 for police, ambulance, or fire rescue. You can dial free from pay phones. For 24-hour **Poison Control**, call 800/222–1222.

Hospitals Baptist Hospital of Miami (✉ 8900 N. Kendall Dr., Miami ☎ 786/596–1960, 786/596–6556 emergency, 786/596–6557 physician referral ⊕ www. baptisthealth.net). **Jackson Memorial Medical Center** (✉ 1611 N.W. 12th Ave., near Dolphin Expressway, Miami ☎ 305/585–1111, 305/585–6901 emergency, 305/547–5757 physician referral ⊕ www.jhsmiami.org). **Mercy Hospital** (✉ 3663 S. Miami Ave., Coconut Grove ☎ 305/854–4400, 305/285–2171 emergency, 305/285–2929 physician referral ⊕ www.mercymiami.org). **Miami Children's Hospital** (✉ 3100 S.W. 62nd Ave., Miami ☎ 305/666–6511 ⊕ www.mch.com). **Mt. Sinai Medical Center** (✉ 4300 Alton Rd., I-195 off Julia Tuttle Causeway, Miami Beach ☎ 305/674–2121, 305/674–2200 emergency, 305/674–2273 physician referral ⊕ www.msmc.com). **Jackson North Medical Center** (✉ 160 N.W. 170th St., North Miami Beach ☎ 305/651–1100, 888/836–3848 physician referral ⊕ www.jhsmiami.org).

Hotlines Abuse Registry (☎ *800/962–2873, 800/453–5145 TTY*). **Drug Helpline** (☎ *800/662–4357*). **Mental Health/Suicide Intervention** (☎ *305/358–4357*). **Missing Children Information Clearing House** (☎ *888/356–4774*). **Rape Treatment Center Hotline** (☎ *305/585–7273*).

TOURS

Coconut Grove Rickshaw centers its operations at CocoWalk. Two-person rickshaws scurry along Main Highway in Coconut Grove's Village Center from 7 PM to midnight. Take a 10-minute ride through Coconut Grove or a 20-minute lovers' moonlight ride to Biscayne Bay; prices start at $5 per person, and you can pick them up curbside.

BOAT TOURS

Duck Tours Miami (✉ *1665 Washington Ave., Miami Beach* ☎ *877/382–5849 or 786/276–8300* ⊕ *www.ducktoursmiami.com*) uses amphibious vehicles to offer daily 90-minute tours of Miami that combine land and sea views. Comedy and music are part of the mix. Tickets are $32 per person, $18 for children 4–12. *Island Queen, Island Lady,* **and** *Pink Lady* (✉ *401 Biscayne Blvd., Miami* ☎ *305/379–5119*) are 150-passenger double-decker tour boats docked at Bayside Marketplace. They offer daily 90-minute narrated tours of the Port of Miami and Millionaires' Row, at a cost of $22 per person, $16 for those under 12. For something a little more private and luxe, **RA Charters** (☎ *305/854–7341 or 305/989–3959* ⊕ *www.racharters.com*) sails out of the Dinner Key Marina in Coconut Grove. Full- and half-day charters include sailing lessons, with extended trips to the Florida Keys. For a romantic night, have Captain Masoud pack some gourmet fare and sail sunset to moonlight while you enjoy Biscayne Bay's spectacular skyline view of Miami. Call for prices and details.

WALKING TOURS

The **Art Deco District Tour** (✉ *1001 Ocean Dr., South Beach, Miami Beach* ☎ *305/531–3484* ⊕ *www.mdpl.org*) operated by the Miami Design Preservation League is a 90-minute guided walking tour that departs from the league's welcome center at the Oceanfront Auditorium. It costs $20 (tax-deductible) and starts at 10:30 AM Tuesday, Wednesday, and Friday–Sunday and 6:30 PM Thursday. Private group tours can be arranged with advance notice. You can go at your own pace with the league's self-guided $15 audio tour, which takes roughly an hour and a half.

Professor Paul George (✉ *1345 S.W. 14th St., Miami* ☎ *305/858–6021*), a history professor at Miami Dade College and historian for the Historical Museum of Southern Florida, leads a variety of walking, bike, and boat tours, as well as tours via Metrorail and Metromover. Pick from tours covering downtown, the Miami River, or neighborhoods such as Little Havana and Coconut Grove. George starts Saturdays at 10 and Sundays at 11 at various locations, depending on the tour; the tours generally last 2–2½ hours. Call for each weekend's schedule and for additional tours by appointment. Tours start at $15 per person, and prices vary by tour and group size.

7

VISITOR INFORMATION

Florida Gold Coast Chamber of Commerce serves the beach communities of Bal Harbour, Bay Harbor Islands, Golden Beach, North Bay Village, Sunny Isles Beach, and Surfside.

Contacts **Coconut Grove Chamber of Commerce** (⊠ *2820 McFarlane Rd., Coconut Grove, Miami* ☎ *305/444-7270* 🖷 *305/444-2498* ⊕ *www.coconutgrove. com*). **Coral Gables Chamber of Commerce** (⊠ *224 Catalonia Ave., Coral Gables* ☎ *305/446-1657* 🖷 *305/446-9900* ⊕ *www.gableschamber.org*). **Florida Tourism Industry Marketing Corporation (Visit Florida)** (☎ *888/7FLA-USA automated* ⊕ *www.visitflorida.com*). **Greater Miami Convention & Visitors Bureau** (⊠ *701 Brickell Ave., Suite 2700, Miami* ☎ *305/539-3000 or 800/933-8448 in U.S.* ⊕ *www. gmcvb.com*). **Key Biscayne Chamber of Commerce & Visitors Center** (⊠ *88 W. McIntyre St., Suite 100, Key Biscayne* ☎ *305/361-5207* 🖷 *305/361-9411* ⊕ *www. keybiscaynechamber.org*). **Miami Beach Chamber of Commerce & Visitors Center** (⊠ *1920 Meridian Ave., Miami Beach* ☎ *305/674-1300 or 800/666-4519* 🖷 *305/538-4336* ⊕ *www.miamibeachchamber.com*). **Sunny Isles Beach Resort Association Visitor Information Center** (⊠ *18070 Collins Ave., Sunny Isles Beach* ☎ *305/947-5826*). **Surfside Tourist Board** (⊠ *9301 Collins Ave., Surfside* ☎ *305/864-0722 or 800/327-4557*).

The Florida Keys

Pelicans, Key West

WORD OF MOUTH

"We stayed at the Casa Marina resort, which has its own private beach, something that is rare in Key West. It's not near Duval, but also not terribly far. Michael's is a great restaurant for dinner and you can't miss Blue Heaven for breakfast. We went there every morning during our stay."

—Njrunr3

WELCOME TO THE FLORIDA KEYS

TOP REASONS TO GO

★ **John Pennekamp Coral Reef State Park:** A perfect introduction to the Florida Keys, this nature reserve offers snorkeling, diving, camping, and kayaking. An underwater highlight is the massive Christ of the Deep statue.

★ **Under the Sea:** Whether you scuba, snorkel, or ride a glass-bottom boat, don't miss gazing at the coral reef and its colorful denizens.

★ **Sunset at Mallory Square:** Sure it's touristy, but just once while you're here you've got to witness the circus-like atmosphere of this daily event.

★ **Duval Crawl:** Shop, eat, drink, repeat. Key West's Duval Street and the nearby roads make a good day's worth of window-shopping and people-watching.

★ **Get on the Water:** From angling for trophy-size fish to zipping out to the Dry Tortugas, a boat trip is in your future. It's really the whole point of the Keys.

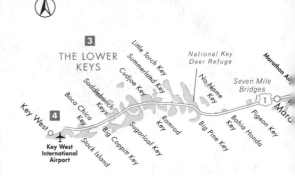

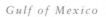

1 **The Upper Keys.** As the doorstep to the islands' coral reefs and blithe spirit, the Upper Keys introduce all that is sporting and sea-oriented about the Keys.

2 **The Middle Keys.** Centered around the town of Marathon, the Middle Keys hold most of the chain's historic and natural attractions outside of Key West.

GETTING ORIENTED

The Florida Keys are the dribble of islands off the peninsula's southern tip. From Miami International Airport, Key Largo is a 56-mile drive along the Overseas Highway. The rest of the keys—Islamorada, Marathon, Bahia Honda Key, Big Pine Key—fall in succession for the 106 miles between Key Largo and Key West. At their north end, the Florida Keys front Florida Bay, which separates it from Everglades National Park. The Middle and Lower Keys front the Gulf of Mexico; the Atlantic Ocean borders the length of the chain on its eastern shores.

8

3 The Lower Keys. Pressure drops another notch in this laid-back part of the region, where wildlife and the fishing lifestyle peak.

4 Key West. The ultimate in Florida Keys craziness, the party town Key West isn't the place for those looking for a quiet retreat.

THE FLORIDA KEYS PLANNER

When to Go

High season in the Keys falls between mid-December and March. November to mid-December crowds are thinner, the weather is wonderful, and hotels and shops drastically reduce their prices. Summer, which is hot and humid, is becoming a second high season, especially among families and European travelers. If you plan to attend the wild Fantasy Fest in October, book your room at least six months in advance. Accommodations are also scarce during the first few weekends of lobster season, which starts in early August and runs through March.

Flying In

In Key West a tiny airport has greeted new arrivals since 1957. But in 2008 a new ticketing, security, and baggage complex more than doubled the size of the terminal at Key West International Airport. The new McCoy Terminal will sit atop a 475-car parking ramp. Besides Key West International Airport, many visitors to the region fly into Miami International Airport, Fort Lauderdale–Hollywood International Airport, and others on the mainland.

About the Restaurants

Seafood rules on the Keys, which are full of chef-owned restaurants. Tropical fruits figure prominently—especially on the beverage side of the menu. Florida lobster should be local and fresh from August to March, and stone crabs from mid-October to mid-May. And don't dare leave the islands without sampling conch, be it in a fritter or in ceviche. Keep an eye out for authentic key lime pie—yellow custard in a graham-cracker crust. If it's green, just say "no." **NOTE:** Particularly in Key West and particularly during spring break, the more affordable and casual restaurants can get loud and downright rowdy, with young visitors often more interested in drinking than eating. Live music contributes to the decibel levels. If you're more the quiet, intimate dining type, avoid such overly exuberant scenes by eating early or choosing a restaurant where the bar is not the main focus.

About the Hotels

Throughout the Keys, the types of accommodations are remarkably varied, from '50s-style motels to cozy inns to luxurious lodges. Key West's lodging portfolio includes historic cottages, restored Conch houses, and large resorts. Most are on or near the ocean, so water sports reign supreme. Some larger properties charge a mandatory daily resort fee of $15 or more, which can cover equipment rental, spa use, and other services. Some guesthouses and inns do not welcome children under 16, and some do not permit smoking.

What It Costs

DINING & LODGING PRICE CATEGORIES				
¢	$	$$	$$$	$$$$
Restaurants				
under $10	$10–$15	$15–$20	$20–$30	over $30
Hotels				
under $80	$80–$100	$100–$140	$140–$220	over $220

Restaurant prices are per person for a main course at dinner. Hotel prices are for a standard double room, excluding 6% sales tax (more in some counties) and 1%–4% tourist tax.

Update by
Chelle Koster
Walton

BEING A CONCH IS A condition of the heart, and foreclosure on the soul. Many throughout the Florida Keys wear that label proudly, yet there is anything but a shared lifestyle here. To the south, Key West has a Mardi Gras mood with Fantasy Festivals, Hemingway look-alike contests, and the occasional threat to secede from the Union. It's an island whose melting-pot character allows crusty natives to mingle (more or less peacefully) with eccentrics and escape artists who lovingly call this 4-mi sandbar "Paradise." Although life elsewhere in the island chain isn't quite as offbeat, it's nearly as diverse. Flowering jungles, shimmering seas, and mangrove-lined islands are also, conversely, overburdened. A river of tourist traffic gushes along U.S. 1 (also called the Overseas Highway), the 110-mi artery linking the inhabited islands. Residents of Monroe County live by diverting the river's flow of dollars to their own pockets. In the process, the fragile beauty of the Keys—or at least the 45 that are inhabited and linked to the mainland by 43 bridges—is paying an environmental price. At the top, nearest the mainland, is Key Largo, becoming more congested as it evolves into a bedroom community and weekend hideaway for residents of Miami and Fort Lauderdale. At the bottom, 106 mi southwest, is Key West, where hundreds of passengers from multiple cruise ships swarm the narrow streets. Offshore is the Florida Keys National Marine Sanctuary, established by Congress in 1990, a wondrous but fragile environment of sea-grass meadows, mangrove islands, and living coral reefs.

The expansion of U.S. 1 to the mainland to four lanes will open the floodgates to increased traffic, population, and tourism. Observers wonder if the four-laning of the rest of U.S. 1 throughout the Keys can be far away. For now, however, take pleasure as you drive down U.S. 1 along the islands. Gaze over the silvery blue-and-green Atlantic and its still-living reef, with Florida Bay, the Gulf of Mexico, and the backcountry on your right (the Keys extend east–west from the mainland). At a few points the ocean and gulf are as much as 10 mi apart. In most places, however, they are from 1 to 4 mi apart, and on the narrowest landfill islands they are separated only by the road. Try to get off the highway. Once you do, rent a boat, anchor, and then fish, swim, or marvel at the sun, sea, and sky. In the Atlantic, dive spectacular coral reefs or pursue grouper, blue marlin, and other deepwater game fish. Along Florida Bay's coastline, kayak and canoe to secluded islands and bays or seek out the bonefish, snapper, snook, and tarpon that lurk in the grass flats and in the shallow, winding channels of the backcountry.

More than 600 kinds of fish populate the reefs and islands. Diminutive Key deer and pale raccoons, related to but distinct from their mainland cousins, inhabit the Lower Keys. And throughout the islands you'll find such exotic West Indian plants as Jamaican dogwood, pigeon plum, poisonwood, satin leaf, and silver-and-thatch palms, as well as tropical birds, including the great white heron, mangrove cuckoo, roseate spoonbill, and white-crowned pigeon. Mangroves, with their gracefully bowed prop roots, appear to march out to sea. Day by day they busily add more keys to the archipelago. With virtually no distracting air pollution or obstructive high-rises, sunsets are a pure, unadulterated spectacle that each evening attracts thousands to waterfront parks, piers, restaurants, bars, and resorts throughout the Keys. Weather is another attraction: winter is typically 10°F warmer than on the mainland; summer is usually 10°F cooler. The Keys also get substantially less rain, around 30 inches annually, compared with an average 55 to 60 inches in Miami and the Everglades. Most rain falls in quick downpours on summer afternoons, except in June, September, and October, when tropical storms can dump rain for two to four days. Winter cold fronts occasionally stall over the Keys, dragging overnight temperatures down to the high 40s.

EXPLORING THE FLORIDA KEYS

Getting lost in the Keys is almost impossible once you understand the unique address system. Many addresses are simply given as a mile marker (MM) number. The markers are small, green, rectangular signs along the side of the Overseas Highway (U.S. 1). They begin with MM 126, a mile south of Florida City, and end with MM 0, in Key West. Keys residents use the abbreviation BS for the bay side of U.S. 1 and OS for the ocean side. From Marathon to Key West, residents may refer to the bay side as the gulf side. The Keys are divided into four areas: the Upper Keys, from Key Largo to the Long Key Channel (MM 106–65) and Ocean Reef and North Key Largo, off Card Sound Road and Route 905, respectively; the Middle Keys, from Conch (pronounced *konk*) Key through Marathon to the south side of the Seven Mile Bridge, including Pigeon Key (MM 65–40); the Lower Keys, from Little Duck Key south through Big Coppitt Key (MM 40–9); and Key West, from Stock Island through Key West (MM 9–0).

THE UPPER KEYS

Diving and snorkeling rule in the Upper Keys, thanks to the tropical coral reef that runs a few miles off the seaward coast. Divers of all skill levels benefit from accessible dive sites and an established tourism infrastructure. Fishing is another huge draw, especially around Islamorada, known for its sports fishing in both deep offshore waters and in the backcountry. Offshore islands accessible only by boat are popular destinations for kayakers. In short, if you don't like the water you might get bored here.

Other nature lovers won't feel shortchanged. Within 1½ mi of the bay coast lie the mangrove trees and sandy shores of Everglades National Park, where naturalists lead tours of one of the world's few saltwater forests. Here you'll see endangered manatees, curious dolphins, and other underwater creatures. Although the number of birds has dwindled since John James Audubon captured their beauty on canvas, birdwatchers will find plenty to see, including the rare Everglades snail kite, bald eagles, ospreys, and a colorful array of egrets and herons. At sunset flocks take to the skies as they gather to find their night's roost, adding a swirl of activity to an otherwise quiet time of day.

The Upper Keys are full of low-key eateries where the owner is also the chef and the food is tasty and never too fussy. The one exception is Islamorada, where you'll find the more upscale restaurants. Restaurants may close for a two- to four-week vacation during the slow season between mid-September and mid-November.

In the Upper Keys, the accommodations are as varied as they are plentiful. The majority of lodgings are in small waterfront complexes with efficiencies and one- or two-bedroom units. These places offer dockage and often arrange boating, diving, and fishing excursions. There are also larger resorts with every type of activity imaginable and smaller boutique hotels where the attraction is personalized service.

Depending on which way the wind blows and how close the property is to the highway, there may be some noise from U.S. 1. If this is an annoyance for you, ask for a room as far from the traffic as possible. In high season, expect to pay $85 to $175 for an efficiency unit; in low season, rates drop to $65 to $155. Some properties require two- or three-day minimum stays during holiday and high-season weekends. Conversely, discounts apply for midweek, weekly, and monthly stays. Campground and RV parks with full hookups charge $25 to $55.

KEY LARGO

56 mi south of Miami International Airport.

The first of the Upper Keys reachable by car, 30-mi-long Key Largo is also the largest island in the chain. Key Largo—named Cayo Largo ("Long Key") by the Spanish—makes a great introduction to the region. This is the gateway to the Keys, and an evening of fresh seafood and views of the sunset on the water will get you in the right state of mind.

The history of Largo reads similar to the rest of the Keys: a succession of native people, pirates, wreckers, and developers. The first settlement on Key Largo was named Planter, back in the days of pineapple and later key-lime plantations. For a time it was a convenient shipping port, but when the railroad arrived Planter died on the vine. Today three communities—North Key Largo, Key Largo, and Tavernier—make up the whole of Key Largo.

What's there to do on Key Largo, besides gaze at the sunset? Not much if you're not into diving or snorkeling. Nobody comes to Key Largo without visiting John Pennkamp Coral Reef State Park, one of the jewels of the state park system. Also popular is the adjacent Key Largo National Marine Sanctuary, which encompasses about 190 square miles of coral reefs, seagrass beds, and mangrove estuaries. If you've never tried diving, Key Largo is the perfect place to learn. Dozens of companies will be more than happy to show you the ropes.

Fishing is the other big draw, and world records are broken regularly in the waters around the Upper Keys. There are plenty of charter companies to help you find the big ones and teach you how to hook the elusive bonefish, sometimes known as the ghost fish.

On land, Key Largo offers all the conveniences of a major resort town, including restaurants that will cook your catch or dish up their own offerings with inimitable style. You'll notice some unusual specialties pop up on the menu, such as cracked conch, spiny lobster, and stone crab. Don't pass up a chance to try the local delicacies, especially the key lime pie.

Most businesses are lined up along U.S. 1, the four-lane highway that runs down the middle of the island. Cars whiz past at all hours—something to remember when you're booking a room. Most lodgings are on the highway, so you'll want to be as far back as possible.

EXPLORING KEY LARGO

Key Largo runs northeast–southwest, with U.S. 1 running down the center. If the highway is your only glimpse of the island, you're likely to feel barraged by its tacky commercial side. Make a point of driving Route 905 in North Key Largo to get a better feel for the island.

American crocodiles, Key Largo wood rats, Key Largo cotton mice, Schaus swallowtail butterflies, and 100 other rare critters and plants call 2,400-acre **Dagny Johnson Key Largo Hammocks Botanical State Park** their home. It's also a user-friendly place to explore the largest remaining stand of the vast West Indian tropical hardwood hammock and mangrove wetland that once covered most of the Keys' upland areas. Interpretive signs describe many of the tropical tree species along a 1¼-mi paved road (2½ mi round-trip) that invites walking, Rollerblading, and biking. Rangers give guided tours and encourage you to taste the fruits of native plants. Pets are welcome if on a leash no longer than 6 feet. You'll also find restrooms, information kiosks, and picnic tables. ⊠ *1 mi north of U.S. 1 on Rte. 905, OS, North Key Largo* ☎ *305/451–1202* ☙ *$1.50* ☼ *Daily 8–sundown. Tours Thurs. and Sun. at 10.*

From the mainland, taking the **Overseas Highway**, rather than Card Sound Road, lands you closer to Key Largo proper, abounding with shopping centers, chain restaurants, and, of course, dive shops.

☽ Where are the best diving and snorkeling sites in the Sunshine State?
Fodor'sChoice **John Pennekamp Coral Reef State Park** is on everyone's list of faves. This
★ underwater gem encompasses 78 square mi of coral reefs, sea-grass beds, and mangrove swamps. Its reefs contain 40 of the 52 species of coral in the Atlantic Reef System and nearly 600 varieties of fish, from the colorful stoplight parrot fish to the demure cocoa damselfish. The park's visitor center has a large floor-to-ceiling fish tank surrounded by smaller ones, so you can get a closer look at many of the underwater creatures. When you want to head out to sea, a concessionaire rents canoes and powerboats, as well as snorkeling and diving equipment. You can also sign up for snorkeling and diving trips ($29 and $50) and glass-bottom-boat rides to the reef ($22). One of the most popular excursions is the snorkeling trip to see Christ of the Deep, the 2-ton underwater

GREAT ITINERARIES

3 DAYS

Spend your first morning diving or snorkeling at John Pennekamp Coral Reef State Park in **Key Largo**. If you aren't certified, sign up for a resort course and you'll be exploring the reefs by the afternoon. Dinner at a bayside restaurant will give you your first look at a fabulous Keys sunset. On Day 2 get an early start to savor the breathtaking views on the two-hour drive to Key West. Along the way make a stop at the natural-history museum that's part of Crane Point Museum, Nature Center & Historic Site in **Marathon**. Another worthwhile detour is Bahia Honda State Park on **Bahia Honda Key**, where you can stretch your legs on a forest trail or snorkel on an off-shore reef. Once you arrive in **Key West**, watch the sunset before dining at one of the island's first-class restaurants. Spend the next morning strolling Duval Street, visiting any of the myriad museums, or taking a walking or trolley tour of Old Town before driving back to the mainland.

4 DAYS

Spend the first day as you would above, overnighting in **Key Largo**. Start Day 2 by renting a kayak and exploring the mangroves of Florida Bay, or take an ecotour of the sandy islands in Everglades National Park. In the afternoon, stop by the Florida Keys Wild Bird Rehabilitation Center before driving down to **Islamorada**. Before day's end, make plans for the next day's fishing. Spend the night in Islamorada. After a morning spent with a rod and reel, stop at one of the many restaurants that is happy to prepare your catch for you. In the afternoon, set off for **Key West**. Enjoy the sunset celebration at Mallory Square.

8

statue of Jesus at Key Largo National Marine Sanctuary. The park also has short nature trails, two artificial beaches, picnic shelters, a snack bar, and a campground. ⊠*MM 102.5, OS, Box 1560,* ☎*305/451–1202* ⊕*www.floridastateparks.org/pennekamp* ✉*$3.50 for 1 person, $6 for 2 people, 50¢ each additional person* ⊗*Daily 8–sunset.*

☺ **Jacobs Aquatic Center.** Take the plunge at one of three swimming pools: an eight-lane, 25-meter lap pool with a diving well; a 3- to 4-foot-deep pool accessible to people with mobility problems; and an interactive play pool with a waterslide, pirate ship, waterfall, and beachfront entry. ⊠*320 Laguna Ave., MM 99.6, OS* ☎*305/453–7946* ⊕*www.jacobsaquaticcenter.org* ✉*$8* ⊗*Weekdays 11–6, weekends 10–7.*

WORD OF MOUTH

"Here's a tip that you can do early. Go to a local dive shop and get a mask, snorkel, and fins. Take them to the local pool (or lake if you have one and it is warm enough) and try them out. Use a dive shop instead of the discount store so you get ones the fit right on you. Take time to get comfortable with them, maybe take an introductory class if one is offered. Then when you get to Key West, you won't waste time trying to learn to breathe with your face in the water and kicking with fins won't be a new chore to learn."

–rm_mn

WHERE TO EAT

★ $$ ✕**The Fish House.** The pan-sautéed black grouper will make you moan with pleasure, but it's just one of many headliners in this nautical eatery. On the fin side, the choices include mahimahi, swordfish, tuna, and yellowtail snapper that can be broiled, blackened, baked, or fried. Prefer shellfish or crustaceans? There are nearly as many choices on the shrimp, lobster, and (from mid-October to mid-May) stone-crab side of the menu. For a sweet ending, try the homemade key lime pie. To ease the long lines, the management added outdoor seating. ✉*MM 102.4, OS* ☎*305/451–4665 or 305/451–0650* ⊕*www.fishhouse.com* ▤*AE, D, MC, V* ⊘*Closed Sept.*

$$ ✕**Snapper's.** "You hook 'em, we cook 'em" is the motto here. Alas, "cleanin' 'em" is not part of the bargain. If you bring in your own ready-for-the-grill fish, dinner here will set you back $13.95 per person. Otherwise, they'll catch and cook you a yellowtail snapper, roasted on a cedar plank with a basil-cream sauce, a grilled tuna steak slathered with Asian barbecue sauce alongside a mound of chipotle mashed potatoes, or a little something from the raw bar. The aromatic steamed mussels are worth the hours of garlic breath, and the ceviche of yellowtail (merrily spiced) wins raves, too. Not for the weak of heart is the Nutty Lobster, a spiny lobster covered with mixed nuts and thrown into the deep fryer. All this is served up in a lively, mangrove-ringed waterfront setting with live music, killer rum drinks, and seating alongside the fishing dock. ✉*139 Seaside Ave.33037* ☎*305/852–5956* ▤*AE, D, MC, V.*

$ ✕**Alabama Jack's.** Calories be damned—the conch fritters here are heaven on a plate. The crab cakes, made from local blue crabs, earn hallelujahs, too. Regulars at this weathered restaurant floating on two roadside barges in an old fishing community include weekend cyclists, relocated retirees, and boaters, who come to admire tropical birds in the nearby mangroves, the occasional crocodile in the canal, or the bands that play on weekend afternoons. Some locals say that Jack's has lost some of its biker-bar feel, but the food's still good and cheap. Jack's closes by 7 or 7:30, when the mosquitoes start biting. ✉*58000 Card Sound Rd., Key Largo* ☎*305/248–8741* ▤*MC, V.*

$ ✕**Mrs. Mac's Kitchen.** Townies pack the counters and booths at this tiny eatery, where license plates are stuck on the walls and folks talk fishing. Got a hankering for tuna casserole or crab cakes? You'll find them here, along with specials like grilled yellowfin tuna. Bring your appetite for the all-you-can-eat fish specials on Tuesday and Thursday. There's also an assortment of tasty burgers and sandwiches, and the chili wins raves. ✉*MM 99.4, BS* ☎*305/451–3722* ▤*AE, D, MC, V* ⊘*Closed Sun.*

$ ✕**Rib Daddy's Steak & Seafood.** You'll swoon after tasting the Memphis-style mesquite-smoked prime rib, beef ribs, and pork baby back ribs flavored with specially formulated rubs and sauces. The menu extends beyond barbecue standards to include steak and seafood. Must-try sides include grilled corn on the cob and sweet-potato casserole. Save room for key lime pie, mango pie, or coconut cake. The kids will love staring at the reef aquarium. ✉*MM 102.2, BS* ☎*305/451–0900* ⊕*www. ribdaddysrestaurant.com* ⌕*Reservations not accepted* ▤*MC, V.*

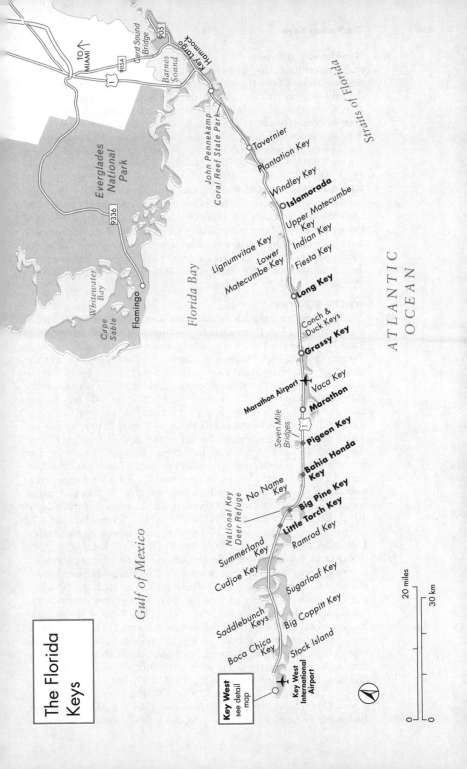

The Florida Keys

TO MIAMI

Card Sound Bridge

905

95A

1

Barnes Sound

Key Largo

Hammock

John Pennekamp Coral Reef State Park

Everglades National Park

9336

Whitewater Bay

Flamingo

Cape Sable

Florida Bay

Gulf of Mexico

Tavernier

Plantation Key

Windley Key

Islamorada

Upper Matecumbe Key

Lignumvitae Key

Lower Matecumbe Key

Indian Key

Fiesta Key

Long Key

Conch & Duck Keys

Grassy Key

Vaca Key

Marathon Airport

Marathon

1

Seven Mile Bridges

Pigeon Key

Bahia Honda Key

No Name Key

Big Pine Key

National Key Deer Refuge

Little Torch Key

Ramrod Key

Summerland Key

Cudjoe Key

Sugarloaf Key

Saddlebunch Keys

Big Coppitt Key

Boca Chica Key

Stock Island

Key West
see detail map

Key West International Airport

Straits of Florida

ATLANTIC OCEAN

20 miles

30 km

0

0

★ $ ✕**Sundowners.** The name doesn't lie. If it's a clear night and you can snag a reservation, this restaurant will treat you to a sherbet-hued sunset over Florida Bay. If you're here in mild weather—anytime other than the dog days of summer or the rare winter cold snap—the best seats are on the patio. The food is excellent: try the key lime seafood, a happy combo of sautéed shrimp, lobster, and lump crab meat swimming in a sauce spiked with Tabasco. Wednesday and Saturday are all about prime rib, and Friday draws the crowds with an all-you-can-eat fish fry. ⊠*MM 104, BS* ☎*305/451–4502* ⊕*sundownerskeylargo.com* ▤*AE, D, MC, V.*

¢ ✕**Harriette's Restaurant.** If you're looking for comfort food—like melt-in-your-mouth buttermilk biscuits—try this refreshing throwback. Little has changed over the years in this yellow-and-turquoise eatery. Owner Harriette Mattson personally greets guests who come for steak and eggs with hash browns or old-fashioned hotcakes with sausage or bacon. At lunchtime, Harriette's shines in the burger department, but there are also specials like meat loaf. ⊠*MM 95.7, BS* ☎*305/852–8689* ▤*No credit cards* ☾*No dinner.*

WHERE TO STAY

$$$$ ▦**Jules' Undersea Lodge.** You can truly sleep with the fishes at this underwater inn. This former research lab has two rooms that sit 5 fathoms (30 feet) below the surface, letting you watch the undersea world through three 42-inch porthole windows. This isn't the place if you're claustrophobic (each of the two rooms is a very cozy 8 by 10 feet) or value your privacy (you share a kitchen and bathroom with the other guests). You also need to be a good swimmer, as the only way to gain access to the lodge is by strapping on scuba gear. You must either be a certified diver or take the hotel's three-hour introductory course (an additional $120). Rates include breakfast and dinner (delivered to your door) and the unlimited use of diving gear. Because of the length of time you'll spend underwater, you can't fly for 24 hours after checking out. The office is open 8 AM to 4 PM. **Pros:** One-of-a-kind experience, unbeatable views. **Cons:** Must be a certified diver or take the special course to stay here, potentially claustrophic accommodations. ⊠*MM 103.2, OS, 51 Shoreland Dr.* ☎*305/451–2353* ⊕*www.jul.com* ↩*2 rooms* ⚭*In-room: kitchen, VCR. In-hotel: pool, diving, no elevator, no kids under 10, no-smoking rooms* ▤*AE, D, MC, V* ▯⚬▯*MAP.*

$$$$ ▦**Key Largo Grande Resort & Beach Club.** Nestled within a hardwood hammock near the southern border of Everglades National Park, this sprawling hotel got a $12 million makeover in 2008. Spacious guest rooms each have a private balcony; most rooms overlook the water or woods, but some face the parking lot. Lighted nature trails and boardwalks lead through the woods to a small beach. Two small pools are separated by a coral rock wall and waterfall. Both restaurants, one of which is very casual, have great views. **Pros:** Nice nature trail on bay side, pretty pools with waterfalls. **Cons:** Pools near the highway, hefty charge for parking. ⊠*MM 97, BS, 97000 Overseas Hwy.* ☎*305/852–5553 or 866/597–5397* ⊕*www.keylargogrande. com* ↩*190 rooms, 10 suites* ⚭*In-room: safe, refrigerators (some). In-hotel: 2 restaurants, room service, bars, tennis courts, pools, gym,*

beachfront, water sports, bicycles, some pets allowed (fee), no-smoking rooms ☰*AE, D, DC, MC, V.*

$$$$

Fodor's Choice

★

🏨 **Kona Kai Resort.** Brilliantly colored bougainvilleas, coconut palms, and guava trees make this 2-acre hideaway one of the prettiest places to stay in the Keys. Each of the intimate cottages has furnishings that add to the tropical feel. Spacious studios and one- and two-bedroom suites—with full kitchens and original art—are filled with natural light. Outside, kick back in a lounge chair or hammock, soak in the hot tub, or contemplate sunset from the deck. The resort also has an art gallery and an orchid house with more than 225 plants. Maid service is every third day to prolong your privacy; however, fresh linens and towels are available at any time. At the pool, help yourself to free bottled water and fruit. **Pros:** Lush landscaping, free use of sports equipment, knowledgeable staff. **Cons:** Expensive rates, some rooms lack privacy. ✉*MM 97.8, BS, 97802 Overseas Hwy.* ☎*305/852–7200 or 800/365–7829* ⊕*www.konakairesort.com* 🛏*8 suites, 3 rooms* ⌂*In-room: no phone, kitchen (some), refrigerator, DVD. In-hotel: tennis court, pool, beachfront, no elevator, concierge, public Internet, public Wi-Fi, no kids under 16, no-smoking rooms* ☰*AE, D, MC, V* �*Closed Sept.*

★ **$$$$**

☺

🏨 **Marriott's Key Largo Bay Beach Resort.** Park the car and toss the keys in the bottom of your bag; there's no need to go anywhere else (except maybe John Pennekamp Coral Reef State Park, just a half mile north). This 17-acre bayside resort has plenty of diversions, from tennis to parasailing to a day spa. Given all that, the pool still rules, so a stroll to the tiki bar could well be your most vigorous activity of the day. The resort's lemon-yellow facade exudes an air of warm, indolent days. This isn't the poshest chain hotel you've ever encountered, but it's fresh-looking and suitably tropical in style. Some of the choicest rooms and suites offer sunset views. **Pros:** Lots of activities, lively atmosphere, lovely pool. **Cons:** Rooms facing highway can be noisy. ✉*MM 103.8, BS, 103800 Overseas Hwy.* ☎*305/453–0000 or 866/849–3753* ⊕*www.marriottkeylargo.com* 🛏*132 rooms, 20 2-bedroom suites, 1 penthouse suite* ⌂*In-room: safe, kitchen (some), Wi-Fi. In-hotel: 3 restaurants, room service, bars, tennis court, pool, gym, spa, beachfront, diving, water sports, bicycles, children's programs (ages 5–13), laundry facilities, laundry service, no-smoking rooms* ☰*AE, D, DC, MC, V.*

8

$$$

🏨 **Azul Del Mar.** The dock points the way to many beautiful sunsets at this adults-only boutique hotel. Advertising executive Karol Marsden and her husband, Dominic, a commercial travel photographer, transformed a run-down mom-and-pop place into this waterfront gem. As you'd expect from innkeepers with a background in the image business, the property offers great visuals, from marble floors and granite countertops to yellow leather sofas and ice-blue bathroom tiles. The owners are crazy about the ocean, so kayaks and other water-sports equipment are plentiful. If you mix business with pleasure, take advantage of the wireless Internet connection on the beach. **Pros:** Great garden, good location, sophisticated design. **Cons:** Smallish beach, not the place for families with young kids. ✉*MM 104.3, BS, 104300 Overseas Hwy., Key Largo* ☎*305/451–0337 or 888/253–2985* ⊕*www.azulkeylargo. com* 🛏*5 suites* ⌂*In-room: no phone, kitchen, refrigerator, VCR, Wi-*

Fi. *In-hotel: beachfront, water sports, bicycles, no elevator, public Wi-Fi, no kids under age 16, no-smoking rooms* ⊟*AE, MC, V.*

$$ 🏨**Coconut Palm Inn.** This low-key inn is set in a quiet residential neighborhood of towering gumbo-limbo and buttonwood trees. Built in the 1930s, the waterfront lodge draws repeat guests with its friendly, relaxed vibe. A 400-foot sandy beach is dotted with the requisite hammocks and swaying palm trees. Screened porches are a welcome touch, letting tropical breezes in and keeping mosquitoes out. Rooms, decorated in West Indies style, vary from one-room efficiencies to one- and two-bedroom suites. No two are alike, although seafoam-green paint is used liberally. **Pros:** Lovely beach, tranquil location. **Cons:** Not much going on here. ⊠*MM 92, BS, 198 Harborview Dr., Tavernier* ☎*305/852-3017* ⊕*www.coconutpalminn.com* 🛏*8 suites, 12 rooms* ⅏*In-room: kitchen (some), refrigerator, VCR (some), Wi-Fi. In-hotel: pool, beachfront, no elevator. laundry facilities, public Wi-Fi, no-smoking rooms* ⊟*AE, MC, V.*

$$ 🏨**Dove Creek Lodge.** Old-school anglers would likely be scandalized by this fishing camp's sherbet-hued paint and plantation-style furnishings. But when they got a load of the massive flat-screen TV, the comfy leather couch, and the stack of fishing magazines in the lobby, they would never want to leave. You can head out on a boat from the marina, chase billfish offshore or bonefish on the flats, and come to brag to your buddies about the one that got away. The surprisingly plush rooms range in size from simple lodge rooms to luxury suites. It's a lively scene—liveliest if you stay in Room 201 or 202, where you'll hear the music from the seafood restaurant next door. **Pros:** Great for fishing enthusiasts, luxurious rooms. **Cons:** Formica countertops in suites, loud music next door. ⊠*147 Seaside Ave.* ☎*305/852-6200 or 800/401-0057* ⊕*www.dovecreeklodge.com* 🛏*14 rooms* ⅏*In-room: safe, kitchen (some), refrigerator, Ethernet. In hotel: pool, public Wi-Fi, airport shuttle, parking (no fee), no-smoking rooms.* ⊟*AE, D, MC, V.*

★ $$ 🏨**Largo Lodge.** When you drive under the dense canopy of foliage at the entrance of Largo Lodge you'll feel like you've gone back in time. Vintage 1950s cottages are tucked amid 3 acres of palm trees, sea grapes, and orchids. Baby-boomer couples seem right at home here in rooms that might call to mind places they stayed as kids. (Young children aren't allowed here, however.) Accommodations—surprisingly spacious—feature small kitchen and dining areas and large screened porches. A lavish swath of bay frontage is perfect for communing with the friendly squirrels and ibises. For swimming, you'll need to drive about 1 mi to John Pennekamp Coral Reef State Park. **Pros:** Lush grounds, great sunset views, affordable rates. **Cons:** No pool, some traffic noise outdoors. ⊠*MM 101.7, BS, 101740 Overseas Hwy.* ☎*305/451-0424 or 800/468-4378* ⊕*www.largolodge.com* 🛏*6 cottages* ⅏*In-room: no phone, kitchen. In-hotel: beachfront, no elevator, no kids under 16* ⊟*MC, V.*

$-$$ 🏨**Coconut Bay Resort & Bay Harbor Lodge.** Some 200 feet of waterfront is the main attraction at this lodge. Coconut palms whisper in the breeze, and gumbo-limbo trees shade the 2½-acre grounds. Nice features abound, like well-placed lounge chairs for gazing out over the water, and kayaks and paddleboats (for when you want to get closer). Everybody shows up on the sundeck or the 30-foot dock to watch the sun slip into Davy Jones's Locker. Easter egg–hued cottages are simply furnished. Ask for Unit 25 and you'll have extra space and a water view. **Pros:** Lush gardens, walking distance to restaurants. **Cons:** A bit dated, no beach. ✉ *MM 97.7, BS, 97770 Overseas Hwy.* ☎ *305/852–1625 or 800/385–0986* ⊕ *www.coconutbaykeylargo.com* ↩ *8 rooms, 5 efficiencies, 1 suite, 1 2-bedroom villa, 6 1-bedroom cottages* ⟐ *In-room: kitchen (some), refrigerator, Wi-Fi (some). In-hotel: pool, beachfront, no elevator, public Wi-Fi, some pets allowed (fee)* ▤ *AE, D, MC, V.*

¢–$ 🖭 **The Pelican.** This 1950s throwback is reminiscent of the days when parents packed the kids into the station wagon and headed to no-frills seaside motels. This is the kind of place where you might see an old-timer fishing off the dock. The owners have spiffed things up and added a beach, but basically it's just a motel, not fancy but comfortable. Guests here don't mind skipping a bit of space and a few frills in favor of homey digs and a low price tag. **Pros:** Free use of kayaks and paddleboats, well-maintained dock, reasonable rates. **Cons:** Some small rooms, needs a little sprucing up. ✉ *99340 Overseas Hwy.* ☎ *305/451–3576 or 877/451–3576* ⊕ *www.hungrypelican.com* ↩ *13 rooms, 4 efficiencies, 4 suites* ⟐ *In-room: no phone, kitchen (some), refrigerator, DVD (some), VCR. In-hotel: beachfront, water sports, no-smoking rooms* ▤ *AE, D, DC, MC, V* 🍽 *CP.*

¢ 🖭 **Seafarer Resort & Dive Center.** It's a budget lodging, but the Seafarer Resort is not without its charms. Outdoors, there's a pond and hammocks. Most rooms boast water views. Rooms 3 and 4 are spacious and best for families. Unit 6, a one-bedroom cottage called the "beach house," has a large picture window with an awesome view of the bay. Some units have private patios. Guests gather at the beachfront picnic table for alfresco dining and on the dock and lounge chairs for sunset-watching. The dive shop offers scuba certification courses. **Pros:** On-site dive shop, sandy beach. **Cons:** Some rooms close to road noise, basic accommodations. ✉ *MM 97.6, BS, 97684 Overseas Hwy.* ☎ *305/852–5349* 🖶 *305/852–0474* ⊕ *www.seafarerresort.com* ↩ *15 units, 7 rooms, 2 studios, 3 1-bedroom cottages, 1 2-bedroom cottage, 2 apartments* ⟐ *In-room: no phone, kitchen (some), refrigerator. In-hotel: beachfront, diving, water sports, bicycles, no elevator, public Internet, no-smoking rooms* ▤ *MC, V.*

★ ☾ ⛺ **John Pennekamp Coral Reef State Park.** Divers and snorkelers won't find a better location in the Upper Keys. Pennekamp's campsites are carved out of hardwood hammock, providing shade and privacy away from the heavy day-use areas. Water laps the shore, providing a soothing lullaby. Activities include boating, fishing, scuba diving and snorkeling, and hiking. There's no restaurant, but there are vending machines for late-night snack attacks. ⟐ *Flush toilets, partial hook-ups (electric and water), dump station, drinking water, showers, fire pits, picnic tables, electricity, public telephone, general store, ranger station, swimming (ocean)* ↩ *47 partial hookups for RVs and tents* ✉ *MM 102.5, OS* ☎ *305/451–1202 park, 800/326–3521 reservations* ⊕ *www.reserveamerica.com* ▤ *AE, D, MC, V.*

8

NIGHTLIFE

The semiweekly *Keynoter* (Wednesday and Saturday), weekly *Reporter* (Thursday), and Friday through Sunday editions of the *Miami Herald* are the best sources of information on entertainment and nightlife. Daiquiri bars, tiki huts, and seaside shacks pretty well summarize Key Largo's bar scene.

Mingle with locals over cocktails and sunsets at **Breezers Tiki Bar** (⊠ *MM 103.8, BS,* ☎ *305/453–0000*), in Marriott's Key Largo Bay Beach Resort. Walls plastered with Bogart memorabilia remind customers that the classic 1948 Bogart-Bacall flick *Key Largo* has a connection with the **Caribbean Club** (⊠ *MM 104, BS,* ☎ *305/451–4466*). It draws beard-and–baseball cap types, happiest while they're shooting the breeze or shooting pool. Postcard-perfect sunsets and live music draw revelers on weekends. **Coconuts** (⊠ *MM 100, OS, 528 Caribbean Dr.* ☎ *305/453–9794*), next to Marina Del Mar Resort, has live music Wednesday to Sunday. The crowd is primarily thirty- and fortysomething, sprinkled with a few more-seasoned townies.

SPORTS & THE OUTDOORS

BIKING

Not as big a pursuit as on other islands, biking can be a little dangerous along Key Largo's main drag.

Tavernier Bicycle & Hobbies (⊠ *MM 91.9, BS, 91958 Overseas Hwy., Tavernier* ☎ *305/852–2859*) rents single-speed adult bikes. Cruisers go for $15 a day, $75 a week. Helmets and locks are free with rental. Closed on Sunday and Monday.

FISHING

Private charters and big head boats (so-named because they charge "by the head") are great for anglers who don't have their own vessel.

Sailors Choice (⊠ *MM 100, OS,* ☎ *305/451–1802 or 305/451–0041* ⊕ *www.sailorschoicefishingboat.com*) has fishing excursions departing twice daily ($40 for half-day trips). The ultramodern 65-foot boat with air-conditioned cabin leaves from the Holiday Inn docks. Rods, bait, and license are included.

SCUBA DIVING & SNORKELING

Much of what makes the Upper Keys a singular dive destination is variety. Places like Molasses Reef, which begins 3 feet below the surface and descends to 55 feet, have something for everyone from novice snorkelers to experienced divers. The *Spiegel Grove*, a 510-foot vessel, lies in 130 feet of water, but its upper regions are only 60 feet below the surface. On rough days, Key Largo Undersea Park's Emerald Lagoon is a popular spot. Expect to pay about $75 for a two-tank, two-site dive trip with tanks and weights, or $35 to $40 for a two-site snorkel outing. Get big discounts by booking multiple trips.

Ocean Divers (⊠*MM 105.5, BS, 522 Caribbean Dr.* ⊠*MM 100, OS, 105800 Overseas Hwy.* ☎*305/451–0037 or 800/451–1113* ⊕*www. oceandivers.com*) operates two shops in Key Largo. Both are PADI five-star facilities and offer day and night dives, a range of courses, and dive-lodging packages. The cost is $80 for a two-tank reef dive with tank and weight rental. Snorkel trips cost $45 with snorkel, mask, and fins. **Amy Slate's Amoray Dive Resort** (⊠*MM 104.2, BS,* ☎*305/451–3595 or 800/426–6729* ⊕*www.amoray.com*) makes diving easy. Stroll down to the full-service dive shop (NAUI, PADI, TDI, and BSAC certified), then onto a 45-foot catamaran. The rate for a two-dive trip is $75.

★ *At John Pennekamp Coral Reef State Park,* **Coral Reef Park Co.** (⊠*MM 102.5, OS* ☎*305/451–6322* ⊕*www.pennekamppark.com*) gives scuba ($29) and snorkeling ($50) tours of the park. Besides the great location and the dependability of this operation, it's suited for water adventurers of all levels.

Conch Republic Divers (⊠*MM90.8, BS* ☎*305/852–1655 or 800/274–3483* ⊕*www.conchrepublicdivers.com*) offers instruction as well as scuba and snorkeling tours of the Pennekamp, Molasses, and other reefs. Two-location dives are $75 with tank and weights.**Quiescence Diving Service** (⊠*MM 103.5, BS* ☎*305/451–2440* ⊕*www.quiescence. com*) sets itself apart in two ways: it limits groups to six to ensure personal attention and offers day and night dives, as well as twilight dives when sea creatures are most active. Two-dive trips start at $59.

WATER SPORTS

Sea kayaking is the fastest-growing water sport in the Keys, thanks in part to the many new outfitters offering tours. Advances in the equipment—such as foot pedals, rudders, and sails—make sea kayaking easier than ever. You can paddle for a few hours or the whole day, on your own or with a guide. Some outfitters even offer overnight trips. The 110-mi Florida Keys Overseas Paddling Trail, part of a statewide system, runs from Key Largo to Key West. You can paddle the entire distance, which takes approximately seven days.

At John Pennekamp Coral Reef State Park, **Coral Reef Park Co.** (⊠*MM 102.5, OS,* ☎*305/451–6325*) has a fleet of canoes and kayaks for gliding around the mangroves or along the coast. It also rents power boats. Rent canoes or sea kayaks from **Florida Bay Outfitters** (⊠*MM 104, BS,* ☎*305/451–3018* ⊕*www.kayakfloridakeys.com*). The company, which helps with trip planning and matches equipment to your skill level, sets up self-guided trips on the Florida Keys Overseas Paddling Trail. It also runs myriad guided tours around Key Largo.

SHOPPING

For the most part, shopping is sporadic in Key Largo, with a couple of shopping centers and fewer galleries than you find on the other big islands. If you're looking to buy scuba or snorkel equipment, you'll have plenty of places from which to choose.

Pick up an old Hemingway novel or the latest tome from a local poet at **Cover to Cover Books** (⊠ *Tavernier Towne Shopping Center, MM 91.2, BS, 91272 Overseas Hwy.* ☎*305/853–2464*). The children's department is especially interesting. There's also a gourmet coffee bar with Internet access. Original works by major international artists—including American photographer Clyde Butcher, sea captain–turned-painter Dirk Verdoorn, local artist John David Hawver, and French sculptor Polles—are shown at the **Gallery at Kona Kai** (⊠*MM 97.8, BS, 97802 Overseas Hwy.* ☎*305/852–7200*), in the Kona Kai Resort. Go into olfactory overload—you'll find yourself sniffing every single bar of soap and scented candle—at **Key Lime Products** (⊠*MM 95.2, BS, 95200 Overseas Hwy.* ☎*305/853–0378 or 800/870–1780* ⊕*keylimeproducts. com*). Take home some key lime juice and bake a pie; the super-easy directions are right on the bottle. You can find lots of shops in the Keys that sell cheesy souvenirs—snow globes, alligator hats, and shell-encrusted anything. **Shellworld** (⊠*MM 97.5,* ☎*305/852–8245*) is the granddaddy of them all. The sprawling building is stuffed with clothing, jewelry, and, yes, delightfully tacky souvenirs.

ISLAMORADA

MM 90.5–70.

True story: Early settlers named this key after their schooner, *Island Home,* but to make it sound more romantic they translated it into Spanish: *Isla Morada.* The chamber of commerce prefers to use its literal translation "Purple Island," which refers either to a purple-shelled snail that once inhabited these shores or to the brilliantly colored orchids and bougainvilleas.

Early maps show Islamorada as encompassing only Upper Matecumbe Key. But the incorporated "Village of Islands" is made up of a string of islands crossed by the Overseas Highway, including Plantation Key, Windley Key, Upper Matecumbe Key, Lower Matecumbe Key, Craig Key, and Fiesta Key. In addition, two islands accessible only by boat—Indian Key and Lignumvitae Key—belong to the group.

Islamorada (locals pronounce it "*eye*-la-mor-*ah*-da") is one of the world's top fishing destinations. For nearly 100 years, seasoned anglers have fished these clear, warm waters teeming with trophy-worthy fish. There are numerous options for those in search of the big ones, including chartering a boat with its own crew or heading out on a vessel rented from one of the plethora of marinas along this 20-mi stretch of the Overseas Highway. More than 150 backcountry guides and 400 offshore captains are at your service.

Islamorada is one of the more affluent resort areas of the Keys. Sophisticated resorts and restaurants meet the needs of those in search of luxury, but there's also plenty for those looking for something more casual and affordable. Art galleries and boutiques make Islamorada's shopping scene the best in the Upper Keys.

EXPLORING ISLAMORADA

Between 1885 and 1915, settlers earned good livings growing pineapples at **Plantation Key,** using Bahamian workers to plant and harvest their crops. The plantations that gave the place its name are long gone, replaced by a dense concentration of homes, businesses, and a public park. ⊠*MM 90.5–86.*

Windley Key is the highest point in the Keys, though at 16 feet above sea level it's not likely to give anyone altitude sickness. Originally two islets, this area was first inhabited by Native Americans, who left behind a few traces of their dwellings, and then by farmers and fishermen who built their homes here in the mid-1800s. Henry Flagler bought the land from homesteaders in 1908 for his Florida East Coast Railway, filling in the inlet between what were then called the Umbrella Keys. His workers quarried coral rock for the rail bed and bridge approaches—the same rock used in many historic South Florida structures, including Miami's Vizcaya and the Hurricane Monument on Upper Matecumbe. Although the Quarry Station was destroyed by the 1935 hurricane, quarrying continued until the 1960s. Today a few resorts occupy the island. ⊠*MM 86–84.*

Islamorada Founder's Park. This public park boasts a palm-shaded beach, swimming pool, marina, and plenty of other facilities. If you want to rent a boat or learn to sail, there are businesses here that are happy to help you out. If you're staying in Islamorada, admission is free. Those staying elsewhere pay $8 to enter the park. Either way, you pay an additional $3 to use the Olympic-size pool. A spiffy new amphitheater hosts concerts, plays, and shows. ⊠*MM 87, BS, Plantation Key* ☎*305/853–1685.*

The fossilized coral reef at **Windley Key Fossil Reef Geological State Park,** dating back about 125,000 years, shows that the Florida Keys were once beneath the ocean. Excavation of Windley Key's limestone bed by the Florida East Coast Railway exposed the petrified reef, full of beautifully fossilized brain coral and sea ferns. The park contains the **Alison Fahrer Environmental Education Center,** with historic, biological, and geological displays about the area. There also are guided and self-guided tours along trails that lead to the railway's old quarrying equipment and cutting pits, where you can make rubbings of the interesting quarry walls. The first Saturday in March is Windley Key Day, when the park sells native plants and hosts environmental exhibits. ⊠*MM 85.5, BS, Windley Key* ☎*305/664–2540* ⊕*www.floridastate parks.org/windleykey* ⊠*Education center free, quarry trails $1.50, ranger-guided tours $2.50* ☉*Education center Thurs.–Mon. 8–5; tours at 10 and 2.*

☾ The second-oldest marine mammal center in the world, **Theater of the Sea** doesn't attempt to compete with more modern, more expensive parks. Even so, it's among the better attractions north of Key West, especially if you have kids in tow. Like the pricier parks, there are dolphin, sea lion, and stingray encounters ($55 to $175, including general admission) where you can get up close and personal with underwa-

8

ter creatures. These are popular, so reserve in advance. Ride a "bottomless" boat to see what's below the waves or take a guided tour of the marine life exhibits. Entertaining educational shows highlight conservation issues. You can stop for lunch at the grill, shop in the boutique, ot sunbathe at a lagoon-side beach. This easily could be an all-day attraction if you're so inclined. ⊠ *MM 84.5, OS, 84721 Overseas Hwy., Windley Key* ☎ *305/664–2431* ⊕ *www.theaterofthesea.com* ⤳ *$26* ⏱ *Daily 9:30–5 (last ticket sold at 3:30).*

Upper Matecumbe Key was one of the earliest of the Upper Keys to be permanently settled. Early homesteaders were so successful at growing pineapples in the rocky soil that at one time the island yielded the country's largest annual crop. However, foreign competition and the hurricane of 1935 killed the industry. Today life centers on fishing and tourism, and the island is filled with bait shops, marinas, and charter-fishing boats. ⊠ *MM 84–79* .

Tucked away behind the library is **Islamorada County Park,** with a small beach on a creek. The water isn't very deep, but it is crystal-clear. Currents are swift, making it unsuitable for young children. Kids can enjoy the grassy fields and the playground. There are also picnic areas and restrooms. ⊠ *MM 81.5, BS, Upper Matecumbe Key* .

OFF THE
BEATEN
PATH

Indian Key Historic State Park. Mystery surrounds 10-acre Indian Key, on the ocean side of the Matecumbe islands. Before it became one of the first European settlements outside of Key West, it was inhabited by Native Americans for several thousand years. The islet served as a base for 19th-century shipwreck salvagers until an Indian attack wiped out the settlement in 1840. Dr. Henry Perrine, a noted botanist, was killed in the raid. Today his plants grow in the town's ruins. In October the Indian Key Festival celebrates the island's heritage. Because of hurricane damage, the Indian Key public dock is closed. Most people kayak or canoe here from Indian Key Fill. Florida Keys Kayak has an office at Robbie's Marina. There are no restrooms or picnic facilities on the island. ☎ *305/664–2540* ⊕ *www.floridastateparks.org/indiankey* ⤳ *Free.* ⏱ *Daily sunrise–sunset.*

Lignumvitae Key Botanical State Park. On the National Register of Historic Places, this 280-acre bayside island is the site of a virgin hardwood forest and the 1919 home of chemical magnate William Matheson. His caretaker's cottage serves as the park's visitor center. Access is by boat—your own, a rented vessel, or a ferry operated by Robbie's Marina at 10 AM and 2 PM Thursday to Monday. (Paddling here from Indian Key Fill, at MM 78.5, is a popular pastime.) The only way to do the trails is by a guided ranger walk, offered Thursday through Monday at 10 and 2. Wear long sleeves and pants, and bring mosquito repellent. On the first weekend in December is the Lignumvitae Christmas Celebration. ☎ *305/664–2540* ⊕ *www.floridastateparks.org/lignumvitaekey* ⤳ *Free; tour $1; ferry $20* ⏱ *Thurs.–Mon. 8–5.*

★ ☺ Prehistoric-looking denizens of the not-so-deep, tarpons congregate around the docks at **Robbie's Marina** on Lower Matecumbe Key. Children—and lots of adults—pay $3 to feed them or $1 just to watch.

Spend some time hanging out at this authentic Keys community, where you can grab a bite to eat, do a little shopping, or charter a boat. ✉*MM 77.5, BS, Lower Matecumbe Key* ☎*305/664–9814 or 877/664–8498* ⊕*www.robbies.com* 🖼*Dock access $1* ⊙*Daily 8–5.*

On Lower Matecumbe Key, **Anne's Beach** is a popular village park whose "beach" (really a typical Keys-style sand flat) is best enjoyed at low tide. The nicest feature here is a ½-mi elevated wooden boardwalk that meanders through a natural wetland hammock. Covered picnic areas along the way give you places to linger and enjoy the view. Restrooms are at the north end. Weekends are packed with Miami day-trippers. ✉*MM 73.5, OS, Lower Matecumbe Key* ☎*305/853–1685.*

WHERE TO EAT

$$$ ✖**Pierre's.** One of the Keys' most elegant restaurants, Pierre's marries British colonial style with South Florida trendiness. Full of Indian and Asian architectural artifacts, the place oozes style, especially the wicker chair–strewn veranda overlooking the bay. Put on your best "tropical chic" duds so you'll be as fabulous as your surroundings. The food, drawn from French and Floridian influences, is layered, brightly colored, and beautifully presented. Among the appetizer choices, few can resist the open-face lobster ravioli or shrimp bisque. The changing list of entrées might include shellfish risotto or pan-seared snapper with roasted corn and pepper hash. The downstairs bar is a perfect vantage point for sunset-watching. ✉*MM 81.5, BS, Upper Matecumbe Key* ☎*305/664– 3225* ♠*Reservations essential* ▤*AE, MC, V* ⊙*Closed Mon.*

Fodor's Choice ★

$$ ✖**Green Turtle Inn.** This landmark dating back to 1928 is a slice of Florida Keys history. Period photographs decorate the wood-paneled walls. Breakfast and lunch options include surprises like smoked-salmon cheesecake with bagel chips and yellowfin tuna tartare. Award-winning chef Andy Niedenthal relies heavily on continental classics tossed with a few Latin touches for his dinner menu. Favorites include turtle chowder (don't gasp; it's made from farm-raised freshwater turtles), churassco steak with yucca hash, and rum-glazed duck with sweet plantain mash. He uses organic produce wherever possible. ✉ *MM 81.2 OC, 81219 Overseas Hwy., Upper Matecumbe Key* ☎*305/664–2006* ⊕*www.greenturtlekeys.com* ♠*Reservations essential.* ▤*AE, D, MC, V.*

★ $$ ✖**Marker 88.** A few yards from Florida Bay, this seafood restaurant has been popular for more than 40 years. Large picture windows offer great sunset views, but the bay is lovely no matter what time of day you visit. Chef Sal Barrios serves such irresistible entrées as grilled yellowfin tuna with wasabi aioli and yellowtail snapper in a delicate meunière sauce. Landlubbers find dishes like Parmesan-crusted filet mignon. If you not that hungry, there's also a long list of sandwiches. The extensive wine list is an oenophile's delight. ✉*MM 88, BS, Plantation Key* ☎*305/852–9315* ♠*Reservations essential* ▤*AE, MC, V.*

⟳ $$ ✖**Morada Bay.** This bayfront restaurant wins high marks for its funky feel, tables planted in the sand, and tiki torches that bathe the evening in romance. "It's great bistro food—original and tasty," as one recent guest put it. Entrées feature alluring combinations like roasted

8

mahimahi with vegetable couscous and caramelized jumbo sea scallops with wild-mushroom risotto. Seafood takes center stage, but you can always get chicken (flavored with lemon) or a steak. The dining room showcases renowned photographer Clyde Butcher's black-and-white photography of the region. Choose a table in the dining room hung with surfboards or outdoors overlooking a beach dotted with kids playing in the sand—as everywhere, they eat faster than their parents. There's nightly live music and a monthly full-moon party. ⊠*MM 81, BS, Upper Matecumbe Key* ☎*305/664–0604* ⊕*www.moradabay-restaurant.com* ⊟*AE, MC, V.*

☺ **$$** ✕**Uncle's Restaurant.** Former fishing guide Joe LePree adds flair to standard seafood dishes by expanding the usual grilled, broiled, or blackened options. Here you can also have them française (in a lemony sauce), milanese (breaded and fried), or LePree (with artichokes, mushrooms, and garden-grown spices). You also can feast on mussels or littleneck clams in a red or white sauce. Specials sometimes combine game (bison, caribou, or elk) with seafood. Portions are huge, so share dishes or take home a doggie bag. Weather permitting, sit outdoors in the garden; poor acoustics make dining indoors unusually noisy. ⊠*MM 81, OS, Upper Matecumbe Key* ☎*305/664–4402* ⊟*AE, D, DC, MC, V* ⊘*Closed Mon.*

★ **$** ✕**Island Grill.** Don't be fooled by appearances, as this shack on the waterfront takes island cuisine up a notch. The eclectic menu tempts you with such dishes as guava barbecue shrimp with pineapple salsa and spicy lobster tacos. Southern-style shrimp and andouille sausage with grits join island-style specialties such as grilled mahimahi with black-bean and corn salsa on the list of entrées. There's an air-conditioned dining room as well as outdoor seating under the trees. Two bars—one indoors and another outdoors—have live entertainment Wednesday to Sunday. ⊠*MM 85.5, OS, Windley Key* ☎*305/664–8400* ⊟*AE, MC, V.*

★ **$** ✕**Kaiyo.** Kaiyo's decor—an inviting setting that includes colorful abstract mosaics, polished wood floors, and upholstered banquettes—almost steals the show. The menu, a fusion of East and West, offers sushi and sashimi and rolls that combine local ingredients with traditional Japanese tastes. The key lime lobster roll is a blend of Florida lobster with hearts of palm and essence of key lime ($13.75). The baby conch roll surrounds tempura conch, ponzu mayo, and kimchee with sushi rice for an inside-out effect. Wash it down with an ice-cold Voss—naturally, hip water is served here—or a top-shelf sake. ⊠*MM 82, OS, Upper Matecumbe Key* ☎*305/664–5556* ⊕*www.kaiyokeys. com* ⊟*AE, MC, V* ⊘*Closed Sun.*

$ ✕**Lorelei Restaurant and Cabana Bar.** Local anglers gather here for breakfast. Lunch and dinner bring a mix of islanders and visitors for straightforward food and yucking good times. Live bands ensure a lively nighttime scene, and the menu staves off inebriation with burgers, guava-barbecued baby back ribs, and whole fried snapper. Sunday afternoon's pig roast gives you a choice of jerk pork, jerk chicken, or pulled pork. Key lime pie comes traditional, frozen, or on a stick.

✉ *MM 82 BS, Upper Matecumbe Key* ☎*305/664–2692* ⊕*www.lore-leifloridakeys.com* ▭*AE, MC, V.*

WHERE TO STAY

$$$$
Fodor's Choice
★

🏨 **Casa Morada.** A trio of hoteliers brought their cumulative 50 years of New York and Miami Beach experience to the Keys. Using their transformative magic, the women turned this place into an all-suites resort worthy of the French Riviera. Lush landscaping, a pool surrounded by a sandy "beach," and lounge chairs at the water's edge are just the start. Complimentary yoga classes, a Zen garden, and a rock waterfall lend a spa-like vibe. Cool tile-and-terrazzo floors invite you to kick off your shoes and step out onto your private patio overlooking the gardens and the bay. Breakfast and lunch are served on the waterside terrace. **Pros:** Cool design, plenty of places to relax, complimentary use of bikes and kayaks. **Cons:** Trailer park across the street, not much of a beach. ✉*MM 82, BS, 136 Madeira Rd., Upper Matecumbe Key* ☎*305/664–0044 or 888/881–3030* ⊕*www.casamorada.com* 🛏*16 suites* ⚘*In-room: safe, DVD. In-hotel: restaurant, room service, bar, pool, bicycles, no elevator, concierge, laundry service, public Wi-Fi, no kids under 16, no-smoking rooms* ▭*AE, MC, V* ⊙*CP.*

★ $$$$

🏨 **Cheeca Lodge & Spa.** Stretching across 27 oceanfront acres, this classic resort has luxurious beachfront bungalows. The West Indies–style furnishings (think mahogany and marble) are a nice contrast with the high-tech touches (42-inch plasma TVs). Rooms have views of ocean, garden, or golf course. Beckoning the grown-ups are the beach with its selection of water-sports equipment and the spa with a wide range of massages, facials, and body treatments. For kids there's Camp Cheeca, a fun and educational program. High season tends to draw lots of families, so Cheeca is not the place to be if you're single or not fond of small fry. **Pros:** Beautifully landscaped grounds, lots of wildlife, plenty of activities. **Cons:** Expensive rates, hefty resort fee for activities, slow service in restaurants. ✉*MM 82, OS, Box 527, Upper Matecumbe Key* ☎*305/664–4651 or 800/327–2888* ⊕*www.cheeca.com* 🛏*135 rooms, 6 suites* ⚘*In-room: safe, refrigerator (some), DVD, Wi-Fi. In-hotel: 2 restaurants, room service, bar, golf course, tennis courts, pools, gym, spa, beachfront, diving, water sports, bicycles, children's programs (ages 5–12), laundry service, concierge, public Wi-Fi, no-smoking rooms* ▭*AE, D, DC, MC, V.*

★ $$–$$$$

🏨 **The Moorings.** This tropical retreat has everything you've dreamed about, from hammocks swaying between towering trees to a sugar-white beach lapped by aqua-green waves. West Indies–style cottages with colorful shutters, private verandas, and wicker furniture are enveloped by a canopy of coconut palms on a residential street off the highway. This is a high-end slice of Old Florida, so don't expect tacky tiki bars. The one-, two-, and three-bedroom cottages all have modern kitchens. Four date back to the 1930s; the others were built in the early '90s. A palm-lined walkway leads to the beach, where a swimming dock awaits. The spa offers massages and beauty treatments. There's a two-night minimum-stay requirement for one-bedroom cottages, a one-week minimum on other lodgings. Often compared to Cheeca Lodge, The Moorings has more of a feeling of privacy. **Pros:** Romantic

8

setting, good dining options, beautiful beach. **Cons:** No room service, extra fee for housekeeping, daily resort fee for activities. ⊠*MM 81.6, OS, 123 Beach Rd., Upper Matecumbe Key* ☎*305/664–4708* ⊕*www. themooringsvillage.com* ⇌*3 cottages, 15 houses* ☾*In-room: kitchen, Wi-Fi. In-hotel: tennis court, pool, spa, beachfront, water sports, no elevator, laundry facilities* ⊟*AE, MC, V.*

$$$ **Chesapeake Resort.** A stem to stern renovation restores this boutique hotel's reputation for step-above-typical accommodations. High-tech gadgets like flat-screen TVs, CD players, and MP3 players give the place an up-to-date feel. Coral stone and dark wood accent the rooms, each of which has a porch or a balcony. Most units are lined up along the long stretch of sand that all but encircles a lagoon; others overlook the tennis court. **Pros:** Oceanfront location, free use of water sports equipment. **Cons:** Dated exterior, mandatory resort fee. ⊠*83409 Overseas Hwy., Upper Matecumbe Key* ☎*305/664– 4662 or 800/338–3395* ⊕*www.chesapeake-resort.com* ⇌*57 rooms, 8 suites* ☾*In room: kitchens, Wi-Fi. In hotel: tennis court, pools, beachfront, watersports, bicycles, laundry facilities, public Wi-Fi.* ⊟*AE, D, MC, V* ⦿*CP.*

$$$ **The Islander Resort.** Although the vintage sign is straight out of a *Happy Days* rerun, this 1050s-era property has undergone a top-to-bottom transformation. The decor is strikingly modern, with white cottage-style furnishings and elegant fabrics. Sunny yellow bedrooms look like pages from a Pottery Barn catalog. Private screened porches lead to a coral-shell beach with palm trees bending in the breeze. Families snap up suites in the oceanfront Beach House; couples looking for more privacy head to rooms set back from the beach. The pools—one saltwater, one freshwater—win raves, as do the full kitchens. A 200-foot dock, lighted at night, adds to the resort feel. **Pros:** Spacious rooms, nice kitchens, eye-popping views. **Cons:** Pricey for what you get, beach has rough sand. ⊠*MM 81.2, OS, Upper Matecumbe Key* ☎*305/664– 2031 or 800/753–6002* ⊕*www.islanderfloridakeys.com* ⇌*114 rooms* ☾*In-room: safe, kitchen, Wi-Fi. In-hotel: restaurant, bar, pools, gym, beachfront, water sports, bicycles, laundry facilities, laundry service, public Wi-Fi* ⊟*AE, D, DC, MC, V* ⦿*CP.*

$$ **White Gate Court.** This small inn is a dog lover's paradise, with plenty of open space for pooches to play. All the sunny yellow cottages have beamed ceilings and spacious floor plans. The backyard has a barbecue and an umbrella-shaded table under palm trees. Rates include use of bicycles, paddleboat, and snorkeling gear. Boaters will appreciate the free docks and ramp. **Pros:** pet-friendly, homey feel, pretty trees. **Cons:** No pool, simple accomodations. ⊠*MM 76, BS, 76010 Overseas Hwy., Upper Matecumbe Key* ☎*305/664–4136 or 800/645–4283* ⊕*www. whitegatecourt.com* ⇌*7 units* ☾*In-room: kitchen, dial-up. In-hotel: beachfront, water sports, bicycles, no elevator, laundry facilities, some pets allowed (fee)* ⊟*MC, V.*

★ $-$$ **Drop Anchor Resort & Marina.** It's easy to find your cottage here, as they are painted in an array of Crayola colors. Immaculately kept, this place has the feel of your college chum's beach house. Inside you'll find soothing West Indies–type furnishings and kitschy-cool, 1950s-era tile in the bathrooms. Welcoming as the rooms may be, you didn't come to the Keys to sit indoors: there's a luscious expanse of white sand awaiting, and you can catch ocean breezes from either your balcony, a comfy Adirondack chair, or a picnic table perched in the sand. There are a fishing pier and boat ramp to accommodate anglers. **Pros:** Colorful, attention to detail, laid-back charm. **Cons:** Noise from the highway, beach is better for fishing than swimming. ⊠ *84959 Overseas Hwy., MM 85, OS, Windley Key* ✑ *Box 222* ☎ *305/664–4863 or 888/664– 4863* ⊕ *www.dropanchorresort.com* ✈ *18 rooms* ⚲ *In-room: kitchen (some), refrigerator. In-hotel: pool, beachfront, no elevator, laundry facilities, public Internet, public Wi-Fi* ☱ *AE, D, DC, MC, V.*

$-$$ ⌂ **Ragged Edge Resort.** Tucked away in a residential area at the ocean's edge, this hotel is big on value but short on style. Ragged Edge draws returning guests who would rather fish off the dock and hoist a brew than loll around in Egyptian cotton sheets. Even those who turn their noses up at the cheap plastic deck furniture and pine paneling admit that the place has a million-dollar setting, with ocean views all around. There's no beach to speak of, but you can ride a bike across the street to Islamorada Founder's Park, where you'll find a nice little beach and water toys for rent. If a bit of partying puts you off, look elsewhere. Plain-Jane though they are, rooms are clean and fairly spacious. Ground-floor units have screened porches; upper units have large decks, more windows, and beam ceilings. **Pros:** Oceanfront location, quiet neighborhood, cheap rates. **Cons:** Dated decor. ⊠ *MM 86.5, OS, 243 Treasure Harbor Rd., Plantation Key* ☎ *305/852–5389 or 800/436– 2023* ⊕ *www.ragged-edge.com* ✈ *10 units* ⚲ *In-room: kitchen, Wi-Fi. In-hotel: pool, bicycles, no elevator, public Wi-Fi* ☱ *AE, MC, V.*

NIGHTLIFE

Islamorada is not known for its raging nightlife, but for local fun, Lorelei's is legendary. Others cater to the town's sophisticated clientele and fishing fervor.

★   Behind a larger-than-life mermaid is the **Lorelei Cabana Bar** (⊠ *MM 82, BS, Upper Matecumbe Key* ☎ *305/664–4656*). This is the kind of place you fantasize about during those long, cold winters up north. It's all about good drinks, tasty pub grub, and sherbet-hued sunsets set to music. Live bands play island tunes and light rock. **Zane Grey Long Key Lounge** (⊠ *MM 81.5, BS, Upper Matecumbe Key* ☎ *305/664–4244*), above the World Wide Sportsman, was created to honor writer Zane Grey, one of the most famous members of the Long Key Fishing Club. The lounge displays the author's photographs, books, and memorabilia. Listen to live blues, jazz, and Motown on a wide veranda that invites sunset watching. **Ziggie & Mad Dog's**(⊠ *MM 83 BS, Upper Matecumbe Key* ☎ *305/664–3391)* the area's glam celebrity hangout, serves appetizers with its happy-hour drink specials.

SPORTS & THE OUTDOORS

BOATING

Marinas pop up every mile or so in the Islamorada area, so finding a rental or tour is no problem. Robbie's Marina is a prime example of a

8

salty spot where you can find it all—from fishing charters and kayaking rentals to lunch and tarpon feeding

Bump & Jump (⊠ *MM 81.2, OS,Upper Matecumbe Key* ☎ *305/664– 9404 or 877/453–9463* ⊕ *www.keysboatrental.com*) is a one-stop shop for windsurfing, sailboat, and powerboat rentals, sales, and lessons. This company delivers to your hotel or house, or drops it off right at the beach. See the islands from the comfort of your own boat (captain's cap optional) when you rent from **Houseboat Vacations of the Florida Keys** (⊠ *MM 85.9, BS, 85944 Overseas Hwy.* ☎ *305/664–4009* ⊕ *www. floridakeys.com/houseboats*). The company maintains a fleet of 42- to 55-foot boats that accommodate up to 10 people and come outfitted with everything you need besides food. (You provision yourself at a nearby grocery store.) The three-day minimum starts at $1,112; one week costs $1,950 and up. Kayaks, canoes, and skiffs suitable for the ocean are also available.**Robbie's Boat Rentals & Charters** (⊠ *MM 77.5, BS, 77520 Overseas Hwy., Lower Matecumbe Key* ☎ *305/664–9814 or 877/664–8498* ⊕ *www.robbies.com*) does it all. The company will deliver your boat to your hotel and give you a crash course on how not to crash it. The rental fleet includes an 18-foot skiff with a 60-horsepower outboard for $135 for four hours and $185 for the day and a 23-foot deck boat with a 130-horsepower engine for $185 for the half day and $235 for eight hours. Robbie's also rents fishing and snorkeling gear (there's good snorkeling nearby) and sells bait, drinks and snacks, and gas. Want to hire a guide who knows the local waters and where the fish lurk? Robbie's offers offshore fishing trips, patch reef trips, and party-boat fishing. Backcountry flats trips are a specialty. Captains Pam and Pete Anderson of **Treasure Harbor Marine** (⊠ *MM 86.5, OS, 200 Treasure Harbor Dr., Plantation Key* ☎ *305/852–2458 or 800/352–2628* ⊕ *www.treasureharbor.com*) provide everything you'll need for a vacation at sea. Best of all, they have excellent advice on where to find the best anchorages, snorkeling spots, or lobstering sites. Vessels range from a 19-foot Cape Dory to a 41-foot Morgan Out Island. Rates start at $160 a day and $700 a week. Hire a captain for $175 to $200 a day. Marina facilities are basic—water, electric, ice machine, laundry, picnic tables, and restrooms with showers. A store sells snacks, beverages, and sundries.

FISHING

Here in the self-proclaimed Sportfishing Capital of the World, sailfish is the prime catch in the winter and dolphinfish in the summer. Buchanan Bank just south of Islamorada is a good spot to try for tarpon in the spring.

Long before fly-fishing became popular, Sandy Moret was fishing the Keys for bonefish, tarpon, and redfish. Now he attracts anglers from around the world with the **Florida Keys Outfitters** (*Green Turtle,* ⊠ *MM 81.2, Upper Matecumbe Key* ☎ *305/664–5423* ⊕ *www.floridakeys outfitters.com*). Weekend fly-fishing classes, which include classroom instruction, equipment, and daily breakfast and lunch, cost $985. Add $1,070 for two additional days of fishing. Guided fishing trips cost $395 for a half day, $535 for a full day. Packages combining fishing and accommodations at Cheeca Lodge are available. The 65-foot party boat **Miss Islamorada** (⊠ *Bud n' Mary's Marina, MM 79.8, OS, Upper Matecumbe Key* ☎ *305/664–2461 or 800/742–7945*) has full-day trips for $60. Bring your lunch or buy one from the dockside deli.

Like other top fly-fishing and light-tackle guides, Captain Geoff Colmes of **Fishabout Charters** (⊠ *105 Palm La., Upper Matecumbe Key,* ☎ *305/853–0741 or 800/741–5955* ⊕ *www.floridakeysflyfish.com*) helps his clients land trophy fish in the waters around the Keys ($500 to $550). But unlike the others, he also heads across Florida Bay to fish the coastal Everglades on three- and four-day trips (from $695 per angler) off his 65-foot mother ship, the *Fishabout*. It has four staterooms, private baths, living room, kitchen, satellite TV, and separate crew quarters. It's ideal when cold, windy weather shuts out fishing around the Keys. Rates include captain, crew, guide fees, lodging, all meals, tackle, and use of canoes for getting deep into shallow Everglades inlets.

SCUBA DIVING & SNORKELING

About 1.25 nautical miles south of Indian Key is the San Pedro Underwater Archaeological Preserve State Park, which includes wreck of a Spanish treasure-fleet ship that sank in 1733. The State of Florida protects the site for divers; no spearfishing or souvenir-collecting is allowed. Resting in only 18 feet of water, it can be seen by snorkelers as well as divers and attracts a colorful array of fish.

Florida Keys Dive Center (⊠ *MM 90.5, OS, Plantation Key* ☎ *305/852–4599 or 800/433–8946* ⊕ *www.floridakeysdivectr.com*) organizes dives from John Pennekamp Coral Reef State Park to Alligator Light. The center has two 46-foot Coast Guard–approved dive boats, offers scuba training, and is one of the few Keys dive centers to offer Nitrox (mixed gas) diving. With a resort, pool, restaurant, lessons, and twice-daily dive and snorkel trips, **Holiday Isle Dive Shop** (⊠ *MM 84, OS, 84001 Overseas Hwy., Windley Key* ☎ *305/664–3483 or 800/327–7070* ⊕ *www.diveholidayisle.com*) is a one-stop dive shop. Rates start at $75 for a two-tank dive.

TENNIS

Not all Keys recreation is on the water. Play tennis year-round at the **Islamorada Tennis Club** (⊠ *MM 76.8, BS, Upper Matecumbe Key* ☎ *305/664–5340* ⊕ *www.islamoradatennisclub.com*). It's a well-run facility with four clay and two hard courts (all lighted), same-day racket stringing, ball machines, private lessons, and a full-service pro shop. Rates are from $25 a day.

WATER SPORTS

Florida Keys Kayak (*Robbie's Marina,* ⊠ *MM 77.5, BS, 77522 Overseas Hwy., Lower Matecumbe Key,* ☎ *305/664–4878*) rents kayaks for trips to Indian and Lignumvitae keys, two favorite destinations for paddlers. Kayak rental rates are $20 per hour for a single, and $27.50 for a double. Half-day rates (and you'll need plenty of time to explore those mangrove canopies) are $40 for a single kayak and $55 for a double.

The company also offers guided two- and three-hour tours ($39 and $49 per person).

SHOPPING

Art galleries, upscale gift shops, and the mammoth World Wide Sportsman (if you want to look the part of a local fisherman, you must wear a shirt from here) make up the variety and superior style of Islamorada shopping.

At the **Banyan Tree** (✉*MM 81.2, OS, 81197 Overseas Hwy., Upper Matecumbe Key* ☎*305/664–3433*), a sharp-eyed husband-and-wife team successfully combines antiques and contemporary gifts for the home and garden with plants, pots, and trellises in a stylishly sophisticated indoor–outdoor setting.At **Down to Earth** (✉*MM 82.2, OS, 82205 Overseas Hwy.,Upper Matecumbe Key* ☎*305/664–9828*), indulge your passion for *objets* that are at once practical and fanciful, such as salad tongs carved from coconut shells or Indonesian furniture with intricate designs. The prices are reasonable, too.The go-to destination for one-of-a-kind gifts is **Gallery Morada** (✉*MM 81.6, OS, 81611 Old Hwy.,Upper Matecumbe Key* ☎*305/664–3650*), where blown-glass objects are beautifully displayed, as are the sculptures, original paintings and lithographs, and hand-painted scarves and earrings by top South Florida artists.Among the best buys in town are the used best-sellers at **Hooked on Books** (✉*MM 82.6, OS, 82681 Overseas Hwy., Upper Matecumbe Key* ☎*305/517–2602*). There are also new titles, audio books, and CDs. **Island Silver & Spice** (✉*MM 82, OS, Upper Matecumbe Key* ☎*305/664–2714*) has tropical-style furnishings, rugs, and home accessories. The shop also stocks women's and men's resort wear and a large jewelry selection with high-end watches and marine-theme pieces. The **Rain Barrel** (✉*MM 86.7, BS, Plantation Key* ☎*305/852–3084*) is a natural and unhurried shopping showplace. Set in a tropical garden of shady trees, native shrubs, and orchids, the crafts village has shops with works by local and national artists and eight resident artists in studios, including John Hawver, noted for Florida landscapes and seascapes. The **Redbone Gallery** (✉*MM 81.5, OS, 200 Industrial Dr., Upper Matecumbe Key* ☎*305/664–2002*), the largest sporting-art gallery in Florida, stocks hand-stitched clothing and giftware, in addition to work by wood and bronze sculptors such as Kendall Van Sant; watercolorists Chet Reneson, Jeanne Dobie, and Kathleen Denis; and painters C.D. Clarke and Tim Borski. Proceeds benefit cystic fibrosis research.

Former U.S. presidents, celebrities, and record holders beam alongside their catches in black-and-white photos on the walls at **World Wide Sportsman** (✉*MM 81.5, BS, Upper Matecumbe Key* ☎*305/664–4615 or 800/327–2880*), a two-level retail center that sells upscale fishing equipment, resort clothing, and gifts. When you're tired of shopping, relax at the Zane Grey Long Key Lounge.

LONG KEY

MM 70–65.5.

Long Key isn't a tourist hot spot, making it a favorite destination for those looking to avoid the masses and enjoy some cultural and eco-logical history in the process. Offering both is **Long Key State Park.** On the ocean side, the Golden Orb Trail leads to a boardwalk that cuts through the mangroves and along-side a lagoon where waterfowl con-gregate. A canoe trail leads through a tidal lagoon, and a broad expanse of shallow grass flats is perfect for bonefishermen. Bring a mask and snorkel to observe the marine life in the shallow water. The park is particularly popular with campers who long to stake their tent at the campground on a beach. Repairs after four hurricanes have left the park with improved facilities, but with very little shade. Replanting efforts are ongoing. Good news: the park has added kayaks to its pad-dle craft rental fleet. Canoes rent for $5 per hour, while kayak rentals start at $17 for two hours.

Across the road from Long Key State Park, beginning at a marker par-tially obscured by foliage, is the free **Layton Nature Trail** (⊠*MM 67.7, BS*). This 20- to 30-minute walk leads through tropical hardwood for-est to a rocky Florida Bay shoreline overlooking shallow grass flats. A marker relates the history of the Long Key Viaduct, the first major bridge on the rail line, and the exclusive Long Key Fishing Camp, which Henry Flagler established nearby in 1906. The camp was washed away in the 1935 hurricane and never rebuilt. ⊠*MM 67.5, OS, Box 776* ☎*305/664–4815* ⊕*www.floridastateparks.org/longkey* ⊠*$3.50 for 1 person, $6 for 2 people, and 50¢ for each additional person in the group* ☉*Daily 8–sunset.*

WHERE TO EAT & STAY

$ ✗**Little Italy.** It's your basic Italian joint that looks like it's been around forever. The menu offers no real surprises—except maybe conch par-migiana and mahimahi with sherry and mushroom sauce. The lunch and dinner menus offer plenty of variety, but few can resist the pull of the pasta. (Maybe it's the garlicky aroma that permeates the place.) The light-bites menu has smaller portions for calorie watchers. Reward those light bites with a slice of decadent chocolate pecan pie. ⊠*MM 68.5, BS* ☎*305/664–4472* ▭*AE, MC, V.* ☉*Closed Wed.*

$ ▦**Lime Tree Bay Resort.** Easy on the eye and the wallet, this 2½-acre resort on Florida Bay is far from the hustle and bustle of the larger islands. You can get a good workout on the water or simply break

a sweat lolling around on the beach or in a hammock in the pleasantly landscaped garden. Walls painted in lovely faux finishes and
hung with tropical arts add a sophisticated look to the rooms. The five
suites are the best places to stay because of the gulf views, followed
by the cottages without gulf views. Four deluxe rooms upstairs have
cathedral ceilings and skylights. The best bet for two couples traveling
together is the upstairs Tree House. Most units have a shared balcony
or porch. **Pros:** Great views, friendly staff, close to Long Key State
Park. **Cons:** Only one restaurant nearby. ⊠*MM 68.5, BS* ☐*Box 839,
Layton* ☎*305/664–4740 or 800/723–4519* ⊕*www.limetreebayresort.
com* ⇦*10 rooms, 11 studios, 8 suites, 5 apartments, 2 cottages.* ⚿*In-
room: kitchen (some), refrigerator, dial-up. In-hotel: tennis court, pool,
beachfront, water sports, bicycles, no elevator, no-smoking rooms*
⊟*AE, D, DC, MC, V.*

**EN
ROUTE**   As you cross Long Key Channel, look beside you at the old **Long Key
Viaduct.** The second-longest bridge on the former rail line, this 2-mi-
long structure has 222 reinforced-concrete arches. The old bridge is
popular with anglers, who fish off the sides day and night.

THE MIDDLE KEYS

Most of the activity for this section of the Florida Kays centers around
the town of Marathon, the region's third-largest metropolitan area. On
either end of it, smaller keys hold resorts, wildlife research and rehab
facilities, a historic village, and a state park. The Middle Keys make
a fitting transition from the Upper Keys to the Lower Keys not only
geographically, but mentally. Crossing Seven Mile Bridge prepares you
for the slow pace and don't-give-a-damn attitude you'll find a little farther down the highway. Fishing is one of the main attractions—in fact,
the region's commercial fishing industry was founded here in the early
1800s. Diving is another popular pastime. There are many beaches
and natural areas to enjoy in the Middle Keys, where mainland stress
becomes an ever more distant memory.

If you get bridge fever—the heebie-jeebies when driving over long
stretches of water—you may need a pair of blinders (or a couple of
tranquilizers) before tackling the Middle Keys. Stretching from Conch
Key to the far side of the Seven Mile Bridge, this zone is home to the
region's two longest bridges: Long Key Viaduct and Seven Mile Bridge,
both historic landmarks.

U.S. 1 takes you from one end of the region to the other in a direct line
that takes in most of the sights, but you'll find some interesting resorts
and restaurants off the main drag.

GRASSY KEY

MM 60–57.

Local lore has it that this sleepy little key was named not for its vegetation—mostly native trees and shrubs—but for an early settler by the name

of Grassy. The key is primarily inhabited by a few families operating small fishing camps and roadside motels. There's no marked definition between it and Marathon, so it feels sort of like a suburb of its much larger neighbor to the south. Grassy Key's sights-to-see tend toward the natural, including a worthwhile dolphin attraction and a small state park.

★ ☾ The 1963 movie *Flipper* popularized the notion of humans interacting with dolphins. The film's creator, Milton Santini, also created the **Dolphin Research Center.** Home to a colony of dolphins and sea lions, the not-for-profit center has tours, narrated programs, and programs that allow you to greet the dolphins from dry land or play with them in their watery habitat. You can even paint a T-shirt with a dolphin—you pick the paint, the dolphin "designs" your shirt ($55). The center also offers five-day programs for children and adults with disabilities. ⊠ *MM 59, BS,* ⬚ *Box 522875, Marathon Shores* ☎ *305/289–1121 or 305/289–0002* ⊕ *www.dolphins.org* ⬚ *Tours $19.50* ☉ *Daily 9–4:30*

OFF THE BEATEN PATH

Curry Hammock State Park. Looking for a slice of the Keys that's far removed from tiki bars? On the ocean and bay sides of U.S. 1, this littoral park covers 260 acres of upland hammock, wetlands, and mangroves. On the bay side, there's a trail through thick hardwoods to a rocky shoreline. The ocean side is more developed, with a sandy beach, a clean bathhouse, picnic tables, a playground, grills, and a 28-site campground open November to May. Locals consider the paddling trails under canopies of arching mangroves one of the best kayaking spots in the Keys. Manatees frequent the area, and it's a great spot for bird-watching. Herons, egrets, ibis, plovers, and sanderlings are commonly spotted. Raptors are often seen in the park, especially during migration periods. ⊠ *MM 57, OS, 56200 Overseas Hwy., Crawl Key, Marathon* ☎ *305/289–2690* ⊕ *www.floridastateparks.org/curryhammock* ⬚ *$3.50 for 1 person, $6 for 2, 50¢ per additional passenger* ☉ *Daily 8–sunset.*

WHERE TO EAT & STAY

$$ ✕**Hideaway Café.** The name says it all—**Hideaway Café is** tucked between Grassy Key and Marathon, easy to miss if you're barnstorming through the middle islands. When you find it (upstairs at Rainbow Bend Resort), you'll discover a favorite of locals who appreciate a well-planned menu, lovely ocean view, and quiet evening away from the crowds. For starters, dig into escargots à la Edison (sautéed with vegetables, pepper, cognac, and cream). Then feast on several specialties, such as a rarely-found chateaubriand, a belly-busting whole roasted duck, or the seafood special combining the catch of the day with scallops and shrimp in a savory sauce. ⊠ *Rainbow Bend Resort, MM 58, OS, Grassy Key* ☎ *305/289–1554* ⊕ *www.hideawaycafe.com* ⬚ *AE, D, DC, MC, V* ☉ *No lunch.*

$ ⬚**Gulf View Waterfront Resort.** "Hey, baby!" may be your greeting at the easygoing Gulf View, but the comment is mostly likely coming from Coco, a white cockatiel. With a flock of 15 birds on property, this homey duplex is part resort, part aviary. Owner-occupied, the Gulf View is decorated with simple wicker furniture, tropical pastels, and ceiling fans. The only jarring design note is the green concrete ledge supporting

8

CLOSE UP

Close Encounters of the Flipper Kind

Here in the Florida Keys, where the 1963 movie *Flipper was filmed*, close encounters of the mammalian kind are an everyday occurrence. There are a handful of facilities that allow you to commune with trained dolphins. In-water programs, where you actually swim with these intelligent creatures, are extremely popular and require advance reservations. All of the programs begin with a course on dolphin physiology and behavior taught by a marine biologist. Afterward you learn a few important dos and don'ts. Finally, you take the plunge, quite literally.

For the in-water programs, the dolphins swim all around you. If you lie on your back with your feet out, they use their snouts to push you around. You can also grab a dorsal fin for an exciting ride. The in-water encounter lasts between 10 to 25 minutes, depending on the program. The entire experience takes about two hours. The best time to go is when it's warm, from March through December. You spend a lot of time in and out of the water, and you can feel your teeth chattering on a chilly day. There's no need to get completely wet, however. Waterside programs let you feed, shake hands, and do tricks with dolphins from a submerged platform. These are great for people who aren't strong swimmers or for youngsters who don't meet a facility's minimum age requirements for in-water programs.

Dolphin Connection. The marine biologists at Hawk's Cay Resort's Dolphin Connection promote conservation. The resort offers three programs, including Dockside Dolphins, a 30-minute encounter from the dry training docks ($50 for resort guests, $60 for non-guests); Dolphin Discovery, an in-water program that lasts about 45 minutes and lets you kiss, touch, and feed the dolphins ($135, $150); and Trainer for a Day, a three-hour session with the animal training team ($275, $285). ⊠ *MM 61, OS, 61 Hawks Cay Blvd., Duck Key* ☎ *888/814–9154* ⊕ *www.dolphinconnection.com.*

Dolphin Cove. This educational program begins during a 30-minute boat ride on adjoining Florida Bay. At the facility's lagoon you have a get-acquainted session from a platform. Finally, you slip into the water for some frolicking with your new dolphin pals. The cost is $165 to $185. For two- to four-year-olds there's a special program that costs $70. ⊠ *MM 101.9, BS, 101900 Overseas Hwy., Key Largo* ☎ *305/451–4060 or 877/365–2683* ⊕ *www.dolphinscove.com.*

Dolphins Plus. Programs here emphasize education and conservation. Costing $125, the Natural Swim program begins with a one-hour briefing; then you enter the water to become totally immersed in the dolphins' world. No touching or interacting is allowed. For that, sign up for the $165 Structured Swim program. ⊠ *MM 99, 31 Corrine Pl., Key Largo* ☎ *305/451–1993 or 866/860–7946* ⊕ *www.dolphinsplus.com.*

Dolphin Research Center. This not-for-profit organization has a colony of bottlenose dolphins and California sea lions. Programs range from a stay-dry Meet the Dolphin program for $25 to get-wet Dolphin Dip ($100), Dolphin Encounter ($180), and Trainer for a Day ($650) programs. You can even paint with a dolphin. ⊠ *MM 59, Marathon Shores* ☎ *305/289–1121 or 305/289–0002* ⊕ *www.dolphins.org.*

the elevated swimming pool. Guests—mostly couples during the winter and families during holidays—appreciate the close proximity to the Dolphin Research Center, practically next door. (The resort offers discount passes.) Canoes, paddleboats, and kayaks are also available for guests for free. **Pros:** Park-like setting, sandy beach area with hammocks, close to restaurants. **Cons:** Ground-level units are dark, some traffic noise. ☒*MM 58.5, BS, 58743 Overseas Hwy.* ☎*305/289–1414* ⊕*www. gulfviewwaterfrontresort.com* ☞*2 rooms, 6 suites, 3 efficiencies* ⌕*In-room: kitchen (some), refrigerator, Wi-Fi. In-hotel: pool, water sports, no elevator, laundry facilities, public Wi-Fi, parking(no fee), some pets allowed (fee), no-smoking rooms* ☰*AE, D, MC, V.*

¢-$　🏨**Bonefish Resort.** Set on a skinny lot bedecked with palm trees, banana trees, and hibiscus plantings, this motel-style hideaway is the best choice among the island's back-to-basics properties. It's not fancy, but it's cheap, clean, and a good base for paddling a kayak, wading for bonefish, and watching the waves roll in from a lounge chair. Rooms are decorated with tropical motifs like the colorful metal lizards on the doors. A narrow gravel courtyard lined with umbrella-shaded tables leads to a small beach and a waterfront pool. The kayaks and paddleboats encourage exploration of the waterfront. The communal deck is scattered with hammocks and chaises. Check-in is at next-door sister property Yellowtail Inn, which has cottages and efficiencies. **Pros:** Decent price for the location, oceanside setting. **Cons:** Decks are small, simple decor. ☒*MM 58, OS, 58070 Overseas Hwy.* ☎*305/743–7107 or 800/274–9949* ⊕*www.bonefishresort.com* ☞*3 rooms, 11 efficiencies* ⌕*In-room: kitchen (some), refrigerator, VCR. In-hotel: beachfront, bicycles, no elevator, laundry facilities, public Wi-Fi, some pets allowed (fee)* ☰*D, MC, V.*

MARATHON

MM 53–47.5.

Marathon is a bustling town, at least compared to other communities in the Keys. As it leaves something to be desired in the charm department, Marathon will probably not be your first choice of places to stay. But there are a surprising number of good dining options, so you'll definitely want to stop for a bite even if you're just passing through on the way to Key West.

Outside of Key West, it has the most historic attractions that merit a visit. Fishing, diving, and boating are the main events here. Throughout the year, it throws tarpon tournaments in March and April, more fishing tournaments in June and September, a birding festival in September, and lighted boat parades around the holidays.

Tucked away from the highway behind a stand of trees, Crane Point—part of a 63-acre tract that contains the last-known undisturbed thatch-palm hammock—is delightfully undeveloped. It's the site of the **Crane Point Museum, Nature Center, & Historic Site.** The facility includes the **Museum of Natural History of the Florida Keys**, which has displays about local wildlife, a seashell exhibit, and a marine-life display that makes you feel you're at the bottom of the sea. Also here is the **Children's Activity Center,** with a replica of a 17th-century galleon and pirate dress-up room where youngsters can play swashbuckler. On the 1-mi indigenous loop trail, visit the Wild Bird Center and the remnants of a Bahamian village, site of the restored **George Adderly House.** It is the oldest surviving example of Bahamian tabby (a concrete-like material created from sand and seashells) construction outside of Key West. A newly recreated Cracker house demonstrates the vernacular housing of the early 1900s. A boardwalk crosses wetlands, rivers, and mangroves before ending at Adderly Village. From November to Easter, docent-led tours, are available; bring good walking shoes and bug repellent during warm weather. Events include a Bahamian Heritage Festival in January. ⊠*MM 50.5, BS, 5550 Overseas Hwy., Box 536* ☎*305/743–9100* ⊕*www.cranepoint.net* ⊠*$8* ☉*Mon.–Sat. 9–5, Sun. noon–5; call to arrange trail tours.*

NEED A BREAK?

If you don't get a buzz from breathing in the robust aroma at Leigh Ann's (More Than Just A) Coffee House (⊠*7537 Overseas Hwy.* ☎*305/743–2001*), order an espresso shot, Cuban or Italian, for a satisfying jolt. Pastries are baked fresh daily, but the biscuits with sausage gravy and the Italian frittata cooked without added fat are among the big movers. Business has been so good that Leigh Ann's is now open for dinner. (Try the risotto, followed by the ultimate seven-layer brownie.) Dinner is served until 9 PM in season. It's closed on Sunday.

Seven Mile Bridge is one of the most-photographed images in the Keys. Actually measuring slightly less than seven miles, it connects the Middle and Lower Keys and is believed to be the world's longest segmental bridge. It has 39 expansion joints separating its various concrete sections. Each April, runners gather in Marathon for the annual Seven Mile Bridge Run. The expanse running parallel to Seven Mile Bridge is what remains of the **Old Seven Mile Bridge,** an engineering and architectural marvel in its day that's now on the National Register of Historic Places. It rested on a record 546 concrete piers. No cars are allowed on the old bridge today, but a 2-mi segment is open for biking, walking, and Rollerblading.

Pleasant, shaded picnic areas overlook a coconut palm-lined grassy stretch and the Atlantic Ocean at **Sombrero Beach.** Separate areas allow swimmers, boaters, and windsurfers to share the narrow cove. Facilities include barbecue grills, showers, and restrooms, as well as a baseball diamond, a large playground, and a volleyball court. Sunday afternoons draw lots of local families toting coolers. The park is accessible for those with disabilities and allows leashed pets. Turn east at the traffic light in Marathon and follow signs to the end. ⊠*MM 50, OS, Sombrero Beach Rd.* ☎*305/743–0033* ⊠*Free* ☉*Daily 8–sunset.*

OFF THE BEATEN PATH

Pigeon Key. There's much to like about this 5-acre island under the Old Seven Mile Bridge. You can reach it by walking across a 2¼-mi section of the bridge or by ferry. Once there, tour the island on your own or join a guided tour. The tour explores the buildings that formed the early-20th-century work camp for the Overseas Railroad that linked the mainland to Key West. Later the island became a fish camp, a state park, and then government administration headquarters. Exhibits in a small museum recall the history of the Keys, the railroad, and railroad baron Henry M. Flagler. Pick up the ferry at the gift shop inside the railroad car on Knight's Key (MM 47, OS). ⊠*MM 45, OS, Box 500130, Pigeon Key* ☎*305/289–0025 general information, 305/743–5999 tickets* ⚏*$11* ☉ *Daily 9:30–4:30; ferryboat departures at 10, 11:30, 1, 2:30.*

WHERE TO EAT

$ ✕**7 Mile Grill.** With its whirling ceiling fans, this old-fashioned restaurant could serve as a location for a film set in the 1950s. The crowd is a mix of visitors charmed by its appearance and anglers from the nearby marina who just want some good grub. At the Marathon end of the Seven Mile Bridge, this restaurant's menu won't wow you, but you can count on friendly servers delivering comfort food for breakfast, lunch, and dinner. Standards on the mostly seafood menu include creamy shrimp bisque, crab cakes, beer-steamed shrimp, and mahimahi served grilled, blackened, or fried. Don't pass up the authentic key lime pie, which regularly wins the local paper's "Best in the Keys" award. Call ahead, as it's sometimes closed in August and September. ⊠*MM 47, BS* ☎*305/743–4481* ⊟*MC, V* ☉*Closed Thurs. mid-Apr.–mid-Nov.*

$ ✕**Barracuda Grill.** Sparsely decorated with fish and bird art and filled
Fodor'sChoice with tables covered with butcher paper, this restaurant is not much to
★ look at. But when it comes to the food, Barracuda Grill delivers. The sophisticated, eclectic menu capitalizes on local seafood (take a test drive with the mangrove snapper), but give equal treatment to aged Angus beef, rack of lamb, and braised pork shank. Smaller entrées such as mini-mahi and baby steak appeal to light appetites. Favorite main courses include Francesca's spicy voodoo stew with scallops, shrimp, and vegetables in a tomato-saffron stock; a 22-ounce cowboy rib eye; and sashimi of yellowfin tuna accompanied by wasabi and tamari. For dessert, slices of oh-so-rich key lime cheesecake fly out of the kitchen. The well-thought-out wine list is heavily Californian. Call ahead, as the owners often close during the off-season. ⊠*MM 49.5, BS, 4290 Overseas Hwy.* ☎*305/743–3314* ⚏*Reservations not accepted* ⊟*AE, MC, V* ☉*No lunch.*

$ ✕**Key Colony Inn.** The inviting aroma of an Italian kitchen pervades this family-owned favorite. As you'd expect, the service is friendly and attentive. For lunch there are fish and steak entrées served with fries, salad, and bread. At dinner you can't miss with traditional dishes like veal Oscar and New York strip, or such specialties as seafood Italiano, a light dish of scallops and shrimp sautéed in garlic butter and served over a bed of linguine. The place is renowned for its Sunday brunch, served from November to April. ⊠*MM 54, OS, 700 W. Ocean Dr., Key Colony Beach* ☎*305/743–0100* ⊟*AE, MC, V.*

★ $ ✕**Keys Fisheries Market & Marina.** From the parking lot, this commercial warehouse flanked by fishing boats barely hints at the restaurant inside. Order at the window outside, pick up your food inside, then

8

dine at one of the waterfront picnic tables under a plastic canopy. Fresh seafood (and a token hamburger) are the only things on the menu. A lobster Reuben ($13.95) served on thick slices of toasted bread is the signature dish. Other delights include the shrimpburger, whiskey-peppercorn scallops, and the Keys Kombo (broiled or grilled lobster, shrimp, scallops, and mahimahi for $25). There's also a 16-flavor ice-cream station and a bar serving beer and wine. ⊠*MM 49, BS, end of 35th St.* ☎*305/743–4353 or 866/743–4353* ⊕*www.keysfisheries.com* ⊟*MC, V.*

¢ ✕**Fish Tales Market and Eatery.** This roadside eatery serves signature dishes such as oysters on a roll and fish of the day on grilled rye with coleslaw and melted cheese. You also can slurp lobster bisque or red conch chowder. Plan to dine early, as it's open only until 6:30. This is a no-frills kind of place with its own seafood market, a couple of picnic tables, and friendly service. ⊠*MM 53, OS, 11711 Overseas Hwy.* ☎*305/743–9196 or 888/662–4822* ⊟*AE, MC, V* ☾*Closed Sun.*

¢ ✕**The Stuffed Pig.** With only eight tables and a counter, this breakfast-and-lunch place is always hopping. The kitchen whips up daily lunch specials like meat loaf or pulled pork with hand-cut fries, but a quick glance around the room reveals that the all-day breakfast is the main draw. You can get the usual breakfast plates, but most newcomers opt for oddities like the lobster omelet, alligator tail and eggs, or "grits and grunts" (that's fish, to the rest of us). On a nice day, make your way to the shady backyard patio. If you can get past the unflattering name, you still might have a tough time swallowing the staff's sometimes surly attitude. ⊠*MM 49, BS, 3520 Overseas Hwy.* ☎*305/743–4059* ⊟*No credit cards.* ☾*No dinner.*

WHERE TO STAY

★ $$$$ ▥**Tranquility Bay.** Ralph Lauren might have designed the rooms at this luxurious beach resort. The 87 two- and three-bedroom town houses have gingerbread trim, white picket fences, and open-floor-plan interiors decorated in trendy cottage style. The picture-perfect theme continues with the palm-fringed pool and the sandy beach edged with a ribbon of blue bay (and echoed in the blue-and-white stripes of the poolside umbrellas). Guests look like models on a photo shoot: attractive young families enjoying themselves at the sunny decks, casual outdoor bar, or elegant restaurant. **Pros:** Secluded setting, gorgeous design, lovely crescent beach. **Cons:** A bit sterile, no real Keys atmosphere. ⊠*MM 48.5, BS, 2600 Overseas Hwy.* ☎*305/289–0888 or 866/643–5397* ⊕*www.tranquilitybay.com* ⇆*87 rooms* ⌂*In-room: kitchen, refrigerator, DVD, Wi-Fi. In-hotel: 2 restaurants, bars, pool, gym, spa, beachfront, water sports, concierge, no-smoking rooms* ⊟*AE, D, MC, V.*

$ ▥**Crystal Bay Resort & Marina.** This resort is a blast from the past. The retro motel has a kitschy miniature golf course, shuffleboard courts, and a self-serve tiki bar. Of the selection of rooms and suites, Room 20 offers the best digs, with a bay view that goes on forever. We're told the Wright Brothers stayed in Unit 29—and who's to argue? The fish stories come fast and furious here. Many folks bring their boats and stay two or three weeks at a time; one guy came and never left. If all this sounds eccentrically charming to you, you'll have a grand old time here. If it sounds weird, stay away. **Pros:** Nice kitchens, friendly staff, casual atmosphere. **Cons:** Some rooms need updating, steep charge for extra guests. ⊠ *MM 49, BS, 4900 Overseas Hwy.* ☎ *305/289–8089 or 888/289–8089* ⊕ *www.crystalbayresort.com* ⚓ *29 rooms* ♿ *In-room: kitchen (some), refrigerator. In-hotel: tennis courts, beachfront, water sports, no elevator, laundry facilities* ⊟ *D, MC, V.*

SPORTS & THE OUTDOORS

BIKING

Tooling around on two wheels is a good way to see Marathon. There's easy cycling on a 1-mi off-road path that connects to the 2 mi of the Old Seven Mile Bridge leading to Pigeon Key.

"Have bikes, will deliver" could be the motto of **Bike Marathon Bike Rentals** (☎ *305/743–3204*), which gets beach cruisers to your hotel door for $45 per week, including a helmet. It's open Monday through Saturday 9 to 4 and Sunday 9 to 2. **Overseas Outfitters** (⊠ *MM 48, BS,* ☎ *305/289–1670*) rents aluminum cruisers and hybrid bikes for $10 to $12 per day. The company also rents tandem bikes and children's bikes. It's open weekdays 9 to 6, Saturday 9 to 5, and Sunday 10 to 3.

BOATING

Sail, motor, or paddle: Whatever your choice of modes, boating is what the Keys is all about. Brave the Atlantic waves and reefs or explore the backcountry islands on the gulf side. If you don't have a lot of boating and chart-reading experience, it's a good idea to tap into local knowledge on a charter.

Captain Pip's (⊠ *MM 47.5, OS* ☎ *305/743–4403 or 800/707–1692* ⊕ *www.captainpips.com*) rents 19- to 24-foot outboards, $145 to $350 per day, as well as tackle and snorkeling gear. You also can charter a small boat with a guide, $620 to $685 for a half day and $875 to $925 for a full day. **Fish 'n' Fun** (⊠ *MM 53.5, OS* ☎ *305/743–2275 or 800/471–3440* ⊕ *www.fishnfunrentals.com*), next to the Boat House Marina, lets you get out on the water on 19- to 26-foot powerboats starting at $140 for a half day, $190 for a full day. The company offers free delivery in the Middle Keys. You also can rent Jet Skis and kayaks. For those who want a live-aboard vacation, **Florida Keys Bareboat Charters** (☎ *305/743–0090* ⊕ *www.floridakeysbareboatchartercompany.com*) rents 27-foot Catalina and Balboa sailboats for $200 a day, $950 a week. The fee includes home-port dockage.

FISHING

For recreational anglers, the deepwater fishing is superb in both bay and ocean. Marathon West Hump, one good spot, has depths ranging from 500 to more than 1,000 feet. Locals fish from a half-dozen bridges, including Long Key Bridge, the Old Seven Mile Bridge (once proclaimed the Eighth Wonder of the World), and both ends of Toms Harbor. Barracuda, bonefish, and tarpon all frequent local waters. Party boats and private charters are available.

Morning, afternoon, and night, fish for mahimahi, grouper, and other tasty catch aboard the 73-foot *Marathon Lady* (⊠ *MM 53, OS, at 117th*

8

St. ☎*305/743–5580* ⊕*www.marathonlady.com*) departs on half-day ($40) excursions from the Vaca Cut Bridge, north of Marathon. Join the crew for night fishing ($50) from 6:30 to midnight from Memorial Day to Labor Day; it's especially beautiful on a full-moon night. Captain Jim Purcell, a deep-sea specialist for ESPN's *The American Outdoorsman,* provides one of the best values in fishing in the Keys.

★ **Sea Dog Charters** (✉*MM 47.5, BS* ☎*305/743–8255* ⊕*www. seadogcharters.net*), next to the 7 Mile Grill, has half- and full-day off-shore, reef and wreck, and backcountry fishing trips, as well as fishing and snorkeling trips aboard 30- to 37-foot boats. The cost is $60 per person for a half day, regardless of whether your group fills the boat, and includes bait, light tackle, ice, and coolers. If you prefer an all-day private charter on a 37-foot boat, he offers those, too, for $850 for up to six people. A fuel surcharge may apply.

GOLF

Key Colony Golf & Tennis (✉*MM 53.5, OS, 8th St., Key Colony Beach* ☎*305/289–1533* ⊕*www.keycolonybeach.net/recreation.html*), a 9-hole course near Marathon, charges $9 for the course ($7 for each additional 9 holes), $3 per person for club rental, and $2 for a pull cart. There are no reserved tee times and there's no rush. Play from 7:30 to dusk. A little pro shop meets basic golf needs. Two lighted tennis courts are open from 7:30 to 10. Hourly rates are $4 for singles, $6 for doubles.

SCUBA DIVING & SNORKELING

Local dive operations take you Sombrero Reef and Lighthouse, the most popular down-under destination in these parts. For a shallow dive and some lobster-nabbing, Coffins Patch, off Key Colony Beach, is a good choice. A number of wrecks such as *Thunderbolt* serve as artificial reefs. Many operations out of this area will also take you to Looe Key Reef.

Hall's Diving Center and Career Institute (✉*MM 48.5, BS, 1994 Overseas Hwy.* ☎*305/743–5929 or 800/331–4255* ⊕*www.hallsdiving.com*) has been training divers for more than 40 years. Along with conventional twice-a-day snorkel and two-tank dive trips ($45 to $55) to the reefs at Sombrero Lighthouse and wrecks like the *Thunderbolt,* the company has more usual offerings like digital and video photography.

Twice daily, **Spirit Snorkeling** (✉*MM 47.5 BS,* ☎*305/289–0614* ⊕*www.spiritsnorkeling.net*) departs on snorkeling excursions to Sombrero Reef and Lighthouse Reef. For $30 a head, refreshments, snacks, and a freshwater shower are provided.

THE LOWER KEYS

Beginning at Bahia Honda Key, the islands of the Florida Keys become smaller, more clustered, and more numerous, a result of ancient tidal water flowing between the Florida Straits and the gulf. Here you're likely to see more birds and mangroves than other tourists, and more refuges, beaches, and campgrounds than museums, restaurants, and hotels. The islands are made up of two types of limestone, both denser than the highly permeable Key Largo limestone of the Upper Keys. As a result, freshwater forms in pools rather than percolating through the rock, creating watering holes that support alligators, snakes, deer, rabbits, raccoons, and migratory ducks. (Many of these animals can be seen in the National Key Deer Refuge on Big Pine Key.) Nature was generous with her beauty in the Lower Keys, which have both Looe Key Reef, arguably the Keys' most beautiful tract of coral, and Bahia Honda State Park, considered one of the best beaches in the world for its fine sand dunes, clear warm waters, and panoramic vista of bridges, hammocks, and azure sky and sea. Big Pine Key is fishing headquarters for a laid-back community that swells with retirees in the winter. South of it, the dribble of islands can flash by in a blink of an eye if you don't take the time to stop at a roadside eatery or check out tours and charters at the little marinas.

BAHIA HONDA KEY

MM 38–36.

Fodor's Choice
★

Most first-time visitors to the region are dismayed by the lack of beaches. But then they discover sun-soaked Bahia Honda Key. The 524-acre **Bahia Honda State Park** sprawls across both sides of the highway, giving it 2½ mi of fabulous sandy coastline—three beaches in all—on both the Atlantic Ocean and the Gulf of Mexico. It's regularly declared the best beach in Florida, and you'll be hard pressed to argue. The sand is baby-powder soft, and the aqua water is warm, clear, and shallow. With their mild currents, the beaches are great for swimming, even with small fry. The snorkeling isn't bad, either; there's underwater life (soft coral, queen conchs, random little fish) just a few hundred feet offshore. Although swimming, kayaking, fishing, and boating are the main reasons to visit, you shouldn't miss biking along the 3½ mi of flat roads or hiking the Silver Palm Trail, with rare West Indian plants and several species found nowhere else in the Keys. Along the way you'll be treated to a variety of butterflies. Seasonal ranger-led nature programs might include illustrated talks on the history of the Overseas Railroad. There are rental cabins, a campground, snack bar, gift shop, 19-slip marina, and facilties for renting kayaks and arranging snorkeling tours. Get a panoramic view of the island from what's left of the railroad—the Bahia Honda Bridge. ⊠*MM 37, OS, 36850 Overseas Hwy.* ☎*305/872–2353* ⊕*www.floridastateparks.org/bahia honda* ⊠*$3.50 for 1 person, $6 for 2 people, plus 50¢ per additional person* ☉*Daily 8–sunset.*

WHERE TO STAY

★ $ 🏠 **Bahia Honda State Park.** Elsewhere you'd pay big bucks for the wonderful water views available at these cabins on Florida Bay. Each two-bedroom unit has a full kitchen and bath and air-conditioning (but no television, radio, or phone). The park also has popular campsites suitable for either tents or motor homes. Some are directly on the beach—

8

talk about a room with a view! Cabins and campsites book up early, so reserve up to 11 months before your planned visit. **Pros:** Great bayfront views, beachfront camping, affordable rates. **Cons:** Books up fast, area can be buggy. ⊠*MM 37, OS, 36850 Overseas Hwy.* ☎*305/872–2353 or 800/326–3521* ⊕*www.reserveamerica.com* ⟋*80 campsites, 48 RV sites, 32 tent sites; 3 duplex cabins* ⚷*In-room: no phone, kitchen, no TV. In-hotel: beachfront, water sports, bicycles, no elevator* ⊟*AE, D, MC, V.*

SPORTS & THE OUTDOORS

Bahia Honda Dive Shop (⊠*MM 37, OS,* ☎*305/872–3210* ⊕*www.bahia hondapark.com*), the concessionaire at Bahia Honda State Park, manages a 19-slip marina; rents wet suits, snorkel equipment, and corrective masks; and operates twice-a-day offshore-reef snorkel trips ($29 plus $6 for equipment). Park visitors looking for other fun can rent kayaks ($10 per hour for a single, $18 for a double) and beach chairs.

BIG PINE KEY

MM 32–30.

In the Florida Keys more than 20 animals and plants are endangered or threatened. Among them is the diminutive Key deer, which stands about 30 inches at the shoulders and is a subspecies of the Virginia ★ white-tailed deer. The 84,351-acre **National Key Deer Refuge** was established in 1957 to protect the dwindling population. These deer once roamed throughout the Lower and Middle Keys, but hunting, destruction of their habitat, and a growing human population caused their numbers to decline to 27 by 1957. The deer have made a comeback, increasing their numbers to between 600 and 750. The best place to see Key deer in the refuge is at the end of Key Deer Boulevard and on No Name Key, a sparsely populated island just east of Big Pine Key. Mornings and evenings are the best time to spot them. Deer may turn up along the road at any time of day, so drive slowly. Feeding them is against the law and puts them in danger. The refuge also has 22 listed endangered and threatened species of plants and animals, including five that are found nowhere else.

The **Blue Hole,** a quarry left over from railroad days, is the largest body of fresh water in the Keys. From the observation platform and nearby walking trail, you might see alligators, turtles, and other wildlife. There are two well-marked trails: the Jack Watson Nature Trail (2/3 mi), named after an environmentalist and the refuge's first warden; and the Fred Mannillo Nature Trail, one of the most wheelchair-accessible places to see an unspoiled pine rockland forest. The visitor center has exhibits on Keys biology and ecology. The refuge also provides information on the Key West National Wildlife Refuge and the Great White Heron National Wildlife Refuge. Accessible only by water, both are popular with kayak outfitters. ⊠*Visitor Center–Headquarters, Big Pine Shopping Center, 28950 Watson Blvd., MM 30.5, BS* ☎*305/872–2239 or 305/872–0774* ⊕*www.fws.gov/nationalkeydeer* ⊠*Free* ☉*Daily sunrise–sunset; headquarters weekdays 8–5.*

WHERE TO EAT & STAY

$ ✕ **No Name Pub.** This no-frills honky-tonk has been around since 1936, delighting inveterate locals and intrepid vacationers who come for the excellent pizza, cold beer, and *interesting* companionship. The decor, such as it is, amounts to the autographed dollar bills that cover every inch of the place. The owners have conceded to the times by introducing a full menu, including a half-pound fried grouper sandwich, spaghetti and meatballs, and seafood baskets. The lighting is poor, the furnishings are rough, and the jukebox doesn't play the latest tunes. This former brothel–bait shop is just before the No Name Bridge. It's a bit hard to find, but worth the trouble if you want a singular Keys experience. ⊠ *MM 30, BS, N. Watson Blvd.* ☎ *305/872–9115* ⊕ *www. nonamepub.com* ⊟ *D, MC, V.*

¢ ✕ **Good Food Conspiracy.** Like good wine, this small natural-foods eatery and market surrenders its pleasures a little at a time. Step inside to the aroma of brewing coffee, and then pick up the scent of fresh strawberries or carrots blending into a smoothie, followed by the earthy odor of hummus. Order raw or cooked vegetarian and vegan dishes, organic soups and salads, and all-natural coffees and teas. Bountiful sandwiches include the popular organic turkey on a whole-wheat pita. If you can't sit down for a bite, stock up on healthful snacks like dried fruits, raw nuts, and carob-covered almonds. Dine early: the shop closes at 7 Monday to Saturday, and at 5 on Sunday. ⊠ *MM 30.2, OS* ☎ *305/872–3945.*

$$$–$$$$ ⬚ **Deer Run Bed & Breakfast.** Key deer wander the grounds of this beachfront B&B, set on a quiet street lined with buttonwoods and mangroves. The "natural beauty" angle is already covered here; innkeepers Jen DeMaria and Harry Appel are now working to elevate the level of lodgings. Two large oceanfront rooms are decorated in soothing earth tones and furnished with mahogany and pecan-wood furnishings. The beach-level unit is decorated in key lime and flamingo-pink, with wicker furnishings, and the garden-view room is an eclectic mix that includes Victorian farmhouse doors serving as the headboard of the queen-size bed. Guests share a living room and a veranda. The animal-friendly atmosphere extends to the kitchen, with a mostly organic breakfast menu suitable for vegetarians. The breakfasts—perhaps flax pancakes with organic fruit or veggie scramble with soy sausage—come with Fair Trade coffee and tea. Guest rooms are stocked with organic cotton towels and cruelty-free toiletries. **Pros:** Quiet location, healthy breakfasts, enthusiastic owners. **Cons:** Exterior is cluttered, price is a bit high. ⊠ *MM 33, OS, 1997 Long Beach Dr.* ☎ *305/872–2015* ⊕ *www.deerrunfloridabb.com* ⇌ *4 rooms* ⌂ *In-room: refrigerator, Wi-Fi. In-hotel: beachfront, water sports, bicycles, no elevator, no kids under 18, no-smoking rooms* ⊟ *D, MC, V* ⍟ *BP.*

★ ¢–$ ⬚ **Big Pine Key Fishing Lodge.** There's a congenial atmosphere at this lively family-owned lodge-campground-marina. It's a happy mix of tent campers (who have the choicest waterfront real estate), RVers (who look pretty permanent), and motel-dwellers who like to mingle at the rooftop pool and challenge each other to a game of poker. Rooms have tile floors, wicker furniture, and doors that allow sea breezes to waft through. A skywalk joins them with the pool and deck. Campsites

8

range from rustic to full hookups. Everything is spotless—even the campground's bathhouse—and the service is good-natured and efficient. The staff will book you a room, sell you bait, or hook you up with a fishing charter. There are plenty of family-oriented activities, so the youngsters will never complain about being bored. Discounts are available for weeklong or longer stays. **Pros:** Local fishing crowd, nice pool, great price. **Cons:** RV park is too close to motel, deer will eat your food if you're camping. ⊠ *MM 33, OS, Box 430513* ☎ *305/872–2351* 🔖 *16 rooms; 158 campsites, 97 with full hookups, 61 without hookups* ⚙ *In-room: kitchen (some), refrigerator (some). In-hotel: pool, no elevator, public Internet* ☐ *MC, V.*

SPORTS & THE OUTDOORS

BIKING

A good 10 mi of paved and unpaved roads run from MM 30.3, BS, along Wilder Road, across the bridge to No Name Key, and along Key Deer Boulevard into the National Key Deer Refuge. Along the way you might see some Key deer. Stay off the trails that lead into wetlands, where fat tires can do damage to the environment.

Marty Baird, owner of **Big Pine Bicycle Center** (⊠ *MM 30.9, BS* ☎ *305/872–0130*), is an avid cyclist and enjoys sharing his knowledge of great places to ride. He's also skilled at selecting the right bike for the journey, and he knows his repairs, too. His old-fashioned single-speed, fat-tire cruisers rent for $8 per half day and $10 for a full day. Helmets, baskets, and locks are included. Although the shop is officially closed on Sunday, join Marty there most Sunday mornings at 8 in winter for a free off-road fun ride.

FISHING

Fish with pros year-round in air-conditioned comfort with **Strike Zone Charters** (⊠ *MM 29.6, BS, 29675 Overseas Hwy.* ☎ *305/872–9863 or 800/654–9560*). Deep-sea charter rates are $600 for a half day, $750 for a full day. It also offers flats fishing in the Gulf of Mexico.

SCUBA DIVING & SNORKELING

Strike Zone Charters (⊠ *MM 29.6, BS, 29675 Overseas Hwy.* ☎ *305/872–9863 or 800/654–9560*) leads dive excursions to the wreck of the 210-foot *Adolphus Busch* ($50), and scuba ($40) and snorkel ($30) trips to Looe Key Reef aboard glass-bottom boats. Strike Zone also offers a five-hour island excursion that combines snorkeling, fishing, and an island cookout for $49 per person. A large dive shop is on-site.

WATER SPORTS

★ **Big Pine Kayak Adventures** (⊠ *Old Wooden Bridge Fishing Camp, MM 30, BS, turn right at traffic light, continue on Wilder Rd. toward No Name Key* ☎ *305/872–7474* ⊕ *www.keyskayaktours.com*) makes it very convenient to rent kayaks by delivering them to your lodging or anywhere between Seven Mile Bridge and Stock Island. The company, headed by *The Florida Keys Paddling Guide* author Bill Keogh, will rent you a kayak and then ferry you—called taxi-yaking—to remote islands with clear instructions on how to paddle back on your own.

Rentals are by the half day or full day. Group kayak tours ($50 for three hours) explore the mangrove forests of Great White Heron and Key Deer National Wildlife Refuges. Custom tours ($125 and up, four hours) transport you to exquisite backcountry areas teeming with wildlife. Kayak fishing charters are also popular.

LITTLE TORCH KEY

MM 29–10.

Little Torch Key and its neighbor islands, Ramrod Key and Summerland Key, are good jumping-off points for divers headed for Looe Key Reef. The islands also serve as a refuge for those who want to make forays into Key West but not stay in the thick of things.

NEED A BREAK? The aroma of rich, roasting coffee beans at Baby's Coffee (⊠ *MM 15, OS, Saddlebunch Keys* ☎ *305/744–9866 or 800/523–2326*) arrests you at the door of "the Southernmost Coffee Roaster." Buy it by the pound or by the cup along with fresh baked goods.

The undeveloped backcountry at your door makes Little Torch Key an ideal location for fishing and kayaking. Nearby **Ramrod Key,** which also caters to divers bound for Looe Key, derives its name from a ship that wrecked on nearby reefs in the early 1800s.

WHERE TO EAT

★ $$$$ ✕ **Little Palm Island Restaurant.** The oceanfront setting calls to mind St. Barth's and the other high-end destinations of the Caribbean. Keep that in mind as you reach for the bill, which can also make you swoon. The restaurant at the exclusive Little Palm Island Resort—its dining room and adjacent outdoor terrace lit by candles and warmed by live music—is one of the most romantic spots in the Keys. The seasonal menu is a melding of French and Caribbean flavors, with exotic little touches. Think hearts of palm and mango salad with pink-pepper vinaigrette as a starter, followed by pan-seared divers scallops in a citrus beurre blanc with potato and lobster pancake. The weekend brunch buffet and the full-moon jazz dinners are very popular. The dining room is open to nonguests on a reservations-only basis. ⊠ *MM 28.5, OS, 28500 Overseas Hwy.* ☎ *305/872–2551* ⚓ *Reservations essential* ⊟ *AE, D, DC, MC, V.*

¢ ✕ **Geiger Key Marina Smokehouse.** There's a hint of the Old Keys at this oceanfront marina restaurant where locals usually outnumber tourists. They come for the daily dinner specials: meat loaf on Monday, pasta on Tuesday, and so on. Weekends are the most popular; the place is packed on Saturday for steak-on-the-grill night and on Sunday for the chicken and ribs barbecue. Local fishermen head here for breakfast before heading out in search of the big ones. ⊠ *MM 10, Geiger Key* ☎ *305/296–3553 or 305/294–1230* ⊕ *www.geigerkeymarina.com* ⊟ *MC, V.*

8

WHERE TO STAY

$$$$ ⚌ **Little Palm Island Resort & Spa.** *Haute tropicale* best describes this lux-
Fodor'sChoice ury retreat, and "second mortgage" might explain how some can afford
★ the extravagant prices. But for those who can, it's worth the price. This
property sits on a 5-acre palm-fringed island 3 mi offshore from Little
Torch Key. The 28 oceanfront thatch-roof bungalow suites have slate-
tile baths, mosquito netting–draped king-size beds, and British colonial–style furnishings. Other comforts include an indoor and outdoor
shower, private veranda, separate living room, and comfy robes and
slippers. Two Island Grand Suites are twice the size of the others and
offer his-and-her bathrooms, an outdoor hot tub, and uncompromising
ocean views. To preserve the quiet atmosphere, cell phones are verbo-
ten in public areas. **Pros:** Secluded setting, heavenly spa, easy wildlife
viewing. **Cons:** Astronomic prices, can be too quiet for some. ⊠*MM
28.5, OS, 28500 Overseas Hwy.* ☎*305/872–2524 or 800/343–8567*
⊕*www.littlepalmisland.com* ⌐*30 suites* ♿*In-room: no phone, safe,
refrigerator, no TV, dial-up. In-hotel: restaurant, room service, bars,
pool, gym, spa, beachfront, diving, water sports, no elevator, concierge,
public Wi-Fi, airport shuttle, parking (no fee), no kids under 16, no-
smoking rooms* ▤*AE, D, DC, MC, V* ⏶*MAP.*

$–$$ ⚌ **Parmer's Resort.** Don't let the behind-the-Jehovah's-Witness-Hall-
location put you off. Almost every room has a view of Pine Channel,
with the lovely curl of Big Pine Key in the foreground. Waterfront cottages, with decks or balconies, are spread out on 5 landscaped acres,
with a heated swimming pool and a five-hole putting green. There are
water sports galore, and the staff will book you a kayak tour, a fishing trip, or a bike excursion, or tell you which local restaurants will
deliver dinner to your room. Value-minded couples (mostly European)
flock here, sharing the landscape with 70-some tropical birds. So what
if the decor feels a little grandma's-house and you have to pay extra if
you want maid services? **Pros:** Bright rooms, pretty setting, good value.
Cons: A bit out of the way, maid service costs extra, little shade around
the pool. ⊠*MM 28.7, BS, 565 Barry Ave.* ☎*305/872–2157* ⊕*www.
parmersresort.com* ⌐*18 rooms, 12 efficiencies, 15 apartments, 1 penthouse* ♿*In-room: no phone, kitchen (some). In-hotel: pool, no elevator, laundry facilities, public Internet, public Wi-Fi, no-smoking rooms*
▤*AE, D, MC, V* ⏶*CP.*

¢–$ ⚌ **Looe Key Reef Resort.** If your Keys vacation is all about diving, you'll
be well served at this scuba-obsessed operation. The closest place to stay
to the stellar reef and affordable to boot, it's popular with the bottom-
time crowd. Rooms are basic, but are perfect for sleeping between dives
and hanging out at the tiki bar. The one suite is equipped with a fridge
and microwave. Single rooms are available. **Pros:** Guests get discounts
on dive and snorkel trips, fun bar. **Cons:** Small rooms, unheated pool,
close to road. ⊠*MM 27.5 OS, Ramrod Key* ☎*305/872–2215 Ext. 2
or 800/942–5397* ⊕*www.diveflakeys.com* ⌐*25 rooms, 1 suite* ♿*In-
room: Wi-Fi. In hotel: bar, pool, no elevator, public Wi-Fi* ▤*MC, V.*

SPORTS & THE OUTDOORS

SCUBA DIVING & SNORKELING

In 1744 the HMS *Looe*, a British warship, ran aground and sank on one of the most beautiful coral reefs in the Keys. Today **Looe Key Reef** (✉*MM 27.5, OS, 216 Ann St., Key West* ☎*305/292–0311*) owes its name to the ill-fated ship. The 5.3-square-nautical-mi reef, part of the **Florida Keys National Marine Sanctuary,** has strands of elkhorn coral on its eastern margin, purple sea fans, and abundant sponges and sea urchins. On its seaward side, it drops almost vertically 50 to 90 feet. In its midst, Shipwreck Trail plots the location of nine historic wreck sites in 14 to 120 feet of water. Buoys mark the sites, and underwater signs tell the history of each site and what marine life to expect. Snorkelers and divers will find the sanctuary a quiet place to observe reef life—except in July, when the annual Underwater Music Festival pays homage to Looe Key's beauty and promotes reef awareness with six hours of music broadcast via underwater speakers. Dive shops and private charters transport hundreds of divers and snorkelers (more than 600 last year) to hear the spectacle, which includes classical, jazz, and New Age, Caribbean music, as well as a little Jimmy Buffett. There are even underwater Elvis impersonators. Rather than the customary morning and afternoon two-location, two-tank trips offered by most dive shops, **Looe Key Reef Resort & Dive Center** (✉*Looe Key Reef Resort, MM 27.5, OS, Box 509, Ramrod Key* ☎*305/872–2215 Ext. 2 or 800/942–5397* ⊕*www.diveflakeys.com*), the closest dive shop to Looe Key Reef, runs a single three-tank, three-location dive ($80 for divers, $40 for snorkelers). The maximum depth is 30 feet, so snorkelers and divers go on the same boat. On Wednesday they run a similar dive that visits wrecks and reefs in the area ($80). The dive boat, a 45-foot Corinthian catamaran, is docked outside the full-service Looe Key Reef Resort.

EN ROUTE The huge object that looks like a white whale floating over Cudjoe Key (MM 23–21) is not a figment of your imagination. It's Fat Albert, a radar balloon that monitors local air and water traffic.

KEY WEST

MM 4–0.

Situated 150 mi from Miami, 90 mi from Havana, and an immeasurable distance from sanity, this end-of-the-line community has never been like anywhere else. Even after it was connected to the rest of the country—by the railroad in 1912 and by the highway in 1938—it maintained a strong sense of detachment. The U.S. acquired Key West from Spain in 1821, along with the rest of Florida. The Spanish had named the island Cayo Hueso, or Bone Key, after the Native American skeletons they found on its shores. In 1823 President James Monroe sent Commodore David S. Porter to chase pirates away. For three decades the primary industry in Key West was wrecking—rescuing people and salvaging cargo from ships that foundered on the nearby reefs. According to some reports, when pickings were lean the wreckers hung out lights to lure ships aground. Their business declined after 1849, when the federal government began building lighthouses.

In 1845 the army began construction on Fort Taylor, which kept Key West on the Union side during the Civil War. After the fighting ended, an influx of Cubans unhappy with Spain's rule brought the cigar industry here. Fishing, shrimping, and sponge-gathering became important industries, as did pineapple canning. Through much of the 19th century and into the 20th, Key West was Florida's wealthiest city in per-capita terms. But in 1929 the local economy began to unravel. Cigar making moved to Tampa, Hawaii dominated the pineapple industry, and the sponges succumbed to blight. Then the Depression hit, and within a few years half the population was on relief.

Tourism began to revive Key West, but that came to a halt when a hurricane knocked out the railroad bridge in 1935. To help the tourism industry recover from that crushing blow, the government offered incentives for islanders to turn their charming homes—many of them built by shipwrights—into guesthouses and inns. The wise foresight has left the town with more than 100 such lodgings, a hallmark of Key West vacationing today. In the 1950s the discovery of "pink gold" in the Dry Tortugas boosted the economy of the entire region. Catching Key West shrimp required a fleet of up to 500 boats and flooded local restaurants with some of the sweetest shrimp alive. The town's artistic community found inspiration in the colorful fishing boats.

Key West reflects a diverse population: Conchs (natives, many of whom trace their ancestry to the Bahamas), freshwater Conchs (longtime residents who migrated from somewhere else years ago), Hispanics (primarily Cuban immigrants), recent refugees from the urban sprawl of mainland Florida, military personnel, and an assortment of vagabonds, drifters, and dropouts in search of refuge. The island was once a gay vacation hot spot, and it remains a decidedly gay-friendly destination. Some of the most renowned gay guesthouses, however, no longer cater to an exclusively gay clientele. Key Westers pride themselves on their tolerance of all peoples, all sexual orientations, and even all animals. Most restaurants allow pets, and it's not surprising to see stray cats, dogs, and even chickens roaming freely through the dining rooms. The chicken issue is one that government officials periodically try to bring to an end, but the colorful fowl continue to strut and crow, particularly in the vicinity of Old Town's Bahamian Village.

Although the rest of the Keys are known for outdoor activities, Key West has something of a city feel. Few open spaces remain, as promoters continue to churn out restaurants, galleries, shops, and museums to interpret the city's intriguing past. As a tourist destination, Key West has a lot to sell—an average temperature of 79°F, 19th-century architecture, and a laid-back lifestyle. Yet much has been lost to those eager for a buck. Duval Street looks like a miniature Las Vegas lined with garish signs for T-shirt shops and tour company offices. Cruise ships dwarf the town's skyline and fill the streets with day-trippers gawking at the hippies with dogs in their bike baskets, gay couples walking down the street holding hands, and the oddball lot of locals, some of whom bark louder than the dogs.

EXPLORING KEY WEST

Key West is the one place in the Keys where you could conceivably do without a car, especially if you plan on staying around Old Town. Even if you've driven the 106 miles down the chain, you're probably ready to abandon your car in the hotel parking lot. Trolleys, buses, bikes, scooters, and feet are more suitable alternatives. To explore on your own, pick up a copy of Sharon Wells' Walking & Biking Guide to Historic Key West. It is organized into 16 different tours according to your areas of interest. To explore the beaches, New Town, and Stock Island, you'll probably need a car.

Numbers in the margin correspond to the Key West map.

OLD TOWN

The heart of Key West, this historic Old Town area runs from White Street to the waterfront. Beginning in 1822, wharves, warehouses, chandleries, ship-repair facilities, and eventually in 1891 the U.S. Custom House sprang up around the deep harbor to accommodate the navy's large ships and other sailing vessels. Wreckers, merchants, and sea captains built lavish houses near the bustling waterfront. A remarkable number of these fine Victorian and pre-Victorian structures have been restored to their original grandeur and now serve as homes, guesthouses, shops, restaurants, and museums. These, along with the dwellings of famous writers, artists, and politicians who've come to Key West over the past 175 years, are among the area's approximately 3,000 historic structures. Old Town also has the city's finest restaurants and hotels, lively street life, and popular nightspots.

8

WHAT TO SEE

6 **Audubon House and Gardens.** If you've ever seen an engraving by ornithologist John James Audubon, you'll understand why his name is synonymous with birds. See his works in this three-story house, which was built in the 1840s for Captain John Geiger and filled with period furniture. It now commemorates Audubon's 1832 stop in Key West while he was traveling through Florida to study birds. A children's room makes his work accessible to youngsters. Docents lead a guided tour that identifies the rare indigenous plants and trees. ✉ *205 Whitehead St., 33040* 📞 *305/294–2116 or 877/294–2470* 🌐 *www.audubon house.com* 💲 *$11* 🕐 *Daily 9:30–5, last tour starts at 4.*

★ **15** **City Cemetery.** You can learn almost as much about a town's history through its cemetery as through its

PELICAN PATH
Pelican Path is a free walking guide to Key West published by the Old Island Restoration Foundation. The guide discusses the history and architecture of 43 structures along 25 blocks of 12 Old Town streets. Pick up a copy at the Chamber of Commerce.

historic houses. Key West's celebrated 20-acre burial place may leave you wanting more, with headstone epitaphs such as "I told you I was sick" and, for a wayward husband, "Now I know where he's sleeping at night." Among the interesting plots are a memorial to the sailors killed in the sinking of the battleship USS *Maine,* carved angels and lambs marking graves of children, and grand aboveground crypts that put to shame many of the town's dwellings for the living. There are separate plots for Catholics, Jews, and refugees from Cuba. You're free to walk around the cemetery on your own, but the best way to see it is on a 60-minute tour given by the staff and volunteers of the Historic Florida Keys Foundation. Tours leave from the main gate, and reservations are required. ⊠*Margaret and Angela Sts., 33040* ☎*305/292–6718* ⊠*$15* ⊗*Daily sunrise–6* PM*, tours Tues. and Thurs. at 9:30; call for additional times.*

🔞 **Dog Beach.** Next to Louie's Backyard, this small beach—the only one in Key West where dogs are allowed—has a shore that's a mix of sand and rocks. ⊠*Vernon and Waddell Sts.* ☎*No phone* ⊠*Free* ⊗*Daily sunrise–sunset.*

★ ⑬ **Eco-Discovery Center.** Walk through a model of Key Largo's Aquarius, the world's only underwater ocean laboratory, to discover what lurks beneath the sea. Opened in 2007, this 6,400-square-foot underwater attraction encourages visitors to venture through a variety of Florida Key habitats, from pinelands, beach dunes, and mangroves to the deep sea. Touch-screen computer displays and live underwater cameras show off North America's only contiguous barrier coral reef. ⊠*35 East Quay Rd., at end of Southard St. in Truman Annex, 33040* ☎*305/809–4750* ⊕ *floridakeys.noaa.gov* ⊠*Free* ⊗*Tues.–Sat. 9–4.*

★ ❶ **Ernest Hemingway Home & Museum.** Amusing anecdotes pepper the guided tours of Ernest Hemingway's home. While living here between 1931 and 1942, Hemingway wrote about 70% of his life's work, including classics like *For Whom the Bell Tolls.* Few of his belongings remain, and there's little about his actual work, but photographs help you visualize his day-to-day life. The supposed descendants of Hemingway's cats— many named for actors, artists, and authors—have free rein of the property. Tours begin every 10 minutes and take 25 to 30 minutes; then you're free to explore on your own. ⊠*907 Whitehead St.* ☎*305/294–1136* ⊕*www.hemingwayhome.com* ⊠*$12* ⊗*Daily 9–5.*

★ ❸ **Fort Zachary Taylor Historic State Park.** Construction of the fort began in 1845, but construction was halted during the Civil War. Even though Florida seceded from the Union, Yankee forces used the fort as a base to block Confederate shipping. More than 1,500 Confederate vessels were detained in Key West's harbor. The fort, finally completed in 1866, was also used in the Spanish-American War. Take a 30-minute guided tour of this National Historic Landmark at noon and 2. In February a celebration called Civil War Heritage Days includes costumed reenactments and demonstrations. From mid-January to mid-April the park serves as an open-air gallery for pieces created for Sculpture Key West. The park's beach is the best in Key West. There's an adjoining picnic

A GOOD TOUR

To cover many sights, take the Old Town Trolley, which lets you get off and reboard a later trolley, or the Conch Tour Train. Old Town is also manageable on foot, bicycle, moped, or golf cart-like electric cars. The area is expansive, so you'll want either to pick and choose from the stops on this tour or break it into two or more days. Start on Whitehead Street at the ❶ **Ernest Hemingway Home & Museum**, and then cross the street and climb to the top of the ❷ **Lighthouse Museum** for a spectacular view. Return to Whitehead Street and follow it north to Angela Street, where you'll turn right. At Margaret Street, the ❶ **City Cemetery** is worth a look for its above-ground vaults and unusual headstone inscriptions. Head north on Margaret Street, turn left onto Southard Street, then right onto Simonton Street. Halfway up the block, ❹ **Nancy Forrester's Secret Garden** occupies Free School Lane. After wandering among the blossoms, head west on Southard Street to Duval Street, turn right, and look at the lovely tiles and woodwork in the ❺ **San Carlos Institute**. Return again to Southard Street, turn right, and follow it through Truman Annex to ❸ **Fort Zachary Taylor State Park**.

Walk west into Truman Annex to see the ❽ **Harry S Truman Little White House Museum**, President Truman's vacation residence. Return east on Caroline and turn left on Whitehead to visit the ❻ **Audubon House and Gardens**, honoring the famed artist and naturalist. Follow Whitehead north to Greene Street and turn left to see the salvaged sea treasures of the ❼ **Mel Fisher Maritime Heritage Society Museum**.

At Whitehead's northern end are the ❿ **Key West Aquarium** and the ❾ **Key West Museum of Art and History**, the historic former U.S. Custom House. By late afternoon you should be ready to cool off with a dip or catch a few rays at the beach. From the aquarium, head east two blocks to the end of Simonton Street, where you'll find the appropriately named ⓮ **Simonton Street Beach**. On the Atlantic side of Old Town is ⓱ **South Beach**, named for its location at the southern end of Duval Street. If you've brought your pet, stroll a few blocks east to ⓲ **Dog Beach**, at the corner of Vernon and Waddell streets. A little farther east is ⓳ **Higgs Beach–Astro City Playground**, on Atlantic Boulevard between White and Reynolds streets. As the sun starts to sink, return to the north end of Old Town and follow the crowds to Mallory Square, behind the aquarium, to watch Key West's nightly sunset spectacle. (Those lucky enough may see a green flash—the brilliant splash of green or blue that sometimes appears as the sun sinks into the ocean on a clear night.) For dinner, head east on Caroline Street to ⓫ **Historic Seaport at Key West Bight**, a renovated area where there are numerous restaurants and bars.

If you're not entirely a do-it-yourselfer, **Key West Promotions** (✉ *422 Fleming St.* ☎ *305/744–9804* ⊕ *www.keywestwalkingtours. com*) offers a variety of guided walking tours, including a pub crawl and restaurant tour.

8

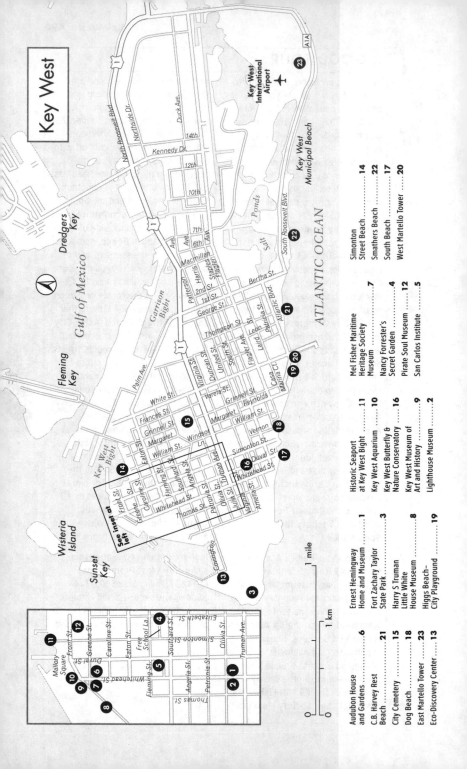

Key West

Audubon House and Gardens **6**
C.B. Harvey Rest Beach **21**
City Cemetery **15**
Dog Beach **18**
East Martello Tower **23**
Eco-Discovery Center **13**

Ernest Hemingway Home and Museum **1**
Fort Zachary Taylor State Park **3**
Harry S Truman Little White House Museum **8**
Higgs Beach–City Playground **19**

Historic Seaport at Key West Bight **11**
Key West Aquarium **10**
Key West Butterfly & Nature Conservatory **16**
Key West Museum of Art and History **9**
Lighthouse Museum **2**

Mel Fisher Maritime Heritage Society Museum **7**
Nancy Forrester's Secret Garden **4**
Pirate Soul Museum **12**
San Carlos Institute **5**

Simonton Street Beach **14**
Smathers Beach **22**
South Beach **17**
West Martello Tower **20**

area with barbecue grills and shade trees, a snack bar, and rental equipment, including snorkeling gear and kayaks. ⊠*End of Southard St., through Truman Annex* ☎*305/292–6713* ⊕*www.floridastateparks. org/forttaylor* ⊠*$3.50 for 1 person, $6 for 2 people, 50¢ per additional person* ⊙*Daily 8–sunset, tours noon and 2.*

NEED A BREAK?

Check out the pretty palm garden next to the Key West Library at 700 Fleming Street, just off Duval. This leafy, outdoor reading area, with shaded benches, is the perfect place to escape the frenzy and crowds of downtown Key West. There's free Internet access in the library, too.

8 **Harry S Truman Little White House Museum.** In a letter to his wife during one of his visits, President Harry S. Truman wrote, "Dear Bess, you should see the house. The place is all redecorated, new furniture and everything." If he visited today, he'd be similarly impressed. There's a photographic review of visiting dignitaries and permanent audiovisual and artifact exhibits on the Florida Keys as a presidential retreat; Ulysses S. Grant, John F. Kennedy, and Jimmy Carter are among the chief executives who passed through here. Tours lasting 45 minutes begin every 15 minutes until 4:15. On the grounds of **Truman Annex**, a 103-acre former military parade grounds and barracks, the home served as a winter White House for presidents Truman, Eisenhower, and Kennedy. ⊠*111 Front St., 33040* ☎*305/294–9911* ⊕*www.trumanlittlewhitehouse.com* ⊠*$12* ⊙*Daily 9–5, grounds sunrise–6; last tour at 4:30.*

🖐 **19** **Higgs Beach–Astro City Playground.** This Monroe County park is a popular sunbathing spot. But bather beware: the Natural Resources Defense Council lists this as one of the Florida beaches that often exceeds acceptable levels of bacteria. A nearby grove of Australian pines provides shade, and the West Martello Tower provides shelter should a storm suddenly sweep in. Kayak and beach chair rentals are available, as is a volleyball net. The beach also has a marker commemorating the gravesite of 295 enslaved Africans who died after being rescued from three South America–bound slave ships in 1860. Across the street, **Astro City Playground** is popular with young children. ⊠*Atlantic Blvd. between White and Reynolds Sts.* ☎*No phone* ⊠*Free* ⊙*Daily 6 AM–11 PM.*

11 **Historic Seaport at Key West Bight.** What used to be a funky—in some places even seedy—part of town is now an 8½-acre historic restoration project of 100 businesses, including waterfront restaurants, open-air bars, museums, clothing stores, bait shops, dive shops, docks, a marina, the Waterfront Market, and the Key West Rowing Club. It's all linked by the 2-mi waterfront **Harborwalk**, which runs between Front and Grinnell streets, passing big ships, schooners, sunset cruises, fishing charters, and glass-bottom boats. Additional construction continues on outlying projects. ⊠*100 Grinnell St.,* ☎*305/293–8309* ⊕*www. keywestseaport.com.*

NEED A BREAK?

Get your morning (or afternoon) buzz at Coffee Plantation (⊠*713 Caroline St.* ☎ *305/295–9808* ⊕ *www.coffeeplantationkeywest.com*), where you can also hook up to the Internet in the comfort of a homelike setting in a circa-

8

CLOSE UP

Hemingway Was Here

In a town where Pulitzer Prize–winning writers are almost as common as coconuts, Ernest Hemingway stands out. Bars and restaurants around the island claim that he ate or drank there (except Bagatelle, where the sign reads "Hemingway Never Liked This Place"), and though he may not have quenched his formidable thirst at all of them, his larger-than-life image continues to grow.

Hemingway came to Key West in 1928 at the urging of writer John dos Passos and rented a house with wife number two, Pauline Pfeiffer. They spent winters in the Keys and summers in Europe and Wyoming, occasionally taking African safaris. Along the way they had two sons, Patrick and Gregory. In 1931 Pauline's wealthy uncle Gus gave the couple the house at 907 Whitehead Street. Now known as the Ernest Hemingway Home & Museum, it's Key West's number-one tourist attraction. Renovations included the addition of a pool and a tropical garden with peacocks.

In 1935, when the visitor bureau included the house in a tourist brochure, Hemingway promptly built the high brick wall that surrounds it today. He wrote of the visitor bureau's offense in a 1935 essay for *Esquire*, saying, "The house at present occupied by your correspondent is listed as number eighteen in a compilation of the forty-eight things for a tourist to see in Key West. So there will be no difficulty in a tourist finding it or any other of the sights of the city, a map has been prepared by the local F.E.R.A. authorities to be presented to each arriving visitor.... This is all very flattering to the easily bloated ego of your correspondent but very hard on production."

During his time in Key West, Hemingway penned some of his most important works, including *A Farewell to Arms, To Have and Have Not, Green Hills of Africa,* and *Death in the Afternoon.* His rigorous schedule consisted of writing almost every morning in his second-story studio above the pool, then promptly descending the stairs at midday. By afternoon and evening he was ready for drinking, fishing, swimming, boxing, and hanging around with the boys.

One close friend was Joe Russell, a craggy fisherman and owner of the rugged bar Sloppy Joe's, originally at 428 Greene Street but now at 201 Duval Street. Russell was the only one in town who would cash Hemingway's $1,000 royalty check. Russell and Charles Thompson introduced Hemingway to deep-sea fishing, which became fodder for his writing. Another of Hemingway's loves was boxing. He set up a ring in his yard and paid local fighters to box with him, and he refereed matches at Blue Heaven, then a saloon at 729 Thomas Street.

Hemingway honed his macho image dressed in cutoffs and old shirts and took on the name Papa. In turn, he gave his friends new names and used them as characters in his stories. Joe Russell became Freddy, captain of the *Queen Conch* charter boat in *To Have and Have Not.*

Hemingway stayed in Key West for 11 years before leaving Pauline for wife number three. Pauline and the boys stayed on in the house, which sold in 1951 for $80,000, 10 times its original cost.

—Jim & Cynthia Tunstall

1890 conch house. Poets, writers, and minstrels sometimes show up to perform while you munch pastries or luncheon sandwiches and wraps and sip your hot or cold espresso beverage.

Key West Aquarium. Feed a nurse shark and explore the fascinating underwater realm of the Keys without getting wet at this kid-friendly aquarium. Hundreds of tropical fish and sea creatures live here. A touch tank enables you to handle starfish, sea cucumbers, horseshoe and hermit crabs, even horse and queen conchs—living totems of the Conch Republic. Built in 1934 by the Works Progress Administration as the world's first open-air aquarium, most of the building has been enclosed for all-weather viewing. Guided tours, included in the admission price, include shark petting and feedings. ⊠*1 Whitehead St.* ☎*305/296–2051* ⊕*www.keywestaquarium.com* ⊠*$11* ⊗*Daily 10–6; tours at 11, 1, 3, and 4:30.*

The Key West Butterfly & Nature Conservatory. This air-conditioned refuge for butterflies, birds, and the human spirit gladdens the soul with hundreds of colorful wings—more than 50 species of butterflies alone—in a lovely glass-encased bubble. Waterfalls, artistic benches, paved pathways, birds, and lush, flowering vegetation elevate this above most butterfly attractions. The gift shop is worth a visit on its own. ⊠*1316 Duval St.* ☎*305/296–2988 or 800/939–4647* ⊕*www.keywestbutterfly. com* ⊠*$10* ⊗*Daily 9–5.*

Key West Museum of Art and History. When Key West was designated a U.S. port of entry in the early 1820s, a custom house was established. Salvaged cargoes from ships wrecked on the reefs were brought here, setting the stage for Key West to become for a time the richest city in Florida. After a $9 million restoration, the imposing redbrick-and-terra-cotta Richardsonian Romanesque–style building has reopened as a museum and art gallery. Smaller galleries have long-term and changing exhibits about the history of Key West, including a Hemingway room and a fine collection of folk artist Mario Sanchez's wood paintings. ⊠*281 Front St.,33040* ☎*305/295–6616* ⊕*www.kwahs.com* ⊠*$10* ⊗*Daily 9–5.*

FodorsChoice
★

Lighthouse Museum. For the best view in town, climb the 88 steps to the top of this 1847 lighthouse. The 92-ft structure has a Fresnel lens, which was installed in the 1860s at a cost of $1 million. The keeper lived in the adjacent 1887 clapboard house, which now exhibits vintage photographs, ship models, nautical charts, and lighthouse artifacts from all along the Key reefs. ⊠*938 Whitehead St.,33040* ☎*305/295–6616* ⊕*www.kwahs.com* ⊠*$10* ⊗*Daily 9:30–5; last admission at 4:30.*

Mel Fisher Maritime Museum. In 1622 two Spanish galleons laden with riches from South America foundered in a hurricane 40 mi west of the Keys. In 1985 diver Mel Fisher recovered the treasures from the lost ships, the *Nuestra Señora de Atocha* and the *Santa Margarita*. Fisher's incredible adventure tracking these fabled hoards and battling the state of Florida for rights is as amazing as the loot you'll see, touch, and learn about in this museum. Artifacts include a gold bar worth $15,000 and a 77.76-carat natural emerald crystal worth almost $250,000. Exhibits

8

on the second floor rotate and might cover slave ships, including the excavated 17th-century *Henrietta Marie,* or the evolution of Florida maritime history. ⊠*200 Greene St.33040* ☎*305/294–2633* ⊕*www. melfisher.org* ▣*$12* ⊘ *Weekdays 8:30–5, weekends 9:30–5.*

❹ Nancy Forrester's Secret Garden. It's hard to believe that this green escape still exists in the middle of Old Town Key West. Despite damage by hurricanes and pressures from developers, Nancy Forrester has maintained her naturalized garden for more than 35 years. Growing in harmony are rare palms and cycads, ferns, bromeliads, bright gingers and heliconias, gumbo-limbo trees strewn with orchids and vines, and a colorful crew of birds, reptiles, cats, and a few surprises. An art gallery has botanical prints and environmental art. One-hour private tours cost $15 per person, four-person minimum. ⊠*1 Free School La.33040* ☎*305/294–0015* ⊕*www.nancyforrester.com* ▣*$10* ⊘*Daily 10–5.*

☾ ⓬ Pirate Soul Museum. Enter if you dare! This $10 million attraction combines an animatronic Blackbeard, hands-on exhibits about buccaneers, and a collection of nearly 500 artifacts, including the only authentic surviving pirate chest in America, dating back to the 1600s. Don't miss the Disney-produced, three-dimensional sound program that takes you below decks into a completely dark mock prison cell. ⊠*524 Front St.33040* ☎*305/292–1113* ⊕*www.piratesoul.com* ▣*$15* ⊘*Daily 9–7.*

❺ San Carlos Institute. South Florida's Cuban connection began long before Fidel Castro was born. The institute was founded in 1871 by Cuban immigrants. Now it contains a research library and museum rich with the history of Key West and 19th- and 20th-century Cuban exiles. Cuban patriot Jose Martí delivered speeches from the balcony of the auditorium, and opera star Enrico Caruso sang in the opera house, which reportedly has exceptional acoustics. It's frequently used for concerts, lectures, films, and exhibits. ⊠*516 Duval St.33040* ☎*305/294–3887* ▣*Free* ⊘*Tues.–Fri. 1:30–7, weekends 11–5.*

⓮ Simonton Street Beach. This small beach facing the gulf is a great place to watch boat traffic in the harbor. Parking, however, is difficult. There are restrooms and a boat ramp. ⊠*North end of Simonton St.* ☎*No phone* ▣*Free* ⊘*Daily 7 AM–11 PM.*

⓱ South Beach. On the Atlantic, this stretch of sand, also known as City Beach, is popular with travelers staying at nearby motels. The Natural Resources Defense Council lists it as one of Florida's beaches that often exceeds accepted levels of bacteria. Enjoy the water, but from afar perhaps. It has limited parking. ⊠*Foot of Duval St.* ☎*No phone* ▣*Free* ⊘*Daily 7 AM–11 PM.*

NEW TOWN

The Overseas Highway splits as it enters Key West, the two forks rejoining to encircle New Town, the area east of White Street to Cow Key Channel. The southern fork runs along the shore as South Roosevelt Boulevard (Route A1A) skirting Key West International Airport. Along the north shore, North Roosevelt Boulevard (U.S. 1) passes the Key West Welcome Center. Part of New Town was created with dredged fill. The island would have continued growing this way had the Army Corps of Engineers not determined in the early 1970s that it was detrimental to the nearby reef.

WHAT TO SEE

㉑ C. B. Harvey Rest Beach. This beach and park were named after Cornelius Bradford Harvey, former Key West mayor and commissioner. It has half a dozen picnic areas, dunes, and a wheelchair and bike path. ✉ *Atlantic Blvd., east side of White St. Pier* ☎ *No phone* ☞ *Free* ☉ *Daily 7* AM*–11* PM.

★ **㉓ East Martello Tower.** This Civil War citadel was *semper paratus,* or "always ready" as the U.S. Coast Guard motto says, but like most of Florida during the war it never saw a lick of action. Today it serves as a museum, with historical exhibits about the 19th and 20th centuries. Among the latter are relics of the USS *Maine,* a Cuban refugee raft, and books by famous writers—including seven Pulitzer Prize winners— who have lived in Key West. The tower, operated by the Key West Art and Historical Society, also has a collection of Stanley Papio's "junk art" sculptures and Cuban folk artist Mario Sanchez's chiseled and painted wooden carvings of historic Key West street scenes. ✉ *3501 S. Roosevelt Blvd.33040* ☎ *305/296–3913* ⊕ *www.kwahs.com* ☞ *$6* ☉ *Weekdays 10-4, weekends 9:30–4:30.*

㉒ Smathers Beach. This beach has nearly 2 mi of sand, plus restrooms, picnic areas, and volleyball courts, all of which make it popular with the Spring Break crowd. Trucks along the road rent rafts, windsurfers, and other beach "toys." Metered parking is on the street. ✉ *S. Roosevelt Blvd.* ☎ *No phone* ☞ *Free* ☉ *Daily 7* AM*–11* PM.

㉔ West Martello Tower. Within the ruins of this Civil War–era fort is the Key West Garden Club, which maintains lovely gardens of native and tropical plants. It also holds art, orchid, and flower shows in March and November and leads private garden tours in March. ✉ *Atlantic Blvd. and White St.33040* ☎ *305/294–3210* ⊕ *www.keywestgarden club.com* ☞ *Donation welcome* ☉ *Tues.–Sat. 9:30–5.*

WHERE TO EAT

Bring your appetite, a sense of daring, and a lack of preconceived notions about propriety. A meal in Key West can mean overlooking the crazies along Duval Street, watching roosters and pigeons battle for a scrap of food that may have escaped your fork, relishing the finest in what used to be the dining room of some 19th-century Victorian home, or gazing out at boats jockeying for position in the marina. And that's just the diversity of the setting. Seafood dominates local menus, but the treatment afforded that fish or crustacean can range from Cuban and New World to Asian and continental.

AMERICAN

$$ ✕**Michael's Restaurant.** White tablecloths, subdued lighting, and romantic music give Michael's the feel of an urban getaway. Garden seating reminds that you are in the Keys. Chef-owner Michael Wilson flies in prime rib, cowboy steaks, and rib eyes from Allen Brothers in Chicago, which has supplied top-ranked steak houses for more than a century. Also on the menu is a melt-in-your-mouth grouper stuffed with jumbo lump crab, veal chop stuffed with mozzarella and prosciutto and topped with a mushroom demi-glace, and a variety of fondue dishes (try the pesto pot, spiked with hot pepper and basil). The Hemingway (mojito-style) and the Third Degree (raspberry vodka and white crème de cacao) top the martini menu. ⊠ *532 Margaret St.* ☎ *305/295–1300* ⊕ *www.michaelskeywest.com* ⊟ *AE, MC, V* ⊘ *No lunch.*

¢   ✕**Lobo's Mixed Grill.** If White Castle has attained national cult status with its burgers, then the equivalent among Key West denizens might very well be Lobo's belly buster. The 7-ounce, charcoal-grilled chunk of ground chuck is thick and juicy and served with lettuce, tomato, and pickle on a toasted bun. The choice of 30 wraps (rib eye, oyster, grouper, and others) is equally popular. The menu includes salads and quesadillas, as well as a fried-shrimp-and-oyster combo. Beer and wine are also served. This outdoor eatery closes at 6, so eat early. Lobo's offers free delivery within Old Town. ⊠ *5 Key Lime Sq., east of intersection of Southard and Duval Sts.* ☎ *305/296–5303* ⊕ *www.loboskeywest. com* ⊟ *No credit cards* ⊘ *Closed Sun. Apr.–early Dec.*

CARIBBEAN

$ ✕**El Meson de Pepe's.** If you want to get a taste of the island's Cuban heritage, this is the place. Perfect for after Mallory Square sunset, you can dine alfresco or in the dining room on refined versions of Cuban classics. Begin with a mega-sized mojito while you enjoy the basket of bread and savory sauces. The expansive menu offers *tostones rellenos* (green plantains with different traditional fillings), *ceviche* (raw fish "cooked" in lemon juice), and more. Choose from Cuban specialties such as roasted pork in a cumin sauce and ropa vieja (shredded beef stew). At lunch, Cuban sandwiches and smaller versions of dinner's most popular entrées are served to an enthusiastic crowd. A salsa band performs outside at the bar during sunset celebration. ⊠ *Mallory Sq., 410 Wall St.* ☎ *305/295– 2620* ⊕ *www.elmesondepepe.com* ⊟ *AE, D, MC, V.*

$ ✕**El Siboney.** Dining at this family-style restaurant is like going to Mom's for Sunday dinner—if your mother is Cuban. The dining room is noisy, and the food is traditional cubanano. There's a well-seasoned black-bean soup, a memorable paella, and local fish served grilled, stuffed, and breaded. Dishes come with plantains, bread, and two sides. To make a good thing even better, the prices are very reasonable. ⊠ *900 Catherine St.* ☎ *305/296–4184* ⊟ *D, MC, V.*

ECLECTIC

$$$ ✕**Café Marquesa.** It's showtime in the display kitchen as Chef Susan **FodorśChoice** Ferry, who trained with Norman Van Aken at his Coral Gables restaurant, works her magic. Ferry presents eight or more entrées each night, **★** and although every dish is a sure bet, frequent guests call attention to the peppercorn-dusted seared yellowfin tuna, the ginger coconut almond–crusted hogfish, and the pan-roasted duck breast. End your meal on a sweet note with key lime napoleon with tropical fruits and berries. There's also a fine selection of wines and a choice of microbrewery beers. Adjoining the intimate Marquesa Hotel, the dining room is relaxed and elegant. ⊠*600 Fleming St.* ☎*305/292–1244* ⊕*www. marquesa.com* ▤*AE, DC, MC, V* ⊘*No lunch.*

$$$ ✕**Louie's Backyard.** Feast your eyes on a steal-your-breath-away view and beautifully presented dishes prepared by executive chef Doug Shook. Once you get over sticker shock on the seasonally changing menu (appetizers cost around $14 to $16; entrées hover around the $35 mark), settle in and enjoy dishes like oven-roasted salmon on a crisp potato cake, grilled tuna with Japanese noodles, or grilled chili-rubbed pork chop with smoked applesauce. Louie's key lime pie has a gingersnap crust and is served with a raspberry coulis. Come for lunch if you're on a budget; the menu is less expensive (but still expect to pay about $17 for your entrée) and the view is just as fantastic. For night owls, the Afterdeck Bar serves cocktails on the water until the wee hours. ⊠*700 Waddell Ave.* ☎*305/294–1061* ⊕*www.louiesbackyard. com* ⌖*Reservations essential* ▤ *MC, V.*

★ **$$$** ✕**Pisces.** Don't be dismayed when you see the sign for Pisces on the Café des Artistes building: Chef Andrew Berman and staff are still there. They've changed the name, updated the menu, and gone contemporary with a stylish granite bar and sparkling mirrors. Some old favorites remain on the menu, such as "lobster tango mango," flambéed in cognac and served with a saffron-basil butter sauce and sliced mangoes. Other dishes include veal chops with wild mushrooms and champagne-braised black grouper. Menu names sounded better when they were in French, but the taste lost nothing in the translation. ⊠*1007 Simonton St.* ☎*305/294–7100* ⊕*www.pisceskeywest.com* ▤*AE, MC, V* ⊘*No lunch.*

$$ ✕**915 Duval.** Twinkling lights draped along the upper and lower porches of this century-old Victorian mansion add an touch. If you like to sample and sip, you'll appreciate the variety of smaller plate selections and wines by the glass. Amply portioned tapas include adventurous combos like the bacon-wrapped dates stuffed with sweet garlic and soy citrus, clams, and chorizo, Thai-style beef salad rolls, and the signature "tuna dome," with fresh crab, lemon-miso dressing, and an ahi tuna sashimi wrapping. There are also larger plates if you're craving something like grilled double pork chops or steak frites. Dine outdoors and people-watch along upper Duval, or sit at a table inside while listening to light jazz. ⊠*915 Duval St.* ☎*305/296–0669* ⊕*www.915duval.com* ▤*AE, MC, V* ⊘*No lunch.*

$$ ✕**Alice's Key West Restaurant.** A rather plain storefront gives way to

Fodor'sChoice a warm and cozy dining room, where chef-owner Alice Weingarten

★ serves her trademark "fusion confusion" fare. Color, zing, and spice are her main ingredients. The spring rolls, for example, are filled with blackened shrimp, fire-roasted corn, and goat cheese. The Brazilian-style pan-seared skirt steak is served with garlicky chimichurri sauce and green-chili and Manchego cheese mashed potatoes, and the Greek-style shrimp is accompanied by kalamata olive-studded mashed potatoes. Save room for her extra special key lime pie made with lime curd and a chocolate lined crust. The place is open for breakfast, too. Eggs, home fries, and toast go for as little as $4. ✉*1114 Duval St.,* ☎*305/292–5733* ⊕*www.aliceskeywest.com* ☰*AE, D, MC, V.*

★ **$$** ✗**Blue Heaven.** The outdoor dining area here is often referred to as "the quintessential Keys experience," and it's hard to argue. There's much to like about this historic restaurant where Hemingway refereed boxing matches and customers cheered for cockfights. Although these events are no more, the free-roaming chickens and cats add that "what-a-hoot" factor. Nightly specials include black-bean soup, seared sea scallops, and sautéed yellowtail snapper in citrus beurre-blanc sauce. Desserts and breads are baked on the premises; the banana bread is a hit during "breakfast with the roosters," and the lobster benedict with key-lime hollandaise is divine. ■**TIP➔Dinner can be crowded and service spotty; your best bet is to come for breakfast or lunch.** ✉*729 Thomas St.* ☎*305/296–8666* ⊕*www.blueheavenkw.com* ⚑*Reservations not accepted* ☰*AE, D, MC, V* ⊘*Closed Labor Day–mid-Oct.*

$$ ✗**Tavern N Town.** Chef Norman Van Aken returned to Key West after making his name synonymous with Miami-style cuisine. Once head chef at Louie's Backyard, he has brought his highly acclaimed brand of new world cuisine to the Beachside Resort. This handsome dual restaurant will ultimately serve an intimate space for a set menu that he designs nightly in back. For now, the only part that is open is the Tavern, a warm room where a friendly bar provides ambience and open kitchen adds lovely aromas from the wood-fired oven. The menu focuses on simply prepared fish and meat dishes, such as pork with smoky plantain cream. Nightly scheduled specials offer affordable favorites such as pasta carbonara. The key lime pie gets extra tang from a pomegranate sauce. The restaurant is also open for breakfast and lunch. ✉*Beachside Resort, 3841 N. Roosevelt Blvd.* ☎*305/296–8100 or 800/546–0885* ⊕*www.beachsidekeywest.com* ⚑*Reservations essential* ☰*AE, D, DC, MC, V.*

★ **$** ✗**The Cafe, A Mostly Vegetarian Place.** You don't have to be a vegetarian to love this New Age café. Local favorites include homemade soup, veggie burgers (order them with a side of sweet-potato fries), portobello mushroom salad, and grilled Gorgonzola pizza. For bigger appetites there are offerings like the Szechuan-style vegetable stir-fry. On Sunday there's a new brunch menu. ✉*509 Southard St.* ☎*305/296–5515* ☰*MC, V.*

FRENCH

★ **$$$** ✗**Café Solé.** Welcome to the self-described "home of the hog snapper." The confusing slogan refers to an award-winning dish of deliciously roasted local fish seasoned with shrimp and red peppers. This little piece of France is concealed behind a high wall and a gate in a residential neighborhood. Inside, Chef John Correa shows culinary wizardry that extends well beyond the hog. Marrying his French training with local ingredients, he creates delicious takes on classics, including Portobello mushroom soup, mangrove snapper with champagne-pesto sauce, and some of the best bouillabaisse that you'll find outside of Marseilles. From the land, there is filet mignon with a wild-mushroom demi-glace. If you can't decide, a three-course tasting dinner costs $27. ✉*1029 Southard St.* ☎*305/294–0230* ⊕*www.cafesole.com* ▤*AE, D, DC, MC, V.*

IRISH

$ ✗**Finnegan's Wake Irish Pub and Eatery.** "Come for the beer. Stay for the food. Leave with the staff," is the slogan of this popular pub. The pictures of Beckett, Shaw, Yeats, and Wilde on the walls and the creaky wood floors underfoot exude Irish country warmth. The certified Angus beef is a bit pricey ($30 for an 18-ounce rib eye), but most of the other dishes are bargains. Traditional fare includes bangers and mash, chicken potpie, and colcannon—rich mashed potatoes with scallions, sauerkraut, and melted white cheddar cheese. Bread pudding soaked with a honey-whiskey sauce is a true treat. There's live music on weekends and daily happy hours from 4 to 7 and midnight to 2 featuring nearly 30 beers on tap. ✉*320 Grinnell St.* ☎*305/293–0222* ▤*AE, D, MC, V.*

ITALIAN

★ $ ✗**Mangia Mangia.** This longtime favorite serves large portions of homemade pastas that can be matched with any of the homemade sauces. Tables are arranged in a brick garden hung with twinkling lights and in a nicely dressed-up dining room in an old house. Everything that comes out of the open kitchen is outstanding, including the *bollito misto di mare* (fresh seafood sautéed with garlic, shallots, and white wine) or the memorable spaghettini "schmappellini," thin pasta with asparagus, tomatoes, pine nuts, and Parmesan. The wine list—with more than 350 offerings—includes old and rare vintages, but also has a good under-$20 selection. ✉*900 Southard St.* ☎*305/294–2469* ⊕*www.mangia-mangia.com* ▤*AE, D, MC, V* ⊗*No lunch.*

★ $ ✗**Salute Ristorante Sul Mare.** This colorful restaurant sits on Higgs Beach, giving it one of the island's best lunch views (and a bit of sand and salt spray on a windy day). The dinner menu includes inventive homemade pasta dishes like cappellini with calamari, capers, olives, and tomatoes, or linguine with shrimp, tomatoes, garlic, and basil. Start with a salad of mixed greens, feta, artichoke hearts, olives, and roasted red pepper or the bean soup with grilled bread. At lunch there are bruschetta, panini, and clams marinara, as well as a fresh-fish sandwich. ✉*1000 Atlantic Blvd., Higgs Beach* ☎*305/292–1117* ▤*AE, MC, V* ⊗*No lunch Sun.*

JAPANESE

$$ ✗**Ambrosia.** Ask any savvy local where to get the best sushi on the island and you'll undoubtedly be pointed to this tiny wood-and-tatami paneled dining room tucked away in a quiet neighborhood. Grab a seat at the sushi bar and watch owner and head sushi chef Masa prepare an impressive array of super-fresh sashimi delicacies. You can't go wrong with the ambrosia special, a sampler of five kinds of sashimi. There's an assortment of lightly fried tempura and teriyaki dishes and a killer bento box at lunch. Enjoy it all with a cup of sake or a cold glass of Sapporo beer. ✉*Santa Maria Resort,1401 Simonton St.* ☎*305/293–0304* ▤*AE, MC, V.*

8

SEAFOOD

$ ✗Half Shell Raw Bar. Smack-dab on the docks, this legendary institution gets its name from the oysters, clams, and peel 'n' eat shrimp that are departure point for its seafood-based diet. It's not clever recipes or fine dining (or even air-conditioning) that packs 'em in; it's fried fish, po'boy sandwiches, and seafood combos. For a break from the deep fryer, try the fresh and light conch ceviche, "cooked" with lime juice. The potato salad is flavored with dill, and the "Pama Rita" is a new twist in Margaritaville. ⊠Lands End Village at Historic Seaport, 231 Margaret St., ☎305/294–7496 ⊕www.halfshellrawbar.com ▭AE, MC, V.

★ $ ✗Seven Fish. A local hot spot, this off-the-beaten-track eatery is good for an eclectic mix of dishes like tropical shrimp salsa, wild-mushroom quesadilla, seafood marinara, and sometimes even an old-fashioned meat loaf with real mashed potatoes. Those in the know arrive early to snag one of the 12 or so tables clustered in the bare-bones dining room. ⊠632 Olivia St. ☎305/296–2777 ⊕www.7fish.com ▭AE, MC, V ⊘Closed Tues. No lunch.

$ ✗Turtle Kraals. Named for the kraals, or corrals, where sea turtles were once kept until they went to the cannery, this place calls to mind the island's history. Today, much smaller box turtles provide live entertainment at 6 on Monday and Friday, when folks cheer on contestants in a turtle race. The menu offers an assortment of marine cuisine that includes seared jerk tuna, seafood enchiladas, and mango crab cakes. The open-walled restaurant overlooks the marina at the Historic Seaport. ⊠231 Margaret St. ☎305/294–2640 ⊕www.turtlekraals.com ▭AE, MC, V.

WHERE TO STAY

Historic cottages, restored century-old Conch houses, and large resorts are among the offerings in Key West, the majority charging between $100 and $300 a night. In high season, December through March, you'll be hard pressed to find a decent room for less than $200, and most places raise prices considerably during holidays. Many guesthouses and inns do not welcome children under 16, and most do not permit smoking indoors. Most tariffs include an expanded continental breakfast and, often, afternoon wine or snack.

GUESTHOUSES

★ $$$$ ⊡Ambrosia Key West. If you desire personal attention, a casual atmosphere, and a dollop of style, stay at these twin inns spread out on nearly 2 acres. Ambrosia is more intimate, with themed rooms such as The Treetop, Sailfish Suites, and Havana Cabana. Ambrosia Too is a delightful art-filled hideaway. Rooms and suites have original work by local artists, wicker or wood furniture, and spacious bathrooms. Each has a private entrance and deck, patio, or porch. Poolside continental breakfast is included, and children are welcome. Pros: Spacious rooms, poolside breakfast, friendly staff. Cons: On-street parking can be tough to come by. ⊠615, 618, 622 Fleming St. ☎305/296–9838 or 800/535–9838 ⊕www.ambrosiakeywest.com ⏎22 rooms, 3 town houses, 1 cottage, 6 suites ⌂In-room: kitchen (some), refrig-

erator. In-hotel: 3 pools, bicycles, no elevator, concierge, public Wi-Fi, parking (no fee), some pets allowed (fee), no-smoking rooms ☰AE, D, MC, V ⭕CP.

$$$$

Fodor'sChoice

★

The Gardens Hotel. Built in 1875, this gloriously shaded property covers a third of a city block in Old Town. Peggy Mills, who bought it as a private estate in 1931, coiffed it with orchids, ponytail palms, and black bamboo. She added walks, fountains, and *tinajones* (earthen pots) imported from Cuba. After her death in 1971, the property was turned into a romantic inn that offers several types of accommodations, from standard rooms with garden and courtyard views to a two-bedroom carriage house suite. Decorated with Bahamian plantation-style furnishings, the quiet and elegant rooms are a luxurious tropical retreat. Most have private verandas. Rates include continental breakfast. **Pros:** Luxurious bathrooms, secluded garden seating, free phone calls. **Cons:** Hard to get reservations. ✉*526 Angela St.* ☎*305/294–2661 or 800/526–2664* ⊕*www.gardenshotel.com* ↪*17 rooms* ⚅*In-room: refrigerator, Wi-Fi. In-hotel: bar, pool, spa, no elevator, concierge, public Wi-Fi, parking (no fee), no kids under 16, no-smoking rooms* ☰AE, D, MC, V ⭕CP.

$$$-$$$$

Azul Key West. The ultramodern—nearly minimalistic—redo of this classic Queen Anne mansion is a break from the sensory overload of Key West's other abundant Victorian guesthouses. The adults-only boutique hotel, 3½ blocks from Duval Street, combines original trim and shiny wood floors with sleek furnishings, including a curved frosted-glass-and chrome check-in desk, leather loungers, and a state-of-the-art sound system. Spacious, serene rooms, some with private verandas, have leather headboards, flat-screen TVs, and remote-controlled fans and lights. **Pros:** Lovely building, marble-floored baths, luxurious linens. **Cons:** On a busy street, weekend surcharge. ✉*907 Truman Ave.* ☎*305/296–5152 or 888/253–2985* ⊕*www.azulhotels. us* ↪*10 rooms, 1 suite* ⚅*In-room: Wi-Fi. In-hotel: pool, bicycles, no elevator, public Wi-Fi, no kids under 21, no-smoking rooms* ☰AE, D, MC, V ⭕CP.

★ $$$-$$$$

Mermaid & the Alligator. An enchanting combination of flora and fauna makes this 1904 Victorian house a welcoming retreat. The property is bathed in palms, banyans, birds of paradise, and poincianas, with cages of colorful, live parrots and swarms of butterflies adding tropical punch. Rooms are Caribbean colonial–inspired, with wood-slat floors, elegant trim, and French doors. The color scheme—key lime, cantaloupe, and other rich colors—couldn't be more evocative of the Keys. Some downstairs rooms open onto the deck, pool, and gardens designed by one of the resident owners, a landscape designer. Upstairs rooms overlook the gardens. An extensive breakfast is served poolside. **Pros:** Inviting hot tub, massage pavilion, island getaway feel. **Cons:** Minimum stay required (length depends on season), dark public areas, cheesy plastic lawn chairs. ✉*729 Truman Ave.* ☎*305/294–1894 or 800/773–1894* ⊕*www.kwmermaid.com* ↪*9 rooms* ⚅*In-room: no phone, no TV, Wi-Fi. In-hotel: pool, no elevator, public Internet, public Wi-Fi, no kids under 16, no-smoking rooms* ☰AE, MC, V ⭕CP.

8

$$$ 🏨 **Courtney's Place.** If you like kids, cats, and dogs, you'll feel right at home in this collection of accommodations ranging from cigar-maker cottages to shotgun houses. The interiors are equally varied in coloring and furnishings, but all rooms have at least a refrigerator, microwave, and coffeepot, if not a full kitchen. The family-owned property is tucked into a residential neighborhood, though within easy walking distance of Duval Street. All rooms are not created equal here; the tiny Room 5 is tucked into an attic space. **Pros:** Near Duval Street, fairly priced. **Cons:** Small parking lot, dated bed linens. ✉*720 Whitemarsh La.* ☎*305/294–3480 or 800/869–4639* 📠*305/294–7019* ⊕*www.courtneysplacekeywest.com* ⌑*6 rooms, 2 suites, 2 efficiencies, 8 cottages* ⚷*In-room: kitchen (some), refrigerator, Wi-Fi. In-hotel: pool, bicycles, no elevator, concierge, laundry facilities, parking (no fee), some pets allowed (fee), no-smoking rooms* ▤*AE, MC, V* ⧖*CP.*

$$$ 🏨 **Heron House Court.** Formerly called Fleur de Key Guesthouse, this circa 1900 inn provides everyone with a warm welcome. Its Conch-style architecture harks back to the property's origins as a boarding-house and cigar-makers' cottages. Standard rooms in the main house are small, so opt for a superior room, slightly more expensive but a great deal larger. Airy, bright rooms have tiled floors and a complementary mix of antiques and reproductions, and are tastefully decorated in tropical colors. The guest rooms are nicer than the public areas, which include a pool and weathered deck. **Pros:** Complimentary weekend wine hours, fluffy bathrobes. **Cons:** Faces noisy Eaton Street, owner's suite smells musty. ✉*412 Frances St.* ☎*305/296–4719 or 888/265–2395* ⊕*www.heronhousecourt.com* ⌑*2 suites, 14 rooms* ⚷*In-room: refrigerator. In-hotel: pool, no elevator, concierge, public Wi-Fi, no kids under 21, no-smoking rooms* ▤*AE, D, MC, V* ⧖*CP.*

$$$ 🏨 **Island City House Hotel.** An oasis with brick walkways, tropical plants, and a canopy of palms sets this convivial guesthouse apart from the pack. The vintage-1880s Island City House has wraparound verandas, pine floors, and charm to spare. Arch House, a former carriage house, has a dramatic entry that opens into a lush courtyard. Although all suites front on busy Eaton Street, only Nos. 5 and 6 face it. A reconstructed cigar factory has become the poolside Cigar House, with spacious rooms, porches, decks, and plantation-style teak and wicker furnishings. The private tropical garden wraps around a spacious pool area. Children are welcome—a rarity in Old Town guesthouses. **Pros:** Private gardens, knowledgeable staff. **Cons:** Spotty Wi-Fi service, no front desk staff at night, some rooms are small. ✉*411 William St.* ☎*305/294–5702 or 800/634–8230* ⊕*www.islandcityhouse.com* ⌑*24 suites* ⚷*In-room: kitchen (some), Wi-Fi (some). In-hotel: pool, bicycles, no elevator, laundry facilities, concierge, public Wi-Fi, no-smoking rooms* ▤*AE, DC, MC, V* ⧖*CP.*

$$$ 🏨 **Key Lime Inn.** This 1854 Grand Bahama–style house on the National Register of Historic Places succeeds by offering amiable service, a great location, and simple rooms with natural-wood furnishings. The cluster of pastel-painted cottages, surrounded by white picket fences, has a residential feel, a bit like a beach colony without the beach, or the backlot of a movie set. The least-expensive Cabana rooms, some with patios,

surround the pool. The Garden Cottages have one room; some include a porch or balcony. Some rooms in the historic Maloney House have a porch or patio. **Pros:** Free parking, some rooms have private patios. **Cons:** Standard rooms are pricey, pool faces a busy street, mulch-covered paths. ✉725 Truman Ave. ☎305/294–5229 or 800/549–4430 ⊕www.keylimeinn.com ➷37 rooms ♨In-room: safe, refrigerator (some), dial-up. In-hotel: pool, no elevator, public Wi-Fi, parking (no fee), no-smoking rooms ▤AE, D, MC, V ⦵CP.

$$$ ⛪**Pearl's Rainbow.** This guesthouse, which caters to lesbians and gay-friendly women, occupies an 1886 cigar factory. It's home to Pearl's Patio, a women-only bar. The Strand restaurant serves breakfast, lunch, and evening snacks. Rooms range from basic to deluxe, and are comfortable, clean, and well appointed. **Pros:** Full breakfast, plenty of privacy. **Cons:** No men allowed, bar attracts late-night partiers. ✉525 United St., 33040 ☎305/292–1450 or 800/749–6696 ⊕www.pearlsrainbow.com ➷32 rooms, 6 suites ♨In-room: refrigerator, kitchen (some), Wi-Fi. In-hotel: restaurant, bar, pools, Internet, public Wi-Fi ▤AE, D, MC, V ⦵BP.

$$-$$$ ⛪**Speakeasy Inn.** During Prohibition, Raul Vasquez made this place popular by smuggling in liquor from Cuba. Today the booze is legal, and there's even a daily happy hour. The Speakeasy Inn is still well known, only now its reputation is for having reasonably priced rooms within walking distance of the beach. Accommodations have bright white walls offset by bursts of color in rugs, pillows, and seat cushions. Queen-size beds and tables are fashioned from salvaged pine. The rooms are basic, but some have nice touches like claw-foot tubs. Room 1 has a deck that's good for people-watching. **Pros:** Good location, reasonable rates, high-quality cigars at the attached cigar store. **Cons:** No pool, basic decor. ✉1117 Duval St. ☎305/296–2680 or 800/217–4884 ⊕www.speakeasyinn.com ➷4 suites, 4 studios ♨In-room: refrigerator, Wi-Fi. In-hotel: bicycles, no elevator, public Internet, public Wi-Fi, no-smoking rooms ▤AE, D, MC, V ⦵CP.

★ $-$$$ ⛪**Popular House/Key West Bed & Breakfast.** Local art—large, splashy canvases, a mural in the style of Gauguin—decorate the walls at this lodging. Handmade textiles (owner Jody Carlson is a talented weaver) drape chairs, couches, and beds. You'll find both inexpensive rooms with shared bath and luxury rooms with all the amenities, as the owners reason that budget travelers deserve the same good style (and lavish tropical continental breakfast) as their well-heeled counterparts. Less-expensive rooms burst with bright colors; the hand-painted dressers add a whimsical flourish. Balconies on the second-floor rooms overlook the gardens. Spacious (and more expensive) third-floor rooms are decorated with a paler palette and original furniture. **Pros:** Feels like an art gallery, tiled outdoor shower, hot tub and sauna area is a welcome hangout. **Cons:** Some rooms are small. ✉415 William St. ☎305/296–7274 or 800/438–6155 ⊕www.keywestbandb.com ➷10 rooms, 6 with bath ♨In-room: no phone, no TV, Wi-Fi (some). In-hotel: pool, bicycles, no elevator, public Internet, public Wi-Fi, no kids under 18, no-smoking rooms ▤AE, D, DC, MC, V ⦵CP.

8

★ $$ ⊡ **Eden House.** From the vintage metal rockers on the streetside porch to the old neon hotel sign in the lobby, this 1920s rambling Key West mainstay hotel is high on character, low on gloss. You'll get a taste of authentic Old Key West, without sacrificing convenience, comfort, or budget. Rooms come in all shapes and sizes, from shared-bath basic to large apartments with full kitchens and private decks or porches. The spacious outdoor area is shaded by towering palms. Grab a book and plop in a hammock in the outdoor library, tucked into a sun-dappled corner with a gurgling waterfall and potted bonsai. **Pros:** Sunny garden, hot tub is actually hot, daily happy hour around the pool. **Cons:** Cutesy signage is overdone. ⊠*1015 Fleming St.* ☎*305/296–6868 or 800/533–5397* ⊕*www.edenhouse.com* ⇆*36 rooms, 8 suites.* ⌂*In-room: kitchen (some), refrigerator (some). In-hotel: restaurant, pool, bicycles, no elevator, public Internet, public Wi-Fi, parking (no fee), no-smoking rooms* ▤*MC, V.*

★ $$ ⊡ **Merlin Guesthouse.** Key West guesthouses don't usually welcome families, but this laid-back jumble of rooms and suites is an exception. If you can live with a few flaws, you'll grab a bargain. Accommodations in the 1930s Simonton House, with four-poster beds, are most suitable for couples. The one- and two-bedroom suites are popular with families. Bright, roomy cottages are perfect if you want a bit more privacy. Get a room in the back if you are bothered by noise. The leafy courtyard and pool area are where guests hang out day and night. **Pros:** Good location near Duval Street, good rates. **Cons:** Neighbor noise, common areas are dated. ⊠*811 Simonton St.* ☎*305/296–3336 or 800/642–4753* ⊕*www.merlinguesthouse.com* ⇆*10 rooms, 6 suites, 4 cottages* ⌂*In-room: no phone, safe, kitchen (some), refrigerator (some), Wi-Fi. In-hotel: pool, no elevator, public Internet, public Wi-Fi, no-smoking rooms* ▤*AE, D, MC, V* ⦿*CP.*

$–$$ ⊡ **Angelina Guest House.** The high rollers and ladies of the night were chased away long ago, but this charming guesthouse revels in its past as a gambling hall and bordello. In the heart of Old Town Key West, it's a home away from home that offers simple, clean, attractively priced accommodations. Accommodations range from small rooms sharing a bath to spacious rooms with king beds and sleeper sofas. Built in the 1920s, this yellow-and-white clapboard building has second-floor porches, gabled roofs, and a white picket fence. The current owners prettied the rooms with flower-print curtains and linens and added homemade cinnamon rolls, which receive rave reviews in the guest book, to the breakfast bar. A lagoon-style pool, fountain, and old-brick walkways accent a lovely garden. **Pros:** Good value, nice garden, friendly staff. **Cons:** Thin walls, basic rooms, shared balcony. ⊠*302 Angela St.* ☎*305/294–4480 or 888/303–4480* ⊕*www.angelinaguesthouse.com* ⇆*13 rooms* ⌂*In-room: no phone, refrigerator (some), no TV. In-hotel: pool, bicycles, no elevator, no kids under 18, no-smoking rooms* ▤*D, MC, V* ⦿*CP.*

HOTELS

$$ ⊡ **Beachside Resort.** The new kid on the block, this hotel vies for convention business with the biggest ballroom in Key West. It also appeals to families with its spacious condo units decorated with impeccable

good taste. Designer furnishings reflect the resort's waterfront location. Frette linens on the beds, real china in the kitchens, and marble hot tubs add touches of luxury. Rooms have spiral staircases down to the gardens and up to the rooftop sundecks. Families enjoy the beach and pool area, while the resort's Norman Van Aken restaurant is a serious perk for the connoisseur crowd. **Pros:** Private beach, shuttle to downtown and the airport, poolside cabanas. **Cons:** Packed with conventions, can't walk to Old Town, cookie-cutter facade. ✉*3841 N. Roosevelt Blvd., New Town* ☎*305/296–8100 or 800/546–0885* ⊕*www.beachsidekeywest.com* ➥*93 rooms, 129 1- to 3-bedroom suites* ⚃*In room: kitchen, Ethernet, Wi-Fi. In hotel: 3 restaurants, room service, bars, pool, gym, concierge, public Wi-Fi, airport shuttle, parking (fee), no-smoking rooms* ▭*AE, D, DC, MC, V.*

★ ⓒ $$$$ 🏨 **Casa Marina Resort.** At any moment, you expect the landed gentry to walk across the oceanfront lawn, just as they did when this 13-acre resort was built back in the 1920s. Set on a private beach, it has the same richly appointed lobby with beamed ceilings, polished pine floor, and original art. Guest rooms are stylishly decorated with armoires and wicker chairs that add a lot of warmth. Fluffy bathrobes and luxurious designer toiletries make it feel like boutique hotel. Two-bedroom loft suites with balconies face the ocean. The main building's ground-floor lanai rooms open onto the lawn, and the pools have a nice view of the Atlantic. **Pros:** The area's nicest resort beach, historic setting, away from the crowds. **Cons:** Long walk to Old Town, showing signs of age. ✉*1500 Reynolds St.* ☎*305/296–3535 or 866/397–6342* ⊕*www.casamarinaresort.com* ➥*239 rooms, 72 suites* ⚃*In-room: safe, dial-up, Wi-Fi. In-hotel: restaurant, room service, bars, tennis courts, pools, gym, spa, beachfront, diving, water sports, bicycles, children's programs (ages 4–12), laundry service, concierge, public Internet, public Wi-Fi, airport shuttle, no-smoking rooms* ▭*AE, D, DC, MC, V.*

$$$$ 🏨 **Hyatt Key West Resort & Spa.** With its own beach, the Hyatt Key West is one of few resorts where you can walk in the sand, then along the streets of Old Town. A top-to-bottom renovation in 2007 transformed this hotel into a tropical escape with plenty of panache. It offers a wide range of water sports, fine dining in two restaurants, and fitness amenities—all with an eye toward keeping green. Rooms are bright and airy, with walk-in showers with rain showerheads, and balconies that overlook the gulf. They pamper you with little extras such as down comforters and fluffy robes. **Pros:** Away from the bustle of Old Town, on the beach, plenty of activities. **Cons:** Beach is small, charge for wireless connections, chain-hotel feel. ✉*601 Front St.,* ☎*305/809–1234* ⊕*www.keywest.hyatt.com* ➥*118 rooms* ⚃*In-room: safe, dial-up, Wi-Fi. In-hotel: 2 restaurants, room service, bars, pool, gym, spa, beachfront, diving, water sports, laundry service, concierge, public Wi-Fi, parking (fee), no-smoking rooms* ▭*AE, D, DC, MC, V.*

$$$$ 🏨 **Marquesa Hotel.** In a town that prides itself on its laid-back luxury,
Fodor's Choice this complex of four restored 1884 houses stands out. Guests—typically
★ shoeless in Marquesa robes—relax among richly landscaped pools, rock waterfalls, and peaceful gardens. Elegant rooms surround a courtyard and have antique and reproduction furnishings, creamy-white and aqua

8

fabrics, and marble baths. The lobby resembles a Victorian parlor, with Audubon prints, vases overflowing with flowers, and photos of early Key West. The clientele is well traveled and affluent 40- to 70-year-olds, mostly straight, but the hotel is very gay-friendly. **Pros:** Elegant setting, romantic atmosphere, deluxe baths. **Cons:** Street-facing rooms can be noisy, expensive rates. ⊠*600 Fleming St.* ☎*305/292–1919 or 800/869–4631* ⊕*www.marquesa.com* ⇔*27 rooms* ☾*In-room: safe, refrigerator, dial-up, Wi-Fi. In-hotel: restaurant, room service, pools, no elevator, laundry service, concierge, public Wi-Fi, no kids under 14, no-smoking rooms* ▤*AE, DC, MC, V.*

★ $$$$ ▦ **Ocean Key Resort.** A pool and lively open-air bar and restaurant sit on Sunset Pier, a perfect place to watch the sun sink into the horizon. Toast the day's end from private balconies that extend from spacious rooms that are both stylish and homey. High ceilings, hand-painted furnishings, sleigh beds, wooden chests, and lavish whirlpool tubs create a personally designed look. This is a full-service resort, with excellent amenities like a great on-site spa. **Pros:** Well-trained staff, lively pool scene, best spa on the island. **Cons:** Confusing layout, too bustling for some. ⊠*Zero Duval St.* ☎*305/296–7701 or 800/328–9815* ⊕*www. oceankey.com* ⇔*75 rooms, 25 suites* ☾*In-room: kitchen (some), refrigerator, dial-up, Wi-Fi. In-hotel: 2 restaurants, room service, bars, pool, spa, diving, water sports, bicycles, laundry service, concierge, public Wi-Fi, parking (fee), some pets allowed, no-smoking rooms* ▤*AE, D, DC, MC, V.*

★ $$$$ ▦ **Pier House Resort & Caribbean Spa.** The staff here goes out of its way to pamper you, and the location—on a quiet stretch of beach at the foot of Duval—is ideal as a buffer from, and gateway to, the action. It's a sprawling complex of weathered gray buildings, including an original Conch house. The courtyard is dotted with tall coconut palms and hibiscus blossoms, and rooms are cozy and colorful, with a water, pool, or garden view. In 2008 the resort opened six top-of-the-line suites extending over the water with sunset views. The rest of the rooms were completely redecorated. Rooms nearest the public areas can be noisy. **Pros:** Beautiful beach, good location, nice spa. **Cons:** Lots of conventions, cookie-cutter feel, poolside rooms are small. ⊠*1 Duval St.* ☎*305/296–4600 or 800/723–2791* ⊕*www.pierhouse.com* ⇔*113 rooms, 29 suites* ☾*In-room: refrigerator, VCR (some), dial-up, Wi-Fi. In-hotel: 2 restaurants, room service, bars, pool, gym, spa, beachfront, bicycles, laundry service, concierge, public Wi-Fi, no-smoking rooms* ▤*AE, D, DC, MC, V.*

★ $$$$ ▦ **Simonton Court.** A small world all its own, this lodging makes you feel deliciously sequestered from Key West's crasser side, but close enough to get there on foot. The "basic" rooms are in an old cigar factory, each with its own unique decor. There's also a restored shotgun house and cottages. But top of the line are the units occupying a Victorian home and the town house facing the property's pool and brick-paved breakfast courtyard. **Pros:** Lots of privacy, well-appointed accommodations, friendly staff. **Cons:** Minimum stays required in high season. ⊠*320 Simonton St., 33040* ☎*305/294–6386 or 800/944–2687* ⊕*www. simontoncourt.com* ⇔*14 rooms, 12 suites* ☾*In room: safe, kitchen* *(some), refrigerator. In-hotel: pools, no kids under age 18, no-smoking rooms* ⊟ *D, DC, MC, V* |◎|CP.

★ $$$$ ⊞**Sunset Key.** This private island retreat feels completely cut off from the world, yet you're just minutes away from the action. Board a 10-minute launch to 27-acre Sunset Key, where you'll find sandy beaches, swaying palms, flowering gardens, and a delicious sense of privacy. A favorite of yacht owners, the hotel has a 40-slip marina. The comforts are first-class at the cluster of one-, two-, and three-bedroom cottages at the water's edge. Baked goods, freshly squeezed juice, and a newspaper are delivered each morning. Each of the accommodations has a kitchen, but you can use the grocery shopping service or hire a private chef (both for a fee, of course). You can use all the facilities at the Westin Key West Resort in Old Town. But be warned that you may never want to leave Sunset Key and its great restaurants, pretty pool, and very civilized beach complete with attendants and cabanas. **Pros:** Peace and quiet, roomy verandas, free 24-hour shuttle. **Cons:** Luxury doesn't come cheap. ⊠*245 Front St.* ☎*305/292–5300 or 888/477–7786* ⊕*www.sunsetkeyisland.com* ⟋*37 cottages* ⑇*In-room: safe, kitchen, DVD, VCR, dial-up. In-hotel: restaurant, bars, room service, tennis courts, pool, gym, beachfront, laundry facilities, laundry service, concierge, public Internet, parking (fee), no-smoking rooms* ⊟*AE, D, DC, MC, V* |◎|CP.

★ $$–$$$ ⊞**Southernmost Hotel & Resorts.** This hotel offers resort-style accommodations at motel prices. Its location on the quiet end of Duval means you don't have to deal with the hustle and bustle of downtown unless you want to (it's within a 20-minute walk). Cookie-cutter rooms are spacious, bright, and airy, and have cottage-style furnishings and the required tropical color schemes. Grab a cold drink from the Tiki Hut bar and join the crowd around the pool, or venture across the street to the beach. Looking for something more upscale and intimate? **Pros:** Pool attracts a lively crowd, access to nearby properties, free parking. **Cons:** Public beach is small. ⊠*1319 Duval St.* ☎*305/296–6577 or 800/354–4455* ⊟*305/294–8272* ⊕*www.southernmostresorts.com* ⟋*127 rooms* ⑇*In-room: safe, refrigerator, dial-up, Wi-Fi (some). In-hotel: bar, pool, beachfront, laundry facilities, public Wi-Fi, parking (no fee), no-smoking rooms* ⊟*AE, D, DC, MC, V* |◎|CP.

NIGHTLIFE

Rest up: Much of what happens in Key West does so after dark. Open your mind and have a stroll. Scruffy street performers strum next to dogs in sunglasses. Characters wearing parrots or iguanas try to sell you your photo with their pet. Brawls tumble out the doors of Sloppy Joe's. Drag queens strut across stages in Joan Rivers garb. Tattooed men lick whipped cream off of women's body parts. And margaritas flow like a Jimmy Buffett tune.

BARS & LOUNGES

No matter your mood, **Durty Harry's** (⊠*208 Duval St. 33040* ☎*305/296–4890*) can fill the bill. The mega-size entertainment complex has live music in a variety of indoor-outdoor bars including Rick's Dance Club Wine & Martini Bar and the tiny Red Garter strip club. Belly up to the bar for a cold mug of the signature Hog's Breath Lager at the infamous **Hog's Breath Saloon** (⊠*400 Front St. 33040* ☎*305/296–4222* ⊕*www.hogsbreath.com*), a must-stop on the Key West bar crawl. Live bands play daily 1 PM –2 AM. **Capt. Tony's Saloon** (⊠*428 Greene St. 33040* ☎*305/294–1838*) was the original Sloppy Joe's in the mid-1930s, when Hemingway was a regular. Later, a young Jimmy Buffett sang here and made this watering hole famous in his song "Last Mango in Paris." Bands play nightly. Pause for a libation at the open-air **Green Parrot Bar** (⊠*601 Whitehead St., at Southard St.* ☎*305/294–6133*). Built in 1890, the bar is said to be Key West's oldest. The sometimes-rowdy saloon has locals outnumbering out-of-towners, especially on weekends when bands play. A youngish, touristy crowd, sprinkled with aging Parrot Heads, frequents **Margaritaville Café** (⊠*500 Duval St.* ☎*305/292–1435*), owned by former Key West resident and recording star Jimmy Buffett, who has been known to perform here. The drink of choice is, of course, a margarita. There's live music nightly, as well as lunch and dinner. Nightlife at the **Pier House** (⊠*1 Duval St.* ☎*305/296–4600 or 800/723–2791*) begins with a steel-drum band to celebrate the sunset on the beach, then moves indoors to the piano bar for live jazz. The **Schooner Wharf Bar** (⊠*202 William St.* ☎*305/292–3302*), an open-air waterfront bar and grill in the historic seaport district, retains its funky Key West charm. Its margarita ranks among Key West's best. There's more history and good times at **Sloppy Joe's** (⊠*201 Duval St.* ☎*305/294–5717*), the successor to a famous 1937 speakeasy named for its founder, Captain Joe Russell. Decorated with Hemingway memorabilia and marine flags, the bar is popular with travelers and is full and noisy all the time. A Sloppy Joe's T-shirt is a de rigueur Key West souvenir, and the gift shop sells them like crazy. The **Top Lounge** (⊠*430 Duval St.* ☎*305/296–2991*) is on the seventh floor of the La Concha Crowne Plaza and is one of the best places in town to view the sunset and enjoy live entertainment.In the best traditions of a 1950s cocktail lounge, **Virgilio's** (⊠*524 Duval St.* ☎*305/296–8118*) serves chilled martinis to the soothing tempo of live jazz and blues nightly.

SPORTS & THE OUTDOORS

Unlike the rest of the region, Key West isn't known for outdoor pursuits. But everyone should devote at least half a day to relaxing on a boat tour, heading out on a fishing expedition, or pursuing some other adventure at sea. The ultimate excursion is a boat or seaplane trip to Dry Tortugas National Park for snorkeling and exploring Fort Jefferson. Other excursions cater to nature-lovers, scuba divers and snorkelers, and folks who would just like to get out in the water and enjoy the scenery and sunset. For those who prefer their recreation land-based, biking is the way to go. Hiking is limited, but walking the streets of Old Town provides plenty of exercise.

Margarita Madness

Mojitos, martinis, and caipirinhas may be the popular drinks in Miami's South Beach, but in Key West the margarita Jimmy Buffett crooned about is still alive and well.

Every bar and club serves them, either the version classic or in dozens of variations. Every bartender claims to make the best. Here are some that rank tops in their category.

At the **Half Shell Raw Bar,** the Raw Bar Rita, made with 1800 Reposado Tequila, has a funky green glow. The Pama Rita, which the menu claims is "for the health nut," is much prettier, dyed and flavored with a splash of red Pama liqueur, and fueled with Herradura Silver. It scores best in the novelty category.

Although **El Meson de Pepe** brags about its mojitos, its Gold Margarita, made with El Jimador Reposado, is no slouch. It goes especially well with a basket of Cuban bread served with addictive red and green dipping sauces. It rates tops for its ability to play well with food.

At Bagatelle's **Toucan Bar,** the Patron's Margarita, named for its brand of top-shelf tequila, gets points for being smooth, almost creamy. It's the perfect balance of tart and sweet. The view of Duval Street adds to the enjoyment.

At **Mangoes,** the Mangorita is naturally the signature drink. Very tropical, but made with Cuervo and Marie Brizard, it ranks in the "tourist drink" category.

The Cabo Rita at **Conch Republic Seafood Company** is named for a type of tequila called Cabo Wabo Reposado (say that three times after sampling a few). It gets bolstered with triple sec, but isn't too sweet. This is a strong contender in the classic category.

At Jimmy Buffett's **Margaritaville** one would expect high competition. Buffett on the stereo makes a margarita go down just right, with or without a shaker of salt. The Herradura Silver tequila is a good start, but the dash of Cointreau makes the Uptown Margarita heavy on the sweet.

Schooner Wharf's Schoonerita takes top rating in the classic class. The bartender shakes the cocktail and squeezes in a healthy dose of real lime juice at the end. Made with Sauza tequila, it comes served in a proper glass birdbath-shaped vessel, although this one has a stem in the shape of a cactus. (South-of-the-border kitsch and margaritas go well together.)

8

BIKING

Key West was practically made for bicycles, but don't let that lull you into a false sense of security. Narrow and one-way streets along with car traffic result in several bike accidents a year. Some hotels rent or lend bikes to guests; others will refer you to a nearby shop and reserve a bike for you. Rentals usually start at about $12 a day, but some places also rent by the half-day. ■TIP➜ Lock up; bikes—and porch chairs!—are favorite targets for local thieves.

Eaton Bikes (✉ *830 Eaton St. 33040* ☎*305/294–8188* ⊕*www.eatonbikes.com*) has tandem, three-wheel, and children's bikes in addition to the standard beach cruisers ($18 for first day) and seven-speed cruisers ($20). It delivers free to all Key West rentals. **Keys Moped & Scooter** (✉*523 Truman Ave. 33040* ☎*305/294–0399*) rents beach cruisers with large baskets for $10 a day. Rates for scoot-

ers start at $30. Look for the huge American flag on the roof. **Moped Hospital** (✉*601 Truman Ave. 33040* ☎*305/296–3344 or 866/296–1625* ⊕*www.mopedhospital.com*) supplies balloon-tire bikes with yellow safety baskets for adults and kids ($12 per day), as well as mopeds ($40) and double-seater scooters ($65). **Paradise Scooter Rentals** (✉*112 Fitzpatrick St.,* ☎*305/923–6063* ⊕*www.paradisescooterrentals.com*) rents bikes for $12 a day and scooters for $60 to $85 a day.

FISHING

Key West Fishing Pro Guides (☎*866/259–4205* ⊕*www.keywestproguides.com*) has several different trips, including flats and backcountry fishing ($400 for a half day) and reef and offshore fishing ($600 for half day). **Key West Bait and Tackle** (✉*241 Margaret St.* ☎*305/292–1961* ⊕*www.keywestbaitandtackle.com*) carries live bait, frozen bait, and fishing equipment. It also has the Live Bait Lounge, where you can sip ice-cold beer while telling fish tales.

GOLF

Key West Resort Golf Course (✉*6450 E. College Rd.* ☎*305/294–5232*) is an 18-hole, par 70 course on the bay side of Stock Island. Greens fees $165.

KAYAKING

Key West is surrounded by marinas, so it's easy to find what you're looking for, whether it's sailing with dolphins or paddling in the mangroves. At **Key West Eco-Tours** (✉ *Historic Seaport 33040* ☎*305/294–7245* ⊕*www.ecokeywest.com*), the sail-kayak-snorkel excursions take you into backcountry flats and mangrove forests. The 4 1/2 hour trip costs $90 per person and includes lunch. Three-hour kayak-only tours costs $75 per single kayak, $120 per double and includes snacks. Sunset sails and private charters are also available.

SCUBA DIVING & SNORKELING

Captain's Corner (✉*Corner of Greene and Elizabeth* ☎*305/296–8865* ⊕*www.captainscorner.com*), a PADI-certified dive shop, has classes in several languages and twice-daily snorkel and dive trips ($40–$45) to reefs and wrecks aboard the 60-foot dive boat *Sea Eagle. Equipment rental is extra.* Safely dive the coral reefs without getting a scuba certification with **Snuba of Key West** (✉*Garrison Bight Marina, Palm Ave. between Eaton St. and N. Roosevelt Blvd.* ☎*305/292–4616* ⊕*www.*

snubakeywest.com). Ride out to the reef on a catamaran, then follow your guide underwater for a one-hour tour of the coral reefs. You wear a regulator with a breathing hose that is attached to a floating air tank on the surface. No prior diving or snorkeling experience is necessary, but you must know how to swim. The $99 price includes beverages.

SHOPPING

On these streets you'll find colorful local art of widely varying quality, key limes made into everything imaginable, and the raunchiest T-shirts in the civilized world. Browsing the boutiques—with frequent pub stops along the way—makes for an entertaining stroll down Duval Street. Cocktails certainly help the appreciation of some goods, such as the figurine of a naked man blowing bubbles out his backside or the swashbuckling pirate costumes that are not just for Halloween anymore.

Where to start? **Bahama Village** is an enclave of spruced-up shops, restaurants, and vendors leading the way in the restoration of the historic district where black Bahamians settled in the 19th century. The village lies roughly between Whitehead and Fort streets and Angela and Catherine streets. Hemingway frequented the bars, restaurants, and boxing rings in this part of town.

ARTS & CRAFTS

Key West is filled with art galleries, and the variety is truly amazing. Much is locally produced by the town's large artist community, but many galleries carry international artists from as close as Haiti and as far away as France. Local artists do a great job of preserving the island's architecture and spirit.

Cuba, Cuba! (⊠*814 Duval St.* ☎*305/295–9442*) stocks paintings, sculptures, and photos by Cuban artists. The **Gallery on Greene** (⊠*606 Greene St.* ☎*305/294–1669*) showcases politically incorrect art by Jeff MacNelly and three-dimensional paintings by Mario Sanchez. This is the largest gallery exhibition space in Key West. The oldest private art gallery in Key West, **Gingerbread Square Gallery** (⊠*1207 Duval St.* ☎*305/296–8900*), represents local and internationally acclaimed artists, including Sal Salinero and John Kiraly, in media ranging from graphics to art glass. Historian, photographer, and painter Sharon Wells opened **KW Light Gallery** (⊠*1203 Duval St.* ☎*305/294–0566*) to showcase her own fine art photography and paintings, as well as the works of other national artists. You can find historic photos here as well. **Lucky Street Gallery** (⊠*1130 Duval St.* ☎*305/294–3973*) sells high-end contemporary paintings. There are also a few pieces of jewelry by internationally recognized Key West–based artists. Changing exhibits, artist receptions, and special events make this a lively venue. **Pelican Poop** (⊠*314 Simonton St.* ☎*305/296–3887*) sells Caribbean art in a tropical courtyard garden. The owners buy directly from Caribbean artisans every year, so the prices are very attractive. Potters Charles Pearson and Timothy Roeder can be found at **Whitehead St. Pottery** (⊠*322 Julia St.* ☎*305/294–5067*), where they display their porcelain stoneware and raku-fired vessels. The setting, around two koi ponds with a burbling fountain, is as sublime as the art. **Glass Reunion** (⊠ *825 Duval St.* ☎ *305/294–1720*) showcases a collection of wild and impressive fine art glass. It's worth a stop in just to see the imaginative and over-the-top glass chandeliers, jewelry, dishes, and platters.

BOOKS

The **Key West Island Bookstore** (⊠ *513 Fleming St.* ☎ *305/294–2904*) is a home-away-from-home for the large Key West writers' community. It carries new, used, and rare titles. It specializes in Hemingway, Tennessee Williams, and South Florida mystery writers.

CLOTHING & FABRICS

Take home a shopping bag full of scarlet hibiscus, fuchsia heliconias, blue parrot fish, and even pink flamingos from the **Seam Shoppe** (⊠ *1114 Truman Ave.* ☎ *305/296–9830*), which has the city's widest selection of tropical fabrics. Since 1964, **Key West Hand Print Fabrics** (⊠ *201 Simonton St.* ☎ *305/294–9535 or 800/866–0333*) has vibrant tropical fabrics and resort wear for men and women. It's in Curry Warehouse, a brick building erected in 1878 to store tobacco. Get beach ready with colorful towels from **Towels of Key West** (⊠ *806 Duval St.* ☎ *305/292–1120 or 800/927–0316*). There are more than 45 unique towel designs, some you'd expect, others more whimsical. All are hand-sewn on the island. Don't leave town without a browse through the legendary **Fairvilla Megastore** (⊠ *520 Front St.* ☎ *305/292–0448*), where you'll find an astonishing array of fantasy wear, outlandish costumes (check out the pirate section), and other "interesting" souvenirs.

FOOD & DRINK

The **Blond Giraffe** (⊠ *802 Duval St.* ☎ *305/293–7874* ⊠ *614 Front St.* ☎ *305/296–2020* ⊠ *1209 Truman Ave.* ☎ *305/295–6776* ⊠ *107 Simonton St.* ☎ *305/296–9174*) turned an old family recipe for key lime pie into one of the island's success stories. You'll often encounter a line out the door waiting for a pie with delicate pastry, sweet-tart custard filling, and thick meringue topping. The key lime rum cake is the best-selling product for shipping home. For a snack on the run, try the pie on a stick. You'll be pleasantly surprised with the fruit wines sold at the **Key West Winery** (⊠ *103 Simonton St.* ☎ *305/292–1717 or 866/880–1717*). Display crates hold bottles of wines made from blueberries, blackberries, pineapples, cherries, mangoes, watermelons, tomatoes, and, of course, key limes. Stop in for a free tasting. **Fausto's Food Palace** (⊠ *522 Fleming St.* ☎ *305/296–5663* ⊠ *1105 White St.* ☎ *305/294–5221*) is a market in the traditional town-square sense. Since 1926 Fausto's has been the spot to catch up on the week's gossip and to chill out in summer—it has groceries, organic foods, marvelous wines, a sushi chef on duty from 8 to 6, and box lunches to go. If you like it hot, you'll love **Peppers of Key West** (⊠ *602 Greene St.* ☎ *305/295–9333 or 800/597–2823* ⊕ *www.peppersofkeywest.com*). The shop has hundreds of sauces, salsas, and sweets guaranteed to light your fire. You'll spend your first five minutes at the family-owned **Waterfront Market** (⊠ *201 William St.* ☎ *305/296–0778*) wondering how to open a franchise in your hometown. The upscale market sells items from around the world, including health food, organic produce, fresh salads, gourmet coffees, imported cheeses, baked goods, and more. Don't miss the fish market, arguably the best in town; there's also a juice bar, sushi, and vegan dishes.

GIFTS & SOUVENIRS

Like a parody of Duval Street T-shirt shops, the hole-in-the-wall **Art Attack** (⊠606 Duval St. ☎305/294–7131) throws in every icon and trinket anyone nostalgic for the days of peace and love might fancy: beads, necklaces, harmony bells, and psychedelic T-shirts. Best sellers are photographic postcards of Key West by Tony Gregory. It's open until 11 nightly. Part museum, part shopping center, **Cayo Hueso y Habana** (⊠410 Wall St., Mallory Sq. ☎305/293–7260 ⊕www.historictours. com/keywest/cayoh.htm) occupies a circa-1879 warehouse with a hand-rolled cigar shop, one-of-a-kind souvenirs, a Cuban restaurant, and exhibits that tell of the island's Cuban heritage. Outside, a memorial garden pays homage to the island's Cuban ancestors. **Fast Buck Freddie's** (⊠500 Duval St. ☎305/294–2007) sells a classy, hip selection of gifts, including every flamingo item imaginable. It also carries such imaginative items as a noise-activated rat in a trap and a raccoon tail in a bag. **Half Buck Freddie's** (⊠920 Caroline St. ☎305/294–2007) is the discount-outlet store for Fast Buck's.

★ For that unique (but slightly overpriced) souvenir of your trip to Key West head to **Montage** (⊠512 Duval St. ☎305/395–9101 or 877/396–4278), where you'll discover hundreds of handcrafted signs of popular Key West guesthouses, inns, hotels, restaurants, bars, and streets. If you can't find what you're looking for, they'll make it for you.

HEALTH & BEAUTY

Key West Aloe (⊠540 Greene St., at Simonton St. ☎305/293–1885 or 800/445–2563) was founded in a garage in 1971. Today it produces some 300 perfume, sunscreen, and skin-care products for men and women.

FLORIDA KEYS ESSENTIALS

TRANSPORTATION

BY AIR

CARRIERS A tiny airport has greeted passengers since 1957. But in 2008 a new ticketing, security, and baggage complex more than doubled the size of the terminal at Key West International Airport. The addition sits atop a 475-car parking lot.

About 500,000 passengers use the airport each year. Up to 100 commercial flights are scheduled daily, operated by five commercial carriers and two commuter airlines.

Flights from Miami, Fort Lauderdale/Hollywood, Fort Myers, West Palm, Atlanta, Naples, Orlando, St. Petersburg, and Tampa are provided by American Eagle, Comair/Delta Connection, Gulfstream/Continental Connection, and US Airways/US Airways Express. However, flights to Key West are frequently canceled because of fuel costs and low passenger counts.

Contacts American Eagle (☎ *800/433–7300* ⊕ *www.aa.com*). **Comair/Delta Connection** (☎ *800/354–9822* ⊕ *www.comair.com*). **Gulfstream/Continental Connection** (☎ *800/523–3273* ⊕ *www.gulfstreamair.com*). **US Airways/US Airways Express** (☎ *800/428–4322* ⊕ *www.usairways.com*).

AIRPORTS &
TRANSFERS
Airporter operates scheduled van and bus pick-up service from all Miami International Airport (MIA) baggage areas to wherever you want to go in Key Largo ($45) and Islamorada ($50). A discount is given to groups of three or more passengers. There are three departures daily; reservations are required. Keys Shuttle runs scheduled service six times a day in 15-passenger vans between Miami Airport and Key West with stops throughout the Keys for $70 to $90 per person. The SuperShuttle charges $101 per passenger for trips to the Upper Keys. To go farther into the Keys, you must book an entire 11-person van, which costs about $250 to Marathon, $350 to Key West. SuperShuttle requests 24-hour notice for transportation back to the airport.

Airport Contacts Key West International Airport (EYW) (☎ *305/296–7223* ⊕ *www.keywestinternationalairport.com*).

Transfer Contacts Airporter (☎ *305/852–3413 or 800/830–3413*).**Keys Shuttle** (☎ *305/289–9997 or 888/765–9997* ⊕ *www.floridakeysshuttle.com*).

Super Shuttle (☎ *305/871–2000* ⊕ *www.supershuttle.com*).

BY BOAT & FERRY

Boaters can travel to and along the Keys either along the Intracoastal Waterway through Card, Barnes, and Blackwater sounds and into Florida Bay or along the deeper Atlantic Ocean route through Hawk Channel. The Keys are full of marinas that welcome transient visitors, but there aren't enough slips for all the boats heading to these waters. Make reservations far in advance and ask about channel and dockage depth—many marinas are quite shallow. For information contact Coast Guard Group for the Florida Keys.

Key West Express operates air-conditioned ferries between the Key West Terminal (Caroline and Grinnell Streets) and Miami, Marco Island, and Fort Myers Beach. The trip from Fort Myers Beach takes at least four hours each way and costs $73 one-way, $128 round-trip. Ferries depart from Fort Myers Beach at 9 AM and from Key West between 5:30 and 6 PM. The Miami and Marco Island ferry costs $53 one-way and $106 round-trip. Departure times are 8:30 or 9:30. The round-trip includes continental breakfast. An up-to-date photo ID is required for each passenger. All bags are subject to search. Advance reservations are recommended.

Contacts Coast Guard Group for the Florida Keys (✉ *Key West,* ☎ *305/292–8856 or 800/368–5647* ✉ *Islamorada,* ☎ *305/664–8077 information, 305/664–4404 emergencies* ✉ *Marathon,* ☎ *305/743–6778 information, 305/743–6388 emergencies*). **Key West Express Ferry** (☎ *239/463–5733 or 866/593–3779* ⊕ *www.seakeywestexpress.com*).

BY BUS

Airporter operates scheduled van and bus service from all Miami International Airport (MIA) baggage areas to wherever you want to go in Key Largo ($45) and Islamorada ($50). A group discount is given for three or more passengers. There are three departures daily, and reservations are required.

Greyhound Lines runs a special Keys shuttle two times a day (depending on the day of the week) from Miami International Airport (departing from Concourse E, lower level) and stops throughout the Keys. Fares run from around $20 for Key Largo (Howard Johnson, MM 102) to around $41 for Key West (3535 S. Roosevelt, Key West International Airport).

Keys Shuttle runs scheduled service six times a day in 15-passenger vans (nine passengers maximum) between Miami Airport and Key West with stops throughout the Keys for $70 to $90 per person.

SuperShuttle charges about $101 per passenger for trips to the Upper Keys. To go farther into the Keys, you must book an entire van (up to 11 passengers), which costs about $250 to Marathon, $350 to Key West. SuperShuttle requests 24-hour notice for transportation back to the airport.

The City of Key West Department of Transportation has six color-coded bus routes traversing the island from 6:30 AM to 11:30 PM. Stops have signs with the international symbol for bus. Schedules are available on buses and at hotels, visitor centers, and shops. The fare is $1 (exact change) or $3 for an all-day pass that you purchase on board.

8

American Coach Lines (formerly the Dade–Monroe Express) provides daily bus service from MM 50 in Marathon to the Florida City Wal-Mart Supercenter on the mainland. The bus stops at major shopping centers as well as on-demand anywhere along the route during daily round-trips on the hour from 6 AM to 9:55 PM. The cost is $1.85 one-way, exact change required.

The Lower Keys Shuttle bus runs from Marathon to Key West ($2 one-way), with scheduled and on-demand stops along the way.

Contacts Airporter ☎305/852–3413 or 800/830–3413. **Greyhound Lines** ☎800/410–5397 or 800/231–2222.**American Coach Lines** ☎305/770–3131. **City of Key West Department of Transportation** ☎305/809–3910. **Keys Shuttle** ☎305/289–9997 or 888/765–9997 ⊕ ⊕www.floridakeysshuttle.com. **SuperShuttle** ☎305/871–2000 ⊕ www.supershuttle.com.**Lower Keys Shuttle** ☎305/809–3910 ⊕ ⊕www.monroecounty-fl.gov.

BY CAR

From MIA, follow signs to Coral Gables and Key West, which put you on Lejeune Road, then Route 836 west. Take the Homestead Extension of Florida's Turnpike south (toll road), which ends at Florida City and connects to U.S. 1. Tolls from the airport run approximately $2.25. The alternative from Florida City is Card Sound Road (Route 905A), which has a bridge toll of $1. Continue to the only stop sign and turn right on Route 905, which rejoins U.S. 1 31 mi south of Florida City.

Except in Key West, a car is essential for visiting the Keys. The best Keys road map, published by the Homestead–Florida City Chamber of Commerce, can be obtained for $5.50 from the Tropical Everglades Visitor Center in Florida City.

The only place in the Keys where parking is a problem is in Old Town Key West. There are public parking lots that charge by the day (some hotels and B&Bs provide parking or discounts at municipal lots). If you arrive early, you can sometimes find spots on side streets off of Duval and Whitehead, where you can park for free—just be sure it's not marked for residential parking only. Your best bet is to bike or take the trolley around town if you don't want to walk. The trolleys and Conch Train allow you to disembark and reboard at will.

Contacts Tropical Everglades Visitor Center (✉ *160 U.S. 1, Florida City, 33034* ☎ *305/245–9180 or 800/388–9669* ⊕ *www.tropicaleverglades.com*).

CAR RENTALS   Unless you plan on staying put, renting a car for at least part of your stay is a necessity. Two- and four-passenger electric cars are an environmentally friendly way to get around Key West. Rent them from Key West Cruisers for $89 to $129 for a half day, $139 to $189 for a full day.

Avis, Budget, and Enterprise serve Marathon Airport. Avis, Alamo, Budget, Dollar, and Hertz serve Key West's airport. Enterprise has offices in Key Largo, Marathon, and Key West. Thrifty Car Rental has an office in Tavernier.

Avoid flying into Key West and driving back to Miami; there are substantial drop-off charges for leaving a Key West car there.

Contacts Alamo (☎ *305/294–6675 or 800/327–9633* ⊕ *www.alamo.com*). **Avis** (✉ *Key West Airport,* ☎ *305/294–4846* ✉ *Marathon Airport,* ☎ *305/743–5428 or 800/331–1212* ⊕ *www.avis.com*). **Budget** (✉ *Key West Airport,* ☎ *305/294–8868* ✉ *Marathon Airport,* ☎ *305/743–3998 or 800/527–0700* ⊕ *www.budget.com*). **Dollar** (✉ *Key West Airport,* ☎ *305/296–9921 or 800/800–4000* ⊕ *www.dollar. com*). **Enterprise** (✉ *2834 N. Roosevelt Blvd., Key West,* ☎ *305/292–0220* 🅜 ⌁ *800/325–8007* ⊕ *www.enterprise.com*). **Hertz** (✉ *Key West Airport,* ☎ *305/294– 1039 or 800/654–3131* ⊕ *www.hertz.com*). **Key West Cruisers** (✉ *500 Truman Ave.* ☎ *305/294–4724 or 888/800–8802*). **Thrifty Car Rental** (✉ *MM 91.8, OS, Tavernier* ☎ *305/852–6088 or 800/847–4389* ⊕ *www.thrifty.com*).

BY TAXI

Contacts Florida Keys Taxi Dispatch (☎ *305/296–6666 or 305/296–1800* ⊕ *www. keywesttaxi.com*). **Luxury Limousine** (☎ *305/367–2329 or 800/664–0124*).

CONTACTS & RESOURCES

EMERGENCIES

Keys Hotline provides information and emergency assistance in six languages. Florida Marine Patrol maintains a 24-hour telephone service to handle reports of boating emergencies and natural-resource violations. The Keys have no 24-hour pharmacies. Hospital pharmacists will help with emergencies after regular retail business hours. Fishermen's Hospital, Lower Florida Keys Health System, and Mariners Hospital have 24-hour emergency rooms.

Contacts Emergencies (☎ *911*). **Fishermen's Hospital** (✉ *MM 48.7, OS, Marathon* ☎ *305/743–5533* ⊕ *www.fishermenshospital.com*). **Florida Marine Patrol/Fish and Wildlife Conservation Commission** (✉ *MM 48, BS, 2796 Overseas Hwy., Suite 100, State Regional Service Center, Marathon* ☎ *305/289–2320, 800/342–5392 after 5* PM ⊕ *www.myfwc.com*). **Lower Florida Keys Health System** (✉ *MM 5, BS, 5900 College Rd., Stock Island* ☎ *305/294–5531*). **Mariners Hospital** (✉ *MM 91.5, BS, Tavernier* ☎ *305/434–3000* ⊕ *www.baptisthealth.net*).

LODGING

The Key West Innkeepers Association is an umbrella organization for dozens of local properties. Vacation Rentals Key West lists historic cottages, homes, and condominiums for rent. Key West Welcome Center gets a lot of walk-in business because of its location on U.S. 1 at the entrance to Key West. Rent Key West Vacations specializes in renting vacation homes and condos for a week or longer. Vacation Key West lists all kinds of properties throughout Key West.

Contacts Key West Innkeepers Association (✉ *Key West, 33040* ☎ *800/492–1911* ⊕ *www.keywestinns.com*). **Vacation Rentals Key West** (✉ *1511 Truman Ave., Key West* ☎ *305/292–7997 or 800/621–9405* 🖷 *305/294–7501* ⊕ *www.keywestvacations.com*). **Key West Welcome Center** (✉ *24746 Overseas Hwy., Summerland Key* ☎ *305/296–4444 or 800/284–4482* ⊕ *www.keywestwelcomecenter.com*). **Rent Key West Vacations** (✉ *1107 Truman Ave., Key West* ☎ *305/294–0990 or 800/833–7368* ⊕ *www.rentkeywest.com*). **Vacation Key West** (✉ *100 Grinnell St., Key West* ☎ *305/295–9500 or 800/595–5397* ⊕ *www.vacationkw.com*).

TOUR OPTIONS

AIR TOURS

Specializing in romantic sunset flights, Conch Air flies out of Marathon Airport in a 1935 Waco biplane for two passengers; scenic rides start at $74 per person.

Fantasy Dan's Airplane Rides depart from Sugarloaf Key Airport; passengers can spot sharks, stingrays, and other reef life on sightseeing rides priced at $20 to $50 per person (sunset and champagne flights are available by special arrangement).

Island Aeroplane Tours flies up to two passengers in a 1941 Waco, an open-cockpit biplane; tours range from an 8-minute overview of Key West ($90 for two) to a 45-minute reef and wreck excursion ($295 for two).

8

Seaplanes of Key West has half- and full-day trips to the Dry Tortugas, where you can explore Fort Jefferson, built in 1846, and snorkel on the beautiful protected reef. Soft drinks and snorkel equipment are included in the $229 half-day, $405 full-day per-person fee, plus a $5 park fee.

Contacts Conch Air (⊟ *Marathon Airport, Marathon, 33050* ☎ *305/395–1117).* **Fantasy Day's Airplane Rides** (⊠ *Sugarloaf Key Airport, MM 17, Sugarloaf Key* ☎ *305/745–2217.* **Island Aeroplane Tours** (⊠ *Key West Airport, 3469 S. Roosevelt Blvd.* ☎ *305/294–8687* ⊕ *www.keywestairtours.com).* **Seaplanes of Key West** (⊠ *Key West Airport, 3471 S. Roosevelt Blvd.* ☎ *305/294–0709 or 800/950–2359* ⊕ *www.seaplanesofkeywest.com).*

BICYCLE TOURS

Lloyd's Original Tropical Bike Tour, led by a 30-year Key West veteran, explores the natural, noncommercial side of Key West at a leisurely pace, stopping on backstreets and in backyards of private homes to sample native fruits and view indigenous plants and trees; at City Cemetery; and at the Medicine Garden, a private meditation garden. The behind-the-scenes tours run two hours and cost $35, including bike rental.

Contacts Lloyd's Original Tropical Bike Tour (⊠ *Truman Ave. and Simonton St., Key West* ☎ *305/304–4700* ⊕ *www.lloydstropicalbiketour.com).*

BOAT TOURS

Captain Sterling's Everglades Eco-Tours operates Everglades and Florida Bay ecology tours ($50 per person) and sunset cruises ($59 per person).

Victoria Impallomeni, a 34-year wilderness guide and marine scientist, invites nature lovers—and especially children—aboard the *Imp II,* a 25-foot Aquasport, for four-hour ($500) and seven-hour ($700) Dancing Dolphin Spirit Charters ecotours that frequently include encounters with wild dolphins. While island-hopping, you visit underwater gardens, natural shoreline, and mangrove habitats. For her Dolphin Day for Humans tour, she pulls you through the water, equipped with mask and snorkel, on a specially designed "dolphin water massage board." Sometimes dolphins follow the boat and swim among participants. Tours also include Sacred Sound Healing Retreats, a self-transformational retreat using vibrations and sounds. All equipment is supplied. Tours leave from Murray's Marina.

Key Largo Princess offers two-hour glass-bottom-boat trips ($25) and sunset cruises on a luxury 70-foot motor yacht with a 280-square-foot glass viewing area, departing from the Holiday Inn docks three times a day.

M/V *Discovery*'s glass-bottom boats have submerged viewing rooms for 360-degree marine watching ($40).

Strike Zone Charters has glass-bottom-boat excursions into the backcountry and Atlantic Ocean. The five-hour Island Excursion ($49 plus fuel surcharge) emphasizes nature and Keys history; besides close encounters with birds, sea life, and vegetation, there's a fish cookout on an island. Snorkel and fishing equipment, food, and drinks are included. This is one of the few nature outings in the Keys with wheelchair access.

For something with more of an adrenaline boost, book with White Knuckle Thrill Boat Ride. The speed boat holds up to 12 people for doing 360s, fishtales, and other on-the-water stunts in the gulf. Cost is $59 each.

Contacts Dancing Dolphin Spirit Charters (⊠ *MM 5 OS at Murray's Marina, 5710 U.S. 1, Key West* ☎ *305/304–7562 or 888/822–7366* ⊕ *www.captain victoria.com).* **Everglades Eco-Tours** (⊠ *Dolphin's Cove, MM 102, BS, Key Largo* ☎ *305/853–5161 or 888/224–6044* ⊕ *www.captainsterling.com).* **Key Largo Princess** (⊠ *MM 100, OS, 99701 Overseas Hwy., Key Largo* ☎ *305/451–4655 or 877/648–8129* ⊕ *www.keylargoprincess.com).* **Murray's Marina** (⊠ *5710 U.S. Highway 1, MM 5, Key West* ☎ *305/296–0364* ⊕ *www.murraymarine.com).* **M/V Discovery** (⊠ *Land's End Marina, 251 Margaret St., Key West* ☎ *305/293–0099 or 800/262–0099* ⊕ *www.discoveryunderseatours.com).* **Strike Zone Charters** (⊠ *MM 29.6, BS, 29675 Overseas Hwy., Big Pine Key* ☎ *305/872–9863 or 800/654–9560).* **White Knuckle Thrill Boat Ride** (⊠ *Hurricane Hole Marina 5130 Overseas Hwy., Key West* ☎ *305/797–0459* ⊕ *www.whiteknucklethrillboatride.com).*

KAYAK TOURS

Captain Bill Keogh (naturalist, educator, photographer, and author of *The Florida Keys Paddling Guide*) operates Big Pine Kayak Adventures, which takes visitors into remote areas of two national wildlife refuges in the Lower Keys to explore mangrove hammocks, islands, creeks, and sponge and grass flats on kayak nature tours, shallow-water skiff eco-tours, backcountry catamaran sailing cruises, and shallow-water fishing expeditions. Prices start at $50 per person for a three-hour tour.

The folks at Florida Bay Outfitters know Upper Keys and Everglades waters well. Take a full-moon paddle, or a one- to seven-day canoe or kayak tour to the Everglades, Lignumvitae, or Indian Key. Trips run $60 to $795.

Lazy Dog Kayak Guides runs four-hour guided sea-kayak-snorkel tours around the mangrove islands just east of Key West. The $60 charge covers transportation, bottled water, a snack, and supplies, including snorkeling gear. A $35 two-hour guided kayak tours is also available.

Contacts Big Pine Kayak Adventures (✑ *Box 431311, Big Pine Key 33043* ☎ *305/872–7474* ⊕ *www.keyskayaktours.com).* **Florida Bay Outfitters** (⊠ *MM 104, BS, 104050 Overseas Hwy., Key Largo* ☎ *305/451–3018* ⊕ *www.kayak floridakeys.com).* **Lazy Dog Kayak Guides** (⊠ *5114 Overseas Highway, Key West* ☎ *305/295–9898* ⊕ *www.lazydog.com).*

WALKING TOURS

In addition to publishing several good guides on Key West, the Historic Florida Keys Foundation conducts tours of the City Cemetery Tuesday and Thursday at 9:30.

As the former state historian in Key West and the current owner of a historic-preservation consulting firm, Sharon Wells of Island City

Strolls knows plenty about Key West. She's authored many works, including the annually revised Walking and Biking Guide to Historic Key West, which has 14 self-guided tours of the historic district. It's available at guesthouses, hotels, and Key West bookstores. If that whets your appetite, sign on for one of her walking or biking tours, including the Famous Writers and Artists of Key West and the Off-the-Beaten-Track Old Town tour, which cost $25, with a four-person minimum.

Key West's Ghosts & Legends offers nightly tours at 7 and 9 ($18), including a visit to the Old City Morgue, haunted Victorian mansions, and the Key West Cemetery to hear fascinating and sometimes bone-chilling stories of real-life events and people. *Tours meet at Duval and Caroline streets.* Reservations are required.

For a more spectacular spiritual experience, tag along with The Original Ghost Tours' 90-minute, lantern-led stroll around Old Town. It departs nightly from the Crowne Plaza La Concha Hotel at 430 Duval Street and costs $15.

For garden lovers, the Orchid Lady takes visitors to three hidden historic and exotic gardens daily in the morning and afternoon. The 90-minute tour costs $25.

Contacts **Historic Florida Keys Foundation** (⊠ *510 Greene St., Old City Hall, Key West* ☎ *305/292–6718*). **Island City Strolls** (⊠ *Box 56, Key West* ☎ *305/294–8380* ⊕ *www.seekeywest.com*). **Key West's Ghosts & Legends Haunted Tour** (⊠ *Tours meet at Duval and Caroline Sts.* ⌂ *Box 1807, Charleston, SC* ☎ *305/294–1713 or 866/622–4467* ⊕ *www.keywestghosts.com*). **The Orchid Lady** (⊠ *410 Caroline St., Key West* ☎ *877/747–2718* ⊕ *www.eorchidlady.com*) **The Original Ghost Tours** (⊠ *6631 Maloney Ave. and 430 Duval St. , Key West* ☎ *305/294–9255* ⊕ *www. hauntedtours.com*).

VISITOR INFORMATION

Contacts **Big Pine and the Lower Keys Chamber of Commerce** (⊠ *MM 31, OS, 31020 Overseas Hwy.,* ⌂ *Box 430511, Big Pine Key* ☎ *305/872–2411 or 800/872–3722* 🖷 *305/872–0752* ⊕ *www.lowerkeyschamber.com*). **Gay and Lesbian Community Center of Key West** (⊠ *513 Truman Ave., Key West* ☎ *305/292–3223* ⊕ *www.glcckeywest.org*). **Greater Key West Chamber of Commerce** (⊠ *402 Wall St., Key West* ☎ *305/294–2587 or 800/527–8539* ⊕ *www. keywestchamber.org*). **Greater Marathon Chamber of Commerce & Visitor Center** (⊠ *MM 53.5, BS, 12222 Overseas Hwy., Marathon* ☎ *305/743–5417 or 800/262–7284* 🖷 *305/289–0183* ⊕ *www.floridakeysmarathon.com*). **Islamorada Chamber of Commerce** (⊠ *MM 83.2, BS, Box 915, Upper Matecumbe Key, Islamorada* ☎ *305/664–4503 or 800/322–5397* ⊕ *www.islamoradachamber.com*). **Key Largo Chamber of Commerce** (⊠ *MM 106, BS, 106000 Overseas Hwy., Key Largo* ☎ *305/451–14747 or 800/822–1088* ⊕ *www.keylargochamber.org*). **Key West Business Guild** (⊠ *513 Truman Ave.,* ⌂ *Box 1208, Key West ,* ☎ *305/294–4603 or 800/535–7797* ⊕ *www.gaykeywestfl.com*). **Key West Welcome Center** (⊠ *24746 Overseas Hwy., Summerland Key* ☎ *305/296–4444 or 800/284–4482* ⊕ *www. keywestwelcomecenter.com*).

The Everglades

Baby alligator, Everglades

WORD OF MOUTH

"April is the best month for the Everglades. The weather is getting a bit warm to hot, but still dry and windy and that keeps the mosquitoes at bay. The main reason for going in April, however, is because gators are out in full force by then. You'll see them sunning themselves and swimming. In the dead of winter, gators hibernate and you'll rarely see them. Even if you did, they would be lethargic in the winter."

—bkluvsNola

WELCOME TO THE EVERGLADES

TOP REASONS TO GO

★ **Fishing:** Cast for some of the world's fightingest game fish—600 species of fish in all—in the Everglades' backwaters.

★ **Birding:** Check hundreds of birds off your life list, including—if you're lucky—the rare Everglades snail kite.

★ **Kayaking:** Do a half-day trip in Big Cypress Preserve or reach for the ultimate—the 99-mile Wilderness Trail.

★ **Swamp Cuisine:** Been hankering for alligator tail and frogs' legs? If that doesn't appeal, you've gotta try the stone crab claws where they're fresh from the traps.

★ **Gator-spotting:** This is ground zero for alligator viewing in the U.S., and you won't leave without spotting your quota.

1 Biscayne National Park. Mostly underwater, here's where the string of coral reefs and islands that are the Florida Keys begins.

2 Everglades National Park. Alligators, Florida panthers, black bears, manatees, dolphins, bald eagles, and roseate spoonbills call this vast habitat home.

GETTING ORIENTED

Florida's Everglades region covers the southernmost tip of the peninsula from the Gulf of Mexico in the west to Florida Bay in the east. It lies west and south of Miami; the Florida Keys front its Florida Bay to the southeast. On the western side, it lies southeast of Naples and Marco Island. Between the two extremes spreads an undeveloped wilderness of mostly protected federal and government lands and waters that include Everglades National Park, Big Cypress National Preserve, and Biscayne National Park.

9

Miccosukee Indian Village

Tamiami Trail

Everglades Gator Park

Hialeah

Miami

Shark Valley

Everglades Safari Park

Coral Gables

Observation Tower **2**

Kendall

1

Biscayne National Park

Everglades National Park

Homestead

Biscayne Bay

Boca Chita Key

Florida's Turnpike Extension

Florida City

Convoy Point

Elliott Key

Adams Key

Barnes Sound

ATLANTIC OCEAN

nake ight

Florida Bay

Florida Keys

Joe Kemp Key

3 Big Cypress National Park. Neighbor to Everglades National Park, it's a sportsman's paradise.

THE EVERGLADES PLANNER

When to Go

Winter is the best time to visit the Everglades, and the busiest. Temperatures and mosquito activity are tolerable, low water levels concentrate the resident wildlife, and migratory birds swell the avian population. In late spring the weather turns hot and rainy, and tours and facilities are less crowded. Migratory birds depart, and you must look harder to see wildlife. Summer brings intense sun and afternoon rainstorms. Water levels rise and mosquitoes descend, making outdoor activity virtually unbearable, unless you swath yourself in netting. Mosquito repellent is a necessity any time of year.

Flying In

Miami International Airport (MIA) is 34 mi from Homestead and 47 mi from the eastern access to Everglades National Park. A number of shuttles run between MIA and Homestead. Southwest Florida International Airport (RSW) in Fort Myers, is the closest major airport to the Everglades' western access. On-demand taxi transportation from the airport to Everglades City is available.

For more flight information see By Air in the Essentials section at the end of this chapter.

About the Restaurants

Dining centers on places that serve home-style food, and small eateries that specialize in: alligator, fish, stone crab, frogs' legs, and fresh Florida lobster from the Keys. Native American restaurants add another dimension, serving local favorites as well as catfish, Indian fry bread (a flour-and-water flatbread), and pumpkin bread. Because of its large Hispanic population, Homestead is home to restaurants specializing in authentic Mexican cuisine. Diners looking for something trendier head to the Keys or Miami. Restaurants in Everglades City, especially those along the river, have the freshest seafood, particularly stone crab. These places can be casual to the point of rustic, and often close for a month or two in the fall. The nearest fine restaurants to Everglades City are in Marco Island and Naples.

About the Hotels

If you're spending several days exploring the East Coast Everglades, stay either in one of the park's campgrounds; 11 mi away in Homestead–Florida City, where there are reasonably priced motels and RV parks; or in the Florida Keys or the Greater Miami–Fort Lauderdale area. Lodgings and campgrounds are also available on the Gulf Coast in Everglades City, Naples, and Marco Island. Florida City's selection is mostly of the chain variety and geared toward business travelers. Accommodations near the parks range from inexpensive to moderate and offer off-season rates in summer, when mosquito populations are rampant.

What It Costs

DINING & LODGING PRICE CATEGORIES

¢	$	$$	$$$	$$$$
Restaurants				
under $10	$10–$15	$15–$20	$20–$30	over $30
Hotels				
under $80	$80–$100	$100–$140	$140–$220	over $220

Restaurant prices are per person for a main course at dinner. Hotel prices are for a standard double room, excluding 6% sales tax (more in some counties) and 1%–4% tourist tax.

Updated by
Chelle Koster
Walton

MIAMI IS THE ONLY CITY in the country that has two national parks and a national preserve in its backyard. Everglades National Park, created in 1947, was meant to preserve the slow-moving River of Grass—a freshwater river 50 mi wide but only 6 inches deep, flowing from Lake Okeechobee through marshy grassland into Florida Bay. Along Tamiami Trail (U.S. 41), marshes of saw grass extend as far as the eye can see, interspersed only with hammocks or tree islands of bald cypress and mahogany, while overhead southern bald eagles make circles in the sky. An assembly of plants and flowers, including ferns, orchids, and bromeliads, shares the brackish waters with river otters, turtles, alligators, and occasionally that gentle giant, the Florida manatee. Not so gentle, though, is the saw grass. Deceptively graceful, these tall, willowy sedges have small, sharp teeth on the edges of their leaves.

Biscayne National Park, established as a national monument in 1968 and 12 years later expanded and designated a national park, is the nation's largest marine park and the largest national park within the continental United States with living coral reefs. A small portion of the park's almost 274 square mi consists of mainland coast and outlying islands, but 95% is under water, much of it in Biscayne Bay. Of particular interest are the mangroves and their tangled masses of stilt-like roots that thicken the shorelines. These "walking trees," as locals call them, have striking curved prop roots, which arch down from the trunk, while aerial roots drop from branches. The trees draw fresh water from saltwater and create a coastal nursery capable of sustaining myriad types of marine life. Congress established Big Cypress National Preserve in 1974 after buying up one of the least-developed watershed areas in South Florida to protect Everglades National Park. The preserve, on the northern edge of Everglades National Park, entails extensive tracts of prairie, marsh, pinelands, forested swamps, and sloughs. Although preservation is the preserve's main purpose, hunting and off-road vehicle use are allowed. Ten Thousand Islands National Wildlife Refuge, accessible only by boat, spreads to the south of Everglades National Park on its gulf side; and Florida Panther National Wildlife Refuge, accessible by two trails, and Fakahatchee Strand Preserve State Park both lie to the northwest.

Miami's backyard is threatened by suburban sprawl, agriculture, and business development. What results is competition among environmental, agricultural, and developmental interests. The biggest issue is water. Starting in the 1930s, a giant flood-control system began diverting water to canals running to the gulf and the ocean. The unfortunate side effect of flood control has been devastation of the wilderness. Park visitors decry diminished bird counts, the black bear population has been nearly eliminated, and the Florida panther once neared extinction. Meanwhile, the loss of fresh water has made Florida Bay saltier, devastating breeding grounds and creating dead zones where pea-green algae have replaced sea grasses and sponges.

The nearly $8 billion, 10-year comprehensive plan worked out between government agencies and a host of conservation groups and industries to restore, protect, and preserve the ecosystem is under way. More than

200 projects tear down levees, fill canals, construct new water-storage areas on land formerly preserved for agriculture or new development, channel water to estuaries and Everglades National Park, and provide flood protection and a reliable water supply. The hope is that new policies and projects implemented over the next decade will go a long way toward reviving the natural system.

EXPLORING THE EVERGLADES

Most sports and activities in both national parks are based on water, on the study of nature, or both. So even when you're on land, be prepared to get a bit damp on the region's marshy trails. Although relatively compact compared with the national parks of the West, these parks still require time to see. The narrow, two-lane roads through the Everglades make for slow travel, whereas sightseeing by boat, a necessity at Biscayne, takes time. The southern tip of the Florida peninsula is largely taken up by Everglades National Park, and land access to it is primarily by two roads. The main park road traverses the southern Everglades from the gateway towns of Homestead and Florida City to the outpost of Flamingo, on Florida Bay. In the northern Everglades, take Tamiami Trail (U.S. 41) east from the Greater Miami area or west from Naples to the western park entrance in Everglades City at Route 29. ■TIP➔In the dry winter season, be careful with campfires and matches; this is when the wildfire-prone saw-grass prairies and pinelands are most vulnerable.

BISCAYNE NATIONAL PARK

Occupying 173,000 acres along the southern portion of Biscayne Bay, south of Miami and north of the Florida Keys, this national park is 95% under water, and its altitude ranges from 4 feet above sea level to 60 feet below. Contained within it are four distinct zones, which from shore to sea are mangrove forest along the coast, Biscayne Bay, the undeveloped upper Florida Keys, and coral reefs. Mangroves line the mainland shore much as they do elsewhere along South Florida's protected bay waters. Biscayne Bay functions as a lobster sanctuary and a nursery for fish, sponges, and crabs. Manatees and sea turtles frequent its warm, shallow waters. Unfortunately, the bay is under assault from forces set on a course of destruction. To the east, about 8 mi off the coast, lie 44 tiny keys, stretching 18 nautical miles north–south and accessible only by boat. There's no commercial transportation between the mainland and the islands, and only a handful can be visited: Elliott, Boca Chita, Adams, and Sands keys. The rest are either wildlife refuges or too small, or have rocky shores or waters too shallow for boats. It's best to explore the Keys between December and April, when the mosquito population is relatively quiescent. Bring repellent just in case. Diving is best in summer, when calmer winds and smaller seas result in clearer waters. Another 3 mi east of the Keys, in the ocean, lies the park's main attraction—the northernmost section of Florida's living tropical coral reefs. Some are the size of a student's desk, others as large as a football field. You can take a glass-bottom-boat ride to see this underwater wonderland, but you really have to snorkel or scuba dive to appreciate it fully. A diverse population of colorful fish—angelfish, gobies, grunts, parrot fish, pork fish, wrasses, and many more—flits through the reefs. Shipwrecks from the 18th century are evidence of the area's international maritime heritage, and a Maritime Heritage Trail is being developed that will string together six of the major shipwreck and underwater cultural sites and is expected to be completed in 2009.

> **WORD OF MOUTH**
>
> "Is the first week of April already bad for mosquitoes at Everglades?" –inor
>
> "Just take a good bug repellent with you to be safe. The Everglades is an unforgettable experience. My first time there was in April, and I had no problems whatsoever." –shaytravels

At press time, three sites, including a 19th-century wooden sailing vessel, have been plotted with GPS coordinates and marked with mooring buoys. Plastic dive cards will be available containing navigational and background information. A Native American midden (shell mound) dating from AD 1000, and Boca Chita Key, listed on the National Register of Historic Places for its 10 historic structures, illustrate the park's rich cultural heritage. More than 170 species of birds have been seen around the park. Although all the Keys are excellent for birding, Jones Lagoon, south of Adams Key, between Old Rhodes Key and Totten Key, is one of the best. It's approachable only by nonmotorized craft.

CONVOY POINT

9 mi east of Florida City, 30 mi south of downtown Miami.

★ The **Dante Fascell Visitor Center** has a wide veranda with views across mangroves and Biscayne Bay. Inside the museum, artistic vignettes and on-request videos explore the park's four ecosystems. Among the facilities are the park's canoe and tour concessionaire, restrooms with showers, a ranger information area, a gift shop, and vending machines. Ranger programs take place daily, along with monthly family festivals and bimonthly narrated paddling trips. Outside are picnic tables and grills. A short trail and boardwalk lead to a jetty and launch ramp. This is the only area of the park accessible without a boat. ⊠*9700 S.W. 328th St., Homestead* ☎*305/230–7275* ⊕*www.nps.gov/bisc* ☑*Free* ☉*Daily 9–5.*

THE OUTDOORS

CANOEING

Biscayne National Underwater Park, Inc. (⊠*Convoy Point Visitor Center, Box 1270, 9710 S.W. 328th St., Homestead* ☎*305/230–1100*), the park's official concessionaire, has canoes and kayaks for rent on a first-come, first-served basis. Canoe prices are $12 an hour, kayaks $16 an hour. Mid-January through April, rangers lead guided paddling trips the second and fourth Saturday of the month. Rentals are available 9–4 daily.

DIVING & SNORKELING

★ **Biscayne National Underwater Park, Inc.** (✉ *Convoy Point Visitor Center, Box 1270, 9710 S.W. 328th St., Homestead* ☎ *305/230–1100*) rents equipment and conducts snorkel and dive trips aboard the 45-foot *Boca Chita*. Three-hour snorkel trips ($26–$35) leave daily at 1:30 and include use of mask, fins, snorkel, and buoyancy vest; and instruction. About one hour is spent on the reef and wrecks. Two-tank scuba trips to shallow reef or

> **DID YOU KNOW?**
>
> Pythons have become a threat to Everglades indigenous wildlife in recent years. Pet owners have been releasing the exotic species in the park, thereby unleashing its predatory powers on native species. In 2005 local papers carried a photograph of a python trying to devour a fully grown alligator. Both creatures died in the mishap.

wall dives depart weekends at 8:30 AM, costing $54, tanks and weights included. Additional trips, including night dives, may be offered according to demand. Complete gear rental ($54 extra, including two tanks) is available. Even with a reservation (recommended), you should arrive one hour before departure to sign up for gear.

BOCA CHITA KEY

★ *10 mi northeast of Convoy Point.*

This island was once owned by the late Mark C. Honeywell, former president of Minneapolis's Honeywell Company. A ½-mi hiking trail curves around the south side of the island. Climb the 65-foot-high ornamental lighthouse (by ranger tour only) for a panoramic view of Miami and surrounding waters. There's no freshwater, access is by private boat only, and no pets are allowed.

WHERE TO STAY

⚠ **Boca Chita Campground.** This small, flat island has a grassy, waterside campground shaded by palm trees that whisper in the breeze. The views are awesome, and a nature trail circles the island. Check with the park concessionaire for drop-off and pick-up service ($38.45 roundtrip). Reservations are required. There's no running fresh water. Campers must carry out all trash. ♿ *Flush toilets, picnic tables* 🍽 *39 sites* ✉ *9700 S.W. 328th St., Homestead* ☎ *305/230–7275, 305/230–1100 transportation* ⊕ *www.nps.gov/bisc* ▤ *No credit cards.*

ELLIOTT KEY

9 mi east of Convoy Point.

This key, accessible only by boat (on your own or from the concessionaire for $35.95 round-trip), has a boardwalk made from recycled plastic and two nature trails with tropical plant life. Take an informal, ranger-led nature walk or hike the 7-mi trail on your own along so-called Spite Highway, a 225-foot-wide swath of green that developers mowed down in hopes of linking this key to the mainland. Luckily the federal government stepped in, and now it's a hiking trail through tropical hardwood hammock. Facilities include restrooms, picnic tables, fresh drinking water, showers (cold), grills, and a campground. Pets are allowed on the island but not on trails. A 30-foot-wide sandy beach about a mile north of the harbor on the west (bay) side of the key is the only one in the national park. Boaters like to anchor off it to swim. For day use only, it has picnic areas and a short trail that follows the shore and cuts through the hammock.

WHERE TO STAY

⚠️**Elliott Key Campground.** The grassy, beachfront tent sites are populated with plenty of native hardwood trees, and there's no light pollution here, so the night sky is brilliant with stars. Spend the day swimming, snorkeling, hiking trails, and fishing. Parties of up to 25 people and six tents can share the group campsite for $25 a night, and leashed pets are welcome. Regular ferry service and boat rental are nonexistent, but the park concessionaire's snorkel boat provides drop-off and pick-up service to campers ($28.45 round-trip). Reservations are required. If you bring a boat, dock in the marina overnight for an additional $5. Bring plenty of insect repellent and try to pick a breezy spot to plant your tent. Keep in mind you must carry out all garbage, and bring some drinking water: the pumps are known to go out on occasion. ⚴ *Flush toilets, drinking water, showers (cold), picnic tables, swimming (bay)* ⟿*40 sites* ✉*9700 S.W. 328th St., Homestead* ☎*305/230–7275, 305/230–1100 transportation, 305/230–1144 Ext. 3074 for group campsite* ⊕*www.nps.gov/bisc* ▱*No credit cards.*

ADAMS KEY

9 mi southeast of Convoy Point.

This small key, a stone's throw from the western tip of Elliott Key, is open for day use and has picnic areas, restrooms, dockage, and a short trail that runs along the shore and through a hardwood hammock. Access is by private boat.

EVERGLADES NATIONAL PARK

11 mi southwest of Homestead, 45 mi southwest of Miami International Airport.

The best way to experience the real Everglades is to get your feet wet either by taking a walk in the muck, affectionately called a "slough slog," or by paddling a canoe into the maze of mangrove islands to stay in a backcountry campsite. Most day-trippers don't want to do that, however. Luckily, there are several ways to see the wonders of the park with relatively dry feet. Take a boat tour in Everglades City or Flamingo, ride the tram or bike the loop road at Shark Valley, or walk the boardwalks that extend out from the main park road. And there's more to see than natural beauty. Miccosukee Indians operate a number of attractions, including a restaurant, and they merit a stop. Admission to Everglades National Park's two pay gates (main entrance and Shark Valley) is valid at both entrances for seven days. Coverage in the following section begins in the southeastern Everglades, followed by the northern Everglades, starting in the east and ending in Everglades City.

THE MAIN PARK ROAD

The main park road (Route 9336) travels from the main visitor center to Flamingo, across a section of the park's eight distinct ecosystems: hardwood hammock, freshwater prairie, pinelands, freshwater slough, cypress, coastal prairie, mangrove, and marine-estuarine. Highlights of the trip include a dwarf cypress forest, the ecotone (transition zone) between saw grass and mangrove forest, and a wealth of wading birds at Mrazek and Coot Bay ponds. Boardwalks, looped trails, several short spurs, and observation platforms allow you to stay dry. Note that facilities at Flamingo are temporarily limited following severe hurricane damage in 2005. The only overnight facilities are in the campground.

> **WORD OF MOUTH**
>
> "Everglades National Park is huge! Shark Valley is not accessible through the Homestead entrance. You must take the Tamiami Trail, which is accessible in the western edge of Miami. Its about a 1-hour-to-1.5-hour drive from Fort Lauderdale."
>
> –MiamiBeachMomma

Numerous interactive exhibits and films make the **Ernest F. Coe Visitor Center** a worthy and important stop during your tour of the region. Stand in a simulated blind and peer through a spyglass to watch birds in the wild; although it's actually a film, the quality is so good you'll think you're outside. Move on to a bank of telephones to hear differing viewpoints on the Great Water Debate. Another exhibit re-creates sights and sounds of the Everglades. The 15-minute film River of Life shows in the theater, plus there is a movie on hurricanes and a 35-minute wildlife film for children available upon request. A schedule of daily ranger-led activities parkwide and information on canoe rentals and boat tours is kept up-to-date on the park's Web site. In the Everglades Discovery Shop, browse through cool nature, science, and kids' stuff and pick up extra insect repellent. Park admission fees permit entry for a seven-day period, including at the Shark Valley access. The Coe Visitor Center, however, has free admission, as it's outside the park gates. ⊠*11 mi southwest of Homestead on Rte. 9336* ☎*305/242-7700* ⊕*www. nps.gov/ever* ⊠*Park $10 per vehicle, $5 per pedestrian, bicycle, or motorcycle* ⊙*Daily 8–5; hrs sometimes shortened in off-season.*

★ A must for anyone who wants to experience the real Everglades, the **Royal Palm Visitor Center** permits

> **WORD OF MOUTH**
>
> "I highly recommend walking along the Anhinga Trail. It's a boardwalk that goes through a portion of the glades, and you will see so many birds, fish, gators, butterflies, etc. It was a hit with everyone in my family, and bring your camera." –like_2travel

Big Cypress National
Preserve & the Everglades
& Biscayne National Parks

GREAT ITINERARY

3 DAYS

With three days, explore all three accesses to the Everglades as well as Biscayne National Park. Start at **Homestead** as your base for exploring Biscayne. Tour the visitor center at **Convoy Point** when you return and finish your day checking out sights in Homestead and **Florida City**. There's an afternoon snorkel trip also, which would give you time to see Florida City and Homestead, have lunch, and learn about the park's ecosystem at the visitor center first. Head to the Everglades on Day 2, following the one-day itinerary

above. Spend the night camping in **Flamingo** or in a Homestead/Florida City hotel. On Day 3, start by driving west along the Tamiami Trail, stopping at **Everglades Safari Park** for an airboat ride; at **Shark Valley** for a tram tour, walk, or bicycle trip; at the **Miccosukee Indian Village** for lunch and a tour; at the **Big Cypress Gallery**; and then at the **Ochopee Post Office**, before ending in **Everglades City**. From here, visit historic **Smallwood Store** on Chokoloskee Island and watch the sunset.

access to the **Anhinga Trail boardwalk**, where in winter spying alligators congregating in watering holes is almost guaranteed. Or follow the neighboring Gumbo Limbo Trail through a hardwood hammock. Do both strolls, as they're short (½ mi) and expose you to two Everglades ecosystems. Rangers conduct daily Anhinga Ambles in season (check for dates by calling ahead or visiting the Web site) starting at 10:30. At 1:30 the Glades Glimpse program takes place daily in season. Ask also about starlight walks and bike tours. The visitor center has interpretive displays, a bookstore, and vending machines. ⊠ *4 mi west of Ernest F. Coe Visitor Center on Rte. 9336* ☎ *305/242–7700* ⊕ *www. nps.gov/ever* ☉ *Daily 8–4.*

HOMESTEAD

30 mi southwest of Miami.

In recent years the Homestead area has redefined itself as a destination for tropical agro- and ecotourism. The emphasis is on "tropical," because as you cross Quail Roost Trail along north Krome Avenue (Route 997) you actually cross latitudes into the tropical zone. Seated at the juncture between Miami and the Keys as well as Everglades National Park and Biscayne National Park, it has the added dimension of shopping centers, residential development, hotel chains, and the Homestead Miami Speedway—when car races are scheduled there, hotels increase rates and have minimum stays. The historic downtown area has become a preservation-driven Main Street. Krome Avenue, where it cuts through the city's heart, is lined with restaurants, an arts complex, antiques shops, and low-budget, but sometimes undesirable, accommodations. West of north–south Krome Avenue, miles of fields grow fresh fruits and vegetables. Some are harvested commercially, and others have U-PICK signs, inviting you to harvest your own. Stands selling farm-fresh produce and nurseries that grow and sell orchids and tropical plants abound. In addition to its agricultural legacy, the town has an eclectic flavor, attributable to its population mix: descendants of pioneer Crackers, Hispanic growers and farm workers, professionals escaping Miami's hustle and bustle, and latter-day northern retirees.

WHAT TO SEE

With a saltwater atoll pool that's flushed by tidal action, **Homestead Bayfront Park,** adjacent to Biscayne National Park, is popular among local families as well as anglers and boaters. Facilities include a sandy beach with lifeguards, a playground, ramps for people with disabilities (including a ramp that leads into the swimming area), and a picnic pavilion with grills, showers, and restrooms. ✉ *9698 S.W. 328th St.* ☎ *305/230–3034* 🏷 *$4 per passenger vehicle, $10 per vehicle with boat, $12 per RV* ☼ *Daily sunrise–sunset.*

★ Because it officially qualifies for tropical status, **Fruit & Spice Park,** in Homestead's Redland historic agricultural district, is the only public garden of its type in the United States. More than 500 varieties of herbs, spices, citrus, and nuts typically grow in the 35-acre park, but it is most famous for its exotic fruits, such as pomelo, carambola, sugar apple, and monstera. There are 70 varieties of bananas alone, plus 70 varieties of avocado, and 140 of mangos. Tours and tastings are available three times daily. ✉ *24801 S.W. 187th Ave.* ☎ *305/247–5727* ⊕ *www.fruitandspicepark.org* 🏷 *$6* ☼ *Daily 10–5; guided tours at 11, 1:30, and 3.*

Enjoy Homestead's fruity bounty in liquid form at **Schnebly Redland's Winery.** Opened to the public in 2005, it began producing fruit wines as a way to avoid wasting thousands of pounds of fruit from the family groves each year, fruit not quite perfect enough for shipping. In 2008 the winery expanded with a spacious reception/tasting indoor area that serves snacks and a lush plaza picnic area framed in coral rock, tropical plants, and waterfalls—topped with an Indian thatched chickee roof. Five bucks buys you a taste of six varieties of surprisingly tasty fruit wines, from the oaky carambola wine to the slightly sweet and acidic passion fruit. For another $5 you can taste the three new sparkling wines. You get to keep your souvenir wineglass and can bring it back anytime for free refills. ✉ *30205 S.W. 217th Ave.* ☎ *305/242–1224 or 888/717–WINE (9463)* ⊕ *www.schneblywinery.com* 🏷 *$5* ☼ *Weekdays 10–5, Sat. 10–6, Sun. noon–5.*

9

☾ Driven by unrequited love, 100-pound immigrant Ed Leedskalnin built **Coral Castle** in the early 1900s out of massive slabs of coral rock, a feat likened to the building of the pyramids. Visitors can learn how he peopled his fantasy world with his imaginary wife and three children, studied astronomy, and built his simple home and elaborate courtyard with no engineering education and tools he mostly fashioned himself. Highlights of the National Register of Historic Places site include the Polaris telescope built to spot the North Star, a working sundial, a 5,000-pound heart-shaped table featured in Ripley's *Believe It or Not,* a banquet table in the shape of Florida, and a playground Ed named "Grotto

of the Three Bears." ✉28655
S. Dixie Hwy. ☎305/248–6345
⊕www.coralcastle.com ✉$9.75
⊘Sun.–Thurs. 8–6, Fri.–Sat. 8–9.

ArtSouth is a groundbreaking project centered on a 3½-acre complex that includes the historic First
Baptist Church, 45 artist studios,
galleries, workshops, sculpture
garden, and stage. Watch artists at
work, take classes, and enjoy con-

> **WITNESS PROTECTION PROGRAM**
>
> Fifteen federally protected threat-
> ened and endangered creatures
> survive within the protection of
> Everglades National Park, includ-
> ing manatees, crocodiles, snail
> kites, and sea turtles.

cert performances. Check Second Saturdays opening exhibits, which
include live entertainment, hands-on art demonstrations, self-guided
tours, and refreshments served from 3 to 7 PM. ✉20 N. Krome Ave.
☎305/247–9406 ⊕www.artsouthhomestead.org ✉Free ⊘Tues.–Fri.
10–6, weekends noon–6.

WHERE TO EAT

★ ¢ ✗ **El Toro Taco.** This simple, saltillo-tiled family-run favorite gets high
marks for its generous portions, homemade tortilla chips (sometimes a
little greasy), and friendly service. Selections include tasty fajitas, enchiladas, and burritos, and other traditional Mexican dishes such as *mole
de pollo,* which combines unsweetened chocolate and Mexican spices
with chicken. Order spicing from mild to tongue-challenging. And if
you're tired of the same old morning fare, consider stopping here for
breakfast, available 10 AM–noon. ✉1 S. Krome Ave. ☎305/245–8182
¢ ▭AE, D, MC, V ⌇BYOB ⊘Closed Mon. ✗ **NicaMex.** Among the
local Latin population, this is a favorite and the lowest priced. It helps
if you speak Spanish, but there are usually staffers who speak English,
and the menu is bilingual. Although they term it *comidas rapidas* (fast
food), the cuisine is not Americanized. You can get authentic huevos
rancheros or *chilaquiles* (corn tortillas cooked in red-pepper sauce) for
breakfast, and specialties such as *chicharron en salsa verde* (fried pork
skin in hot green-tomato sauce) and shrimp in garlic all day. Seafood
and beef soups are best-sellers and have generous amounts of vegetables and seafood or meat. Choose a domestic or imported beer, pop a
coin into the Wurlitzer jukebox, select a Latin tune, and escape to a
foreign land. ✉32 N.W. 1st St., across from the Krome Ave. bandstand
☎305/246–8300 ▭AE, D, MC, V.
¢ ✗ **Sam's Country Kitchen.** For good old Southern-style home cooking,
Sam's is the choice of the local population. Burgers, sandwiches, and
dinners—including chicken livers, country-fried chicken, and fried
clams—come with fresh-baked corn bread and a daily selection of sides
such as okra with tomatoes, turnip greens, pickled beets, or onion
rings. Don't miss out on the changing selection of homemade soups
and desserts. All this goodness comes cheaply, but at the expense of an
anything-but-glamorous dining area and often slow service. ✉1320 N.
Krome Ave. ☎305/246–2990 ▭MC, V ⊘Closed for dinner Sun.

WHERE TO STAY

★ $ -$$ Redland Hotel. Of downtown Homestead's smattering of mom-and-pop motels, this is the most desirable and has the most character. When it opened in 1904, the inn was the town's first hotel. It later became the first mercantile store, the first post office, the first library, and the first boardinghouse. Today, each room has a different layout and furnishings, and some have access to a shared balcony. The style is Victorian, with lots of pastels and reproduction antique furniture. The pub is popular with locals, and there are good restaurants and antiques shops nearby. A coffee shop–Internet café with free Wi-Fi connections was added in 2006. **Pros:** Historic character, convenient to downtown, well maintained. **Cons:** Traffic noise, small rooms, ugly street location. ⊠ *5 S. Flagler Ave.* ☎ *305/246–1904 or 800/595–1904* ⊕ *www.redlandhotel.com* ⬥ *13 rooms* ⚙ *In-room: VCR, Ethernet, dial-up. In-hotel: restaurant, room service, bar, public Wi-Fi, no-smoking rooms* ⊟ *AE, D, MC, V.*

★ $ Grove Inn Country Guesthouse. Away from downtown but close to Homestead's agricultural attractions, Grove Inn derives much of its personality from co-owner Paul, a former show man. The garden is lush with organic, tropical fruit trees and native plants (instead of a guest book there's a live autograph tree in the courtyard, where people sign the leaves) and the rooms are decorated fussily with antique furnishings and table settings. The owners go out of their way to pamper you, starting with a country breakfast using local produce, served family-style in a dining room done in deep Victorian florals. They offer behind-the-scenes tours of orchid nurseries and farms not otherwise open to the public. A vending machine dispenses complimentary cold drinks. **Pros:** Fresh fruit, privacy, delicious breakfast, rural location. **Cons:** Far from downtown and national parks, no restaurants nearby, not suited to families. ⊠ *22540 S.W. Krome Ave., 6 mi north of downtown* ☎ *305/247–6572 or 877/247–6572* ⊕ *www.groveinn.com* ⬥ *13 rooms, 1 2-bedroom suite, 1 cottage* ⚙ *In-room: kitchen (some), refrigerator, dial-up. In-hotel: pool, laundry facilities, some pets allowed, no-smoking rooms* ⊟ *AE, D, MC, V* ⑩ *BP.*

SPORTS & THE OUTDOORS

AUTO RACING

The **Homestead Miami Speedway** (⊠ *1 Speedway Blvd.* ☎ *305/230–7223* ⊕ *www.homesteadmiamispeedway.com*) is a state-of-the-art facility with 65,000 grandstand seats and two tracks: a 2.21-mi continuous road course and a 1.5-mi oval. There's a schedule of year-round manufacturer and race-team testing, club racing, and other national events.

BOATING

Boaters give high ratings to the facilities at **Homestead Bayfront Park.** The 174-slip marina has a ramp, dock, bait-and-tackle shop, fuel station, ice, dry storage, and boat hoist, which can handle vessels up to 50 feet long if they have lifting rings. The park also has a tidal swimming area. ⊠ *9698 S.W. 328th St.* ☎ *305/230–3033* ⊠ *$4 per passenger vehicle, $10 per vehicle with boat, $10 per RV, $10 hoist* ⊙ *Daily sunrise–sunset.*

SHOPPING

In addition to Homestead Boulevard (U.S. 1) and Campbell Drive (Southwest 312th Street and Northeast 8th Street), **Krome Avenue** is popular for shopping. In the heart of Old Homestead, it has a brick sidewalk, art galleries, and antiques stores. The **Antique Mall** contains six dealer shops plus a cafe.

FLORIDA CITY

2 mi southwest of Homestead.

The Florida Turnpike ends in this southernmost town on the peninsula, spilling thousands onto U.S. 1 and eventually west to Everglades National Park, east to Biscayne National Park, or south to the Florida Keys. Florida City and Homestead run into each other, but the difference couldn't be more noticeable. As the last outpost before 18 mi of mangroves and water, this stretch of U.S. 1 is lined with fast-food eateries, service stations, hotels, bars, dive shops, and restaurants. Hotel rates increase significantly during NASCAR races at the nearby Homestead Miami Speedway. Like Homestead, Florida City is rooted in agriculture, with hundreds of acres of farmland west of Krome Avenue and a huge farmers' market that processes produce shipped nationwide.

WHERE TO EAT

$$$ ✕ **Mutineer Restaurant.** Families and older couples prefer the quirky yet well-dressed setting of this roadside steak-and-seafood restaurant with an indoor-outdoor fish-and-duck pond. It was built to look like a ship in 1980, back when Florida City was barely on the map. Etched glass divides the bi-level dining rooms, with velvet upholstered chairs, an aquarium, and nautical antiques. The big menu has 12 seafood entrées, including stuffed grouper (a favorite), Florida lobster tails, and snapper Oscar, plus another half-dozen daily seafood specials, as well as poultry, ribs, and steaks. At lunch there are burgers and seafood sandwiches, and there's a happy-hour buffet all day until 7 PM in the lounge for $2.25 and the purchase of a drink. Friday and Saturday are dance nights with live entertainment. ⊠ *11 S.E. 1st Ave. (U.S. 1), at Palm Dr.* ☎ *305/245–3377* ⊕ *www.mutineer.biz* ⊟ *AE, D, DC, MC, V.*

$$ ✕ **Capri Restaurant.** Locals have been coming here for affordable Italian food in a wide selection since 1958. Outside it's a rock-walled building with a big parking lot that fills up nightly. The interior has dark-wood paneling with redbrick accents and heavy wooden furniture. A pleasant courtyard affords outdoor dining. The tasty fare ranges from pizza with a light, crunchy crust and ample toppings to spaghetti 16 different ways, and broiled steaks and seafood-pasta classics. This is traditional Italian-American cuisine with no surprises and little flourish. Bargain hunters have two choices: the daily early-bird entrées, 4:30 to 6:30 for $12 to $14, which include soup or salad and potato or spaghetti, and the Tuesday family night (after 4 PM), which has all-you-can-eat pasta with salad or soup for $6.95. Specialty martinis and fruity cocktails supplement the international wine list. ⊠ *935 N. Krome Ave.*

☎*305/247–1542* ⊕*www.the-capri.com* ▭*AE, D, MC, V* ⊘*Closed for lunch Sun.*

$$ ✗**Captain's Restaurant and Seafood Market.** A comfortable place where the chef knows how to do seafood with flair, this is one of the town's best bets. Locals and visitors alike gather in the cozy dining room or outdoors on the patio. Blackboards describe a varied menu of sandwiches, pasta, seafood, steak, and nightly specials. Inventive offerings include lobster Reuben sandwich, crawfish pasta, and pan-seared tuna topped with balsamic onions and shallots. ⊠*404 S.E. 1st Ave.,* . ☎*305/247–9456* ▭*AE, MC, V.*

★ **$** ✗**Farmers' Market Restaurant.** Although it's in the farmers' market and serves fresh vegetables, seafood figures prominently on the menu of home-cooked specialties. A family of fishermen runs the place, so fish and shellfish are only hours from the sea. Catering to the fishing and farming crowd, it opens at 5:30 AM, serving pancakes, jumbo eggs, and fluffy omelets with home fries or grits in a pleasant dining room with checkered tablecloths on the edge of town. The lunch and dinner menus have fried shrimp, seafood pasta, country-fried steak, roast turkey, and fried conch, as well as burgers, salads, and sandwiches. ⊠*300 N. Krome Ave.* ☎*305/242–0008* ▭*MC, V.*

$ ✗**Gusto's Grill & Bar.** This fun and friendly place is mostly about drinking and watching sports on TV, yet it's also good for catching a reasonably priced meal, especially during happy hour (4 to 7 PM), when there's a free buffet (with a two-drink minimum). Sit indoors or out (televisions are situated throughout) to order your honey garlic wings, shrimp corn chowder, pasta, burgers, pizza, steak, cashew salmon, and crab cakes from the extensive menu. Shoot pool and sip a Razzeberri Mojito while you wait. ⊠*326 S.E. 1st Ave.* ☎*786/243–9800* ▭*AE, D, MC, V.*

★ ¢ ✗**Rosita's Restaurante.** With its population of immigrant farm workers, this area can boast the real thing in Mexican, a flavor you just don't get in the Tex-Mex chains. Order à la carte specialties or dinners and combos with beans and rice, and salad. Forty-three breakfast, lunch, and dinner entrées are served all day and range from Mexican eggs, enchiladas, and taco salad to stewed beef, shrimp rancheros style, and fried pork chop. The food is on the spicy side, and if you like more fire, each table comes prepared with fresh-tasting salsa, pickled jalapeños, and bottled habañero sauce. Clean (with lingering faint whiffs of bleach to prove it) and pleasant, with an open kitchen, take-out counter, and Formica tables, it's a favorite with locals and budget-minded guests at the hostel across the street. ⊠*199 W. Palm Dr.* ☎*305/246-3114* ▭*AE, MC, V.*

WHERE TO STAY

$$$ ▦**Best Western Gateway to the Keys.** If you want easy access to Everglades and Biscayne national parks as well as the Florida Keys, you'll be well placed at this pretty, modern, two-story motel two blocks off the Florida Turnpike. Standard rooms, done in tropical colors, have two queen-size beds or one king-size bed. Rooms around the lushly landscaped pool cost the most. There's high-speed Internet access available in the rooms, plus wireless access in the lobby. All rooms are no-smoking. **Pros:** Convenient to national parks and Keys, business services, pretty pool area. **Cons:** Traffic noise, generic rooms, fills up fast during high season. ⊠*411 S. Krome Ave.* ☎*305/246–5100 or 888/981—5100* 🖶*305/242–0056* ⊕*www.bestwestern.com/gateway-tothekeys* 📠*114 rooms* ⌂*In-room: refrigerator, Ethernet, dial-up. In-hotel: pool, no elevator, laundry facilities, Wi-Fi, no-smoking rooms* ⊟*AE, D, DC, MC, V* ⑩*CP.*

$-$$$ 🏨**Fairway Inn.** Two stories high with a waterfall pool, this motel has some of the area's lowest chain rates, and it's next to the chamber of commerce. Rooms, with either one king-size bed or two doubles, have tiled bathrooms and closet areas. **Pros:** Affordability; convenient to restaurants, parks, and raceway; free wireless connections in room. **Cons:** No character, plain rooms, small rooms. ⊠*100 S.E. 1st Ave.* ☎*305/248–4202 or 888/340–4734* 📠*160 rooms* ⌂*In-room: refrigerator, dial-up, Wi-Fi. In-hotel: pool, laundry facilities, no-smoking rooms* ⊟*AE, D, MC, V* ⑩*CP.*

¢-$$$ 🏨**Travelodge.** This bargain motor lodge is close to the Florida Turnpike, Everglades and Biscayne national parks, the Florida Keys, and the Homestead Miami Speedway. In fact, most of the racers stay here, which makes it difficult to get a room when any track events are scheduled. Clean and colorful rooms are smallish, but they have more amenities than usually found in this price range, including complimentary breakfast and newspaper, coffeemaker, hair dryer, iron with ironing board, high-speed Internet access, and voice mail. Fast-food and chain eateries, gas stations, and a visitor's bureau are within walking distance. **Pros:** In-room refrigerator and microwave, convenience to U.S. 1, complimentary breakfast. **Cons:** Lack of character, small rooms, busy location. ⊠*409 S.E. 1st Ave.* ☎*305/248–9777 or 800/758–0618* 🖶*305/248–9750* ⊕*www.tlflcity.com* 📠*88 rooms* ⌂*In-room: safe, refrigerator, Ethernet, dial-up, Wi-Fi. In-hotel: pool, laundry facilities* ⊟*AE, D, DC, MC, V* ⑩*CP.*

$$ 🏨**Comfort Inn.** Rooms are large, have contemporary tropical furnishings, and are on one of two floors (there's no elevator). They're outfitted with irons, hair dryers, and coffeemakers. Continental breakfast and newspapers are free. In-room Internet connections are high-speed. It's in an asphalt complex of hotels, gas stations, and restaurants just off U.S. 1. **Pros:** Free continental breakfast, close to restaurants and services, in-room conveniences. **Cons:** No elevator, noisy location, nondescript rooms. ⊠*333 S.E. 1st Ave.,* ☎*305/248–4009 or 888/352–2489* 🖶*305/248–7935* 📠*124 rooms* ⌂*In-room: safe, refrigerator, Ethernet, dial-up. In-hotel: pool, no elevator, laundry facilities, public Wi-Fi, no-smoking rooms* ⊟*AE, D, DC, MC, V* ⑩*CP.*

$-$$ 🏨**Econo Lodge.** Close to the Florida Turnpike and with access to the Keys, this is a good pullover spot for an overnight. The rooms are uncramped, with attractive bedspreads, and have coffeemakers and data ports. The pool sits in the middle of the parking lot, but tall ficus hedges separate it from busy Highway 1. There's a $1 daily charge to use the refrigerators that are in the rooms. **Pros:** Convenient location, business services, microwaves and refrigerators for rent. **Cons:** Urban-ugly location, noisy, lack of character. ⊠*553 N.E. 1st Ave.* ☎*305/248–9300 or 800/553–*

2666 ⌨305/245–2753 ⊕www.
econolodge.com ⟲42 rooms ♿In-
room: refrigerator, dial-up, Wi-Fi.
In-hotel: pool, no elevator, laundry
facilities, public Internet, public Wi-
Fi, no-smoking rooms ▤AE, D,
DC, MC, V ⦿|CP.

★ $ 🖳**Ramada Inn.** Racing fans can
hear the engines roar from this
two-story motel next to an outlet
mall and within 15 minutes of the
raceway and Everglades and Bis-

> ### ALL BARK, NO BITE?
>
> Only four out of the Everglades'
> 27 species of snakes are venom-
> ous: cottonmouths, diamondback
> rattlesnakes, dusky pigmy rattle-
> snakes, and coral snakes. Wear
> sturdy boots when hiking in
> wooded or grassy areas to
> avoid bites.

cayne national parks. If you're looking for an upgrade from the other
chains, this one offers more amenities and comfort, such as 37-inch
plasma TVs, closed closets, and stylish furnishings. Carpeted rooms are
bright and clean and have upholstered chairs, a coffeemaker, and an
iron and ironing board. Included are a continental breakfast with some
hot items, and local calls. **Pros:** Extra room amenities, business clientele perks, convenient location. **Cons:** Busy location, chain anonymity.
✉124 E. Palm Dr. ☎305/247–8833 or 800/426–7866 ⌨305/247–
6456 ⊕www.hotelfloridacity.com ⟲123 rooms ♿In-room: refrigerator (some), dial-up, Wi-Fi. In-hotel: pool, no elevator, laundry service,
public Internet, no-smoking rooms ▤AE, D, DC, MC, V ⦿|CP.

¢ 🖳**Everglades Hostel.** Stay in clean and spacious private or dorm-style
rooms (generally six to a room; bring your own linen); relax in indoor
and outdoor quiet areas; watch videos or TV on a big screen; and take
affordable airboat, hiking, biking, and sightseeing tours. This HI-AYH
facility is in a minimally restored Art Deco building on a lush, private
acre between Everglades and Biscayne national parks, 20 mi north
of Key Largo. At mealtime, enjoy a free all-you-can-make pancake
breakfast in the communal kitchen, pitch in for a communal dinner
(according to demand, $5 each), or walk to a nearby restaurant. Pets
are welcome. You can make free domestic long-distance calls from the
phone in the lobby. **Pros:** Affordability, Everglades tours, free services.
Cons: Communal living, no elevator, old structure. ✉20 S.W. 2nd
Ave. ☎305/248–1122 or 800/372–3874 ⌨305/245–7622 ⊕www.
evergladeshostel.com ⟲46 beds in dorm-style rooms with shared
bath, 2 private rooms with shared bath ♿In-room: no a/c (some), no
phone, no TV. In-hotel: water sports, bicycles, no elevator, laundry
facilities, public Internet, public Wi-Fi, some pets allowed, no-smoking rooms ▤MC, V.

SHOPPING

Prime Outlets—Florida City (✉250 E. Palm Dr. ☎888/545–1798
⊕www.primeoutlets.com) has nearly 50 discount stores plus a small
food court.

Divers Supply (✉402 S.E. First Ave. ☎305/247–3483 ⊕www.divers-
supply.com) For good deals on diving equipment before you get to the
Keys' more costly shops, stop here. It carries everything from snorkels
to dive kayaks.

9

★ **Robert Is Here** (✉ *19200 Palm Dr. [S.W. 344th St.]* ☎ *305/246–1592* ⊕ *www.robertishere.com*), a remarkable fruit stand, sells vegetables, fresh-fruit milk shakes (the key lime shake is fabulous), 10 flavors of honey, more than 100 flavors of jams and jellies, fresh juices, salad dressings, and some 30 kinds of tropical fruits, including (in season) carambola, lychee, egg fruit, monstera, sapodilla, dragonfruit, genipa, sugar apple, and tamarind. The stand started in 1960, when seven-year-old Robert sat at this spot selling his father's bumper crop of cucumbers. Now Robert ships around the world, and everything is first quality. Seconds are given to needy area families. An odd assortment of animals out back—from goats to emus—adds to the entertainment value. The stand opens at 8 and never closes earlier than 7. It does shut down, however, during September and October.

FLAMINGO

38 mi southwest of Ernest F. Coe Visitor Center.

Here at the far end of the main road lies a marina (from which sightseeing tours and fishing charters into Everglades National Park depart), a visitor center, and a campground on Florida Bay. The marina also rents kayaks and motorboats. Before Hurricanes Katrina and Wilma washed them away in 2005, a lodge, cabins, and restaurants provided Everglades National Park's only accommodations. At press time, no information was available about the rebuilding of Flamingo Lodge. Nearby is Eco Pond, one of the most popular wildlife observation areas. Recovery efforts continue, so check ⊕ *www.nps.gov/ever* for a facilities update before you visit.

The **Flamingo Visitor Center** provides an interactive display and has natural-history exhibits in the small Florida Bay Flamingo Museum. Check the schedule for ranger-led activities, such as naturalist discussions, evening programs in the campground amphitheater, and hikes along area trails. Some of the park's best birding is at nearby Eco Pond. ☎ *239/695–2945* ⊘ *Exhibits are always open; staffed hours: 8–4:30 mid-Nov. through mid-Apr..*

WHERE TO STAY

For an intense stay in the "real" Florida, consider one of the 45 backcountry campsites deep in the park, many inland, with some on the beach. You'll have to carry your food, water, and supplies in; take care to carry out all your trash. You'll also need a site-specific permit, available on a first-come, first-served basis from the Flamingo or Gulf Coast Visitor Center. These sites cost $10 for a permit plus $2 per person per night with a 14-night limit.

⚠ **Everglades National Park.** About 12 mi southwest of Florida City, the park has two developed campsites available through a reservation system from mid-November through mid-April; the rest of the year they're first-come, first-served. Six miles west of the park's main entrance, **Long Pine Key** has no-permit hiking, though you will need separate permits for freshwater and saltwater fishing. ♿ *Flush toilets, dump station,* *drinking water, picnic tables, public telephone* ⮑*108 drive-up sites* ☎*800/365–2267 campsite reservations, 305/242–7873 Long Pine Key, 305/242–7700, 239/695–2945 park information in Flamingo* ⊕*www. recreation.gov* ▭*D, MC, V.*

★ Thirty-eight miles southwest of the park's main entrance, ⚠️ **Flamingo** has hiking and nature trails. Of its 234 drive-in sites, most have a view of the bay; nine of its 40 walk-in sites are on the water. ♿*Flush toilets, dump station, drinking water, showers (cold), general store* ⮑*234 drive-up sites, 40 walk-in sites, 20 on the water* ☎*800/365–2267 campsite reservations, 305/242–7700, 239/695–2945 park information* ⊕*reservations.nps.gov* ▭*D, MC, V.*

THE OUTDOORS

BOATING

★ The marina at **Flamingo Lodge, Marina & Outpost Resort** (☎*239/695–3101*) rents 17-foot power skiffs for $155 per day (if returned by 4 pm), $100 per half day, $65 for two hours. Several private boats are also available for charter. A small store sells food, camping supplies, bait and tackle, propane, and fuel. A concessionaire rents rods, reels, binoculars, and coolers by the half and full day.

CANOEING & KAYAKING

Everglades has well-marked canoe trails in the Flamingo area, plus the southern end of the 99-mi Wilderness Trail from Everglades City to Flamingo.

★ **Flamingo Lodge, Marina & Outpost Resort** (☎*239/695–3101*) rents canoes in two sizes: small (up to two paddlers) and family-size (up to four). Small canoes rent for $8 per hour; family-size run $10. Daily and overnight rates also available. Saltwater crocodiles like to hang out around the marina on Buttonwood Canal, so you're practically guaranteed a sighting.

FISHING

★ **Flamingo Lodge, Marina & Outpost Resort** (☎*239/695–3101*) helps arrange two-person charter fishing trips on weekends. The cost is $450 a day for one or two people, $350 for a half day. Cost per person over two is $25 each. Cost includes tackle, ice, and license.

TAMIAMI TRAIL

141 mi from Miami to Fort Myers.

In 1915, when officials decided to build an east–west highway linking Miami to Fort Myers and continuing north to Tampa, it made sense to call it the Tamiami Trail. In 1928 the road became a reality, cutting

9

through the Everglades and altering the natural flow of water and the lives of the Miccosukee Indians, who eked out a living fishing, hunting, farming, and frogging here.

Today the highway's traffic streams through Everglades National Park, Big Cypress National Preserve, and Fakahatchee Strand Preserve State Park. The landscape is surprisingly varied, changing from hardwood hammocks to pinelands, then abruptly to tall cypress trees dripping with Spanish moss and back to saw-grass marsh. Those who slow down to take in the scenery are rewarded with glimpses of alligators sunning themselves along the banks of roadside canals and in the shallow waters, and hundreds of waterbirds, especially in the dry winter season. The man-made landscape has chickee huts, Native American villages, and airboats parked at roadside enterprises.

> ## OK, KILL JAWS MUSIC
>
> One thing you won't see at Shark Valley is sharks. The name comes from the Shark River, also called the River of Grass, which flows through the area. Several species of shark swim up this river from the coast (about 45 mi south of Shark Valley) to give birth. The young sharks aren't able to tolerate saltwater, and need to experience the waters of the slough before they can swim out to sea.

Businesses along the trail give their addresses either based on their distance from Krome Avenue, Florida Turnpike, and Miami on the east coast or Naples on the west coast. Between Miami and Naples the road goes by several names, including Tamiami Trail, U.S. 41, Ninth Street in Naples, and, at the Miami end, Southwest 8th Street.

WHAT TO SEE

A perennial favorite with tour-bus operators, **Everglades Safari Park** has an arena that seats up to 300 people to watch an educational alligator show and wrestling demonstration. Before and after the show, get a closer look at the alligators and crocodiles on Gator Island, walk through a small wildlife museum, follow the jungle trail, or climb aboard an airboat for a 30-minute ride on the River of Grass (included in admission). There's also a restaurant, a gift shop, and an observation platform that looks out over the Glades. Small, private airboat tours are available for an extra charge and last 20 minutes to 2½ hours. ✉*26700 Tamiami Trail, 15 mi west of Florida Tpke.* ☎*305/226–6923 or 305/223–3804* ⊕*www.evsafaripark.com* ⊠*$20* ☉*Daily 9–5.*

After visiting **Everglades Gator Park** you can tell your friends you came face-to-face with—and even touched—an alligator, albeit a baby one. You can also squirm in a "reptilium" of venomous and nonpoisonous native snakes or learn about Native Americans of the Everglades through a reproduction of a Miccosukee village. The park also has wildlife shows with native and exotic animals, 45-minute airboat tours, and RV campsites, as well as a gift shop and restaurant. The last airboat ride departs 45 minutes before sunset. ✉*24050 Tamiami Trail, 12 mi west of Florida Tpke.* ☎*305/559–2255 or 800/559–2205* ⊕*www. gatorpark.com* ⊠*Tours, wildlife show, and park $20* ☉*Daily 9–6.*

★ ☺ It takes a bit of nerve to walk the paved 15-mi loop in **Shark Valley**, because in the winter months alligators lie on and alongside the road, basking in the sun—most, however, do move quickly out of the way. You can also ride a bicycle or take a tram tour (reservations recommended in winter). Stop at the halfway point to climb the concrete observation tower's ramp, which spirals skyward 50 feet. From there the River of Grass spreads as far as the eye can see. Observe waterbirds as well as alligators and, if you're lucky, river otters crossing the road, and follow a short trail into the habitat. Just behind the bike-rental area a short boardwalk trail meanders through the saw grass and another one passes through a tropical hardwood hammock. A small visitor center has rotating exhibits, a bookstore, and park rangers ready to answer questions. An underwater live camera in the canal behind the center lets visitors sporadically see the alligators and otters from the gift shop. Shark Valley is the national park's north entrance; however, no roads here lead directly to other parts of the park. ⊠ *23½ mi west of Florida Tpke.* ☎ *305/221–8455, 305/221–8776 tram tours* ☞ *Park $10 per vehicle, $5 per pedestrian, bicyclist, or motorcyclist* ☯ *Visitor center daily 9:15–5:15 (8:45–5:15 from late Dec. through late March); gate daily 8:30–6.*

★ ☺ The cultural center at **Miccosukee Indian Village** showcases the Miccosukee's foods, crafts, skills, and lifestyle. It also presents cultural alligator shows, which explain how the animals and Native Americans have historically interacted, and crafts demonstrations. Narrated 30-minute airboat rides take you into the heart of the wilderness to which these Native Americans escaped after the Seminole Wars and Indian Removal Act of the mid-1800s. In modern times the Miccosukee clans have relocated to this village along Tamiami Trail, but most still maintain their hammock farming and hunting camps. The village's museum shows a film and displays chickee structures and artifacts that explain this ancient culture. Guided tours are available throughout the day. The Everglades Music & Craft Festival falls on a July weekend, and the weeklong Indian Arts Festival is in late December. There's a restaurant and gift shop on-site. ⊠ *Just west of Shark Valley entrance, 25 mi west of Florida Tpke. at Mile Marker 70* ☎ *305/223–8380* ⊕ *www.miccosukeetribe.com* ☞ *Village $10, rides $10* ☯ *Daily 9–5.*

The **Oasis Visitor Center** is a welcome respite along the Tamiami Trail. If you blow by here as you speed between Miami and Naples, you'll miss out on an opportunity to learn about the surrounding preserve. The biggest attraction is the huge gators you can view from the boardwalk in front. Inside the center are a small exhibit area, an information center, a bookshop, and a theater that shows a dated but informative 15-minute film on the preserve and Big Cypress Swamp. The center also has myriad seasonal ranger-led and self-guided activities, such as campfire and wildlife talks, hikes, slough slogs, and canoe excursions. The 8-mi Turner River Canoe Trail begins nearby and crosses through Everglades National Park before ending in Chokoloskee Bay, near Everglades City. Rangers lead four-hour canoe trips on most Wednesdays, Saturdays, and Sundays in season beginning at 9:30 AM. Two-hour ranger swamp

9

walks take place most Saturdays beginning at 1 PM and Mondays at 10 AM. Reservations are required (☎239/695–1201) for ranger programs up to 14 days in advance. Hikers on their own can join the Florida National Scenic Trail, which begins in the preserve and is divided in three segments 6.5 to 28 mi each. Two 5-mi trails, Concho Billy and Fire Prairie, can be accessed a few miles east off Turner River Road. Turner River Road and Birdon Road form a 17-mi gravel loop drive that's excellent for birding. Bear Island has about 32 mi of scenic, flat, looped trails that are ideal for bicycling. Most trails are hard-packed lime rock, but a few miles are gravel. Cyclists share the road with off-road vehicles, which are most plentiful during General Gun Hunting season, from mid-November through December. To see the best variety of wildlife from your car, follow 26-mi Loop Road, south of U.S. 41 and west of Shark Valley, where alligators, raccoons, and soft-shell turtles crawl around right beside the gravel road and swallowtail kites and brown-shouldered hawks swoop. Stop at H. P. Williams Roadside Park, west of the Oasis, and walk along the boardwalk to spy gators, turtles, and garfish in the river waters. ⊠24 mi east of Everglades City, 50 mi west of Miami, 20 mi west of Shark Valley ☎239/695–1201 ⊕www.nps.gov/bicy ⊠Free ⊗Daily 9–4:30.

The tiny **Ochopee Post Office** is the smallest in North America. Buy a picture postcard of the little one-room shack and mail it to a friend, thereby helping to keep this picturesque spot in business. ⊠4 mi east of Rte. 29, Ochopee ☎800/275–8777 ⊗ Weekdays 10–noon and 1–4:30, Sat. 10–11:30.

☾ A classic Florida roadside attraction, **Wooten's Airboat Tours** offers a typical Everglades array of alligators, snakes, panthers, and other creatures in addition to airboat and swamp-buggy tours. See wild-life and an old fishing camp complete with a moonshine still on the swamp-buggy tour. Visit the animal exhibits separately or as part of a tour combo. ⊠Tamiami Trail, 1½ mi east of Rte. 29, Ochopee ☎239/695–2781 or 800/282–2781 ⊕www.wootenseverglades.com ⊠$25 for half-hour tour, $8 for animal exhibits ⊗Daily 8:30–5 (last ride departs at 4:30).

Since it opened in 1989, **Florida Panther National Wildlife Refuge** has remained off-limits to human access to protect the endangered cougar subspecies. In 2005, driven by public input, the refuge opened two short loop trails in a region lightly traveled by panthers so visitors could get a taste of the wet prairies, tropical hammocks, and pine uplands where panthers range and wild orchids thrive. The trails, less than 2 mi total, range from muddy in spots in winter to thigh-high under water in summer, and may be closed when particularly flooded. If you look closely, you may see signs of deer, black bear, and even panthers, but sightings are rare. ⊠Off Rte. 29, ½ mi north of I–75 Exit 80 ⌂3860 Tollgate Blvd., Suite 300Naples ☎800/344–9453 ⊕floridapanther. fws.gov ⊠Free ⊗Daily dawn–dusk; trails may be closed July–Nov. because of rain.

★ The ½-mi boardwalk at **Fakahatchee Strand Preserve State Park** gives you an opportunity to see rare plants, bald cypress, nesting eagles, and North America's largest stand of native royal palms and largest concentration and variety of epiphytic orchids, including 31 varieties of threatened and endangered species that bloom most extravagantly in the hot months. It's particularly famous for its ghost orchids, which are visible only on guided hikes. You can drive through the 12-mi-long (one-way) W. J. Janes Memorial Scenic Drive and hike the spur trails that lead off it. Rangers lead swamp walks and canoe trips November through April. ⊠ *Boardwalk on north side of Tamiami Trail 7 mi west of Rte. 29. W. J. Janes Scenic Dr. ¾ mi north of Tamiami Trail on Rte. 29; ranger station on W. J. Janes Scenic Dr., Box 35, Everglades City* ☎ *239/695–4593* ⊕ *www.floridastateparks.org/fakahatcheestrand* ⊠ *Free* ☉ *Daily 8–sunset.*

> ## CROCS OR GATORS?
>
> You can tell you're looking at a crocodile, not an alligator, if you can see its lower teeth protruding when its jaws are shut. Gators are much darker in color—a grayish black—compared with the lighter tan color of crocodiles. Alligators' snouts are also much broader than their long, thin crocodilian counterparts.

★ Nature trails, biking, camping, and canoeing into Everglades territory make **Collier-Seminole State Park** an easy introduction to this often forbidding land. Of historical interest, a Seminole War blockhouse has been re-created to hold the interpretative center, and one of the "walking dredges"—invented to carve the Tamiami Trail out of the muck—adorns the grounds. ⊠ *20200 E. Tamiami Trail, Naples* ☎ *239/394–3397* ⊕ *www.floridastateparks.org/collier-seminole* ⊠ *$4 per car* ☉ *Daily 8–sunset.*

WHERE TO EAT

$ ✕ **Coopertown Restaurant.** Make this pit stop for local color and cuisine fished straight from the swamp. For more than a half century this small, casual eatery inside an airboat concession storefront has attracted the famous and the humbly hungry. House specialties are frogs' legs and alligator tail prepared cornmeal-breaded and deep-fried, served simply on paper ware with a lemon wedge and Tabasco. Also choose from more conventional selections, such as catfish, shrimp, or sandwiches. ⊠ *22700 S.W. 8th St., 11 mi west of Florida Tpke., Miami* ✉ *Box 940176* ☎ *305/226–6048* ⊕ *www.coopertown-airboats.com* ⊟ *AE, MC, V.*

$ ✕ **Empeek Aaweeke.** Whether you're staying at the Miccosukee Resort or just spending the day at the slot machines, the all-day buffet will bolster you with salads, cold cuts, chicken, fish, meat dishes, and desserts. There's a Friday night seafood buffet. The restaurant's bright Art Deco furnishings and tribal art murals are in keeping with the rest of the resort. Kids under age six eat free; ages six to 11 eat half-price. ⊠ *500 S.W. 177th Ave., 6 mi west of Florida Tpke., Miami* ☎ *305/925–2555 or 877/242–6464* ⊕ *www.miccosukee.com* ⊟ *AE, D, MC, V.*

9

★ ¢ ✕**Miccosukee Restaurant.** For a taste of local culture at a reasonable price, this restaurant at the Miccosukee Indian Village overlooking the River of Grass provides the best variety of food along Tamiami Trail in Everglades territory. A mural depicting Native American women cooking and men engaged in a powwow and a view of the River of Grass with outdoor seating provide atmosphere in this roadside cafeteria setting; servers wear traditional Seminole patchwork vests. Favorites are catfish and frogs' legs breaded and deep-fried, Indian fry bread, pumpkin bread, and Indian burgers and tacos, but you'll also find more common fare, such as huge burgers, fish, and Hispanic dishes. Try the Miccosukee Platter ($22.95) for a sampling of local favorites, including gator bites. Breakfast and lunch are served daily. ✉*25 mi west of Florida Tpke.* ☎*305/223–8380 Ext. 2374* ⊟*AE, D, MC, V.*

☙ ¢ ✕**Pit Bar-B-Q.** At the edge of Miami, this old-fashioned roadside eatery is a holdout from the Everglades' backwoods heritage and a popular, affordable option for families. Order at the counter, pick up your food, and eat at one of the picnic tables indoors on the screened porch or outdoors. Specialties include barbecued chicken and ribs with a tangy sauce, french fries, coleslaw, and a fried biscuit, plus burgers and fish sandwiches. The whopping double-decker beef or pork sandwich with slaw requires at least five napkins. Locals flock here, bringing the kids on weekends for pony rides. ✉*16400 Tamiami Trail, 5 mi west of Florida Tpke., Miami* ☎*305/226–2272* ⊟*AE, D, MC, V.*

WHERE TO STAY

$$$ ▦**Miccosukee Resort & Convention Center.** Big-name entertainers, major sporting events, and gaming draw crowds to this nine-story resort at the crossroads of Tamiami Trail and Krome Avenue. Like an oasis on the horizon, it's the only facility for miles, and it's situated to attract the attention of travelers going to the Everglades, driving across the state, or looking for casino action. The casino occupies the lobby, making for a cigarette-smoky welcome as visitors enter to check in. Most units have a view of Everglades saw grass and wildlife. In addition to an enormous indoor play area for children and a game arcade for teens and 'tweens, there are tours to Everglades National Park and the Miccosukee Indian Village, shuttles to area malls, and a golf course about 9 mi away. **Pros:** Casino, most modern resort in these parts, golf. **Cons:** Cigarette smell in lobby, parking lot fills with gamblers, doesn't feel compatible with the Everglades. ✉*500 S.W. 177th Ave., 6 mi west of Florida Tpke., Miami* ☎*305/925–2555 or 877/242–6464* ⊕*www. miccosukee.com* ☚*256 rooms, 46 suites* ♿*In-room: safe, dial-up. In-hotel: 3 restaurants, bars, golf course, pool, gym, spa, children's programs (ages 0–12), laundry service, airport shuttle, public Internet, no-smoking rooms* ⊟*AE, D, DC, MC, V.*

⚠**Everglades Gator Park.** At an airboat tour facility in the heart of the Everglades, this RV park is especially popular with snowbirds, as it's close to the Port of Miami and Miami airport and offers short-term RV storage. Campers are surrounded by the sounds of alligators, birds, and frogs by night, departing and arriving airboats by day. There's a restaurant inside the park. ♿*Restaurant, flush toilets, full hookups, drinking water, electricity, public telephone, general store* ☚*20 full hookups,*

20 partial hookups ✉*24050 S.W. 8th St., Miami* ☎*Box 787, Miami* ☎*305/559–2255 or 800/559–2205* 🖷*305/559–2844* ⊕*www.gator-park.com* ⊟*AE, D, DC, MC, V.*

🐊 **Trail Lakes Campground.** Closer to Everglades City and Big Cypress Preserve, Trail Lakes is near a canoe launch and has the added attraction of a nature park and wildlife exhibits. The complex's owner, David Shealy, is the self-proclaimed expert on the Skunk Ape, the Everglades version of Big Foot, and often appears on national television. RV and tent campsites circle a small lake and front the River of Grass. ﴾*Flush toilets, full hookups, drinking water, electricity, dump station, public telephone, general store* ◆*80 RV sites, 25 tent sites* ✉*40904 Hwy. 41 E, Ochopee* ☎*305/695–2275* 🖷*305/695–2275* ⊕*www.skunkape. info* ⊟*MC, V.*

THE OUTDOORS

★ **Shark Valley Tram Tours** (✉*Shark Valley* ☎*305/221–8455*) rents one-speed, well-used bikes daily 8:30–4 (last rental at 3; bikes must be returned by 4) for $6.50 per hour.

SHOPPING

The shopping alone should lure you to the **Miccosukee Indian Village** (✉*25 mi west of Florida Tpke., just west of Shark Valley entrance* ☎*305/223–8380*). Wares include Native American crafts such as beadwork, moccasins, dolls, pottery, baskets, and patchwork fabric and clothes.

EVERGLADES CITY

35 mi southeast of Naples, 83 mi west of Miami.

Aside from a chain gas station or two, this is perfect Old Florida. No high-rises (other than an observation tower) mar the landscape at this western gateway to Everglades National Park, just off the Tamiami Trail. It was developed in the late 19th century by Barron Collier, a wealthy advertising man. Collier built it as a company town to house workers for his numerous projects, including construction of the Tamiami Trail. It grew and prospered until the Depression and World War II. Today it draws people to the park for canoeing, fishing, and bird-watching excursions. Airboat tours, though popular with visitors, are banned within the preserve and park because of the environmental damage they cause to the mangroves. The annual Seafood Festival, held the first weekend of February, draws 60,000 to 75,000 visitors to eat seafood, hear nonstop music, and buy crafts. At other times, dining choices are limited to a handful of basic eateries. The town is small, fishing-oriented, and unhurried, making it excellent for boating and bicycling. Pedal along the waterfront on a 2-mi ride along the strand out to Chokoloskee Island.

The best place to find information about Everglades National Park's watery western side is at the **Gulf Coast Visitor Center.** During the winter season, it's filled with canoeists checking in for trips to the Ten Thousand Islands and 99-mi Wilderness Waterway Trail, visitors viewing

9

interpretive exhibits about local flora and fauna while they wait for the departure of a naturalist-led boat trip, rangers answering questions, and backcountry campers purchasing permits. In season (Christmas through Easter), rangers lead bike tours and canoe trips. There are no direct roads from here to other sections of the park. ⊠*Rte. 29* ☎*239/695–3311* 🖃*Park free* ☉*Mid-Nov.–mid-Apr., daily 8–4:30; mid-Apr.–mid-Nov., daily 9–4:30.*

You can climb 108 steps to the top of the **Observation Tower** (across the road from the visitor center entrance), which was built in 1984 and recently reopened to visitors behind the chamber of commerce office. The office does not have regular hours, so call ahead to see when you can visit. ⊠*905 Copeland Ave.* ☎*239/695–3172* 🖃*$2* ☉*Call for hrs.*

Through artifacts and photographs at the **Museum of the Everglades,** meet the Native Americans, pioneers, businesspeople, and fishermen who played a role in the development of southwest Florida. Exhibits and a film chronicle the tremendous feat of building Tamiami Trail through the mosquito- and gator-infested Everglades wetlands. The only unaltered structure original to the town of Everglades, where it opened in 1927 as the town's laundry, the building is on the National Register of Historic Places. In addition to the permanent displays, there are occasional rotating exhibits and works by local artists. ⊠*105 W. Broadway* ☎*239/695–0008* ⊕*www.colliermuseum.com* 🖃*Free* ☉*Tues.–Fri. 9-5, Sat. 9–4.*

OFF THE BEATEN PATH

Smallwood Store. Ted Smallwood pioneered this last American frontier in 1906 and built a 3,000-square-foot pine trading post raised on pilings on Chokoloskee Bay. Smallwood's granddaughter Lynn McMillin reopened it in 1989, after it had been closed for several years, and installed a small gift shop and a museum chock-full of goods from the store, including historic photographs and original store ledgers; Native American clothing, furs, and hides; and area memorabilia. An annual festival in March celebrates the century-long relationship the store has had with local Native Americans. ⊠*360 Mamie St., Chokoloskee Island* ☎*239/695–2989* 🖃*$3* ☉*Dec.–Apr., daily 10–5; May–Nov., daily 11–5.*

WHERE TO EAT

$$$ ✕**Rod and Gun Club.** The striking, polished pecky-cypress woodwork in this historic building dates from the 1920s, when wealthy hunters, anglers, and yachting parties from around the world came for the winter season. The main dining room holds the overflow from the popular enormous screened porch that overlooks the river. Like life in general here, servers move slowly and upkeep is minimal. Fresh seafood dominates a menu that includes stone crab claws in season, a turf-and-surf combo of steak and grouper, a swamp-and-turf combo of frogs' legs and steak, seafood and pasta pairings, and yummy key lime pie. If you lack the nerve to go native for your entrée, you can sample frogs' legs or gator nuggets as an appetizer. Arrive by boat or land. ⊠*200 Riverside Dr.* ☎*239/695–2101* ⊕*www.evergladesrodandgun. com* 🖃*No credit cards.*

$$ ✕**Everglades Seafood Depot.** Come for affordable, scenic breakfast, lunch, or dinner to this storied 1928 Spanish-style stucco structure on Lake Placid. It began its life as the original Everglades depot, was part of the University of Miami, appeared in the film *Winds across the Everglades,* and has housed several restaurants. Today's menu has a wide selection of well-prepared seafood—from shrimp and grouper to frogs' legs and alligator—and combinations thereof. For big appetites, there are generously portioned entrécs of steak and fish specials and combination platters that include warm, fresh-baked biscuits. Weekly specials include a taco bar one day and all-you-can-eat specials others. Ask for a table on the back porch overlooking the lake or a window seat. ⊠ *102 Collier Ave.* ☎ *239/695–0075* ▤ *AE, D, MC, V.*

🐚 $$ ✕**Oyster House Restaurant.** One of the town's oldest and most old-fashioned fish houses, it serves all the local staples—shrimp, gator tail, frogs' legs, oysters, stone crab, and grouper—in a lodge-like setting where mounted wild animals decorate the walls and rafters. Shrimp scampi and grouper smothered in tomatoes are among the few exceptions to fried preparation. But deep-frying is an art in these parts, so if you're going to indulge, do it here. Try to dine at sunset. ⊠ *Hwy. 29 S.* ☎ *239/695– 2073* ⊕ *www.oysterhouserestaurant.com* ▤ *AE, D, MC, V.*

$ ✕**Triad Seafood.** Along the Barron River, seafood houses, fishing boats, and crab traps populate one shoreline; mangroves the other. Some of the seafood houses, selling fresh off the boat, added picnic tables and eventually grew into restaurants. Triad is one, with a deck overhanging the river and holding about nine outdoor tables where you can enjoy the view and fresh seafood during stone crab season, October 15 to May 15. Nothing fancy, but you won't find a better grouper sandwich anywhere. Roughly from 6 AM to 2:30 PM the house also serves breakfast, fried shrimp, oyster, crab cake, and soft-shell blue crab baskets, plus Reubens, hamburgers, Philly cheesesteak sandwiches, and, on Friday, smoked ribs. ⊠ *401 School Dr.* ☎ *239/695–0722* ▤ *AE, MC, V* ⊙ *Closed May 16–Oct. 15.*

¢ ✕**Havana Café.** Cuban specialties are a tasty change from the shanty seafood houses of Everglades City; brightly painted walls and floral tablecloths make this little eatery and its 10 indoor tables and four porch tables a cheerful spot. Service is order-at-the-counter for breakfast and lunch (until 3 PM). Start the day with the sweet punch of café con leché and a pressed egg sandwich. For lunch, you'll find the ubiquitous Cuban sandwich, burgers, and shrimp, grouper, steak, and pork plates with rice and beans and yucca. ⊠ *Chokoloskee Mall* ☎ *239/695–2214* ▤ *No credit cards* ⊙ *Closed Mon No Dinner.*

WHERE TO STAY

$–$$ ⊞**Ivey House.** A remodeled 1928 boardinghouse originally for workers
Fodor's Choice building the Tamiami Trail, the Ivey House today fits many budgets.
★ One part is a friendly bed-and-breakfast bargain with shared baths and a cottage. The newer inn, connected to the B&B by a ramp, has rooms with private baths—some of Everglades City's plushest accommodations. Most inn rooms surround the screen-enclosed pool and courtyard. Display cases of local flora and fauna decorate the inn, as do

9

photographs of the Everglades and Ten Thousand Islands. The layout is designed to promote camaraderie, but there are secluded patios with chairs and tables for private moments. Rates include breakfast (hot breakfast in season). The Ivey House is run by the owners of NACT-Everglades Rentals & Eco Adventures, so stay here before or after the ecotours and save 20% on canoe and kayak rentals and tours. **Pros:** Canoe and kayak rentals and tours, pleasant atmosphere, affordability. **Cons:** Not on the water, small rooms, sparse amenities, breakfast for guests only. ✉107 Camellia St. ☎239/695–3299 🖨239/695–4155 ⊕www.iveyhouse.com 🛏31 rooms, 18 with bath; 1 2-bedroom cottage ♿In-room: refrigerator (some), dial-up. In-hotel: restaurant, room service, pool, laundry facilities, public Wi-Fi, no-smoking rooms ➟MC, V ☉Lodge closed Apr.–Sept. ⦿BP.

$ ▦**Glades Haven Cozy Cabins.** Bob Miller wanted to build a Holiday Inn next to his Oyster House Restaurant on marina-channel shores. When that didn't go through, he sent for cabin kits and set up mobile home–size units around a pool on his property. Guests who rent these cabins get free boat docking. A full cabin, done up in wood, tin roof, and polished floor, has a full kitchen and separate bedroom with screened porch. Duplex cabins—one of the best deals in town—come with a small fridge and microwave, with or without a screened porch. **Pros:** Convenient to ENP boating, good food options, marina. **Cons:** Crowded trailer-park feel, no phones. ✉801 Copeland Ave. ☎239/695–2746 or 888/956–6251 ⊕www.gladeshaven.com 🛏24 cabins, 5 3-bedroom houses ♿In-room: no phone, kitchen (some). In-hotel: 2 restaurants, pool, laundry facilities ➟AE, D, MC, V.

★ ⛺**Outdoor Resorts.** This clean, amenity-rich RV resort, set at the water's edge on secluded Chokoloskee Island, has sunny sites with concrete pads. Tropical vegetation adds shade and color. All sites have a water view. The property has boat rentals, tennis and shuffleboard, a marina, and a bait shop. A TV hookup and use of a recreation hall and health club are included in the rates and help while the hours away on rainy days. A motel accommodates those who come without an RV. ♿Pools, flush toilets, full hookups, drinking water, guest laundry, showers, electricity, general store 🛏283 sites, 8 efficiencies with kitchens ✉Rte. 29, 6 mi south of Tamiami Trail ⬛Box 39, Chokoloskee Island ☎239/695–3788 🖨239/695–3338 ⊕www.out-door-resorts.com/ci ➟MC, V.

THE OUTDOORS

BOATING

Glades Haven Marina (✉801 S. Copeland Ave. ☎239/695–2628 ⊕www.gladeshaven.com) can put you on the water to explore the Ten Thousand Islands in 16-foot Carolina skiffs and 24-foot pontoon boats. Rates start at $150 a day, with half-day and hourly options. It also rents kayaks, canoes, and fishing tackle, and has a 24-hour boat ramp and dockage for vessels up to 24 feet long.

CANOEING & KAYAKING

Everglades National Park Boat Tours (⊠ *Gulf Coast Visitor Center* ☎ *239/695–4731 or 866/628–7275*) rents 17-foot canoes for day and overnight use. Rates are $25.44 per day, including tax. Car-shuttle service is available, for an additional fee for canoeists paddling the Wilderness Trail in season, and travelers with disabilities can be accommodated. Reservations are strongly suggested from December through April.

Fodor'sChoice **NACT-Everglades Rentals & Eco Adventures** (⊠ *Ivey House, 107 Camel-*
★ *lia St.* ☎ *239/695–3299* ⊕ *www.evergladesadventures.com*) is an established source for canoes, sea kayaks, and guided Everglades trips (November through April). Canoes cost from $35 the first day, $27 for each day thereafter, and kayaks are from $45 for the first day. Half-day rentals from 1 to 5 PM are available. Shuttles deliver you to major launching areas in the region, such as the Turner River ($30 for up to two people) and Collier-Seminole State Park ($60).

BIG CYPRESS NATIONAL PRESERVE

Through the 1950s and early 1960s, the world's largest cypress-logging industry prospered in the Big Cypress Swamp. The industry died out in the 1960s, and the government began buying parcels. Today, 729,000 acres, or nearly half of the swamp, have become this national preserve. The word "big" in its name refers not to the size of the trees but to the swamp, which juts down into the north side of Everglades National Park like a piece in a jigsaw puzzle. Its size and strategic location make it an important link in the region's hydrological system, in which rainwater first flows through the preserve, then south into the park, and eventually into Florida Bay. Its variegated pattern of wet prairies, ponds, marshes, sloughs, and strands provides a wildlife sanctuary, and thanks to a policy of balanced land use—"use without abuse"—the watery wilderness is devoted to research and recreation as well as preservation. The preserve allows—in limited areas—hunting, off-road vehicle (airboat, swamp buggy, four-wheel-drive vehicles) use by permit, and cattle grazing. Compared with Everglades National Park, the preserve is less developed and has fewer visitors. That makes it ideal for naturalists, birders, and hikers who prefer to see more wildlife than humans. Several scenic drives link off Tamiami Trail; some require four-wheel-drive vehicles, especially in wet summer months. A few lead to camping areas. Roadside picnic areas are off the Tamiami Trail. There are three types of trails—walking (including part of the extensive Florida National Scenic Trail), canoeing, and bicycling. All three trail types are easily accessed from the Tamiami Trail near the preserve's visitor center, and one boardwalk trail departs from the center. Canoe and bike equipment can be rented from outfitters in Everglades City, 24 mi west, and Naples, 40 mi west.

9

CAMPING

⚠ **Big Cypress National Preserve.** There are four no-fee primitive camp-grounds within Big Cypress National Preserve along the Tamiami Trail and Loop Road. One of them, Burns Lake, is open September through January 6 and camping is free. Others may close seasonally for repairs or because of flooding, so check ahead. A fifth site, Monument Lake Campground, has restrooms, a cold shower, an amphitheater, and activities and seasonal programs (mid-December through March). Campers can use the dump station on Dona Drive in Ochopee. The sixth, Midway, is the only one with RV electrical hookups and an on-site dump station, which is free to campers. It is tidily maintained and an improvement upon private campgrounds in the area. ⟐ *Flush toilets, dump station, running water, showers (cold)* ⇥*40 sites at Burns Lake; 10 tent, 26 RV or tent sites at Monument Lake; 10 tent, 26 RV or tent sites at Midway* ⊠*Tamiami Trail (Hwy. 41), between Miami and Naples* ⌖*HCR 61, Box 110, Ochopee* ☎*239/695–1201* ⊕*www.nps.gov/bicy* ⊟*No credit cards.*

THE EVERGLADES ESSENTIALS

TRANSPORTATION

BY AIR

Miami International Airport (MIA) is 34 mi from Homestead and 83 mi from Flamingo in Everglades National Park. *For airline carriers to MIA, refer to the Miami chapter.* Airporter runs shuttle buses three times daily that stop at the Ramada Inn in Florida City on their way between MIA and the Florida Keys. Shuttle service, which takes about an hour, runs 6:10 AM to 5:20 PM from Florida City, 7:30 AM to 6 PM from the airport. Reserve at least 24 hours in advance. Pick-ups can be arranged for all baggage-claim areas. The cost is $30 one-way. SuperShuttle operates 11-passenger air-conditioned vans to Homestead. Service from MIA is available around the clock; booths are outside most luggage areas on the lower level. For the return to MIA, reserve 24 hours in advance. The one-way cost is $51 per person. Southwest Florida International Airport (RSW) in Fort Myers, about an hour away from Everglades City, is the closest major airport to the Everglades western access. For carrier information, see *the Lower Gulf Coast chapter.* On-demand taxi transportation from the airport to Everglades City runs about $100.

Contacts Miami International Airport (MIA) (☎*305/876–7000* ⊕*www.miami-airport.com*). **Southwest Florida International Airport (RSW)** (☎*239/768–1000* ⊕*www.flylcpa.com*). **Airporter** (☎*800/830–3413*). **SuperShuttle** (☎*305/871–2000* ⊕*www.supershuttle.com*).

BY BUS

Metrobus travels daily through the Miami–Homestead–Florida City area on weekdays. Regular fare is $1.50. The Dade-Monroe Express provides daily bus service from the Florida City Wal-Mart Supercenter to Mile Marker 50 in Marathon. The bus makes several stops in Florida City and the Keys, during daily round-trips on the hour from 6 AM to 10 PM. The cost is $1.85 each way.

Contacts Dade-Monroe Express (☎ *305/770–3131* ⊕ *www.miamidade.gov/transit).* **Metrobus** (☎ *305/770–3131* ⊕ *www.miamidade.gov/transit*).

BY CAR
From Miami the main highways to the area are U.S. 1, the Homestead Extension of Florida Turnpike, and Krome Avenue (Route 997). To reach Biscayne National Park from Homestead, take U.S. 1 or Krome Avenue to Route 9336 (Palm Drive) and turn east. Follow Palm Drive for about 8 mi until it becomes Southwest 344th Street and follow signs to the park headquarters. To reach Everglades National Park's Ernest F. Coe Visitor Center and Flamingo, head west on Palm Drive in Florida City and follow signs. From Florida City the Ernest F. Coe Visitor Center is 11 mi; Flamingo is 49 mi. The north entrance of Everglades National Park at Shark Valley is reached by taking the Tamiami Trail about 20 mi west of Krome Avenue. To reach the west entrance of Everglades National Park at the Gulf Coast Visitor Center in Everglades City, take Route 29 south from the Tamiami Trail.

CAR RENTAL Agencies in the Homestead area include Budget and Enterprise Rent-a-Car.

Contacts Budget (✉ *30260 S. Dixie Hwy., Homestead* ☎ *305/248–4524 or 800/527–0700).* **Enterprise Rent-a-Car** (✉ *29130 S. Dixie Hwy., Homestead* ☎ *305/246–2056 or 800/736–8222).*

CONTACTS & RESOURCES

EMERGENCIES
In national parks, rangers answer police, fire, and medical emergencies. The Florida Fish and Wildlife Conservation Commission, a division of the Florida Department of Natural Resources, maintains a 24-hour telephone service for reporting boating emergencies and natural-resource violations. The Miami Beach Coast Guard Base responds to local marine emergencies and reports of navigation hazards. The base broadcasts on VHF-FM Channel 16. The National Weather Service supplies local forecasts.

Contacts Emergencies (☎ *911).* **Hospital emergency line** (☎ *305/596–6556).* **Homestead Hospital** (✉ *975 Baptist Way, Homestead* ☎ *305/248–3232, 305/596–6557 physician referral).* **Florida Fish and Wildlife Conservation Commission** (☎ *305/956–2500).* **Miami Beach Coast Guard Base** (✉ *100 MacArthur Causeway, Miami Beach* ☎ *305/535–4300 or 305/535–4314).* **National Parks** (☎ *305/247–7272).* **National Weather Service** (☎ *305/229–4522).*

TOURS
Many Everglades-area tours operate only in season, roughly November through April. The National Park Service has free programs, typically focusing on native wildlife, plants, and park history. At Biscayne National Park, for example, rangers give informal tours of Elliott and

Boca Chita keys, which you can arrange in advance, depending on ranger availability. Contact the respective visitor center for details. Wings Ten Thousand Islands Aero-Tours operates scenic, low-level flight tours of the Ten Thousand Islands National Wildlife Refuge, Big Cypress National Preserve, Everglades National Park, and the Gulf of Mexico in an Alaskan floatplane. On the 20- to 90-minute flights, see saw-grass prairies, Native American shell mounds, alligators, and wading birds. Prices start at $35 per person with a group of three or four. For an all- or multiday outing, opt for flights across the gulf to the Florida Keys or Dry Tortugas. Wooten's Everglades Airboat Tours runs airboat and swamp-buggy tours ($25) through the Everglades. (Swamp buggies are giant tractorlike vehicles with oversize rubber wheels.) Tours last approximately 30 minutes. Combination tours, including a visit to the animal sanctuary, cost $53. Southwest of Florida City near the entrance to Everglades National Park, Everglades Alligator Farm runs a 4-mi, 30-minute tour of the River of Grass with departures 20 minutes after the hour. The tour ($19) includes free hourly alligator, snake, and wildlife shows, or take in the shows only ($13.50).

From the Shark Valley area, Buffalo Tiger's Florida Everglades Airboat Ride is operated by a former chairman of the Miccosukee tribe, who, at almost 90 years old, greets his guests when he can. Indian guides narrate the 40-minute trip from the perspective of the Native Americans, who have lived there since the 1800s. Trips run on the north side of Tamiami Trail, where there's more water and wildlife, and include a stop at an old Native American camp. Tours cost $25 each for two people and operate 10 to 5 daily. Reservations are not required. Coopertown Airboat Ride operates the oldest airboat rides in the Everglades (since 1945). The 35- to 40-minute tour ($19) takes you 9 mi to hammocks and alligator holes. Everglades Gator Park offers 45-minute narrated airboat tours ($18, including park tour and wildlife show). Everglades Safari Park runs 40-minute airboat rides for $20 and small, private airboat tours for an extra charge; they last 40 minutes to 2½ hours. The price includes a show, natural museum admission, and gator tour. The Miccosukee Indian Village 30-minute narrated airboat ride stops at a 100-year-old family camp in the Everglades to hear tales and allow passengers to walk around and explore ($10).

Tours at Biscayne National Park are run by people-friendly Biscayne National Underwater Park, Inc. Daily trips (at 10, with a second trip at 1 during high season, depending on demand) explore the park's living coral reefs 10 mi offshore on *Reef Rover IV*, a 53-foot glass-bottom boat that can carry 48 passengers. On days when the weather is unsuitable for reef viewing, an alternative three-hour, ranger-led interpretive tour visits Boca Chita Key. (Rangers also conduct the Boca Chita tour on certain Sundays in season.) Reservations are recommended. The cost is $24.45, and you should arrive at least one hour before departure.

Flamingo Marina Boat Tours is the official concession operating sightseeing excursions through Everglades National Park. The two-hour backcountry *Pelican* cruise ($18) is the most popular. The boat winds under a heavy canopy of mangroves, revealing abundant wildlife— from alligators, crocodiles, and turtles to herons, hawks, and egrets.

Starting at the Shark Valley visitor center, Shark Valley Tram Tours follows a 15-mi loop road, especially good for viewing gators, into the interior, stopping at a 50-foot observation tower. Two-hour narrated tours cost $15.25 and depart hourly 9 to 4 December through April; the rest of the year tours run every two hours from 9:30 to 3. Reservations are recommended December through April. On the west side, Everglades National Park Boat Tours operates 1½-hour trips ($26.50) through the Ten Thousand Islands National Wildlife Refuge and mangrove wilderness, where passengers often see dolphins, manatees, bald eagles, and roseate spoonbills. In the height of the season, four tour boats run four times daily. One boat can accommodate large parties and wheelchairs (not electric) and all have drink concessions. Everglades Rentals & Eco Adventures leads one-day to seven-night Everglades paddling tours November through April. Highlights include bird and gator sightings, mangrove forests, no-man's-land beaches, relics of the hideouts of infamous and just-plain-reclusive characters, and spectacular sunsets. Included in the cost of overnight tours ($800 for two nights to $1,300 for six nights) are canoe or kayak rental, all necessary equipment, a guide, meals, and lodging for the first night at the Ivey House. There's a two-person minimum.

Contacts **Biscayne National Underwater Park, Inc.** (⊠ *Convoy Point, east end of North Canal Dr., 9710 S.W. 328th St.* ⬠ *Box 1270, Homestead* ☎ *305/230–1100* ⊕ *www.nps.gov/bisc).* **Buffalo Tiger's Florida Everglades Airboat Ride** (⊠ *5 mi. east of Shark Valley* ☎ *305/382–0719).* **Coopertown Airboat Ride** (⊠ *11 mi west of Florida Tpke. on Tamiami Trail* ☎ *305/226–6048* ⊕ *www.coopertownairboats. com).* **Everglades Alligator Farm** (⊠ *40351 S.W. 192nd Ave.* ☎ *305/247–2628* ⊕ *www.everglades.com).* **Everglades Gator Park** (⊠ *12 mi west of Florida Tpke. on Tamiami Trail* ☎ *305/559–2255 or 800/559–2205* ⊕ *www.gatorpark.com).* **Everglades National Park Boat Tours** (⊠ *Gulf Coast Visitor Center, Everglades City* ☎ *239/695–2591 or 866/628–7275* ⊕ *www.nps.gov/ever).* **Everglades Rentals & Eco Adventures** (⊠ *Ivey House, 107 Camellia St.* ⬠ *Box 5038, Everglades City* ☎ *239/695–3299* ⊕ *www.evergladesadventures.com).* **Everglades Safari Park** (⊠ *26700 Tamiami Trail, 15 mi west of Florida Tpke.* ☎ *305/226–6923 or 305/223–3804* ⊕ *www.evsafaripark.com).* **Flamingo Lodge, Marina & Outpost Resort Boat Tours** (⊠ *1 Flamingo Lodge Hwy., Flamingo* ☎ *239/695–3101* ⊕ *www. flamingolodge.com).* **Miccosukee Indian Village** (⊠ *25 mi west of Florida Tpke. on Tamiami Trail* ☎ *305/223–8380* ⊕ *www.miccosukeetours.com).* **Shark Valley Tram Tours** (⬠ *Box 1739, Tamiami Station, Miami* ☎ *305/221–8455* ⊕ *www.nps. gov/ever/visit/tours.htm.* **Wings Ten Thousand Islands Aero-Tours** (⊠ *Everglades Airport, 650 Everglades City Airpark Rd.* ⬠ *Box 244, Chokoloskee* ☎ *239/695–3296* ☾ *Nov.–May).* **Wooten's Everglades Airboat Tours** (⊠ *Wooten's Alligator Farm, 1½ mi east of Rte. 29 on Tamiami Trail* ☎ *239/695–2781 or 800/282–2781* ⊕ *www. wootensairboats.com).*

9

VISITOR INFORMATION

Contacts **Big Cypress National Preserve** (⌂ *HCR 61, Box 11, Ochopee 34141* ☎ *239/695–1201* ⊕ *www.nps.gov/bicy*). **Biscayne National Park** (*Dante Fascell Visitor Center,* ✉ *9700 S.W. 328th St., Homestead* ☎ *305/230–7275* ⊕ *www.nps. gov/bisc*). **Everglades Area Chamber of Commerce** (✉ *Rte. 29 and Tamiami Trail* ⌂ *Box 130, Everglades City* ☎ *239/695–3172* ⊕ *www.florida-everglades. com/chamber*). **Everglades National Park** (*Ernest F. Coe Visitor Center* ✉ *40001 Rte. 9336, Homestead* ☎ *305/242–7700* ⊕ *www.nps.gov/ever*). **Flamingo Visitor Center** (✉ *1 Flamingo Lodge Hwy., Flamingo* ☎ *239/695–2945*). **Gulf Coast Visitor Center** (✉ *Rte. 29, Everglades City* ☎ *239/695–3311* ⊕ *www.nps.gov/ever*). **Tropical Everglades Visitor Center** (✉ *160 U.S. 1, Florida City* ☎ *305/245–9180 or 800/388–9669* ⊕ *www.tropicaleverglades.com*).

The Lower Gulf Coast

Naples

WORD OF MOUTH

"Sanibel is lovely, but because the island lies east–west, you won't actually see the sunset on most of the Sanibel beaches. [On] Sanibel you really need a car. Rates are still high on Sanibel til the first of May. All that said, Sanibel is my favorite."

—luvtravl

WELCOME TO
THE LOWER GULF COAST

TOP REASONS TO GO

★ **Heavenly Beaches:** Whether you go to the beach to sun, swim, gather shells, or watch the sunset, the region's Gulf of Mexico beaches rank among the best.

★ **Edison & Ford Winter Estates:** A rare complex of two famous inventors' winter homes comes complete with botanical research gardens, Edison's lab, and a museum.

★ **Island-Hopping:** Rent a boat or jump aboard a charter for lunch, picnicking, beaching, and shelling on a subtropical island adrift from the mainland.

★ **Naples Shopping:** Flex your buying power in downtown Naples' charming shopping districts or in lush outdoor centers around town.

★ **Watch for Wildlife:** On the edge of Everglades National Park, the region protects vast tracts of fragile land and water where you can see alligators, manatees, dolphin, roseate spoonbills, and hundred of other birds.

1 Fort Myers Area. Don't miss the Edison & Ford Estates along royal-palm-lined McGregor Boulevard. For museums, theater, and art, the up-and-coming downtown River District rules.

2 The Coastal Islands. Shells and wildlife refuges bring nature-headed types to Sanibel and Captiva Islands. Fort Myers Beach is known for its lively clubs and shrimp fleet. For true seclusion, head to the area's unbridged island beaches.

3 Naples Area. Some of the region's best shopping and dining take up residence in historic buildings trimmed with blossoms and street sculptures in Old Naples. Hit Marco Island for the boating lifestyle and funky fish-village character.

GETTING ORIENTED

The Lower Gulf Coast of Florida, as its name suggests, occupies a stretch of coastline along southernmost West Florida, bordered by the Gulf of Mexico. It lies south of Tampa and Sarasota, directly on the other side of the state from West Palm Beach and Fort Lauderdale. In between the two coasts stretch heartland agricultural areas and Everglades wilderness. The region encompasses the major resort towns of Fort Myers, Fort Myers Beach, Sanibel Island, Naples, and Marco Island, along with a medley of suburban communities and smaller islands.

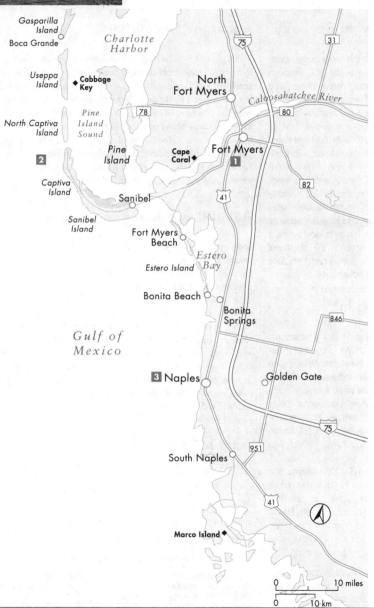

Gasparilla
Island

Boca Grande

*Charlotte
Harbor*

Useppa
Island

◆ **Cabbage
Key**

North
Fort Myers

Caloosahatchee River

*Pine
Island
Sound*

North Captiva
Island

2

Pine
Island

**Cape
Coral** ◆

Fort Myers

1

Captiva
Island

Sanibel

*Sanibel
Island*

Fort Myers
Beach

*Estero
Bay*

Estero Island

Bonita Beach

Bonita
Springs

*Gulf of
Mexico*

3 Naples

Golden Gate

10

South Naples

Marco Island ◆

78

75

31

80

41

82

846

75

951

41

0   10 miles
0   10 km

LOWER GULF COAST PLANNER

When to Go

In winter this is one of the warmest areas of the U.S., although occasionally temperatures drop below freezing in December or January. From February through April you may find it next to impossible to find a hotel room. Numbers drop off-season, but visitors within driving range and convention clientele still keep things busy. Temperatures and humidity soar, but discounted room rates make summer attractive. Summer, however, is rainy season, but most storms occur in the afternoon. Hurricane season runs from June through November.

Flying In

Southwest Florida International Airport (RSW) is the major airport for the region. Airlines serving RSW include Air Canada, AirTran Airways, American, Cape Air, Comair, Continental, Delta, Frontier, jetBlue, LTU International Airways, Midwest, Northwest, Southwest, Spirit, Sun Country, Sunwing, United, US Airways, USA 3000 Airlines, and WestJet. Delta Connection and a couple of private charters service Naples Municipal Airport. Private pilots land at both RSW and Page Field in Fort Myers. North Captiva Island has a private airstrip.

For more flight information see By Air in Essentials at the end of this chapter.

About the Restaurants

In this part of Florida fresh seafood reigns supreme. Succulent native stone crab claws, a particularly tasty treat, in season from mid-October through mid-May, are usually served hot with drawn butter or chilled with tangy mustard sauce. Supplies are typically steady, since these crabs are not killed to harvest their claws and their limbs regenerate in time for the next season. Other seafood specialties include fried grouper sandwiches and Sanibel pink shrimp. In Naples's highly hailed restaurants, mingle with locals, winter visitors, and other travelers and catch up on the latest culinary trends.

About the Hotels

Lodging in Fort Myers, the islands, and Naples can be pricey, but there are affordable options even during the busy winter season. If these destinations are too rich for your budget, consider visiting in the off-season, when rates drop drastically. Beachfront properties tend to be more expensive; to spend less, look for properties away from the water. In high season—Christmas through Easter—always reserve ahead for the top properties. Fall is the slowest season: rates are low and availability is high, but this is also the prime time for hurricanes. New resorts are popping up around the region. Naples Bay Resort, an 85-unit luxury hotel, rental cottage, and marina complex, opened in February 2008. In Cape Coral, The Resort at MarinaVillage plans to open by early 2010.

What It Costs

DINING & LODGING PRICE CATEGORIES

¢	$	$$	$$$	$$$$
Restaurants				
under $10	$10–$15	$15–$20	$20–$30	over $30
Hotels				
under $80	$80–$100	$100–$140	$140–$220	over $220

Restaurant prices are per person for a main course at dinner. Hotel prices are for a standard double room, excluding 6% sales tax (more in some counties) and 1%–4% tourist tax.

Updated by
Chelle Koster
Walton

WITH ITS SUBTROPICAL CLIMATE AND beckoning family-friendly beaches, the Lower Gulf Coast, also referred to as the state's southwestern region, is a favorite vacation spot of Florida residents as well as visitors. There's lots to do in addition to the sun and surf scene throughout its several distinct travel destinations. Small and historic downtown Fort Myers, dubbed the River District, rises inland along the Caloosahatchee River, and the rest of the town sprawls in all directions. It got its nickname, the City of Palms, from the hundreds of towering royal palms that inventor Thomas Edison planted between 1900 and 1917 along McGregor Boulevard, a historic residential street and site of his winter estate. Edison's idea caught on, and more than 2,000 royal palms now line 15 mi of McGregor Boulevard. Museums and educational attractions are the draw here, as downtown diligently tries to shape itself as an entertainment destination and makes slow but sure headway. Across the river, Cape Coral has evolved from a mostly residential community to a resort destination for water-sports enthusiasts. Off the coast west of Fort Myers are more than 100 coastal islands in all shapes and sizes—among them Sanibel and Captiva, two thoughtfully developed resort islands. Connected to the mainland by a 3-mi causeway, Sanibel is known for its superb shelling, fine fishing, beachfront resorts, and wildlife refuge. Here and on Captiva, to which it is connected by a short bridge, multimillion-dollar homes line both waterfronts, but the gulf beaches are readily accessible. Just southwest of Fort Myers is Estero Island, home of busy Fort Myers Beach, and farther south, Lovers Key State Park and the growing area of Estero and Bonita Springs.

Farther down the coast lies Naples, once a small fishing village and now a thriving and sophisticated town, a smaller, more understated version of Palm Beach with fine restaurants, chichi shopping areas, and—locals will tell you—more golf holes per capita than anywhere else in the world. There's a lovely small art museum in the 1,473-seat Naples Philharmonic Center, which is the west-coast home of the Miami City Ballet. The beaches are soft and white, and access is relatively easy. East of Naples stretch the Big Cypress National Preserve and Everglades National Park, and a half hour south basks Marco Island, which people visit mostly for beaches and fishing. See a maze of pristine miniature mangrove islands when you take a boat tour departing from the island's marinas into Ten Thousand Islands National Wildlife Refuge. Although high-rises line much of Marco's waterfront, natural areas have been preserved, including the tiny fishing village of Goodland, an outpost of Old Florida that tries valiantly to stave off new development.

10

EXPLORING THE LOWER GULF COAST

In this region vacationers tend to spend most of their time outdoors—swimming, sunning, shelling, fishing, boating, and playing tennis or golf. Fort Myers is the only major inland destination; it has several interesting museums and parks. The barrier islands vary from tiny and undeveloped to sprawling and chockablock with hotels and restaurants.

Be aware that the destination's growing popularity, especially during winter, means traffic congestion at peak times of day. Avoid driving when the locals are getting to and from work and visitors are getting to and from the beach.

FORT MYERS AREA

In Fort Myers, old Southern mansions and their modern-day counterparts peek out from behind stately palms. Views over the broad Caloosahatchee River, which borders the city's small but businesslike cluster of office buildings downtown, soften the look of the area. These days, it's showing the effects of age and urban sprawl, but planners work at reviving what has been termed the River District. North of Fort Myers are small fishing communities and new retirement towns, including Boca Grande on Gasparilla Island; Englewood Beach on Manasota Key; Port Charlotte, north of the Peace River; and Punta Gorda, at the convergence of the Peace River and Charlotte Harbor.

FORT MYERS

90 mi southeast of Sarasota, 140 mi west of Palm Beach.

The inviting city core lies inland along the banks of the Caloosahatchee River, a half hour from the nearest beach. The town is best known as the winter home of inventors Thomas A. Edison and Henry Ford.

WHAT TO SEE

Majestic palms, some planted by Thomas Edison, line **McGregor Boulevard,** one of the city's most scenic streets. It runs from downtown to Summerlin Road, which takes you to the barrier islands.

Fodor'sChoice ★ **Edison & Ford Winter Estates,** Fort Myers's premier attraction, pays homage to two of America's most ingenious inventors: Thomas A. Edison, who gave the world the stock ticker, the incandescent lamp, and the phonograph, among other inventions; and his friend and neighbor, automaker Henry Ford. Donated to the city by Edison's widow, his 12-acre estate is a remarkable place with three homes, a laboratory, botanical gardens, and a museum. The laboratory is just as Edison left it when he died in 1931. Edison traveled south from New Jersey and devoted much of his time here to inventing things (there are 1,093 patents to his name), experimenting with rubber for friend and frequent visitor Harvey Firestone, and planting some 600 species of plants collected around the world. Next door to Edison's two identical homes is Ford's "Mangoes," the more modest seasonal home of Edison's fellow inventor. It's said that the V-8 engine in essence was designed on the back porch. The property's oldest building, the Caretaker's House, dates to 1860. Research garden renovation is ongoing. Tours are guided or audio self-guided. One admission covers both homes; laboratory-museum-only

GREAT ITINERARIES

2 DAYS

Fort Myers is a good base for a short visit. It's not directly on the beach, but its central location makes day trips easy. On the morning of your first day, visit Edison & Ford Winter Estates, in downtown Fort Myers, and then take McGregor Boulevard and Summerlin Road to **Sanibel Island**. There, stop by the Bailey-Matthews Shell Museum and the J.N. "Ding" Darling National Wildlife Refuge before heading to Bowman's Beach for shelling, swimming, and its famous sunset. The next day drive down Interstate 75 to **Naples**. If you have a heart for art, stop by the **Naples Museum of Art** before hitting Old Naples for some shopping and relaxing on the nearby beach. Check out the subtropical plants and exotic animals at **Naples Zoo**.

4 DAYS

Stay near the water on **Sanibel Island**. Spend your first day shelling and swimming, taking a break from the beach for a stop at the Bailey-Matthews Shell Museum. On Day 2, head into **Fort Myers** to Edison & Ford Winter Estates and, if you have kids, the hands-on Imaginarium nearby. Spend your third day back on Sanibel, dividing your time between the beach and the J.N. "Ding" Darling National Wildlife Refuge; go kayaking or try bird-watching in the early morning or evening. On Day 4, drive south to **Naples**—and the sights mentioned in the two-day itinerary, or for even more wildlife, head to the Corkscrew Swamp Sanctuary, a nature preserve east of **Bonita Springs**.

tickets are also available. ✉ *2350 McGregor Blvd.* ☎ *239/334–3614* ⊕ *www.efwefla.org* 🎫 *$20* ◷ *Guided tours daily 9–4; closes at 5.*

In a restored railroad depot, the **Southwest Florida Museum of History** showcases the area's history dating to 800 BC. Displays include prehistoric Calusa artifacts, a reconstructed *chickee* hut, canoes, clothing and photos from Seminole settlements, historical vignettes, changing exhibits, and a replicated Florida Cracker house. A favorite attraction is the *Esperanza*, a private railcar from the 1930s. ✉ *2300 Peck St.* ☎ *239/332–5955* ⊕ *www.cityftmyers.com/museum* 🎫 *$9.50* ◷ *Tues.–Sat. 10–5.*

★ ☺ Kids can't wait to get their hands on the wonderful interactive exhibits at the **Imaginarium Hands-On Museum,** a lively museum-aquarium combo that explores the environment, physics, anatomy, weather, and other science and lifestyle topics. Check out the marine life in the aquariums, the touch pool, the living-reef tank, and the outdoor lagoon; visit tarantulas, a kinkajou, snakes, a juvenile alligator, and other live critters in the Animal Lab; dig for dinosaur bones; slap a hockey puck; watch a 3-D movie in the theater or a hands-on show; then prepare to get blown away in the Hurricane Experience. ✉ *2000 Cranford Ave.* ☎ *239/337–3332* ⊕ *www.cityftmyers.com/imaginarium* 🎫 *$8* ◷ *Mon.–Sat. 10–5, Sun. noon–5.*

10

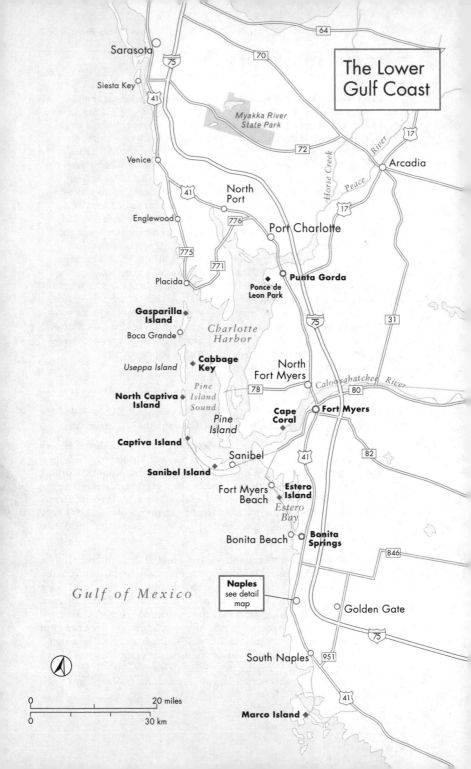

Sarasota

Siesta Key

75

41

Venice

41

North
Port

Englewood

776

Placida

775

771

Gasparilla
Island

Boca Grande

Useppa Island

North Captiva
Island

Captiva Island

Sanibel Island

Myakka River
State Park

72

Horse Creek

Peace River

Arcadia

17

17

31

Port Charlotte

Punta Gorda

Ponce de
Leon Park

Charlotte
Harbor

Cabbage
Key

Pine
Island
Sound

Pine
Island

Cape
Coral

75

North
Fort Myers

78

Caloosahatchee River

80

Fort Myers

Sanibel

Fort Myers
Beach

Estero
Island

Estero
Bay

Bonita Beach

41

82

Bonita
Springs

846

Naples
see detail
map

Golden Gate

75

Gulf of Mexico

South Naples

951

41

Marco Island

The Lower
Gulf Coast

64

70

0   20 miles

0   30 km

For a look at exhibits on wildlife, fossils, and Florida's native animals and habitats, head to the **Calusa Nature Center and Planetarium.** Boardwalks lead through subtropical wetlands, a birds-of-prey aviary, a butterfly house, and a re-created Seminole Indian village. There are snake, alligator, and other live-animal demonstrations several times daily. The 90-seat planetarium has astronomy shows daily and special laser shows. ⊠*3450 Ortiz Ave.* ☎*239/275-3435* ⊕*www.calusanature.com* 💲*Nature center and planetarium $9* ⊙*Mon.–Sat. 9–5, Sun. 11–5; call for astronomy and laser show schedule.*

★ ☺ At **Manatee Park** you may glimpse Florida's most famous marine mammal. When Gulf waters are cold—usually from November to March—the gentle sea cows congregate in these waters, which are warmed by the outflow of a nearby power plant. Pause at any of the three observation decks and watch for bubbles. Hydrophones allow you to eavesdrop on their songs. Periodically one of the mammoth creatures—mature adults weigh hundreds of pounds—will surface. The park rents kayaks in winter and on summer weekends, and kayaking clinics and free guided walks are available. ⊠*1½ mi east of I–75 Exit 141 at 10901 Rte. 80* ☎*239/694-3537* ⊕*www.leeparks.org* 💲*Parking $1 per hr to maximum of $5 per day* ⊙*Daily 8–sunset. Gates lock automatically and promptly at closing time. Visitor center daily 9–4.*

WHERE TO EAT

$$$ ✕**Biddle's Restaurant & Piano Bar.** Refined, intimate surroundings, an outdoor patio, and a karaoke piano bar set the mood for seafood, pasta, and chops infused with flavor and accompanied with creative sides and sauces. Start with the award-winning seafood martini. For dinner entrées, seafood pasta comes with brandy-tomato cream sauce, chicken breast stuffed with prosciutto, lobster ravioli with blood-orange beurre blanc, and seafood Wellington topped with lobster cream sauce. The glamorous chocolate piano dessert brings the meal to a fitting end. Lunch offering range from duck salad and Greek chicken wrap to chicken marsala and petite veal chops. ⊠*20351 Summerlin Rd.* ☎*239/433-4449* ⊕*www.biddlesrestaurant.com* ▤*AE, D, MC, V.*

★ $$$ ✕**Bistro 41.** Shoppers and business folk meet here for some of the town's most dependable and inventive cuisine. Amid brightly painted, textured walls and a display kitchen, the menu roams from meat loaf and rotisserie chicken to pasta dishes and pan-seared snapper topped with proscuitto and goat cheese. To experience the kitchen at its imaginative best, check the night's specials, which often include daringly done seafood (crabmeat-crusted tripletail fish with caramelized plantains and passion-fruit beurre blanc, for instance) and usually cost more than regular menu items. When weather permits, ask for a table on the patio. On Sunday there's a limited menu available. ⊠*13499 S. Cleveland Ave.* ☎*239/466-4141* ⚐*Reservations recommended for dinner* ⊕*www.bistro41.com* ▤*AE, D, MC, V*

★ $$$ ✕**The Veranda.** Restaurants come and go quickly as downtown reinvents itself, but this one has endured since 1979. A favorite of business and government bigwigs, it serves imaginative continental fare with a trace of a Southern accent. Notable are tournedos with smoky

10

sour-mash whiskey sauce, rack of lamb with rosemary merlot sauce, herb-crusted honey grilled salmon, and a grilled seafood sampler with saffron cream fettucine, all served with homemade honey-drizzled bread and muffins with pepper jelly. The restaurant is a combination of two turn-of-the-20th-century homes, with a two-sided central brick fireplace, and sconces and antique oil paintings on its pale-yellow walls. Ask for an outdoor courtyard table when weather permits. ⊠ *2122 2nd St.* ☎ *239/332–2065* ⊕ *www.verandarestaurant.com* ⊟ *AE, MC, V* ⊘ *Closed Sun. No lunch Sat.*

$$ ✕ **French Roast Café.** Irish omelet, Belgian waffles, steak au poivre, Vietnamese sea bass, Waldorf chicken salad: French Roast clearly travels farther abroad than its name implies. And it does it with utmost taste and flavor, as its faithful local clientele will attest. The best deals are the lunchtime Vietnamese and early-bird (4:30 to 5:30) meals. It offers three-course Vietnamese or Parisian dinners for $30. Leave room for crepes à la Grand Marnier tableside or something from the bakery, and a cup of fresh-roasted coffee (hence the second part of its name). The interior poses a soothing surprise in a busy part of town with a water feature, fireplace, and classic columns. ⊠ *12995 S. Cleveland. Ave. #118* ☎ *239/936–2233* ⊟ *AE, D, MC, V* ⊘ *Closed Mon. and Wed.–Fri. for breakfast, Mon. in summer.*

★ $$ ✕ **Mille Saporé.** If you're looking for finely crafted, flavorful (its name means "a thousand flavors") Mediterranean interpretations in a range from gourmet pizza to fine seafood and grilled meats, this intimate, candlelit corner belies its strip-mall location. Fans—shoppers and local business folk—rave about its seafood pizza, Brie calzone, red snapper with sour oranges, vegetable pasta, and nightly specials. ⊠ *15880 Summerlin Rd. 33908* ☎ *239/437–5040* ⊟ *AE, D, MC, V* ⊘ *No lunch.*

$ ✕ **Cibo.** When Cafe Cibo recently moved down a few doors to a bigger space and dropped the "café" in its name, it kept the flavor-bursting Italian food that has made loyal fans who relish the Italian propensity for fresh, quality ingredients. In contrast to the sophisticated black-and-white setting, the menu comes in colors from classic Caesar salad with shaved grana padano and Mama's spaghetti and meatballs with pomodoro sauce to lobster française and New York strip with braised cannelloni beans and baby broccolini. The lasagna Napoletana is typical of the standards set here—a generous square of pasta layered with fluffy ricotta, meat ragu, mozzarella, and the totally fresh-tasting, garlicky pomodoro sauce. ⊠ *12901 McGregor Blvd.* ☎ *239/454–3700* ⊟ *AE, MC, V* ⊘ *No lunch Sat.–Mon.*

♻ $ ✕ **Shrimp Shack.** Seafood lovers flock to these two locations with their vivacious staff, bustle, and tropical color. There's a wait for lunch in winter season and a brisk take-out business at both addresses. Southern-style deep frying prevails—whole-belly clams, grouper, shrimp, onion rings, hush puppies, and pork loin planks—though you can get some selections broiled or blackened. Create your own basket by selecting two or three fried, broiled, or blackened choices. This is your place if you like your seafood simple. The Colonial location has outdoor seating. ⊠ *13361 Metro Pkwy.* ☎ *239/561–6817* ⊠ *Royal Palm Sq., 1400 Colonial Blvd. #57* ☎ *239/277–5100* ⊟ *AE, D, DC, MC, V.*

¢ ✗**Chile Ranchero.** The local gringo population converges regularly on this authentic little corner of Mexicana along busy Tamiami Trail. You can't beat the prices or the portions. The staff speak Spanish and so does the menu, with English subtitles. Dishes appeal to American and Latin palates, with a range from chorizo sandwiches and steak ranchero to liver tacos and excellent nachos con ceviche. ⊠*11751 S. Cleveland Ave. #18* ☎*239/275–0505* ⊟*AE, D, MC, V.*

★ ¢ ✗**Philly Junction.** From the bread (Amorosa rolls) to the beer (Yuengling), it comes from Philadelphia. Not only are the Philly cheesesteaks delicious and authentic, but the burgers and other sandwiches are excellent—and the prices are among the lowest around. Stay for an old-fashioned sundae, or join the Philly natives for pork roll and scrapple at breakfast. The café occupies two rooms sided with natural wood board-and-bead paneling in a strip mall. Signs at every table humorously reveal "25 Ways To Tell You're From Philly." ⊠*4600 Summerlin Rd.* ☎*239/936–6622* ⊟*MC, V* ⊗*No dinner Sun.*

WHERE TO STAY

🕓 $$$$ 🏨**Sanibel Harbour Resort & Spa.** Families and business folk who want
Fodor's Choice luxury without Sanibel Island price tags flock to this high-rise resort
★ complex. It is not on Sanibel proper but instead towers over the bay at the last mainland exit before the causeway. Choose from three lodging options—a concierge club–style inn, the hotel, and condos—all with sweeping views of island-studded San Carlos Bay. There's also tennis, the best resort spa in the Fort Myers area, restaurants (one of which is a buffet-dining yacht), the gorgeous circular windowed Charley's Bar, and a large free-form pool, among other facilities and activities. Rent a kayak, take a wildlife-viewing cruise, or go fishing. The beach is small and bayside, but transportation to Sanibel's beaches is free. **Pros:** Luxury accommodations, full amenities, great views. **Cons:** Daily amenities fee added to rate, unspectacular beach, high rates. ⊠*17260 Harbour Pointe Dr., Fort Myers* ☎*239/466–4000 or 800/767–7777* 🖷*239/466–6050* ⊕*www.sanibel-resort.com* ⮐*279 rooms, 69 suites, 39 condominiums* &*In-room: safe, Ethernet, Wi-Fi (some). In-hotel: 6 restaurants, room service, bars, tennis courts, pools, gym, spa, beachfront, children's programs (ages 5–12), executive floor, public Wi-Fi, no-smoking rooms* ⊟*AE, D, DC, MC, V.*

$$$–$$$$ 🏨**Hilton Garden Inn.** This compact, prettily landscaped low-rise is near Fort Myers's cultural and commercial areas, and a business clientele favors it for its convenience. Rooms, done in florals and light-color wood, are spacious, with marble vanities in the bath, and have high-speed Internet access and free HBO. A huge aquarium in the lobby adds a nice Florida feel for vacationers. **Pros:** Near performing arts center, enjoyable restaurant, large and convenient rooms. **Cons:** Chain feel, small pool, at busy intersection. ⊠*12600 University Dr.* ☎*239/790–3500* 🖷*239/790–3501* ⊕*www.hilton.com* ⮐*109 rooms, 17 suites* &*In-room: refrigerator, Ethernet, dial-up. In-hotel: restaurant, bar, pool, laundry facilities, laundry service, Wi-Fi* ⊟*AE, DC, MC, V.*

$$$ 🏨**Ambassador Riverfront Hotel.** Towering 24 stories over the city harbor downtown, this hotel, formerly a Ramada Inn, caters equally to business and pleasure travelers with an elegant marble atrium lobby, mez-

10

zanine restaurant, two swimming pools, and easy access to downtown's street parties and clubs. Shuttles take you to the Edison & Ford Winter Estates, the mall, and the airport. The best rooms have views of the harbor; all are done up tropical-style, with bright bedspreads and white walls and furnishings. **Pros:** River views, convenient to downtown's restaurants and attractions, roomy accommodations. **Cons:** Unstable (it changes hands often). ⊠*2500 Edwards Dr.* ☎*239/337–0300 or 800/833–1620* 🖷*239/337–1530* ⊕*www.ambassadorfl.com* ⇨*216 rooms, 195 suites* ⚫*In-room: refrigerator (some), dial-up, Wi-Fi. In-hotel: restaurant, room service, bar, tennis court, pools, gym, public Wi-Fi, airport shuttle, some pets allowed (fee)* ▱*AE, D, DC, MC, V.*

NIGHTLIFE & THE ARTS

THE ARTS

The **Barbara B. Mann Performing Arts Hall** (⊠*Edison Community College, 13350 Edison Pkwy., off College Pkwy.* ☎*239/481–4849* ⊕*www.bbmannpah.com*) presents Broadway plays, concerts, musicals, and comedians.

★ The **Broadway Palm Dinner Theater** (⊠*1380 Colonial Blvd.* ☎*239/278–4422* ⊕*www.broadwaypalm.com*) serves buffet dinners along with some of Broadway's best comedies and musicals. There's also a 90-seat black-box theater that plays smaller-scale comedies and musicals.

★ In the restored circa-1920 Arcade Theatre downtown, **Florida Repertory Theatre** (⊠*12267 1st St.* ☎*239/332–4488 or 877/787–8053* ⊕*www. floridarep.org*) stages professional entertainment, from Neil Simon shows to musical revues.

NIGHTLIFE

Lively every night in season (Thursday through Sunday the rest of the year), **Bahama Breeze** (⊠*14701 Tamiami Trail* ☎*239/454–9234*) sways tropical with calypso, soca, and other island sounds.

★ **Dwyer's Prime** (⊠*13851 S. Cleveland Ave.* ☎*239/425–0782*) hosts jazz and blues performers every Thursday, Friday, and Saturday night. **Laugh In Comedy Café** (⊠*College Plaza, 8595 College Pkwy.* ☎*239/479–5233*), south of downtown, has comedians Friday and Saturday. **Stevie Tomato's Sports Page** (⊠*11431 S. Cleveland Ave.* ☎*239/939–7211*) has big-screen TVs and good munchies.

SPORTS & THE OUTDOORS

BASEBALL

The **Boston Red Sox** (⊠*2201 Edison Ave.* ☎*239/334–4700* ⊕*www.red-sox.com*) train in Fort Myers every spring. The **Minnesota Twins** (⊠*Lee County Sports Complex, 14100 Six Mile Cypress Pkwy.* ☎*239/768–4210*) play exhibition games in town during March and early April. From April through August, the Miracle, a Twins single-A affiliate, play home games at the Complex.

BIKING

The longest bike path in Fort Myers is along Summerlin Road. It passes commercial areas, and close to Sanibel through dwindling wide-open spaces. Linear Park, which runs parallel to Metro Parkway, offers more natural, less-congested views. A trailhead park is in the planning stages for parking and bike trails access. For a good selection of rentals, try the **Bike Route** (⊠*8595 College Parkway Suite B-1* ☎*239/481–3376* ⊕*thebikeroute.com*).

FISHING

Anglers head for the gulf, its bays, and estuaries for saltwater fishing—snapper, sheepshead, mackerel, and other species. The Caloosahatchee River, Orange River, canals, and small lakes offer freshwater alternatives.

GOLF

★ The driving range and 18-hole course at the **Eastwood Golf Club** (⊠*4600 Bruce Herd La.* ☎*239/275–4848*) are affordable, especially if you don't mind playing at unfavorable times (midday in summer, for example). Many golfers enjoy the lack of development around the course, which poses challenges with its water hazards and doglegs. Fees include cart and tax; fees without cart included are available at certain times. Greens fee $30/$30. The **Fort Myers Country Club** (⊠*3591 McGregor Blvd.* ☎*239/936–2457*), with 18 holes, challenges golfers with its small greens. It's the town's oldest course. Lessons are available. Greens fee $55/$20 Head to the **Shell Point Golf Club** (⊠*16401 On Par Blvd.* ☎*239/433–9790*) for an 18-hole course and a driving range. Greens fee $99/$56 (including cart).

SAILING

★ **Southwest Florida Yachts** (⊠*3444 Marinatown La. NW* ☎*239/656–1339 or 800/262–7939* ⊕*www.swfyachts.com*) charters sailboats and offers lessons.

SHOPPING

★ **Bell Tower Shops** (⊠*Cleveland Ave. and Daniels Pkwy.* ☎*239/489–1221* ⊕*www.thebelltowershops.com*), an open-air shopping center, has about 40 stylish boutiques and specialty shops, a Saks Fifth Avenue, and 20 movie screens. **Edison Mall** (⊠*Colonial Blvd. at Cleveland Ave.*) is the largest air-conditioned indoor mall in Fort Myers, with several major department stores and more than 150 specialty shops. Along its boardwalks, **Sanibel Tanger Factory Outlets** (⊠*McGregor Blvd. and Summerlin Rd.* ☎*888/471–3939* ⊕*www.tangeroutlet.com*) has outlets for Dexter, Van Heusen, Maidenform, Coach, Liz Claiborne, and Samsonite, among others. Just east of Fort Myers, more than 900 vendors sell new and used goods at **Fleamasters Fleamarket** (⊠*1 mi west of I–75 Exit 138 on Rte. 82* ⊕*www.fleamall.com*), Friday through Sunday between 8 and 4.

10

CAPE CORAL & NORTH FORT MYERS

Cape Coral is 13 mi from downtown Fort Myers via North Fort Myers, just across the river (1 mi) from south Fort Myers.

Four bridges cross from Fort Myers to Cape Coral and its eastern neighbor, North Fort Myers. Families especially find fun in these residential communities and their rural backyards, including undiscovered Pine Island.

Sun Splash Family Waterpark is the place to cool off when summer swelters. It has a dozen wet and dry attractions, including seven thrill waterslides; the Lilypad Walk, where you step from one floating "lily pad" to another; an arcade; a family pool and Tot Spot; and a river tube ride. ⊠*400 Santa Barbara Blvd.* ☎*239/574–0557* 🎟*$17* ☯*Mid-Mar.–Sept., call or visit the Web site for hrs.*

FodorśChoice
★

Shell Factory & Nature Park, once a shopping attraction and a survivor from Florida's roadside-attraction era, is an entertainment complex where you'll find restaurants, bumper boats, miniature golf, and a musical lighted fountain show (7:30 and 8:30 nightly). Admission is $5 for each attraction, open 11–7. The Nature Park (🎟*$10* ☯*10–7*) contains a petting zoo with camels, llamas, and goats; a walk-through aviary; an EcoLab with reptiles and small animals; a prairie dog habitat; and a gator slough. Shell Factory also hosts annual events such as the Gumbo Fest in January and the Chili & Rib Fest in February. ⊠*2787 N. Tamiami TrailNorth Fort Myers* ☎*239/995–2141 or 800/282–5805* ⊕*www.shellfactory.com* 🎟*$5–$10 per attraction* ☯*Mid-Mar.–Sept., call or visit the Web site for hrs.*

**OFF THE
BEATEN
PATH**

ECHO Global Farm & Nursery. Educational Concerns for Hunger Organization is a small Christian ministry group striving to end world hunger via creative farming. A fascinating 90-minute tour of its working farm takes you through five simulated tropic-zone gardens and has you tasting leaves and berries, walking through rain-forest habitat, visiting farm animals, stopping at a simulated Haitian school, witnessing urban gardens grown inside tires on rooftops, and learning all about ECHO's mission. The edible landscape nursery and gift shop sell fruit trees and the same seeds ECHO distributes to impoverished tropical farmers in 180 countries. ⊠*17391 Durrance Rd., North Fort Myers* ☎*239/543–3246* ⊕*www.echonet.org* 🎟*$8* ☯*Tours Jan.–Mar., Tues.–Fri. at 10 and 2, Sat. at 10; Apr.–Dec., Tues., Fri., and Sat. at 10; or by appointment. Nursery open Mon.–Sat. 9–noon.*

WHERE TO EAT

Cape Coral determinedly moves from its pigeon hole as a residential community to attract tourism with its downtown reconfiguration and the happy appearance of destination restaurants at the Cape Harbour residential marina development. Early 2010, The Resort at MarinaVillage, a separate 184-unit property, is scheduled to open and drastically change the face of Cape Coral tourism.

★ **$$** ✕**Rumrunners.** Cape Coral's best casual cuisine is surprisingly affordable, considering the luxury condo development that rises around it and the size of the yachts that pull up to the docks. Caribbean in spirit, with lots of indoor and outdoor views of a mangrove-fringed waterway, it serves bistro specialties such as seafood potpie, pork marinated with rum and orange juice, bronzed salmon, and a warm chocolate bread pudding that is addictive. ⊠ *5848 Cape Harbour Dr. at the Marina at Cape Harbour, off Chiquita Blvd.* ☎ *239/542–0200* ▤ *AE, D, MC, V* ⚓ *Reservations suggested.*

$ ✕ **Siam Hut.** Lunch and dinner menus at this Cape Coral fixture let you design your own stir-fry, noodle, or fried-rice dish. Dinner specialties include fried crispy frogs' legs with garlic and black pepper, a sizzling shrimp platter, fried whole fish with curry sauce, salads, and pad thai (rice noodles, shrimp, chicken, egg, ground peanuts, and vegetables). Get your food fiery hot or extra mild. Two traditional Thai tables allow you to sit on floor pillows (conveniently with backs) or you can opt for a more conventional table or booth. ⊠ *4521 Del Prado Blvd.* ☎ *239/945–4247* ▤ *MC, V* ⊘ *Closed Sun. No lunch Sat.*

★ ¢ ✕ **Bert's Bar & Grill.** Looking to hang out with the locals on Pine Island? You get that, cheap eats, live entertainment, a pool table, and a water view to boot at Bert's. Speaking of boots, you're likely to see much of the clientele wearing white rubber fishing boots, known here as Pine Island Reeboks. Order pizza, a burger, fried oysters, or grouper Reuben from the no-nonsense menu. ⊠ *4271 Pine Island Rd., Matlacha* ☎ *239/282–3232* ▤ *MC, V.*

WHERE TO STAY

$$ ▦ **Casa Loma Motel.** Stay at this pretty little motel, 15 minutes from Fort Myers at the end of the Croton Canal, to be close to Cape Coral's attractions and escape the sticker shock of the beaches. All units are efficiencies with a porch or balcony, some overlooking the canal. **Pros:** Affordable, kitchen facilities, canal access. **Cons:** Far from beaches, on a busy street, must drive to restaurants. ⊠ *3608 Del Prado Blvd.,* ☎ *239/549–6000 or 877/227–2566* 📠 *239/549–4877* ⊕ *www.casa lomamotel.com* ⇆ *48 efficiencies, 1 suite* ⚒ *In-room: kitchen, dial-up. In-hotel: pool, no elevator, laundry facilities, no-smoking rooms* ▤ *AE, D, MC, V.*

$$ ▦ **Tarpon Lodge Sportsman Inn.** If you're looking for no-frills escape and fishing, this aptly named lodge, built in 1926 on a sweep of green lawn with magnificent views out to sea, may do the trick. Rooms are small and simple, and the sunny restaurant dishes up creative surprises. It's in the fishing village of Pineland, on the edge of Pine Island Sound, settled in the 16th century by Calusa Indians and near an archaeological site and trail. **Pros:** Waterfront view, historic, great restaurant. **Cons:** Old digs, far from other restaurants, far from beach. ⊠ *13771 Waterfront Dr., Pineland* ☎ *239/283–3999* 📠 *239/283–7658* ⊕ *www.tarponlodge. com* ⇆ *21 rooms, 2 cottages* ⚒ *In-room: no phones. In-hotel: restaurant, bar, pool, no elevator, public Wi-Fi* ▤ *AE, MC, V* ⊙| *CP.*

SPORTS & THE OUTDOORS

GOLF

Coral Oaks Golf Course (⊠ *1800 N.W. 28th Ave.* ☎ *239/573–3100*) has an 18-hole layout and a practice range. Arthur Hill designed the cham-

10

pionship par-72 course, which has lots of lakes, ponds, wildlife, and mammoth live oaks. After 2 pm you can save money by walking the course. Greens fee $59/$69 (including cart).

TENNIS

Cape Coral Yacht and Racquet Club (✉ *5819 Driftwood Pkwy.* ☎ *239/574–0808*) has five lighted hard courts. Guest fees apply.

THE COASTAL ISLANDS

A maze of islands in various stages of habitation fronts Fort Myers mainland, separated by the Intracoastal Waterway. Some are accessible via a causeway; to reach others, you need a boat. If you cut through bay waters, you have a good chance of being escorted by bottlenose dolphins. Mostly birds and other wild creatures inhabit some islands, which are given over to state parks. Traveler-pampering hotels on Sanibel, Captiva, and Fort Myers Beach give way to rustic cottages, old inns, and cabins on quiet Cabbage Key and Pine Island, which have no beaches because they lie between the barrier islands and mainland. Others are devoted to resorts. When exploring island beaches, keep one eye on the sand: shelling is a major pursuit in these parts.

GASPARILLA ISLAND (BOCA GRANDE)

43 mi northwest of Fort Myers

Before roads to the lower Gulf Coast were even talked about, wealthy Northerners came by train to spend the winter at the **Gasparilla Inn**, built in 1912 in Boca Grande on Gasparilla Island, named, legend has it, for a Spanish pirate who set up headquarters in these waters. Although condominiums and modern sprawl creep up on the rest of Gasparilla, much of the town of Boca Grande looks like another era. The mood is set by the Old Florida homes and tree-framed roadways. The island's calm is disrupted in the spring when anglers descend with a vengeance on Boca Grande Pass, considered among the best tarpon-fishing spots in the world. Boca Grande is accessible by car, but is more than an hour's drive from Fort Myers. Day-trippers can catch a charter boat or rent a boat, dock at Boca Grande Marina, and rent a bike or golf cart for a day of exploring and lunching. North of it stretches a long island, home to Don Pedro Island State Park and Palm Island Resort, both accessible only by boat, then the off-the-beaten-path island of Manasota Key and its fishing resort community of Englewood Beach.

The island's beaches are its greatest prize, and lie within **Gasparilla Island State Park and Boca Grande Lighthouse Museum** at the south end. The long, narrow beach ends at Boca Grande Pass, famous for its deep waters and tarpon fishing. The pretty, two-story, circa-1890 lighthouse once marked the pass for mariners. In recent years it has been restored as a museum that explores the island's fishing and railroad heritage in rooms once occupied by the lighthouse keeper. ✉ *Boca Grande* ☎ *941/964–0060* ⊕ *www.barrierislandparkssociety.org/museum.html* 💲*$2 per* *vehicle; $1 suggested donation to lighthouse* ☉ *Park daily 8–sunset; lighthouse Nov.–May, Mon.–Sat 10–4, Sun. 12-4; June–Oct., Wed.– Sat. 10–4, Sun. 12-4; closed Aug.*

WHERE TO EAT & STAY

★ $$$ ✕**Boca Bistro.** Part of the island's new Boca Grande Resort complex, the bistro brings to Boca a new level of creative dining with an elevated waterside view. Red lacquered walls threaded with gold and copper leaf frame a bank of windows on the second-story restaurant. Nightly specials complement a menu including ceviche, poached lobster tail with orange buerre blanc, duo of duck (confit leg and seared breast) with hoisin barbecue and orange peppercorn sauces, and grouper with lime-dill butter. ⊠*5800 Gasparilla Rd., Boca Grande* ☎*941/964–8020* ▤*AE, D, MC, V* ☉*No lunch. Closed Mon. No dinner Sun. (brunch only). Seasonal closings vary; call ahead between Easter and Thanksgiving.*

> ### KING FISHERS
>
> Pine Island Sound and Boca Grande Pass spawned the sport of tarpon-fishing in the late 1880s. A wealthy Chicago streetcar mogul built the Izaak Walton Club on Useppa Island in 1911 for the famed and wealthy who descended to capture the "Silver King."

★ $$$$ ▦**Gasparilla Inn.** Social-register members such as the Vanderbilts and DuPonts still winter at the gracious pale-yellow wooden hotel built by shipping industrialists in the early 1900s. Lodge rooms are not lavishly decorated by today's standards, but received a face-lift in recent years to coordinate with the inn's feminine, Victorian air. The cottage rooms spread around the inn in charming historic digs. The inn takes up much of the town of Boca Grande with its rich-blooded amenities—sprawling lawns, a golf course, croquet, and a beach club with a 10-room spa. In recent years the inn has gone from a mandatory meal plan in high season to more flexible packages customized to guests' desires— from full meals to none year-round. (Rates represented here are for full American Plan in winter.) Gentlemen are required to wear a jackets in the main dining room during the winter season. **Pros:** Historic property, newly painted and upgraded. **Cons:** Expensive, the quirks of a very old building. ⊠*500 Palm Ave., Boca Grande* ☎*941/964–2201 or 800/996–1913* ⊕*www.gasparillainn.com* ▤*941/283–1384* ⬥*142 rooms* ⚭*In-room: Ethernet (some), Wi-Fi (some). In-hotel: 3 restaurants, golf course, tennis courts, pools, gym, spa, beachfront* ▤*AE, D, MC, V* ⏣*FAP.*

SPORTS & THE OUTDOORS

BIKING

Boca Grande's erstwhile railroad bed has been paved for a 7-mi bike path that golf cart drivers also share. **Island Bike 'N Beach** (⊠*333 Park Ave., Boca Grande* ☎*941/964–0711*) rents bikes as well as golf carts.

CANOEING & KAYAKING

☽ **Grande Tours** (⊠*12575 Placida Rd., Placida* ☎*941/697–8825* ⊕*www. grandetours.com*) leads kayaking ecotours along the creeks and open waters around Charlotte Harbor. Cost is $50 for two hours. Also available are kayaking lessons, kayak fishing excursions, kids kayak camp, and rentals.

NORTH CAPTIVA ISLAND

3 mi south of Cabbage Key.

No bridges lead to this 750-acre island, and most visitors arrive by prearranged water taxi from Pine Island. They come for the isolation and complete absence of "civilization." Some of the private houses can be rented through **North Captiva Island Club Resort** (☎ *239/395–1001 or 800/576–7343* ⊕ *www.northcaptiva.com*). The complex has two pools and a sauna, which you're free to use, plus bike, kayak, and golf cart (the main mode of motorized transportation on the island) rentals and two restaurants and a pool bar that serve food. The island also holds another public restaurant outside the resort. It's a good idea to bring your own groceries; there's only one small store, and it's quite pricey. Walk to secluded beaches at the south end, where Hurricane Charley split the island in two in 2004.

SANIBEL & CAPTIVA ISLANDS

23 mi southwest of downtown Fort Myers.

Sanibel Island, accessible from the mainland via the Sanibel Causeway (toll $6 round-trip), is famous as one of the world's best shelling grounds, a function of the unusual east–west orientation of the island's south end. Just as the tide is going out and after storms, the pickings can be superb, and shell seekers with the telltale "Sanibel stoop" patrol every beach carrying bags of conchs, whelks, cockles, and other bivalves and gastropods. (Remember, it's unlawful to pick up live shells.) Away from the beach, flowery vegetation decorates small shopping complexes, pleasant resorts and condo complexes, mom-and-pop motels, and casual restaurants. But much of the narrow road down the spine of the island is bordered by nature reserves that have made Sanibel as well known among bird-watchers as it is among seashell collectors.

Captiva Island, connected to the northern end of Sanibel by a bridge, is quirky and engaging. At the end of a twisty road lined with million-dollar mansions lies a delightful village of shops and eateries.

At Sanibel's southern tip, the frequently photographed **Sanibel Lighthouse,** built in 1884, before the island was settled, guards **Lighthouse Beach.** Although the lighthouse is not open to the public, the area around it has been a wildlife refuge since 1950. A fishing pier, nature trail, and restrooms are available. ⊠ *Periwinkle Way, Sanibel* ☎ *239/472–6477* 🅿 *Parking $2 per hr.*

★ The charming **Sanibel Historical Village and Museum** shows off buildings from the island's past—a 1927 post office, a garage housing a Model T Ford, the Old Bailey general store, a teahouse, a 1925 winter vacation cottage, a 19th-century one-room schoolhouse, and the 1913 Rutland House Museum, with old documents and photographs and a Calusa

Indian exhibit. ✉ *950 Dunlop Rd., Sanibel* ☎ *239/472–4648* 💲 *$5* ⊙ *Nov.–Apr., Wed.–Sat. 10–4; May–mid-Aug., Wed.–Sat. 10–1; closed mid-Aug.–Oct.*

The beach in **Gulfside Park** is quiet, safe from strong currents, and good for solitude and shells. There are restrooms and picnic tables and long stretches to stroll. ✉ *Algiers La. off Casa Ybel Rd., Sanibel* ☎ *239/472–6477* 💲 *Parking $2 per hr.*

Tarpon Bay Beach is centrally located and safer for swimming than beaches at the passes, where waters move swiftly. It is, however, one of the more populated beaches, lined with low-rise condos and resorts. You can walk for miles in either direction. ✉ *Tarpon Bay Rd. off Sanibel–Captiva Rd., Sanibel* ☎ *239/472–6477* 💲 *Parking $2 per hr.*

To help you identify your Sanibel Island beach finds, stop at the **Bailey-Matthews Shell Museum,** where a shell-finder display identifies specimens from local waters in sizes ranging from tiny to huge. Thirty-five vignettes and exhibits explore shells in the environment, art, and history, including a life-size display of native Calusa and how they used shells for tools and food. Handle shell specimens and play games in the colorful kids' lab. A 6-foot globe at the center of the museum rotunda highlights shells from around the world. ✉ *3075 Sanibel–Captiva Rd., Sanibel* ☎ *239/395–2233 or 888/679–6450* ⊕ *www.shellmuseum.org* 💲 *$7* ⊙ *Daily 10–5.*

Fodor's Choice ★

More than half of Sanibel is occupied by the subtly beautiful **J. N. "Ding" Darling National Wildlife Refuge,** 6,300 acres of wetlands and lush, jungly mangrove forests named after a conservation-minded Pulitzer Prize–winning political cartoonist, who fathered the federal Duck Stamp program. The masses of roseate spoonbills and ibis and the winter flock of white pelicans here make for a good show even if you're not a die-hard bird-watcher. Birders have counted some 230 species, including herons, ospreys, and the timid mangrove cuckoo. Raccoons, otters, alligators, and a lone American crocodile also can be spotted. The 4½-mi Wildlife Drive is the main way to explore the preserve; drive, walk, or bicycle along it, or ride a specially designed open-air tram with a naturalist on board. There are also a couple of short walking trails, including one to a Calusa shell mound. Or explore from the water via canoe or kayak (guided tours are available). The best time for bird-watching is in the early morning about an hour before or after low tide, and the observation tower along the road offers prime viewing. Interactive exhibits in the center, at the entrance to the refuge, demonstrate the refuge's various ecosystems and explain its status as a rest stop along a major bird migration route. Because Wildlife Drive is closed to vehicular traffic on Friday, try to time your visit for another day. ✉ *1 Wildlife Dr., off Sanibel–Captiva Rd. at MM 2, Sanibel* ☎ *239/472–1100, 239/472–1351 tram* ⊕ *www. fws.gov/dingdarling* 💲 *$5 per car, $1 for pedestrians and bicyclists, tram $13, Education Center free* ⊙ *Education Center Jan.–Apr., daily 9–5; May–Dec., daily 9–4; Wildlife Drive Sat.–Thurs. 7:30–8.*

Fodor's Choice ★

10

For a good look at snowy egrets, great blue herons, alligators, and other inhabitants of Florida's wetlands, follow the 4½ mi of walking trails at the 1,800-acre wetlands managed by the **Sanibel–Captiva Conservation Foundation.** See island research projects and nature displays, visit a butterfly house, and touch sea creatures. Guided walks are available on and off property; the beach walk is especially enjoyable and easily educational. ⊠ *3333 Sanibel–Captiva Rd., Sanibel* ☎ *239/472–2329* ⊕ *www.sccf.org* ⊠ *$3* ⊘ *Oct.-May., weekdays 8:30–4; June-Sept., weekdays 8:30–3; Dec.-Apr., also open Sat. 10–3.*

Long, wide **Bowman's Beach,** on Sanibel's northwest end, is the island's most secluded strand. Walk the length of it and leave humanity behind, finding some of the greatest concentrations of shells along the way. The sunsets at the north end are spectacular—try to spot the green flash said to occur just as the sun sinks below the horizon. Here's where, you may have heard, nudists once sunbathed—but current laws prohibit it, and local officials police against it. ⊠ *Bowman Beach Rd., Sanibel* ☎ *239/432–2006* ⊠ *Parking $2 per hr.* ■TIP→Red tide, a common natural beach occurrence that kills fish, also has negative effects on the human respiratory system. It causes scratchy throats, runny eyes and noses, and coughing. Although the effects are not long-term, it's a good idea to avoid the beach when red tide is in the vicinity (look for posted signs).

Turner Beach is the sunset-watching spot on the southern tip of Captiva. Strong currents through the pass make swimming tricky, and parking is limited. Surfers head here when winds whip up the waves. ⊠ *Captiva Dr., Captiva* ⊠ *Parking $2 per hr.*

Captiva Beach, is acclaimed as one of the nation's most romantic beaches for its fabulous sunsets—the best view on Sanibel and Captiva. The parking lot is small, so arrive early. Facilities are limited to portable restrooms, but stores and restaurants are nearby. ⊠ *Captiva Dr., Captiva* ⊠ *Parking $2 per hr.*

WHERE TO EAT

⊘ $$$ ✕**Bubble Room.** This lively, kitschy favorite is fun for families and nostalgic types with fat wallets. Servers wear scout uniforms and funny headgear. Electric trains circle overhead, glossies of 1940s Hollywood stars line the walls, and tabletops showcase old-time toys. After grazing your basket of cheesy bubble bread and sweet, yeasty sticky buns, go for aged prime rib or the grouper steamed in a paper bag. It's more about the atmosphere than the food here, but the homemade triple-layer cakes, delivered in hefty wedges, are stand-out. The red velvet is a classic favorite. Be prepared to wait for a table in season. ⊠ *15001 Captiva Dr., Captiva* ☎ *239/472–5558* ⊕ *www.bubbleroomrestaurant.com* ⚠ *Reservations not accepted* ☰ *AE, D, DC, MC, V.*

★ $$$ ✕**Traders Store & Cafe.** In the midst of a warehouse-size import store, this bistro, accented with artifacts from Africa and other exotic places, is a favorite of locals. The marvelous sesame-seared tuna lunch salad with Asian slaw and wasabi vinaigrette exemplifies the creative fare. For dinner, go for the barbecued baby back ribs, macadamia-crusted grouper, or any of the day's finely crafted specials. A local crooner entertains two nights a week. The bar serves light nibbles and happy hour two-fers. ⊠*1551 Periwinkle Way, Sanibel* ☎*239/472-7242* ▭*AE, D, MC, V.*

$$ ✕**Green Flash.** Good food and second-story, sweeping views of quiet waters and a mangrove island keep boaters and others coming back to this casual indoor-outdoor restaurant. Seafood dominates, but there's a bit of everything on the menu, from shrimp in beer batter and grilled swordfish to pork tenderloin Wellington. For lunch, try the Green Flash sandwich (smoked turkey and prosciutto or vegetables, both with cheese on grilled focaccia). On cool, sunny days, grab a table out back dockside. ⊠*15183 Captiva Dr., Captiva* ☎*239/472-3337* ▭*AE, D, DC, MC, V.*

$$ ✕**McT's Shrimphouse and Tavern.** In this informal Sanibel landmark, the menu predictably spotlights fresh seafood. The baked oysters make great starters. If you're a seafood fiend, go for the Sanibel steamer or all-you-can-eat shrimp and crab. Besides more than 15 shrimp entrées, ribs, prime rib, and Cajun-style chicken are available. Few can resist the Sanibel mud pie, an enormous ice-cream concoction heavy on the Oreo crumbs. Stop in for a before- or after-dinner drink in the bar with the upside-down tree forest. ⊠*1523 Periwinkle Way, Sanibel* ☎*239/472-3161* ⚔*Reservations not accepted* ▭*AE, D, MC, V.*

$ ✕**Redfish Bluefish.** Despite the whimsical name and brightly painted, garbage-art decor, there's nothing frivolous about the food. There's not a green egg to be found on the dinner menu in this intimate spot, which lists three courses of well-designed dishes shrunk to taster size and concentrated with multilevel flavor, such as the shrimp tostado, bison meat loaf, and porterhouse of spring lamb. ⊠*Behind Tower Gallery, 751 Tarpon Bay Rd., Sanibel* ☎*239/472-1956* ▭*AE, D, MC, V* ☺*Closed Mon. No lunch.*

¢ ✕**Amy's Over Easy Café.** Locals head to this bright, chicken-decorated eatery for breakfast and lunch. Kick-start the day with the egg Reuben sandwich, veggie Benedict, or a custom omelet made with whole eggs, whites only, or egg substitute. The lunch menu includes salads, a vegetarian wrap, burgers, grilled mahimahi, and blackberry cobbler. If there's a wait for breakfast, spend it browsing and sipping free coffee at the café's gift shop. Early dinner is served Tuesday–Saturday. ⊠*630-1 Tarpon Bay Rd., Sanibel* ☎*239/472-2625* ⚔*Reservations not accepted* ▭*AE, D, MC, V* ☺*No dinner Sun. and Mon.*

☾ ¢ ✕**Lazy Flamingo.** At two Sanibel locations, this is the friendly neighborhood hangout enjoyed by locals and visitors alike. The original in Santiva (between Sanibel and Captiva) is small, with counter service only; the other is larger (but there's still often a wait) and provides table service. Both have a funky nautical look à la Key West and a popular following for their "Dead Parrot Wings" (Buffalo wings coated with tongue-scorching hot sauce), grouper sandwiches, burgers, and steamer pots. ⊠*6520C Pine Ave., Sanibel* ☎*239/472-5353* ⊠*1036 Periwinkle Way, Sanibel* ☎*239/472-6939* ⊕*www.lazyflamingo.com* ⚔*Reservations not accepted* ▭*AE, D, MC, V.*

10

WHERE TO STAY

☺ $$$$ **Casa Ybel Resort.** At this time-share resort, palms, ponds, a footbridge, and gazebos set the mood on 23 acres of gulf-facing grounds. Inside the two-floor stilt buildings, the one- and two-bedroom apartments are roomy and contemporary, with full kitchens, wicker furniture, tasteful patterns, and big screened-in porches that look out to the beach. The respected Thistle Lodge restaurant is in a re-created historic home with a beach view. **Pros:** On the beach, good restaurants, lots of recreational opportunities. **Cons:** Spa treatments in-room only or beachside, minimum stay requirement. ⊠ *2255 W. Gulf Dr., Sanibel* ☎ *239/472–3145 or 800/276–4753* 🖷 *239/472–2109* ⊕ *www.casaybelresort.com* ⇱ *40 1-bedroom units, 74 2-bedroom units* ⚘ *In-room: safe, kitchen, DVD, VCR, Ethernet. In-hotel: 2 restaurants, bars, tennis courts, pool, beachfront, children's programs (ages 4–11)* 🖃 *AE, D, DC, MC, V.*

$$$$ **Sanibel's Seaside Inn.** Tucked among the subtropical greenery, right on the beach, this quiet inn is a pleasant alternative to the area's larger resorts. Cottage suites are done up in charming island cottage style with rattan, and have full kitchens and flat-screen TVs. Rooms come with a handy wet-bar area stocked with dishware, a coffeemaker, toaster, microwave, and small fridge. Continental breakfast and bike use are complimentary, and DVDs are on hand to borrow. You may use amenities at Sundial Beach Resort and the Dunes Golf Club. **Pros:** intimate, lots of character, beautiful beachfront. **Cons:** pool not conducive to families, no restaurant or lounge on property. ⊠ *541 E. Gulf Dr., Sanibel* ☎ *239/472–1400 or 888/295–4560* 🖷 *239/481–4947* ⊕ *www.seasideinn.com* ⇱ *22 rooms, 10 cottage suites* ⚘ *In-room: kitchen (some), refrigerator, VCR, Wi-Fi. In-hotel: pool, beachfront, bicycles, laundry facilities, public Wi-Fi, no-smoking rooms* 🖃 *AE, D, DC, MC, V* ⦿*CP.*

☺ $$$$ **South Seas Island Resort.** This massive 330-acre resort closed for about
Fodor's Choice   a year and a half after extensive hurricane damage in August 2004. It
★   partially reopened in March 2006 under new ownership with all-new, upgraded guest accommodations, 19 swimming pools, reinvented private restaurants and shops, and a remodeled 9-hole golf course with lush water features. The resort is now operating full swing and at its best ever. As in the past, stylish, low-rise hotel rooms, villas, and houses are all over the property but are concentrated at either end, near the marina and, to the south, near the entry gate and the small shopping complex. Dunes fringe a pristine 2½-mi beach, and mangroves edge the single main road. Entry gates and water on three sides give the resort a delicious seclusion, but trolleys take you around the property and into Captiva village. A new Golden Door Spa is expected to open in 2008. **Pros:** Full-service amenities, security, isolation, exclusivity, car-free transportation. **Cons:** High rates, isolation (a pro for some, con for others), spread out. ⊠ *5400 Plantation Rd.Captiva 33924* ☎ *239/472–5111 or 800/965–7772* 🖷 *239/481–4947* ⊕ *www.southseas.com* ⇱ *138 rooms, 482 suites* ⚘ *In-room: kitchen. In-hotel: 2 restaurants, room service, bars, golf course, tennis courts, pools, gym,*

spa, beachfront, water sports, bicycles, children's programs (ages 3–18) ⊟AE, D, DC, MC, V.

★ ☪ $$$$ ▦ **Sundial Beach & Golf Resort.** Sanibel's largest resort encompasses 400 privately owned, individually decorated one- and two-bedroom condos, about 260 of which are in its rental program. It caters to groups in fall, families in winter. The latter hang around the main pool with its seashell slide, the shell-strewn beach, and the Eco-Center, where they can pet live shells and sign up for family activities and kids' camp. **Pros:** Full-service amenities, great beach. **Cons:** Conference crowds, crowded pool area. ⊠1451 Middle Gulf Dr., Sanibel ☎239/472–4151 or 866/565–5093 ⎙239/472–8892 ⊕www.sundialresort.com ➷1300 1-bedroom units, 130 2-bedroom units ⚭In-room: safe, kitchen, VCR, dial-up, Wi-Fi. In-hotel: 2 restaurants, bars, tennis courts, pools, gym, beachfront, water sports, bicycles, children's programs (ages 4–12), public Wi-Fi, no-smoking rooms ⊟AE, D, DC, MC, V.

$$$-$$$$ ▦ **Shalimar.** Well-maintained grounds and an inviting beach are the appeal of this small property. Units occupy tin-roof two-story cottages and a two-story motel set back from the beach amid palm trees and other subtropical greenery. The small pool is in the courtyard, and there are barbecue grills. **Pros:** On the beach, intimate, free Wi-Fi, variety of accommodations. **Cons:** No restaurants or shopping on property or nearby. ⊠2823 W. Gulf Dr., Sanibel ☎239/472–1353 or 800/472–1353 ⎙239/472–6430 ⊕www.shalimar.com ➷20 efficiencies, 11 1-bedroom units, 2 2-bedroom units ⚭In-room: kitchen, VCR, dial-up, Wi-Fi. In-hotel: pool, beachfront, bicycles, laundry facilities, public Internet, public Wi-Fi. ⊟AE, D, MC, V.

$$$-$$$$ ▦ **Waterside Inn.** Palm trees and white sand set the scene at this quiet beachside vacation spot made up of white one- and two-story buildings. Rooms and efficiencies are modestly furnished, with bright cobalt-blue-and-white interiors, and have balconies or patios and at least a partial view of the gulf. Single-story cottages are named for apricot, kiwi, raspberry, and other fruits and painted appropriately. **Pros:** Beachfront, intimate, small pets allowed. **Cons:** No restaurants on-site or within walking distance. ⊠3033 W. Gulf Dr., Sanibel ☎239/472–1345 or 800/741–6166 ⎙239/472–2148 ⊕www.watersideinn.net ➷4 rooms, 10 efficiencies, 13 cottages ⚭In-room: kitchen (some), refrigerator, dial-up, Wi-Fi. In-hotel: pool, beachfront, bicycles, laundry facilities, public Wi-Fi, some pets allowed (fee) ⊟AE, D, MC, V.

$$$ ▦ **'Tween Waters Inn.** Besides its great beach-to-bay location, this inn has historic value. In the 1930s, Pulitzer Prize–winning cartoonist and conservationist "Ding" Darling, namesake of Sanibel's refuge, stayed in its historic cottages, which are the most charming of the property's accommodations. Water-sports enthusiasts especially like all the available rentals and charters out of the marina. The pool bar and Crow's Nest lounge, both of which serve food, are popular with locals and visitors alike. **Pros:** Great views, lots of water-sports options, free Wi-Fi. **Cons:** Beach is across the road from accommodations, rooms are bland. ⊠Captiva Dr., Captiva ☎239/472–5161 or 800/223–5865 ⎙239/481–0249 ⊕www.tween-waters.com ➷32 rooms, 24 efficiencies, 40 suites, 4 2-bedroom suites, 2 3-bedroom suites, 19 cottages

10

♿*In-room: kitchen (some), Wi-Fi (some). In-hotel: restaurant, bar, tennis courts, pool, gym, spa, beachfront, bicycles, laundry facilities, public Internet, public Wi-Fi, no-smoking rooms* ⊟*AE, D, DC, MC, V* ⦿⎮*CP.*

SPORTS & THE OUTDOORS

BIKING

Everyone bikes around flat-as-a-pancake Sanibel and Captiva—on bikeways that edge the main highway in places, on the road through the wildlife refuge, and along side streets. Free maps are available at bicycle liveries. On Sanibel, rent by the hour or the day at **Billy's Bikes** (⊠*1470 Periwinkle Way, Sanibel* ☎*239/472–5248* ⦿*www.billysrentals.com*), which also rents motorized scooters and conducts Segway tours. On Captiva, bikes are available at **Jim's Rentals** (⊠*11534 Andy Rosse La., Captiva* ☎*239/472–1296* ⦿*www.yolo-jims.com*).

BOATING

The Boat House (⊠*Sanibel Marina, 634 N. Yachtsman Dr., Sanibel* ☎*239/472–2531*) rents 21-foot powerboats starting at $132.50 for a half day for up to three people. **Sweet Water Boat Rental** (*'Tween Waters Marina,* ⊠*15951 Captiva Dr., Captiva* ☎*239/472–6336*) can set you up with a 19-foot center-console powerboat starting at $200 for a half day.

CANOEING & KAYAKING

★ One of the best ways to scout out the wildlife refuge is by paddle. Rent a canoe or kayak from the refuge's official concessionaire, **Tarpon Bay Explorers** (⊠*900 Tarpon Bay Rd., Sanibel* ☎*239/472–8900* ⦿*www.tarponbayexplorers.com*). Guided tours are also available.

FISHING

Local anglers head out to catch mackerel, pompano, grouper, reds, snook, snapper, tarpon, and shark. To find a charter captain on Sanibel, ask around at its main public marina, **Sanibel Marina** (⊠*634 N. Yachtsman Dr., Sanibel* ☎*239/472–2723*). On Captiva, the place to look for guides is **'Tween Waters Marina** (⊠*15951 Captiva Dr., Captiva* ☎*239/472–5161*).

GOLF

Rent clubs and take lessons as well as test your skills against the water hazards on the 18-hole course at the **Dunes Golf & Tennis Club** (⊠*949 Sandcastle Rd., Sanibel* ☎*239/472–2535*), greens fee $110/$42.

TENNIS

At the **Dunes Golf & Tennis Club** (⊠*949 Sandcastle Rd., Sanibel* ☎*239/472–3522*) there are seven clay courts and two pros who give lessons.

SHOPPING

Sanibel is known for its art galleries, shell shops, and one-of-a-kind boutiques; the several small open-air shopping complexes are inviting, with their tropical flowers and shady ficus trees. The largest cluster of complexes is **Periwinkle Place** (⊠*2075 Periwinkle Way, Sanibel*

@*www.periwinkleplace.com*), with nearly 30 shops. At **She Sells Sea Shells** (✉*1157 Periwinkle Way, Sanibel* ☎*239/395–2266*), everything imaginable is made from shells, from decorative mirrors and lamps to Christmas ornaments. The owner wrote the book on shellcraft, and you can buy it there.

Fodor'sChoice
★ Expect the unexpected in wildlife art at **Jungle Drums** (✉*11532 Andy Rosse La., Captiva* ☎*239/395–2266* @*www.jungledrumsgallery.com*), where fish, sea turtles, and other wildlife are depicted with utmost creativity and touches of whimsy.

ESTERO ISLAND (FORT MYERS BEACH)

18 mi southwest of Fort Myers.

Crammed with motels, hotels, and restaurants, this island is one of Fort Myers's more frenetic gulf playgrounds. Dolphins are frequently spotted in Estero Bay, part of the Intracoastal waterway, and marinas provide a starting point for boating adventures, including sunset cruises, sightseeing cruises, and deep-sea fishing. At the southern tip, a bridge leads to Lovers Key State Park.

☺ At the 17-acre **Lynn Hall Memorial Park,** in the commercial northern part of Estero Island, the shore slopes gradually into the usually tranquil and warm gulf waters, providing safe swimming for children. And since houses, condominiums, and hotels line most of the beach, you're never far from civilization. There are picnic tables, barbecue grills, playground equipment, and a free fishing pier. A bathhouse with restrooms, a pedestrian mall, and a number of restaurants are nearby. Parking is metered; 25¢ buys only eight minutes and meters are closely surveyed. ✉*Estero Blvd.* ☎*239/463–1116* ◷*Daily 7* AM*–11* PM.

OFF THE BEATEN PATH
Lovers Key State Park. Once a little-known secret, this out-of-the-way park encompassing 1,616 acres on four barrier islands and several uninhabited islets is gaining popularity among beachers and birders. Bike, hike, or walk the park's trails; go shelling on its 2½ mi of white-sand beach; take a boat tour; or rent a canoe, kayak, or bike. Trams run regularly 9 to 5 to deliver you and your gear to South Beach. The ride is short but often dusty. North Beach is a five-minute walk from the concession area and parking lot. Watch for osprey, bald eagles, herons, ibis, pelicans, and roseate spoonbills, or sign up for an excursion to learn fishing or cast-netting. Weddings often take place at the gazebo on the beach. There are also restrooms, picnic tables, a snack bar, and showers. On the bayside, playgrounds and another picnic area cater to families. ✉*8700 Estero Blvd.* ☎*239/463–4588* @*www.floridastateparks.org/loverskey* ▱*$5 2–8 people in 1 vehicle, $3 for 1 person in 1 vehicle, $1 for pedestrians and bicyclists* ◷*Daily 8–sunset.*

10

WHERE TO EAT

$$$ ✕**The Sandy Butler.** Visitors to Fort Myers Beach now can find fine dining if they're willing to drive a few miles off the island. This huge complex of gourmet market and fresh cuisine may be a bit ambitious for the area, but it has survived for a couple of years to become a favor-

ite of foodies from Sanibel and Fort Myers. At dinner, a wide range of prices appeals to different budgets—from a delicious Beef Rotollo (fresh pasta rolled with Bolognese sauce, spinach, and mozzarella; $14) to the tender bone-in pork chop with Stilton and port glaze ($26) or chateaubriand for two ($70). The trio of crèmes brulées is a true treat—especially the cayenne chocolate selection. ☒ *17650 San Carlos Blvd.,* ☎*239/482–6765* ▤*AE, D, MC, V.*

$$ ✗**Matanzas Inn.** Watch boats coming and going whether you sit inside or out at this rustic Old Florida–style restaurant right on the docks alongside the Intracoastal Waterway. When the weather cooperates, tables outdoors, under umbrellas, provide the best ambience. Inside, a rustic shack gives way to a more formal dining area in the back; there's a bar upstairs with sweeping views. You can't miss with shrimp from the local fleets—delicately cornmeal-breaded, stuffed, or done Alfredo with scallops. The Matanzas Steamer (market price), a house specialty, heaps on the fish and shellfish. This is true Fort Myers Beach style, meaning service can be a bit gruff—and slow. ☒*416 Crescent St.* ☎*239/463–3838* ⊕*www.matanzasrestaurant.com* ⌁*Reservations not accepted* ▤*AE, D, MC, V.*

$$ ✗**Parrot Key Caribbean Grill.** For something more contemporary than Fort Myers Beach's traditional shrimp and seafood houses, head to San Carlos Island on the east side of the high bridge where the shrimp boats dock. Parrot Key sits marina-side near the shrimp docks and exudes merriment with its flair for Floribbean cuisine and island music. The all-day menu takes tropical cues with dishes such as habanero (hot chili) wings, chicken sandwich with kiwi-strawberry-mango barbecue sauce, filet au poivre with a brandy-mango demi-glace, and fried oysters with creole mustard. There's live entertainment weekends from 7 to 10 PM. ☒*2400 Main St.* ☎*239/463–3257* ⊕*www.myparrotkey.com* ⌁*Reservations not accepted* ▤*AE, D, MC, V.*

¢ ✗**Plaka.** A casual long-timer and a favorite for a quick breakfast, lunch breaks, and sunset dinners, Plaka—Greek for "beach"—has typical Greek fare such as moussaka, pastitsio, gyros, and roast lamb, as well as burgers, hot dogs, sandwiches, fried seafood, and strip steak. It lies along a row of casual sidewalk restaurants in a pedestrian mall near the beach. There's indoor dining, but grab a seat on the porch or under an umbrella on the patio. ☒*1001 Estero Blvd.* ☎*239/463–4707* ⌁*Reservations not accepted* ▤*AE, D, MC, V.*

WHERE TO STAY

$$$$ ⊡**DiamondHead.** This 12-story, all-suites resort sits on the beach, and many rooms, especially those on higher floors, have stunning views. Units are done in rich fall tones but show a little wear and tear. Each has a living room with queen-size sleeper sofa, a separate bedroom, and a kitchenette. The well-organized children's programs include everything from crafts to scavenger hunts to sand golf. **Pros:** Right on beach, walking distance to Times Square, kitchen facilities. **Cons:** Heavy foot and car traffic, very small fitness center, not the best value on the beach. ☒*2000 Estero Blvd.* ☎*239/765–7654 or 888/765–5002* ▤*239/765–1694* ⊕*www.diamondheadfl.com* ⇱*124 suites* ⌁*In-room: kitchen,*

Ethernet, dial-up, Wi-Fi. In-hotel: 2 restaurants, bar, pool, gym, beach-front, children's programs (ages 4–14), laundry facilities, public Wi-Fi ☒*AE, D, MC, V.*

★ $$$$ 🏨**Lovers Key Beach Club & Resort.** Views can be stupendous from upper floors in this 14-story waterfront resort just north of Lovers Key State Park. The gulf seems to stretch forever, and dolphins and manatees in the estuary put on quite a show. Most of the plantation-style condominiums have spa bathtubs with a window view. All of the one- and two-bedroom units have full kitchens and handsome decor that continues the lobby theme of bamboo, palms, and pineapples. The lagoon-style waterfall pool sits bayside, where a narrow strip of protected sand constitutes the beach. **Pros:** Excellent views, off the beaten path, spacious accommodations. **Cons:** Not a true beach, far from shopping, limited amenities. ☒*8771 Estero Blvd.* ☎*239/765–1040 or 877/798–4879* 📠*239/765–1055* ⊕*www.loverskey.com* 🛏*100 condominiums* ⚙*In-room: kitchen, dial-up, Wi-Fi. In-hotel: restaurant, pool, gym, beachfront, laundry facilities, public Internet, public Wi-Fi* ☒*AE, D, DC, MC, V.*

$$$ 🏨**Pierview Hotel & Suites.** In the thick of things at Fort Myers Beach's so-called Times Square, this three-story property, formerly a Ramada Inn, has pretty gingerbread trim. Inside, cheery florals and wallpaper borders along the ceiling make the rooms homey, and all have a porch or balcony. The new private owner has plans to tear the old building down and start over, so call ahead to learn the status of the hotel. **Pros:** Near all the action, right on the beach, affordable. **Cons:** Old building, limited amenities, no Internet access. ☒*1160 Estero Blvd.* ☎*239/463–6158 or 800/544–4592* 📠*239/765–4240* 🛏*56 rooms, 14 suites* ⚙*In-room: safe, kitchen (some), dial-up. In-hotel: bar, pool, beachfront, laundry facilities, some pets allowed (fee), no-smoking rooms* ☒*AE, D, MC, V.*

☪ $$–$$$ 🏨**Outrigger Beach Resort.** On a wide gulf beach, this casual resort has rooms and efficiencies with configurations to suit different families and budgets. The standard rooms offer your basic motel setup; efficiencies are roomier and work well for families. All open up to a shared porch or balcony. You'll also find a broad sundeck, tiki cabanas, sailboats, and a beachfront pool with a popular tiki bar. **Pros:** Beautiful beach, cabana and water-sports rentals, family-friendly. **Cons:** Can be noisy, crowded pool area, old-school look and feel. ☒*6200 Estero Blvd.* ☎*239/463–3131* ⊕*www.outriggerfmb.com* 🛏*74 rooms, 68 efficiencies* ⚙*In-room: safe, kitchen (some), refrigerator, dial-up. In-hotel: 2 restaurants, bar, pool, beachfront, bicycles, public Internet, public Wi-Fi, no-smoking rooms* ☒*AE, MC, V.*

SPORTS & THE OUTDOORS

BIKING

Fort Myers Beach has no designated trails, so most cyclists ride along the road. **Fun Rentals** (☒*1901 Estero Blvd.* ☎*239/463–8844* ⊕*www.funrentals.org*) advertises bike-rental rates anywhere from two hours to a week. Rent bikes in Lovers Key State Park through **Nature Recreation Management** (☒*8700 Estero Blvd., Fort Myers Beach* ☎*239/314–0110* ⊕*www.naturerecreationmanagement.com*). Fees are $10 for a full day.

10

CANOEING

Lovers Key State Park offers both kayak rentals and guided kayaking tours of its bird-rich estuary. The concessionaire, **Nature Recreation Management** (⊠ *8700 Estero Blvd., Fort Myers Beach* ☎ *239/314–0110* ⊕ *www.naturerecreationmanagement.com*), charges $35 for its guided tour, which is offered Monday, Wednesday, and Saturday. Rentals begin at $20 for a half day, $30 for a full day.

FISHING

Getaway Deep Sea Fishing (⊠ *18400 San Carlos Blvd.* ☎ *800/641–3088 or 239/466–3600* ⊕ *www.getawaymarina.com*) rents fishing equipment, sells bait, and can arrange half- and full-day charters. Rates start at $47 for a half day and include bait, license, and equipment.

GOLF

The **Fort Myers Beach Golf Course** (⊠ *4200 Bay Beach La., off Estero Blvd.* ☎ *239/463–2064*) has 18 holes and a practice range in the midst of a condo community but filled with birds. Greens fee $50/$25.

NAPLES AREA

As you head south from Fort Myers on U.S. 41, you soon come to Estero and Bonita Springs, followed by the Naples and Marco Island areas, which are sandwiched between Big Cypress Swamp and the Gulf of Mexico. East of Naples the land is largely undeveloped and mostly wetlands, all the way to Fort Lauderdale. Here, along the northern border of the Florida Everglades, there are stunning nature preserves and parks. Tours and charters out of Everglades City explore the mazelike Ten Thousand Islands National Wildlife Refuge. These waters are full of fish and wildlife. Between Naples and Everglades City, acres of breeze-swept saw grass stretch off to the horizon. Keep your eyes peeled and you may even spot alligators in the waterways alongside the road. Naples itself is a major vacation destination that has sprouted pricey high-rise condominiums and golfing developments, plus a spate of restaurants and shops to match. A similar but not as thorough evolution has occurred on Marco Island, the largest of the Ten Thousand Islands.

ESTERO/BONITA SPRINGS

10 mi south of Fort Myers.

Towns below Fort Myers have started to flow seamlessly into one another since the opening of Florida Gulf Coast University in San Carlos Park and as a result of the growth of Estero and Bonita Springs, agricultural communities until not long ago. In recent years the area has become a shopping mecca of mega outdoor malls mixing big-box stores, smaller chains, and restaurants. Bonita Beach, the closest beach to Interstate 75, has evolved from a fishing community into a strip of upscale homes and beach clubs built to provide access for residents of inland golf developments.

★ Tour one of Florida's quirkier chapters from the past at **Koreshan State Historic Site.** Named for a religious cult that was active at the turn of the 20th century, Koreshan preserves a dozen structures where the group practiced arts, worshipped a male-female divinity, and created its own branch of science called cosmogony. The cult floundered when leader Cyrus Reed Teed died in 1908, and in 1961 the four remaining members deeded the property to the state. Rangers lead tours, and the grounds are lovely for picnicking and camping. Canoeists paddle the Estero River, fringed by a forest of exotic vegetation the Koreshans planted. ⊠ *Tamiami Trail, Estero* ☎ *239/992–0311* ⊕ *www.floridastateparks.org/koreshan* ☞ *$4 per vehicle with up to 8 passengers; $3 for a single driver; $1 per bicyclist, pedestrian, or extra passenger* ⊙ *Daily 8 AM–sunset.*

☾ Opened in 1936 and one of the first attractions of its kind in the state, **Everglades Wonder Gardens** captures the beauty of untamed Florida. The old-fashioned, rather cramped zoological gardens have Florida panthers, black bears, crocodiles and alligators, tame Florida deer, flamingos, and trained otters and birds. There's also a funky natural-history museum. Tours, which include an otter show and alligator feedings, run continuously, the last starting at 4. The swinging bridge over the alligator pit is a real thrill. ⊠ *27180 Old U.S. 41* ☎ *239/992–2591* ☞ *$15* ⊙ *Daily 9–5.*

Bonita Springs Public Beach, at the south end of Bonita Beach, has picnic tables, beach concessions, and a restaurant next door. As far as local beaches goes, it's the easiest to access and the most popular south of Fort Myers Beach. ⊠ *Hickory Blvd. at Bonita Beach Rd.* ☎ *239/461–7400* ☞ *Parking $1 per hr up to $5 per day.*

★ The 342-acre **Barefoot Beach Preserve** is a quiet, out-of-the-way place, accessible via a private neighborhood road around the corner from the buzzing public beach. It has picnic tables, a nature trail and learning center, a butterfly garden, a canoe trail, and refreshment stands. Gopher tortoises often cross the road right in front of your car, so drive slowly. Park rangers lead nature walks and canoe trips. ⊠ *Lely Beach Rd.* ☎ *239/591–8596* ☞ *$5.*

OFF THE
BEATEN
PATH
Fodor's Choice
★
☾

Corkscrew Swamp Sanctuary. To get a feel for what this part of Florida was like before civil engineers began draining the swamps, drive 13 mi east of Bonita Springs (30 mi northeast of Naples) to these 11,000 acres of pine flatwood and cypress, grass-and-sedge "wet prairie," saw-grass marshland, and lakes and sloughs filled with water lettuce. Managed by the National Audubon Society, the sanctuary protects North America's largest remaining stand of ancient bald cypress, 600-year-old trees as tall as 130 feet, as well as endangered birds, such as wood storks, which often nest here. This is a favorite destination for serious birders, and in 2006 was designated the gateway to the new Great Florida Birding South Trail. If you spend a couple of hours to take the 2¼-mi self-guided tour along the boardwalk, you'll spot ferns, orchids, and air plants, as well as wading birds and possibly alligators and river otters. A nature center educates you about this precious, unusual habi-

10

tat with a dramatic re-creation of the preserve and its creatures in the Swamp Theater. ✉ *375 Sanctuary Rd. W., 16 mi east of I–75 on Rte. 846* ☎ *239/348–9151* ⊕ *www.audubon.org* ✍ *$10* ⊙ *Oct. 1–Apr. 10, daily 7–5:30; Apr. 11–Sept. 30, daily 7 AM–7:30 PM.*

WHERE TO EAT & STAY

$$$ ✕ **Blue Water Bistro.** For the convenience of shoppers at the new Coconut Point, several excellent restaurants cluster in the midst of the shopping center. Most are hooked to a chain. This one, although part of a Naples-Bonita Springs dining dynasty, has a personality all its own with a suave indoor-outdoor bar scene and seafood that's anything but timid. Its specialty is grilled fish from around the globe that you can mix and match with a choice of sauces and sides. For instance, try Clear Springs trout with wasabi citrus soy sauce and onion rings with chipotle barbeque. Other specials include a classic burger, king crab alfredo, and grouper kung pao. ✉ *23151 Village Shops Way, Ste. #109, Coconut Point, Estero* ☎ *239/949–2583* ⚖ *Reservations accepted.* ⊕ *www.bluewaterbistro.net* ▤ *AE, MC, V* ⊙ *No lunch.*

¢ ☕ ✕ **Doc's Beach House.** Right next door to the public beach access, Doc's has fed hungry beachers for decades. Come barefoot and grab a quick libation or meal downstairs, outside on the beach, or in the courtyard. When the thermometer reaches "searing," take refuge on the air-conditioned second floor, with its great view of beach action. Basic fare on the breakfast and all-day menu includes a popular Angus burger, pizza, and seafood plates. ✉ *27908 Hickory Blvd., Bonita Springs* ☎ *239/992–6444* ⚖ *Reservations not accepted* ⊕ *www.docsbeachhouse.com* ▤ *No credit cards.*

$$$$ ☕ 🏨 **Hyatt Coconut Point Resort & Spa.** This secluded luxury Hyatt, with its
Fodor's Choice marble-and-mahogany lobby and 18 floors, makes a lovely sanctuary
★ for golfers, families, and conferences. Man-made water features include a slide pool, lap pool, lazy-river pool, and fountain-waterfall pool. For nature-made water features, catch a ferry to the hotel's private island beach. Handsomely appointed rooms overlook the water or the golf course. Its spa is known for its rare Watsu (water shiatsu) pool, and an interpretive center showcases natural and prehistoric history. **Pros:** Luxury amenities, top spa, great ceviche bar in one restaurant. **Cons:** Boat shuttle to the beach, expensive restaurants and no others very close by. ✉ *5001 Coconut Rd., Bonita Springs* ☎ *239/444–1234 or 800/554–9288* 🖷 *239/390–4277* ⊕ *www.coconutpoint.hyatt.com* ⇥ *426 rooms, 30 suites* ⚘ *In-room: safe, refrigerator, VCR, Ethernet, dial-up, Wi-Fi. In-hotel: 5 restaurants, room service, bars, golf course, tennis courts, pools, gym, spa, beachfront, concierge, children's programs (ages 3–12), executive floor, public Internet, public Wi-Fi, no-smoking rooms* ▤ *AE, D, DC, MC, V.*

$$$ 🏨 **Trianon Bonita.** Convenient to Bonita Springs' best shopping and dining at The Promenade shopping center, this branch of a downtown

Naples favorite feels European in its peaceful, sophisticated way. It's very similar to its predecessor Naples property, and has a new poolside-lakeside alfresco bar and grill. Rooms are oversize and the lobby has a vaulted, coved ceiling and marble columns. Cocktails and complimentary breakfast are served in the library, where a fireplace and baby grand piano dominate. **Pros:** Shops and restaurants within walking distance, intimate atmosphere, refined amenities. **Cons:** Sometimes less-than-friendly front desk staff, far from beach, slightly stuffy. ✉*3401 Bay Commons Dr., Bonita Springs* ☎*239/948–4400 or 800/859–3939* 🖷*239/948–4401* ⊕*www.trianon.com* ✑*100 rooms* ⏃*In-room: safe, refrigerator (some), dial-up, Wi-Fi. In-hotel: pool, public Internet, public Wi-Fi, no-smoking rooms* ▤*AE, D, DC, MC, V* ⦿*CP.*

SPORTS & THE OUTDOORS

BIKING

Rent bicycles by the day or by the week at **Bonita Bike & Baby** (✉*No physical address; by cell phone and delivery only* ☎*239/947–6377*).

BOATING

Bonita Beach Resort Motel & Boat Rental (✉*26395 Hickory Blvd.* ☎*239/992–2137*) rents pontoon boats for a minimum of two hours or by the half and full day.

CANOEING

The meandering Estero River is pleasant for canoeing as it passes through Koreshan State Historic Site to the bay. **Estero River Outfitters** (✉*20991 Tamiami Trail S, Estero* ☎*239/992–4050* ⊕*www.esteroriver outfitters.com*) provides rental canoes, kayaks, and equipment.

DOG RACING

Greyhounds race year-round at the **Naples/Fort Myers Greyhound Track** (✉*10601 Bonita Beach Rd. SE* ☎*239/992–2411* ⊕*www.naplesfort myersdogs.com*).

SHOPPING

★ **Miromar Outlets** complex (✉*Corkscrew Rd. at I–75 Exit 123 in Estero, near Germain Arena* ☎*239/948–3766* ⊕*www.miromaroutlets.com*) includes Adidas, Nike, Nautica, Off 5th Saks Fifth Avenue, and more than 140 other stores and eateries. **Gulf Coast Town Center** (✉*Airways Blvd. and Marathon Way* ⊕*www.gulfcoasttowncenter.com*) is a mega-spread of stores and chain restaurants including a 123,000-square-foot Bass Pro Shops, Borders, Best Buy, Costco, and movie theaters. **Coconut Point Town Center** (✉*23106 Fashion Dr., Estero* ☎*239/992–4259*), a 500-acre planned community, tops Gulf Coast with even more stores and restaurants, some of which are non-chain. The **Promenade at Bonita Bay** (✉*South Bay Dr.*) in the Bonita Bay subdivision is Bonita Springs' chic shopping venue, with an upscale collection of shops and restaurants.

10

NAPLES

21 mi south of Bonita Springs.

Poised between the Gulf of Mexico and the Everglades, Naples belies its wild setting and Indian-post past with the trappings of wealth—neo-Mediterranean-style mansions, neatly manicured golfing developments, revitalized downtown streets lined with galleries and one-of-a-kind shops, and a reputation for lively and eclectic dining. Visitors come for its luxury hotels—including two Ritz-Carltons—its fabulous white-sand beaches, fishing, shopping, theater and arts, and a lofty reputation for golf. Yet with all the highfalutin living, Naples still appeals to families, especially with a new water park and a Children's Museum slated to open there in spring 2009 at North Collier Regional Park.

❶
Fodor'sChoice
★
The well-maintained 166-acre **Delnor-Wiggins Pass State Park** has one of Naples's best beaches, barbecue grills, picnic tables, a boat ramp, an observation tower, restrooms with wheelchair access, bathhouses, showers, boat ramps, and lots of parking. Fishing is best in Wiggins Pass, at the north end of the park. Rangers conduct sea-turtle programs in summer, and birding and other programs year-round. ✉ *11100 Gulf Shore Dr. N, at Rte. 846* ☎ *239/597–6196* ⊕ *www.floridastateparks. org/delnor-wiggins* ✑ *$5 per vehicle with up to 8 people, $3 for single driver, $1 for pedestrians and bicyclists* ⊙ *Daily 8–sunset.*

❿
The **Sun-N-Fun Lagoon** brings splashy fun to a county park east of town. Interactive water features such as water pistols and dumping buckets are designed for children age seven and under. The whole family will go for the lazy river and slides. ✉ *15000 Livingston Rd. at North Collier Regional Park* ☎ *239/254–4021* ⊕ *www.colliergov.net* ✑ *$10* ⊙ *Call or visit Web site for hours.*

❷
Fodor'sChoice
★
The cool, contemporary **Naples Museum of Art**, around the corner from the Waterside Shops in the Naples Philharmonic Center for the Arts, displays provocative, innovative pieces, including American miniatures, antique walking sticks, modern American and Mexican masters, and traveling exhibits. Dazzling installations by glass artist Dale Chihuly include a fiery cascade of a chandelier and an illuminated ceiling layered with many-hued glass bubbles, glass corkscrews, and other shapes that suggest the sea; alone, this warrants a visit. ✉ *5833 Pelican Bay Blvd.* ☎ *239/597–1900 or 800/597–1900* ⊕ *www.the phil.org* ✑ *$8* ⊙ *Tues.–Sat. 10–4, Sun. noon–4 Oct.-June; closed Mon. and July-Oct.*

❸
Kayak through the mangroves or into the surf at **Clam Pass Beach Park.** Next to the Naples Grande Resort, a ¾-mi boardwalk winds through the mangrove area to the beach. Convenient for north-end Naples residents and hotel guests, it provides tram service down the boardwalk. ✉ *Next to the Naples Grande Resort on Seagate Dr.* ☎ *239/353–0404* ✑ *Parking $6* ⊙ *Daily 8–sunset.*

❹
The lush and entertaining 52-acre **Naples Zoo**, established in 1919 as a botanical garden, today draws visitors curious to see lions, African wild dogs, tigers, lemurs, antelope, and monkeys. Central exhibits include

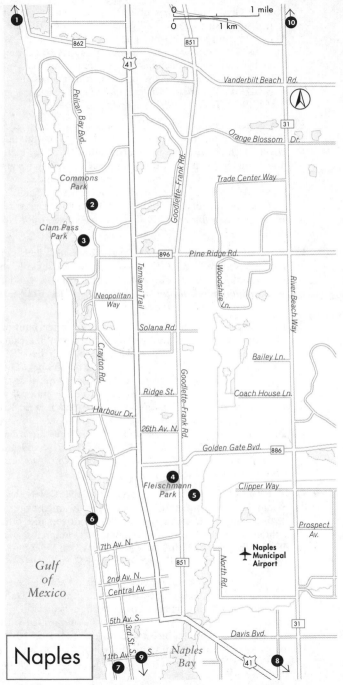

Panther Glade and its new in 2007 Leopard Rock, but it's the shows that distinguish this nationally accredited zoo. The presentations in Planet Predator and Serpents: Fangs & Fiction star the extreme in wild animals. The Primate Expedition Cruise takes you through islands of monkeys and lemurs. Youngsters can amuse themselves in three separate play areas, and there are meet-the-keeper times and alligator feedings. ⊠ *1590 Goodlette Rd.* ☎ *239/262–5409* ⊕ *www.napleszoo.com* ☞ *$15.95* ⊙ *Daily 9:30–5:30; gates close at 4:30.*

5 On 14 acres bordering a tidal lagoon teeming with wildlife, the **Naples Nature Center** includes an aviary, a wildlife rehabilitation clinic, a Discovery Center with a serpentarium, and a 3,000-gallon sea-turtle aquarium. Short trails are dotted with interpretive signs, and there are free (with paid admission) guided walks and boat tours on the mangrove-bordered Gordon River several times daily. Canoes and kayaks are available for rent. ⊠ *1450 Merrihue Dr.* ☎ *239/262–0304* ⊕ *www.conservancy.org* ☞ *$9* ⊙ *Mon.–Sat. 9–4:30; Nov.–Apr. also Sun. noon–4.*

6 Stretching along Gulf Shore Boulevard, **Lowdermilk Park** is great for families. It has more than 1,000 feet of beach as well as volleyball courts, a playground, restrooms, showers, vending machines, and picnic tables. ⊠ *Gulf Shore Blvd. at Banyan Blvd.* ☎ *239/213–3029* ☞ *Parking 25¢ per 15 min* ⊙ *Daily 7–sunset.*

7 Houses in 19th-century South Florida were often built of a concrete-like material made of sand and seashells. For a fine example of such tabby construction, stop by **Palm Cottage,** built in 1895 and one of the Lower Gulf Coast's few surviving tabby homes. The historically accurate interior contains simple furnishings typical of the period. In 2007 the Norris Gardens opened next to the cottage. It was designed to reflect turn-of-the-last-century garden trends with Palm, Pioneer, and Edible gardens and more. Docents give guided tours of the home and, for $15, a historic walking tour of the area. Touring the gardens is self-guided. ⊠ *137 12th Ave. S* ☎ *239/261–8164* ⊕ *www.naples historicalsociety.org* ☞ *$8* ⊙ *Guided tours Nov.–Apr., Tues.–Sat. 1–4; May–Oct., Wed. and Sat. 1–4.*

★ **8** To get a feel for local history, stop by the **Collier County Museum,** where a Seminole chickee hut, native plant garden, swamp buggy, reconstructed 19th-century fort, steam logging locomotive, and other historical exhibits capture important developments from prehistoric times to the World War II era. ⊠ *3301 Tamiami Trail E.* ☎ *239/774–8476* ⊕ *www. colliermuseum.com* ☞ *Free* ⊙ *Weekdays 9–5, Sat. 9–4.*

★ **9** Developing in phases, the **Naples Botanical Garden** is worth a visit even as it grows. Self-guided tours take in a lovely Date Palm Allée backdropped by an artistic mosaic wall, a fruit and spice garden, a fragrance garden, and the Pollination Pavilion filled with butterflies, bees, geckos, hummingbirds, and lories. By late 2010 the attraction plans to add Florida, children's, Brazilian, Caribbean, and Asian gardens. ⊠ *4820 Bayshore Dr.* ☎ *239/643–7275* ⊕ *www.naplesgarden.*

org 🎫*$7* ⊙*Oct. –May, Wed.–Sat. 10–4, Sun. noon–4; June–Sept., Thurs.–Sat. 10–2.*

WHERE TO EAT

$$$$
Fodor'sChoice
★

✕**Artisans in the Dining Room.** The crème de la crème of Naples dining, the Ritz's main restaurant is equally rich in food and decor. Exquisite moldings, solid European furnishings, tranquil piano or harp music, and large framed artworks, plus a new concept in menu that addresses diners' shrinking appetites, are its hallmarks. The menu is divided by protein type and offers each item in full portion or in half portion for smaller appetites or mix-match tapas-style dining. Signature dishes include lobster salad, Kobe beef, grilled tuna and shrimp, and the soufflé du jour. ✉*280 Vanderbilt Beach Rd.* ☎*239/598–3300* ✍*Reservations essential* ▭*AE, D, DC, MC, V* ⊙*No lunch. Closed June–Oct.*

$$$$
✕**Cote d'Azur.** Capturing the essence of its namesake in the French Riviera region, Cote d' Azur offers a blend of country fare, exotic ingredients, and slow-cooked goodness with a menu that executes French technique with perfection and joie de vivre. The narrow dining room, with yellow striped awnings and windows inset with mirrors and decorated with flower boxes, suggests a French provincial sidewalk café. The whole fish of the day comes directly from Europe, plus there's much to intrigue on the regular menu, including halibut with eggplant, pine nuts, raisins, and pesto; and roasted duck with sun-dried currants and cherries, green peppercorn port sauce, and roasted pear. ✉*11224 Tamiami Trail N.* ☎*239/597–8867* ⊕*www. cotedazurrestaurant.com* ▭*AE, D, MC, V* ⊙*No lunch. Closed Mon. Sometimes closes for Sept.*

$$$
✕**Aura.** At the Naples Grande Resort, it breaks all the rules with a chic wall-less lobby setting and a short menu of multidimensional and artistically plated creations in a style termed New American Bistro. Diners can order appetizers and "plates" lunch and dinner. After 6 PM a handful of entrées satisfy hardier appetites. Start with mushroom bisque with truffle foam, sample a plate or two—grown-up grilled-cheese sandwich with tomato soup and vegetable risotto and smoked shrimp, perhaps—or go for lacquered grouper with wasabi mashed potatoes or a mixed grill of skirt steak, chorizo, and pork tenderloin. Save room for the delightfully innovative dessert shooters. Breakfast is also served. ✉*475 Seagate Dr., Naples Grande Resort* ☎*239/597–3232* ⊕*www.naplesgrande.com* ▭*AE, D, DC, MC, V.* , jgrace@luxuryresorts.com->

★ $$$
✕**Bha! Bha!** Classic and fusion Middle Eastern cooking—some of Naples's finest ethnic food—fill the menu with wonderful, adventurous taste treats. Specialties include dried-plum lamb, garlic eggplant chicken, mango-ginger shrimp, and spicy beef in saffron sauce with cucumber yogurt. Ocher walls, stuffed ottomans, and exotic tapestries confirm the "Persian bistro" on the restaurant's sign. The service lags at times, but intrepid palates still declare it worth finding (hidden in a strip mall) and waiting for. A belly dancer entertains certain nights. ✉*847 Vanderbilt Rd.* ☎*239/594–5557* ⊕*www.bhabhapersianbistro. com* ▭*AE, MC, V.*

10

$$$ ✕ **Chops City Grill.** Count on high-quality cuisine that fuses, as its name reflects, a personality split between chopstick cuisine and fine cuts of meat. Ultrasophisticated yet resort-wear casual, it draws everyone from young business folk to the local retired population. Sushi and Pacific Rim inspirations such as beef satay and teriyaki-glazed sea bass represent its Asian persuasion; dry-aged T-bone, fillets, and beef porterhouse for two, its meaty side. They come together in the Asian barbecue pork porterhouse. Dine inside with a view of the kitchen or, at the Bonita Springs branch, alfresco in the courtyard. ⊠ *837 5th Ave. S.* ☎ *239/262–4677* ⊠ *Hwy. 41 at Brooks Grand Plaza, Bonita Springs* ☎ *239/992–4677* ⚑ *Reservations essential* ⊕ *www.chopsbonita.com* ⊟ *AE, DC, MC, V* ⊘ *No lunch.*

Fodor's Choice
★

WORD OF MOUTH

"We go to Bha! Bha! every time we are in Florida (twice a year). It is a gem hidden in a strip mall. Despite the strip-mall setting, the outdoor patio is nice in the evenings. The food is excellent."

–BetsyinKY

$$$ ✕ **Tommy Bahama's Tropical Café.** Here Naples takes a youthful curve. Island music sounds on the umbrella-shaded courtyard at this, the prototype for the chain. It has that trademark rattan look that identifies the Tommy Bahama label in clothing and furniture stores across the nation. Indoors and out, everybody's munching sandwiches, salads, and grilled seafood and meats with a tropical flair (tuna pan-seared with a lemongrass crust, blackberry brandy barbecued ribs) and sampling Tommy's Bungalow Brew beer. ⊠ *1220 3rd St. S* ☎ *239/643–6889* ⊕ *www.tommybahama.com* ⊟ *AE, MC, V.*

$ ✕ **Cilantro Tamales.** The salsa and chips alone are worth a visit to this bright and lively little spot, with slabs of clay tile for placemats. The signature dish, smoked Gouda–stuffed tamales, sets an example for freshness, authenticity, and a flair of creativity. Imaginative touches are also added to other Tex-Mex standards, including enchiladas, fajitas, rellenos, and a Mexican rice bowl. ⊠ *10823 N. Tamiami Trail* ☎ *239/597–5855* ⊕ *www.cilantrotamales.com* ⊟ AE, MC, V ⊘ *Closed Mon. Aug. –Sept.*

☾ ¢–$ ✕ **Aurelio's Is Pizza.** Transplanted from Chicago, the pizza here is steeped in tradition and flavor. The selections are typical, with a few show-offs such as shrimp barbecue, BLT, and the low-cholesterol spinach Calabrese. There's also pasta with homemade sauces and chicken Parmesan or Alfredo. Red-and-white tablecloths and old Illinois license plates accent this neighborhood-style strip-mall café. ⊠ *590 N. Tamiami Trail* ☎ *239/403–8882* ⊕ *aureliosofnaples.com* ⊟ *AE, MC, V* ⊘ *Closed Mon. No lunch Sat. and Sun.*

¢ ✕ **Old Naples Pub.** Local blue- and white-collar workers gather with visitors for affordable sandwiches and seafood in the courtyard of this 20-year-old traditional pub, tucked away from shopping traffic at 3rd Street Plaza. It strikes one as an everybody-knows-your-name kind of place, with jars of pickles on the tables and friendly bartenders. Taste some 20 kinds of beer and order fried grouper sandwiches, burgers, crispy chicken salad, and nachos, as well as such not-so-traditional pub snacks as sesame seared ahi tuna and fried gator tail. There's musical entertainment nightly between Thanksgiving and Easter. ⊠*255 13th Ave. S* ☎*239/649–8200* ⊕*www.naplespubs.com* ▤*AE, D, MC, V.*

WHERE TO STAY

★ **$$$$** ⊞**Bellasera.** It is "off 5th" just enough (less than two blocks) for privacy and convenience. Right off a Tuscany postcard, it feels quite villa-like with its red-tile roofs and burnt-gold stucco. The privately owned studios and one- to three-bedroom suites, keeping in theme with earthy hues and terra-cotta tiles, huddle three-story high around a beautifully tiled pool, fountain, and courtyard. Private cabanas line the pool on two sides and Zizi restaurant spills out onto the patio on another. The studios have in-room whirlpool tubs with plantation shutters opening onto the master bedroom so you can watch TV from your bubble bath. **Pros:** Near shops and restaurants, spacious rooms, screened patio or balcony. **Cons:** Must take shuttle to beach, on a busy highway, average restaurant. ⊠*221 9th St. S,* ☎*239/649–7333 or 888/612–1115* 🖷*239/649–6233* ⊕*www.bellaseranaples.com* ↩*10 studios, 30 1-bedroom suites, 48 2-bedroom suites, and 12 3-bedroom suites* ⚅*In-room: kitchen(some), refrigerator, Wi-Fi. In-hotel: restaurant, room service, bar, pool, gym, concierge, public Internet, public Wi-Fi* ▤*AE, D, DC, MC, V.*

★ **$$$$** ⊞**Edgewater Beach Hotel.** This compact waterfront seven-story hotel anchors the north end of fashionable Gulf Shore Boulevard. The one- and two-bedroom suites are decorated in a clean Art Deco style and have coffee and espresso machines, fully-equipped kitchens (but no stoves), and gingerbread-trimmed patios or balconies, many with exquisite gulf views. Have meals by the pool or in the elegant restaurant in the newly renovated lobby. You'll also find the small fitness center and business facilities on the same floor. Guests have certain dining and recreational privileges (including golfing) at the Naples Grande Resort, a sister property. **Pros:** Beautiful beach, convenient and spacious accommodations, fabulous restaurant. **Cons:** 2 mi from shopping, expensive, no tubs in some rooms. ⊠*1901 Gulf Shore Blvd. N,* ☎*239/403–2000, 800/821–0196, 800/282–3766 in Florida* 🖷*239/403–2100* ⊕*www.edgewaternaples.com* ↩*97 1-bedroom suites, 28 2-bedroom suites* ⚅*In-room: safe, kitchen, Ethernet, dial-up, Wi-Fi. In-hotel: 2 restaurants, bars, pool, gym, beachfront, bicycles, public Wi-Fi* ▤*AE, D, DC, MC, V.*

$$$$ ⊞**Inn on Fifth.** To plant yourself in the heart of Naples nightlife and shopping, you can't beat this swank property whose rooms are well soundproofed to shut out the activity when you're ready to wrap yourself in the provided robe and seclude yourself in comfort. When you're not, slide open the French doors and tune in to 5th Avenue from the balcony. A spa completes a list of urban amenities that also includes a lively Irish pub, a popular crab restaurant, a rooftop pool, and an arched, columned marble lobby with crystal chandeliers and a dramatic sweeping staircase. A theater is next door, and the beach is six blocks away. The pub is ultrafriendly, but the front desk staff is known to be less than helpful. **Pros:** Near shopping and restaurants, metro vibe, very comfortable rooms. **Cons:** A little bustly if you prefer quiet,

10

pool is eye-level with power lines, not on the beach. ✉ *699 5th Ave. S,* ☎ *239/403–8777 or 888/403–8778* 🖷 *239/403–8778* ⊕ *www.innon-fifth.com* 🛏 *76 rooms, 11 suites* ⚺ *In-room: safe, dial-up, Wi-Fi. In-hotel: restaurant, bar, pool, gym, spa, concierge, laundry service, public Internet, public Wi-Fi.* ▤ *AE, D, DC, MC, V* ⎁ *CP.*

$$$$
Fodor's Choice
★
 ⊡ **LaPlaya Beach & Golf Resort.** LaPlaya bespeaks posh and panache down to the smallest detail—custom-designed duvet covers, marble bathrooms, and a palm-tree-patterned teddy bear on the pillow, for instance. The boutique resort features a Thai-style spa, rock-waterfall pools, a tony Miami-style beachfront restaurant, and a casual tiki bar that serves food. Of its 189 units, 141 are beachfront with private balconies. Some have jetted soak tubs with a view of the gulf. **Pros:** Right on the beach, high-end amenities, beautiful rooms. **Cons:** Golf course is off-property, no locker rooms in spa. ✉ *9891 Gulf Shore Dr.* ☎ *239/597–3123 or 800/237–6883* 🖷 *239/567–8283* ⊕ *www. laplayaresort.com* 🛏 *180 rooms, 9 suites* ⚺ *In-room: Ethernet, dial-up. In-hotel: restaurant, bars, golf course, pools, gym, spa, concierge, public Wi-Fi, no-smoking rooms* ▤ *AE, D, MC, V.*

☾ **$$$$**
 ⊡ **Naples Beach Hotel and Golf Club.** Family-owned and -managed for more than 50 years, this beach resort is a piece of Naples history. On a prime stretch of powdery sand, it stands out for its par-72, 18-hole championship golf course, the first resort course in the state with a pro shop and golf school. The hotel's lobby has skylights, a coral rock fireplace, an aquarium, and a baby grand piano. Rooms, decorated in light colors, are in six high- and mid-rise pink buildings, and packages make an extended stay affordable. **Pros:** Terrific beach, good recreational amenities. **Cons:** Expensive, shows its age in places, have to cross street to reach spa and golf facilities. ✉ *851 Gulf Shore Blvd. N* ☎ *239/261–2222 or 800/237–7600* 🖷 *239/261–7380* ⊕ *www. naplesbeachhotel.com* 🛏 *264 rooms, 42 suites, 12 efficiencies* ⚺ *In-room: kitchen (some), dial-up, Wi-Fi. In-hotel: 3 restaurants, bars, golf course, tennis courts, pool, gym, spa, beachfront, children's programs (ages 5–12), laundry service, public Internet, public Wi-Fi, no-smoking rooms* ▤ *AE, D, DC, MC, V.*

$$$$ ☾
Fodor's Choice
★
 ⊡ **Naples Grande Resort & Club.** A beach, full amenities, and top-shelf luxury: formerly the Registry Resort, its new branding reflects its golf-club focus. And if the links aren't your thing, a recently opened Golden Door Spa just might be. Rooms are spacious and comfortable at this high-rise hotel. One of the glories of the property—at least for families—is the immense free-form family swimming pool, with zero entry (water begins at a depth of zero feet), and a 100-foot waterslide. The hotel sits behind dusky, twisted mangrove forests; to get to the 3 mi of powdery white sand, it's a short walk or tram ride. Indigenous cypress and pines frame the Naples Grande Golf Club, the hotel's 18-hole Rees Jones layout, a short drive away. **Pros:** Great tennis and golf, top-notch restaurant. **Cons:** Not right on the beach, high room rates with resort fee. ✉ *475 Seagate Dr.* ☎ *239/597–3232 or 800/247–9810* 🖷 *239/566–7919* ⊕ *www.naplesgrande.com* 🛏 *395 rooms, 79 suites* ⚺ *In-room: Ethernet, dial-up. In-hotel: 4 restaurants, room service, bars, golf course, tennis courts, pools, gym, spa, beachfront, water*

sports, bicycles, children's programs (ages 4–12), laundry service, public Wi-Fi ⊟*AE, DC, MC, V.*

★ $$$$ ⊡**Ritz-Carlton Golf Resort.** Ardent golfers with a yen for luxury will find their dream vacation at Naples's most elegant golf resort. Ritz style prevails all the way but in a more contemporary verve than at its sister resort, the Ritz-Carlton, Naples. The lobby is done up in rich upholstery, with floor-to-ceiling windows looking out onto greens and grounds manicured like a French château's. Rooms are regal, with marble bathrooms and color schemes in shades of greens and burgundies; half of them have balconies with links views. The golf academy can help you polish your skills, and you have access to the spa, kids' program, and other amenities of the beachside Ritz-Carlton, which is nearby. Dining at Tuscan-style Lemonia is divine, especially for Sunday brunch. The cigar bar next door is inviting, with its billiards and fireplace. **Pros:** Great golfing, fine dining, very elegant. **Cons:** Must take shuttle bus to beach, expensive. ⊠*2600 Tiburón Dr.* ☎*239/593–2000 or 800/241–3333* 🖷*239/593–2010* ⊕*www.ritzcarlton.com* 🛏*258 rooms, 37 suites* ♿*In-room: safe, dial-up, Wi-Fi. In-hotel: 4 restaurants, room service, bars, golf course, tennis courts, pool, concierge, children's programs (ages 5–12), laundry service, executive floor, public Internet, public Wi-Fi, parking (fee), some pets allowed (fee), no-smoking rooms* ⊟*AE, D, DC, MC, V.*

$$$$ ⊡**Ritz-Carlton, Naples.** This is a classic Ritz-Carlton, awash in marble, **Fodor's**Choice antiques, and 19th-century European oil paintings. In the rooms, the ★ comforts of home prevail—assuming your home is a palace. Outside, steps away, the beach is soft, white, and dense with seashells. Given the graciousness of the staff, you quickly get over the incongruity of traipsing through the regal lobby in flip-flops, clutching a plastic bag of beach finds. It doesn't hurt that the kitchen is a wonder as well, making meals at Artisans in the Dining Room and the clubby Grill, and even dessert in the lobby, just a little bit special. Then there's the elegant spa, one of the first and largest under the Ritz-Carlton brand with a complete menu of indulgences including its new eco-room. **Pros:** Very luxurious, flawless service, great beach. **Cons:** Valet parking only, short walk to the beach. ⊠*280 Vanderbilt Beach Rd.* ☎*239/598–3300 or 800/241–3333* 🖷*239/598–6691* ⊕*www.ritzcarlton.com* 🛏*450 rooms, 35 suites* ♿*In-room: safe, Wi-Fi. In-hotel: 7 restaurants, room service, bars, tennis courts, pools, gym, spa, beachfront, concierge, children's programs (ages 5–12), laundry service, executive floor, public Internet, public Wi-Fi, parking (fee), some pets allowed (fee), no-smoking rooms* ⊟*AE, D, DC, MC, V.*

$$$–$$$$ ⊡**Trianon Old Naples.** Oh so Euro in feel, this boutique hotel is just enough removed from 5th Avenue's traffic to feel private while convenient. Wrought-iron balconies and shade trees set the stage outside; inside, the elegant lobby has high ceilings, a working granite fireplace, plush furnishings, and a library that doubles as a wine-and-beer bar and breakfast room. Rooms are large and lavishly furnished, with heavy draperies. **Pros:** Close to stores and restaurants, elegant setting, spacious rooms. **Cons:** Limited facilities, must drive to beach. ⊠*955 7th Ave. S,* ☎*239/435–9600 or 877/482–5228* 🖷*239/261–0025*

10

⊕*www.trianon.com* ⬤*55 rooms, 3 suites* ⬥*In-room: safe, dial-up, Wi-Fi. In-hotel: bar, pool, public Internet, public Wi-Fi* ⊟*AE, D, DC, MC, V* ⚋*CP.*

$$-$$$ ⬛**Holiday Inn.** Although this two-story motel is on a major highway, it's set back from the road and the rooms are quiet because most of them are behind the restaurant and pool. Decorated with dark wood and goldenrod-tone carpeting and bedspreads, they're also clean and comfortable. Landscaping is well maintained, and the location is convenient if you plan to sightsee. Handsome Pate's Steak House, a big name to local meat eaters, is on-site. **Pros:** Free Wi-Fi, nice steak house, fair rates. **Cons:** 15-minute drive to beach, on busy highway, not conducive to walking to restaurants and shopping. ⬛*1100 9th St. N,* ☎*239/263–3434 or 800/325–1135* ⬛*239/261–3809* ⊕*www.hi naples.com* ⬤*137 rooms* ⬥*In-room: dial-up, Wi-Fi. In-hotel: restaurant, bar, pool, public Internet, public Wi-Fi* ⊟*AE, D, DC, MC, V.*

NIGHTLIFE & THE ARTS

THE ARTS

★ Naples is the cultural capital of this stretch of coast. The **Naples Philharmonic Center for the Arts** (⬛*5833 Pelican Bay Blvd.* ☎*239/597–1900 or 800/597–1900* ⊕*www.thephil.org*) has a 1,473-seat performance center with plays, concerts, and exhibits year-round. It's home to the 85-piece Naples Philharmonic, which presents both classical and pop concerts. The Miami Ballet Company performs here during its winter season. The **Naples Players** (⬛*Sugden Community Theatre, 701 5th Ave. S* ☎*239/263–7990* ⊕*www.naplesplayers.org*), on 5th Avenue, performs musicals and dramas year-round; winter shows often sell out well in advance.

NIGHTLIFE

Downtown's 5th Avenue South is the scene of lively nightclubs and sidewalk cafés. **McCabe's Irish Pub** (⬛*699 5th Ave. S* ☎*239/403–7170*) hosts Irish bands most weekends and some weeknights. Audiences often join in on the lusty lyrics. Hit **Ultra Naples** (⬛*15495 U.S. 41 N* ☎*239/514–3790*) for DJ music and dancing Thursday through Saturday.

SPORTS & THE OUTDOORS

BIKING

Try **Clint's Bicycle Shoppe of Naples** (⬛*8789 Tamiami Trail N* ☎*239/566–3646*) for rentals by the week or month, starting at $30 a week. For daily rentals, try **Naples Cyclery** (⬛*813 Vanderbilt Beach Rd. at Pavilion Shopping Center* ☎*239/566–0600* ⊕*www.naplescyclery.com*), where rates range from $6 to $40 for two hours and selections include recumbent bikes, two- and four-passenger surreys, tandems, and more.

BOATING

Naples Watersports at Port-O-Call Marina (⬛*550 Port-O-Call Way* ☎*239/774–0479*) rents 19-foot pontoon boats and 21-foot deck boats starting at $75 for one hour.

FISHING

The *Lady Brett* (⊠*Tin City, 1200 Fifth Ave. S* ☎*239/263–4949* ⊕*www.tincityboats.com*) makes half-day fishing trips twice daily at $70 each. Take a guided boat and learn to cast and tie flies at **Mangrove Outfitters** (⊠*4111 E. Tamiami Trail* ☎*239/793–3370 or 888/319–9848* ⊕*www.mangrove-outfitters.com*).

GOLF

★ **Tiburón Golf Club** (⊠*Ritz-Carlton Golf Resort, 2600 Tiburón Dr.* ☎*239/593–2000*)has two 18-hole Greg Norman–designed courses, the Black and the Gold, and a golf academy. Challenging and environmentally pristine, the links include narrow fairways, stacked sod wall bunkers, coquina sand, and no roughs. Greens fee $280/$105. At **Lely Flamingo Island Club** (⊠*8004 Lely Resort Blvd.* ☎*239/793–2600* ⊕*www.lely-resort.net*), there are three 18-hole courses—the Classics, Flamingo Island, and the Mustang—plus a golf school. Mustang is the easiest and most wide open. Greens fee $165/$39. **Naples Beach Hotel & Golf Club** (⊠*851 Gulf Shore Blvd. N* ☎*239/435–2475* ⊕*www.naplesbeachhotel.com*) has 18 holes, a golf school, and a putting green. The region's oldest course, a par 72, it was built in 1929 and last renovated in 1998. Greens fee (includes cart): $145 (balls included)/$50. At affordable **Riviera Golf Club** (⊠*48 Marseille Dr.* ☎*239/774–1081*) there are 18 holes. Greens fee $58/$34 (includes cart).

TENNIS

Cambier Park Tennis Center (⊠*775 8th Ave. S* ☎*239/213–3060*) offers clinics and play on 12 Hydro-Grid lighted clay courts for members and visitors.

SHOPPING

Old Naples encompasses two distinct shopping areas marked by historic buildings and flowery landscaping: 5th Avenue South and 3rd Street South. Both are known for their abundance of fine-art galleries and monthly musical entertainment. Near 5th Avenue South, **Old Marine Market Place at Tin City** (⊠*1200 5th Ave. S* ⊕*www.tin-city.com*), in a collection of tin-roof former boat docks along Naples Bay, has more than 30 boutiques, eateries, and souvenir shops, with everything from jewelry to T-shirts and seafood. At the classy **Village on Venetian Bay** (⊠*4200 Gulf Shore Blvd.* ⊕*www.venetianvillage.com*), nearly 60 shops and restaurants have been built at water's edge.

★ Only in South Florida can you find something like **Waterside Shops** (⊠*Seagate Dr. and U.S. 41* ⊕*www.watersideshops.net*), four-dozen stores plus eateries wrapped around a series of waterfalls, waterways, and shaded open-air promenades, all renovated in 2006. Saks Fifth Avenue is one of the anchors. **Gattle's** (⊠*1250 3rd St. S* ☎*239/262–4791 or 800/344–4552*) stocks pricey, beautifully made linens. **Marissa Collections** (⊠*1167 3rd St. S* ☎*239/263–4333*) showcases designer women's wear. At the **Mole Hole** (⊠*1201 3rd St. S* ☎*239/262–5115*), gift items large and small, from glassware to paperweights to knick-knacks, cover every surface.

★ Among 5th Avenue South's upscale selection, **Regatta** (⊠*750 5th Ave. S* ☎*239/262–3929*) sells personal and home accessories with a sense of humor and style. Naples's ladies-who-lunch often donate their year-old Armani castoffs and fine collectibles to a spate of terrific thrift shops such as **Options** (⊠*968 2nd Ave. N* ☎*239/434–7115*). The most upscale clothes sometimes go to consignment shops such as **New to You** (⊠*933 Creech Rd.* ☎*239/262–6869*).

Encore Shop (⊠*3105 Davis Blvd.* ☎*239/775–0032*) carries designer furniture, paintings, decorative items, and collectibles. For more bargains, hit **Prime Outlets Naples** (⊠*Rte. 951 west of Marco Island* ☎*239/545–7196 or 877/466–8853*), home to more than 40 factory outlets.

MARCO ISLAND

20 mi south of Naples.

High-rises line part of the shore of Marco Island, which is connected to the mainland by two bridges. Yet it retains an isolated feeling much appreciated by those who love this corner of the world. Some natural areas have been preserved, and the down-home fishing village of Goodland is resisting change. Fishing, boating, sunning, swimming, and tennis are the primary activities.

★ ⟲ In the midst of 110,000-acre Rookery Bay National Estuarine Reserve, **Rookery Bay Environmental Learning Center** interprets the Everglades environment and local history with interactive models, aquariums, original art, a film, and classes. It's on the edge of the estuary, about five minutes east of Marco's north bridge on Collier Boulevard. A new audio tour option was initiated in 2007 for a nominal fee. In 2009 the center is scheduled to debut a million-dollar, 250-foot pedestrian bridge that will span the reserve's creek from the center's second floor. ⊠*300 Tower Rd.* ☎*239/417–6310* ⊕*www.rookerybay.org* ⊠*$5* ⟲*Mon.–Sat. 9–4* ⟲*Closed Sat. May-Oct.*

⟲ **Tigertail Beach** is on the southwest side of the island, 2,500 feet along both developed and undeveloped areas. Once gulf-front, in recent years a sand spit known as Sanddollar Island has formed, which means the beach, especially at the north end, has become mud flats—great for birding. Facilities include playgrounds, volleyball, a butterfly garden, free use of a beach wheelchair, a concession stand, restrooms, and showers. Sailboat and kayak rentals are available, and rangers conduct nature programs. ⊠*490 Hernando Ct.* ☎*239/353–0404, 239/591–8596 for ranger programs* ⊠*Parking $6* ⟲*Daily 8–sunset.* ■**TIP→**The **Conservancy of Southwest Florida** conducts free educational beach walks at Tigertail Beach every weekday from 8:30 to 9:30 am January–mid-April.

Marco Island was once part of the ancient Calusa kingdom. The Marco Cat, a statue found in 1896 excavations, has become symbolic of the island's prehistoric significance. A replica of the original, which is kept by the Smithsonian Institution, is among displays illuminating ancient past to modern present at the **Marco Island Historical Society Museum**. Both it and its unstaffed branch location interpret local history through vignettes, video, and artifacts. ⊠*140 Waterway Dr. at Bald Eagle Dr.* ☎*239/642–7468* ☏*Free* ⊙ *Weekdays 9–4* ⊠*Shops of Olde Marco, 168 Royal Palm Dr., 2nd fl.* ☎*239/389–6447* ☏*Free* ⊙*Daily 7–7* ⊕*www.themihs.org.*

WHERE TO EAT

★ $$$$ ✕**Sale e Pepe.** Marco's best dining view comes also with some of its finest cuisine. The name means "salt and pepper," an indication that this palatial restaurant with terrace seating overlooking the beach adheres to the basics of home-style Italian cuisine. Pasta, sausage, and ice cream are made right here in the kitchen; all products are local or imported from Italy. Simple dishes, such as veal ravioli, risotto, yellow pepper and shrimp soup, sautéed salmon with basil sauce, roasted grouper with lobster sauce, and grilled lamb chops explode with home-cooked, long-cooked flavors. For a gourmet adventure, splurge on the chef's tasting menu for $85 ($45 extra with wine pairings). Breakfast, lunch, and dinner are served here. ⊠*Marco Beach Ocean Resort, 480 S. Collier Blvd.* ☎*239/393–1600* ⊕*www.sale-e-pepe.com* ▭*AE, D, DC, MC, V.*

$$$ ✕**Arturo's.** This place is huge, with expansive Romanesque dining
Fodor'sChoice rooms and more seating on the patio. Still it fills up year-round with
★ a strong following that appreciates the attitude of fun and serious Italian cuisine done comprehensively and traditionally. Start with the plump mussels marinara, then choose from three pages of classic Italian entrées. The stuffed pork chop, a nightly special, is a winner, as is the New York–style cheesecake. ⊠*844 Bald Eagle Dr.* ☎*239/642–0550* ⚑*Reservations essential* ⊕*www.arturosmarcoisland.com* ▭*AE, D, DC, MC, V.*

$$$ ✕**Café de Marco.** This cozy, cottagelike little bistro with cheery yellow walls and elegantly draped windows serves fresh local fish with original preparations, and there are always good daily specials. Try stuffed Florida lobster, sautéed frogs' legs, or the broiled seafood platter. Steaks, chicken, and a vegetarian dish are also available. For a taste of the café without the sticker shock, dine 5–5:45 for $13.95. ⊠*244 Palm St.* ☎*239/394–6262* ⊕*www.cafedemarco.com* ▭*AE, MC, V* ⊙*Closed Sun. Easter–Christmas. No lunch.*

$$$ ✕**Olde Marco Island Inn.** Dating from the turn of the 20th century, this inn lends grace to intimate meals. Continental style heavily influences the menu, which includes scallops Saint Jacques in a sherry mushroom sauce, Florida lobster tails (market price), duck with ginger Grand Marnier sauce, and prime rib. The inn serves dinner only; early-bird specials run from 5–6, featuring some regular menu items priced $13.95–$24.95. The cottagelike veranda room feels pleasantly Florida, but the more formal back rooms are gorgeous. A piano player entertains Wednesday, Friday, and Saturday nights. ⊠*100 Palm St.* ☎*239/394–3131 or 877/475–3466* ⊕*www.oldemarcorestaurant.com* ▭*AE, D, MC, V* ⊙*No lunch; closed Sun. after Mother's Day through Jan. 1.*

$$$ ✕**Verdi's.** There's a Zen feel to this American bistro with a devoted clientele built on creative American-Italian-Asian fusion cuisine. You might start with steamed littleneck clams in garlic butter or duck pot-stickers, then move on to entrées such as grilled swordfish, crispy duck, or the New Zealand rack of lamb. Cuban coffee crème brûlée and deep-

10

dish apple strudel are among the tempting desserts. ⊠*Sand Dollar Plaza, 241 N. Collier Blvd.* ⊕*www.verdisbistro.com* ☎*239/394–5533* ⊟*D, DC, MC, V* ⊗*No lunch.*

$$ ✕**Old Marco Lodge Crab House.** Built in 1869, this waterfront restaurant is Marco's oldest landmark, and boaters often cruise in and tie up dockside to sit on the veranda and dine on local-seafood and pasta entrées. The all-you-can-eat salad bar is a popular lunch option. For dinner, start with a wholesome bowl of vegetable crab soup. Crab entrées come in four varieties—stone, snow, soft-shell blue, and king—but the menu includes all manner of shellfish, pasta, grouper, steak, and sandwiches. Save room for the authentic key lime pie. A game room keeps antsy kids occupied. ⊠*1 Papaya St., Goodland* ☎*239/642–7227* ⊕*www. oldmarcolodge.com* ⊟*AE, D, MC, V* ⊗*Closed Sept.; Mon. and Tues. May–Aug.; and Mon. Oct.–mid-Dec.*

$ ✕**The Crazy Flamingo.** Burgers, seafood, finger foods such as conch fritters and chicken wings, and late-night hours are the draw at this neighborhood bar, where there's counter service only and seating indoors and outdoors on the sidewalk. Try the seafood steamer pot, mussels marinara, or grouper sandwich. ⊠*Marco Island Town Center, 1035 N. Collier Blvd.* ☎*239/642–9600* ⚑*Reservations not accepted* ⊟*No credit cards.*

$ ✕**Sunset Grille.** Head to this popular spot, formerly Tide Beachfront Bar & Grill, for the best casual dining with a view of the beach and a menu of sandwiches, burgers, New Jersey–style thin-crust pizza (after 5 PM), wings, and seafood. The lively sports-bar scene adds to the fun indoors; a porch accommodates alfresco diners with the most inexpensive dining view in Marco. Just beware if you leave your table: the porch has no screens and the local gulls are thieves. ⊠*Apollo Condominiums, 900 S. Collier Blvd.* ☎*239/393–8433* ⊟ *D, MC, V.*

WHERE TO STAY

$$$$ ⛱**Hilton Marco Island Beach Resort.** This 11-story beachfront hotel is smaller and more conservative than the Marriott, and it seems less busy and crowded. All rooms are spacious and have private balconies with unobstructed gulf views, a sitting area, a dry bar, bathrobes, and a mini-refrigerator. Since 2005 the resort has been undergoing heavy renovation that will result in a new stand-alone spa by 2009. **Pros:** Gorgeous wide beach, complete business services, exclusive feel. **Cons:** A little stuffy, charge for Wi-Fi, business focus. ⊠*560 S. Collier Blvd.* ☎*239/394–5000 or 800/394–5000* ⊟*239/394–8410* ⊕*www.hilton marcoisland.com* ⚓*271 rooms, 26 suites* ⚒*In-room: safe, refrigerator, Ethernet, dial-up, Wi-Fi. In-hotel: 2 restaurants, bar, tennis courts, pool, gym, spa, beachfront, water sports, children's programs (ages 5–12), public Wi-Fi* ⊟*AE, D, DC, MC, V.*

$$$$
FodorśChoice
★
⛱**Marco Beach Ocean Resort.** One of the island's first condo hotels, this 12-story class act has one- and two-bedroom suites done in royal blues and golds. All rooms face the gulf and the property's crescent-shaped rooftop pool (on the fifth floor). The bathrooms are full of marble. The Sale e Pepe Tuscan-style restaurant wins raves and awards. Golf and tennis are nearby. **Pros:** Top-rate dining, beach location, full amenities with a boutique feel. **Cons:** High-priced, a rather squeezed feel, near

big, busy resort. ✉️*480 S. Collier Blvd.* ☎️*239/393–1400 or 800/260–5089* 📠*239/393–1401* 🌐*www.marcoresort.com* ⌨️*87 1- and 16 2-bedroom suites* ♿*In-room: kitchen, dial-up, Ethernet, Wi-Fi (some). In-hotel: restaurant, bars, tennis courts, pool, gym, spa, beachfront, concierge, public Internet, public Wi-Fi* ▤*AE, D, DC, MC, V.*

★ $$$$ 🏨**Marco Island Marriott Resort, Golf Club & Spa.** A circular drive and
☾ manicured grounds front this beachfront resort made up of two 11-story towers. In 2007, it completed a massive, three-year renovation that includes a new spa. It's delightfully beachy outside, where Marco's crescent beach reaches its widest, yet the interior is elegant, with many shops and restaurants, a polished marble lobby, and large, plush rooms with good to exceptional water views. The stand-alone spa is massive and ultra-pampering. Kids love the zero-entry rock-waterfalls pool with slides. The hotel's golf course is 10 minutes away by tram. **Pros:** Terrific beach, top-notch amenities, great spa. **Cons:** Huge size, lots of convention business, parking across the street in uncovered lot. ✉️*400 S. Collier Blvd.* ☎️*239/394–2511 or 800/438–4373* 📠*239/642–2672* 🌐*www.marcoislandmarriott.com* ⌨️*727 rooms, 54 suites* ♿*In-room: refrigerator, Wi-Fi. In-hotel: 6 restaurants, bars, golf course, tennis courts, pools, gym, spa, beachfront, water sports, bicycles, concierge, children's programs (ages 5–12), laundry service, public Internet* ▤*AE, DC, MC, V.*

$$–$$$ 🏨**Boat House Motel.** For a great location at a good price, check into this two-story motel. Modest but appealing with its white facade and turquoise trim, it's at the north end of Marco Island, on a canal close to the gulf. Units are light and bright and furnished with blond woods, rattan, and tropical-print fabrics. All have a balcony or walled-in terrace, and some have great water views. You can fish from the motel's dock. **Pros:** Away from busy beach traffic, affordable, boating docks and access. **Cons:** No beach, hard to find, tight parking area. ✉️*1180 Edington Pl.* ☎️*239/642–2400 or 800/528–6345* 📠*239/642–2435* 🌐*www.theboathousemotel.com* ⌨️*20 rooms, 3 condominiums, 1 2-bedroom house* ♿*In-room: kitchen (some), refrigerator, dial-up, Wi-Fi. In-hotel: pool, no elevator, public Wi-Fi, some pets allowed (fee)* ▤*MC, V.*

SPORTS & THE OUTDOORS

BIKING

Rentals are available at **Scootertown Island Bike Shop** (✉️*845 Bald Eagle Dr.* ☎️*239/394–8400*) for use on the island's bike path along beachfront condos, resorts, and residential areas. Charges begin at $5 an hour, but you can also rent by the day, week, and month.

FISHING

Sunshine Tours (✉️*Rose Marco River Marina, 951 Bald Eagle Dr.* ☎️*239/642–5415* 🌐*www.sunshinetoursmarcoisland.com*) operates deep-sea ($99 per person for half day) and backcountry ($59 per person for three hours) fishing charters.

THE LOWER GULF COAST ESSENTIALS

TRANSPORTATION

BY AIR

CARRIERS Southwest Florida International Airport (RSW) is served by Air Canada, AirTran Airways, American, Cape Air, Comair, Continental, Delta, Frontier, jetBlue, LTU International Airways, Midwest, Northwest, Southwest, Spirit, Sun Country, Sunwing, United, US Airways, USA 3000 Airlines, and WestJet. Delta Connection and a couple of private charters service Naples Municipal Airport.

Contacts **Air Canada** (☎ 888/247–2262). **AirTran Airways** (☎ 800/247–8726). **American** (☎ 800/433–7300). **Cape Air** (☎ 800/352–0714). **Comair** (☎ 800/221–1212). **Continental** (☎ 800/525–0280). **Delta** (☎ 800/221–1212). **Frontier Airlines** (☎ 800/432–1359). **jetBlue Airways** (☎ 800/538–2583). **LTU International Airways** (☎ 866/266–5588). **Midwest Airlines** (☎ 800/452–2022). **Northwest** (☎ 800/225–2525). **Southwest Airlines** (☎ 800/435–9792). **Spirit** (☎ 800/772–7117). **Sun Country** (☎ 800/359–6786). **Sunwing** (☎ 800/761-1711). **United** (☎ 800/241–6522). **US Airways** (☎ 800/428–4322). **USA 3000 Airlines** (☎ 877/872–3000). **WestJet** (☎ 888/937–8538).

AIRPORTS & TRANSFERS Southwest Florida International Airport is about 12 mi southwest of Fort Myers and 25 mi north of Naples. An on-demand taxi for up to three passengers to Fort Myers, Sanibel, or Captiva costs about $21 to $68, and it's about $64 to $95 to Naples. Extra people are charged at $10 each. Other transportation companies include Aaron Airport Transportation, Boca Grande Limo, Charlotte Limousine Service, and Sanibel Island Taxi. The Naples Municipal Airport is a small facility east of downtown principally serving Delta Airlines, private planes, commuter flights, and charters. Once you have arrived, call Naples Taxi.

Airport Contacts **Naples Municipal Airport** (☎ 239/643–0733 ⊕ www.flynaples. com). **Southwest Florida International Airport** (☎ 239/768–1000 ⊕ www.fly lcpa.com). **Aaron Airport Transportation** (☎ 239/768–1898 or 800/998–1898). **Boca Grande Limo** (☎ 941/964–0455 or 800/771–7433). **Charlotte Limousine Service** (☎ 941/627–4494 or 800/208–6106). **Naples Airport Shuttle** (☎ 239/430–4747 or 888/569–2227 ⊕ www.naplesairportshuttle.com). **Naples Taxi** (☎ 239/643–2148). **Sanibel Island Taxi** (☎ 239/472–4160).

BY BOAT

Key West Shuttle operates a ferry from Marco Island (from Thanksgiving through May) and Fort Myers Beach (year-round) to Key West. The cost for the round-trip (four hours each way) from Fort Myers Beach is $128, from Marco Island $106.

Contact **Key West Shuttle** (☎ 239/394–9700 or 888/539–2628 ⊕ www.key westshuttle.com).

BY BUS

Greyhound Lines has service to Fort Myers and Naples. LeeTran serves most of the Fort Myers area. In Naples and Marco Island, Collier Area Transit (CAT) runs regular routes.

Contacts **Greyhound Lines** (☎ 800/231–2222 ✉ 2250 Peck St., Fort Myers ☎ 239/334–1011 ✉ 2669 Davis Blvd., Naples ☎ 239/774–5660 ⊕ www.greyhound.

com). **LeeTran** (☎239/275–8726 ⊕ www.rideleetran.com). **Collier Area Transit (CAT)** (☎239/596–7777 ⊕ www.colliergov.net).

BY CAR

Interstate 75 spans the region from north to south. Once you cross the Georgia border into Florida, it's about six hours to Fort Myers and another half hour to Naples. Alligator Alley, a section of Interstate 75, is a toll road ($2 to enter) that runs from Fort Lauderdale through the Everglades to Naples. The trip takes about three hours. U.S. 41 also runs the length of the region. Also known as the Tamiami Trail, U.S. 41 goes through downtown Fort Myers and Naples and is also called Cleveland Avenue in the former and 9th Street in the latter. McGregor Boulevard (Route 867) and Summerlin Road (Route 869), Fort Myers's main north–south city streets, head toward Sanibel and Captiva islands. San Carlos Boulevard runs southwest from Summerlin Road to Fort Myers Beach, and Pine Island–Bayshore Road (Route 78) leads from North Fort Myers through northern Cape Coral onto Pine Island. In Naples, east–west trunks exiting off Interstate 75 include, from north to south, the Immokalee Road (Route 846) at the north edge of town, Pine Ridge Road (Route 896), and Route 951, which takes you also to Marco Island.

CAR RENTAL

Contacts Alamo (☎800/462–5266). **Avis** (☎800/331–1212). **Budget** (☎800/527–7000). **Hertz** (☎800/654–3131). **National** (☎800/227–7368).

CONTACTS & RESOURCES

EMERGENCIES

Ambulance or Police (☎911).

VISITOR INFORMATION

The Marco Island Area Chamber of Commerce is open to the public weekdays 9 to 5 and in season also Saturday 10 to 3. The Naples Area Chamber of Commerce also opens Saturday 9 to 5. The Sanibel & Captiva Islands Chamber of Commerce opens daily 9 to 5. The Lee County Visitor and Convention Bureau and Naples, Marco Island, Everglades Convention and Visitors Bureau do not have visitors centers.

Contacts Lee County Visitor & Convention Bureau (✉12800 University Dr., Suite 550, Fort Myers ☎239/338–3500 or 800/237–6444 ⊕ www.fortmyers-sanibel.com). **Marco Island Area Chamber of Commerce** (✉1102 N. Collier Blvd., Marco Island ☎239/394–7549 or 800/788–6272 ⊕ www.marcoislandchamber.org). **Naples, Marco Island, Everglades Convention and Visitors Bureau** (✉3050 N. Horseshoe Dr., #218, Naples ☎239/403–2425 ⊕ www.paradisecoast.com). **Sanibel & Captiva Islands Chamber of Commerce** (✉1159 Causeway Rd., Sanibel ☎239/472–1080 ⊕ www.sanibel-captiva.org).

10

The Tampa Bay Area

Downtown Tampa skyline

WORD OF MOUTH

"Definitely visit the Dalí museum in downtown St. Pete—the masterworks can't be seen anywhere else."

—Gekko

WELCOME TO THE TAMPA BAY AREA

TOP REASONS TO GO

★ **Art Gone Wild:** Whether you take the guided tour or chart your own course, experience the one-of-a-kind collection at the Salvador Dalí Museum in St. Petersburg.

★ **Cuban Roots:** You'll find great food and engaging shops in historic Ybor City, which is just east of downtown Tampa.

★ **Endangered Marine Mammals:** Swimming with West Indian manatees in Crystal River is a breathtaking experience.

★ **Historic Smokehouse:** Ted Peters Famous Smoke Fish near St. Petersburg has '50s-era charm and a menu bursting with flavor.

★ **Culture Fix:** If you love the arts, there's no finer offering in the Bay Area than at the Florida State University Ringling Center for the Cultural Arts in Sarasota.

1 North & West of Tampa Bay. State-of-the-art zoos and museums promise to broaden your imagination, while some of Florida's best beaches tempt you with sparkling waters.

2 The Nature Coast. The name says it all, particularly in coastal areas of Hernando and Citrus counties, where vast preserves give glimpses of wild Florida and many of its rare creatures, including West Indian manatees.

3 South of Tampa Bay. Barrier islands lure travelers to another battery of white-sand beaches, but Sarasota's cultural treasures are the true magnet for many of its visitors.

GETTING ORIENTED

On the east side of the bay, industry- and business-oriented Tampa also offers attractions such as Busch Gardens. To the west, St. Petersburg and Clearwater use beaches and barrier islands as calling cards. Moving to the south, Sarasota's cultural offerings are among the finest in Florida. And to the north, the Nature Coast is home to manatees and other wild things.

TAMPA BAY AREA PLANNER

When to Go

Winter and spring are high season, and the level of activity is double what it is in the off-season. In summer there are huge afternoon thunderstorms, and temperatures hover around or above 90°F during the day. Luckily the mercury drops to the mid-70s at night, and beach towns have a consistent on-shore breeze that starts just before sundown, which enabled civilization to survive here before air-conditioning arrived.

Flying In

Tampa International Airport, the area's largest and busiest with 18 million passengers a year, is served by most major carriers and offers ground transportation to surrounding cities. **Sarasota-Bradenton International** also offers several options, including air service from most big-name domestic carriers. **St. Petersburg-Clearwater International Airport** is much smaller, with lesser known airlines and service to and from fewer places.

For more flight information see By Air in Essentials at the end of this chapter.

About the Restaurants

Fresh gulf seafood is plentiful, and raw bars serving oysters, clams, and mussels are everywhere. Tampa's many Cuban and Spanish restaurants serve spicy paella with seafood and chicken, boliche (stuffed eye-round roast) with black beans and rice, ropa vieja and other treats. Tarpon Springs adds classic Greek specialties. In Sarasota the emphasis is on ritzier dining, but many restaurants offer extra-cheap early-bird menus for seatings before 6 PM.

About the Hotels

Many convention hotels in the Tampa Bay area double as family-friendly resorts—taking advantage of nearby beaches, marinas, spas, tennis courts, and golf links. However, unlike Orlando and some other parts of Florida, the area has been bustling for more than a century, and its accommodations often reflect a sense of its history. You'll find a turn-of-the-20th-century beachfront resort where Zelda and F. Scott Fitzgerald stayed, a massive all-wood building from the 1920s, plenty of Art Deco, and throwbacks to the Spanish-style villas of yore. But one thing they all have in common is a certain Gulf Coast charm.

What It Costs

DINING & LODGING PRICE CATEGORIES

¢	$	$$	$$$	$$$$
Restaurants				
under $10	$10–$15	$15–$20	$20–$30	over $30
Hotels				
under $80	$80–$100	$100–$140	$140–$220	over $220

Restaurant prices are per person for a main course at dinner. Hotel prices are for a standard double room, excluding 6% sales tax (more in some counties) and 1%–4% tourist tax.

Updated by
Jim Tunstall
and Christina
Tourigny

11

PLANNING AND AN ABUNDANCE OF preserves have partially shielded the Tampa Bay area from the overdevelopment that saturates much of the Atlantic Coast. While this is one of the state's largest metro areas, it is less fast-lane than Miami. Granted, Tampa has Florida's third-busiest airport and a vibrant business community, but to counter that St. Petersburg, Clearwater, and Sarasota have exceptional beaches, and the entire bay area has superior hotels and resorts that make this an excellent place to spend a week or more.

Native Americans were the sole inhabitants until Spanish explorers such as Juan Ponce de León, Pánfilo de Narváez, and Hernando de Soto passed through in the mid-1500s. Less than a century after the U.S. Army and civilian settlers arrived in 1824, industrialist Henry Plant created an economic momentum that was sustained into the third millennium. A military presence remains in Tampa at MacDill Air Force Base, the U.S. Operations Command.

Today the region embraces old and new Florida. Terrain ranges from the pine-dotted northern reaches to the coast's white-sand beaches and barrier islands. Tampa is a full-fledged city, with a modest high-rise skyline and highways jammed with traffic. Across the bay, St. Petersburg's compact downtown has interesting restaurants, shops, and museums on the southeast side of the Pinellas County peninsula. The county's western periphery is rimmed by barrier islands with beaches, quiet parks, and little, laid-back beach towns. To the north, communities such as Tarpon Springs, settled by Greek sponge divers, celebrate their ethnic heritage. Farther north, you will find land dotted with crystal-clear rivers, springs, and nature preserves, and to the south lie resort towns, including Sarasota, which, like the Pinellas County beaches, fill up in winter with snowbirds escaping the cold.

EXPLORING THE TAMPA BAY AREA

Whether you feel like strolling along white-sand beaches, testing your nerve on thrill rides, or wandering through upscale shopping districts, there's something to your liking in the diverse Bay Area. Bright, modern Tampa is the area's commercial center. Peninsular St. Petersburg lies across the bay. Tarpon Springs, to the northwest, is still Greek in flavor. The Nature Coast, to the north, remains somewhat rural, with extensive preserves. To the south, Sarasota is a sophisticated resort town.

NORTH & WEST AROUND TAMPA BAY

The core of the northern bay comprises the cities of Tampa, St. Petersburg, and Clearwater. A semitropical climate and access to the gulf make Tampa an ideal port for the cruise industry. The waters around Clearwater and St. Petersburg are often filled with pleasure and commercial craft, including boats with day and night trips featuring gambling in international waters. It's fitting that an area with a thriving international port should also be populated by a wealth of nationalities. The center of the Cuban community is the east Tampa enclave of Ybor City, whereas north of Clearwater, in Dunedin, the heritage is Scottish. North of Dunedin, Tarpon Springs has supported a large Greek population for decades and is the largest producer of natural sponges in the world. Inland, to the east and north of Tampa, it's all suburban sprawl, freeways, shopping malls, and—the main draw— Busch Gardens.

TAMPA

84 mi southwest of Orlando.

Tampa, the west coast's business and commercial hub, has numerous high-rises and heavy traffic. Amid the bustle is a concentration of restaurants, nightlife, stores, and cultural events.

Numbers in the margin correspond to the Downtown Tampa map.

While eels, sharks, and stingrays are the headliners, the **Florida Aquarium** is much more than a giant fishbowl. This is a dazzling architectural landmark with an 83-foot-high multitier glass dome and 200,000 square feet of air-conditioned exhibit space. It has more than 10,000 aquatic plants, and animals representing species native to Florida and the rest of the world. The major exhibit areas reflect the diversity of Florida's natural habitats—Wetlands, Bays and Beaches, and Coral Reef. Creature-specific exhibits are the No Bone Zone (lovable invertebrates) and Sea Hunt, with predators ranging from sharks to exotic lion fish. The aquarium's most impressive single exhibit is the Coral Reef Gallery, in a 500,000-gallon tank ringed with viewing windows, including an awesome 43-foot-wide panoramic opening. Part of the tank is a walkable tunnel, almost giving the illusion of venturing into underwater depths. There you see a thicket of elkhorn coral teeming with tropical fish. A dark cave reveals sea life you would normally see only on night dives. For $75, visitors six and up can swim with fish, and for $150 certified divers 15 and up can dive with sharks. If you have two hours, try *Bay Spirit,* Wild Dolphin Ecotour, which takes up to 49 passengers onto Tampa's bay in a 64-foot catamaran for an up-close look at bottlenose dolphins and other wildlife. The outdoor Explore A Shore exhibit, which gives younger kids a chance to release some energy, is an aquatic playground with a waterslide, water jet sprays, and a climbable replica pirate ship. Last but not least, two black-footed African penguins make twice daily appearances in the aquarium lobby. ✉ *701 Channelside Dr., Downtown* ☎ *813/273–4000* ⊕ *www.flaquarium. org* ✎ *Aquarium $17.95, Ecotour $19.95; Aquarium/Ecotour combo $32.95; parking $5* ☉ *Daily 9:30–5.*

Downtown Tampa's **Riverwalk** connects some developed-area waterside entities such as the Marriott Waterside, the Channelside shopping and entertainment complex, and the Florida Aquarium. **Cotanchobee Fort Brooke Park** includes a wall of bronze plaques telling the story of Tampa's Seminole War fort from the Seminole perspective. The landscaped park is 6 acres and extends along the Garrison cruise-ship chan-

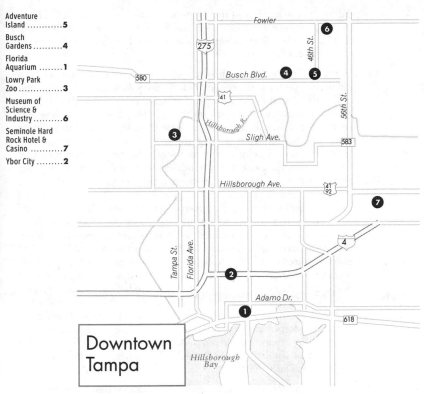

**Downtown
Tampa**

nel and along the Hillsborough River downtown. The walkway is being expanded as waterside development continues.

Lively **Ybor City**, Tampa's Latin quarter, is one of only four National Historic Landmark districts in Florida. It has antique-brick streets and wrought-iron balconies. Cubans brought their cigar-making industry to Ybor (pronounced *ee*-bore) City in 1886, and the smell of cigars— hand-rolled by Cuban immigrants—still wafts through the heart of this east Tampa area, along with the strong aroma of roasting coffee. These days the neighborhood is emerging as Tampa's hot spot, as empty cigar factories and historic social clubs are transformed into trendy boutiques, art galleries, restaurants, and nightclubs that are a microcosm of Miami's sizzling South Beach. Take a stroll past the ornately tiled **Columbia** restaurant and the stores lining 7th Avenue. Step back into the past at **Centennial Park** (⊠ *8th Ave. and 18th St.*), which re-creates a period streetscape and hosts the Fresh Market every Saturday. Ybor City's destination within a destination is the dining and entertainment palace **Centro Ybor** (⊠ *1600 E. 7th Ave.*). It has shops, trendy bars and restaurants, a 20-screen movie theater, and GameWorks, an interactive playground developed by Steven Spielberg. The **Ybor City Museum State Park** provides a look at the history of the cigar industry. Admission includes a tour of La Casita, one of the shotgun houses occupied by cigar workers and their families in the late 1890s. ✉*1818 E. 9th Ave., between Nuccio Pkwy. and 22nd St., from 7th to 9th Ave.* ☎*813/247–6323* ⊕*www.ybormuseum.org* ✉*$3* ⊙*Daily 9–5; walking tours Sat. 10:30, $6.*

❸ Natural habitat exhibits such as the white tiger clubs and clouded leopards in Asia Gardens make the 56-acre **Lowry Park Zoo** one of the best small-scale animal parks in the country. Safari Africa is the home of Tamani, a young African elephant (born in October 2005), while residents of the nearby Ituri Forest include cheetahs and lovably plump pygmy hippos. The stars at Primate World range from cat-size red-ruffed lemurs to a colony of heavyweight Bornean orangutans that love to ham for the camera. For hands-on experiences, Lowry has more options than most large parks, including chances to ride a camel, feed a giraffe, or serve as a perch for energetic lorikeets. Majestic red-tailed hawks and other raptors are displayed in the Birds of Prey Center, and you can come face-to-face with American alligators, Florida panthers, black bears, and red wolves at the Florida Wildlife Center. Kookaburras and kangaroos populate the Wallaroo Station children's zoo, and gentle creatures of another kind star at the Manatee Aquatic Center. Speaking of manatees, they are among the occasional sights on the Hillsborough River Odyssey Ecotour ($14, Wed.–Sun.), where you also may spot wild hawks and herons. This zoo is particularly attuned to night events: parties range from food and beer tastings for adults to chaperoned sleepovers for children ages six and up. Additionally, there are water-play areas, rides, shows, and restaurants. ✉*1101 W. Sligh Ave., Central Tampa* ☎*813/935–8552* ⊕*www.lowryparkzoo.com* ✉*$18.95* ⊙*Daily 9:30–5.*

❹ Nearly 4½ million vacationers and locals flock to **Busch Gardens** each year. The hook: Five roller coasters are an irresistible lure for thrill-ride jockeys. But this state-of-the-art attraction also is a world-class zoo with more than 2,000 animals and a live entertainment venue that provides a full day (or more) of entertainment for the whole family. The 335-acre adventure park's habitats offer views of some of the world's most endangered and exotic animals. You can experience up-close animal encounters ($33.99–$119.99 plus regular admission) on the **Serengeti Plain,** a 65-acre free-roaming habitat that is home to reticulated giraffes, Grevy's zebras, white rhinos, bongos, impalas, and more. **Myombe Reserve: The Great Ape Domain** allows you to view lowland gorillas and chimpanzees in a lush, tropical-rain-forest environment. The Broadway-style theater extravaganza **KaTonga: Tales from the Jungle** is a 35-minute celebration of animal folklore, and the hapless Leslie Nielsen leads a bumbling band of buccaneers on the big screen in *Pirates 4-D.* **SheiKra,** North America's first dive coaster, opened in mid-2005. On the wings of an African hawk, riders fly through a three-minute journey 200 feet up, then (gulp!) plunge 90 degrees straight down at 70 mi per hour. As if that is not enough to tighten your fanny pack, attraction workers removed the floor in 2007, so riders' feet dangle far above ground. The park's coaster lineup also includes steel giants **Kumba** and **Montu,** a double wooden roller coaster called **Gwazi,** and

FodorsChoice
★

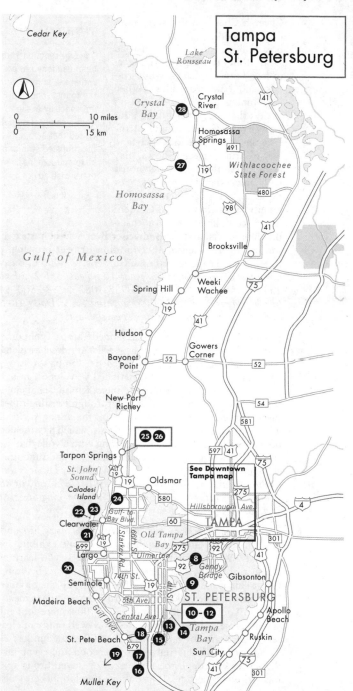

Cheetah Chase—a five-story family coaster full of hairpin turns and breathtaking dips. The off-road safari **Rhino Rally** brings you face-to-face with elephants, white rhinos, and Nile crocodiles. (When it's running properly, which isn't always the case, a flash flood adds a river-raft element.) **Land of the Dragons** is a 4-acre kids' playland that has rides, special shows, play areas, and a three-story tree house with towers and stairways. For those 21 years or older, the **Hospitality House** in the Bird Gardens offers complimentary Anheuser-Busch products, and the **Budweiser Beer School** hosts a 30-minute lesson in the art, science, and tradition of beer brewing. Allow six to eight hours to experience Busch Gardens. ⊠ *3000 E. Busch Blvd., 8 mi northeast of downtown Tampa and 2 mi east of I–275 Exit 50, Central Tampa* ☎ *813/987–5000, 813/987-5082 or 888/800–5447* ⊕ *www. buschgardens.com* ☎ *$64.95; parking $9* ⊙ *Daily 10–6; sometimes earlier, later in summer during special events.*

From spring until mid-fall, rides named Tampa Typhoon, Gulf Scream, and Key West Rapids promise heat relief at **Adventure Island,** a corporate cousin and neighbor of Busch Gardens. Tampa's most popular "wet" park features waterslides and artificial wave pools in a 30-acre package. One of the attraction's headliners, Riptide, challenges you to race three other riders on a sliding mat through twisting tubes and hairpin turns. Planners of this park also took the younger kids into account, with offerings such as Fabian's Funport, which has a scaled-down wave pool and interactive water gym. Along with a volleyball complex and a surf pool, there are cafés, snack bars, picnic and sunbathing areas, and changing rooms. ⊠ *1001 Malcolm McKinley Dr., less than 1 mi north of Busch Gardens, Central Tampa* ☎ *813/987–5660 or 888/800–5447* ⊕ *www.adventureisland.com* ☎ *$35.95; parking $6* ⊙ *Mid-Mar.–late Oct., daily 10–5.*

The **Museum of Science and Industry (MOSI)** is a fun and stimulating scientific playground, though at times some exhibits aren't working properly. When it's hitting on all cylinders, you learn about Florida weather, anatomy, flight, and space by seeing *and* by doing. At the Gulf Coast Hurricane Exhibit, you can experience what a hurricane and its 74-mph winds feel like, though crowds sometimes mean a long wait. The BioWorks Butterfly Garden is a 6,400-square-foot engineered ecosystem project that demonstrates how wetlands can clean water plus serve as a home for butterflies. The 100-seat Saunders Planetarium—Tampa's only planetarium—has afternoon and evening shows, one of them a trek through the universe. For adventurous spirits, there's a high-wire bicycle ride 30 feet above the floor. There's also an impressive IMAX theater, where films are projected on a hemispherical 82-foot dome (special films $10.95, others free with admission). Kids in Charge, a 40,000-square-foot science center with interactive exhibits aimed at the 12-and-under set, opened in 2005, complete with a flight simulator ($3.50 additional charge). Disasterville, an exhibit about—you guessed it—natural disasters, opened in mid-2006, giv-

> **WORD OF MOUTH**
>
> "For a really good steak, you must try Bern's Steak House. It is a Tampa fixture and gets ranked as one of the top steak houses in the world! The wine list is one of the most extensive anywhere."
>
> –nolefan1

ing visitors a chance to walk through a simulated town hit by natural disasters. ✉ *4801 E. Fowler Ave., 1 mi north of Busch Gardens, Northeast Tampa* ☎ *813/987–6100 or 800/995–6674* ⊕ *www.mosi. org* 🎫 *$20.95* 🕐 *Mon. –Fri. 9–5; Sat.-Sun. 9–6.*

❼ The latest buzz at the **Seminole Hard Rock Hotel & Casino** is about the much-anticipated upgrade that may add blackjack and baccarat to the gaming areas. Until the formalities are addressed (including legislative action and a possible legal challenge) gamers can still get their kicks at the casino's poker tables, slot machines, and video gaming machines. The casino lounge serves drinks 24 hours a day. Floyd's restaurant has dinner and nightlife. ✉ *5223 N. Orient Rd., off I–4 at N. Orient Rd. Exit* ☎ *813/627–7625 or 866/502–7529* ⊕ *www.seminolehardrock. com* 🎫 *Free* 🕐 *Daily 24 hrs.*

WHERE TO EAT

$$$–$$$$
Fodor'sChoice
★

✗ **Bern's Steak House.** For those who love meat, this is one of Florida's finest steak houses, an elegant eatery with the air of an exclusive club. Rich mahogany paneling and ornate chandeliers define the legendary Bern's, where Laxer ages his own beef, grows his own organic vegetables, roasts his own coffee, and maintains his own saltwater fish tanks. Cuts of topmost beef are sold by weight and thickness. There's a 60-ounce, 3-inch porterhouse that's big enough to feed your pride (of lions), but for our taste the veal loin chop or 8-ounce Chateaubriand is more than enough. The wine list includes some 6,500 selections (with 1,800 dessert wines). After dinner, tour the kitchen and wine cellar before having dessert upstairs in a cozy booth. Casual business attire is recommended. ✉ *1208 S. Howard Ave., Hyde Park* ☎ *813/251–2421 or 800/282–1547* ⊕ *www.bernssteakhouse.com* ⌂ *Reservations essential* 🍽 *AE, D, MC, V*

$$–$$$$
✗ **Castaway.** The specialty of this midprice casual restaurant with bay views is local seafood—grilled, broiled, or blackened—but the menu also includes grilled steaks, such as New York strip, and several pasta dishes, making it popular with mainstream diners, including locals. Entrées change frequently, but favorites have included Cantonese-style shrimp with snow peas, baby corn, and shiitake mushrooms. Dine inside or on the expansive deck, popular for lunch and a sunset view over the bay. The jets dipping down over the bay on their final approach are just far enough away to avoid a noise problem. Don't be in a rush at

peak meal times when service often grinds to a halt. ✉ *7720 Courtney Campbell Causeway, east side, 1 mi west of Tampa International Airport, Airport Area* ☎ *813/281–0770* ⊕ *AE, D, DC, MC, V.*

★ $$–$$$$ ✗ **Mise en Place.** Chef Marty Blitz and his wife, Maryann, have delighted upscale downtown diners for more than two decades with an inventive, ever-changing menu that has made this one of Tampa's most celebrated restaurants. On the top end of the price chart, you might find a nicely outfitted mustard-and-pecan crusted rack of lamb with double onions (rings and bourbon-glazed shallots) and an accompanying dollop of white cheddar grits (pronounced gree-its by true Southerners). Most fowl fans will love the roast duck in a ragout of spinach and cauliflower. Those of you who want to leave the decision to the chef can opt for the rotating "Get Blitzed" tasting menu ($65 with wine, $45 without). ✉ *442 W. Kennedy Blvd., entrance off Grand Central Pl., Central Tampa* ☎ *813/254–5373* ⊕ *www.miseonline.com* ⊟ *AE, D, DC, MC, V* ⊙ *Closed Sun. and Mon. No lunch Sat.*

$$–$$$$ ✗ **Roy's.** Chef Roy Yamaguchi's Hawaiian fusion restaurant has fresh ingredients flown in daily from around the Pacific. Some menu items change daily, so you might just call ahead if you don't want to be surprised (or disappointed because your favorite was served yesterday). Regular dishes include roasted macadamia-nut-crusted mahimahi with lobster-essence sauce and blackened ahi tuna with spicy soy-mustard sauce. The kitchen also presents a prix-fixe menu, usually around $35 per person for an appetizer, entrée, and dessert. Speaking of something for after the main event, choices include a melting chocolate soufflé and a fresh-fruit cobbler. ✉ *4342 Boy Scout Blvd., Airport Area* ☎ *813/873–7697* ⊕ *www.roysrestaurant.com* ⊟ *AE, D, DC, MC, V.*

$$–$$$ ✗ **Bella's Italian Cafe.** Carnivores are not slighted, but we love to go meatless when we visit this SoHo (South Howard Avenue) eatery, which had its coming out in 1986. The lasagna napoletana is bursting with four kinds of cheese and the garlicky basil-tomato sauce gives it just the right bite. The grouper alla calabrese (lightly battered and sautéed with red wine, capers, olives and onions) is another memory maker. Already moderately priced, Bella's is not too highbrow to ignore pizza and calzones—there are dozens of options. ✉ *1413 S. Howard Ave., Hyde Park* ☎ *813/254–3355* ⊕ *www.bellasitaliancafe.com* ⚎ *AE, D, MC, V*

$$–$$$ ✗ **Restaurant BT.** Local restaurateur B.T. Nguyen has earned quite a following since opening her first two eateries here more than two decades ago. The service, pastel accents, and white-cloth tables lend intimacy to her latest restaurant, which specializes in French-Vietnamese cooking. Bo Tai Chanh (filet tartare infused with lime juice, chili, ginger, and herbs) makes a great beginning. If sweet-and-sour is in your game plan, sea bass in a tomato-pineapple sauce makes a great entrée. Ditto for shaken beef (cubed filet mignon seared in cognac) that comes on a bed of watercress with jasmine rice. And vegetarians get more than token attention here; they can dig into monk's ragout (tofu with snow peas, bamboo shoots, black mushrooms, carrots, and baby corn), among others. Even the bar menu is inventive, with 11 martinis ranging from lychee to lemongrass-lime. ✉ *133 W. Snow Ave.* ☎ *813/258–1916* ⊕ *www.restaurantbt.com* ⊟ *AE, D, DC, MC* ⊙ *Closed Sun.*

$-$$$ ✕**Byblos Cafe.** Good grub, a friendly crowd, and belly dancers on Friday and Saturday evenings make Byblos—named for an ancient city in Phoenicia—a fun addition to almost any itinerary. If you are new to Greek and Lebanese cooking (or just cannot make up your mind), try the Taste of Lebanon ($30), which includes mezah (starters) like hummus and grape leaves, among others, and entrées like kebabs and kafta (ground meat with onions and spices). The mainstream menu is dotted with lamb chops, gyros, curried chicken or beef, and other treats. By the way, you can join the dancers—if you have the bravado. ⊠ *2832 S. MacDill Ave., South Tampa* ☎*813/805–7977* ▭*www.bybloscafe.com* ▭*AE, MC, V.*

$-$$$ ✕**Columbia.** Make a date for some of the best Latin cuisine in Tampa.
Fodor's Choice A fixture since 1905, this magnificent structure with an old-world air,
★ spacious dining rooms, and a sunny courtyard takes up an entire city block and seems to feed the entire city—locals as well as travelers—throughout the week, but especially on weekends. The paella, bursting with seafood, chicken, and pork, arguably is the best in Florida, and the 1905 salad—with ham, olives, cheese, and garlic—are legendary. The menu has Cuban classics such as *boliche criollo* (tender eye of round stuffed with chorizo sausage), *ropa vieja* (shredded beef with onions, peppers, and tomatoes), and *arroz con pollo* (chicken with yellow rice). The flamenco dancing show (Monday–Saturday evenings, $6 cover) is a must. ⊠*2117 E. 7th Ave., Ybor City* ☎*813/248–4961* ⊕*www. columbiarestaurant.com/ybor.asp* ▭*AE, D, DC, MC, V.*

$-$$$ ✕**Café Dufrain.** Dogs can tag along if you dine on the patio at pet-friendly Café Dufrain, a riverside eatery popular with an upscale crowd. For a little something that will bring your taste buds alive, try the red chile-marinated filet mignon delivered with sweet-corn risotto and tomato salsa. You'll also enjoy Dufrain's cioppino, a delightful dish inhabited by sea bass, lobster, shrimp, and chorizo. Seal the deal with the mango cheesecake. In mild weather, opt for the waterfront view of downtown Tampa—even if you don't have Fido in tow. ⊠*707 Harbour Post Dr., Downtown* ☎*813/275–9701* ⊕*www.cafedufrain. com* ▭*AE, D, MC, V.*

$-$$ ✕**Kojak's House of Ribs.** Few barbecue joints can boast the staying power of this family-owned and –operated pit stop, which had its debut in 1978. In the last three decades, it has earned a following of sticky-fingered regulars who have turned it into one of the most popular barbecue stops in central Florida. It could pass for a century-old Cracker house complete with veranda, pillars supporting the overhanging roof, and red-brick steps. Day and night, three indoor dining rooms and an outdoor dining porch have a steady stream of hungry patrons digging into tender barbecued pork spareribs that are dry-rubbed and tanned overnight before visiting the smoker for a couple hours. Then they're bathed in the sauce of your choice. Chicken also is made with the same Oklahoma recipe and, on the side, 'slaw and 'tater salad are among several choices. Kojak's also has a nice selection of sandwiches, including sloppy chicken and country-style sausage. ⊠*2808 Gandy Blvd., South Tampa* ☎*813/837–3774* ⊕*www.kojaksbbq.com* ☰*AE, D, MC, V* ⊙*Closed Mon.*

$-$$ ✕ **Stumps Supper Club.** The menu is as lively as the entertainment at one of Tampa's more popular restaurant-nightclub combos. Southern vittles are the house specialty, and they're reminiscent of Sunday dinner at one of our aunts' houses. The Brunswick stew (chicken mingling with butter beans and veggies in tomato broth) is close to perfection. The meat loaf comes under a creamy ham gravy, and the obligatory country-fried steak does not disappoint. Sides include corn bread, cheese grits, black-eyed peas, and collard greens. Decorated in flea-market chic, Stumps takes food quite seriously. Friday and Saturday nights after 9 you'll bump into Jimmy James & The Velvet Explosion, a six-piece band that relives Elvis, Abba, Motown, and KC & the Sunshine Band. Speaking of bumping, that's guaranteed on a dance floor usually crowded with 20- to 40-somethings beyond sane capacity. Validated parking is $1.50 for three hours; $1 per hour thereafter. ⊠*615 Channelside Dr., Downtown* ☎*813/226–2261* ⊕*www.stumpssupperclub. com* ☰*AE, D, DC, MC, V* ⊙*No lunch weekdays.*

¢ ✕ **Mel's Hot Dogs.** Talk about a tubular experience. Visitors as well as passersby usually are greeted by a red wiener-mobile parked on the north side of the highway—just east of Busch Gardens. Those lucky enough to venture inside find walls dotted with photos from fans and a hot-diggity menu that's heaven for tube-steak fans. You can order a traditional dog, but try something with a little more pizzazz, such as a bacon-cheddar Reuben-style bow-wow on a poppyseed bun or the Mighty Mel, a quarter-pounder decked out with relish, mustard, and pickles. To avoid lunch crowds, arrive before 11:30 or after 1:30. Mel's is a true roll-up-your-sleeves place that's popular with the workday crowd as well as travelers wanting to step outside of the theme park for a bite. ⊠*Central Tampa, 4136 E. Busch Blvd., Tampa* ☎*813/985–8000* ⊕*www.melshotdogs.com* ☰ ⊙*Closed Sun.*

WHERE TO STAY

★ $$$-$$$$ ▦ **Casita de la Verdad.** The home of a cigar worker in the factory district, this inn is one of the most intimate places to stay in the Bay area. In the heart of Ybor City, it has the same kind of clapboard siding and picket fences that were originally part of the home. Inside, you'll find hardwood and marble floors, a claw-foot tub, and two queen-size beds. There's also a full kitchen and a grill-equipped deck that's ideal for searing a steak, but don't let them stop you from going out for a traditional breakfast—*café cubano* or *café con leche* with a wedge of buttered Cuban bread. **Pros:** Romantic, nostalgic. **Cons:** Sense of isolation. ⊠*1609 E. 6th Ave., Ybor City* ☎*813/654–6087* ⊕*www. yborcityguesthouse.com* ⟿*1 room* ⚫*In-room: kitchen, refrigerator, Ethernet* ☰*AE, MC, V.*

★ $$$-$$$$ ▦ **Saddlebrook Resort Tampa.** If you can't get enough golf and tennis, here's your fix. Saddlebrook is one of west Florida's premier resorts of its type, largely because it has so many things in one spot—36 holes of championship golf, the Arnold Palmer Golf Academy, 45 clay, grass, and artificial-surface tennis courts, a Harry Hopman tennis program, a full-service spa, a fitness center, and a kids' club. Varied accommodations include one- and two-bedroom suites; wireless high-speed Internet access is available throughout the hotel. There's also a 5-acre executive challenge course. **Pros:** Heavily wooded grounds are a nice buffer from urban sprawl; great choice for the fitness-minded. **Cons:** Isolated at 12 mi from the heart of Tampa's action. ⊠ *5700 Saddlebrook Way, Wesley Chapel* ☎ *813/973–1111 or 800/729–8383* 🖷 *813/973–4504* ⊕ *www.saddlebrookresort.com* 🛏 *800 rooms, 420 suites* ⚘ *In-room: kitchen (some), Ethernet, Wi-Fi. In-hotel: 4 restaurants, room service, bars, golf courses, tennis courts, pools, gym, spa, bicycles, no elevator, children's programs (ages 4–12), laundry service, concierge, public Wi-Fi* ☰ *AE, D, DC, MC, V* ⏺*MAP.*

$$$-$$$$ 🖼 **Tampa Marriott Waterside.** Across from the Tampa Convention Center, downtown Tampa's Marriott was built for conventioneers but is also convenient to tourist spots such as the Florida Aquarium, the St. Pete Times Forum (concerts and sports), and the Channelside, Hyde Park, and Ybor City entertainment and shopping districts. At least half the rooms and most of the suites overlook the channel to Tampa Bay, which has sparse boat traffic except on weekends; the bay itself is visible from the higher floors of the 27-story hotel. The pillared lobby has real palm trees growing out of the gleaming tile floors and the coffee bar overlooks the water. Il Terrazzo is the hotel's formal, Italian dining room. **Pros:** Great downtown location. **Cons:** Traffic gridlock during rush hour, streets unsafe on foot after dark. ⊠ *700 S. Florida Ave., Downtown* ☎ *888-268-1616* ⊕ *www.marriott.com* 🛏 *681 rooms, 36 suites* ⚘ *In-room: safe, kitchen (some), Ethernet. In-hotel: 3 restaurants, room service, bars, pool, gym, spa, laundry facilities, laundry service, concierge, executive floor, public Wi-Fi, parking (fee), no-smoking rooms* ☰ *AE, D, DC, MC, V.*

$$$-$$$$ 🖼 **Westin Tampa Harbour Island.** Few folks think of the islands when visiting Tampa, but this 12-story hotel on a 177-acre man-made islet in the Bay is just an eight-minute walk or short drive from downtown Tampa, the St. Pete Times Forum, and the convention center. The rooms are decorated in whites and bright colors and many have terrific views of the water or the downtown skyline. Service is attentive. There's a marina, and you may use the extensive health and fitness center and 20 tennis courts at the Harbour Island Athletic Club, next door, for $17 daily. **Pros:** Close to downtown but doesn't feel like it; trolley from hotel to the convention center or to the electric streetcar (TECO) station (from which you can travel to Channelside, the Florida Aquarium, or Ybor City). **Cons:** Not the best choice if you want the freedom to roam the Bay area. ⊠ *725 S. Harbour Island Blvd., Harbour Island* ☎ *813/229–5000* 🖷 *800/937–8461* ⊕ *www.starwoodhotels.com/ westin* 🛏 *299 rooms, 19 suites* ⚘ *In-room: safe, refrigerator (some), Ethernet, Wi-Fi. In-hotel: restaurant, room service, bar, pool, laundry service, airport shuttle, parking (fee), some pets allowed, no-smoking rooms* ☰ *AE, DC, MC, V.*

$$$ 🖼 **Equus Meadow Inn.** Horse lovers won't find a better bunkhouse than this lovely, two-unit (cottage and suite) bed-and-breakfast. The Car-

riage House Cottage has a bedroom and sitting room with a woody Victorian decor and modern trimmings such as satellite television. The Meadowlook Suite has a balcony, a parlor, a claw-foot tub, and inside or outside stairway access, ruling it out for guests with mobility problems. It, too, has satellite TV. Both units have private baths (the suite's is down a hall) and daily breakfast. For $35–$40 per hour you can rent one of the inn's six steeds for a guided Western trail ride. Kids under 18 are not permitted unless a parent or guardian signs a release or accompanies them. There is no Internet service, but laptop users can take advantage of wireless at a nearby Starbucks. **Pros:** Intimate, nice escape, horses. **Cons:** Charm may be lost on non–horse lovers. ✉*6812 George Rd., North Tampa Area* ☎*813/806–5566* ⊕*www. equusmeadowinn.com* ⌨*2 units* ⟐*In-room: kitchen (one), small refrigerator, no elevator* ⊟*MC, V.*

★ $$-$$$ 🏨 **Don Vicente de Ybor Historic Inn.** Built as a home in 1895 by town founder Don Vicente de Ybor, this inn shows that the mainly working-class cigar city had an elegant side, too. From the beige stucco exterior to the white marble staircase in the main lobby, this boutique hotel is an architectural tour de force. Rooms have parquet floors, canopied beds, and private baths; most have wrought-iron balconies. Common areas have crystal chandeliers, Tiffany lamps, and Persian carpets. **Pros:** Elegant, rich in history, within walking distance of Ybor City's salsafied nightlife. **Cons:** Things can get a bit rowdy outside on weekend nights, though many of Ybor City's clubs have closed in recent times. ✉*1915 Republica de Cuba, Ybor City* ☎*813/241–4545 or 866/206–4545* 🖷*813/241–6104* ⊕*www.donvicenteinn.com* ⌨*13 rooms, 3 suites* ⟐*In-room: Ethernet. In-hotel: restaurant, bar, laundry service, public Wi-Fi* ⊟*AE, D, DC, MC, V* ⑩*BP.*

NIGHTLIFE & THE ARTS

THE ARTS

Occupying 9 acres along the Hillsborough River, the 345,000-square-foot **Tampa Bay Performing Arts Center** (✉*1010 W.C. MacInnes Pl., Downtown* ☎*813/229–7827 or 800/955–1045* ⊕*www.tbpac.org*) is the largest such complex south of the Kennedy Center in Washington, D.C. Among the facilities are the new 200-seat Teco Theater, the 2,500-seat Carol Morsani Hall, a 1,047-seat playhouse, a 300-seat cabaret theater, and a 120-seat black-box theater. Opera, concerts, drama, and ballet performances are presented here. In a restored 1926 movie palace, the **Tampa Theatre** (✉*711 N. Franklin St., Downtown* ☎*813/274–8982* ⊕*www.tampatheatre.org*) has films, concerts, and special events.

NIGHTLIFE

While there are more boarded storefronts than in the past, the biggest concentration of nightclubs, as well as the widest variety, is found along 7th Avenue in Ybor City. It becomes a little like Bourbon Street in New Orleans on weekend evenings. Popular **Adobe Gilas** (✉*1600 E. 8th Ave., Ybor City* ☎*813/241–8588*) has live music Thursday through Sunday nights and a balcony overlooking the crowds on 7th Avenue. There's a large selection of margaritas and more than 30 brands of tequila, and food is served until 2 AM. Considered something of a dive—but a lovable one—by a loyal and young local following that ranges from esteemed jurists to nose ring–wearing night owls, the **Hub** (✉*719 N. Franklin St., Downtown* ☎*813/229–1553*) is known for one of Tampa's best martinis and one of its most eclectic jukeboxes. **The Tampa Improv** (✉*Centro Ybor, 1600 E. 8th Ave., Ybor City* ☎*813/864–4000* ⊕*www.improvtampa.com*) stars top comedians in performances Wednesday through Sunday.   Catch comedians Wednesday through Sunday nights at **Side Splitters** (✉*12938 N. Dale Mabry Hwy., Central Tampa* ☎*813/960–1197* ⊕*www.sidesplitters comedy.com*). **Skippers Smokehouse** (✉*910 Skipper Rd., Northeast Tampa* ☎*813/971–0666* ⊕*www.skipperssmokehouse.com*), a junkyard-style restaurant and oyster bar, has live reggae Wednesday, Grateful Dead night on Thursday, blues on a rotating schedule, and great smoked fish every night. **Stumps Supper Club** (✉*615 Channelside Dr., Downtown* ☎*813/226–2261* ⊕*www.stumpssupperclub.com*) serves Southern food, and has live dance music daily and a DJ and Jimmy James and the Velvet Explosion on Friday and Saturday. **Blue Martini Lounge** (✉*2323 N. Westshore Blvd., West Tampa* ☎*813/873–2583*) at International Plaza has live entertainment nightly except Monday and a menu of killer martinis à la *Sex and the City.*

 International Plaza's **Bay Street** (✉*2223 N. West Shore Blvd., Airport Area*) has become one of Tampa's dining and imbibing hot spots.

SPORTS & THE OUTDOORS

BASEBALL

Locals and tourists flock each March to see the **New York Yankees** (✉*Legends Field, 1 Steinbrenner Dr., near corner of Dale Mabry Hwy. and Martin Luther King Jr. Blvd., off I–275 Exit 41B, Central Tampa* ☎*813/879–2244 or 813/875–7753*) play about 17 spring-training games at Legends Field, a 10,382-seat replica of Yankee Stadium. Call for tickets. From April through September, the stadium belongs to a Yankee farm team, the **Tampa Yankees,** who play 70 games against the likes of the Daytona Cubs and the Sarasota Red Sox.

CANOEING

In northeast Tampa, **Canoe Escape** (✉*9335 E. Fowler Ave., ½ mi east of I–75* ☎*813/986–2067* ⊕*www.canoeescape.com*) arranges guided or self-guided trips from two hours to all-day duration on the upper Hillsborough River, abounding with alligators, ibises, hawks, and other wildlife. They also rent canoes and kayaks.

DOG RACING

Tampa Greyhound Track (✉*8300 N. Nebraska Ave.* ☎*813/932–4313* ⊕*www.tampadogs.com*) holds dog races from early June to December.

FISHING

Captain Jim Lemke of **Light Tackle Adventures** (✉*8613 Beth Ct., Odessa* ☎*813/917–4989 or 813/920–5460* ⊕*www.lighttackleadventures. com*) is an outfitter who arranges bay, backwater, offshore, and flats-fishing trips for everything from snook to tarpon.

FOOTBALL

Seeing the National Football League's **Tampa Bay Buccaneers** (⊠ *Raymond James Stadium, 4201 N. Dale Mabry Hwy., Central Tampa* ☎ *813/879–2827 or 800/282–0683* ⊕ *www.buccaneers.com*) play isn't easy without connections, since the entire stadium is booked by season-ticket holders years in advance. But tickets can be found in the classifieds of newspapers such as the Tampa Tribune and St. Petersburg Times. The Arena Football League **Tampa Bay Storm** (⊠ *St. Pete Times Forum, 401 Channelside Dr., Downtown* ☎ *813/301–6900* ⊕ *www. tampabaystorm.com*) plays about 16 games in its March-to-June season. The Storm has a hot rivalry with the Orlando Predators.

GOLF

Babe Zaharias Golf Course (⊠ *11412 Forest Hills Dr., Northeast Tampa* ☎ *813/631–4374*) is a challenging 18-hole public course with water hazards on 8 holes; greens fee $17/$32. A pro is on hand to give lessons. **Bloomingdale Golfers Club** (⊠ *4113 Great Golfers Pl., Southeast Tampa* ☎ *813/685–4105*) has 18 holes, a two-tiered driving range, a 1-acre putting green, and a restaurant; greens fee $30/$80. **The Claw at USF** (⊠ *13801 N. 46th St., North Tampa* ☎ *813/632–6893*) is named for its many dog-legged fairways. The 18-hole par-71 course is on a preserve with moss-draped oaks and towering pines, and is free of any on-course housing developments; greens fee $31/$53. **The Club at Eaglebrooke** (⊠ *1300 Eaglebrooke Blvd., Lakeland* ✛ *Polk County, 30 mi from Tampa* ☎ *863/701–0101*) is an 18-hole course; greens fee $59/$69. Ten miles north of Tampa International Airport, **Westchase Golf Club** (⊠ *11602 Westchase Golf Dr., Tampa* ☎ *813/854–2331*) has a wooded 18-hole course with bridges and bulkheads; greens fee $25/$89. Golfers rotate from the back 9 holes to the front 9. The **Saddlebrook Resort** (⊠ *5700 Saddlebrook Way, Wesley Chapel* ☎ *813/973–1111*) has 36 holes; greens fee $55/145. There's also a driving range, golf shop, on-site pro, and resort spa. The public, 18-hole course at **Tournament Players Club of Tampa Bay** (⊠ *5300 W. Lutz Lake Fern Rd., Lutz* ☎ *813/949–0090*), 15 mi north of Tampa, was designed by Bobby Weed and Chi Chi Rodriguez; greens fee $69/$162.

HORSE RACING

Tampa Bay Downs (⊠ *Race Track Rd., off Rte. 580, Oldsmar* ☎ *813/855–4401* ⊕ *www.tampadowns.com*) holds Thoroughbred races from December to May, plus simulcast TV broadcasts of other Thoroughbred races at tracks around the nation. Live poker tournaments also are held.

TENNIS & RACQUETBALL

The **City of Tampa Tennis Complex at HCC** (⊠ *3901 W. Tampa Bay Blvd., Central Tampa* ☎ *813/223–8602*), across from Raymond James Stadium and immediately north of Tampa International Airport, has 12 clay courts and 16 hard courts ($5 an hour for clay courts; $2.50 an hour for hard courts). All courts are lighted. The complex also has four racquetball courts. The **Sandra Freedman Tennis Complex** (⊠ *59 Columbus Dr., Central Tampa* ☎ *813/259–1664*)

SHOPPING

For the mildly unusual to the downright bizarre, stop at **Squaresville** (⊠ *508 S. Howard Ave., Near Downtown* ☎*813/259–9944*), which stocks everything from Cuban clothing to Elvis posters to Betty Page clocks. The **Channelside shopping and entertainment complex** (⊠ *615 Channelside Dr., Downtown*) offers movie theaters, shops, restaurants, and clubs; the official Tampa Bay visitor center is also here. If you want to grab something at Neiman Marcus or Nordstrom on your way to the airport, the upscale **International Plaza** (⊠ *2223 N. Westshore Blvd., Airport Area*) mall, which includes Betsey Johnson, J. Crew, L'Occitane, Louis Vuitton, Tiffany & Co., and many other shops, is immediately south of the airport. Bay Street, the mall's dining "district," is one of Tampa's hot spots. **Old Hyde Park Village** (⊠ *Swan Ave. near Bayshore Blvd., Hyde Park*) is a gentrified shopping district like the ones you find in every major American city. Williams-Sonoma and Brooks Brothers are mixed in with bistros and sidewalk cafés. More than 120 shops, department stores, and eateries are in one of the area's biggest market complexes, **Westfield Brandon** (⊠ *Grand Regency and Rte. 60, Brandon*), an attractively landscaped complex near Interstate 75, about 20 minutes east of downtown by car. If you are shopping for hand-rolled cigars, head for 7th Avenue in **Ybor City,** where a few hand-rollers practice their craft in small shops. One of the more popular stops is the King Corona Cigar Factory (⊠ *1523 E. 7th Ave., Ybor City*).

ST. PETERSBURG

21 mi west of Tampa.

St. Petersburg and the Pinellas Coast form the thumb of the hand that juts out of Florida's west coast and grasps Tampa Bay. There are two distinct parts of St. Petersburg: the at-times snobbish downtown and cultural area, centered on the bay, and the more laid-back but pricey beach area, a string of barrier islands that faces the gulf and includes St. Pete Beach, Treasure Island, and Madeira Beach. Causeways link beach communities to the mainland peninsula.

Numbers in the margin correspond to the Tampa St. Petersburg map.

❽ If you can't decide whether to go in-line skating or saltwater fishing, do both at once (depending on your level of athleticism) on Tampa Bay's car-free **Friendship TrailBridge,** formerly the Gandy Bay Bridge (U.S. Highway 92), which connects Tampa and St. Petersburg. The trail runs parallel to the newer Gandy Bridge and can be accessed from either city. The 2½-mi span has no facilities except for portable potties that have been placed at either end of the two-lane concrete structure. The recreational-trail experience is like going to sea on foot. Long wooden decks on each side of the bridge (open 24 hours) are reserved for anglers, and the former traffic lanes of the bridge are open sunrise to sunset to runners, walkers, bicyclists, and in-line skaters. ☎*727/549–6099.*

❾ **Sunken Gardens** is a 100-year-old botanical paradise. Check out photos of its colorful past in the gift shop. Explore the cascading waterfalls and koi ponds, and walk through the butterfly house and exotic gardens where more than 50,000 tropical plants and flowers thrive amid groves of some of the area's most spectacular palm trees. You can arrange a guided tour (no charge, Sundays at 1:30), and there are special events and workshops year-round. The on-site restaurant, open for dinner, and Great

WORD OF MOUTH

"Our departing day, we had an afternoon flight, so we snuck in a trip to Sunken Gardens. It took a good hour and half and our daughter enjoyed the butterfly garden and flamingoes."—miller20621.

Explorations, a hands-on kids' museum (ask for the dual-admission ticket and save $2), make this place a family favorite. ⊠ *1825 4th St. N* ☏ *727/551–3102* ⊕ *www.sunkengardens.org* ✆ *$8* ⊙ *Mon.–Sat. 10–4:30, Sun. noon–4:30.*

⑭ "Don't touch" are words never spoken at **Great Explorations**. The museum is hands-on through and through, with a Robot Lab, Climb Wall, Lie Detector, Fire House, Vet's Office, and other interactive play areas, including the new Tree House. Smart exhibits like the Tennis Ball Launcher, which uses compressed air to propel a ball through a series of tubes, and Sounds Waves, where Styrofoam pellets in a clear tube show differences in sound frequencies, employ low-tech to teach kids (and parents) high-tech principles. ⊠ *1925 4th St. N* ☏ *727/821–8992* ⊕ *www.greatexplorations.org* ✆ *$9* ⊙ *Mon.–Sat. 10–4:30, Sun. noon–4:30.*

⑫ Downtown St. Petersburg gets a massive infusion of vibrancy from **BayWalk,** a shopping, dining, and entertainment mall in a square-block complex incorporating California mission–style design and courtyard areas lined with trendy eateries, bars, shops, and a 20-screen movie theater. It's best for adults to stroll the plaza and restaurants in the afternoon and early evening, since teenagers overtake BayWalk at night. Among the restaurants at 2nd Avenue North and 2nd Street (off I–275 Exit 23A) are Dan Marino's Fine Food & Spirits; dish; Johnny Rockets, of hamburger-chain fame; and Wet Willies, a see-and-be-seen bar. ⊠ *Bordered by 2nd St. N, 2nd Ave. N, 1st St. N, and 3rd Ave. N.* ☏ *727895–9277* ⊕

⑩ The downtown **Florida Holocaust Museum** is the fourth-largest museum of its kind in the United States. It has the permanent History, Heritage, and Hope exhibit, an original boxcar, and an extensive collection of photographs, art, and artifacts. One compelling display includes portraits and biographies of Holocaust survivors. The museum, which also has a series of rotating exhibits, was conceived as a learning center for children, so many of the exhibits avoid overly graphic content; parents are warned before entering a gallery if any of the subject matter is potentially too intense for kids. ⊠ *55 5th St. S* ☏ *727/820–0100* ⊕ *www.flholocaustmuseum.org* ✆ *$10* ⊙ *Daily 10–5.*

⑪ One of the city's cornerstones, the **Museum of Fine Arts** is a gorgeous Mediterranean Revival structure that houses outstanding collections of

European, American, pre-Columbian, and Asian art. Here, you'll find major works by American artists ranging from Whistler to O'Keeffe to Rauschenberg and Lichtenstein, but the museum is known for its collection of French artists, including Fragonard, Cézanne, Monet, Rodin, Gauguin, and Renoir. There are also photography exhibits that draw from a permanent collection of more than 1,200 works. Docents give narrated gallery tours. Admission prices and museum hours are sometimes increased for special exhibits. It's located on the waterfront, one block from the Pier. ⊠ *255 Beach Dr. NE* ☎ *727/896–2667* ⊕ *www. fine-arts.org* ☞ *$8* ⊙ *Tues.–Sat. 10–5, Sun. 1–5.*

❸ The Spanish surrealist certainly had a different way of viewing our
Fodor'sChoice world, as evidenced by exhibits at the **Salvador Dalí Museum,** which holds
★ the world's most comprehensive collection of his work. The mind-expanding paintings in this downtown headliner include Eggs on a Plate without a Plate, The Hallucinogenic Toreador, and more than 90 other oils. You'll also discover more than 100 watercolors and drawings, and 1,300 graphics, sculptures, photographs, and objets d'art displayed. Frequent hour-long tours are led by well-informed docents (no additional charge). How did the collection end up here? A rich industrialist and friend of Dalí's, Ohio magnate A. Reynolds Morse, was looking for a museum site after his huge Dalí collection began to overflow his mansion. The people of St. Petersburg vied admirably for the collection, and the museum was established here as a result. ⊠ *1000 3rd St. S* ☎ *727/823–3767 or 800/442–3254* ⊕ *www.salva-dordalimuseum.org* ☞ *$15* ⊙ *Mon.–Wed. 9:30–5:30, Thurs. 9:30–8, Fri. 9:30–6:30, Sat. 9:30–5:30, Sun. noon–5:30.*

★ ❺ **Bayside Tours** is a fun way to see downtown St. Petersburg, the park system, and the Tampa Bay waterfront while a tour leader tickles your brain with local history. This is different from most tours because you are not going by bus or boat—your self-guided chariot is a motorized Segway. Each tour starts with an easy 15- to 20-minute training session. Much of the trick is simply a matter of leaning—forward to reach warp speed of about 12 mph, backward to slow down or brake, and sideways to turn. Tours are 60 or 90 minutes and are offered up to three times daily. Reservations are required. ⊠ *335 N.E. 2nd Ave.* ☎ *727/896–3640* ⊕ *www.gyroglides.com* ☞ *Tours $35–$50* ⊙ *Tues.–Sat. 10:30 and 2, Sun. 12:30 and 2, Mon. 12:30, 2:30, and 4:30.*

ℂ ❻ Spread over five small islands, or keys, 1,136-acre **Fort De Soto Park** lies at the mouth of Tampa Bay. It has 7 mi of beaches, two fishing piers, a 4-mile hiking-skating trail, picnic and camping grounds, and a historic fort that kids of any age can explore. The fort for which it's named was built on the southern end of Mullet Key to protect sea lanes in the gulf during the Spanish-American War. Roam the fort or wander the beaches of any of the islands within the park. ⊠ *3500 Pinellas Bayway S, Tierra Verde* ☎ *727/582–2267* ☞ *Free* ⊙ *Beaches, daily sunrise–sunset; fishing and boat ramp, 24 hrs.*

❼ **Pass-A-Grille Beach,** at the southern end of St. Pete Beach, has parking meters, a snack bar, restrooms, and showers. It and Clearwater Beach are two of the area's most popular saltwater swimming holes. ✉ *Off Gulf Blvd. (Rte. 699), St. Pete Beach.*

🔟⑱ **Treasure Island** (✉ *11260 Gulf Blvd.*) is a free beach north of Pass-A-Grille with dressing rooms, metered parking, and a snack bar.

⑲ In the middle of the mouth of Tampa Bay lies a small (350 acres), largely unspoiled but critically eroding island, **Egmont Key,** now a state park, national wildlife refuge, national historic site, and bird sanctuary. On the island are the ruins of Fort De Soto's sister fortification, **Fort Dade,** built during the Spanish-American War to protect Tampa Bay. The primary inhabitants of the less-than-2-mi-long island are the threatened gopher tortoise and box turtles. Shelling and nature-viewing are rewarding. The only way to get here, however, is by boat. **Dolphin Landings Tours** (☎ *727/367–4488* ⊕ *www.dolphinlandings.com*) does a four-hour shelling trip, a two-hour dolphin-sighting excursion, back-bay fishing or party-boat fishing, and other outings.

WHERE TO EAT

★ $$$-$$$$ ✕ **Marchand's Bar & Grill.** Opened in 1925 and once known as the Pompeii Room, this wonderful Vinoy Hotel eatery has frescoed ceilings and a spectacular view of Tampa Bay and the nearby boat docks. Upscale and special-occasion diners are drawn to Marchand's by an imaginative and ever-changing menu. A one-time visit might offer a deliciously rare lamb duo (T-bone and double chop) with cheese and pesto-smashed spuds, halibut poached in vanilla-bean olive oil, or lump crab-and-cheese ravioli with crunchy duck cracklings. The wine list is extensive, including a number of by-the-glass selections. There's live jazz Friday and Saturday nights. ✉ *Renaissance Vinoy Resort, 501 5th Ave. NE* ☎ *727/894–1000* ⊟ *www.marchandsbarandgrill. com* ⊟ *AE, D, DC, MC, V.*

$$-$$$ ✕ **Salt Rock Grill.** It's not the same scene as the eateries on Miami's South Beach, but tourists and locals who want to see and be seen flock to this beachside hangout, attesting to its good-time atmosphere. (A band plays Saturday and Sunday nights during summer, and couples get close on the patio bar and beach.) But the rock-solid, if slightly less-than-imaginative, menu is the best reason to come. Don't believe the "monster" Caribbean lobster is as billed—at 1¼ pounds it's chicken lobster size, but it's twice cooked including a finish on the grill and quite tasty. The showstopper is the cioppino (shrimp, king crab, lobster, mussels, fish, and clams with a sourdough crust). In fair weather, dine on the dock; otherwise ask for a table with a view of the water. ✉ *19325 Gulf Blvd.* ☎ *727/593–7626* ⊕ *www.saltrockgrill.com* ⊟ *AE, MC, V.*

$-$$ ✕ **Hurricane Seafood Restaurant.** Sunsets and gulf views are the bait that hooks regulars as well as travelers who find their way to this somewhat hidden St. Pete Beach pit stop. Dating to 1977, it's mainly heralded as a watering hole where you can hoist a cold one while munching on one of the area's better grouper sandwiches. (Speaking of this sweet white fish, it's the real deal here, which isn't a guarantee in some restaurants recently exposed for selling cheaper fish billed as grouper.) The Hurricane also has a range of seafood and steak entrees. The aforementioned sunsets are best seen from the rooftop sundeck. ✉ *807 Gulf Way, St. Pete Beach* ☎ *727/360–9558* ☰ *www. thehurricane.com* ☰ *AE, D, MC, V.*

$$–$$$ ✗ **Spoto's Italian Grille.** Simple formula here: aged Angus beef expertly prepared and pasta cooked to perfection equal a 30-year tour in a business that sees far more casualties than success stories. The restaurant serves about every cut of beef one can imagine, from a huge porterhouse to a petit fillet to a three-quarter pound veal chop. And if red meat is not your thing, grouper piccata, smoked salmon in a basil-tomato cream and, our favorite, Long Island duck in ginger-brandy sauce are some of the other specialties. Dishes are served with hot bread, fresh vegetables, and soup or salad. ✉ *4871 Park St. N* ☎ *727/545–9481* ⊕ *www.spotossteakjoint.com* ✉ *1280 Main St., Dunedin* ☎ *727/734–0008* ☰ *AE, D, MC, V* ☉ *No lunch.*

$–$$ ✗ **Crabby Bill's.** Nothing fancy about the crab man's place—just some of the area's tastiest Florida seafood served family-style (picture long picnic-style tables) and in a friendly atmosphere. The fried grouper sandwich is as fine as the Hurricane's offering (⇨ above), or order it grilled, broiled, or blackened. But crustaceans are the house specialty. That means your choice of blue, softshell, king, and, from October to May, delicious though costly stone crabs, among others. There's also a good selection of other treats, including flounder, bay scallops, and farm-raised oysters. Diners usually dress in the official uniform of Florida beaches: shorts, T- or polo shirts, and flip-flops or slip-ons. ✉ *5300 Gulf Blvd.* ☎ *727/360–8858* ⊕ *www.crabbybills.com* ☰ *D, MC, V.*

$$–$$$$ ✗ **The Lobster Pot.** There's no dearth of seafood restaurants along the Gulf Coast, so it takes more than the usual fried, broiled, and raw suspects to keep one around for three decades. Faithful regulars have consistently kept the Lobster Pot on top of the fish chain. Inside its wood-plank-over-frame walls, expect white-tablecloth service and entrées such as sweet sautéed snapper capped with crab, asparagus, and a dollop of Hollandaise. First-timers may not want to detour from the house specialties—marine cuisine—but recently the grilled rack of lamb has received raves. For starters, don't miss mussels with a different twist. They're sautéed with coconut milk and basil. ✉ *17814 Gulf Blvd.* ☎ *727/391–8592* ⊕ *www.lobsterpotrestaurant.com* ☰ *AE, D, DC, MC, V* ☉ *No lunch.*

¢–$$ ✗ **Ted Peters Famous Smoked Fish.** Picture this: flip-flop–wearing anglers and beach-towel clad bathers lolling on picnic benches, soaking up a beer or three, and devouring flavorful oak-smoked salmon, mullet, and mackerel. Everything comes to the table with heaped helpings of German potato salad or coleslaw. If you're industrious enough to have hooked your own fish, the crew will smoke it for about $1.50 per pound. If not, there's always what many consider to be the best burger in the Tampa Bay region. The popular smoked-fish spread is available to go. There's also indoor seating at Ted's, which has been a south side fixture for more than six decades. Closing time is 7:30 PM. ✉ *1350 Pasadena Ave. S, South Pasadena* ☎ *727/381–7931* ⚠ *Reservations not accepted* ☰ *No credit cards* ☉ *Closed Tues.*

Fodor'sChoice ★

¢ ✗ **Brisket Basket.** You can dine in (counter and picnic tables only), drive up, or holler for delivery, but make sure you dig into the pulled or sloppy-style beef brisket. What makes it special? It's rubbed with sweet and hot paprika, then slow-cooked all night. There's a nice selection of side dishes, including hominy, slaw, chili, brisket chowder, and German potato salad with a rich helping of bacon. And, if you're feeding a small army or at least a hungry quartet, you can order brisket or meat loaf by the pound. ⊠ *2500 5th Ave. N, St. Petersburg* ☎ *727/327–9712* ⊕ *www.brisketbasket.com* ⊟ *Reservations not accepted* ⊟ *MC, V* ⊗ *closed Sun.*

¢–$ ✕ **TooJay's.** Kippered salmon and roast brisket with potato pancakes are the mainstays at this kosher-style deli with a busy dining room at breakfast, lunch, and dinner. Other selections include salmon cakes, shepherd's pie, and shrimp salad. Don't miss the éclair, a house specialty. The restaurant is nothing fancy, but it's bright and friendly, and management ensures you're waited on promptly. Everything on the menu is available for takeout. ⊠ *141 2nd Ave. N, BayWalk, St. Petersburg* ☎ *727/823–3354* ⊕ *www.toojays.com* ⚲ *Reservations not accepted* ⊟ *AE, D, DC, MC, V.*

WHERE TO STAY

$$$–$$$$
Fodor'sChoice
★
Don CeSar Beach Resort. You gotta love the story—real or imagined—about Thomas Rowe's ghost. As legend has it, the man who built this Roaring 20s–era hotel came back after death to meet his beloved. Some guests and staff swear they see the couple occasionally having a rendezvous in the garden; others say Rowe appears in corridors and rooms. On a more documented level, the Don once was a favorite of F. Scott and Zelda Fitzgerald, Babe Ruth, and Clarence Darrow. Today the "Pink Palace," as it's called thanks to its paint job, is a Gulf Coast landmark with remarkable architecture. Its exterior and public areas have turn-of-the-last-century elegance. Ditto for the rooms, and the staff is known for old-world service—if some are at times a bit chilly. The restaurant, Maritana Grille, specializes in Florida seafood and is lined with huge fish tanks. The more casual Beach House Suites by the Don CeSar, less than ½ mi from the main building, has one-bedroom condos and a great little beach bar. **Pros:** Romantic, great beach, great dining options. **Cons:** Quite pricey. ⊠ *3400 Gulf Blvd., St. Pete Beach* ☎ *727/367–6952 or 800/282–1116* ⊜ *727/363–5034* ⊕ *www.don cesar.com* ⊠ *Resort: 277 rooms, 40 suites; Beach House: 70 condos* ⌂ *In-room: safe (some), Ethernet, Wi-Fi. In-hotel: 3 restaurants, room service, bars, pools, gym, spa, beachfront, children's programs (ages 5–12), laundry service, concierge, parking (fee), some pets allowed, no-smoking rooms* ⊟ *AE, D, DC, MC, V.*

$$$–$$$$
Inn at the Bay. Here's a charmer set in a three-story 1910 Victorian home that's near downtown and a short distance from the museums and the Pier. Rooms have four-poster beds and antique furniture. The Sailboat Suite has a fireplace and whirlpool bath. A full hot breakfast is served at your leisure. Like most B&Bs, it doesn't have an elevator, but there is a wheelchair ramp, and there are rooms on the lower floor. **Pros:** Quiet, tree-lined neighborhood but still close to downtown. **Cons:** B&Bs aren't for those who like seclusion. ⊠ *126 4th Ave. NE,* ☎ *727/822–1700 or 888/873–2122* ⊜ *727/896–7411* ⊕ *www.innat thebay.com* ⊠ *7 rooms, 5 suites* ⌂ *In-room: Ethernet, Wi-Fi. In-hotel:*

parking (no fee), no kids under 9, no-smoking rooms ⊟*AE, D, DC, MC, V* ⏑*BP.*

$$$-$$$$
FodorśChoice
★

⊞ **Renaissance Vinoy Resort & Golf Club.** Built in 1925, making it the same vintage as the Don CeSar, the Vinoy is a luxury resort in a quiet, quaint neighborhood not far from downtown St. Petersburg's attractions. The resort's $93 million renovation in the early 1990s allowed it to keep its yesteryear glamour and place on the National Register of Historic Places. Some of the units are cramped by today's standard, so ask for one of the spacious

rooms for more comfort; all have cheery, modern decorations. The resort overlooks Tampa Bay, and a tiny bayside beach several blocks away is good for strolling (though unswimmable). Transportation is provided to Gulf beaches 30 minutes away. Other offerings include access to a Ron Garl–designed golf course with a stunning clubhouse, a big marina, and pool attendants who deliver drinks. The hotel is convenient to downtown museums, the Pier, or BayWalk and service tends to be a bit friendlier than at the Don. **Pros:** Charm, history, proximity to downtown museums. **Cons:** Pricey, not beachfront. ✉*501 5th Ave. NE* ☎*727/894–1000* ⊟*727/822–2785* ⊕*www.vinoyrenaissance resort.com* ⬷*345 rooms, 15 suites* ♿*In-room: Ethernet. In-hotel: 5 restaurants, room service, bars, golf course, tennis courts, pools, gym, spa, laundry facilities, laundry service, concierge, no-smoking rooms* ⊟*AE, D, DC, MC, V.*

☾ $$$-$$$$

⊞ **TradeWinds Islands Resort.**Most rooms have a view of the beach, though you may have to crane your neck to see the Gulf in some. Furnishings are modern if a bit pedestrian in standard rooms. The TradeWinds is very popular with business, European, and Latin American guests, and it has some of the showmanship of an Orlando hotel, with a man-made waterway inside the complex, complete with paddleboats. It's also one of the few pet-friendly resorts in the area, boasting a play area and room-service menu for dogs and cats ($7–$13 for pork chops, salmon, and more). There are on-site swimming lessons for children and adults. **Pros:** Great beachfront location, close to several outside restaurants. **Cons:** Heavy convention trade. ✉*5500 Gulf Blvd., St. Pete Beach* ☎*727/363–2212* ⊟*727/363–2222* ⊕*www. tradewindsresort.com* ⬷*434 rooms, 310 suites (Island Grand: 378 rooms, 207 suites; Sandpiper: 56 rooms, 103 suites)* ♿*In-room: safe, kitchen, refrigerator, Ethernet, Wi-Fi. In-hotel: 11 restaurants, bars, tennis courts, pools, gym, spa, beachfront, children's programs (ages 4–15), laundry facilities, laundry service, concierge, parking (fee), no-smoking rooms* ⊟*AE, D, DC, MC, V.*

$$$-$$$$

⊞ **Mansion House Bed & Breakfast Boutique Inn.** A pleasant 15-minute walk from the Pier, Mansion House B&B is actually two 20th-century next-door-neighbor wood-frame mansions in charming Arts and Crafts style. One house is said to have been home to the first mayor of St. Petersburg. The first and second floors of each house have inviting, individually decorated rooms; the most appealing might be the Carriage Room, which has a cathedral ceiling and an old-fashioned, custom-made, built-in four-poster bed. Wi-Fi is accessible throughout the property, including poolside. **Pros:** Within walking distance of pier, restaurants, shops, and art galleries. **Cons:** Not wheelchair accessible, kids must be nine and older. ⊠*105 5th Ave. NE* ☎*727/821–9391 or 800/274–7520* 🖷*727/821–6906* ⊕*www.mansionbandb.com* ➾*12 rooms, 1 carriage house* ⌂*In-room: Ethernet, Wi-Fi. In-hotel: pool, no elevator, Wi-Fi, parking (no fee), some pets allowed (fee), no kids under 9, no-smoking rooms* ☰*AE, D, MC, V* ⬚❘*BP.*

$$$–$$$$ 🏠**Island's End Resort.** Sunrise and sunset views are part of the charm of this 1950s-vintage motel, which offers one- and three-bedroom cottages. Outdoors, the grounds are dotted with huge live oaks, sea grapes, teak deck chairs, and a weathered fishing pier that adds to the resort's character. The property is nicely landscaped, and it's an easy walk to the beach, restaurants, and shops. Grills are available if you want to barbecue. The small resort makes a great place for families who want to enjoy the beach life. Continental breakfast is served on Tuesday, Thursday, and Saturday. **Pros:** Good value, nice views, nice location, and very reminiscent of 1950s Florida charm. **Cons:** Access via a narrow road with creeping traffic. ⊠*1 Pass-A-Grille Way, St. Pete Beach* ☎*727/360–5023* 🖷*727/367–7890* ⊕*www.islandsend. com* ➾*6 cottages* ⌂*In-room: kitchen, DVD, VCR, Wi-Fi. In-hotel: laundry facilities, some pets allowed* ☰*MC, V* ⬚❘*CP.*

NIGHTLIFE

Carlie's (⊠*7020 49th St. N* ☎*727/527–5214* ⊕*www.carlieslounge. com*) is hopping Thursday–Sunday with plenty of dancing to local bands. At **Cha Cha Coconuts** (⊠*The Pier* ☎*727/822–6655*), crowds catch live contemporary music Friday through Sunday year-round. **Coliseum Ballroom** (⊠*535 4th Ave. N* ☎*727/892–5202*) has ballroom dancing and group lessons on most Wednesday afternoons and Saturday nights. Call ahead. At **Marchand's** (⊠*501 5th Ave. NE* ☎*727/894–1000*), a fine-dining spot inside the posh Vinoy Hotel, sophisticated locals and well-informed out-of-towners gather at the bar for after-dinner cocktails and dancing to top-notch jazz bands Friday and Saturday. It's the most genteel place in town for a nightcap. The **Rare Olive** (⊠*300 Central Ave., corner of 3rd St.* ☎*727/822–7273* ⊕*www. rareolive.com*) adds a touch of class to an otherwise jeans-and-T-shirt nightlife scene with martinis, banquettes, and an assortment of bands and DJs. It also has Texas Hold 'Em tournaments. **Stormy's at the Hurricane** (⊠*807 Gulf Way, Pass-A-Grille Beach* ☎*727/360–9558*) is a fine place to watch the sunset and then dance to DJ music every Friday and Sunday.

SHOPPING

One of the state's more notable bookstores is **Haslam's** (⊠*2025 Central Ave.* ☎*727/822–8616*), a family-owned emporium that's been doing business just west of downtown St. Petersburg for more than 70 years. The store carries some 300,000 volumes, from cutting-edge best-sellers to ancient tomes. If you value a good book or simply like to browse, you could easily spend an afternoon here. Designer boutiques, movie theaters, and trendy restaurants can be found at the downtown shopping plaza **Florida Craftsmen Galleries** (⊠*501 Central Ave.* ☎*727/822–4294*), which gives 125 homegrown craftsmen a chance to exhibit glassware, jewelry, furniture, and more. **John's Pass Village and Boardwalk** (⊠*12901 Gulf Blvd., Madeira Beach*) is a collection of shops and restaurants in an old-style fishing village, where you can pass the time watching pelicans cavorting and dive-bombing for food. A five-story structure on the bayfront, the **Pier** (⊠*800 2nd Ave. NE*), near the Museum of Fine Arts, looks like an inverted pyramid. Inside are numerous shops and eating spots. More than 150 art dealers sell their wares at **Art & Antiques** (⊠*Beach Street between 1st and 2nd Aves.*).

CLEARWATER

12 mi north of St. Petersburg.

Residential areas are a buffer between the commercial areas that center on U.S. 19 and the beach, which is moderately quiet during winter, but buzzing with life during Spring Break and summer. There's a semi-quaint downtown area on the mainland, just east of the beach.

Numbers in the margin correspond to the Tampa St. Petersburg map.

⓴ When pelicans and other birds become entangled in fishing lines, locals sometimes carry them to the nonprofit **Suncoast Seabird Sanctuary,** founded by Ralph Heath and dedicated to the rescue, repair, recuperation, and release of sick and injured birds. At times there are hundreds of land and sea birds in residence, including egrets, herons, gulls, terns, sandhill cranes, hawks, owls, and cormorants. ⊠*18328 Gulf Blvd., Indian Shores* ☎*727/391–6211* ⊕*www.seabirdsanctuary. org* ⊠*Donation welcome* ☉*Tours Wed. and Sun. at 2.*

㉑ South of Clearwater Beach, on Sand Key at Clearwater Pass, **Sand Key Park** (⊠*1060 Gulf Blvd.* ☎*727/588–4852*) has a lovely beach, plenty of green space, a playground, and a picnic area.

㉒ The **Clearwater Marine Aquarium** is a laid-back attraction offering an opportunity to participate in the work of saving and caring for endangered marine species. Many of the sea turtles, dolphins, and other animals living at the aquarium were brought there to be rehabilitated from an injury or saved from danger. The aquarium conducts tours of the bays and islands around Clearwater, including a daily ecocruise on a pontoon boat (you might just see a dolphin or two), and kayak tours of Clearwater Harbor and St. Joseph Sound. ⊠*249 Windward Passage* ☎*727/441–1790* ⊕*www.cmaquarium.org* ⊠*$9* ☉ *Mon.—Sat. 9–5, Sun. 10–5.*

㉓
Fodor's Choice
★

Connected to downtown Clearwater by Memorial Causeway, **Clearwater Beach** (⊠ *Western end of State Rd. 60, 2 mi west of downtown Clearwater*) is on a narrow island between Clearwater Harbor and the gulf. It has a widespread reputation for beach volleyball. There are lifeguards here as well as a marina, concessions, showers, and restrooms. Around Pier 60 there's a big, modern playground. This is the site of a nightly sunset celebration complete with musicians and artisans. It's one of the area's nicest and busiest beaches, especially on weekends and during Spring Break, but it's also one of the costliest in terms of parking fees, which can reach $1.25 per hour.

**OFF THE
BEATEN
PATH**

Pinewood Cultural Park. Three out-of-the-way but worthwhile attractions grace this space. **Florida Botanical Gardens** (⊠ *12175 125th St. N, Largo* ☏ *727/582–2200* ⊕ *www.flbg.org* ⊠ *Free* ☉ *Daily 7–7*) welcomes you to 150 acres of native and exotic ornamental plants. Demonstrations teach environmentally friendly gardening techniques. The University of Florida Pinellas County Extension maintains the gardens. More than 27 historic local structures are gathered at **Heritage Village** (⊠ *11909 125th St. N, Largo* ☏ *727/582–2123* ⊠ *Donations accepted* ☉ *Tues.–Sat. 10–4, Sun. 1–4*), including a log cabin and Victorian-era home, tracing local history back to the 1850s. **Gulf Coast Museum of Art** (⊠ *12211 Walsingham Rd., Largo* ☏ *727/518–6833* ⊠ *www.gulfcoastmuseum. org* ⊠ *$8* ☉ *Tues.–Sat. 10–4, Sun. noon–4*) completes the complex with permanent showings of Florida artists and visiting exhibits.

WHERE TO EAT

$$–$$$ ✕ **Bob Heilman's Beachcomber.** The Heilmans have fed hungry diners since 1920 at their Florida Trend magazine Hall of Fame eatery. Although it's very popular with tourists, you'll also rub shoulders with a number of devoted locals. Despite the frequent crowds, the service is fast and friendly. The sautéed chicken is an American classic—arriving with mashed spuds, gravy, veggie du jour, and fresh baked bread. Or try the black grouper with a delicious twist—it's griddled with a citrus-mango vinaigrette. The family also owns the neighboring **Bobby's Bistro & Wine Bar.** ⊠ *447 Mandalay Ave., Clearwater Beach* ☏ *727/442–4144* ⊕ *www.heilmansbeachcomber.com* ⊟ *AE, DC, D, MC, V.*

$–$$ ✕ **Frenchy's Rockaway Grill.** Quebec native Mike "Frenchy" Preston runs four eateries in the area, including the fabulous Rockaway. The headliner here is a killer grouper sandwich that's moist and not battered into submission. (It's also real grouper, something that's not a given these days in Florida, because of fishing restrictions.) Mike also gets a big thumbs-up for his she-crab soup and, on the march-to-a-different-drummer front, the cheddar-stuffed shrimp. In mild weather, eat on the deck, though the screaming yellow and turquoise paint job can be nearly as blinding as the sun. ⊠ *7 Rockaway St.* ☏ *727/446–4844* ⊕ *www.frenchysonline.com* ⊟ *AE, MC, V.*

WHERE TO STAY

$$$–$$$$ ⊞ **Safety Harbor Resort & Spa.** While it's not for everyman, those who enjoy old-school pampering love the 50,000-square-foot Aveda-concept spa, which has the latest in therapies and treatments. The pleasant hamlet of Safety Harbor is also a point of interest, with charming shops along the nearby main street. The resort was built over hot springs on Tampa Bay in 1926, but little of the original architecture remains. The springs still function, however, feeding into pools, the spa, and water coolers. The property has on-site golf and tennis instruction, and golf courses are 5 mi away. **Pros:** Charm, good choice for spa lovers. **Cons:** Far from local attractions, staff can be chilly. ✉ *105 N. Bayshore Dr., Safety Harbor* ☎ *727/726–1161 or 888/237–8772* 🖷 *727/724–8772* ⊕ *www.safetyharborspa.com* 🛏 *189 rooms, 4 suites* 🖧 *In-room: Ethernet, Wi-Fi. In-hotel: restaurant, tennis courts, pools, gym, spa, laundry facilities, laundry service, some pets allowed, no-smoking rooms* ▤ *AE, D, DC, MC, V.*

$$$–$$$$ 🏨 **Sheraton Sand Key Resort.** Expect something special—a modern property and one of the few uncluttered beaches in the area at this chain landing zone. The nine-story, T-shaped resort is set on 10 well-manicured acres, and many rooms have excellent Gulf views, others keep an eye over an adjacent park. All rooms have balconies or patios. Considered one of the top corporate-meeting and convention hotels in the Clearwater area, the resort has amenities—such as a beautiful private beach—that make it ideal for leisure travelers, too. **Pros:** Private beach, great views. **Cons:** Clearwater Beach crowds just off-property. ✉ *1160 Gulf Blvd., Clearwater Beach* ☎ *727/595–1611* 🖷 *727/596–8488* ⊕ *www.sheratonsandkey.com* 🛏 *375 rooms, 15 suites* 🖧 *In-room: Ethernet. In-hotel: 4 restaurants, room service, bars, tennis courts, pool, gym, beachfront, water sports, children's programs (ages 3–15), public Wi-Fi, some pets allowed, no-smoking rooms* ▤ *AE, D, DC, MC, V.*

$$–$$$ 🏨 **Belleview Biltmore Resort & Spa.** Built by railroad magnate Henry Plant, the exterior and public areas of this huge 1896 Victorian resort look like a *Great Gatsby* movie set. It is one of the world's largest wooden structures and is on the National Register of Historic Places. Units range from cozy little rooms to spacious suites that lie off long, creaky corridors. Furnishings lean toward mahogany with floral appointments. The 21 acres overlook a narrow part of Clearwater Bay. The spa matches the Victorian opulence of the rest of the hotel, with the convenience of modern facilities. The hotel staff conducts daily historical tours. **Pros:** Nostalgic, off the beaten tourist path. **Cons:** In addition to being creaky it's also a bit musty. ✉ *25 Belleview Blvd.* ☎ *727/373–3000 or 800/237–8947* 🖷 *727/441–4173* ⊕ *www.belleviewbiltmore.com* 🛏 *226 rooms, 40 suites* 🖧 *In-room: Ethernet, Wi-Fi. In-hotel: 3 restaurants, bars, golf course, tennis courts, pools, gym, spa, bicycles, some pets allowed, no-smoking rooms* ▤ *AE, D, DC, MC, V.*

THE ARTS

Ruth Eckerd Hall (✉*1111 N. McMullen Booth Rd.* ☎*727/791–7400* ⊕*www.rutheckerdhall.com*) hosts many national performers of ballet, opera, and pop, classical, or jazz music.

SPORTS & THE OUTDOORS

BASEBALL

The **Philadelphia Phillies** (✉*Bright House Networks Field, 601 N. Old Coachman Rd.* ☎*727/441–8638, 727/442–8496 tickets*) get ready for the season with spring training here (February–March). The stadium also hosts the Phillies' farm team.

BIKING

Lou's Bicycle Center (✉*8990 Seminole Blvd., Largo* ☎*727/398–2453*) rents bikes, does quick repairs, and sells new bikes. There's an access point to the Pinellas Trail a couple of blocks west of Lou's on 86th Avenue Southwest.

The **Pinellas Trail** is a 35-mi paved route that spans Pinellas County. Once a railway, the trail runs adjacent to major thoroughfares, no more than 10 feet from the roadway, so you can access it from almost any point. You get the flavor of neighborhoods and an amalgam of suburbs along the way. The trail, also popular with in-line skaters, has spawned trailside businesses such as repair shops and health-food cafés. There are also many lovely rural areas to bike through and plenty of places to rent bikes. Be wary of traffic in downtown Clearwater and on the congested areas of the Pinellas Trail, which still needs more bridges for crossing over busy streets. To start riding from the route's south end, park at Trailhead Park (37th Street South at 8th Avenue South) in St. Petersburg. To ride south from the north end, park your car in downtown Tarpon Springs (East Tarpon Avenue at North Stafford Avenue). The 2½-mi car-free **Friendship Trail** is part of the Pinellas Trail system. It's accessible from either Tampa or St. Petersburg, immediately adjacent to the Gandy Bridge. ☎*727/464–8201* ⊕*www.pinellascounty. org/trailgd/default.htm.*

GOLF

Clearwater Executive Golf Course (✉*1875 Airport Dr.* ☎*727/447–5272*) has 18 holes and a driving range; greens fee $16/$39.

MINIATURE GOLF

The live alligators advertised on the roadside sign for **Congo River Golf** (✉*20060 U.S. 19 N* ☎*727/797–4222*) are not in the water traps, just in a small, fenced-off lagoon adjacent to the course. The reptiles do, however, add a Florida touch to this highly landscaped course tucked into a small parcel of land adjacent to Clearwater's busiest north–south thoroughfare. Admission is $6.50–$7. Closed mid-October–April, weekends only April, May, October.

TENNIS
Shipwatch Yacht & Tennis Club (⊠*11800 Shipwatch Dr., Largo* ☎*727/596–6862*) has 11 clay courts, three of which are lighted for night play, and two hard courts.

DUNEDIN

㉔ *3 mi north of Clearwater.*

If the sound of bagpipes and the sight of men in kilts appeals to you, head to this town, named by two Scots in the 1880s. In March the Highland Games and in November the Celtic Festival pay tribute to the town's heritage. Dunedin also has a nicely restored historic downtown area—only about five blocks long—that has become a one-stop shopping area for antiques hunters and is also lined with gift shops and good, non-chain eateries.

WHERE TO EAT

$$–$$$$ ✗**Bon Appetit.** Known for its creative fare, this waterfront restaurant has a menu that changes as frequently as twice a month and offers salads and light entrées as well as such selections as broiled rack of lamb in herbed walnut crust and sautéed veal sweetbreads with mushrooms in brown butter. The roasted grouper in garlic and lemon butter gets well-deserved plaudits from many patrons. Bon Appetit is another eatery with staying power—serving at the same location for more than three decades. It's a great place to catch a sunset over the Gulf of Mexico. There's a pianist Wednesday–Sunday evenings and a Sunday brunch. ⊠*148 Marina Plaza* ☎*727/733–2151* ▤*www.bonappetitrestaurant. com* ▤*AE, D, DC, MC, V.*

★ **$–$$** ✗**Casa Tina.** Vegetarians get special attention with a menu literally brimming with fun food.Try the enchiladas (with vegetables or chicken) or chiles rellenos, roasted cheese-stuffed peppers. Cactus salad won't prick your tongue, but the tantalizing flavor created by tender pieces of cactus, cilantro, tomatoes, onions, lime, and *queso fresco* (a mild white cheese) might prick your taste buds. There also are tamales, tacos, and tortillas prepared dozens of ways. The place is often crowded, and service can be slow, but it's worth it. ⊠*369 Main St.* ☎*727/734–9226* ⊕*www.casatinas.com* ▤*AE, D, MC, V* ☉*Closed Mon.*

OFF THE BEATEN PATH
Caladesi Island State Park. Quiet, secluded, and still wild, this 3½-mile-long barrier island is one of the best shelling beaches (scallops, nautilus, baby's ear, and various other varieties) on the Gulf Coast, second only to Sanibel. The park also has plenty of sights for birders—from common sandpipers to majestic blue herons to rare black skimmers—and miles of trails through scrub oaks, saw palmettos, and cacti (with tenants such as armadillos, rabbits, raccoons, and rattlesnakes). The landscape also features mangroves and dunes, and the gradual slope of the sea bottom makes this a good swim for novice swimmers and kids. You have to get to Caladesi Island by private boat (there's a 108-slip marina) or through its sister park, Honeymoon Island State Recreation Area, where you take the 15-minute ferry ride across to Caladesi. The park has the only section of beach north of Venice where it's okay to bring your pets—on a leash. ⊠*Dunedin Causeway to Honeymoon*

Island, then board ferry ☎*727/734–5263 ferry information, 727/469–5942 or 727/734-1501 parks information* 🚗*Honeymoon $5 per car, ferry $9* 🕐*Daily 8–sunset; ferry hourly 10–4:30 in fair weather.*

SPORTS & THE OUTDOORS

BASEBALL

The **Toronto Blue Jays** (✉*Knology Park, 373 Douglas Ave., north of State Rd. 580* ☎*727/733–9302*) play about 18 spring training games here in March.

GOLF

Dunedin Country Club (✉*1050 Palm Blvd.* ☎*727/733–7836*), a semi-private course, has 18 holes, a driving range, and a pro shop; greens fee $50/$55.

TARPON SPRINGS

10 mi north of Dunedin.

Tucked into a little harbor at the mouth of the Anclote River, this growing town was settled by Greek immigrants at the end of the 19th century. They came to practice their generations-old craft of sponge diving. Although bacterial and market forces seriously hurt the industry in the 1940s, sponging has had a modest return, mostly as a focal point for tourism. The docks along Dodecanese Boulevard, the main waterfront street, are filled with sweet old buildings with shops and eateries. Tarpon Springs' other key street is Tarpon Avenue, about a mile south of Dodecanese. This old central business district has become a hub for antiques hunters. The influence of Greek culture is omnipresent; the community's biggest celebration is the annual Greek Orthodox Epiphany celebration in January, in which teenage boys dive for a golden cross in Spring Bayou, a few blocks from Tarpon Avenue, during a ceremony followed by a street festival in the town's central business district.

㉕ **St. Nicholas Greek Orthodox Cathedral** is a replica of St. Sophia's in Istanbul and an excellent example of New Byzantine architecture. It's the home of a weeping icon that received national and international headlines in the 1970s. ✉*36 N. Pinellas Ave.* ☎*727/937–3540* 🎫*Donation suggested* 🕐*Daily 9–4.*

㉖ **The Sponge Factory** is a shop, museum, and cultural center that reveals more than you ever imagined about how a lowly sea creature, the sponge, created the industry that built this village. See a film about these much-sought-after creatures from the phylum *porifera* and how they helped the town prosper in the early 1900s. You'll come away converted to (and loaded up with) natural sponges and loofahs. ✉*510 Dodecanese Blvd., off Rte. 19* ☎*727/938–5366* 🎫*Free* 🕐*Daily 10–6.*

WHERE TO STAY

★ $$$–$$$$ 🏨**Westin Innisbrook Golf Resort.** A massive pool complex with a 15-foot waterslide and a sand beach are part of the allure of this sprawling, 1,100-acre resort. But 72 holes of golf, including the Copperhead

11

course (home of March's PODS Championship), are the real magnets. The resort's grounds are beautifully maintained, and guest suites are in 24 two- and three-story lodges tucked among the trees between golf courses. Some of the roomy junior, one-bedroom, and two-bedroom suites have balconies or patios. Innisbrook has enough restaurants and lounges to make it self-contained, though today the area around it offers a little competition. **Pros:** Great for serious golfers, varied dining options. **Cons:** Removed from other attractions. ✉ *36750 U.S. 19 N, Palm Harbor* ☏ *727/942–2000 or 800/456–2000* 🖷 *727/942–5576* ⊕ *www.innisbrookgolfresort.com* ⇌ *600 suites* ⚭ *In-room: kitchen (some), Ethernet. In-hotel: 4 restaurants, bars, golf courses, tennis courts, pools, gym, bicycles, laundry facilities, laundry service, concierge, public Wi-Fi, no-smoking rooms* ▭ *AE, D, DC, MC, V.*

THE NATURE COAST

The coastal area north of Tampa is sometimes called the Nature Coast, and aptly so. Flora and fauna have been well preserved in this area, and West Indian manatees are show-stoppers. These gentle vegetarian marine mammals, distantly related to elephants, remain an endangered species, though their numbers have grown to about 3,500 or more today. Many manatees have massive scars on their backs from run-ins with boat propellers. Extensive nature preserves and parks have been created to protect them and other wildlife indigenous to the area, and these are among the best spots to view manatees in the wild. Although they are far from mythical beauties, it is believed that manatees inspired ancient mariners' tales of mermaids. U.S. 19 and the Suncoast Parkway, a toll road, are the prime routes through this rural region, and traffic flows freely once you've left the congestion of St. Petersburg, Clearwater, and Port Richey. If you're planning a day trip from the bay area, pack a picnic lunch before leaving, since most of the sights are outdoors.

HOMOSASSA SPRINGS

31 *20 mi north of Weeki Wachee.*

At the **Homosassa Springs Wildlife State Park** you can see many manatees and species of fish through a floating glass observatory known as the Fish Bowl—except in this case the fish are outside the bowl and you are inside it. The park's wildlife-walk trails lead you to excellent manatee, alligator, and other animal programs. Among the species are bobcats, a western cougar, white-tailed deer, a black bear, pelicans, herons, snowy egrets, river otters, whooping cranes, and even a hippopotamus named Lucifer, a keepsake from the park's days as an exotic-animal attraction. Boat cruises on Pepper Creek lead you to the Homosassa wildlife park (which takes its name from a Creek Indian word meaning "place where wild peppers grow"). ✉ *4150 S. Suncoast Blvd. (U.S. 19)* ☏ *352/628–2311 or 352/628–5343* ⊕ *www.citrusdirectory.com/hsswp/main.html* 🎟 *$9* ⊙ *Daily 9–5:30; boats run every ½ hr 9:15–3:15.*

WHERE TO EAT & STAY

¢-$ ✕**Dan's Clam Stand.** Four reasons to go: the fried grouper sandwich, the clam "chow-da," anything else seafood, and the beef burgers. This is a small, divelike place about 2 mi east of Homosassa Springs State Wildlife Park and U.S. 19, but it's very popular among locals—just check out the packed parking lot at lunch and dinner. New England seafood is a house specialty, including whole-belly clams and "lob-sta," but the grouper and mahimahi are homegrown, and Dan's won't bust your budget. ⊠*7364 Grover Cleveland Blvd.* ☎*352/628–9588* ⊠*2315 N. Sunshine Path/off Highway 44, Crystal River* ☎*352/795–9081* ▭*Debit only* ⊘*Closed Sun.*

$-$$ ⊡**Homosassa Riverside Resort.** Five villas with multiple guest rooms fill this big (by Homosassa standards) complex. There's a marina with boat and scuba-equipment rentals, a restaurant and bar that overlook the river, and an island where monkeys cavort in the trees. (Don't go near it; they bite!) Resort grounds cover 9 acres of semitropical forest along the riverfront. **Pros:** Right on the river, basic but clean. **Cons:** Out of the way, and fishing, boating, and swimming are the only reasons to stay in Homosassa. ⊠*5297 Cherokee Way* ☎*352/628–2474 or 800/442–2040* ⊟*352/628–5208* ⊕*www.riversideresorts.com* ⋗*43 suites* ⚒*In-room: kitchen (some), refrigerator (some). In-hotel: restaurant, bar, laundry facilities, no-smoking rooms* ▭*D, MC, V.*

CRYSTAL RIVER

7 mi north of Homosassa Springs.

❸❷ The **Crystal River National Wildlife Refuge** is a U.S. Fish and Wildlife Service sanctuary for the endangered manatee. Kings Spring, around which manatees congregate in winter (generally from November to March), feeds crystal-clear water into the river at 72°F year-round. This is one of the best sure-bet places to see manatees in winter, since as many as 350 congregate near this 40-acre refuge. The small visitor center has displays about the manatee and other refuge inhabitants. In warmer months, when most manatees scatter (about 80 stay here year-round), the main spring is fun for a swim or scuba diving. Though accessible only by boat, the refuge provides neither tours nor boat rentals. For these, contact marinas in the town of Crystal River, such as the **American Pro Diving Center** (⊠*821 S.E. Hwy. 19* ☎*352/563–0041 or 800/291–3483* ⊕*www.americanprodiving.com*) or the **Crystal Lodge Dive Center** (⊠*Behind Best Western, 614 N.W. U.S. 19 N* ☎*352/795–6798* ⊕*www.manatee-central.com*). ⊠*1502 S. Kings Bay Dr.* ☎*352/563–2088* ☞*Free* ⊘*Mid-Nov.–mid-Mar., daily 8–4; mid-Mar.–mid-Nov., weekdays 8–4.*

WHERE TO EAT & STAY

$-$$ ✕**Crystal River Wine & Cheese Co.** Excellent salads and good wine at affordable prices make this a very popular eatery, but the service can be a tad tardy, and the limited seating coupled with lingering diners make it difficult to park your keister during prime time, especially weekends. ⊠*734 S.E. U.S. 19* ☎*352/795–0008* ▭*AE, D, MC, V.*

11

$$-$$$ ⊡**Best Western Crystal River Resort.** Divers favor this cinder-block roadside motel close to Kings Bay and its manatee population. Dive boats depart for scuba and snorkeling excursions from the marina. The property was renovated in 2004, and the rooms are nestled under large oak trees that make the place feel like the Old South. **Pros:** Great Kings Bay location. **Cons:** Pretty standard chain motel. ⊠*614 N.W. U.S. 19* ☎*352/795–3171 or 800/435–4409* 🖷*352/795–3179* ⊕*www.crystalriverresort.com* ⇄*114 rooms, 18 efficiencies* ⚭*In-room: kitchen (some), Wi-Fi. In-hotel: restaurant, bar, pool, diving, water sports, laundry facilities, public Wi-Fi, no-smoking rooms* ▤*AE, D, DC, MC, V.*

$$-$$$ ⊡**Plantation Inn & Golf Resort.** On the shore of Kings Bay, this two-story plantation-style resort is on 232 acres near several nature preserves and rivers. Although the resort's exterior looks like that of a huge Southern mansion, the rooms are more comfortable than palatial, with blond-wood furniture and wall-to-wall carpeting. Some rooms have patios. Condos and villas have views of the golf course. The Plantation is popular among upscale, older Yuppies. **Pros:** Good location for golfers and boaters. **Cons:** Stuffy old-Southern-club feel. ⊠*9301 W. Fort Island Trail* ☎*352/795–4211 or 800/632–6262* 🖷*352/795–1368* ⊕*www.plantationinn.com* ⇄*126 rooms, 2 suites, 5 condos, 12 villas* ⚭*In-room: kitchen (some), refrigerator (some), dial-up. In-hotel: 2 restaurants, bars, golf course, tennis courts, pool, diving, public Internet, public Wi-Fi, no-smoking rooms* ▤*AE, D, DC, MC, V.*

SPORTS & THE OUTDOORS

GOLF

The **Plantation Inn & Golf Resort** (⊠*9301 W. Fort Island Trail* ☎*352/795–7211 or 800/632–6262*), open to the public, has 27 holes, a driving range, and a putting green; greens fee $21/$55.

SOUTH OF TAMPA BAY

Sarasota anchors the southern end of Tampa Bay. A string of barrier islands borders the two cities with fine beaches. Sarasota County has 35 mi of Gulf beaches, as well as two state parks, 22 municipal parks, and more than 30 golf courses, many open to the public. Sarasota has a thriving cultural scene dating to circus magnate John Ringling, who chose this area for the winter home of his circus and his family.

SARASOTA

65 mi south of Tampa.

A sophisticated resort town, Sarasota is traditionally the home of some ultra-affluent residents, dating to John Ringling of circus fame. Cultural events are scheduled year-round, and there is a higher concentration of upscale shops, restaurants, and hotels than in much of the Tampa Bay area. Across the water from Sarasota lie the barrier islands of **Siesta Key**, **Longboat Key,** and **Lido Key,** with myriad beaches, shops, hotels, condominiums, and houses.

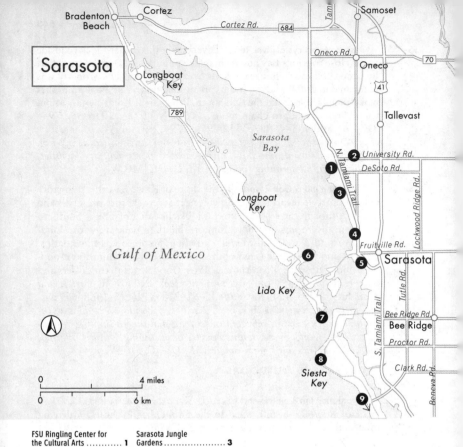

Sarasota

Decades ago, circus tycoon John Ringling found this area an ideal spot for his clowns and performers to recuperate from their months of travel while preparing for their next journey.

Numbers in the margin correspond to the Sarasota map.

🖐 ❶ **Florida State University Ringling Center for the Cultural Arts.** Along Sara-
Fodor'sChoice sota Bay, Ringling built a grand home called *Cà d'Zan* ("House of
★ John," in Venetian dialect), patterned after the Palace of the Doges in Venice, Italy. This exquisite mansion of 32 rooms, 15 bathrooms, and a 61-foot Belvedere Tower was completed in 1925, restored in 2002, and is a must-visit today. Its 8,000-square-foot terrace overlooks the dock where Ringling's wife, Mable, moored her gondola. The **John and Mable Ringling Museum of Art** is the State Art Museum of Florida and houses 500 years of art, including a world-renowned collection of Rubens paintings and tapestries. The **Ringling Circus Museum** displays circus memorabilia from its ancient roots to modern day. The Tibbals Learning Center, which opened in early 2006, focuses on the American circus and the collection of Howard Tibbals, master model-builder, who spent 40 years building the world's largest miniature circus. This impressive to-scale replica of the circa 1920s and '30s Ringling Bros. and Barnum & Bailey Circus is authentic from the number of pancakes the circus cooks are flipping, to the exact likenesses and costumes of the performers (painstakingly re-created from photography and written accounts), to the correct names of the animals marked on the miniature mess buckets. Tibbals's passion to re-create every exact detail continues in his on-site workshop, where kids can ask him questions and watch him carving animals and intricate wagons. ⊠ *U.S. 41, ½ mi west of Sarasota-Bradenton Airport* 🕾 *941/359–5700* ⊕ *www.fsu. edu/~ringling or www.ringling.org* 🎟 *$19* ⊙ *Daily 10–5:30.*

❷ On display at the **Sarasota Classic Car Museum** are 100 restored antique, classic, and muscle cars—including Rolls-Royces, Pierce Arrows, and Auburns. The collection includes rare cars and vehicles that belonged to famous people, such as John Lennon and John Ringling. ⊠ *5500 N. Tamiami Trail* 🕾 *941/355–6228* ⊕ *www.sarasotacarmuseum.org* 🎟 *$8.50* ⊙ *Daily 9–6.*

🖐 ❸ One of Florida's better throwback attractions, **Sarasota Jungle Gardens** fills 10 acres with native and exotic animals as well as tropical plants. The lush gardens date to 1936, and still have the small-world feel of yesterday's Florida. You'll find native species such as red-tailed hawks and great-horned owls in the birds of prey show, Burmese pythons and other snakes in the reptile encounter and bugs of many varieties in a show called Critters and Things. You can talk to trainers in the Meet the Keeper show and get to know such plants as the rare Australian nut tree and the Peruvian apple cactus in the gardens. Also on-site are flocks of flamingos, reptiles, and a butterfly garden. ⊠ *3701 Bayshore Rd.* 🕾 *941/355–5305* ⊕ *www.sarasotajunglegardens.com* 🎟 *$14* ⊙ *Daily 9–5.*

🖐 ❹ Kids and parents alike love state-of-the-art **G.WIZ** *(the Hands-on Science Museum)*. Exhibits teach visitors about sight, sound, motion, magnetism, electricity, and more. Included are the ExploraZone, a butterfly garden, and the ecozone with snakes, a kids' lab, a technology gallery, and other exhibits. The museum also hosts a series of temporary exhibits, such as the recent "Bodies Revealed" and "Tutankhamun the Boy King." ✉*1001 Blvd. of the Arts* ☎*941/309–4949* ⊕*www. gwiz.org* ✉*$9, higher for special exhibits* ☉*Mon.–Thu. 9–7, Fri. –Sat. 9–8, Sun. 10–6.*

⑤ **Marie Selby Botanical Gardens** and her home are a don't-miss attraction for plant and flower lovers. You can stroll through the Tropical Display House with orchids and colorful bromeliads, and wander the garden pathway past plantings of bamboo, under ancient banyans, and through the mangrove along Little Sarasota Bay with spectacular views of downtown. There are rotating exhibits of botanical art and photography in a 1924 restored mansion. Enjoy lunch at the Selby Café in the historic Selby House. Shop at the Banyan Treasures Store for unique gifts as well as the Rainforest Store, specializing in orchids and tropical plants. ✉*811 S. Palm Ave.* ☎*941/366–5731* ⊕*www.selby. org* ✉*$12* ☉*Daily 10–5.*

⑥ The 135,000-gallon shark tank at **Mote Marine Aquarium** lets you view its inhabitants from above and below the water's surface. Additional tanks show off eels, rays, and other marine creatures native to the area. There's also a touch tank where you can get friendly with horseshoe crabs, conchs, and more. Hugh and Buffett are the resident manatees that have lived at the aquarium since 1996 and are part of a research program. There's also a permanent sea-turtle exhibit. Many visitors take the 105-minute boat trip onto Sarasota Bay, conducted by **Sarasota Bay Explorers** (☎*941/388–4200* ⊕*www.sarasotabayexplorers.com*). The crew brings marine life on board in a net, explains what it is, and throws it back to swim away. You are almost guaranteed to see bottlenose dolphins. Reservations are required for the excursion. ✉*1600 Ken Thompson Pkwy., City Island, Sarasota* ☎*941/388–4441* ⊕*www. mote.org* ✉*Aquarium $17, boat excursion $26, combined ticket $36* ☉*Aquarium daily 10–5; boat tours daily 11, 1:30, and 4.*

⑦ **South Lido Park,** at the southern tip of the island, has one of the best beaches in the region, but also no lifeguards. The sugar-sand beach offers little for shell collectors, but try your luck at fishing, take a dip in the gulf, roam the 100-acre park, or picnic as the sun sets through the Australian pines into the water. Facilities include nature trails, a canoe trail and kayak launch and trail, volleyball court, playground, horseshoe pits, restrooms, and picnic grounds. ✉*2201 Ben Franklin Dr., Lido Key, Sarasota.*

⑧ **Siesta Beach** and its 40-acre park have nature trails, a concession stand, Fodor'sChoice fields for soccer and softball, picnic facilities, a playground, restrooms,
★

a fitness trail, and tennis and volleyball courts. In 1987 this beach was recognized internationally as having the whitest and finest sand in the world, a powdery, quartz-based compound that squeaks under your feet. ⊠*948 Beach Rd., Siesta Key, Sarasota.*

❾ Only 14 acres, **Turtle Beach** is a beach-park that's popular with families and is more secluded than most gulf beaches. It doesn't have the soft, white sand of Siesta Beach, but it does have boat ramps, a canoe and kayak launch, fishing from both the bay and Gulf, horseshoe pits, picnic and play facilities, a recreation building, restrooms, and a volleyball court. ⊠*8918 Midnight Pass Rd., Siesta Key, Sarasota.*

OFF THE BEATEN PATH

Fodor's Choice
★

Myakka River State Park. With 28,900 acres, this outstanding wildlife preserve is absolutely, lovely and is great for bird-watching and gator-sighting. Hour-long tram tours explore hammocks, airboat tours whiz over the lake, and there are hiking trails and bike rentals. A 100-foot-long canopy walkway gives you a bird's-eye view from 25 feet above ground. If you care to stay awhile, the park rents cabins that have kitchens, fireplaces, and air-conditioning. There's also a campground. Reservations are essential for cabins and camping. ⊠*Rte. 72, 9 mi southeast of Sarasota* ☎*941/365–0100 tours, 941/361–6511 camping, 800/326–3521 cabin reservations* ⊕*www.myakkariver.org* ⊠*$5 per vehicle up to 8 people; tours $10; cabins $60 per night* ⊗*Daily 8 AM–dusk; boat tours daily at 10, 11:30, 1, and 2:30.*

WHERE TO EAT

$$$–$$$$ **✕Café L'Europe.** Located in a neighborhood meant to impress big spenders, this sidewalk and indoor café has a courteous staff and a menu that's respectable if not spectacular. Popular entrées range from potato-crusted grouper to brandied duckling to Dover sole meunière. There's also a nice choice of wines by the glass. In mild weather the outdoor tables are a great place to people watch. Indoors, the decor is complemented by arches, hanging plants, and fine linens. ⊠*431 St. Armands Circle* ☎*941/388–4415* ⊕*www.cafeleurope.net* ⊟*AE, DC, D, MC, V.*

$$$–$$$$ **✕Ophelia's on the Bay.** The menu changes nightly at this intimate waterfront spot, which has hung around nearly two decades. Beyond the view of Little Sarasota Bay and its mangroves, the entrées might include Kobe flat iron steak with heart-of-palm rice, black grouper with coconut-and-cashew crust with papaya jam and habanero mashed potatoes; mushroom and asiago ravioli; and free-range chicken breast with sausage and walnut stuffing. ⊠*9105 Midnight Pass Rd., Siesta Key* ☎*941/349–2212* ⊕*www.opheliasonthebay.net* ⊟*AE, D, DC, MC, V* ⊗*No lunch.*

$$–$$$$ **✕Euphemia Haye.** Named for its original owner, this refueling stop is
Fodor's Choice a pleasant find with good food, a friendly staff, and intimate lighting,
★ though the prices can cause credit cards of the unsuspecting to light up. Treats include Grecian lamb shank braised in a red-wine garlic sauce, crispy barbecue duckling in a sweet and spicy sauce, and a very tasty pistachio-crusted red snapper. The upstairs Haye Loft, once the home of the original owner's grandson, has been converted into a lounge and

dessert room. ✉ *5540 Gulf of Mexico Dr., Longboat Key* ☎ *941/383–3633* ⊕ *www.euphemiahaye.com* ▭ *AE, D, MC, V.*

$$–$$$$ ✗ **Michael's on East.** Forget the fact that it's located in a shopping center—this is a trendy, elegant Sarasota dining spot that's popular with the after-theater set. The fare ranges from chicken bow-tie pasta with sun-dried tomatoes and shiitake mushrooms to porcini-rubbed rack of lamb and veal osso buco with eggplant and leeks. Desserts, such as a key lime tart with graham-cracker crust, are standouts here. A light menu is served in the intimate bar, where there's often piano music or jazz in the evening. The lunch menu includes sandwiches such as fire-roasted chicken. ✉ *1212 East Ave. S* ☎ *941/366–0007* ⊕ *www.michaelsoneast. com* ⊙ *Closed Sun. No lunch Sat.* ▭ *AE, D, DC, MC, V.*

$$–$$$ ✗ **Columbia.** On trendy St. Armands Circle, this eatery isn't as good as the original landmark in Ybor City, which celebrated its 100th birthday in 2005, yet it is still worth a visit. The menu reflects Spanish and Cuban cooking, and includes three versions of Spanish paella and a superb black-bean soup. A house specialty is pompano papillote (pompano with shrimp, crabmeat, and artichoke in a white-wine sauce, baked in parchment), and the 1905 salad is deserving of its cult status. ✉ *411 St. Armands Circle, Lido Key* ☎ *941/388–3987* ⊕ *www.columbia restaurant.com* ▭ *AE, D, DC, MC, V.*

$–$$$ ✗ **Café Baci.** For 14 straight years its northern Italian cuisine has earned Café Baci the best restaurant award from *Sarasota Magazine, a sign that locals love it. But savvy travelers come here, too.* Menu highlights include veal osso buco braised in red wine, stock, and veggies; red snapper à la Baci, cooked with tomatoes, black olives, rosemary, and white wine; and ravioli du jour. The interior is not as enticing as the entrées, but resembles an English garden, with splashes of green and white and slightly outdated floral accents. ✉ *4001 S. Tamiami Trail* ☎ *941/921–4848* ⊕ *www.cafebaci.net* ▭ *AE, D, DC, MC, V.*

$–$$$ ✗ **Patrick's.** A longtime favorite among locals, this upscale restaurant with a sports bar attracts crowds that belly up to the bar after work and end up staying for steak sandwiches, juicy cheeseburgers, pizza, pasta, char-grilled steaks, pot roast, and chicken potpie. Local *Sarasota Magazine* continually ranks the burgers here as the best in the area. ✉ *1400 Main St.* ☎ *941/952–1170* ⊕ *www.patricksofsarasota. com* ⚎ *Reservations not accepted* ▭ *AE, D, DC, MC, V.*

¢–$$ ✗ **The Old Salty Dog.** A view of New Pass between Longboat and Lido keys and affordable eats make this a popular stop, especially for visitors to Mote Marine Aquarium. It's open-air but comfortable even in summer, thanks to a pleasant breeze. Quarter-pound hot dogs, fish-and-chips, wings, and burgers set the menu's tone. Locals hang out at the beer bar, shaped from the hull of an old boat. ✉ *1601 Ken Thompson Pkwy., City Island* ☎ *941/388–4311* ⊕ *www.theoldsaltydog.com* ✉ *5023 Ocean Blvd., Sarasota* ☎ *941/349–0158* ⚎ *Reservations not accepted* ▭ *MC, V.*

¢–$ ✗ **TooJay's.** A sister deli to its St. Petersburg location, TooJay's is bright and cheerful and has warm wood tones. Breakfast offers fetching omelets, waffles, French toast, and blintzes. The lunch and dinner menus showcase a variety of sandwiches such as Reubens, pizzas, and finger foods as well as soup du jour and chili. ⌧ *Westfield Shopping-town-Southgate, 3501 S. Tamiami Trail* ☎*941/362–3692* ⊕*www. toojays.com* ⌲*Reservations not accepted* ▤*AE, D, DC, MC, V.*

¢–$ ✗**Yoder's.** Pies—key lime, Dutch apple, egg custard, strawberry rhubarb, and others—are among the main events at this Amish family restaurant in the heart of Sarasota's Amish community, but don't miss enjoying at least one meal here. Entrées, served family style—feeding two to three people—typically include meat loaf, liver and onions, turkey and dressing, a wonderful goulash, and other hearty dishes, and breakfasts include big stacks of pancakes. The desserts might be the best part of the meal, particularly the pies. The place gets crowded around noon and early evening. ⌧*3434 Bahia Vista* ☎*941/955–7771* ⊕*www.yodersrestaurant.com* ⌲*Reservations not accepted* ▤*MC, V* ⊘*Closed Sun.*

WHERE TO STAY

$$$$ ⊡**Hyatt Sarasota on Sarasota Bay.** Popular among business and upscale travelers, the Hyatt is contemporary in design and in the heart of the city, across from the Van Wezel Performing Arts Hall. All the spacious rooms overlook Sarasota Bay or the marina and the lagoon-style pool and hot tub, which have waterfalls flowing into them. Your concierge will arrange fishing, golfing, and babysitting if you desire. Pros: Great location and view. Cons: Still a chain, if higher-end. ⌧*1000 Blvd. of the Arts* ☎*941/953–1234 or 800/233–1234* ▤*941/952–1987* ⊕*www. sarasota.hyatt.com* ⇖*294 rooms, 12 suites* ⌂*In-room: Ethernet, Wi-Fi. In-hotel: 2 restaurants, room service, bars, pool, gym, bicycles, laundry facilities, laundry service, concierge, Wi-Fi, airport shuttle, some pets allowed, no-smoking rooms* ▤*AE, D, DC, MC, V.*

$$$$ ⊡**Longboat Key Club and Resort.** This beautifully landscaped 410-acre property is one of *the* places to golf in the state and one of the top tennis resorts in the country. Water is the test on both golf courses, which have excellent pro shops, lessons, and clinics. Tennis courts are Har-Tru–surfaced. Hobie Cats, kayaks, Sunfish, deep-sea charters, and ecology trips are also available. All rooms have balconies overlooking a golf course, beach, or private lagoon where manatees and bottlenose dolphins are occasionally seen. Golf and dining facilities are for resort guests and club members only. Pros: Trendy and appealing to the upscale getaway folks. Cons: Can be a bit uncomfortable and snooty if you're an everyman or -woman. ⌧*301 Gulf of Mexico Dr., Longboat Key* ☎*941/383–8821, 800/237–8821, or 888/237–5545* ▤*941/383–0359* ⊕*www.longboatkeyclub.com* ⇖*23 rooms, 95 suites* ⌂*In-room: kitchen (some), refrigerator, Ethernet. In-hotel: 5 restaurants, room service, bars, golf course, tennis courts, pool, gym, beachfront, bicycles, children's programs (ages 5–12), laundry facilities, concierge, Wi-Fi, no-smoking rooms* ▤*AE, DC, MC, V.*

★ $$$$ ⊡**Ritz-Carlton, Sarasota.** Developers like to say that this hotel is circus magnate John Ringling's realized dream, and it certainly has a style Ringling would have coveted. Fine artwork and fresh-cut flowers decorate marble-floored hallways. Rooms have marble bathrooms, and private balconies with views of Sarasota Bay, the marina, or the downtown skyline. In late 2005 the Ritz opened a private 18-hole

Tom Fazio–designed golf course 12 mi northeast of the property on the Braden River. A European-style spa and guest-and-members-only beach facility on Lido Key, about 4 mi away, make this city resort full-service. Vernona restaurant serves regional organic cuisine, and overlooks yachts in the marina. **Pros:** Ritz-glitz. **Cons:** Separation of some amenities, such as the golf course and beach facility ⊠*1111 Ritz-Carlton Dr.* ☎*941/309–2000 or 800/241–3333* 🖷*941/309–2100* ⊕*www. ritzcarlton.com/resorts/sarasota* ↩*266 rooms, 30 suites* ♨*In-room: safe, Wi-Fi. In-hotel: 2 restaurants, room service, bars, golf course, tennis courts, pool, gym, spa, children's programs (ages 5–12), laundry service, concierge, executive floor, Wi-Fi, some pets allowed, no-smoking rooms* ⊟*AE, D, DC, MC, V.*

$$$$ 🏨 **Turtle Beach Resort.** Reminiscent of a quieter, friendlier time, many of the cottages here date to the 1940s, a romantic plus for yesteryear lovers, especially given that they are well maintained. In all, there are two studios, two one-bedroom units, and six two-bedroom cottages with full kitchens. Some units have courtyards. The grounds are private, shielded by high wooden fences and palms, bougainvilleas, and other tropical foliage. The inn sits on Sarasota Bay and is named for the sea-turtle nesting sites that lie across the street. If you really want to escape, use one of the resort's canoes or kayaks to paddle a short distance south to a beach dotted with sand dunes and sea oats. **Pros:** Nice location. **Cons:** Inconvenient to the area's cultural attractions. ⊠*9049 Midnight Pass Rd., Siesta Key* ☎*941/349–4554* 🖷*941/312–9034* ⊕*www.turtlebeachresort.com* ↩*20 cottages and rooms with hot tubs* ♨*In-room: kitchen, refrigerator, DVD (some), VCR, Wi-Fi. In-hotel: pools, no elevator, laundry facilities, parking (no fee), no-smoking rooms* ⊟*D, MC, V.*

★ $$$–$$$$ 🏨 **Colony Beach & Tennis Resort.** If tennis is your game, this is the place to stay—it's one of Florida's best racquet clubs, and tennis greats such as Björn Borg have made the Colony their home court. Ten of its courts are clay hydrosurfaced (the other 11 are hard), and the pros are all USPTA-certified. They run clinics and camps at all levels, and with the guaranteed match-making program, you can play with a pro when no one else is available. There are even rackets and lessons for children, plus excellent free kids' programs. The Colony dining room has a reputation for good food and wine. Suites sleep up to eight. Among the suites are a two-story penthouse as well as three private beach houses that open onto sand and sea. The exterior of the lodging buildings could stand to be updated. **Pros:** *The* place for tennis fans, just 3 mi from St. Armands Circle, the Rodeo Drive of Florida's West Coast. **Cons:** Pricey, not a good choice for nonplayers. ⊠*1620 Gulf of Mexico Dr., Longboat Key* ☎*941/383–6464 or 800/426–5669* 🖷*941/383–7549* ⊕*www.colonybeachresort.com* ↩*235 suites* ♨*In-room: safe, kitchen, Ethernet. In-hotel: 2 restaurants, bars, tennis courts, pool, gym, spa, beachfront, water sports, bicycles, children's programs (ages 3–17), laundry facilities, laundry service, concierge, public Wi-Fi, no-smoking rooms* ⊟*AE, D, DC, MC, V.*

★ $$$–$$$$ 🏨 **The Cypress, a Bed & Breakfast Inn.** The only B&B in downtown Sarasota, the inn has a delightful assortment of themed rooms. The Martha Rose Suite has French accessories with a balcony overlooking the Gulf, a sitting area, and a separate powder room. French doors in the Mango Suite open onto a garden, and the furnishings include a couch, armchair, and Victorian writing desk. Aptly named Kathryn's Garden Room has a floral feel with wicker furnishings, a sitting area, and views of live oaks and mango trees. The Victorian-style Elizabeth Brittany Suite has an oak high-back bed and tropical sitting room. And the Essie Leigh Key West Room has a front-porch view of the bay, a pewter-and-brass bed, and private entrance. All have private baths. Rates include full breakfast and afternoon hors d'oeuvres and refreshments. Guests under 21 aren't permitted. Pros: Friendly staff, convenient to downtown, a five-minute drive from the beaches at Lido Key. Cons: No in-room phones. ⊠ *621 Gulfstream Ave. S* ☎ *941/955–4683* ⊕ *www. cypressbb.com* ♥ *5 rooms* ⌂ *In-room: no phone, Wi-Fi. In-hotel: concierge, public Wi-Fi, parking (no fee), no kids under 21, no-smoking rooms* ⊟ *AE, D, MC, V* ⌸ *BP.*

$$–$$$$ ⌨ **A Beachfront Sea Castle Accommodations.** The 10 buildings that make up this property are two-story in the Old Florida style, and all rooms lead out to the beach at Siesta Key. Rooms are bright and decorated in tasteful pastel colors, and have balconies with lounge chairs. During high season (mid-December–April), the owners mainly rent out weekly. Pros: beachfront. Cons: 1950s Florida rustic isn't for everyone. ⊠ *1001–1019 Seaside Dr., Siesta Key* ☎ *941/349–8858 or 800/720–6885* ⊕ *www.sea-castle.com* ♥ *40 rooms, 10 apartments* ⌂ *In-room: kitchen (some), refrigerator, VCR (some), dial-up (some). In-hotel: pool, beachfront, no elevator, laundry facilities, parking (no fee), no-smoking rooms* ⊟ *D, MC, V (varies by building).*

$$–$$$$ ⌨ **Lido Beach Resort.** Superb gulf views can be found at this classy beachfront resort. The South Tower was completed in May 2002, and the majority of rooms there have beach and gulf views. There are two free-form pools and three Jacuzzis, all right on the beach. The resort is equipped with Wi-Fi hot spots. Pros: Gulf views, beachfront. Cons: Bland furnishings. ⊠ *700 Ben Franklin Dr., Sarasota* ☎ *941/388–2161 or 800/441–2113* 🖷 *941/388–3175* ⊕ *www.lidobeachresort.com* ♥ *158 rooms, 64 suites* ⌂ *In-room: kitchen (some), refrigerator, Ethernet. In-hotel: 2 restaurants, bars, pools, beachfront, children's programs (ages 8–13), laundry facilities, laundry service, concierge, public Wi-Fi, no-smoking rooms* ⊟ *AE, D, DC, MC, V.*

$$–$$$ ⌨ **Gulf Beach Resort.** Lido Key's first motel has been named a historic property by the county. The resort is beachfront and is composed of condominium units that are rented out as motel rooms; since each unit is individually owned, renovations at the property are continuous. Rooms are bright and each has a different decor—many return visitors have their favorite rooms and book several years in advance. Pros: Just 2 mi from St. Armands Circle, well maintained. Cons: Pretty basic motel. ⊠ *930 Ben Franklin Dr., Lido Key* ☎ *941/388–2127 or 800/232–2489* 🖷 *941/388–1312* ⊕ *www.gulfbeachsarasota.com* ♥ *8 rooms, 41 suites* ⌂ *In-room: dial-up. In-hotel: pool, beachfront, no elevator, laundry facilities, no-smoking rooms AE, D, DC, MC, V.*

$-$$$ ⊡ **Best Western Midtown.** Here's a three-story motel that's comfortable, and very affordable during its off-season, from mid-April through early February. Set back from U.S. 41 and somewhat removed from traffic noise, it's within walking distance of a shopping center and several restaurants—including the popular Michael's on East—and is central to area attractions and downtown. Rooms have sitting areas. **Pros:** Central location. **Cons:** Bland chain feel. ⊠*1425 S. Tamiami Trail,* ☎*941/955–9841 or 800/937–8376* 🖶*941/954–8948* ⊕*www. bwmidtown.com* ⇨*100 rooms* ⚠*In-room: refrigerator (some), Ethernet. In-hotel: pool, laundry facilities, no-smoking rooms* ⊟*AE, D, DC, MC, V* ⦶*CP.*

NIGHTLIFE & THE ARTS

THE ARTS

Sarasota has free cultural events most Friday nights. The first Friday of each month, historic Palm Avenue downtown has **Art Walks** from 6 to 9. Members of the Palm Avenue Arts Alliance open their galleries to the public and entertain with dancing and singing. The third Friday of each month, from 6 to 10, **Towles Court Artists Colony** (⊠*1938 Adams La., Downtown* ⊕*www.towlescourt.com*) hosts an evening for folks to wander in and out of its galleries, ask the artists about their work, and enjoy wine and cheese. The fourth Friday night (October to May, 6–9 PM) brings **Smooth Jazz on St. Armands Circle.** Musicians perform in the center of the circle; bring a blanket, relax, and enjoy refreshments from on-site kiosks.

Among the many theaters in Sarasota, the $5 million **Asolo Repertory Theatre** (⊠*5555 N. Tamiami Trail* ☎*941/351–8000 or 800/361–8388* ⊕*www.asolo.org*) mounts rotating-repertory productions November through mid-June. Performers at the **Florida West Coast Symphony Center** (⊠*709 N. Tamiami Trail* ☎*941/953–4252* ⊕*www.fwcs.org*) include the Florida West Coast Symphony, Florida String Quartet, Florida Brass Quintet, Florida Wind Quintet, and New Artists Piano Quartet. **Golden Apple Dinner Theatre** (⊠*25 N. Pineapple Ave.* ☎*941/366–5454* ⊕) serves a standard buffet along with musicals. A long-established community theater, **The Players Theatre** (⊠*838 N. Tamiami Trail U.S. 41 and 9th St.* ☎*941/365–2494*), launched such actors as Montgomery Clift and Paul Reubens. The troupe performs comedies, special events, live concerts, and musicals. The **Sarasota Concert Band** (⊠*1345 Main St.* ☎*941/364–2263*), which celebrated its 50th anniversary in 2005, has 50 players, many of them full-time musicians; performance venues change with each event. The **Van Wezel Performing Arts Hall** (⊠*777 N. Tamiami Trail* ☎*941/953–3368 or 800/826–9303* ⊕*www.vanwezel. org*) is easy to find—just look for the purple shell rising along the bay front. It hosts some 200 performances each year, including Broadway plays, ballet, jazz, rock concerts, symphonies, and children's shows.

The **Sarasota Film Society** (⊠*Burns Court Cinema, 506 Burns La.* ☎*941/364–8662, 941/955–3456 theater* ⊕*www.filmsociety.org*) shows foreign and art films daily. Call the theater for film titles and show times, and see the society's Web site for detailed descriptions of films.

Celebrating its 46th season in 2005, the **Sarasota Opera** (⊠ *The Edwards Theater, 61 N. Pineapple Ave.* ☎ *941/366–8450 or 888/673–7212)* performs from February through March in a historic 1,033-seat downtown theater. Internationally known artists sing the principal roles, supported by a professional chorus of 24 young apprentices.

NIGHTLIFE

The **Gator Club** (⊠ *1490 Main St.* ☎ *941/366–5969)*, in a classy, historic building downtown, has live music and dancing 365 days a year.

SPORTS & THE OUTDOORS

BASEBALL

The **Cincinnati Reds** (⊠ *Ed Smith Stadium, 2700 12th St.* ☎ *941/954–4101)* have spring training here in March.

BIKING

CB's Saltwater Outfitters (⊠ *1249 Stickney Point Rd., Siesta Key* ☎ *941/349–4400* ⊕ *www.cbsoutfitters.com)* rents boats, fishing gear, and bikes hourly or by the day.

DOG RACING

The greyhounds run from late November through mid-April at the **Sarasota Kennel Club** (⊠ *5400 Bradenton Rd.* ☎ *941/355–7744* ⊕ *www. sarasotakennelclub.com)*.

FISHING

Flying Fish Fleet (⊠ *U.S. 41, on the bay front at Marina Jack* ☎ *941/366–3373* ⊕ *www.flyingfishfleet.com)* has several boats that can be chartered for deep-sea fishing and has daily group trips on its "party" fishing boat.

GOLF

Bobby Jones Golf Course (⊠ *1000 Circus Blvd.* ☎ *941/955–8097)* has 45 holes and a driving range; greens fee $11/$51. **Bobcat Trail Golf Club** (⊠ *1350 Bobcat Trail, North Port* ☎ *941/429–0500)* is a semiprivate 18-hole course 35 mi from Sarasota; greens fee $29/$75. Semiprivate **Forest Lakes Golf Club** (⊠ *2401 Beneva Rd.* ☎ *941/922–1312)* has a practice range and 18 holes; greens fee $27/$50. Fifteen miles from Sarasota, **Heron Creek Golf & Country Club** (⊠ *5303 Heron Creek Blvd., North Port* ☎ *941/423–6955 or 800/877–1433)* has a semiprivate 27-hole course; greens fee $30/$90. There are 27 holes at the Ron Garl-designed **University Park Country Club** (⊠ *7671 Park Blvd., University Park* ☎ *941/359–9999)*; greens fee $60/$125. This club is private, but does allow nonmembers limited play after 11 AM.

KAYAKING

Siesta Sports Rentals (⊠ *6551 Midnight Pass Rd., Siesta Key* ☎ *941/346–1797* ⊕ *www.siestasportsrentals.com)* rents kayaks, bikes, beach chairs, scooters, and beach wheelchairs and strollers. Guided kayaking trips are also available.

SHOPPING

St. Armands Circle (✉*John Ringling Blvd. [Rte. 789] at Ave. of the Presidents*) is a cluster of oh-so-exclusive shops and restaurants just east of Lido Beach. The **Ringling Art Museum Store** (✉*5401 Bay Shore Rd.* ☎*941/359–5700* ⊕*www.ringling.org/museum_store.asp*) is a fun place to pick up clown noses, circus poster-books, T-shirts, and more.

Downtown Sarasota has many unique boutiques and eateries. **Sarasota News & Books** (✉*1341 Main St., Downtown* ☎*941/365–6332*) is an independent bookstore that carries a good selection of books and periodicals, hosts author-signing events, and has a café with outdoor tables. **Lotus** (✉*1451 Main St., Downtown* ☎*941/906–7080* ⊕*www. lotussarasota.com*) is a home-decor and clothing boutique, specializing in shoes, accessories, Bliss cosmetics, and cotton bedding. They also display and sell works by local artists. **Rousseau's** (✉*1385 Main St., Downtown* ☎*941/365–1072*) has fun and unusual women's clothing and jewelry in a SoHo-style boutique. **Whole Foods** (✉*1451 1st St. at Lemon Ave., Downtown* ☎*941/955–8500*) carries organic produce, has a specialty wine-and-cheese market, and offers a deli with prepared meals that make great picnic lunches for the beach.

THE TAMPA BAY AREA ESSENTIALS

TRANSPORTATION

BY AIR

CARRIERS Many carriers serve Tampa International Airport. Sarasota's airport is served by major carriers. Scheduled service to St. Petersburg–Clearwater International is limited, and from many areas of the country you have to supply your own plane. American TransAir connects to U.S. cities, and Air Transat flies from Toronto.

AIRPORTS & TRANSFERS Central Florida Limousine provides Tampa International Airport service to and from Hillsborough (Tampa, Plant City) and Polk (east of Tampa-Lakeland) counties, and Super Shuttle serves Pinellas County (St. Pete Beach, St. Petersburg, Clearwater). Expect taxi fares to be about $12 to $25 for most of Hillsborough County and about twice that for Pinellas County. Transportation to and from Sarasota–Bradenton Airport is provided by West Coast Executive Sedan. The average cab fare between the airport and downtown is $12 to $25.

Airport Contacts Tampa International Airport (✉*5503 Spruce St., 6 mi from downtown Tampa* ☎*813/870–8700* ⊕*www.tampaairport.com*). **St. Petersburg–Clearwater International Airport** (✉*14700 Terminal Blvd., off Rte. 686, 9 mi from downtown St. Petersburg* ☎*727/453–7800* ⊕*www.fly2pie.com*). **Sarasota–Bradenton International Airport** (✉*600 Airport Circle, off U.S. 41, just north of Sarasota* ☎*941/359–2777* ⊕*www.srq-airport.com*).

Transfer Contacts Super Shuttle (☎*727/572–1111 or 800/282–6817* ⊕*www. supershuttle.com*). **West Coast Executive Sedan** (☎*941/359–8600*).

11

BY BUS

Service to and throughout the state is provided by Greyhound Lines. Around Tampa, the Hillsborough Area Regional Transit (HART) serves the county, and the TECO Line Streetcars replicate the city's first electric streetcars, transporting cruise-ship passengers to Ybor City. Around St. Petersburg, Pinellas Suncoast Transit Authority serves Pinellas County. The Looper trolley operates to downtown area attractions. In Sarasota the public transit company is Sarasota County Area Transit (SCAT). Fares for local bus service range from 50¢ to $2.50 (for an all-day pass), and exact change is required.

Contacts Greyhound Lines (☎ 800/231–2222 ⊕ www.greyhound.com). **Greyhound Sarasota** (✉ 575 N. Washington Blvd., Sarasota ☎ 941/955–5735). **Greyhound Clearwater** (✉ 2811 Gulf-to-Bay Blvd., Clearwater ☎ 727/796–7315). **Greyhound St. Petersburg** (✉ 180 9th St. N, St. Petersburg ☎ 727/898–1496). **Greyhound Tampa** (✉ 610 E. Polk St., Tampa ☎ 813/229–2174). **Hillsborough Area Regional Transit** (HART) ☎ 813/254–4278 ⊕ www.hartline.org). **Pinellas Suncoast Transit Authority** (PSTA) ☎ 727/540–1900 ⊕ www.psta.net). **Sarasota County Area Transit** (SCAT) ☎ 941/316–1234). **TECO Line Street Cars** (☎ 813/254–4278).

BY CAR

Interstate 75 and 275 span the bay area from north to south. Once you cross the Florida border from Georgia, it should take about 4½ hours to reach Tampa and another hour to reach Sarasota. Interstate exits are numbered according to mileage from their southern terminus, rather than sequentially. Coming from Orlando, you're likely to drive west into Tampa on Interstate 4. Along with Interstate 75, U.S. 41 (which runs concurrently with the Tamiami Trail for much of the way) stretches the length of the region. U.S. 41 links the business districts of many communities, so it's best to avoid it and all bridges during rush hours (7–9 AM and 4–6 PM). U.S. 19 is St. Petersburg's major north–south artery; traffic can be heavy, and there are many lights, so use a different route when possible. One viable option is the Veterans Expressway and Suncoast Parkway (both toll roads), which runs from west Tampa to northern Hernando County. Interstate 275 heads west from Tampa across Tampa Bay to St. Petersburg, swings south, and crosses the bay again on its way to Terra Ceia, near Bradenton. Along this last leg—the Sunshine Skyway and its stunning suspension bridge—you'll get a bird's-eye view of bustling Tampa Bay. The Gandy Bridge (Highway 92) also yields a spectacular view of Tampa Bay, and Route 679 takes you along two of St. Petersburg's most pristine islands, Cabbage and Mullet keys. Route 64 connects Interstate 75 to Bradenton and Anna Maria Island. Route 789 runs over several slender barrier islands, past miles of blue-green Gulf waters, beaches, and waterfront homes. The road does not connect all the islands, however; it runs from the village of Anna Maria off the Bradenton coast south to Lido Key, then begins again on Siesta Key and again on Casey Key south of Osprey, and runs south to Nokomis Beach.

BY TRAIN

Amtrak trains run from the Northeast, Midwest, and much of the South to the Tampa station.

Contacts Amtrak (⊠ *Tampa Union Station, 601 N. Nebraska Ave., Tampa* ☎ *800/872–7245 or 813/221–7600* ⊕ *www.amtrak.com*).

CONTACTS & RESOURCES

EMERGENCIES

There are 24-hour emergency rooms at Bayfront Medical Center, Manatee Memorial Hospital, Sarasota Memorial Hospital, and University Community Hospital.

Contacts Emergencies (☎ *911*). **Bayfront Medical Center** (⊠ *701 6th St. S, St. Petersburg* ☎ *727/893–6100*). **Manatee Memorial Hospital** (⊠ *206 2nd St. E, Bradenton* ☎ *941/745–7559*). **Sarasota Memorial Hospital** (⊠ *1700 S. Tamiami Trail, Sarasota* ☎ *941/917–9000*). **University Community Hospital** (⊠ *3100 E. Fletcher Ave., Tampa* ☎ *813/971–6000*).

TOURS

The *American Victory* Mariners Memorial & Museum Ship offers weekend day trips aboard the restored World War II–era merchant marine vessel with historical reenactments of life aboard during its wartime service. Gourmet meals and a stunning view of the Tampa skyline are available aboard StarShip Cruises, with lunch and dinner cruises aboard its namesake *StarShip,* which seats up to 350 people in the dining room.

On Captain Memo's Pirate Cruise, crew members dressed as pirates take you on sightseeing and sunset cruises in a replica of a 19th-century sailing ship. Dolphin Landings Charter Boat Center has daily four-hour cruises to unspoiled Egmont Key at the mouth of Tampa Bay. Aboard the glass-bottom boats of St. Nicholas Boat Line, you take a sightseeing cruise of Tarpon Springs' historic sponge docks and see a diver at work. The *Starlite Princess,* an old-fashioned paddle wheeler, and *Starlite Majesty,* a sleek yacht-style vessel, make sightseeing and dinner cruises.

Contacts *American Victory* **Mariners Memorial & Museum Ship** (⊠ *705 Channelside Dr., Berth 271, behind Florida Aquarium, Tampa* ☎ *813/228–8766* ⊕ *www.americanvictory.org*). **Captain Memo's Pirate Cruise** (⊠ *Clearwater Beach Marina, Clearwater Beach* ☎ *727/446–2587*). **Dolphin Landings Charter Boat Center** (⊠ *4737 Gulf Blvd., St. Pete Beach* ☎ *727/360–7411*). **St. Nicholas Boat Line** (⊠ *693 Dodecanese Blvd., Tarpon Springs* ☎ *727/942–6425*). **Starlite Princess and Starlite Majesty** (⊠ *Clearwater Beach Marina, at the end of Rte. 60, Clearwater Beach* ⊠ *Corey Causeway, 3400 S. Pasadena, South Pasadena* ☎ *727/462–2628* ⊕ *www.starlitecruises.com*). **StarShip Cruises** (⊠ *603 Channelside Dr., Tampa* ☎ *813/223–7999 or 877/744–7999*).

VISITOR INFORMATION

Contacts Bradenton Area Convention & Visitors Bureau Tourist Information Center (⊠ *1 Haven Blvd., Palmetto* ⊠ *Kiosk in Prime Outlets Ellenton, 5461 Factory Shops Blvd., Ellenton* ☎ *941/729–9177* ⊕ *www.floridasgulfislands.com*). **Cedar Key Chamber of Commerce** (⊠ *525 2nd St., Box 610, Cedar Key* ☎☎ *352/543–5600* ⊕ *www.cedarkey.org*). **Clearwater Regional Chamber of Commerce** (⊠ *1130 Cleveland St., Clearwater* ☎ *727/461–0011* ⊕ *www.clearwaterflorida.org*). **Greater Dunedin Chamber of Commerce** (⊠ *301 Main St., Dunedin* ☎ *727/733–3197* ⊕ *www.dunedin-fl.com*). **Greater Tampa Chamber of Commerce** (⊠ *615 Channelside Dr., Box 420, Tampa* ☎ *813/228–7777, 813/223–1111 Ext. 44 for Visitors Information Department* ⊕ *www.tampachamber.com*). **Sarasota Convention and Visitors Bureau** (⊠ *655 N. Tamiami Trail, Sarasota* ☎ *941/957–1877 or 800/522–9799* ⊕ *www.sarasotafl.org*). **St. Petersburg Area Chamber of Commerce** (⊠ *13850 58th St. N, Suite 2200, St. Petersburg* ☎ *727/821–4069* ⊕ *www.stpete. com*). **St. Petersburg/Clearwater Area Convention & Visitors Bureau** (⊠ *14450 46th St. N, Suite 108, St. Petersburg* ☎ *727/464–7200 or 877/352–3224* ⊕ *www. floridasbeach.com*). **Tampa Bay Beaches Chamber of Commerce** (⊠ *6990 Gulf Blvd., St. Pete Beach* ☎ *727/360–6957 or 800/944–1847* ⊕ *www.tampabay beaches.com*). **Tampa Bay Convention and Visitors Bureau** (⊠ *400 N. Tampa St., Suite 2800, Tampa* ☎ *800/368–2672 or 813/223–1111* ⊕ *www.visittampa bay.com*). **Tarpon Springs Chamber of Commerce** (⊠ *11 E. Orange St., Tarpon Springs* ☎ *727/937–6109* ⊕ *www.tarponsprings.com*). **Ybor City Chamber Visitor Bureau** (⊠ *1600 E. 8th Ave., Suite B104,* ☎ *813/248–3712* ⊕ *www.ybor.org*).

11

Florida Essentials

PLANNING TOOLS, EXPERT INSIGHT, GREAT CONTACTS

There are planners and there are those who, excuse the pun, fly by the seat of their pants. We happily place ourselves among the planners. Our writers and editors try to anticipate all the issues you may face before and during any journey, and then they do their research. This section is the product of their efforts. Use it to get excited about your trip to Florida, to inform your travel planning, or to guide you on the road should the seat of your pants start to feel threadbare.

GETTING STARTED

We're really proud of our Web site: Fodors.com is a great place to begin any journey. Scan "Travel Wire" for suggested itineraries, travel deals, restaurant and hotel openings, and other up-to-the-minute info. Check out "Booking" to research prices and book plane tickets, hotel rooms, rental cars, and vacation packages. Head to "Talk" for on-the-ground pointers from travelers who frequent our message boards. You can also link to loads of other travel-related resources.

▌ RESOURCES

ONLINE TRAVEL TOOLS

The state of Florida is very visitor-oriented and has a terrific Web site—⊕*www.visitflorida.com*—with superb links to help you find out all you want to know. It's a wonderful place to learn about everything from fancy resorts to camping trips to car routes to beach towns.

All About Florida **Visit Florida** (⊕www.visit florida.com).

VISITOR INFORMATION

For general information about Florida's attractions, contact the office below; welcome centers are on Interstate 10, Interstate 75, Interstate 95, and U.S. 231 (near Graceville), and in the lobby of the New Capitol in Tallahassee. *For regional tourist bureaus and chambers of commerce see individual chapters.*

Contacts **Visit Florida** (⊠2540 W. Executive Center Circle, Suite 200, Tallahassee ⊘Box 1100, Tallahassee ☎850/488–5607 ⊕www.visitflorida.com).

▌ THINGS TO CONSIDER

GOVERNMENT ADVISORIES

If you travel frequently, look into the TSA's Registered Traveler program (⊕www.tsa.gov). The program, which is still being tested in several U.S. airports, is designed to cut down on gridlock at security checkpoints by allowing pre-screened travelers to pass quickly through kiosks that scan an iris and/or a fingerprint. How sci-fi is that?

If you are visiting Florida during the June through November hurricane season and a hurricane is imminent, be sure to follow directions from local authorities.

GEAR

The northern part of the state is much cooler in winter than the southern part, and you'll want to take a heavy sweater if you plan on traveling north in winter months. Even in summer, ocean breezes can be cool, so always take a sweater or jacket just in case.

Miami and the Naples–Fort Myers areas are warm year-round and often extremely humid in summer months. Be prepared for sudden storms all over Florida in summer, but keep in mind that plastic raincoats are uncomfortable in the high humidity. Often storms are quick and the sun comes back in no time.

Dress is casual throughout the state, with sundresses, jeans, or walking shorts appropriate during the day; bring comfortable walking shoes or sneakers for theme parks. A few restaurants request that men wear jackets and ties, but most do not. Be prepared for air-conditioning working in overdrive.

You can generally swim year-round in peninsular Florida from about New Smyrna Beach south on the Atlantic

Coast and from Tarpon Springs south on the Gulf Coast. Be sure to take a sun hat and sunscreen—the sun can be fierce even in winter and even if it's chilly or overcast. Don't leave valuables on your beach blanket while you walk the beach or go for a dip.

TRIP INSURANCE

What kind of coverage do you honestly need? Do you even need trip insurance at all? Take a deep breath and read on.

We believe that comprehensive trip insurance is especially valuable if you're booking a very expensive or complicated trip (particularly to an isolated region) or if you're booking far in advance. Who knows what could happen six months down the road? But whether or not you get insurance has more to do with how comfortable you are assuming all that risk yourself.

Comprehensive travel policies typically cover trip-cancellation and interruption, letting you cancel or cut your trip short because of a personal emergency, illness, or, in some cases, acts of terrorism in your destination. Such policies also cover evacuation and medical care. Some also cover you for trip delays because of bad weather or mechanical problems as well as for lost or delayed baggage. Another type of coverage to look for is financial default—that is, when your trip is disrupted because a tour operator, airline, or cruise line goes out of business. Generally you must buy this when you book your trip or shortly thereafter, and it's available to you only if your operator isn't on a list of excluded companies.

If you're going abroad, consider buying medical-only coverage at the very least. Neither Medicare nor some private insurers cover medical expenses anywhere outside of the United States besides Mexico and Canada (including time aboard a cruise ship, even if it leaves from a U.S. port). Medical-only policies typically reimburse you for medical care (excluding that related to preexisting conditions) and hospitalization abroad, and provide for evacuation. You still have to pay the bills and await reimbursement from the insurer, though.

Expect comprehensive travel insurance policies to cost about 4% to 7% of the total price of your trip (it's more like 12% if you're over age 70). A medical-only policy may or may not be cheaper than a comprehensive policy. Always read the fine print of your policy to make sure that you are covered for the risks that are of most concern to you. Compare several policies to make sure you're getting the best price and range of coverage available.

■ TIP→OK. You know you can save a bundle on trips to warm-weather destinations by traveling in rainy season. But there's also a chance that a severe storm will disrupt your plans. The solution? Look for hotels and resorts that offer storm/hurricane guarantees. Although they rarely allow refunds, most guarantees do let you rebook later if a storm strikes.

BOOKING YOUR TRIP

ONLINE

You really have to shop around. A travel wholesaler such as Hotels.com or Hotel-Club.net can be a source of good rates, as can discounters such as Hotwire or Priceline, particularly if you can bid for your hotel room or airfare. Indeed, such sites sometimes have deals that are unavailable elsewhere. They do, however, tend to work only with hotel chains (which makes them just plain useless for getting hotel reservations outside of major cities) or big airlines (so that often leaves out upstarts like jetBlue and some foreign carriers like Air India). Also, with discounters and wholesalers you must generally prepay, and everything is nonrefundable. And before you fork over the dough, be sure to check the terms and conditions, so you know what a given company will do for you if there's a problem and what you'll have to deal with on your own.

■ TIP➜To be absolutely sure everything was processed correctly, confirm reservations made through online travel agents, discounters, and wholesalers directly with your hotel before leaving home.

Booking engines like Expedia, Travelocity, and Orbitz are actually travel agents, albeit high-volume, online ones. And airline travel packagers like American Airlines Vacations and Virgin Vacations—well, they're travel agents, too. But they may still not work with all the world's hotels.

An aggregator site will search many sites and pull the best prices for airfares, hotels, and rental cars from them. Most aggregators compare the major travel-booking sites such as Expedia, Travelocity, and Orbitz; some also look at airline Web sites, though some also compare other travel products, including complex packages—a good thing, as you can sometimes get the best overall deal by booking an air-and-hotel package.

WITH A TRAVEL AGENT

If you use an agent—brick-and-mortar or virtual—you'll pay a fee for the service. And know that the service you get from some online agents isn't comprehensive. For example Expedia and Travelocity don't search for prices on budget airlines like jetBlue, Southwest, or small foreign carriers. That said, some agents (online or not) *do* have access to fares that are difficult to find otherwise, and the savings can more than make up for any surcharge.

A knowledgeable brick-and-mortar travel agent can be a godsend if you're booking a cruise, a package trip that's not available to you directly, an air pass, or a complicated itinerary including several overseas flights. What's more, travel agents that specialize in a destination may have exclusive access to certain deals and insider information on things such as charter flights. Agents who specialize in types of travelers (senior citizens, gays and lesbians, naturists) or types of trips (cruises, luxury travel, safaris) can also be invaluable.

A top-notch agent planning your trip to Russia will make sure you get the correct visa application and complete it on time; the one booking your cruise may get you a cabin upgrade or arrange to have a bottle of champagne chilling in your cabin when you embark. And complain about the surcharges all you like, but when things don't work out the way you'd hoped, it's nice to have an agent to put things right.

■ TIP➜Remember that Expedia, Travelocity, and Orbitz are travel agents, not just booking engines. To resolve any problems with a reservation made through these companies, contact them first.

■ ACCOMMODATIONS

Florida has every conceivable type of lodging—from tree houses to penthouses, mansions for hire to hostels. Even with occupancy rates inching above 70%, there are almost always rooms available, except maybe at Christmas and other holidays.

Children are welcome generally everywhere in Florida. Pets are another matter, so inquire ahead of time if you're bringing an animal with you.

In the busy seasons—over Christmas and from late January through Easter in the southern half of the state, during the summer along the Panhandle and around Jacksonville, and all over Florida during holiday weekends in summer—always reserve ahead for the top properties. Fall is the slowest season: rates are low and availability is high, but this is also the prime time for hurricanes. St. Augustine stays busy all summer because of its historic flavor. Key West is jam-packed for Fantasy Fest at Halloween. If you're not booking through a travel agent, call the visitors bureau or the chamber of commerce in the area you'll be visiting to check whether a special event is scheduled for the period of your trip.

Most hotels and other lodgings require you to give your credit-card details before they will confirm your reservation. If you don't feel comfortable e-mailing this information, ask if you can fax it (some places even prefer faxes). However you book, get confirmation in writing and have a copy of it handy when you check in.

Be sure you understand the hotel's cancellation policy. Some places allow you to cancel without any kind of penalty—even if you prepaid to secure a discounted rate—if you cancel at least 24 hours in advance. Others require you to cancel a week in advance or penalize you the cost of one night. Small inns and bed-and-breakfasts are most likely to require you to cancel far in advance. Most hotels allow children under a certain age to stay in their parents' room at no extra charge, but others charge for them as extra adults; find out the cutoff age for discounts.

■TIP➔Assume that hotels operate on the European Plan (EP, no meals) unless we specify that they use the Breakfast Plan (BP, with full breakfast), Continental Plan (CP, continental breakfast), Full American Plan (FAP, all meals), or Modified American Plan (MAP, breakfast and dinner), or are all-inclusive (AI, all meals and most activities).

APARTMENT & HOUSE RENTALS

Contacts (⌂Box 1133, Captiva 33924 ☎800/547–0127 ⊕www.captiva-island.com). **Florida Keys Rental Store/Marr Properties** (⌂Box 600, ✉99980 Overseas Hwy., Key Largo ☎800/585–0584 or 305/451–3879 ⊕www.floridakeysrentalstore.com). **Florida Sunbreak** (☎800/786–2732 or 305/532–1516 ⊕www.floridasunbreak.com). **Freewheeler Vacations** (✉85992 Overseas Hwy., MM 86, Islamorada ☎866/664–2075 or 305/664–2075 ⊕www.freewheeler-realty.com). **Interhome** (☎954/791–8282 or 800/882–6864 ⊕www.interhome.us). **ResortQuest International** (✉35000 Emerald Coast Pkwy., Destin ☎877/588–5800 ⊕www.resortquest.com). **Sand Key Realty** (✉2701 Gulf Blvd., Indian Rocks Beach ☎866/353–8911 or 727/595–5441 ⊕www.sandkey.com). **Suncoast Realty** (✉224 Franklin Blvd., St. George Island ☎800/341–2021 ⊕www.uncommonflorida.com). **Vacation Home Rentals Worldwide** (☎201/767–9393 or 800/633–3284 ⊕www.vhrww.com). **Villas International** (☎415/499–9490 or 800/221–2260 ⊕www.villasintl.com). **Wyndham Vacation Resorts** (✉5259

Coconut Creek Pkwy., Margate ☎800/251–8736 ⊕www.fairfieldresorts.com).

BED & BREAKFASTS

Small inns and guesthouses are increasingly numerous in Florida, but they vary tremendously, ranging from economical places that are plain but serve a good home-style breakfast to elegantly furnished Victorian houses with four-course breakfasts and rates to match. Many offer a homelike setting. In fact, many are in private homes with owners who treat you almost like family; others are more businesslike. It's a good idea to make specific inquiries of B&Bs you're interested in. The association listed below offers descriptions and suggestions for B&Bs throughout Florida.

Reservation Services Bed & Breakfast.com (☎512/322–2710 or 800/462–2632 ⊕www.bedandbreakfast.com) also sends out an online newsletter. **Bed & Breakfast Inns Online** (☎800/215–7365 ⊕www.bbonline.com). **BnB Finder.com** (☎212/432–7693 or 888/547–8226 ⊕www.bnbfinder.com). **Florida Bed and Breakfast Inns** (☎800/524–1880 ⊕www.florida-inns.com). **Daytona Beach Convention and Visitors Bureau** (✉126 E. Orange Ave., Daytona Beach ☎800/854–1234 or 386/255–0415).

HOTELS

Wherever you look in Florida, it seems, you'll find lots of plain, inexpensive motels and luxurious resorts, independents alongside national chains, and an ever-growing number of modern properties as well as quite a few timeless classics. In fact, since Florida has been a favored travel destination for some time, vintage hotels are everywhere: there are grand edifices like the Breakers in Palm Beach, the Boca Raton Resort & Club in Boca Raton, the Biltmore in Coral Gables, and the Casa Marina in Key West; and smaller, historic places, like the Governors Inn in Tallahassee and the New World Inn in Pensacola.

All hotels listed have private bath unless otherwise noted.

▌RENTAL CARS

When you reserve a car, ask about cancellation penalties, taxes, drop-off charges (if you're planning to pick up the car in one city and leave it in another), and surcharges (for being under or over a certain age, for additional drivers, or for driving across state or country borders or beyond a specific distance from your point of rental). All these things can add substantially to your costs. Request car seats and extras such as GPS when you book.

Rates are sometimes—but not always—better if you book in advance or reserve through a rental agency's Web site. There are other reasons to book ahead, though: for popular destinations, during busy times of the year, or to ensure that you get certain types of cars (vans, SUVs, exotic sports cars).

■TIP→**Make sure that a confirmed reservation guarantees you a car. Agencies sometimes overbook, particularly for busy weekends and holiday periods.**

Car rental is highly recommended for travelers in Florida, since public transportation is limited and restrictive. In-season rates in Miami begin at $36 a day and $170 a week for an economy car with air-conditioning, automatic transmission, and unlimited mileage. Rates in Orlando begin at $35 a day and $149 a week. Rates in Fort Lauderdale begin at $36 a day and $159 a week. Rates in Tampa begin at $34 a day and $149 a week. This does not include tax on car rentals, which varies from county to county. Bear in mind that rates fluctuate tremendously—both above and below these quoted figures—depending on demand and the season.

In the past, major rental agencies were at the airport, whereas cheaper firms weren't. Now, however, all over Florida, even the majors might be off airport property. Speedy check-in and frequent shuttle buses make off-airport rentals almost as convenient as on-site service. However, it's wise to allow a little extra time for bus travel between the rental agency and the airport.

TRANSPORTATION

▌ BY AIR

Flying times to Florida vary based on the city you're flying to, but typical times are 3 hours from New York, 4 hours from Chicago, 2¾ hours from Dallas, 4½ to 5½ hours from Los Angeles, and 8 to 8½ hours from London.

Airlines & Airports Airline and Airport Links.com (⊕ www.airlineandairportlinks. com) has links to many of the world's airlines and airports.

Airline Security Issues Transportation Security Administration (⊕ www.tsa.gov) has answers for almost every question that might come up.

Air Travel Resources in Florida Better Business Bureau (☎ 703/276-0100 ⊕ www.bbb. org). Florida Attorney General (☎ 850/414-3300 ⊕ http://myfloridalegal.com/consumer).

AIRPORTS

Both major and regional airports are plentiful in Florida so you can usually pick one quite close to your destination and often choose from a couple of nearby options. If you're destined for the north side of Miami-Dade County (metro Miami), or are renting a car at the airport, consider flying into Fort Lauderdale–Hollywood International; it's much easier to use than Miami International, and often—if not always—cheaper. The airports are only 40 minutes apart by car.

▌TIP➔Long layovers don't have to be only about sitting around or shopping. These days they can be about burning off vacation calories. Check out ⊕ www.airportgyms. com for lists of health clubs that are in or near many U.S. and Canadian airports. There are several participating gyms within 15 minutes of Florida's major airports. All offer a $8 to $12 day pass. Miami International has a gym in the airport.

Airport Information Daytona Beach International Airport (DAB) (☎ 386/248-8069 ⊕ www.volusia.org/airport). **Fort Lauderdale–Hollywood International (FLL)** (☎ 954/359-6100 ⊕ www.broward. org/airport). **Jacksonville International Airport (JAI)** (☎ 904/741-4902 ⊕ www. jaa.aero). **Miami International Airport (MIA)** (☎ 305/876-7000 ⊕ www.miami-airport.com). **Orlando International (MCO)** (☎ 407/825-2001 ⊕ www.orlandoairports. net). **Palm Beach International (PBI)** (☎ 561/471-7420 ⊕ www.pbia.org). **Sarasota Bradenton International Airport (SRQ)** (☎ 941/359-2777 ⊕ www.srq-airport.com). **Southwest Florida International Airport (FMY)** (☎ 239/590-4800 ⊕ www.flylcpa.com). **St. Petersburg–Clearwater International Airport (PIE)** (☎ 727/453-7800 ⊕ www. fly2pie.com). **Tampa International (TPA)** (☎ 813/870-8700 ⊕ www.tampaairport.com).

GROUND TRANSPORTATION

SuperShuttle has service to and from Miami International, Palm Beach International, and Tampa International airports. Downtown Miami to Miami International Airport is typically $15 and takes 30 minutes. Downtown Miami to Palm Beach International Airport is typically $92 and takes 1½ hours. Downtown St. Pete to Tampa International Airport is approximately $20; the shuttle will pick you up three hours before your scheduled departure. There is no shared-shuttle service from downtown Tampa to Tampa International Airport, but SuperShuttle can book you with their car-service operators: Exclusive, which costs $92 from downtown to the airport; or ExecuCar, which runs approximately $55 from downtown to the airport. It is best to book your reservations with SuperShuttle at least two days in advance. They will pick you up from a hotel, office, or residence. There are hubs inside the airports where you can obtain SuperShuttle tickets to take you from the airport to your desired local destination.

Taxis are available at Miami International's arrival zone; flat rates vary by the zone you will be traveling to, but run between $19 and $52 in the immediate Miami area—the flat rate to Miami Beach is $32. Yellow Cab taxis from Orlando International to downtown Orlando run approximately $35. Yellow Cab and United Cab have service to and from downtown Tampa and have a flat rate of $22.

FLIGHTS

Airline Contacts Air Canada (☎888/247–2262 ⊕ www.aircanada.com). **Alaska Airlines** (☎800/252–7522 ⊕ www.alaskaair.com). **American Airlines** (☎800/433–7300 ⊕ www.aa.com). **Continental Airlines** (☎800/523–3273 for U.S. and Mexico reservations, 800/231–0856 for international reservations ⊕ www.continental.com). **Delta Airlines** (☎800/221–1212 for U.S. reservations, 800/241–4141 for international reservations ⊕ www.delta.com). **jetBlue** (☎800/538–2583 ⊕ www.jetblue.com). **Northwest Airlines** (☎800/225–2525 ⊕ www.nwa.com). **Southwest Airlines** (☎800/435–9792 ⊕ www.southwest.com). **Spirit Airlines** (☎800/772–7117 ⊕ www.spiritair.com). **United Airlines** (☎800/864–8331 for U.S. reservations, 800/538–2929 for international reservations ⊕ www.united.com). **USAirways** (☎800/428–4322 for U.S. and Canada reservations, 800/622–1015 for international reservations ⊕ www.usairways.com).

Smaller Airlines AirTran (☎800/247–8726 ⊕ www.airtran.com) to Miami, Fort Lauderdale, Fort Myers, Jacksonville, Orlando, Sarasota, Tampa, and West Palm Beach. **jetBlue** (☎800/538–2583 ⊕ www.jetblue.com) to Tampa, Fort Lauderdale, Sarasota, Fort Myers, West Palm Beach, and Orlando. **Midwest Airlines** (☎800/452–2022 ⊕ www.midwestairlines.com) to Fort Lauderdale, Fort Myers, Orlando, and Tampa. **Southwest Airlines** (☎800/435–9792 ⊕ www.southwest.com) to Fort Lauderdale, Fort Myers, Jacksonville, Orlando, Tampa, and West Palm Beach.

▌BY BUS

Greyhound passes through practically every major city in Florida. For schedules and fares, contact your local Greyhound Information Center.

Using a major credit card, you can purchase Greyhound tickets online or by using the carrier's toll-free phone numbers. You can also purchase tickets—using cash, traveler's checks, or major credit cards—at any Greyhound terminal where tickets are sold or through one of the many independent agents representing Greyhound. A complete state-by-state list of agents is available at the Greyhound Web site.

Bus Information Greyhound Lines (☎800/231–2222 or 800/229–9424 ⊕ www.greyhound.com).

▌BY CAR

Three major interstates lead to Florida. Interstate 95 begins in Maine, runs south through the Mid-Atlantic states, and enters Florida just north of Jacksonville. It continues south past Daytona Beach, the Space Coast, Vero Beach, Palm Beach, and Fort Lauderdale, ending in Miami.

Interstate 75 begins in Michigan at the Canadian border and runs south through Ohio, Kentucky, Tennessee, and Georgia, then moves south through the center of the state before veering west into Tampa. It follows the west coast south to Naples, then crosses the state through the northern section of the Everglades, and ends in Fort Lauderdale.

California and most southern states are connected to Florida by Interstate 10, which moves east from Los Angeles through Arizona, New Mexico, Texas, Louisiana, Mississippi, and Alabama; it enters Florida at Pensacola and runs straight across the northern part of the state, ending in Jacksonville.

ROADSIDE EMERGENCIES

If you need emergency assistance while traveling on roads in Florida, dial 911 or *FHP from your cell phone.

Emergency Services Florida Highway Patrol (☎911 or *FHP ⊕ www.dot.state.fl.us); their Web site provides real-time traffic information—including areas congested with construction or accidents.

RULES OF THE ROAD

Speed limits are 60 mph on state highways, 30 mph within city limits and residential areas, and 70 mph on interstates and Florida's Turnpike. Be alert for signs announcing exceptions.

In Florida you must strap a child six or younger into a child-restraint device: children aged through three years must be in a separate carrier or child seat, and children four through six can be secured in a separate carrier, integrated child seat, or by a seat belt. The driver will be held responsible for passengers under the age of 16 who are not wearing seat belts. All front-seat passengers are required to wear seat belts.

Florida's Alcohol/Controlled Substance DUI Law is one of the toughest in the United States. A blood alcohol level of .08 or higher can have serious repercussions, even for the first-time offender.

ON THE GROUND

■ COMMUNICATIONS

INTERNET

Wi-Fi is widely available in Florida's high-end hotels and even B&Bs. Most hotels have at least an Internet room in their business-service center or in-room data ports in guest rooms. Wi-Fi is usually accessible in certain hot spots of the hotel, such as the main floor or in the lobby. In-room data ports generally cost $10 for 24 hours of use. Some hotels charge you by 15-minute increments (fees vary by hotel) to use the Internet in the business-service center, whereas other hotels offer this as a complimentary service. Many U.S. cities are instituting Wi-Fi hot spots in downtown areas.

Contacts **Cybercafes** (⊕ www.cybercafes. com) lists more than 4,000 Internet cafés worldwide.

■ EATING OUT

An antismoking amendment endorsed in 2002 by Florida voters bans smoking statewide in most enclosed indoor workplaces, including restaurants. Exemptions are permitted for stand-alone bars where food takes a backseat to the libations.

A cautionary word: raw oysters have been identified as a potential problem for people with chronic illness of the liver, stomach, or blood, or who have immune disorders. Since 1993 all Florida restaurants serving raw oysters have been required to post a notice in plain view of all patrons, warning of the risks associated with consuming them.

FLORIBBEAN FOOD

A trip to the Tampa area or South Florida is incomplete without a taste of Cuban food. The cuisine is heavy, with pork dishes like *lechon asado,* served in garlic-based sauces. The two most typical dishes are *arroz con frijoles* (the staple side dish

of rice and black beans) and *arroz con pollo* (chicken in sticky yellow rice). Key West is a mecca for lovers of key lime pie (the best is found here) and conch fritters, another local favorite. Stone crab claws, another South Florida delicacy, can be savored from November through May.

MEALS & MEALTIMES

Unless otherwise noted, the restaurants listed in this guide are open daily for lunch and dinner.

RESERVATIONS & DRESS

Regardless of where you are, it's a good idea to make a reservation if you can. In some places (Hong Kong, for example), it's expected. We mention them specifically only when reservations are essential (there's no other way you'll ever get a table) or when they are not accepted. For popular restaurants, book as far ahead as you can (often 30 days), and reconfirm as soon as you arrive. (Large parties should always call ahead to check the reservations policy.) We mention dress only when men are required to wear a jacket or a jacket and tie.

Online reservation services make it easy to book a table before you even leave home. OpenTable covers most states, including 20 major cities, and has limited listings in Canada, Mexico, the United Kingdom, and elsewhere. DinnerBroker has restaurants throughout the United States as well as a few in Canada.

Contacts **OpenTable** (⊕ www.opentable.com). **DinnerBroker** (⊕ www.dinnerbroker.com).

WINES, BEER & SPIRITS

Beer and wine are usually available in Florida's restaurants, whether you're dining first-class or at a beachside bistro. A few chain restaurants in the major cities are also microbreweries and have a variety of premise-made beers that change with the season. Liquor is generally available at fine-dining establishments only.

▌ HEALTH

SPECIFIC ISSUES IN FLORIDA

If you are unaccustomed to strong subtropical sun, you run a risk of sunburn and heat prostration, even in winter. So hit the beach or play tennis, golf, or another outdoor sport before 10 or after 3. If you must be out at midday, limit strenuous exercise, drink plenty of liquids, and wear a hat. If you begin to feel faint, get out of the sun immediately and sip water slowly. Even on overcast days, ultraviolet rays shine through the haze, so use a sunscreen with an SPF of at least 15, and have children wear a waterproof SPF 30 or higher.

While you're frolicking on the beach, steer clear of what look like blue bubbles on the sand. These are Portuguese men-of-war, and their tentacles can cause an allergic reaction. Also be careful of other large jellyfish, some of which can sting.

If you walk across a grassy area on the way to the beach, you'll probably encounter sand spurs. They are quite tiny, light brown, and remarkably prickly. You'll feel them before you see them; if you get stuck with one, just pull it out.

▌ HOURS OF OPERATION

Many museums in Florida are closed Monday, but offer extended hours on another weekday and are usually open on weekends. Some museums reserve a day of the week for free admission. Popular visitor attractions are usually open daily, with the exception of Thanksgiving and Christmas Day.

▌ MONEY

Prices throughout this guide are given for adults. Substantially reduced fees are almost always available for children, students, and senior citizens.

CREDIT CARDS

Throughout this guide, the following abbreviations are used: **AE**, American Express; **D**, Discover; **DC**, Diners Club; **MC**, MasterCard; and **V**, Visa.

It's a good idea to inform your credit-card company before you travel, especially if you're going abroad and don't travel internationally very often. Otherwise, the credit-card company might put a hold on your card owing to unusual activity—not a good thing halfway through your trip. Record all your credit-card numbers—as well as the phone numbers to call if your cards are lost or stolen—in a safe place, so you're prepared should something go wrong. Both MasterCard and Visa have general numbers you can call (collect if you're abroad) if your card is lost, but you're better off calling the number of your issuing bank, since MasterCard and Visa usually just transfer you to your bank; your bank's number is usually printed on your card.

Reporting Lost Cards American Express (☎800/992–3404 in U.S. or 336/393–1111 collect from abroad ⊕www.americanexpress.com). **Diners Club** (☎800/234–6377 in U.S. or 303/799–1504 collect from abroad ⊕www.dinersclub.com). **Discover** (☎800/347–2683 in U.S. or 801/902–3100 collect from abroad ⊕www.discovercard.com). **MasterCard** (☎800/622–7747 in U.S. or 636/722–7111 collect from abroad ⊕www.mastercard.com). **Visa** (☎800/847–2911 in U.S. or 410/581–9994 collect from abroad ⊕ www.visa.com).

▌ SAFETY

Stepped-up policing of thieves who prey on tourists in rental cars has helped address what was a serious issue in the early 1990s. Still, visitors should be especially wary when driving in strange neighborhoods and leaving the airport, especially in the Miami area. Don't assume that valuables are safe in your hotel room; use in-room safes or the hotel's safety deposit boxes. Try to use ATMs only during the day or in brightly lighted, well-traveled locales.

▌**TIP➔Distribute your cash, credit cards, IDs, and other valuables between a deep front pocket, an inside jacket or vest pocket, and a hidden money pouch. Don't reach for the money pouch once you're in public.**

BEACH SAFETY
Before swimming, make sure there's no undertow. Rip currents, caused when the tide rushes out through a narrow break in the water, can overpower even the strongest swimmer. If you do get caught in one, resist the urge to swim straight back to shore—you'll tire before you make it. Instead, stay calm. Swim parallel to the shoreline until you are outside the current's pull, then work your way in to shore.

▌ TAXES

Florida's sales tax is 6% or higher depending on the county, and local sales and tourist taxes can raise what you pay considerably, especially for certain items, such as lodging. Miami hoteliers, for example, collect roughly 12.5% for city and resort taxes. It's best to ask about additional costs up front, to avoid a rude awakening.

▌ TIME

The western portion of the Panhandle is in the Central time zone, but the rest of Florida is in the Eastern time zone.

▌ TIPPING

Whether they carry bags, open doors, deliver food, or clean rooms, hospitality employees work to receive a portion of your travel budget. In deciding how much to give, base your tip on what the service is and how well it's performed.

In transit, tip an airport valet $1 to $3 per bag, a taxi driver 15% to 20% of the fare.

For hotel staff, recommended amounts are $1 to $3 per bag for a bellhop, $1 to $2 per night per guest for chambermaids, $5 to $10 for special concierge service, $1 to $3 for a doorman who hails a cab or parks a car, 15% of the greens fee for a caddy, 15% to 20% of the bill for a massage, and 15% of a room-service bill (bear in mind that sometimes 15% to 18% is automatically added to room-service bills, so don't add it twice).

In a restaurant, give 15% to 20% of your bill before tax to the server, 5% to 10% to the maître d', 15% to a bartender, and 15% of the wine bill for a wine steward who makes a special effort in selecting and serving wine.

INDEX

NOTES

NOTES

NOTES

NOTES

ABOUT OUR WRITERS

After being hired sight unseen by a South Florida newspaper, Fort Lauderdale-based freelance travel writer and editor **Lynne Helm** arrived from the Midwest anticipating a few years of palm-fringed fun. Well, more than a quarter century later (after covering the state for several newspapers, consumer magazines, and trade publications), she's still enamored of Florida's sun-drenched charms.

Jennie Hess is a travel and feature writer based in Orlando. When she's not checking out the latest Disney show or attraction, she's looking for ways to take the Orlando experience to the next level. Formerly a publicist for Walt Disney World Resort, Jennie enjoys sharing noteworthy gems ranging from the hottest live entertainment at Epcot to the newest Audio-Animatronics figures at Pirates of the Caribbean. She gives us the inside scoop on the evolving Disney kingdom and "don't miss" attractions beyond the theme parks, with added insights gleaned from her husband and two teenage sons.

Snowbird **Susan MacCallum-Whitcomb** spends as much time as possible in the Sunshine State. Little wonder: winters in her Nova Scotian hometown can be *loooong*. Having already worked on Fodor's *Bermuda*, *Boston*, *Budapest* and *California* guides, she jumped at the chance to update the Experience chapter for Florida.

Gary McKechnie, who reported on the Panhandle, knows a lot about his native Florida, having worked as a Walt Disney World ferryboat pilot, Jungle Cruise skipper, steam-train conductor and double-decker bus driver. He is author of *Great American Motorcycle Tours*.

Alicia Callanan Mandigo, our Disney Shopping updater, is a freelance broadcast journalist and writer. Though technically a transplant, she considers herself a Central Florida native. Alica worked at Epcot while she was in college, and she still considers it the best job she's ever had.

Julia Neyman, who updated the Miami & Miami Beach chapter, is in her first year at Columbia Law School, where she is studying international law and foreign policy. But before locking herself in the law library, Julia spent two years living in Miami and writing for the *Miami Herald* and the *South Florida Business Journal*.

A Yankee by birth, Northeast writer **Kerry Speckman** moved to Jacksonville in the early 1980s and has been basking in the sun and Southern hospitality ever since. She's a freelance travel writer who has written for *Zagat* and *AAA Going Places* and is a contributing writer to *Jacksonville Magazine*.

Good meals stick to your ribs; great meals stick in your mind. That's the belief of **Rowland Stiteler,** who has served as editor and dining critic of *Orlando* and *Central Florida* magazines. During the past 10 years he's researched more than 500 Florida hotels and restaurants for travel publications and the convention and resort industry.

Palm Beach/Treasure Coast writer **Mary Thurwachter,** a Florida resident since 1979, writes travel stories for *The Palm Beach Post* and authors its popular Bed, Breakfast & Beyond and INNside Scoop columns. As The *Post*'s Sunshine State travel expert, she has cased all sorts of Florida joints, from the Panhandle to the Keys.

Homegrown Floridians **Jim Tunstall** and **Christina Tourigny** grew up in the Tampa Bay area and have spent much of their lives tasting the state's treasure. Today, they live with their flock of critters in a radar blip called Lecanto. They added their very personal touch to our Tampa/ St. Petersburg chapter.

From her home of more than 25 years on Sanibel Island, **Chelle Koster Walton**—author of the Keys, Everglades, and Lower Gulf Coast chapters—has written and contributed to a dozen guidebooks, two of which have won Lowell Thomas Awards. She has penned thousands of articles about Florida and the Caribbean for *Miami Herald, USA Today, Concierge.com,* and other print and electronic media.